Odoo 10 Implementation Cookbook

Explore the capabilities of Odoo and discover all you need to implement it

Mantavya Gajjar

Packt

BIRMINGHAM - MUMBAI

Odoo 10 Implementation Cookbook

First published: October 2017

Production reference: 1031017

Published by Packt Publishing Ltd.
Livery Place
35 Livery Street
Birmingham
B3 2PB, UK.

ISBN 978-1-78712-342-7

www.packtpub.com

Credits

Author

Mantavya Gajjar

Reviewer

Nikunj Jani

Commissioning Editor

Kunal Parikh

Acquisition Editor

Nitin Dasan

Content Development Editor

Lawrence Veigas

Technical Editor

Mehul Singh

Copy Editor

Karuna Narayanan

Project Coordinator

Prajakta Naik

Proofreader

Safis Editing

Indexer

Pratik Shirodkar

Production Coordinator

Nilesh Mohite

About the Author

Mantavya Gajjar has 10+ years of experience in Odoo, starting from TinyERP and OpenERP. He started his career as a developer and has developed many features in TinyERP, OpenERP, and Odoo. He initiated a mobile application project at the Indian office. He has a graduate and postgraduate degrees in computer science from Gujarat Vidyapith. He completed his studies in May 2006. On 1st June 2006, he started working for Axelor and TinyERP at Ahmedabad.

He was the first international employee, appointed to establish a branch of Tiny ERP in India (Ahmedabad, Gujarat). He has done everything, from registering a legal company to setting up the physical office and recruitment. He has interviewed more than 8,000 candidates in the past 10 years, selecting 300 candidates and training them for the Indian branch. Most professionals working on Odoo in India are trained by him. As a result, today India (Ahmedabad, Gujarat) is called the *Hub of Odoo Developers*. Today, there are over 1,000 Odoo developers in Gujarat alone.

Mantavya is actively engaged with many universities to prepare and review the syllabus for computer applications and computer science courses. As a reviewer, he has reviewed thousands of academic student projects. Being an alumnus of the Gujarat Vidyapith Computer Science Alumni Association, he contributes his free time to various social activities. He also plays the role of a trustee member and treasurer at Gujarat Vidyapith Computer Science Alumni Association. He has been a reviewer for the book, *Working with OpenERP*, by Packt.

In his spare time, he likes to play cricket with friends and drives to new destinations by road with his wife and daughter.

I would like to thank my wonderful daughter, Hetvi, and wife, Minal, for all their love and support. I would also like to thank my mom, a lifelong housewife, for having encouraged me always to keep moving forward in life, and my father for being my guru and philosopher, and for always being there to support me.

Many thanks to the great team at Odoo.

Also, many thanks to all the reviewers, the great people at Packt, and the Odoo community for all their support.

About the Reviewer

Nikunj Jani earned a masters degree in computer applications from Gujarat, India. He began his career in 2007 as a software engineer with an MNC called SATYAM COMPUTERS. In 2009, he joined TinyERP, a division of Odoo, S.A. in India as a team lead. During his tenure of 8+ years with Odoo, he has worked with several versions, including 5.0, 6.0, 6.1, 7.0, 8.0, 9.0, 10.0, and 11.0. He has worked as a functional consultant (business analyst), training manager, and project manager.

Currently, he is the product owner and heads a usability and testing team at Odoo (India) for the upcoming versions. Nikunj is an open source enthusiast who has given 35+ international functional trainings/consultancies to Odoo partners, prospects, and end customers.

Nikunj has a total of 10 years of IT experience, and his specialties include training, consultancy, analysis, project management, usability, and testing new features of Odoo.

www.PacktPub.com

For support files and downloads related to your book, please visit www.PacktPub.com.

Did you know that Packt offers eBook versions of every book published, with PDF and ePub files available? You can upgrade to the eBook version at www.PacktPub.comand as a print book customer, you are entitled to a discount on the eBook copy. Get in touch with us at service@packtpub.com for more details.

At www.PacktPub.com, you can also read a collection of free technical articles, sign up for a range of free newsletters and receive exclusive discounts and offers on Packt books and eBooks.

Mapt

https://www.packtpub.com/mapt

Get the most in-demand software skills with Mapt. Mapt gives you full access to all Packt books and video courses, as well as industry-leading tools to help you plan your personal development and advance your career.

Why subscribe?

- Fully searchable across every book published by Packt
- Copy and paste, print, and bookmark content
- On demand and accessible via a web browser

Customer Feedback

Thanks for purchasing this Packt book. At Packt, quality is at the heart of our editorial process. To help us improve, please leave us an honest review on this book's Amazon page at `https://www.amazon.com/dp/1787123421`. If you'd like to join our team of regular reviewers, you can email us at `customerreviews@packtpub.com`. We award our regular reviewers with free eBooks and videos in exchange for their valuable feedback. Help us be relentless in improving our products!

Table of Contents

Preface

Odoo 10 Implementation Cookbook provides a list of essential recipes and steps to configure and implement Odoo for your business, either on the Odoo online (SaaS) platform or installed locally on your hardware. This book will help you understand the value of Enterprise Resource Planning (ERP) systems and the best practices and approaches for getting a system configured and using it in your organization. This book is only focused on the implementation of the Odoo applications in an organization. For new users or already experienced users, it can be a complete reference to major Odoo applications, such as sales, purchase, inventory, finance, and accounting, and manufacturing. New users or already experienced users can use this book to configure and implement the Odoo application— the Odoo Studio, an application used to configure existing views, reports, and automated business processes. It allows you to create a new application from scratch without entering any code; a non-developer can create and configure a new application using this studio.

Out of the two implementation approaches available, the big-bang approach is suitable for an enterprise with more than 50 users. For an enterprise with less than 50 users, Odoo offers an out-of-the-box approach on its online (SaaS) platform to implement Odoo using the Odoo Studio, by configuring the available enterprise application and customizing the views or reports if required for localization.

In this book, we have tried our best to cover most features of the Odoo enterprise applications that you are likely to use in your business. Unfortunately, there are just not enough pages to cover all topics. In Appendix, we have included an additional recipe that helps you install Odoo 10 on Ubuntu Linux, for using it onsite for customer needs, which cannot be achieved on Odoo online using the Odoo studio.

After the book is released, make sure to check for online updates in which we cover more advanced subjects.

Packt also offers other Odoo books that cover more advanced Odoo topics.

What this book covers

`Chapter 1`, *Getting Started with Odoo Online*, guides you how to set up your online instance without any setup; you just need a web browser, and you can create an instance later that can be accessed on Android tablet or mobile. The chapter covers the management of the online instances and managing the users and features for the instances. The chapter then guides you through setting up your website theme and email integration. At the end of the chapter, it also guides you on how you can move from an onsite to an online instance, or download the database from an online instance and start using it locally on your server.

`Chapter 2`, *Quickstart Implementation Methodology*, shows you how to activate the new features and installing an application in your instance. Next, the chapter guides you through the implementation planner; using this, you will be guided to implement the Customer Relationship Management application. The later part of the chapter describes how to customize a view, create new fields, and add them to the view. The chapter also guides you to create a new application using Odoo Studio and shows you how you can export and import a customization into your instance.

`Chapter 3`, *Traceability – Leads to Cash*, begins with creating and managing customers, and managing your leads and opportunities. The chapter guides you to create a proposal and send it to the customer for online negotiation and approval. The chapter ends with describing the steps to deliver the product and service, prepare an invoice based on the delivered product, and get paid by the customer.

`Chapter 4`, *Modern Way of Doing Sales and Managing Sales Contracts*, starts with a detailed configuration of the product, preparing and sending a sales quotation, applying a discount, and calculating the margin. This chapter also guides you through the configuration of the delivery cost and how to add this to the sales quotation. To speed up the sales process, the chapter also guides you through the preparation of an online quotation using templates, sending it to the customer, getting online approval, and negotiating. The chapter ends with the management of the recurring sell and invoicing through sales contracts.

`Chapter 5`, *Time Tracking and Invoicing Policy*, begins with the configuration of the product to track the delivery of the service and material, and the configuration of the invoice policy to create an invoice based on the delivery of time and material. The chapter also shows you how to track the delivery of the service using the timesheet application and how to create an invoice based on the delivery of time and material. It also shows how to create an advance invoice before the delivery of the service.

`Chapter 6`, *Start Selling Online with Odoo eCommerce*, guides you to activate the Odoo eCommerce application and configure your online shop, configure prices for the products and their variants that are created automatically using a combination of attributes. The chapter also shows you how you can integrate the payment gateway and shipping services to automate the shipping and payment process. The chapter ends with configuring the checkout process, and in case you would like to add an extra step to the checkout process, you will be shown how to access the orders and their payments from the eCommerce control panel.

`Chapter 7`, *Setting up Financial Management with Odoo*, starts with activating the full accounting feature on top of the invoicing application, along with a detailed customer invoice and receipt of payment through cash, bank cheque, and bank reconciliation. The chapter also demonstrates the configuration of tax, printing the tax invoice, and how to get the tax report. The chapter also demonstrates the management of vendor bills, due dates for payment, and paying vendor bills by cheque printing. The chapter also gives you details about how to access the financial statements, along with closing and opening a new financial year.

`Chapter 8`, *Scale Your Business*, shows you in-depth features related to accounting, beginning with activating and configuring multi-currency and multi-company features, managing invoicing and payment in different currencies, and grouping financial statements from multiple companies. The chapter also demonstrates the management of cost centers using analytic accounts and helps you to compute profit and loss by customer or project. The chapter also describes the management of assets by category and computing depreciation and allows you to see revenue recognition to manage advances.

`Chapter 9`, *Purchase Management*, begins with the purchase cycle, starting from a request for a quotation to the receipt and payment of vendor bills. You will see the two different ways of making a purchase using a standard purchase or the purchase through a tender. The chapter also demonstrates the management of multiple units of measuring and controlling the vendor bills.

`Chapter 10`, *Warehouse and Inventory Management*, covers the setting up of a warehouse and locations within the warehouse, initializing the inventory, and verifying the inventory periodically. You will also see efficient ways of managing delivery orders and incoming shipments. The chapter also demonstrates traceability using serial or lot numbers. You will see the most efficient ways of managing the warehouse operation through a single screen called a barcode interface, and using just a barcode scanner you will be able to manage all inventory operations.

`Chapter 11`, *Advance Warehouse Management*, demonstrates product costing and valuation method in the beginning of the chapter. The chapter also guides how the transportation cost can be added to the incoming shipment to calculate the actual cost of product purchased and shows the quality control in the warehouse to help you set up the quality test and check the quality of the product in incoming shipments.

`Chapter 12`, *Setup your Manufacturing Process*, begins with setting up the bill of material, creating the first manufacturing order, and processing it. The chapter also describes the configuration of the assembly line and work centers and computes the cost of the manufactured product. You will see an efficient way of managing procurements through the master production schedule. The chapter also demonstrates selling and purchasing kit products that combine multiple products into a single product without a manufacturing process.

`Chapter 13`, *Product Life Cycle Management and Maintenance*, explains the engineering change order and getting approval on the change for a bill of materials or assembly line. The chapter also demonstrates corrective and preventive maintenance plans for equipment and computes overall equipment efficiency.

`Chapter 14`, *Implement Project Management*, explains the setting up of the project management application and managing the tasks in the project pipe. The chapter also shows how to create forecasting for long-term projects, for better planning and availability of resources. It demonstrates how to manage the project issues and ratings on the issues.

`Chapter 15`, *Implement Human Resource Applications*, demonstrates launching recruitment, receiving an application, and scheduling interviews. The chapter also demonstrates leave allocation for employees or group of employees, leave requests and approval, and checks the leaves statics at the end. The chapter also describes the management of employee expenses and reimbursements and how to re-invoice employee expenses to the customer.

`Appendix`, *Installation of Odoo on Ubuntu*, demonstrates the installation of the Odoo on an Ubuntu server operating system in a step by step fashion. This is important as it is recommended to setup the Odoo server on a Linux operating system.

What you need for this book

In order to successfully practice what is demonstrated in this book, you will need the following:

- Odoo Version 10.0 (Online)
- Odoo Version 10.0 (Enterprise/Onsite)
- Odoo Version 10.0 (Community)

Who this book is for

This book is targeted at Odoo functional users and project managers who would like to use it for their organization. No expertise in Odoo is expected or assumed.

Sections

In this book, you will find several headings that appear frequently (Getting ready, How to do it…, How it works…, There's more…, and See also). To give clear instructions on how to complete a recipe, we use these sections as follows:

Getting ready

This section tells you what to expect in the recipe, and describes how to set up any software or any preliminary settings required for the recipe.

How to do it…

This section contains the steps required to follow the recipe.

How it works…

This section usually consists of a detailed explanation of what happened in the previous section.

There's more…

This section consists of additional information about the recipe in order to make the reader more knowledgeable about the recipe.

See also

This section provides helpful links to other useful information for the recipe.

Conventions

In this book, you will find a number of text styles that distinguish between different kinds of information. Here are some examples of these styles and an explanation of their meaning. Code words in text, database table names, folder names, filenames, file extensions, pathnames, dummy URLs, user input, and Twitter handles are shown as follows: "Create a new user for JIRA in the database and grant the user access to the `jiradb` database we just created using the following command." A block of code is set as follows:

```
<Contextpath="/jira"docBase="${catalina.home}
/atlassian- jira" reloadable="false" useHttpOnly="true">
```

Any command-line input or output is written as follows:

```
mysql -u root -p
```

New terms and **important words** are shown in bold. Words that you see on the screen, for example, in menus or dialog boxes, appear in the text like this: "Select **System info** from the **Administration** panel."

Warnings or important notes appear like this.

Tips and tricks appear like this.

Reader feedback

Feedback from our readers is always welcome. Let us know what you think about this book-what you liked or disliked. Reader feedback is important to us as it helps us develop titles that you will really get the most out of. To send us general feedback, simply e-mail `feedback@packtpub.com`, and mention the book's title in the subject of your message. If there is a topic that you have expertise in and you are interested in either writing or contributing to a book, see our author guide at `www.packtpub.com/authors`

Customer support

Now that you are the proud owner of a Packt book, we have a number of things to help you to get the most from your purchase.

Downloading the example code

You can download the example code files for this book from your account at `http://www.packtpub.com`. If you purchased this book elsewhere, you can visit `http://www.packtpub.com/support` and register to have the files e-mailed directly to you. You can download the code files by following these steps:

1. Log in or register to our website using your e-mail address and password.
2. Hover the mouse pointer on the **SUPPORT** tab at the top.
3. Click on **Code Downloads & Errata**.
4. Enter the name of the book in the **Search** box.
5. Select the book for which you're looking to download the code files.
6. Choose from the drop-down menu where you purchased this book from.
7. Click on **Code Download**.

You can also download the code files by clicking on the **Code Files** button on the book's webpage at the Packt Publishing website. This page can be accessed by entering the book's name in the **Search** box. Please note that you need to be logged in to your Packt account. Once the file is downloaded, please make sure that you unzip or extract the folder using the latest version of:

- WinRAR / 7-Zip for Windows
- Zipeg / iZip / UnRarX for Mac
- 7-Zip / PeaZip for Linux

The code bundle for the book is also hosted on GitHub at `https://github.com/PacktPublishing/Odoo-10-Implementation-Cookbook`. We also have other code bundles from our rich catalog of books and videos available at `https://github.com/PacktPublishing/`. Check them out!

Errata

Although we have taken every care to ensure the accuracy of our content, mistakes do happen. If you find a mistake in one of our books-maybe a mistake in the text or the code-we would be grateful if you could report this to us. By doing so, you can save other readers from frustration and help us improve subsequent versions of this book. If you find any errata, please report them by visiting `http://www.packtpub.com/submit-errata`, selecting your book, clicking on the **Errata Submission Form** link, and entering the details of your errata. Once your errata are verified, your submission will be accepted and the errata will be uploaded to our website or added to any list of existing errata under the Errata section of that title. To view the previously submitted errata, go to `https://www.packtpub.com/books/content/support` and enter the name of the book in the search field. The required information will appear under the **Errata** section.

Piracy

Piracy of copyrighted material on the Internet is an ongoing problem across all media. At Packt, we take the protection of our copyright and licenses very seriously. If you come across any illegal copies of our works in any form on the Internet, please provide us with the location address or website name immediately so that we can pursue a remedy. Please contact us at `copyright@packtpub.com` with a link to the suspected pirated material. We appreciate your help in protecting our authors and our ability to bring you valuable content.

Questions

If you have a problem with any aspect of this book, you can contact us at `questions@packtpub.com`, and we will do our best to address the problem.

1
Getting Started with Odoo Online

In this chapter, we will cover the following recipes:

- Creating, activating, and using Odoo online instances
- Accessing Odoo on your Android mobile and tablet
- Accessing, duplicating, and renaming an instance
- Managing features and users
- Setting up your domain name and website theme
- Email integration
- Moving your instance from onsite to online
- Downloading database backup from Odoo online

Introduction

Odoo (**On Demand Open Object**) is an open source suite of business applications; it became the world's most downloaded and used business application software; with 2 million users worldwide. On a standard installation of Odoo, you will see the Apps icon that allows you to install the apps you need. Odoo has a great apps architecture that allows you to install new apps on demand.

Today, more and more companies are choosing to host their business applications on an online cloud platform. It is too costly for the companies to host their business applications on local hardware. This approach requires not only a lot of capital to buy hardware and software licenses, but also creates a lot of responsibility and risk in backing up data and ensuring the stability of the business application. The best thing about the Odoo online platform is that you can start using Odoo online instance in a few clicks. You don't have to choose the operating system or perform installation steps.

Creating, activating, and using Odoo online instance

Accessing the Odoo online version is simpler than all its previous versions. You can start with a single application, which is free for unlimited users. The instance created with the first application needs to be activated, as it expires in 4 hours if it is not activated, and all the changes made in the instance will be lost. You will not be able to go back to the free subscription plan on the installation of the second application; you will be notified when you are about to install the second application.

Getting ready

We assume that you are ready and have a computer with an internet connection, and you have connected to the Odoo cloud platform at `https://www.odoo.com`. You will be asked for your name, email, company name, and contact information, which will be used to create an Odoo instance.

> The first application is free, so select it carefully if you wish to use it for free for unlimited users. You can add more applications later, once your instance is ready.

How to do it...

1. Open your browser and navigate to `https://www.odoo.com/trial`.
2. Choose the first application you would like to start with. Clicking on that application will redirect you to the signup form in case you are not logged in at odoo.com. For our example, let's start with the Odoo CRM application:

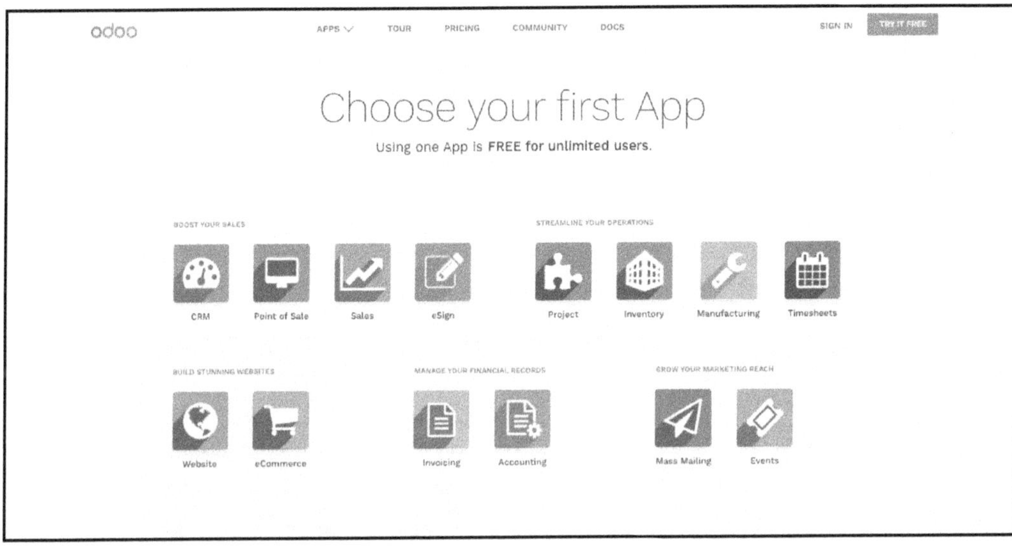

3. You will be asked for your name, email, company name, and contact information, which will be used to create an Odoo instance. Fill the required information in on the signup form and click on the **START NOW** button:

> The signup form information is used to create your instance; your email address will be your username and on activation of your email you will be asked to set a new password at Odoo. Details filled on this form can be changed later at `https://odoo.com/my/home`.

The instance is ready with **Discuss**, **Calendar**, and **CRM** applications. You can manage internal and external communication using chatter, calendar to manage the meetings with customers, and your sales activity using leads and opportunities in the CRM application:

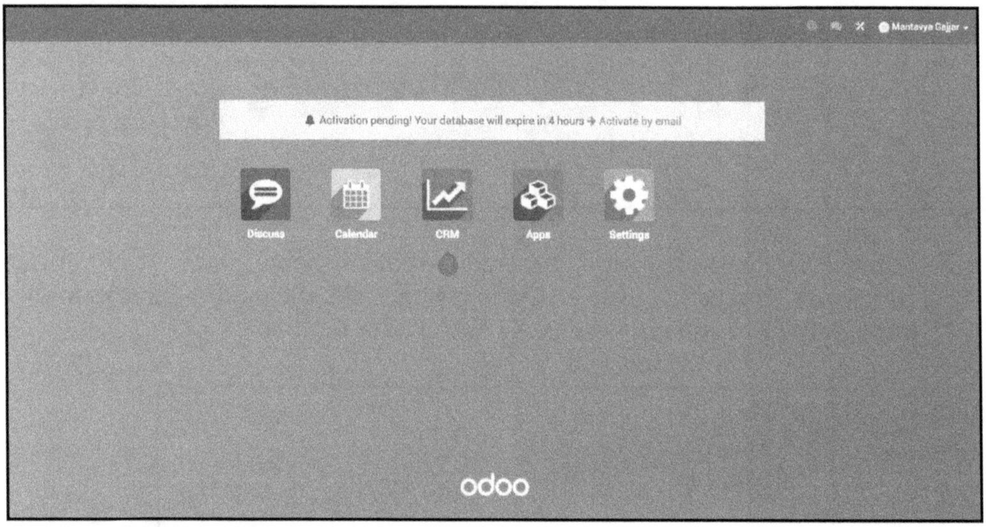

We will discuss the CRM application in detail in `Chapter 3`, *Traceability – Leads to Cash.*

> This is an Odoo trial instance; it will be available for only 4 hours. If you close the browser, you will lose changes made to the instance and you will have to start again.

4. At the top of the application icons, you will see a message that informs you how long your trial version will run before you need to activate it. You should not see this message if you have successfully verified your email address; you should get an email with an activation link in your inbox, to activate your Odoo instance. It is possible to lose the Odoo instance before the time runs out:

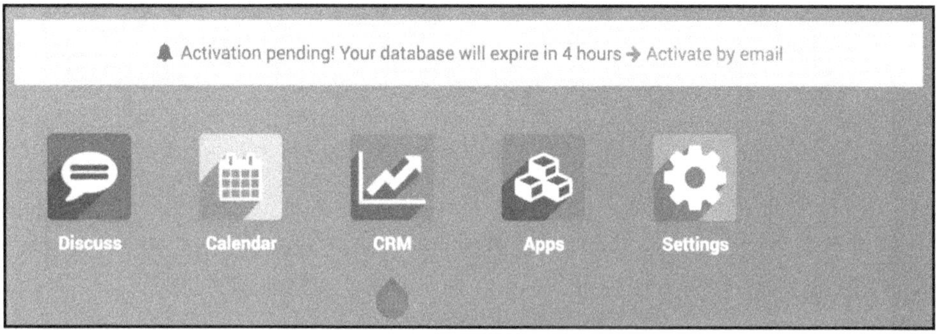

5. If you don't receive an email, you can click on the **Activate by email** link to resend the activation email. You will get a popup to confirm your email address or change it, in case you entered the wrong email address at the time of creating an online instance:

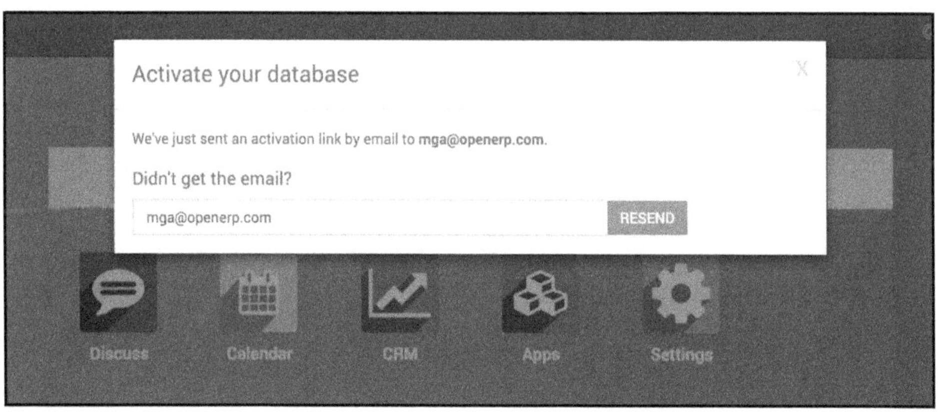

6. As soon as you receive an email in your mailbox, clicking on the **Click to activate your database** button will redirect you to your instance. It should be activated, and if you have installed only one application it will be free for lifetime use, or for 15 days only if you have installed more than one application:

7. To subscribe to Odoo online and continue using it, click on the **Subscribe to keep it running!** the link at the top of the page:

You will be redirected to a payment page; where you can see the current plan you are about to opt for; it is monthly when you start your subscription, but later it can be switched to yearly to avoid monthly bills:

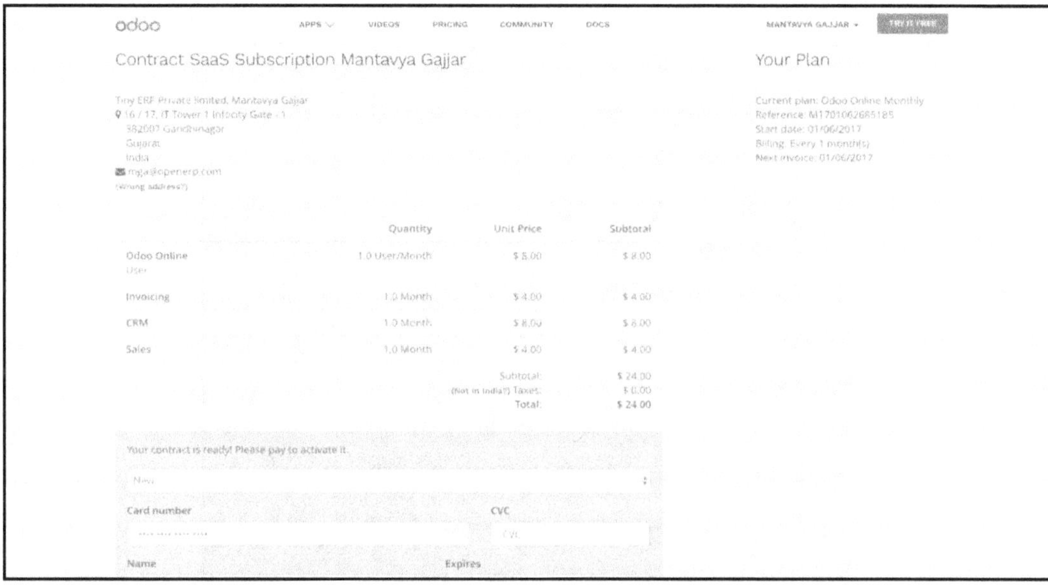

It can be quite convenient to have an Odoo subscription, so you can focus on the implementation, rather than setting up the production environment and maintaining it.

8. If your online instance is deactivated, you can still get back the last changes you made and continue using it until Odoo permanently drops your instance. Typing the URL `yourcompany.odoo.com` will redirect you to the blocked instance page as follows:

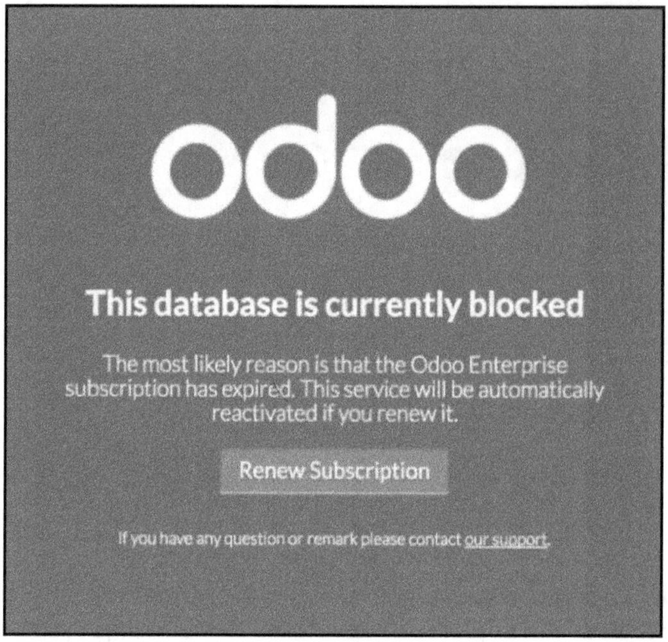

9. Clicking on **Renew Subscription** will redirect you to a payment page; on confirmation of payment your instance will be unblocked and you can continue using it or download the backup in case you would like to move it onsite.

There's more...

All the instances created with the first app are running under the free subscription plan for unlimited users. However, on the installation of the second application, your instance will be converted to a non-free instance. You will be notified when you are about to install the second application:

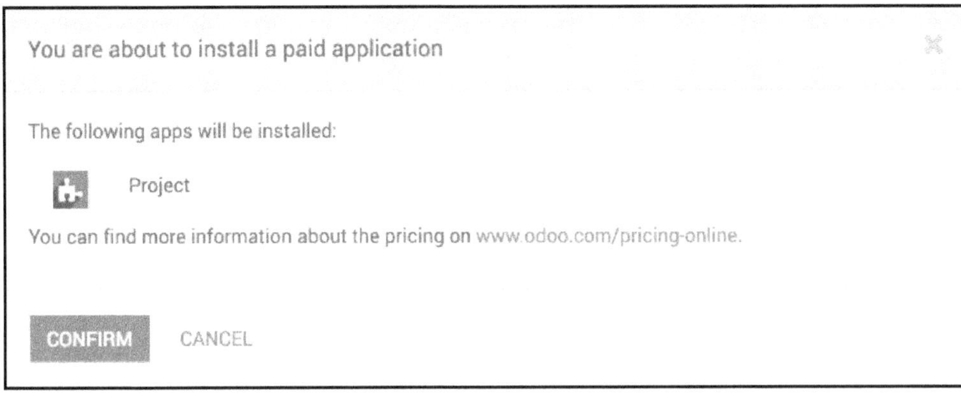

On the installation of the second application, your instance will lose the free subscription plan and convert to billing-based subscription. You will get 15 days to subscribe for your instance—once your 15 days run out, you will lose your Odoo online instance.

Before you proceed with the payment, please identify the number of active users within your organization and the number of applications you have installed. The following screenshot is the **Odoo online pricing** calculator for the month of January--2017. You can locate the Odoo online pricing at `https://www.odoo.com/pricing-online`, which you can use to calculate the approximate price that the online subscription will cost you:

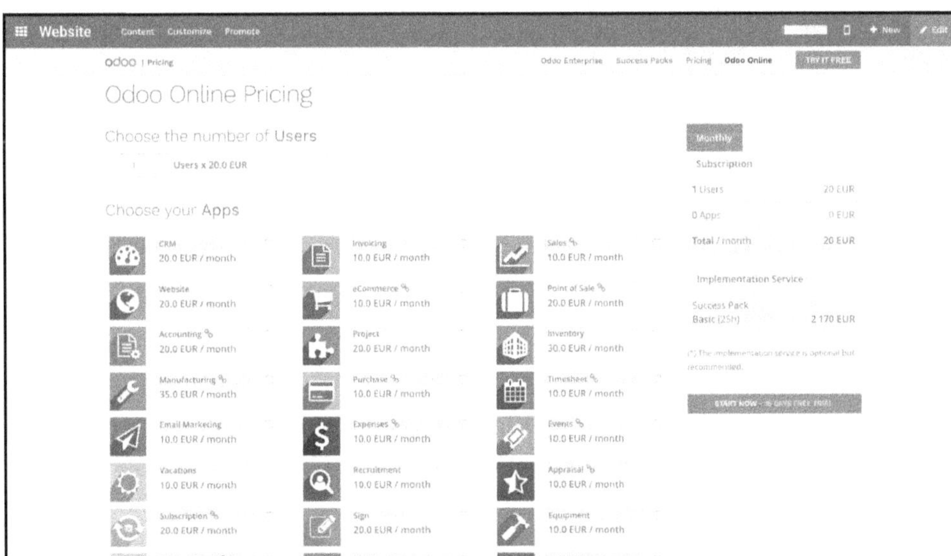

Depending on your needs, an Odoo subscription might be a good decision to start with. Installing and maintaining an Odoo instance on your server requires deep knowledge and has a high risk for the production system. You must maintain adequate disaster recovery procedures in case your server crashes or in case of hard drive failure. There is also complexity in applying the bug fixes and in migration to a new version of Odoo.

> The price for the Odoo online instance is payable depending on the customer location. Asian customers pay $16 per month, while customers from the USA pay $25 per month. European and the Middle East customers pay €20 per month.

Accessing Odoo on your Android mobile and tablet

Odoo has released an official Android mobile application along with the release of version 10. At the beginning of Odoo 9, Odoo started to use mobile compatible design. Apps and menus were designed to flow and format properly on mobiles and tablets. You can download the Odoo official mobile application from the Google Play store.

> The Odoo team is working on the development of the iOS application for iPhone and iPad; it will be available on Apple app store with the release of Odoo version 11.

Getting ready

We assume that you have created and activated your online instance successfully.

How to do it...

1. Open the Play store on your mobile and search for Odoo; you will be able to see the first application developed by Odoo - S.A. is the correct one. Install that application on your mobile. It takes a few seconds depending on your network speed.

The Odoo mobile official application looks like the following screenshot:

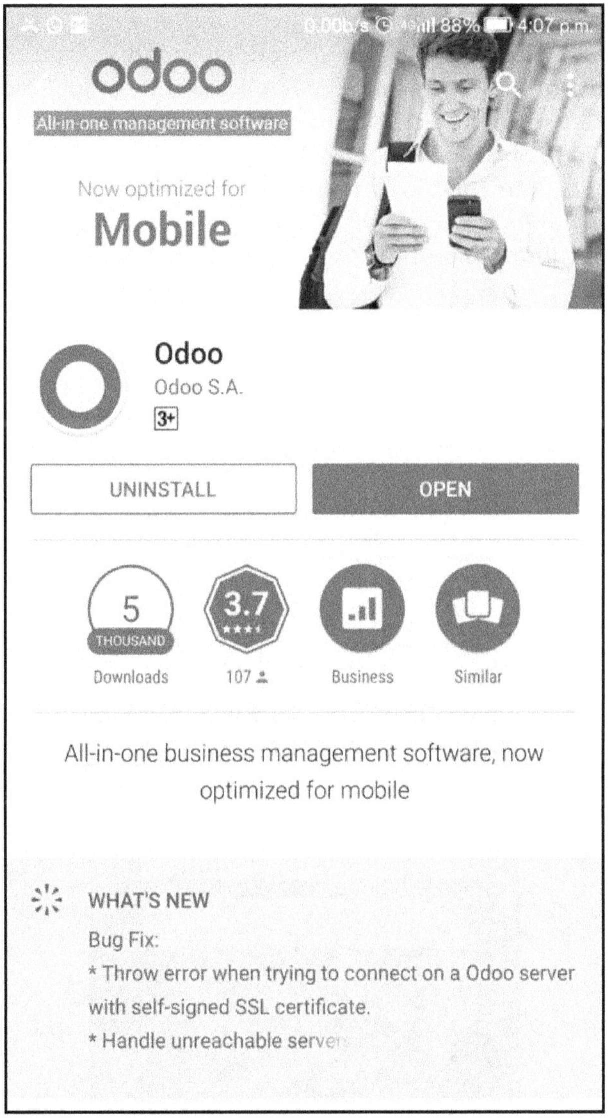

Downloading the app may incur mobile data charges; we advise you to connect to a Wi-Fi network before installing or connecting.

The application size is comparatively small; it should not take more than a minute to install. The application is compatible with Android Ice Cream Sandwich 4.0 and above. Lastly, the application was updated on 27th October 2016 at the time of writing. The Odoo mobile application works well for Odoo Enterprise version 10. It will also work for Odoo version 9, but some legacy features; such as push notifications and optimizing view for mobile may not be supported.

2. Run the Odoo mobile application and get ready to connect to your Odoo instance. You will be asked for the URL, username, and password in order to connect to your instance. You can connect to any Odoo instance provided it is running on Odoo online. Make sure you use the correct URL `https://yourcompany.odoo.com` to connect to the Odoo instance:

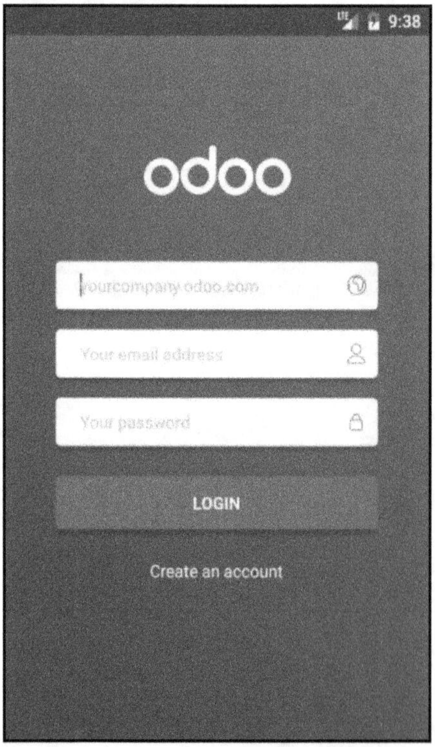

You may create a new online instance from the Odoo mobile application too - we advise you to connect to an existing instance with a valid username, password, and connection URL.

3. On successful login, you will get all your Odoo applications on your mobile including the custom applications that you may have installed:

Odoo mobile takes a few minutes the first time you connect to Odoo instance. Once it is connected you can keep the application in memory using Android settings, so it will load faster later.

There's more...

Odoo has developed a native application for mobile which connects to the Odoo instance and fetches the web application. Integration with mobile components makes Odoo useful even on small devices on the go.

> This is the biggest advantage of the Odoo mobile application you don't need any development skills on mobile to make it compatible with customization you have done through Odoo Studio.

Real-time push notifications

Odoo mobile provides real-time notifications using the Google cloud notification platform. For online users, it is already activated:

When you see the device registration message on the related partner for the login user, it confirms that your device is successfully registered to obtain the real-time push notifications from your instance.

> Push notifications are dependent on your devices and on Android; most of the standard devices get the notifications even if the application is not running. On some devices, you will get notifications only if the Odoo mobile application is running in the background. If your phone is rooted, and you have installed the custom Android without the Google Play service, notifications may not work.

Built-in barcode scanner

Odoo mobile supports scanning barcodes on picking lists. The barcode scanning works for the Warehouse Management Barcode Scanning apps; it manages your inventory movement using a barcode scanner.

Click on the barcode app icon and you will be able to get the barcode scanning interface. This screen is based on the device from which it is accessed. It is different on desktops - on mobile you will get the button to **TAP TO SCAN**. By clicking on that, the camera will be activated and you can scan barcodes on the picking list; the same picking operation will be open on mobile:

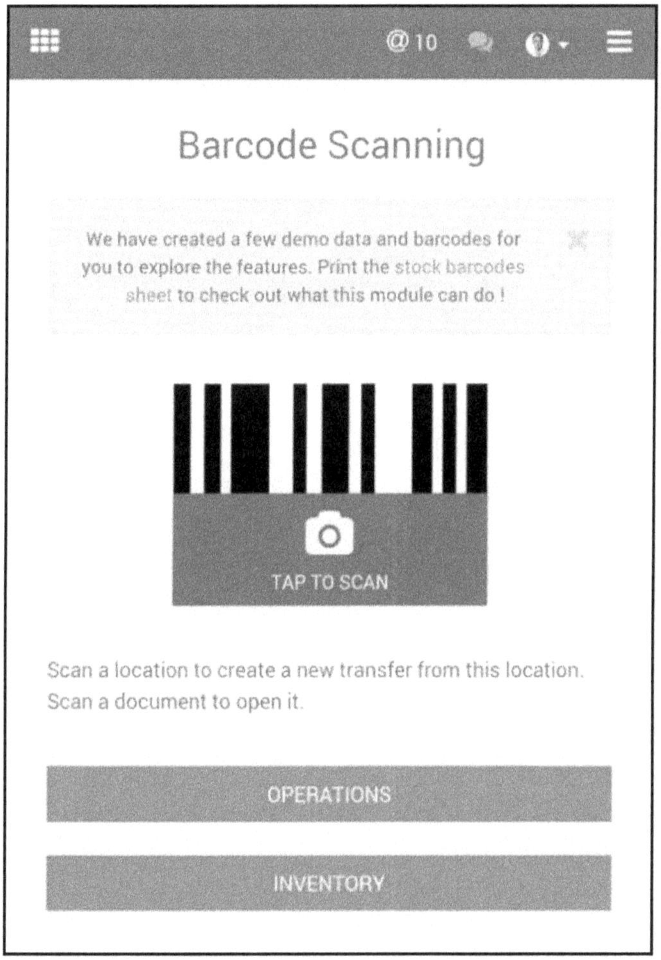

Sync contacts

You can add your Odoo contacts to your mobile address book using the Odoo mobile application. To add a contact to your mobile, click on the **Contacts** app and open the contact you would like to add to mobile. You will get the **Add to Contact** button beside the **Active** button:

Click on the **Add to Mobile** button; on successful contact creation on mobile, you will be notified below the screen. Click on **View** to open the created contact in your mobile phone book.

Multiple account support

You may connect with multiple Odoo instances on the same mobile device. When you connect to an instance the first time, the Android application creates an account on mobile. To connect with other Odoo instances you have to log out; you will be redirected to select the account or given the option to create a new account:

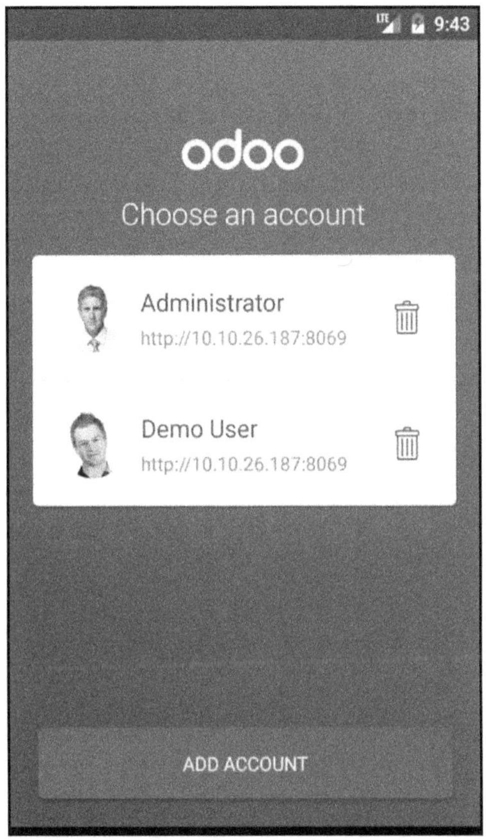

Accessing, duplicating, and renaming an instance

You may have multiple instances created on the Odoo online platform. Odoo's customer portal is designed in such a way that it can be used by customers to manage their instances or by Odoo partners to manage their customers' instances.

On the database management page, you can control access to other instances you were connected to, or you may revoke your access with those instances when they are no longer in use.

How to do it...

1. Managing your Odoo instance requires you to signin to the Odoo customer portal. Visit `https://www.odoo.com/web` and enter your username and password to manage your instances. Visit the **My Databases** page at `https://accounts.odoo.com/my/databases`. You will be able to see other instances as well, such as help and apps, besides your own instance:

As I am connected to the **HELP** and **ODOO** apps, they appeared in my databases; there are some instances hosted by Odoo to manage their online forum and the Odoo app store.

> Odoo supports single sign-in to connect to Odoo instances; by clicking on an instance you will enter into your instance and you will not be asked for the username and password.
>
> Odoo considers one instance as equal to one database. You can see the instances you have created or connected to, or you can create a new instance too, from your portal account.

Clicking on **MANAGE YOUR DATABASES** will redirect you to the database management page:

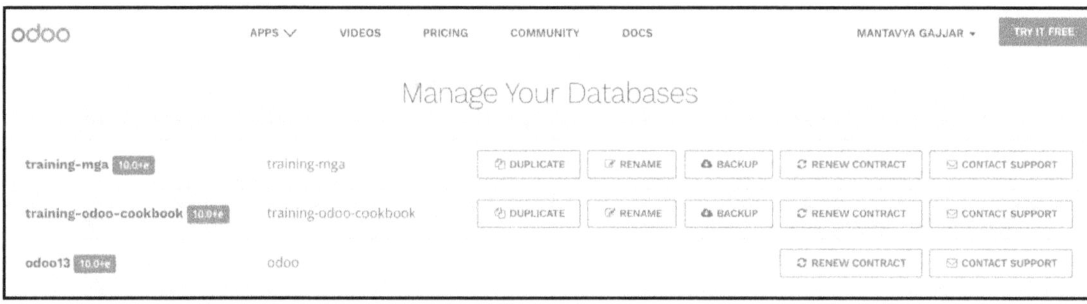

2. Make sure you select the correct instance in the preceding image to duplicate it. Click on the **DUPLICATE DATABASE** button available to the right of the name to create a duplicate instance, enter the suffix name for the duplicated instance, and click on the **DUPLICATE DATABASE** button:

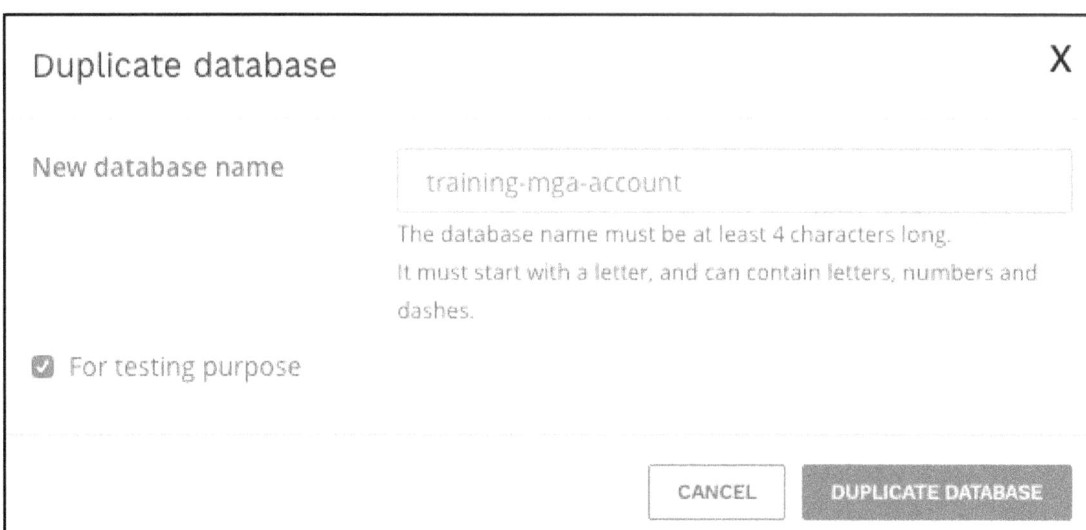

Choose the purpose of the new database. If you select **For testing purpose** it will create a test database, otherwise, you will have a new master database.

A duplicated database has the same behavior as a real one:
1. Emails are sent
2. Payments are processed (in e-commerce, for example)
3. Delivery orders (shipping providers) are sent

It is strongly advised to test behavior using sample customers/products (with a disposable e-mail address, for example).

3. Similar to duplicating an instance, renaming an instance can be performed from the same page. Click on **RENAME DATABASE**, enter the new name of the instance, and click on **Rename Instance**; it is as simple as duplicating an instance:

There's more...

When you log into your duplicated database, you will notice that the URL uses the same name you chose for your duplicated database. Duplicate databases expire automatically after 15 days:

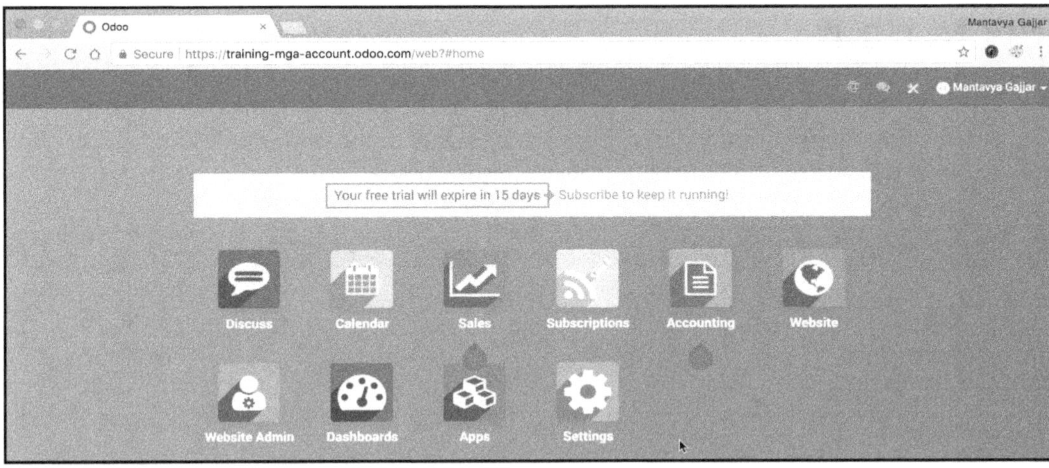

Instance duplication and renaming instance features are not available to free customers for Odoo online instances.

Managing features and users

As the administrator of your database, you are responsible for its usage. This includes the apps you install as well as the number of users currently in use. Odoo is many things (ERP, CMS, CRM application, e-commerce backend, and so on) and there is an application for every need, but it is not a smartphone. You should apply caution when adding/removing features, especially applications on your database, since this may impact your subscription amount significantly, or switch you from a free account to a paying one on the online platform.

Getting ready

Before carrying out any of these procedures, we strongly advise you to test them on a duplicated database. That way, if something goes wrong, your day-to-day business will not be impacted.

How to do it...

1. In your Odoo instance, click on **Settings**; in this application, you will be able to see how many applications you have installed. Look at the following screenshot; in my instance, there are 11 applications installed:

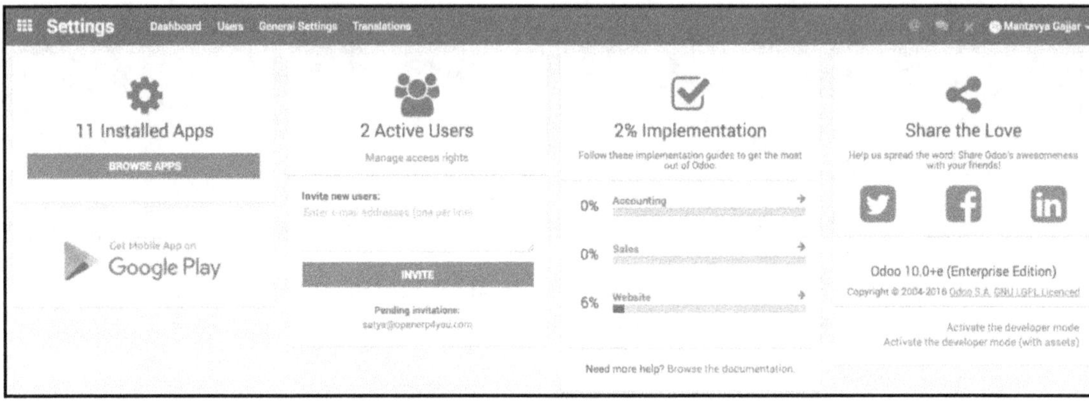

2. Click on **Browse Apps** to access the list of your installed applications. You will see all the applications available in your instance; those that are installed or available to install. To get the list of installed applications applies the **Installed** filter:

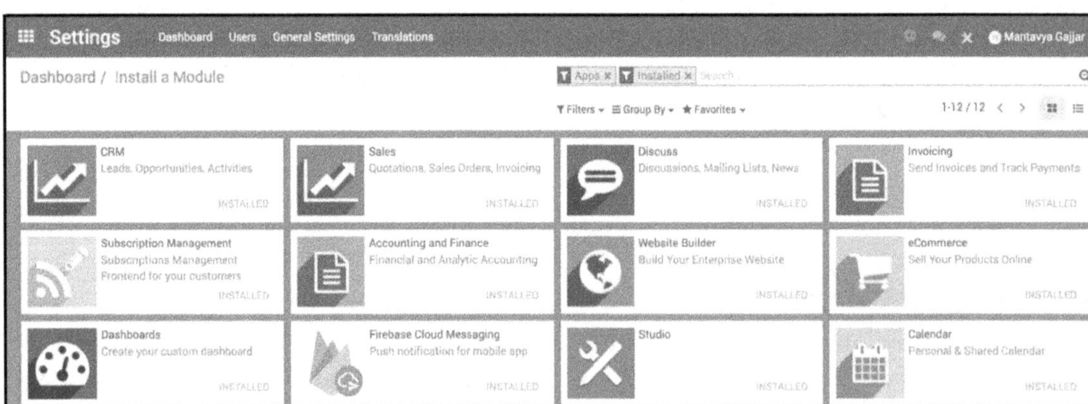

3. Click on the application you want to uninstall; I want to uninstall the **Sales** application. Then, on the form view of the application, click on the **UNINSTALL** button:

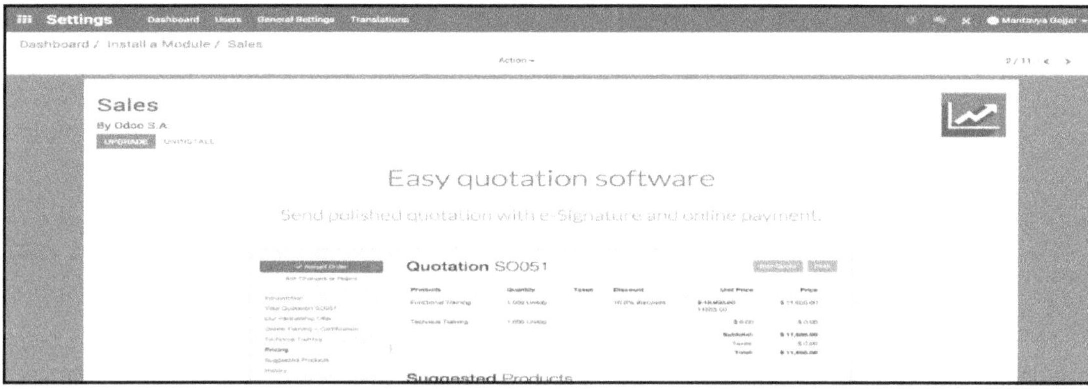

4. Some applications have dependencies, like invoicing, e-commerce, and so on. Therefore, the system will give you a warning message to advise you of what is about to be removed. If you uninstall your application, all its dependencies will be uninstalled as well and the data in them will permanently disappear. If you are sure you still want to uninstall it, then click **CONFIRM**:

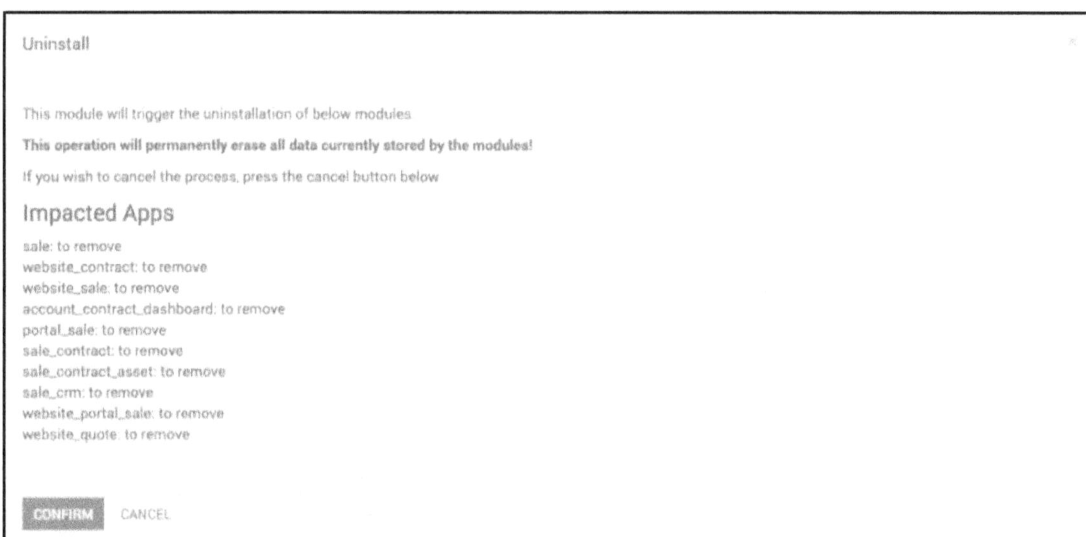

Look at the preceding screenshot; it is asking you to check and confirm the number of applications that are going to be uninstalled.

> The data will be lost for the uninstalled applications, so make sure that you have taken the data backup before you uninstall the application.

5. In your Odoo instance, click on **Settings**. You will have a section showing you the active users on your database. Click on **Manage access rights**:

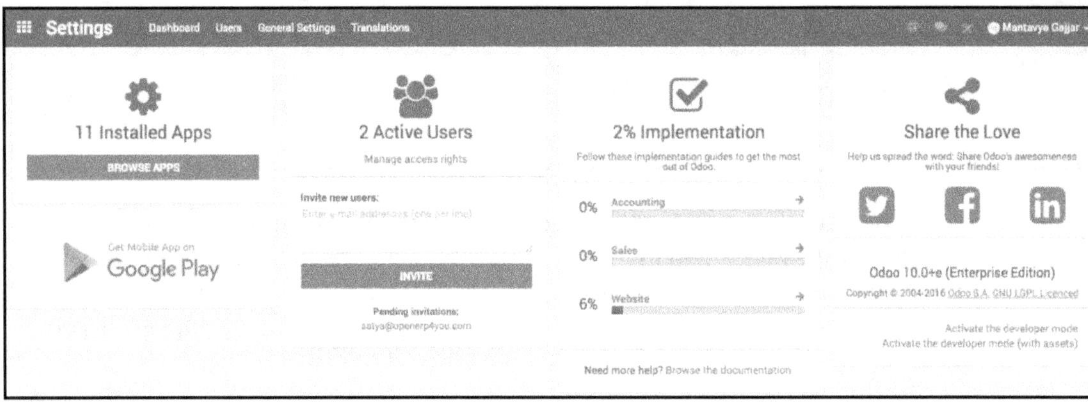

6. You'll then see the list of your active users:

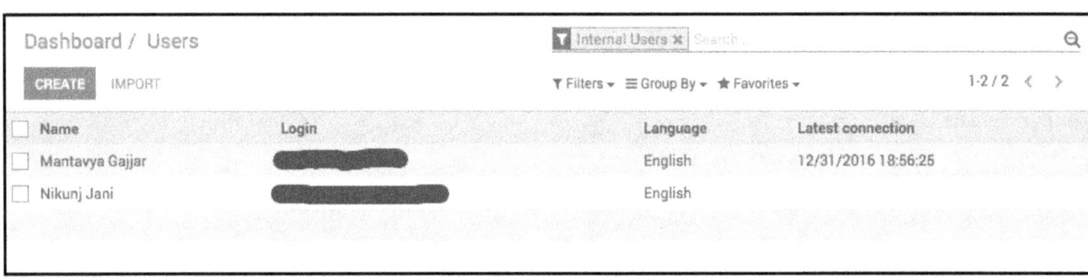

> The pre-selected filter **Internal Users** shows you are paying users (different from **Portal Users** which are free). If you remove this filter, you'll get all your users (the ones you pay for and the portal ones).

7. In your list of users, click on the user you want to deactivate:

8. As soon as you are on the user form, go with your mouse cursor to the status **Active** (top right). Click on **Active** and you will notice that the status will change to **Inactive** immediately.

TIP: Never deactivate the main user in your instance. Inactive users are not able to log into the instance.

There's more...

Odoo releases a long-term support version every 12 to 18 months. A long-term support release comes with bugfixes, improvements, usability, and features. Odoo considers every major release such as V7, V8, V9, and V10 as long-term supported versions and provides support for latest 3 long-term releases under the Odoo enterprise contract in parallel. Odoo supports V8, V9, and V10 at the time of writing:

Odoo	8.0	September 18, 2014	Revamped Inventory and WMS, Support for CMS: Website builder, e-commerce, point of sale and business intelligence
	9.0	October 1, 2015	Revamped Accounting features, Odoo Community split from Odoo Enterprise [20]
	10.0	October 5, 2016	Revamped Manufacturing features

Odoo online customers benefit from the long-term release cycle as they have an early access to new features on Odoo subscription before they get released under the long-term version for enterprise customers. Odoo keeps its online version up-to-date. On the Odoo online platform the new version releases every 3 months with bug fixes, usability improvements and sometimes new apps, it will be available immediately for the online customers while onsite customers get those features when Odoo releases its long-term stable version. The long-term stable release will be available every 12 to 18 months.

The Odoo LTS version will be named as Odoo 9, Odoo 10, while the SaaS version will be named as saas~14, saas~15, and so on, Odoo supports last three LTS versions under maintenance and migration.

These are great benefits for companies running their business with standard needs; you can evolve quickly with the fast evolution of the Odoo online version.

Setting up your domain name and website theme

Odoo has many enterprise social features. It performs many activities online such as sending email, inviting your customers to a portal and sending a document to get it signed online. All these activities bring users or visitors to your instance. By default, Odoo assigns a sub-domain name based on your company name filled-in at the time of creating an Odoo instance: `https://yourcompany.odoo.com`.

Odoo allows you to personalize your instance, you can set up your personal domain name and website theme on the online instance. Once a visitor accesses your website by typing your company's domain name, `https://yourcompany.com`, they are immediately redirected to your instance.

Getting ready

We assume that you have access to the Odoo online customer portal to access your instances and that you already bought your domain name If not, look at the recommended domain name provider here,
`http://www.mytipshub.com/top-ten-best-domain-registrar/`.

To change your website theme, you should have access to the administrator account for the instance you are going to change the theme on. If you have not selected the theme, please go to `https://www.odoo.com/apps/themes` and choose the theme you would like to apply.

How to do it...

1. Go to your domain manager's website and search for the DNS Zones management page. Create a **CNAME** record that points to your domain (for example, `www.yourcompany.com`) and to your Odoo database (`yourcompany.odoo.com`). Please see your domain manager for specific directions on how to complete this task.
2. Access the database manager at `https://accounts.odoo.com/my/databases`. Click on **DOMAINS** to the right of the database you would like to redirect. A database domain prompt will appear. Type your custom domain (for example, `www.yourcompany.com`) and press **ADD**. Then click **OK**:

> Setting up a custom domain does not mean you will lose your sub-domain set by Odoo. You can use both `www.yourcompany.com` and `yourcompany.odoo.com` simultaneously.

3. To test the settings, open your web browser and type `yourcompany.odoo.com` and go. You will see your instance page if all the settings are applied correctly.

> It may take some time to apply changes depending on how your DNS propagates the changes.

4. If you have not installed the Odoo website application, let's go to the Odoo application list, search for the **Website Builder** application, and click on **Install it**:

5. On successful installation of the **Website Builder** application, it will redirect you to choose the website theme available on the Odoo online platform. You can look at the live preview before selecting the theme. There are twenty-five themes available to choose from, in various types of business categories:

Each theme comes with various out of the box snippets and customization options to change colors, fonts, layouts, and backgrounds. We will look into the theme controls in more detail in `Chapter 6`, *Start Selling Online with Odoo eCommerce*.

6. The only way to change the theme is to search for the **Website Theme Install** application responsible for proposing, installing, and replacing the website theme:

Upgrading the **Website Theme Install** application will redirect you to the theme selection view, allowing you to choose the new theme and install it.

> **TIP:** It is advisable to select and set the theme you would like to keep for production use, as changing your theme after uploading the content to the website may mean losing some of the content format and may require re-working.

Email integration

Your incoming and outgoing emails are activated at the online instance; your default email domain is `@yourcompany.odoo.com`. As it is, it may not suit your company name, but you can change it to `@yourcompany.com`, and start getting and sending emails on your own domain. Let's see how you can configure your own domain in your online instance.

Getting ready

Refer to your server configuration to create the catch-all email address on your mail server. Refer to `https://support.google.com/a/answer/33962` to configure the catch-all email address, in case you are using a Google business email application as your email server. What you need is the `catchall@yourcompany.com` email address and password.

> Catch all email address refers to all those email addresses which do not exist on the email server. The email server pushes all emails to catch all, which are sent to the email address not existing on the server.

How to do it...

1. Activate the developer mode from **Settings**; clicking on **Activate the developer mode** will reload the page and your URL will be changed to `https://yourcompany.odoo.com/web?debug#home`:

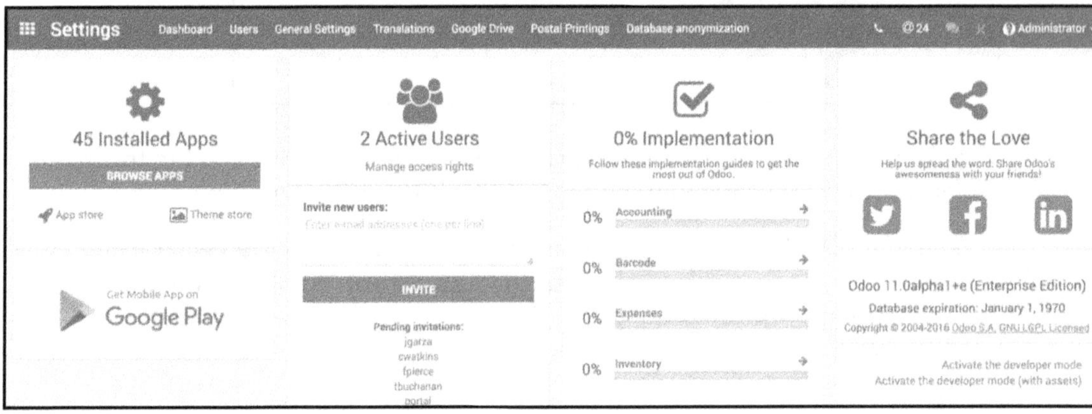

2. Open the **General Settings** page from **Settings** | **General Settings** to change the default domain; on your instance, it will be `yourcompany.odoo.com`, so each email alias created in Odoo will use that domain. Look at the following screen; you have to change to `yourcompany.com` instead of `yourcompany.odoo.com`:

3. Next is to create an incoming email server; to read email coming to your domain. Use a catchall email address and password to read all emails coming to your domain. Go to **Settings** | **Technical** | **Emails** | **Incoming Mail Servers** and click on the **New** button to create a new incoming server:

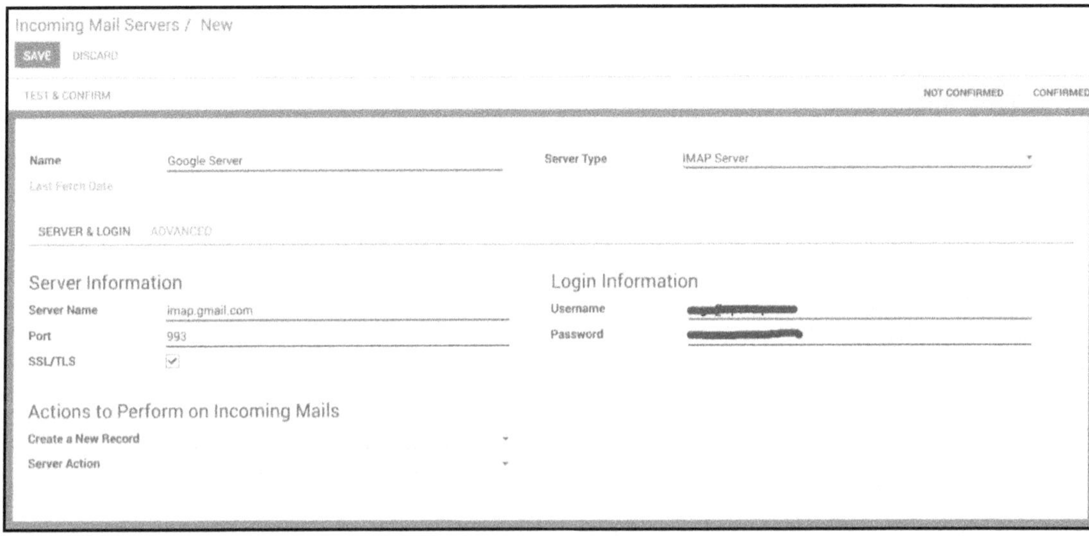

4. To test your email server settings, send an email to `sales@yourcomapny.com`. If everything works well, you should get an opportunity in your direct sales team, as your alias for your direct sales team is `sales@yourcompany.com`:

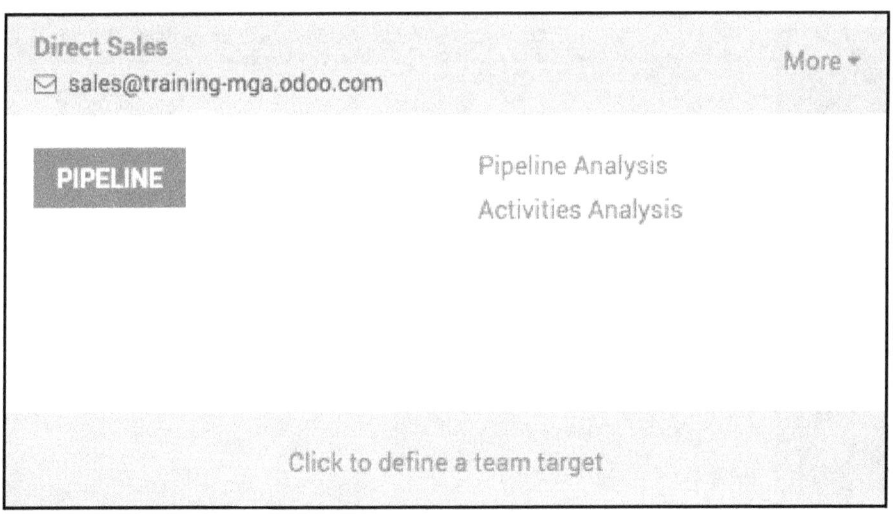

It may take 3 to 5 minutes to reflect the new opportunity in the system, as the Odoo server reads your incoming email periodically every 3 to 5 minutes.

With the default configuration, you will start getting emails on `@yourcompany.odoo.com`. To test it, send an email to `sales@yourcompany.odoo.com` address; it will create an opportunity in the **Direct Sales** team.

There's more...

Working with a traditional mailbox requires a minimum of 1 hour a day to process the inbox. To overcome this problem, Odoo has developed a new way of communication. The way emails are integrated in Odoo makes them the backbone of the whole communication system. It has changed the way people work with emails, as each email is not just information, but a to-do list for you:

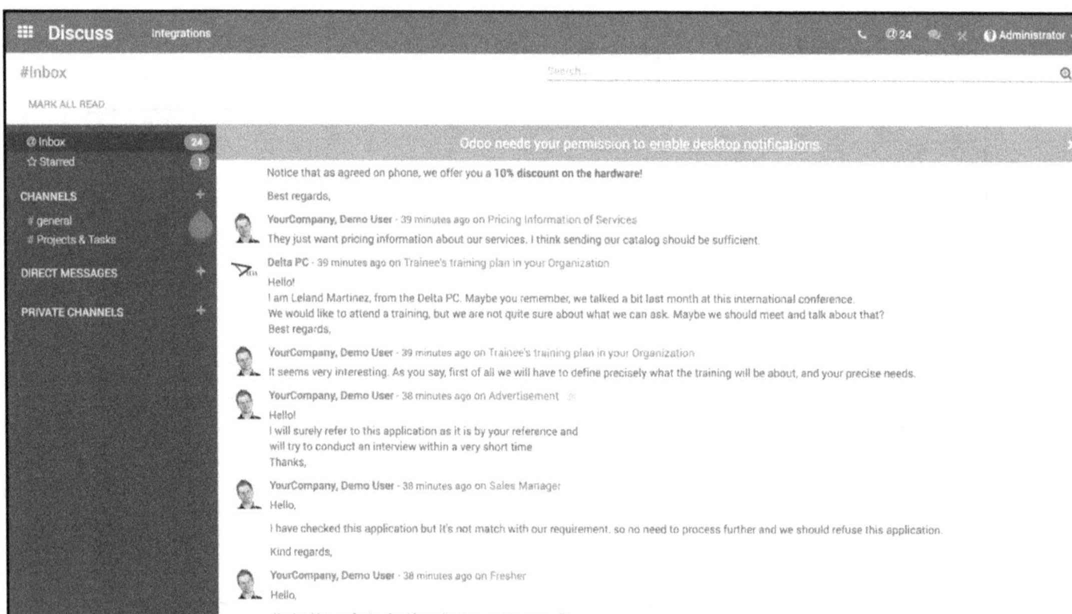

To process your inbox, you have to pass through the linked document on each email, marked as read. You can also reply straight away on the document, and the reply email will be sent to all the followers of that document.

Moving your instance from onsite to online

Looking at the benefits of the Odoo online platform over the onsite instance, you may be interested in moving your instance to the Odoo online platform. It is too difficult for small and medium-scale companies to create an industry standard in-house infrastructure. It is possible to migrate the local Odoo instance of version 7 or above to the Odoo online platform.

How to do it...

1. Create a backup up of your database from your local instance; visit `https://your-local-domain/web/database/manager`. You will be able to see all the databases available on your local instance. You may have more than one database if you keep production and test databases on the same instance:

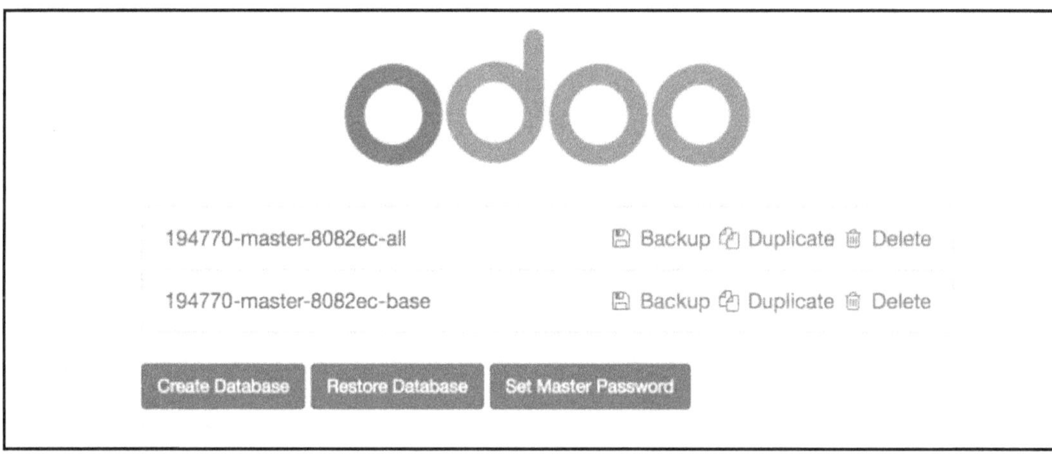

2. Click on the **Backup** button to the right of the database you want to take the backup of. You will be asked for the master password. Enter the master password, select the format **zip (includes filestore)**, and click on the **Backup** button:

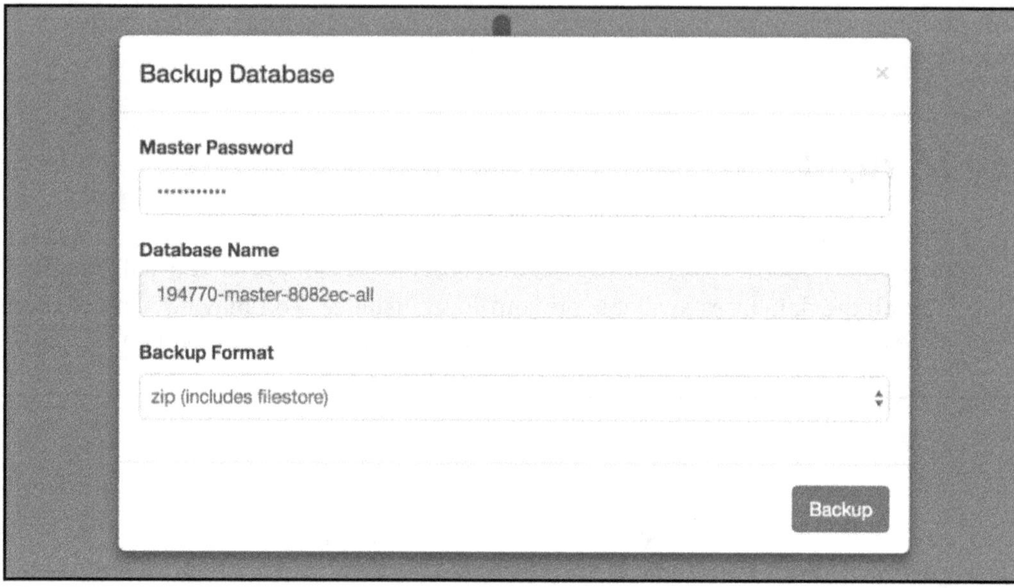

The download will start on the input of the correct master password; depending on the size of the database and filestore, it may take time. You will get the `.zip` file containing the database backup and the folder containing the attachments you have uploaded to your instance:

3. Open the Odoo upgrade website `https://upgrade.odoo.com/database/upload` to upload your database for the automated migration, and upload your database:

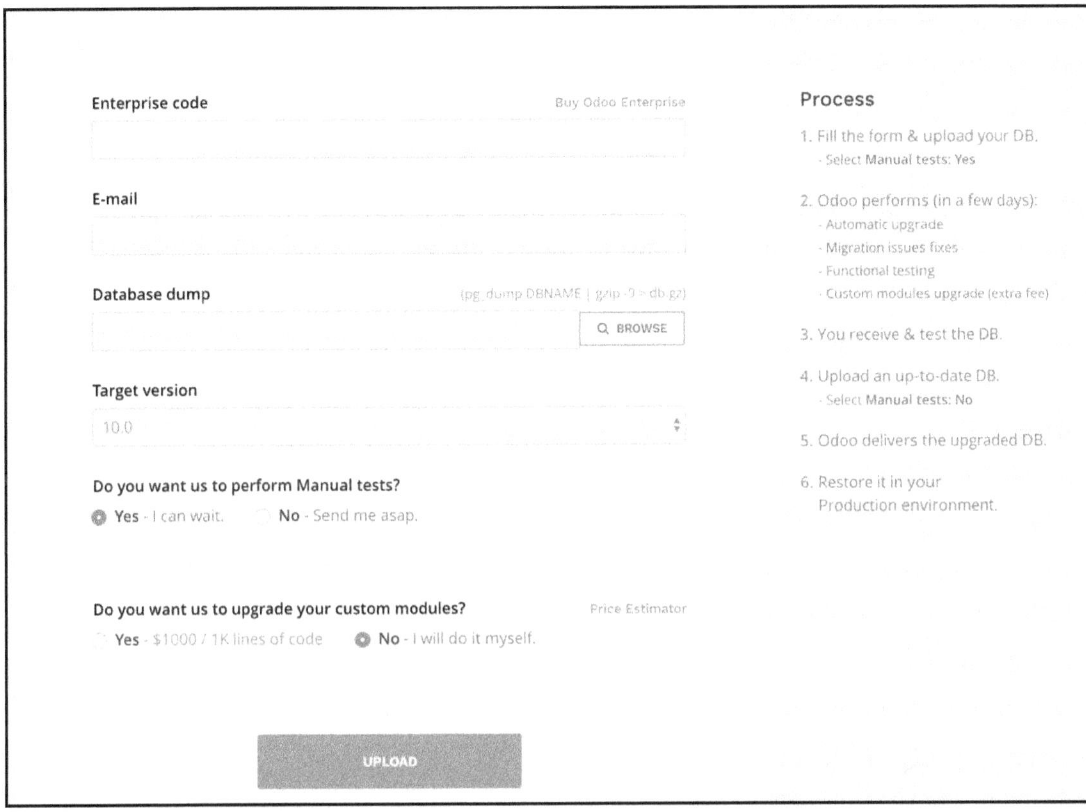

4. Send an email to `help@odoo.com` to make the special request that you would like to move to the Odoo online platform.

> The migration server is an automated platform for migrating databases from older versions to newer versions, offered by the Odoo migration team. Moving from onsite to online takes a week. Migration and using Odoo on the cloud is a paid service offered by the Odoo team.

There's more...

There is no configuration involved to ensure you get the best service level on Odoo. You are getting a high level of service on Odoo to ensure 99% uptime, security, and backups.

Running a business application on your premises involves lots of complexity in terms of choosing the correct hardware and setting up the backup and recovery, power, and internet backup. All these are complex and difficult for small and medium companies to get started with.

Odoo online subscription takes care all those complexities for end users, allowing you to get started with Odoo online in one click. Online subscription manages bug fixes, security patches, and automatic upgrades to ensure you are always using the newest version of Odoo. All the new features are released for online users prior to the onsite users, in order to give a great user experience to end customers.

Uptime

Customer databases are hosted in the closest Odoo data center. EMEA—France, Americas—Canada, APAC—Hong Kong. Each customer instance is replicated in real-time on a hot-standby system located in the same data center. Odoo works with different hosting providers worldwide (and can switch at any time), but they always deliver at least a 99.9% uptime guarantee. So they can guarantee a minimum of 99.9% uptime (3 nines, excluding planned maintenance). This corresponds to a maximum unplanned downtime of 1.44min/24h or 8h/year. Odoo usually delivers much better uptime than this (100% most months), and their providers always deliver a much better uptime than their SLA, too.

The data centers where Odoo is hosted are Tier-III certified or equivalent, with N+1 redundancy for power, network, and cooling. Each customer database is replicated in real-time on a hot-standby server located in the same data center.

Security

The safety of data is very important to Odoo; they design their systems and procedures to guarantee it. There are various security aspects taken care of, and they are as below.

- **SSL**: All web connections to client instances are protected with 256-bit SSL encryption HTTPS with a 2048-bit modulus SSL certificate, and running behind Grade A SSL stacks. All Odoo's certificate chains are using SHA-2 already.
- **Reliable platform**: Servers with full hardware guarantee, redundant data storage, network and electrical supplies.
- **Passwords**: Customer passwords are protected with industry-standard PBKDF2+SHA512 encryption, salted + stretched for thousands of rounds.

- **Safe system**: Servers run recent Linux distribution with up-to-date security patches, with firewall and intrusion countermeasures.
- **Isolation**: Client data is stored in dedicated databases, there is no sharing of data between clients, and no access possible from one database to another.

Backups

Odoo keeps 14 full backups for up to 3 months: 1/day for 7 days, 1/week for 4 weeks, and 1/month for 3 months. Backups are replicated on at least three different machines in different data centers. Users can download manual backups of their live data at any time.

For a permanent disaster impacting one server only, Odoo has Disaster Recovery Plan, which has the following metrics:

- **Recovery Point Objective**: 5 minutes, that is, losing a maximum of 5 minutes of work
- **Recovery Time Objective**: 30 minutes, that is, the service will be back online after a maximum of 30 minutes, standby promotion time and DNS propagation time included

For data center disasters where one entire data center is completely and permanently down, Disaster Recovery Plan has these metrics:

- **Recovery Point Objective**: 24 hours, that is, you can lose a maximum of 24 hours of work if the data cannot be recovered and you need to restore the last daily backup
- **Recovery Time Objective**: 24 hours, that is, the service will be restored from the backup within 24 hours in a different data center.

Download database backup from Odoo online

You may wonder if you are locked into the service once you start using Odoo online subscription, as all your data is stored on the Odoo cloud platform.

You are wrong! The Odoo online platform allows you to move from, and enter into it at any time. You can set up your local server with the same code used on Odoo cloud, and you will get the backup of your database for download at any time.

How to do it...

1. Access your instances at `https://accounts.odoo.com/my/databases`. Click on **Manage your Databases**:

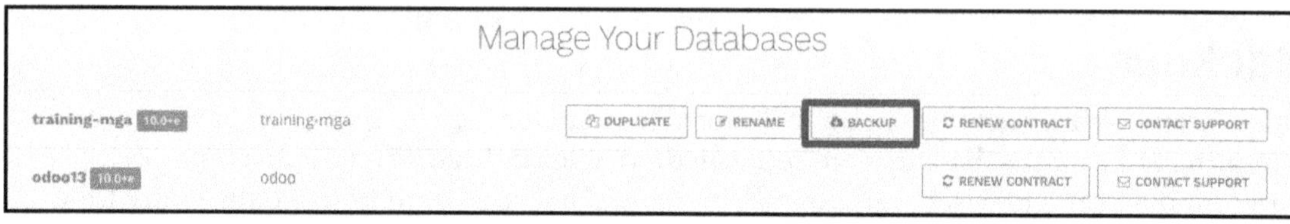

2. Click on the **Backup** button to the right of the database name to start backup and downloading within a second. You will get the `.zip` file containing the backup of the database and a copy of the filestore.
3. Download and install the Odoo Enterprise latest version from `https://www.odoo.com/page/download/`. For details about the installation of Odoo on Linux please refer to Appendix A, *Installation of Odoo on Linux*, at the end of this book.
4. Restore the database to your local instance by typing `http://localhost:8069/web/database/manager` into the browser to open a database management page:

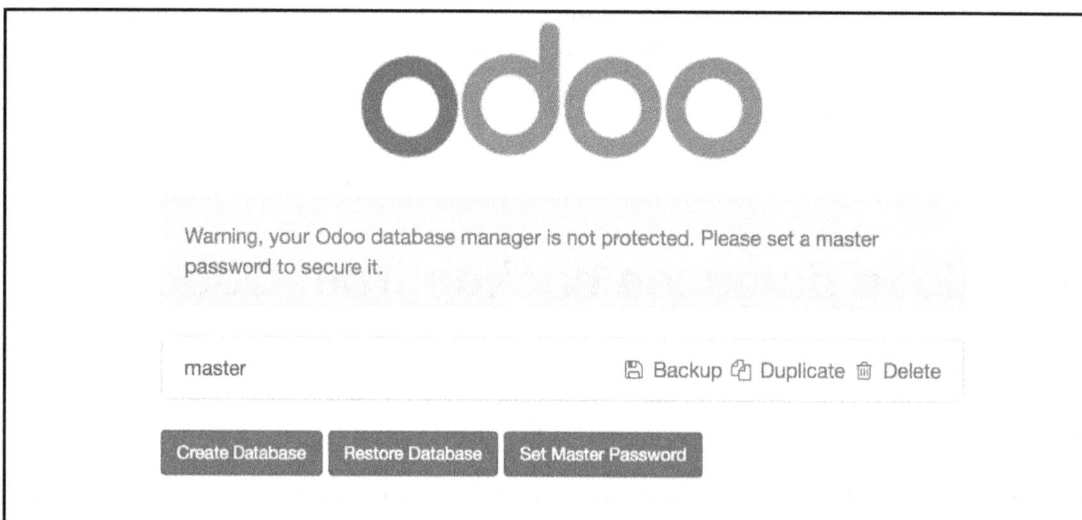

5. Click on the **Restore Database** button to restore the database you have downloaded from the Odoo online platform. It will ask you to select the database backup file and master password, if you have set it, and click on the **Restore** button:

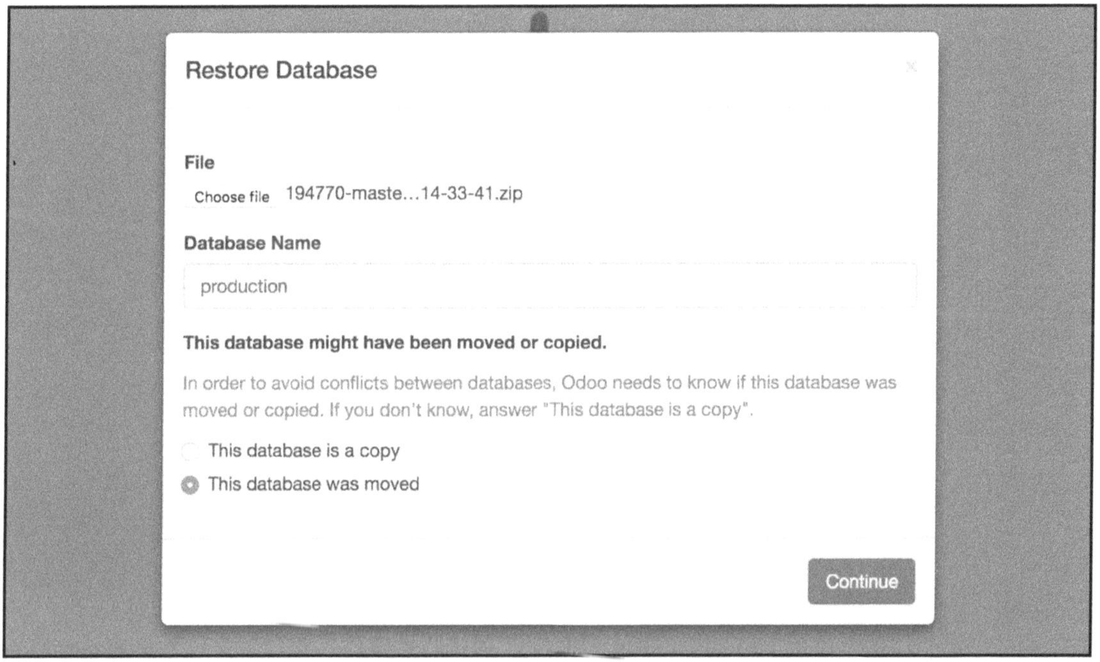

6. Select the option **This database was moved**. This will keep your instance running with the same subscription key you have on the online instance. You have to renew your subscription from `https://www.odoo.com/buy` later.

> Moving from online to onsite, you may lose the website theme which was used on the online version, but you may buy that theme from the Odoo app store to use it onsite.

2

Quickstart Implementation Methodology

In this chapter, we will cover the following recipes:

- Installing a new application and enabling additional features
- Implementing Odoo CRM using the Odoo implementation tool
- Installing Odoo studio and adding new fields to a view
- Creating a new business application using Odoo studio
- Exporting and importing a custom application

Introduction

Commonly, there are two methodologies popular for the implementation of Odoo business applications. Large scale project implementation methodology is a big-bang approach followed by the Odoo official partner network, and the Quickstart implementation is offered by the Odoo team and some partners on the cloud platform.

Large scale projects are a solution to specific business needs and provide customization, a long sales cycle, and an implementation cycle, as well.

The Quickstart approach is useful for small and medium sized companies who would like to adapt a standard business process. This is available in Odoo, out-of-the-box, to help you to go live as quickly as possible. According to the Odoo team, a project can go live in 100 hours after implementing four major applications: **Sales**, **Purchasing**, **Stocks**, and **Accounting**.

Odoo offers this service under the name**Implementation Service**, computed based on the number of applications selected. Look at the following screen computed, based on the four major applications:

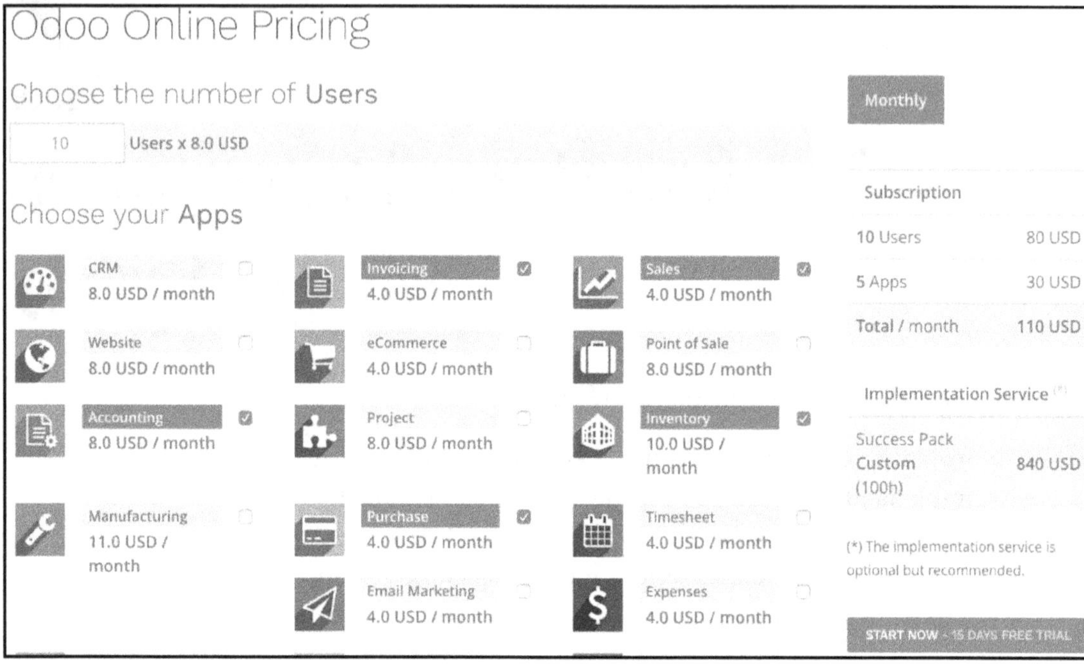

In this chapter, we will go through the self-implementation methodology to help you to start using Odoo CRM by yourself, which can save the cost of the implementation service.

Installing a new application and enabling additional features

Odoo is a suite of business applications. The software is designed with a perfect modular approach and allows the user to start with one application and keep on adding new applications when the business grows. All the applications are installed later and will be integrated by default.

Odoo focuses on a great user experience for the first run, and it keeps the business flow as simple as possible. A user can start using it confidently, but on the first run, you may not get all the features; however, additional features can be activated once you install the new application.

Let's try to install the **Salesapp** and enable a pricelist for a product based on specific customer segments.

Getting ready

Create your online instance at `https://www.odoo.com` if you have not created it yet. Go through the recipe*Creating Odoo online instance* in `Chapter 1`, *Getting Started with Odoo 10*, for detailed instructions on how to create your online instance.

> **TIP**
> It is always preferred that before you do any operations on a master instance, such as installing or uninstalling a new application, or activating new features, that you duplicate the instance. To duplicate the instance, go through the recipe*Accessing, duplicating, and renaming an instance* in `Chapter 1`, *Getting Started with Odoo 10*. If everything goes well, you can apply it to your master instance.

We assume that you have created a duplicate instance to test the installation and activation of new features.

How to do it...

1. In your Odoo instance, click on **Settings**; in this application, you will be able to see how many applications you have installed. Look at the following screenshot. In my instance there are 11 applications installed:

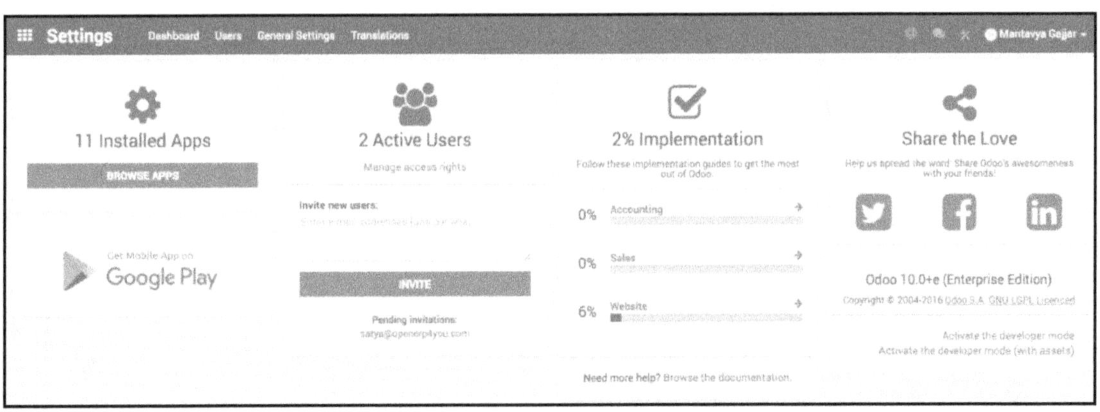

2. Click on **BROWSE APPS** to access the list of applications available to your instance:

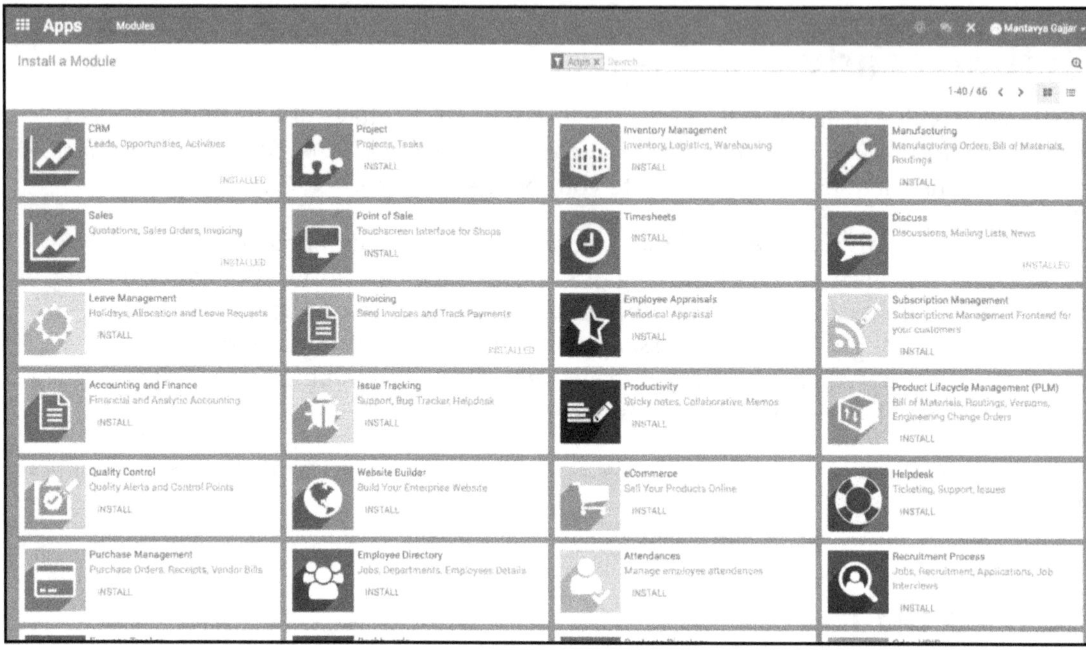

3. Click on the **INSTALL** button for an application you would like to install. It may take some time depending on the application you choose to install. Odoo computes the dependency of the application and selects the list of dependent applications to install:

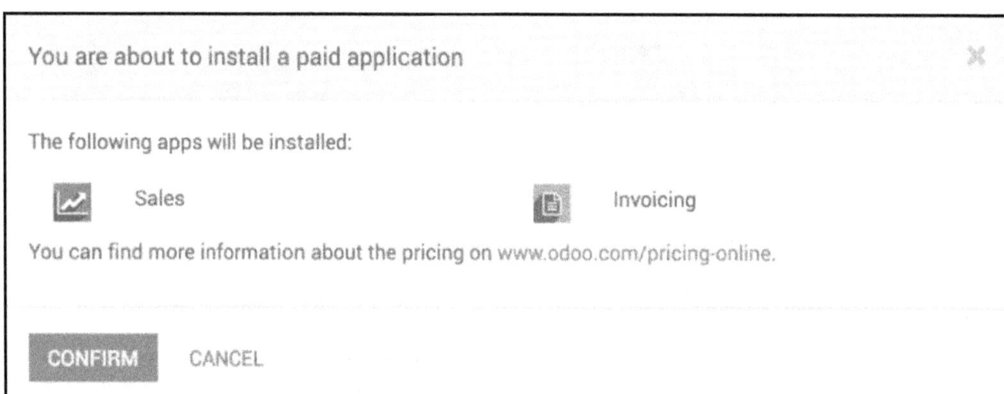

I chose to install the **Sales** application to manage my sales activity.

To enable the additional features for the **Sales** application, visit the **Settings** page from **Sales** | **Configuration** | **Settings**:

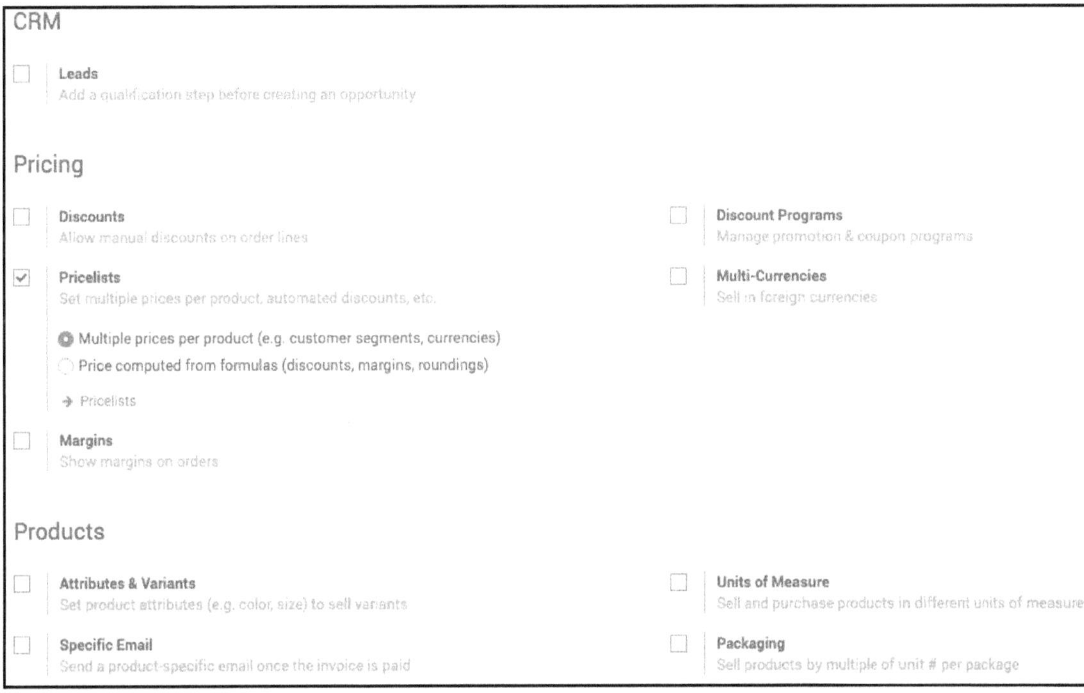

Choose the feature you would like to enable. I am going to enable the **Pricelists** options, as I would like to set **Multiple prices per product**. Select the options and click on the **Save** button.

> This operation may take some time depending on the features activated. Odoo may have to enable the features by applying the correct group of users or may need to install a new application.

4. The advance pricelist is activated; now you can set multiple prices for the same products depending on your customer segment. Go to the **Product** page, **Sales** | **Sales** | **Products**:

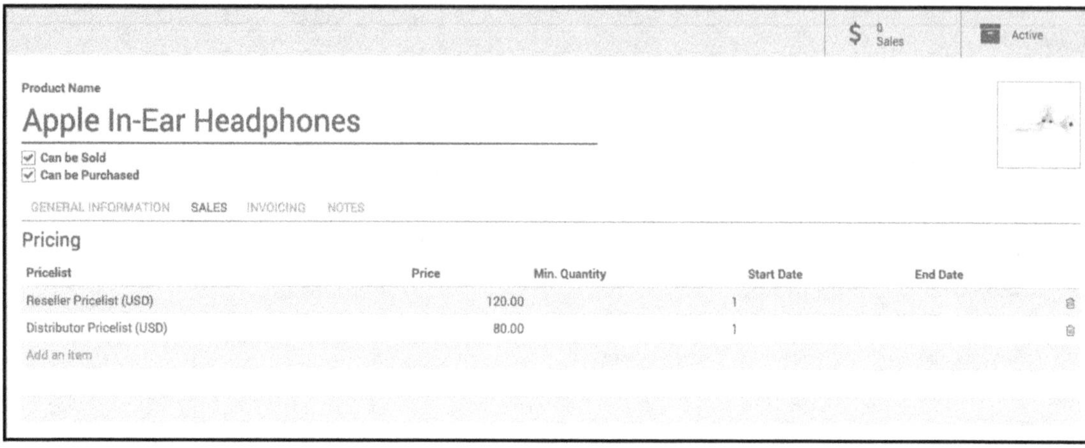

5. Click on the product you would like to change the price for. Click on the **EDIT** button, go to the **Sales** tab, and click on **Add an item** to add a new price policy. Look at the preceding screen. I have added two different prices for **Online customer** and **Regular customer**.

There's more...

Odoo as an application runs in different modes; the default mode is simple and usable for normal users to have a great user experience. Odoo runs in three different modes:

- **Normal user mode**: The default mode; most users are in this mode for production use.
- **Developer mode**: The name itself suggests something related to technical stuff. You can enter the complex configuration of the application and Odoo's internal system, as well.
- **Developer mode with assets**: In addition to the developer mode, this loads all the resources such as JavaScript, CSS files, and images separately, instead of loading them in a bundle. This mode may be slower than the other modes.

Entering the technical settings

There are many advanced technical settings and options not available in the default mode, however, these can be accessed from the advanced technical mode. To activate the advanced technical mode from the user interface, go to **Settings**and click on the link**Activate the developer mode**, available in the last box:

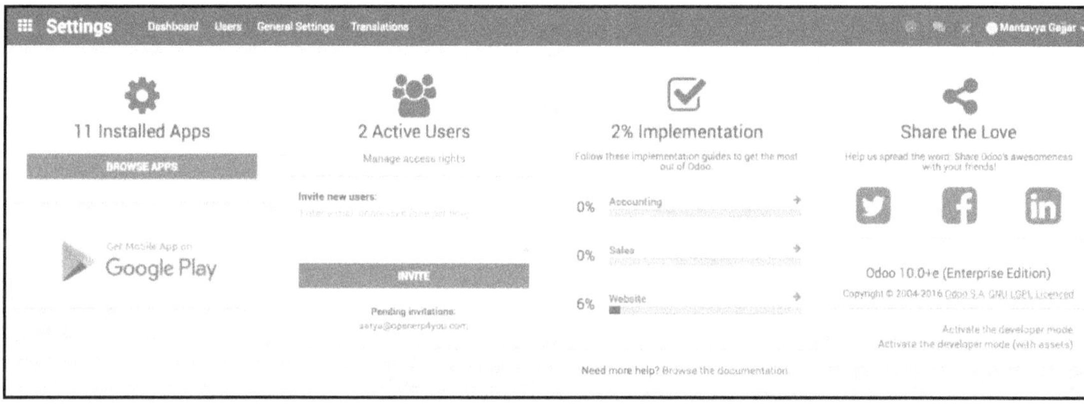

A page will be loaded and you have a new URL, as shown, in your browser:

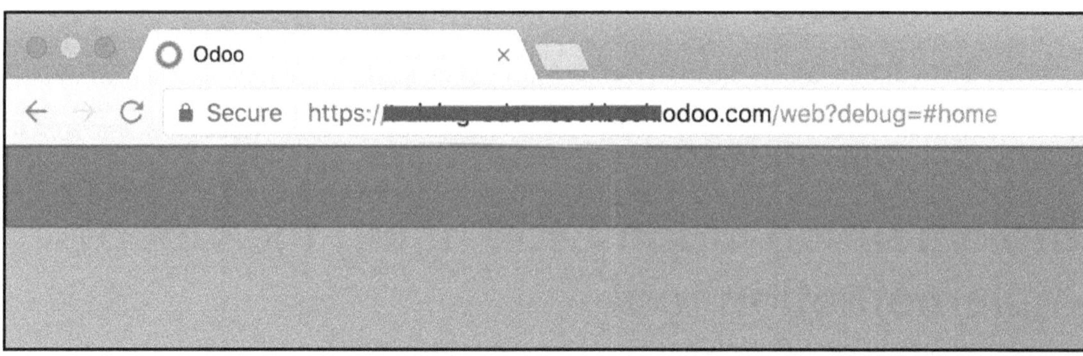

The advanced technical mode can be activated by entering the `debug` keyword in between the `?` and `#` characters in the URL, as shown in the preceding screenshot.

Once you enter into the advanced technical mode, you will be able to see the detailed configuration for the sales application. Look at the following screenshot for the configuration of **Sales** after entering into the advanced technical mode:

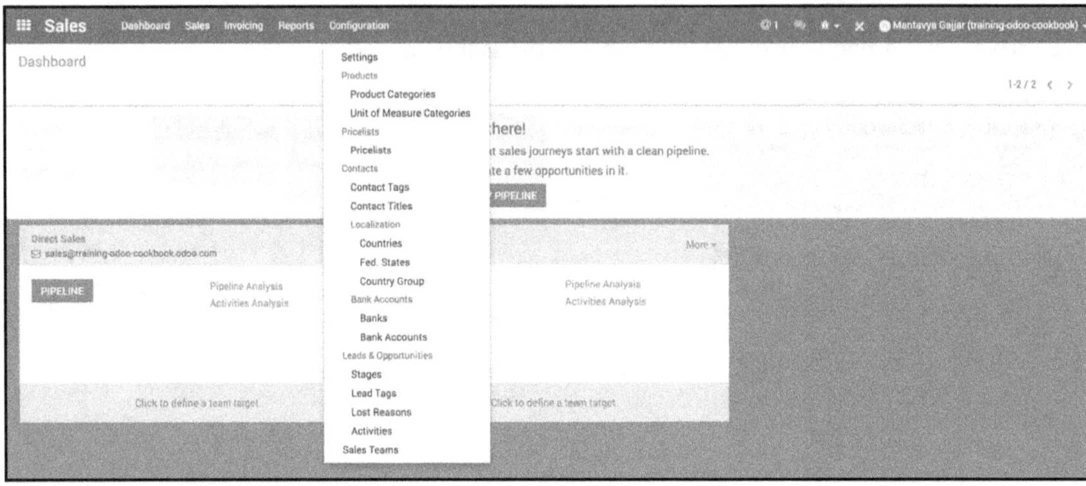

There's more...

- Uninstalling an application can be found in `Chapter 1`, *Getting Started with Odoo Online.*

Implementing Odoo CRM using the Odoo implementation tool

The Odoo implementation guide is a useful tool for small and medium scale companies who want to implement a business application by themselves. One can follow the steps and get the implementation done by themselves. You can implement Odoo by yourself without using the implementation service offered by Odoo.

The Sales Planner is a useful step-by-step guide created to help you implement your sales funnel and define your sales objectives easier.

We strongly recommend you go through every step of the tool the first time you use Odoo CRM and to follow the requirements. Your input is strictly personal and intended as a personal guide and mentor for your work. As it does not interact with the backend, you are free to adapt any detail whenever you feel it is needed.

Getting ready

It is assumed that you have created your online instance with Odoo CRM as your first application and activated your online instance. As it is advisable to make the duplicated database before making any changes for testing, once everything goes well, you can apply the same changes to the production instance. Make sure you are working on the duplicated instance.

How to do it...

1. An implementation tool can be accessed within the application on top, that implementation plan is for the current application only:

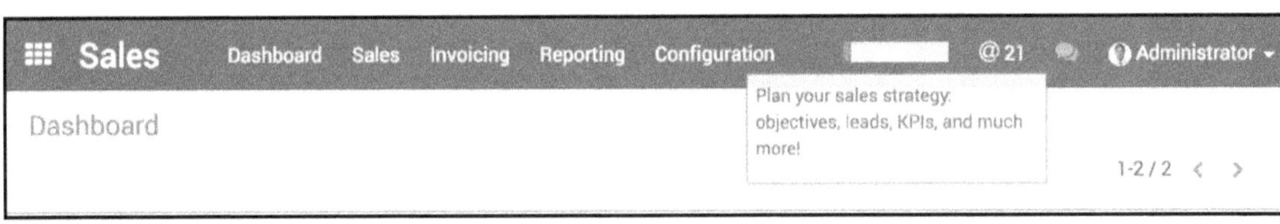

Implementation plans for all the applications can be accessed from **Settings**. Click on **Settings**. On the dashboard you can see the implementation progress for all the installed applications:

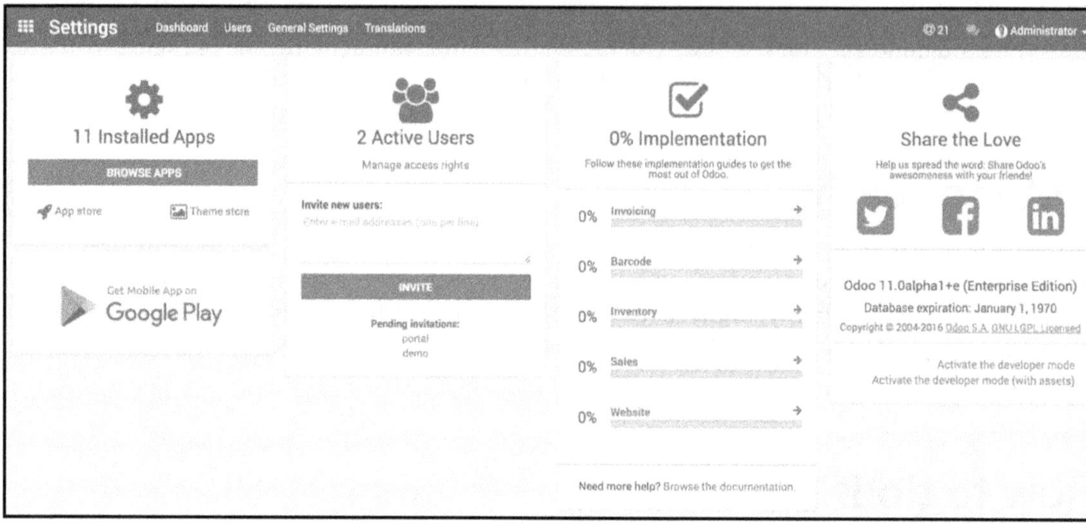

Here, you can see the status of the implementation plan for all the applications installed in your instance.

2. Click on the **Sales** application to enter the implementation plan for the sales implementation. The first screen you can see is a welcome message from Fabien Pinckaers, Founder:

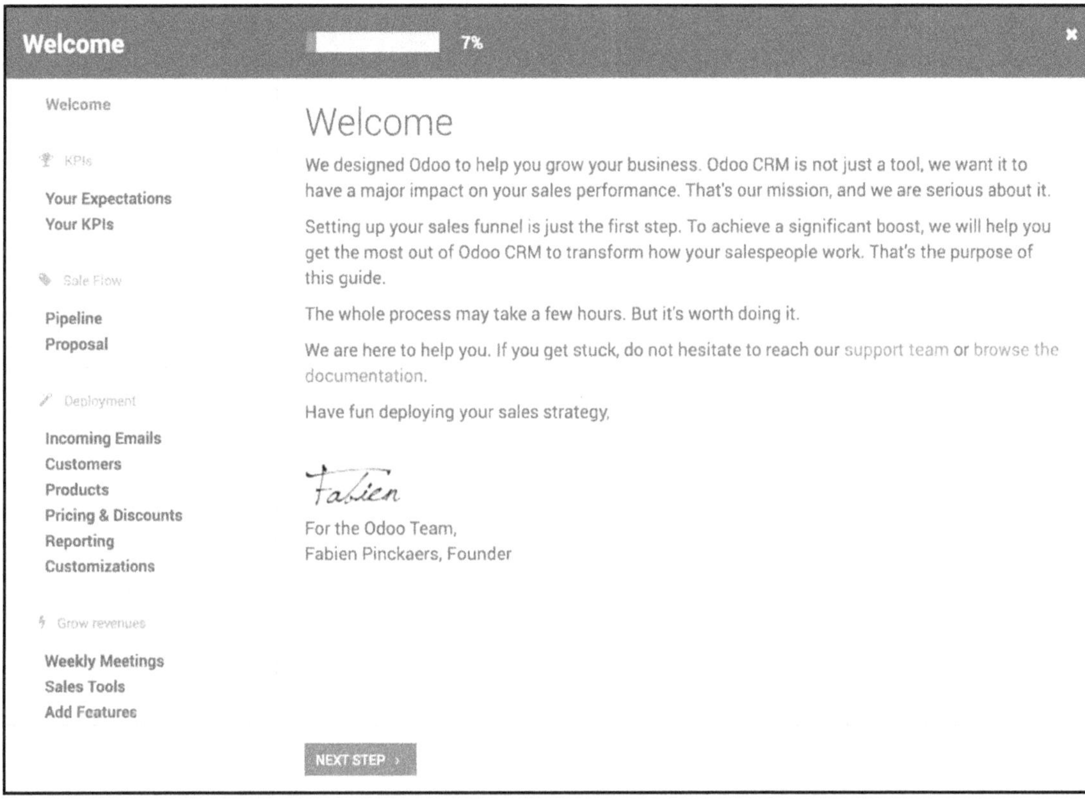

3. Click on **NEXT STEP** to start the implementation process. This wizard will answer all your questions related to the implementation of the Odoo CRM application:

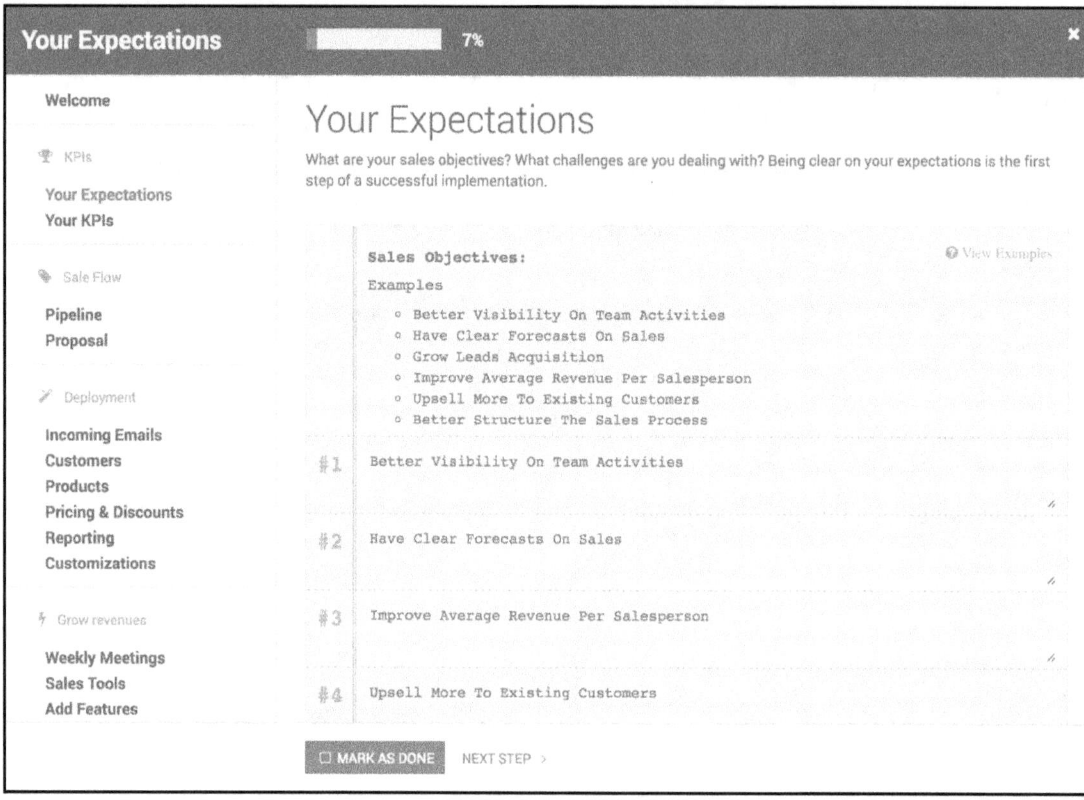

In this step, you have to define your sales objectives. What challenges are you dealing with? Being clear on your expectations is the first step of a successful implementation. Click on **View Examples** to see standard sales objectives.

Once you define the sales objectives, click on **MARK AS DONE** to set this step as completed. Clicking on **MARK AS DONE** will change the overall progress of the sale implementation. At the end of the deployment process, your expectations should be reached. If not, our CRM experts are available to help you achieve your KPIs.

4. Click on **NEXT STEP** to move forward and define, what the main KPIs you need to track for your sales activities are. Click on **View Examples** to see some of the standard KPIs that every sales manager wants to achieve:

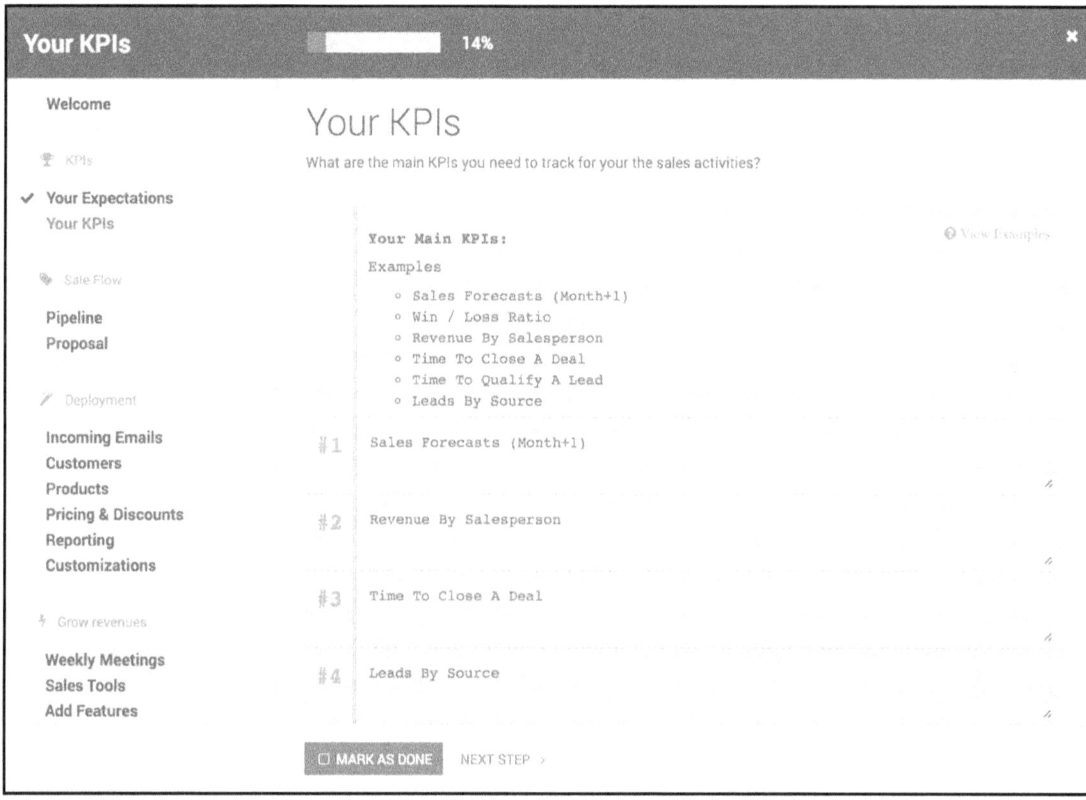

5. Click on **MARK AS DONE** once you define the KPIs you want to track in the system. Changes applied to this wizard will not change anything in the system, these changes are recorded for information purposes.

6. Click on **NEXT STEP** to move forward and define how you would like to streamline your sales pipe. You can choose some of the best sales pipes or you can create your own sales pipe:
   - A good pipeline should have between 5 and 7 stages
   - The first stage is usually **New** and the last one is **Won**

- Don't use stages to qualify opportunities, use tags instead
- Every stage should be a step forward in the buyer's decision-making, not a task to carry out

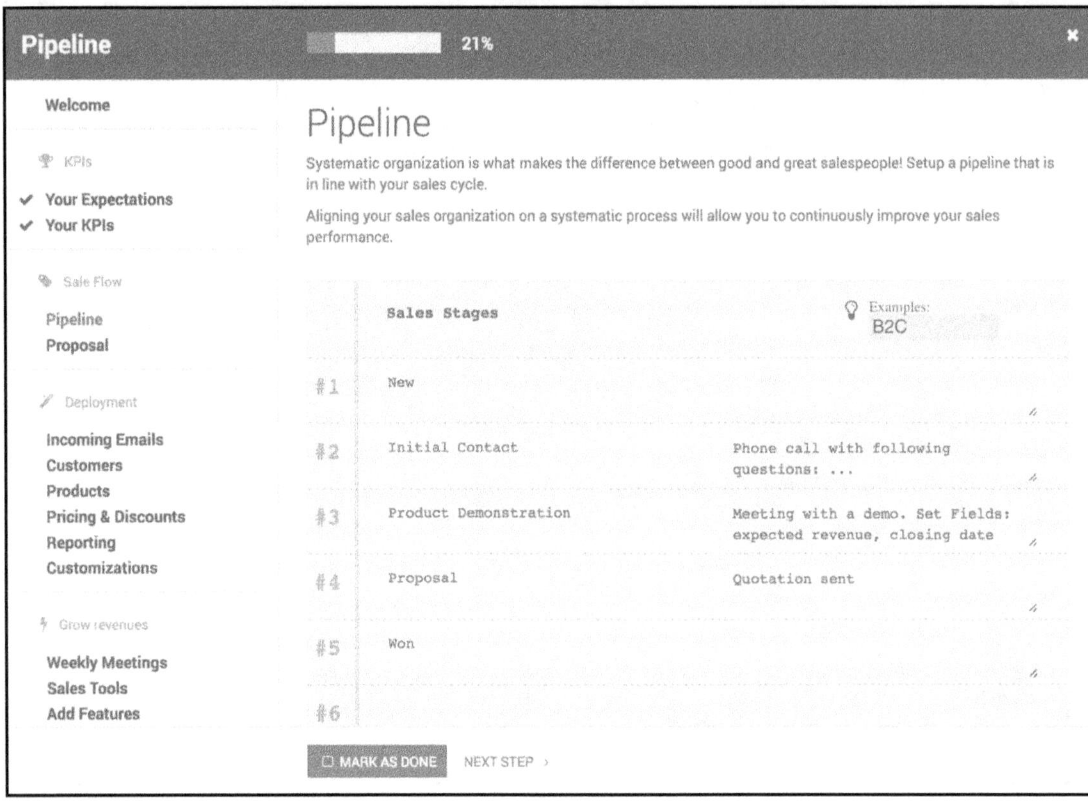

Great pipelines have stages aligned with the buyer's buying process, not your selling process:

	Example: Qualified stage		Example: Negotiation stage
👍	**The customer** understood his pain points and proposed the next step in the buying process	👍	**The prospect** started to discuss your offer
👎	**You** understand the customer's needs and pain points, and you have a fairly good idea of his budget to spend	👎	**You** called the prospect for a follow up on your offer

Follow the recommended actions available in this step. Go to your sales pipe and create the sales stages for your sales team.

> Using the sales planner, we can implement the CRM application. This is an excellent tool that can be used as training tools to train the new members in the team as it has clearly defined the KPI's and Goals we want to achieve from the sales team.

7. Click on **NEXT STEP** to move forward and choose what kind of proposals you usually send to your customers. Depending on your customer target and the products you are offering them, you should choose a proposal method and install the module accordingly:

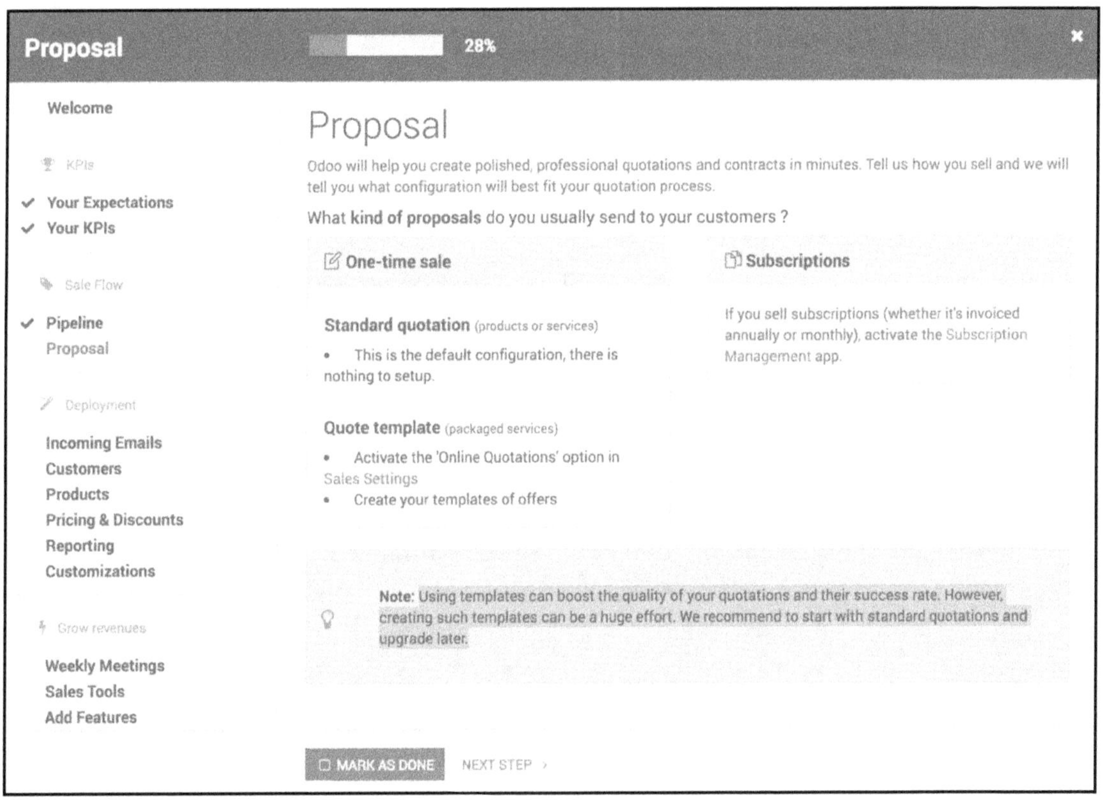

Subscription will be the best choice if you are selling a website hosting service, where you need to manage the website hosting subscriptions for the customers and generate recurring bills every year.

When you do one-time sales, you can use the standard quotation or quotation template when you sell packaged products, including product and service.

> Using templates can boost the quality of your quotations and their success rates. However, creating such templates can be a huge effort. We recommend starting with standard quotations and upgrading later to a quotation template.

8. The next step is to set up what you want to create in the CRM when you receive emails at your single point of contact. The default single point of contact is `info@yourcompany.odoo.com`, by default, it will create an opportunity in CRM:

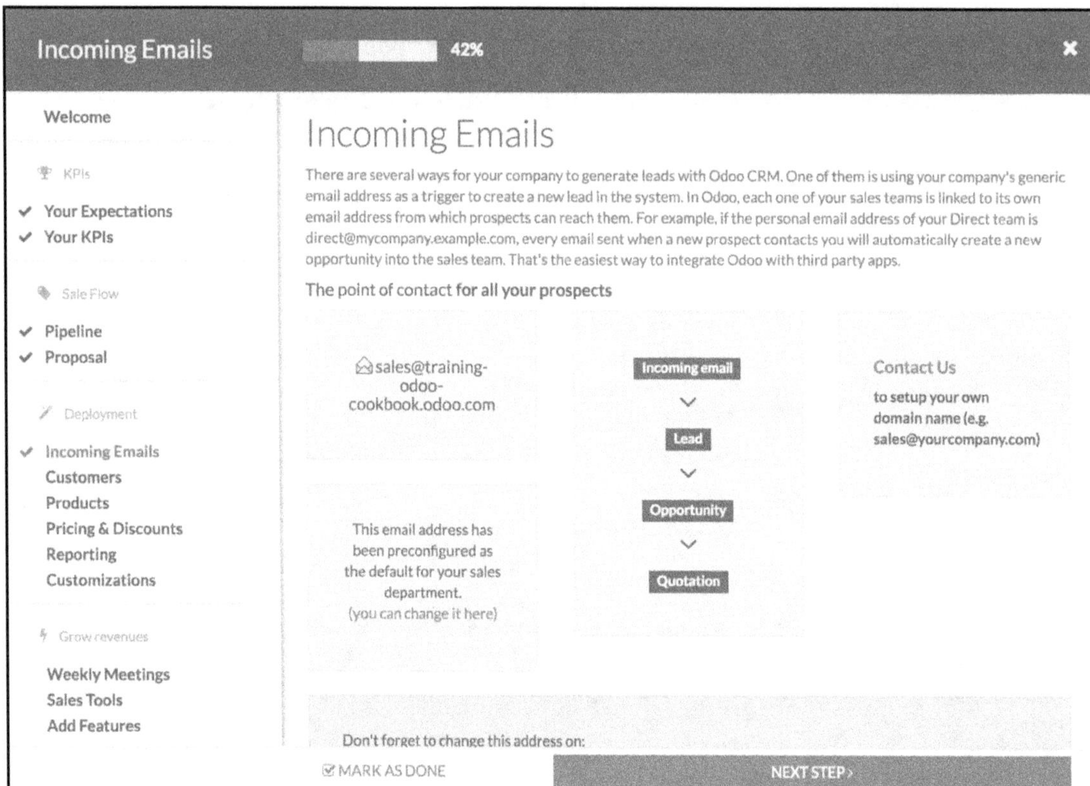

What you are supposed to change here is your single point of contact address that triggers the creation of opportunity or leads in the system.

The second thing you are asked to configure is whether you need a lead passed through the qualification process and converted to opportunity for the sales team to start working on.

> Create a lead, when you receive many emails per day, you can activate an automated qualification process to convert them to opportunity else keep as it is to generate the opportunity for the sales team to directly start working on.

9. Moving forward, click on **NEXT STEP** to add products and customers to CRM. Unless you are starting a new business, you probably have a list of products, customers, and vendors you'd like to import. It is recommended to use the templates for customers, vendors, and product to import them with a single click:

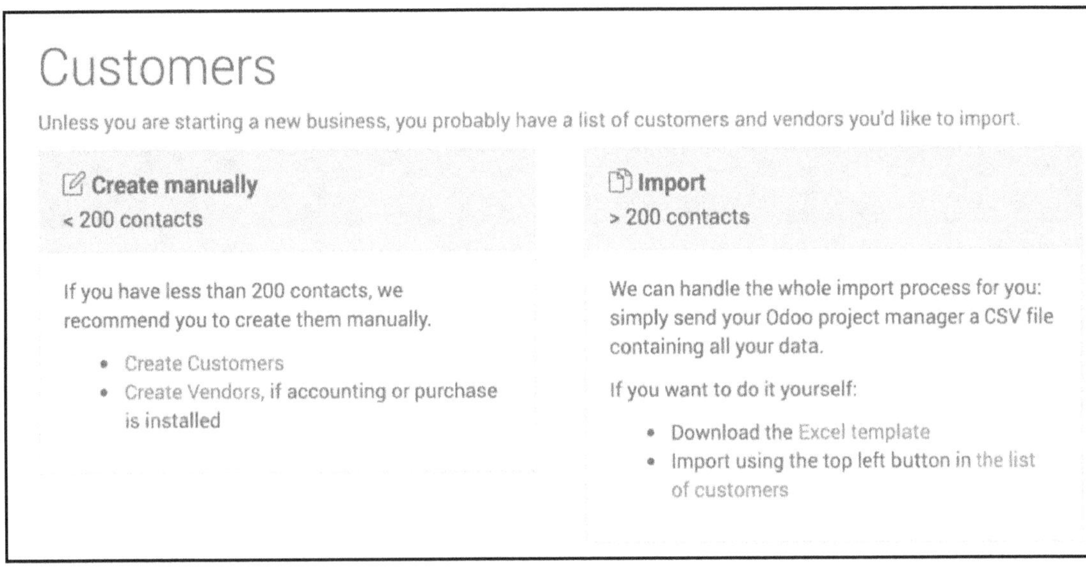

Download the template to import customers and vendors from this step.

Fill in your customers, vendors, and products in the downloaded templates. To import customers and vendors, go to **Sales** | **Sales** | **Customer**, to import products go to **Sales** | **Sales** | **Products**, click on the **Import** button and load the files you have created with the template.

The import/export feature is activated by default on the online platform, if it is not activated, go to**Settings** | **General Setting**, select**Allow users to import and export date from CSV/XLS/XLSX/ODS files**. When you are in a customer or product form, switch to list view mode to get the **Import** button.

For complex imports (>5000 items, product variants, pictures, and so on), use the Odoo API to import scripts, visit`https://www.odoo.com/documentation/9.0/api_integration.html`.

10. Moving forward to the most important configuration to define the pricing and discounts strategy for the products. In Odoo, there are three different ways to manage your prices as follows:
    - **Unique Price (default)**
    - **Specific Price per Audience**
    - **Rules & Formulas**

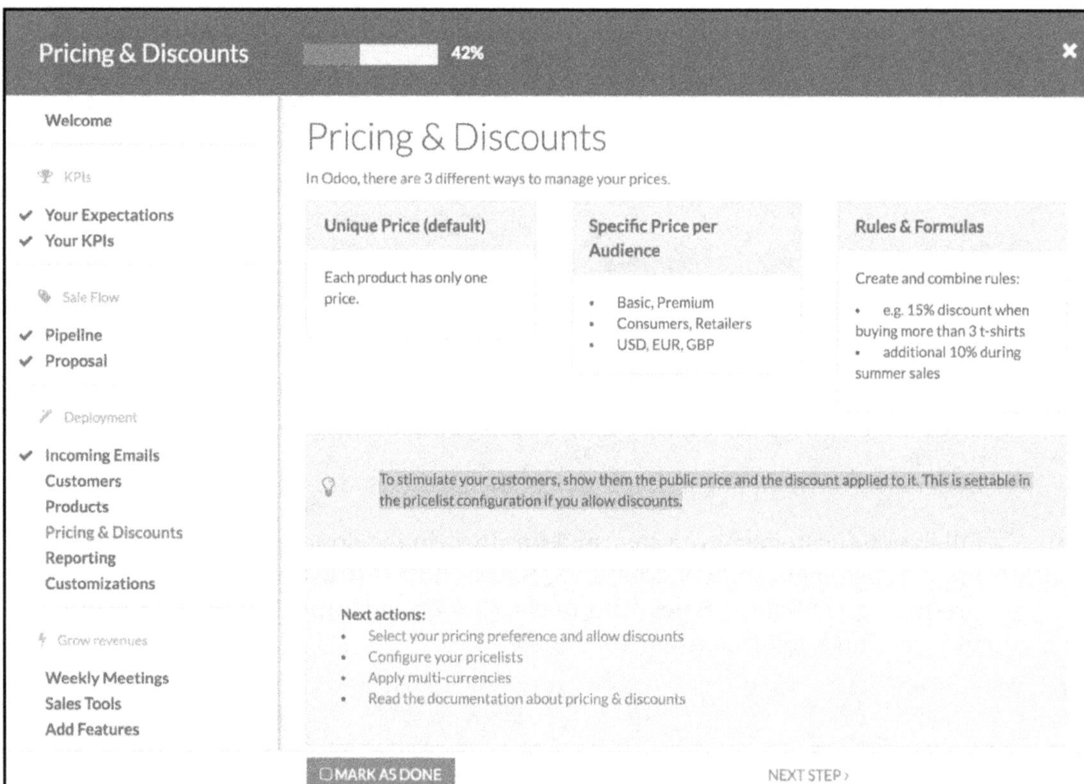

11. To configure the pricelist, go to **Sales** | **Configuration** | **Settings**, the most recommended option is to choose **Specific prices per customer segment, currency, etc**. You can define a price on a product for a customer segment, you can also have multiple currency pricelists too when you activate the multi-currency from **Settings** | **General Settings**.
12. The last step is to check the reports in order to track and validate the KPIs set up by you at the beginning of the implementation. Most of the reports are generated from**Sales** | **Reports** | **Pipeline**:

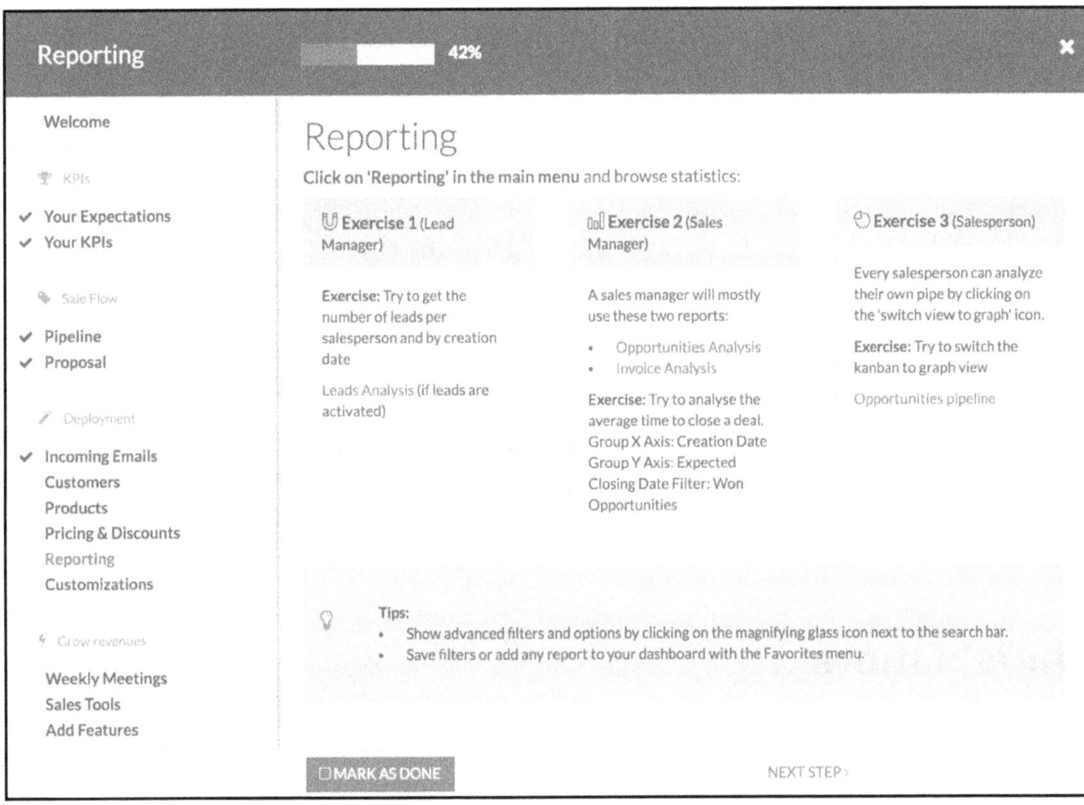

13. Follow the exercise to generate the sample reports and you'll quickly learn to generate the reports that are required to track your KPIs.

 You can generate the custom reports using advanced filters, and group by options. Once you generate the required reports, you can save them using **Favorites | Save current search**:

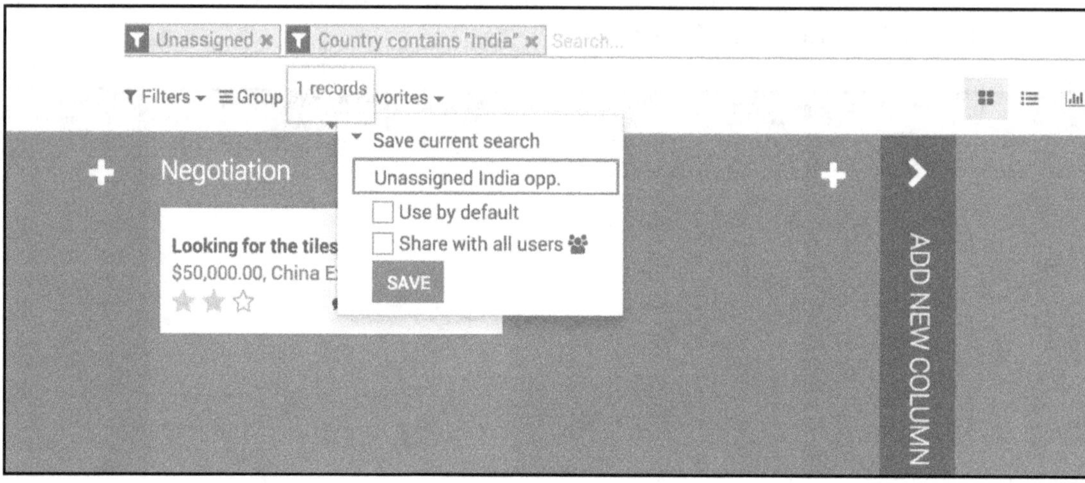

 If you are able to generate the reports for your KPIs to track, you succeed in the implementation of the Odoo CRM. If not, check the detailed process of working with sales pipe in the *Generate and qualify leads, convert to opportunity, and follow-ups*, recipe in `Chapter 3`, *Traceability - Marketing Campaign to Order and Cash.*

There's more...

Following an implementation tool step by step, follow the instructions, perform the required activities, and when you are done with the step, mark that as done. At the end, you will be notified of the successful completion of the implementation process:

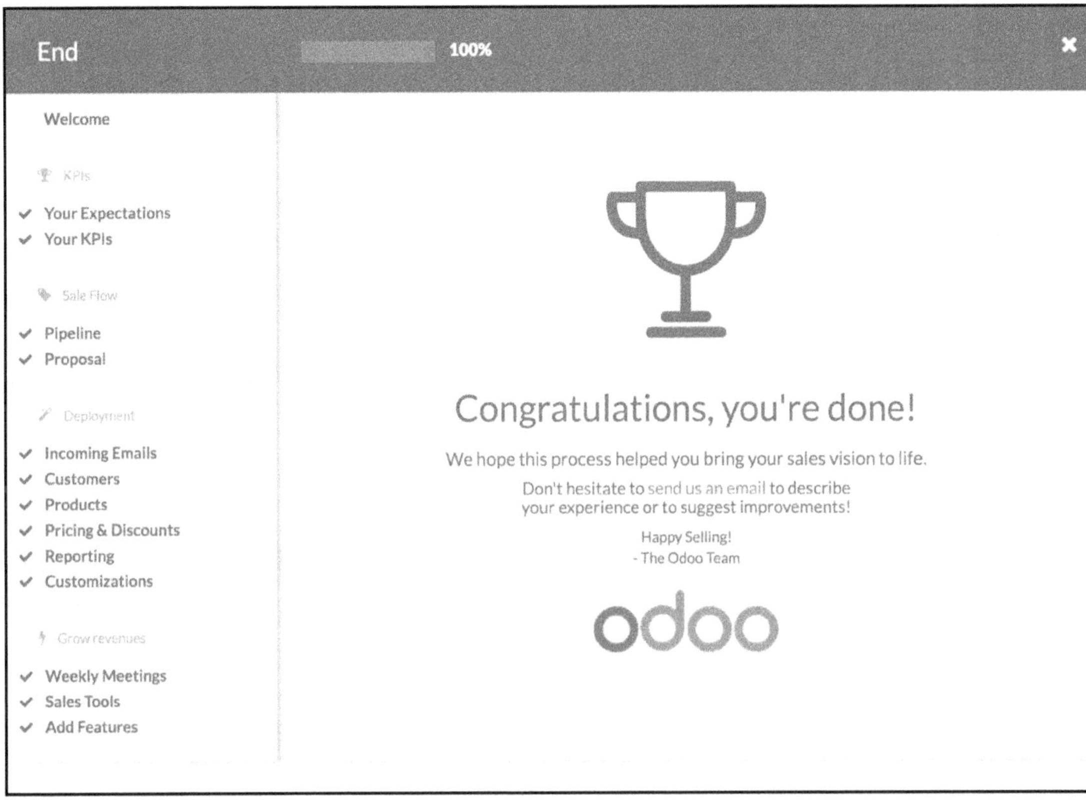

The end of a successful implementation of Odoo CRM.

> **TIP:** The best and recommended approach to implement any business application in Odoo is to follow the step by step implementation tool. Related users and teams can also use the same tool to get trained for the respective application by reading the KPIs section.

Adding more features

Odoo is the world's only software to have a full integration of **Marketing Apps** for your sales channel—insight sales, point of sale, and e-commerce. To boost your leads acquisition, you should have a look at the marketing apps:

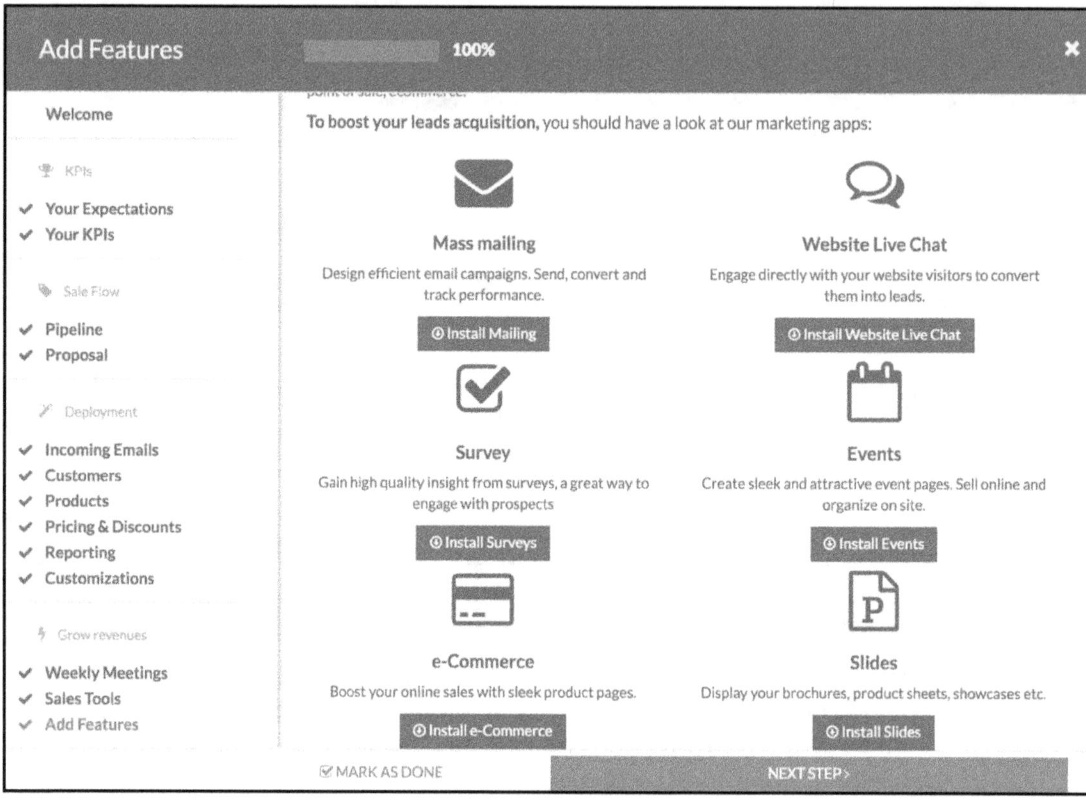

Customization using Odoo studio

Every business is different, you will find many features available as a standard in the Odoo, however, if any feature is missing or need changes such as missing fields, change views or reports, using Odoo studio it can be added. It is advisable to customize the screen and reports. You can do the customization yourself without writing a single line of source. The following recipe is about customization using Odoo studio.

Managing your implementation to-do list

In order to manage your implementation to-do list and collaborative implementation, it is suggested that you install the Odoo Notes application, which will help you track the changes done by your responsible team members:

This module allows you to manage your to-do lists and share it with your team to collaborate efficiently. Get acquainted with all the generic tools of Odoo: Messaging, Discussion Groups, Kanban Dashboard, and so on:

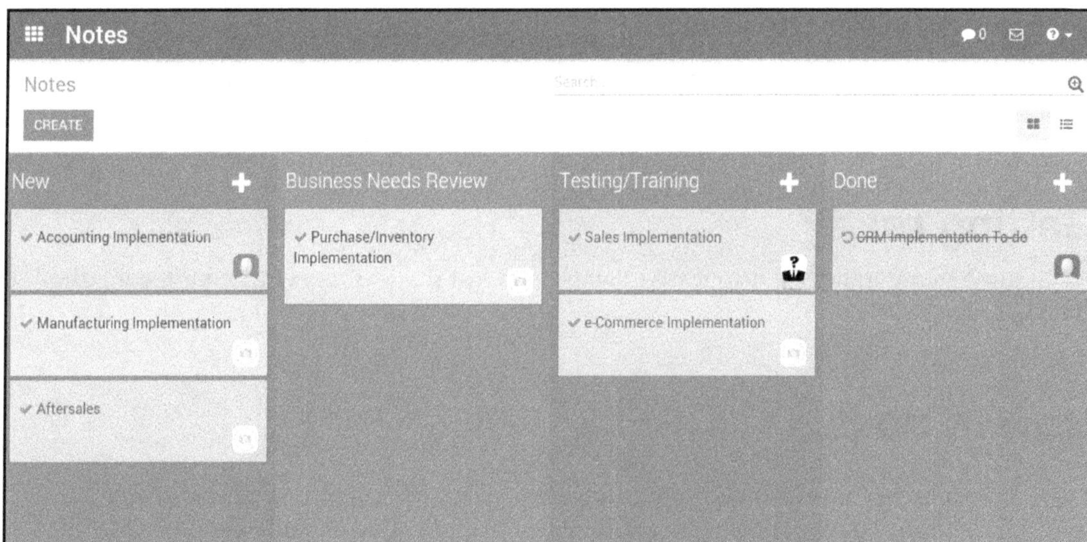

This application is even compatible with the Etherpad platform (`http://etherpad.org`). To use these collaborative pads rather than standard Odoo Notes, install the following add-on: **Memos Pad**.

Each time you plan to implement an application, it is better to plan with Odoo Notes, assign responsibility on each note, and post a message in the chatter to start the implementation process. This will help you to define the goals, track activity, and get up-to-date implementation statuses.

Installing Odoo studio and adding a new field to a view

Odoo Studio was recently launched along with Odoo version 10. You can customize screens and reports, add new fields to model, create an automated action or create a new business application from scratch without any development skills. You can design awesome reports and create some automated business workflows too using Odoo studio.

Customizations done in Odoo Studio can be exported as an Odoo module. Developers or consultants can use Odoo Studio to bootstrap new modules or to create a prototype model of the proposed application.

Let's see how it will be easy for the non-Odoo developers to apply the customization without development.

Getting ready

We assume that you have a duplicated database to test the features without affecting the master database.

How to do it...

1. Odoo Studio is a module like any other Odoo app. Go to **Apps** and search for studio. You will be able to see the Studio application as follows:

You can also click on the customization tool available beside the chatter. If studio is installed, you will enter customization mode, or it will ask you to install the Studio first:

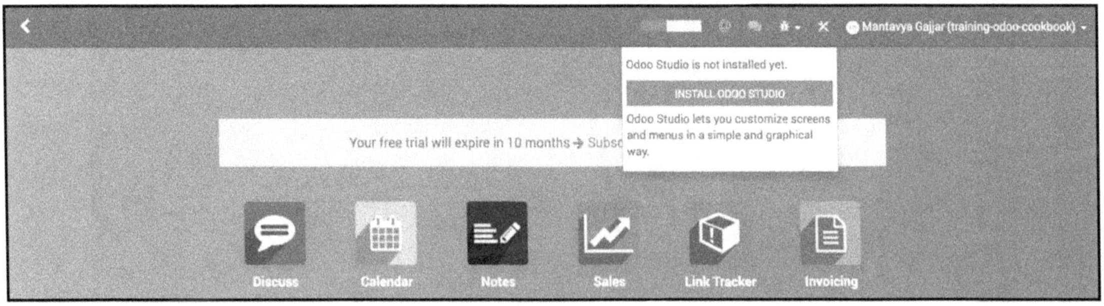

2. Click on the**Install** or **Install Odoo Studio** button to install the Studio app in your instance.

Installation of a studio application may incur additional charges to your Odoo online subscription. Only administrators are allowed to do modifications using the Studio application.

3. Studio mode can be activated from the customization tool icon. Click on theCustomizations tool icon and you will enter into studio mode, and by clicking on the **CLOSE** button you can exit the studio mode:

4. Click on **Notes** to create a pad on odoo.com, used to make a note of changes applied on this instance. You can create a short note about the customization applied on an instance for future reference:

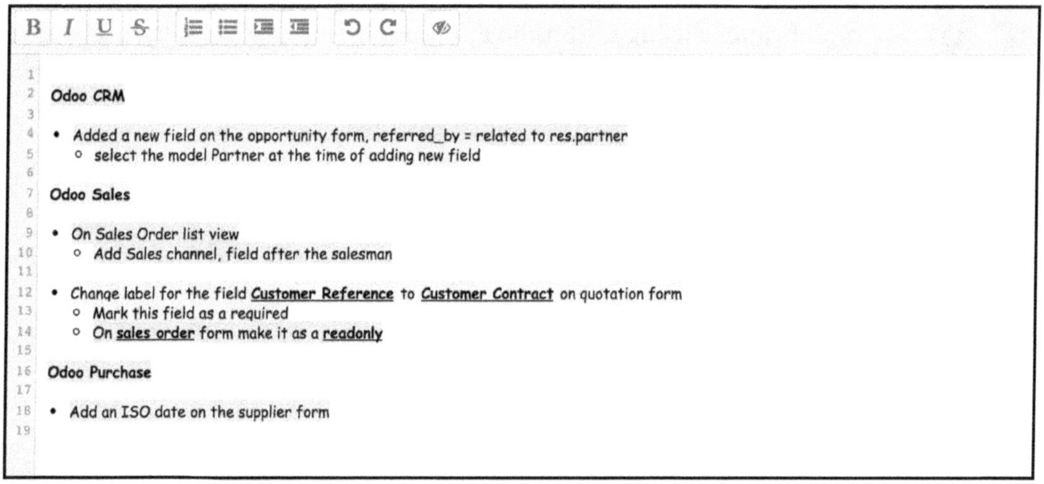

Odoo pad is hosted and maintained by Odoo, you can use a kind of tool that can be shared and writable among your team members.

The Odoo CRM application is already installed, let's add a new field with labeled **Referred By** on opportunity Form View with a linked contact details, that is, Name, Contact Number, Email, and Website, so on, this field will replace the existing field having just a text information. Click on **Sales** | **My Pipeline**. You will get the opportunity pipe, you will be redirected to the form view by clicking on any opportunity:

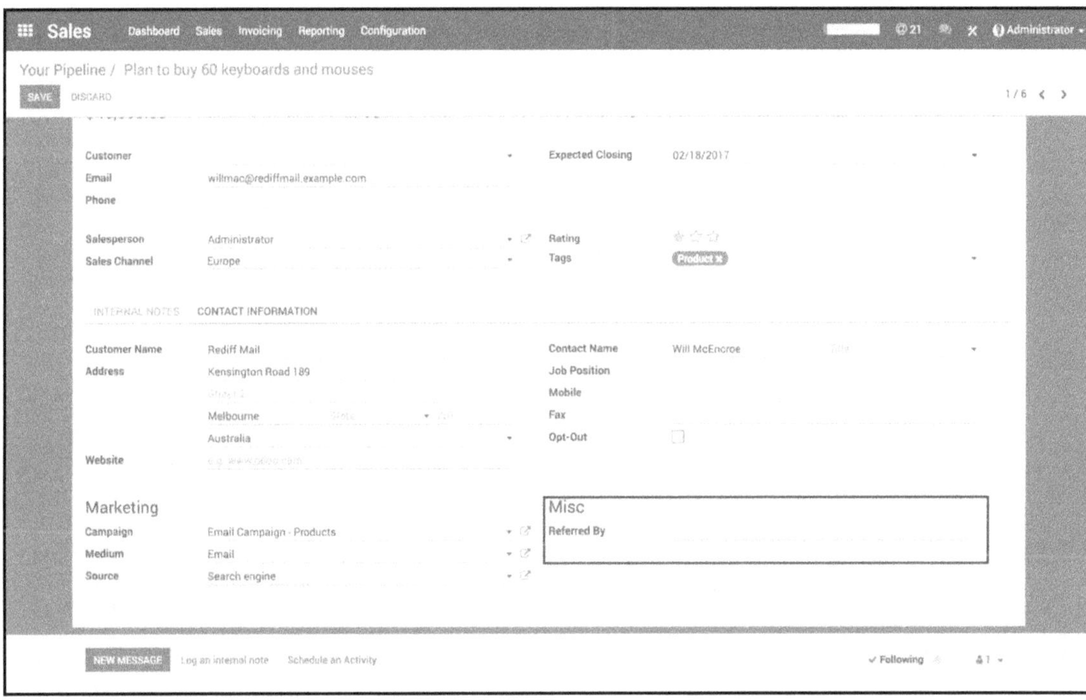

On the **Contact Information** tab, under the **Misc**. section, you will see the **Referred By** field, we will add a new field above this existing one.

To start customization, click on the customization icon and enter studio mode:

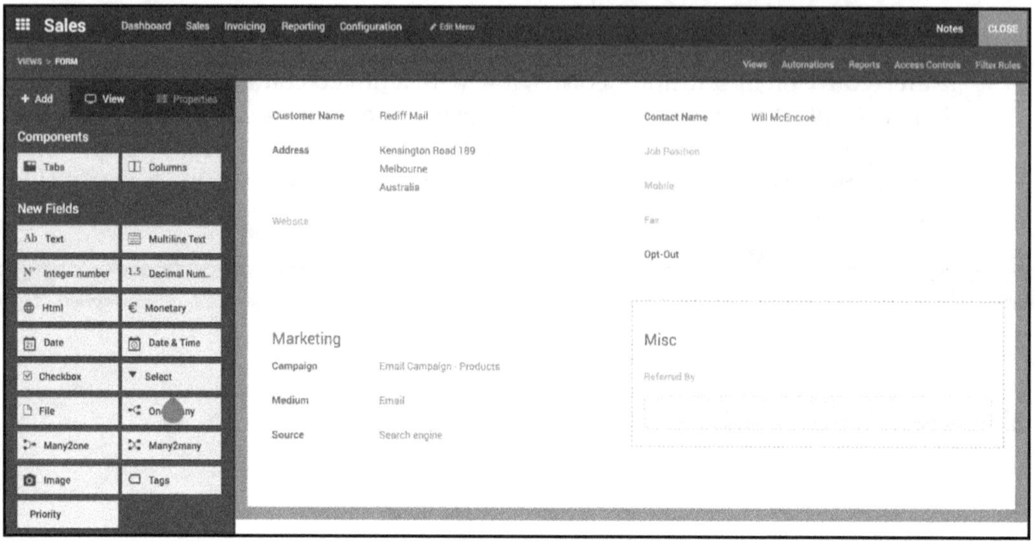

You will see a sidebar that has three tabs, **+Add**, **View**, and **Properties**. A list of field types available to create a new field are on the **+Add** tab.

Drag a field of type **Many2one** and drop it above the **Referred by** the existing field on the form. A pop-up will appear asking you to select the related model for this field:

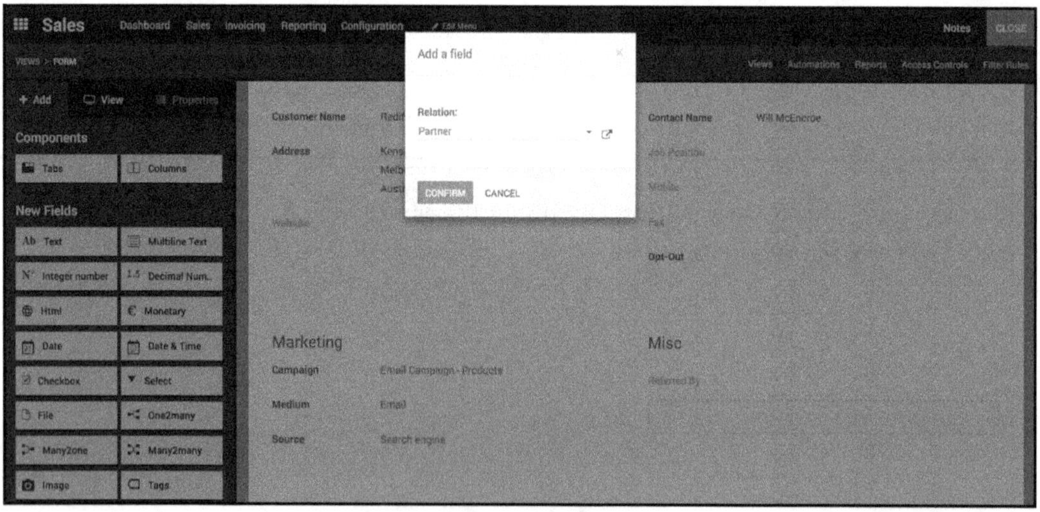

Select an existing model **Partner**, search for the technical name `res.partner`. You will see **Partner** as a result, select it and click on the**CONFIRM** button.

You have successfully added a new field to store a reference for the opportunity.

Some of the information, such as a label of the field might not be suitable. To change the label, select a field on the left panel, and the property tab will be activated. It has a list of properties that can be changed for a selected field. The properties are as follows:

- **Invisible**: You would like to have a field on the form view for reference, but not visible to end users.
- **Required**: User must enter the value in the field.
- **Read only**: Users are not allowed to change the value.
- **Label**: It is a label for the field. In our case, set it to **Referred By**.
- **Help tooltip**: It provides a help text that explains what the user should enter in the field.
- **Placeholder**: It is an alternative text for the field, applicable for text field only.
- **Widgets**: It is used to select how the field should look.
- **Default Value**: It sets the default value for the field.
- **Domain**: It is a technical setting that allows you to set the filter on field values.
- **Context**: It is a technical setting that allows you to pass the specific values to the server.
- **Limited visibility to group**: It is a field that is visible to the selected groups only. You can select multiple groups:

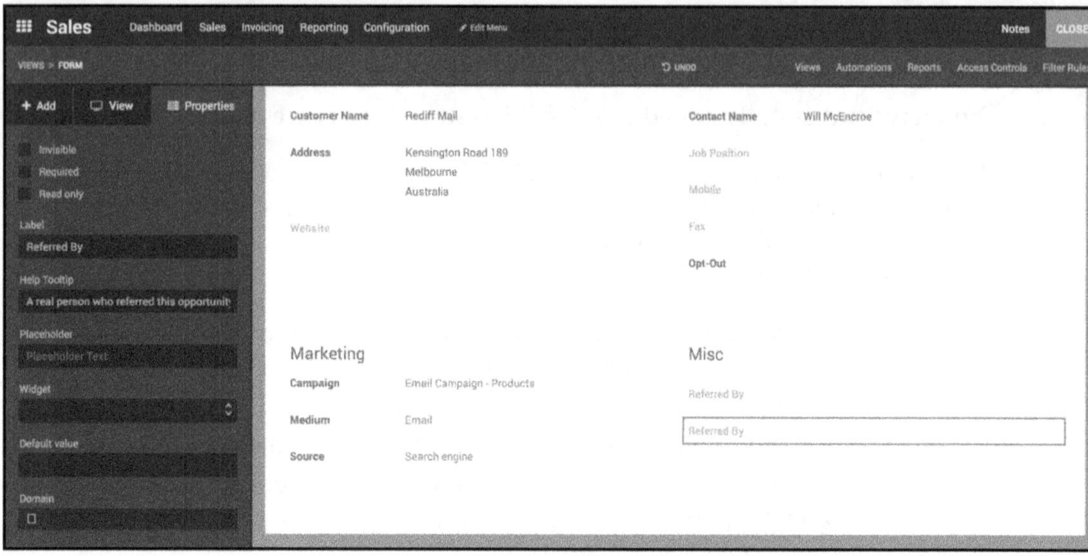

5. Change the label, **Help Tooltip** for the selected field. To exit studio mode, click on the **Close** button:

6. The Odoo Sales application is already installed, let's go to **Sales Channel**to add the **Sales** team field in the list view after the **Salesman** field. Drag the **Sales Channel (team_id)** field and drop it after the salesman field, and you are done:

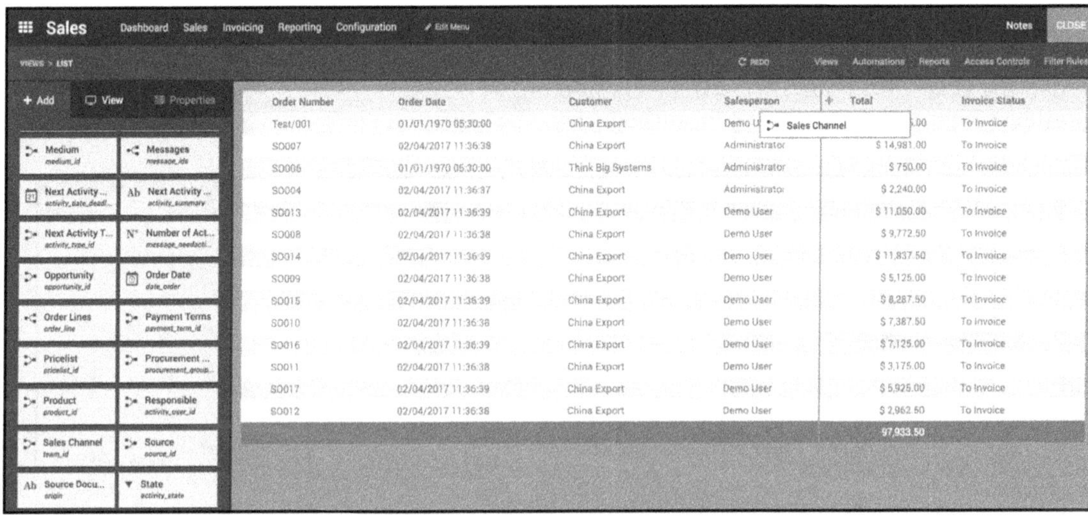

7. You have successfully added the **Sales Channel** field, click on the **CLOSE** button to exit studio mode.

There's more...

Odoo Studio is quite an impressive tool for non-developers, but sometimes, developers are impressed with this tool too. The developers can get an advantage to use the Odoo Studio, they can get the access to the Code Editor to write a Python code or XML views, they can write the complex stuff with the editor.

Debug mode

The developers sometimes want to debug the JavaScript in browser, by default, Odoo creates the asset bundles to pack web resources such as JavaScript and Cascading Style Sheets. When they are minified and packed into the bundle it will not be easy to debug them into the browser.

The debug mode is dedicated to enter into the debugging of the assets, and getting access to the technical features and complex features. There are some complex features available on the view, but they are marked as **Technical Setting**, you have to enter into the debug mode to access those features.

The debug mode, also known as the **Developer** mode sometimes, it can be activated from the **Settings**. Enter into the **Settings** and clicking on **Activate the developer mode**, it will reload the page and your URL will be changed to `https://yourcompany.odoo.com/web?debug=#home`:

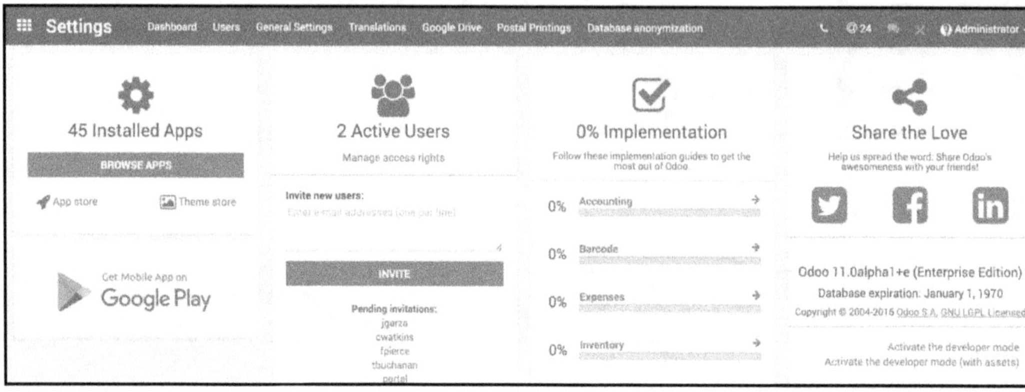

If it is too frequent for you to get access to the debug mode, the another simple way is to install the Google Chrome plugin, so every time you click on the debug icon in Chrome, you will automatically enter into the debug mode. To install the Odoo debug plugin, go to the Chrome apps store and search for Odoo, you will find approximately three apps. Install the Odoo Debug plugin:

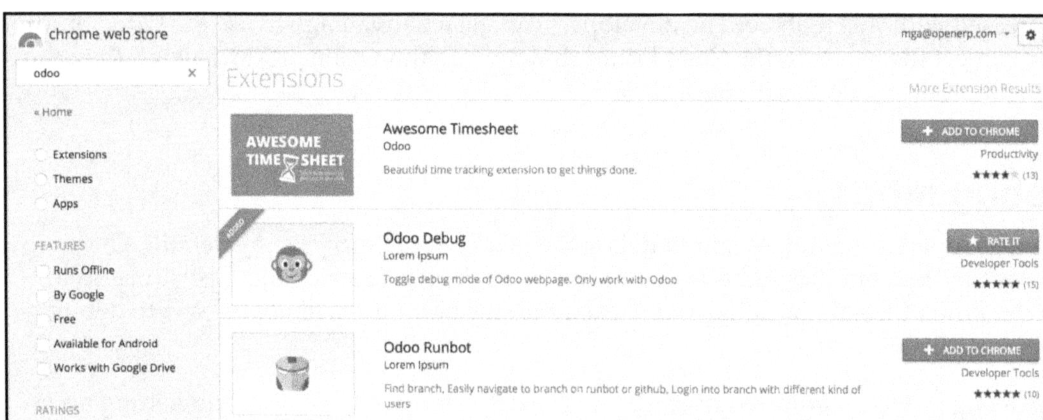

When you are on any page within the Odoo application, by clicking on the plugin, you can toggle the debug mode to access the technical feature. By double-clicking the plugin, you can enter debug mode with assets.

Creating a computed field

Technically, computed fields are the function fields that compute the values based on the value of other fields. You will be able to write the Python code to compute the value of the field at the time of creating a computed field using Odoo Studio.

> **TIP:** Make sure you are in debug mode before you enter studio mode, it will be easy for us to get the technical name of any field from the tooltips available on the field.

Let's take a simple example to add a balance field, that computes the difference of**Total Receivable** and **Total Payable** for customer.

Go to the customer's form view, enter into studio mode, drag and drop the **Monitory** field below the **Tags** fields, and change the label of the field to **Balance to Receive**:

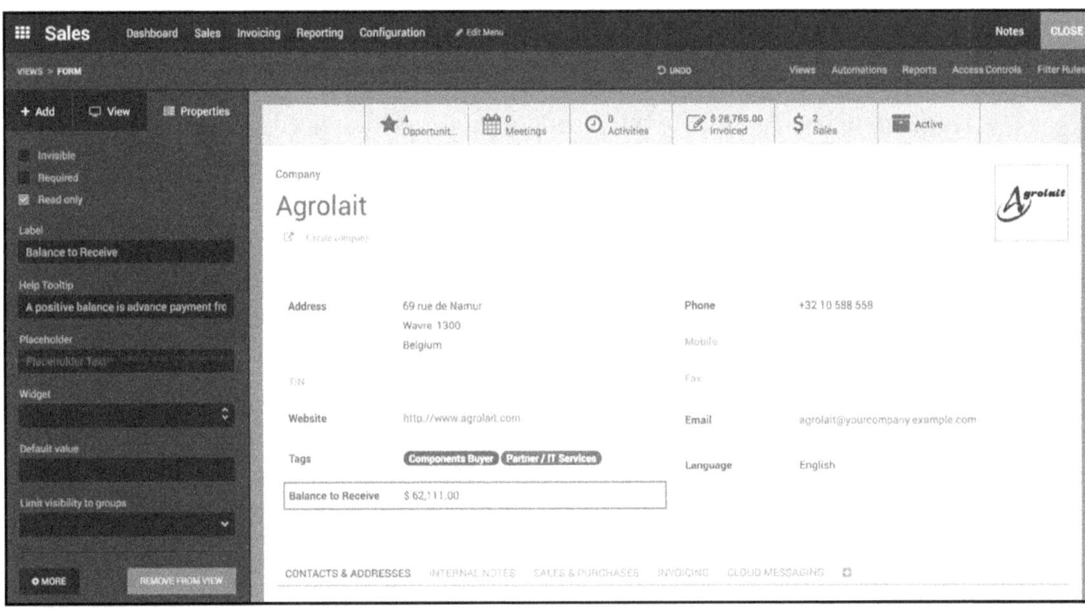

Enter `A positive balance is advance payment from the customer and negative balance is receivable form customer` in the **Help Tooltip** field to give a clear message to end-users.

To write the code to compute the balance, select field and on the left panel, click on **More**. You will be recited to the details of the field, as shown in the following screenshot:

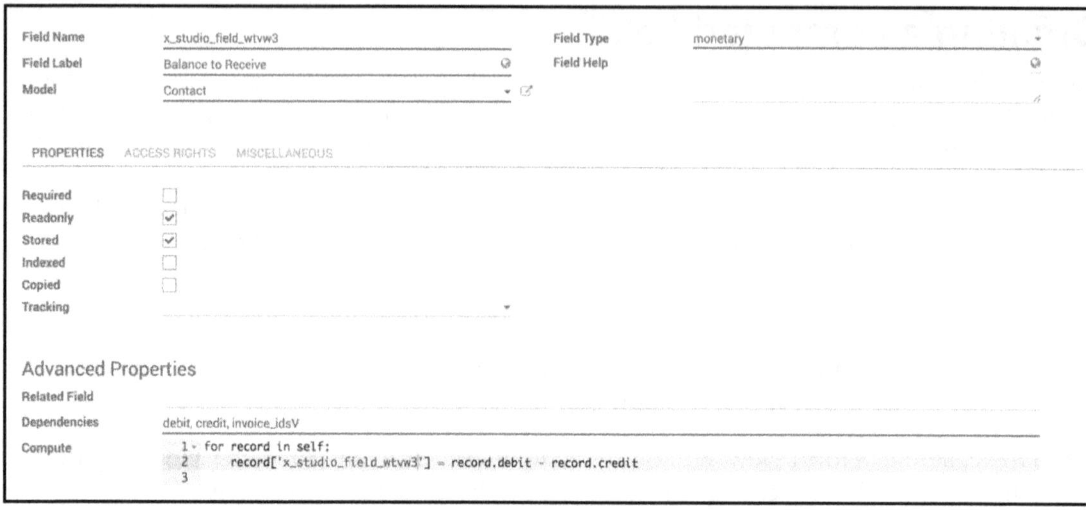

There are three important fields that you have to configure as follows:

- **Stored**: If it is set to **False**, by default it is set to **True**
- **Dependencies**: To execute the compute process Odoo needs either a field or list of fields comma separated, when the value of those fields changes, the compute methods triggers on that record
- **Compute**: We can write the Python code that will be executed to compute the value of the field

In our case, the value of the **dependency** fields will be `debit`, `credit`, and `invoice_ids`. Write the following code in the `compute` method:

```
for record in self:
record['x_studio_field_wtvw3'] = record.debit - record.credit
```

Once you are done with the configuration, create some customer and vendor bills for the same customer. The balance will be computed automatically; a small piece of code generates this big feature in Odoo.

Organizing the menu structure

Let's assume that your salesman wants quick access to the **Quotation** menu from the **Sales** menu. You can organize a menu hierarchy using Odoo Studio. Click on the **Sales** application, enter studio mode, and you will have an **Edit Menu** button on the top, besides the configuration menu.

Click on the **Edit Menu** button and a popup will appear that has the menu structure of the **Sales** application:

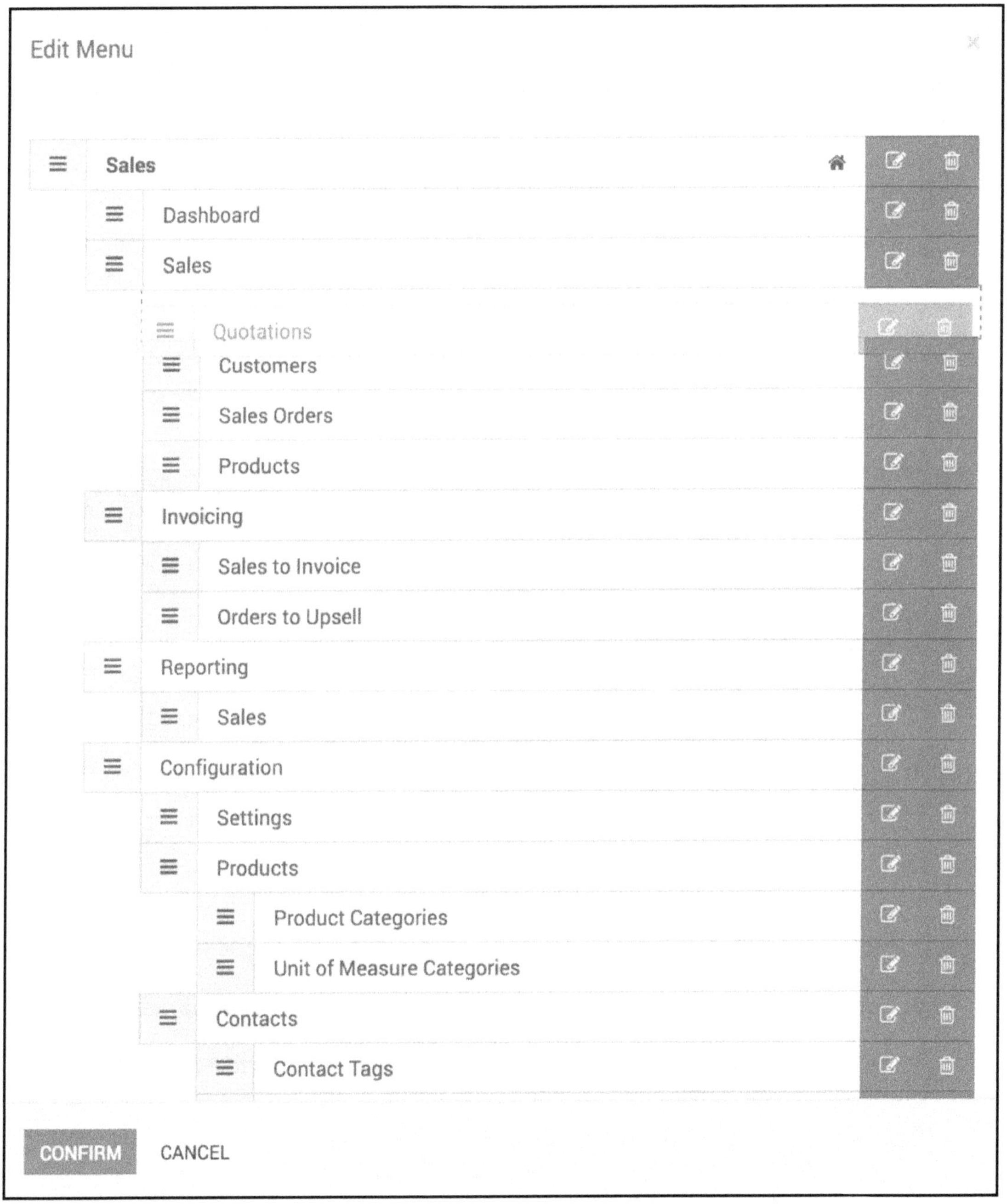

You can drag and drop the menus to organize the order. You can see in the preceding image, I have dragged **Quotation** from its position, and I'm about to drop it just below **Sales**. The indentation of the menu is important to define the parent-child relation of the menus.

Gaining access to the code editor

For the non-developer, it is quite difficult to understand the code written behind Odoo. For developers, gaining access to the editor would be quite impressive.

Let's do an example based on the previous one. The **Balance to Receive** fields should be visible only if someone is set to customer and vendor, or else hide the field. Enter debug mode before you enable studio mode.

Go to the customer form, enter studio mode, click on the view on the left panel, and at the bottom, you will see the **XML** button. By clicking on that field, you will have access to the code editor:

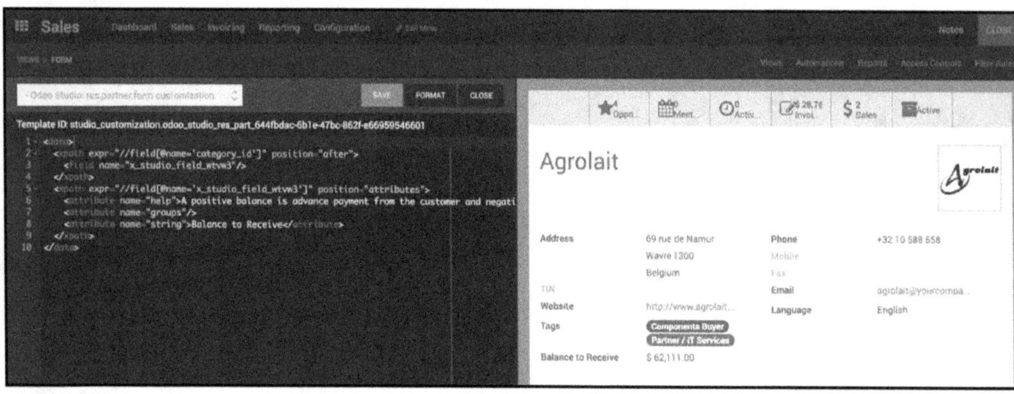

Select the correct view from the drop-down box to the left of the **SAVE** button, the name should be `Odoo Studio : res.parner.form customization`:

Add a new attribute for the field. The only way to understand the correct field is by the label. Add the following small piece of code below the label attribute:

```
<attribute name="attrs">{'invisible': ['|',
 ('customer','=',False), ('supplier','=',False)]}  </attribute>
```

> **TIP:** To get the name of the field used in the expression, move your mouse over that field and a tooltip will give you all the technical details about that field.

Make sure your code looks as follows after applying the changes:

```
<data>
  <xpath expr="//field[@name='category_id']" position="after">
    <field name="x_studio_field_wtvw3"/>
  </xpath>
  <xpath expr="//field[@name='x_studio_field_wtvw3']" position="attributes">
    <attribute name="help">A positive balance is advance payment from the customer and negative balance is receivable form customer</attribute>
    <attribute name="groups"/>
    <attribute name="string">Balance to Receive</attribute>
    <attribute name="attrs">{'invisible': ['|', ('customer','=',False), ('supplier','=',False)]}</attribute>
  </xpath>
</data>
```

Click on **Save** and **Close** to exit from the editor. Click **Close** in the upper-right to exit from the studio. The **Balance to Receive** will be visible only if **Is a Customer** and **Is a Supplier**fields are selected under **SALES & PURCHASE** tab.

Creating a new business application using Odoo Studio

The job of Odoo Studio does not end with adding new fields, or changing the views. Using Odoo Studio you can create a new application from scratch without being a developer. Using Odoo Studio you can create beautiful application, design awesome reports, customize advanced screens, automate business workflows, and the great things are everything you developed using studio is also accessible on Odoo mobile.

Getting ready

It is assumed that you have a clear specification for the new application you are going to develop. I am going to develop the module, **Odoo Academy** app, I have to create a course, a new model, for student and teacher, and I will use the existing model, **Partner** (**res.partner**).

TIP: The best approach to customization is to duplicate the database each time and implement the feature. Export the customization and import into the master.

How to do it...

1. Go to your instance home page, enter into studio mode by clicking on the customization icon, and you will get, as soon as you are into studio mode, a **+ New App** icon is visible at last:

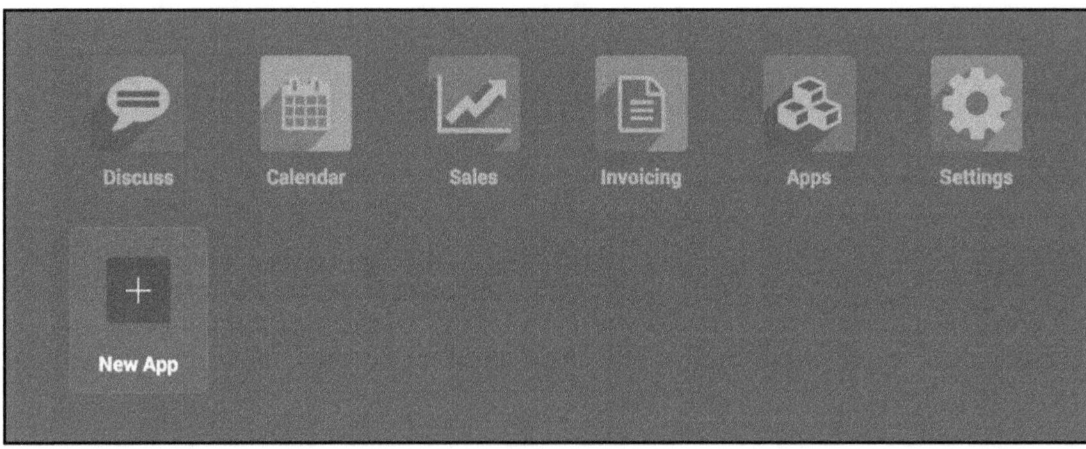

2. Click on the **New App** icon, you will jump into the new application wizard:

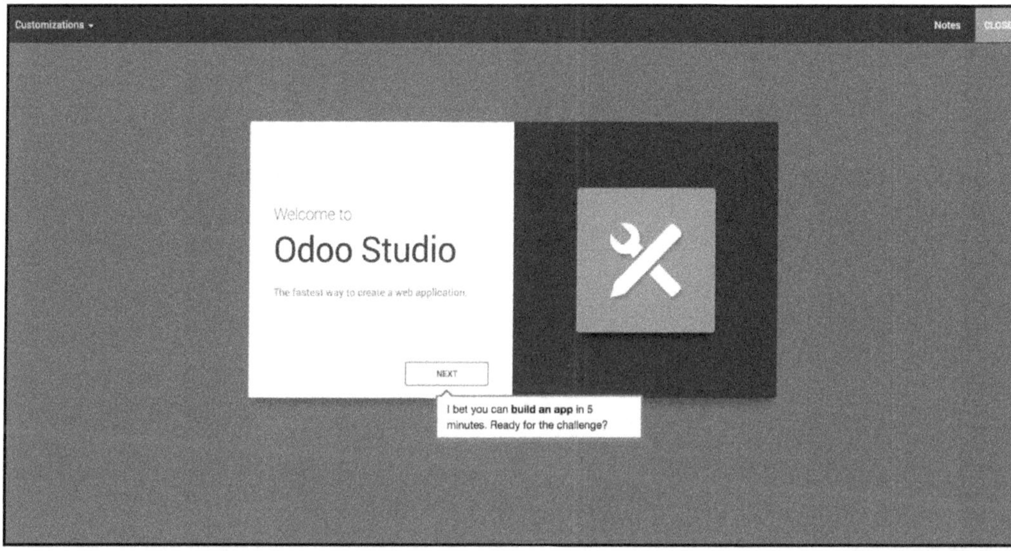

3. Click on **Next**, you have to create an icon for your app. Select the background color, frontend color, and icon. If you do not like the way Odoo allows you to create an icon, you can upload your custom icon instead:

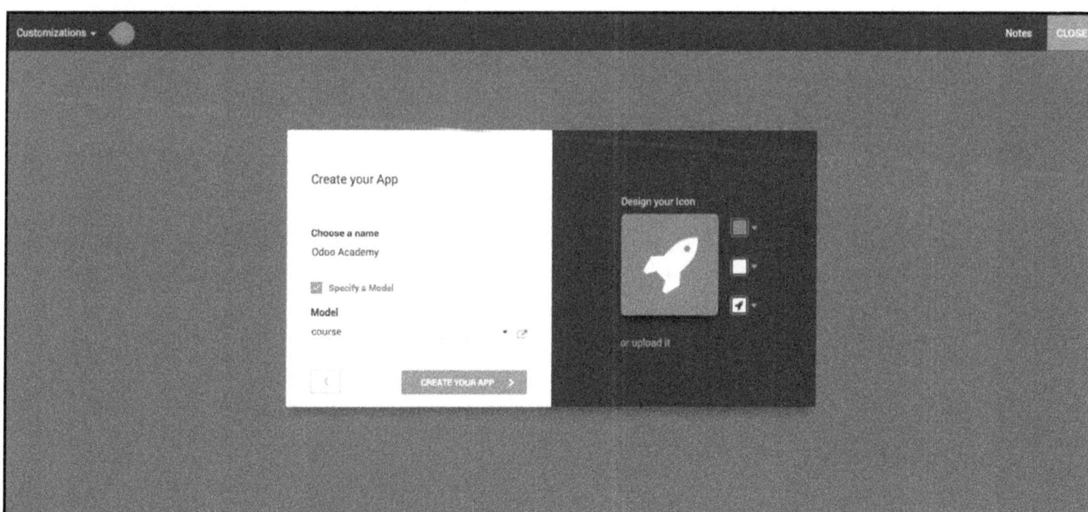

Select **Model**, you can select or create a new model here. I have to create a new mode course, write a course, and select **Create "course"**.

4. Finally, click on the **CREATE YOUR APP**button to create your application.

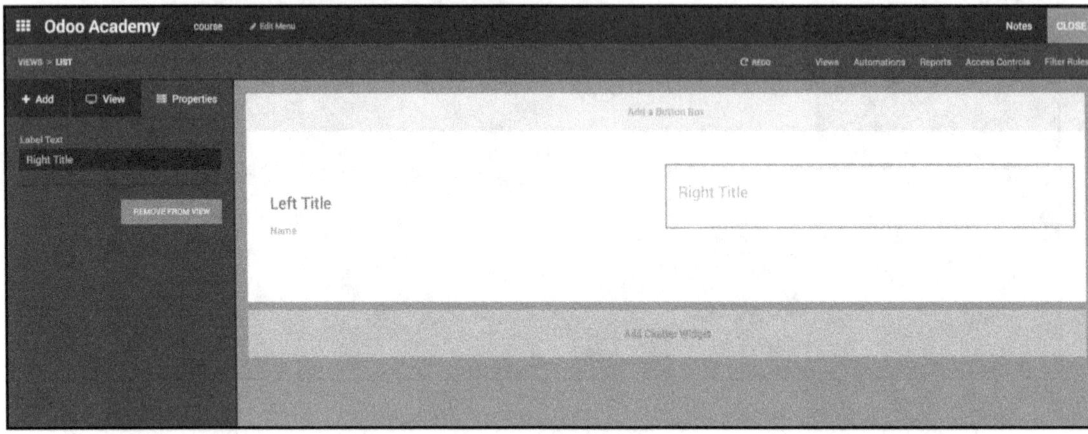

Your application is created and you will directly jump to the form view of your **Course** model. According to the standard Form view of Odoo the name field has to be on the top of the form and not inside the column components.

Select the **Name** field, drag and drop on the top of the form.

Select the **Right Title** section, remove the label from the left panel, and do the same for the **Left Title** section, keep only the name field which is added by default.

5. There are various types of fields and components that can be added on the Form view. They can be added from the **Add** tab visible on the left panel, drag the **Column** component and drop it below the name field:

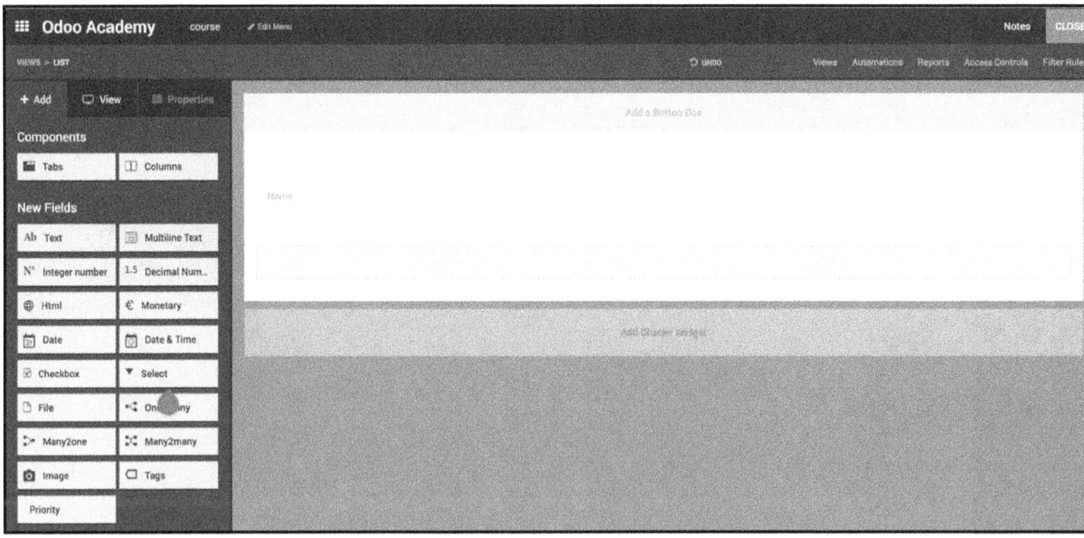

6. Select the **Left Title** section and change the label to **Trainer**, select the **Right Title** section and change it to **Information**. Drag a new **Many2one** field from the left panel and drop inside the **Trainer** section, a popup will appear asking you to select the related model. Enter `res.partner`, the technical name of the Partner model and select it. Select the field and change the label to **Trainer**:

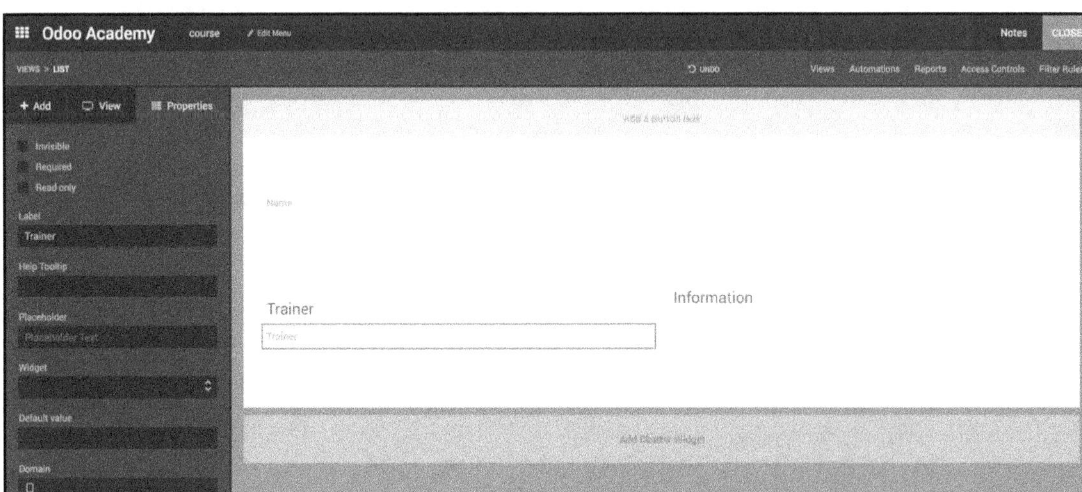

7. On the right **Information** panel, add a **Quarter** field. Drag and drop the field from the right panel to add the **Created on** field and drag the **Created on** field from the existing fields.
8. Click on the **Add chatter** widget, to add a chatter widget to the course mode so that you can track communication for the course:

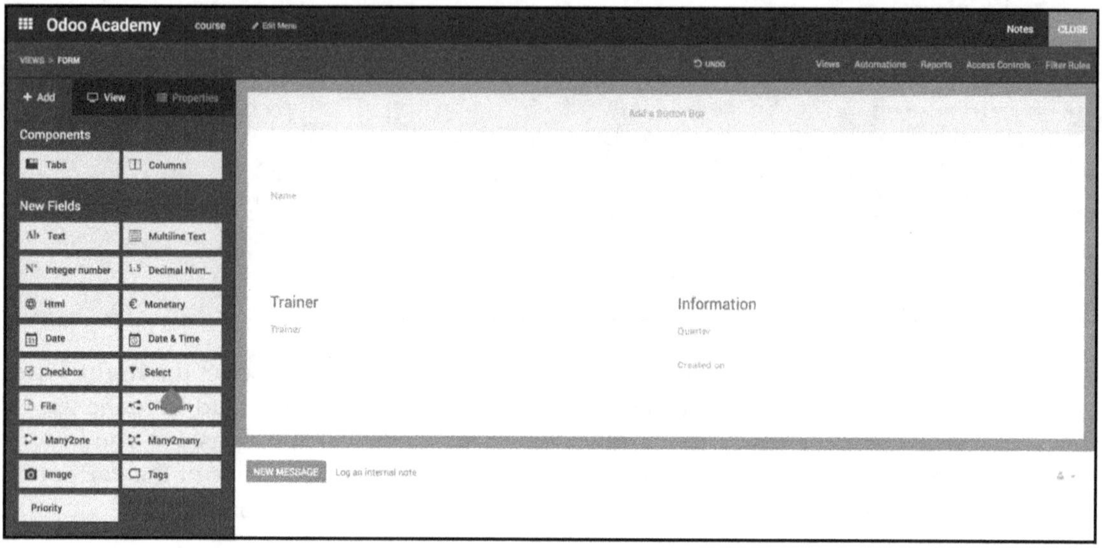

9. Exit from studio mode and your course form should look as follows:

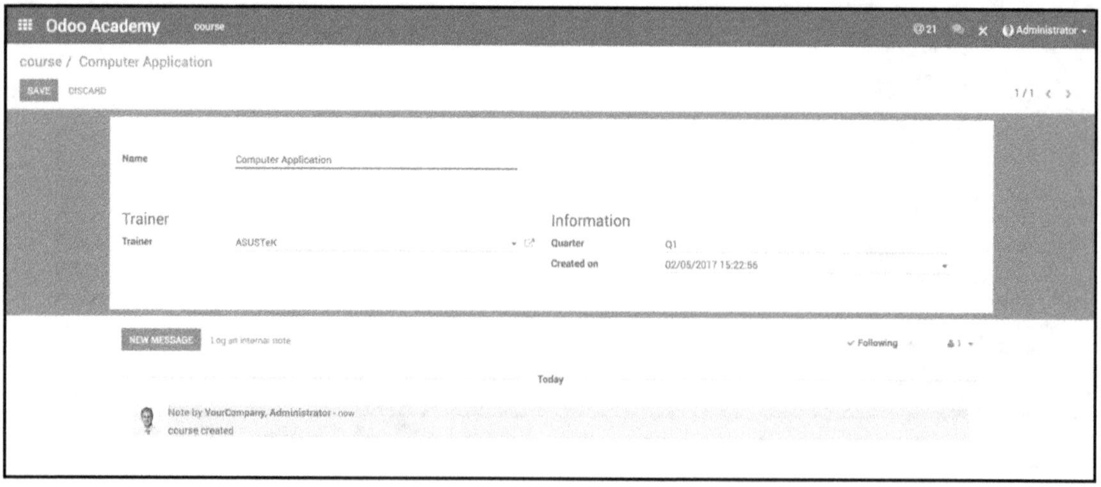

10. Let's organize menus on the application. Change course to **Course**, add a new menu, **Students** to the application. Enter studio mode and click on the **Edit Menu** button on the top.

    To change the label of a course, click the edit button beside it, change the label, and click on confirm:

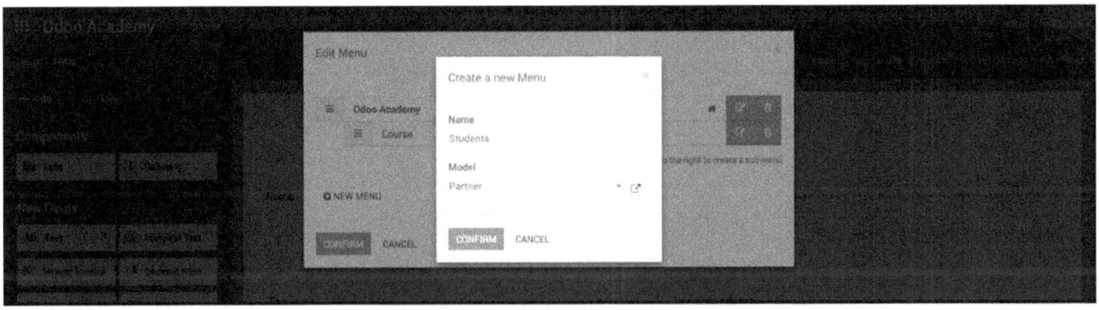

11. Let's create the menu for the student. To create a new menu, click on **New Menu**, enter**Name,**select **Partner** in model, and click on **CONFIRM**.

    Click on **Confirm** in the **Edit Menu** dialog and you will have two menus at the top, **Course** and **Students**:

Click on **Student** on the menu and you will see all the contacts, open a form view. Let's add a new field to associate students with the course. Enter Odoo Studio mode, drag and drop the **Many2one** field below **Tags**; this will prompt a popup to ask for the related model name, select the **Course** as a model. Select the newly added field and change the label to **Course**:

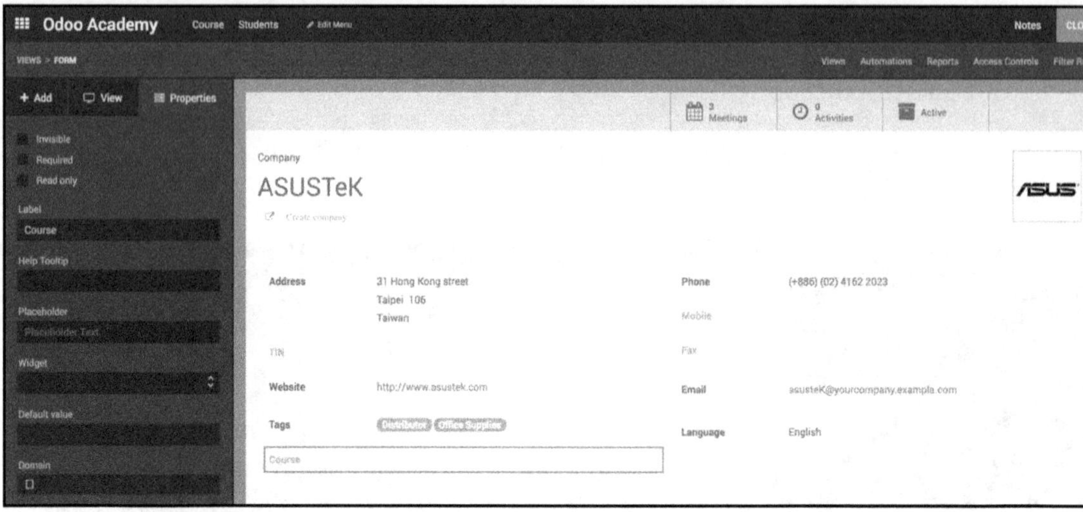

12. Exit from studio mode and you can select the course on the student form view:

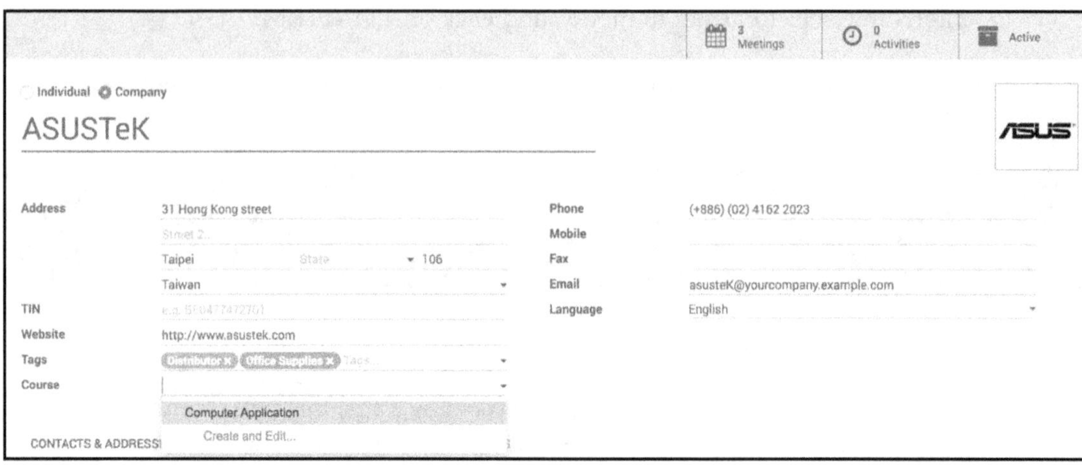

13. Now, go to the **Course** form view, so that you can add the related buttons that will open the list of students associated with the course. Enter studio mode and at the top of the form view, click on the **+ button** to add a new action button, a popup will appear asking you to enter **Label**, select the icon and the related field to create an action button:

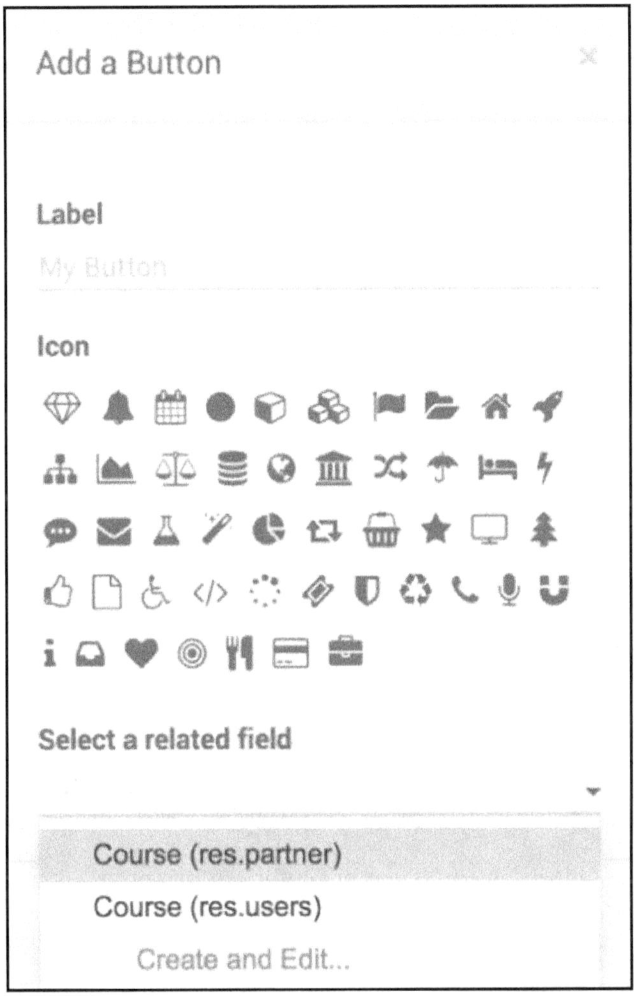

Enter the label **Student**and select **Icon** and **Partner (res.partner)** in **Select a related field**.

14. Click on **Confirm**, your action button is added to the form and it will display the number of students who have followed the **Computer Application** course:

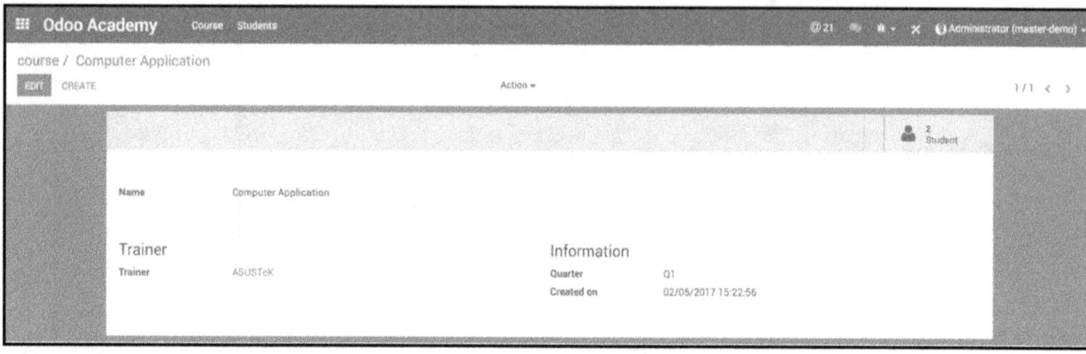

Clicking on the**Students** action button, you will be redirected to the list of student, who have opted for the **Computer Application** course.

There's more...

You have successfully created an Odoo Academy application without writing a single line of code. This application also appears on the home screen of your instance:

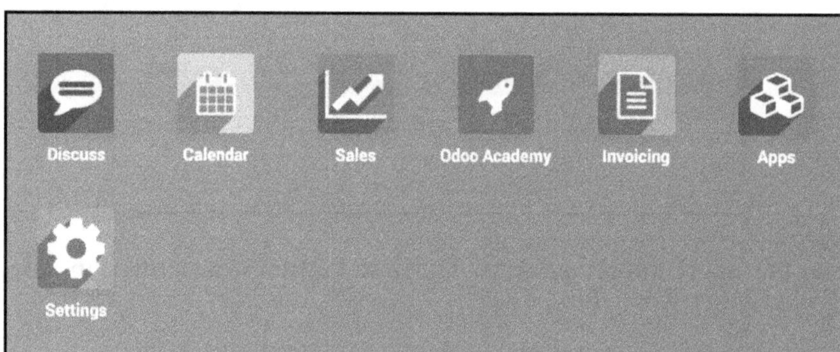

Setting the default view

By clicking on the Odoo Academy application, you will jump into the application, the first screen you will see is the course list. Let's assume that instead of a list view, you want to see the Kanban view.

Click on the application, enter studio mode, and you can see all the views available.

Views that are not activated yet are displayed as an inactive view, the activated views are displayed as a dark image. A home button is displayed on the view, which indicates that list view is the main view for the course model.

Click on the **Kanban** view to activate it, **Set as Default** from the context menu on **Kanban** view, look at the following screenshot:

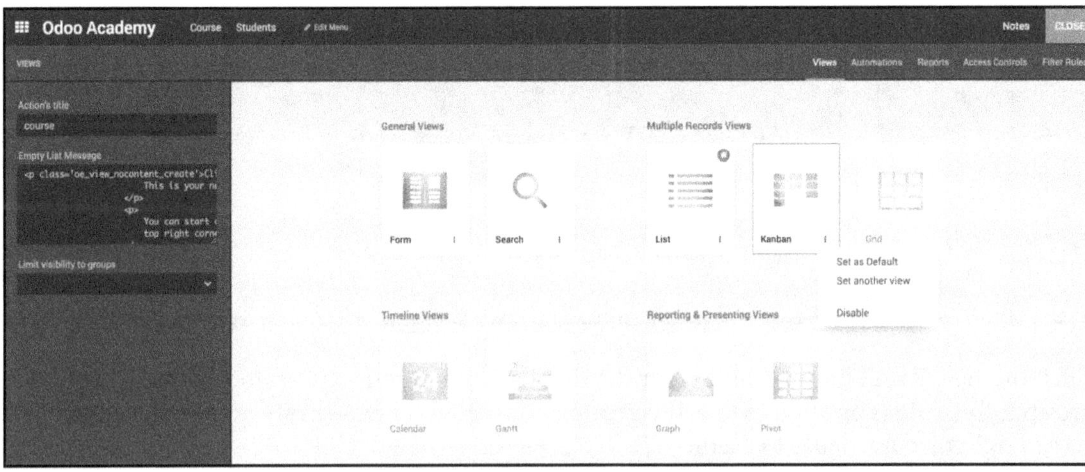

Next time when you jump to the **Odoo Academy** application, you will get the Kanban view for the course:

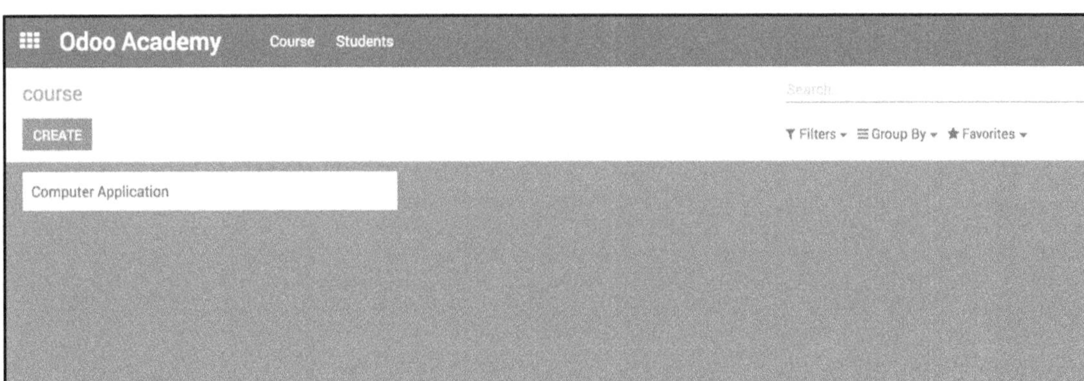

You can customize the **Kanban** view by entering into the studio mode.

Setting up an access control list

Security is an important concern while developing a new application. Who can access various parts of the business should be a part of your implementation strategy.

You can set up the access rights by using existing groups/role linked on the access control list or you can create a new group.

Go to the **Odoo Academy** application, enter studio mode, click on the **Access Control Lists**tab, and you will get the list of access controls defined for that model:

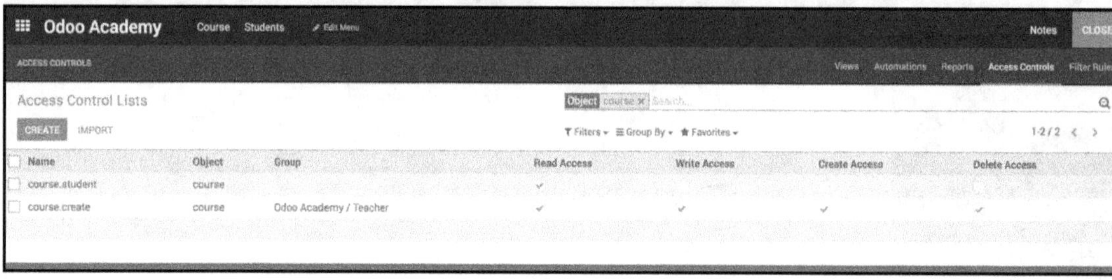

Click on the **CREATE**button and enter the details. Enter a self-explanatory name, choose a group if this rule is applied to specific groups of users else keep empty, and choose what access rights are available to them.

You can assign a correct group on the user form later, to apply the correct access control:

Exporting and importing a custom application

Once you implement the application on the duplicated database, you are ready to move those settings and customizations to the production database.

How to do it...

1. Go to the home page of your instance, enter studio mode, and click on the **Export** menu in the upper-left **Customization** menu. Look at the following screenshot:

Odoo will create a new application by incorporating all the changes in a structured way so that it can be loaded on the destination instance like other Odoo applications.

The download will begin once the module creation is completed by Odoo. The default filename will be `customization.zip`:

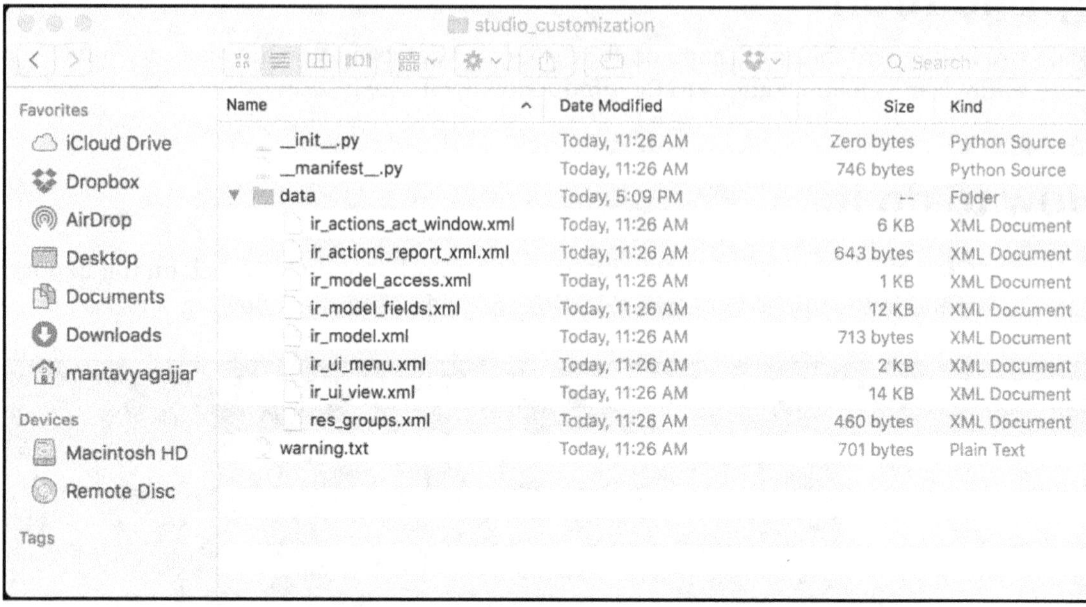

All customization is exported in the form of XML files including Python code, if you write for the computed fields.

2. Change a few things before you import this customization to a production instance. Extract the `customization.zip` file, open the `__manifest__.py` file, and change the value of name and description to make it a realistic module. Change the directory name to `module_name`, one you would like to keep.
3. Create a ZIP file again. Once you have completed the changes in that module, create a `module_name.zip` file so that it will be easy for you to separate the features by application on the production instance.

4. To import and install the app created with Odoo studio, connect to your production database, enter studio mode, and click on the **Import** menu in the upper-left **Customization** menu.

   A popup will appear asking you to upload your module created with the Odoo Studio. Click on the upload module button and select the module to upload:

   By clicking on the **Install** button, Odoo uploads your module to an apps list and installs the module.

3
Traceability - Leads to Cash

In this chapter, we will cover the following recipes:

- Creating and managing your customers
- Generate, qualify leads, convert to opportunity and follow-ups
- Getting customer's approval online for a sales proposal
- Invoice to your customer and get paid

Introduction

Getting traceability in business is always an important factor while implementing enterprise software to automate various business activities. The definition of traceability changed time to time as the business evolve, during 20th century the traceability in business were to track an incoming lot, stock in warehouse and delivery. The main challenge for the business was to integrate sales, purchase, inventory and manufacturing to the accounting software, so that consolidated accounting statement can be generated.

Today the challenge is changed, as the companies are getting modern, the customer became real challenge for companies as they are not integrated. Business use plenty of non-integrated software for customer related activities, such as POS, mass mailing, lead tracking, eCommerce, sales consolidation, after sales service, and communication tools. Companies cannot offer an amazing and unified customer experience without integration. You may lose lots of time and money just to understand you are running business without profit without integrated software.

Odoo approach is different, and that's what modern company need, to put the customer in the center of all the business activities, you want to know the revenue generated for the marketing campaign, when you spent money, you want to get return on that, most of the companies they don't do that. The result, a poor customer experience and a complex system to manage with non-integrated software.

Let's move forward, and see how Odoo can convert your company into modern company. Install sales application, getting started with lead, opportunity, create quotation, get it confirmed, send invoice and get paid. Using Odoo you can track your pipe form lead to cash.

Creating and managing your customers

Customer is the real challenge for modern companies. To improve the customer experience and better after-sales service you have to integrate your customers to every business operations. Odoo is managing the customers in such way that you have centralized communication history recorded for various business operations for all your customers, vendors or employees.

Let's install Odoo Sale application and create customer and understand the importance of some fields which helps to configure the real-world business needs.

Getting ready

We assume that you are ready with the requirement specification to answers some of the questions listed below:

- How you would like to categorize your customers?
- Code system to generate the code for customer, vendors and employee to search quick
- Differentiates the customers between tax paying and tax exempted
- Credit limit and payment terms for the customers

Those are some sample questions; you should have clear requirements before you start crating your customers.

How to do it...

1. Go to **Apps** and search for the **Sales** application; click on **Install** button to install that app. Odoo sales app use to manage your sales activities in Odoo:

On successful installation of **Sales** application, you will be redirect to homepage and you can get the **Sale** app on your screen; refer the following screen:

2. Click on **Sales** | **Sales** | **Customers** to jump on the customer list. A help message will be appeared to guide you further, the help message will be visible when you do not have record:

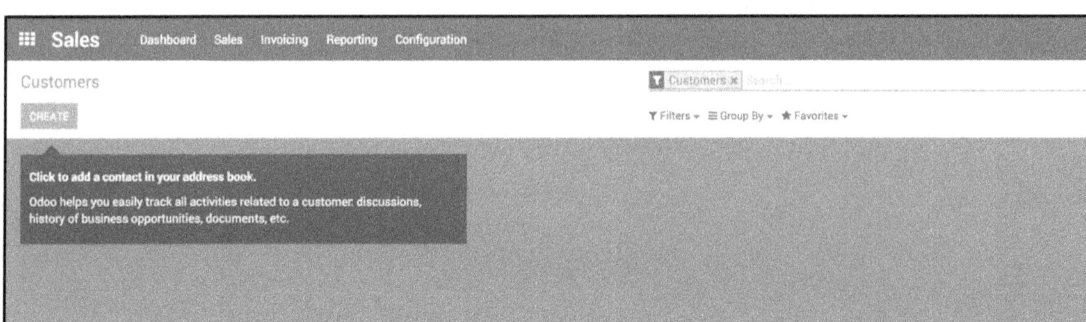

3. Click on **CREATE** button to create a new customer. The first thing to decide is, a customer type. Is the customer a walk-in retail customer or a company, select **Individual** if you creating walk-in customer.

   When your target customer is consumers, you can set your customer as **Individual**. In our case the customer is a legal company so, **Company** is selected:

   Enter **Name**, **Address**, **Email**, **Website**, **Phone** and **Mobile**. Except **Name,** all other are optional fields, you can enter name and click on the **Save** button to quick create customer.

   Create a `tag` depending on how you would like to categorized your customers, I have created `components Buyer and Partner / IT Services`, as I would like to categorized my customer as `Wholesaler`, `Distributors`, `Sellers`, and `Consumers`. You can set the color for tag, to identify these more easily on the Kanban view, look at the following screen:

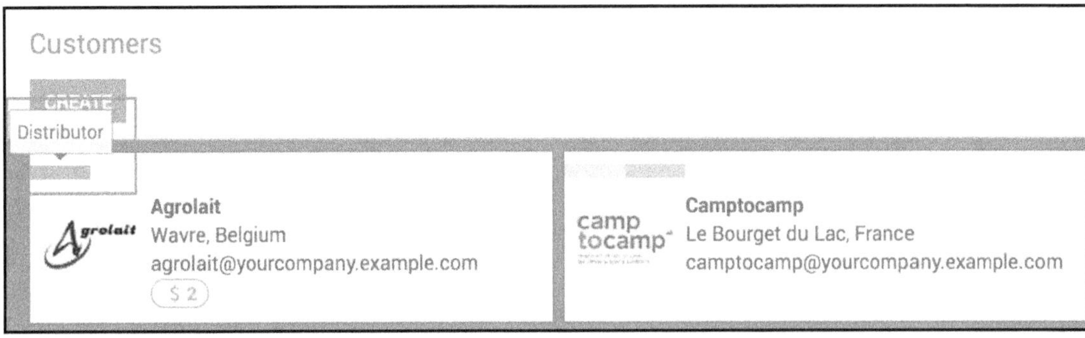

Select the language on customer, it is preferred language for customer to get all the documents to be printed in this language, Odoo does all the communication with the customer in their preferred language, also printing all the reports in customer's preferred language.

> **TIP**
> Odoo support multiple languages, the on-screen language is based on the user preference, and the language for reports can be set on the customer form. New language can be loaded form **Settings | Translations | Load a Translation**

4. Multiple addresses for the customer can be created form **CONTENT & ADDRESSES** Tab.

Assume you have to deliver the products with delivery slip to manager in warehouse and invoice should goes account manager in account office. Click on **CREATE** button to add new contact or address:

A popup will appear, depending on the address type you choose, fields on the form will be changed. You will be asked to fill the **Address**, **Email**, **Phone**, **Mobile** and **Notes** for **Invoice**, **Shipping** and **Other** address type:

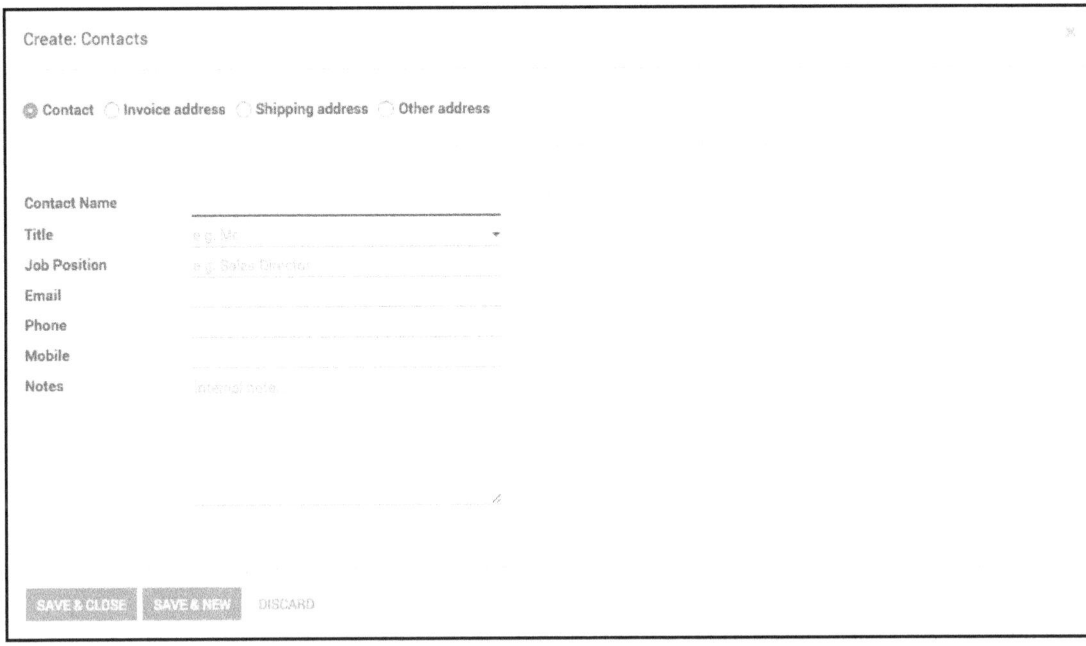

However, if you choose a **Contact** type, you will be asked for the **Contact Name**, **Email**, **Mobile** and **Phone**.

5. **Notes**, is textbox, you can enter any text you would like to store for the future reference.

TIP

A good practice is to post an internal note on chatter for any future reference, users can not change information on the Chatter while internal notes can be changed without track.

6. Under the **Sales & Purchase** tab you will find the settings related to the Sale and Purchase:
    - **Is a Customer**: check if your mark as customer
    - **Is a Vendor**: check if you want to mark as vendor
    - **Salesperson**: a single point of contact in organization
    - **Internal Reference**: A short code for the customer, that helps to find the customer quickly.

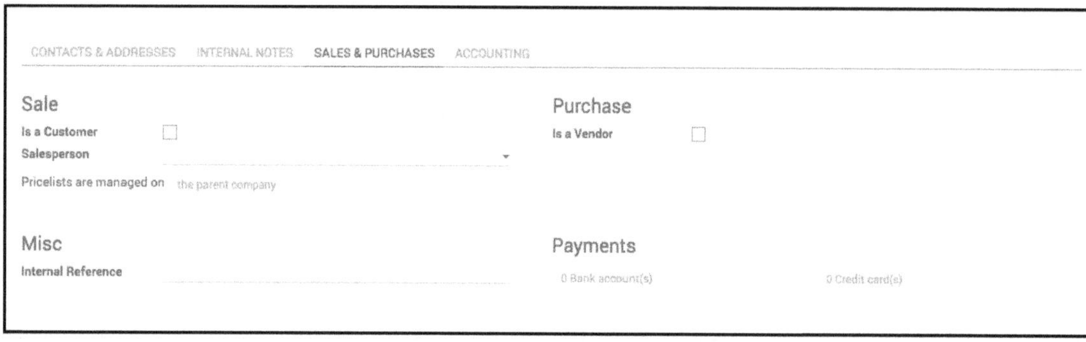

All the contacts created are marked as a **Customers** by default; it can be changed to **Vendors** if you want to create vendors. You can select both in case your vendor is your customer.

7. **ACCOUNTING** tab contains the settings related to the invoices and billing. Make sure you configure **Customer Payment Terms** correctly; it impacts on the credit limit and due dates for the customer invoices.

   The default payments terms are:

    - **15 Days:** a due date will be exact after 15 days from the date of invoice.
    - **30 Net Days:** a due date will be exact after 30 days from the date of invoice.
    - **Immediate Payment**: a due date will be same as the invoice date; no credit days will be given.

   The **Fiscal Position** is used to differentiate your tax paying and tax exempted customers. By default, choose nothing to keep all customers as tax paying.

I have installed only Sale App, the configuration on customer form will be depending on the number of application and features you have activated

There's more...

A quick start methodology suggests using the best out of available features. There are some features available in Odoo, which can be used effectively with the help of configuration. Let's go through some of the features that help you to efficiently managing the communication, portal access, and searching the customers, vendors and employees.

Searching a customer

Accessing a correct customer quickly from the list of customers requires unique customer identification. You can define the code system that helps you to generate and retrieve the customer, vendor or employees based on the code quickly.

Here is an example of customer Agrolait, the code `AGL` is generated based on the customer name `Agrolait`; when you type `AGL` in Customer field on Sales order or invoice the customer `Agrolait` will be searched quickly.

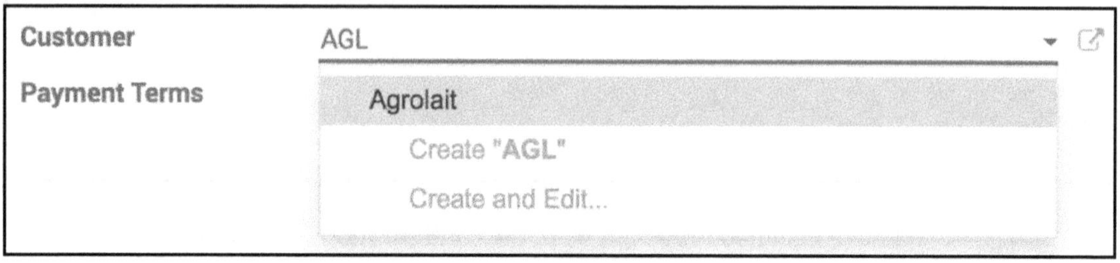

It is advisable to create a short code for the frequent customer or supplier and assign into **Internal Reference**, this will help us search them quickly.

Achieve and restore your customer

It's suggested to archive some of the customers, who haven't placed any order since long. How frequently you should check and archive those customers is part of the business strategy. Archiving unused customers helps you to focus on the important ones and helps to improve the performance of the system.

To achieve a customer, search and open the customer you want to archive, click on the **Archive** button, and customer will be archived, look at the following screen:

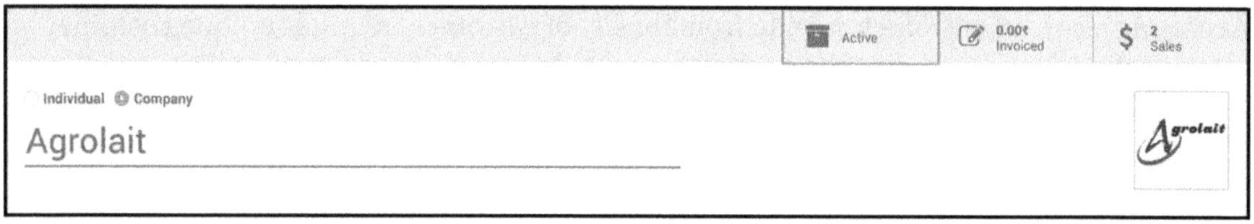

Next time, when you open the customer list, an archive customers will not be appeared in the list. The archived customers can be accessed or restored from **Sales** | **Sales** | **Customers**, click on the **Filters** and select the **Archived** filter. You will get a list of archived customers, as **Customers** filter is applied by default.

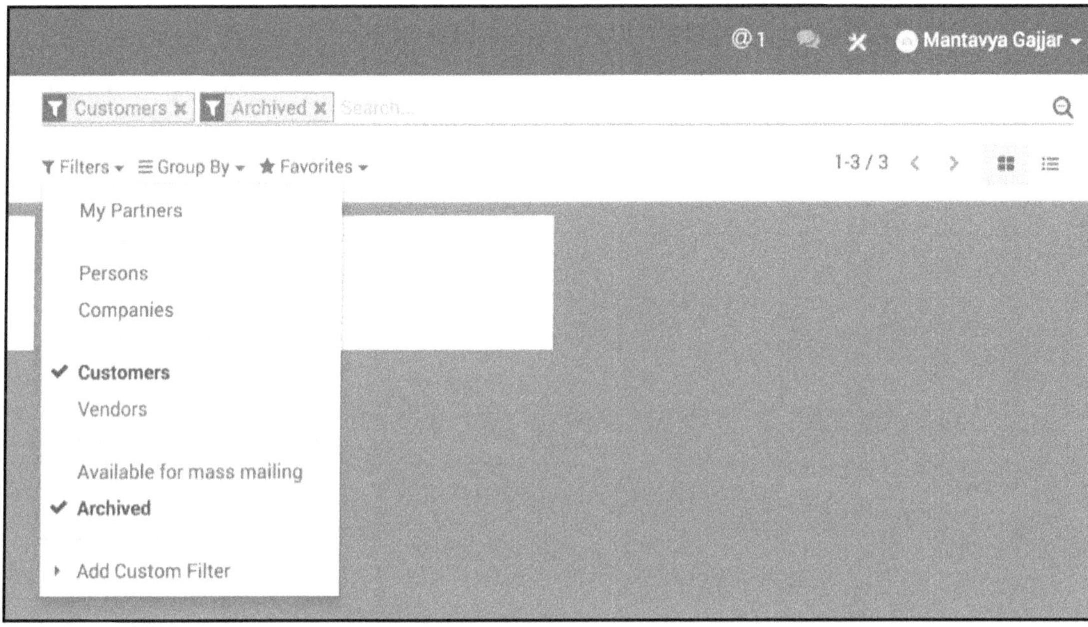

Select the customer you want to restore; you can see the button **Archived** in red colour, as soon as you move the mouse over the button, the label will be changed to **Unarchive.**

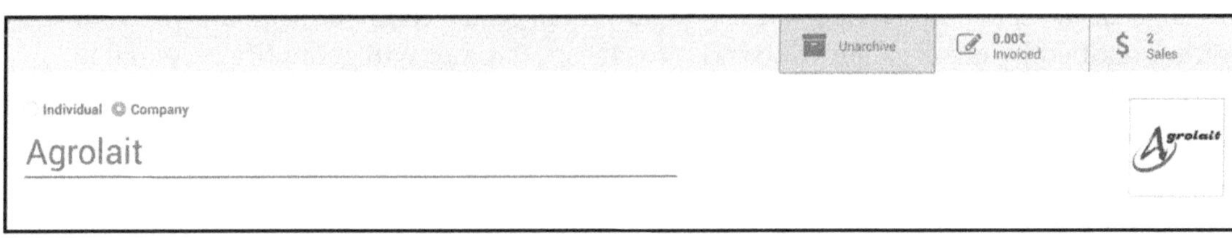

See the button **Unarchive**, the customer will be restored back and it will be available in default customer list.

Communication history on customer

As the customer is in center of business, accessing the communication history of a customer helps us serve better and helps us to get the good customer feedback for the service provided. The communication history can be found below the customer information; this includes not only the chat history but you can attach document to each message.

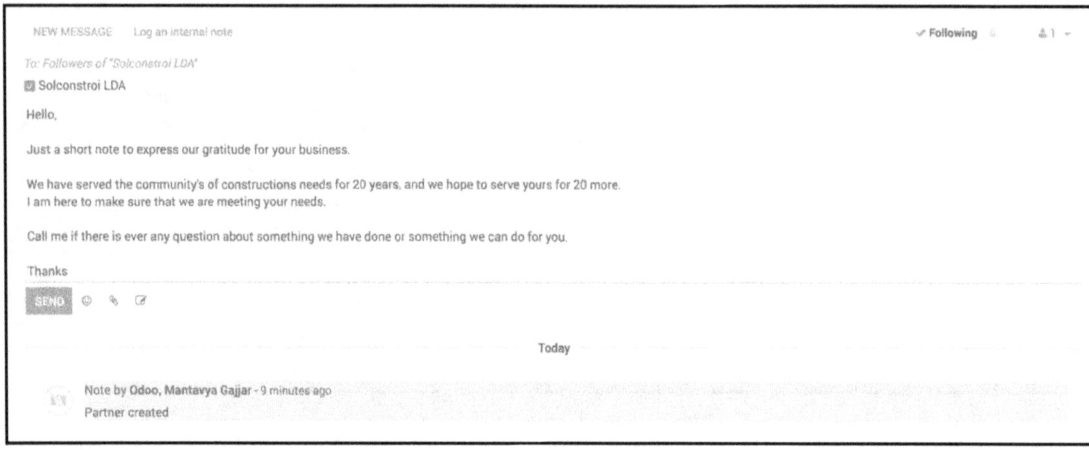

Click on the **NEW MESSAGE** button to compose a message to customer, you can enter the message, at the same time Odoo ask you to add them on the follower list. Followers are getting notified by email when you send messages, customer will get notify by email in their email box, look at the following email how email looks like in customer mailbox sent form Odoo:

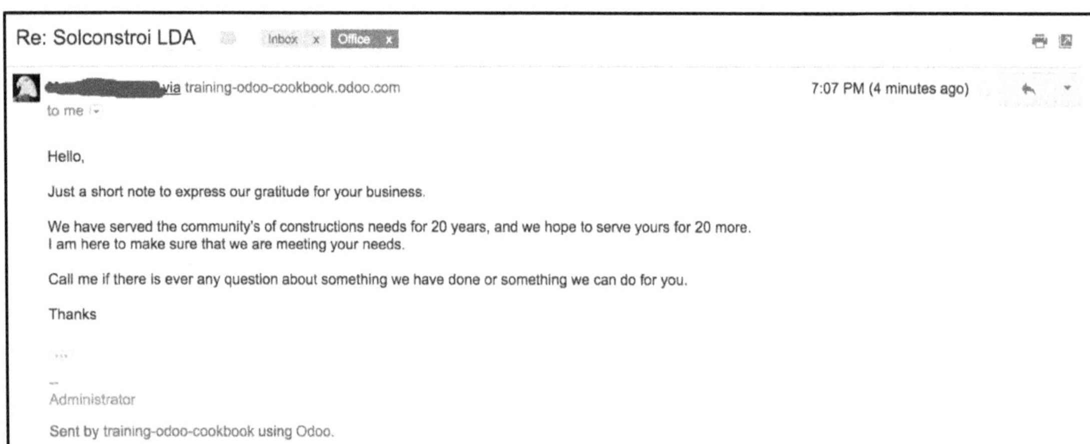

When customer replies you on the same email, you will get notify in chatter below the customer information:

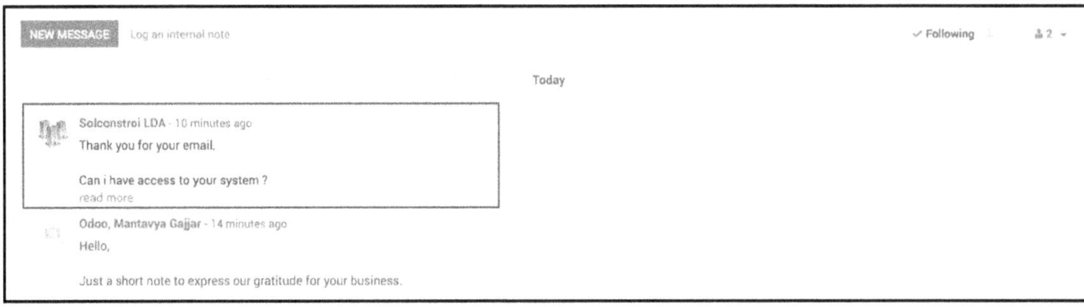

Invite your customer to online portal

Customer portal is such a tool allows your customer to stay connected with your business. You can invite your customer to access the useful resources and business documents related to them such as quotations, sales orders, invoice and payment details.

Open the related customer to issue a customer portal access and click on the **Action** button to open the popup menu having a possible list of actions for the customer.

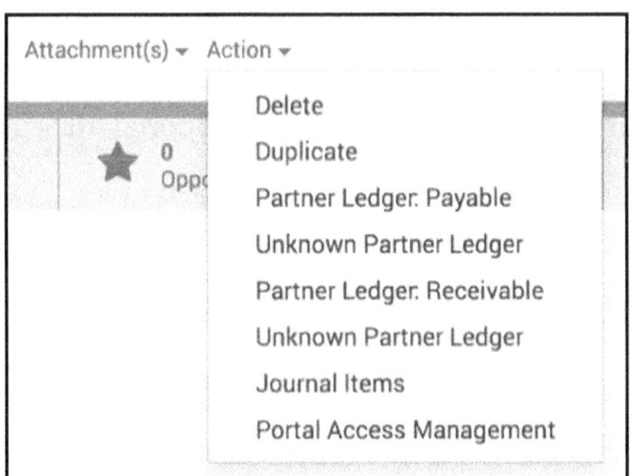

Click on the **Portal Access Management**, a popup will appear to confirm which email address you can issue a portal access.

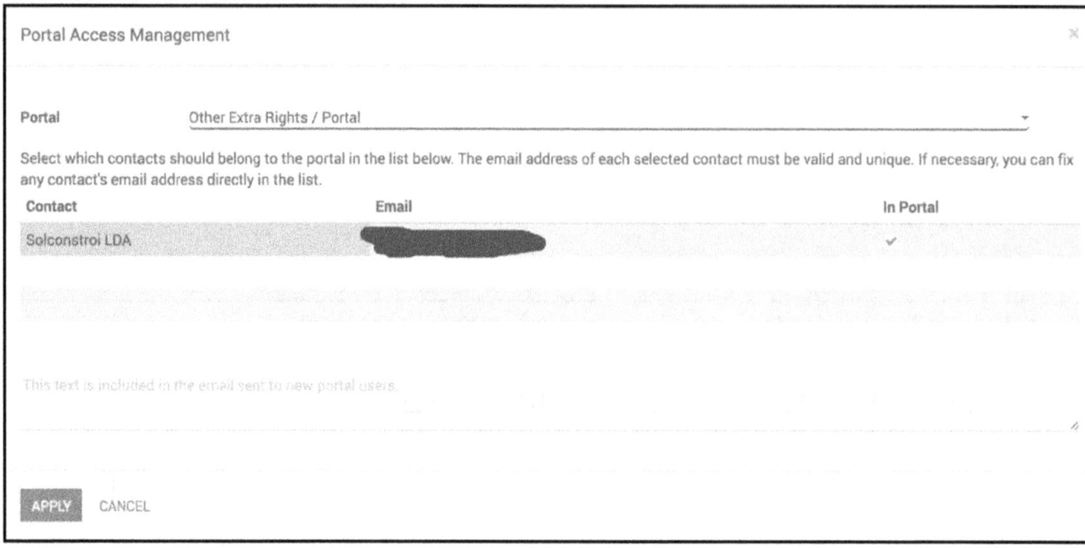

Select **In Portal** checkbox beside the correct email address on which you are going to issue the portal access and click on **APPLY** button. Customer will get an invitation email with the signup instructions.

Following the signup instruction, the customer will be asked to set the password and email address will be set as a username. By entering into the portal, the customer will get access to their documents in an online portal.

Generate and qualify leads, convert to opportunity and follow-ups

Imagine a bucket full of business card. They show an interest in your products is normally called leads. The lead contains valuable information to realize a further sales opportunity. The lead has to be qualified enough before a salesman started to be working on. While the lead represents the first contact with the prospect yet to be qualified, a sales opportunity represents a potential customer. The salesman pays attention to each opportunity for the proposition, negotiation and confirms or cancels the sales.

Let's see how you can organize your sales activity and follow-up using Odoo CRM.

Getting ready

You have to choose the way, how your team will work, and you have to follow any one approach; either **start with opportunity** or **start with leads**. Odoo by default follows the **start with opportunity** approach, as small companies they do not have many leads, so they do not have to pass-through the qualification process. They can start with the opportunity.

We assume that you have duplicated your database before you install the CRM application, start working with sample data to test the flow and process of lead generation, qualification and working with opportunity.

How to do it...

1. Go to **Apps**, search for **CRM**, click on the **install** button.

Previously, we have already installed the **Odoo Sales** application to manage sales activities, but, when you install CRM you can get the feature that, generating leads, qualifying them, follow-ups on opportunity, and sales forecasting:

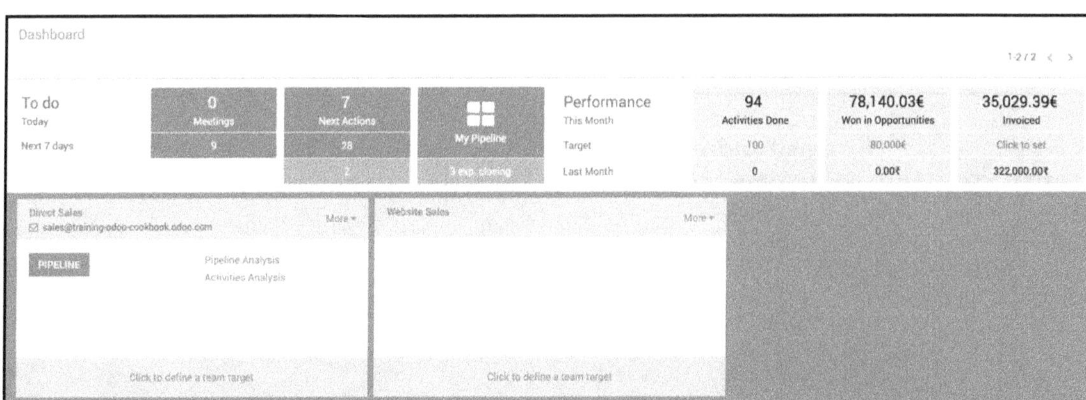

You will find salesman dashboard, having an action to do, meeting to attend today and in next 7 days, on the left and performance measure on the right having targets versus achieved.

2. After installation of Odoo **CRM** application, the first thing you have to do is change the approach; **start with leads** instead of opportunity. Click on the **Sales** | **Configuration** | **Settings;** you will be redirected to setting page:

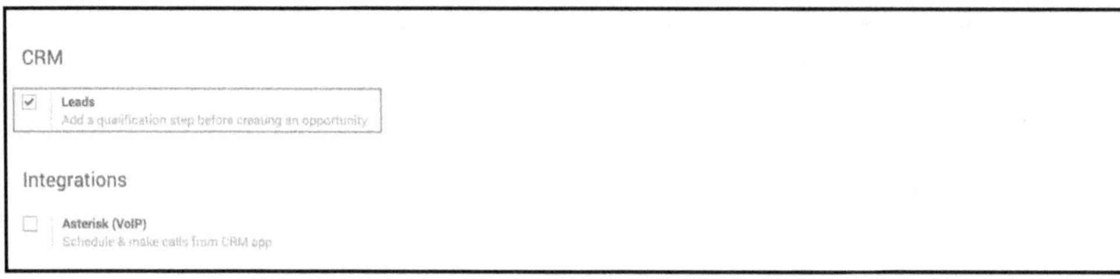

3. Find the setting option for **Leads** and select the checkbox, it will Add a qualification step before creating an opportunity. The current email address is `sales@yourcompany.odoo.com`, it can be changed to `info@yourcompany.odoo.com` from the Sales team setting page, that creates a lead in the Sales team, you can set the one you want, It can be sales, contacts or callback:

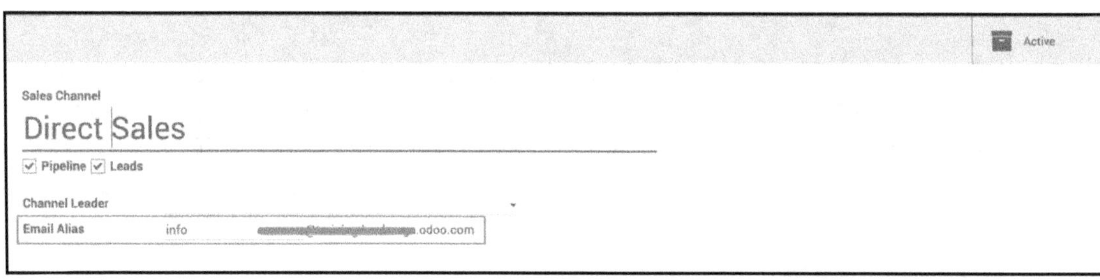

Use email address setup on the leads setting on your business card, website, email signature, that helps you to get more leads.

To test it, send an email to your default email address that should create leads. In this case, the address is `info@yourcompany.odoo.com`.

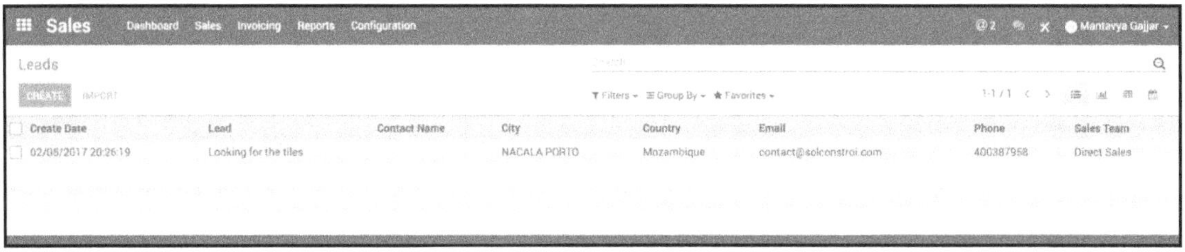

Most of the information's are filled, as it links customer based on the email address, the customer will be linked automatically based on the email address and contact information filled too:

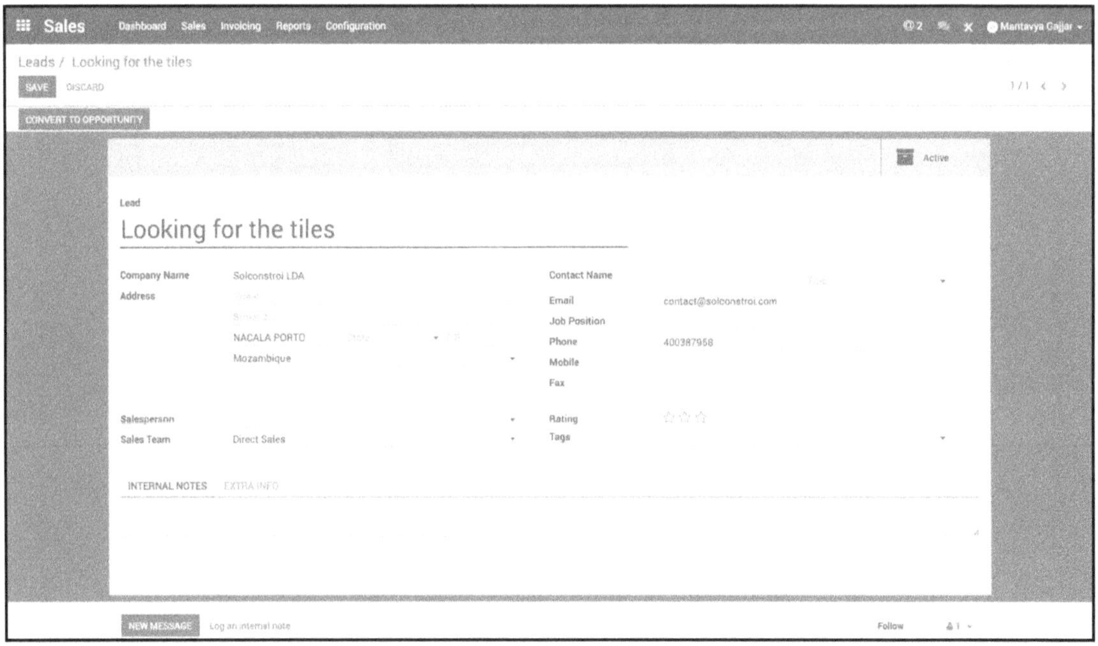

The Email subject will be set on the Lead name, at the bottom of the Lead form, you can see the content of the email sent by the prospect:

4. To qualify the lead, let's send the first email; and ask for the contact details such as phone number or direct mobile number, if we did not get those details in the first email, it will be easy for the salesman to make a call to discuss the requirements in detail:

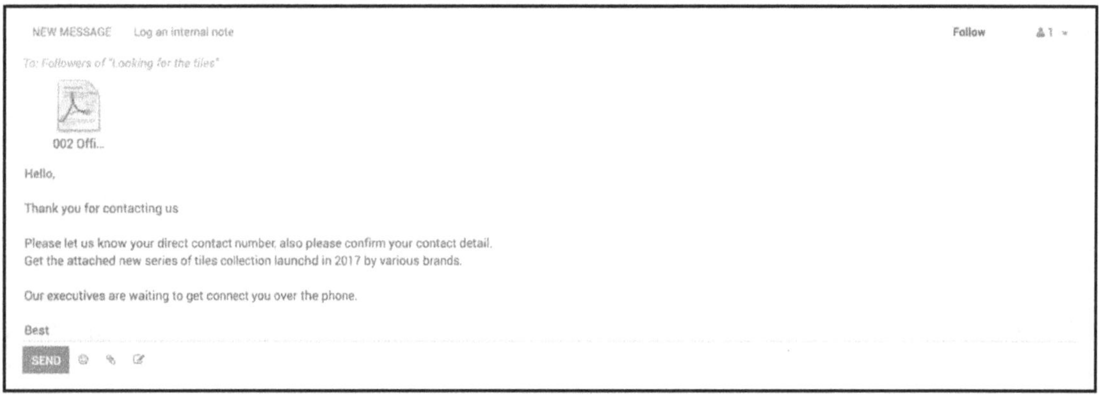

To send an email click on the **NEW MESSAGE** button, type the message, click on the "attachment icon" to attach the tiles broacher, by clicking on **SEND** button the email will be sent to prospects.

> **TIP:** To send email to many leads go to **List View**, apply a filter on the leads, select all those leads and click on action **Lead/Opportunity Mass Mail** from **Action** menu.

5. Convert to opportunity, once you get the reply on lead, every day you should check the leads having a reply or unread messages. From the Filters on **Leads** list view, click on **Unread Messages** from the filter to get the list of leads you got the reply from prospects.

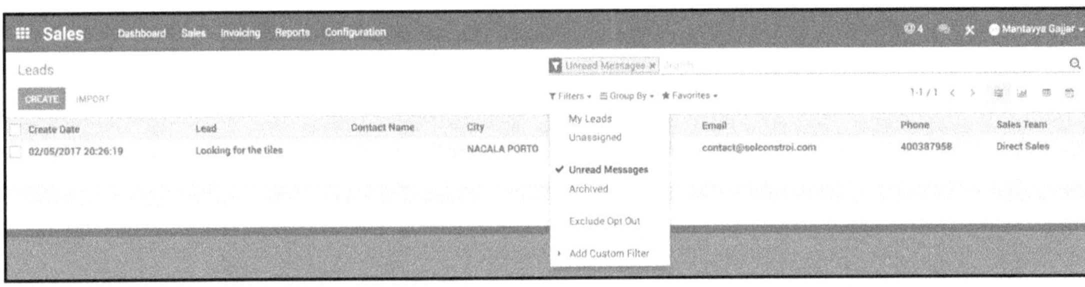

Select all the leads, prospects replied on, click on the **Convert to opportunities button**, from **Action** menu.

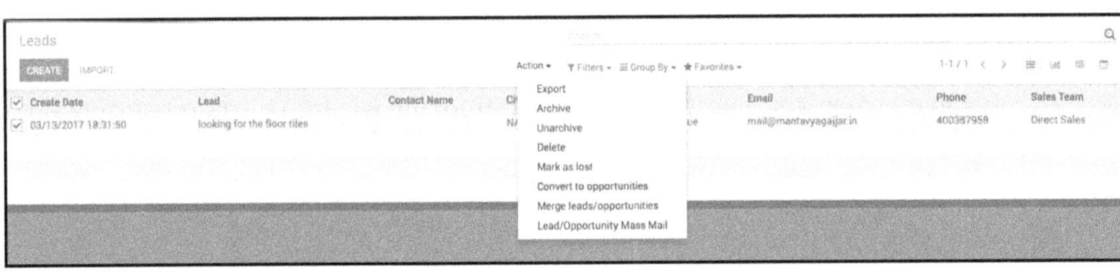

The wizard will appear to guide you on further.

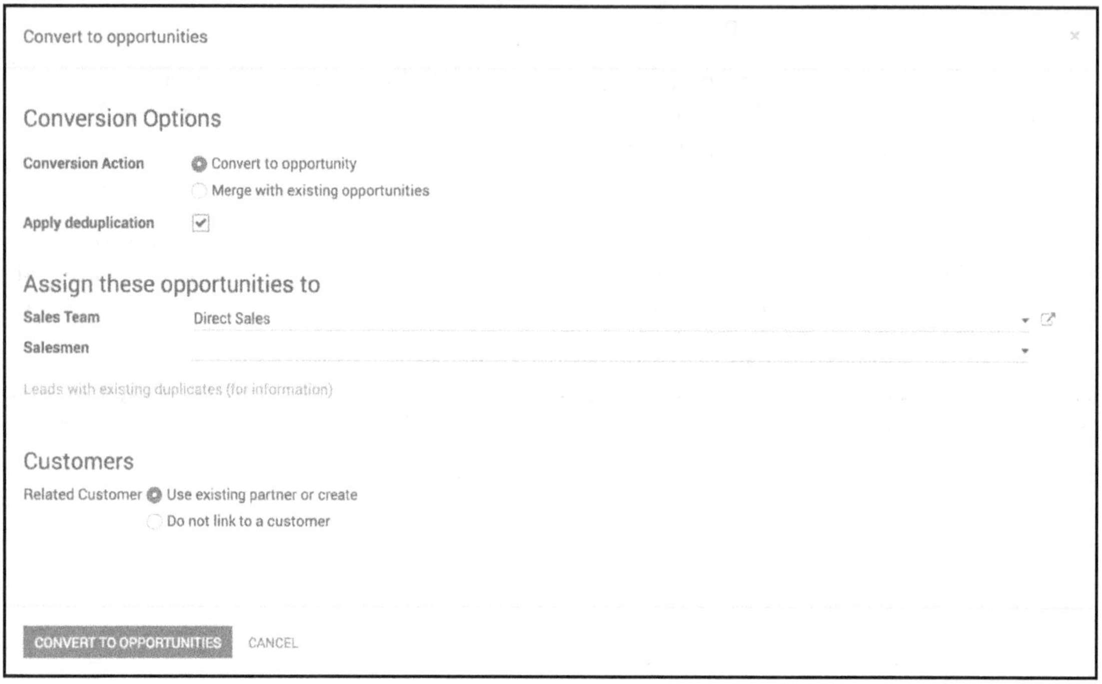

The Convert to opportunity wizard used to convert a lead to new opportunity or link with the existing opportunity, choose to **Convert to opportunity** if you want to create a new opportunity or select **Merge with existing opportunity** if an opportunity already.

However, when you select **Apply Duplication**, the wizard will automatically find the duplicate opportunity based on the contact number or email address for each partner and merge with them automatically.

At the end the leads converted to opportunities, let's choose the **Sales Team** and **Salesmen** to whom we would like to assign the opportunity created. I have chosen **Direct Sales** team and keep the Salesman field empty, the manager of the team is responsible to assign the opportunities to **Salesman** to work on.

We may have a possibility that Customer may be linked on the Lead based on the email address or we have a Contact information, let's choose how the customer will be set on the opportunity.

There are two ways either keep the customer field empty on opportunity by selecting option **Do not link to a customer** or select option **Lead choose Use existing partner or create** to set the customer on opportunity by creating a new customer based on the contact details or use the customer which was linked on lead.

By clicking on **CONVERT TO OPPORTUNITIES** button an opportunity will be created from the leads and you will be redirected to the opportunity for the view.

Leads will be disappeared from the list of **Leads** as soon as you convert that into Opportunity, the information of the leads still available on the opportunity form view under **MORE INFORMATION** tab.

The single lead can be converted to opportunity form the lead form view, by clicking on the **CONVERT TO OPPORTUNITY** button.

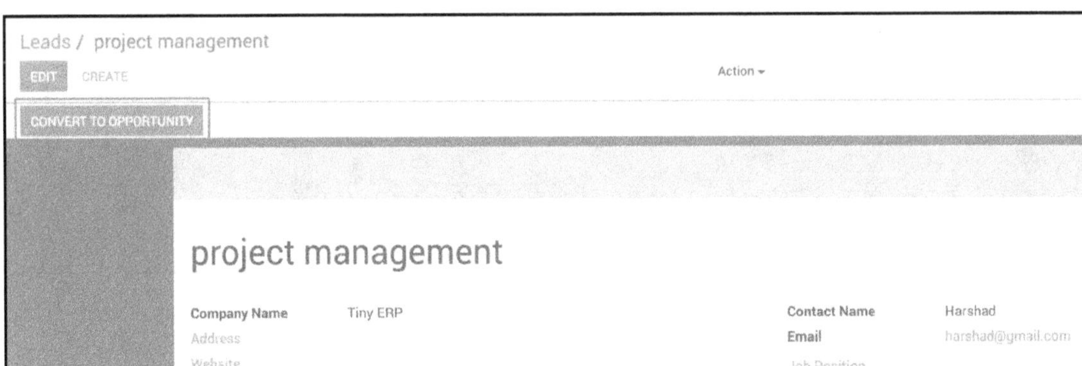

6. As a manager of **Direct Sales** team, your responsibility is to assign the unassigned opportunity to salesman within the team.

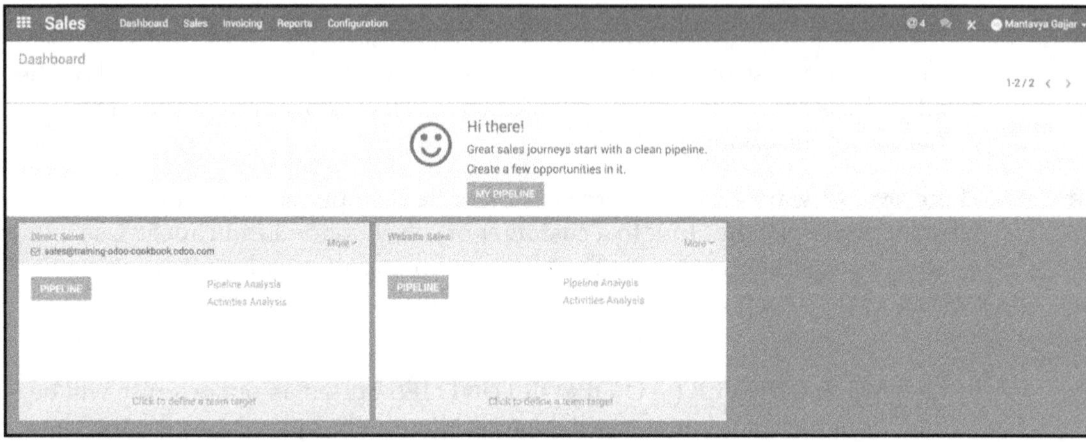

Click on the **PIPELINE** on the **Direct Sales** team from sales **Dashboard.** On opportunity pipe, click on the **Unassigned** Opportunity from the filter to get the list of unassigned opportunities in the team.

Click on the opportunity, assign a salesman and click on **SAVE** button.

7. As soon as the opportunities assigned to a salesman, as a salesman you have to start working on the opportunities. Salesman can access their opportunities by clicking on the **MY PIPELINE** button from the dashboard, click on the opportunity to work on.

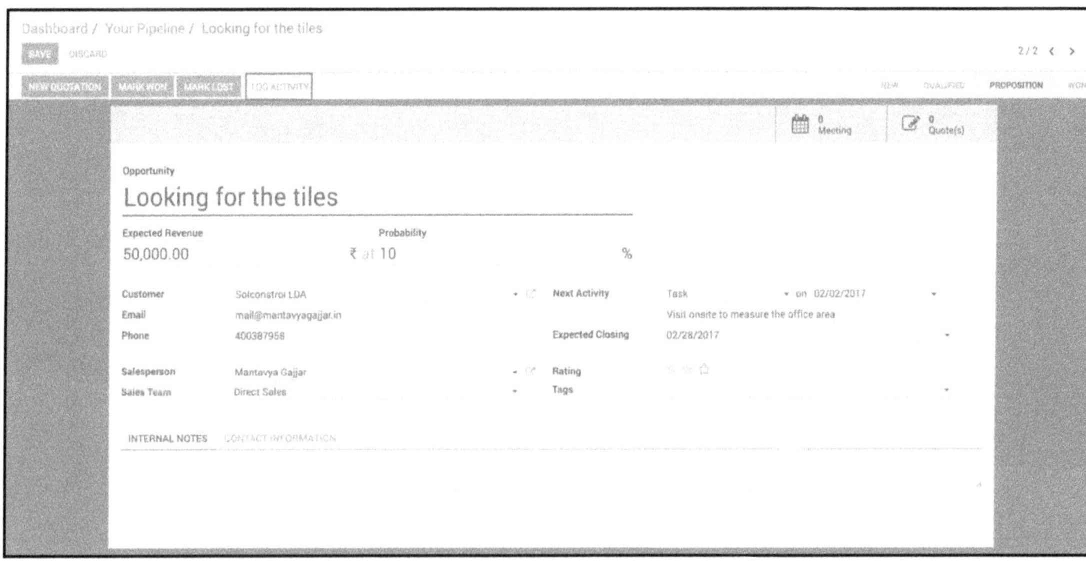

The first task is to call the prospect if you have a correct contact number, discuss the requirement in details, and make a call log by clicking on the **Log Activity** button:

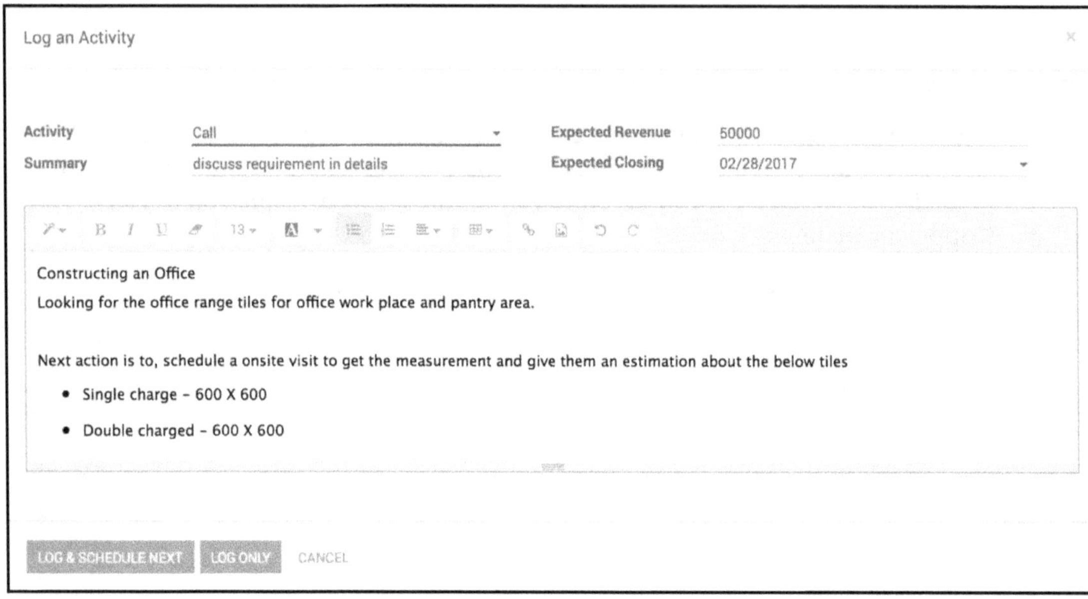

Enter the summary and notes about the call; also, enter the **Expected Closing** date and **Expected Revenue** if you get an idea about the deals after discussing with the prospect.

Click on the **LOG & SCHEDULE NEXT** activity.

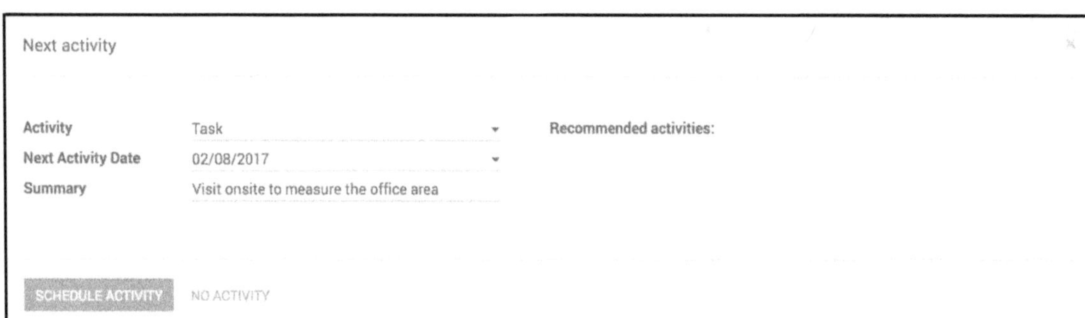

Select the next activity to be performed in the **Activity** field, enter the **Next Activity Date**, enter the activity details in the **Summary** field. By clicking on the **SCHEDULE ACTIVITY** button, the next activity is set and your opportunity will be updated with **Next Activity Date** and **Summary**.

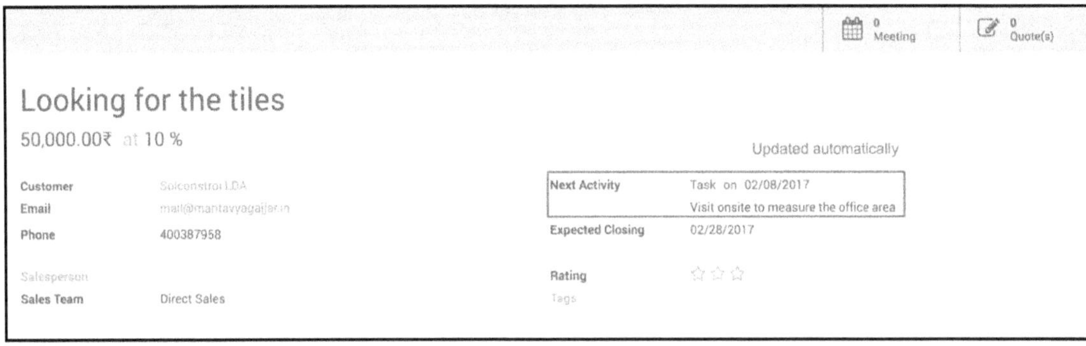

Every time you perform an activity, do not forget to make a log activity and schedule the next activity, so you can efficiently do a follow-up on opportunity and get the best out of it.

As soon as you complete the first call and schedule the next activity, the chatter has been updated to keep a full track of all the activities performed on opportunity:

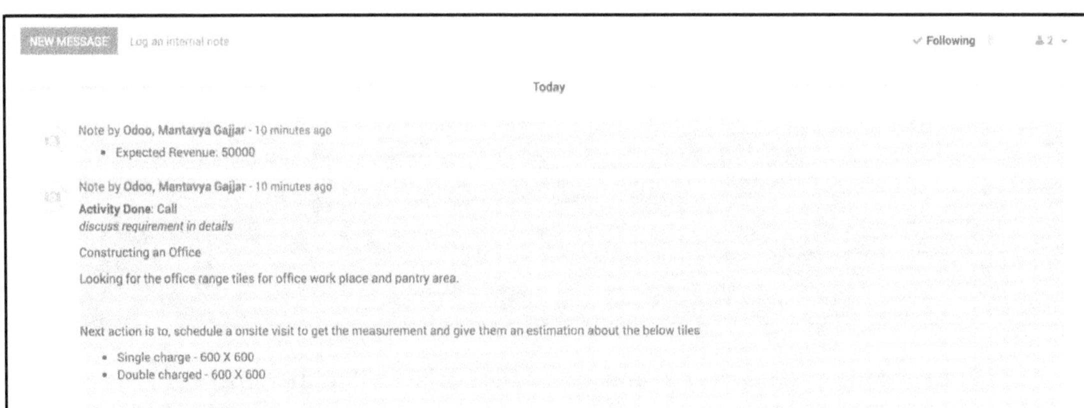

8. It's a best practice to manage your agenda using calendar; do not forget to schedule a meeting invite prospect in your agenda once you confirm to visit prospect's place to measure the office area:

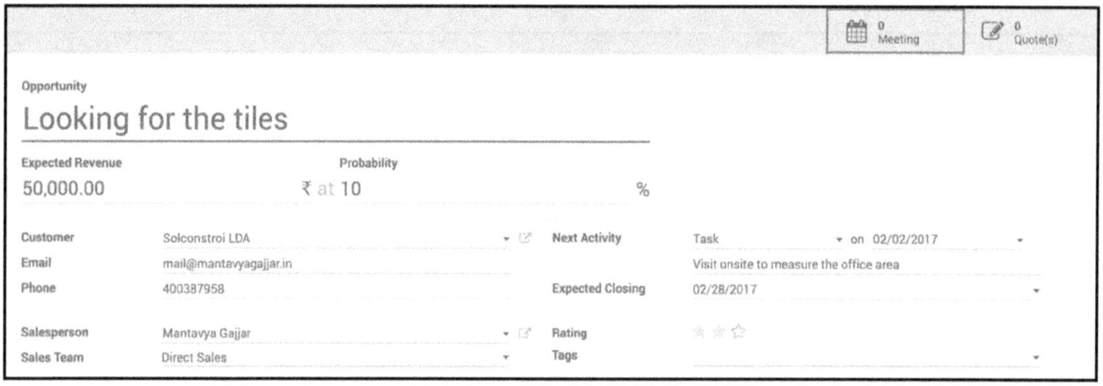

Click on the **Meeting;** by default, it will open **Week** agenda view. To create a meeting, click on start time on a particular date and drag up to end time. A popup will appear asking you the **Summary** of the meeting, enter the summary and click on **CREATE** button:

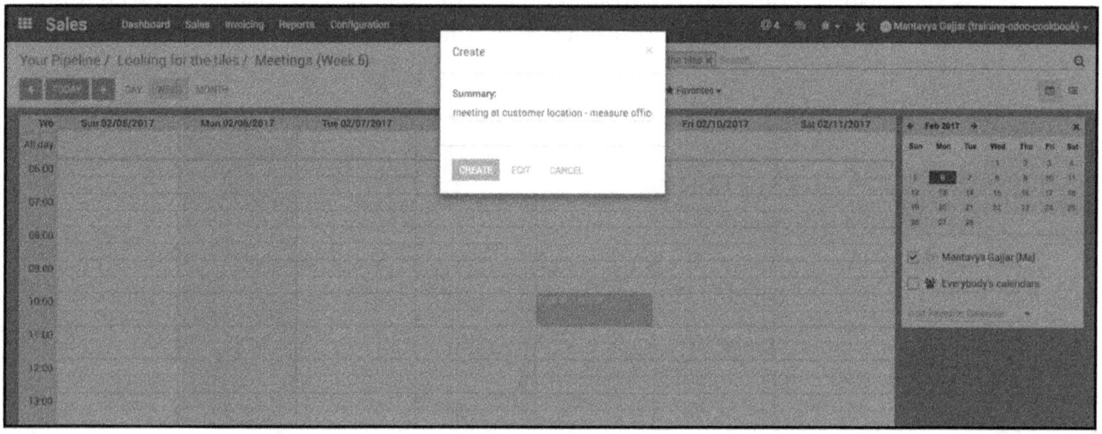

The meeting will be created and an email will be sent to the prospect.

9. The reminder can be set for the meeting. Odoo will remind you prior to the meeting. To set the reminder click on meeting and a popup will appear, as follows:

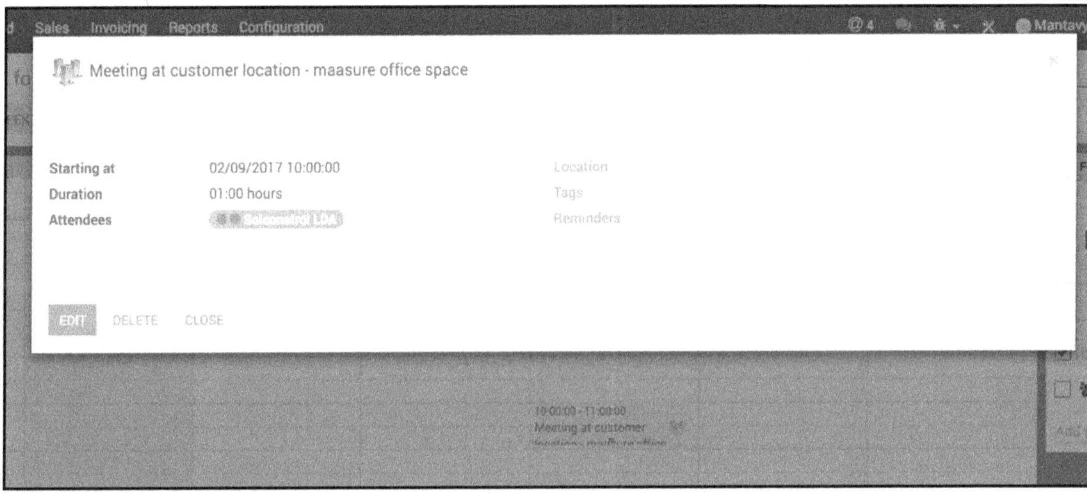

Click on **EDIT** button; full details of the event will be opened; select **15 minute(s)** in the **Reminders** field and click on the **SAVE**:

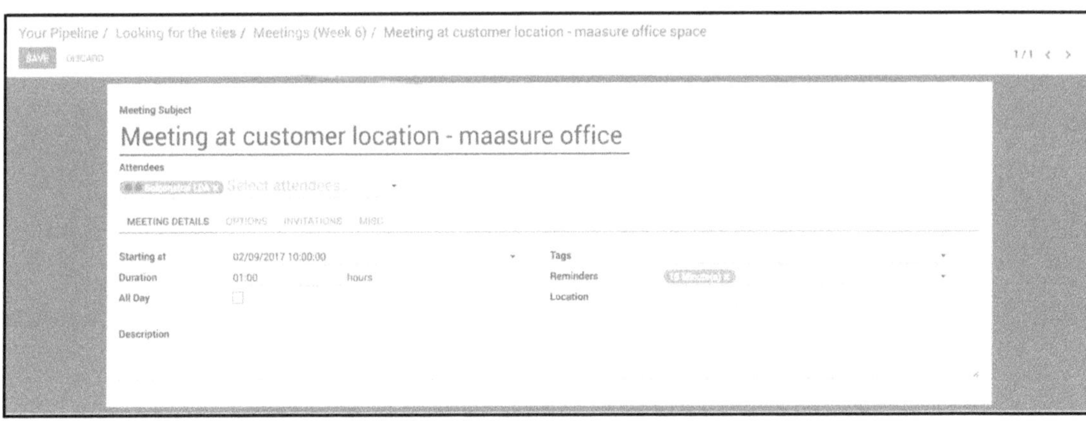

The reminder is set successfully and you will be notified prior to the 15 minutes of the meeting in Odoo and it will also send you an email:

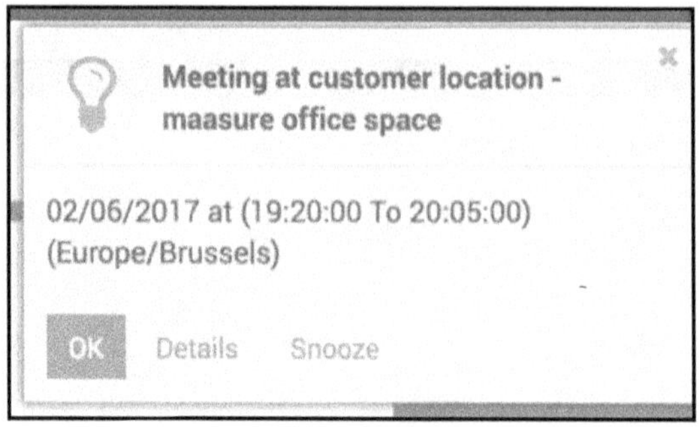

> TIP
>
> You can set more than one reminder for the meeting by selecting the multiple reminders on **Reminders** field.

10. As your opportunity gets qualified, the prospect is interested in our products; you can move opportunity from **New** to **Qualified** stage; drag an opportunity form **New** to **Qualified** stage:

11. We have to perform the follow-up activity based on the next action date. To check what are the opportunities you have to work on today, go to **Kanban** view and apply the filter **Today Activity**. You will get your to-do list for today, as shown in the following image:

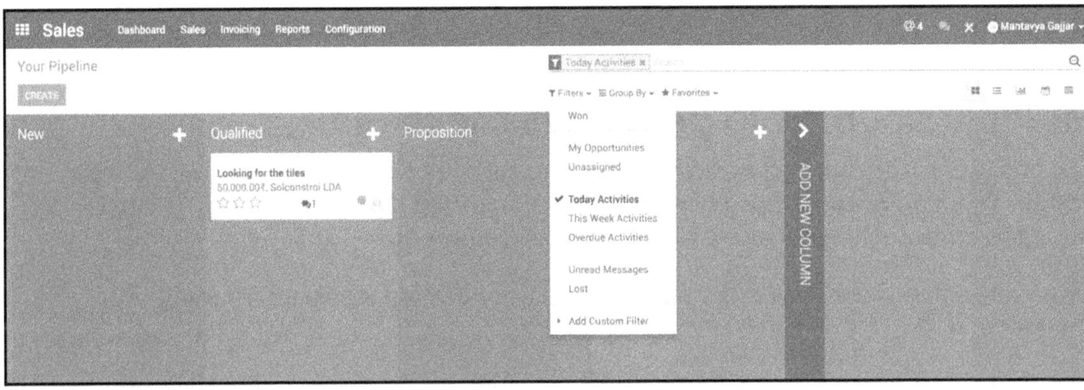

All the opportunity having the red circle on the bottom right indicates opportunities delayed to process according to the next action date.

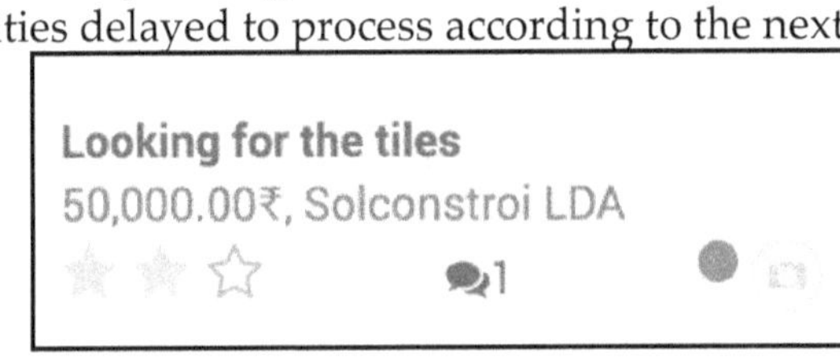

Those opportunity having an unread message has to be processed before you start working on the today's opportunity.

There's more...

There are many additional applications and features available to generate leads, qualify them, create reusable emails templates can be configured and used to process the opportunity faster, and manage the activity schedule. Let's see some of these useful features in how to active and use to make salesman's life simple.

Multiple sources to generates the leads

The business cards collected during the event or road shows are always treated as leads besides that, you can also buy a list of contact details of those who are using or looking for, the simpler product then you are selling; you can import those list as leads.

Odoo offers two more ways to generate the leads, which is a real need for modern companies. Using Odoo you can generate the leads using two methods listed as follows;

- Use an email alias like `info@yourcompany.odoo.com` or `info@yourcompany.com`
- Activate the website **Contacts Us** page, so that customer can directly contact you with contact details and query.

Generating the leads using email is already activated on your instance; you need to set up the correct email alias on your sales team. To activate the **Contact us** page to generate the leads, go to **Apps**, remove the application filter, search for `contact`, install the **Contact Form** application.

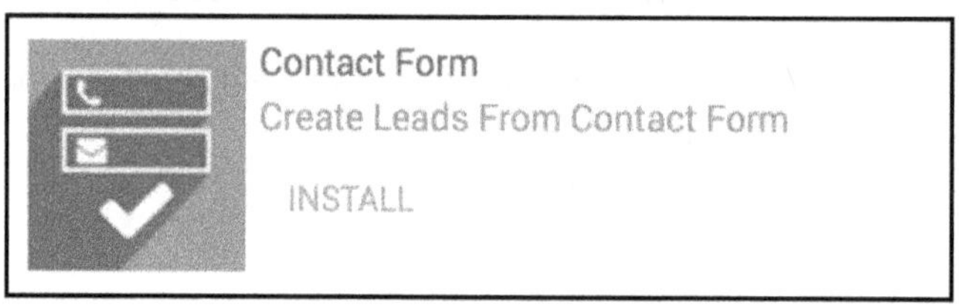

You will be redirected to contact us page at `http://yourdomain.odoo.com/page/contactus`

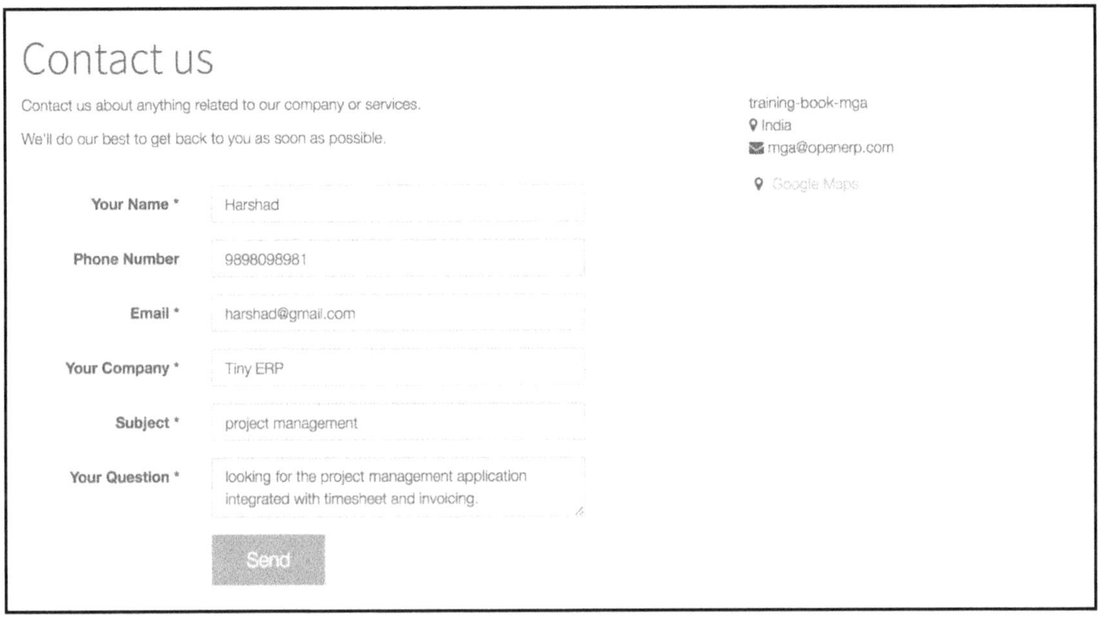

The Tanks message will have appeared as soon as visitor fill the **Contact Us** form and click on **Send** button, you will get a lead created in CRM, as follows:

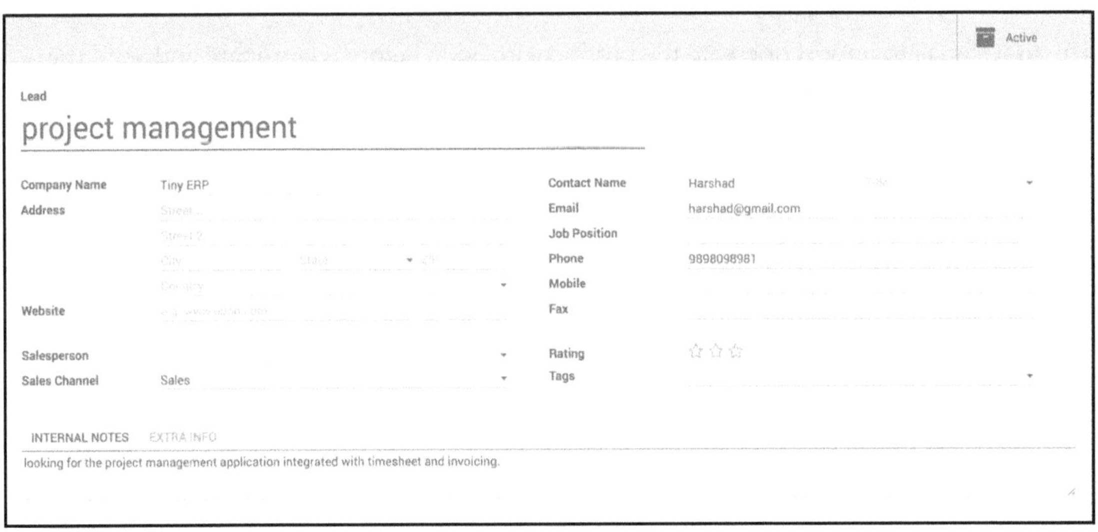

Along with information filled in by the customer, you will also get many other details like pages accessed by the visitor before sending an inquiry.

Getting customer's approval online for a sales proposal

It's a moment, the salesman is waiting for when the prospect gets interested in the product and start a discussion about the product feature and pricing. An opportunity moved forward to proposition stage as prospect starts a discussion about the product pricing, the salesman should identify the decision makers, requirement about the products and its features, the delivery time so that salesman can do the better negotiation on him a later stage.

Let's create the products, and send the first proposal to prospects, start negotiating on the proposal and get it confirmed online with customer's signature.

Getting ready

The first step is to import or create the products in Odoo before we prepare and send the proposal to the customer. To create a product, go to **Sales** | **Sales** | **Products**. Click on the **CREATE** button.

Enter `Laguna light white - 600 X 600` in the **Product name** field, 400 in the **Sales price** field, 250 in **Cost price** field, select *Consumable* in **Product Type** field, as shown in the following image:

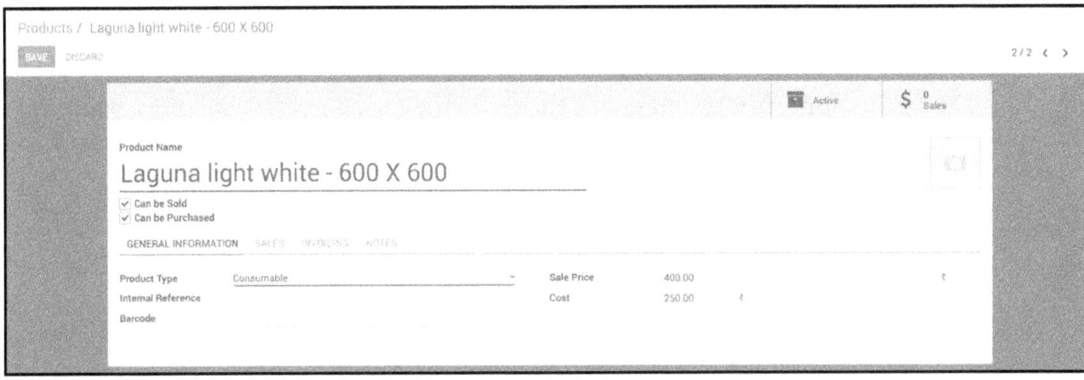

The second important field to configure is, **Invoicing Policy** under **Invoicing** tab. Select **Delivered quantities** in the **Invoicing Policy** field.

Choose **Invoicing Policy** based on your business policy, selecting **Ordered quantities** will allow you to raise an invoice based on the quantity in sold in sale order while selecting **Delivered quantities** will allow you to raise an invoice based on quantity delivered.

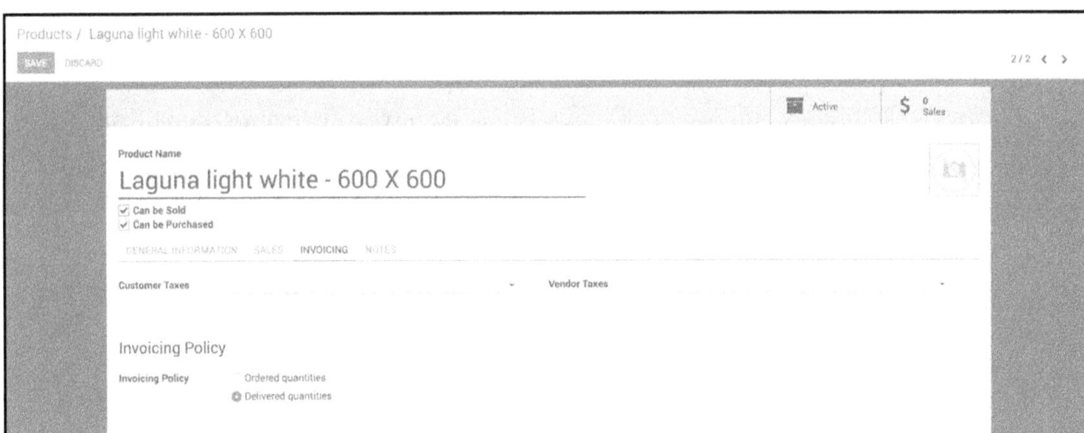

You are done with the product configuration.

How to do it...

1. Let's go to opportunity and create the first proposal, based on the office space measured during the onsite visit. Click on **Sales** | **Sales** | **My Pipeline**, search for the opportunity, and click on it to open the form view:

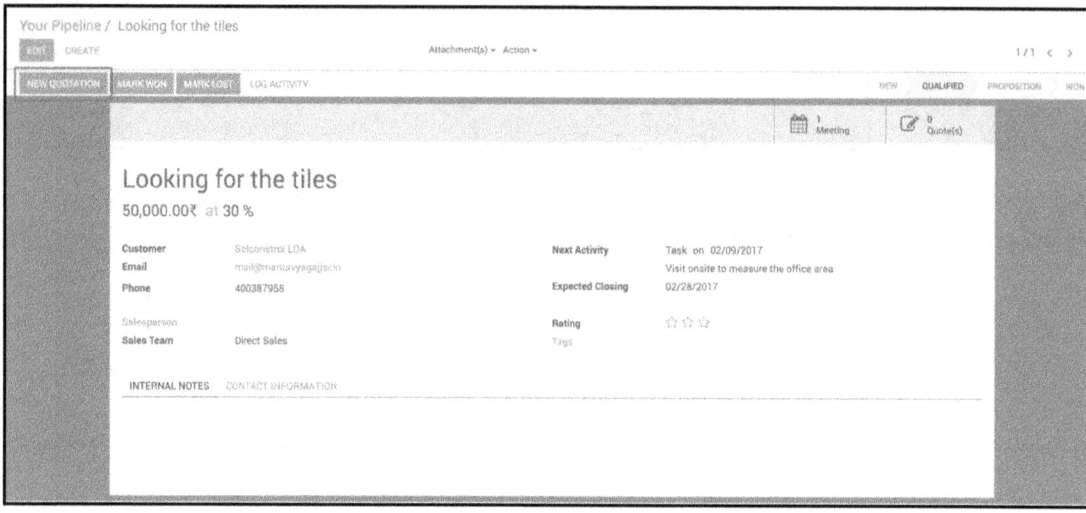

The quotation can be created by clicking on the **NEW QUOTATION** button on opportunity form view, add the quotation line by clicking on **Add an Item** link, select the product `Laguna light white - 600 X 600`, and enter `500` in **Quantity** field.

The **Proposal Date** and **Expatiation Date** has to be set on the quotation, along with the Payment Term, enter the appropriative dates before we send the proposal to the customer.

Look at the following screen of the sales quotation:

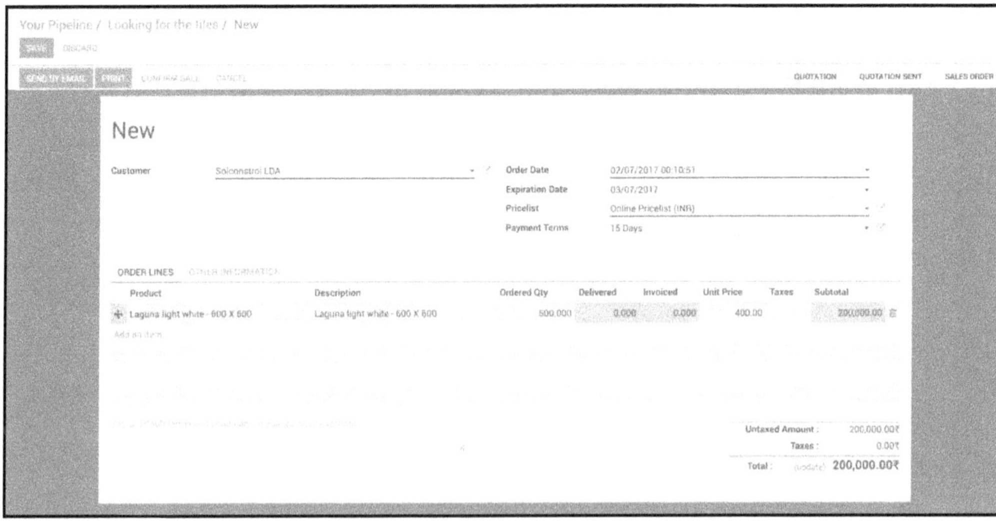

Click on the **SEND BY EMAIL** button to send the copy of the proposal to the customer by email.

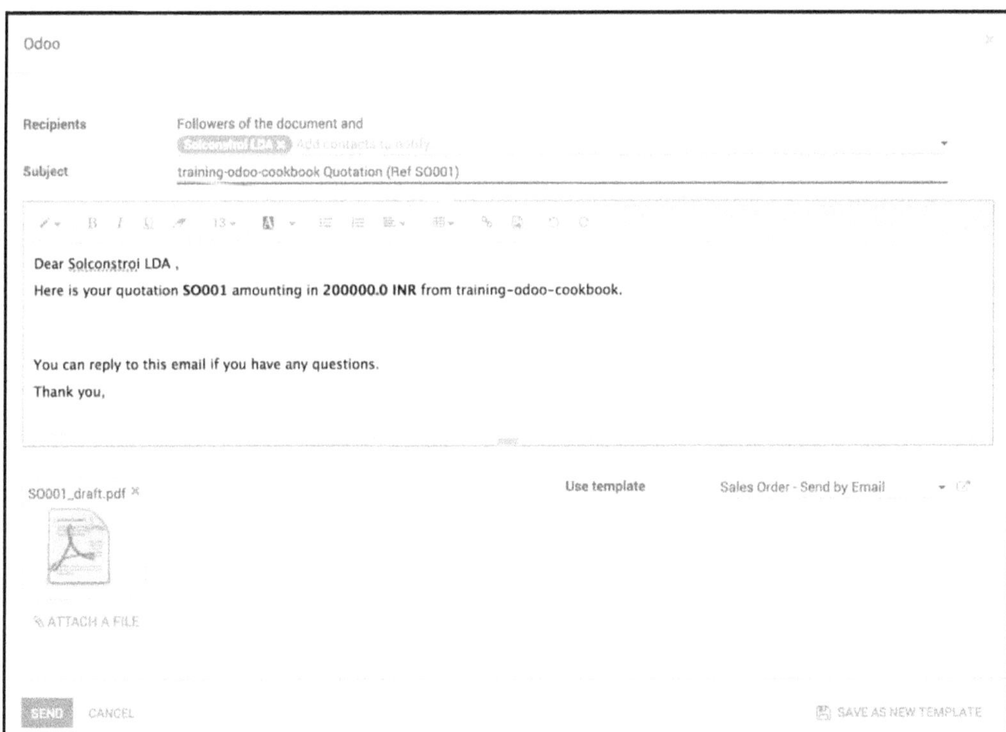

The email will be generated based on the predefined email template, however, the content of the email can be changed, a quotation will be generated and attached to the email, click on the **SEND** button to send the proposal to prospect.

2. Once the quotation sent to the prospect, it's time to move opportunity forward from **QUALIFIED** to **PROPOSITION** stage. You can jump to opportunity from sales quotation **SO001**, by clicking on the opportunity title in breadcrumb:

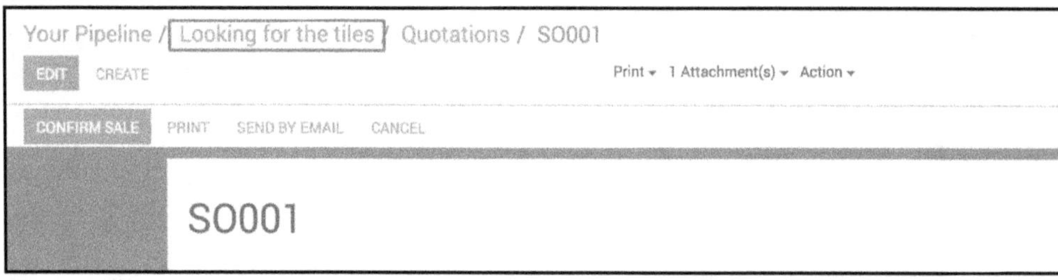

3. To move opportunity to proposition stage, click on the **PROPOSITION** stage on the status bar.

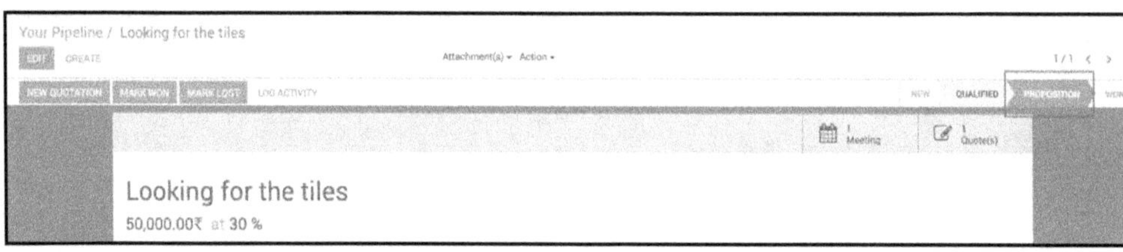

Clicking on the **Quotation(s)** action button, you can jump to the list of quotations, prepared and sent to this opportunity. As soon as a customer asked for the quotation for a new product, you can click on the **NEW QUOTATION** button, add product line and send through the email, instead of changing the existing quotation.

4. Customer gets an email in their mailbox, the quotation will be available as an attachment on the email, the quotation will be in PDF format:

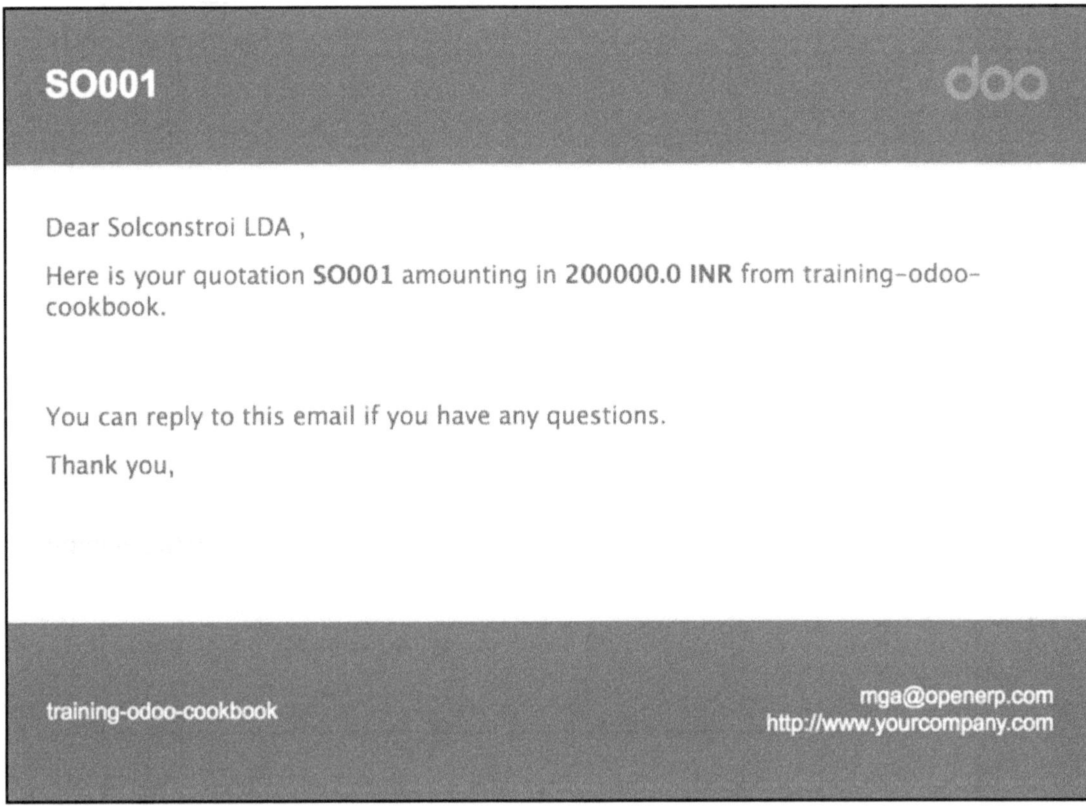

Click on proposal attached in the email and prospect will get a detailed quotation, look at the following image:

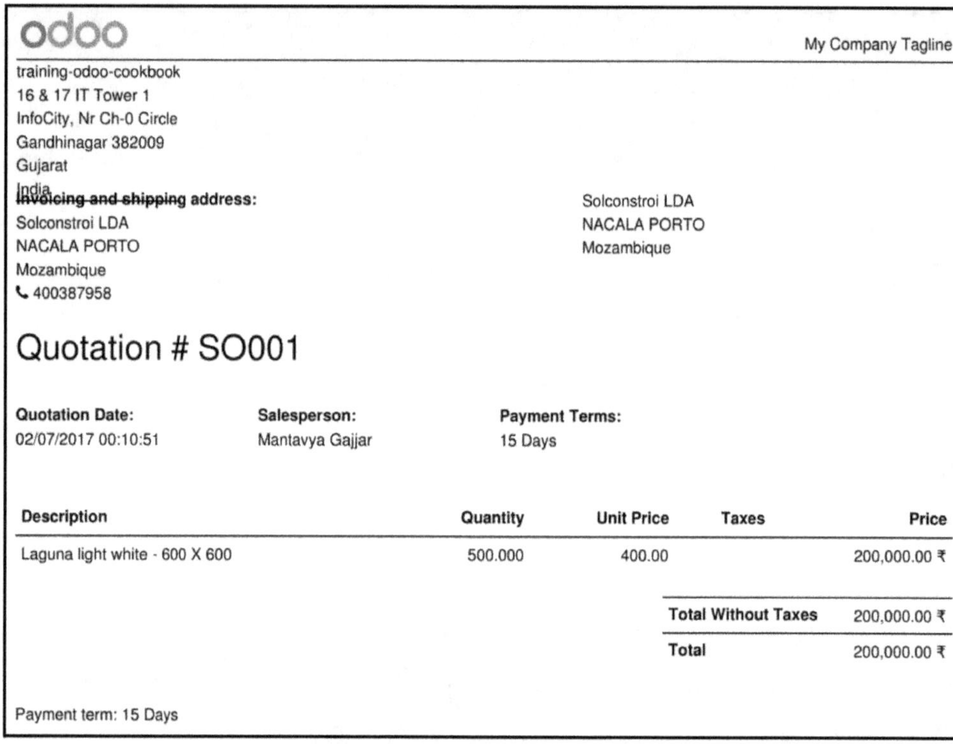

odoo

My Company Tagline

training-odoo-cookbook
16 & 17 IT Tower 1
InfoCity, Nr Ch-0 Circle
Gandhinagar 382009
Gujarat
India

Invoicing and shipping address:
Solconstroi LDA
NACALA PORTO
Mozambique
400387958

Solconstroi LDA
NACALA PORTO
Mozambique

Quotation # SO001

Quotation Date:	Salesperson:	Payment Terms:
02/07/2017 00:10:51	Mantavya Gajjar	15 Days

Description	Quantity	Unit Price	Taxes	Price
Laguna light white - 600 X 600	500.000	400.00		200,000.00 ₹

Total Without Taxes	200,000.00 ₹
Total	200,000.00 ₹

Payment term: 15 Days

We will have a message just below the sales quotation, when a customer replies to this email. Assume that customer reply on the proposal email we send to starts discussion on the pricing:

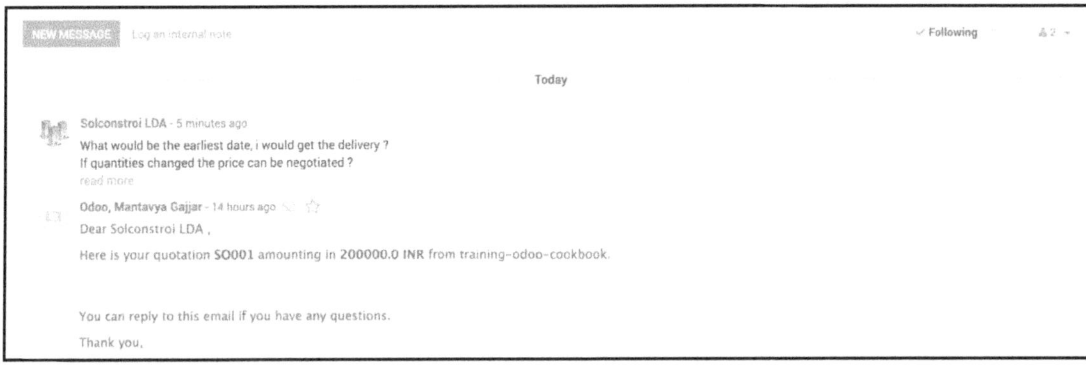

As customer starts a discussion about the pricing, let's change the stage of the opportunity into CRM, so that sales manager has a clear view of the sales channel.

5. Go to **Sales | Sales | My Pipeline** and search for the opportunity you just started negotiation on, you can start negotiation in proposition stage or add a new stage negotiation will help you to track the opportunities easily. Let's add a new stage negotiation and move it before the **Won** stage. Click on **ADD NEW COLUMN**, and a column will be replaced by the input box; enter *Negotiation* as a value and click on **ADD** button:

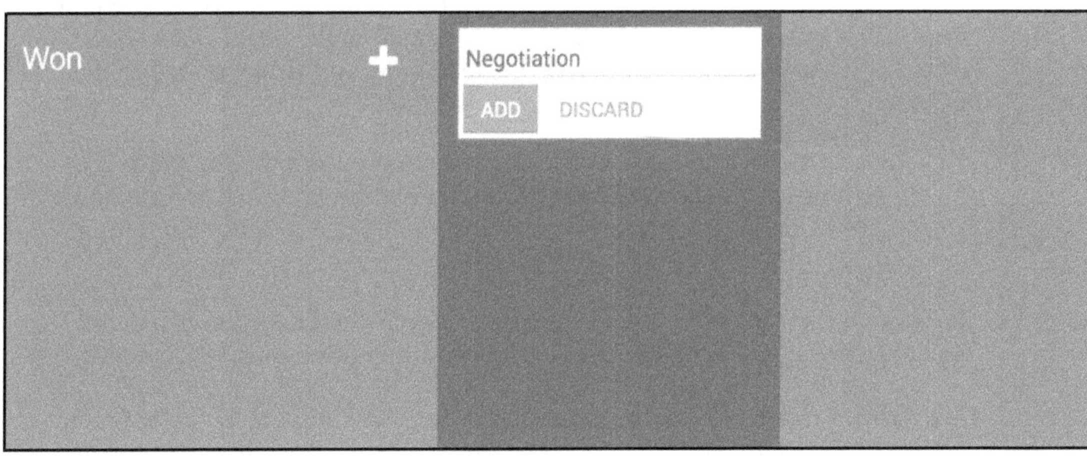

Once you are ready with the Negotiation stage, move opportunity form **PROPOSITION** to **NEGOTIATION** stage using drag and drop.

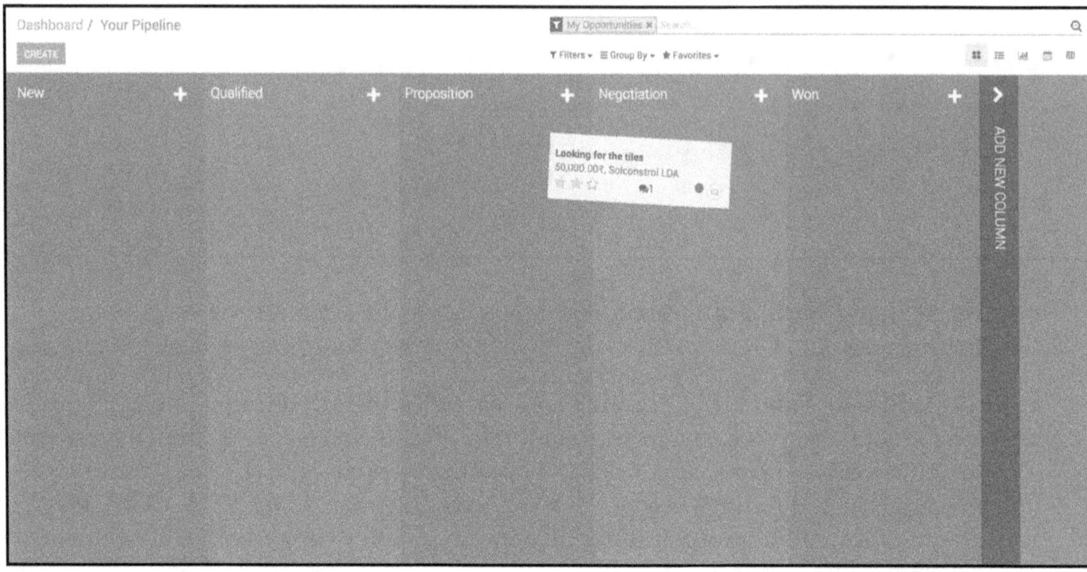

You can discuss the pricing along with other factors like logistics cost and other charges. It is advisable to use the Terms and condition field available at the bottom of sales quotation, mention all the **terms and condition** related to the quotation.

> **TIP**
> The default terms and condition can be setup form the company settings, available at **Setting** | **General Setting** and click on **Configure Your Company Data**, and you will be redirected to company setting.

6. The sales order can be confirmed as soon as the customer is agreed to move forward, he is agreed to all the terms and conditions along with the pricing.

   Go to **Sales** | **Sales** | **Quotation**, search for the *SO001* and open the quotation, click on **CONFIRM SALES** button to confirm the quotation:

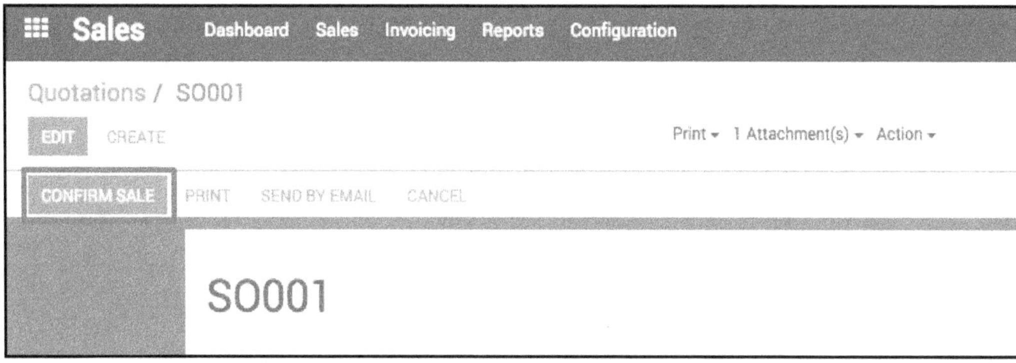

The quotation is confirmed and converted to Sales Order.

7. The delivery of the product can be processed on the Sales Order, go to the Sales Order SO001, click on EDIT button to enter into edit mode, enter delivered quantity on the order line.

> The **Invoicing Policy** we set to *Based on the delivery* on the product. It means the invoice can be created once the delivery of the order has been processed.

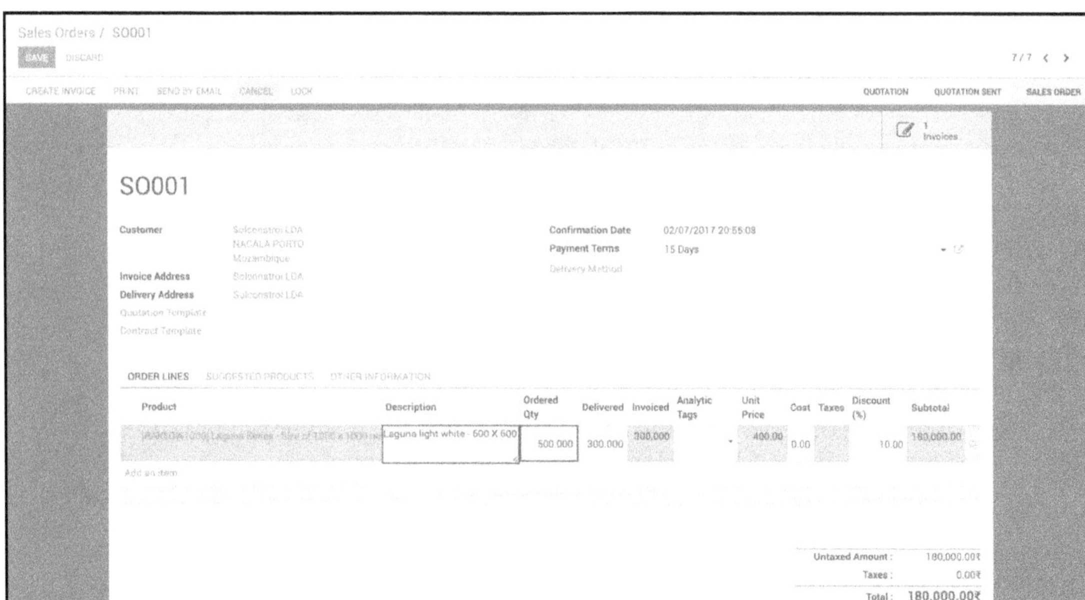

8. As soon as you enter the quantity in **Delivered** field to indicate that products are delivered manually, the line color will be changed to blue, indicates that the line is ready to invoice, and **CREATE INVOICE** button will be activated too.

> TIP: If the Odoo stock module is installed, the **Delivered** quantity will be marked as read-only and it computes the delivered quantities based on the delivery orders in the warehouse.

Invoice to your customer and get paid

Send an invoice to the customer is the responsibility of the accounting department, Odoo invoicing is super flexible and you can manage almost all the business, some of the business cases which is managed by the Odoo invoicing application is as follows:

- Invoice based on the ordered quantities
- Invoice based on the delivery
    - Single invoice for single delivery
    - Single invoice for multiple deliveries
- Advance invoice before delivery
    - Invoice based on the percentage of the total invoice amount
    - Invoice with fixed amount
- Create single invoice for multiple orders for the same customer

Let's go to the sales order, make delivery either full or partial and send an invoice based on the delivered quantity.

How to do it...

1. All the sale orders which are ready for the invoicing, either full or partial, it can be found at **Sales** | **Invoicing** | **Sales to Invoice** menu:

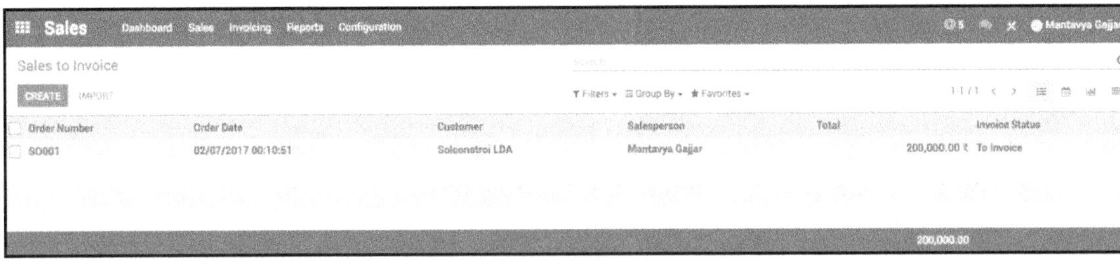

2. To create an invoice for the sales order, click on the order enter into the form view, and click on the **CREATE INVOICES** button, a wizard will be appearing to guide you further:

Keep the default option selected; the default options will be selected depending on the situation, however you can change the option, please go through the following list of options to understand when to select which option.

- **Invoiceable lines** - create an invoice for all the blue lines on sales order
- **Invoiceable lines (deduct the down payment)** - create an invoice for the blue lines and deduct the advance payment, if an advance invoice created to get the advance payment
- **Down payment (percentage):** create an invoice based on the fixed amount.
- **Down payment (fixed amount):** create an invoice based on the percentage of the invoice total amount.

The quantity to invoice will be computed when option **Invoicable lines** is selected, `Quantity to Invoice = Quantity Delivered - Quantity Invoiced.`

3. You can create a single invoice for multiple orders-- from the list view, go to **Sales** | **Invoicing** | **Sales to Invoice**, select customer under the **Group By** menu, expand the customer group for which invoice has to be created, click on the checkbox to select all the record.

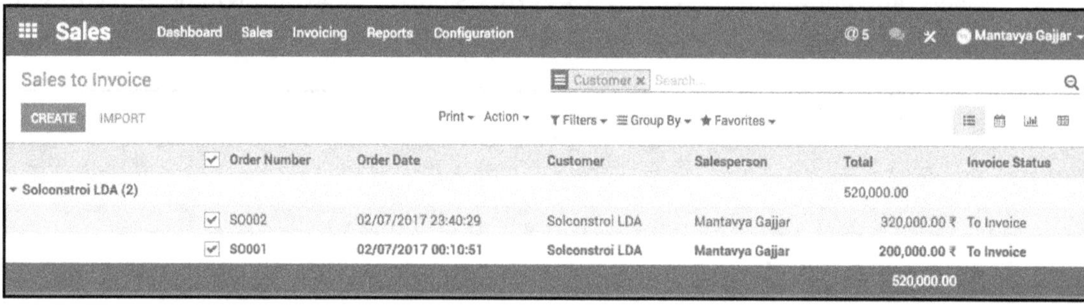

From the **Action drop-down** menu, click on the **Invoice Order**, to create an invoice for the selected orders in the list view.

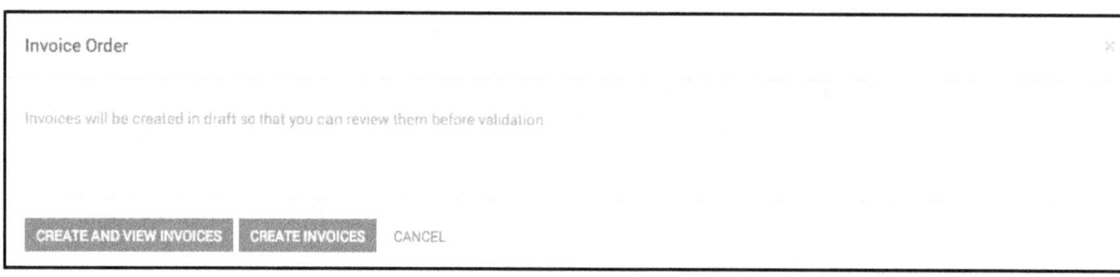

If you select multiple orders for the different customer, you are allowed to create an invoice and Odoo will create one invoice per customer.

4. All the invoices are created will stay in **DRAFT;** those invoices have to be reviewed by an accountant before sending to customers. An accountant may review the invoice one by one and confirm them or it is possible to confirm the multiple invoices at once, from the list view.

It is advisable to review invoice one by one, but still, some companies have to process many invoices every day, they choose to confirm multiple invoices at once:

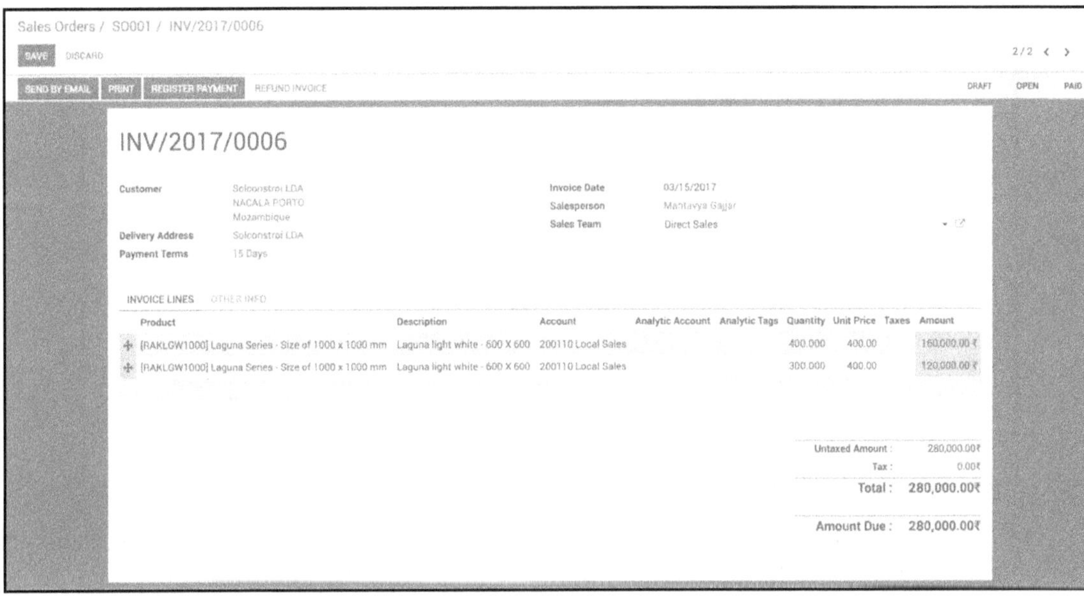

Once the invoice is validated, an invoice goes to **OPEN** state and an invoice number will be generated. We can send the invoice to the customer by clicking on the **SEND BY MAIL** button, or use **REGISTER PAYMENT** button to make the payment on the invoice.

The invoice can be printed and can be sent to the customer by courier, click on the **PRINT** button to print the invoice, it will look like the following screen:

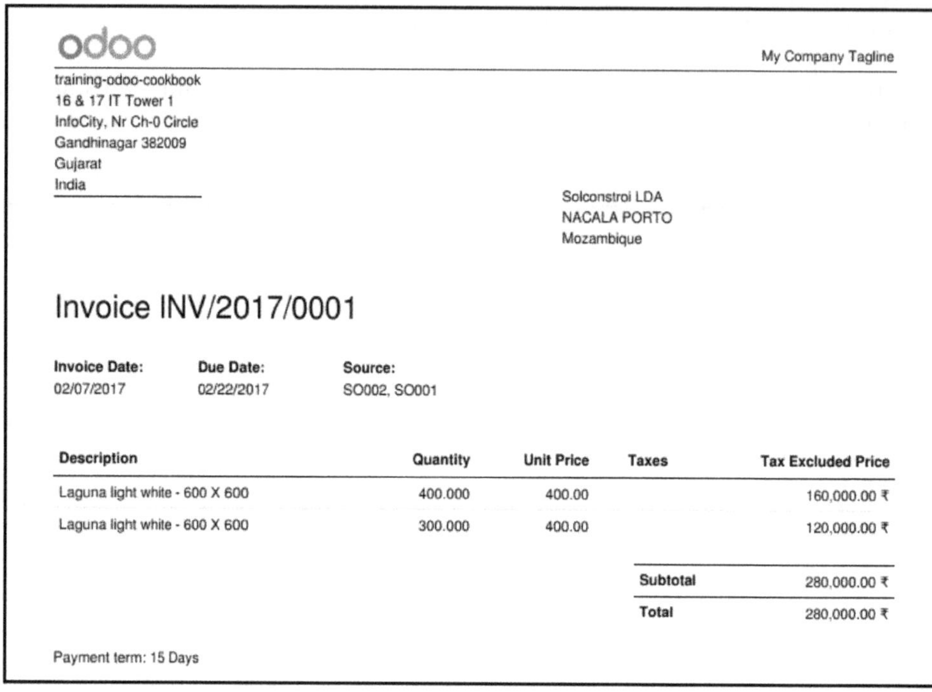

odoo

My Company Tagline

training-odoo-cookbook
16 & 17 IT Tower 1
InfoCity, Nr Ch-0 Circle
Gandhinagar 382009
Gujarat
India

Solconstroi LDA
NACALA PORTO
Mozambique

Invoice INV/2017/0001

Invoice Date:	Due Date:	Source:
02/07/2017	02/22/2017	SO002, SO001

Description	Quantity	Unit Price	Taxes	Tax Excluded Price
Laguna light white - 600 X 600	400.000	400.00		160,000.00 ₹
Laguna light white - 600 X 600	300.000	400.00		120,000.00 ₹
			Subtotal	280,000.00 ₹
			Total	280,000.00 ₹

Payment term: 15 Days

5. As soon as the payment received it can be registered on the invoice. The payment can be received through Bank / Cash or online transfer. The easiest way to register the payment is, to open the invoice and click on the **REGISTER PAYMENT** button.

The payment wizard will be a popup and guide you through the payment process:

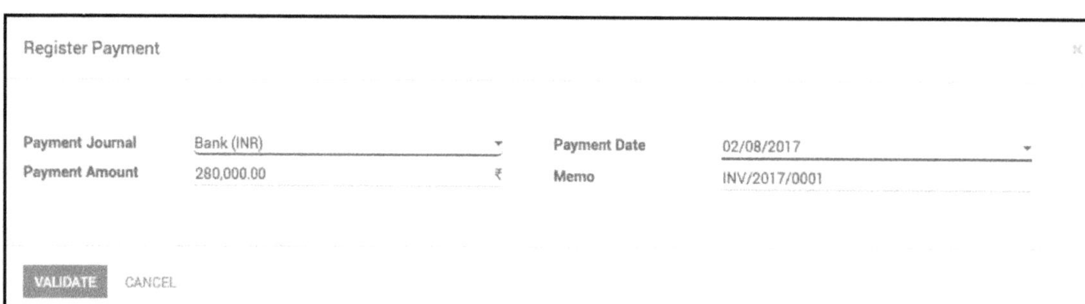

Select the payment journal based on the payment mode, select Bank if we receive the check, online transfer or select Cash if cash received. Enter the **Payment Amount** you received, confirmed **Payment Date** and click on the **VALIDATE** payment button:

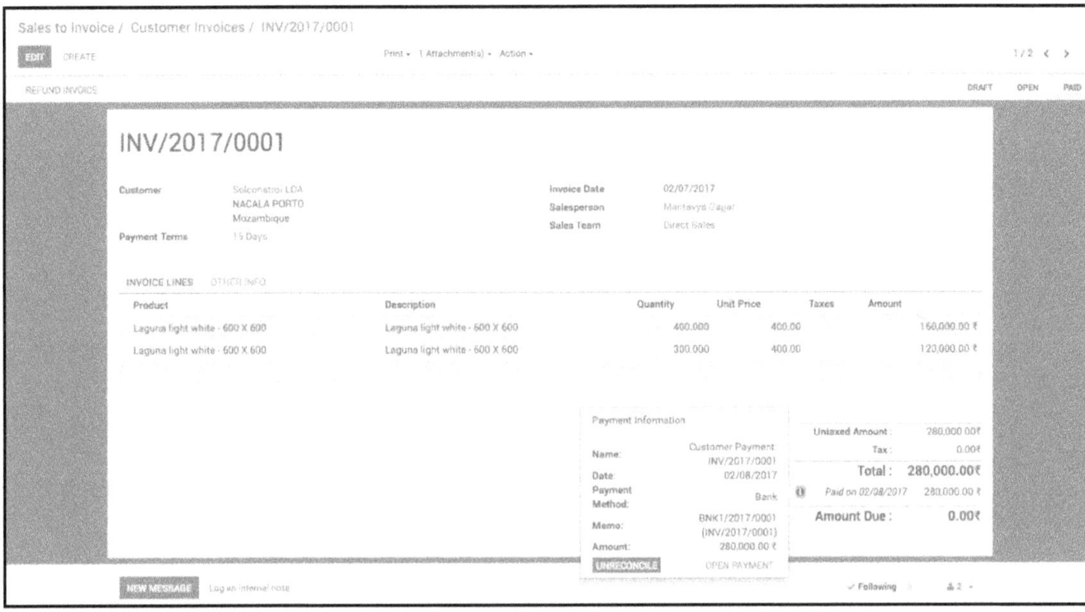

As soon as you click on the **VALIDATE** button, the payment has been registered against the invoice and you can see the full detail of the payment. When payment received is equal to the invoice **Total**, your invoice will go to the **Paid** state else it will start open and **Amount Due**, will be computed.

> The payment register against the invoice is reconciled against the invoice, still, you need to reconcile your bank with your bank statement, we will see in detail about the reconciliation in `Chapter 8`, Scale Your Business.

4

Modern way of doing sales and managing sales contracts

In this chapter we will cover the following recipes:

- Create and configure your products
- Managing your sales quotation
- Adding delivery cost to quotation
- Getting approval of order online
- Setup recurring sales and invoicing

Introduction

Traditional companies spend lots of time just preparing quotations, sending them to customers by courier, and negotiating over email and phone calls, it takes a long time to get confirmation of the order. Modern companies need an integrated application that allows them to prepare and send the quotation in a minute by email, negotiate on quotations in real-time text chatting, and allows customers to confirm and sign the order and pay online.

Let's see in detail, how you can convert your traditional company to a modern company by using sales and supporting applications in Odoo.

Create and configure your products

The most important thing in Odoo is to configure the product before you start selling. A product is used to define the stockable product, consumable product, or a service.

Other than the types of product there are many tricky configurations available on the product form that is required by the different applications, such as Income, Expense, and Tax configuration form Accounting application, routes and the barcode required by the Inventory application.

> The product configuration may change depending on the list of the application installed, on your instance. In my case, I have installed only Sales application.

Let's create a consumable and service type product to see how Odoo treats them and execute the business flow accordingly.

Getting ready

We assume that you are working on the duplicated instance, if not, create a duplicate instance and try to configure products on that.

How to do it...

1. To create the product, go to **Sales** | **Sales** | **Products**. Click on the **Create** button
2. Enter the **Product name**, select **Can be Sold** if you are going to sell this product and **Can be Purchased** if you purchase this product from vendors. You will not be able to get the product on purchase and sales order form when **Can Be Sold** and **Can Be Purchased** are not checked.

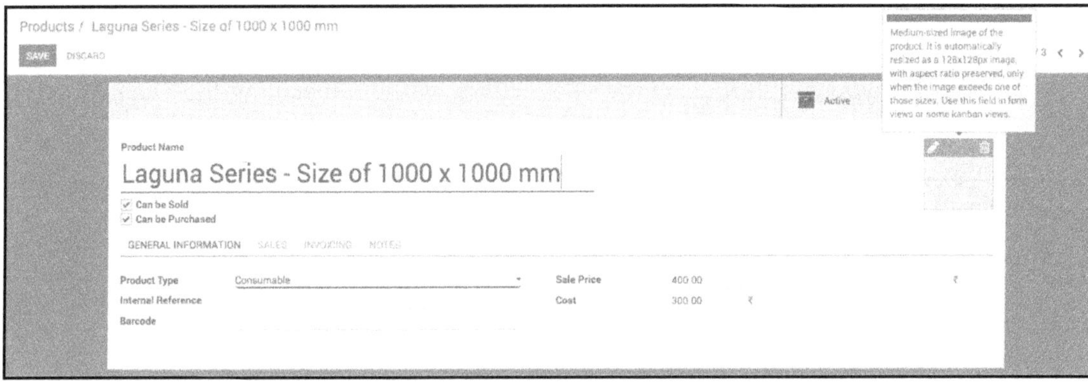

You can check only **Can be Sold** checkbox on the product form when you configure the service type of products and you are not outsourcing that service.

3. To change the product image, take the mouse on the image control, you will get the option to remove the current image or replace by clicking on the pencil icon. Click on pencil icon you will be asked to select new image, choose an image, and click on the **Open** button, the image will be updated on the product page:

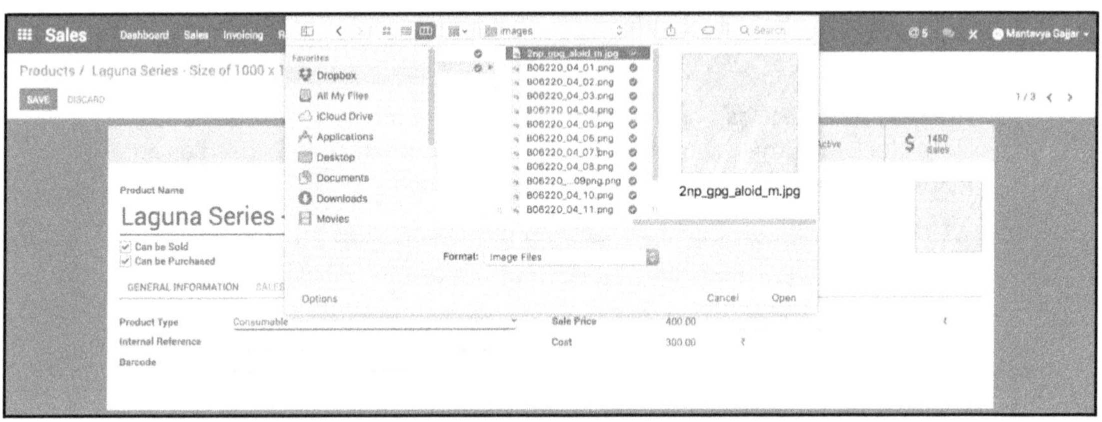

4. In **General information** tab, select the **Product type** as **Consumable**, you won't get a **Stockable** option as we have not installed stock module yet. Odoo is super flexible; you can start using the sales activity without installing the **Stock** application:

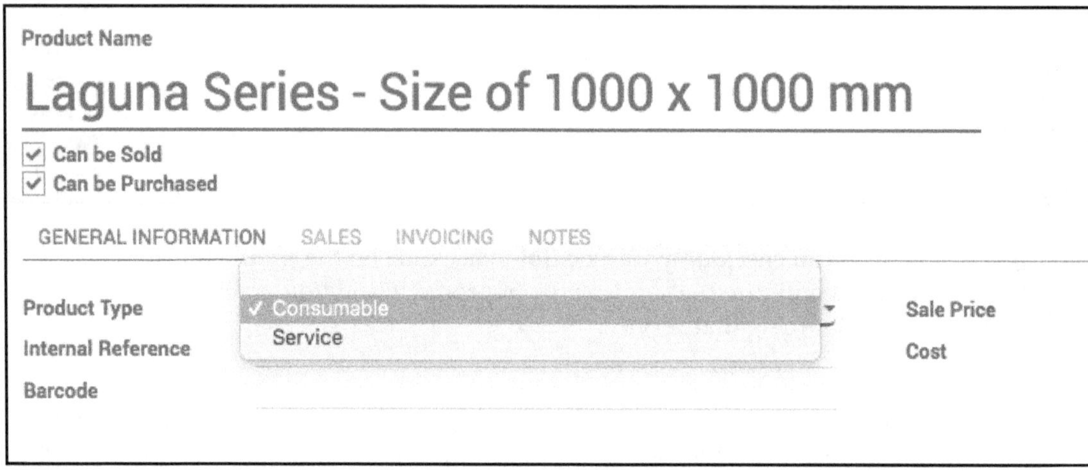

Go to **Apps**, search for the stock application, click on **Install** button to install the stock application, on successful installation you will get the third option **stockable** in product type list.

5. **Internal reference** can be a product technical name; you may use this field to store stock keeping the unit code, commonly known as SKU used as an identification code for the warehouse or product:

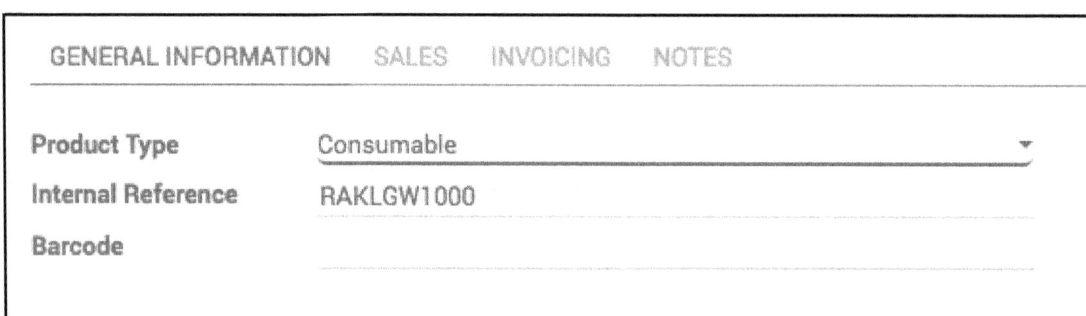

6. The pricing for the product can be set under the **General information** tab, the **Sales price** is used to define the price for customer and **Cost** is the price at which the product can be purchased from a vendor:

Price entered on product form is the fixed price and can be changed in sale or purchase order for the specific order.

> The advance sale price computation can be managed using the Pricelist option while cost price can be computed using standard, average and real time.

7. The barcode field is used to define the international article number used for product information. Enter the barcode number either manually or attach the barcode scanner to the computer, keep your curser on **Barcode** field and scan the barcode, the number will be entered automatically:

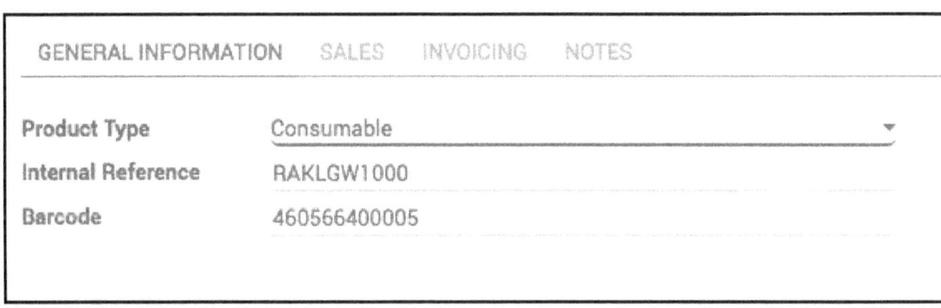

8. The same barcode will be used to print the product label. You can print the label form:

9. Until you activate or install any other application you will not have any configuration under the Sales tab. Let's go to **Sales** | **Configuration** | **Setting** and activate the P**ricelist** option **Specific prices per customer segment, currency, etc**:

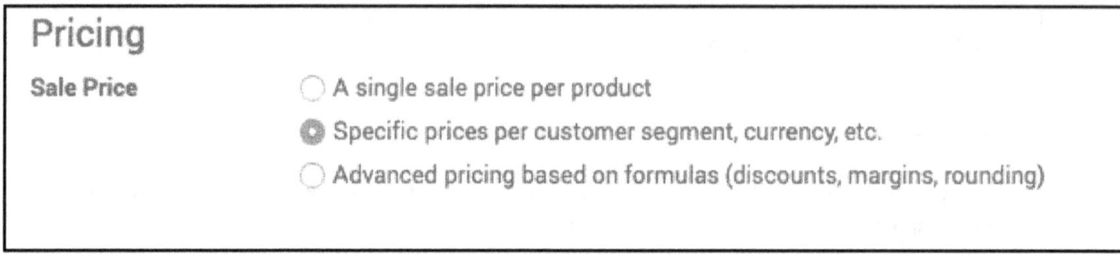

As the Pricelist feature is now activated, you can see the pricing option on a product. You can create the price per customer segment by creating a new line on the **Pricelist** field. Click on Add an Item link, by selecting the **Pricelist** and setting the Price it's done. We have created three different pricelist **Walk-in Customer, Online Pricelist** and **Distributor pricelist** with three different prices:

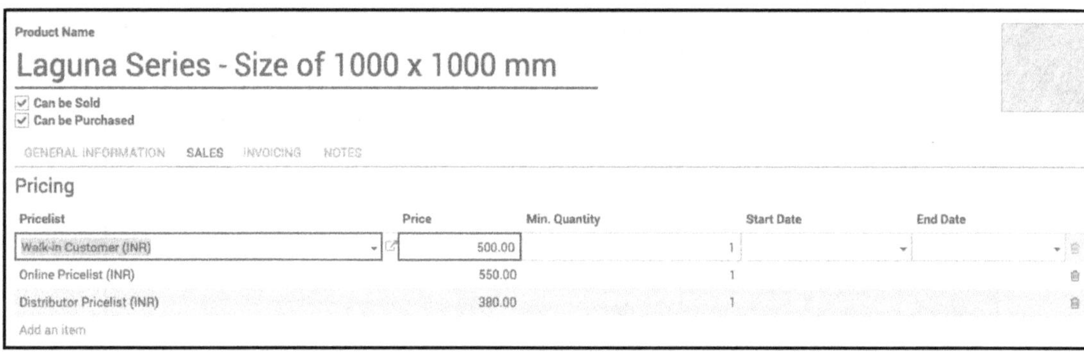

10. The invoicing related configure can be found under **Invoice** Tab. **Customer tax** and **Vendor tax** are the default tax applied in sales and purchaser order:

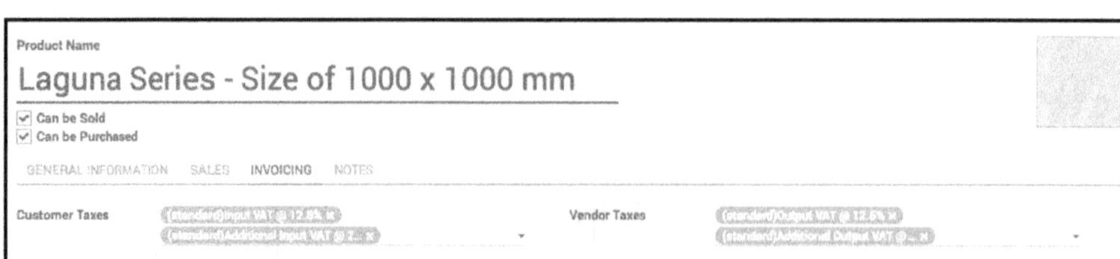

Usually, the customer tax and vendor tax are the same.

> The sales taxes are the default taxes applied to all customers, however, taxes can be changed depending on the customer location using a fiscal position. We will see recipe *Apply tax based on customer location* in `Chapter 7`, *Setup Financial Management with Odoo*

11. The invoicing policy defines how the invoice will be created from sales order. Select **Delivered quantities** in the **Invoicing Policy** field:

> Choose **Invoicing Policy** based on your business policy, selecting **Ordered quantities** to raise an invoice based on quantity sold in order irrespective of delivered quantity. Select invoice based on **Delivered quantities** to raise an invoice based on quantity delivered and not based on the quantity in order.

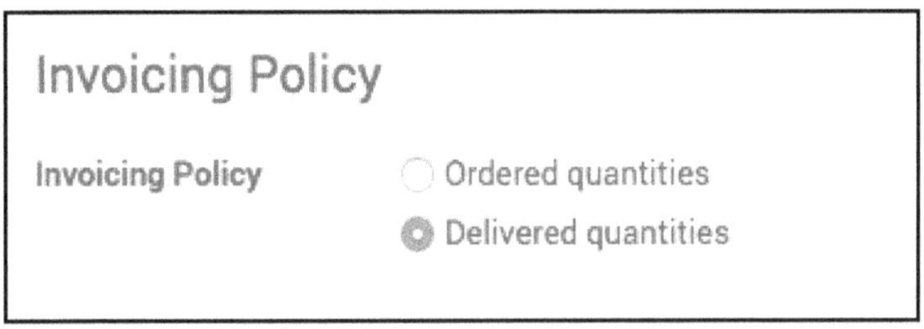

The last configuration, the **Notes tab**, defines the product description that will appear on the sales order line in the product description:

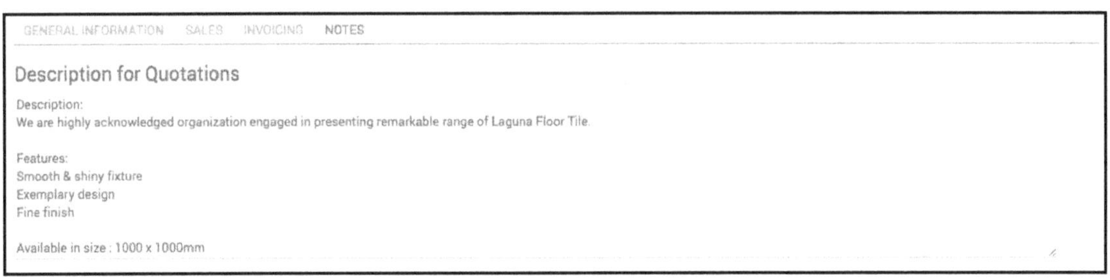

How it works...

You are almost done with the product configuration. To test the product configuration, create sale quotation, select **Customer** and select the **Product**:

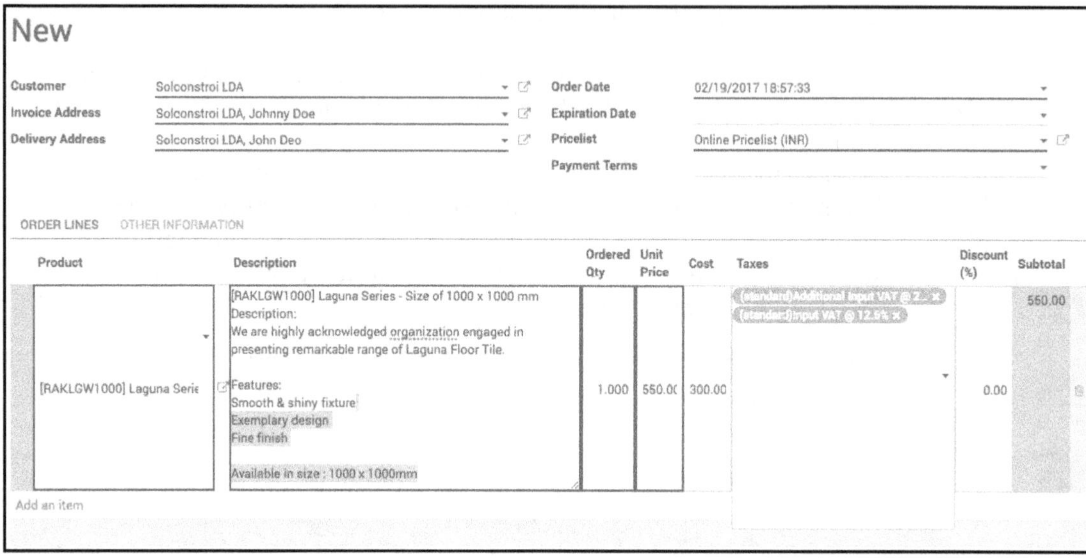

The **Description, Unit price, Taxes** will be selected and applied automatically based on the product configuration. However, you are allowed to change for the specific order.

There's more...

Let's look at testing the Pricelist. To test the **Pricelist**, create a new order, go to **Sales** | **Sales** | **Sales Quotation** select the **Customer**, the default **Pricelist** will be selected, change the **Pricelist** to **Distributor Pricelist (INR)** and click on **Add an item** on the sales order line to create a new order line:

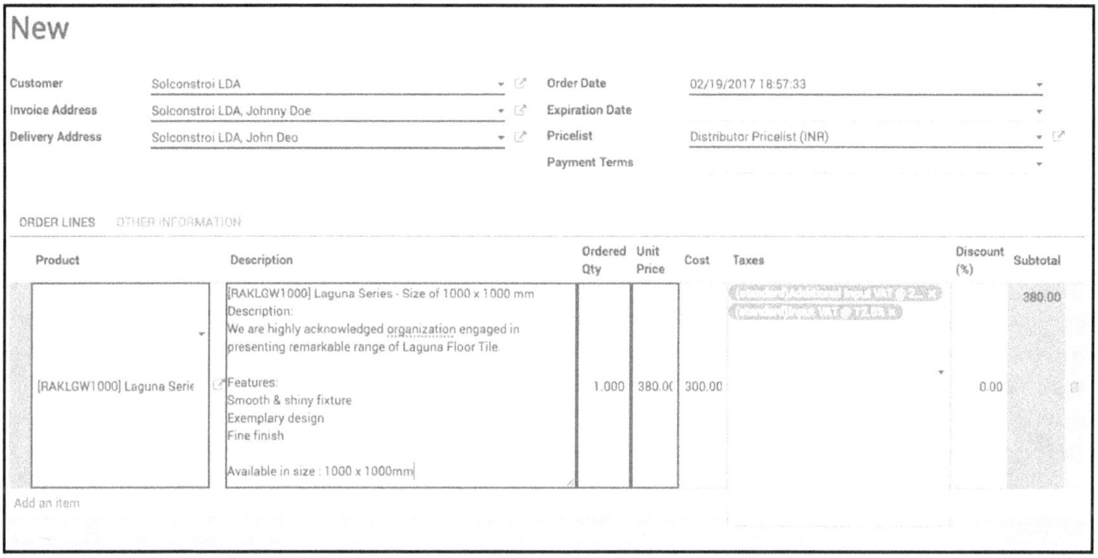

You should get the price `380` specified in the **Distributor pricelist**.

Managing your sales quotation

Quotations are documents sent to customers to offer an estimated cost for a particular set of goods or services. The customer can accept the quotation, in that case, the seller will have to issue a sales order, or refuse it.

For example, Group Lucky company sells building material products and their client Solconstroi LDA showed interest in Laguna light white - 600 X 600 tiles of 500 piece for their office. We would like to send them a quotation for those Laguna light white - 600 X 600 tiles with a sales price of 400 USD with a 5% discount.

How to do it...

1. To create the quotation, click on **Sales** | **Sales** | **Quotations**, you will be taken to a list of quotations and confirmed orders.

2. Click on **CREATE** button to create a new quotation, you will be taken to the form view of quotation:

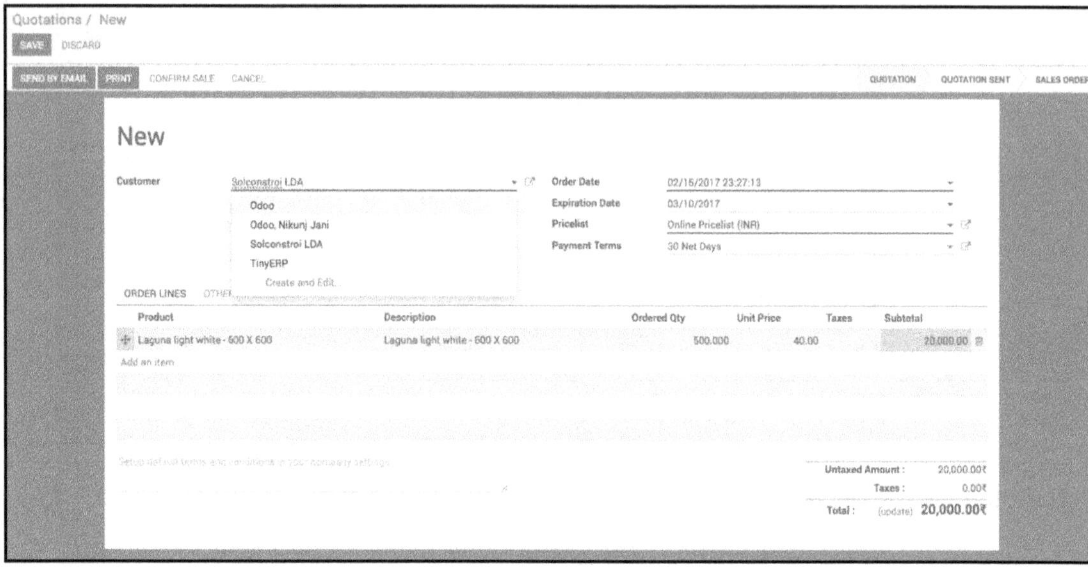

Select the **Customer** first, **Order Date**, **Pricelist** and **Payment Terms** will be selected automatically depending on the selected customer.

Pricelist and **Payment terms** should be changed depending on the customer you choose on the quotation. You may change those fields other than default selected when you change pricelist or payment term it will change only for the current order.

3. Add a new line on the quotation, select the **Product**, change the **Description** to describe the product specification, **Ordered Qty**, **Unit Price** will be filled automatically, but you may change the price per qty. You can see this in the following image:

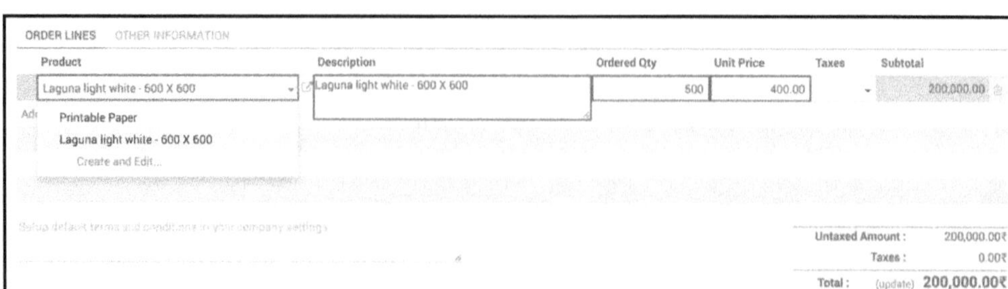

Taxes will be applied automatically. **Subtotal** and **Total** will be computed when you change anyone from **Ordered Qty**, **Price** or **Taxes** on any line.

4. The proposal should have the **Order Date**, the **Expiration Date** of the proposal and **Payment Terms**.

Click on the **SEND BY EMAIL** button to send the proposal to the customer by email:

The quotation will be saved and an automated email will be generated with a PDF copy of the quotation attached to the email. Click on the SEND button to send the quotation to a customer.

5. Customer will receive an email in his/her mailbox with pdf quotation report attached in the email:

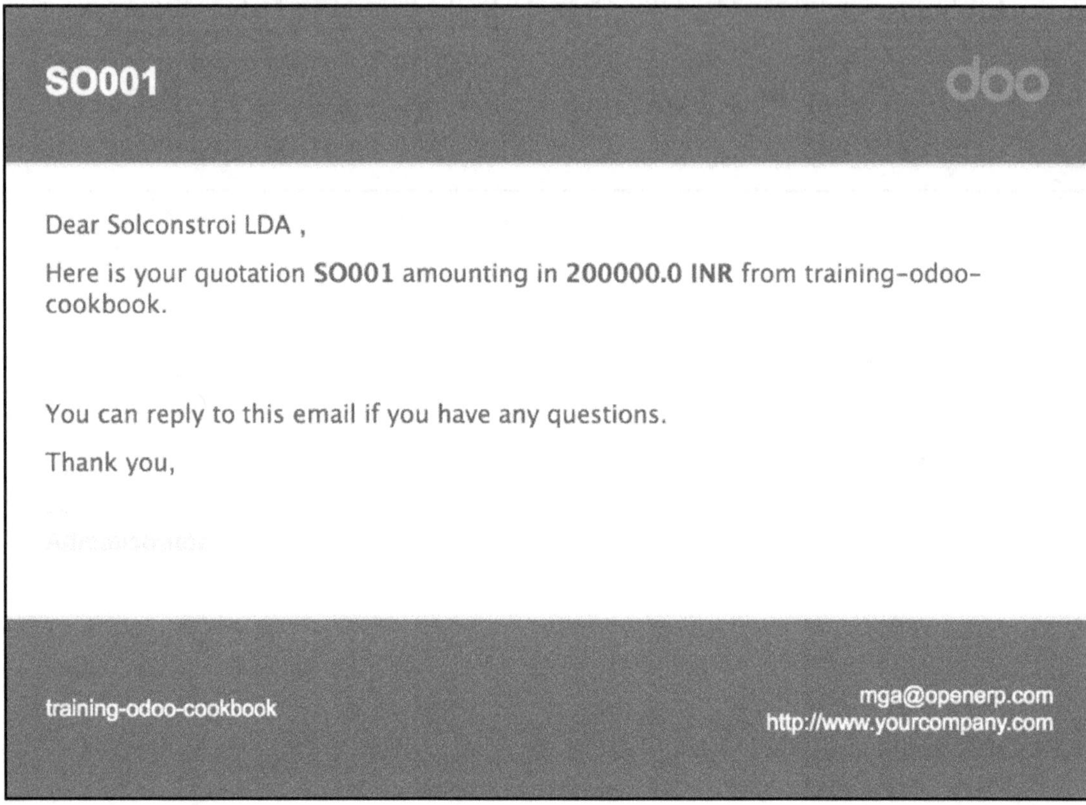

Click on quotation attached in the email, the customer will get a detailed quotation. Look at the following image:

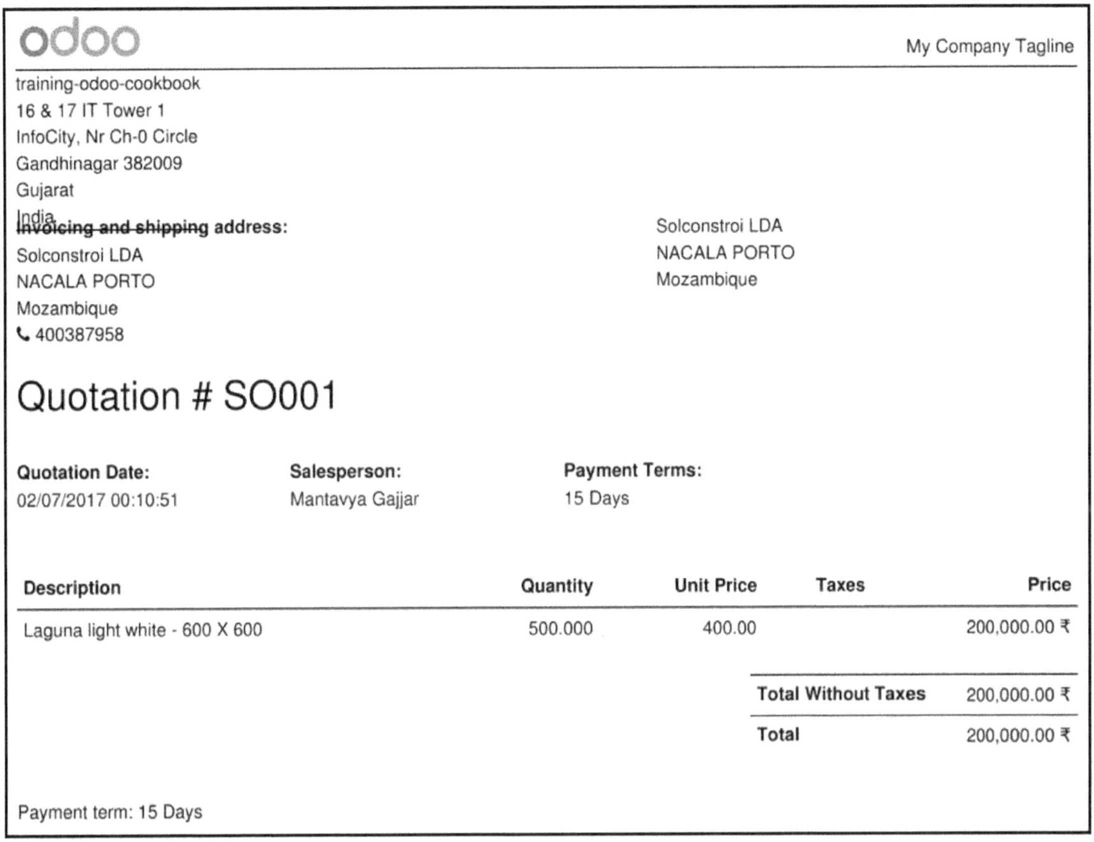

odoo

My Company Tagline

training-odoo-cookbook
16 & 17 IT Tower 1
InfoCity, Nr Ch-0 Circle
Gandhinagar 382009
Gujarat
India

Invoicing and shipping address:

Solconstroi LDA
NACALA PORTO
Mozambique
400387958

Solconstroi LDA
NACALA PORTO
Mozambique

Quotation # SO001

Quotation Date: 02/07/2017 00:10:51
Salesperson: Mantavya Gajjar
Payment Terms: 15 Days

Description	Quantity	Unit Price	Taxes	Price
Laguna light white - 600 X 600	500.000	400.00		200,000.00 ₹
		Total Without Taxes		200,000.00 ₹
		Total		200,000.00 ₹

Payment term: 15 Days

When customer replies to this email, we will have a message just below the same quotation. Let's assume that customer start a discussion on the pricing part, just by replying to the email:

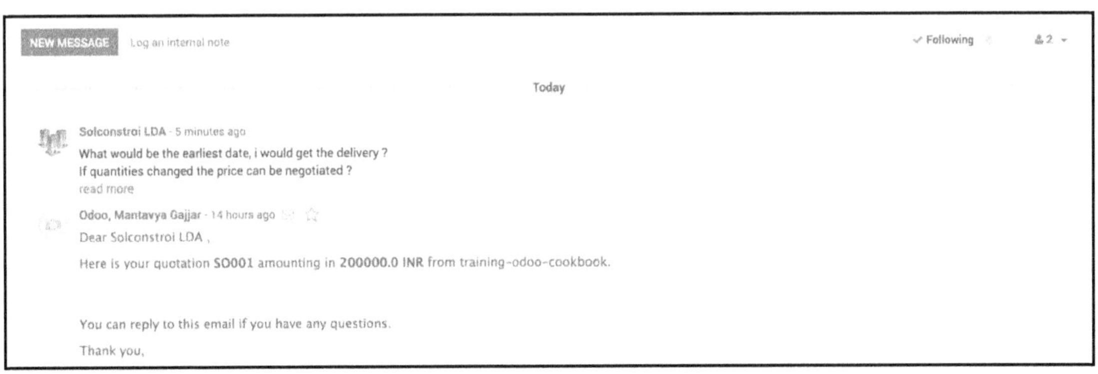

As customer starts discussing the pricing, let's trigger a positive signal to the quotation, click on **Confirm Sale** to confirm the quotation and convert to the confirmed sales order.

6. Customer may ask to change the quantities after confirmation of the quotation, this is the standard business case when a customer like your products and wanted to increase the ordered quantities:

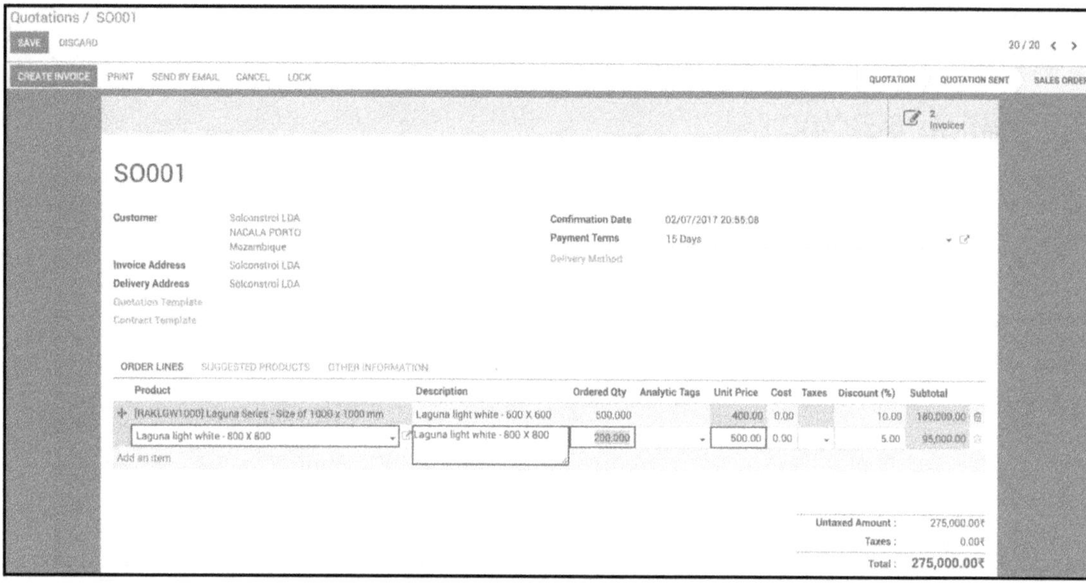

With Odoo you can simply click on **EDIT** to edit the confirmed order, change the quantities and click on the **SAVE** button. Odoo manages all the business cases while editing the confirmed sales order.

> You can lock the order by clicking on the **LOCK** button on order when you do not want to allow the salesman to change the order details, however, we can process the delivery and invoice creation can be done when the order goes to **LOCK** stage.

7. To enable the discount feature on quotation, go to **Sales** | **Configuration** | **Settings** and change **Discount** setting to **Allow discounts on sales order lines.**

The discount column will be activated on the quotation; you can enter the manual discount if needed. The discount is always in percentage (%) on the sales order line, you can offer different discounts rates for different products and quantities.

> The discount can be offered manually or computed automatically if you applied on Pricelist and will be displayed online. Advance discount can be computed using the advance **pricelist** option.

There's more...

Odoo has many features on quotation and sales order to answer the real business requirements. Let's see some of the cases to solve some case such as mention customer, delivery, and invoice address, three different address on quotation, setup terms and conditions, display margins on the quotations.

Multiple addresses on quotation

Let's consider a customer is a legal company and has requested us to send an invoice to their account office while delivery of the order at their warehouse with delivery slip. You can change the address setting on sale order to have a separate invoice and delivery address from settings:

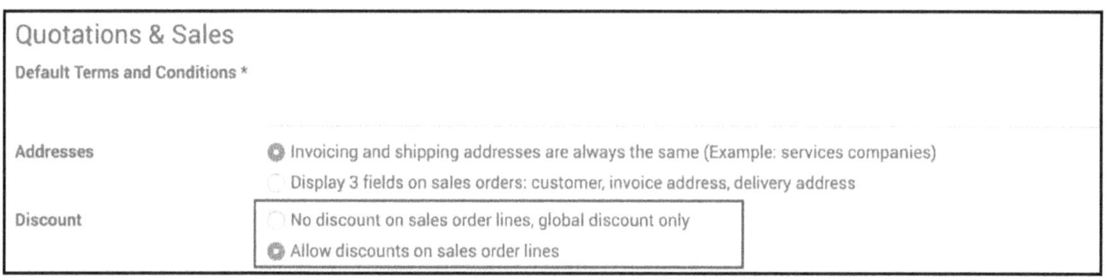

Go to **Sales** | **Configuration** | **Setting** and change the address setting to **Display 3 fields on sales orders, customer, invoice address, delivery address**. In case of Service Company, the default setting will be ok.

To define the invoice and delivery address for the customer go to **Customer** and create a new contact address from **CONTACTS & ADDRESSES** tab.

Now, when you select the customer on sales order, the other two addresses will be selected automatically on the sales quotation:

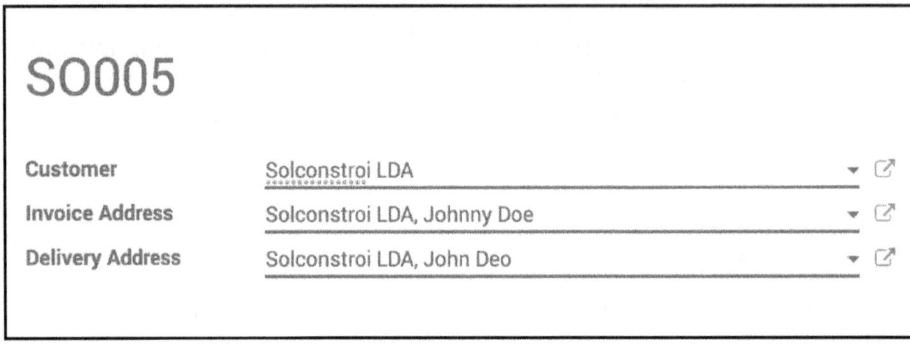

You can change the invoice or delivery address if a customer has multiple accounts or warehouse address. When you print the quotation, it has clear information about the shipping and invoice address:

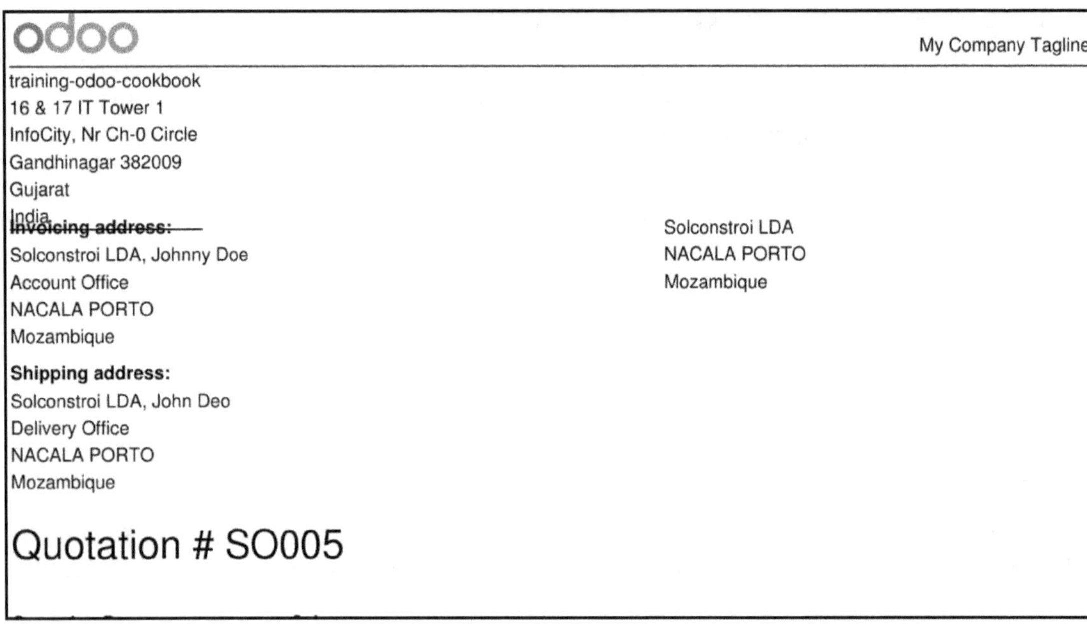

Set up terms and conditions

The commercial proposal has to be clear on the many other aspects besides the product quantity and pricing. Usually, all the commercial aspects have to be given below the proposal in terms of Terms and conditions. With Odoo you can define the terms and conditions, can be applied to all the quotations by default, when you create.

> The terms and condition normally have the payment terms information, transportation specification, specific services have to be taken care for the transportation. Let's see how to setup the default terms and conditions to be applied for the quotation, later it can be changed for quotations if needed.

Go to **Sales** | **Configuration** | **Settings**, enter the **Default Terms and Conditions** can be applied to all the proposals.

Click on the **Save** button to apply the setting. Now the default terms and conditions will be applicable for the quotation created after applying setting:

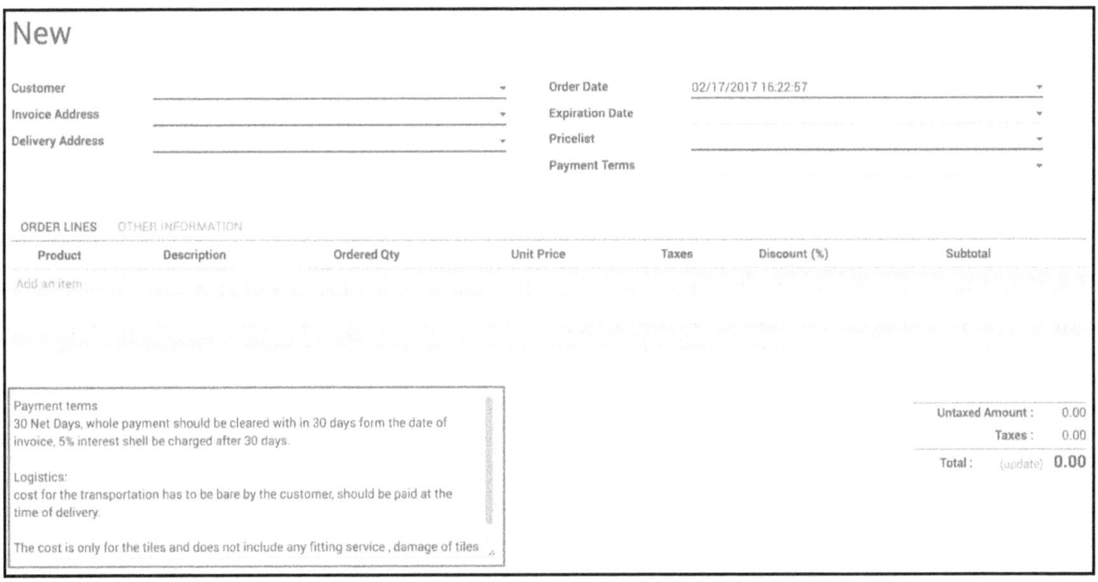

TIP

You will get the default terms and conditions below the quotation, you can change it, and the changes will be applied only to the current quotation.

Compute margins on the quotation

As a sales manager, your job is to control and execute the deals. You can negotiate better when you know the margins on each sale order during the negotiation. The margin is the actual profit that can be calculated as the difference between the sale price and cost price.

To activate the feature to compute the real-time margin on quotation go to **Sales** | **Configuration** | **Setting** and activate to **Display Margins On Quotations And Sales Orders**:

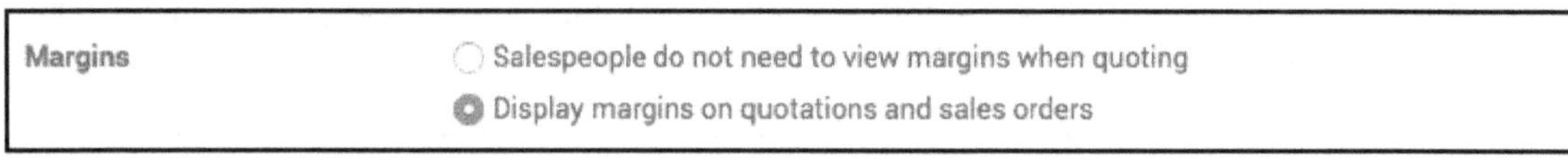

Click on **Apply** button to apply the setting.

To test the feature, go to **Sales** | **Sales** | **Quotation**, click on **Create** button to create a new quotation. Above the **Terms and Condition** field, you can see the **Margin** field. The margin will be computed when you add some order lines.

Select **Customer** and add some order lines, on the selection of the product, **Unit price** and **Cost** are filled automatically. **Unit price** is product sale price while **Cost** is product cost price. You can change the cost price on order without changing the product cost price to compute the margin correctly for the current order.

Sale Order Modification

By default, the confirmed sales order is allowed to modify the ordered quantities and other information until its mark as locked by clicking on the **Lock** button. The advantage is to manage the real-time business case such as when the customer asked to increase or decrease the quantities or adding of removing the products from confirmed order.

However, you can prevent to modify the confirmed sales order, by changing the sales application setting. Go to **Sales** | **Configuration** | **Setting** and search for the option **Sale Order Modification** the default option selected is **Allow to edit sales order from the 'Sales Order' menu (not from the Quotation menu)** switch to **Never allow to modify a confirmed sales order**, click on the **Apply** button:

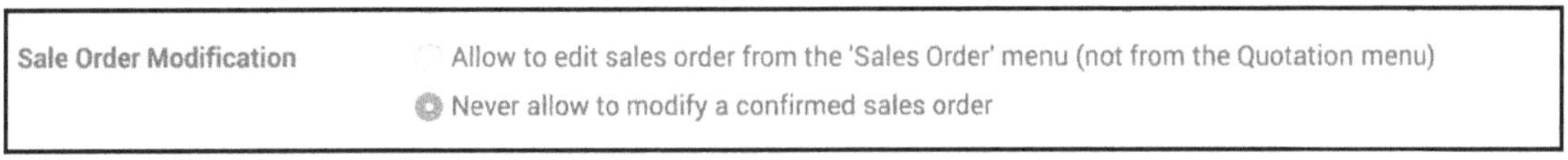

When you confirm the order, by default the order will go to **LOCK** stage and not allow too many any modification to the confirmed order, such as the products, its quantity, price or terms and conditions of the order.

Adding delivery cost to quotation

The most common requirement for business is to add the delivery charges with the quotation, the delivery charges have to be computed based on some formula or rules given by the delivery company.

Delivery cost, in case of wholesale, is paid by either customer or supplier depending on the negotiation and most of the time cost of the delivery it is given by the shipping company as the shipping consignments are huge, the cost of the delivery cannot be estimated in advance.

Odoo have a built-in delivery computation framework that allows you to configure the delivery rules, to compute the delivery cost based on distance, weight, volume, sale price of the product or you can integrate with delivery service provider such as DHL, FedEx, UPS, USPS, to get the delivery price in real time. Such delivery providers are useful when you have an e-commerce store and your customer wants to choose delivery cost by themselves.

Getting ready

We assume that you are working on the duplicated instance, if not, create a duplicate instance and try to install, and test the delivery cost.

How to do it...

1. The first thing is to install the delivery module, go to Apps, search for the `Delivery Costs` application and click on the **Install** button to install the **Delivery Costs** application. As **Delivery Costs** is not the main application, you have to remove the **Apps** filter:

> Installing the delivery cost application will automatically install the stock module, so now you should have stock application also available on your screen.

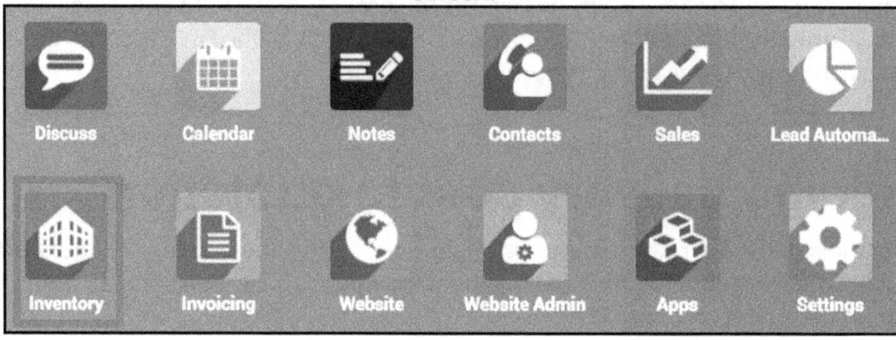

2. Delivery method and cost can be configured from the **Sales** | **Configuration** | **Delivery Methods**. Click on the **Delivery Methods** to create new or configure the existing delivery methods:

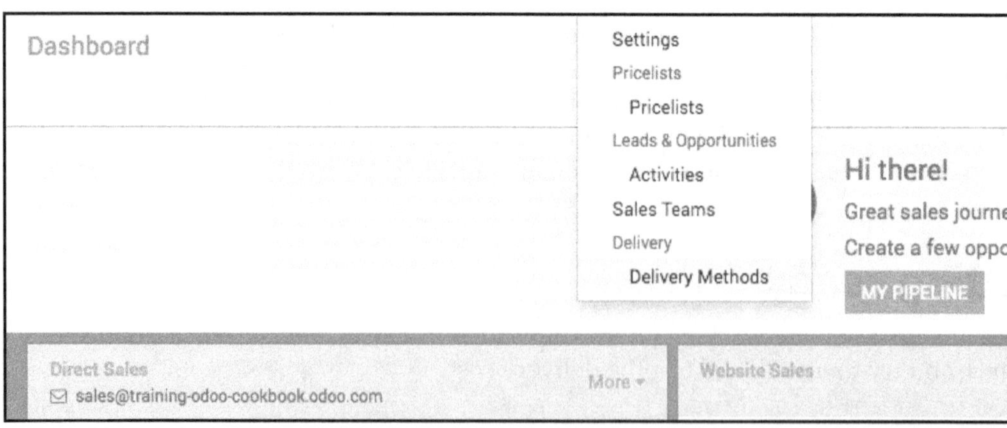

3. As soon as you arrive at the list of delivery methods, you will see only one delivery method available by default called **Free delivery charges** which will allow you to mention the delivery provider free of delivery cost.
4. To create a new delivery method, click on **Create** button, create the rules based on the delivery service provider. Enter the name of the service provider and keep **Fixed Price** for the **provider**:

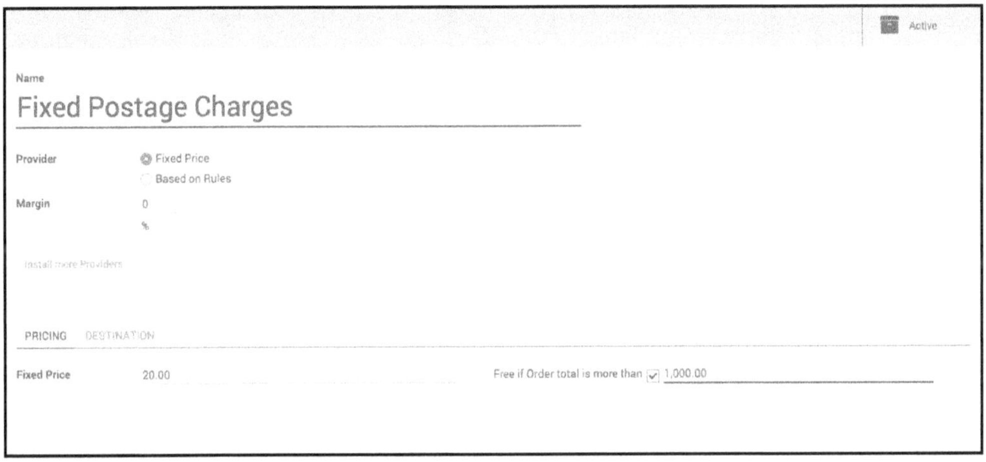

The **Fixed Price** can be entered in the **Pricing** tab below the form. You can avoid the delivery cost and make it **Free if Order total is more than** a certain amount, select the checkbox and enter the amount.

A new product is added to the product list when you create a new delivery method. The name of the product will be same as the delivery method name and product will be set as service.

When you add the margin on the delivery method, it charges customer always higher than the cost of the standard delivery service.

5. To test the delivery cost, create a new quotation add some product line, and select the **Delivery Method - Fixed Postage charges** to apply for the order.

On selection of the delivery method, a delivery cost will be updated and by clicking on the **Set Price** link, a new sales order line will be added for the delivery cost:

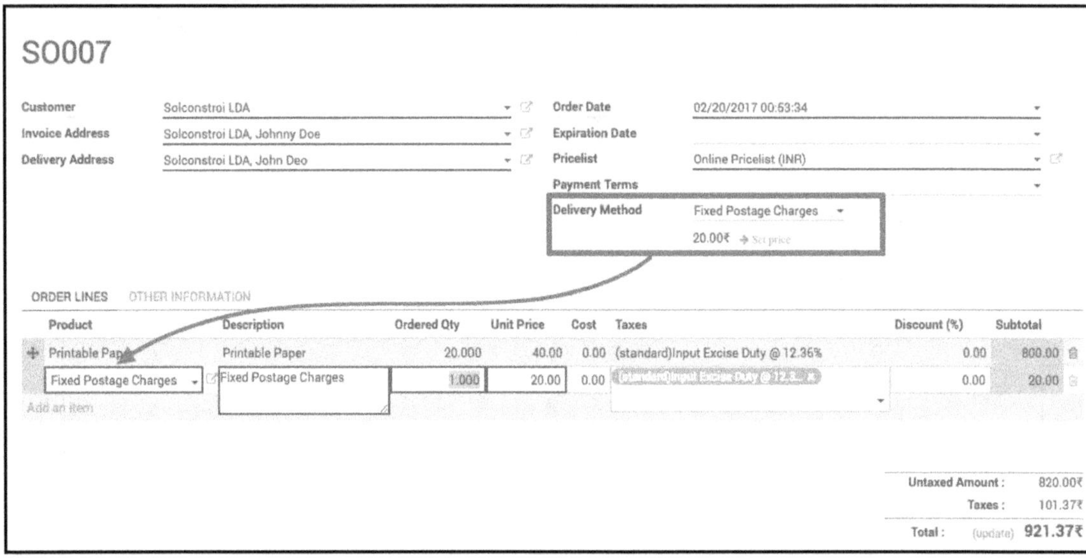

If the order total price is more than `1000` excluding tax amount, the delivery cost will be set to `0`. You can still add delivery charges line to order. It is going to charge you but you make it free for the customer, so your margin on the order will be decreased by the cost of delivery.

As the delivery service is a product, you will get the other setting applied automatically, such as default tax. When you add the correct cost and sale price you can also have the margin calculated for the delivery service too.

If you do not want to add the margin on top of the delivery cost, keep the sale price equal to the cost price on the delivery method.

6. Let's create a Speed Post-Delivery method, this will be the complex delivery rule that computes the delivery cost based on the weight and price divide into several slabs of the weight. Let's set prices according to the following rules:
   - if weight <= 5.0 then fixed price 10.0
   - if weight <= 10.0 then fixed price 20.0
   - if weight <= 50.0 then 15.0 times weight
   - if weight <= 100.0 then 20.0 times weight

7. Let's create a new delivery method. To create the delivery method click on **CREATE** button, enter *Speed Post Delivery* in **Name** field, select *Based on Rules* for the **Provider** field. As soon as you select the option **Based on Rules**, the rule list will appear under the **PRICING** tab which allows you to enter the pricing rules:

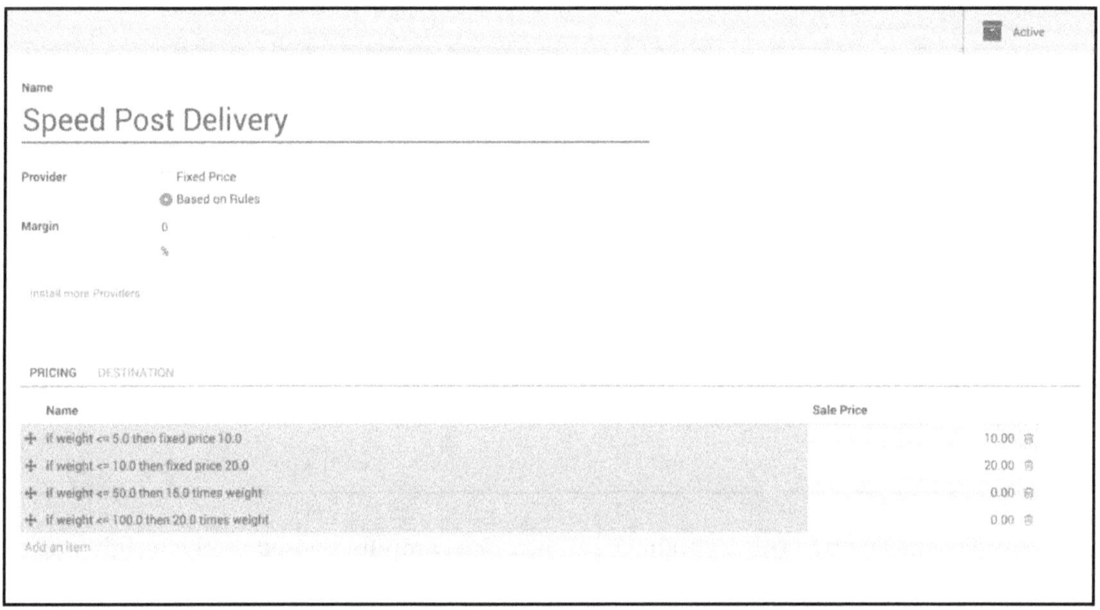

To add the price computation rules, click on the Add an item, a popup will be appeared to create the price rules, to create the condition `weight <= 5`, the first operand has to be selected from parameters *weight, volume, volume * weight, price* or *quantity*, then select the comparison operator and second operand has to be entered digits to compare with. Look at the following screen:

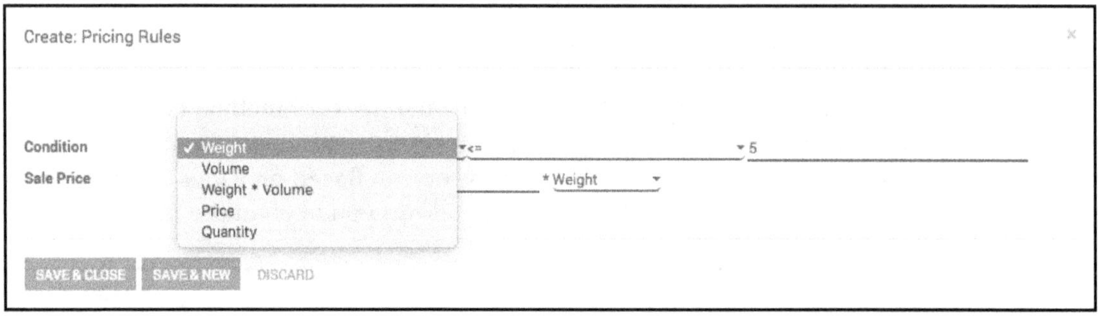

Click on the **SAVE & NEW** button and create other rules. Your rules should ideally look as follows:

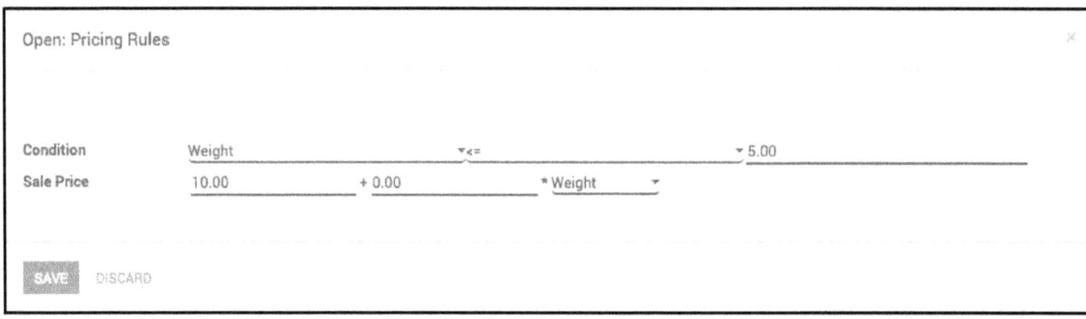

For the last two rules, you have set the price computed based on the weight and not the fixed price. Create the price computation rules as follows to compute the sale price based on the product attributes such as **weight**, **volume**, **weight * volume, price**, and **quantity**.

8. To test the rules, let's set the product weight first on the product form. Open the **Product Lagune Series - Size of 1000 X 1000mm** and set the weight on it:

9. Let's create the sales order. Add two quantities of tiles having weight `4.5` each and try to add the delivery cost. It should add `20` as the delivery cost:

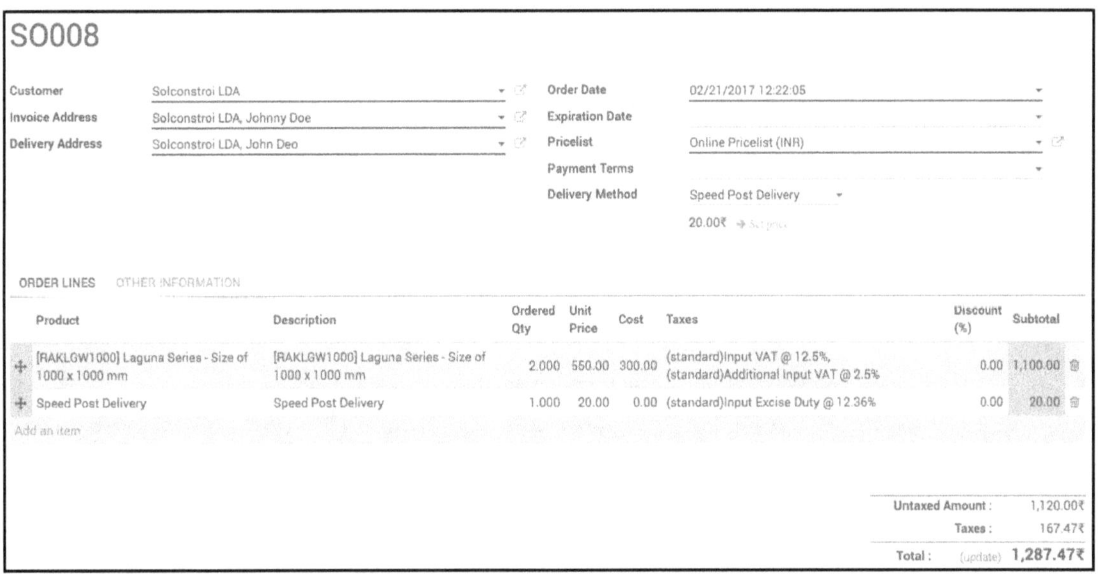

10. Change the quantity to `100`, the weight will be recomputed for the order. The total weight will be 450 kg, save the quotation, you will not get the delivery charges as the rules do not cover the cost for weight above 100 kg. If you still try to add the delivery cost, a warning message will be raised as shown in the following image:

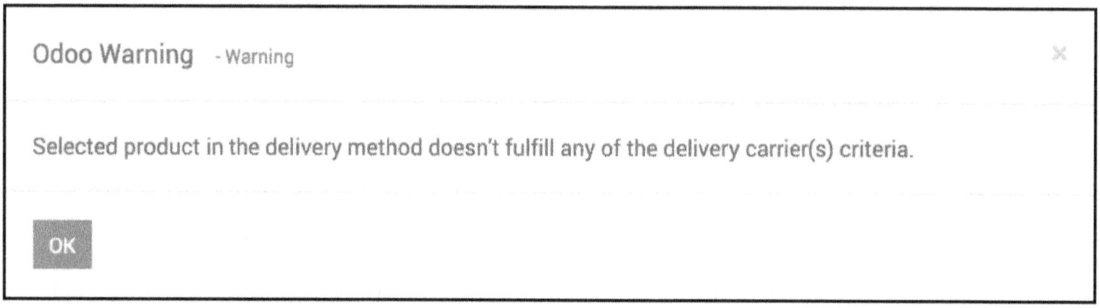

11. Let's open the delivery method **Speed Post Delivery** and add a new line in the **PRICING** rules at the end of the rules, which takes care for the weight greater than 100kg, look at the following screen of new rule added:

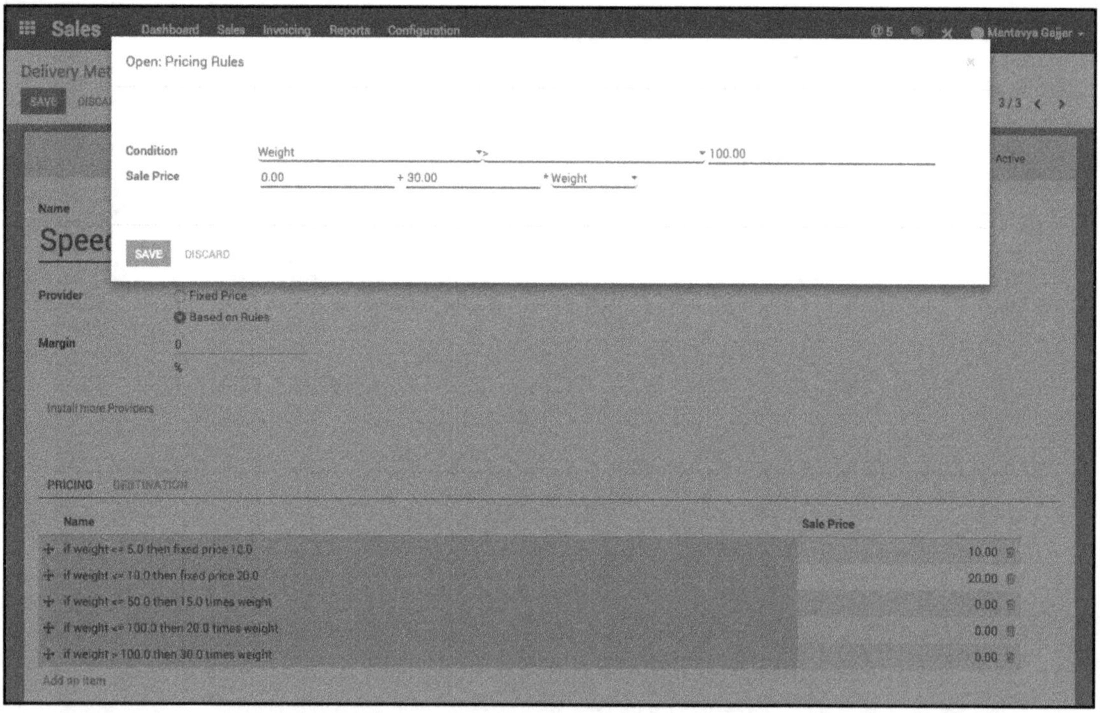

12. Now change **Ordered Qty** to `10.0` and **Save** the quotation, the delivery cost should be updated on the quotation, click on **Set price** link to apply the delivery price on the quotation:

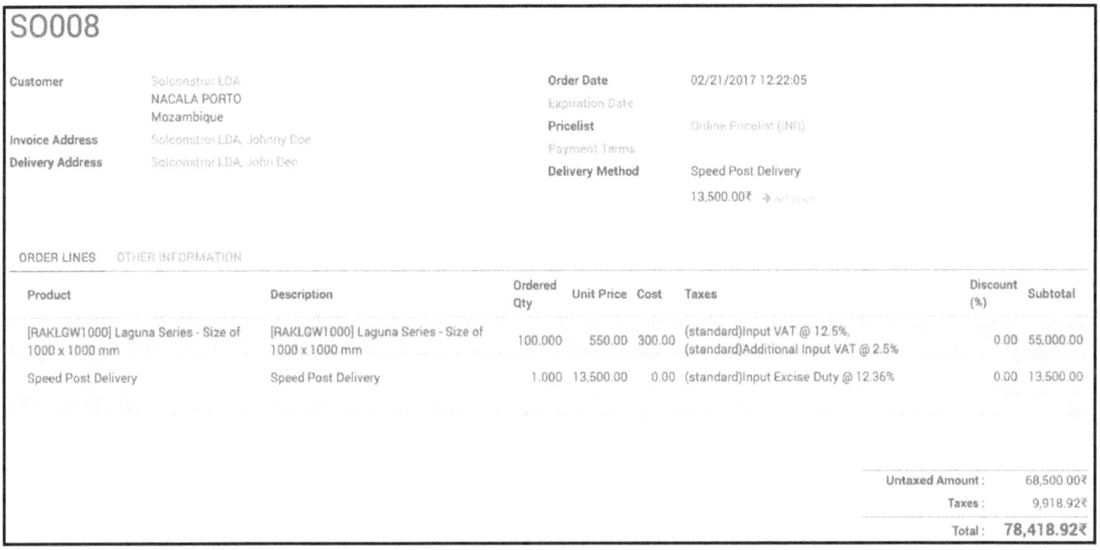

Getting approval of order online

Preparing the quotation, printing it, sending and negotiating with the prospect, get the approval of the proposal by courier was the traditional way of doing business. Today modern companies need much more than that, they want to create the proposal in a minute, send to the prospect online, track the customer activity with the proposal, negotiation online on the proposal and get online approval.

Assume that you are selling the combo product that is made-up with multiple products, in my case we sell a **Modular Kitchen – Basic**, which is made-up with the materials such as Microwave oven, Double door refrigerator, Some stones, and cabinets. Using Odoo Online proposal application you can create a beautiful proposal using ready-made templates, send it online, negotiate real-time on the quotation and get it confirmed online with customer signature.

Let's install the **Online proposal** application, create a template of the proposal, prepare a quotation using the template, send it to prospect, negotiate on the proposal and get it confirmed and signed online.

How to do it...

1. To install the **Online Proposals** application, go to **Apps** and search for the `online proposal`, you have to remove the default **Apps** filter as an online proposal is not a primary application. Click on the **INSTALL** button. On successful installation of the application, you will be taken to the homepage.
2. Go to **Sales** | **Configuration** | **Quotation Templates** and click on **Create** button to create a new quotation template. Using quotation template a salesman can create a beautiful template in a minute and send to the prospect for the approval.

   Let's create a quotation template of `Modular kitchen - basic` pack that consists of platform stone, **Double door refrigerator**, **Microwave oven**, **Drawer set** and **Low height cabinet:**

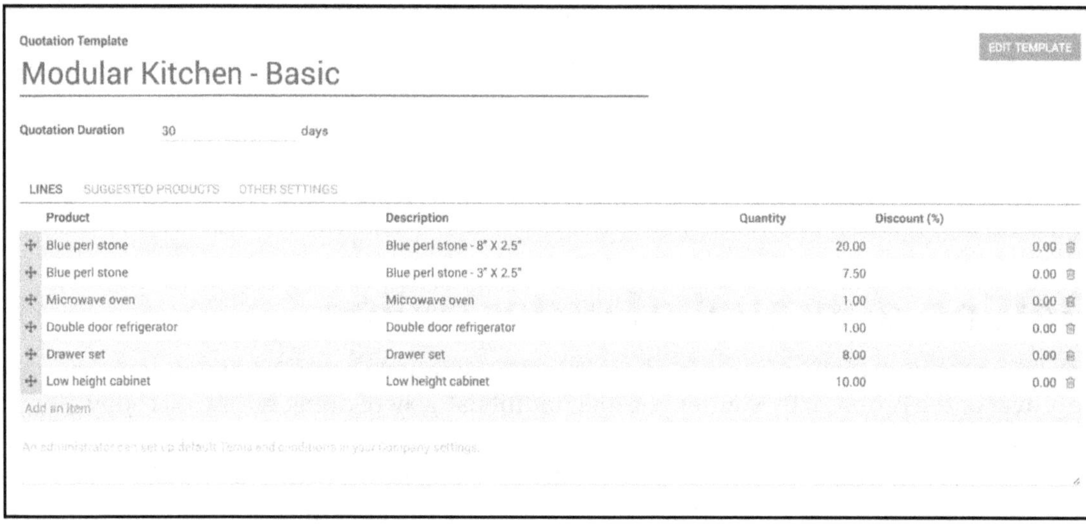

You can add the **Suggested Product** to the quotation template so that prospect can add to the proposal by themselves during the buying process. We will cover this in the *There's more...* section.

On the **Other setting** tab, you can find the **Payment** option, **Confirmation Mail**, and terms and conditions that will be applied to the quotation:

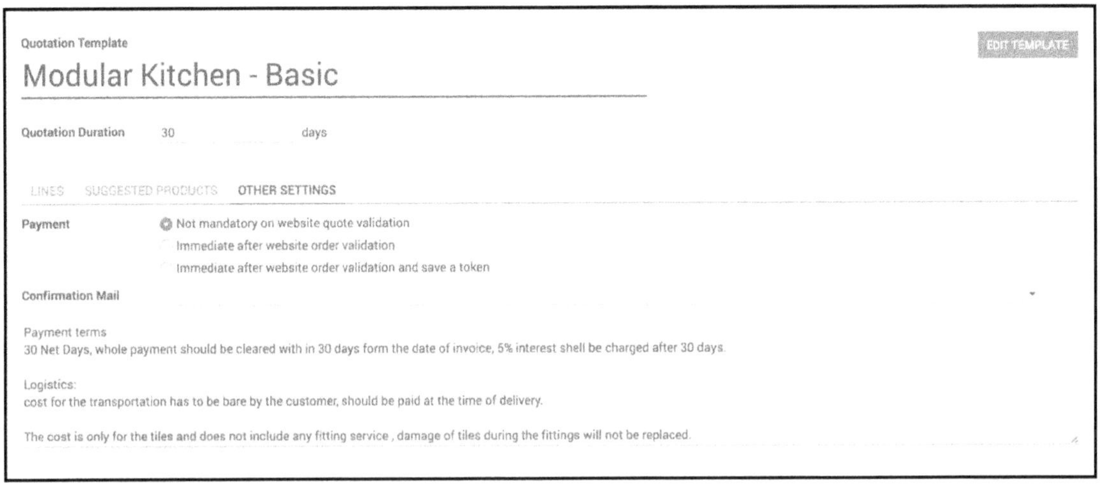

3. To make the proposal more attractive, click on the **EDIT TEMPLATE** button, you will be redirected to the online view of quotation with three predefined section, **About us**, **Our Offer** and **Terms & Conditions**.

 Jump down to the **Our Offer**, you can see many sections, each section represents one product added to the quotation, you can make it more interactive by adding the content below each section:

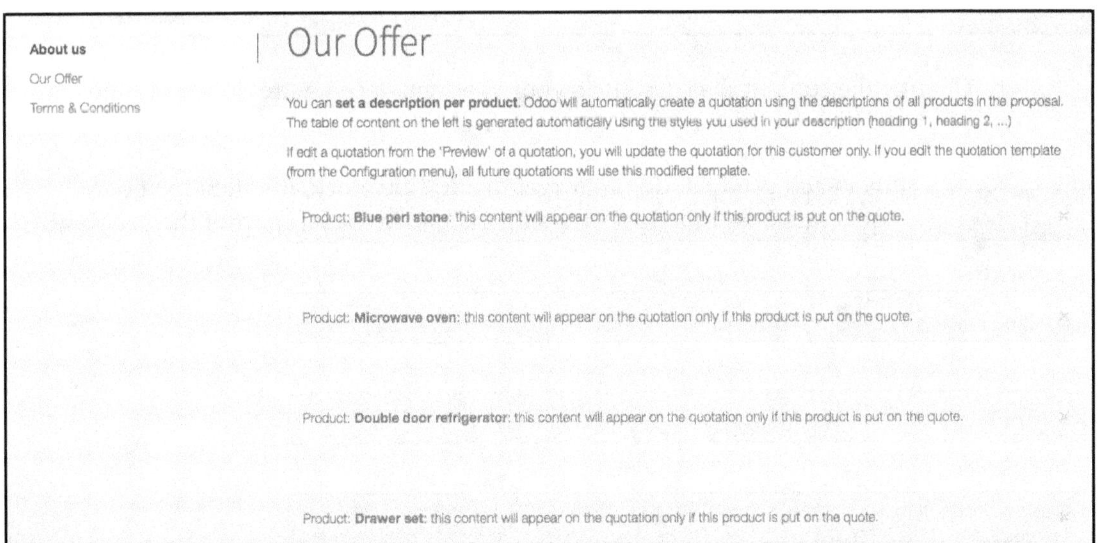

4. Clicking on the **EDIT** button on the right top corner, you will be entering into the edit mode, left panel will be visible with the predefined building blocks, you can drag and drop the building blocks to define the beautiful product information block:

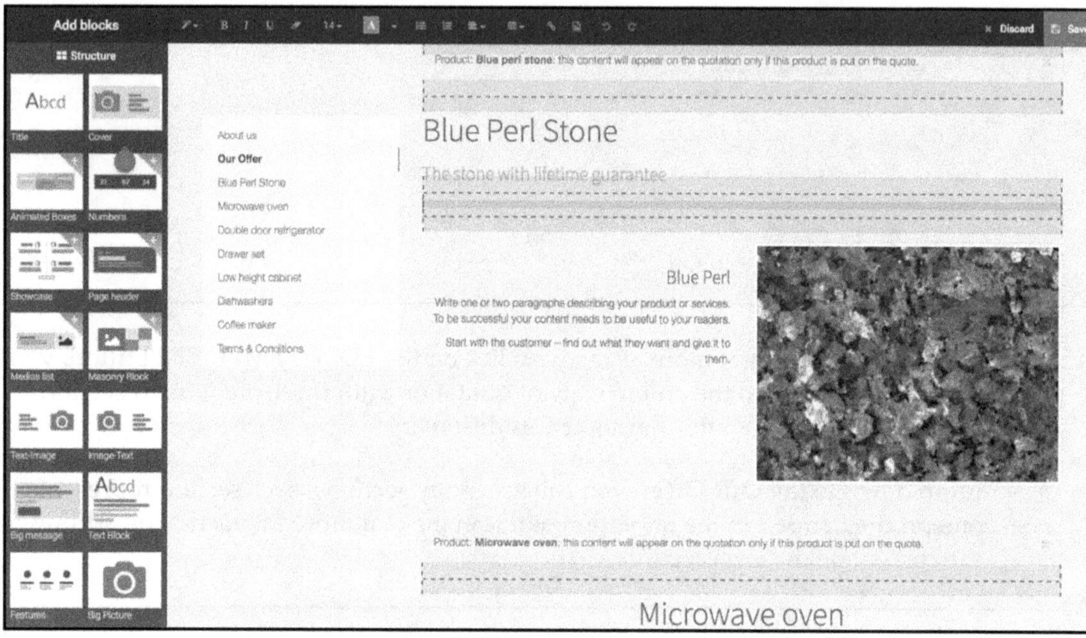

5. Change the content that describes your product, once you're done with the entire product, click on the **Save** button on the right top corner:

> **TIP**
> For each product, do not forget to add title block, it will help you to generate better navigation menu visible on the left part of the proposal.

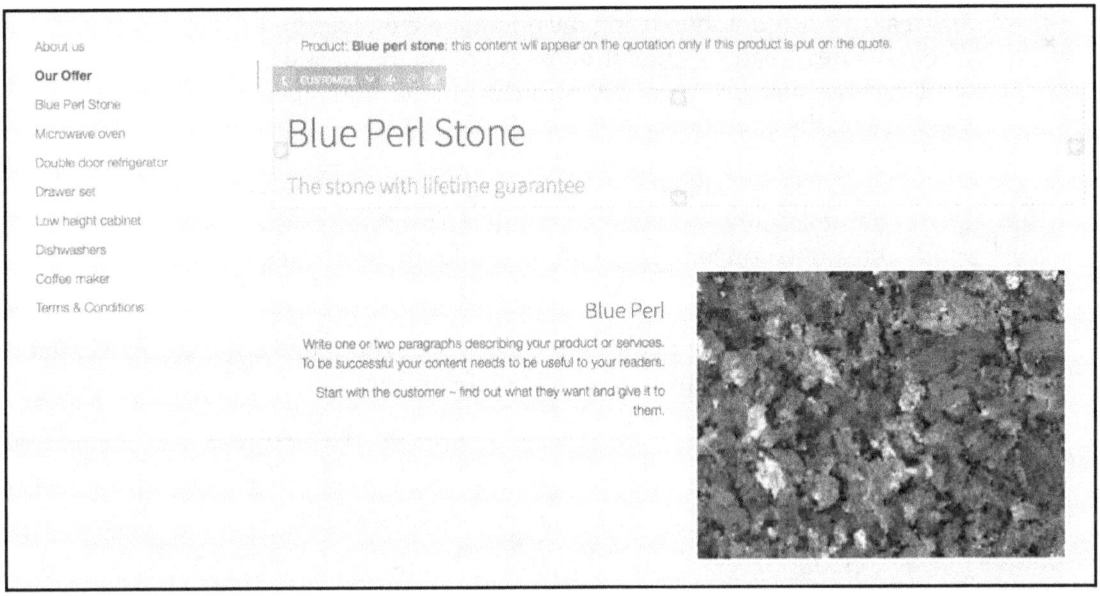

6. Once you're done with all the product description, your left navigation menu should look like the following screenshot. Clicking on the product name you will be taken to the product information:

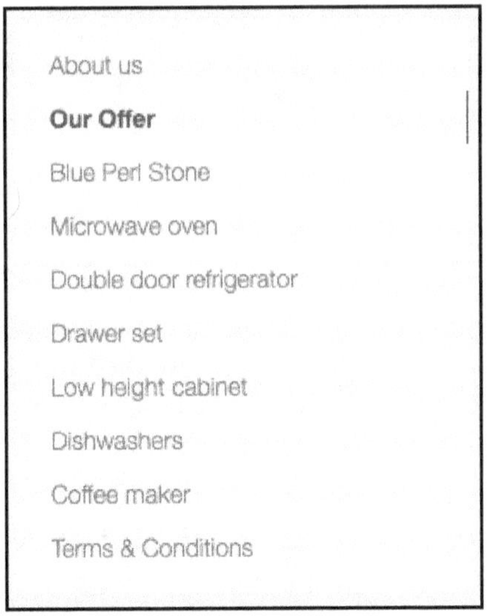

7. To create a new quotation using the quotation template, go to quotation list through **Sales** | **Sales** | **Quotation** and click on the **Create** button. Select the quotation template from the list, according to the template you will get the list of products on the quotation.

> If you have just one quotation template, that will be selected automatically and you will see all the products that you have added to the quotation template with their sales price on the quotation.

8. Select the **Customer**, the **Expiration Date** will be computed automatically based on the validity days defined on quotation template:

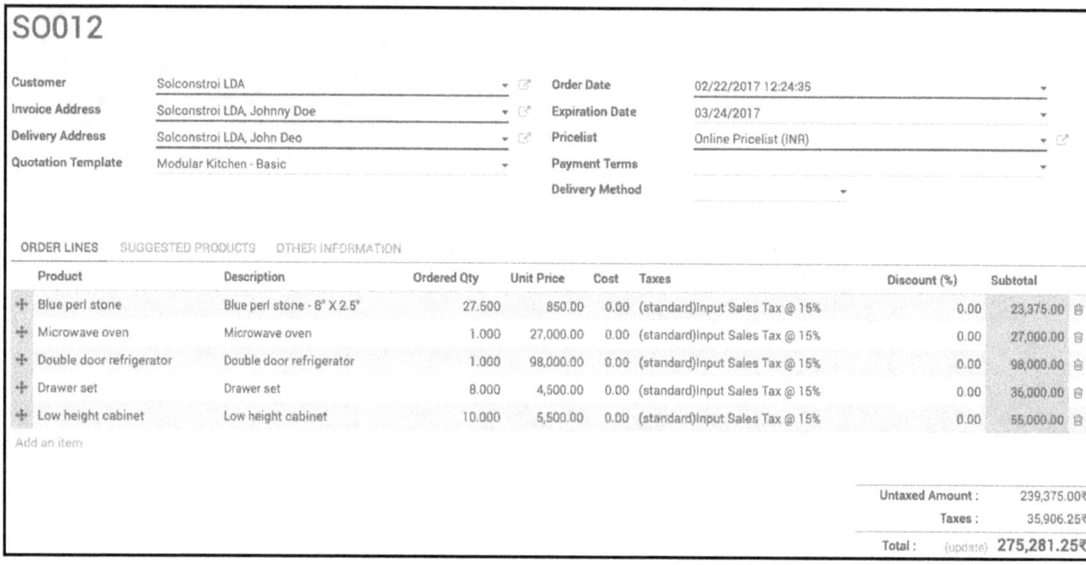

Just in a single click, the salesman can create a quotation. Before you send quotation to the customer you can preview the quotation, by clicking on the **Preview** button, you will be redirected to the online view of quotation.

On the online quotation, you can see:

- Customer, invoice and shipping address
- Salesman contact details
- Buttons to accept or reject or ask changes to the proposal

- Expiration date, the last date till the proposal is valid
- Product details with the pricing and terms and conditions
- Discussion history between prospect and salesman
- Suggested product at the end of the proposal, prospect can add to the proposal by them self

You have a possibility to change the proposal before you send to the customer:

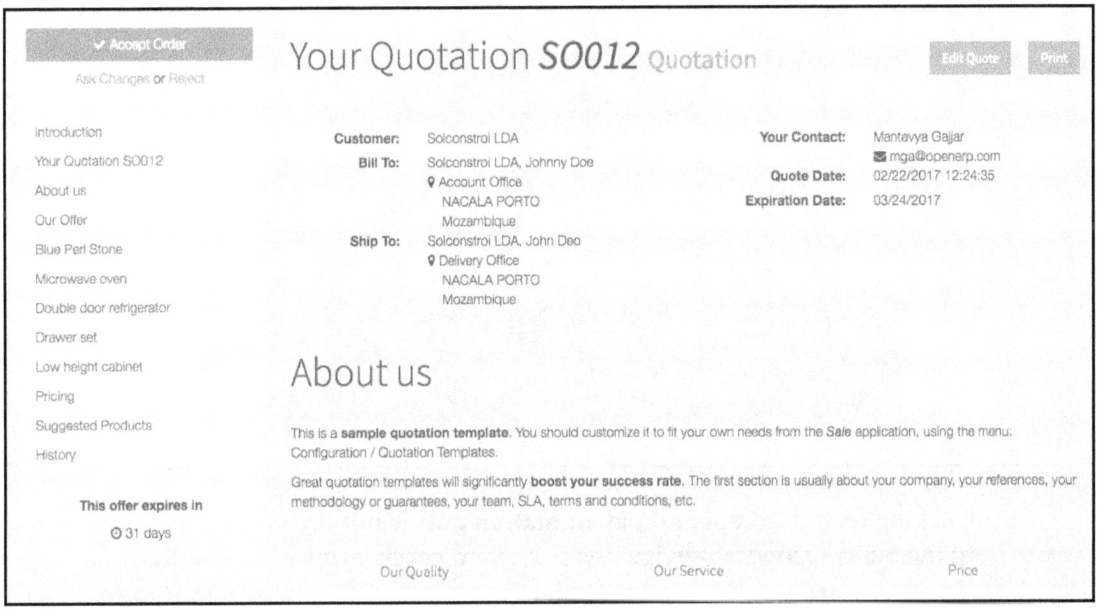

9. By clicking on the **Edit Quote** button, you will be taken to the quotation in the backend. Click on the **Send by Email** button, a popup will appear that allows you to send the online proposal with an attached copy of the PDF proposal.

10. The customer will be notified by the email, with attached copy of the proposal:

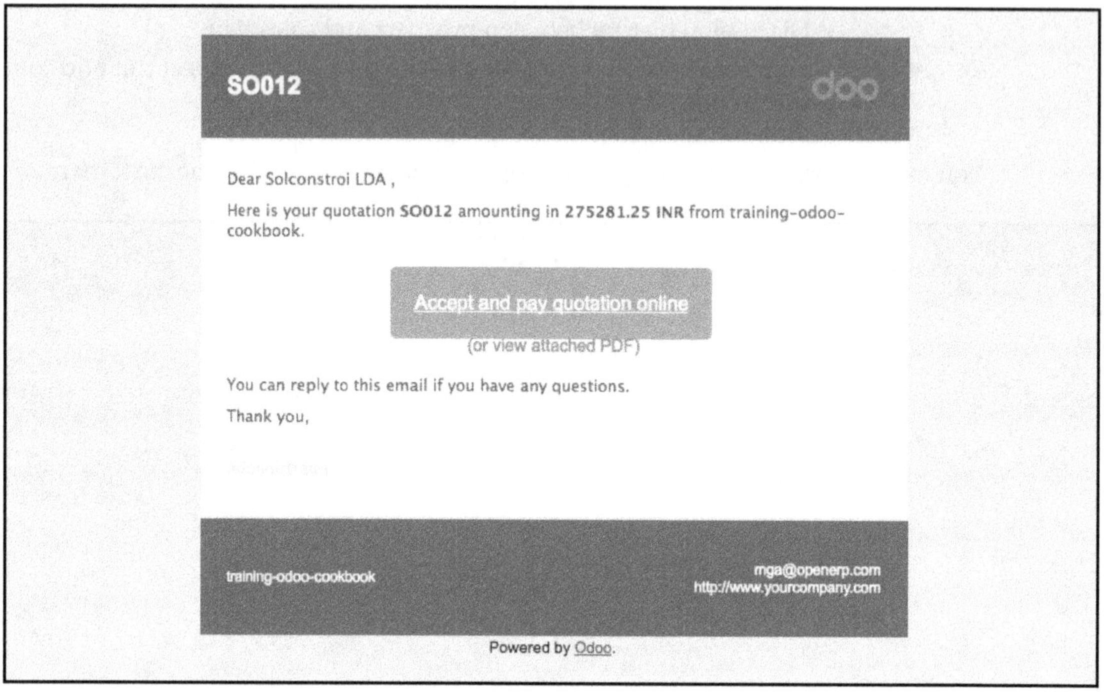

11. Clicking on the **Accept and pay quotation online** button, you will be redirected to the online proposal, review the price, and check terms and conditions.
12. You can start negotiation on the proposal real time, scroll down to **History** section, type message and click on **Send** button to post the message on the proposal.
13. Salesman or manager will also get notified about the new message on the sales quotation, they can also track the prospect activity like when they viewed the proposal online:

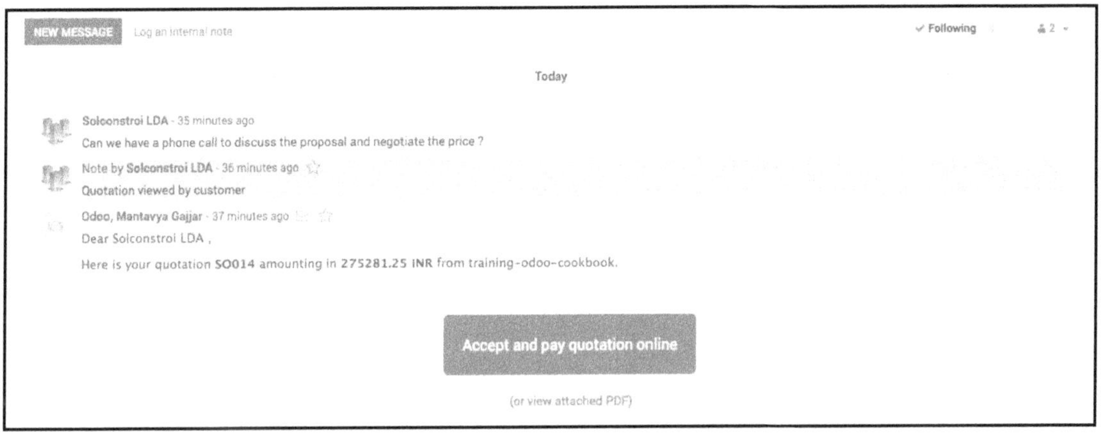

14. Let's assume that customer is going to confirm and sign the order, salesman or sales manager get notify about this activity in Odoo:

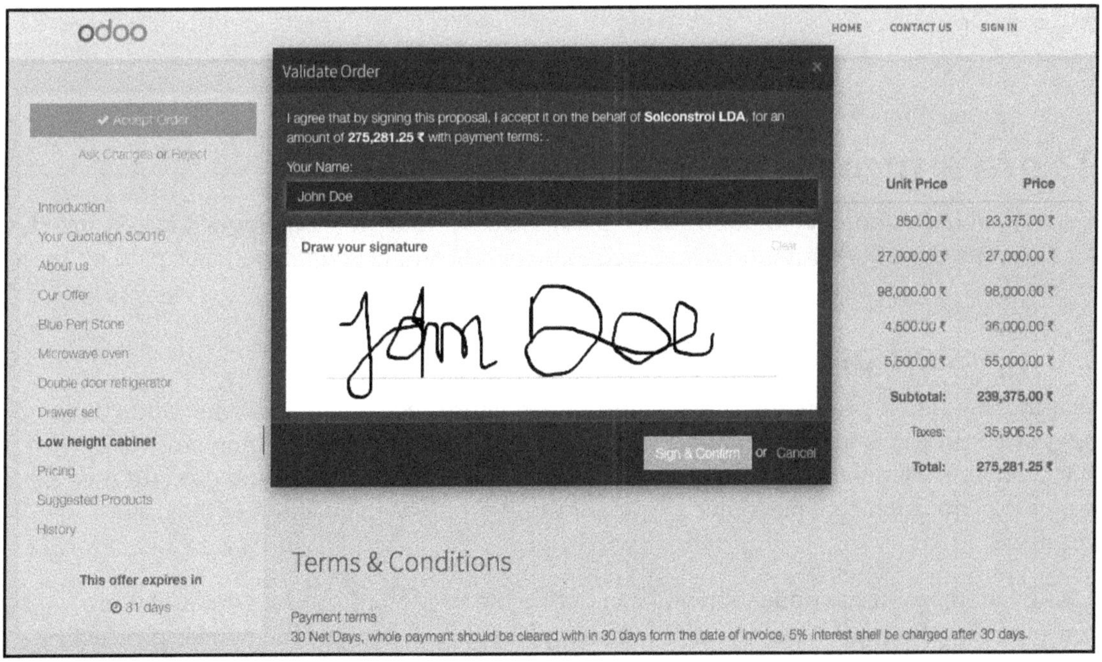

Salesman or sales manager will get notified about the order status with a signature attached in the chatter, they can proceed further to process the order delivery and invoicing:

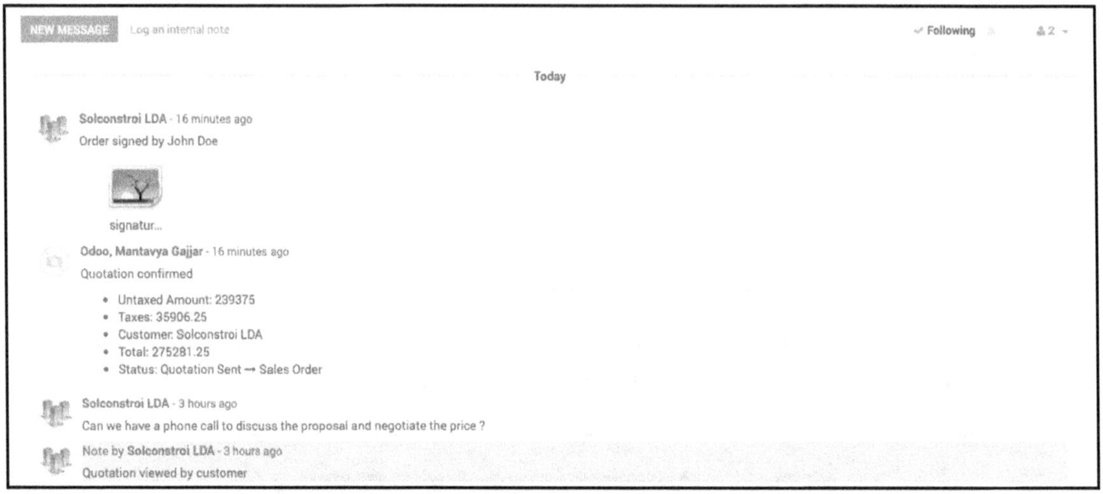

There's more...

Using a modern approach of doing sales using Odoo online proposal application, your sales team can prepare the quotation faster, negotiate online and get confirmed and paid online.

Suggested products

Adding suggested product in the quotation, there more chance that customer adds those suggested products in the quotation to buy them. It is a good way of doing cross-selling to the prospects. While defining the products on the quotation template you can add the suggested products that customer may need those products in addition to the base products.

Using Odoo proposal application you can define the suggested product on quotation template, creating quotation based on the template always suggest the related product to the customer. It is useful and ease of use, salesman does not have to remember which product they have to add as a suggested on the quotation as it is defined once on the quotation template.

Go to **Sales** | **Configuration** | **Quotation template**, open quotation template `Modular Kitchen - Basic`, click on the **Suggested Product** tab, add the list of products you would like to mention as suggested products. Those products will appear in the suggested product list on quotation. Look at the following screen of suggested product:

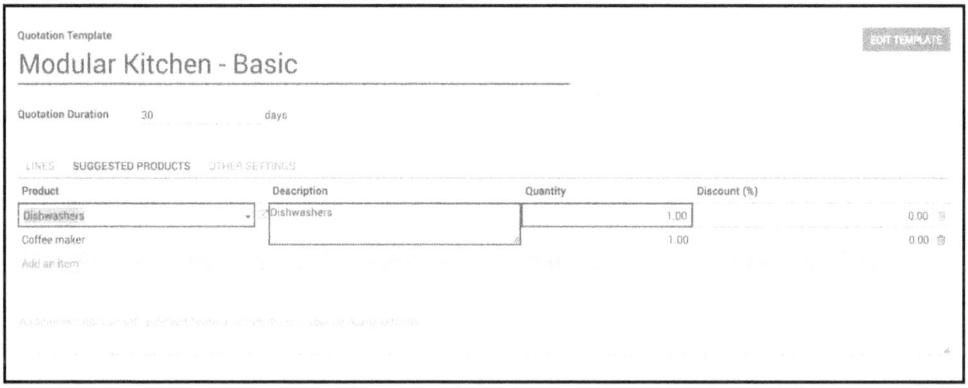

Create a quotation using the quotation template and click on the **SUGGESTED PRODUCTS** tab, you will see that the suggested products will be automatically added to the quotation from the quotation template.

The price and discount can be changed for the suggested product. Changing the products price and discount will not affect the quotation template specification:

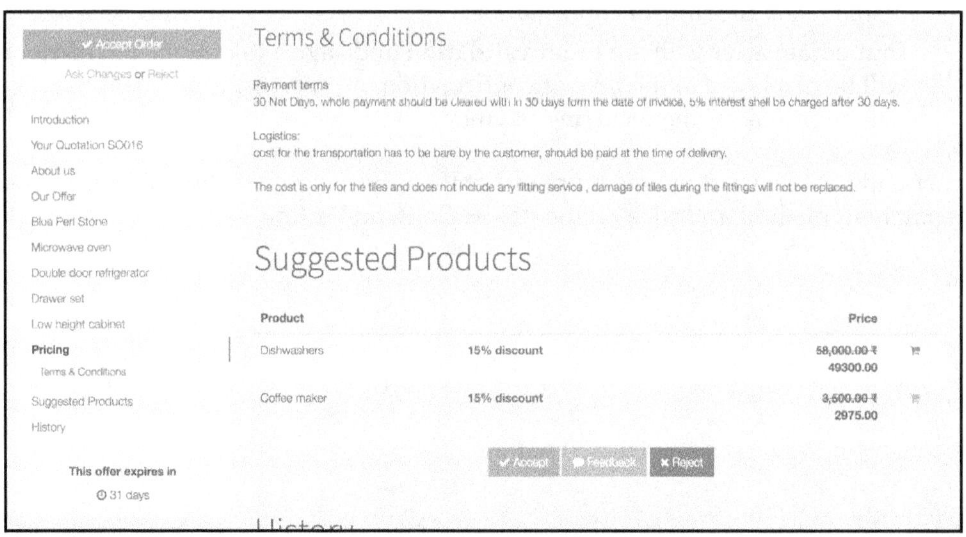

Customer can add the suggested product to the quotation by themselves by clicking on the cart icon right to the product name.

> TIP
> The suggested product can be added by the prospect, to remove the product from the quotation you need the assistance of a salesman or sales manager.

Payment option

Getting order confirmed online is a modern way of doing sales by the customer themselves, an online buyer on e-commerce store pays through credit card or net-banking, with Odoo online proposal you can not only send the online proposal, but you can also get paid online through various payment options such as Wire Transfer, Paypal, Ogone, etc...

To configure the payment option, go to **Sales** | **Configuration** | **Quotation template**, open quotation template `Modular Kitchen - Basic`, click on the **Other Settings** tab, to configure the payment options.

The payment options are as the following:

- **Not mandatory on website quote validation**, do not ask for the payment at the time of confirmation
- **Immediate after website order validation**, the payment options will be displayed at the time of confirmation.
- **Immediate after website order validation and save a token**, the payment options will be displayed at the time of confirmation, on successful payment the token will be stored for the recurring payment.

Customer will get the list of payment options at the time of confirmation of order, select the correct payment method and click on the **Pay & Confirm** button:

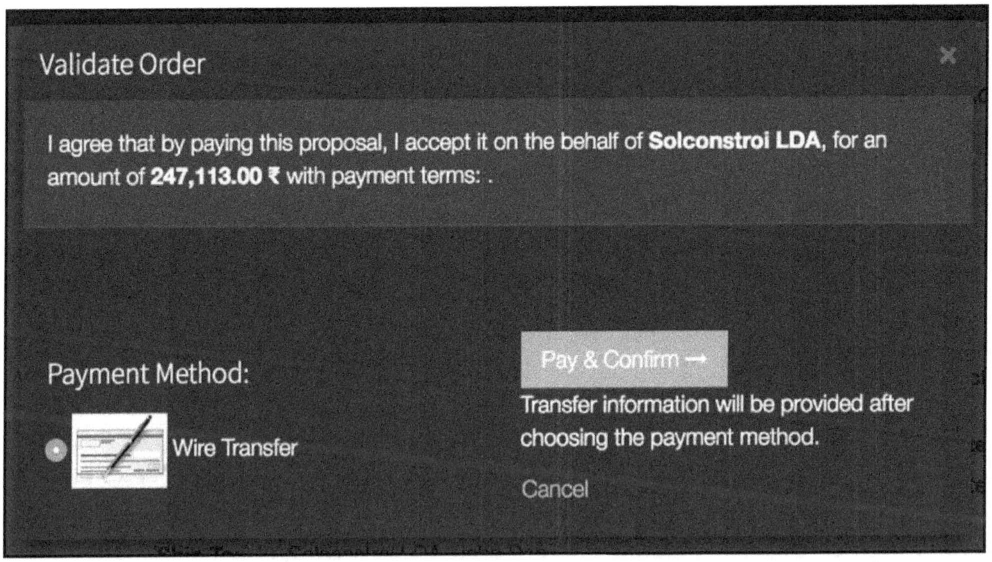

The payment methods will be displayed based on the payment options enabled on the instance. The payment method can be enabled from the **Accounting** | **Configuration** | **Settings**, click on the **Configure payment acquiring methods** link right to the payment option.

You will get the list of payment methods, click on the **Install** button and configure the options.

The payment options **Immediate after website order validation and save a token** will work only with the payment provider which support server to server payment process.

Setup recurring sales and invoicing

Odoo helps you to create professional quotation in minute, by default Odoo support one-time sale with standard quotation to sale products or services. This is the default configuration, there is nothing to setup, to sale the packaged product or services you need to activate the online quotation feature of sales application.

Many businesses provide regular services to their customers, manage accounts and track the record of services provided, generate the recurring bills on regular intervals, the simple example of the recurring service is the annual maintenance contract. As a business, you want to know monthly recurring revenue, non-recurring revenue, revenue per customer, annual run rate, analysis reports by the sales person, and you can get the cohort analysis by contract or by revenue.

You can use subscription application to generate the recurring bills based on the service provided. The subscription may include-- annual maintenance contract, a monthly subscription to a service, etc.

Getting ready

Before you proceed for the activation of subscription feature we assume that you have prepared the subscription plans that you are going to offer. Beside that plan, you have to decide few points, such as: To define and generate the recurring bills you should have:

- How frequently you are generating the bills
- Customer can switch from one plan to another plan
- Payment can be acquired automatic or manual
- You want to activate the customer self-service

How to do it...

1. To activate the subscription plans and recurring bill go to **Sales** | **Configuration** | **Setting** and go to the **Subscriptions** setting to **manage subscriptions and recurring invoicing**, select the checkbox and click on the **Apply** button to activate the feature. You will be redirected to the home page, as soon as the subscription feature is activated.

2. Click on the **Subscriptions** application, you will be taken into the subscription application. Here, you will see the list of subscriptions.

3. To configure the subscription application, we have to create two things, first subscription product, and subscription template.

   Let's create the subscription product first. To create the subscription product, go to **Subscriptions | Subscription Products** under the **Subscriptions** application and click on the **CREATE** button to create a new product:

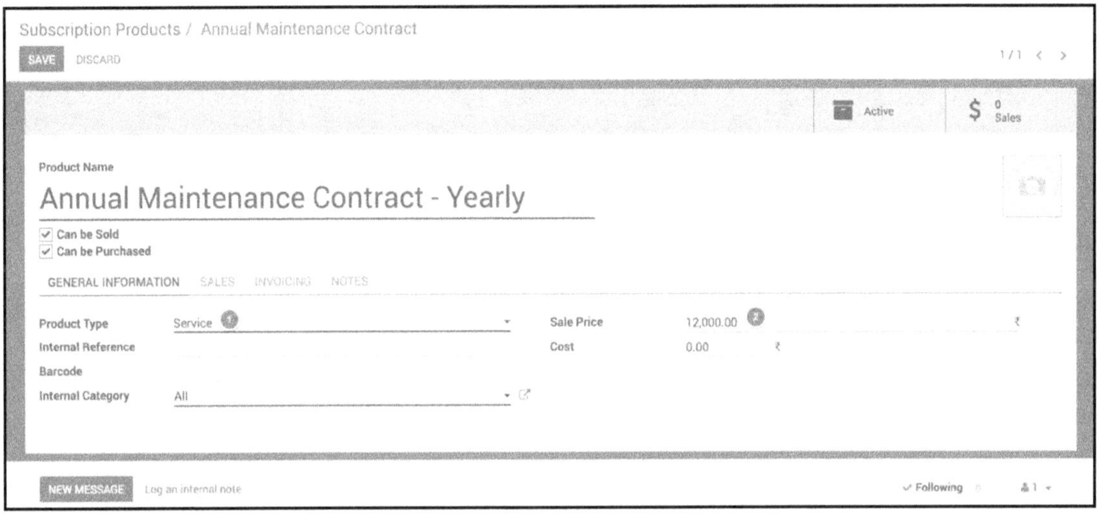

   The **Product Type** set to **Service** and **Sale Price** are two important fields which have to be filled on the product form. The most important is to select **Subscription Product** checkbox available under the **SALES** Tab.

4. The second step is to create a subscription template that helps us to create and start the subscription quickly. The subscription template is a blueprint of the products list that we are offering the subscription service and terms & conditions related to the subscription.

The subscription plan can be created from **Subscriptions | Subscription Template**, click on **CREATE** button to create a new template. Look at the following screen for the **Annual Maintenance Contract**:

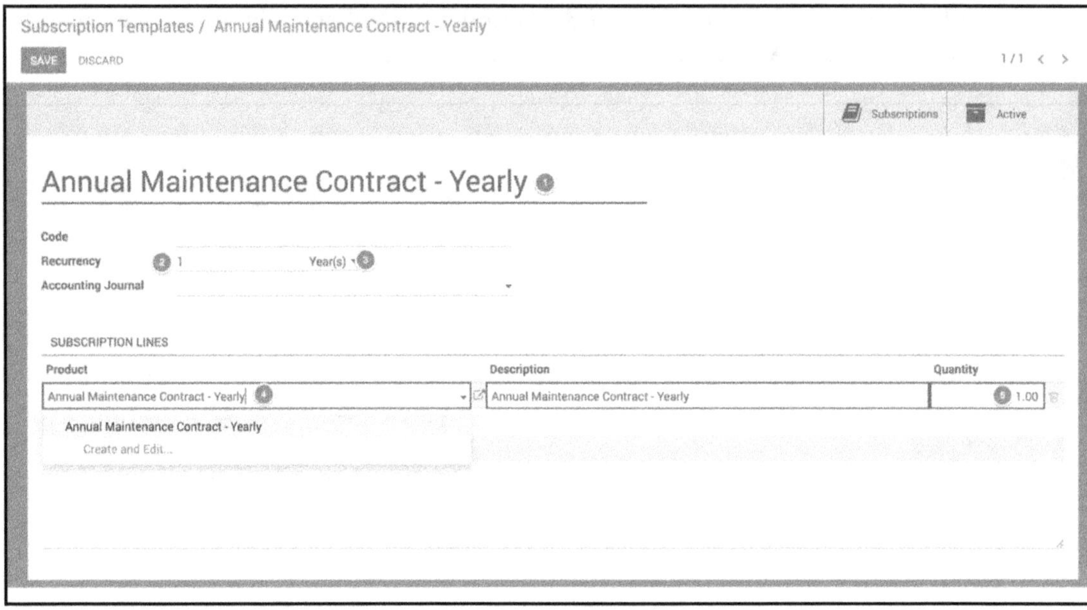

Enter `Annual Maintenance Contract - Yearly` in the **Name** field. Set `1` for **Year(s)** in the **Recurrency** field. Click on **Add an item** on the **SUBSCRIPTION LINES.** Select **Annual Maintenance Contract - 1 Year** in the **Product** field. Enter **Description** and set **Quantity** to 1 on the line.

In our case, the quantity refers to the number of air-conditioners (as per the screenshot above) installed and stated in the subscription for the maintenance contract. This quantity can be changed at the time of creating the service contract.

5. There are two ways to start the subscription plan for the air-conditioners contract. The simplest way is to create the subscription using the subscription template. To create a new subscription, go to the **Subscription** application and you will see the empty subscription list, click on the **CREATE** button to create a new subscription. Look at the following subscription created for 1 year:

Select the customer. As soon as you select the **Subscription Template**, the **SUBSCRIPTION LINES** will be filled automatically. Set 5 in the **Sold quantity** field as the customer has bought it for the service of 5 air-conditioners. **Pricelist** will be filled automatically based on the selection of the customer. Name of the subscription will be generated automatically.

The Actual Quantity is the quantity used by the customer onsite. In our case, when we do the first air-conditioners service onsite, we will come to know how many air-conditioners are actually installed by the customer. It can be less than the Sold Quantity or if they are more, we have a potential to upsell for the additional quantity.

The **Start date** is the date when the subscription starts. The contract has to be renewed on the **Date of next invoice**. On this date, the invoice has to be generated and sent to the customer to request a payment.

6. The first invoice has to be generated and sent to the customer before we started the subscription. Click on the **Generate Invoice** link to create the first invoice. Confirm the Invoice and send it to the customer for the payment. Look at the following invoice we created:

7. The subscription can be started as soon as the payment is confirmed. It can be started by clicking on **START SUBSCRIPTION** button on the subscription:

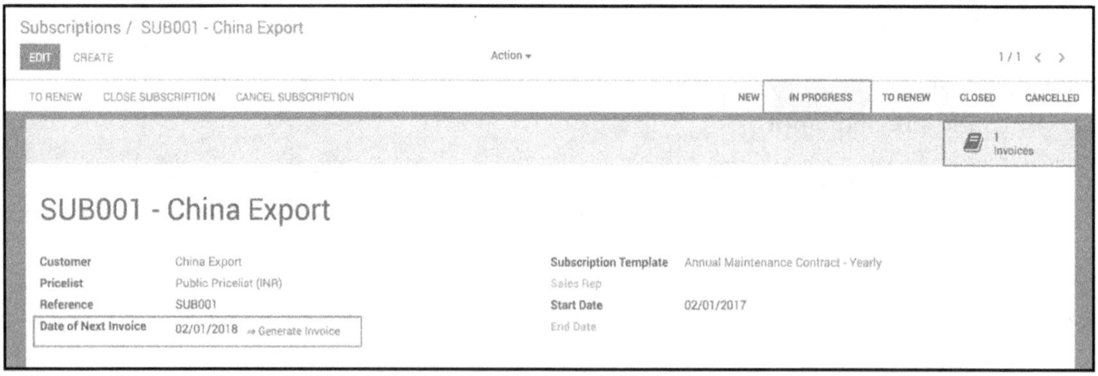

8. The subscription will go to the **TO RENEW** stage as soon as it expires. The renewal of the contract can be done either by creating the next invoice or by sending a renewal quotation.

   If you are sure about the customer renewal and the payment, click on **Generate Invoice**, or send the Renewal Quotation by clicking on the **Renewal Quotation** link.

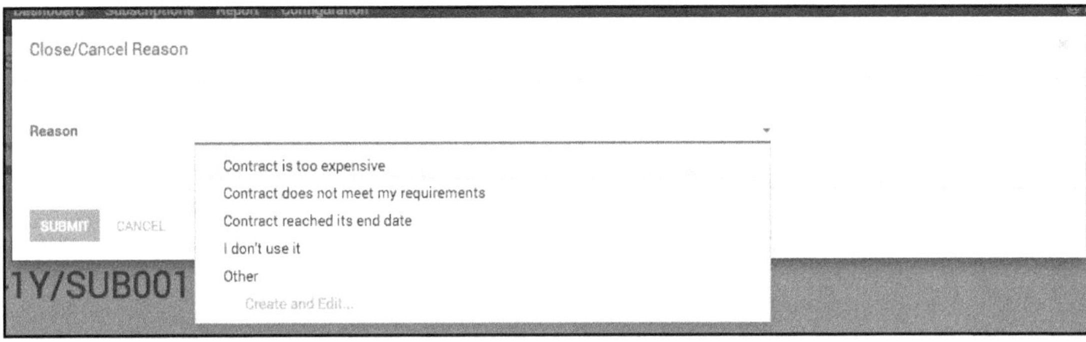

Click on the **Submit** button to close the contract:

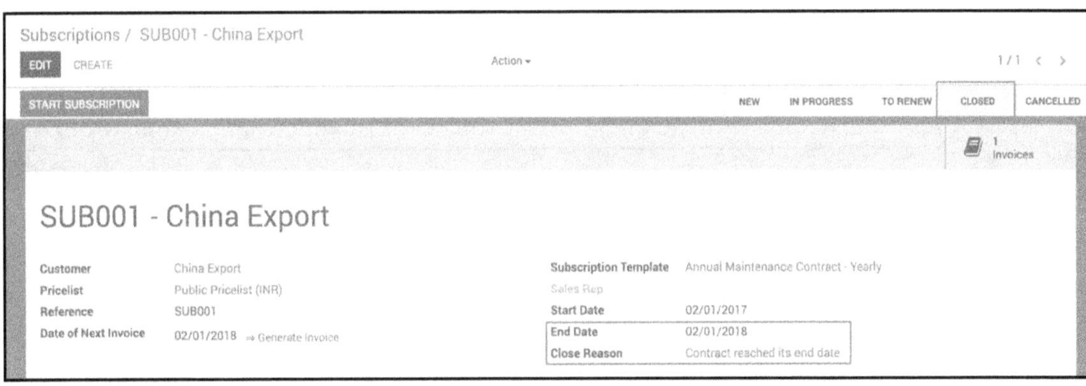

The contract will be updated; **End date** and **Close reason** will be set on the contract selected on the closing wizard.

There's more...

Odoo subscription feature manages the different types of contract templates. Creating a subscription manually from the subscription template or automatically through a typical sales process. You can create an invoice for upselling or renewal on the expiration of the subscription contract.

There are many other features available with Odoo subscription application, some of those important features involve allowing users to manage their subscriptions, switch between different subscription plans, and closing contracts through the customer portal. These are some of the important features; let's jump into the details of those features.

Create subscription from sales order

The typical sales cycle starts from leads or an opportunity. The quotation will be sent. Now enter into a negotiation and confirm the sales quotation to convert it into a sales order. The subscription will be created automatically as soon as the order is confirmed.

Let's see in detail how the subscription can be created automatically through a typical sales process:

1. To have this feature we have to activate the full subscription application to activate the subscription creation through the typical sales cycle. Go to Apps and search for the **Subscription Management** full features application:

2. The second step is to configure the **Quotation Template**, that helps the salesman to create a beautiful quotation quickly. Go to **Sales** | **Configuration** | **Quotation templates** and click on the **CREATE** button. Now, enter `Annual Maintenance Contract` in **Name** field and then go to **OTHER SETTING** tab and select the **Annual Maintenance Contract- Yearly** in **Contract Template** field:

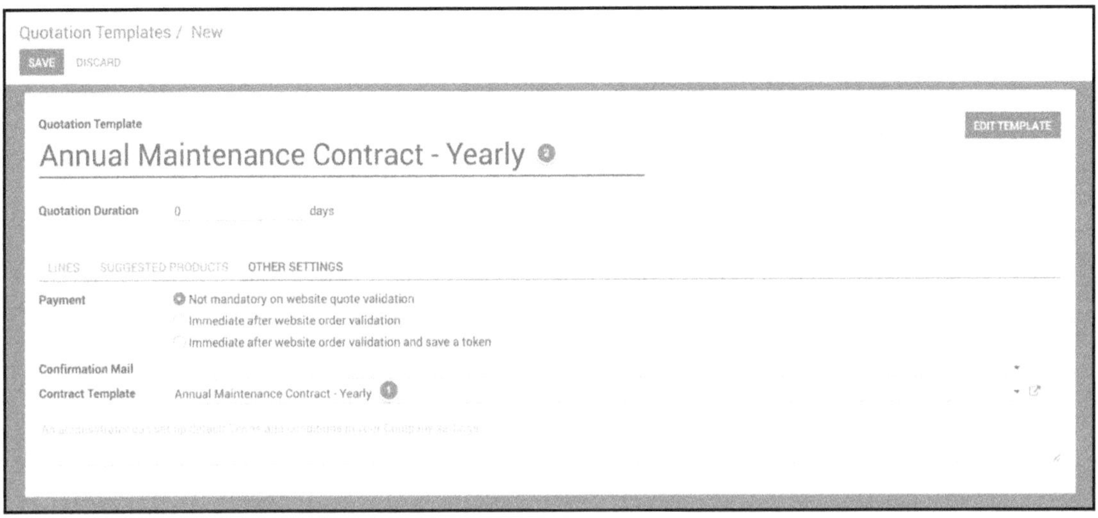

Refer recipe *Getting approval of order online* using Odoo online in the current chapter to design a beautiful quotation template by clicking on the **Edit Template** button.

3. Now, we are ready to create the proposal and sell the first subscription through a typical sales cycle. As a salesman, go to **Sales** | **Sales** | **Quotations** to create the proposal.

Click on **CREATE** button, select the customer, select **Annual Maintenance Contract** in the **Contract Template** field. The quotation will be filled with product added from the subscription. You can change the **Order quantity** as shown in the following screenshot:

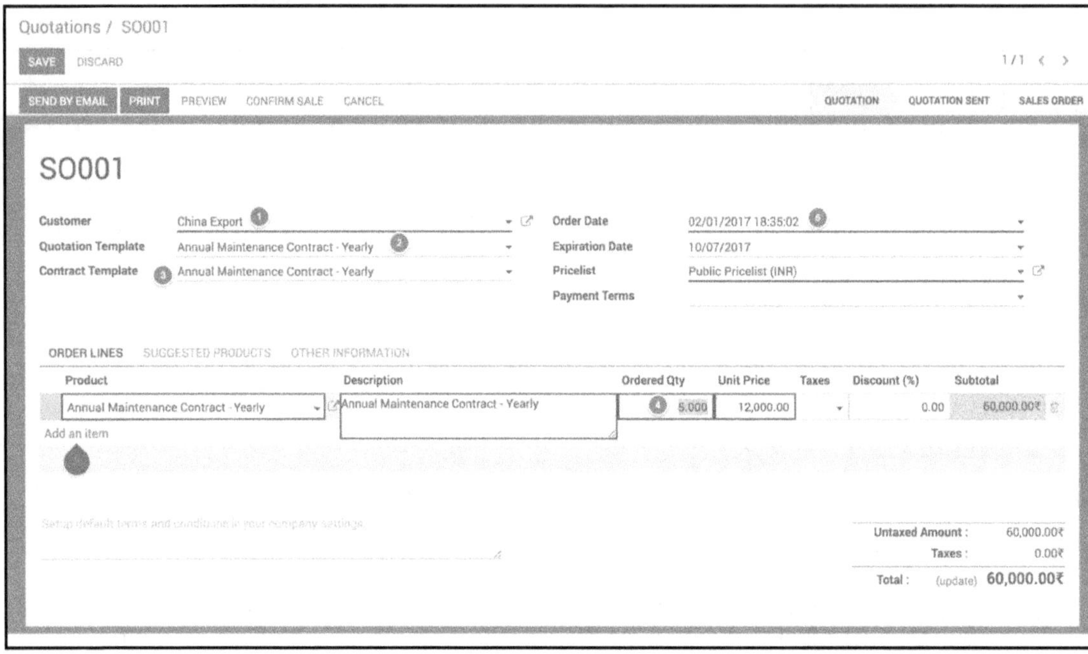

The quotation can be confirmed online by the customer or on behalf of the customer a salesman can confirm the order by clicking on the **CONFIRM ORDER** button.

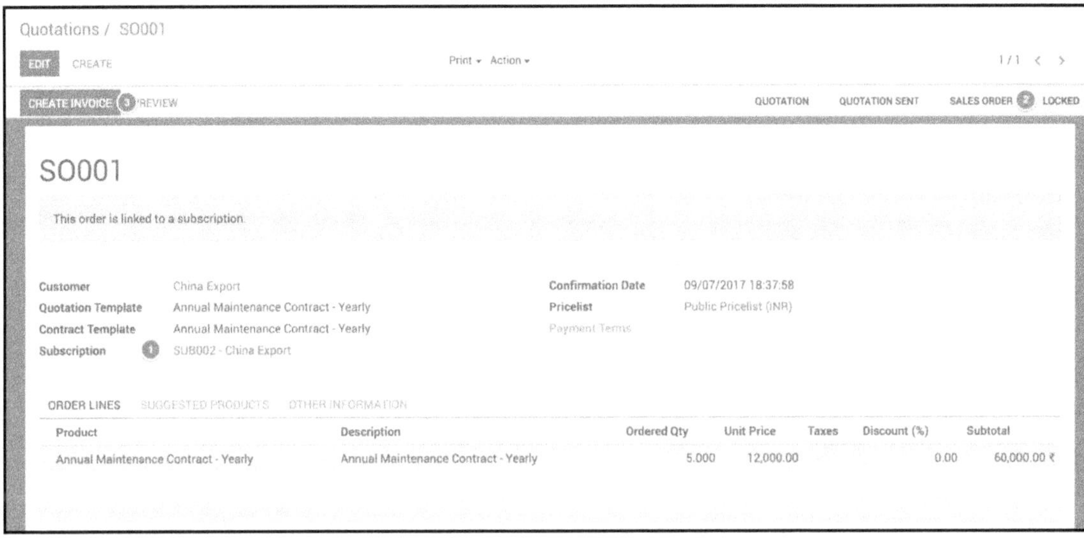

The sales order will be set to **LOCKED** and no more changes are allowed. The subscription will be created, linked to the sales order and set to **IN PROGRESS** mode automatically.

4. You are ready to create the first invoice, as the line on the sales order is highlighted in blue color. Look at the preceding screen. All the invoices created will be linked to the subscription automatically.

Look at the subscription created in the following screen, the **Date of Next Invoice** is set to the one year later, as the first invoice was already created from the sales order.

When you sell the subscription through a typical sales process, the first invoice will be generated through the sales order.

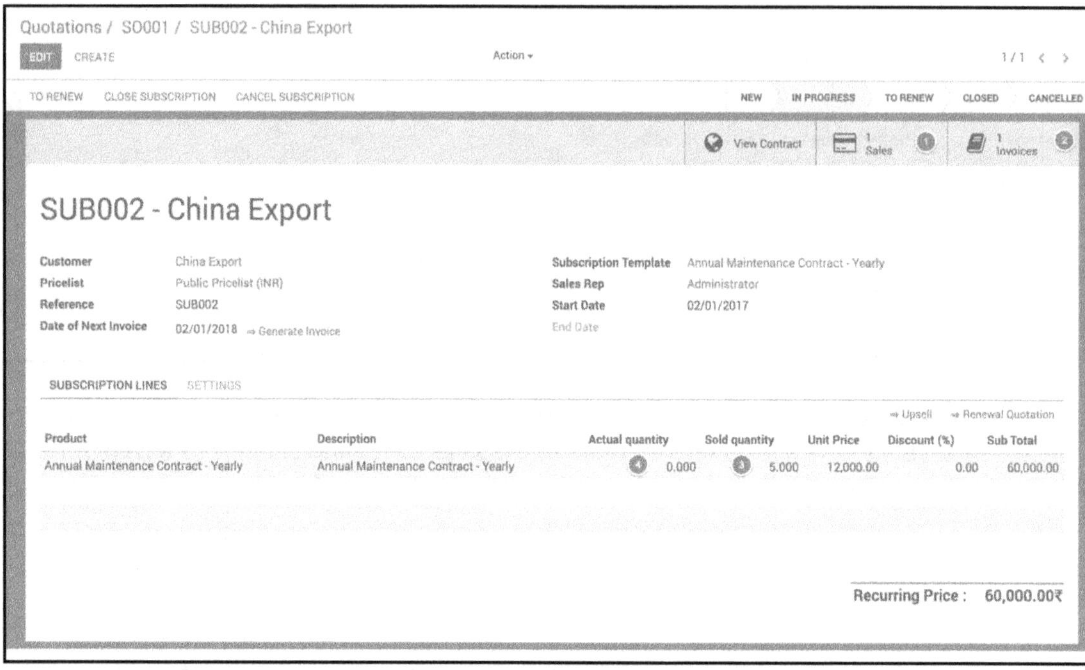

We can see the **Sales** and **Invoices** created for the subscription. These can be tracked from the **Action** button available on the top of the form. Make sure that **Sold quantity** will be same as the quantity sold on sales order, the **Actual quantity** can be updated after the completion of the first service at the customer site.

5. The renewal process remains the same; you can track all the subscription having the status **TO RENEW**, go to **Subscriptions** | **Subscriptions To Renew** under the Subscription application.

Subscription is set **TO RENEW** state automatically depending on the **Date of Next Invoice**, to continue running the subscription make sure that the invoice has been created and validated before it gets expired.

Open the contract and send the renewal quotation or create an invoice depending on the customer demand. On the confirmation of payment receipt, you can start the contract by clicking on **Start Subscription** button.

Upselling in subscription

It is a normal business case, that sometimes a customer wants to add new units in the service and maintenance contract. Let's assume that customer wants to add few more air-conditioners to the existing subscription contract **SUB002 – China Export** form 1st August 2017.

You can add those new air-conditioners to the existing contract without creating a new contract. Also, create an invoice for the remaining time from *1st August 2017*. The upsell feature also computes the price based on the remaining time from the date of upsell.

To add new air-conditioners to the existing contract, open the contract and click on the **Upsell** link. A wizard will pop up, asking you to select the product you want to add and the date:

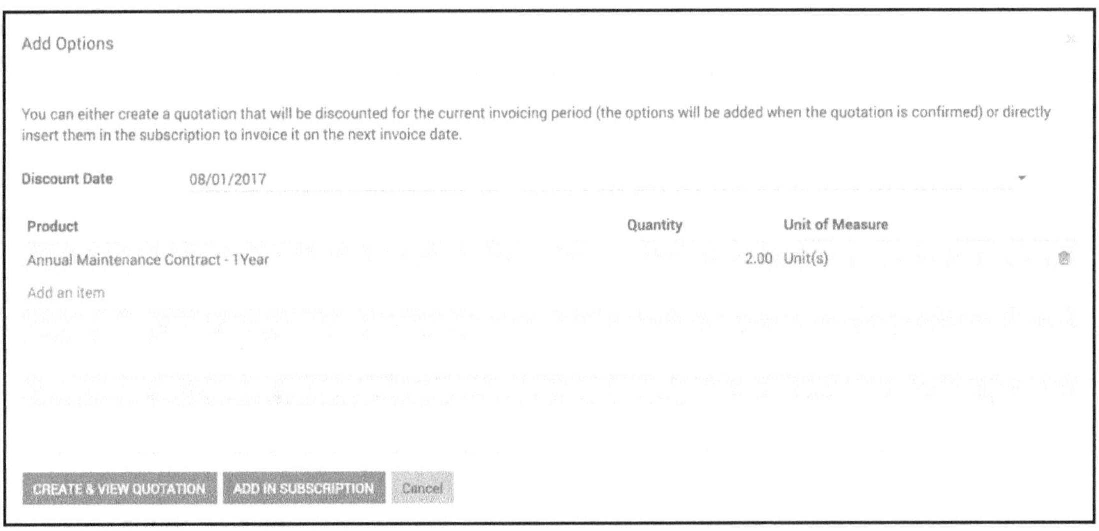

Select the **Discount date**, it is an actual date from where new air-conditions are to be added. This will compute the cost on the prorate base instead of full 12 months. Select the product that we are going to offer, enter 2 in quantity as the customer is going to add 2 new air-conditioners for the maintenance.

The discount on the invoice will be computed based on this date to adjust the price for the remaining time for the contract.

There are two ways to add additional products to the existing subscription. You can either add them directly or through the typical sales cycle by creating **Quotations**, get it confirm, create an invoice and get paid. Let's click on **CREATE AND VIEW QUOTATION** button. You will be redirected to the quotation created just now:

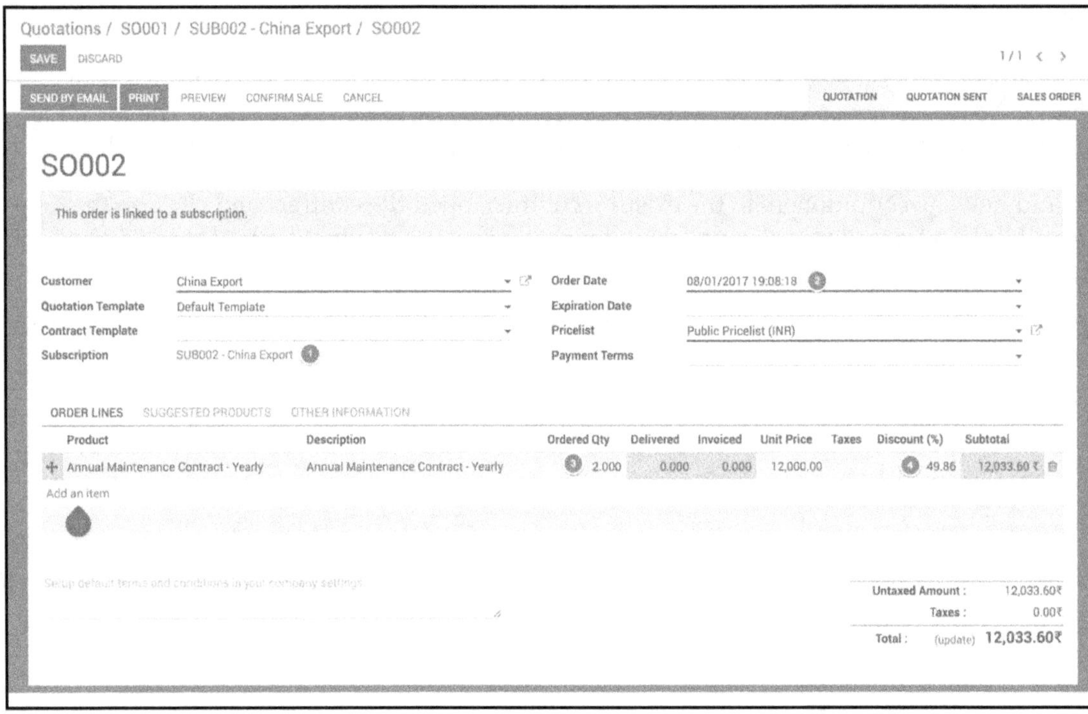

Make sure that the **Quantity Ordered** is updated correctly on the quotation. Also, **Discount (%)** should be applied correctly based on the **Order Date**. Follow the sales cycle, send quotation to the customer by email or courier. As soon as the customer confirms the sales order, click on the **CONFIRM ORDER** button and create an invoice. Register the payment received from the customer.

Let's check the subscription **SUB002 - China Export**, the Upsell quantity is added to the **Sold quantity.** Look at the following screen of subscription, after upselling 2 quantity from *1st August 2017*.

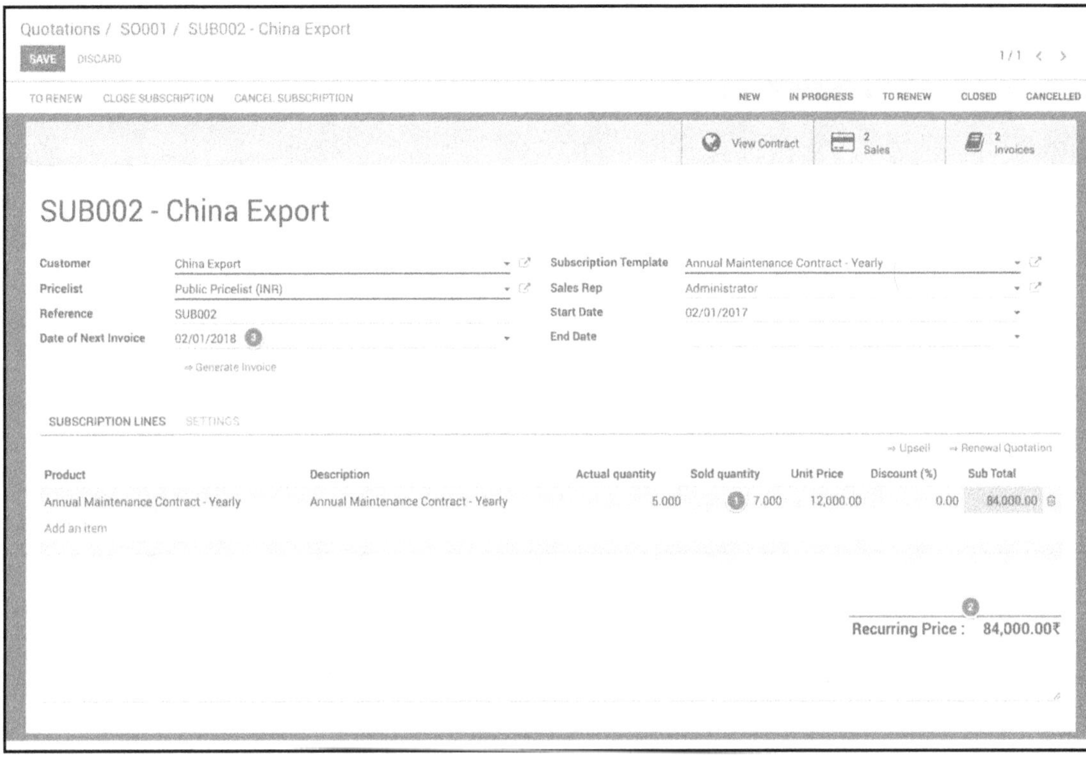

As soon as the **Sold quantity** is updated. The **Recurring Price** on the subscription can be calculated again based on the new quantity. The next renewal invoice will be generated for the **Recurring Price** on 1st February 2018 for total 7 quantity.

Change contracts through customer portal

Selling services, creating recurring invoices and getting paid is made easy by Odoo **Subsection** application. The customer can manage their subscriptions for an online customer through the portal. It will be a great experience for the customers when they are able to manage, change the subscription plans by themselves on the customer portal. They can also add the valued products or services themselves.

We have already gone through the portal feature in `Chapter 3`, *Traceability – Leads to Cash*, refer *Invite your customer to online portal* recipe to activate the invite user to access their documents online on the customer portal.

As soon as customers log into the portal account, they will be redirected to the homepage. Click on your username on the right top corner, and jump to **My Account**.

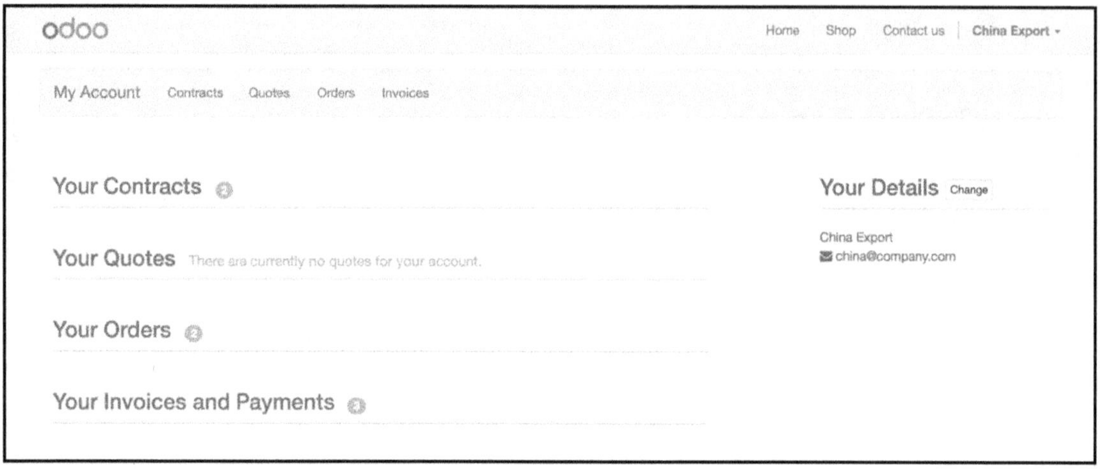

1. You can see contracts under the **Your Contracts** section. Clicking on the link, you will be redirected to the contracts list. You can filter the contracts based on the status -- **renew, in progress**, **closed** or **all contracts**, you can also sort the contract by name or newest first.:

Look at the preceding screenshot, we can filter the contract by its **State**, by **Month**, or short by **Name** or **Date**.

2. Click on the contract to get more details. You will be redirected to contract details having contract description, recurring price. Look at the contract details page, it will look like the following screenshot:

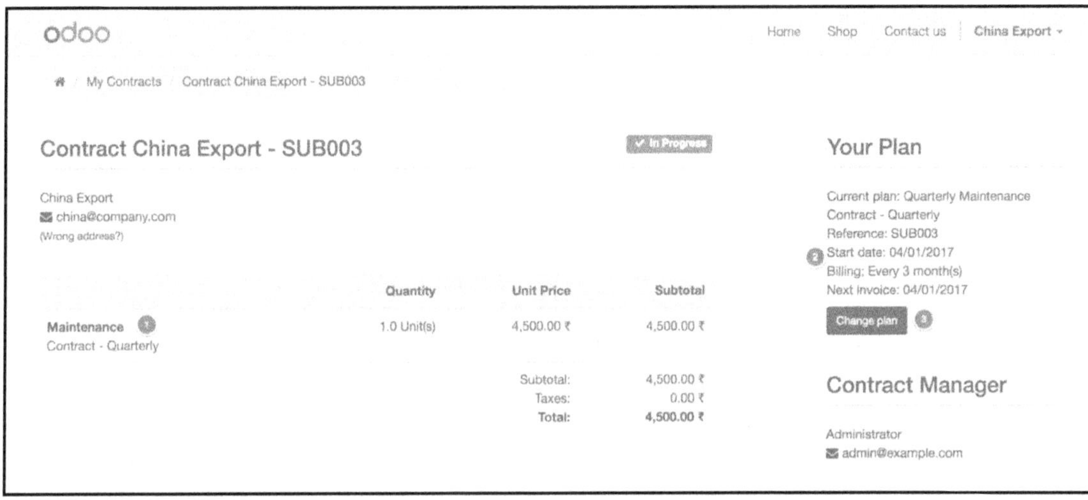

On the right side of the contract details, you can see the invoicing and details of contract dates, such as start date, invoice cycle and next invoice date.

3. Assume that we have customers with a Quarterly Recurring plan and they would like to switch to the yearly plan which will cost them 12,000 instead of 18,000 monthly recurring plan. Click on the **Change plan** button to get the list of plans available to make the switch. You can see the current plan in the following screenshot:

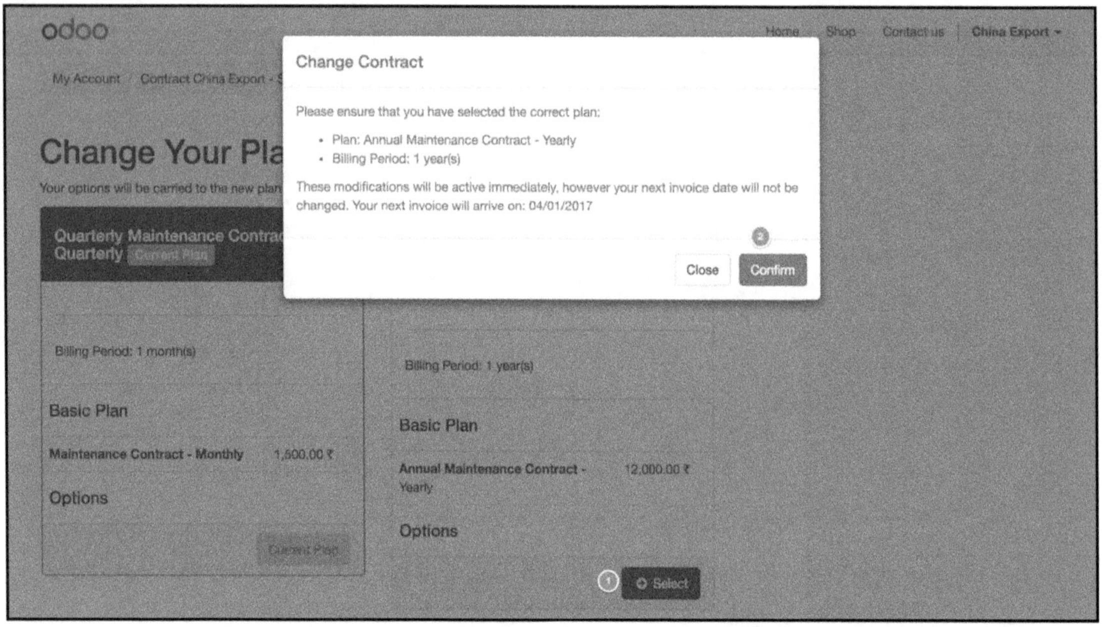

You will be notified about the next invoice date and plan details. Click on the **Confirm** button if you would like to switch to the new plan.

4. As the first invoice is already generated, the plan will be switched to from the next invoice date. The next invoice will be generated according to the selected plan.

The customer can switch between the different subscription plans only if the subscription plans are configured to allow for the selection by the customer. There are two fields which need to be configured in order to allow customers to switch between plans. It is advisable to configure the **Subscription Templates** instead of configuring the individual subscription plans.

The first configuration is to select **Allow Online Order** field available on the subscription template. Select **Allow Online Order** field on all the templates which can be available to the user:

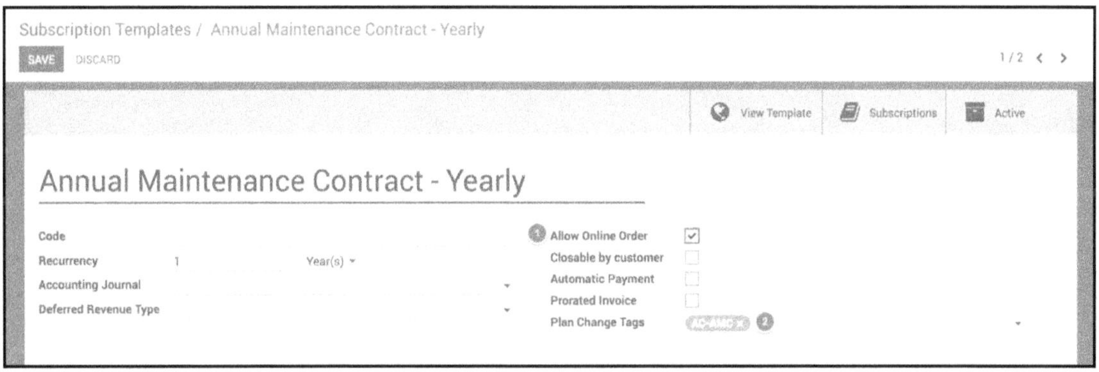

The second field to configure is **Plan Change Tags.** Select the same Tags on the similar plan which can be switched from each other. Select the tags **AC-AMC** on **Annual Maintenance Contract – Yearly** and **Maintenance Contract – Monthly** subscription template.

Adding products to subscription

Similar to switching between the subscription plans, we can also offer additional valued services or products, which customers can add to the plan by themselves through the online portal.

Let's assume that there is some service which can be offered additionally to the contract such as Gas refill, Vacuumed Pipe Cleaning, and so on. These are additional services which can be added to the standard air-conditioners service.

Let's go through following steps to see how a customer can add the additional product or service himself/herself through the online portal:

1. Sign-in using the customer account, and go to the **My Account**. Open the existing and running subscription. Go to the portal account, and jump to the contract on which you want to add the additional service:

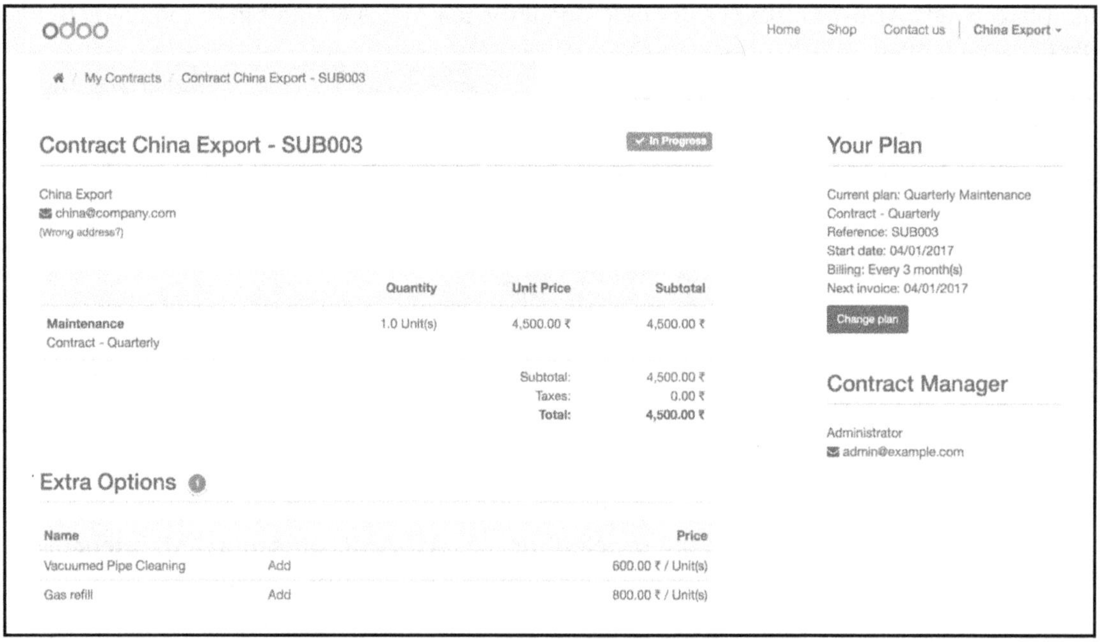

2. Below the contract details, you will get a list of additional products or service that can be added to the existing contract. Clicking on the **Add** link. You will be asked to confirm the addition of the optional service to the current contract.

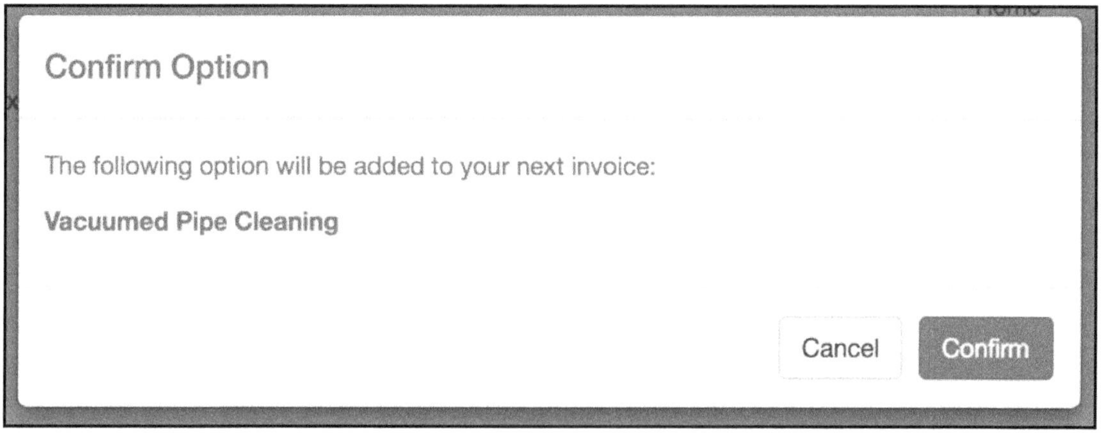

3. By clicking on the **Confirm** button, the additional service will be added to the existing subscription plan. From the next invoice, we will have the charges for the subscription plan plus the additional service added to the contract. Look at the following screen:

>

Let's see how to configure and offer the additional products on the subscription plans.

The additional product added to the subscription can be removed too. It can be managed by the customer through the online customer portal.

Addition of the additional product or service can be done based on the additional product configuration available on the **OPTION LINES** tab on the subscription template:

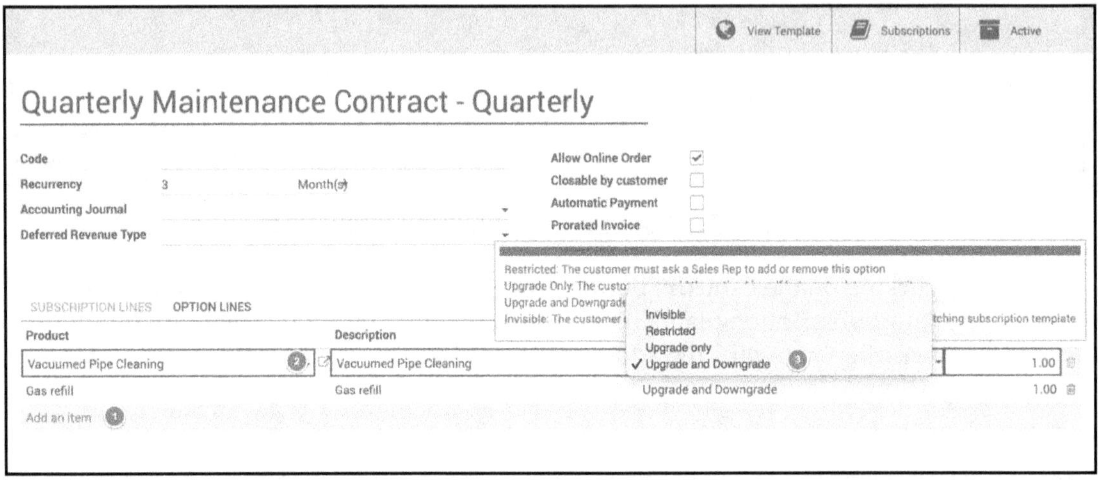

TIP

The customer is sometimes allowed or not allowed to remove the additional products or service by themselves once it has been added to the contract. This configuration depends on the additional product's configuration available on subscription template under the **OPTION LINES** tab.

Depending on the configuration of **Portal Access** field, a customer is allowed to add or remove the additional products from the subscription plan. The values of **Portal access** field are as follows:

- **Invisible** - accessible only to the salesperson to add or remove to the contract.
- **Restricted** - portal customer can see the additional product line. To add them to the subscription, they have to ask the salesperson.
- **Upgrade only** - the customer can add those products by themselves. However, they are not allowed to remove it from the subscription through the portal.
- **Upgrade and downgrade** - the customer can add or remove the additional product through the customer portal.

Closing contract through portal

Using customer portal, the contracts can be managed by the customer themselves. They can perform actions like adding or removing new products or services, switching between the different plans. The customer can close the subscription plan if he/she is allowed to close it. Look at the following configuration of the subscription template, to allow a customer to close the contract by themselves:

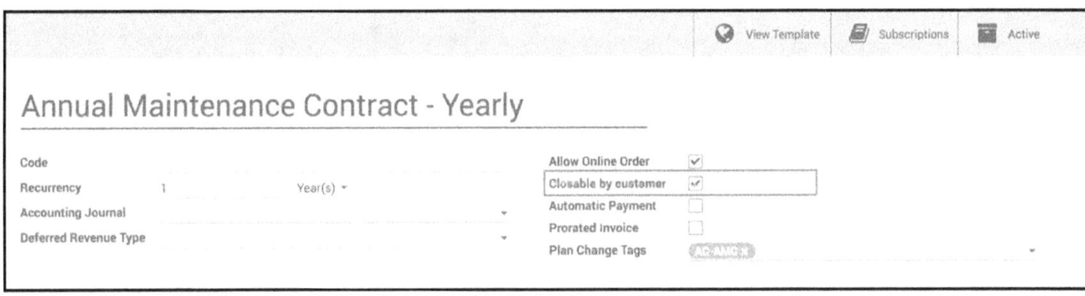

Select the **Closable by customer** field available on the subscription template so that customer can close the subscription by themselves on the portal.

The customer can get the **Close Your Account** button on the right panel of the contract. This button is allowed only when subscription template is configured accordingly:

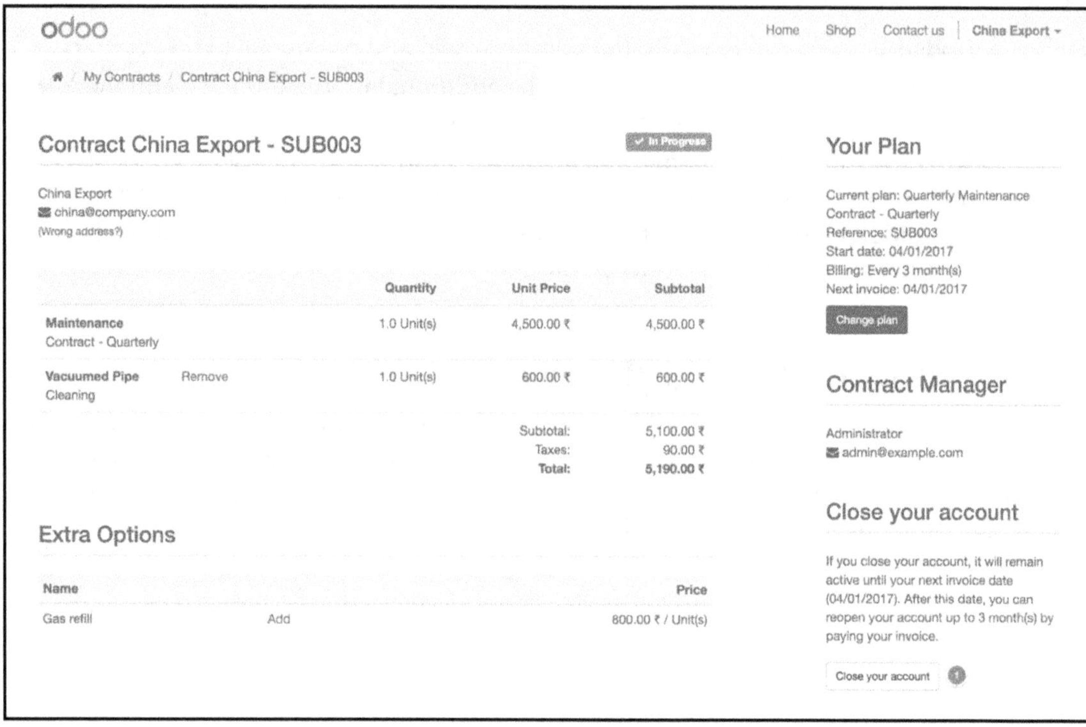

After clicking on the **Close your account** button, you will be asked to provide the reason for closing your subscription, you will also be asked for your feedback:

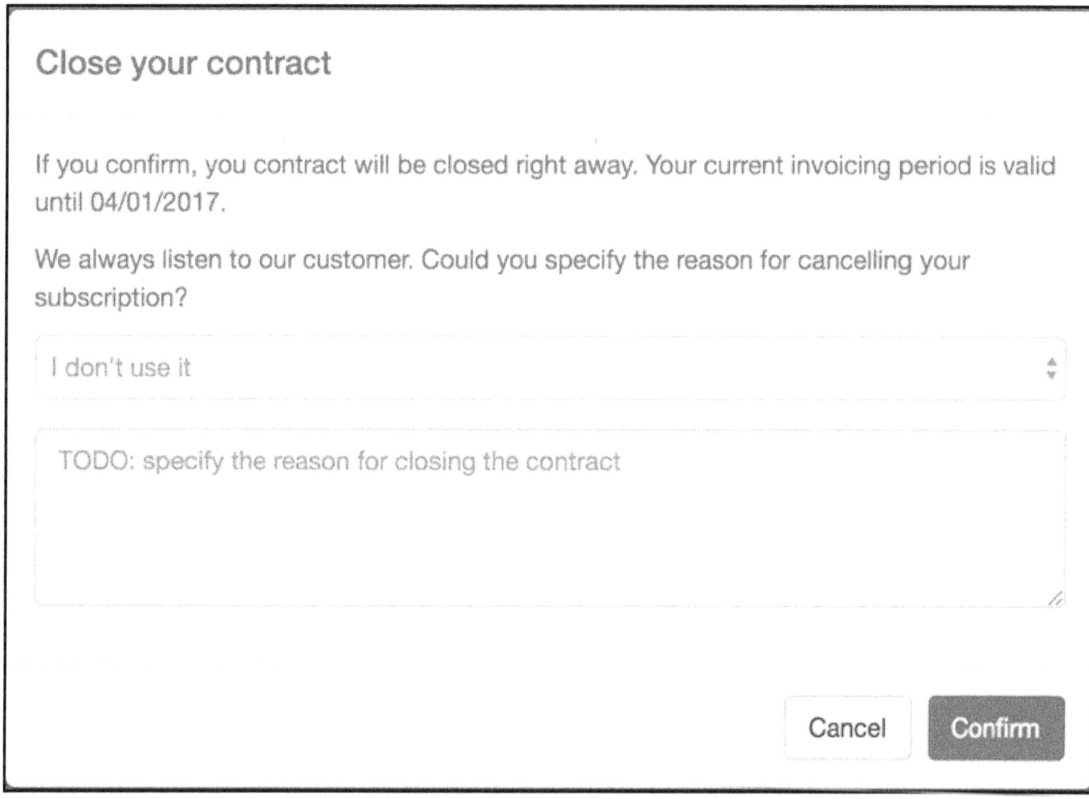

Clicking on the **Confirm** button, the contract will be closed right away and the invoice will not be generated anymore. Contract status is moved to the "**Closed**" stage.

5
Time Tracking and Invoicing Policy

In this chapter, we will cover the following recipes:

- Set up the product to track time and invoice policies
- Time tracking while delivering a service
- Working with the Timesheet application
- Invoicing based on time and materials
- Advance invoicing before delivery

Introduction

Tracking the service delivered is always a challenging and difficult job for the service-based company when they have to do billing based on the time spent to deliver the service. It takes a long time when they have two different software for accounting and project management. Until they consolidate the time spent on project management software, they cannot create an invoice.

Each time you create an invoice, you have to track the invoicing policy committed to the customer, whether a full invoice for the number of hours sold or an invoice depending on the time planned for the task or time spent on the task.

Odoo has time-tracking control, using its Timesheet application, which is also integrated with project management, sales, and accounting. You can sell a time-based project or fixed cost consulting service, and using timesheet, you can track the time spent on the project or service, in the case of time-based projects, you can create an invoice based on the time spent on each task in a project.

Let's see in detail how your team can use the Timesheet application, that allows you to create an accurate time-based invoice for your customer.

Set up the product to track time and invoice policies

The product has already been configured in `Chapter 4`, *Modern way of doing sales and managing sales contracts*, the time-tracking configuration on the product is a key configuration when you would like to track the service given by your team through timesheet, or task and create an invoice based on the time reported by the team.

Product in Odoo can be defined as a service when you are selling consulting days or projects.

Getting ready

We assume that you are working on the duplicated instance; if not, create a duplicate instance and try to configure products and follow the steps on that.

How to do it...

1. To get the time-tracking configuration option on the product form, you have to install the Timesheet application. To install the Timesheet application, go to **Apps** and search for timesheet. Click on the **Install** button on the **Timesheet** application to install it.

   On successful installation of the Timesheet application, you will get the two applications installed on your instance, **Timesheet** and **Project**, as the Timesheet application is dependent on the project.

2. To create a new service-type product, go to the product through **Sales** | **Sales** | **Products**, and click on the **CREATE** button. Enter the product name `Prepaid consulting`, select the product type as **Service**, and cost price and sale price have to be entered according to the service offered. To change the **Invoicing Policy**, go to the **INVOICING** tab.

There are two important parameters that have to be configured carefully, **Invoicing Policy** and **Track Service**:

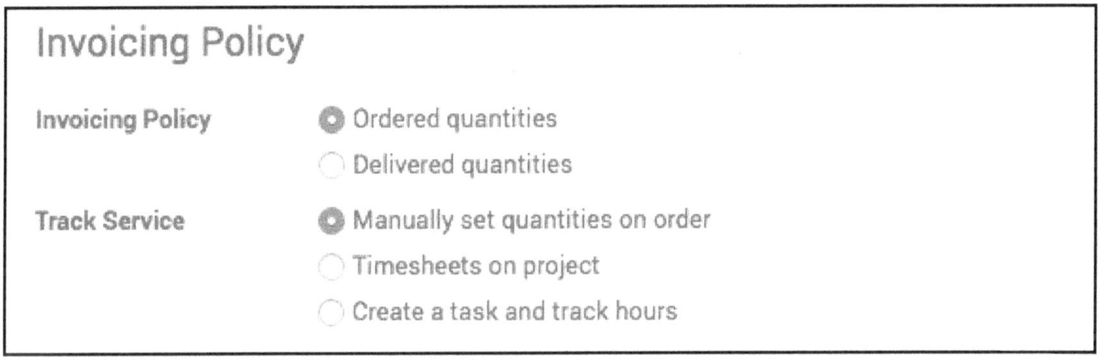

Here, I have configured it to track the service through timesheet and invoice based on what has been sold in the sales order.

3. Let's test the configuration. Create a sales order by going to **Sales** | **Sales** | **Quotation** and click on the **CREATE** button. Select the customer and click on **Add an item**. Select **Prepaid consulting** in the product, and the rest will be filled in automatically:

4. Confirm the quotation by clicking on the **CONFIRM SALE** button. As soon as you click on the button, the quotation converts to sales order and goes to the **SALE ORDER** stage:

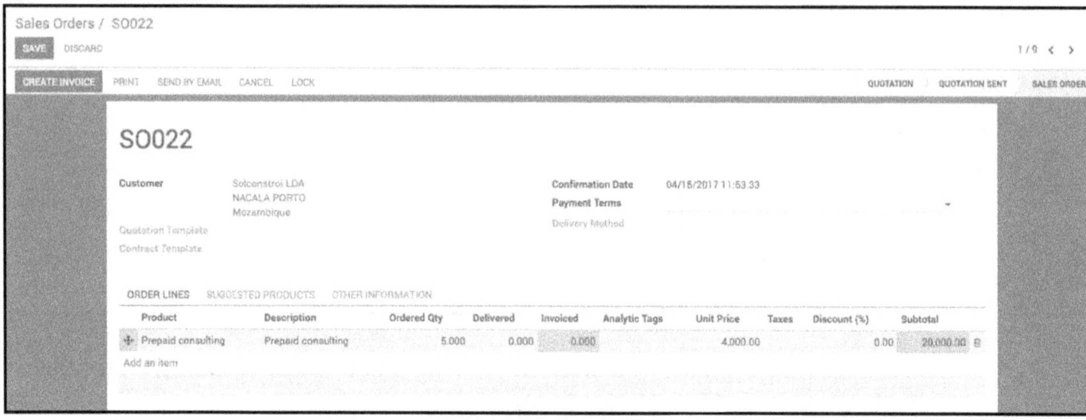

The **Invoicing policy** is based on the **Ordered quantity**; you can create an invoice without waiting for the delivery of the service, The blue color of the sale order line indicates; the order line can be invoiced to the customer.

> TIP
>
> When you change **Invoicing policy** to **Delivered quantities**, you cannot create an invoice until you deliver the service. The quantities you can invoice will not be more than the delivered quantities.

5. Click on the **CREATE INVOICES** button to create an invoice. A wizard will appear with the correct option selected. Keep that options as is and click on **CREATE AND VIEW INVOICES** to jump to the created invoice to confirm it, or click on **CREATE INVOICES** just to create a draft invoice:

6. Click on **CREATE AND VIEW INVOICES**. You will see the created invoice:

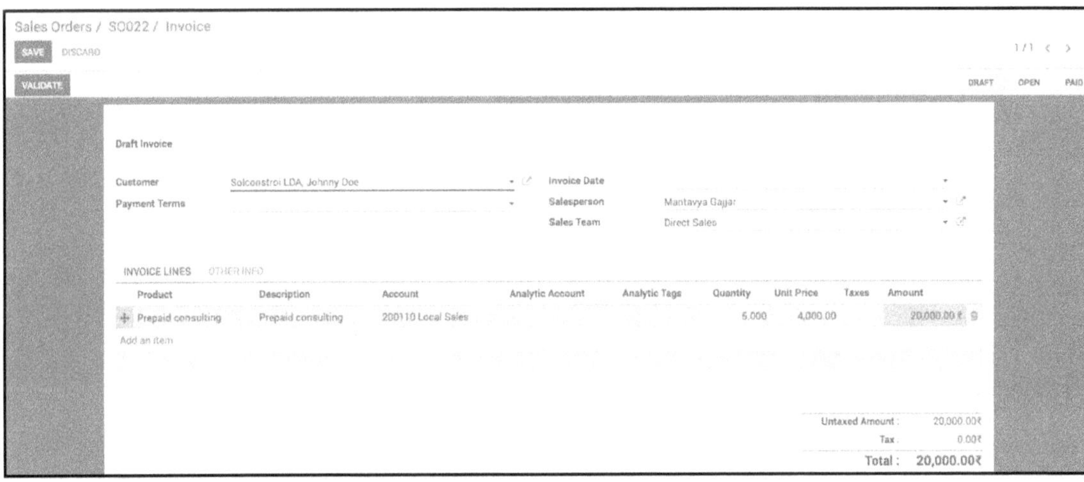

Review the invoice and click on the **VALIDATE** button if you would like to confirm and send the invoice to the customer.

7. The delivery of the service is not done yet. You can see the indication on the sale order. The invoiced quantity is set to `5`, but the delivered quantity is `0`:

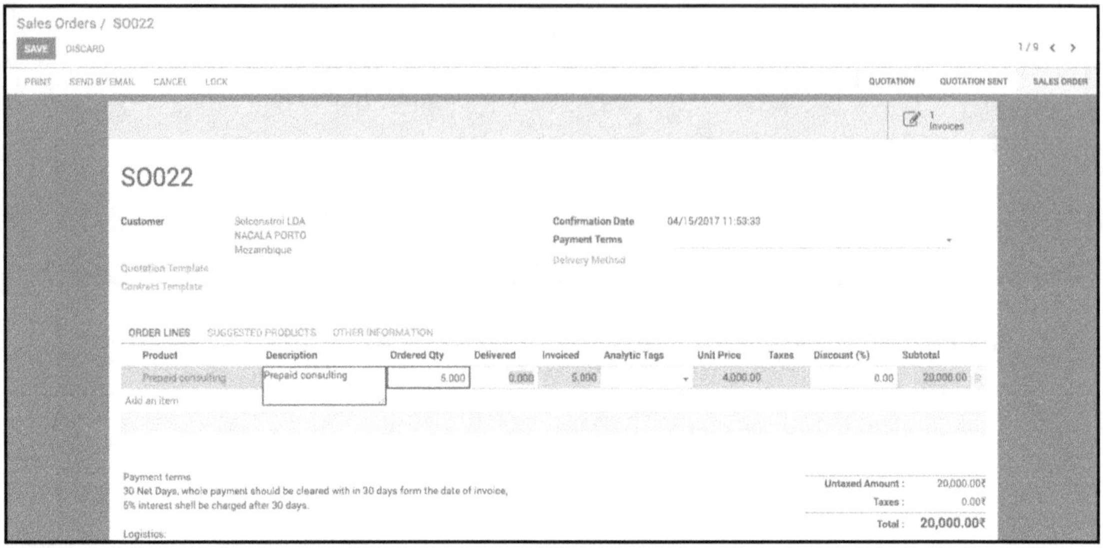

As the **Track Service** is set to **Manually set quantities on order** to track the service delivered. Let's edit the sales order, and you can enter the quantities delivered manually.

How it works...

There are two important parameters when you working with the service product, one is to track the service and other is the way to create an invoice. With the combination of these two parameters you can achieve all the business cases, please go through the following list of all the possibilities (*Expected behavior)* for the combination of *Invoicing policy* and *Track service* fields.

Invoicing Policy	**Track Service**	**Expected behavior**
Ordered quantities	Manually set quantities on order	• Invoice can be raised before delivery based on the quantity ordered • Project or task will not be created • Tracking of quantity will be done directly on the order

Ordered quantities	Timesheets on project	• Invoice can be raised before delivery based on the quantity ordered • Project will be created with the same name as order number • Tracking of time can be done on the project using timesheet
Ordered quantities	Create a task and track hours	• Invoice can be raised before delivery based on the quantity ordered • A task will be created in the project created • Tracking of time can be done on the project using timesheet
Delivered quantities	Manually set quantities on order	• Invoice can be raised after the delivery quantity (time spent to be set manually on the sales order) • A task or project will not be created • Time spent can be directly entered on the sales order
Delivered quantities	Timesheets on project	• Invoice can be raised based on the delivered quantities • Project will be created with the same name as the order number • Tracking of time can be done on the project using timesheet
Delivered quantities	Create a task and track hours	• Invoice can be raised based on the delivered quantities • A task will be created in the project created • Tracking of time can be done on the project using timesheet

Time tracking while delivering a service

The delivery of the stockable product is managed by the warehouse, while delivery of the service can be done by the team. It's important to track the service as we may need the details later to prepare the invoice.

Let's create a consulting service product and see how your service company can manage the delivery of the service and invoice based on that.

How to do it...

1. The Timesheet application is installed, and the **Track Service** option is available under the **Invoicing Policy** configuration on the product. Create a new product by going to **Sales** | **Sales** | **Products**. Enter the name as `Consulting Service`, enter the cost price and sale price of the service, and do not forget to select the product type as **service**.

   To configure **Invoicing Policy,** click on the **INVOICING** tab, select **Delivered quantities** for **Invoicing Policy** and **Timesheets on project** for **Track Service**:

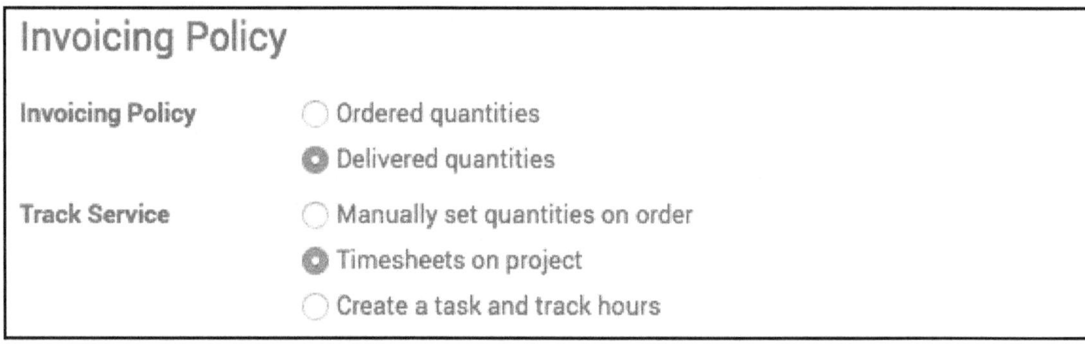

   Using this configuration does the following:

   - Invoices based on actual hours spent on the consulting work
   - Project will be created with the name same as the order number
   - Tracking of time can be done on the project using timesheet

2. Let's create a sales order by going to **Sales** | **Sales** | **Quotation** and click on the **CREATE** button. Select the customer and click on **Add an item**. Then, select the **Consulting Service** product; the rest will be filled in automatically.
3. Click on the **CONFIRM SALE** button to confirm the sales order. As soon as you confirm the order, the project will be created the same as the order number and linked to the order; in our case, it is `SO023`. All the time spent on this customer has to be encoded on the timesheet for this project only:

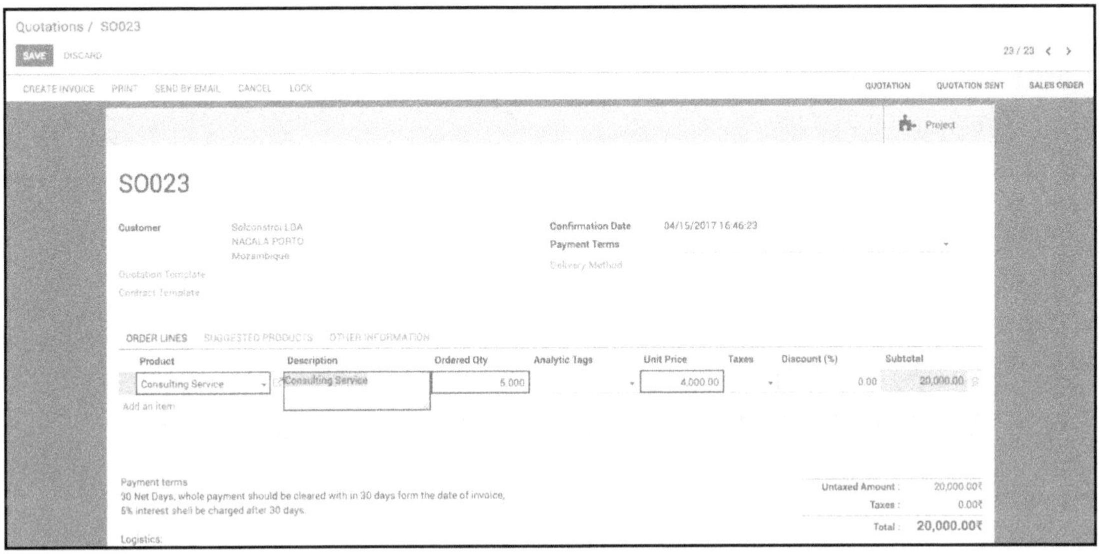

If you cannot see the project link on the confirmed sales order, check your product confirmation. The **Invoicing Policy** needs to be configured correctly on the product.

4. As the invoicing policy is based on the delivered quantities, and the delivery of the service is tracked by the timesheet, all the time reported to the timesheet for the project `SO023` will be invoiceable time.

   Click on the **Timesheets** application. Then, you will be directed to your timesheet:

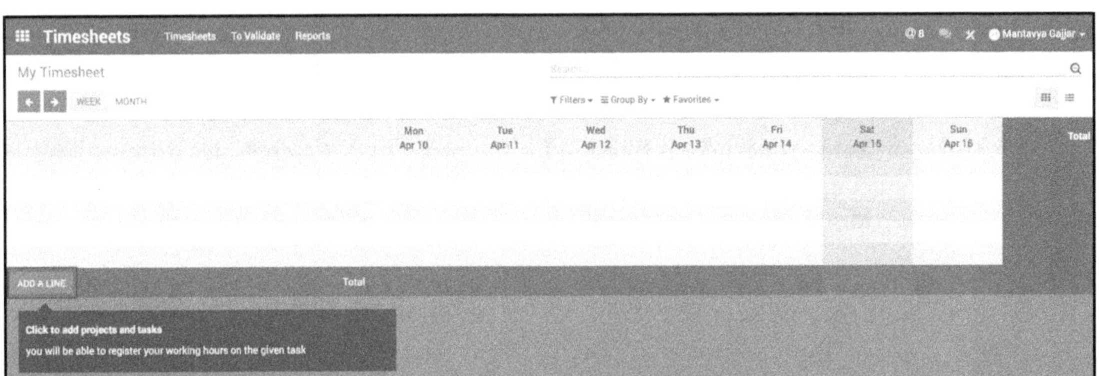

Click on the **ADD A LINE** button to add a timesheet line. A popup will appear. Select the project the same as your sale order number. Enter the time spent and a description of the service delivered. The project is created automatically when you confirm the order:

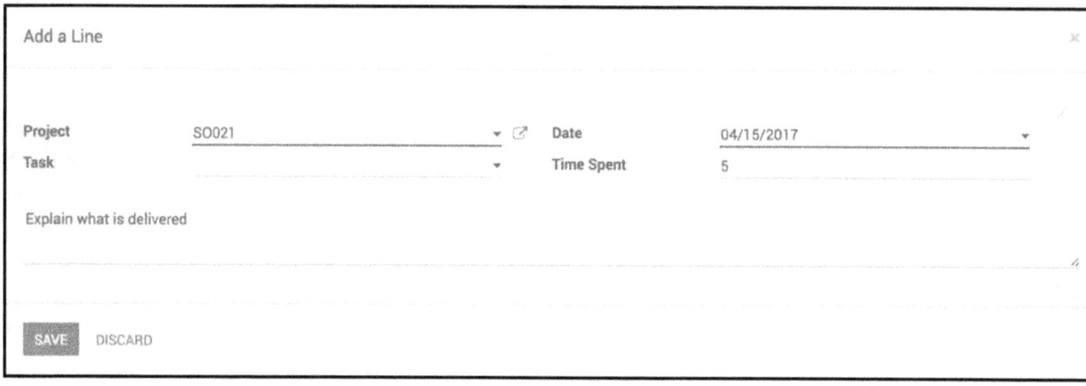

All the numbers encoded on the timesheet will be in hours.

Click on the **SAVE** button to add the timesheet line onto your timesheet. It will be linked to the project and sales order. The delivered quantity should be set to `5` as we have encoded the timesheet for 5 hours for the project.

You can create multiple tasks for the project, assign them to consultants to work on. Consultants will work on assigned tasks and fill the timesheet entries. The **Delivered quantity** will get updated as soon as the timesheet entries created for the project. All the Delivered quantities will be used later to create an invoice.

5. As soon as the timesheet is filled in for the project `SO023`, the sales order is ready for invoicing. The line on the sales order will become blue, indicating that the line is ready for invoicing. The timesheet and project get linked automatically on the sales order:

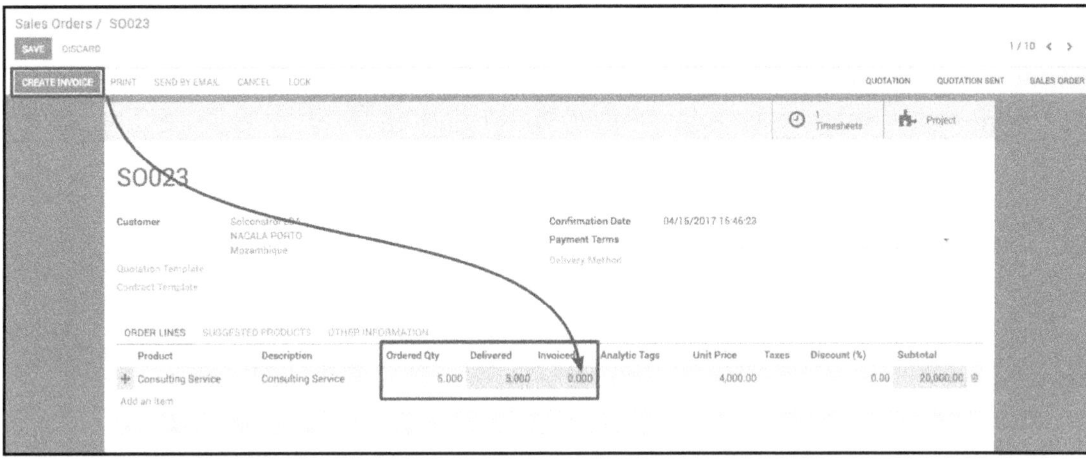

The **CREATE INVOICE** button will be highlighted as the order has something to invoice. Click on the **CREATE INVOICES** button to create an invoice based on the delivered quantity. When you click on the button, a popup will appear. Keep the option selected on the wizard as is. It will be the best option selected as per the current invoice:

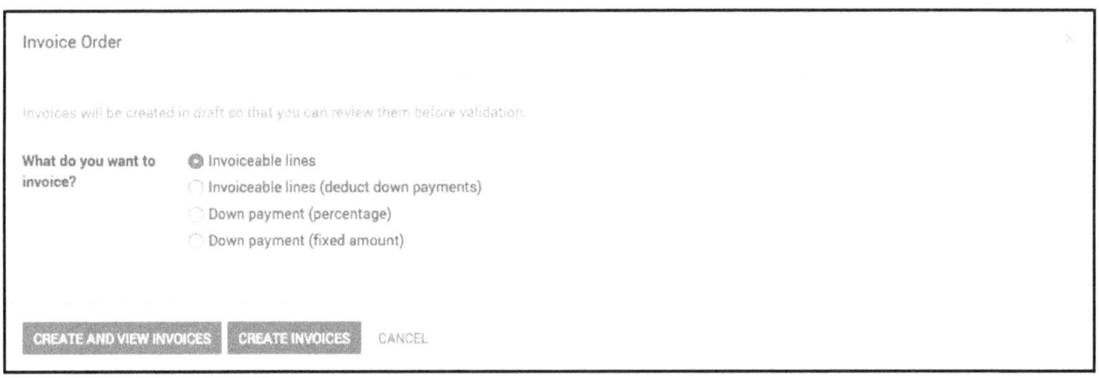

Clicking on the **CREATE AND VIEW INVOICES** button will create an invoice and open the created invoice. **CREATE INVOICE** will create an invoice. I have clicked on the **CREATE AND VIEW INVOICES** button:

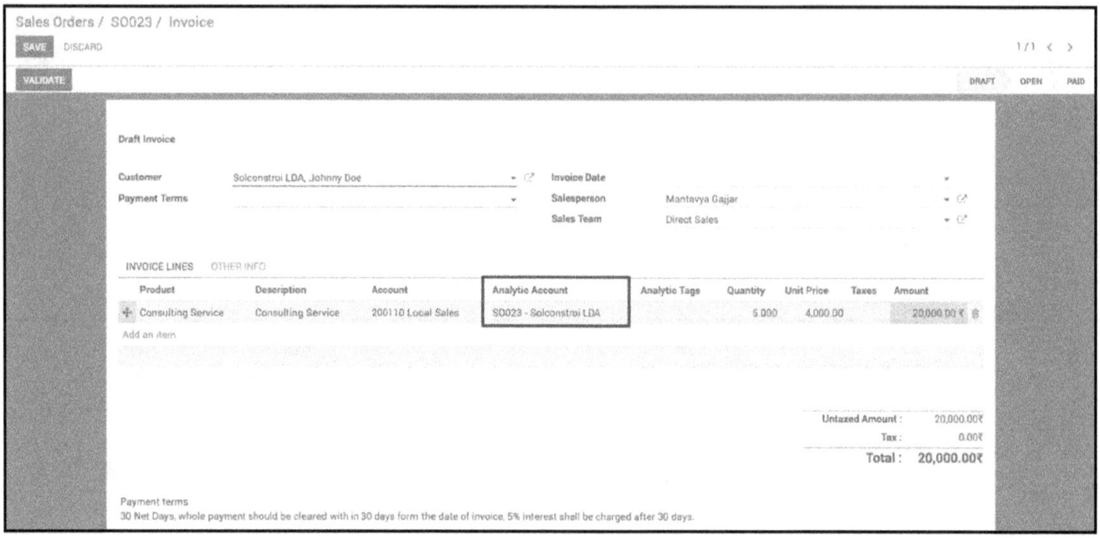

Validate the invoice by clicking on the **VALIDATE** button. Make sure that **Analytic account** is linked to the invoice line to compute the correct cost.

6. Your order is ready to be locked now if you do not have any changes in the service or invoicing part. By clicking on the **LOCK** button, you can lock the sales order. Once the order is locked, you cannot modify the order; however, you will be able to process the invoice and delivery of services or goods:

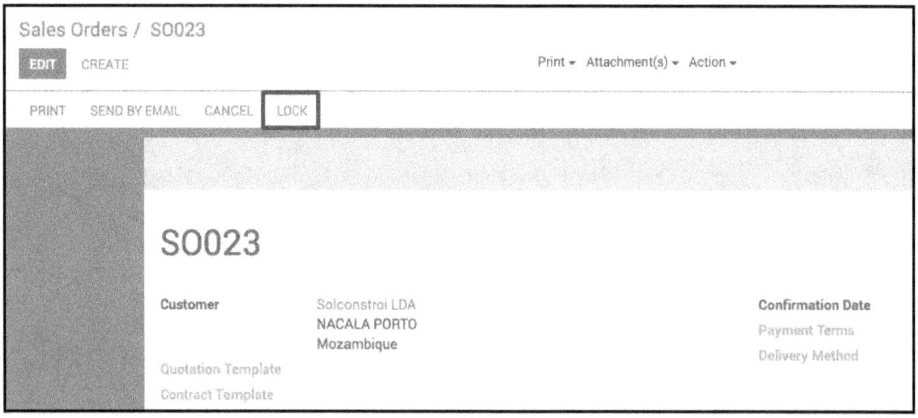

7. You can track the time spent by your team of consultants to deliver the services. To do this, click on the **Timesheets** icon from the action bar:

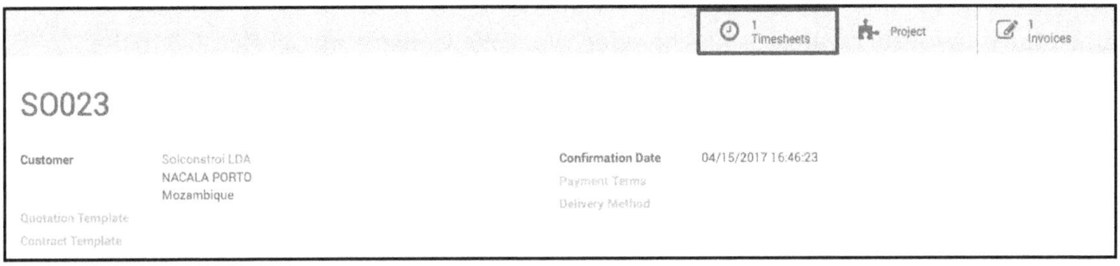

You will see the list of timesheet entries; as it is a standard Odoo list view, you can generate various analytical reports by applying **Filters** and **Group By** options:

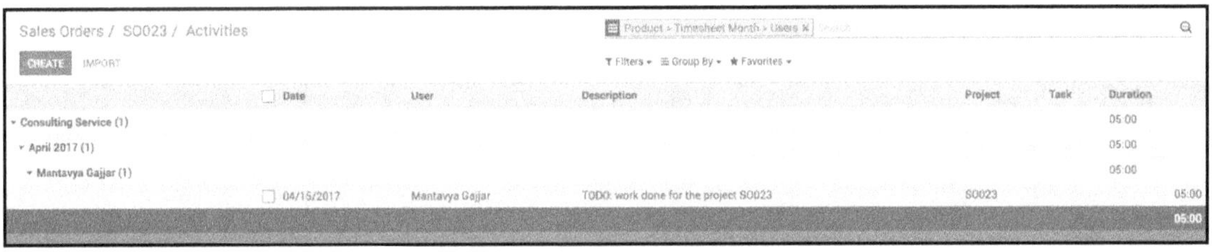

There's more...

There are two approaches to track the service, **Track by Project** and **Track by Task**; both approaches are used depending on the business case you have.

Working with projects and tasks

Track by Project can be activated by setting the second option **Timesheets on project** for **Track Service** on product configuration under **Invoicing Policy**. Using this configuration on the product, a new project will be created when the service product will be sold. It is useful when you have to create an invoice based on multiple users timesheets, working on the different tasks for the project.

In a long-term project, where project stages are important to maintain the flow and quality of each task, you can have a new task on the sales of service instead of creating a new project. This approach is called **Track by Task**.

Let's see how to create a long-term project to track the task flow with stages. Each time you sell a service, you will have a task. The newly created task can be assigned to a team member.

Open the previously created product having the name **Consulting Service**. Go to the **INVOICING** tab and the **Invoicing Policy** configuration:

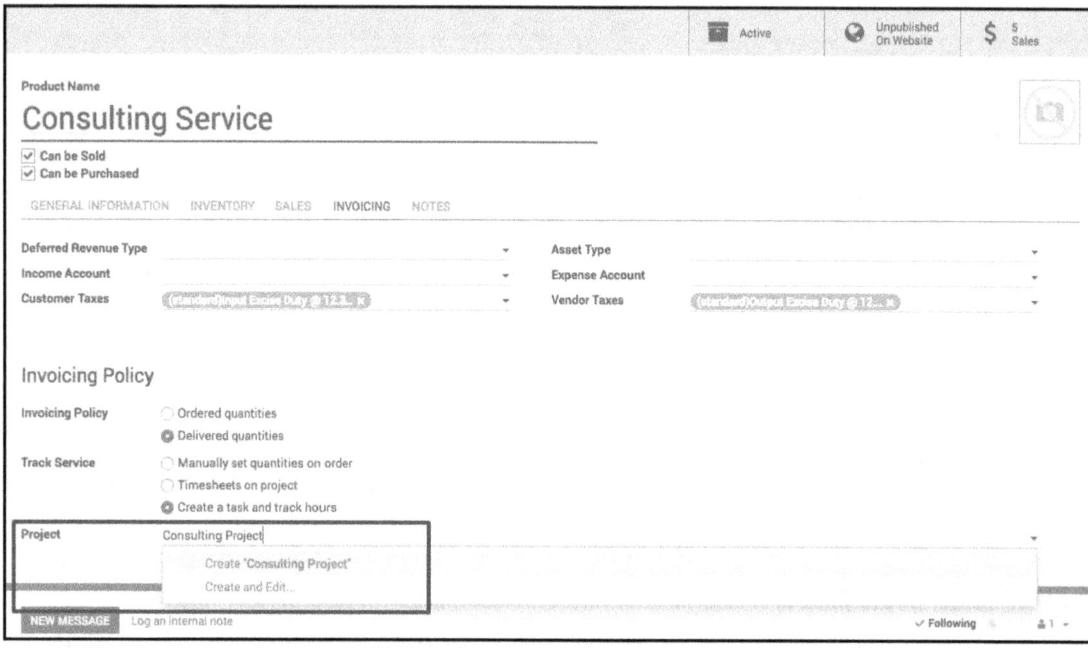

Select **Create a task and track hours** for the **Track Service** field. As soon as you select that option, you will be asked for the default project to link to the newly created task. Either select the existing project or create a new project just by typing the name `Consulting Project` and select the **Create "Consulting project"** option on the list. Save the product form.

The second thing to configure is the project stages. Go to the **Project** application and click on **Consulting Project**:

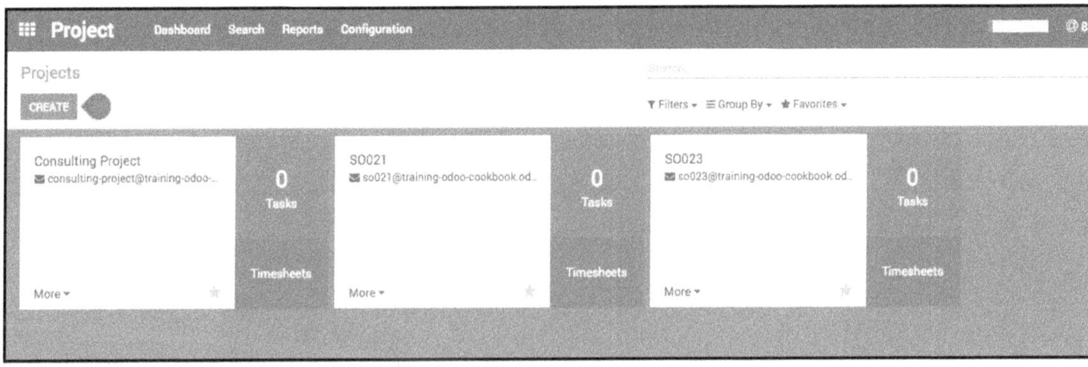

You will be jumped to the project stages. Currently, it's empty; click on **ADD NEW COLUMN**, You will be asked for a stage name, Enter the name to create a stage, click on **Add** button to create the stage:

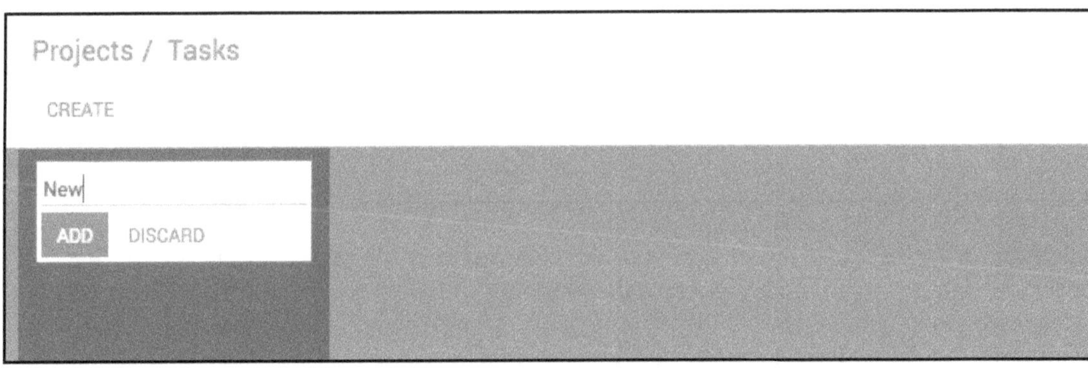

Once you create all the stages, your project pipe will look like this:

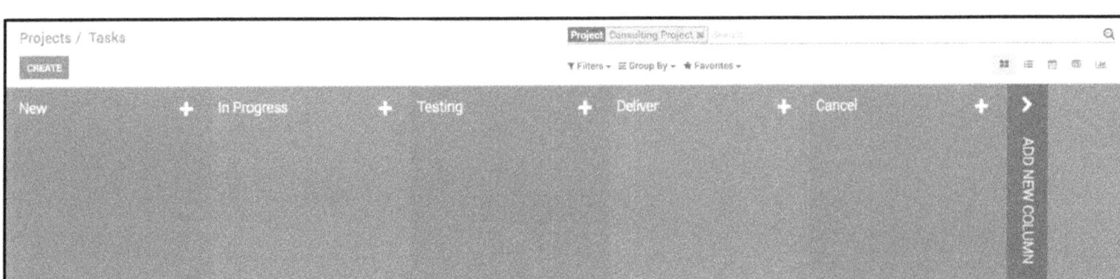

You are ready to sell a **Consulting Service** that is managed through **Consulting Project**.

Go to **Sales** | **Sales** | **Quotations** to create a new quotation, select the customer, and select **Consulting Service** as the product on the quotation line.

Save the order and click on **CONFIRM SALE** to confirm the order. As soon as you confirm the order, a task will be created and linked to the sales order. Look at the following screenshot:

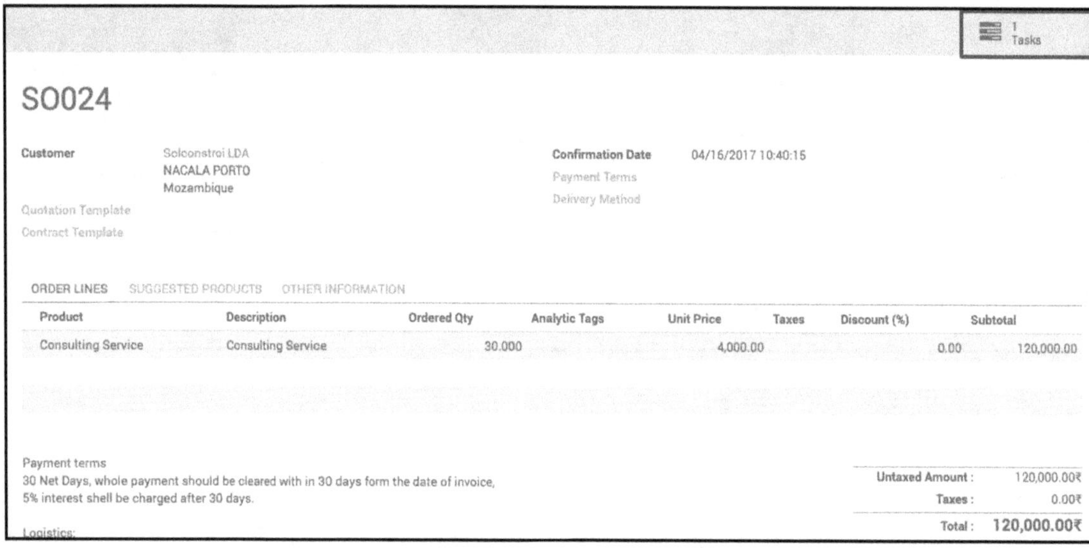

Clicking on the **Tasks** action button you will be jumped to the task associated with the order. By default, it will be assigned to the manager of the project. The **Initial Planned Hours** are same as the **Ordered Qty** on the order, **Deadline** will be computed based on the Delivery Lead Time defined on the Service type product.

The description of the task will be the same as the product description defined for the product. The same description will be available on the order line:

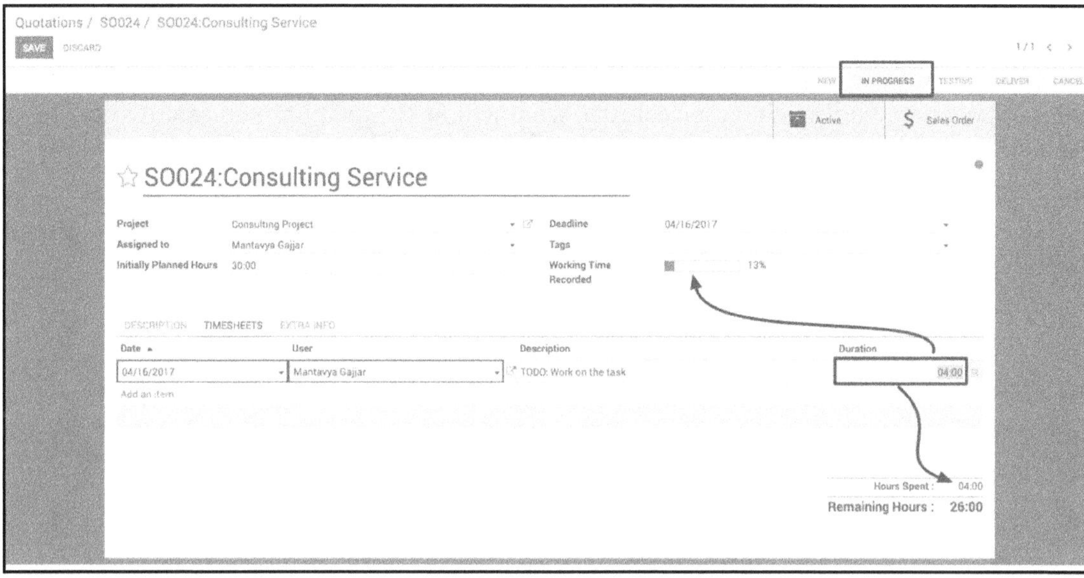

As soon as a consultant starts working on the task, the consultant marks the task stage as **In Progress** and the time spent on the task will fill as a timesheet entry. It computes the time remaining and consumed, and the overall progress of the task.

Depending on the **Invoicing policy** set on **Consulting Service,** invoicing can be done in advance at once for sold quantities or if it is based on **Delivered quantities**. The accountant or account manager will go to **Sales** | **Invoicing** | **Sales to Invoice** at regular intervals to check for the invoiceable order:

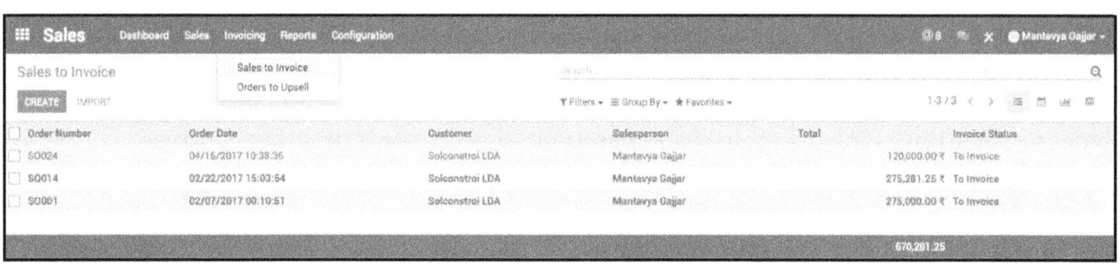

The sales order listed under the **Sales to Invoice** menu is ready to raise an invoice to customer. Create an invoice either order by order or select all the orders having the same customer and choose the **Invoice Order** option from the action menu from the top of the list.

I am going to raise invoice order by order. Go to **sales to invoice** menu available under the **Sales** application, you will have a clear idea what will be the quantity you can invoice against the ordered quantity:

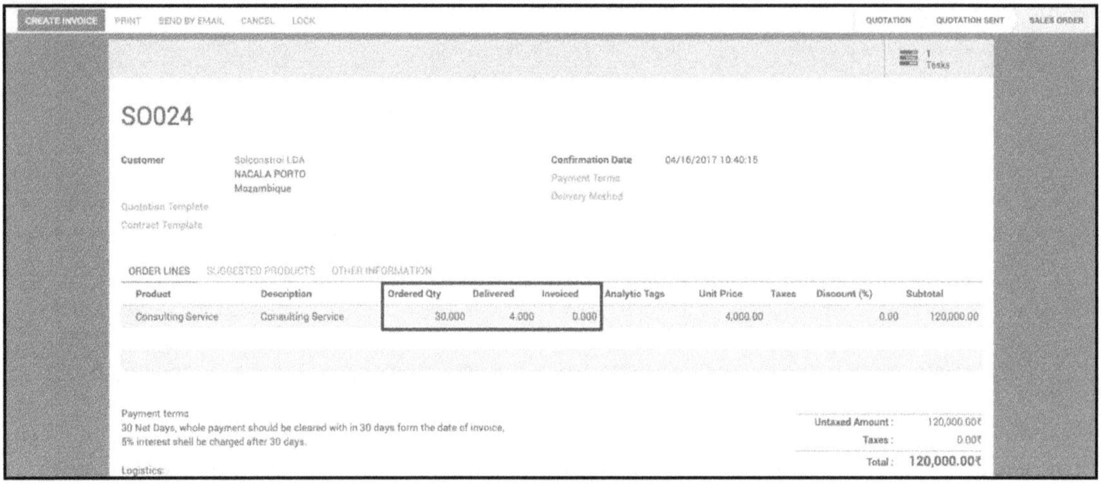

The invoicing process is as simple as we have seen in this recipe, click on the **CREATE INVOICE** button the follow the steps, you will be redirected to the invoice created.

Working with timesheet

Timesheet is a great tool that helps you manage the daily activities and workforce. Get an overview of your billable time. Track all the resources allocated to your project and see your profits and losses. Keep your projects under control. It also helps you automatically generate one-time or recurring invoices based on expenses and timesheet entries.

Timesheet view

Timesheet is an application that can be used by integrating with Sales, Project, and Invoicing applications, or independent of those applications. Clicking on the **Timesheet** application from home will show you your current timesheet:

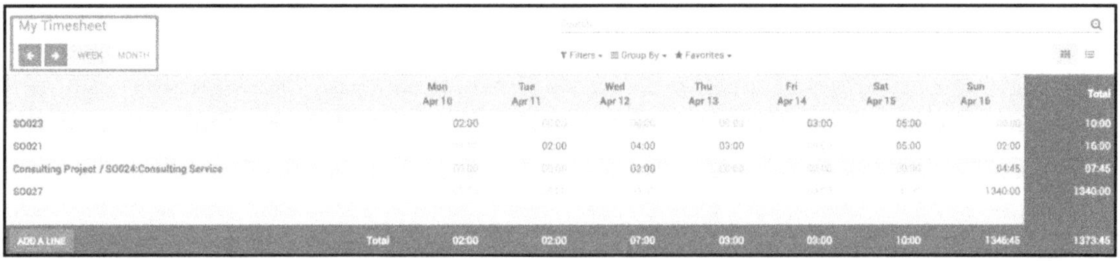

In the top left corner, you can move to the next **WEEK** or **MONTH** depending on the current view. The timesheet can be viewed in the **WEEK** view or the **MONTHY** view.

Filters and **Group By** also works on the timesheet. The default view mode is a grid you can switch to list view, where you can actually see the detailed activities.

Entering the timesheet entry

By default, on the row, you can see all the projects you worked on during the week. A working hour can be registered on the timesheet by selecting the right project and date:

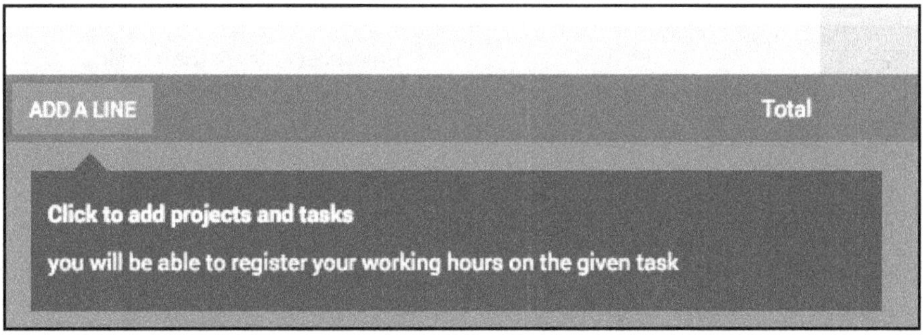

When you start a new week, you have to add the project to your timesheet by clicking on the **ADD A LINE** button:

A popup will appear to select **Project** and **Task**. Enter the time spent and a description of the task performed. Click on **SAVE** to add it to your timesheet.

Every time you make a change to the timesheet, a new activity will be generated, and you can get work done for each activity. Let's take an example you worked on two activities for the same project on 17th April, you update the time twice on the timesheet.

After some time, you complete another activity for the same project; you change to `6` hours instead of `3` hours:

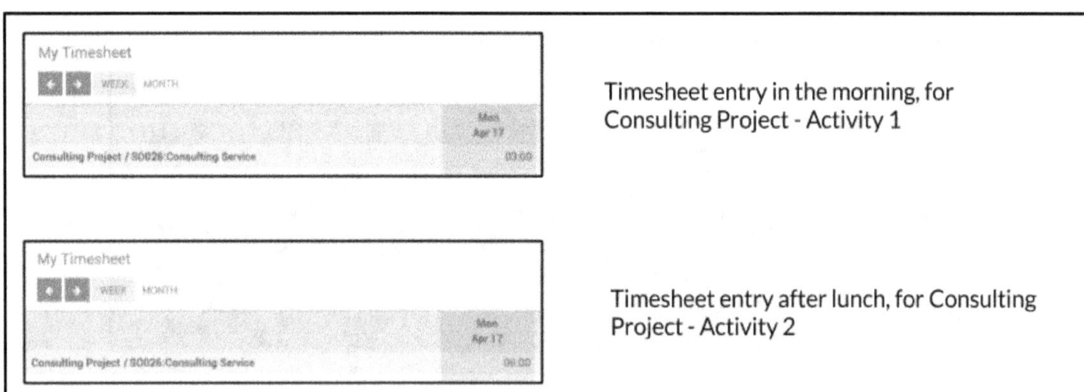

There will be two different activities generated based on these two modifications. Click on the hours to see the detailed activities behind those hours with the breakdown of the hours and description:

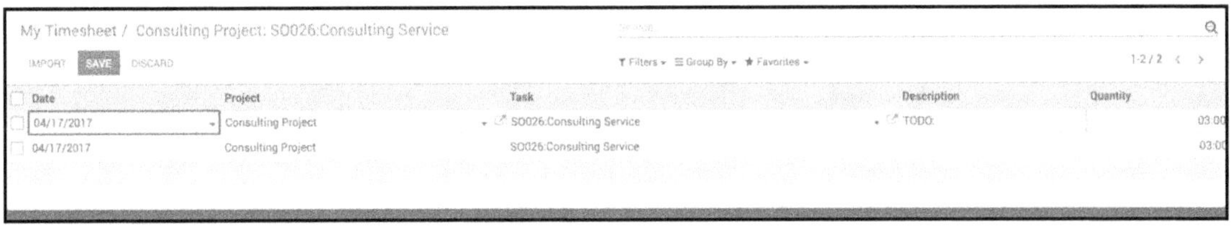

Click on the **Description** field and change it. Click on the **SAVE** button to save it.

Timesheet validation

Timesheet can be validated by the project manager or someone else responsible in the company. The validation can be done by month or by week. Go to **Timesheet** | **To Validate** | **Last Week**, and you will be shown all the timesheets waiting for validation:

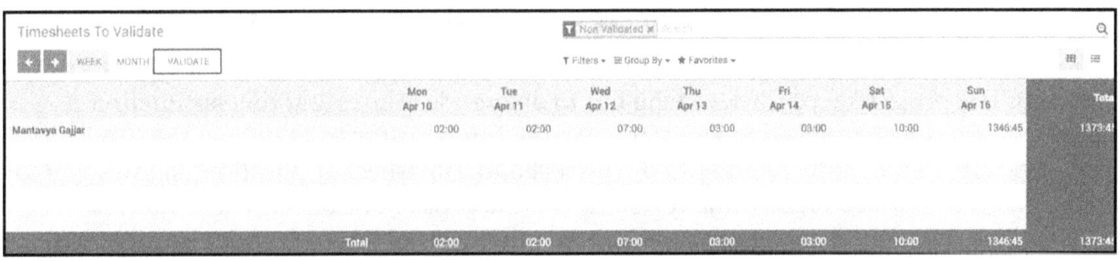

Clicking on **VALIDATE** button you will be asked to choose the list of users to validate their timesheet on the popup wizard.

As soon as you select the list of users, click on the **VALIDATE** button to confirm the timesheet for the selected users.

Invoicing the timesheet

By default, the invoice will be created. Based on all the timesheet entries the user entered, either they are validated or not validated lines. You can control the timesheet lines to create an invoice from the configuration. Go to **Sales** | **Configuration** | **Setting** and search for the **Invoice Timesheets** field:

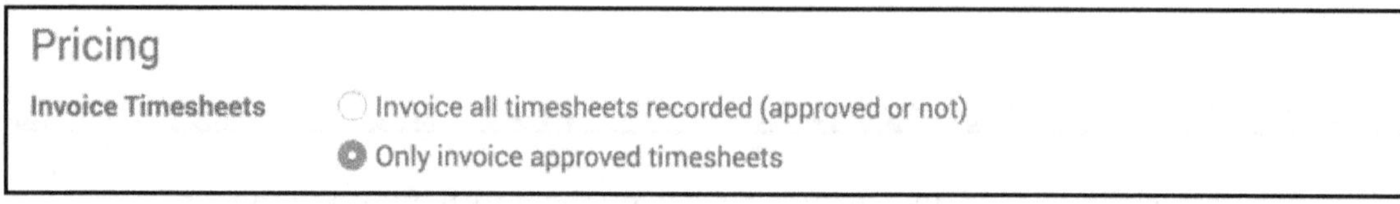

The default option selected is **Invoice all timesheets recorded (approved or not)**. Change this setting to **Only invoice approved timesheets**, and click on **APPLY** to save the setting. Now, the timesheet in charge has to validate all the timesheets before the invoice gets prepared.

Working with the Timesheet application

Odoo made it simple to raise an invoice based on the time spent on the delivery of the order (project). The project keeps track of who has to deliver deadlines and time estimations, while the Timesheet application keeps track of the time consumed to deliver the service. The sales application, integrated with the project and Timesheet applications, allows you to create an invoice based on the time registered on the project timesheet. The team can efficiently manage their timesheet as a Chrome plugin or on any mobile device anywhere, anytime:

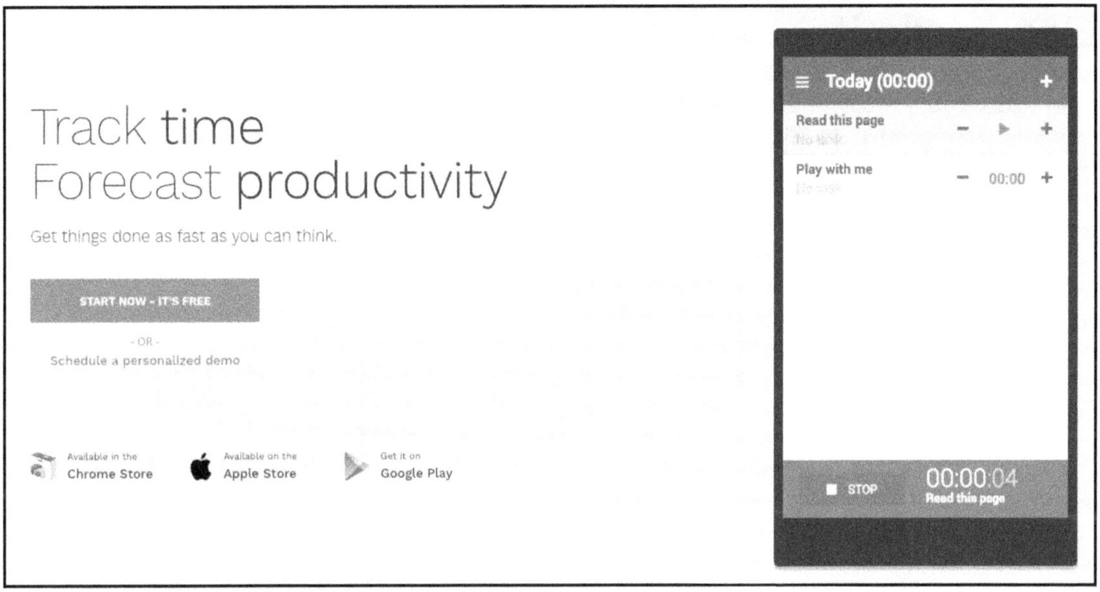

Using the Timesheet application, users can:

- Plan the daily activities
- Track time for ongoing tasks
- Enter the timesheet entries
- Get the daily and weekly statistical reports
- Get integrated with the Odoo instance

Let's see how your team can benefit from the Timesheet application to plan and manage timesheet activities on the go.

Getting ready

We assume that you have already installed the application on a mobile device. To install the application, you have to go to your mobile's respective app store.

Besides the mobile application, you should have your instance URL, username, and password handy to connect with the Odoo instance later.

How to do it...

1. You should get the **Awesome Timesheet** application on your mobile up on successful installation of the application from the Play Store. Click on the icon to open the application:

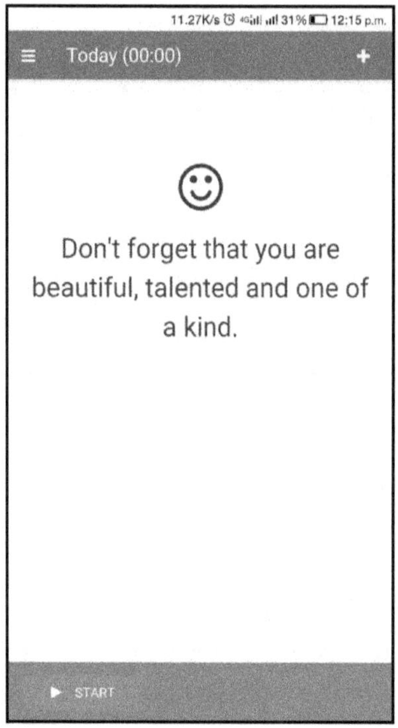

The first screen you see is today's activity. As you still haven't linked the application with your Odoo instance, you won't be able to fetch any data.

> The Odoo mobile application can work in two ways, whether it is connected to Odoo or not. If it is connected to Odoo, it will sync data with the instance, or if not, it will store the data on mobile, and when you connect with Odoo instance, it will push all your local data to the Odoo instance. You will never lose any of your data if you start using the mobile app without connecting to the Odoo instance.

2. The next step is to install the timesheet synchronization application on the Odoo instance. Go to **Apps**, search for `timesheet`, remove the **Apps** filter, and install the application, having the title **Synchronization with the external timesheet application** :

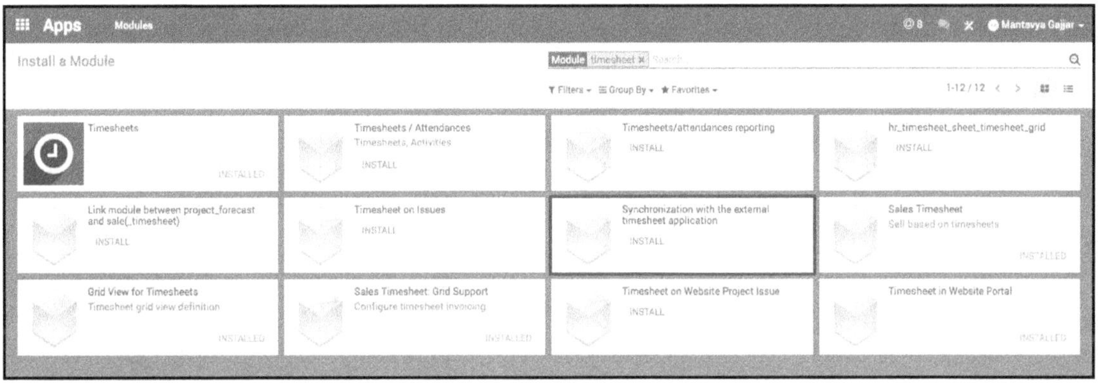

This application will provide the interface for the external timesheet application to synchronize the data. It will take care of the security while synchronization of the project and timesheet data.

3. Let's connect the mobile application with Odoo instance to fetch the data from. From the left menu select the **Synchronize** option to connect your device to Odoo:

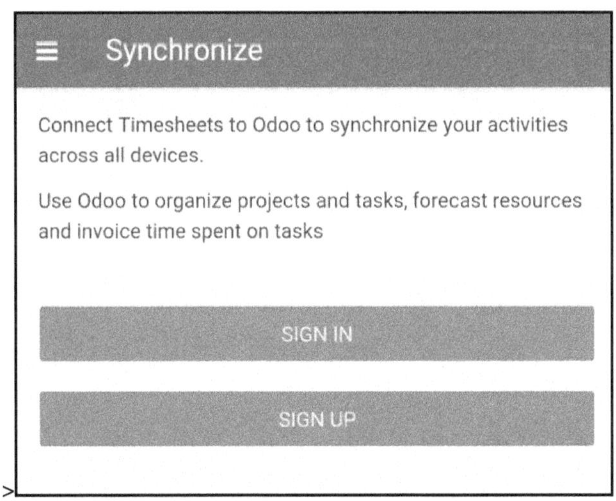

You can either connect or create a new instance from the application. Let's connect with the existing instance. Keep **Use an Odoo.com account** if your instance is on Odoo cloud; otherwise, click on **Reset** to enter the local instance URL:

If not, just reset the default configuration from the bottom of the screen. As soon as you use the *Odoo.com* account, you will be asked to log in, and then, you'll be guided to follow the steps as follows:

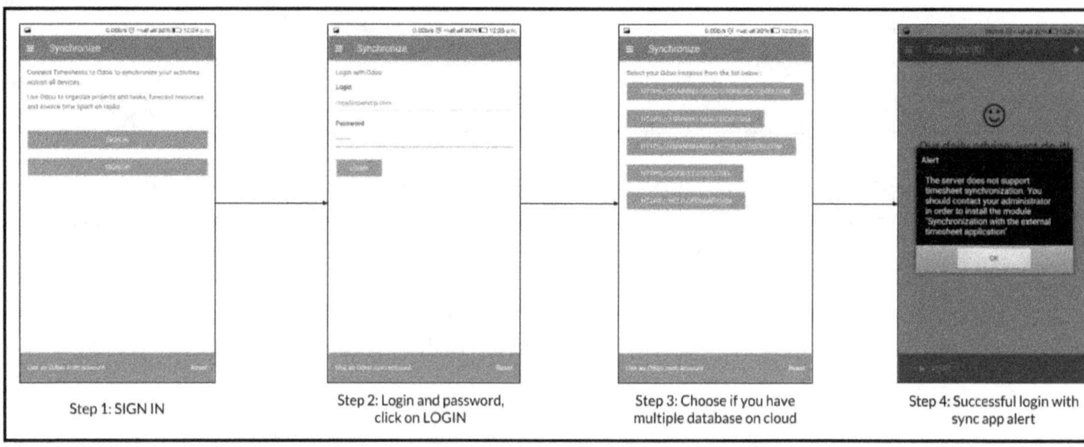

On successful login, you will be prompted for the local data, which you can keep or discard. If you keep it, it will be in sync with the Odoo instance:

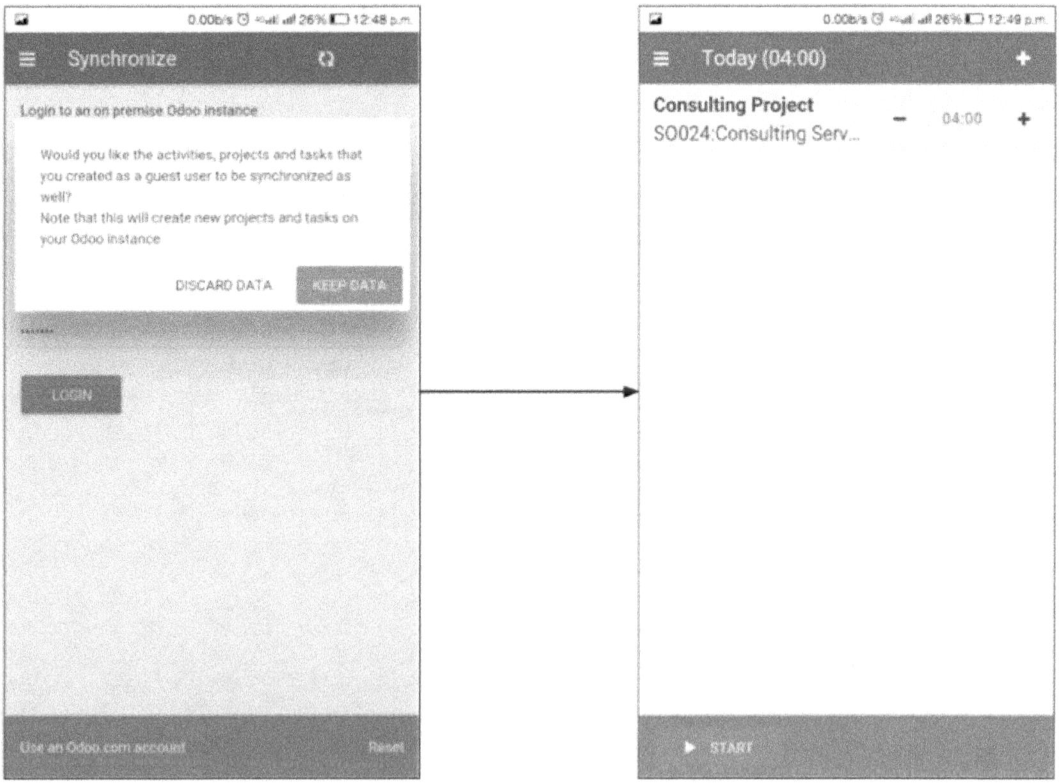

Successful login, asked you keep the local data or discard it

Your today's activity sync form the Odoo instacne

The first screen you get up on successful login is today's activity you performed.

4. Now you can start another activity by clicking on the **START** button. The application starts computing the time and as soon as you click on **STOP**, you will be redirected to a screen to fill in the timesheet details, You will be asked to select the **Project** and **Task** and enter the **Work Summary** details, the **Time Spent** will be filled in automatically. You can change the hours manually before clicking on the **SAVE** button on the Activity:

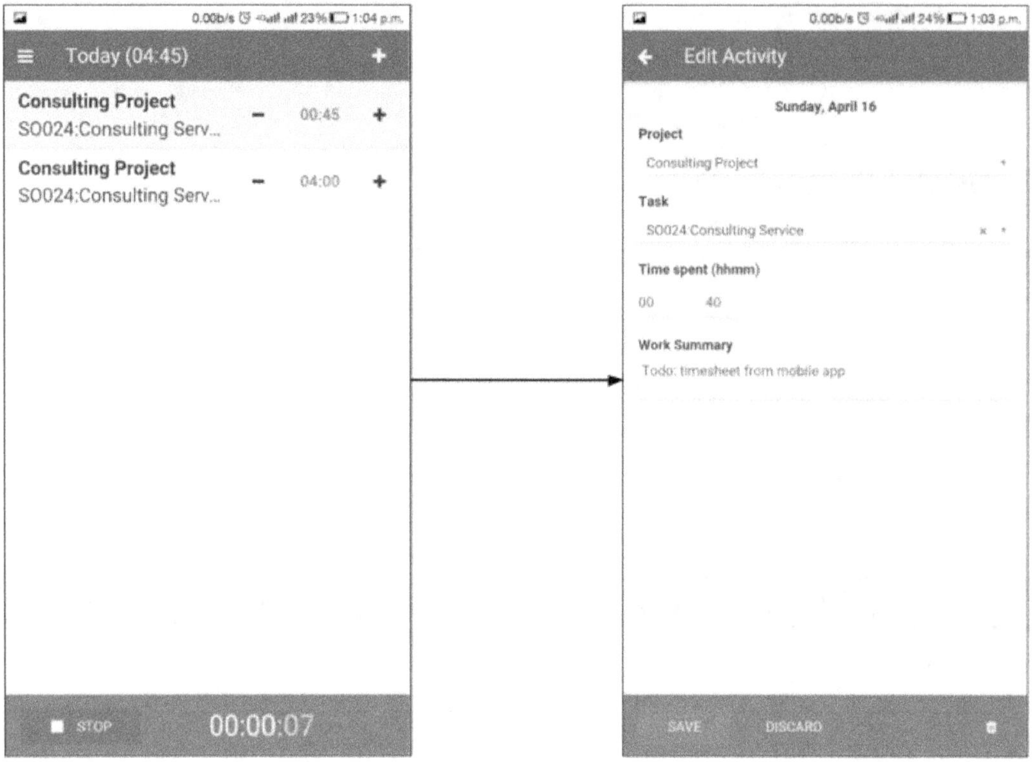

Start your next activity by clicking on the START button

Fill and SAVE the timesheet entry on STOP

Click on the **SAVE** button to save the timesheet entry. It will periodically synchronize with the Odoo instance. You can do it manually from the **Synchronize** menu by clicking on the **SYNC NOW** button.

5. You can plan today's tasks at the beginning of every day from the **Today's Plan** menu. Go there to plan your day. You will get all the tasks that are waiting to start:

Step 1: Jump to Today's Plan, Select the task plan for today

Step 2: Task planned in today's list

Step 3: increase or decrease the hours on task

You can choose the task to scheduled and that's all. The task is scheduled in your daily plan. Once you finish the task, change the working hours using the + or - sign beside the task, and that's done. If you wish to enter a **Work Summary**, click on the task, change the details, and click on the **SAVE** button.

6. You can get the weekly statistical report for the timesheet from the **Statistics** menu. Click on the menu and you can change to the previous or next week using the left and right arrows available on the top of the screen:

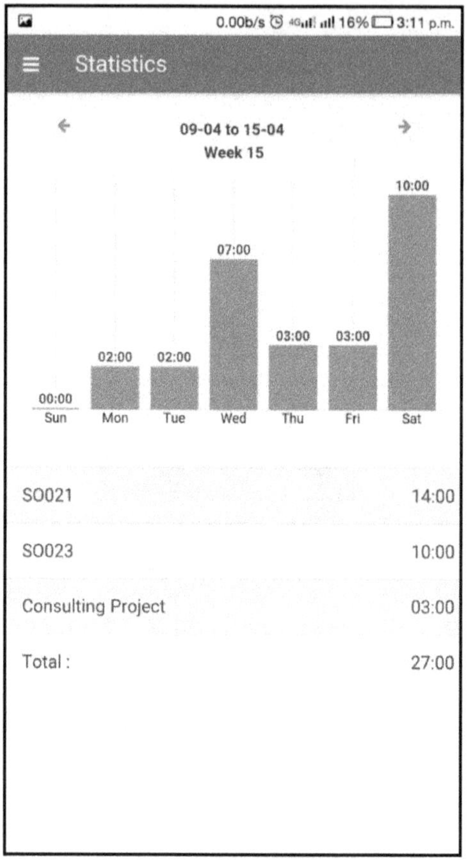

There's more...

Like the mobile application, you can also install and use this application on Google Chrome browser. To install the plugin, go to the Chrome Web Store and search for `Odoo`:

Click on the + ADD TO CHROME button to install the plugin to your browser. Follow the same steps as we did on our mobile device to log into the application. On successful login, you will get today's tasks on the application:

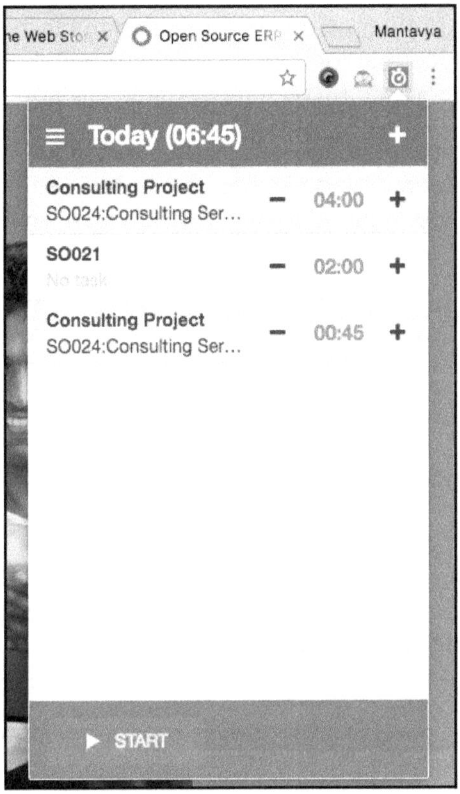

During the sign-in process, the app will automatically detect if you're already logged into *odoo.com*. If it detects this, the same account will be used to log into your instance. If you have multiple accounts on *odoo.com*, the current login account will be detected and connected.

Invoicing based on time and material

The most common business case is where the supplier has to supply material and services to complete the order. Everything has to be planned and tracked in the ongoing project. It may become super complex. When your software either manages the delivery and invoicing of stockable product (material) or the service, it will become nearly impossible to manage the planning, delivery, and invoicing with multiple applications.

In the previous recipe, we have seen how we made the delivery of the service and tracked it using the Timesheet application on mobile. Let's see in this recipe how we can make the quotation have the service and material to deliver and create an invoice based on the delivery of the material and service.

Getting ready

We assume that you are ready with the material and service type product created in `Chapter 3`, *Traceability - Leads to Cash*. In my case, I will use the existing product, which is **Laguna Series - Size of 1000 x 1000 mm** and **Tiles fitting service**, which are already created in my instance.

Make sure that you have enough stock in the warehouse for the **Laguna Series - Size of 1000 x 1000 mm** product. To update the quantity on hand for the product, open the product from view and click on the **UPDATE QTY ON HAND** button, the popup window will appear as shown in the following screenshot:

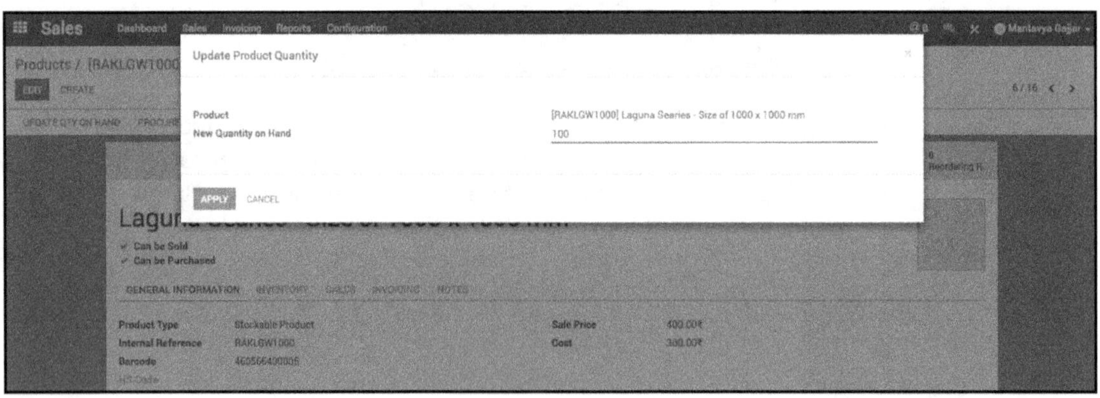

Click on the **Save** button. You should see the **On Hand** quantity on the action bar.

Tiles fitting service is a *service*-type product, configured to **Track Service** by *Timesheet on Project*, and **Invoicing Policy** will be based on the *Delivered quantities*.

How to do it...

1. Go to the quotation by going to **Sales** | **Sales** | **Quotations**. Click on the **CREATE** button to create a new quotation, select the customer, and add the quotation lines. First, select **Laguna Series - Size of 1000 x 1000 mm** and enter `400` in quantity. For the second item, select **Tiles fitting service** and enter `1312` in quantity:

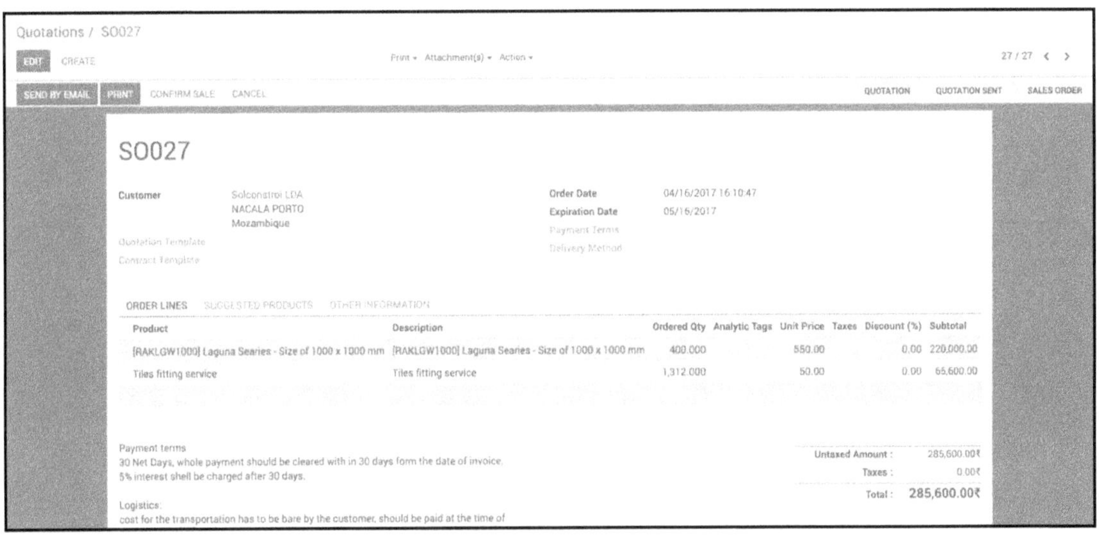

2. Confirm the quotation by clicking on the **CONFIRM SALE** button. As soon as you confirm the order, you will see that **Delivery** and **Project** are linked, as shown in the following screenshot:

Delivery is the material to be delivered to the warehouse, and **Project** is the service that has to be delivered by the team.

> TIP: Quantity for the **Tiles fitting service** represents the square feet of tile-fitting work to be done. This is approximately the billing to be done based on the actual measurements represented by the quantity delivered.

3. To deliver the tiles (material), click on the **Delivery** action button. You will see the delivery order screen as follows:

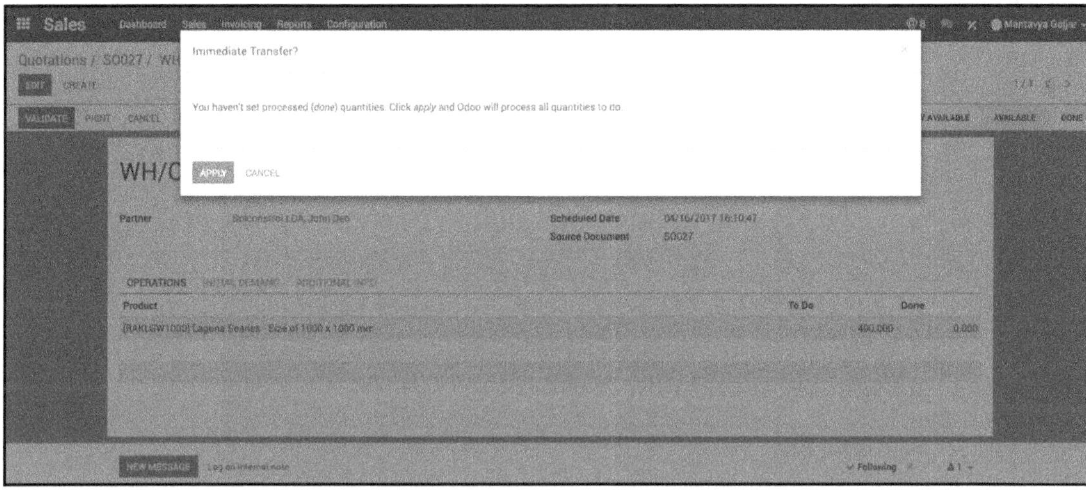

Click on the **VALIDATE** button to process the delivery order. A popup will appear to confirm and transfer all the requested quantities. Click on **APPLY** to process the delivery order. As soon as you process the delivery order, it will be marked as **Done**.

The line having a **[RAKLGW1000] Laguna Series - Size of 1000 x 1000 mm** product on the sales order will be ready to invoice. You will be notified when its color changes to blue:

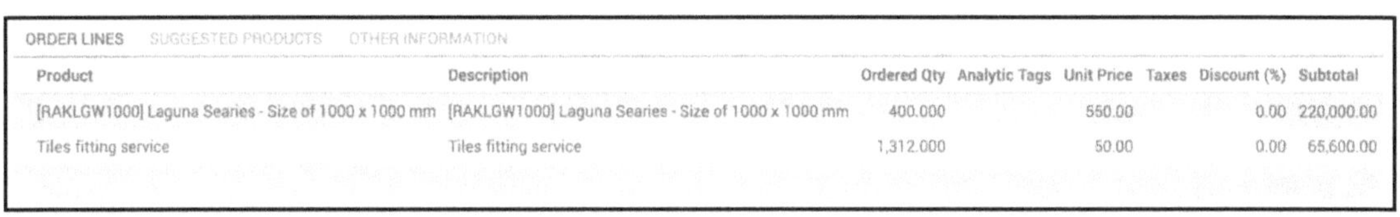
ORDER LINES SUGGESTED PRODUCTS OTHER INFORMATION

Product	Description	Ordered Qty	Analytic Tags	Unit Price	Taxes	Discount (%)	Subtotal
[RAKLGW1000] Laguna Searies - Size of 1000 x 1000 mm	[RAKLGW1000] Laguna Searies - Size of 1000 x 1000 mm	400.000		550.00		0.00	220,000.00
Tiles fitting service	Tiles fitting service	1,312.000		50.00		0.00	65,600.00

4. **The Tiles fitting service** can be marked as delivered when physically the service will be delivered onsite, and the timesheet will be filled based on the actual hours of service delivered.

To fill in the timesheet line, go to the **Timesheet** app and create a timesheet line, as follows:

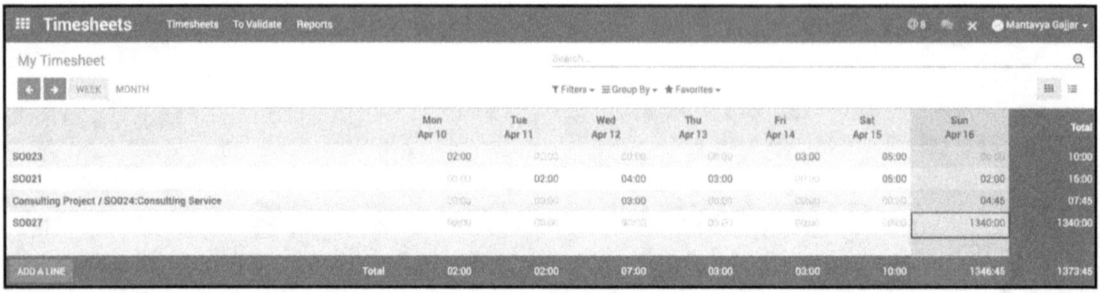

5. Check the sales order `SO027`. The timesheet entry linked to the sales order and both the lines should be ready to raise the invoice:

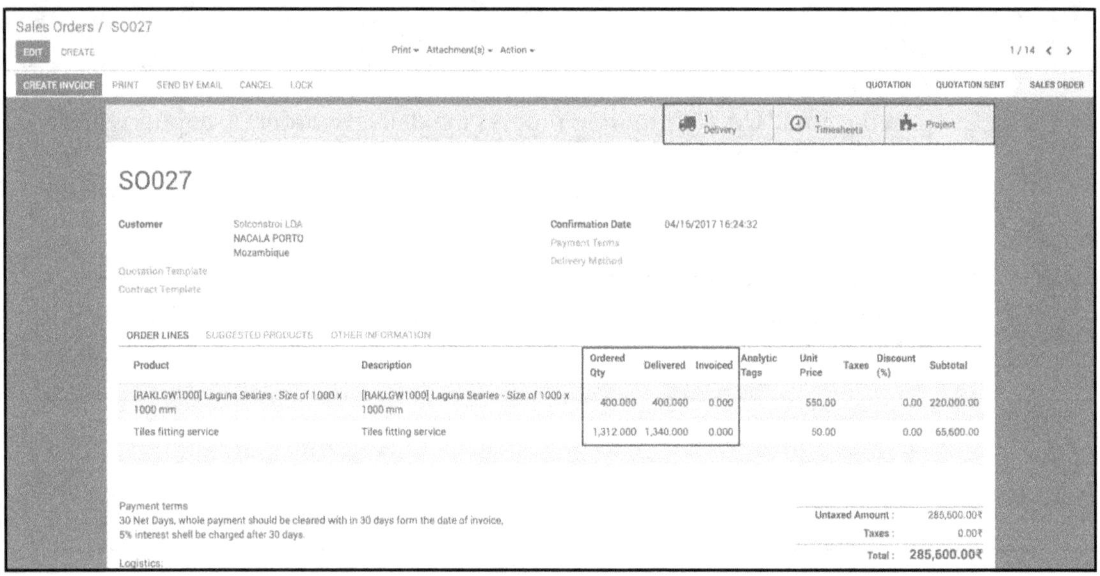

Delivered Qty on the sales order can be different from **Ordered Qty**. The quantity on the invoice can be either **Ordered Qty** or **Delivered Qty** depending on the **Invoicing Policy** configured on the product.

As soon as you create the invoice, it gets linked to the sales order, and the quantity is updated in the **Invoiced** field:

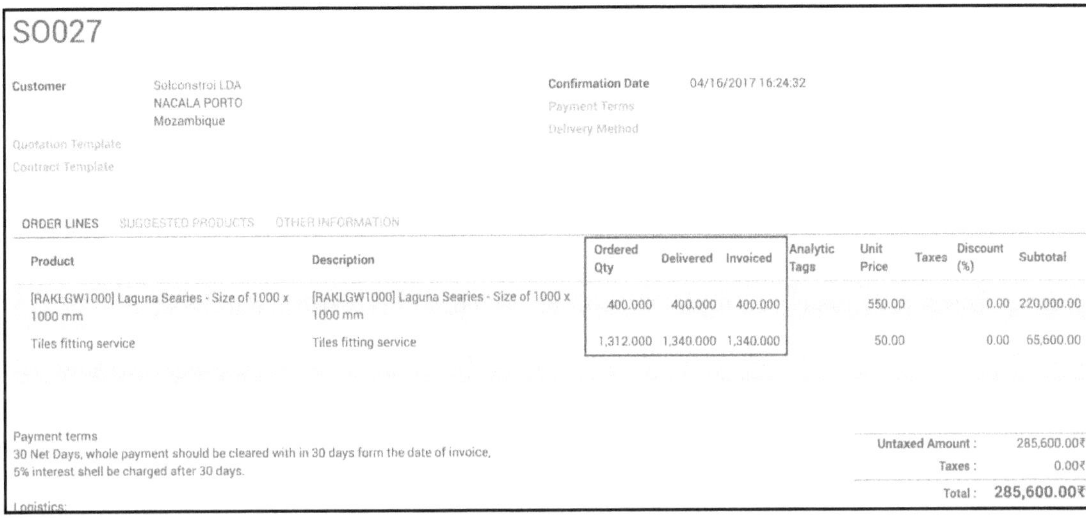

Finally, the order can be marked as **LOCK,** as delivery and invoicing is done for the order.

Advance invoicing before delivery

Getting an advance payment before the delivery is a standard business case. Advance invoicing is required when your invoicing policy is set to **Delivered quantities**. If it is set to **Ordered quantities**, you can create a final invoice just after the confirmation. You can ask for advance payment just after the confirmation of the order, and when the actual invoice is created, the advance invoice and payment will be adjusted against it. The advance invoice can be fixed price or a percentage of the invoice amount.

With Odoo, you can manage advance invoice easily. Let's create a quotation, confirm the order, and raise an invoice for advance payment. Adjust the advance against the final invoice.

Getting ready

We assume that you are clear with the product configuration **Invoicing Policy** and **Track Service** options and the combined effect on the sales order. If you are not clear on these concepts, go through the first recipe, *Setup the product to track time and invoice policies,* of this chapter.

How to do it...

1. Create a quotation by going to **Sales** | **Sales** | **Quotations**. The advance invoicing option works for any kind of product, whether it is consumable, stockable, or a service. I have added the stockable product to my order:

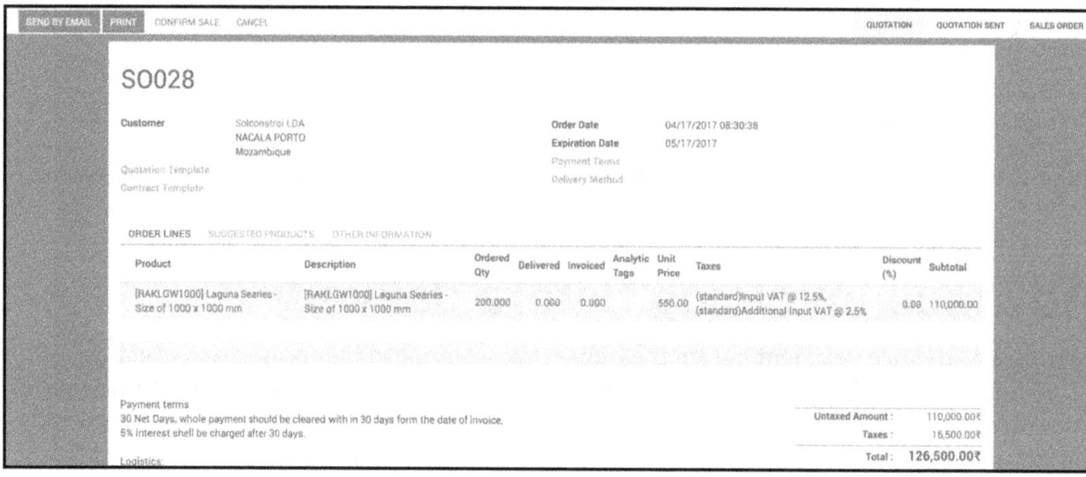

2. Click on the **CONFIRM SALE** button to confirm the quotation. The delivery order should be linked to the order:

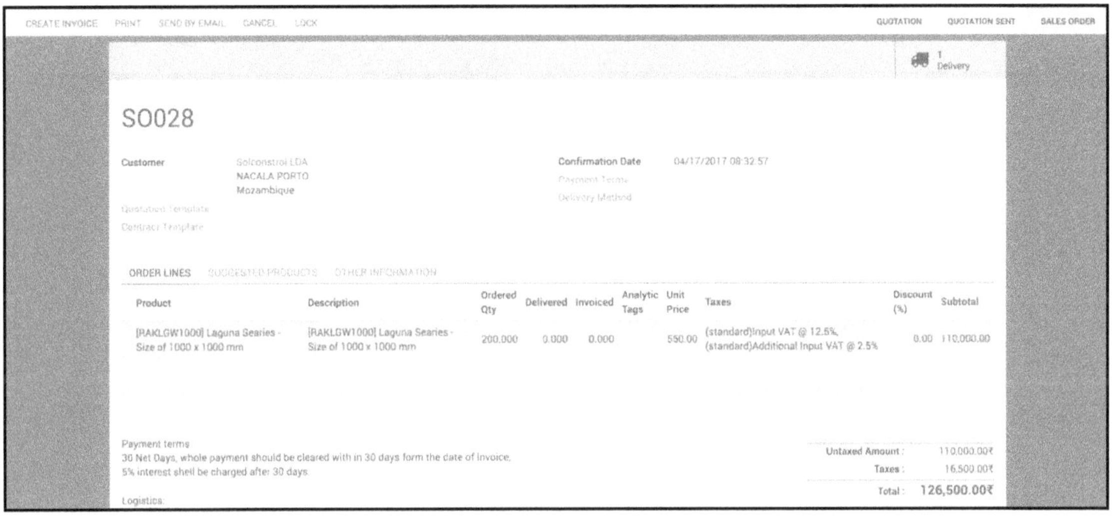

As my order invoicing policy is based on **Delivered quantities**, the line is waiting for the delivery. This means that first, you have to process the delivery in order to raise an invoice according to the standard flow.

3. The **CREATE INVOICE** button is still highlighted; it indicates that there is not any line ready for the invoicing or waiting for the delivery first or proposed action on this sales order. However, you are still able to click on the **CREATE INVOICE** button to create an invoice:

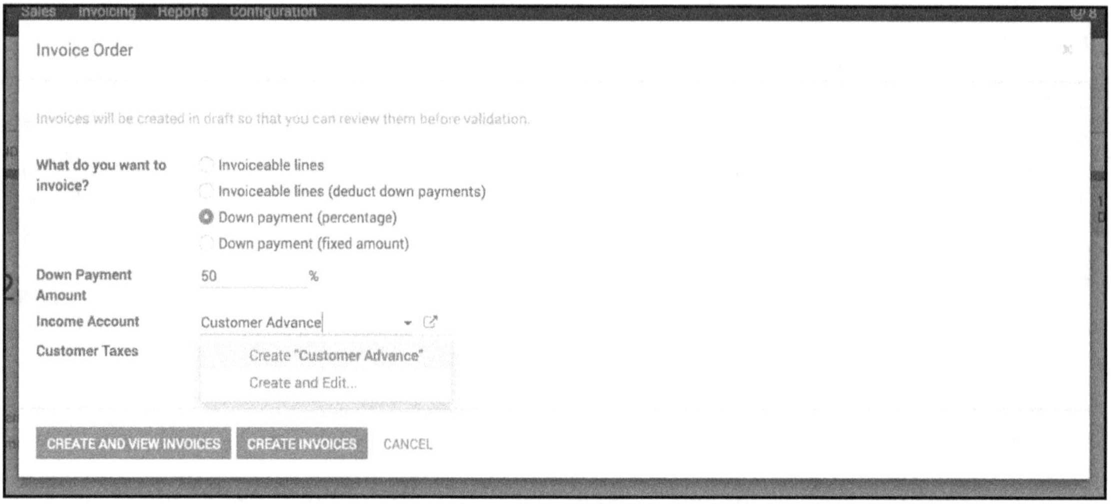

Odoo is smart enough to understand that you would like to create an invoice before the delivery; it will select the appropriate options on the **Down payment (percentage)** wizard. You have to enter the percentage. The **Income Account** and **Customer Tax** accounts will be asked for only the first time.

If the **Customer Advance** account is not available on your chart of account, quickly create a new account with the **Current Liability** account type. We will see the accounting configuration in `Chapter 7`, *Setting Financial Management with Odoo*.

4. Click on **CREATE AND VIEW INVOICES**. A new invoice will be created. When you analyze the invoice closely, you will notice that the product on the invoice is **Down payment** and not the one you sold:

Down payment is saved as part of the configuration; you will not be asked to set it during the creation of the invoice. If you would like to change it, go to **Sales** | **Configuration** | **Settings**, find the **Deposit product** option, change the product to **Down payment**, and click on the **APPLY** button to save the settings:

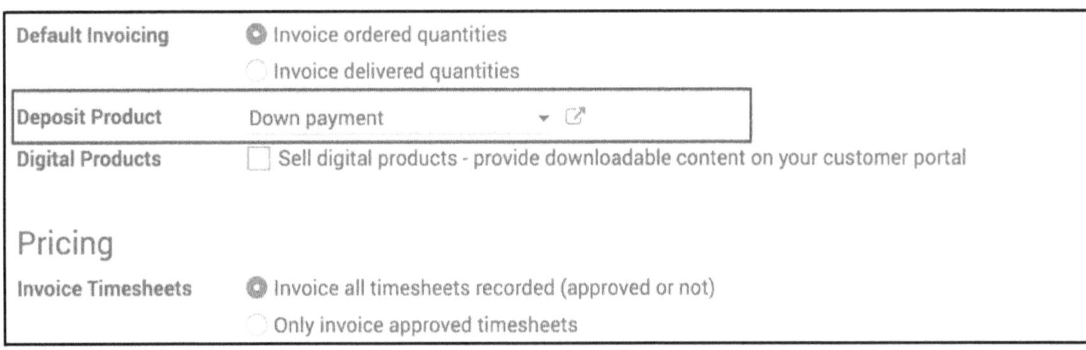

5. The sales order also tracks the advance invoices raised against the order. A new line will be added to the order, which does not impact the order amount:

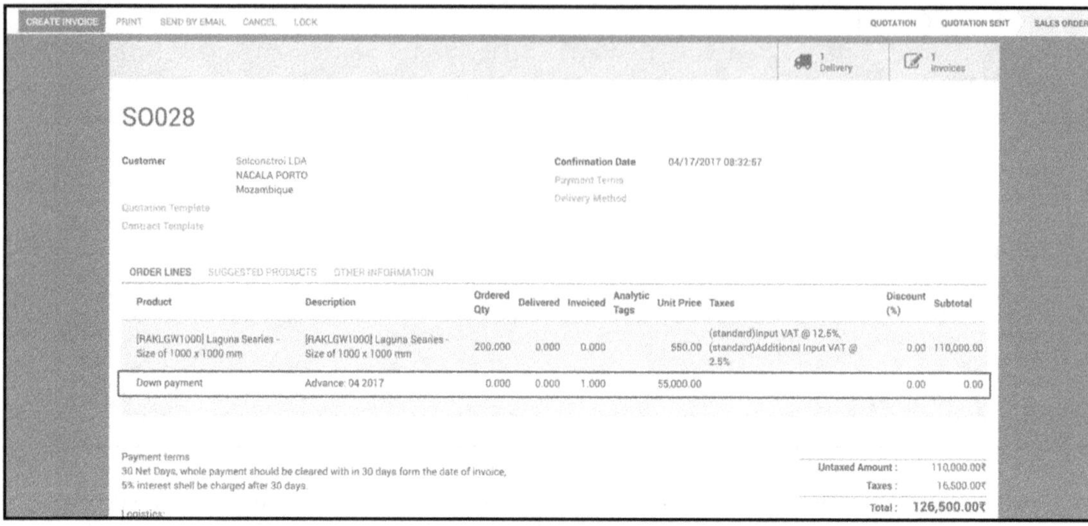

The purpose of adding this line is to keep track of the advance on screen and on the printed sales order. The same line will appear on the printed report.

6. Let's assume the delivery has been done. Both the lines are in blue for the actual product sold and the **Down payment.** Now, we are about to create the final invoice. Click on the **CREATE INVOICE** button. The default option selected on the wizard is **Invoiceable lines (deduct down payments)**. Click on the **CREATE AND VIEW INVOICES** button.

There will be two invoices linked to the sales order, and you will be shown the list of invoices attached to the order:

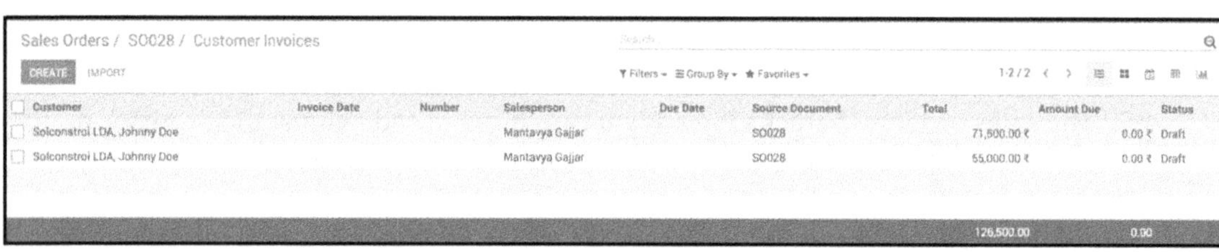

The final invoice is created, having two lines--**[RAKLGW1000] Laguna Series - Size of 1000 x 1000 mm,** with the total amount, and **Down payment** deducted from the invoice amount. The total of all the invoices raised against the order is the same as the order value.

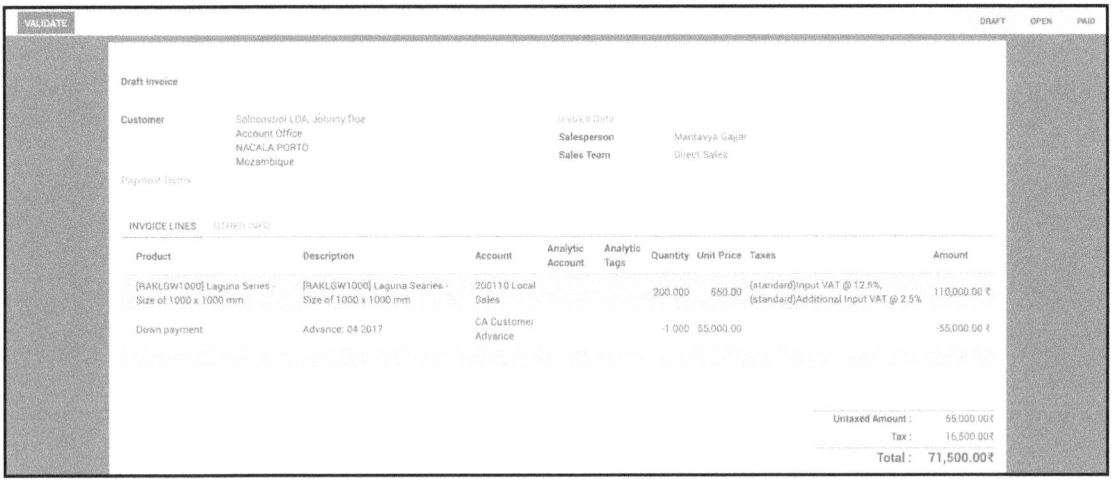

How it works...

Create an invoice wizard smart enough to understand the current order and propose the option to create an invoice based on that. You can create an invoice for the invoiceable lines, or invoice for the down payment or the final invoice, that adjusts the down payment:

- **Invoiceable lines**: This option will be selected when any of the lines are invoiceable on the sales order
- **Invoiceable lines (deduct down payments)**: This option will be selected when any of the lines are invoiceable and at least one down payment line exists on the sales order.
- **Down payment (percentage)**: Select this option if you would like to create an invoice to ask for the advance payment. You will be asked to enter the percentage of the sales order amount to create an invoice
- **Down payment (fixed amount)**: Select this option if you would like to create an invoice to ask for the advance payment. You will be asked to enter the fixed amount to create an invoice.

6
Start Selling Online with Odoo eCommerce

In this chapter, we will cover the following recipes:

- Set up and configure an online shop
- Configure products and their variants
- Set up delivery integration and payment gateway
- Review and checkout order
- Access orders and payments

Introduction

Today, the challenge of modern companies is to get a business application with Omni sales channel support, whereby customers are in the center of the system so it doesn't matter from which channel customer buy the product. Every customer is important to business whether they are a wholesaler, dealer, or consumer end customer. They should get the pricing based on their customer level whether they buy online or onsite.

Odoo is the only business software which provides the real-time integration between business applications such as Customer Relationship Management, Accounting, Inventory, Back Office Sales Management and eCommerce applications. Odoo integrates all those business applications smartly by keeping customers in the middle of the business. The security layer that allows the user to read the information based on the user type such as visitor may have a limited access to the shop, while a login user gets an access can access and their orders, invoices, and track the order status.

Odoo has a built-in eCommerce application that allows you to publish the product catalog, accept the online order and process the payment through various payment gateways, we can also integrate various shipping connectors to ensure the on-time delivery of the customer order.

Let's see how you can set up and start an online shop in a few clicks, integrate shipping and payment connectors to provide better and quality service, and get the real-time order status, make it easy for the accountant to match the invoice and payment.

Set up and configure an online shop

Working with Odoo Website and eCommerce has a great advantage. A new application installed on the instance will automatically integrate with your existing applications. For example, when you install an eCommerce, you don't need to worry about the integration between Sales, Inventory, and Accounting. All the products you have made available in the sales application will be available in the online shop, of course, you can control the visibility of the shop and all the orders placed on online shop will be available in the sales application.You can configure the products, it's category and pricing strategy for the online customers.

Let's go to the Odoo instance; install the online shop (eCommerce) application; set up the online shop, product catalog, and user-friendly categories.

Getting ready

Odoo eCommerce is an application extension to the Odoo website. It is dependent on the website application. The website application was already installed when we activated the online proposal in `Chapter 4`, *Modern way of doing sales and managing sales contracts*.

We assume that you have played with the website builder. If not, go to the website by clicking on the **Website** application and follow the pink signs to build your website in a few minutes:

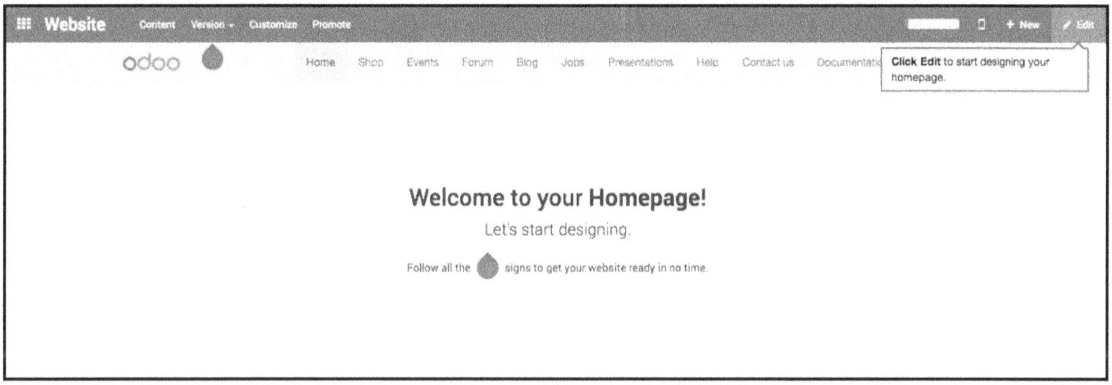

How to do it...

1. Odoo eCommerce can be installed from the Odoo **Apps**. Go to **Apps** and search for `eCommerce`. Then, click on the **INSTALL** button to install the application:

On successful installation, you will be redirected to the online shop page, `https://yourcompany.odoo.com/shop`. All the applications of Odoo are integrated with each other and share the products, category and pricing strategy between them. We will get all the products displayed on the shop page automatically. However, all these products are inactive and not published on the shop yet. You need to review all those products in order to publish them on the shop:

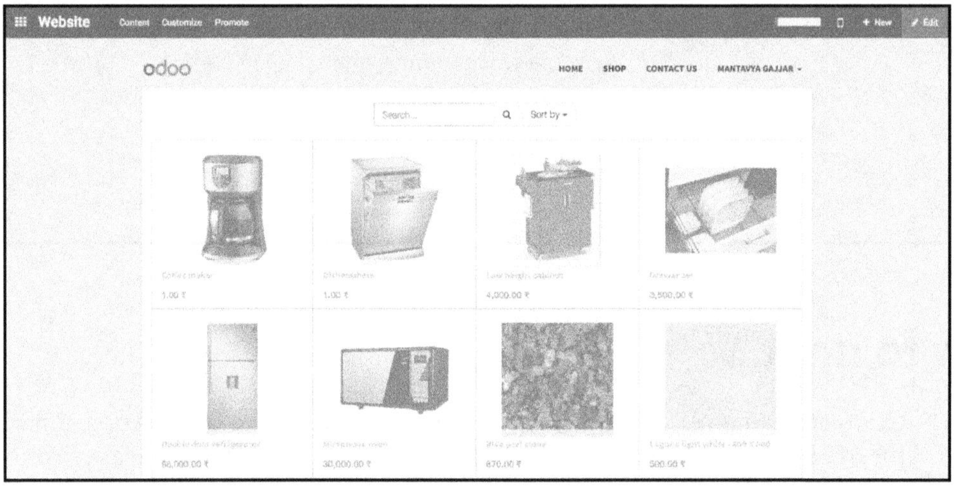

The shop page will be displayed depending on the theme you choose. To change the current theme, click on **Customize** or follow the steps explained in `Chapter 1`, *Getting started with Odoo Online, Setting up your domain name and website theme* section:

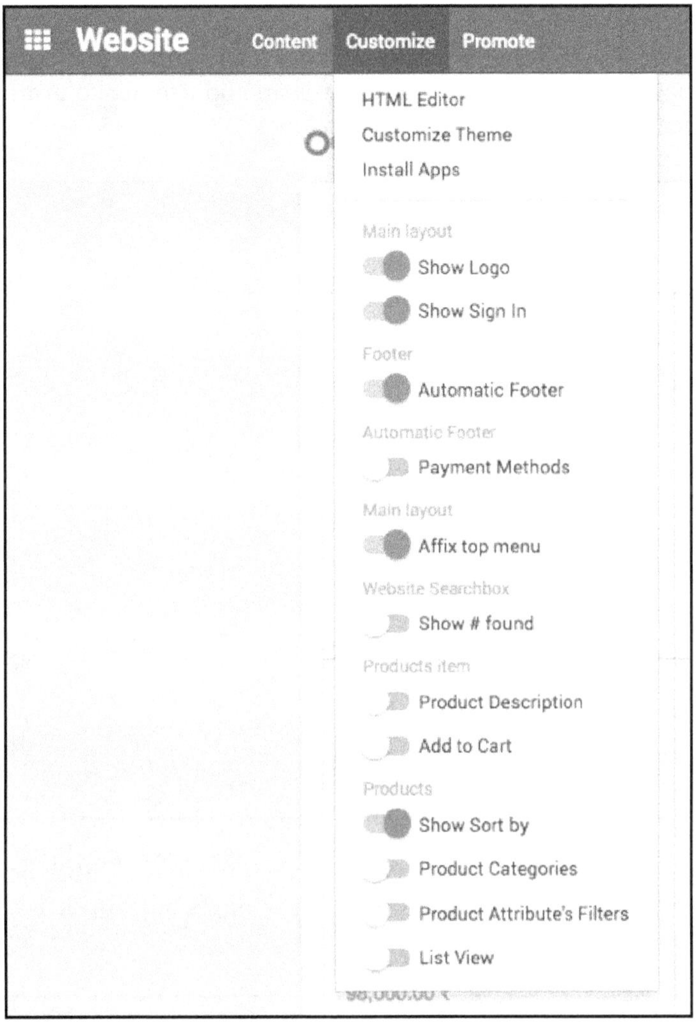

Beside **Customize Theme**, you may also find other key configurations for the shop, such as **Product Item** and **Products**. You can also configure **Main layout**, **Footer**, **Product Search** and **Payment Methods** for your website. The **Customize** options will be changed depending on the theme you choose and the page on which you are.

2. The shop layout can be changed to list view. Go to **Customize** | **Products** | **List View**. The page will be refreshed, and box view will be converted to list view. Both box view and list view are super clean and usable; you can choose any one to showcase our products on the shop page:

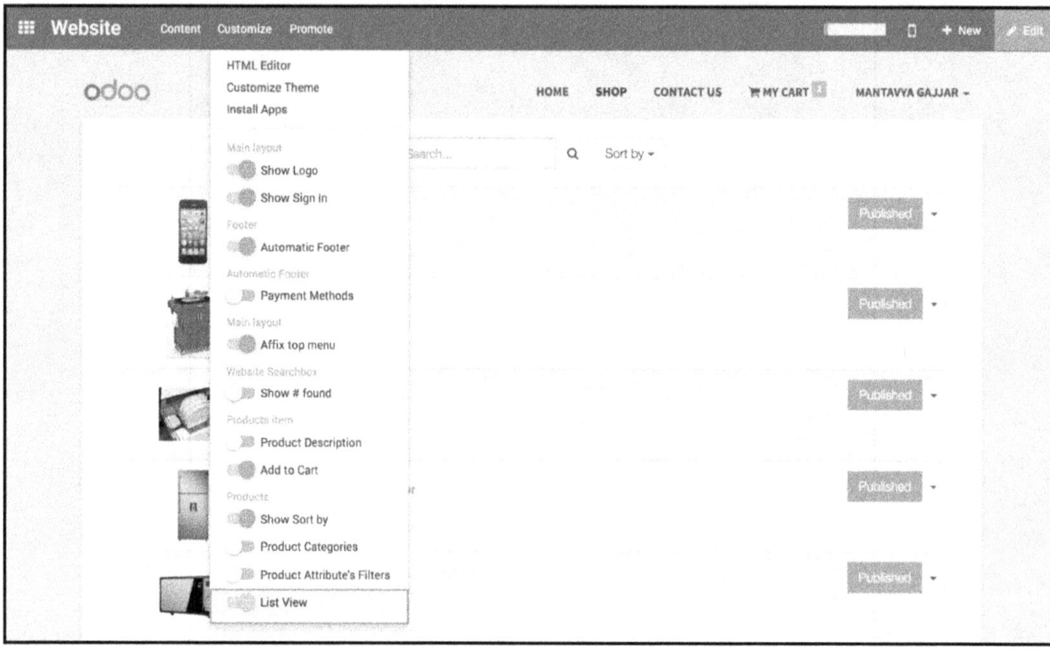

3. The visibility of the product can be managed using the **Published/Unpublished** button available beside each product. It's a toggle button; clicking on the button swaps the visibility state:

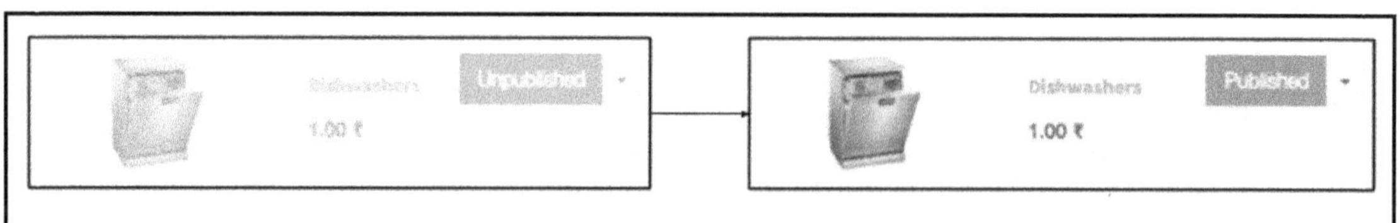

Click on Unpublished button to publish the product on online shop

List view would be the view you are looking for when you have to manage the visibility of your products on the shop page. You can **Publish/Unpublished** them quickly from the List View screen.

4. A user can filter the specific product by its category. Displaying the product category on the shop page is essential when the shop sells multiple types of product; in our case, we sell building materials, home appliances, furniture, and many other types of products.

   Categorization of the product can be activated by going to **Customize** | **Products** | **Product Categories**:

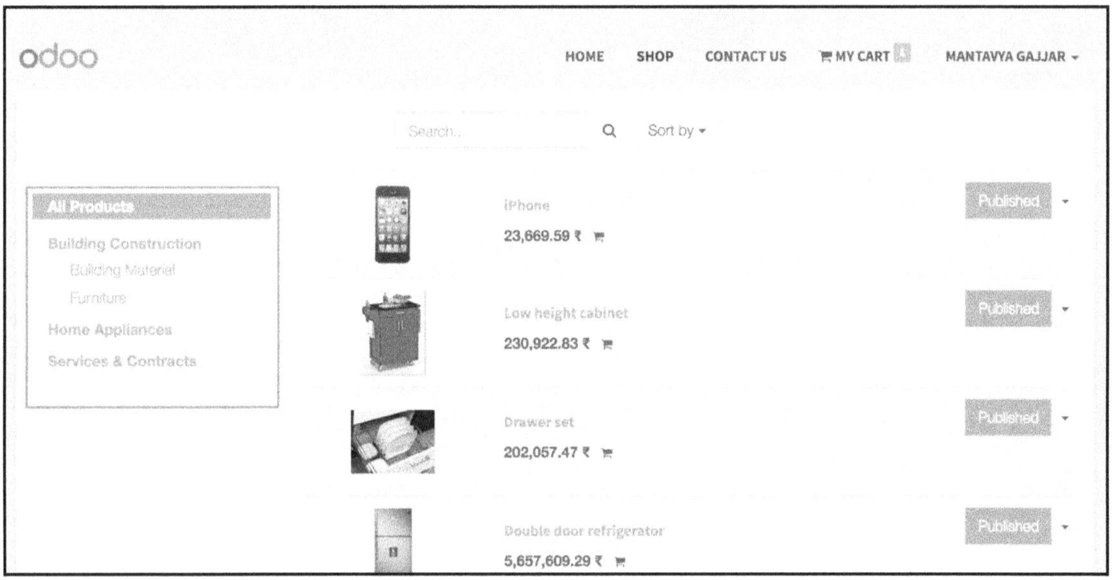

5. As soon as the **Product Category** feature is enabled, you will get the additional configuration to select the way to display product category. By default, it's a list of categories or a collapsible list view. Change the category view by going to **Customize | Product Categories | Collapsible Category List**:

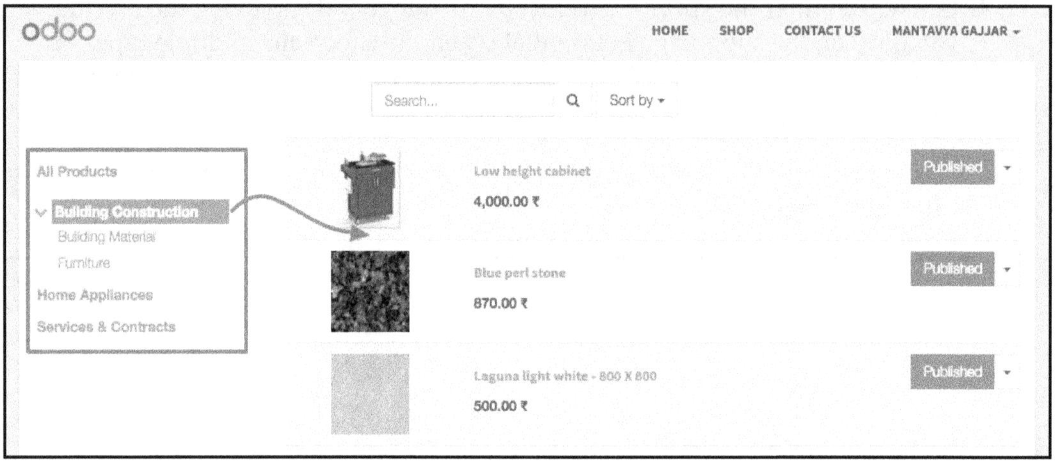

The product category hierarchy can be created from the backend. Go to **Website Admin | Configuration | Website Product Category** and you can create the parent/child category by setting the **Parent Category** field:

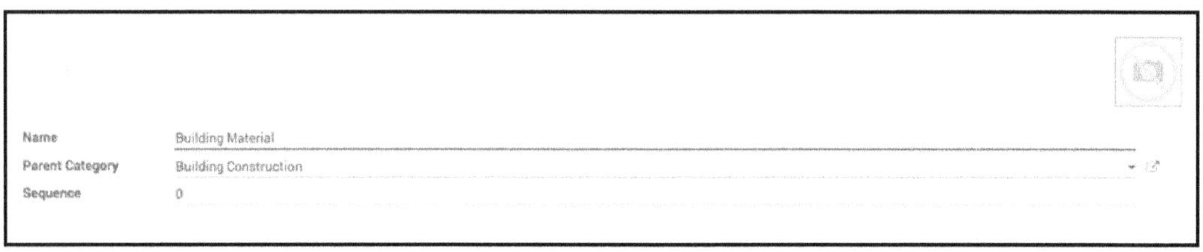

You can activate the product description on the shop page by clicking on **Product description** from **Customize | Product item** menu:

The product description can be set on the product form. Enter the description in the **Description for Quotations** field under the **NOTES** tab.

Like the description, the quick cart icon can be activated on the product catalogue from the **Add to Cart** menu from **Customize** | **Product item**.

Click on the **Add to Cart** option. The cart icon will appear beside the product price on the product list.

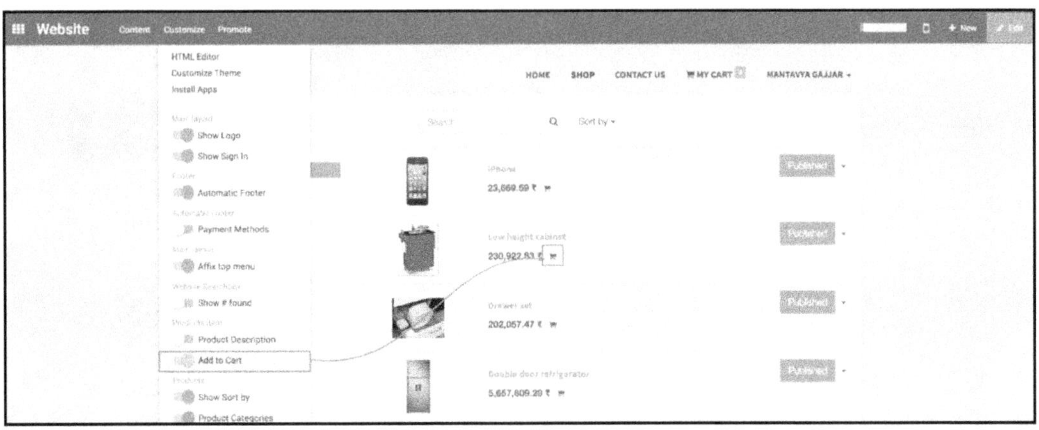

When you click on the cart icon, the product will be added to the cart, and you will be redirected to the checkout process:

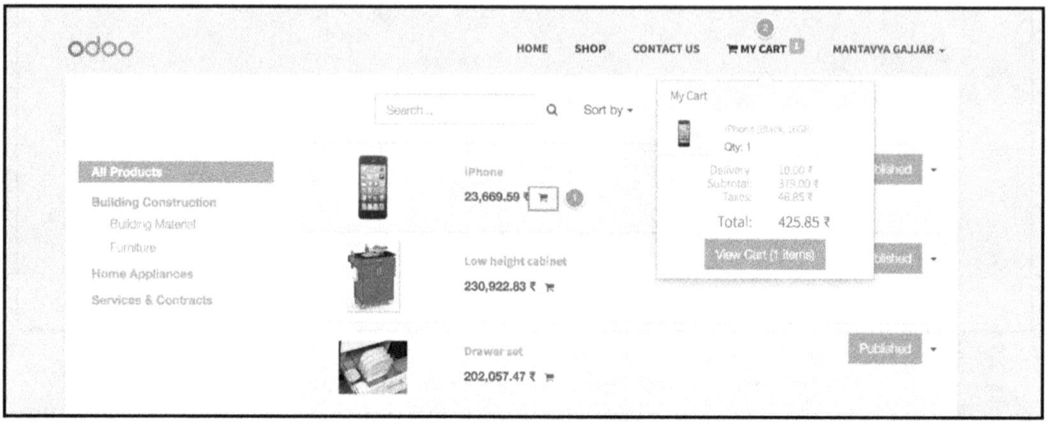

6. You can switch between box view and list view by deactivating **List view** previously activated in step 2. You will switch to box view without losing any other configuration such as product category, add to cart button. Look at the following screen after switching to **Box View:**

7. Like the shop page, you can also configure the view of the product page. By clicking on the product, you will be redirected to the product page. Check the **Customize** options; you will find many useful options to configure the product page.

   Almost all the minimum options are activated in the product catalog. There are some advanced options that can be enabled to have the advanced product catalog such as Product Variants filter, Discussion, and Ratings on the Product; the advanced options are available under the Customization menu. You will see product variants in the next recipe, *Configure products and their variants*, of this chapter.

8. The product page will look like the following image after activating Discussion and Ratings on the Product:

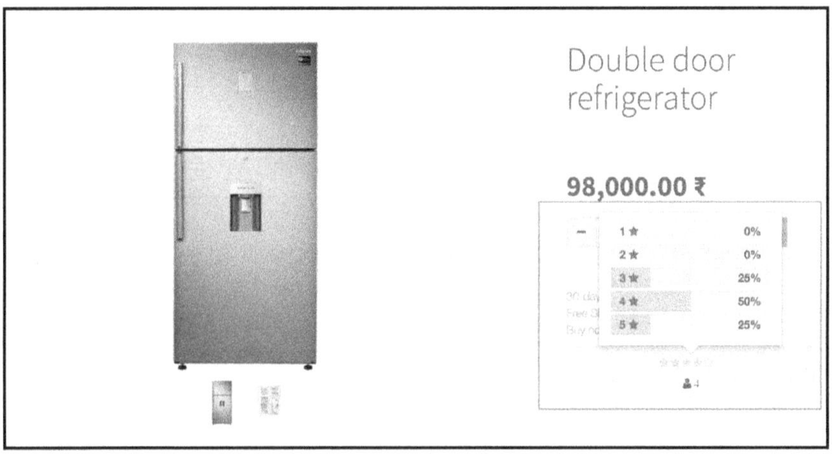

   The chatter can be found below product information. Only login users can post the comments and submit ratings on the product.

There's more...

The product page can be designed like a website page. Click on the **EDIT** button on the top-right corner. The page will become editable; the left panel will appear with the building blocks to build the page. Drag and drop the building blocks on the page, change the details, and click on **SAVE** to save the product page.

Multiple product images

You can activate the multiple images for the product. With multiple images, the user can understand the product and its features easily. Go to backend by clicking on the top-left application icon. You will be shown our instance home page:

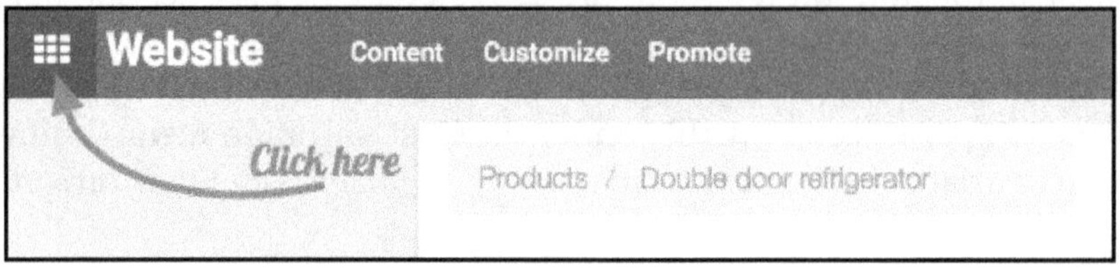

To activate the feature, go to **WebsiteAdmin** | **Configuration** | **Settings**, search for the **Multi Images** option, and select **Several images per product**. Click on the **APPLY** button to save the setting:

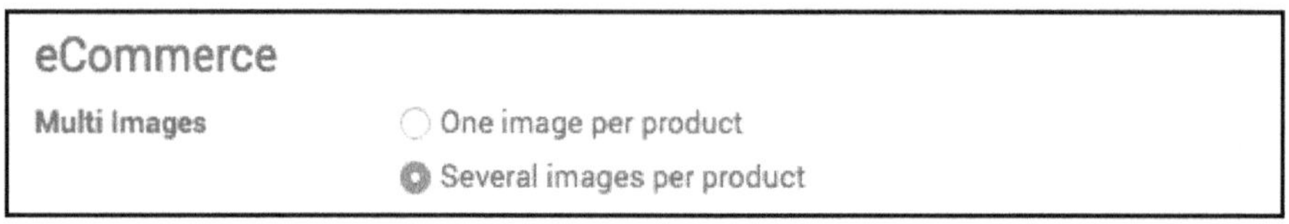

As soon as the settings are saved, you will be redirected to our instance home screen. Go to **Website Admin** | **Catalog** | **Products** and open the product to add multiple images. The new tab **IMAGES** will be added to the product form:

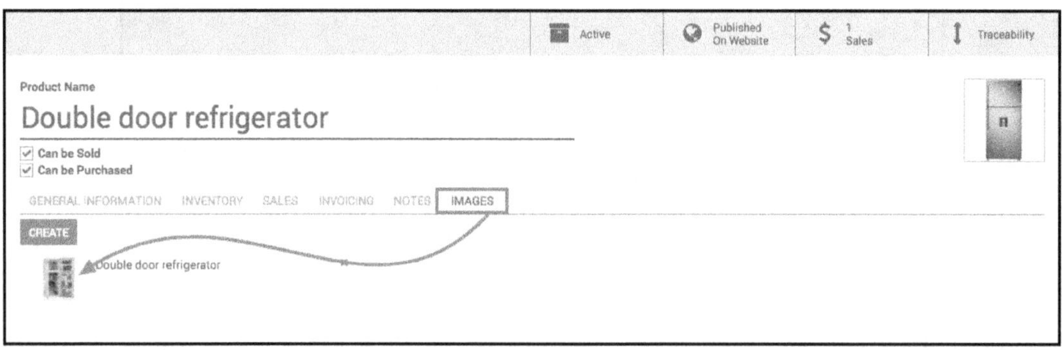

Click on the **CREATE** button to add the image. The pop-up form will appear; fill the name and select the image. Click on **SAVE & NEW** if you would like to add another image or click on **SAVE & CLOSE** to save the added image:

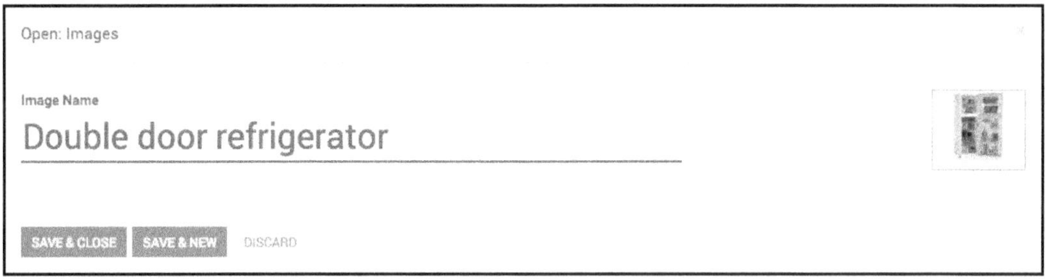

Add multiple images for the product. Click on the **Published** button on the **Product** form.

You will be redirected to the product page. It will look like this:

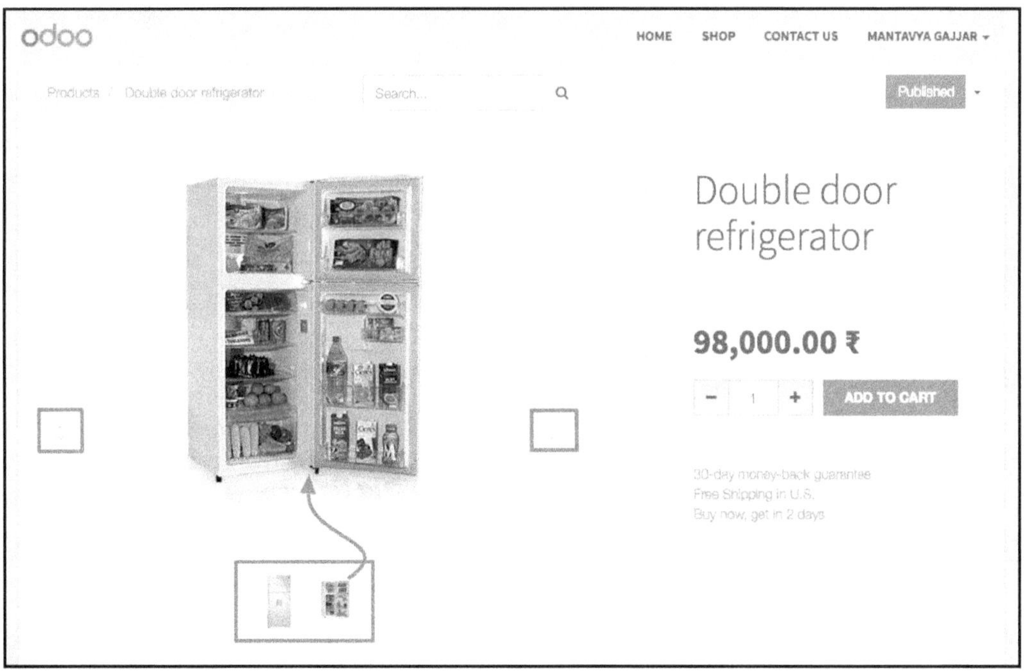

The product image converted to the image-sliding control. You will be able to see all the attached images. Click on the next or previous arrow to move through a set of images, or click on the image from the image list here.

The Product Catalogue and Cart can have an advanced feature that helps you to increase sales by suggesting an Alternative Products or Accessory Products on the Cart page; we will go through all those features in the upcoming recipe *Review and checkout order*.

Magnify image

The image magnification feature is activated by default. You can check it by going to **Customize | Product | Activate Magnify**.

The mouse icon is converted into a magnification icon as soon as we hover the mouse over the image. When you click on the image, you will enter magnification mode. Move the mouse from left to right and top to bottom to move around the magnified image:

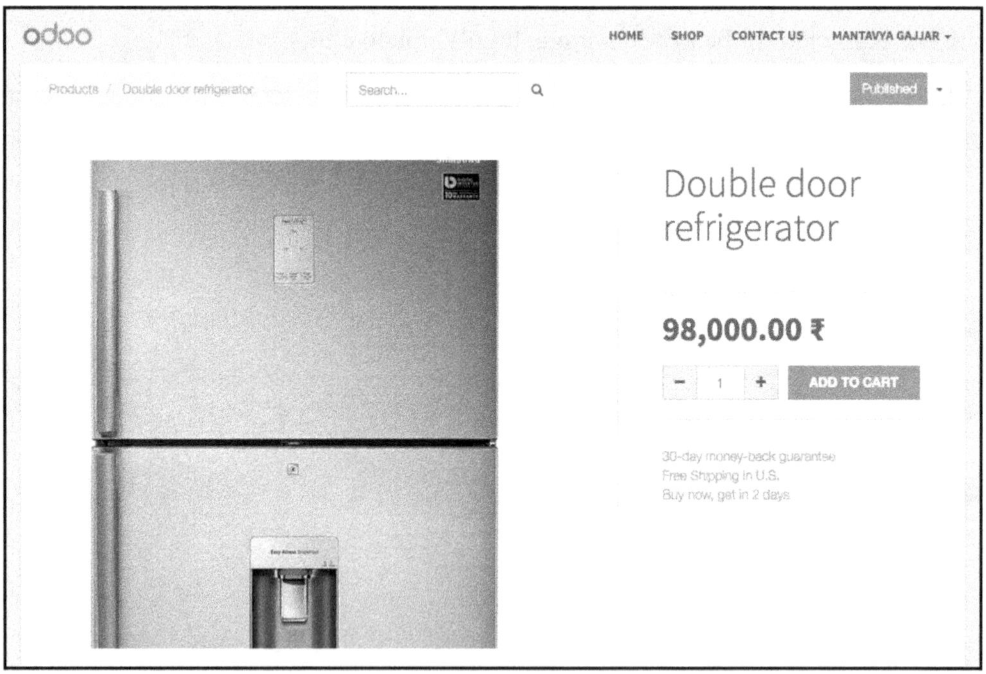

In the case of multiple images, first select an image to magnify and enter the magnify mode by clicking on it.

Configure products and their variants

It is a standard business need to create variations of the Product by its color, shape, size, or the technology behind the same product. The iPhone is the easiest example to understand the product variant; it has many variations in capacity of the internal storage, such as 32GB, 64GB, 128GB, and 256GB on and the color of the phone such as Black, Jet Black, Gold, Rose Gold, Silver, and Red. The variations of the iPhone will be created based on these two attributes: internal storage and color.

There are four types of internal storage and six types of color available, the total number of variety created is equal to the multiplication of the total number of attributes, in our case 24 variations will be created.

Let's see how we can enable the product variant feature in Odoo, define the product attributes and their values, and create the product variants. The price can be increased or decreased based on the product attributes, let's see how to set the product variants price by setting the additional price for the attributes, we can increase or decrease the price by attribute. Finally, we will see how to display product variants on the product page and choose the correct variant, get the price for selected variant and add to the cart. Odoo also allows us to filter the product by its attribute on the product catalog page.

Getting ready

Working with product and its variants requires knowledge of the product and some of its important fields, such as Product Type, Sales Price, and Cost.

As always it is advisable to duplicate the database before you perform any configuration changes in order to not lose master configuration.

TIP

I am not sure there will be a limit on creating a number of duplicated database on the Odoo online platform.

How to do it...

1. Go to **Sales** | **Configuration** | **Setting** and enable the option **Products can have several attributes, defining variants (for example—size, color, and so on)** and click on the **APPLY** button to activate the Product variant feature.
2. When the variant feature is enabled successfully, you will find a new **VARIANTS** tab added to the product form.

   Go to **Sales** | **Sales** | **Products** and select the product for which you would like to create the variants. Let's take an example of iPhone 7. It has a variety in terms of color and memory capacity:

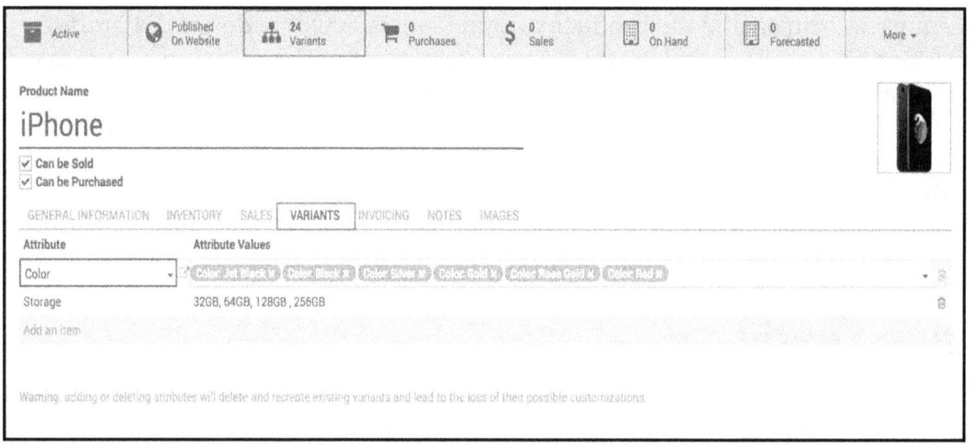

   You can add **Attribute** and **Attribute Values** to create the product variants. The attribute is Color in our case and Jet Black, Black, Silver, Gold, Rose Gold, and Red are the attribute values.

3. The product's Attribute **Type** has to be configured correctly when you are going to use the product attribute on the product web page. The Attribute **Type** can be a type of **Radio**, **Select**, **Color**, or **Hidden**.

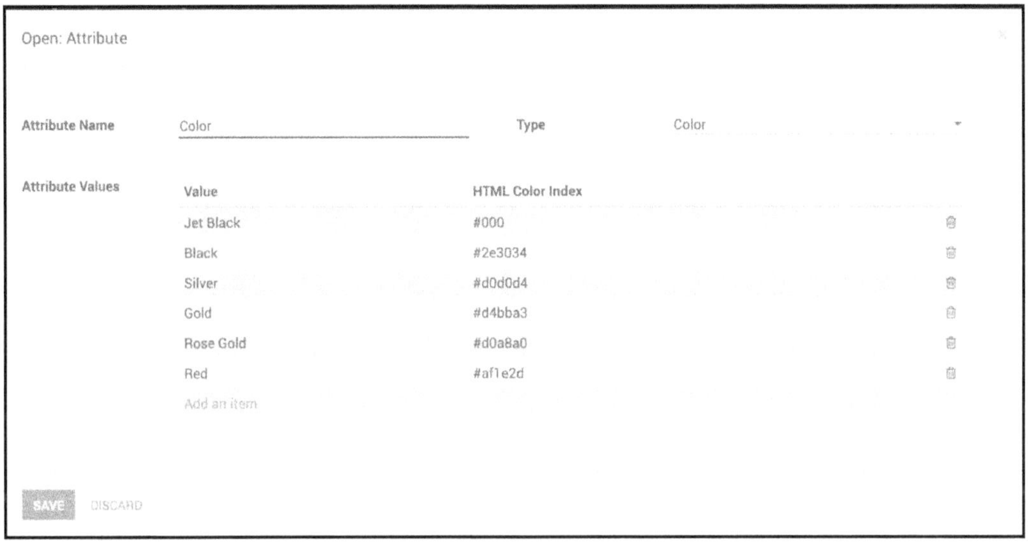

The Attribute **Type** field is used to define, how the attribute will be displayed on the product page:

- **Radio**: You can see all the options but choose only one. Choose this when you have a maximum of two or three options.
- **Selection**: You have a drop-down selection box to choose the options from. Choose this when you have more than three attribute values to choose from.
- **Color**: Select color when your attribute values have to display the color on the page.
- **Hidden**: This attribute value will not be displayed on the product page for the selection.

4. As soon as you created the variant lines and defined the Attribute and Attribute Values, click on the **SAVE** button to save the product configuration. Product variants will be created with a combination based on the attributes and attribute values:

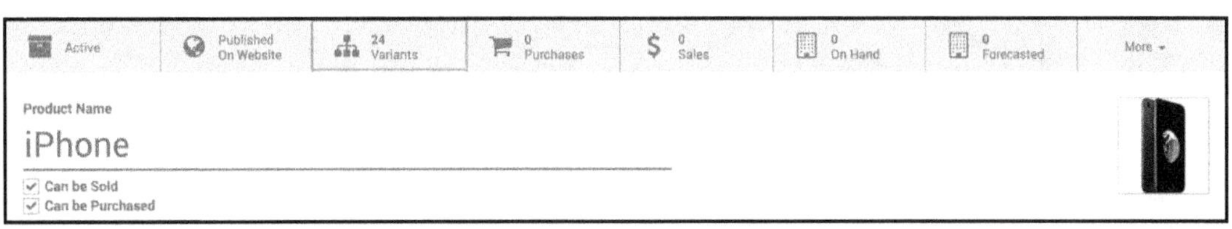

The number of variants will be displayed beside the **Variants** button. When you click on the button, you will go to product variants created based on the attribute and its values. A total of 24 variant products are created with the combination of four storage and six color attributes:

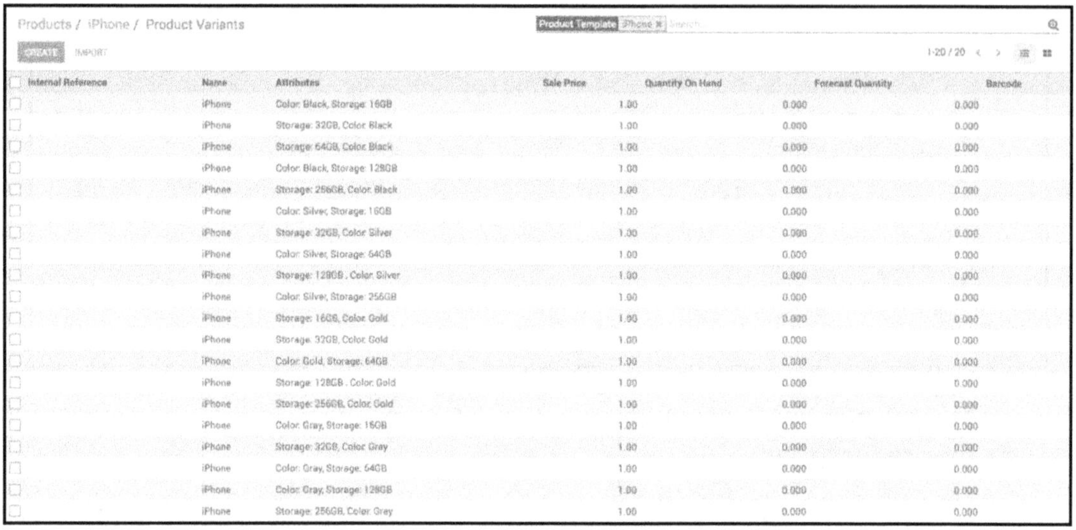

Information such as **Barcode, Cost price**, and **Image** can be set directly on the product variant. Click on any product to open its form view and set the value:

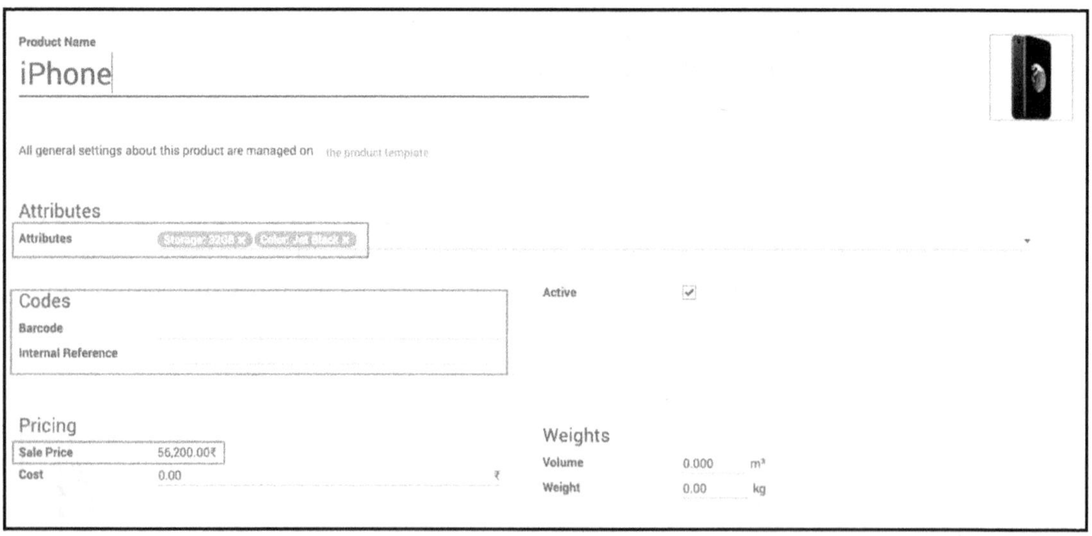

The sale price of the variant products is computed based on the main product and additional price is defined per variant attribute. The formula to compute the price is the sale price for the product plus additional cost per variant attribute.

It is advisable to uncheck the Active field on the Product variant form if any of the Attribute combination is available as a product.

5. To set the additional price for the variants, first go to product form view and set **Sale price** for **iPhone**:

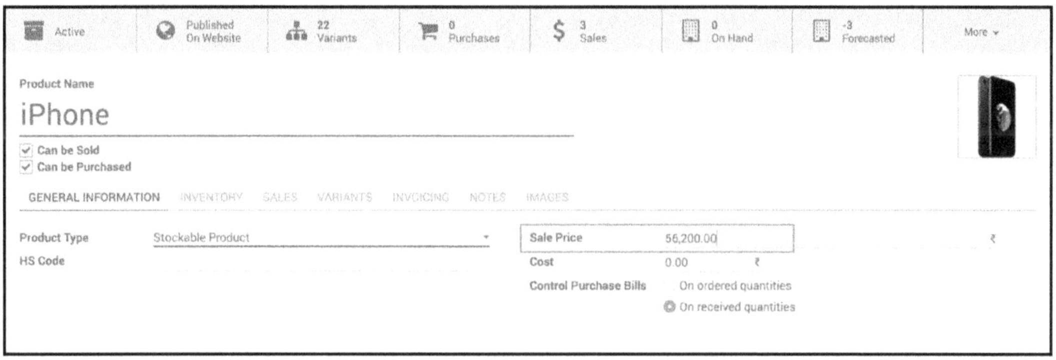

6. Click on the **VARIANT PRICE** button. Go to the variant price list, where you can set the additional price per variant:

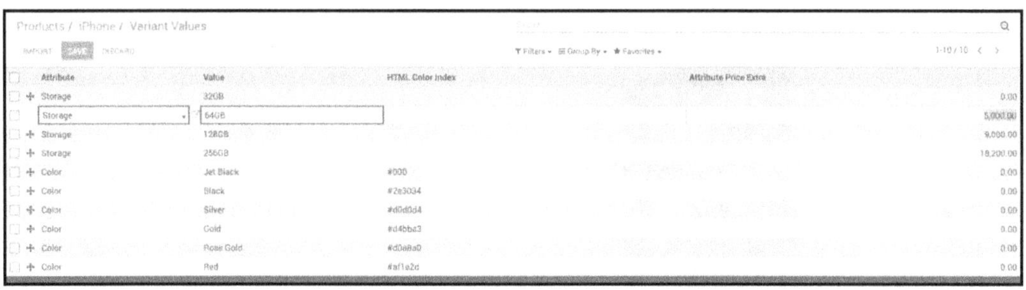

7. Click on the **SAVE** button to save the price updated on variants. Go back to **iPhone** and click on **Variants** to get the list of variants. You can see the sale price computed for all the variants of **iPhone**:

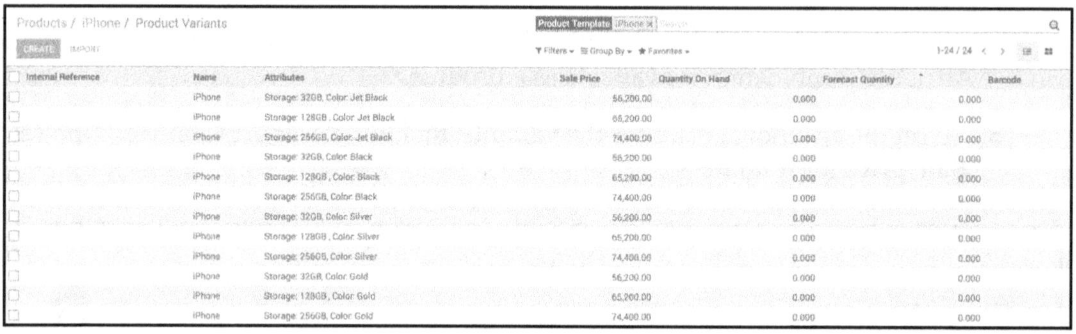

The iPhone's with Storage of 128GB and 256GB has a higher price than the 32GB store capacity phone; the color attribute is not adding any extra price, only the storage capacity adds an additional cost to the final price.

8. You are ready to go to frontend and check the configuration of variants on the Product page. Click on the **Published on Website** button to view the online product page. On the right panel, the product name appears; below the product name, you can see all the product attributes and values.

9. To make the product page more interactive, you can select the attribute value and change the photo of the product. Let's select the Rose Gold color on the Color Attribute: click on the EDIT button on the page, by clicking on the image a popup will appear, choose the relevant photo for the Rose Gold color.

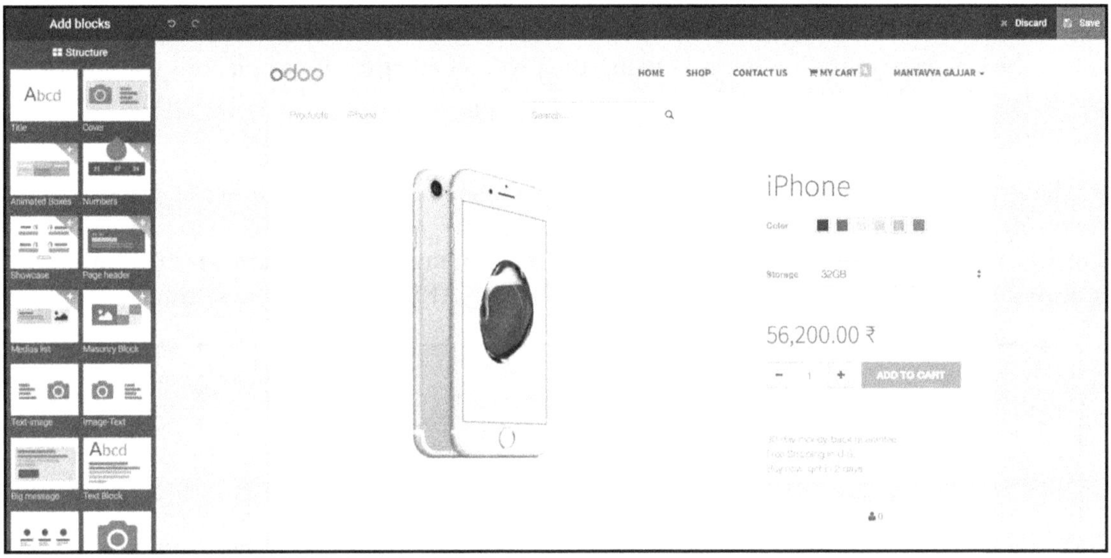

Save the changed image by clicking on the SAVE button. Now when you click on the Black Color you can see the iPhone in black; the photo will change when you click on the Rose Gold color on the Color Attribute.

There's more...

There are two important features an online shop should have when they want products with its attributes to be displayed on the product catalog page, it is good to have filters on product attributes to search for the specific product, the second feature is to have the price variation based on the product attributes.

Odoo creates a variant for all the possibilities based on the product attributes. You can choose the pricing strategy for the variant by adding the additional cost or use the pricelist to set the price for the product variants depending on the business case.

Use Pricelist to compute the variants price

The price variation can be set on the variant attribute; you can increase or decrease the price for the final product using the **Attributes Price Extra** field available on the Attribute Value. The price computation for the variants can be done in two ways: either using the variants attribute additional price or using the pricelist feature of Odoo.

Using the price computation method using the product attribute is simple, but we cannot create conditional pricing rules. The pricelist is giving you the freedom to compute or set the price to apply any business rules.

We have already gone through the price feature in `Chapter 4`, *Modern way of doing sales and managing sales contracts,* under the recipe *Create and configure your products*. Go to **Sales** | **Configuration** | **Settings** and select the **Advanced pricing based on formulas (discounts, margins, rounding)** options for **Price list** and click on **APPLY** to save the setting:

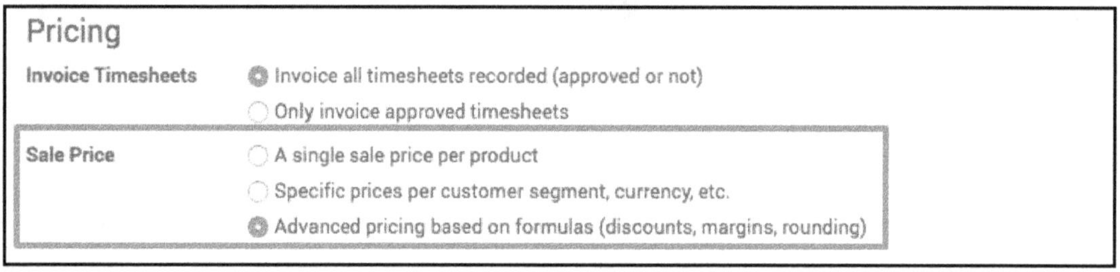

The advance pricing allows you to define the price for the variants. You can set the fixed price or compute the price based on the percentage. Go to **Sales** | **Configuration** | **Pricelists**, and you will get the pricelist created:

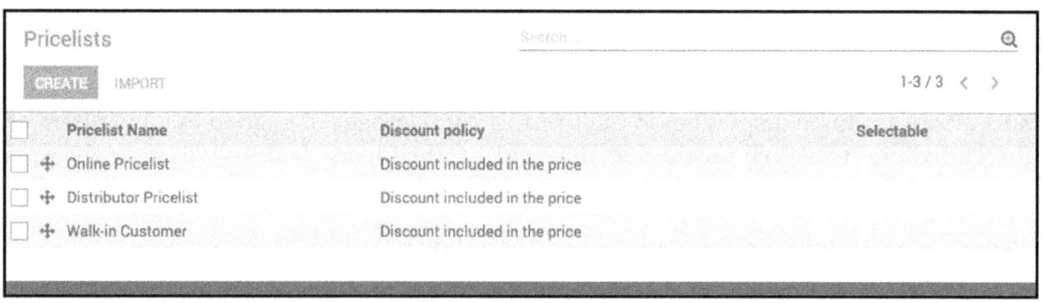

The pricelist in Odoo is common for the frontend and backend; you can apply the price strategy on the website, which you have in your back office. You can also have the customer-oriented product price on the website when registered by customers online:

Select the **Selectable** checkbox when you want your customers or visitors to choose the best pricelist or schemas on the website. By creating **Country Groups**, you can set the pricelist for the international customers. You may have the possibility to create a multi-currency pricelist and set the pricing depending on the country.

The price computation can be done by adding a new line to **Pricelist Items**. Click on **Add an Item** to add the new price computation rule:

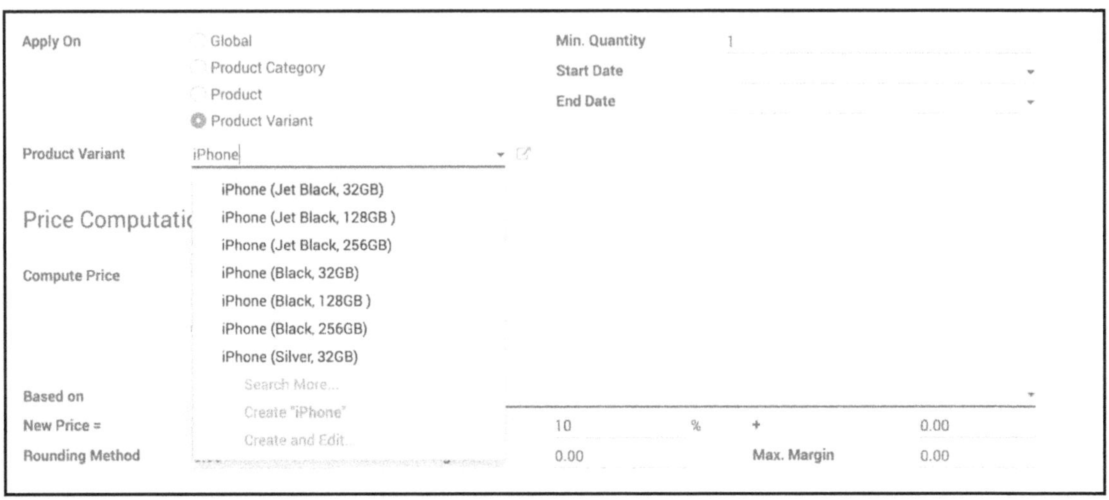

A popup will appear. Select **Product variant** on **Apply On**. This will let you choose the product variant to compute the price. Choose the variant to compute the price. Price can be computed based on the fixed percentage or formula; please go through the price computation methods listed as follows to understand how they compute the price:

- **Fixed Price**: The Fixed Price will override the Product Sale Price. Fixed price will come instead of Product Sale Price on Sales quotation or Product page.
- **Percentage (discount)**: By default, the discount will be considered. Set the amount in percentage. Set the negative value to increase the price instead of the percentage.
- **Formula**: A complex way to compute the price. You can set the base price to compute the price. It can be **Sale price**, **Cost price**, or **Other price list**. You can control the discount, additional fixed price, and minimum and maximum margins while computing the price.

Let's create pricelist rules that increase the price of the iPhone (Jet Black, 32GB) by 10 percent; select the *Product Variant* in the **Apply On** field. Select *iPhone (Jet Black, 32GB)* in the **Product Variant** field, select the *Formula* option for **Compute Price** field and to increase the price *-10* has to be entered on the **Price Discount** field. Look at the following screen:

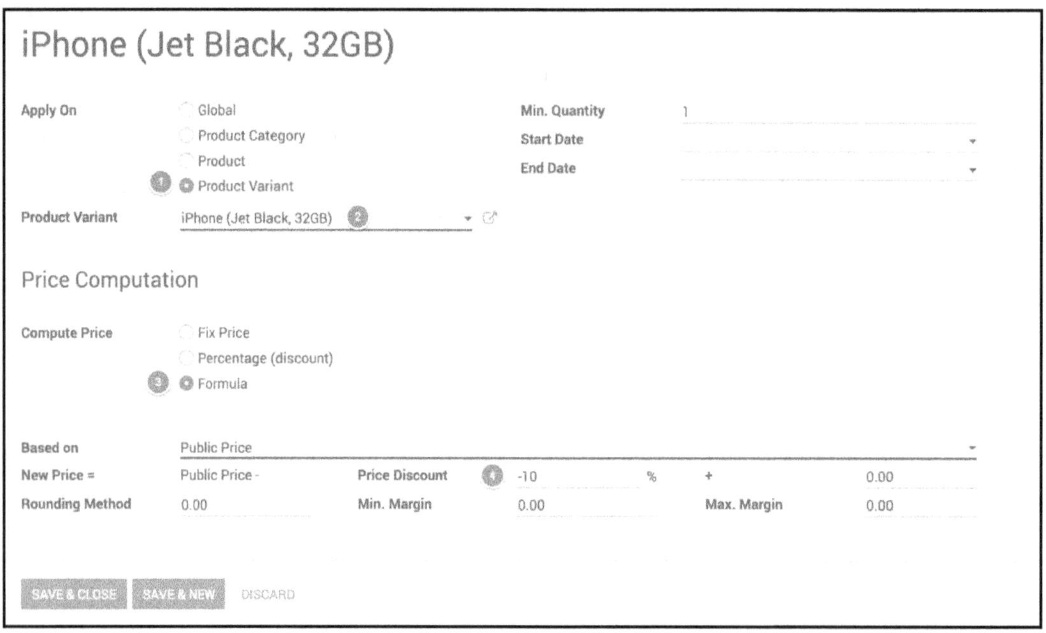

We have increased the price for *iPhone (Jet Black, 32GB)* by 10 percent. The updated price can be checked on the iPhone product page: select Jet Black on the Color and select 32 GB on the Storage. The old price was 56,200. After applying the pricelist the price has been increased by 10%. Look at the following image:

TIP

We have computed the price for variants using attribute addition cost plus pricelist. You can use both or any one depending on the need. First, the variant sale price will be computed and pricelist rules will be applied on top of that.

Search product by its attributes

It is recommended to give search features to the visitor or customer to search products by its attributes and its values. This feature is worth adding to the product catalog when products share common attributes. Let's take an example whereby a customer would like to search for the iPhone based on the Color or Storage capacity.

The feature of the product attribute filter can be activated by clicking on the Product Attribute's Filters available under the Customization menu. As soon as you click on the menu the filter will appear in the left top corner of the product catalog page as shown in the following screenshot:

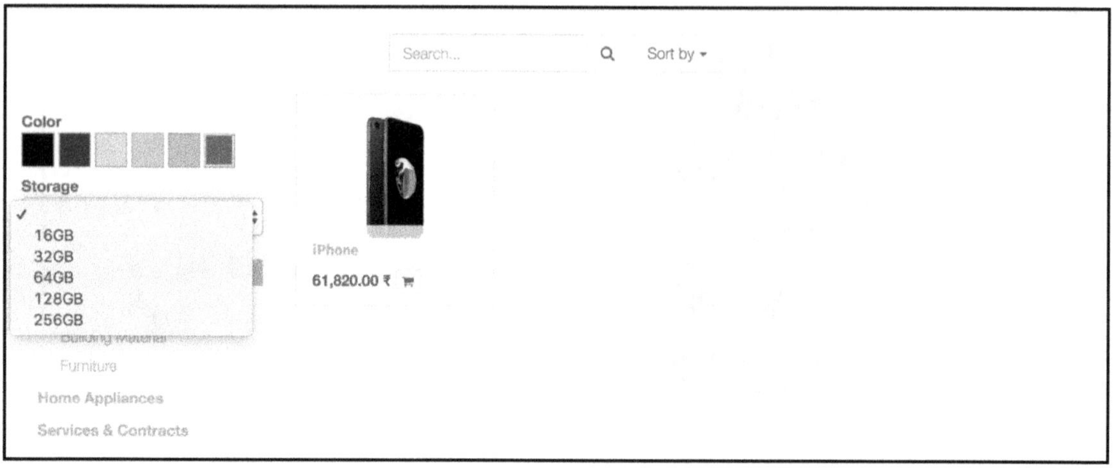

The attributes are coming from the different products available in the catalog. We can apply the filter by selecting one or more attribute values, such as the Black and Red color to search for the iPhone available in Black and Red color.

The filter will be applied based on the value selected for the multiple attributes. We can select values for two attributes to search for the iPhone with Red color and storage capacity of 128 GB.

Deactivate some variants

Let's take a real-life example. When iPhone launched with the Red color, it was only available with a storage capacity of 128 GB and 256 GB, other than that the Red color was not available.

Odoo creates a variant for all the possibilities based on the product attributes. You can choose later which are the available variants and deactivate the variant which is not as per the product specification.

To deactivate some product variants which are not available as per the product specification, go to product page, click on the **Product Variant** button, you will reach the variant list. Open the form view of the specific variant you want to deactivate, in our case we have to deactivate two variants: Storage—32 GB, Color—Red, and Storage—64 GB, Color—Red, as shown below.

Uncheck the Active field available on the Variant form and click on the **SAVE** button. Let's check on the product page, how it will restrict the user to select the 32 GB with Red color iPhone, look at the following screen:

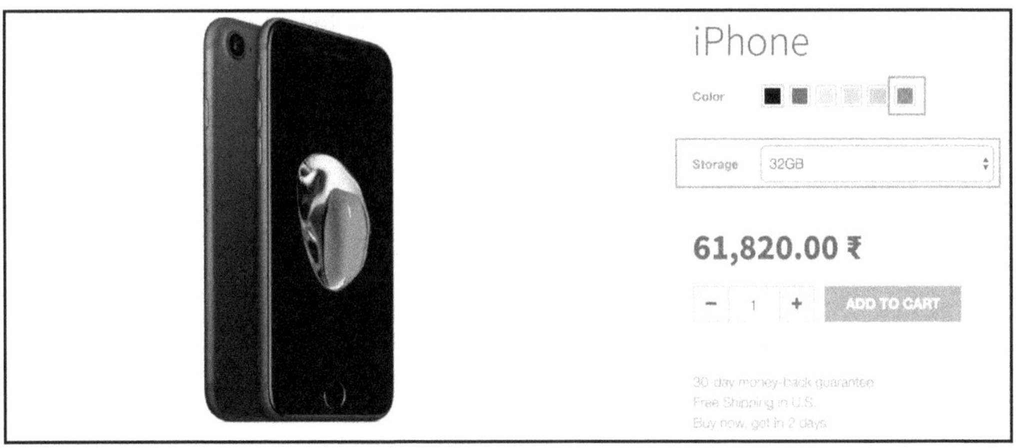

As soon as the user selects either 32GB or 64GB in storage capacity, the Red color will be disabled and not allow selection by the user as this combination of the product is not available as per the product specification.

Set up delivery integration and payment gateway

Allow your customer to pay online and select the fastest delivery option on your e-commerce store to give the best user experience to your customer. Setting up the delivery and payment gateway is the most important task before you set up the online shop. You cannot give a great experience to your customer if you are not connected to the fastest and cost-effective delivery and payment acquire connector.

Wire transfer is the default payment method available in Odoo as a payment option on the website. This is very easy to start with but it is slow and not an efficient process to collect the payment for the online shop. Choose a suitable payment gateway to integrate the online shop, configure the credential, and you can start collecting an online payment as soon as you put them in production.

Odoo has a built-in delivery framework to compute the delivery cost based on the weight and volume and to set the cost on the sales quotation. The default option is used to set up the delivery price grid given by the delivery service provider. We have already gone through the recipe *Adding delivery cost to quotation* recipe in `Chapter 4`, *Modern way of doing sales and managing sales contracts.*

If you are using or plan to use the delivery service providers such as FedEx, UPS, and USPS, Odoo also supports an integration with those services to get the real-time price.

Let's see how you can configure the payment gateway to process the online payment. Delivery connectors give the price in real time and label printing for the delivery. Integration of payment and delivery gives a great user experience to your online customers.

Getting ready

We assume that you are already aware of the delivery connectors and payment gateways Odoo has already integrated with. We advise you to identify and choose from the list of the following payment gateways and shipping connectors, which provide good quality of service in our country:

- Payment Gateways:
    - SEPA Credit Transfer – *Single Euro Payments Area (SEPA)*
    - Adyen Payment Acquirer
    - Authorize.Net Payment Acquirer
    - Buckaroo Payment Acquirer

    - Ingenico Payment Acquirer
    - Paypal Payment Acquirer
    - PayuMoney Payment Acquirer
    - Sips Payment Acquirer
- Delivery Connectors:
    - UPS integration
    - Fedex integration
    - Temando integration
    - USPS integration
    - DHL integration

How to do it...

1. Let's first activate the delivery connector on the website. Go to **Website Admin** | **Configuration** | **Settings** and search for the **Shipping Management** option. Choose the **Delivery methods are selectable on the website: the customer pays for shipping costs** option. As soon as you choose the option and click on the **APPLY** button, Odoo will install the delivery connector framework:

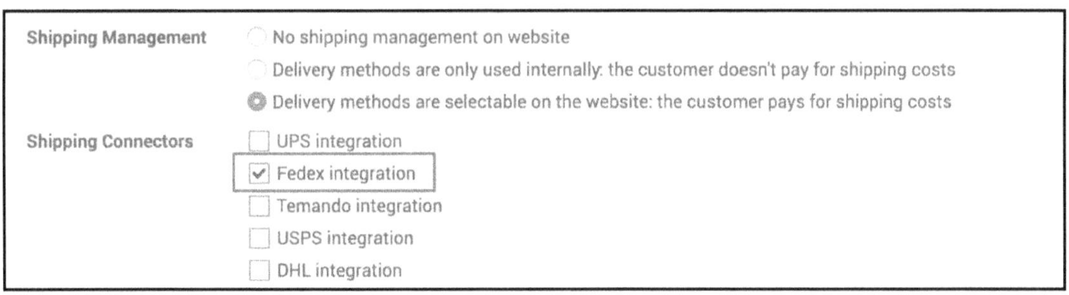

You are ready to install the delivery connector framework. Choose any delivery connector from the list of **Shipping Connectors**. Click on **APPLY** to save the settings. Odoo will install the connector application. On successful installation, you will be redirected to the home page of your instance.

2. Go to **Admin** | **Configuration** | **Delivery Methods**; you will see two new delivery methods added: **Fedex US** and **Fedex International**.

The first thing you have to set up is the credential for FedEx. It includes developer key, password, account number, and meter number. That information is used to communicate with the FedEx service in order to get the cost price based on the weight:

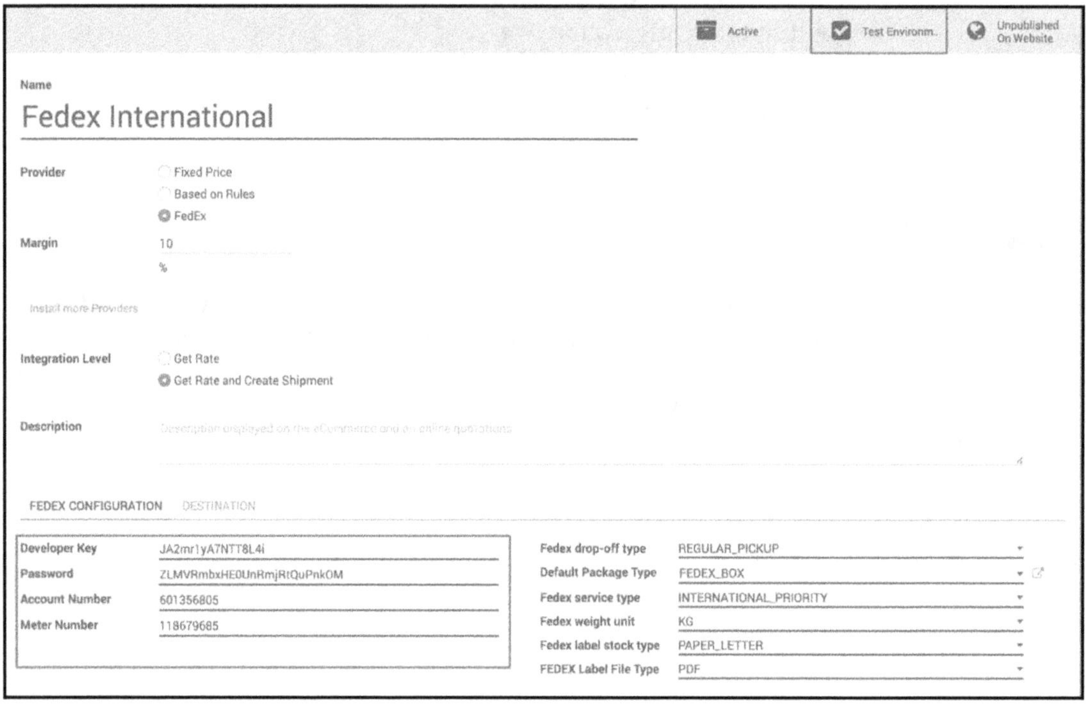

The real-time pricing starts working perfectly when you are in the production environment. Sometimes you may not get the correct price when the delivery connector is in the **Test Environment;** as soon as you move your mouse over the **Test Environment** button, it changes the label to **Switch to production**. Click on the button and you can switch to the production environment.

3. All set. Let's publish it on the website to be used by the customers to choose the provider to ship their products. Open **FedEx International** and click on the **Unpublished On Website** button to publish it on the website.

> Make sure you published delivery methods that are ready to use in production. Keeping testing methods on the system may bring down the system performance. It is advisable to unpublish by clicking on the **Unpublished** button, and deactivate it by clicking on the **Deactivate** button for those methods.

4. You have a possibility to add the **Margin** to the cost price on top of the provider price. You can add the margin percentage on top of the delivery cost, you can increase the delivery cost by 10 percent on top of the cost price provided by the delivery provider:

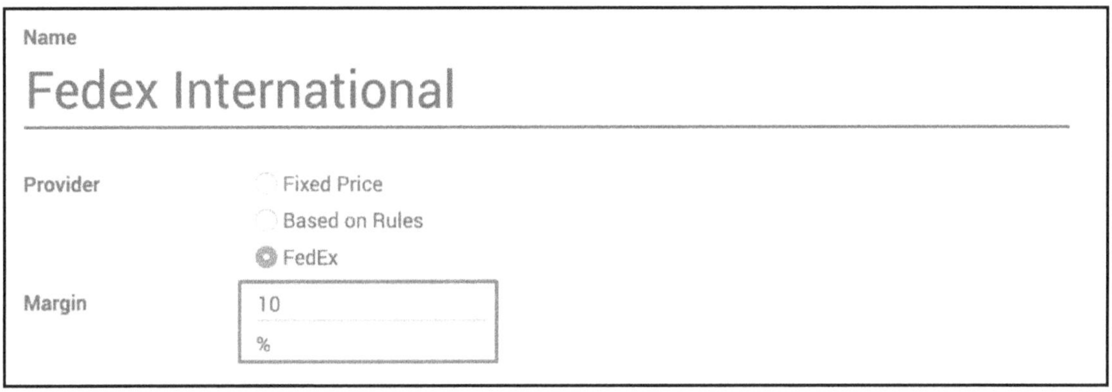

The cost of the delivery price will be computed or received from the delivery provider; we will increase it by 10 percent and display on the Sales quotation or Checkout Page.

5. You can choose the level of integration. Use the **Get Rate** option on the provider to get real-time prices based on the weight and the later part of the shipment, and other things will be managed manually. Alternatively, you can have a full integration starting from getting the price in real time to place an order for the delivery and getting a barcode label for the shipment. Choose the **Get Rate and Create Shipment** option to activate the full integration:

6. You are done with the configuration for the integration part. Now, you can set the filters to select the provider depending on the provider's delivery criteria. Let's assume that the provider does the delivery only in India. The business rules to allow or restrict the region can be set under the **DESTINATION** tab.

   You can choose **Zip From**, **Zip To**, **States**, or **Countries** where the provider accepts and delivers the consignment:

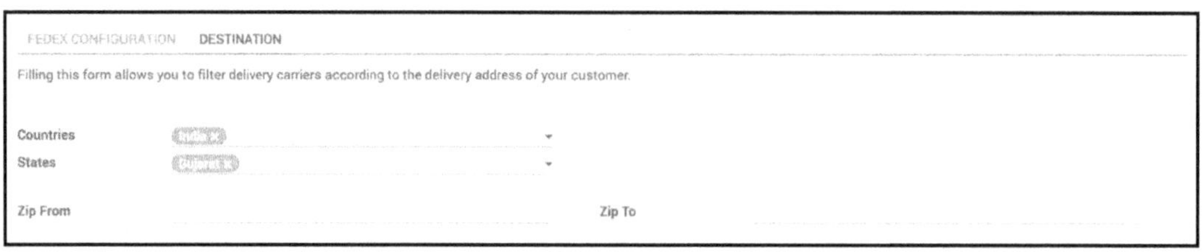

   I have applied the filter on **State** to restrict the delivery only in Gujarat. As soon as I select Gujarat, the **Country** filter is set to India automatically.

> When you leave all the fields empty, it's evaluated, as the delivery can be done across the world. Make sure that you define your area of business and choose the best delivery service accordingly. Set the same business area on the delivery provider so that other than those areas, the customer gets a clear message that you are not delivering the products.

7. You are ready with the delivery provider configuration. Make sure that all your products have the correct weight entered on the product page. To check the Weight information, go to **Website Admin** | **Catalogue** | **Products**. Switch to product from view by clicking on the product. The **Weight** field appears under the **INVENTORY** tab:

Review all your products for the Weight field, and you are done with the configuration. You will not get the **Weight** and **Volume** fields for some products, as that product has the variants, and you can find those fields on the product variant form.

8. Let's activate the payment gateway on the online shop. To activate the payment gateway go to **Accounting** | **Configuration** | **Setting.** You will find the **Payments** options under **Invoicing and Payments**. By default, there is only one payment acquirer which is active, it is **Wire Transfer**. You can make that provider as default by selecting it in **Default Acquirer**:

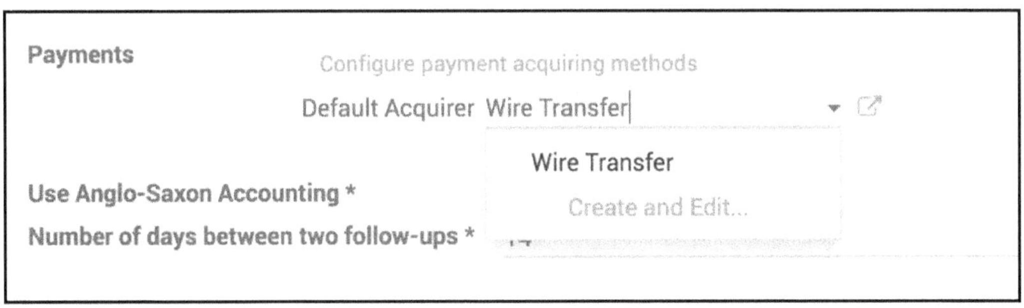

9. Click on the **Configure payment acquiring methods** link. You will be redirected to the list of payment acquirers. Click on the **INSTALL** button to activate the payment acquirer:

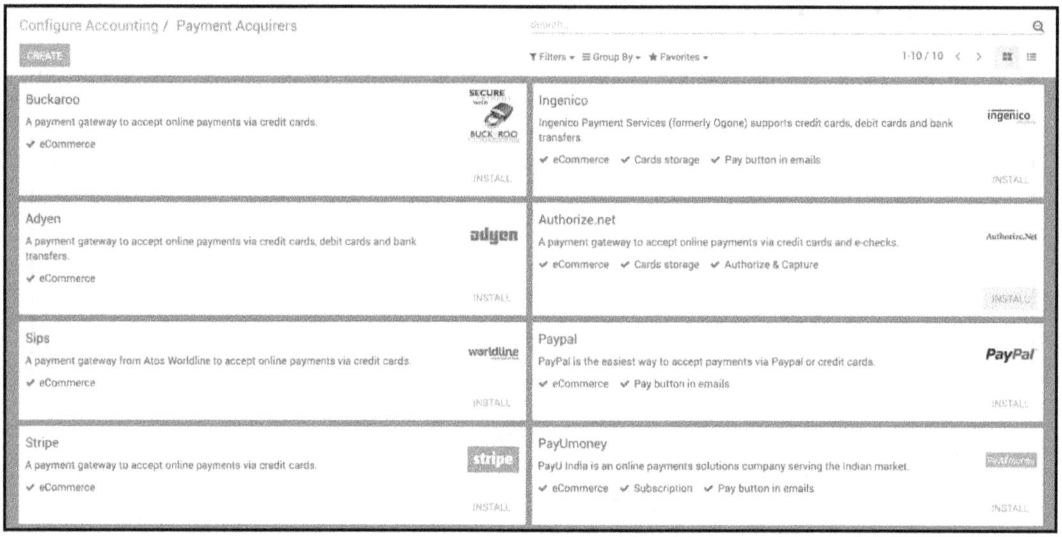

I have activated the **Authorize.net** payment provider.

10. As soon as the payment provider is installed successfully, you will be redirected to payment provider configuration. You have to enter **API Login key** and **API Transaction Key**, which should be acquired from the respective payment gateway account. You will find a link to **How to configure your Authorize.Net account (look for Getting Started Guide)**. You will get the guide for almost all the payment gateways:

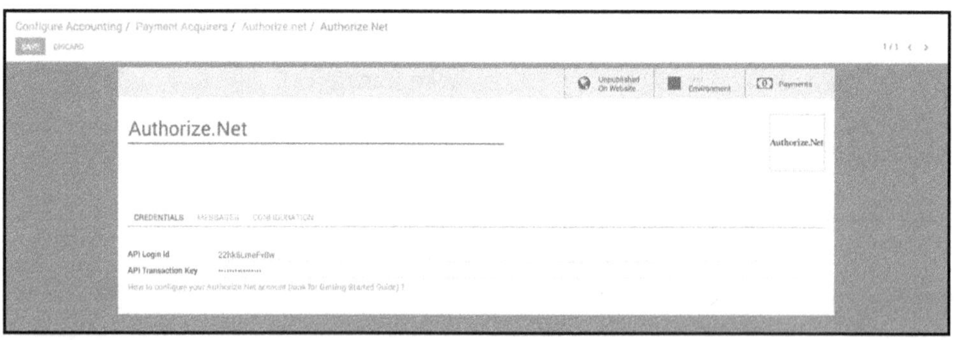

11. There are different types of messages given during the payment processing, such as **Help Message**, **Thanks Message**, **Pending**, **Done**, **Cancel**, and **Error Message**. The default messages are given; you can change the message under the **MESSAGES** tab if you want a custom message:

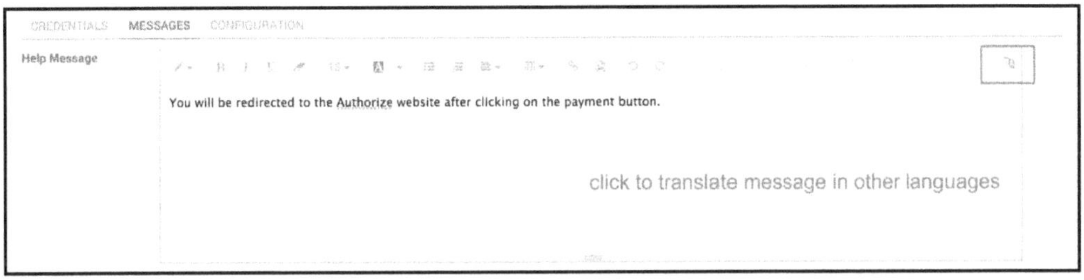

Click on the icon available in the message box at the top-right corner. You can set the message in other languages activated in Odoo.

12. The next step is to set up **Order Confirmation** and **Store Card Data**. You will find these options under the **CONFIGURATION** tab:

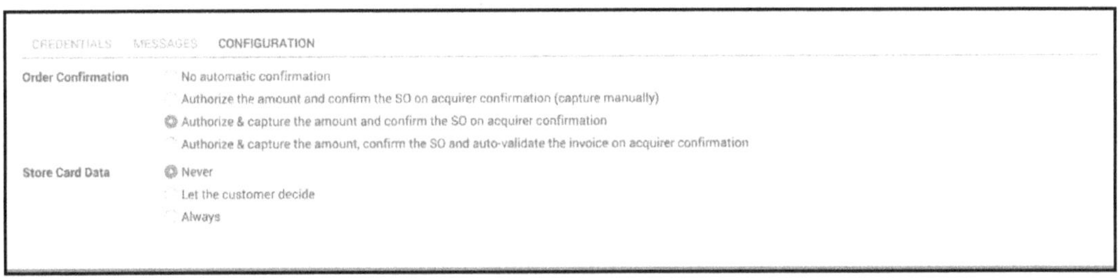

13. **Order Confirmation** is about the order getting confirmed. You can set any option from the ones listed here:
    - No automatic confirmation. When you choose this option, the payment transaction will be created with an Acquirer Reference number and set to **DONE** stage on a successful online payment process. The payment will link to the Sales order, but the sales order will stay in the draft stage, it has to be processed manually.
    - Authorize the amount and confirm the SO on acquirer confirmation (capture manually). When you choose this option, the payment transaction will be created and stay in the **AUTHORISED** stage on successfully online payment process. The payment will link to the Sales order, and sales order will be confirmed, the payment will be linked to the sales.

- Authorize and capture the amount and confirm the SO on acquirer confirmation. When you choose this option, the payment transaction will be created and go to the **DONE** stage on a successful online payment process. The payment will link to the Sales order, and sales order will be confirmed, the payment will be linked to the sales.
- Authorize and capture the amount, confirm the SO and auto-validate the invoice on acquirer confirmation. When you choose this option, the payment transaction will be created and stay in the **DONE** stage on a successful online payment process. The payment will link to the Sales order, and sales order will be confirmed, the invoice will be created from the sales order and it will be validated automatically.

Usually, any eCommerce store does not store the card information; the default option set on **Store Card Data** is set to *Never* in Odoo. However, if needed for recurring payment processing, Odoo store the token given by the payment provider at the first transaction.

Review and checkout order

Customers can have a great experience with online shopping. Starting from selecting the product to selecting the delivery method and payment options during the checkout process. A seamless integration between ERP application, e-commerce, delivery platform, and payment gateway is a huge effort. It requires a huge team and effort required to keep the eCommerce application alive and running that is integrated with Inventory, Accounting, Payment Gateway and Shipping Gateway.

Odoo does this integration seamlessly like any other application, just by installing the eCommerce application your instance starts offering products an online shop. We have gone through the setup of the shop, products, and their variants and their pricing. We have also integrated the payment gateway and delivery method on the online shop.

Let's see how customers can check out the order in a few clicks, get the cost for the delivery from delivery providers, and process payment on the payment gateway. You can also introduce a new step in the checkout process if required.

Getting ready

We assume that you have already set up your online shop, configured its view options from the customization, and your shop is integrated with the delivery connectors and ready to take the payment online through the payment gateways.

Setting up an online shop begins with the installation of the eCommerce application on Odoo instance. Refer to the *Setup and configure online shop* recipe to set up. You can configure the view by the customization options available on the shop page. Refer to Configure products and its variants recipe to set up the products and their variants on the shop page. You can enable the Filters based on the variant attributes. The last setting to be done before you go live is to enable the payment and shipping gateway; refer to the *Setup delivery integration and Payment gateway* recipe to do so.

Once you are done with the preceding configuration, you are ready to accept the first online order.

I choose Authorize.Net as a payment gateway to process the online payment and FedEx as the delivery integrator; the order will be delivered through the FedEx delivery method. I have also set the pricelist currency to USD, to be compatible with the online payment provider; look at the following screen of my pricelist confirmation.

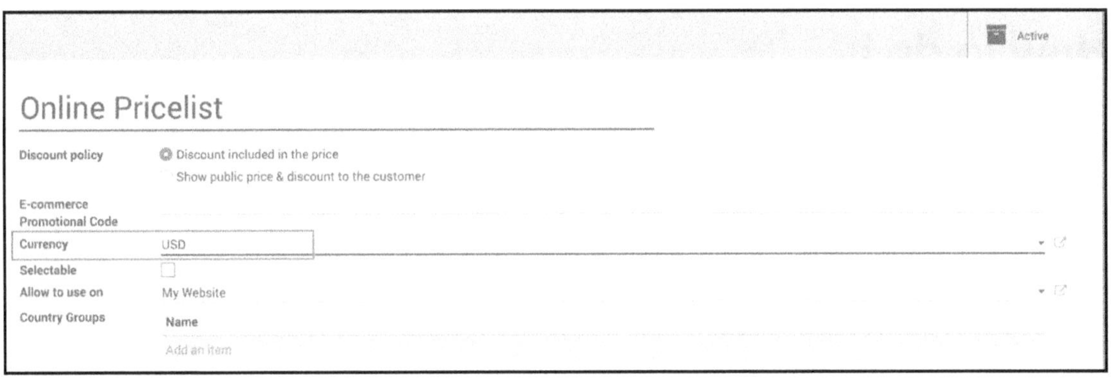

The pricelist can be accessed from **Configuration** | **Pricelist** under the **Sales** Application. As soon as the pricelist currency set to USD your product price will be converted to USD as follows:

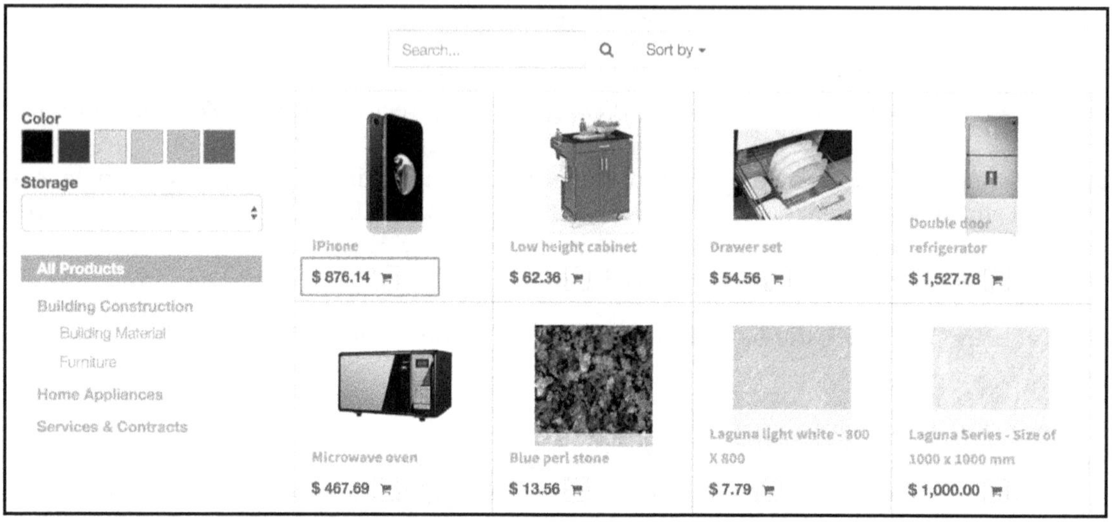

How to do it...

1. The product can be added to the cart by clicking on the cart icon beside the product price. You will be redirected to the cart page, having the product added to the cart. Look at the following screenshot:

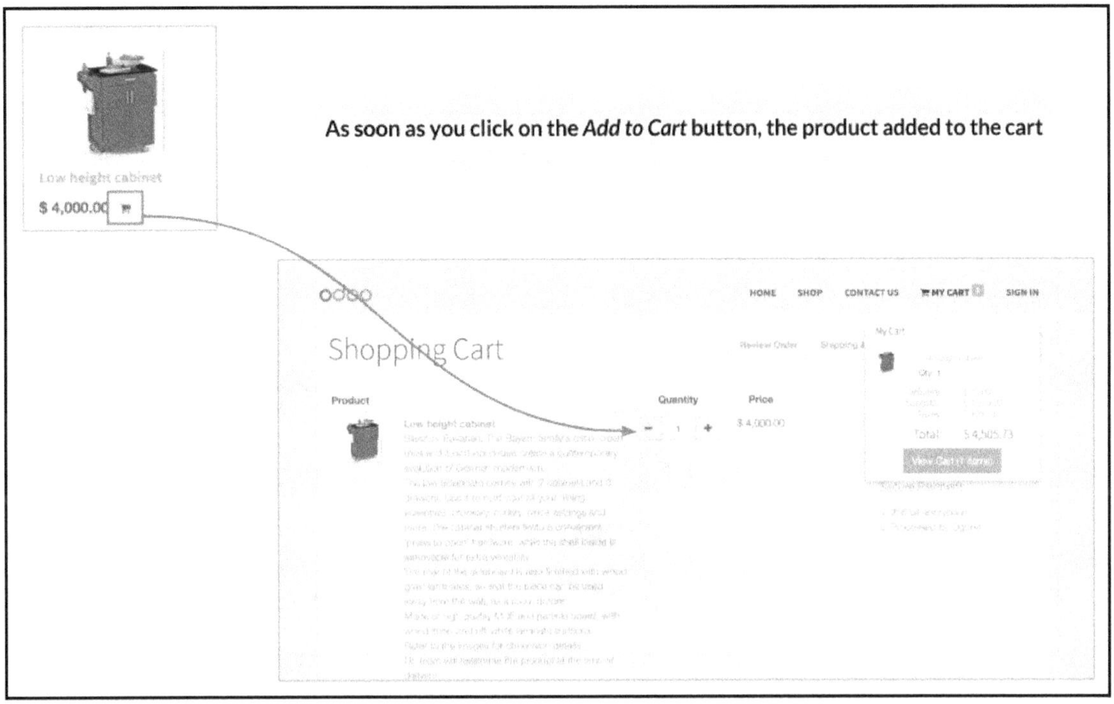

You can continue shopping by clicking on the **Continue shopping** button. Click on **View Cart (1 items)** to start the checkout process. By clicking on the quantity increase or decrease button, you can change the product quantity.

2. Don't be surprised if you arrive at the product page for some product, when you click on the **ADD TO CART** button:

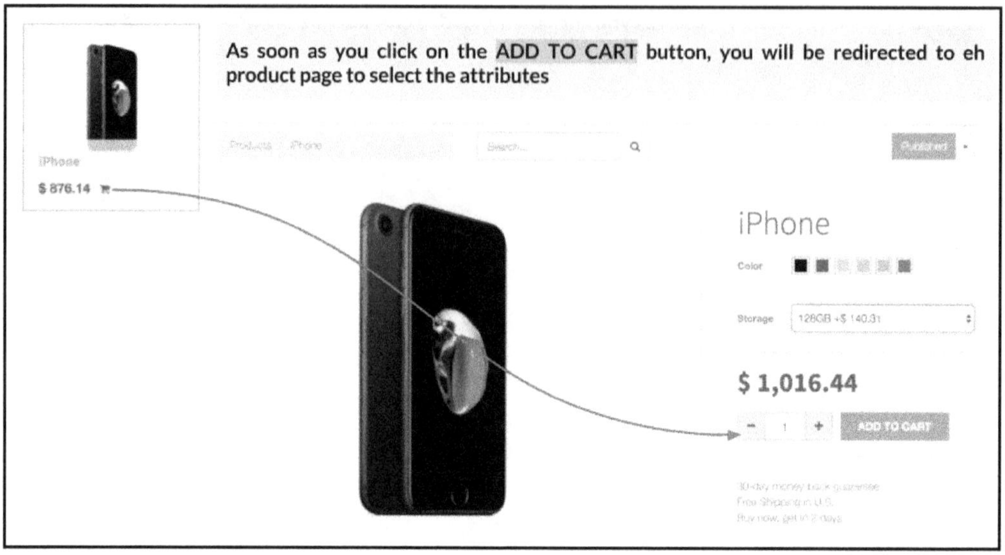

Some products may have a product variant. The variant attribute should be chosen on the product page in order to place the order. Select the attribute and click on the **ADD TO CART** button. As soon as the product is added to the cart, you will be redirected to the cart page:

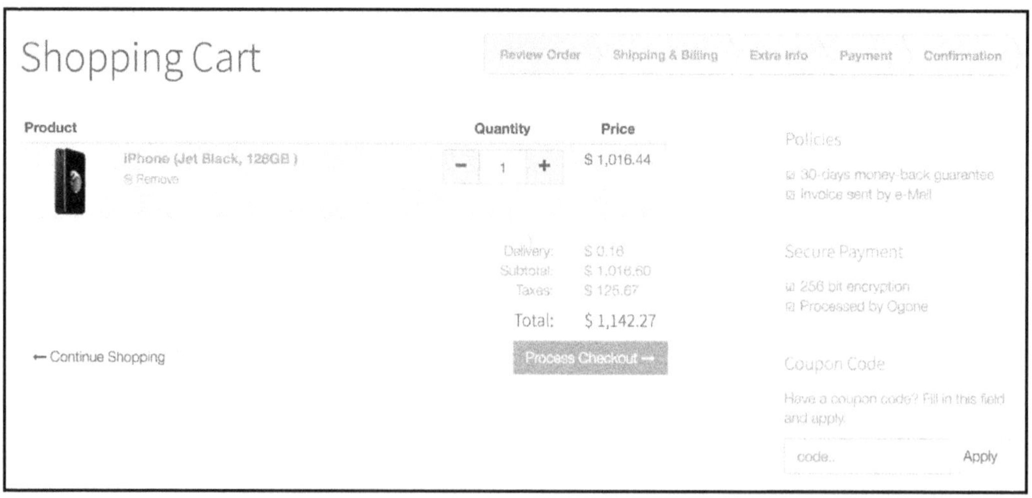

3. Click on the **Process Checkout** button to process the order. You will be asked to fill **Your address**, which will be the shipping and billing addresses, or click on **Log in** to choose from the existing addresses:

The entered address will be chosen as **Billing Address** and **Shipping address**. However, you can change the billing address or create a new one:

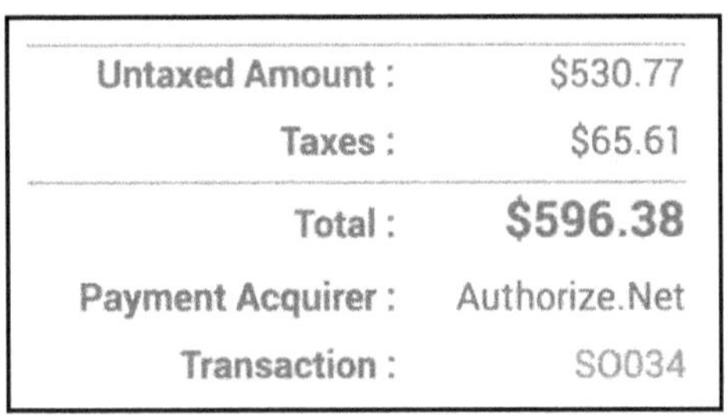

4. Click on the **Confirm →** button. It may take some time, as it tries to get the delivery charges from different providers. It will check with all the delivery methods installed on the Odoo.

It proposes two delivery methods that are delivering to an international address. Depending on the customer address, the delivery method will be suggested on this page:

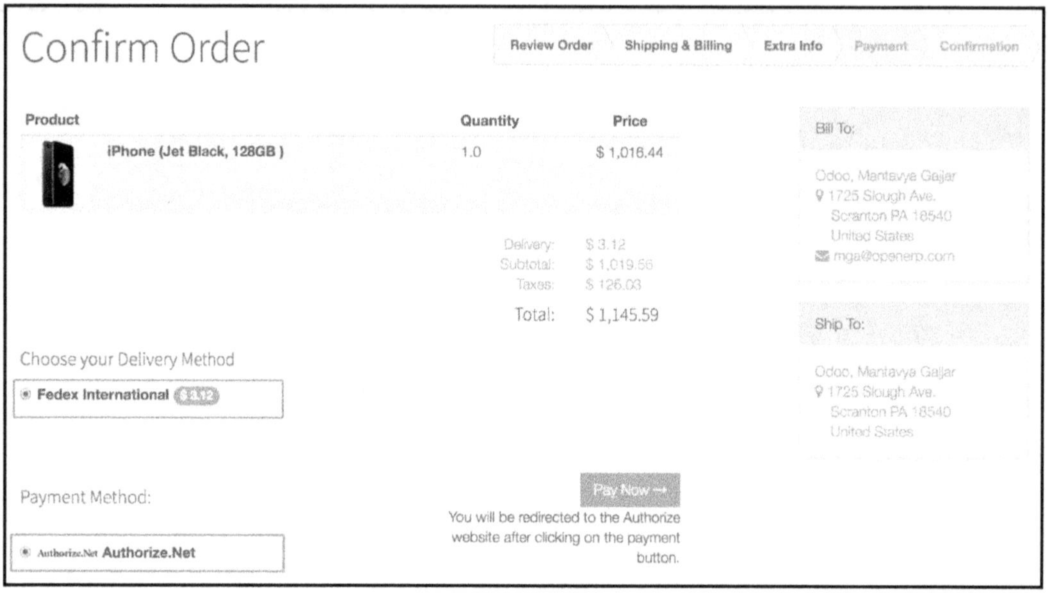

The changes are depending on the distance weight and delivery time. You can change the delivery method from **Speed Port Delivery** to **FedEx International** to get fast delivery. The delivery cost will be changed when you change the delivery method.

5. The default payment method will be selected on this page. As we have activated **Authorised.Net**, it is selected. If you plan to choose any other method, you can change it and click on the **Pay Now →** button.

Let's choose the **Authorised.Net** payment acquirer and click on the **Pay Now →** button to process the payment. You will be redirected to the authorized payment processing page shown in the following screenshot:

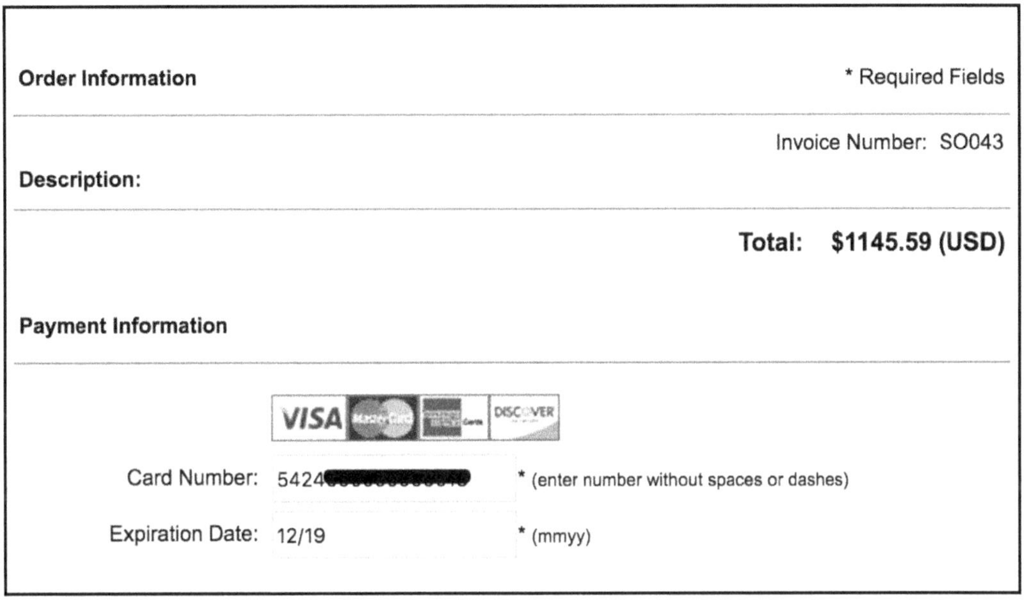

Enter **Card Number** and **Expiration Date** and click on the **Confirm Payment** button at the bottom of the page. The billing and shipping will be copied from Odoo shop and it will be available below the **Payment Information** block; you may allow changing the address if you want; it will look like the following screenshot:

6. You will be redirected back to the payment confirmation page. The status of the payment is passed to the confirmation page. You will see **Payment Information** and the message depending on the information coming from the payment provider:

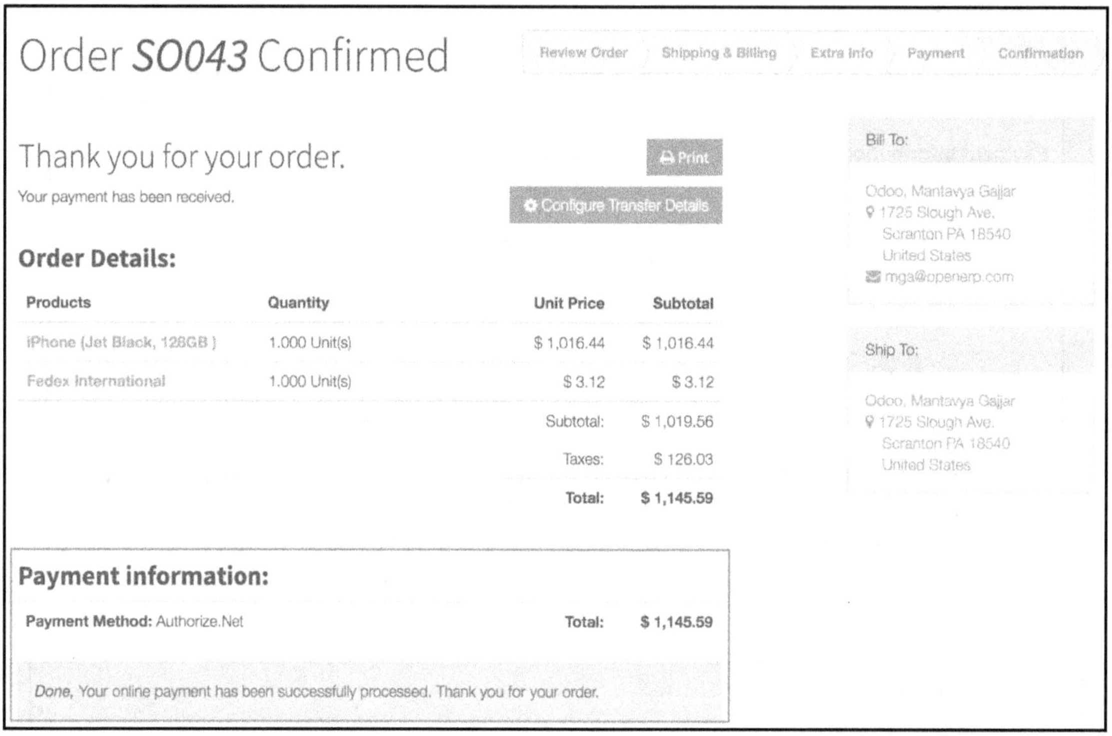

7. The order processing will be done based on the option selected on the payment acquirer. I have set the **Authorize & capture the amount and confirm the SO on acquirer confirmation on the payment** option acquire method:

My Company Tagline

training-odoo-cookbook
1725 Slough Ave.
Scranton PA 18540
United States

Invoicing and shipping address:
Odoo, Mantavya Gajjar
1725 Slough Ave.
Scranton PA 18540
United States

Odoo, Mantavya Gajjar
1725 Slough Ave.
Scranton PA 18540
United States

Order # SO043

Date Ordered: 08/25/2017 15:50:52

Payment Terms: Immediate Payment

Description	Quantity	Unit Price	Taxes	Price
iPhone (Jet Black, 128GB)	1.000	1,016.44	(standard)Input Excise Duty @ 12.36%	$ 1,016.44
Fedex International	1.000	3.12	(standard)Input Excise Duty @ 12.36%	$ 3.12

Total Without Taxes	$ 1,019.56
Taxes	$ 126.03
Total	$ 1,145.59

Payment Information	Total
Payment Method: Authorize.Net **Payment Status:** *Done*, Your online payment has been successfully processed. Thank you for your order.	$ 1,145.59

8. The order will be confirmed on successful payment; otherwise, the order will be in draft only, waiting for the payment confirmation:

On successful payment, the status will be updated on the order itself, below **Total**. **Payment Acquirer** and **Transaction** will be linked to the order.

There's more...

Seamless integration between Sales, eCommerce, Payment Acquirer, and Delivery methods give the best user experience. Just in a few clicks, users can shop and check out the cart, get the delivery price, and make the payment online. Behind the scenes, there are many different applications working to gather track and update the status on the order and respective statement.

Let's see what are the other statements that get updated behind the scenes during the checkout and payment process. Lets' check how we can add an extra step to the checkout process.

Payment status

Customers will be notified of the Odoo eCommerce application by an automated e-mail for the order:

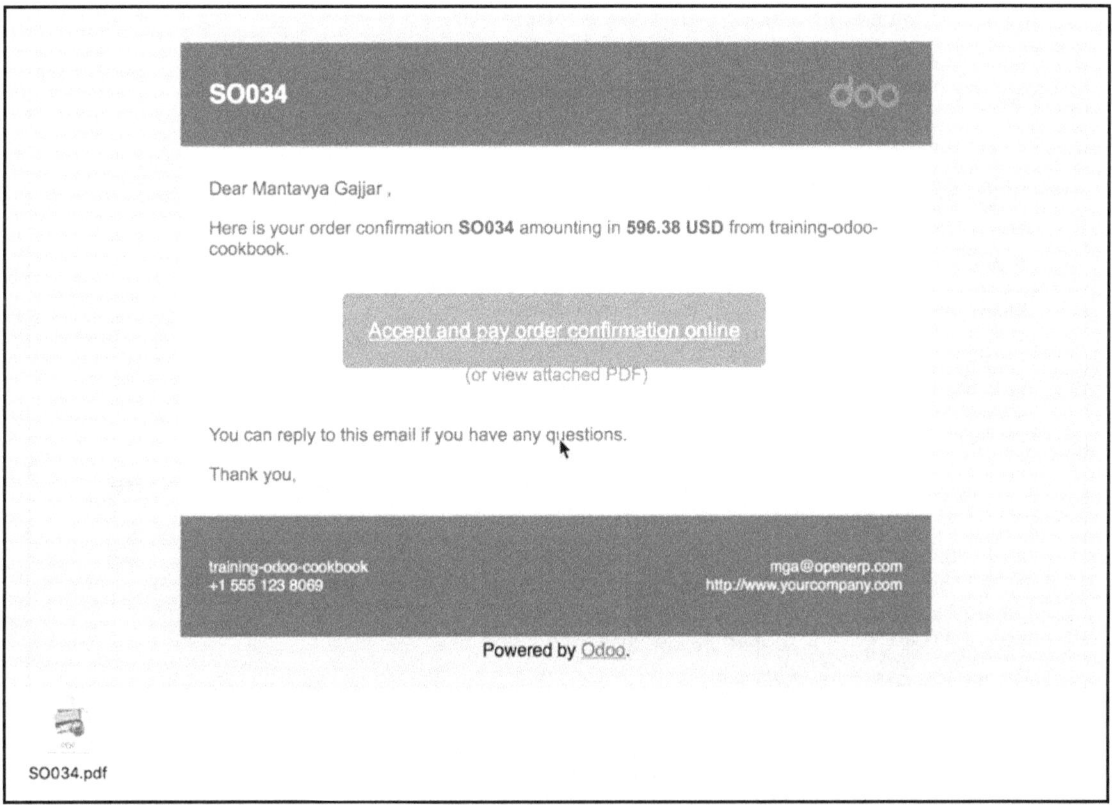

When a customer proceeds and pays online, an e-mail will be sent from the payment acquirer about the status of the payment:

Auto-Receipt

Transaction Receipt from for $1145.59 (USD)

To: Mantavya Gajjar (MGA),

Reply-To:

Order Information

Description:	Goods or Services
Invoice Number	SO043

Billing Information
Mantavya Gajjar
1725 Slough Ave.
Scranton, PA 18540
United States
mga@openerp.com

Shipping Information
Mantavya Gajjar
1725 Slough Ave.
Scranton, PA 18540
United States

Total: $1145.59 (USD)

Payment Information

Date/Time:	25-Aug-2017 3:21:49 PDT
Transaction ID:	60028561158
Payment Method:	MasterCard xxxx0015
Transaction Type:	Purchase
Auth Code:	VQKSHK

Merchant Contact Information

The payment status will be attached to the order too when the customer chooses to pay through the online payment gateway. You can see which payment gateway has been chosen by the customer to pay online, and the payment transaction will be attached below the order:

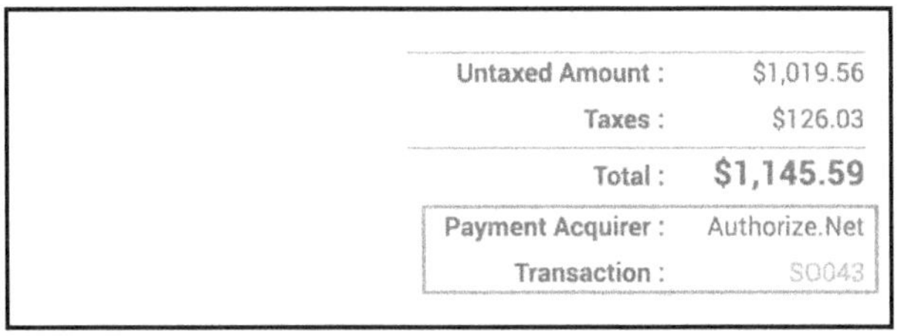

The details of the transaction give the exact details about the payment, stating whether it was a success or failure. The transaction code is also attached to the payment transaction. Click on the *SO043* link to the **Transaction** field. You will see the details of the payment:

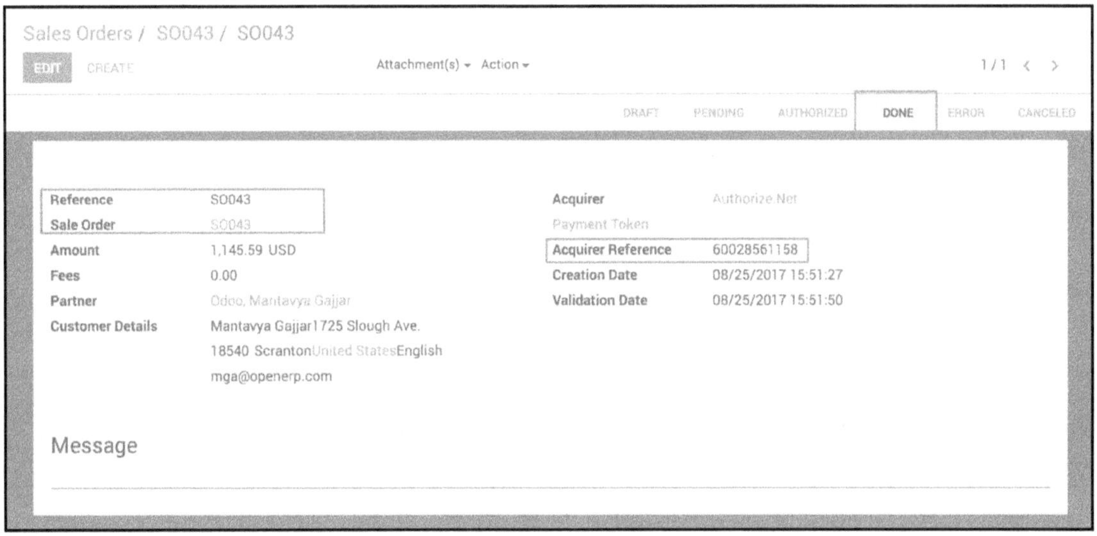

On the left-hand side, you will find the order details, and on the right-hand side, you will see the payment details. **Order Reference**, **Amount,** and **Acquirer Reference** are the important fields used for matching the payment with the order.

The **Payment Token** will be available customer pay for the order which requests to deduct the payment on a recurring basis. The Payment Token is used to request payment on the next payment date, this is usually needed when we get the payment for a subscription order.

The unique reference number given by **Acquirer** identified as payment reference is **Acquirer reference**. **Creation Date** is the date when the transaction begins, and **Validation Date** represents the transaction end date. The status of the transaction displayed on the top-right status bar shows **DONE** in our case.

Print delivery label and track shipment

The shipping connectors are integrated with the Odoo. There are two ways of integration: either to get just the price or to get the price and generate the consignment on the shipping provider. **Integration Level** can be set on the delivery method setting:

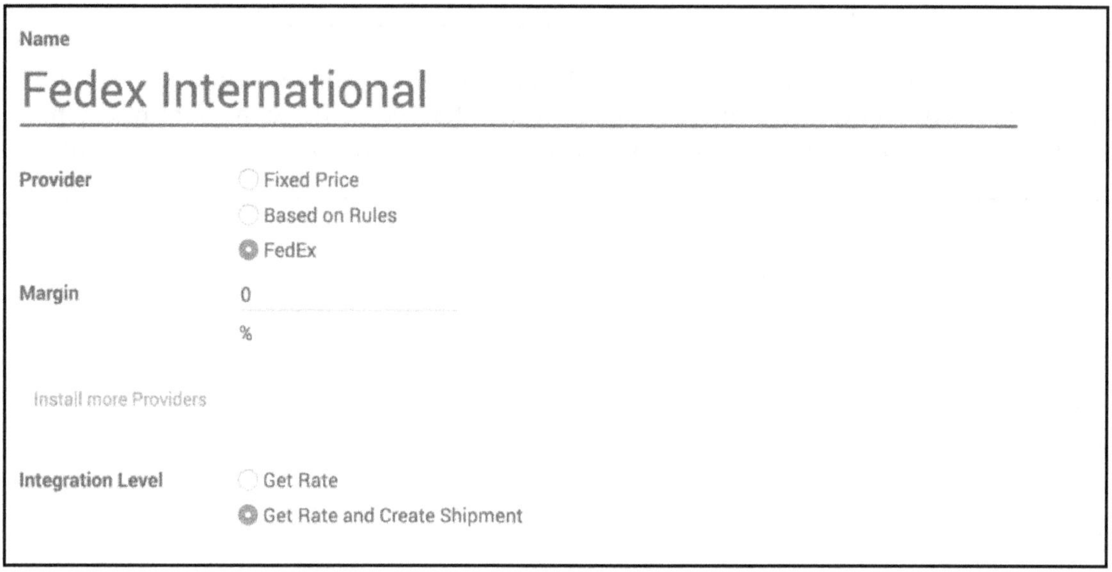

We have set **Integration Level** to **Get Rate and Create Shipment**; it will get the rates and create shipment on the confirmation of the delivery order.

Go to **Sales Orders**, open the sales order; go to **Delivery**, and confirm the delivery order. As soon as the delivery order is confirmed, the delivery label is also fetched from the carrier website and attached to **Delivery Order**. The attachment can be found on the **Attachments** menu, or you will found it on the chatter:

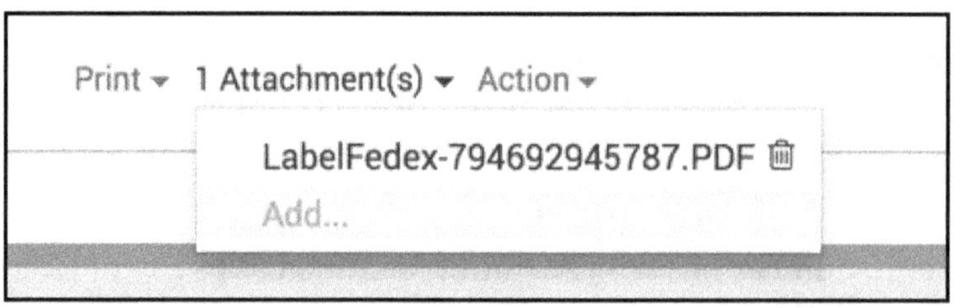

Click on the document to download it:

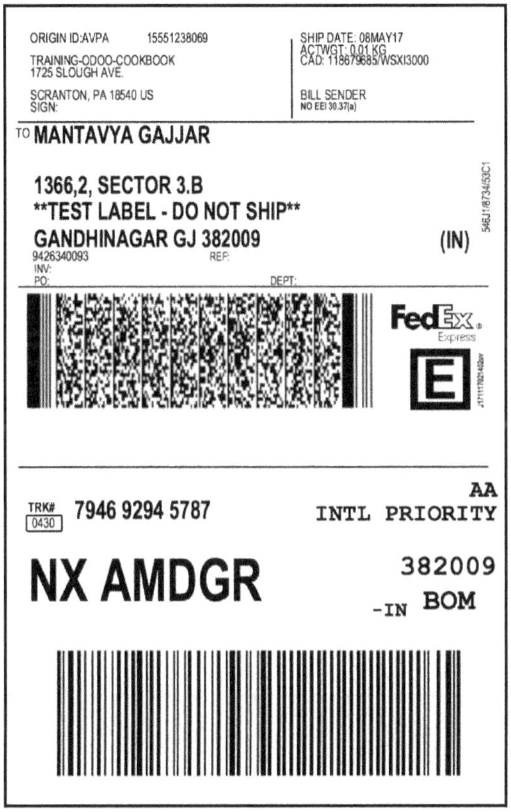

You can print it and affix to the package before the delivery.

You will get the tracking information attached to the delivery order under **Delivery Information**. You will have **Carrier** and **Tracking Reference** attached to the order. Look at the following screenshot:

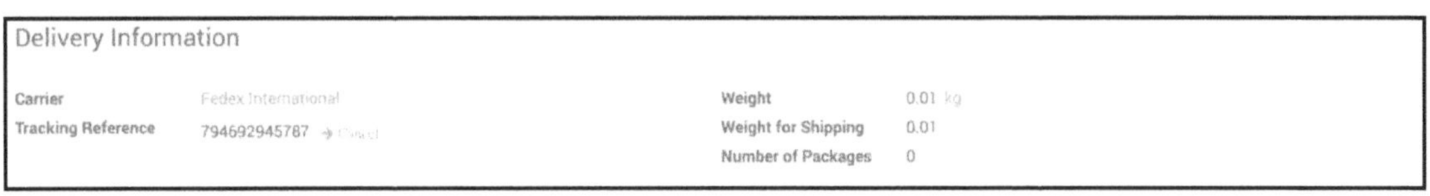

The weight of the product, **Number of Packages**, and **Weight for Shipping** are displayed on the order. The shipment can be canceled, by clicking on the **Cancel** link available beside **Tracking Reference**. The shipment can be tracked by clicking on the **Tracking** button in the top-right corner:

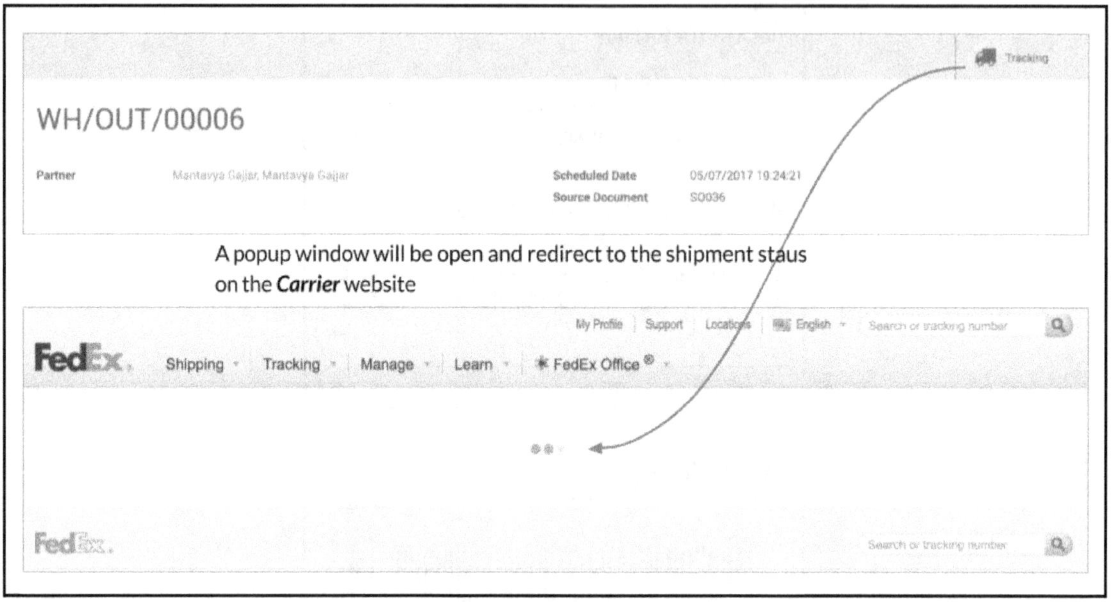

Discount coupon

The most exciting field for the customer is to apply the discount or coupon code in the shopping cart. Many of the online shopping websites announce schemes to attract the customers. The customer will have a code. They will apply it to the cart that internally computes the discount on the order or specific products within the order.

Odoo simply uses the Pricelist to compute and apply the discount on the order. You have to create a Pricelist that computes the special price with a fixed or percentage of discount. Enter the code that you would like to announce as an offer:

Set the **E-commerce Promotional Code** option. It is text fixed. Define the marketable easy-to-remember code. The best part of using the price list is you can set the price for the product template, category, or specific variants of products. You can set the fixed price or compute the percentage. The **Start Date** and **End Date** values are used to limit the offer period.

On the eCommerce frontend, you just need to activate the **Coupon Code** feature where customers can apply the code. This feature can be activated on the cart page. Go to the cart page and activate the **Coupon Code** feature from the **Customize** menu:

Assuming that, as a customer, we have a coupon code to get the 10 percent discount during the month of May 2017:

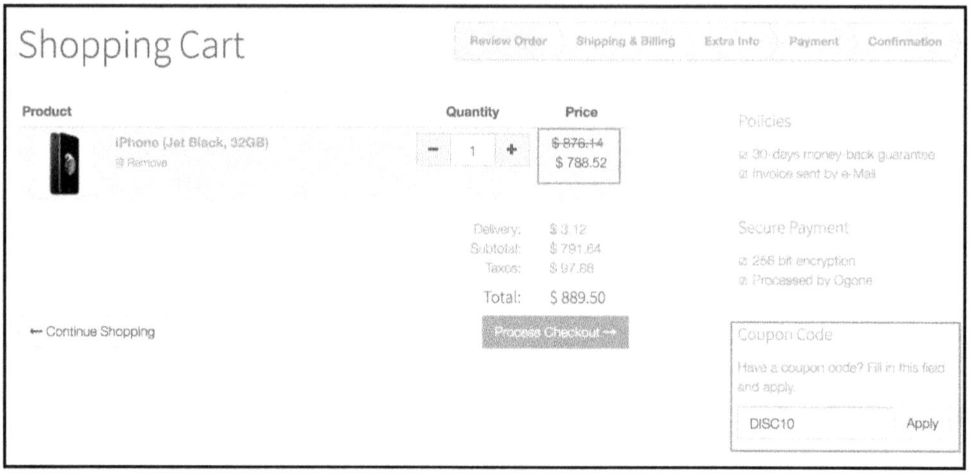

You will get the fields to apply the coupon to the order which is available in the right-bottom corner: enter *DISC10* and click on the **Apply** button. The price will be changed on the order as per the discount schemes configured on the Pricelist.

> The code can be applied only once. When you try to apply code more than once on the same order, it will be toggled and the order will be switched back to the old product price.

To cover all the businesses, a more complex coupon feature is in development; it will be released in Odoo 11.

Extra step to checkout process

The shopping cart has the capability of delivering the customized product or service on demand. Almost all those shopping carts need customer input in order to process the order.

Let's take an example of a t-shirt printing website. Once the t-shirt size gets confirmed, users have to upload the photo or input the text that has to be printed on the t-shirt.

Using Odoo, you can have only standard steps during the checkout process. You can add new steps without any development; it's a part of Odoo's standard feature. Check the Customize options when you enter the checkout process. You will find a feature to enable **Extra Step Option** under **Wizard Checkout**:

An **Extra Step** will be added in the checkout process. Continue to the checkout process. You will arrive at the **Extra Step**. The default form will be available with three fields: **Your Reference**, **Give us your feedback...**, and **A document to provide?** You can change the label of those fields to adapt according to your requirements:

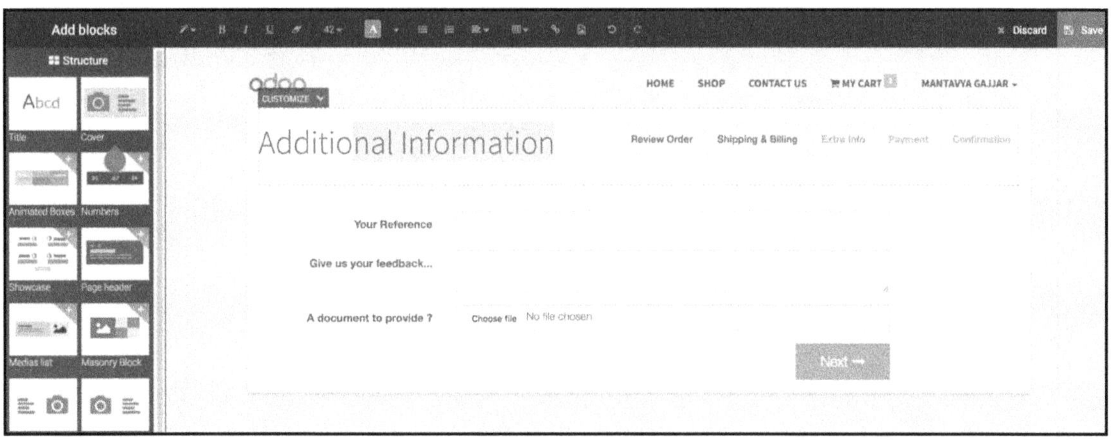

Once the view is ready, you can click on the **SAVE** button to publish it onto the production. All the information filled in the extra fields will appear in the chatter of the sales order.

Access orders and payments

Integration is always a painful task. Working with an eCommerce application that is not connected to the business is like driving a car without full control. You cannot have a clear view of the business when your ERP and eCommerce are not integrated. Your customer does not have an amazing experience until you consolidate the sales figures from all the channels. By the time you do this, it may be too late to take the decision.

All the applications installed on Odoo instance are integrated by default. For example, an order generated from back-office sales and orders placed online on the website is the same and can be found under the **Sales** application.

Let's see how you can analyze the sales generated from the different channels, back office, and eCommerce.

How to do it...

1. Like other applications of Odoo, **Website Admin** is an application, and it's got its own dashboard. As soon as you enter into the application, the first screen you get is the application dashboard:

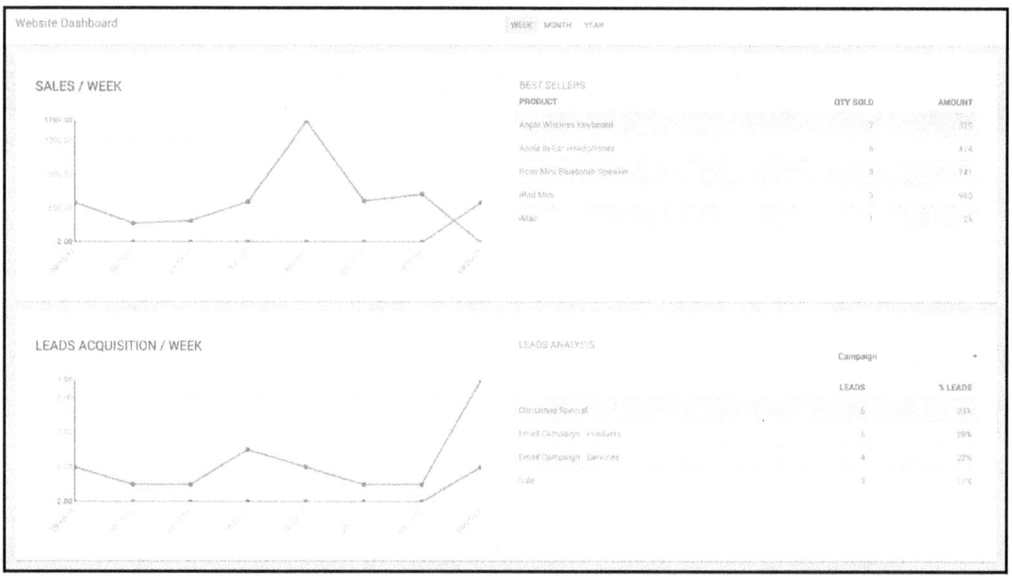

Make sure that you have installed the **Contact Form** application from the Apps menu to enable the LEADS ACQUISITION analysis report.

You can track visitors and their activity on the website; generated revenue per campaign; leads acquisition; and sales by the week, month or year. You have to link Google analytic account in order to get the visits analysis in Odoo.

2. **Website Admin** represents the eCommerce application in Odoo. You can access all the documents such as product catalog, orders, invoices, and website Pricelist within the application. The orders can be accessed by going to **Website Admin** | **Orders** | **Orders**. All the orders placed online on the eCommerce site are accessible here:

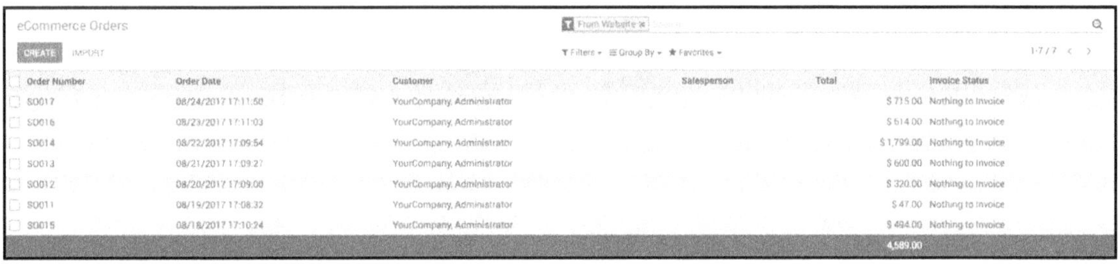

3. Don't be surprised if you find many orders under **Website Admin** | **Orders** | **Abandoned Orders**. All the orders are those created by the customer on the online store by adding an item to the cart; somehow the customer did not initiate the payment or did not succeed to pay online. Those orders will be marked as canceled after some time and will be marked an abandoned order.

Usually, online stores wait for 1 hour to get the payment transfer. It does not receive payment in an hour after the order created, the order will be marked as canceled after marked as **Abandoned Orders**:

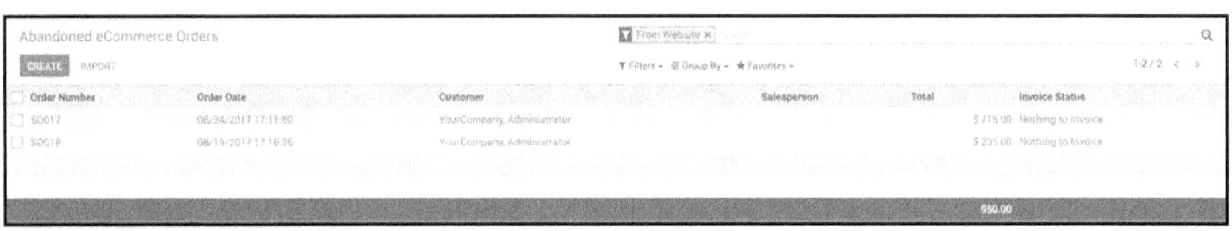

Periodically check for all those orders; you can delete those orders as they were left just after creating them.

4. The order confirmed online, but still waiting for the payment can be found in the **Unpaid Orders** menu. Go to **Website Admin** | **Orders** | **Unpaid Orders**:

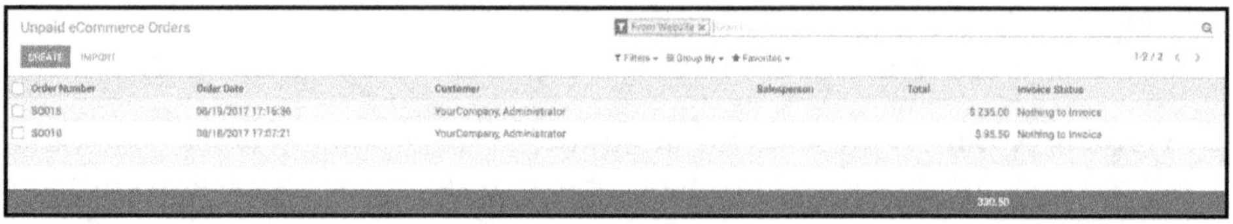

You will find orders that have failed to process the payment. Please check whether you keep the **Write Transfer** payment activated or not. If yes, all the orders that have selected that payment option will stay as unpaid orders.

5. The payment related to the sales order can be found on the order itself, go through *Payment status* in the *Review and checkout order* recipe in `Chapter 6`, *Start Selling Online with Odoo eCommerce*. The payment made is either successful or unsuccessful.

7
Setting up Financial Management with Odoo

In this chapter, we will cover the following recipes:

- Setting up financial management in Odoo
- Customer invoices and payments
- Getting paid through a bank or cash and reconciliation
- Create and configure tax, apply on invoice, and print tax report
- Managing vendor bills and payments
- Closing the financial year and printing financial reports

Introduction

Like the other major applications of Odoo such as CRM, Sales, E-commerce, Project and Timesheet applications, Invoicing and Accounting are built-in applications. They are integrated with other applications as accounting is the heart of any business application.

Accounting is an important part of any business, ten years ago the challenge was to integrate all the group of company's financial data into a single document, such as a Profit and Loss and Balance sheet. Today the challenge is how to integrate accounting with different applications, such as Marketing, E-commerce, Customer Relationships, Help Desk, other than the core applications, such as Sales, Inventory, and Manufacturing.

In Odoo the accounting application is divided into two different applications—Invoicing and Accounting and Finance. The Invoicing application takes care of the customer invoices and vendor bills, with some detailed configuration such as Taxes, Payment Terms, Fiscal Position, and Multi-currency while the full accounting scope is covered by the Accounting and Finance application.

We have already worked with the Invoicing application in `Chapter 4`, *Modern Way of Doing Sales and Managing Sales Contract* and `Chapter 5`, *Time Tracking and Invoicing Policy*. Throughout this chapter, we will see the full scope of accounting and finance, from configuring a chart of accounts to generating financial statements such as profit and loss and balance sheet statements.

Let's see how we can configure and adapt an Odoo Accounting and Finance application for any country worldwide. Odoo has the chart of account for more than 40 countries. Next, in the chapter we will see how to create the customer invoice and vendor bills, adding payment terms in the invoice and bills and managing the follow-ups and payments, at last, we will go through the tax creation and tax computation.

At the end of a financial year, we will close the profit and loss account and carry forward the profit or loss to the balance sheet in order to start the new financial year.

Setting up financial management in Odoo

Finance is the heart of an organization; it is connected to all the core activities of a business such as Sales, Purchase, Manufacturing, Projects, and so on. Odoo has a great modular approach, and that's the reason you can choose either to use only the Invoicing application; or the full Financial Accounting application. Invoicing is an integrated application with Sales and Purchase; and is used to create an invoice and track payments, while the Financial Accounting application supports full accounting features, from the configuration of the chart of accounts to printing legal reports such as Profit and Loss Accounts, and Balance sheets.

Let's activate the fully featured Financial Accounting application, configure company information, install a chart of accounts and configure it, and import the opening balance for an each account. To import the opening balance, we have to import the accounts closing from the balance sheet and the customer ledger of customers and suppliers with their due dates.

Getting ready

The backbone of an accounting system is the chart of accounts. Every country has its own chart of accounts depending on the business type or yearly turnover.

> It is recommended you start the accounting system from the new financial year. You just need to import the balance sheet; it is advisable to not work on importing the old accounting entries.

Keep handy the last balance sheet to import. If you have an unaudited balance sheet before the audit is complete, you can skip the import process and start working with the new financial year entries in the accounting module. Import the balance sheet as soon as you get the final balance sheet after the audit is completed.

How to do it...

1. The Odoo online platform is smart enough to detect the country you belong to, and selects the chart of accounts depending on the country, and when the accounting module is installed, it will automatically install the appropriate chart of account.

> When you are onsite, at the time of creating a database, you will be asked to fill the country, depending on which the chart of accounts will be installed.

When you install **Sale** or **Purchase** as your first application, the **Invoicing** application will be installed as a dependency. **Invoicing** is a minimal set of accounting features to start working with the customer invoices and vendor bills.

With the invoicing application, you can create customer invoices and vendor bills, and you are able to analyze the invoices. In order to activate the full accounting package with the chart of accounts configuration and the statuary reports based on countries, you can install the **Accounting & Finance** application from **App**.

2. Let's go to **App** to verify that the **Accounting and Finance** application is installed; install it if not installed. It is not always the case, but if you are onsite and did not select the country field at the time of creating a database, you will be asked to browse all the charts of account of all the countries and install the appropriate one:

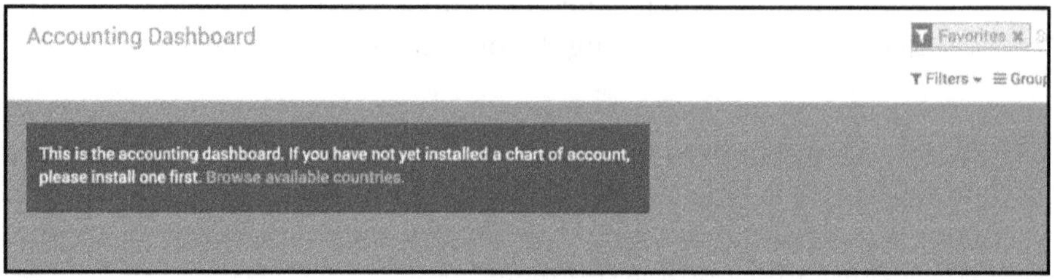

For the onsite users, make sure that the country field is selected at the time of creating a new database. Please refer to `Appendix`, *Installation of Odoo 10* on Ubuntu Linux, to install Odoo locally and create a new database. If the country field was not selected, the accounting or invoicing application will be installed but the chart of account won't be available, and it has to be installed manually like other Odoo applications from Apps.

3. Click on **Browse available countries** to select the correct chart of account, and install it:

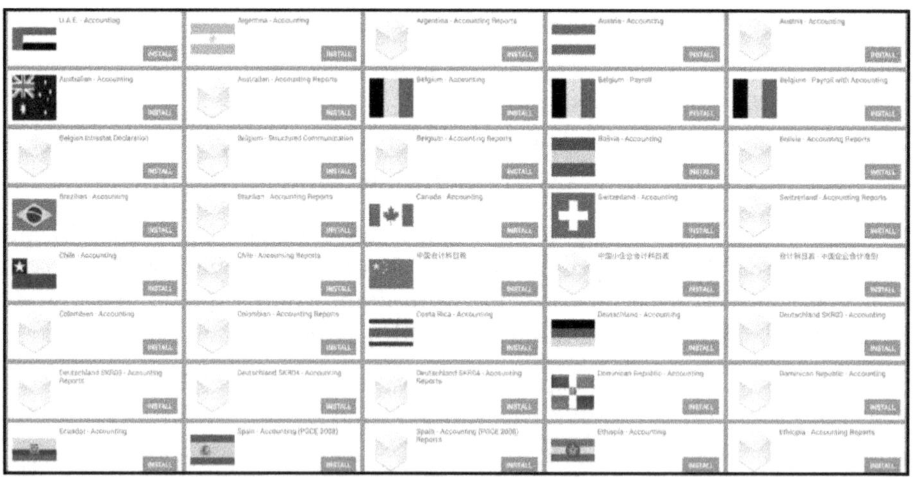

> The default chart of account is **Generic - Account**. When Odoo doesn't find the chart of account for your country, the Generic chart of account can be install.

4. As soon as the **Accounting and Finance** application is installed, verify the chart of account, which is available at **Accounting** | **Adviser** | **Chart of Accounts**. To verify the chart of account, apply **Group by** on the *Account Type* field. This is the easiest way, as we will be able to find the account by its type:

Mark as **Deprecated** if any account is not useful; click on the form view to deprecate the account.

5. If the account does not exist on the chart of account, click on the **CREATE** button to create a new account:

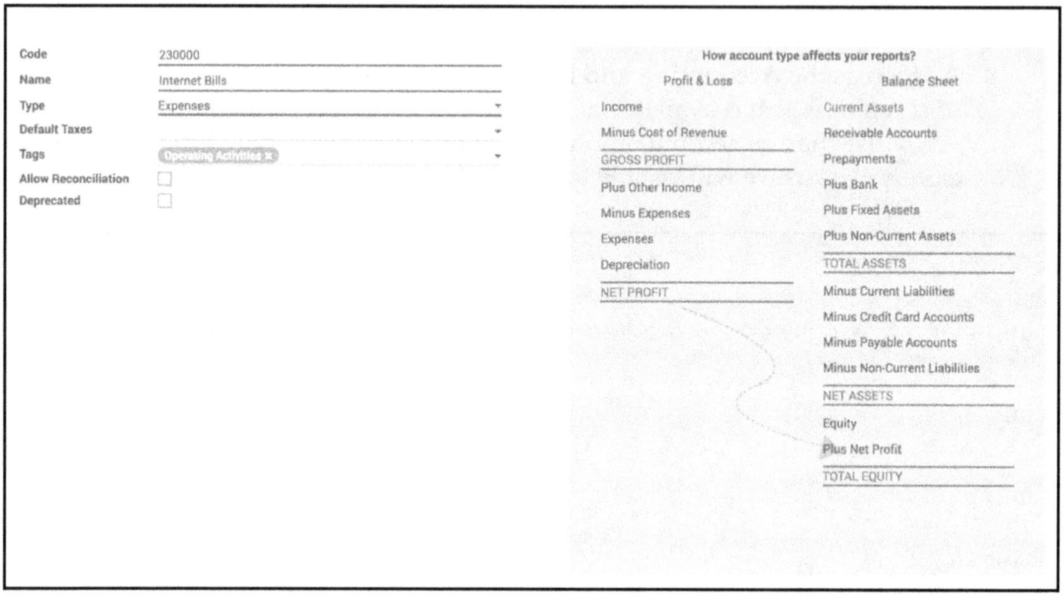

Code is an important field; the hierarchy in a chart of account can be created with the code. The following screen represents the **Current Assets** hierarchy:

	As of 01/31/2017			
	Initial Balance	Debit	Credit	Total
Class 1		$ 36,400.00		
10		$ 184,900.00		
100		$ 98,000.00		
100000 Fixed Asset Account	$ 0.00	$ 98,000.00		$ 98,000.00
101		$ 85,900.00		
101110 Stock Valuation Account	$ 0.00	$ 39,800.00		$ 39,800.00
101200 Account Receivable	$ 0.00	$ 300.00		$ 300.00
101401 Bank	$ 0.00	$ 13,000.00		$ 13,000.00
101501 Cash	$ 0.00	$ 32,800.00		$ 32,800.00
102		$ 1,000.00		
102012 Advance Rant	$ 0.00	$ 1,000.00		$ 1,000.00

Enter the name of the account; the same name will be printed on the report and depending on the type, the account will be linked to the respective heads--either to **Expense** or **Income** under the **Profit** and **Loss** account or to **Assets** or **Liability** under the balance sheet.

6. You are ready to import the opening balance for an account; an opening balance can be entered in the chart of accounts by creating a journal entry with the account and its respective balance. Look at the following sample balance sheet:

Assets			Liabilities	
Current Assets			Current Liabilities	
Cash		32,800	Accounts Payable	49,000
Accounts Receivable		300	Accrued Expenses	450
Prepaid Rent		1,000	Unearned Revenue	1,000
Inventory		39,800	Total Current Liabilities	50,450
			Long-term Liabilities	99,500
Total Current Assets		73,900	**Total Liabilities**	149,950
			Owner's Equity	
Long-term Assets			Owner's Equity	
Leasehold Improvements	100,000		Retained Earnings	11,950
Accumulated Depreciation	(2,000)	98,000	Common Stock	10,000
Total Long-term Assets		98,000	Total Owner's Equity	21,950
Total Assets:		171,900	**Total Liabilities and Owner's Equity**	171,900

Accounts Receivables and **Accounts Payables** need a ledger to identify with which customer or supplier you have outstanding receivables and payables and what will be the due date.

7. Go to **Accounting** | **Advisory** | **Journal Entry**, click on the **CREATE** button to create a new journal entry. Select the journal or keep the default miscellaneous journal, enter **OPENING** in the `Reference field`.

To create a journal item, click on the **Add an item** link on the **JOURNAL ITEMS** field. Select the account, the partner should be selected if the account is payable or receivable, enter the label, and enter the debit or credit balance.

The due date has to be set on all the journal items. Journal items which belong to accounts payable or receivable have an actual due date while other lines have the due date as the first day of the new financial year has to be set:

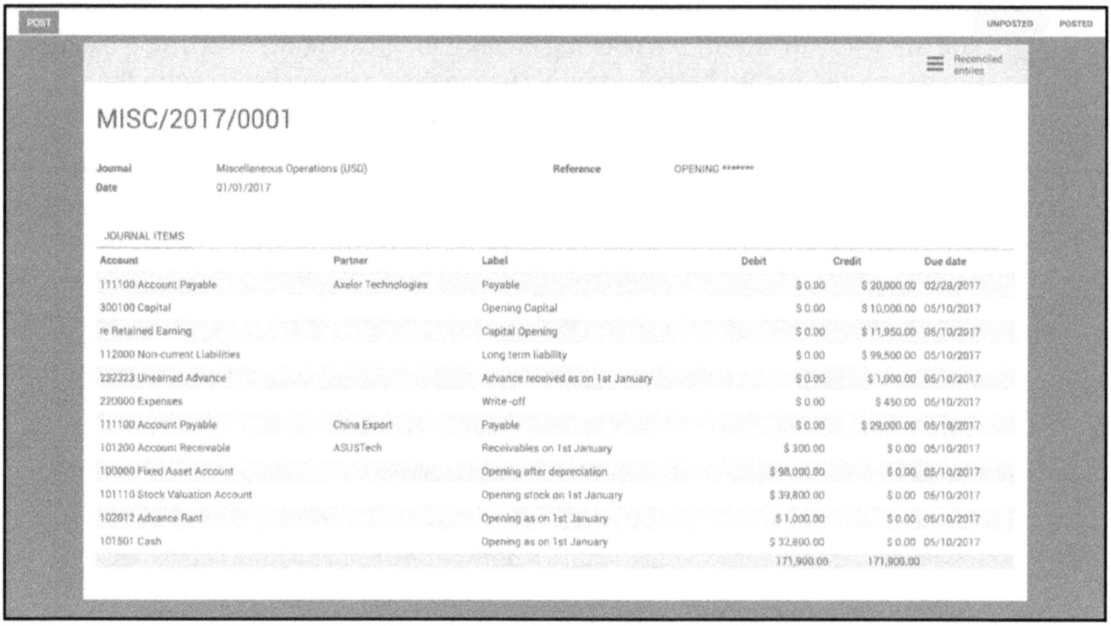

The debit total should be equal to the assets, and the credit total should be equal to the liability. Both the debit total and credit total entries should match to save the entries in Odoo. Before you post the entries, verify **Due date** for all the entries. The **Partner Aged** balance report will be computed depending on **Due date**. Click on **POST** to post the entries.

8. As soon as we post the *OPENING* journal entry, all the accounts are set with the respective opening balance; you can have the same balance in the balance sheet report. To verify the account and its balance in the balance sheet, go to **Accounting** | **Reports** | **Balance Sheet**:

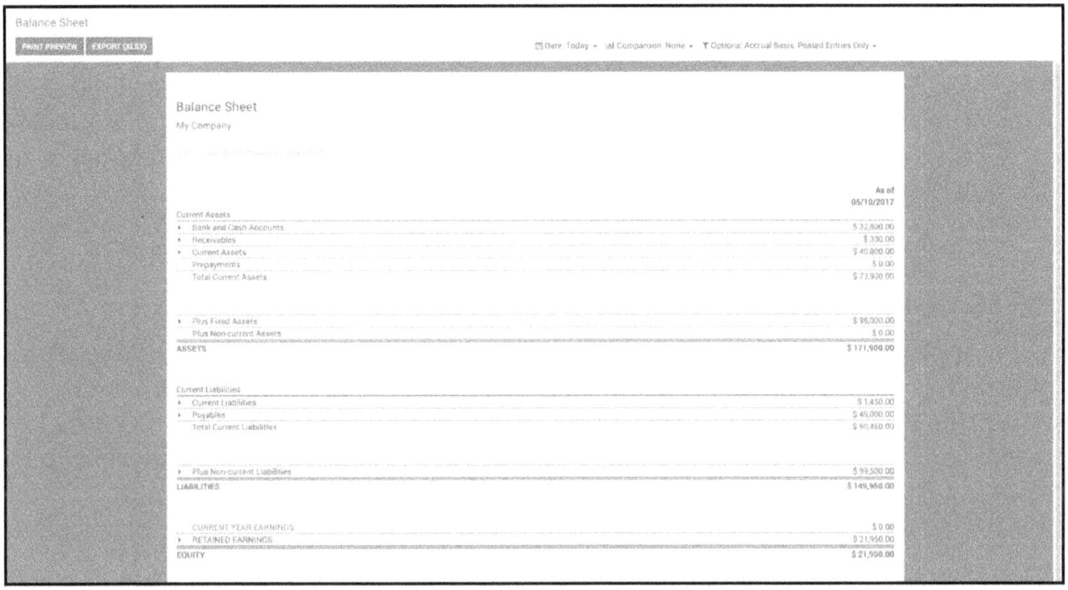

If the balance sheet printed from Odoo does not match with your balance sheet, make sure that you selected the correct account during the opening entry, and set the correct type on the account you created.

9. You are ready to start the financial year in Odoo. Before you start the transaction, let's go and check the financial year configuration. This configuration is company-specific. The **Fiscal Year Last Day** field has to be defined once, and it represents the closing month and day of the financial year:

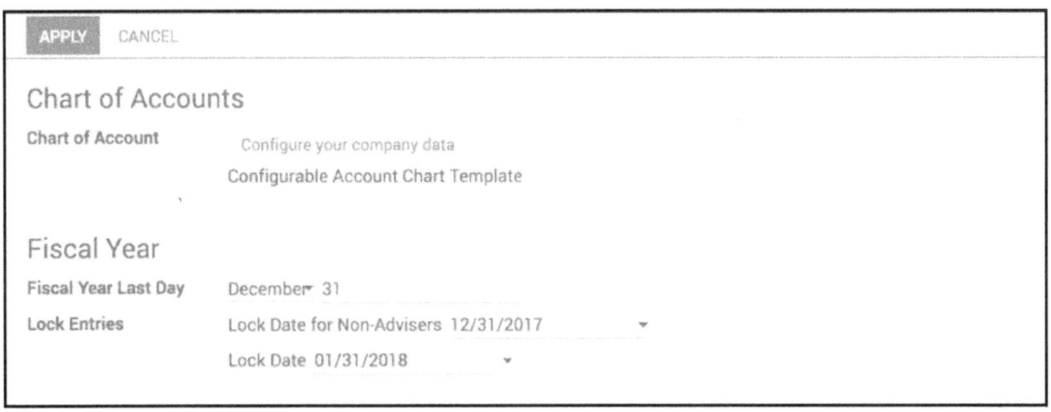

At the end of every financial year, the old accounting entries can be locked through **Configuration | Settings**. There are two different levels of locking: one for an accountant and one for an adviser. To lock an entry for the accountant, enter the date in the **Lock Date for Non-Advisers** field. The auditor can still make the modifications, and once the audit process completes you can enter **Lock Date**, which locks modification of entries before the entered dates.

There's more...

As every application has its own dashboard in Odoo, the **Accounting** application has a dashboard too. The dashboard is not available when only the **Invoicing** application is installed. The dashboard will be installed when the full-featured Financial Accounting is installed. The **Invoicing** application will be replaced by **Accounting**, and by clicking on the **Accounting** application, you can enter into the application and see the accounting dashboard.

Let's see how to configure the dashboard according to the needs of an accountant or account office. The dashboard can be configured by creating and adding the accounting journals on it or hiding the existing journals.

Odoo Localization

Getting started with Odoo online is much easier compared to Odoo onsite, as the chart of account is selected automatically depending on the country you are from. Let's say if you create an instance and select India as your country. The Indian chart of account will be installed automatically.

The account localized module contains the following configuration:

- Chart of account specific to the country
- Tax configuration and computation
- Chart of tax—used to generate the tax chart and tax report
- Localized financial reports

The localized accounting module available in the core is taken care of by the accounting team available in Odoo; they try to update the specification on every new release.

Accounting Dashboard

The default dashboard is generated based on the chart of account installed. The most common journals that can be found on the dashboard are the following:

- **Customer Invoices**
- **Vendor Bills**
- **Bank**
- **Cash**

When you remove the **Favorite** filter, you may find two more journals:

- **Exchange Difference**
- **Miscellaneous Operations**

The dashboard looks like the following screenshot:

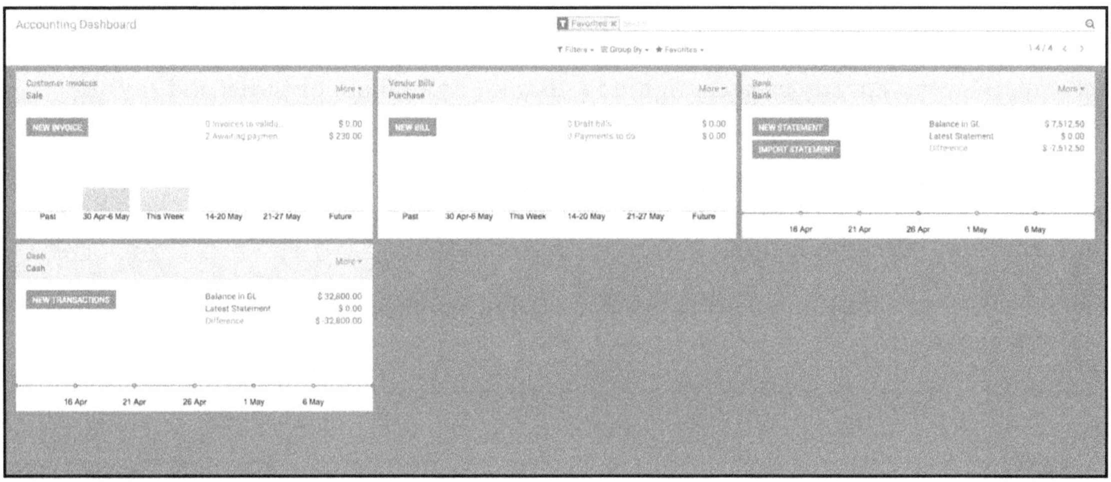

You can change the name of the journals, like **Bank** to **State Bank of India**—click on **More** | **Settings**, the form view will be opened for the journal:

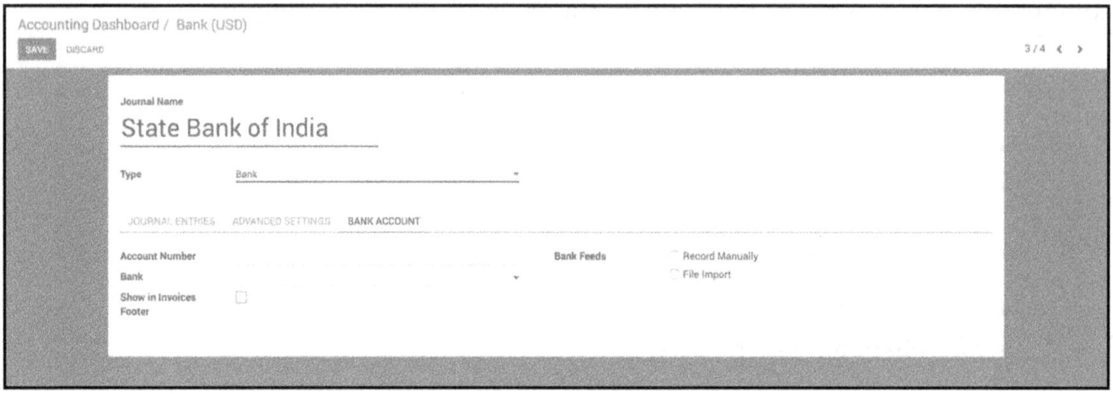

Change **Journal Name**, click on **SAVE**, and it's done. Almost all the minor needs of the company can be solved with the set of journals given as standard in Odoo online. However, if you want, you may add as many journals as needed. Let's assume your company has two accounts. One has already been configured as **Bank** | **State Bank of India**, and say, the other account is **Axis Bank**.

Go to **Accounting** | **Configuration** | **Accounting** | **Journals**. You will see the available journals; click on **CREATE** to create a new journal. Enter the minimum details asked for in the form view, select the **Type** as `Bank`, and click on **SAVE**.

The types of journals we can have in Odoo are **Sales**, **Purchase**, **Bank**, **Cash**, and **Miscellaneous**:

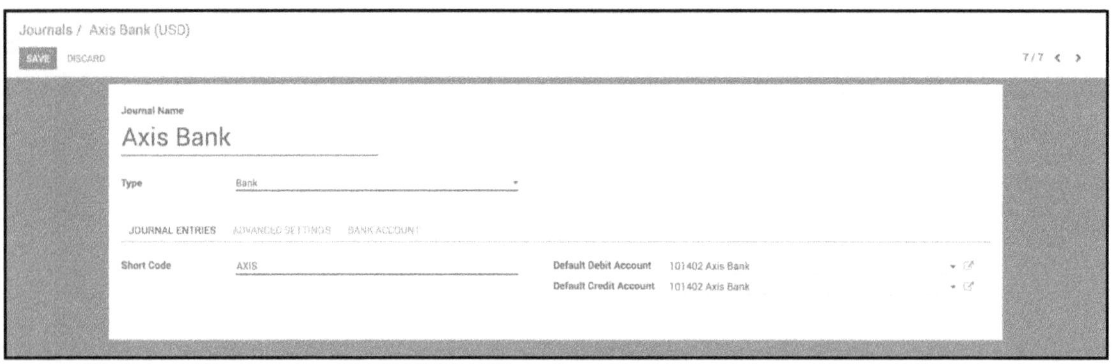

The journal created just now, will be available on **Accounting Dashboard**. If you want to remove it from the dashboard, click on the **More** button, and remove the star to hide it from the dashboard.

Bank synchronization

Depending on the types of journal, an additional setting will appear. The **BANK ACCOUNT** tab is visible when *Bank* is selected in the **Journal Type** field:

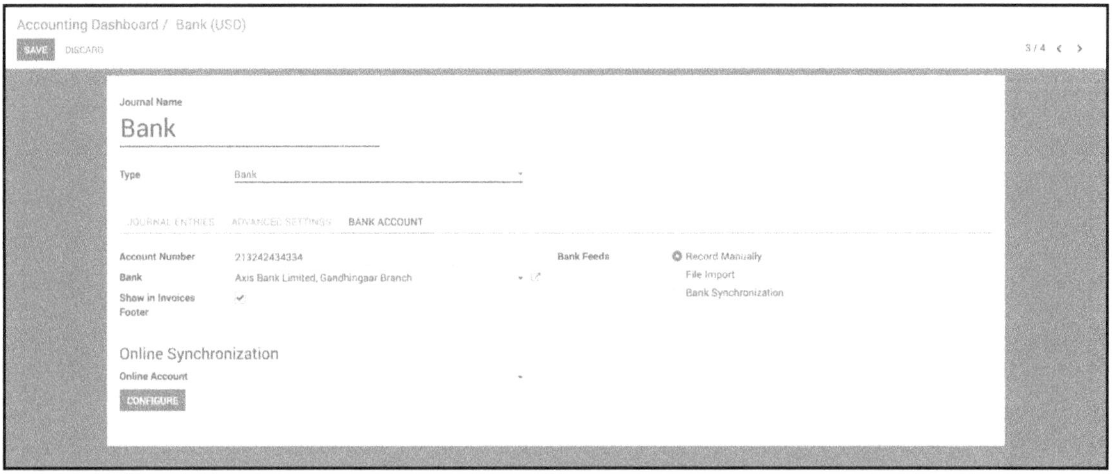

Enter **Account Number. Bank** is the address of the bank where we have our bank account. **Bank Feed** is a method by which the bank statement will be created in Odoo.

Following are the options you will see in the Bank Feed section:

- **Record Manually**: Every bank transaction is recorded manually.
- **File Import**: This imports files given by the bank; Odoo supports QIF, OFX, SEPA, and CSV.
- **Bank Synchronization**: It connects with your bank through the Yodlee bank interface. It supports 16000+ banks worldwide. Check the supported banks worldwide at `https://www.odoo.com/page/accounting-features`.

To synchronize your bank statement in Odoo, click on the **CONFIGURE** button under the **Online Synchronization** option:

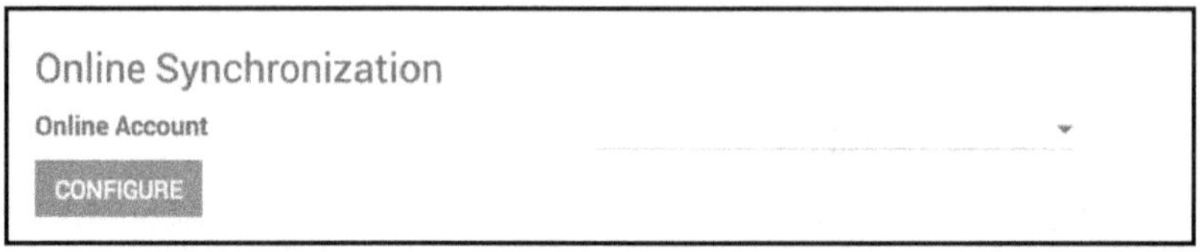

In the popup that appears, click on the link **Add a new bank to your system**, and you will get a search box to search for your bank; enter the name, and click on the search icon:

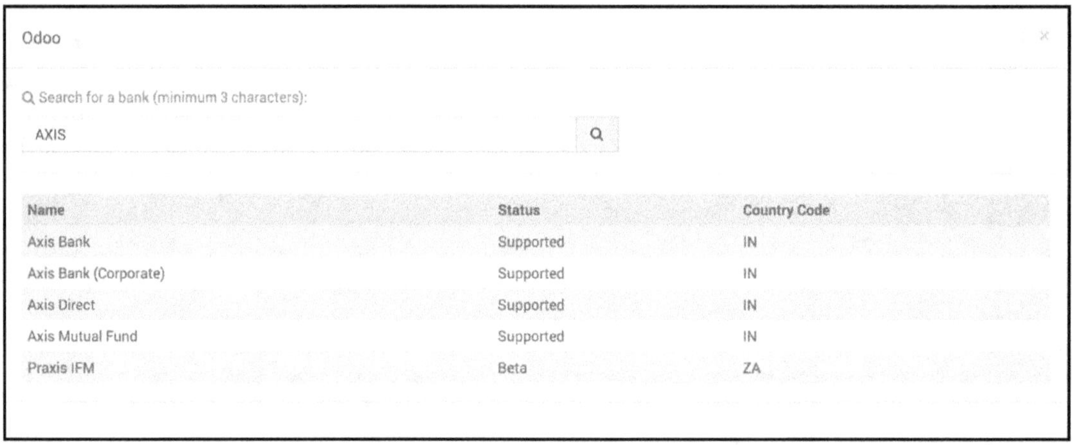

You will see the list of banks available by country. Select the bank if your bank appears in the list. Odoo will confirm the bank with you; you will be asked to enter the username, password, and other security questions. You have to pass through the bank's security system to connect to your bank. As soon as you select the bank and confirm, it will ask you for the username and password and guide you through further security checks:

On successfully passing through the security gateway, you will get access to the bank statement. The statement will be updated in Odoo periodically. We will see how to reconcile the bank statement in the recipe *Get paid through a bank or cash and reconciliation* of this chapter.

Customer invoices and payments

Odoo is a suite of business applications; those applications can either be used alone, they can be used together and work in an integrated way. The business flow is completely dependent on the number of modules installed on your instance. Let's take an example of invoicing--the invoice will be created from the sales order if the sales application is installed. However, if you have installed the subscription application, the invoice can be created from the contract too.

So, there are many different ways of creating an invoice depending on the module installed. Here are the different ways to create an invoice:

- **Sales Order | Invoice**
- **Sales Order | Delivery Order | Invoice**
- **eCommerce Order | Invoice**
- **Regular Contracts | Invoices**
- **Recurring Contracts | Invoices**

The following are the different ways to create invoices manually:

- Create a refund invoice
- Give a discount
- Modify the invoice prepared from a sales order
- Create an invoice for a non-core business

The Odoo accounting application is integrated with all the other applications you use on your instance. Let's see how you can create a direct invoice, and send it to the customer by email.

How to do it...

1. An invoice can be created either from **AccountingDashboard** or **Accounting | Sales | Customer Invoice**. You will be taken to a list of invoices. Click on the **CREATE** button to create a new invoice. As we are creating an invoice manually, we have to enter all the information such as **Customer, Invoice Lines**, and so on:

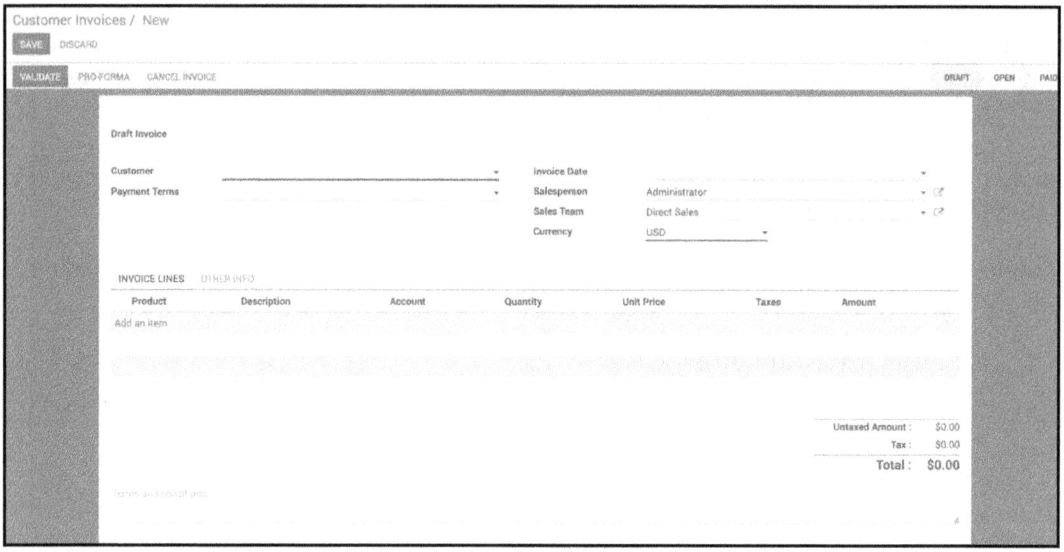

2. **Payment Term** will be filled automatically based on the customer selected on the invoice. However, that can be changed from order to order manually. To set **Payment Terms** on the customer, open the customer form view; and set the field **Customer Payment Terms** under the **ACCOUNTING** tab:

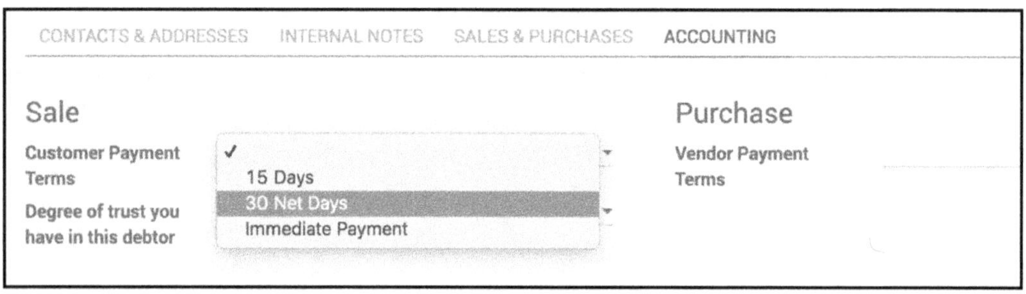

Select the option from the list of existing terms, and click on **SAVE**.

3. The currently logged user will be set in the **Salesperson** field; however, it can be changed; if the sale has to be registered for another salesperson. **Sales Team** will be set automatically, depending on **Salesman**; this can be changed too in some business cases.

   These fields are used to generate the statistical reports to measure the sales by a team or a salesman or to compute the incentives.

4. By default, **Invoice Date** is not set. It can either be set manually, or it will be set automatically when the invoice is confirmed.

   The income will be considered in the month depending on the date it was registered; **Invoice Date** will be copied to the journal entries in accounting when the invoice gets confirmed.

5. Let's create an invoice line that actually describes the invoice detailing part--it can be a product or service with **Quantity**, **Unit Price**, and **Taxes**:

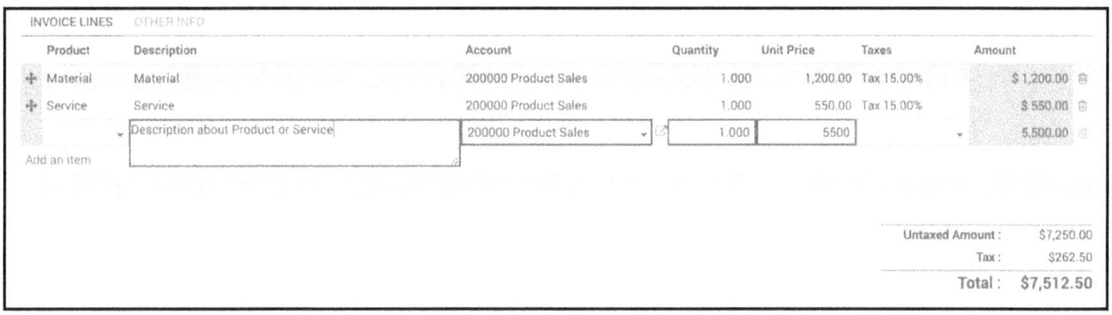

   Product is not a required field when you are working with invoices. You have to enter **Description**, **Quantity**, and **Unit Price**. The default **Account** will be selected where the income will be registered; you can change it to another account if you want the income to be registered in another account.

6. **Terms and conditions** can be defined on the invoice; look at the bottom of the invoice, you will find a textbox to enter text information. It will be printed on the invoice as it is at the end of the invoice.

7. In business, it's sometimes required to send the **PRO-FORMA** invoice before we validate the invoice. You can activate the feature that allows you to create a **PRO-FORMA** invoice from **Accounting | Configuration | Settings**. Select the option **Allow pro-forma invoices**, and click on **APPLY** to activate the feature:

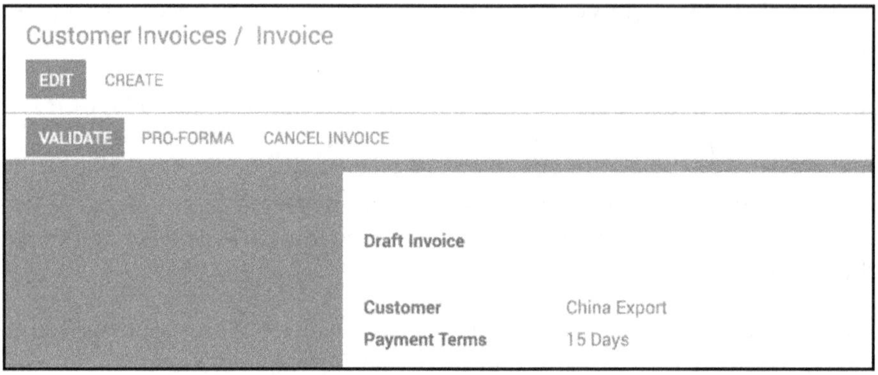

As soon as the feature is activated, you can see the button **PRO-FORMA** in **Invoice**, to create a **PRO-FORMA** invoice. Click on the button. The invoice goes to the **PRO-FORMA** state, and now you are ready to send the Pro-forma invoice to the customer:

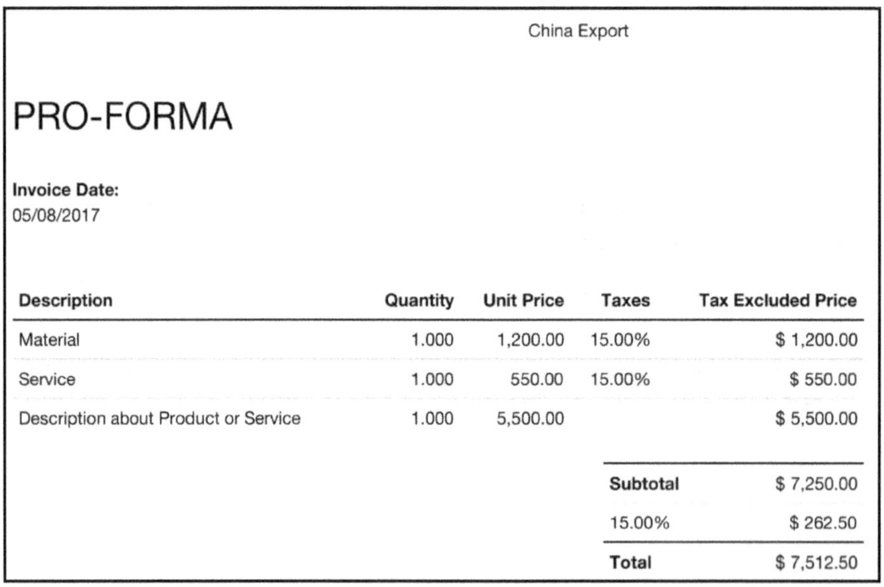

China Export

PRO-FORMA

Invoice Date:
05/08/2017

Description	Quantity	Unit Price	Taxes	Tax Excluded Price
Material	1.000	1,200.00	15.00%	$ 1,200.00
Service	1.000	550.00	15.00%	$ 550.00
Description about Product or Service	1.000	5,500.00		$ 5,500.00

Subtotal	$ 7,250.00
15.00%	$ 262.50
Total	$ 7,512.50

8. The invoice can be confirmed before we send it to the customer; click on the **VALIDATE** button to confirm the invoice. The invoice number will be generated as soon as the invoice gets confirmed. You can print the invoice and send it to the customer. Here is the final invoice ready to print and send to the customer either by courier or by email:

The value of the **Amount Due** field is computed as soon as you confirm the invoice. It is equal to the difference between the total of the invoice and the payment received against the invoice.

You can send the invoice to the customer by clicking on **SEND BY EMAIL** or print the invoice by clicking on the **PRINT** button.

9. Let's assume that the customer pays the invoice by check; you can register the check payment by clicking on **REGISTER PAYMENT**. A pop-up wizard will appear, and ask you to fill the payment information:

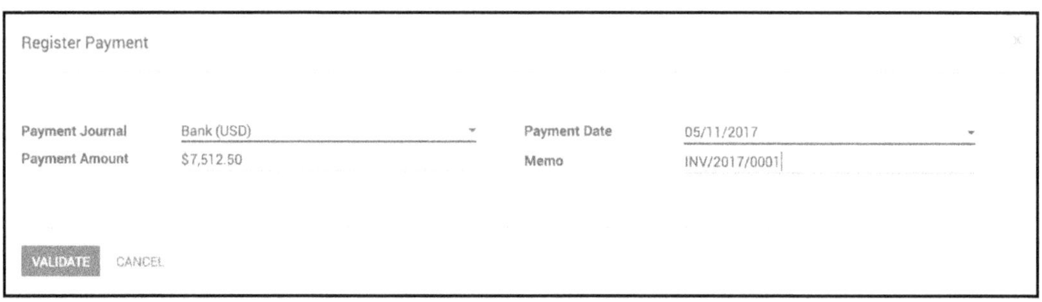

Select *Bank (USD)* in the **Payment Journal** field, **Payment Amount** will be the amount written on the check, **Payment Date** will be the date mentioned on the check, and the **Memo** field can be the free text where you can enter the check number along with the invoice number. Click on **VALIDATE** to register the payment:

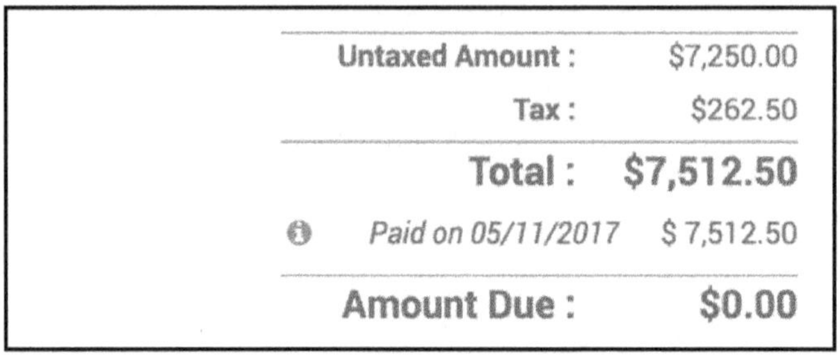

As soon as the payment is registered, the payment details are updated on the invoice, and **Amount Due** has computed again before the invoice goes to the **PAID** state, as in the preceding screen.

There's more...

Customer invoice is a way more simplified way to create a sales entry in the sales book. Creating an invoice is faster than writing journal entries into the sales journal where you have to compute the different lines by **Due Date** based on **Payment Terms**. Let's look at this in detail.

Payment Terms

The payment term is a time period that is used to define and calculate payment instalments and their respective dates, that is, 50 percent in advance and the balance in 30 days means that the customer has to pay 50 percent on confirmation of invoice and the remaining 50 percent within 30 days from the date of invoice.

The payment terms can be created from **Accounting** | **Configuration** | **Management** | **Payment Terms**. You will see the default payment terms available: **15 Days**, **30 Net Days**, and **Immediate Payment**. Let's create a new payment term, `50% Immediate, Balance after 30 Days`; click on the **CREATE** button:

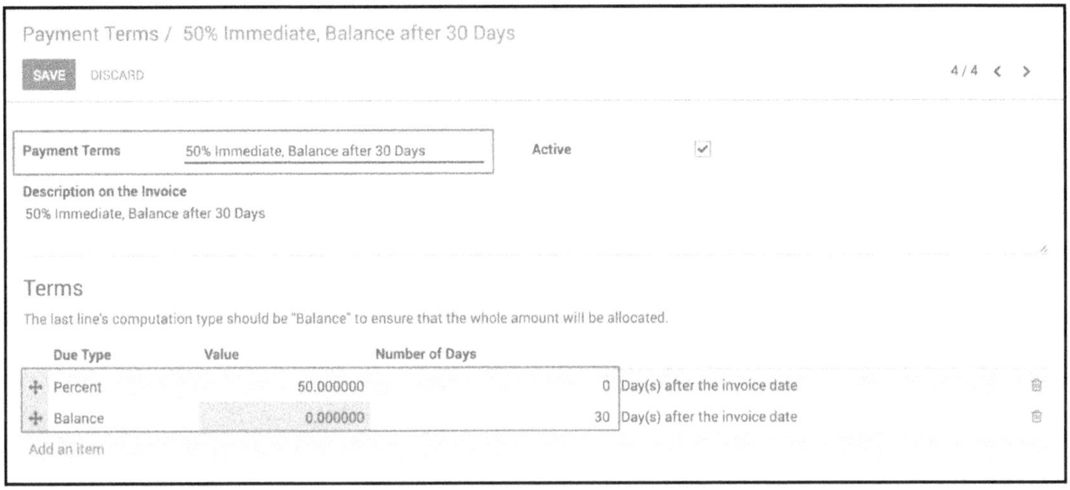

Enter `50% Immediate, Balance after 30 Days` in the **Payment Terms**. Enter clear payment terms information in **Description on the Invoice**; it will be visible on the invoice.

There is a default line with the label **Balance**, **Value** is `0.0000`, **Number of Days** is `0`, **Day(s) after the invoice date**. Click to edit the default line to label **Balance**, keep Balance selected in **Type**, and enter `30` in the **Number of Days** field. The last date will be computed based on this line to clear the full payment.

To compute the date for 50 percent immediate payment, let's create a new line; by clicking on **Add an item.** A popup will appear as follows:

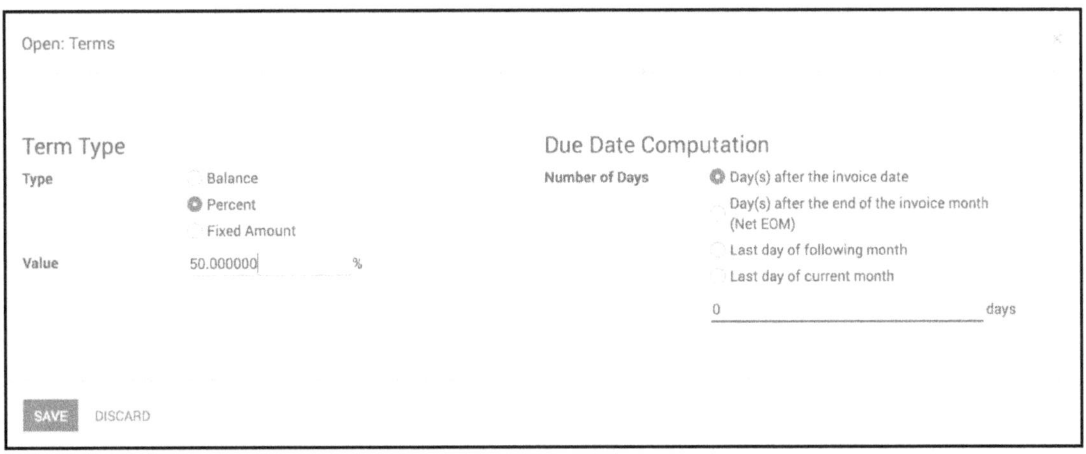

Select **Percent** in the **Type** section set it to `50.000000`% in the **Value** field, keep the option **Day(s) after the invoice date** selected for **Number of Days**, and `0` in **days**. Click on **SAVE** to create a new line:

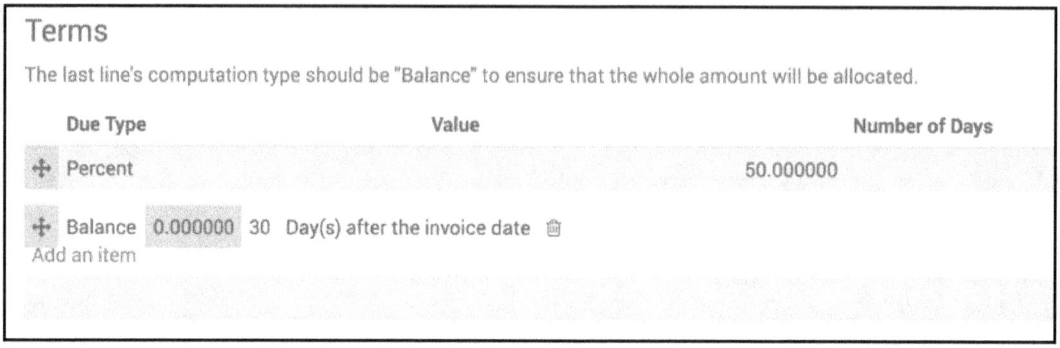

The new line will be added after the **Balance** line. When you try to SAVE you might get a warning message as follows:

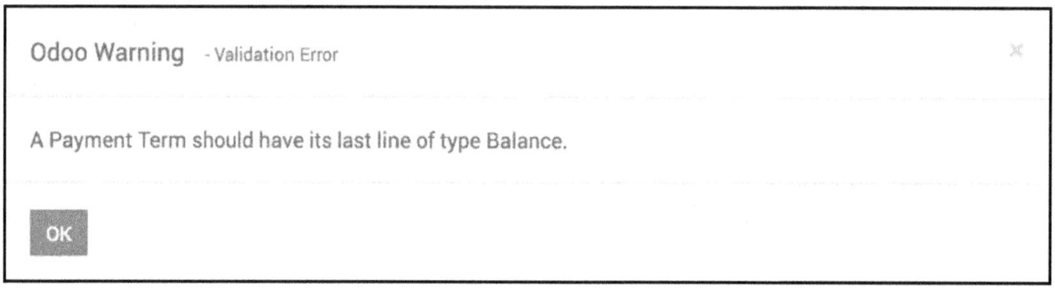

Use the sequence handler to arrange the order of the payment terms line, and save **Payment term**.

The payment term is ready to use; you can set this payment term on the customer, or directly use it on the invoice; let's check how this works. Create an invoice and select the payment term. Change the **Invoice Date** to *1st May 2017*, and confirm the invoice.

As soon as you confirm the invoice, the accounting line will be created with respect to the payment term selected on the invoice. It computes two installments with their due dates to clear the payment base on the invoice date, that is, *1st May 2017*. You can go to the accounting entries linked to the invoice from the **OTHER INFO** tab:

Click on the **Journal Entry** link *INV/2017/0002*; you will be directed to the journal entries created for the invoice, as seen in the following screenshot:

A total sum of 115 $ is receivable from the customer, where 50 percent of the amount should be paid on the same day of generating the invoice, and 50 percent within 30 days.

Payment follow-ups

As soon as you allow your customer to pay later or in installments, you have to keep track of the dates by which your debt will get cleared. Odoo has a feature that can help you to track and follow up the payments. The follow-up can be manual or automatic. The payment follow-up feature can be activated from **Accounting** | **Configuration** | **Settings**:

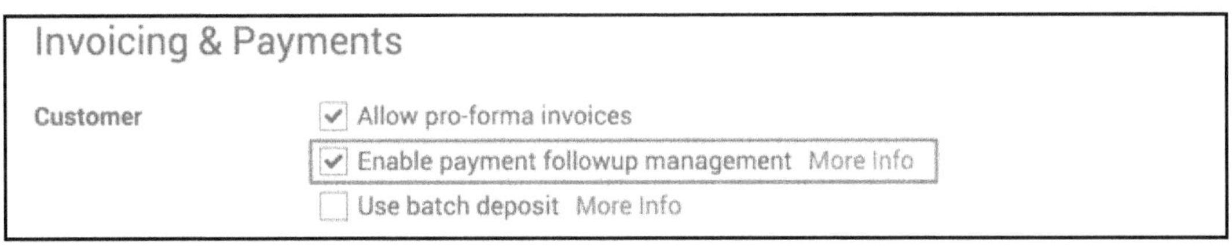

Search for `Enable payment followup management`, under the **Invoicing & Payment** section, select it and click on the **APPLY** button.

To check the receivables from the customer by invoices, go to **Accounting** | **Sales** | **Customers Statement**, where you will see the customers with the list of invoices waiting for payments.

> If you do not find any customers in the **Customer Statement**, it means that none of your customers have an overdue invoice to pay.

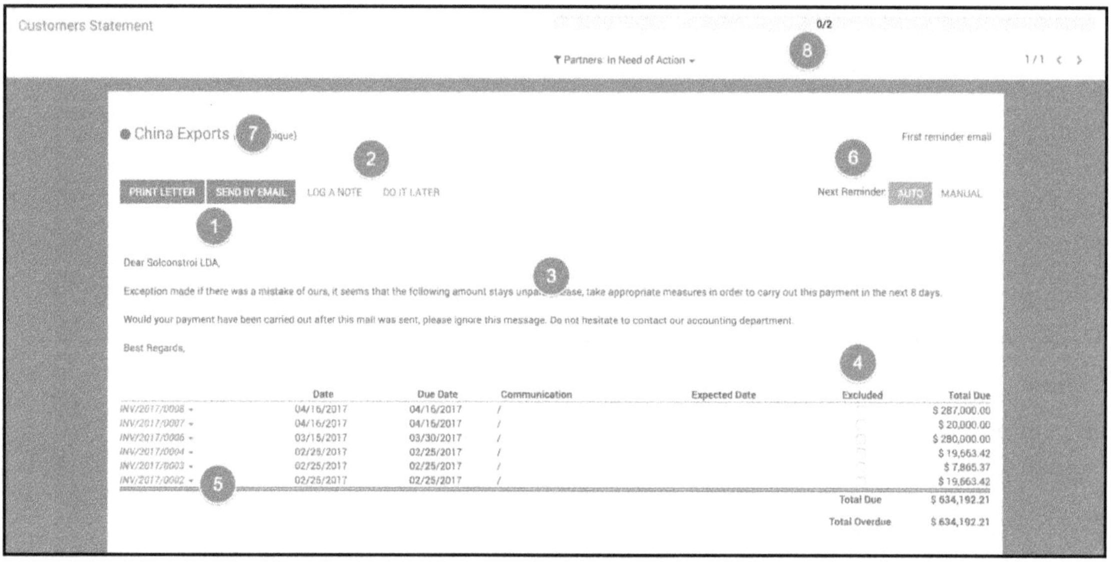

The **Customers Statement** has a nice interface; it is integrated with many business processes such as sending a reminder email, printing a letter, making a note of the customer or invoice regarding payment follow-ups. These are the options available to you:

1. You can either print the follow-up letter or send it by email. Do not forget to select the list of invoices given to include in the follow-up letter or email.
2. You can click on the **LOG A NOTE** button; a popup will appear from where you can choose a quick date until which no follow-ups will be initiated by clicking on **ONE WEEK**, **TWO WEEKS**, **ONE MONTH**, or **TWO MONTHS**:

Enter a reason or commitment given by the customer to clear the dues in **Note** field and click on the **SAVE** button to save it. This will create a chatter history on the customer form view.

3. You can customize the follow-up message; click on the pencil icon to change the message text.
4. Select the list of invoices to be excluded in the follow-up email or printed letter.
5. If you would like to make a note on an individual invoice or mention the expected date to receive the payment, you can open the details of the invoice or journal entries:

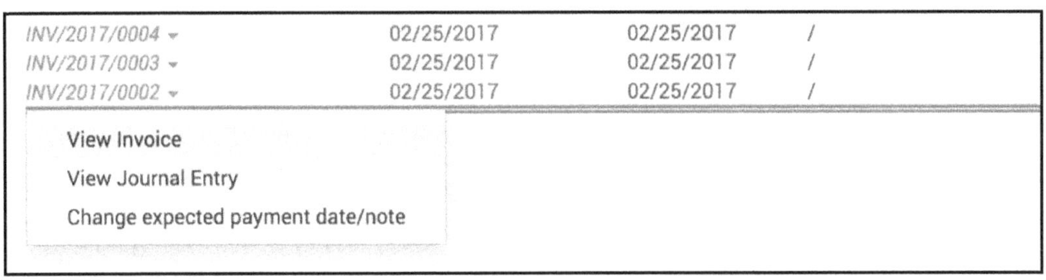

6. You can set the next follow-up mode; it can be set to **MANUAL** or **AUTO**. If set to manual, this will appear in the **Customer Statement**, we have to do the follow-up manually, else an email will be sent automatically when it's set to **AUTO**.
7. You can set the customer status beside the name of the customer:

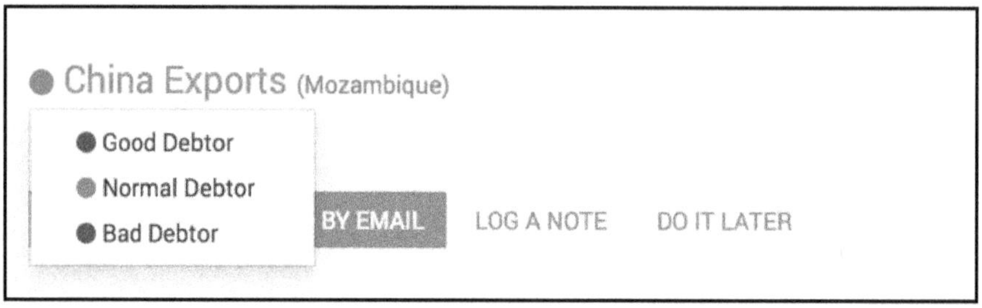

Choose the customer status; this will help you to recognize the customer level during the follow-up and in the future sales.

8. The progress bar shows you the number of follow-ups that are yet to be done, and the number of follow-ups completed.

The follow-up activity done for the customer or for an individual invoice are registered on the customer and invoice under the chatter.

Get paid through a bank or cash and reconciliation

Getting a payment and keeping track of which invoice the payment is received against, is complex stuff to manage. A customer may make a partial payment pay partial invoice, or pay an invoice in advance. The payment can be received through the bank or as cash. There are many combinations of the payment processing system. Odoo is capable of managing all such business cases out of the box using the Bank or Cash statement.

Let's see how easy it is to manage the statement; for the bank or cash. Create a statement, encode the entries, match the statement with the bank or cash balance, reconcile the entries with the outstanding, and close the statement at the end.

Getting ready

Bank or Cash are managed in Odoo by statements, for the bank transactions, the bank will be provided by a statement that has to be matched with the statement prepared in Odoo. In the statement, you have an opening balance list of transactions (debit or credit), and at the end, you have a closing balance. Usually, we receive a statement from the bank every month or whenever we have requested to receive the statement. With Odoo, we can manage a statement by month, half month, week or a day, depending on what you want.

We assume that you are ready with the Journals in Odoo as per the list of banks you have. For each bank, you have to decide how to import the statement. If you choose the statement synchronization from the bank, it would be an excellent option, as the statement will be imported automatically in Odoo.

If your bank is not available in the bank synchronization in Odoo, try to check the formats are given by the bank as an importable bank statement in Odoo. Odoo supports the QIF, OFX, SEPA, and CSV formats to import the bank statement.

Go for manual statement encoding when your bank does not support any of the automatic methods, such as synchronization, or import the statement.

How to do it...

1. Open **Accounting Dashboard**, you will see all the journals that we have created: **State Bank of India** and **Axis Bank**:

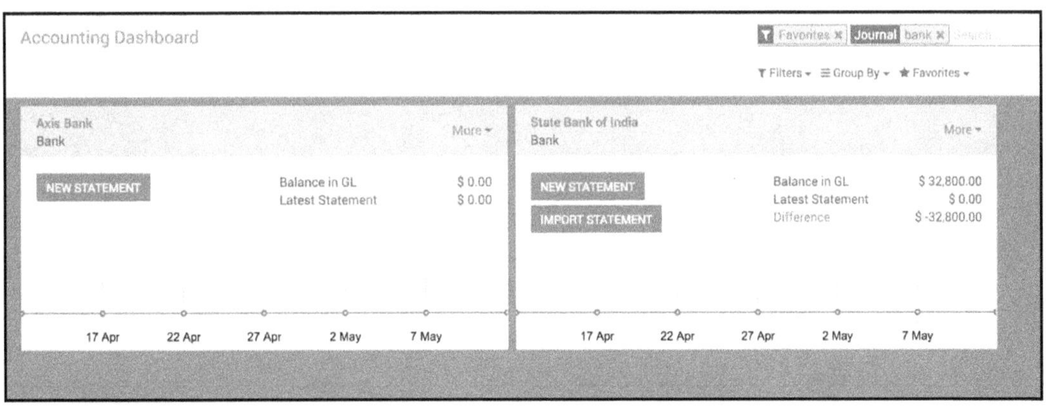

The Axis Bank journal is newly created, and we do not have a balance initialized in the Odoo journal. But for **State Bank of India**, we have initialized the balance in the opening entries. This is the reason behind the difference of **32,800** which you can see in the preceding screenshot.

There are two balances displayed in the Bank or Cash journals: **Balance in Ledger** and balance according to the **Last Statement**:

- **Balance in GL**: 32,800
- **Last Statement**: 0

This means that the statement is not yet initialized with the balance. Let's initialize the statement with the balance as per the General Ledger.

2. Click on the **NEW STATEMENT** button to create a new bank statement; the default configuration on the bank journal to **Feed Statement** is set to **Manual**. Enter the following values on the new statement created:
    - **Reference**: January 2017 (first statement in the new financial year)
    - **Date**: 1st January 2017
    - **Starting Balance**: 32,800
3. The **Starting Balance** field has to be initialized only once when you move to Odoo. From the next statement, the closing balance of the last statement will be carried forward as an opening balance in the new statement:

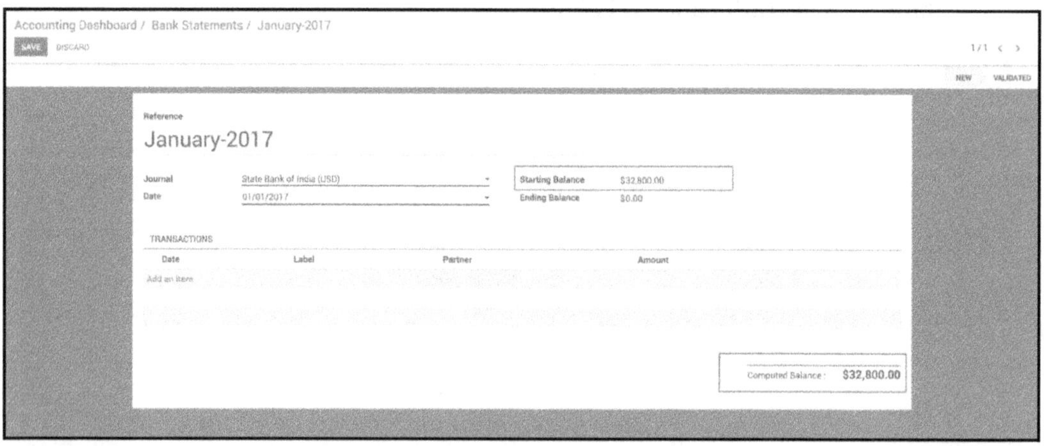

When you go back to **Accounting Dashboard**, you can see now there is no difference anymore, and both the balances match.

4. Let's assume that in order to open a new account, we have to issue a check from **State Bank of India** to **Axis bank**. It will be an internal transfer from one bank to another bank. Click on the **More** option in the **State Bank of India** journal:

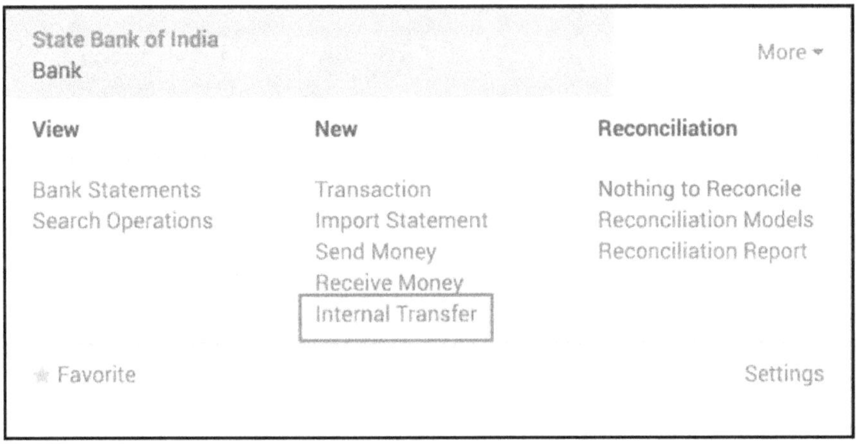

The next step is to make **Internal Transfer** from **State Bank of India** to **Axis Bank**:

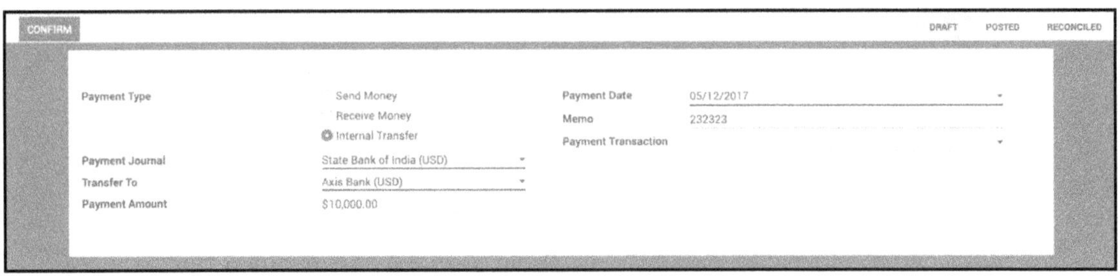

5. The transfer form is easy to understand--in **Payment Journal**, select **State Bank (USD)**, and in **Transfer To**, select **Axis Bank (USD).** Enter the amount and **Memo** for reference. Click on the **CONFIRM** button to confirm the internal transfer:

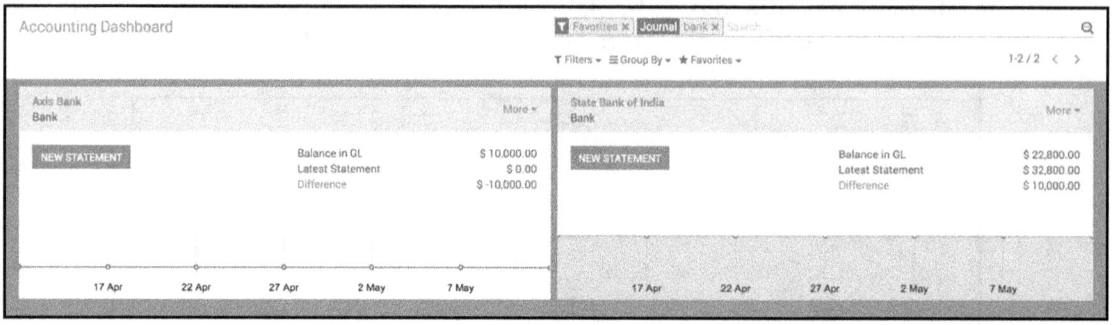

6. The difference is visible in both the bank journals. The **General Ledger** is updated in both the banks, but the latest statement has to be updated in both the banks. Create a statement in both the banks. In **State Bank of India**, enter the negative amount, which indicates withdrawal:

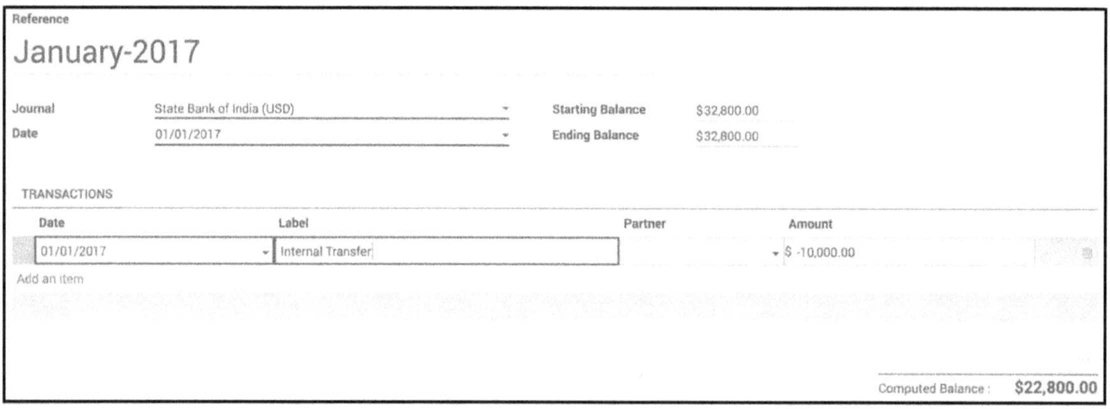

7. Create a statement for **Axis bank**--for the **Internal Transfer** label, the amount will be + `10,000`. As soon as you create the statement for Axis bank, the balance problem will be solved for both the bank accounts. The remaining part would be reconciling the statement:

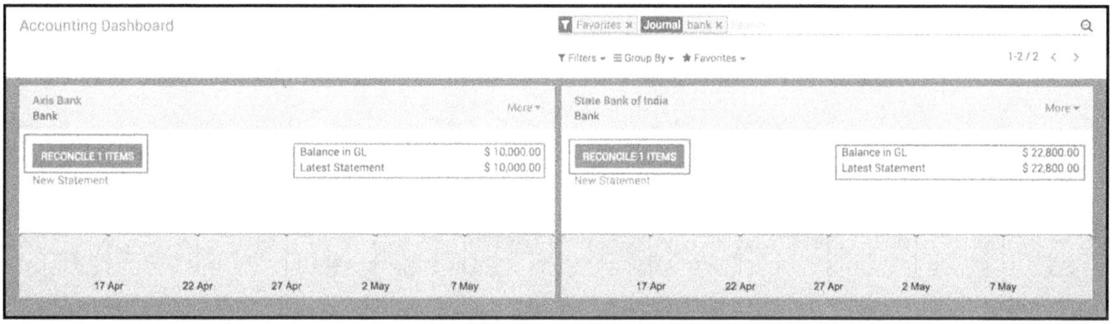

8. Click on the **RECONCILE 1 ITEMS** button to reconcile the bank statement; the reconciliation can be started with any bank, either Axis or **State Bank**, that is, the order of reconciliation can be anything. Let's initiate the reconciliation process for Axis bank:

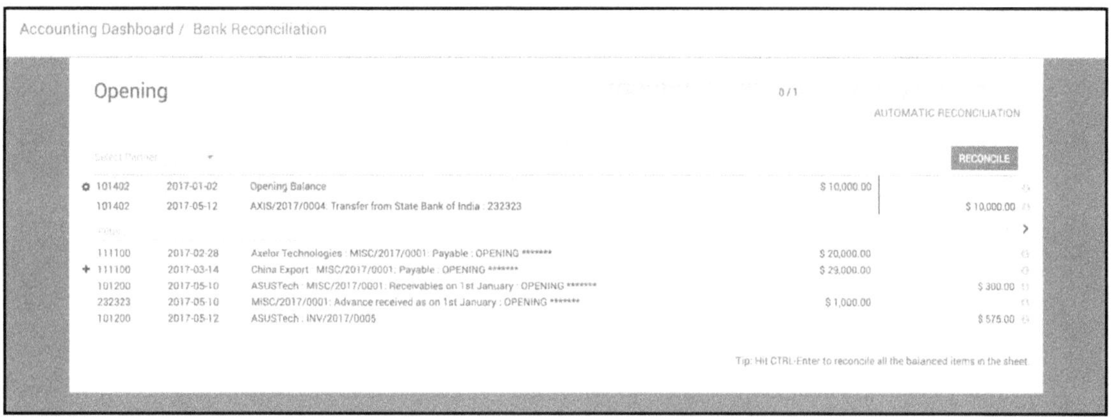

The matching entries will be selected automatically, and ask you to process and reconcile the line. Click on the **RECONCILE** button to process it:

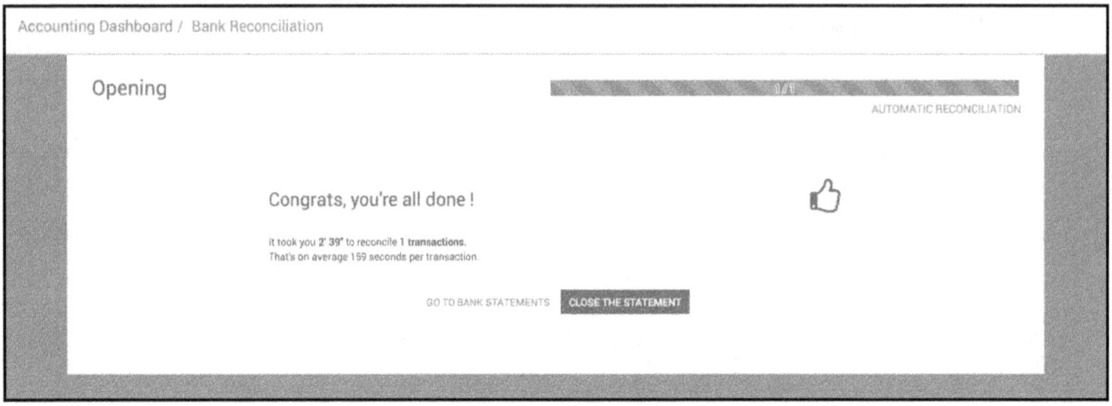

Do the same for State Bank. This is the easiest way to make an internal transfer between bank or cash accounts; you can also make a transfer between a bank and petty cash.

9. Let's assume that you receive a check from a customer, **China Export**, against an invoice waiting for payment. You can record a check before you deposit it into the bank. To record the check receipt, go to **Accounting** | **Sales** | **Payments**, and create a new customer payment:

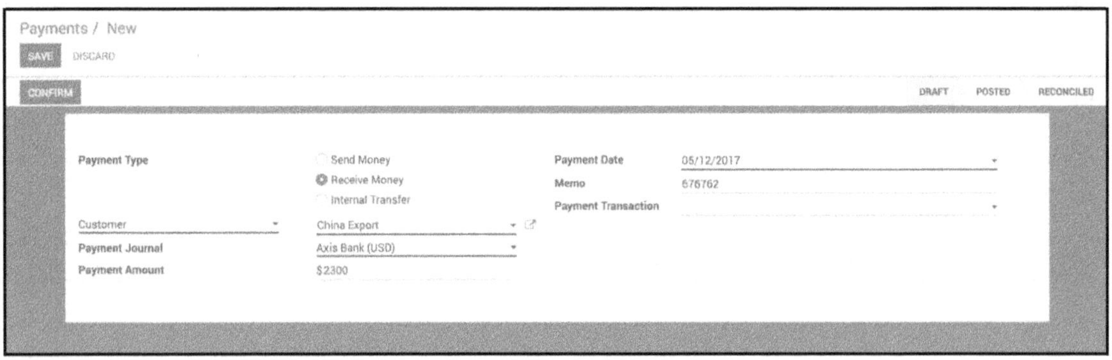

By default, the **Receive Money** option is selected for the field **Payment Type**; select the customer, choose the bank in which you are going to deposit this check, enter the check number in the **Memo** field for future reference, and enter the check amount.

10. As soon as you click on the **CONFIRM** button, the General Ledger will be updated, and you will have a difference between **Balance as per the General Ledger** and **Balance as per the Statement**:

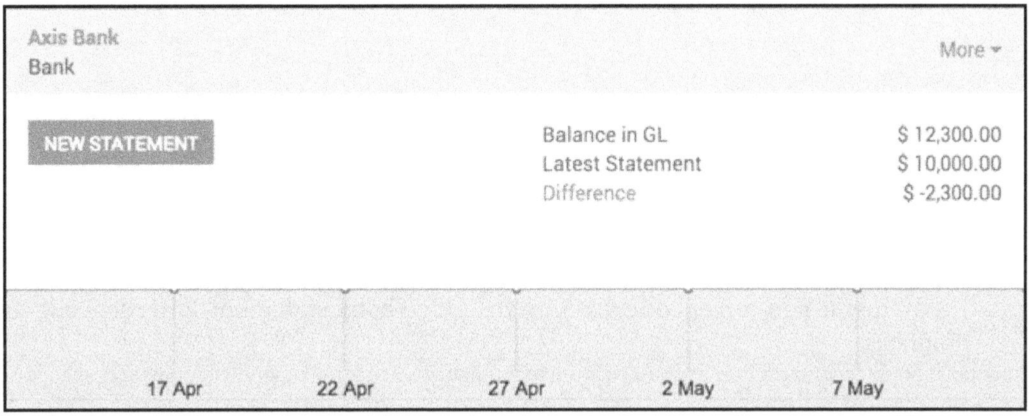

11. Periodically, you have to check for **Manual Invoices & Payments Matching**, the payment received by check should match with the invoices waiting for the money. You can run the process from **Accounting** | **Adviser** | **Manual Payments & Invoices Matching**. You can use **AUTOMATIC RECONCILIATION** when the payment and invoice amount match. When most of the customers pay exactly the same as the invoice amount, it is quite convenient to match automatically. When you receive a different amount compared to that on the invoice, you have to match them manually:

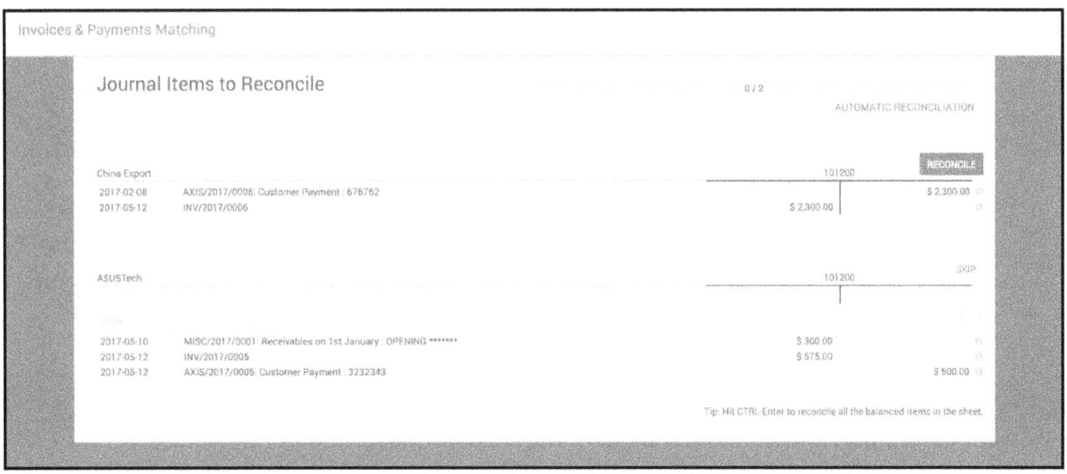

12. Reconcile manually and match the entries. On successful reconciliation of the check with the invoice, you will find that most of the invoices go to the paid stage where the full amount is received:

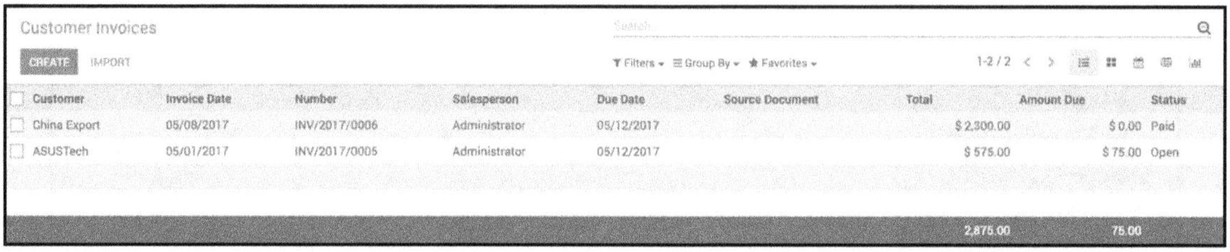

13. On the next day, the checks get cleared and this is reflected in the bank online statement. You can encode this into the Odoo bank statement, and reconcile those entries:

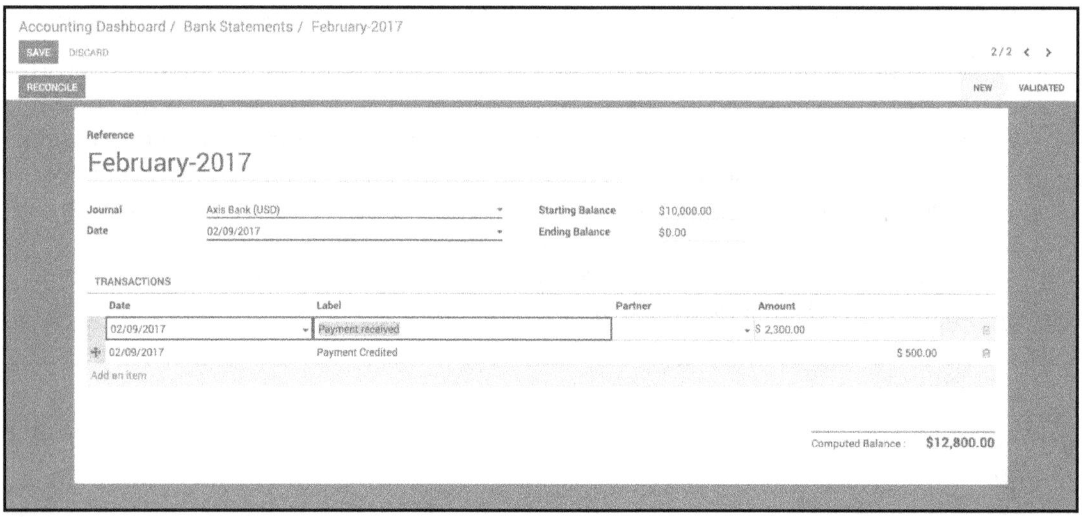

14. If you get the name of the customer, enter it on the statement line, otherwise, leave that blank—Odoo is smart enough to identify the correct entry and match automatically. Click on the **RECONCILE** button to actually reconcile the bank check and payment received in the bank:

15. You can go for **AUTOMATIC RECONCILIATION** as, most of the time, checks deposited in the bank are cleared with the same amount. So, it will be easy for you and Odoo to match the entries automatically:

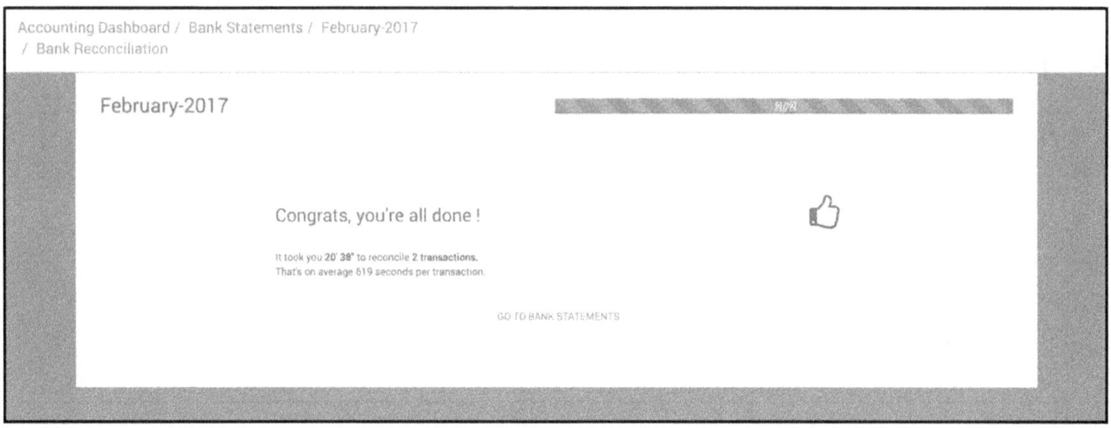

That's done. All the entries are matched, and if you check the status of the invoice, the payment goes to both paid and reconciled respectively.

16. You can click on **GO TO BANK STATEMENT**, and enter the closing balance as per the bank statement. Your computed closing balance and, theoretically, the closing balance should match—you can validate the statement when both match. Click on the **VALIDATE** button to validate the statement.

There's more...

Working with bank statements is super easy with the Odoo bank statement. When you work with the manual feeding of statements, you have to enter each and every entry manually to the statement. You can import the statement given by the bank in any of the Odoo-supported formats. The reconciliation process is the same as we have just been through; the only benefit is that the accountant does not have to encode the statement manually.

Import Bank Statement

Check with your bank to download the bank statement in a digital format such as CSV, QFX or QIF. Once you get the statement file, check at Odoo supports the file format to import as a bank statement or not. Go to **Configuration & Settings** page under the **Accounting** application and check under the available import formats under the **Bank & Cash** section:

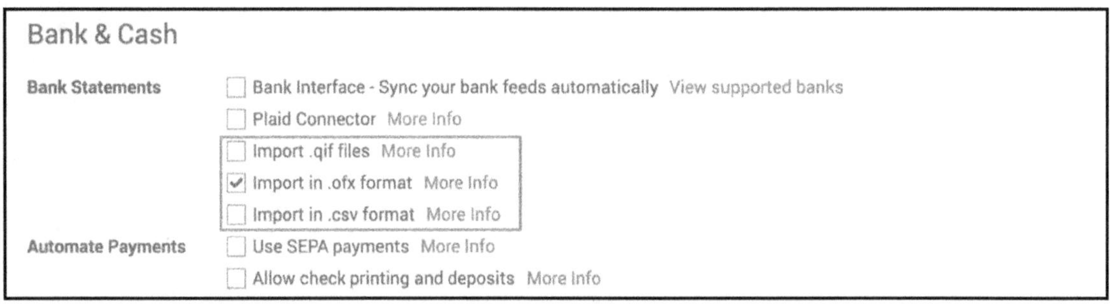

Odoo supports QIF, QFX, and CSV file formats. Select the appropriate format and activate the feature by clicking on the **APPLY** button on the setting page. You are ready to import bank statements in Odoo. Let's see how to import it, match the entries and reconcile.

1. Go to **Accounting Dashboard**, and click on the **More** option on the bank journal to import the statement:

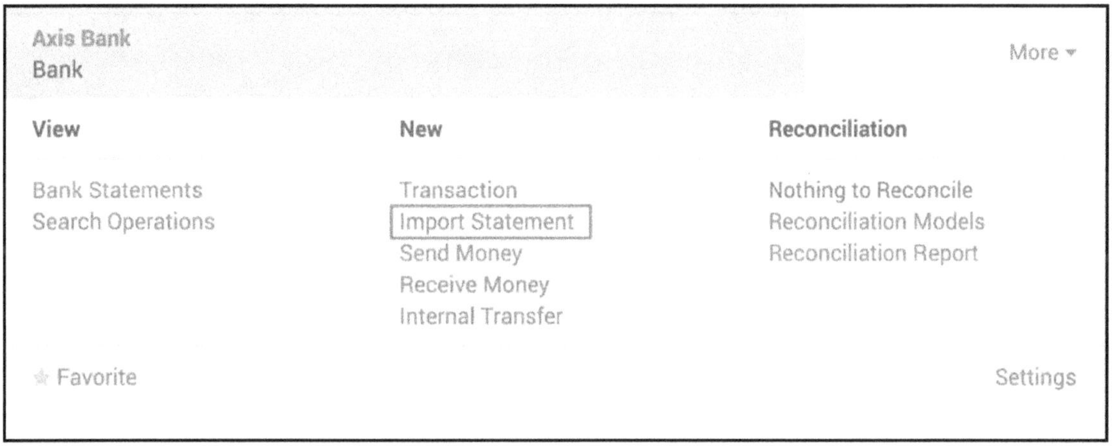

2. Click on **Import Statement**. A popup wizard will appear and ask you to select the file to upload, as seen in the following screenshot:

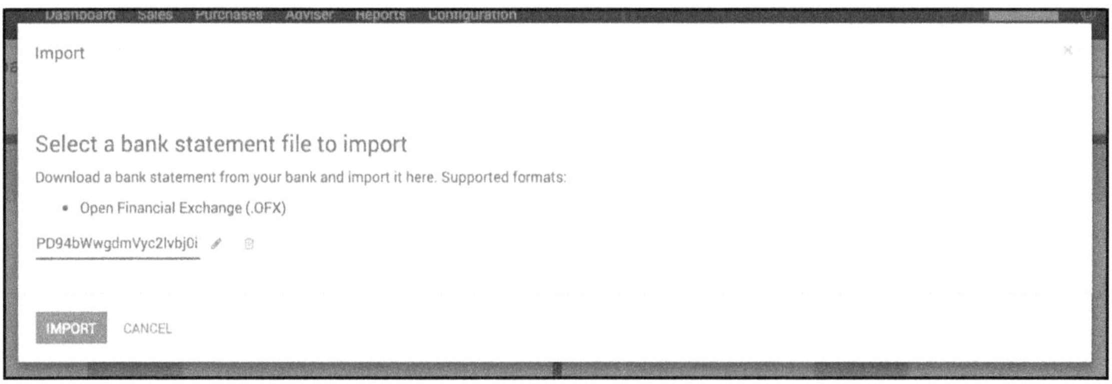

3. Click on **UPLOAD YOUR FILE**, select the file, and click on the **IMPORT** button. As soon as the file is imported to Odoo, it will create new statement import entries and process the reconciliation. You will be taken to the **Bank Reconciliation** page. Most of the entries match automatically, and in those few entries where the partner does not match, like bank charges, review the entries and click on the **RECONCILE** button for each entry:

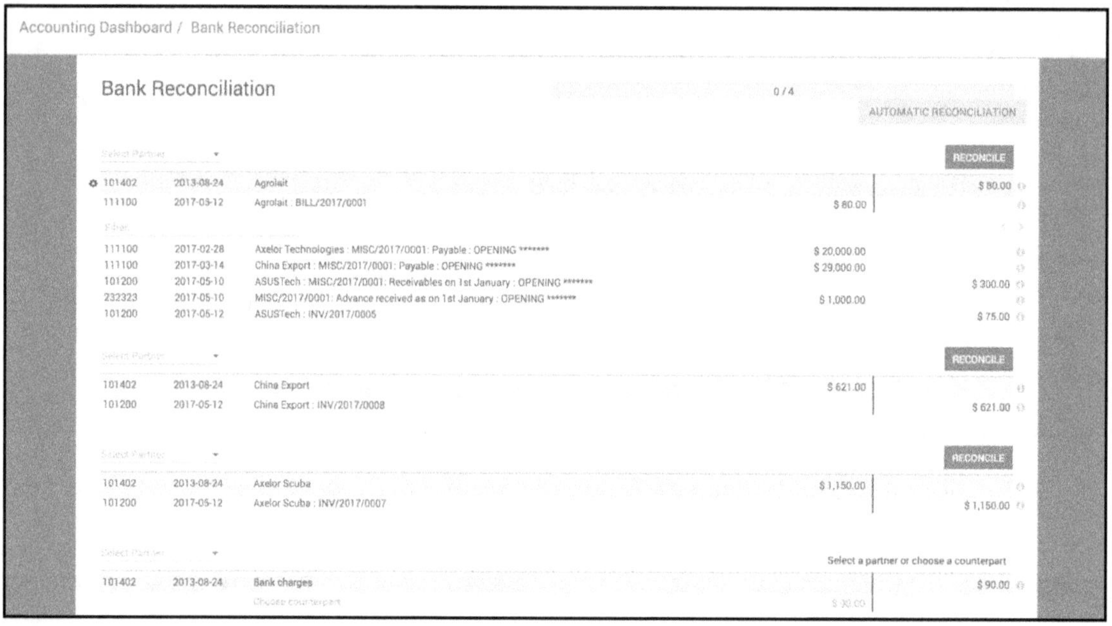

Fixing the counterpart manually

Sometimes, Odoo is not able to identify the counterpart entry for the payment received or deducted in the bank, for example, bank charges or customer advance, without notification.

You can actually define the counterpart during the reconciliation process. Every time you have to click on **Choose Counterpart**, the entry form will appear with some fields like **Account**, **Label**, **Amount**, and **Tax**.

Select the correct account for the counterpart--in our case, **Bank Charges** is an expense so the **Expense** account is selected in counterpart:

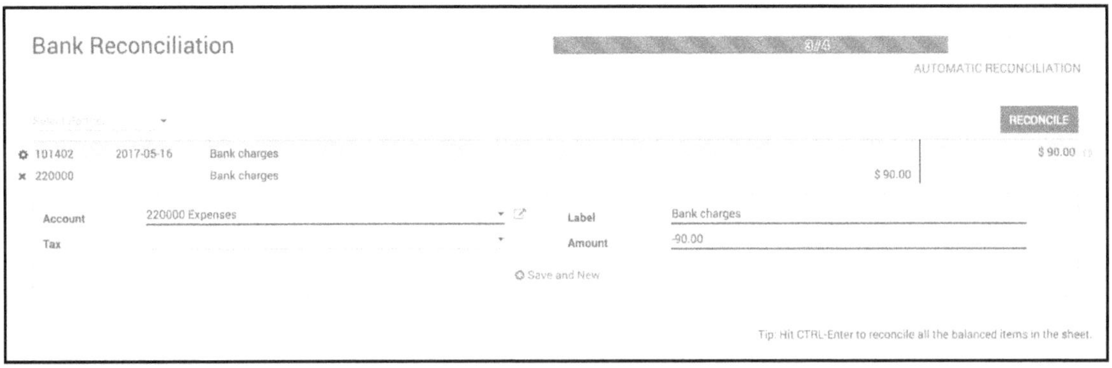

Click on the **RECONCILE** button, an entry will be created for the expense, and that will be reconciled with the bank charges.

Advance payment and invoicing

Sometimes in business, you may receive a payment in advance from a customer, or you may have to pay an advance to your vendors before you place an order. As soon as you receive the payment in the bank, create a bank statement and reconcile it, as it is a payment in advance from the customer; don't select the counterpart at reconciliation.

When you have a partner linked to the entry without a counterpart, you will get the **VALIDATE** button instead of the **RECONCILE** button. Click on the **VALIDATE** button to process those entries; that will be considered as an advance from the customer or to the vendors. Let's take an example where I receive `5000` from **China Export** as an advance. Now take a look at the following screenshot:

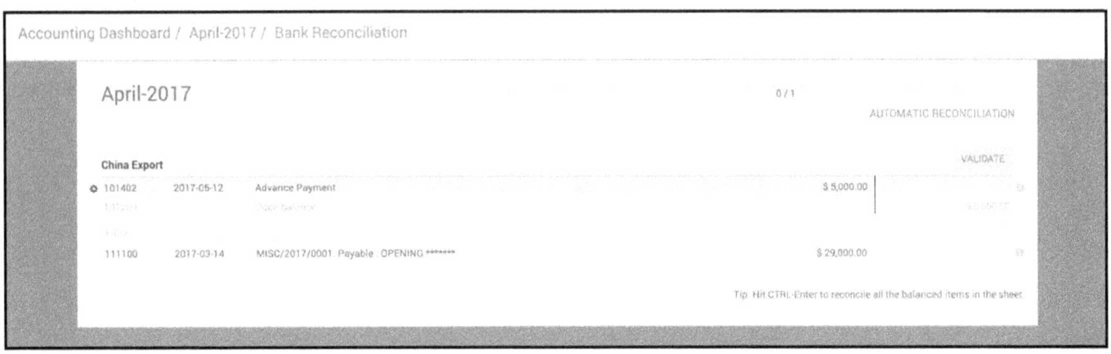

Assume that after a few days the customer places an order after the payment is received. Create **Customer Invoice**, as soon as you confirm the invoice. At the top of the invoice, you will get the message **You have outstanding payments for this customer. You can allocate them to mark this invoice as paid.**

Odoo will let you know the balance available for the customer that you can assign to the current invoice:

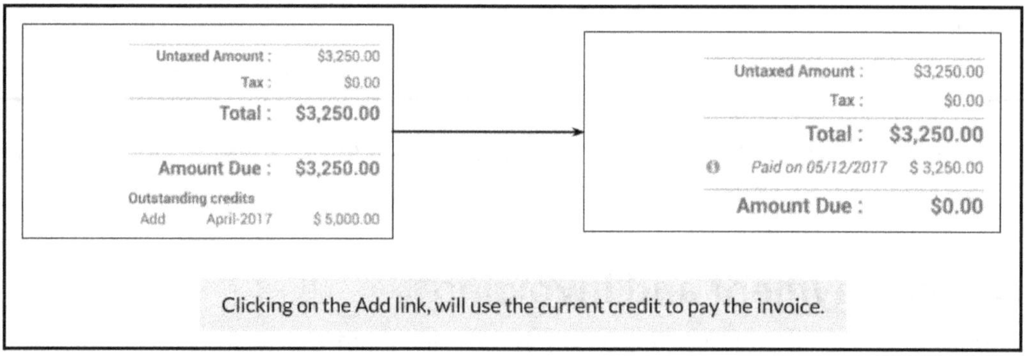

Clicking on the Add link, will use the current credit to pay the invoice.

Until the `5000` credit is not consumed completely, you will get a message on each invoice to consume the outstanding credit. As soon as you pay the invoice with the outstanding credit, the invoice will go to the **PAID** state.

Cash discount - Reconciliation model

Usually, cash discounts are given to customers who clear their payment on or before the due date. The cash discount policy helps a lot to maintain cash flow in a business. For example, normally, a 2 percent cash discount is given if a customer clears the payment within a week, otherwise, the customer can pay within 30 days from the date of the invoice. So, you should be able to identify whether the customer eligible for a cash discount now; is eligible, you can process the bank reconciliation with the cash discount.

The reconciliation model can help you to speed up the process. You can create a reconciliation model from **Accounting Dashboard**: click on the **More** link for the bank where you want to allow the cash discount and choose **Reconciliation Model** to create a new reconciliation model:

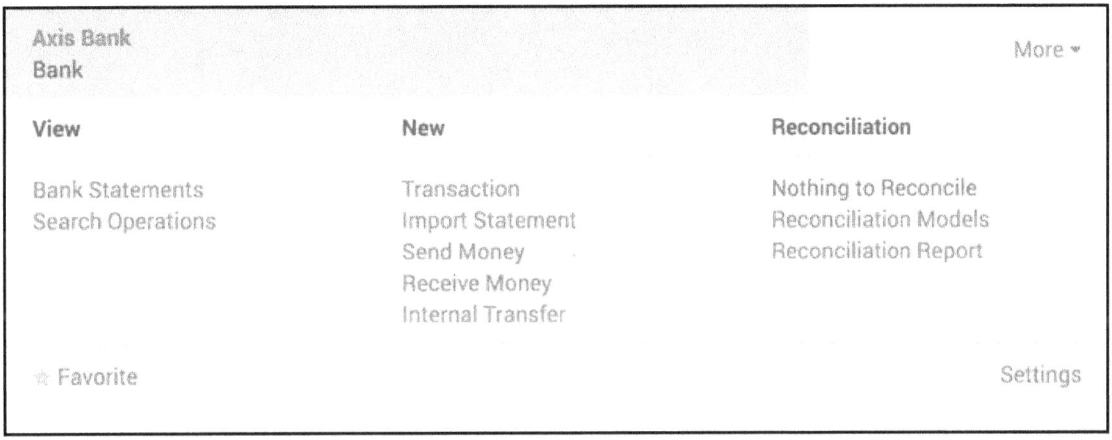

The steps to create a cash discount model are as follows:

1. Create a new model for cash discounts as follows:

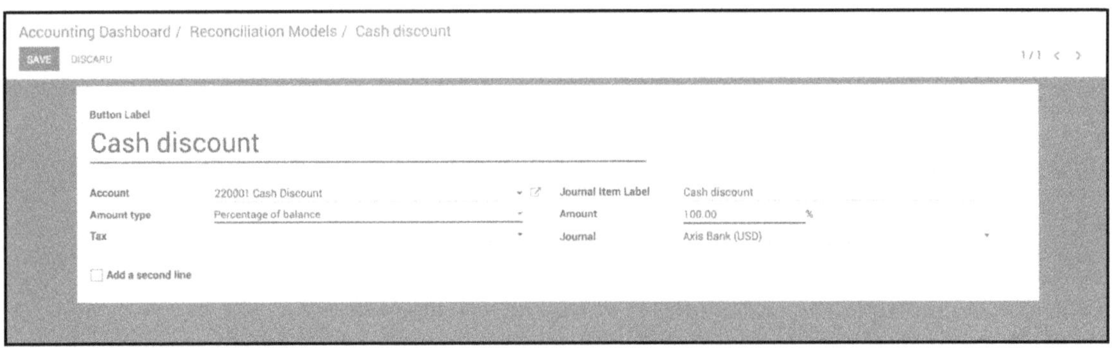

2. Before creating an invoice, let's create the payment terms to attach to the invoice. Please go through the recipe *Customer invoice and payments* from this same chapter to create payment terms. The payment terms created looks like the following screenshot:

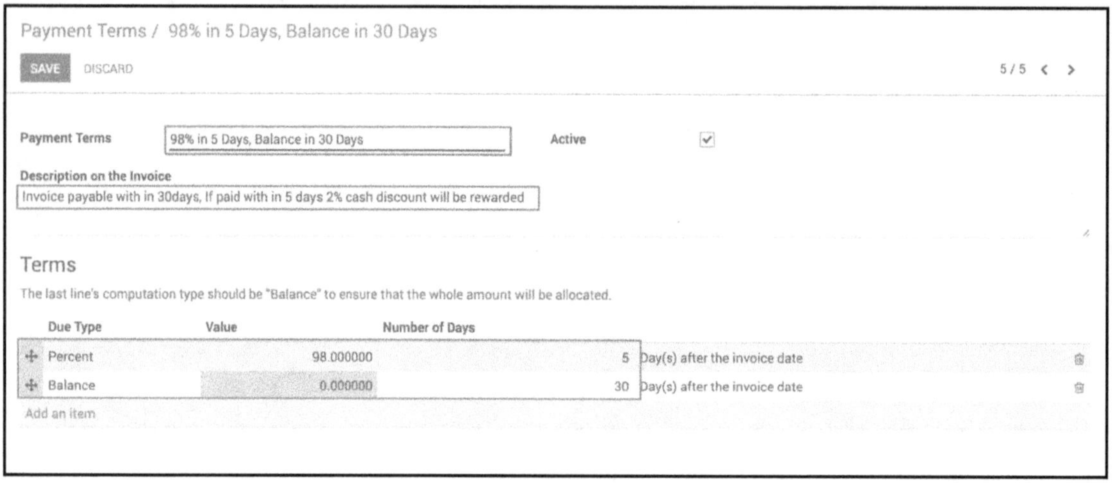

3. To make it clear that it's not a payment term but a cash discount, don't forget to set a clear description that will appear on the invoice.
4. Let's create an invoice for **China Export** of `100`, attach the payment term, and create a payment to encode the check received from the customer having the value 98.
5. Go to **Manual Invoices & Payments Matching**, you will get the payment line and invoice line with `98` matched for **China Export**. Select the remaining invoice line with 2, and add a new line by clicking on the **CASH DISCOUNT** button on the counterpart:

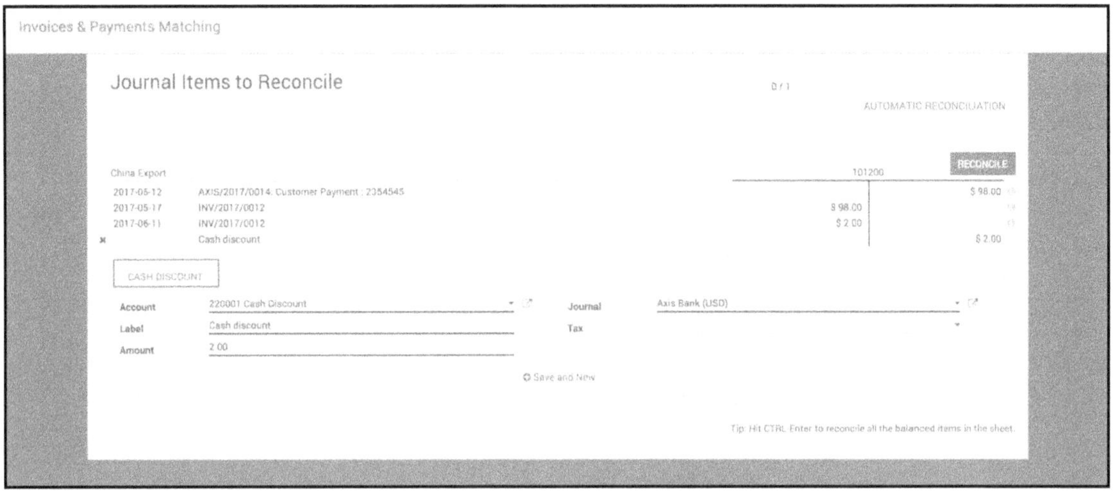

6. If the customer pays the invoice after five days, where a cash discount is not applicable, you can still reconcile the payment line of 100 with two invoice lines 98 and 2, as displayed in the following screenshot:

The Reconciliation Model can be used for many different purposes, for example, deduction of TDS can be configured with the Reconciliation Model.

Batch Deposit

There are some business cases where the company receives many checks or payment instructions on a daily basis, such as when receiving a credit card payments at the cash counter; all those transactions will be credited by the bank in a single instruction per day.

For the checks, the bank asks for the deposit slips to be filled with the list of checks or cash deposit. The bank statement will have a single line for the total of all the checks or cash deposited in a batch instead of an individual check. Odoo helps you to prepare and print the batch deposit. Later, it can be selected at the time of bank reconciliation.

The **Batch Deposit** feature can be activated from **Configuration** | **Settings** under the Accounting application. Check the feature, **Use batch deposit**, and click on **APPLY** to save the settings:

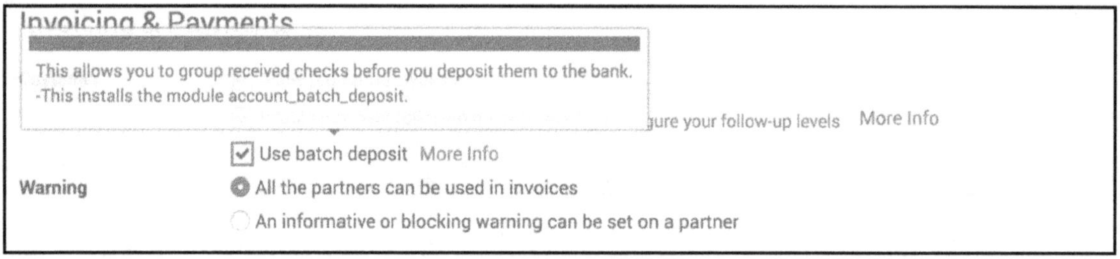

Once the feature is activated, Odoo automatically activates the batch deposit on all the active bank or cash journals that you have. To control the batch deposit feature, it can be active or inactive on some bank accounts. Go to the list of journals, search for the list of bank journals, and select or remove the **Batch Deposit** option for **Debit Method** under the **Miscellaneous** section available in **Advance Settings**:

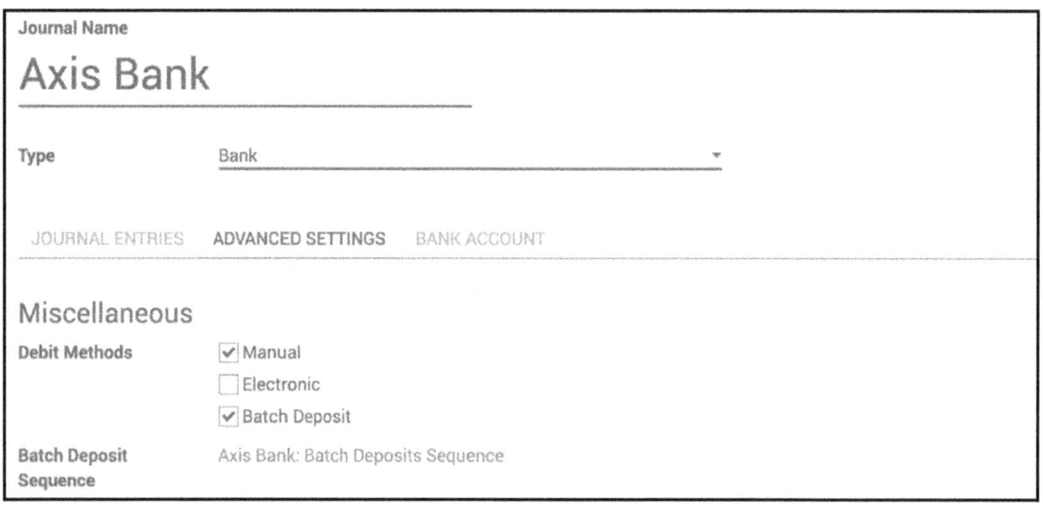

The sequence for **Batch Deposit** can be changed from **Batch Deposit Sequence**; click on the link **Axis Bank: Batch Deposits Sequence** to change it.

At the time of recording the payment, select the payment journal of the bank in which you plan to deposit the checks. As soon as you select the bank, you will be able to see the **Batch Deposit** options--select it if you plan to deposit in a batch:

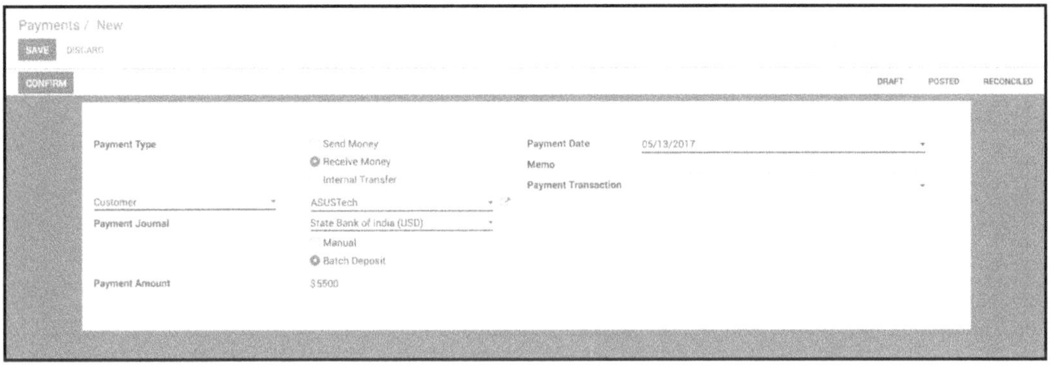

At the beginning of each day, create a batch deposit that has the transactions for the previous day, which can be submitted to the bank. To create a batch deposit, go to **Sales** | **Batch Deposit** under the **Accounting** application. Select the bank for which you are creating a batch, and select the list of checks to be deposited in the batch.

By default, Odoo offers you all the checks that have not been deposited yet. So, you can verify them and deposit them in the bank:

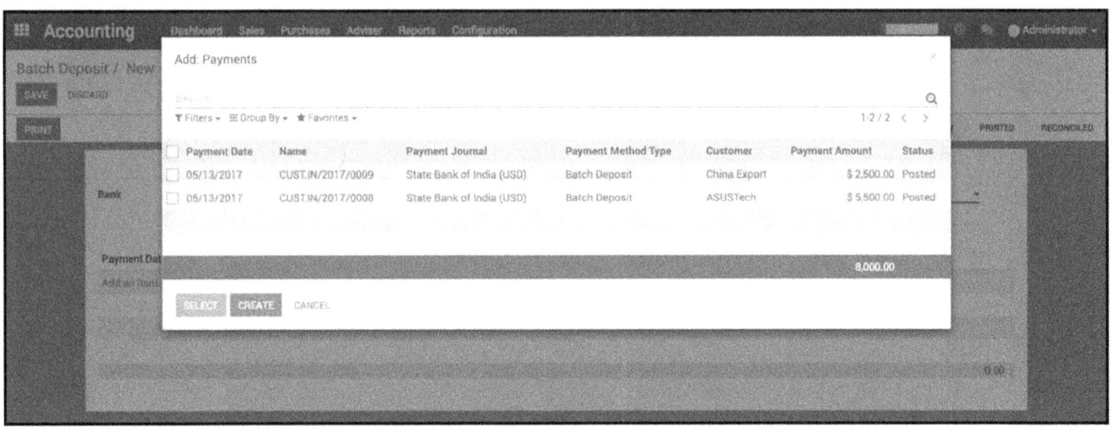

You can then print the batch deposit. It will be very useful to have prepared the deposit slip that the bank usually requires you to complete.

The final deposit statement looks like the following screenshot:

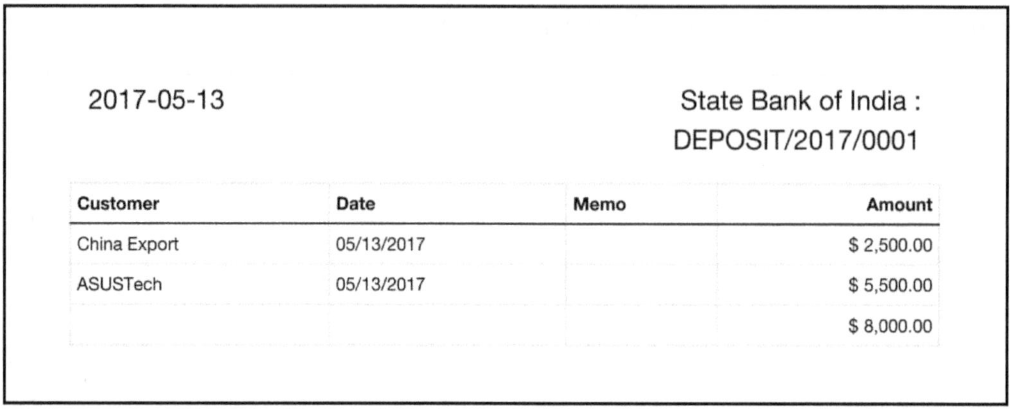

2017-05-13

State Bank of India :
DEPOSIT/2017/0001

Customer	Date	Memo	Amount
China Export	05/13/2017		$ 2,500.00
ASUSTech	05/13/2017		$ 5,500.00
			$ 8,000.00

A batch deposit can be created from the customer payments; go to the list view, and select the checks to be deposited together. From the **Action** tab, select the **Create Batch Deposit** option. You have to carefully select the lines to make sure that you do not mix the checks to be deposited in different banks.

When you receive a bank statement, you can see the line that refers to the batch deposit number; create a bank statement line and reconcile the statement. When the reconciliation process is run, the user will be able to select the batch deposit that matches with the bank statement line.

Select the batch deposit from the available list of deposits against the payment received in the bank that refers to the deposit slip, as shown in the following screenshot:

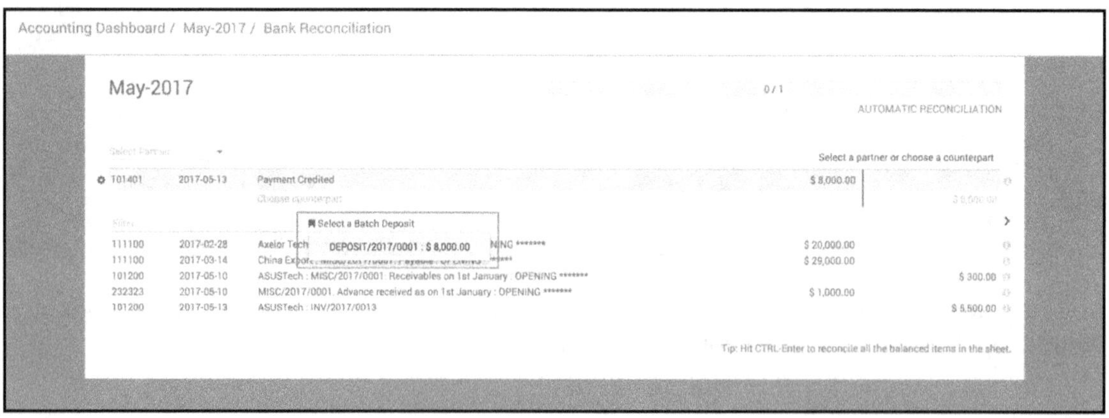

When you select a batch deposit, Odoo automatically fills all the checks contained in this deposit for the matching ones. There were two checks in this batch deposit, as seen in the following example:

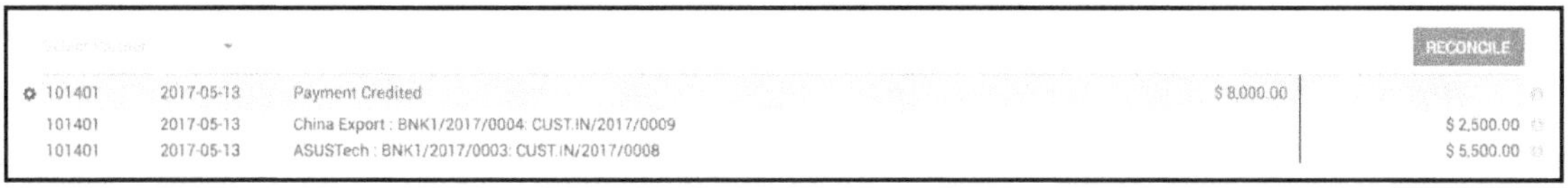

Create and configure tax, apply on invoices and print tax report

The tax engine in Odoo is very flexible and supports many different types of taxes: value-added tax (VAT), eco-taxes, federal/state/city taxes, retention, withholding tax, and so on. For most countries, your system is preconfigured with the right taxes when you start using Odoo online. The changes to the tax computation rules can be done in Odoo if your countries chart of account is not configured as per the current rules.

Let's see how to create a new tax, configure it to adapt the computation, how to choose default tax at the time of a product sale, and the most important how to choose different taxes for the local and export customer, at the end let's see how to get the tax report.

How to do it...

1. The taxes applied in your country are installed automatically for most localizations. The default taxes will be appearing on sales orders and invoices coming from each product's **Invoicing** tab.

The taxes selected on the product form are the default taxes applied for sales and purchase of that product:

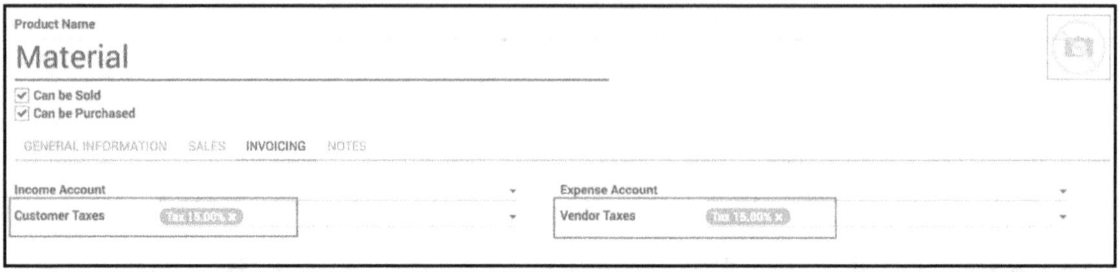

2. The default taxes set on the product at the time of creating a new product are coming from the account default configuration. To change the default taxes set for any new product created, go to **Accounting** | **Configuration** | **Settings**:

   Change the tax configuration for two fields **Default Sales Tax** and **Default Purchase Tax**. Normally **Default Sales** and **Purchase Tax** is same. Look at the following screen of the default tax configuration:

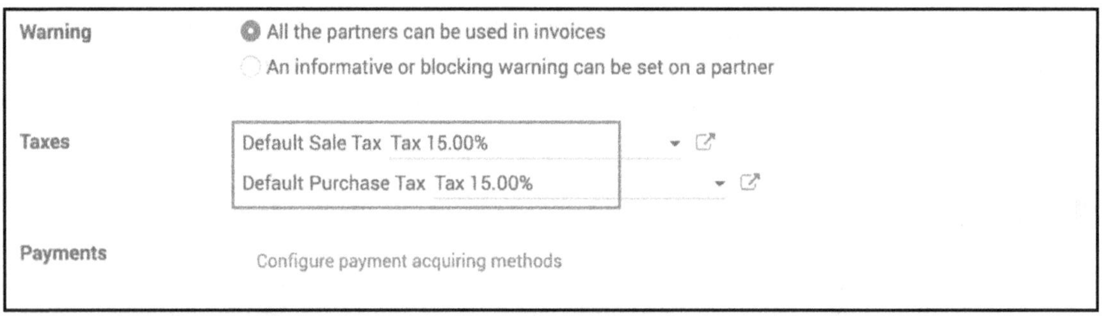

   Change the Tax and click on **APPLY** button to save the tax. The new tax will be applied on the product created after setting the default taxes.

3. When the tax is not available as part of the standard Chart of Tax, you can create a new one from **Configuration** | **Taxes** under the **Accounting** application. You can create a tax that can be a sales tax or purchase tax. Let's create a new tax, *VAT 5%,* which will be applicable by default on all the products instead of *Tax 15%:*

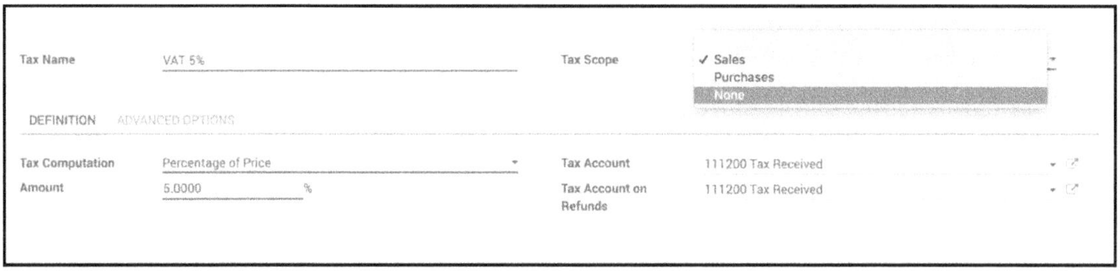

4. Enter `VAT 5.0%` in **Tax Name**. **Tax Scope** will be `Sales`. Select **Tax Scope** as `Purchase` if you want to create the purchase tax, or set `None` when you create a tax as a part of some other tax. Tax created with **Tax Scope** as `None`, cannot be applied either on Sale or Purchase order.

   Select **Percentage of Price** in **Tax Computation.** Enter `5.0000`% in **Amount**. Link tax with the account so the ledger will be generated based on the tax transactions. You can select this new tax, VAT 5 percent, as the default tax under the **Configuration** | **Settings of Accounting** application.

5. The new tax created and set as default will be applied to all the new products created. Look at the following screenshot, *5% VAT* is applied when creating a new product called **Material**:

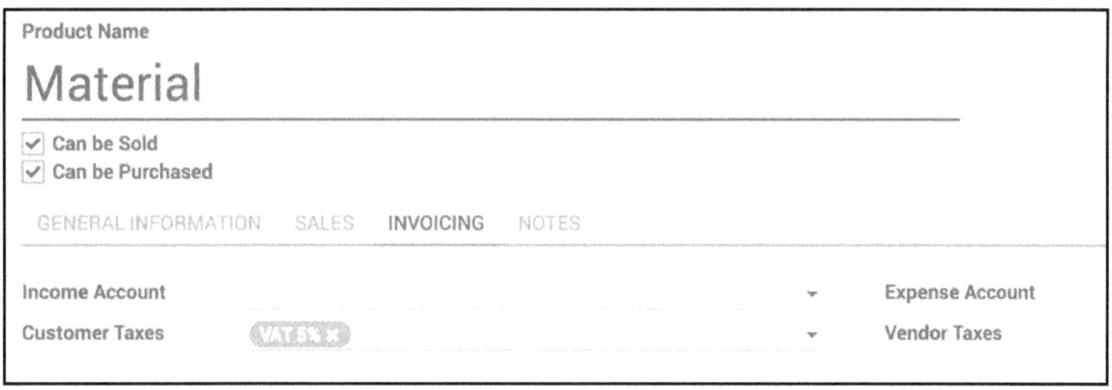

6. Let's create an invoice and select the **Material** product; the default tax applied to the material is *VAT 5%*:

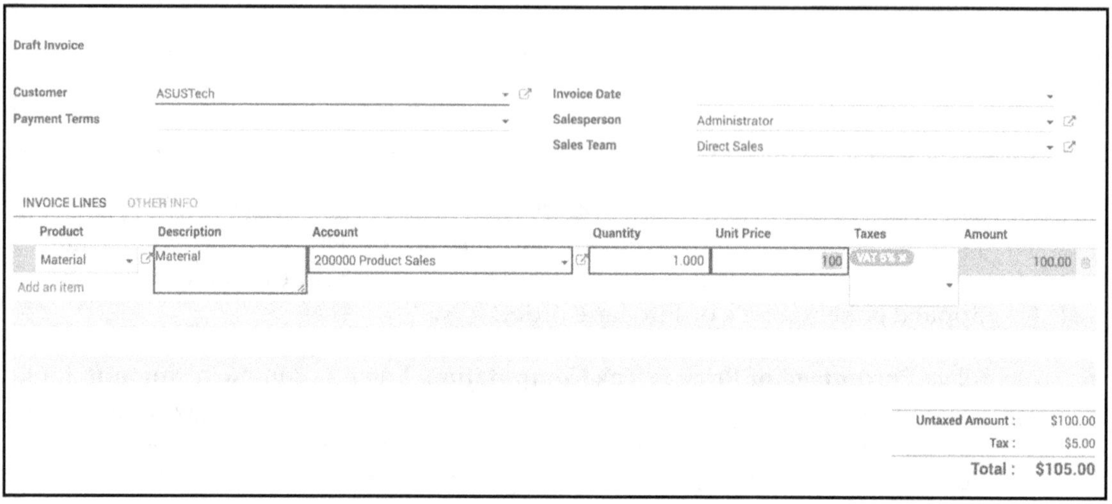

7. The taxes are computed correctly on the invoice, the detailed computation of the tax can be found under the **OTHER INFO** tab on the invoice. Look at following screen to see the tax computation:

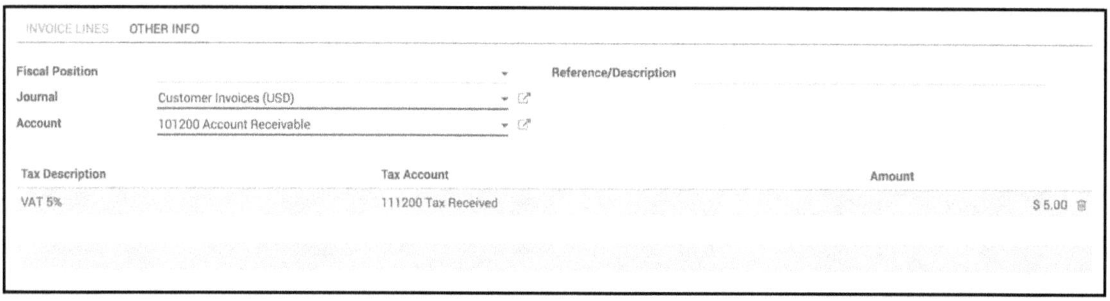

We can see only one line which computes the *VAT 5 percent*. You will be finding multiple tax liens if you have multiple taxes applied on different products.

8. As soon as the invoice is confirmed, the accounting entries will be created, which generates the general ledger entries for the **Sales**, **Accounting Receivable**, and **Tax Received** account. Look at the following screenshot that shows the accounting entries created when an invoice gets confirmed:

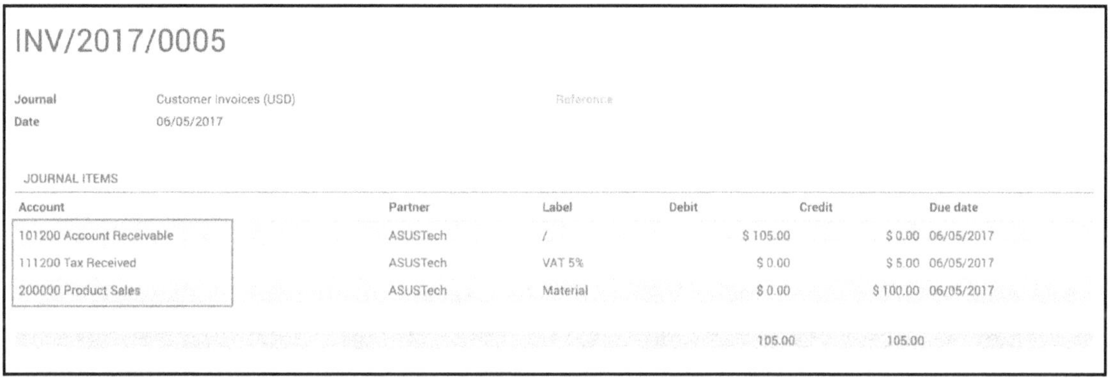

There's more...

There are different types of computations that need to be performed depending on the country or type of business, such as computing tax based on the group of tax or especially for the retail business; the tax should be included in the product price. In some countries, the tax can be applied and computed based on the customer location--countries like the USA have a specific tax computation application called Tax Cloud which takes care of the latest rules to apply and computes the tax based on the product category and customer location. It also allows their customers to pay the online tax to the government.

Let's see some of the application of tax to manage the complex rules and regulations.

Group of taxes

There is more than one tax which may be applicable on some of the products; as soon as you select a product on the invoice, a single tax is applied, but internally it computes more than one tax to maintain the different tax accounts.

Let's create a new tax, VAT 15%, that will be a combination of VAT 12.5% and **Add**. VAT 2.5%. Create two separate taxes: VAT 12.5% and Add. VAT 2.5%, as follows:

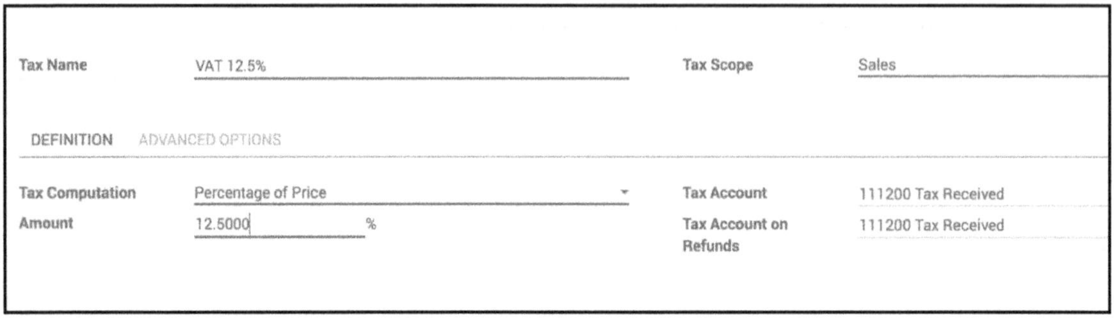

Create **Add**. VAT 2.5% the same as VAT 12.5%. As soon as you are ready with the two separate taxes, create a group of taxes using VAT and **Add**. VAT, which is VAT 15%. Create a new tax, select **Group of Taxes** in **Tax Computation**, and add the two different taxes, as shown in the following screenshot:

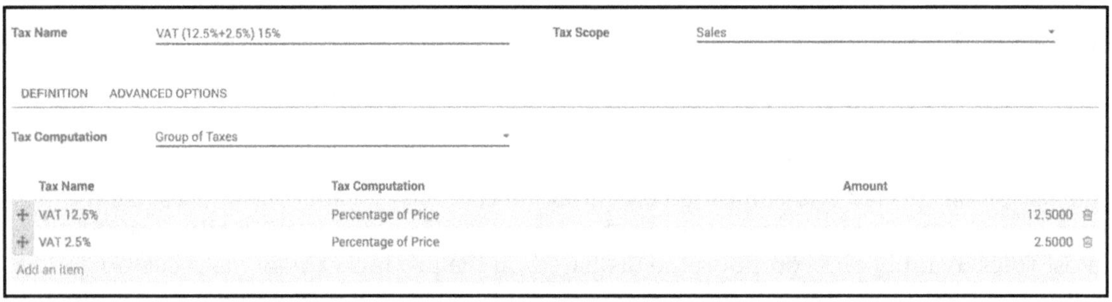

The group of taxes helps us to apply the multiple taxes under the same name, sometimes it also known as a composite tax. You can see that when I created a composite taxes VAT (12.5%+2.5%) 15%, when we apply VAT (12.5%+2.5%) 15%, it will compute two different taxes 12.5% and 2.5% separately on the invoice.

Tax grouping on an invoice

There may be a possibility that while creating a customer invoice, different types of products may have different tax applied may be selected. The tax may have been computed correctly; it is visible on the invoice too. Look at the following screenshot having the products **Service** and **Material** with VAT and **Service Tax** applied on it:

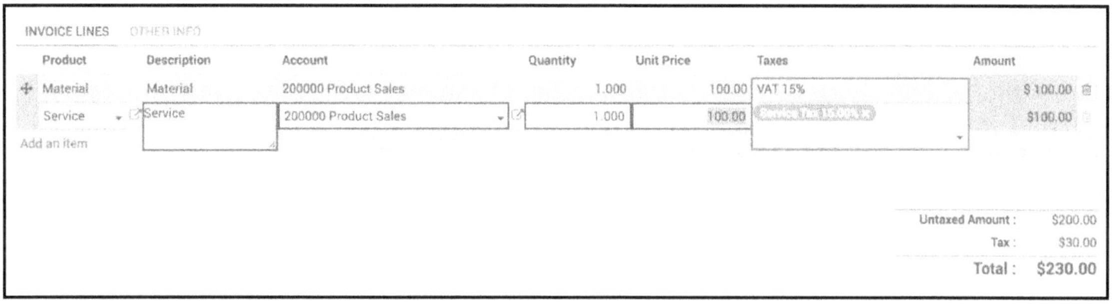

The tax computed on the product and service are correct, the same is visible in the tax lines on the **OTHER INFO** tab, as seen in the following screenshot:

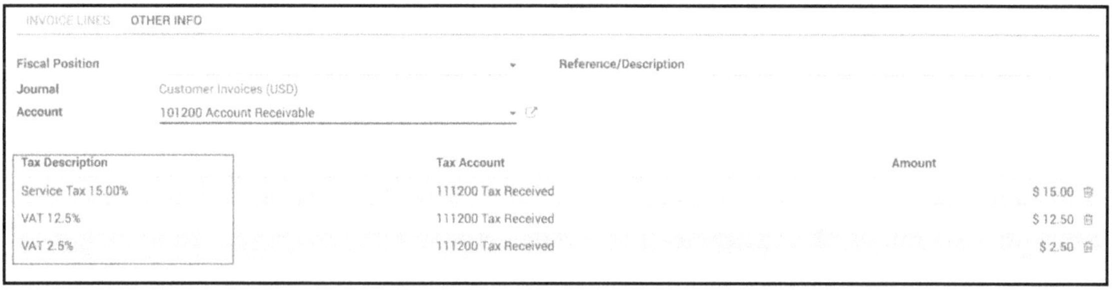

When you print an invoice, it shows the tax computation as correct on the tax lines, but **Taxes** under the invoice **Subtotal** create a confusion about the tax applied on the invoice. You cannot have a clear view on what tax is computed, as you cannot see the total **Service Tax** and **VAT**. Look at the following printed invoice--under the subtotal, you can see only **Taxes**:

Description	Quantity	Unit Price	Taxes	Tax Excluded Price
Material	1.000	2,203.00	VAT 15%	$ 2,203.00
Service	1.000	3,029.00	TS. 15%	$ 3,029.00
			Subtotal	$ 5,232.00
			Taxes	$ 784.81
			Total	$ 6,016.81

You can create a group for related taxes to separate the tax amount on the invoice. The **Tax Group** is a field available on the tax configuration part under **ADVANCE OPTION**. Open the configuration, and change the **Tax Group** field as shown in the next screenshot for all the **VAT** taxes (12.5% and 2.5%), and set the **Tax Group** to **VAT**. For service tax, create a group **Service Tax**; look at the following screen for the **Tax Group** configuration:

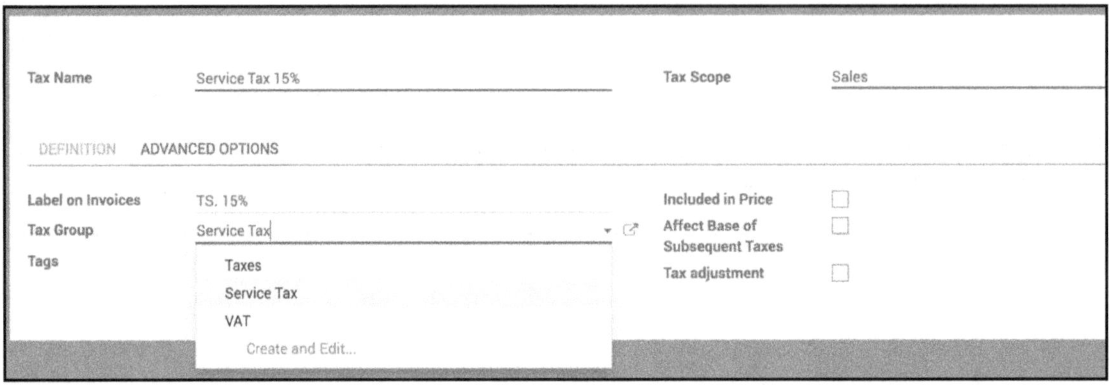

Print an invoice and you will get the tax total by the group of tax clearly, as the **Taxes** field is now divided into **VAT** and **Service Tax**, as shown here:

Description	Quantity	Unit Price	Taxes		Tax Excluded Price
Material	1.000	2,203.00	VAT 15%		$ 2,203.00
Service	1.000	3,029.00	TS. 15%		$ 3,029.00
				Subtotal	$ 5,232.00
				VAT	$ 330.46
				Service Tax	$ 454.35
				Total	$ 6,016.81

Tax included in price

Sometimes, a business needs to have the tax included in the product price, mostly for the retail business or it is also known as business to customer. Retail sales need the tax to be included in the product price. There are two ways to configure the product price included in tax as follows:

- Add the tax additionally on top of the product
- Compute the product price including tax in it

To enable the tax to be included in the price, the tax has to be configured. Open the tax configuration you would like to include in the product price, and select the **Included in Price** checkbox available under the **ADVANCE OPTIONS** tax:

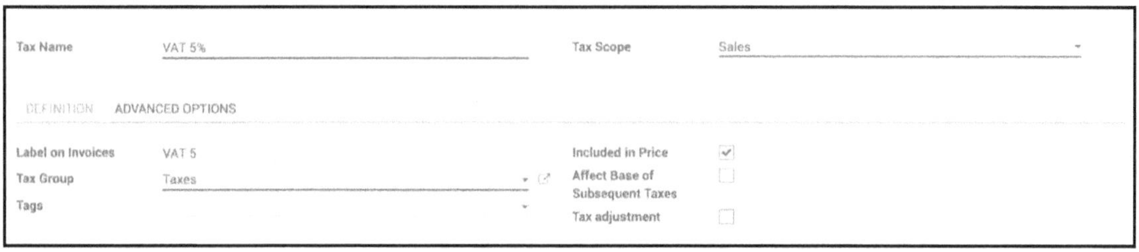

The tax amount will be detected from the product price as we have configured the tax included in the product price.

When you create an invoice for amount `105`, the tax, which is `5`, will be deducted from the product price, and the product price is computed based on this tax deduction, which is `100`, as seen in this screenshot:

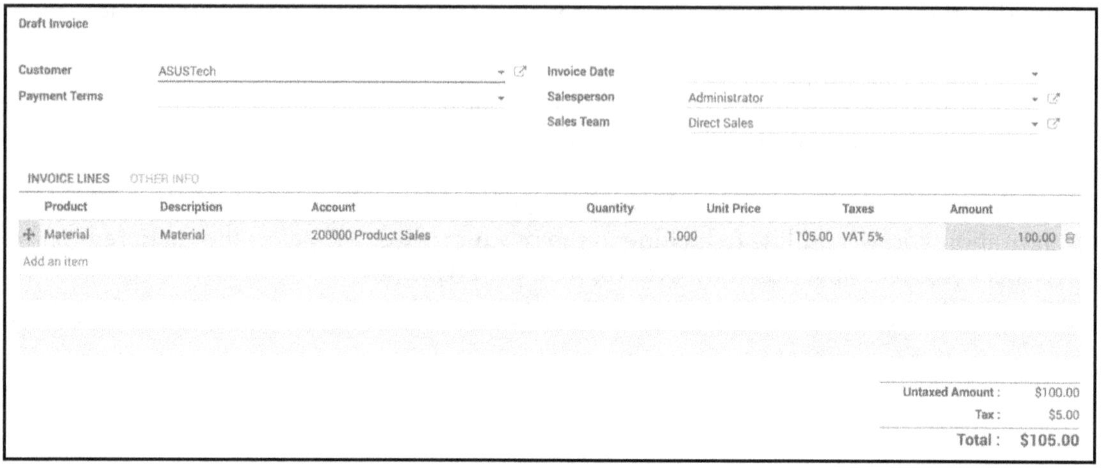

Apply tax based on customer location

The tax computation is quite complicated in some countries; tax percentages applied will be based on customer location. For example, when you sell a product to the customer within the state, the tax applicable is 15%. But for the same product when it sold to the customer outside the state the tax applicable is 5%.

It is difficult to check the customer location and change the tax on an invoice for every customer, as Odoo applies the default tax on the product. Odoo has a feature called fiscal position. By using this feature, we can change not only **Tax** but also **Accounts**, depending on the customer location.

To set up **Fiscal Position**, go to **Configuration** | **Fiscal Position** under the **Accounting** application. Create a new position and set the name to **Outside State**, and then set **TAX MAPPING**. For example, replace 5% with the 15%. Check the following screenshot:

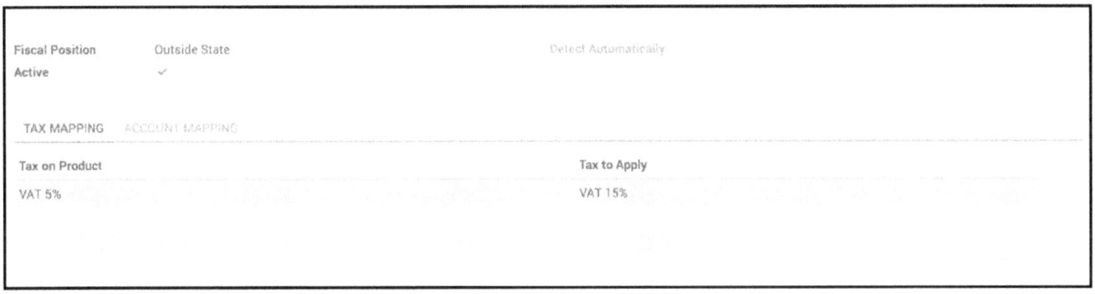

Apply **Fiscal Position** on the customers who are outside the state; you will find that field under the **ACCOUNTING** tab.

> Create a fiscal position to set as the default for the entire list of customers who are located within the state. Name it **Default Position** or **Local Customer**. So, all customers should have a fiscal position--if they are local, apply the default tax, if outside the state, then apply a different tax, and if outside the country, another tax will be applicable.

The right fiscal position will be applied automatically when you create a customer. The **Detect Automatically** option helps you to configure **Country Group** and **Country** with the **Zip** range. When creating a customer, the right fiscal position will be applied automatically:

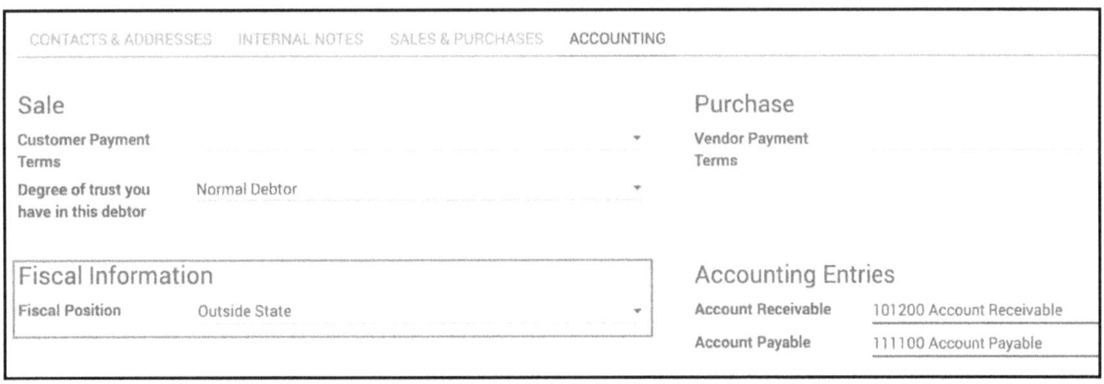

Let's create an invoice for a customer who is outside the state, and check what tax Odoo will apply and compute on the sale of **Material**. The default tax is **VAT 15%**; this will be replaced with **VAT 5%** when you have a customer located outside the state.

Tax report and auditing

The tax reports will be generated automatically as soon as you confirm the customer invoice or vendor bills:

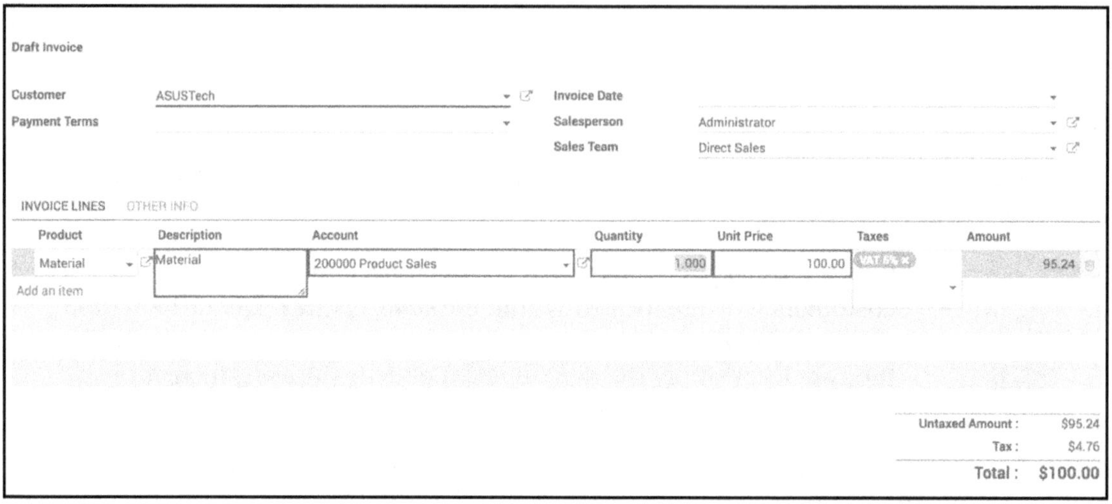

The **Tax Report** can be accessed from **Reports** | **Tax Reports** under the **Accounting** application.

The **Base Amount** and **Tax** values will be displayed on the screen for this month, it can be changed to **This Quarter**, **This Financial Year** or Start Date and End date can be applied to the Custom filter.

You can also compare the sales and purchase tax with the last period as well. Look at the following screen for the default tax report:

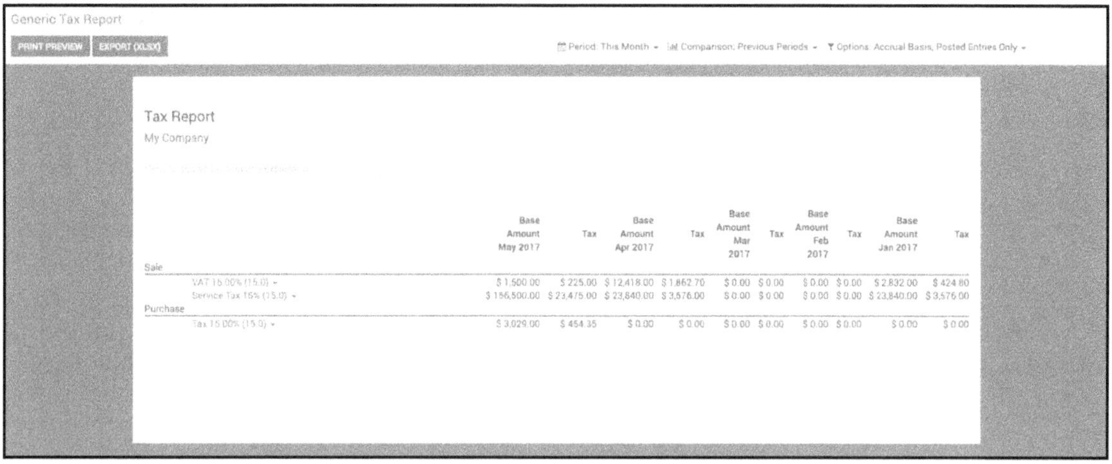

The period I have chosen is the current month; if you enable comparison with the last four periods, Odoo will automatically select the last four months.

As soon as you click on the drop-down arrow beside **Tax**, you can analyze the entries behind it. The entries can be a **Net** amount (base amount based on that the tax is computed) and a **Tax** amount. If you click on **Tax Audit**, you will be presented with a list of tax entries created based on the sales transactions, look at the following screen of tax lines:

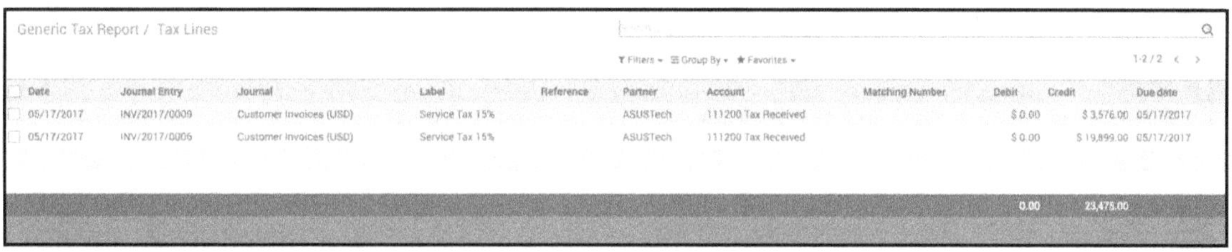

You can select those entries and export them for further reporting or tax filing.

Manage vendor bills and payments

A company may have many types of purchases such as purchase, of goods from a supplier, purchase of a stationery item for office use, purchase of an asset, vendor bills for electricity or telephone, or water expense, and so on. Usually, vendor bills are controlled by the purchase process. The purchase application confirms the rates and delivery of the goods or service based on which the vendor bills are created in accounting. Please go through `Chapter 11`, *Purchase Management*, to set up the purchase process.

Here is the standard workflow after installation of the **Purchase** application in Odoo:

- The request for quotation is created and sent to vendors.
- The vendor confirms the rates and the RFQ are converted into a Purchase Order.
- An incoming shipment is generated by the purchase order for the stockable and consumable items.
- As soon as the vendor bill is received, validate the bill with the product received to process further.

However, if you plan to use the accounting as an application, you can create a vendor bill into accounting. Let's create the vendor bills manually in **Accounting**, set up the due date on the bill, and plan the cash flow using **Aged Payable**.

How to do it...

1. The Vendor bill can be created from **Purchases | Vendor Bills** under the **Accounting** application or click on the **NEW BILL** button available under the Vendor Bills section on Accounting dashboard.
2. Select the **Vendor**, enter **Bill Date**. **Due Date** is the last day to pay the bill, and **Vendor Reference** can be a vendor's bill number:

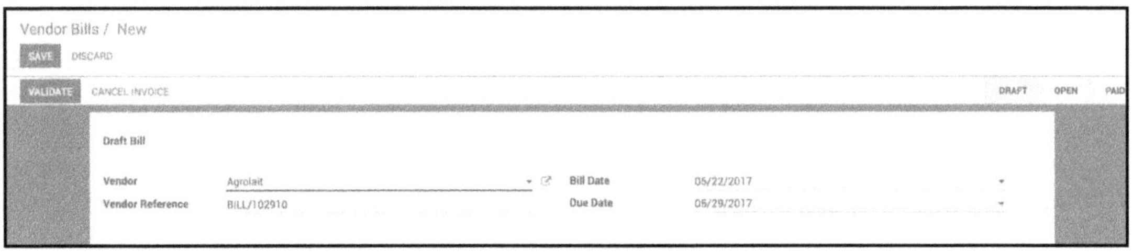

Make sure that you have checked the **Is a Vendor** checkbox on the partner form; this can be the only reason why your desired vendor may not be available on **Vendor Bills**:

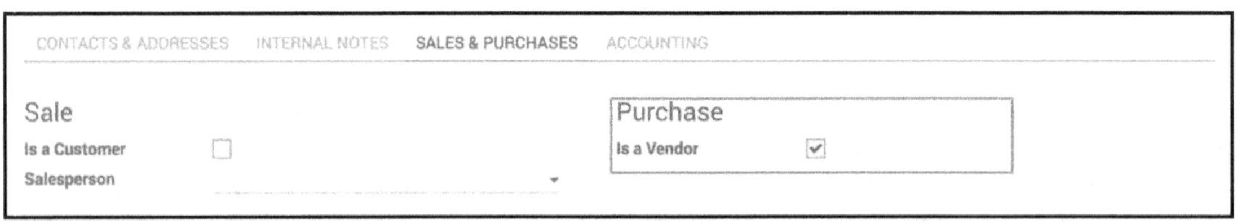

Select **Is a Vendor** check box and click on the **SAVE** button.

3. The bill items have to be added manually in case the **Purchase** application is not installed. Let's create the bill lines manually, enter a product or just a description if you do not want to create consumable products. Just select the correct expense or capital account depending on the product bought; enter the quantity, amount, and tax if applicable:

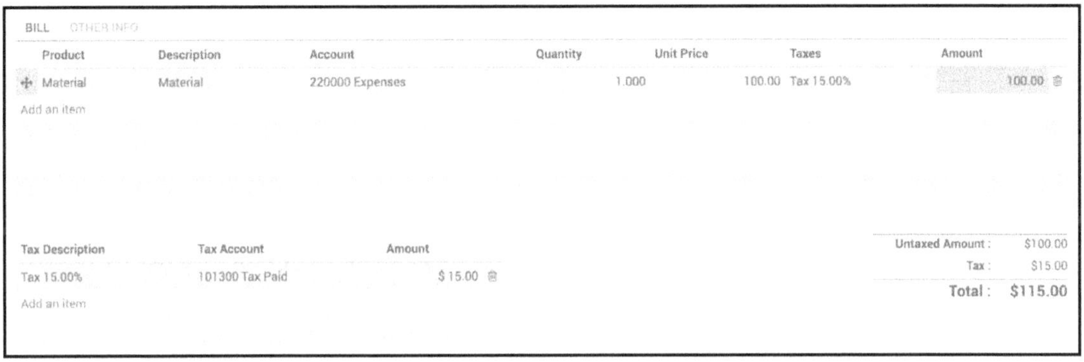

When the **Purchase** application is installed, you will get the field to select the purchase order to prepare the vendor bill automatically:

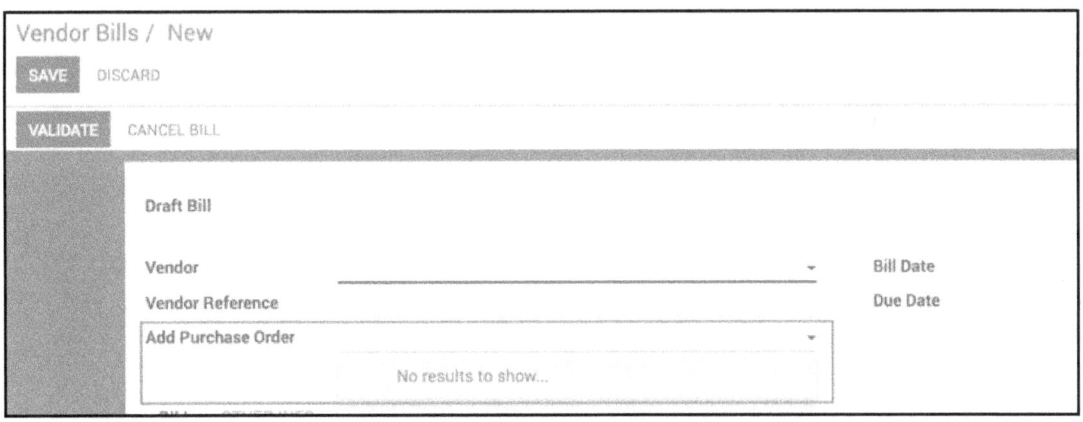

As soon as you select the purchase order, the billable lines will be added automatically to the bill.

4. **Bill Date** is the date on which the bill is prepared by the vendor--in our accounting, it may be reflected on the same date, or we can change the date if it is not a current month expense:

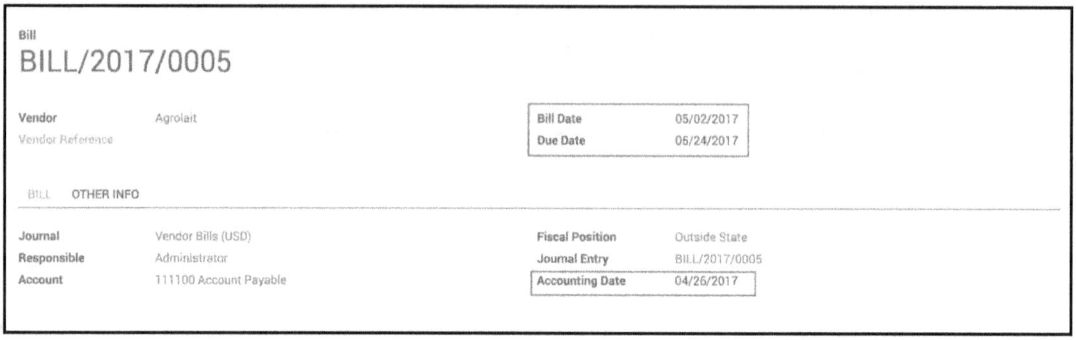

If you don't change **Accounting Date** on the **OTHER INFO** tab, by default, **Bill Date** will be applied as **Accounting Date**; if changed manually, the new date will be considered.

5. Click on the **VALIDATE** button to validate the invoice. The payment can be registered either from **Vendor Bill** or **Purchase | Payment** from the **Accounting** application.

> When the payment has been registered on the vendor bills, by clicking on the **REGISTER PAYMENT** button, you don't need to match the payment entry with a vendor bill.

6. Let's make the payment for **Vendor Bill** from **Purchase | Payment** under the Accounting application. Create a payment entry, select **Payment Type** to **Send Money, Vendor** as an **Agrolait**. The payment can be a bank, enter **Payment Amount**. Verify the payment transaction, and **CONFIRM** the payment. The payment entry looks as follows:

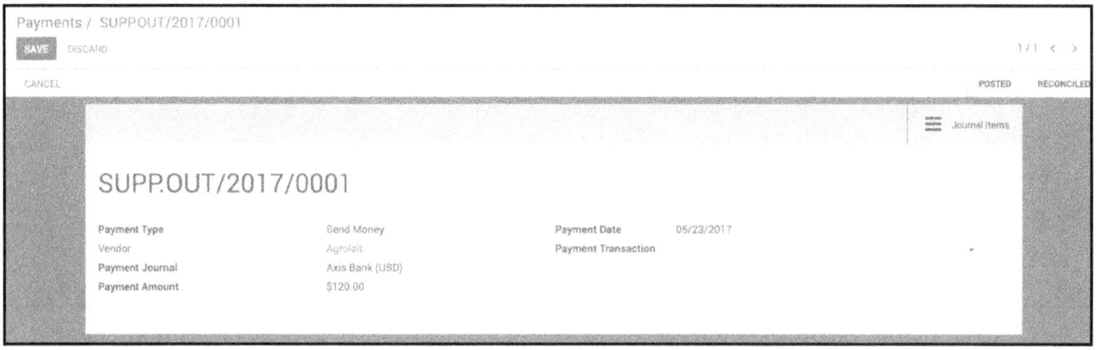

7. As the payment is done using **Purchase | Payment**, it will not match with the vendor bill. Let's match the payment with the vendor bill entries from the **Manual Payments & Invoices Matching** menu available under the **Advisor** menu:

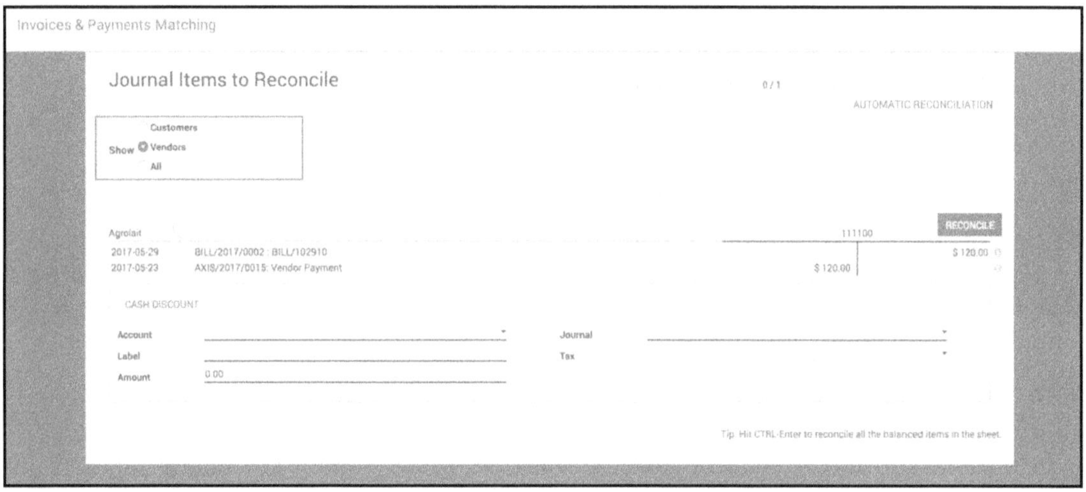

The filters can be applied to get only **Customers** payments or **Vendor** payments to match the payment entry with invoices or bills. Select **All** to see all the payment entries. Click on the **RECONCILE** button to match the payment entries with the vendor bill. Look at the bill after matching the payment. It should go to the paid state.

8. Create a bank statement, create a vendor bill payment entry--make sure that the payment amount is entered with the negative sign, click on **RECONCILE**, and the rest of the process remains the same:

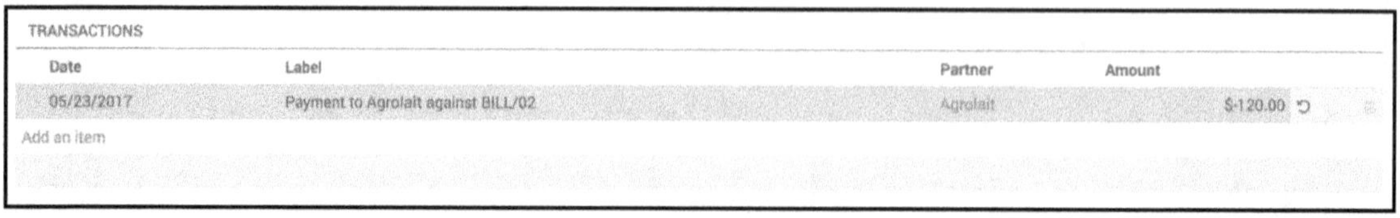

There's more...

Vendor bill is a single interface used to record the purchase of stockable products, consumable materials, capital expenses, and expenses for other services. Depending on the account selected on the bill line, the types of purchase will be decided. The payment process has to be done through bank or cash. Either register payment on the bill or create the payment and later, the payment can be matched manually with the bills. Let's see some additional features that you can activate with the vendor bills, and its payment process.

Manual tax computation on vendor bills

Depending on the type of business, you need a tax registration to collect the tax and the account (ledger) has to be maintained for such taxes. The tax payable has to be computed at a specific interval and paid to the government regularly. In such cases, the taxes have to be created and configured correctly to maintain the tax ledger.

Assume that some of the taxes are not having the tax registration account for those taxes it is not compulsory to maintain the tax ledger as we are not going to get the input tax credit in such case. Odoo allows you to manage those kinds of taxes manually on the vendor bills instead of creating those taxes.

On the vendor bills, the taxes can be entered manually by creating a tax line below the bill lines. Click on **Add an Item**, enter the description, select the account (usually, it's the same account), then select expense on the bill line, and simply enter the tax amount. Look at the following screenshot for reference:

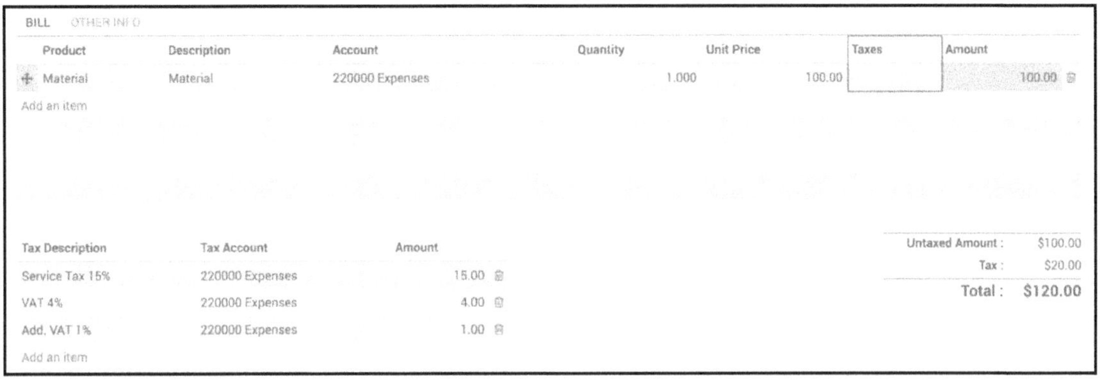

You can see that **Taxes** are not applied on the bill line; the taxes lines are created manually, with **Tax Description**, **Tax Account**, and **Amount**.

Asset management

Registering a capital expense while registering a vendor bill creates an asset. An asset has to be managed in order to count the depreciation. Apply that on the balance sheet to have the correct value. Depreciation needs to be counted depending on the provision and classification of assets. We will see in detail about managing assets, computing depreciation, and the end of managing the life of an asset in `Chapter 8`, *Scale Your Business*.

Check printing

Once you choose to pay the vendor bills by check, you can select to pay by check, and the checks can be printed in batch. At the end, the bank reconciliation process will match the checks you sent to the suppliers with actual bank statements.

Activate the feature **Allow check printing and deposits** from **Accounting** | **Configuration** | **Settings**:

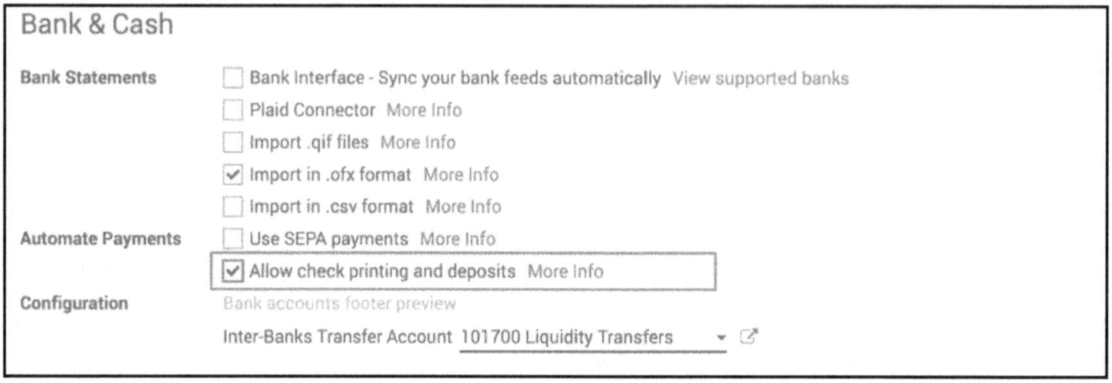

To pay a check to vendors, you have to activate the **Check** payment method on the bank journals. Open the bank journal settings. In the **Payment Method** field, select the **Check** payment method. The following screenshot shows payment method activation:

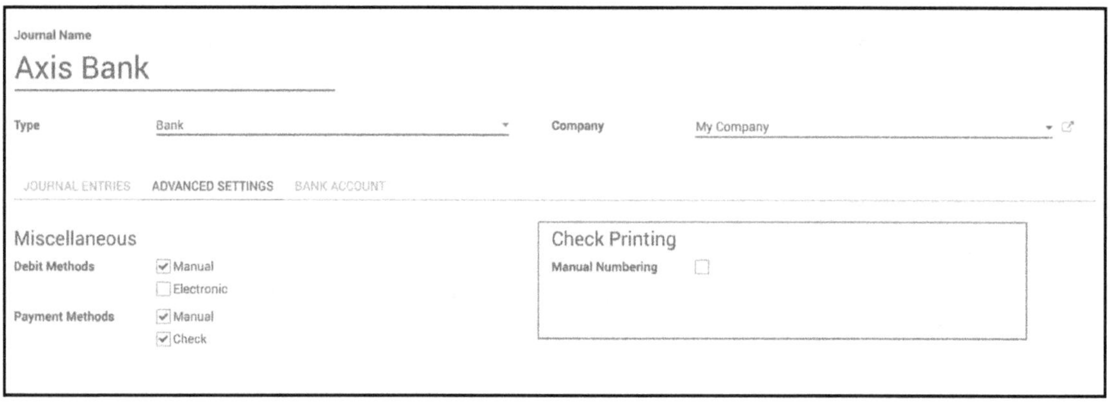

The check number can be maintained on the payment entry in two ways, either entered manually at the time of printing the check or can be generated automatically using the sequence number. Select **Manual Numbering**, if you plan to generate the check number generated manually using the sequence.

If you want to maintain the check numbers for pre-printed checks, do not select this option. You will be asked for the check number at the time of printing the check.

By default, Odoo supports three different formats for printing the checks, however, you can also customize check printing if you have any other printing format other than the available formats through customization:

- Checks at the top, and details in the middle and bottom
- Checks in the middle, and details at top and bottom
- Checks at the bottom, and details at the top

The supplier payment can be processed in three steps, listed as follows:

1. Registering a payment on the vendor bill, you'd pay.
2. Printing a check in a batch or individually for all the registered payments.
3. Reconciling the bank statements.

The payment can be registered on the vendor bills or through payments under a vendor bill. Let's create a payment entry. The payment methods will be changed according to the **Payment Journal** selected. Select the **Axis Bank** journal, select **Checks** as the payment method, and **VALIDATE** the payment. Look at the following screenshot to see how the payment dialogue looks like:

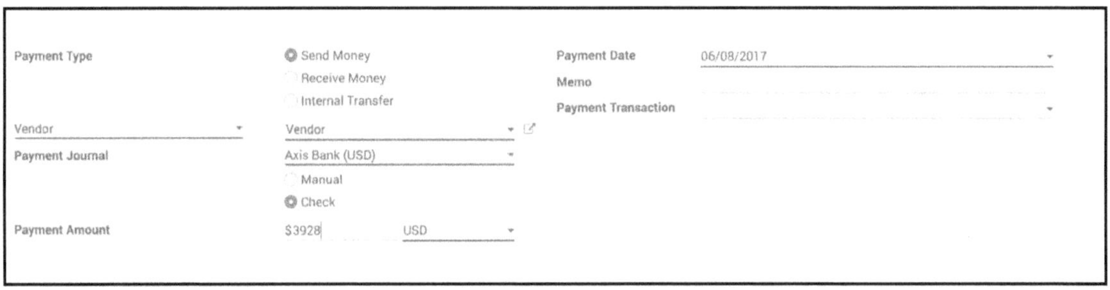

As soon as you confirm the payment entry, it goes to the **POSTED**; state and you are ready to print the check. The **PRINT CHECK** button will appear on the form that allows you to print the single check just after the payment confirmation.

If you plan to issue some checks for all the pending vendor bills, create the payment entries and print all the checks at the end of the day; you can see the number of checks to be printed on the dashboard on the related bank journal:

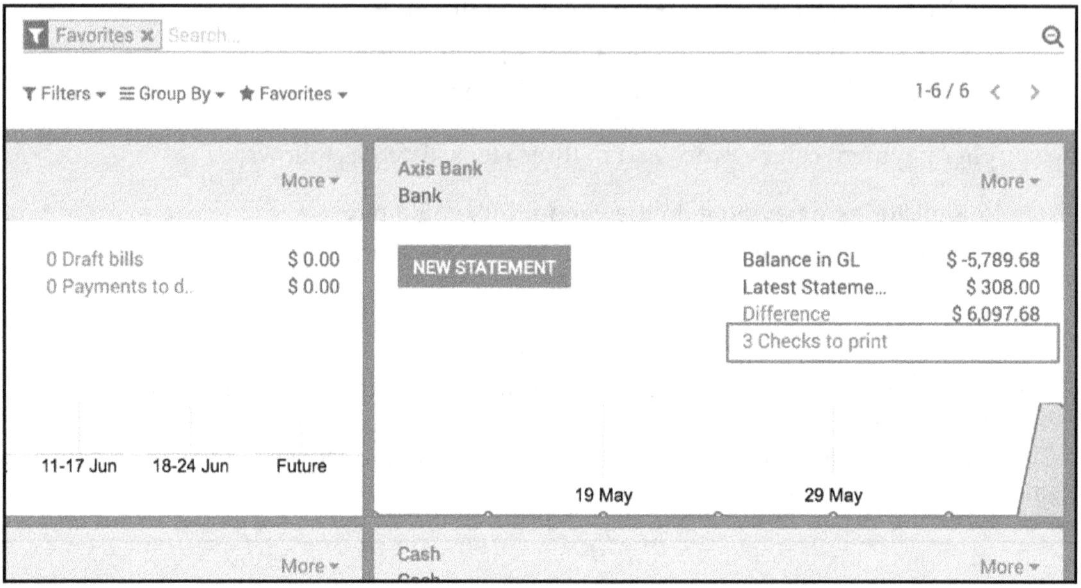

By clicking on the link to print the checks, you will be redirected to the list of checks to be printed. You can print all the checks at once by selecting them, or review each check and print them individually.

Let's print the checks. Click on the **PRINT CHECK** button, a popup will appear asking you to enter the check number printed on the check:

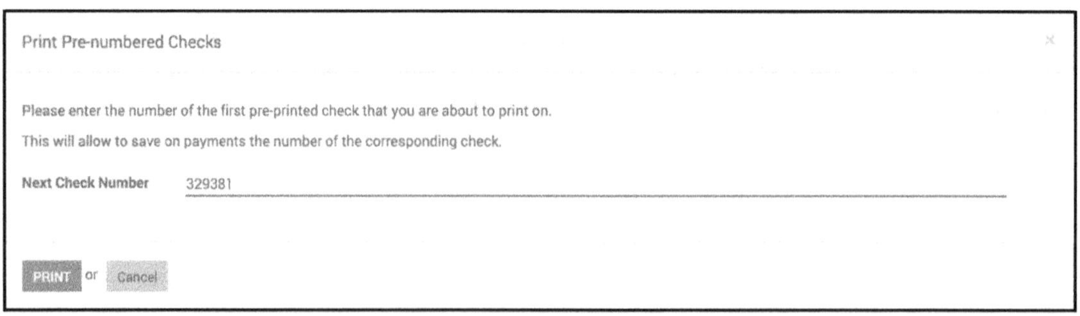

Enter the check number, and click on the **PRINT** button to print the check.

> To print all the checks in a batch, select all the payments from the list view and click on **Print Check** from the top **Print** menu.

As soon as the bank statement is received, the check entry will be matched with the statement entry automatically, and the payment entry will be marked as **RECONCILED**.

Closing financial year and printing financial reports

Before going ahead to close the current fiscal year, there are a few steps one should, typically, take to ensure that your accounting is correct, up to date, and accurate. Odoo allows you to do an internal and external audit seamlessly. During the audit, you can check the financial reports available in your localization module. Besides that, a few very useful generic and dynamic reports are available for all countries.

The best part is, you can compare values with another period within the same financial year or the previous financial year. And you can choose how many periods you want to compare.

> You can annotate every report to print them, and report to your adviser. Export to XLS to manage extra analysis. Drill down into the reports to see more details (payments, invoices, journal items, and so on).

Let's see how to close the current financial year, start a new financial year, and look at some important, yet generic, reports available in Odoo built to use for the audit process such as Balance Sheet, Profit and Loss, Chart of Account, Executive Summary, General Ledger, and so on.

Getting ready

We assume that like every financial year, you have decided how you would like to distribute the profit or subtract the loss from reserve and surplus. The audit process has to be completed before you close the financial year. Make sure to check and verify the following points during the accounting audit process:

- All the accounting entries in all the bank accounts are reconciled correctly
- All the customer invoices have been entered and approved
- All the vendor bills are entered and approved
- All the expenses, their accounting dates, and accuracy are validated

How to do it...

1. Odoo reports are generated in real time and do not require a special treatment or condition to generate any of the financial reports.

   Before closing the financial year, let's check the current year's earning or loss after the audit process completed. The report is available at **Accounting | Reporting | Profit and Loss**. Look at the following screen of an audited profit and loss account:

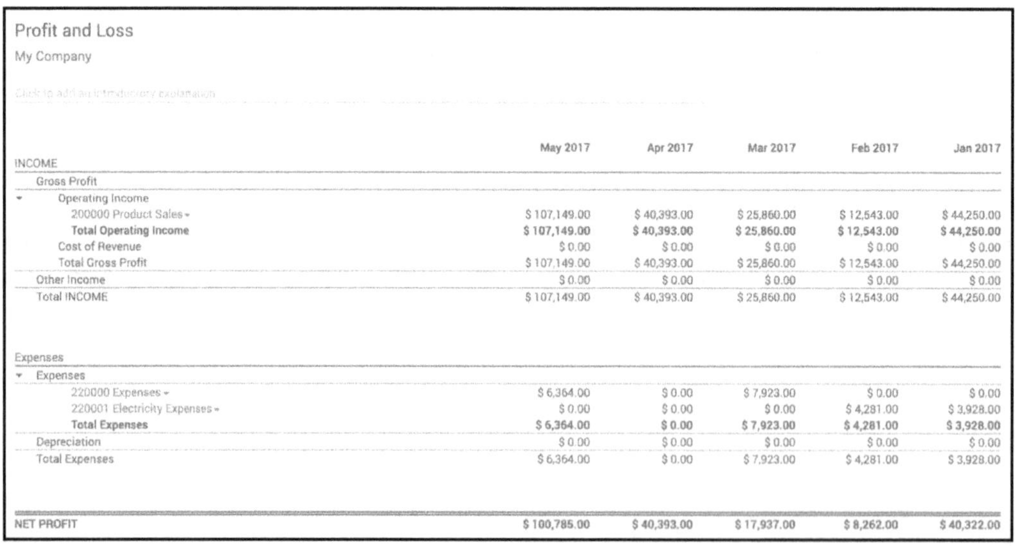

Profit and Loss

My Company

	May 2017	Apr 2017	Mar 2017	Feb 2017	Jan 2017
INCOME					
Gross Profit					
Operating Income					
200000 Product Sales	$ 107,149.00	$ 40,393.00	$ 25,860.00	$ 12,543.00	$ 44,250.00
Total Operating Income	**$ 107,149.00**	**$ 40,393.00**	**$ 25,860.00**	**$ 12,543.00**	**$ 44,250.00**
Cost of Revenue	$ 0.00	$ 0.00	$ 0.00	$ 0.00	$ 0.00
Total Gross Profit	$ 107,149.00	$ 40,393.00	$ 25,860.00	$ 12,543.00	$ 44,250.00
Other Income	$ 0.00	$ 0.00	$ 0.00	$ 0.00	$ 0.00
Total INCOME	$ 107,149.00	$ 40,393.00	$ 25,860.00	$ 12,543.00	$ 44,250.00
Expenses					
Expenses					
220000 Expenses	$ 6,364.00	$ 0.00	$ 7,923.00	$ 0.00	$ 0.00
220001 Electricity Expenses	$ 0.00	$ 0.00	$ 0.00	$ 4,281.00	$ 3,928.00
Total Expenses	**$ 6,364.00**	**$ 0.00**	**$ 7,923.00**	**$ 4,281.00**	**$ 3,928.00**
Depreciation	$ 0.00	$ 0.00	$ 0.00	$ 0.00	$ 0.00
Total Expenses	$ 6,364.00	$ 0.00	$ 7,923.00	$ 4,281.00	$ 3,928.00
NET PROFIT	$ 100,785.00	$ 40,393.00	$ 17,937.00	$ 8,262.00	$ 40,322.00

> TIP
>
> As per the statement, we have positive in the **NET PROFIT**, which shows that we have a profit during the financial year. The loss will be represented by the negative balance under the **NET PROFIT** section.

2. As soon as the statement finalizes after the auditing, the second step is to transfer the **NET PROFIT** or **NET LOSS** from the **Profit and Loss** account to the **Balance sheet**, in most of the companies it's a **Reserve and Surplus** account. The actual profit will be distributed later among the stack holders. Let's check the balance sheet. It shows the profit under the CURRENT YEAR EARNINGS section, as the following screen:

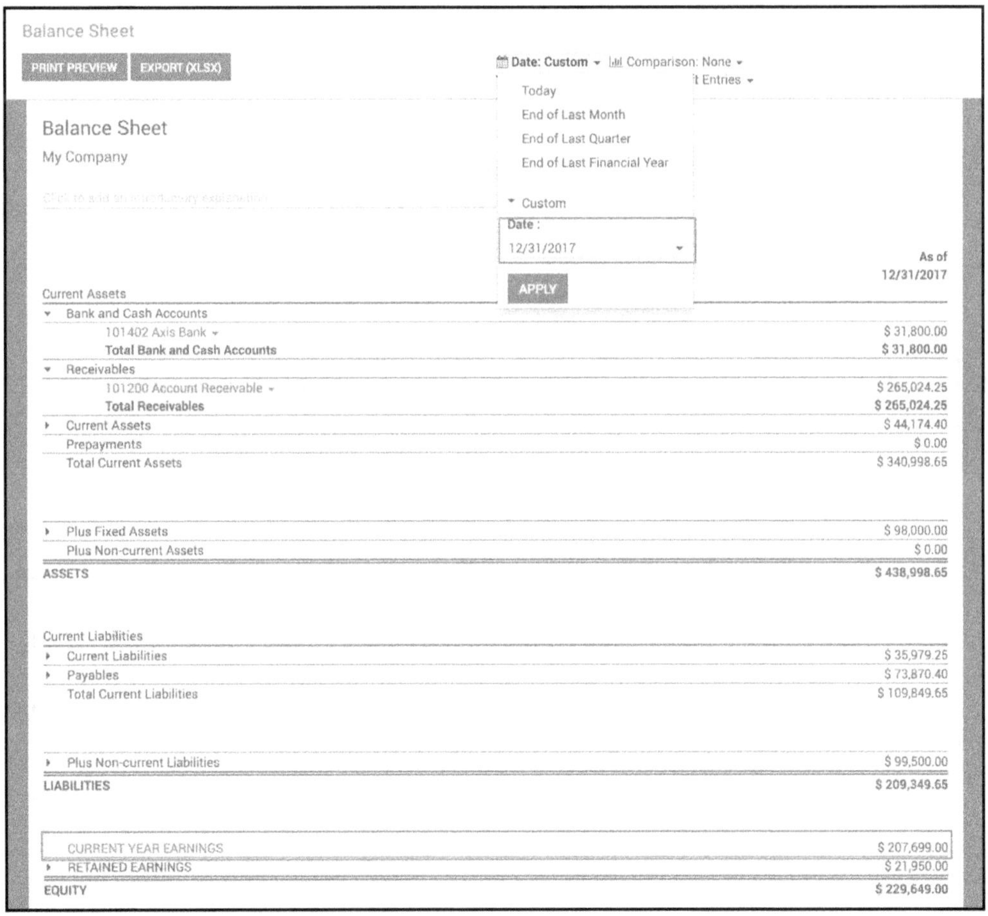

Create a journal entry, as shown in the next screenshot, to transfer the profit or loss to the reserve and surplus account. Every chart of account has a special account called **Undistributed Profits/Losses** with the account code 999999, which holds the current year's profit or loss:

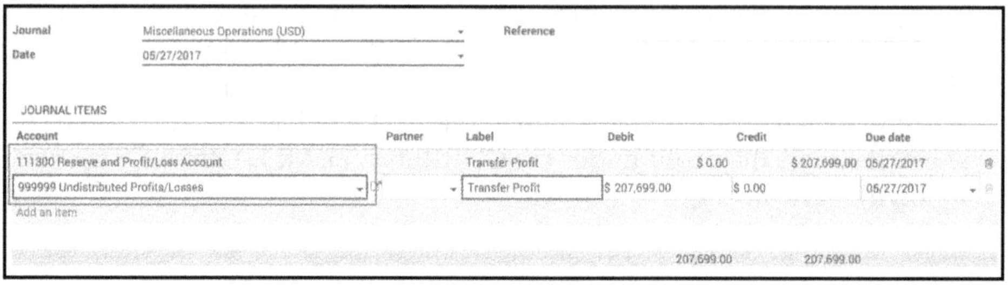

Post the journal entry to confirm the transfer of profit or loss to the reserve and surplus account.

3. Check the **Profit and Loss** account and balance sheet reports after posting the journal entry. You should see the **Profit and Loss** account initialized for a new financial year as follows:

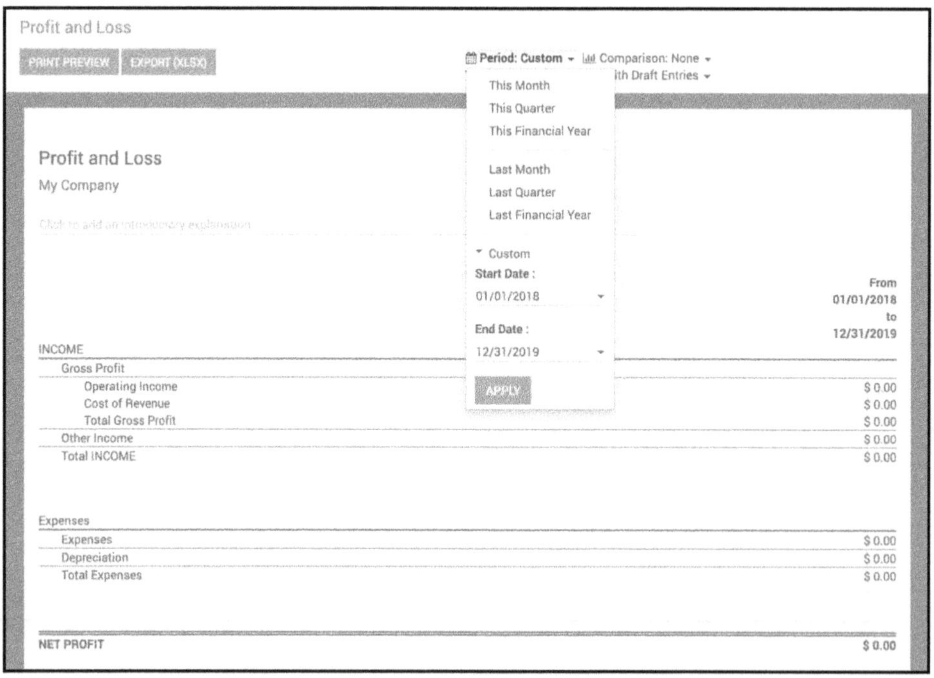

4. The **CURRENT YEAR EARNINGS** in the balance sheet is set to 0 as the profit is transferred to the **Reserve and Profit/Loss** account. Look at the balance sheet report after the entry:

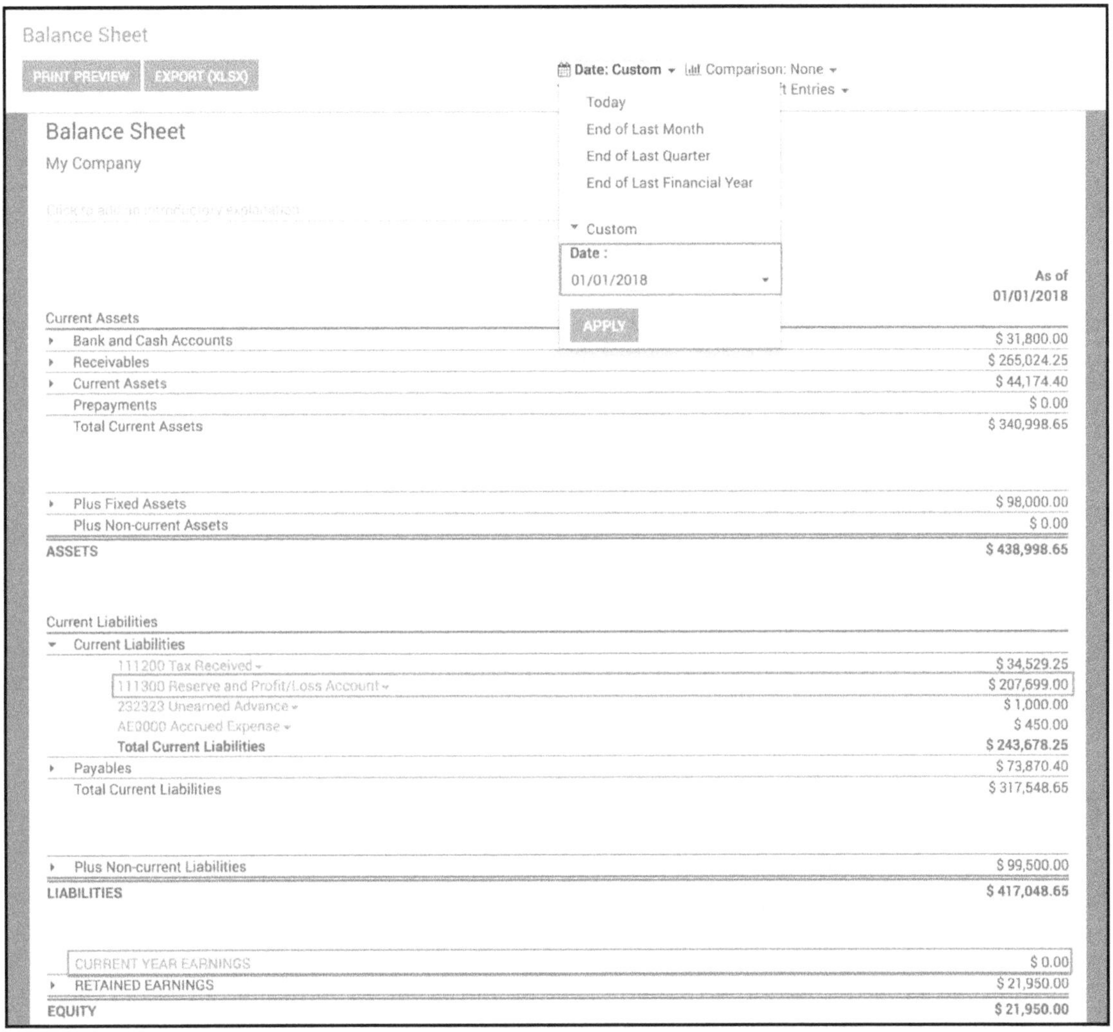

5. Once the profit or loss has transferred correctly, we are ready to close the financial year by setting the dates under the **Lock Entries** section available in the **Accounting** | **Configuration** | **Settings** page. Look at the following screen:

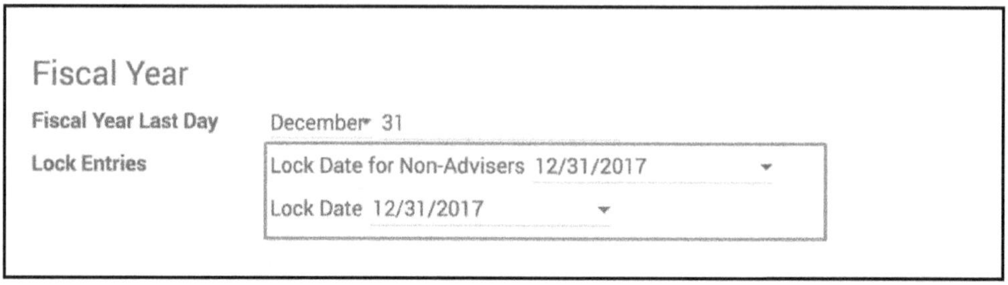

Setting **Lock Date for Non-Advisers** has to be set before the audit or year-end closing process starts as once the date is passed the accountant should not change the past year entries.

The **Lock Date** is important as once this date is set no one, including an advisor, can make changes or creating a new entry before Lock Date, in our case either accountant or adviser cannot change or create a new entry before the date 31/12/2017.

Setting to the Lock Date is referred to the closing financial year process in Odoo. The new financial year starts automatically, so we do not have to perform any process for that.

There's more...

The Odoo accounting application comes with many powerful reports available built in. Besides the built-in reports, some country-specific reports are also available from the localization module.

The **Profit and Loss** and **Balance Sheet** reports are the standard reports available in Odoo have already been gone through during the year-end process. Let's see in detail what the other standard reports available in Odoo are.

All the standard reports are available under the **Reporting** menu in the **Accounting** application.

Chart of account report

A listing of all your accounts, also known as **Chart of Account** or **Trial Balance**, is displayed grouped by class in some countries. In some countries, it can be displayed in a hierarchy format as well; the hierarchy is generated based on the account codes:

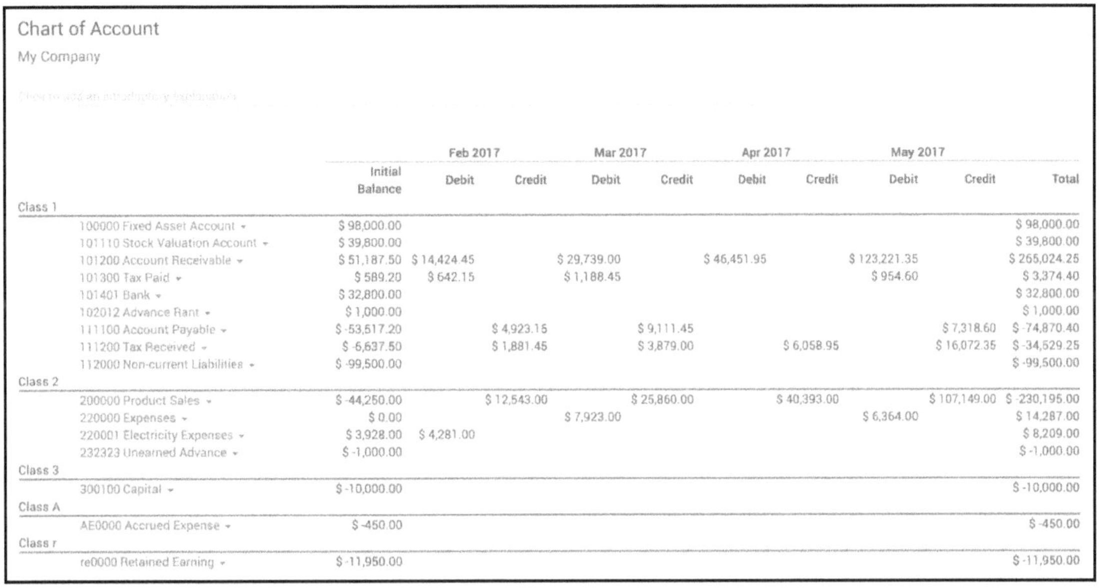

Chart of Account
My Company

	Initial Balance	Feb 2017 Debit	Feb 2017 Credit	Mar 2017 Debit	Mar 2017 Credit	Apr 2017 Debit	Apr 2017 Credit	May 2017 Debit	May 2017 Credit	Total
Class 1										
100000 Fixed Asset Account	$ 98,000.00									$ 98,000.00
101110 Stock Valuation Account	$ 39,800.00									$ 39,800.00
101200 Account Receivable	$ 51,187.50	$ 14,424.45		$ 29,739.00		$ 46,451.95		$ 123,221.35		$ 265,024.25
101300 Tax Paid	$ 589.20	$ 642.15		$ 1,188.45				$ 954.60		$ 3,374.40
101401 Bank	$ 32,800.00									$ 32,800.00
102012 Advance Rant	$ 1,000.00									$ 1,000.00
111100 Account Payable	$ -53,517.20		$ 4,923.15		$ 9,111.45				$ 7,318.60	$ -74,870.40
111200 Tax Received	$ -6,637.50		$ 1,881.45		$ 3,879.00		$ 6,058.95		$ 16,072.35	$ -34,529.25
112000 Non-current Liabilities	$ -99,500.00									$ -99,500.00
Class 2										
200000 Product Sales	$ -44,250.00		$ 12,543.00		$ 25,860.00		$ 40,393.00		$ 107,149.00	$ -230,195.00
220000 Expenses	$ 0.00			$ 7,923.00				$ 6,364.00		$ 14,287.00
220001 Electricity Expenses	$ 3,928.00	$ 4,281.00								$ 8,209.00
232323 Unearned Advance	$ -1,000.00									$ -1,000.00
Class 3										
300100 Capital	$ -10,000.00									$ -10,000.00
Class A										
AE0000 Accrued Expense	$ -450.00									$ -450.00
Class r										
re0000 Retained Earning	$ -11,950.00									$ -11,950.00

To change the trial balance view from classic to hierarchical, click on the **Options** tab, and select **Hierarchical and Subtotals**. The view will be changed to hierarchical view:

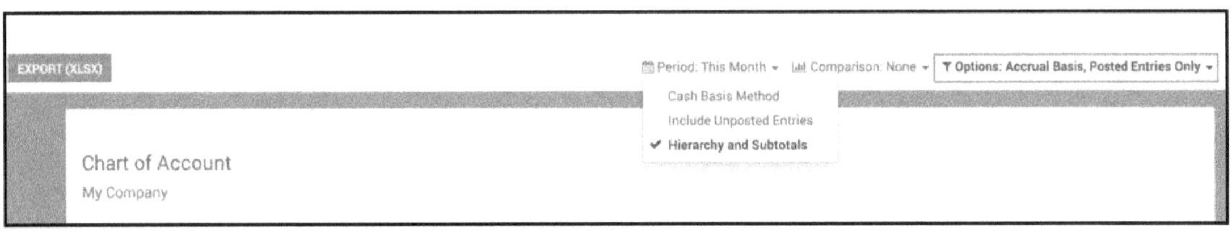

Compare profit and loss account

The **Profit and Loss** report (or **Income / Expense Statement**) shows your organization's net income or loss by deducting the expenses from the income for the report period selected on it.

Make sure that you have applied all the income and expense entries including depreciation on the assets at the end of the year to get the correct reports.

The **Profit and Loss** account can be found in the menu **Reports** | **Legal Statements** under the **Accounting** application.

The comparison of the reports can be activated from the **Comparison** menu, the default companies option selected is **No Comparison**. There are three ways to make the comparison explained as follows:

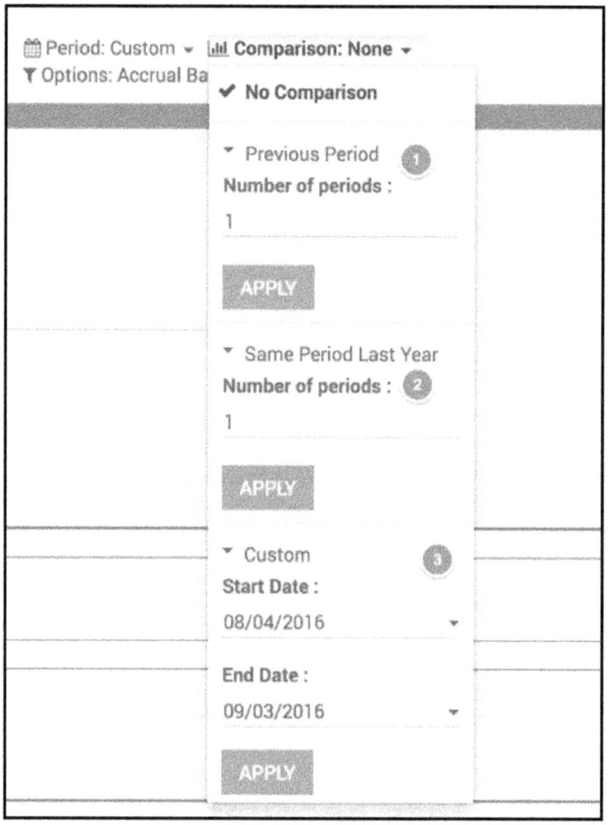

The comparison is always in respect to Period (*This Month, This Quarter, This Financial Year,* etc...). The following screenshot shows a profit and loss account of the last five months for the same financial year, as *This Month* is selected in **Period:**

Profit and Loss

My Company

	May 2017	Apr 2017	Mar 2017	Feb 2017	Jan 2017
INCOME					
Gross Profit					
Operating Income					
200000 Product Sales	$ 107,149.00	$ 40,393.00	$ 25,860.00	$ 12,543.00	$ 44,250.00
Total Operating Income	**$ 107,149.00**	**$ 40,393.00**	**$ 25,860.00**	**$ 12,543.00**	**$ 44,250.00**
Cost of Revenue	$ 0.00	$ 0.00	$ 0.00	$ 0.00	$ 0.00
Total Gross Profit	$ 107,149.00	$ 40,393.00	$ 25,860.00	$ 12,543.00	$ 44,250.00
Other Income	$ 0.00	$ 0.00	$ 0.00	$ 0.00	$ 0.00
Total INCOME	$ 107,149.00	$ 40,393.00	$ 25,860.00	$ 12,543.00	$ 44,250.00
Expenses					
Expenses					
220000 Expenses	$ 6,364.00	$ 0.00	$ 7,923.00	$ 0.00	$ 0.00
220001 Electricity Expenses	$ 0.00	$ 0.00	$ 0.00	$ 4,281.00	$ 3,928.00
Total Expenses	**$ 6,364.00**	**$ 0.00**	**$ 7,923.00**	**$ 4,281.00**	**$ 3,928.00**
Depreciation	$ 0.00	$ 0.00	$ 0.00	$ 0.00	$ 0.00
Total Expenses	$ 6,364.00	$ 0.00	$ 7,923.00	$ 4,281.00	$ 3,928.00
NET PROFIT	$ 100,785.00	$ 40,393.00	$ 17,937.00	$ 8,262.00	$ 40,322.00

We can compare by the previous period of the same financial year. The same period of the last financial year or by custom dates. From this comparison, an accountant can get a clear indication of any unexpected income or loss.

Compare balance sheets

The balance sheet report shows the company situation starting from the date of company incorporation. The balance sheet report can be printed from **Reporting** | **Legal Statements** under the **Accounting** application.

Like the profit and loss account comparison, the comparison for balance sheets can be enabled from the **Comparison** menu. The comparison can be done in three ways. Look at the following screen of comparison options:

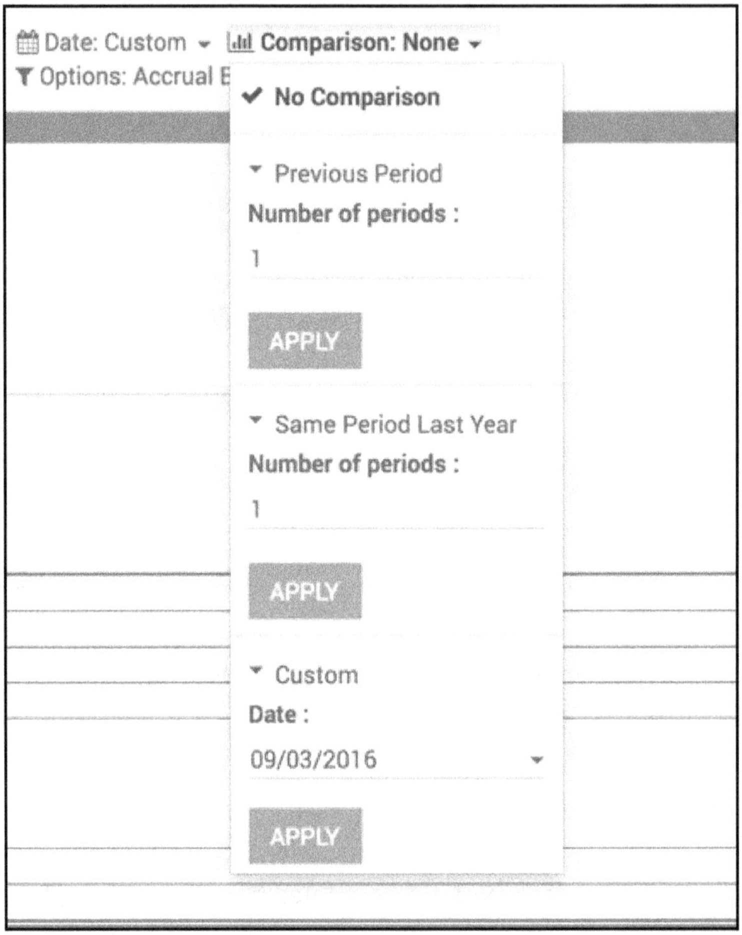

The default option selected for the comparison is *No Comparison*, other than that there are three other options available.

The comparison is always in respect to Period (*Today, End of the Month, End of Last Quarter or End of Last Financial Year*). The following screenshot shows a balance sheet of the last five months for the same financial year, as *Today* is selected in **Period**.

Current Liabilities					
Current Liabilities					
111200 Tax Received	$ 34,529.25	$ 18,456.90	$ 12,397.95	$ 8,518.95	$ 6,637.50
232323 Unearned Advance	$ 1,000.00	$ 1,000.00	$ 1,000.00	$ 1,000.00	$ 1,000.00
AE0000 Accrued Expense	$ 450.00	$ 450.00	$ 450.00	$ 450.00	$ 450.00
Total Current Liabilities	**$ 35,979.25**	**$ 19,906.90**	**$ 13,847.95**	**$ 9,968.95**	**$ 8,087.50**
Payables					
111100 Account Payable	$ 74,870.40	$ 67,551.80	$ 67,551.80	$ 58,440.35	$ 53,517.20
Total Payables	**$ 74,870.40**	**$ 67,551.80**	**$ 67,551.80**	**$ 58,440.35**	**$ 53,517.20**
Total Current Liabilities	$ 110,849.65	$ 87,458.70	$ 81,399.75	$ 68,409.30	$ 61,604.70
Plus Non-current Liabilities					
112000 Non-current Liabilities	$ 99,500.00	$ 99,500.00	$ 99,500.00	$ 99,500.00	$ 99,500.00
Total Plus Non-current Liabilities	**$ 99,500.00**	**$ 99,500.00**	**$ 99,500.00**	**$ 99,500.00**	**$ 99,500.00**
LIABILITIES	$ 210,349.65	$ 186,958.70	$ 180,899.75	$ 167,909.30	$ 161,104.70
CURRENT YEAR EARNINGS	$ 207,699.00	$ 106,914.00	$ 66,521.00	$ 48,584.00	$ 40,322.00
RETAINED EARNINGS					
300100 Capital	$ 10,000.00	$ 10,000.00	$ 10,000.00	$ 10,000.00	$ 10,000.00
re0000 Retained Earning	$ 11,950.00	$ 11,950.00	$ 11,950.00	$ 11,950.00	$ 11,950.00
Total RETAINED EARNINGS	**$ 21,950.00**	**$ 21,950.00**	**$ 21,950.00**	**$ 21,950.00**	**$ 21,950.00**
EQUITY	$ 229,649.00	$ 128,864.00	$ 88,471.00	$ 70,534.00	$ 62,272.00

We can compare with the previous period of the same financial year. The same period of the last financial year or by custom dates.

From this comparison, an accountant can get a clear indication of any unexpected ups and downs in the increase of liabilities or decrease of assets.

The Executive Summary report

The **Executive Summary** report allows you to take a quick look at all the important figures you need to run your company, such as cash, profitability, payables and receivables, and statistics on the credit period. Look at the following sample report that shows you a number with a comparison of last four months:

Executive Summary

My Company

Click to add an introductory explanation

	May 2017	Apr 2017	Mar 2017	Feb 2017	Jan 2017
CASH					
Cash received	$ 0.00	$ 61,428.40	$ 0.00	$ 15,062.55	$ 32,800.00
Cash spent	$ 0.00	$ 0.00	$ 0.00	$ 0.00	$ 0.00
Cash surplus	$ 0.00	$ 61,428.40	$ 0.00	$ 15,062.55	$ 32,800.00
Closing bank balance	$ 109,290.95	$ 109,290.95	$ 47,862.55	$ 47,862.55	$ 32,800.00
PROFITABILITY					
Income	$ 107,149.00	$ 40,393.00	$ 25,860.00	$ 12,543.00	$ 44,250.00
Cost of Revenue	$ 0.00	$ 0.00	$ 0.00	$ 0.00	$ 0.00
Gross profit	$ 107,149.00	$ 40,393.00	$ 25,860.00	$ 12,543.00	$ 44,250.00
Expenses	$ 6,364.00	$ 0.00	$ 7,923.00	$ 4,281.00	$ 3,928.00
Net Profit	$ 100,785.00	$ 40,393.00	$ 17,937.00	$ 8,262.00	$ 40,322.00
BALANCE SHEET					
Debtors	$ 188,533.30	$ 65,311.95	$ 80,288.40	$ 50,549.40	$ 51,187.50
Creditors	$ -74,870.40	$ -67,551.80	$ -67,551.80	$ -58,440.35	$ -53,517.20
Net assets	$ 229,649.00	$ 128,864.00	$ 88,471.00	$ 70,534.00	$ 62,272.00
PERFORMANCE					
Gross profit margin (gross profit / operating income)	100.0%	100.0%	100.0%	100.0%	100.0%
Net profit margin (net profit / income)	94.1%	100.0%	69.4%	65.9%	91.1%
Return on investments (net profit / assets)	22.9%	12.8%	6.7%	3.5%	18.1%
POSITION					
Average debtors days	52.8	46.9	93.1	108.8	34.7
Average creditors days	21.0	48.5	78.4	125.8	36.3
Short term cash forecast	$ 113,662.90	$ -2,239.85	$ 12,736.60	$ -7,890.95	$ -2,329.70
Current assets to liabilities	1.6	1.2	0.9	0.8	0.8

The following terms, which are used in the reports, are explained as follows:

- **Performance**:
    - **Gross profit margin**: This is the total sales achieved in the business less the direct cost to achieve those sales (that is, labor, materials, and so on)
    - **Net profit margin**: This refers to the gross profit less the overhead costs to achieve the sale (that is, office rent, electricity, taxes and duties, and so on)
    - **Return on investment (p.a)**: This is the ratio of the net profit achieved compared to the assets used to make that profit

- **Position**:
    - **Average debtor days**: The average number of days that your customers took to pay all invoices in full
    - **Average creditor days**: The average number of days you took to pay all vendor bills in full
    - **Short term cash forecast**: The cash is expected to come in this month and go out of the organization in the next month, that is, the difference between sales and purchases in the month.
    - **Current assets to liabilities**: This is, typically, used to measure a company's ability to clear its debt. It is also called current ratio--the ratio of the current assets to the current liabilities.

The General Ledger report

All the transactions are written in the accounting journals during the financial year. All those transactions can be printed in a ledger format; the **General Ledger** reports allow you to do that. The journals and the date period you choose, based on that the general ledger print the opening balance and transactions:

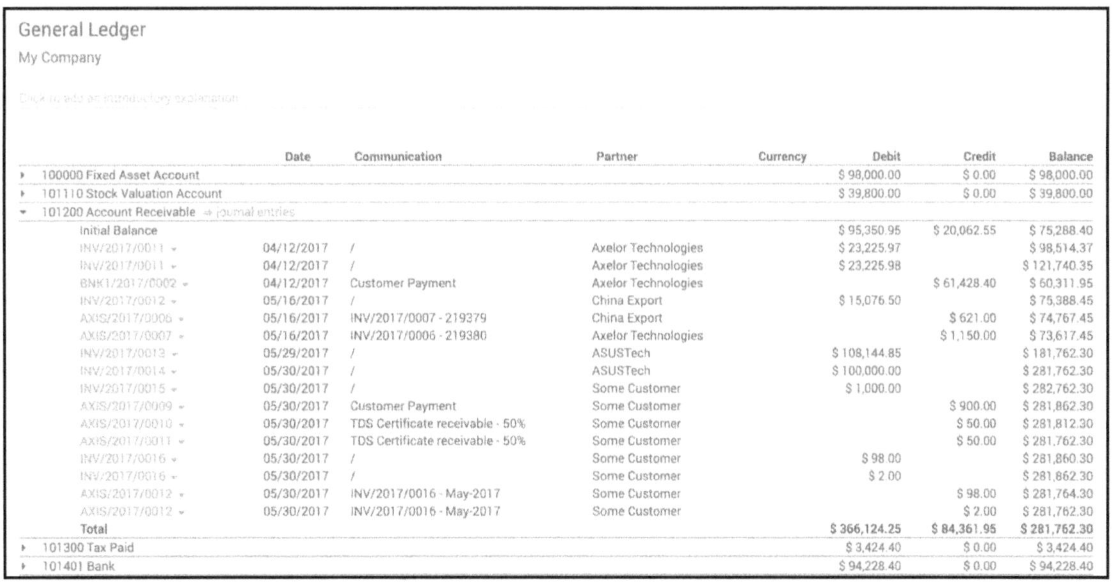

General Ledger

My Company

	Date	Communication	Partner	Currency	Debit	Credit	Balance
100000 Fixed Asset Account					$ 98,000.00	$ 0.00	$ 98,000.00
101110 Stock Valuation Account					$ 39,800.00	$ 0.00	$ 39,800.00
101200 Account Receivable ⇒ journal entries							
Initial Balance					$ 95,350.95	$ 20,062.55	$ 75,288.40
INV/2017/0011	04/12/2017	/	Axelor Technologies		$ 23,225.97		$ 98,514.37
INV/2017/0011	04/12/2017	/	Axelor Technologies		$ 23,225.98		$ 121,740.35
BNK1/2017/0002	04/12/2017	Customer Payment	Axelor Technologies			$ 61,428.40	$ 60,311.95
INV/2017/0012	05/16/2017	/	China Export		$ 15,076.50		$ 75,388.45
AXIS/2017/0006	05/16/2017	INV/2017/0007 - 219379	China Export			$ 621.00	$ 74,767.45
AXIS/2017/0007	05/16/2017	INV/2017/0006 - 219380	Axelor Technologies			$ 1,150.00	$ 73,617.45
INV/2017/0013	05/29/2017	/	ASUSTech		$ 108,144.85		$ 181,762.30
INV/2017/0014	05/30/2017	/	ASUSTech		$ 100,000.00		$ 281,762.30
INV/2017/0015	05/30/2017	/	Some Customer		$ 1,000.00		$ 282,762.30
AXIS/2017/0009	05/30/2017	Customer Payment	Some Customer			$ 900.00	$ 281,862.30
AXIS/2017/0010	05/30/2017	TDS Certificate receivable - 50%	Some Customer			$ 50.00	$ 281,812.30
AXIS/2017/0011	05/30/2017	TDS Certificate receivable - 50%	Some Customer			$ 50.00	$ 281,762.30
INV/2017/0016	05/30/2017	/	Some Customer		$ 98.00		$ 281,860.30
INV/2017/0016	05/30/2017	/	Some Customer		$ 2.00		$ 281,862.30
AXIS/2017/0012	05/30/2017	INV/2017/0016 - May-2017	Some Customer			$ 98.00	$ 281,764.30
AXIS/2017/0012	05/30/2017	INV/2017/0016 - May-2017	Some Customer			$ 2.00	$ 281,762.30
Total					$ 366,124.25	$ 84,361.95	$ 281,762.30
101300 Tax Paid					$ 3,424.40	$ 0.00	$ 3,424.40
101401 Bank					$ 94,228.40	$ 0.00	$ 94,228.40

Look at the preceding screenshot having a General Ledger of account receivable.

Cash flow statement report

The cash flow report shows the cash advance paid to vendors and the advance received from customers, which shows the cash flow for operating activities. You can also track the cash spent and received against a capital sale or purchase, the cash spent and received against financing activities such as bank changers, interest on loans, and so on, and finally, you can track the cash or equivalent cash in hand. Look at the following screenshot of the cash flow for the last four months:

	June 2017	May 2017	Apr 2017	Mar 2017
Cash flows from operating activities				
Advance Payments received from customers	$ 0.00	$ 0.00	$ 0.00	$ 0.00
▸ Cash received from customers	$ 0.00	$ 2,740.00	$ 93,809.00	$ 0.00
Advance payments made to suppliers	$ 0.00	$ 0.00	$ 0.00	$ 0.00
▸ Cash paid for	$ 0.00	$ -2.00	$ 0.00	$ 0.00
Total Cash flows from operating activities	$ 0.00	$ 2,738.00	$ 93,809.00	$ 0.00
Cash flows from investing & extraordinary activities				
Cash in	$ 0.00	$ 0.00	$ 0.00	$ 0.00
Cash out	$ 0.00	$ 0.00	$ 0.00	$ 0.00
Total Cash flows from investing & extraordinary activities	$ 0.00	$ 0.00	$ 0.00	$ 0.00
Cash flows from financing activities				
Cash in	$ 0.00	$ 0.00	$ 0.00	$ 0.00
▸ Cash out	$ 0.00	$ -90.00	$ 0.00	$ 0.00
Total Cash flows from financing activities	$ 0.00	$ -90.00	$ 0.00	$ 0.00
Cash flows from unclassified activities				
Cash in	$ 0.00	$ 0.00	$ 0.00	$ 0.00
▸ Cash out	$ 0.00	$ -69.57	$ 0.00	$ 0.00
Total Cash flows from unclassified activities	$ 0.00	$ -69.57	$ 0.00	$ 0.00
Minus previously recorded advance payments (already in the starting balance)	$ 0.00	$ 20.57	$ -32,380.60	$ 0.00
Net increase in cash and cash equivalents	**$ 0.00**	**$ 2,599.00**	**$ 61,428.40**	**$ 0.00**

In just one screen, you can have a full report for cash, whether it's received or paid, and the balance at the end in terms of liquidity.

The Aged Payable and Aged Receivable report

The **Aged Payable** and **Aged Receivable** reports always show the payment due as of today and to be received or paid in the coming days.

Look at the following report of **Aged Payable** that shows you the amount which is due as of today; you can drill down by individual vendors, and then, by vendor bills later:

Aged Payable

My Company

	Not due on 2017-05-27	0 - 30	30 - 60	60 - 90	90 - 120	Older	Total
Axelor Technologies							
MISC/2017/0001				$ 20,000.00			
Total	$ 0.00	$ 0.00	$ 0.00	$ 20,000.00	$ 0.00	$ 0.00	$ 20,000.00
China Export							
MISC/2017/0001				$ 29,000.00			
Total	$ 0.00	$ 0.00	$ 0.00	$ 29,000.00	$ 0.00	$ 0.00	$ 29,000.00
The Electricity Company							
BILL/2017/0004	$ 7,318.60						
BILL/2017/0001					$ 4,517.20		
BILL/2017/0002				$ 4,923.15			
BILL/2017/0003			$ 9,111.45				
Total	$ 7,318.60	$ 0.00	$ 9,111.45	$ 4,923.15	$ 4,517.20	$ 0.00	$ 25,870.40
Total	$ 7,318.60	$ 0.00	$ 9,111.45	$ 53,923.15	$ 4,517.20	$ 0.00	$ 74,870.40

The same as the **Aged Payable** report, the **Aged Receivable** reports show the customer due as of today and in the coming days. You can drill down by the individual customer, and later, invoices:

Aged Receivable

My Company

	Not due on 2017-05-27	0 - 30	30 - 60	60 - 90	90 - 120	Older	Total
ASUSTech							
AXIS/2017/0004					$ -15,062.55		
INV/2017/0009			$ 14,762.55				
MISC/2017/0001		$ 300.00					
INV/2017/0006		$ 2,344.85					
Total	$ 0.00	$ 2,644.85	$ 14,762.55	$ 0.00	$ -15,062.55	$ 0.00	$ 2,344.85
Axelor Technologies							
INV/2017/0010			$ 14,976.45				
INV/2017/0011			$ 23,225.97				
BNK1/2017/0002			$ -61,428.40				
INV/2017/0008		$ 7,607.25					
INV/2017/0011		$ 23,225.98					
INV/2017/0006		$ 48,542.65					
Total	$ 0.00	$ 79,375.88	$ -23,225.98	$ 0.00	$ 0.00	$ 0.00	$ 56,149.90
China Export							
INV/2017/0012		$ 15,076.50					
INV/2017/0007		$ 6,817.20					
Total	$ 0.00	$ 21,893.70	$ 0.00	$ 0.00	$ 0.00	$ 0.00	$ 21,893.70
Total	$ 0.00	$ 103,914.43	$ -8,463.43	$ 0.00	$ -15,062.55	$ 0.00	$ 80,388.45

Tax Report

Tax Report shows you the tax collected on sales and the tax paid on purchases in a single screen:

Tax Report

My Company

Click to add an introductory explanation

	Base Amount May 2017	Tax	Base Amount Apr 2017	Tax	Base Amount Mar 2017	Tax	Base Amount Feb 2017	Tax	Base Amount Jan 2017	Tax
Sale										
Tax 15.00% (15.0)	$ 107,149.00	$ 16,072.35	$ 40,393.00	$ 6,058.95	$ 25,860.00	$ 3,879.00	$ 12,543.00	$ 1,881.45	$ 44,250.00	$ 6,637.50
Purchase										
Tax 15.00% (15.0)	$ 6,364.00	$ 954.60	$ 0.00	$ 0.00	$ 7,923.00	$ 1,188.45	$ 4,281.00	$ 642.15	$ 3,928.00	$ 589.20

You can get the net amount and tax amount by ledger, and compute the tax which is payable in the end.

8
Scale Your Business

In this chapter, we will cover the following recipes:

- Manage multi-currency transactions
- Multi-company and intercompany transactions and rules
- Analytic accounting and reporting
- Revenue recognition
- Asset management and depreciation

Introduction

Odoo has a powerful accounting application with a modular approach that attracts various kinds of user base. Users can actually use invoicing-only or full-feature accounting application depending on their needs. There are some advanced features such as managing multiple currencies, multiple companies, profit center, and depreciation or revenue recognition when you would like to scale your business with multiple branches or start selling in the international market.

Computing depreciation is quite a complicated job. When you have many different types of assets, you may want to track the types of assets and their current value, compute the depreciation, and scrap the assets at the end of their life.

Let's see how you can implement the accounting features that you need to scale your business, and manage advanced accounting features such as cost centers, assets, and depreciation for multiple categories of assets, and recognition of periodic revenue in the case of advance sales.

Manage multi-currency transactions

As soon as you grow your business, you start selling in multiple currencies. Shipping internationally requires lots of formalities to be performed, with clean documents such as invoices in their native currency. Let's assume that you start selling to Europe and you need to raise an invoice in EUR. However, all your accounting has to be done in USD as you are in the USA. You raise an invoice in EUR, which is susceptible to change on a daily basis. You should be able to track and encode the business impact between the rate on which the invoice is raised and the rate on which the payment is received in your bank.

Let's see how to activate the multi-currency feature in Odoo, how to enable new currency and their rates, and how to compute the foreign exchange gain or loss while dealing with multiple currencies.

Getting ready

We assume that you are ready with the list of currencies to activate in Odoo. Odoo allows you to manage the rates for the currency either manually or through synchronization from the European Central Bank or Yahoo finance service. Decide after reading how you would like to update the rates and how frequently the exchange rate has to be updated.

How to do it...

1. Odoo works in single-currency mode by default. You can activate the multi-currency mode by going to **Configuration** | **Setting** under the **Accounting** application. Search for `Multi Currencies` and activate the **Allow multi currencies** feature, as shown in the following screenshot:

As soon as you activate the feature, you will be asked to select the **Rate Difference Journal**. It is the journal that is used to record the foreign exchange gain or loss transaction during payment reconciliation. It will be selected by default as a part of the chart of account configuration.

You can also configure how frequently and from where you would like to configure the currency rates. Look at the **Live Currency Rates** option.

2. New currency can be activated by going to **Configuration** | **Multi-Currencies** | **Currencies** under the **Accounting** application. You will get a list of currencies available in Odoo. Click on the currency you would like to activate; let's activate the **EUR** currency:

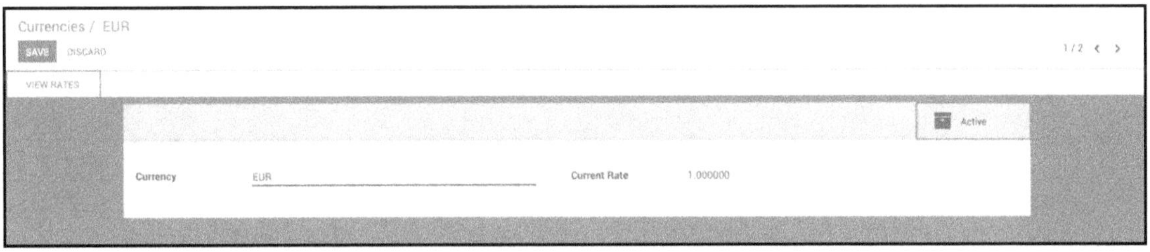

By clicking on the **Active** button, the current rate was set to `1` by default. You can change the rates for the currency by clicking on the **VIEW RATES** button. Create a new rate that should be with respect to the base currency. Normally, the base currency is the one that is set on the company currency:

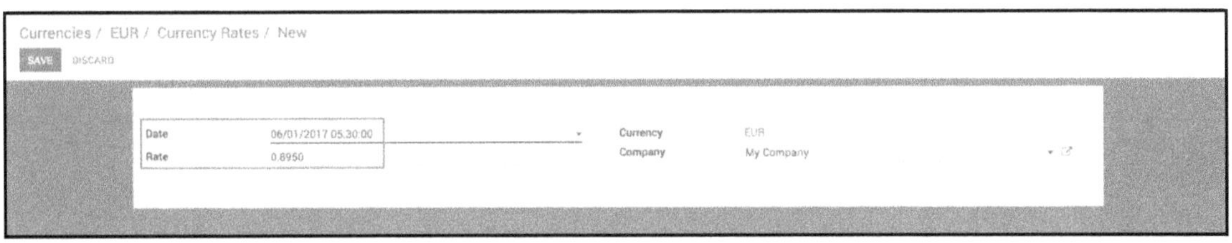

3. The currency field has been activated on the invoice to raise an invoice in a different currency than the company currency. Make sure that you select the currency just after selecting the customer, and then start adding the invoice lines:

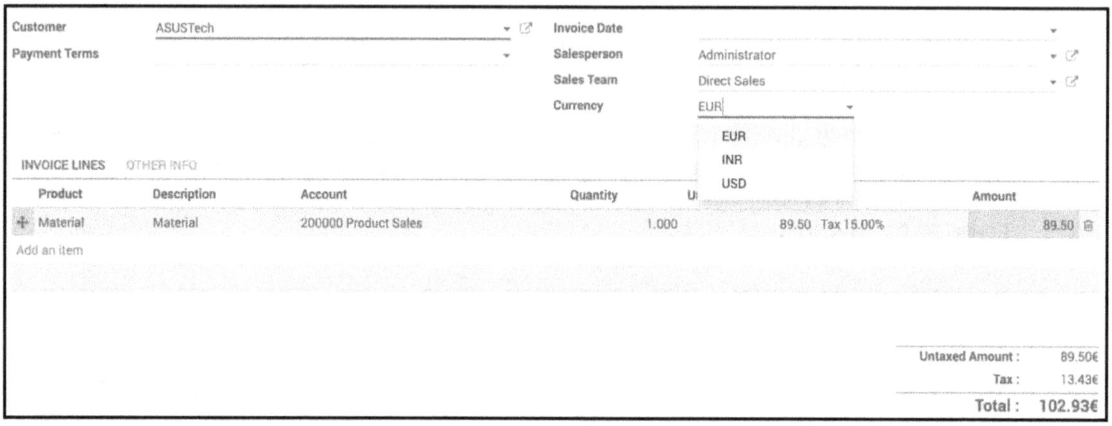

The position of the currency symbol changes depending on the currency. The $ symbol will appear before the amount, while € will appear after the amount. This can be changed in the currency configuration by entering the **Debug** mode.

4. In my case, the sale price for the material is **$100** as my company currency is USD. When I create an invoice for a European customer in EUR, it computes to **89.50€** based on the exchange rate of 1$ being equal to 0.895€. Confirm the invoice and look at the journal entry linked to the invoice. The transaction takes place in a different currency, but the accounting entry is written in USD ($):

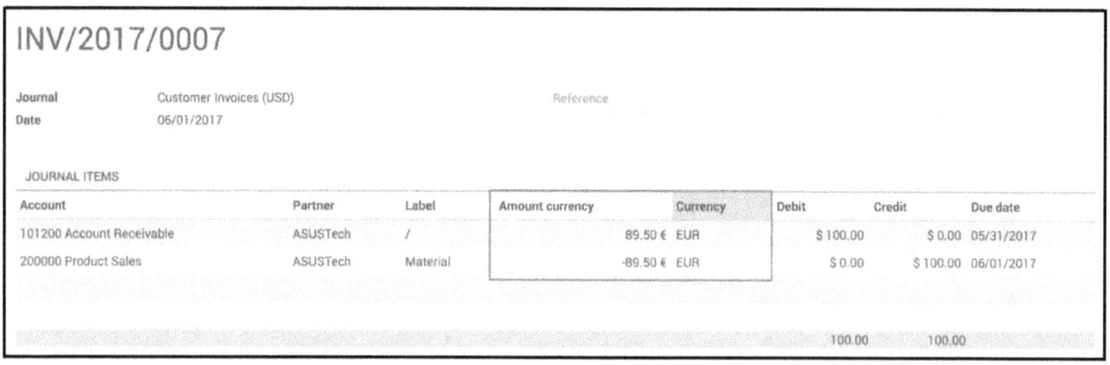

The accounting transaction is always recorded in the company currency. If it is a multi-currency transaction, the **Amount Currency** and **Currency** fields hold the currency information.

5. The customer initiates the payment in EUR from their bank, and the customer transfers the payment receipt. Let's register the payment receipt in Odoo. Look at the following screenshot to register the EUR transaction in a bank account:

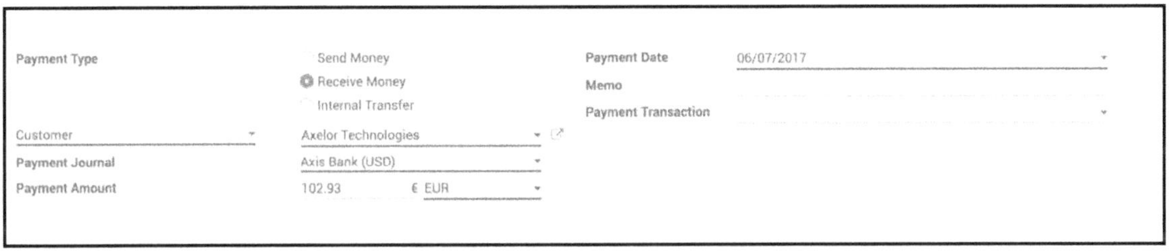

6. Match the invoice entry with the payment entry manually. Look at the following screenshot. The payment entry matches with the invoice entry in EUR currency as we get the instruction from the customer in EUR:

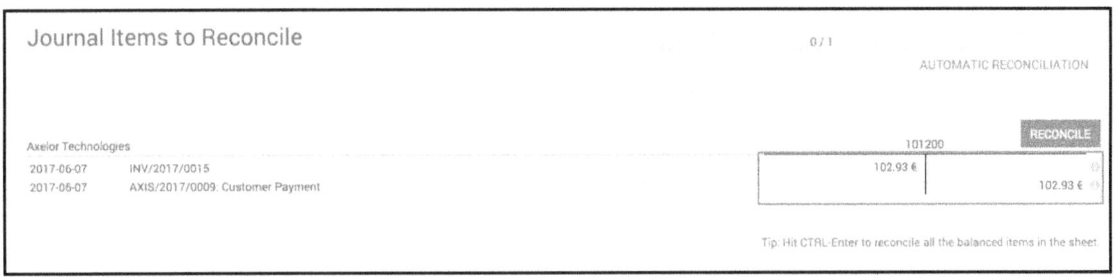

7. Click on the **RECONCILE** button to reconcile the entry. It computes the exchange gain or loss and creates an entry during the reconciliation process. We received $1.28 less as the exchange rate changed. Look at the following entry for the foreign exchange loss:

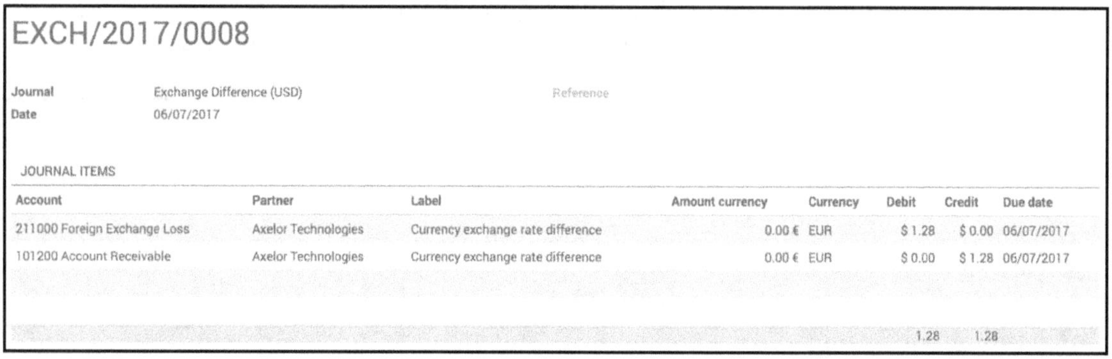

There's more...

You may find the **Currency** field on almost every screen related to accounting, such as **Invoice**, **Vendor Bill**, **Payments**, **Bank Statement**, and so on, on every transaction. You can define the transaction currency and conversion to the company currency for accounting. Several topics such as multi-currency journal entry, managing Forex bank account, multi-currency pricelist, and foreign exchange gain or loss have to be understood in detail while setting up the multi-currency environment.

Multi-currency journal entry

While working with multi-currency transactions, you will get the **Currency** field on every screen. You can actually encode the journal ledger in a different currency than the company currency. Let's take an example where you get the capital funding from foreign investors through bank transfers. The transfer you got was in EUR, and your company currency is in USD.

To create the journal entry, go to **Adviser** | **Journal Entries** under the **Accounting** application. Click on the **CREATE** button to create a new entry, select the **Miscellaneous Operations (USD)** journal, select the date of the transaction, enter details in **Reference**, and create a transaction line as follows:

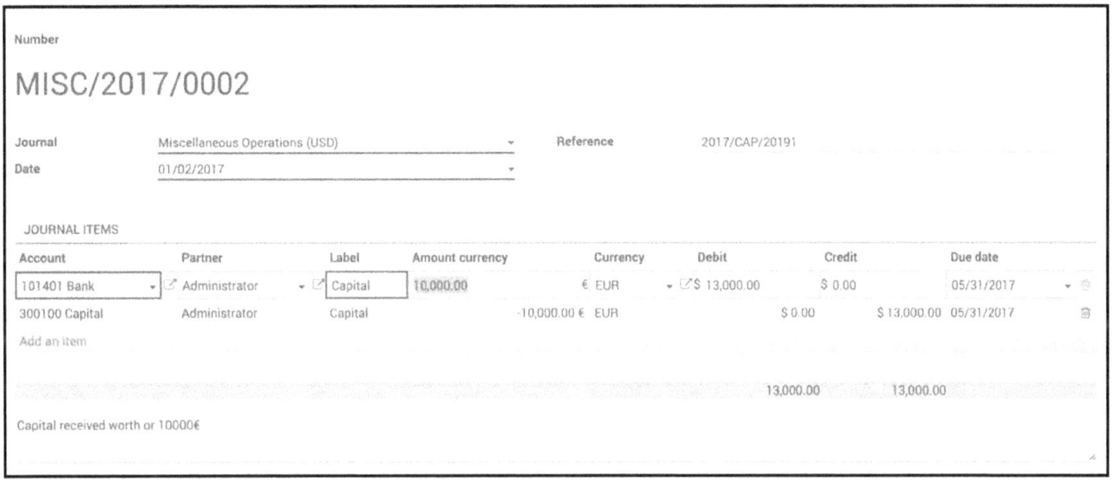

As soon as you post the entry, you will find the difference in the amount. Create a bank statement and reconcile. Check the balance sheet report at the end. You should see that your capital account has been increased by $13,000.

Forex bank account

In some countries, businesses can hold foreign currency in a bank by opening a foreign currency account. It is a special bank that operates for a foreign currency, that is, the company in the USA can open the bank account to hold the EUR currency.

Odoo can manage your bank account that holds the foreign currency in the bank. You can also make the transaction in the foreign currency to receive or send the money. Let's see how Odoo can help you to manage it.

Create a new Bank journal. Go to **Configuration** | **Accounting** | **Journals** in the **Accounting** application. Create a new bank journal. You will find the **Currency** field. Select the foreign currency you hold in the bank. In this case, it is **EUR**. Now, click on **SAVE** to save the journal:

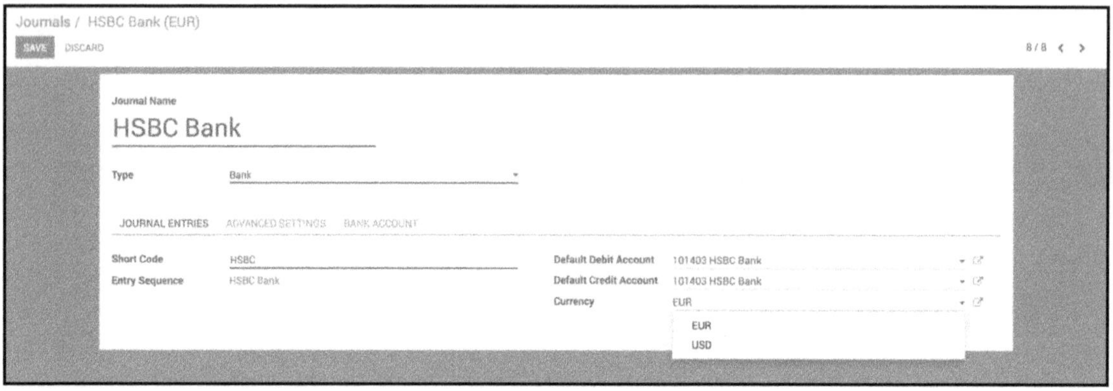

You will find the **Currency** field set to **EUR** on the default Debit and Credit account created automatically and linked on the journal. Once you save the bank journal, you are ready to either create or import the statement in the journal.

Let's assume that you are waiting for the customer invoice that was raised in EUR, and you receive a payment from the customer in EUR. To encode the payment, let's create a bank statement and enter the transaction of the payment receipt first. The amount you entered is in EUR as your bank account currency is in EUR. The reconciliation can be done at the end of the month when the bank statement is received; look at the reconciliation of the bank payment received against the invoice.

Let's check the balance sheet report to be sure that our accounting system produces all the figures and reports in USD only, even if we have a bank account in foreign currency:

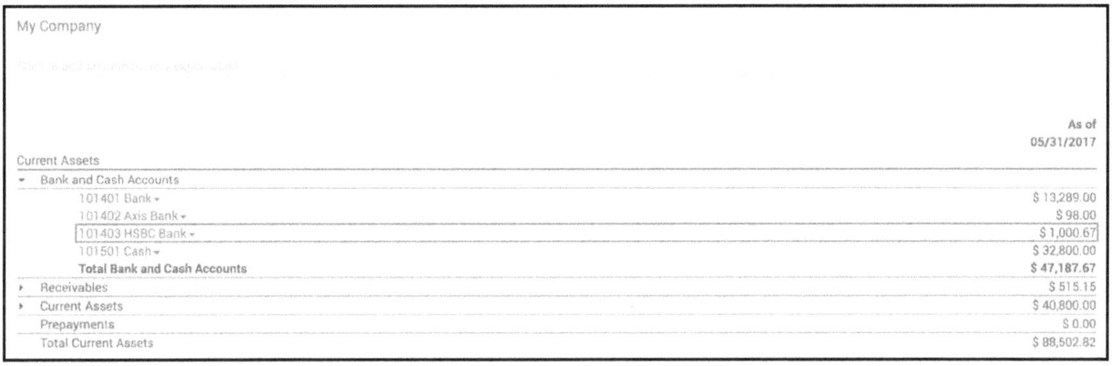

My Company

	As of 05/31/2017
Current Assets	
▾ Bank and Cash Accounts	
101401 Bank ▾	$ 13,289.00
101402 Axis Bank ▾	$ 98.00
101403 HSBC Bank ▾	$ 1,000.67
101501 Cash ▾	$ 32,800.00
Total Bank and Cash Accounts	**$ 47,187.67**
▸ Receivables	$ 515.15
▸ Current Assets	$ 40,800.00
Prepayments	$ 0.00
Total Current Assets	$ 88,502.82

Odoo converts the currency to the base currency using the latest exchange rates available, and stores them on the transaction. The foreign exchange gain or loss has to be computed and entered manually for the Forex bank account at regular intervals.

The balance for the Forex bank account will not change on the balance sheet as soon as the currency rate changes.

Multi-currency Pricelist

Pricelist is a great feature of Odoo to define special pricing rules for a set of customers. However, this feature is available only on the **Sales** application. You can use a **Pricelist** on the sales quotation. Go through recipe `Chapter 4`, *Modern way of doing sales and managing sales contracts*, under the recipe *Create and configure your products* to understand how pricelist works in Odoo.

The conversion of price between multiple currencies will be done by the multi-currency engine. Let's taken an example of the **Material** product we have. The sale price is $100. When we sell in Europe we will raise an invoice in EUR; this computes the price to 89.74€ based on the rate. However, some business cases do not require the price conversion, but a fixed price that is not based on the rate conversion, such as where the price of a t-shirt in the USA is $100 while the same t-shirt sold in Europe is 90€, which is not a conversion between USD to EUR.

The only way is to create a **Pricelist**, for EUR currency and set the fixed price on the product. You can get the price of the product depending on the **Pricelist** and not based on the currency conversion:

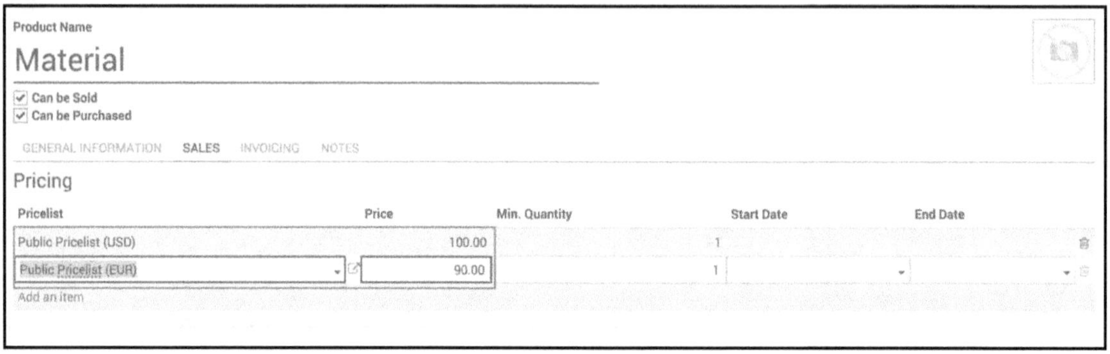

Create a sales quotation in EUR. Try to sell the **Material** product. Instead of rate conversion, you should get the price of 90€. Look at the sales order screen here:

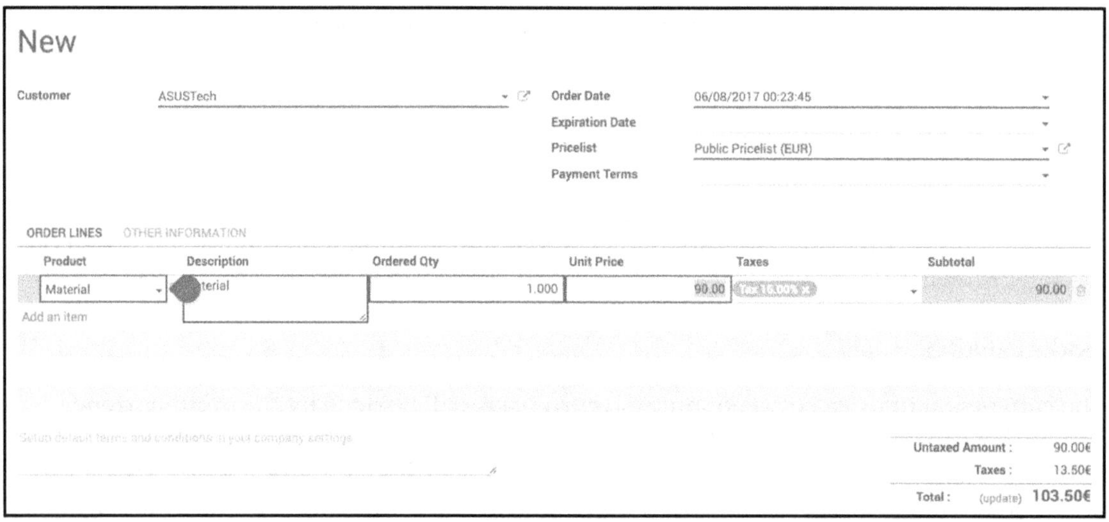

Foreign exchange gain or loss

It is normal in business to receive more or less amount when you sell and receive payment in foreign currency. Such difference should be recorded under the special account called a foreign exchange gain or loss account that impacts the net loss or net profit.

We have already seen how foreign exchange gain or loss works. Make sure that you are continuously updating the exchange rates for the currency you are dealing with to compute the correct exchange difference.

Multi-company and intercompany transactions and rules

Starting a new company in a different country is a way to scale the business. Scaling a business will bring more revenue to the business. At the same time, if you don't track the financial activity, it can be converted to a big loss too. There are many challenges to overcome in managing a subsidiary company. Some challenges are listed here:

- Setup, that is, working with a different chart of accounts and different fiscal period
- Localization reports for the parent and subsidiary companies
- Consolidation of numbers in different reports (Profit and Loss and Balance Sheet are the main reports)
- Managing an intercompany transaction (a transaction in one company will be recorded to the other company automatically)
- Managing intercompany access rights

There are many such challenges to be addressed in order to succeed in setting up and working in a multi-company environment.

Let's see how Odoo can manage all your challenges to scale business and get consolidation and control over multi-company environments. Odoo also supports automation for the inter-company transaction rules while working in a multi-company environment.

Getting ready

Staring a subsidiary company is the same as starting a new company. You have to set up the company's legal information, install the chart of account, and add the missing account depending on the country where the subsidiary started, set up the bank statement feed, and so on.

The most important configuration is to decide who will work under which company: not physically, but who will have access to both the companies. You have to prepare the list of users to allow them such access.

How to do it...

1. In order to set up multiple companies in Odoo, the multi-company feature has to be activated. Go to **Settings** | **General Settings**, search for the **Manage multiple companies** option, and enable it:

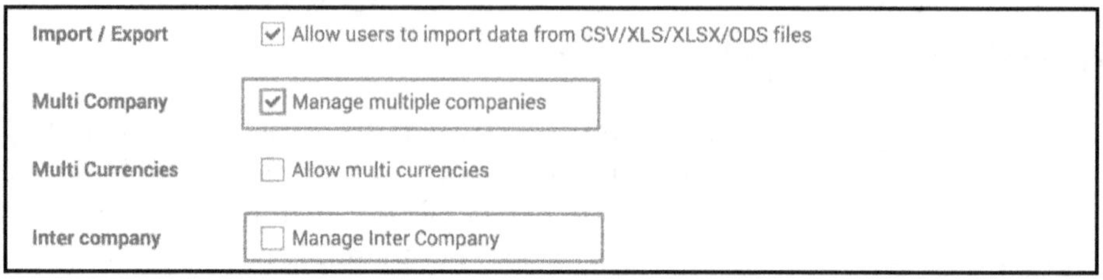

As soon as you select the **Manage multiple companies** option, the **Manage Inter Company** option will appear, and you can select it if you want to automate intercompany transaction based on the rules. Click on **APPLY** to save the setting.

> TIP: If you do not plan to use either **Sales** or **Purchase** or **Inventory** application, it is suggested to not activate the **Manage Inter Company** feature as it will install **Sales**, **Purchase** and **Inventory** application, which may cost you on a recurring basis.

2. As soon as multi-company is enabled, go to **Settings** | **Users** | **Companies** and create a new company. Enter the company information. Look at the following screenshot of the new company:

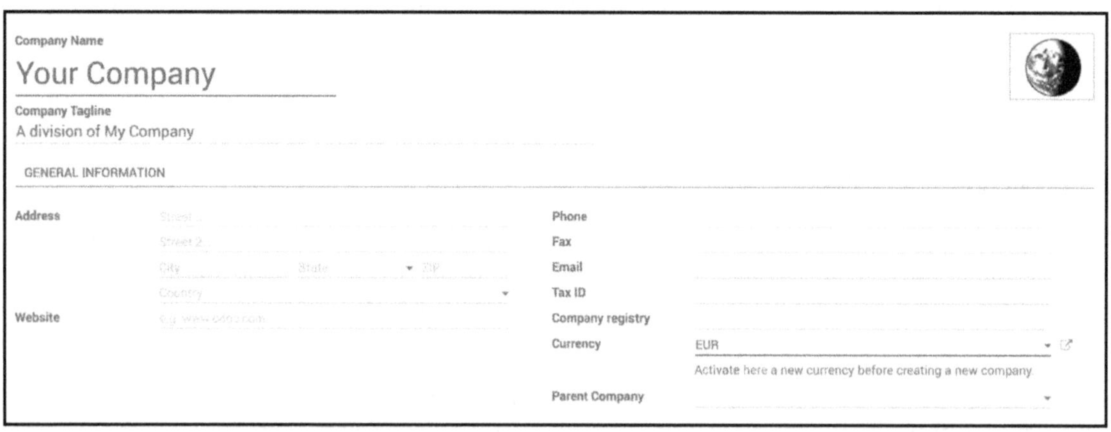

Make sure that besides the company information, the currency set by the company is correct.

3. To set up localized company information, users have to connect to that company. Let's choose the list of users who can connect to your company. Go to users through **Settings** | **Users** | **Users**. Open **Users** and add **Your Company** to the **Allowed Company** field on that user form:

Save the user and reload the page. As soon as the page reloads, you can see the company selector at the top, beside the current username. When you click on that, you will see the list of companies to which the current users have an access to connect. Users can enter that company by clicking on the company name from the menu. Look at the following screenshot:

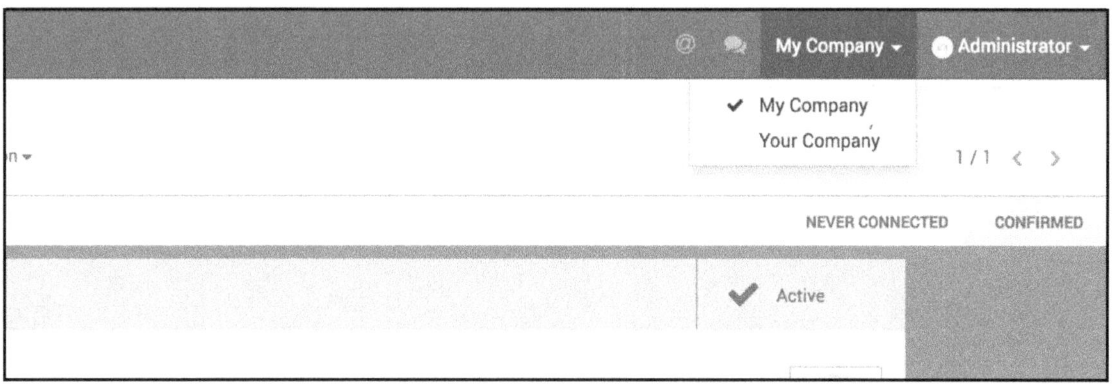

4. Now, it's time to set up the localization information for the new company, such as chart of account, the rate for the base, and other currencies. Let's go to **Configuration** | **Settings** and then go to the **Accounting** application:

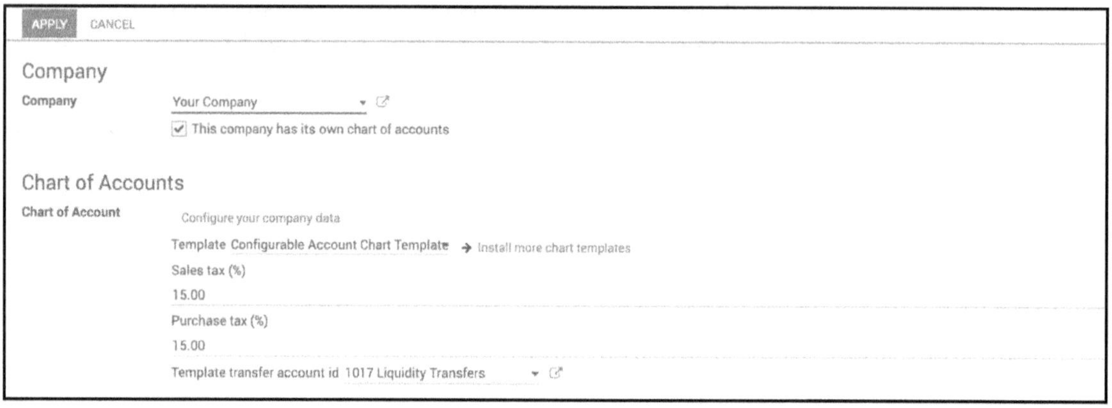

Changes made on this settings page will be updated for the current currency company selected on the page. Here, in my case, it is **Your Company**. To load the chart of an account, either select it from the list or install the template by clicking on the **Install more chart of templates** link. If you install a country-specific module, the rest of all the setup will be done automatically.

5. Before we do any transaction, let's check the currency and their rates by going to **Configuration** | **Currencies**. Filter only **Active** currency from the **Filters** option. Look at the screen here. Both currencies have the rate `1.000000`, which is not normal:

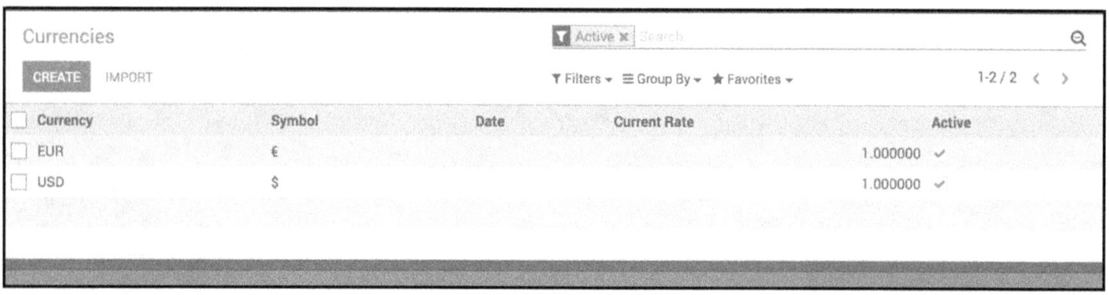

According to the current company, EUR is a base currency; so, the rate for EUR should be `1.00000`. The rates for other currencies should be updated with respect to EUR. Update the rates for USD with respect to EUR. After that, it should be displayed as shown here:

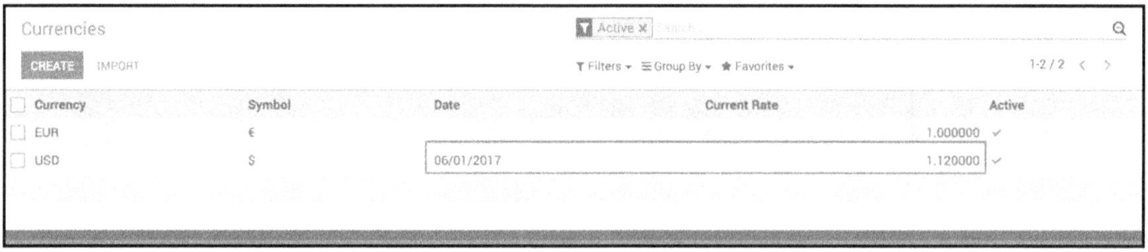

6. You are still in your company and the company's currency is in EUR. Let's create an invoice as your company is ready for transactions with the product of your company. Look at the following screenshot of the invoice created in EUR currency:

It is always advisable to separate the product when you are working under the multi-company and multi-currency environment.

You can be sure by verifying that the invoice being created belongs to **Your Company** only. Check on the **OTHER INFO** tab; you will find **Your Company** in the **Company** field:

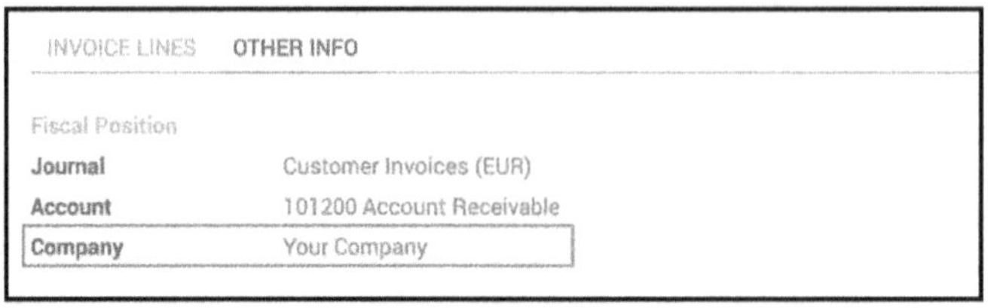

Every document, not just the invoice, that has to be separate from the other company has a **Company** field.

There's more...

The reason behind starting a new company is to get tax benefits or really expand a business across multiple countries. In most cases, the role of the subsidiary company is to buy from the company and sell to the local market. After all, the role of the head office is to track and control the expenses of subsidiary companies, get the profitability for each company, and generate the global profit and loss statement and balance sheet at the end of the financial year.

Let's see how we can consolidate the profit and loss statement and balance sheet, allow the chief finance officer to see and control the subsidiary and set up the intercompany invoicing between subarray companies.

Consolidation of the profit and loss statement and balance sheet

The most difficult job is to consolidate the financial statements across multiple companies, especially when you are working across multiple companies in different countries, which means managing their accounting in different currencies. Odoo manages this in a smart way, without defining the parent-child relationship between those companies.

A user can have access to the data from multiple companies in reporting based on the **Allowed Companies** field. Users can consolidate the data into reports from the list of companies defined in **Allowed Companies**. If you have not configured the **Allowed Companies** field properly, have a look at the following screenshot and change the configuration accordingly:

Once the **Allowed Companies** field is configured correctly, let's go to the **Balance Sheet** report under the **Accounting** application and try to print the report. No matter which company you are connected to, the report will be prepared based on the current company's currency, but the accounting entries will be fetched from all the companies selected in the report. The list of companies will be available in the report for selection based on the **Allowed Companies** field in the user form. Take a look at the following **Balance Sheet** account report:

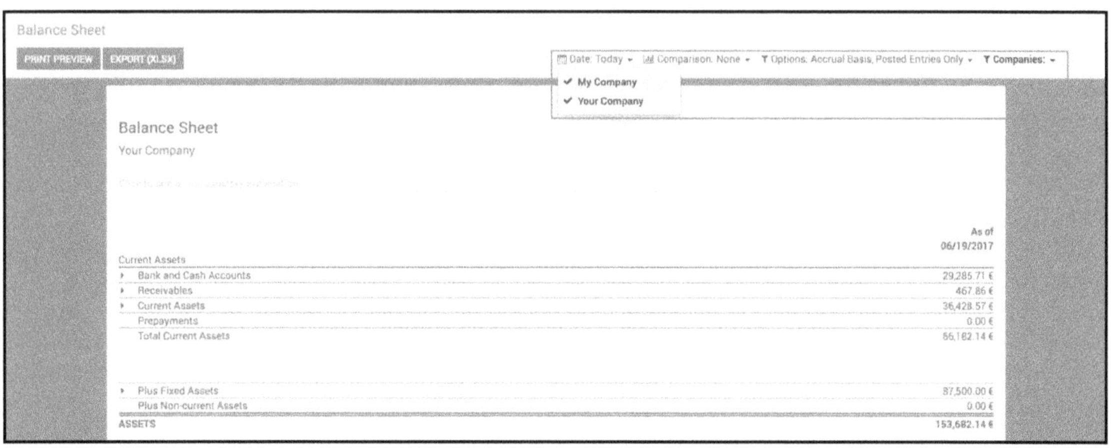

Now, switch to **My Company** and try to print the same report. The report will be available in USD, and all the figures will be available in USD:

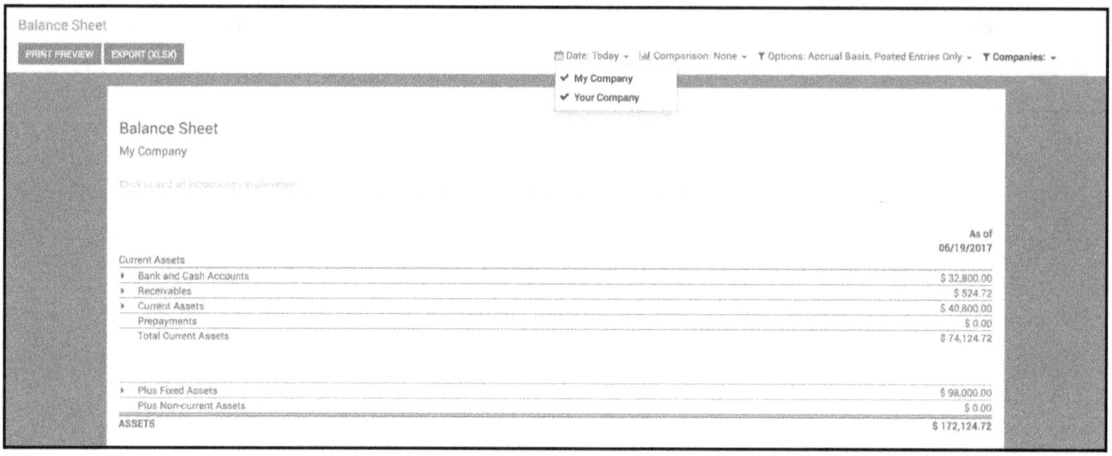

The printing of any reports works out of the box in a multi-company and multi-currency environment. You can choose which company is to be included in the reports.

Make sure that the currency and its rates are up to date to get the correct reports.

Subsidiary company

In most cases, the multi-company needs to be set up for subsidiary companies. What they need is a consolidation of the balance sheet at the end of the financial year, even though there is no parent-child relationship between companies.

In some cases, finance offices want to see ongoing transactions for the entire subsidiary without switching between companies. Odoo allows you to switch between companies, and you can get the information for that company.

The ongoing transactions can be available to the finance officer. Just by defining the parent-child relationship between companies, the officer can track and manage the approval and rejection of the invoices or any other documents:

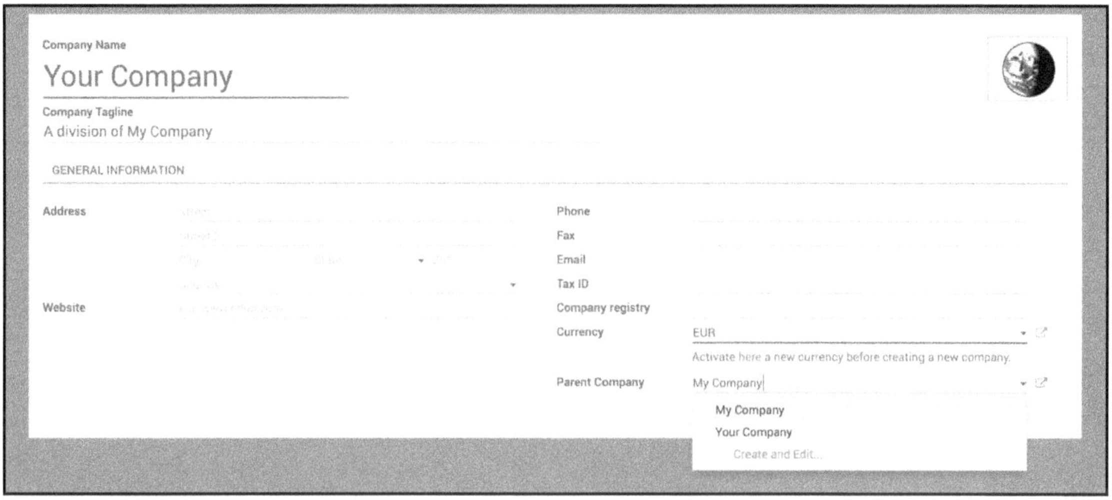

Look at the preceding screenshot. It shows you how to configure **Your Company** as a child company by selecting **My Company** in **Parent Company** field.

Inter-company invoicing

An intercompany transaction is a primary need when you have multiple companies. Subsidiary companies are usually purchasing from the parent company and selling to the local market. There are lots of invoices or sales orders to be created for the purchases made by all the subsidiaries.

An intercompany transaction can be set up at two levels, either at **Sales** or **Purchase** application or directly at the invoicing level.

The intercompany transaction rules can be activated by going to **Settings** | **General Settings**. Look at the following screenshot. Select the **Create Invoice/Refunds when encoding invoice/refunds** option to set up intercompany transactions at the invoice level:

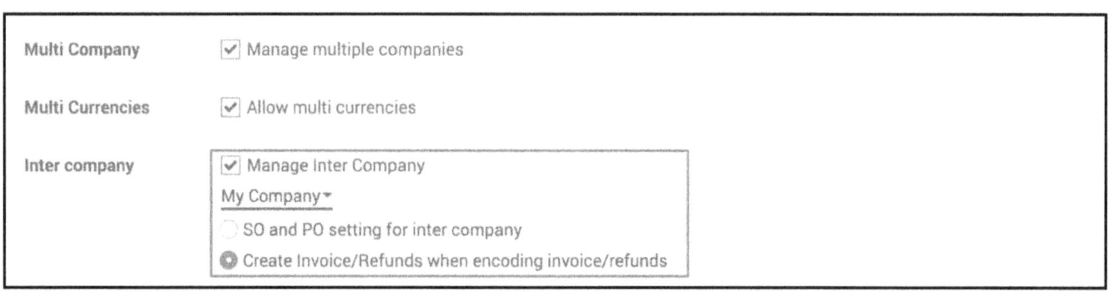

When the parent company (**My Company)** creates customer invoices, the vendor bill will be created automatically for the child company (**Your Company**). Look at the following screenshot. It shows an invoice created for **Your Company**:

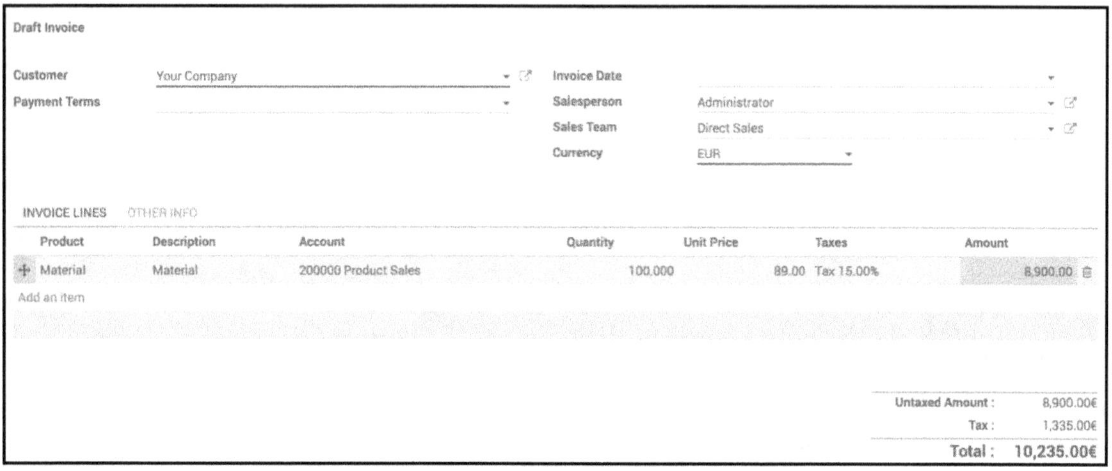

The vendor bill will be created in **Your Company** automatically when the customer invoice is confirmed in **My Company**. Look at the screenshot here:

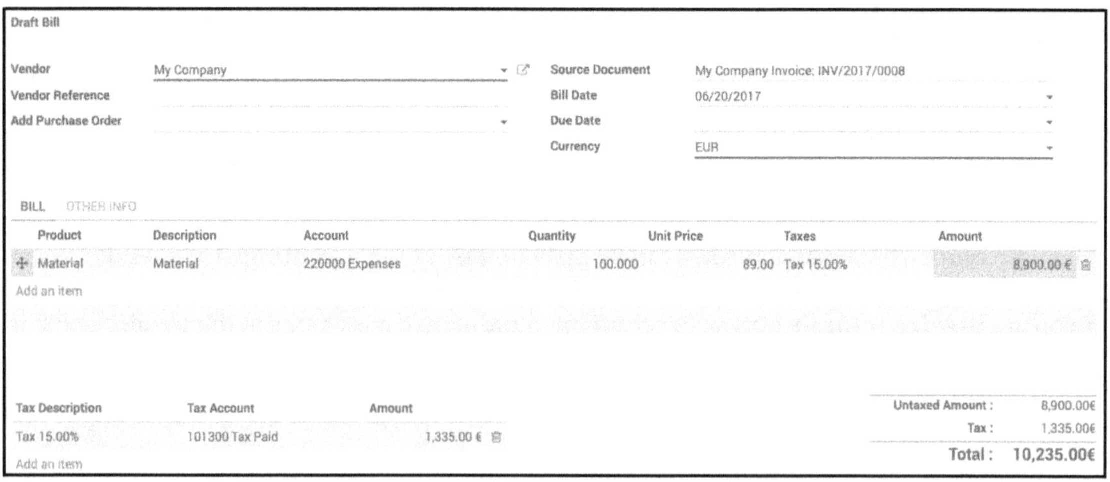

The taxes have to be verified and applied manually based on the customer invoice; they will not be applied by default. You can choose to integrate at the **Sales** or **Purchase** level if you need advanced rules for the intercompany transaction.

Analytic accounting and reporting

Analytic accounting is also known as the cost/profit center. It is used to group various accounts to calculate the difference between cost and revenue and know whether we can expect income or expense. The analytic account can be used to assess the profitability of projects, track and control regular expenses, and so on.

Odoo manages the cost center or profit center using an analytic account. It is a special single-entry accounting system where debit entry is represented by negative amounts and credit entry represent by positive amounts. It can be linked with every financial transaction that should be included in the costing or profit center.

The analytic accounting entry can be created either automatically or manually. Usually, an analytic entry can be created automatically from sales invoices, vendor bills, projects, or a timesheet. Let's see how can we can enable this feature and calculate the costing or profitability of using analytic account through the invoicing directly.

How to do it...

1. The analytic accounting feature can be enabled from the **Configuration | Settings** page of the **Accounting** application. Search for **Analytic accounting** under the **Accounting and Finance**, features group. Select it and click on the **APPLY** button to enable it:

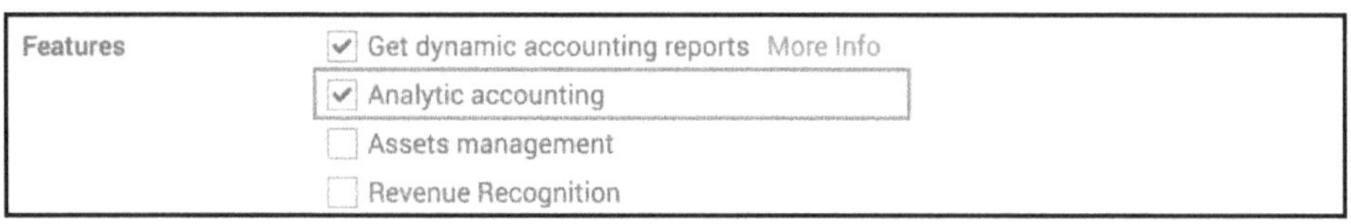

2. The cost center / analytic account can be created by going to **Advisor** | **Analytic Accounting** under the **Accounting** application. You will find the list of analytic accounts created. Click on **CREATE** to create a new one.

   Enter the name in the **Analytic Account** field. Fill the **Reference** field and the **Customer** field if it is related to a specific customer:

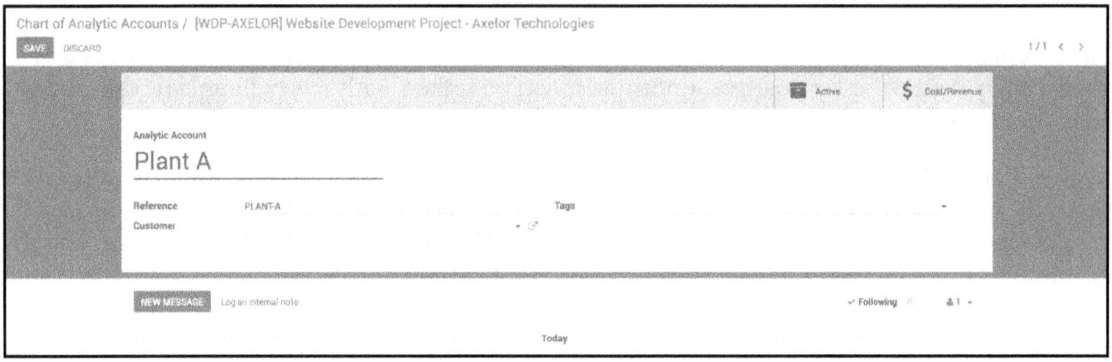

3. The team working on the project will fill the timesheet. Purchase of any material dedicated to this project can be entered as a cost, and sales registered to this project can be registered as an income for this project. It will be done automatically. Just select the analytic account at the time of purchase or enter the timesheet entry:

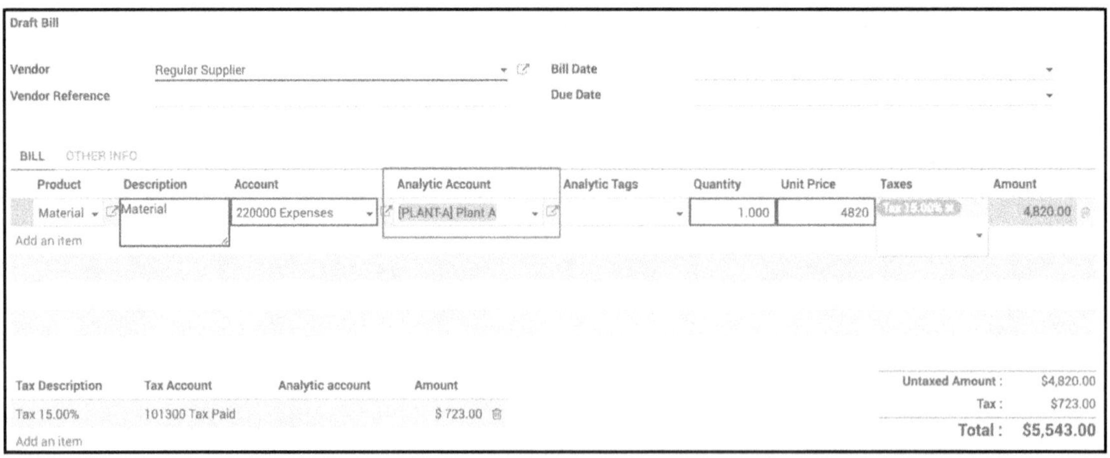

   Look at preceding screenshot. The project is selected during the purchase of the material.

4. Link an analytic account at the time of creating an invoice for the project, like with the expense. An income will be registered with the analytic account, and the difference between the revenue and cost will be either profit or loss:

As soon the customer invoice gets confirmed, the analytic entries will be created automatically.

Let's check the analytic accounts. On the list, you can see the total **Debit** and **Credit**, and the difference between them as **Balance**.

Debit represents the expense; **Credit** represents the income. If the balance is positive, it will be profit; otherwise, a negative balance represents the loss. Look at the following screenshot for the list of analytic accounts:

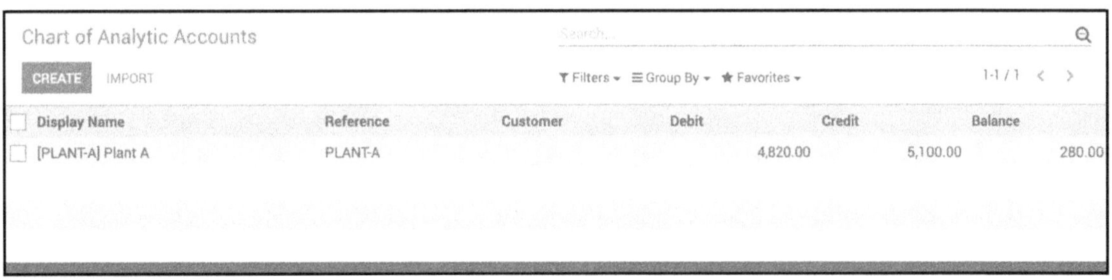

Like other Odoo views, you can also apply the filter and grouping to generate the statistical reports.

5. The detailed list of the income and expense entries can be viewed for the analytic account. Open the form view of the analytic account and click on the **Cost / Revenue** action button. The reports can be generated from the list view by applying the **Group By** options, with the default group options applied by month. Look at the screenshot here:

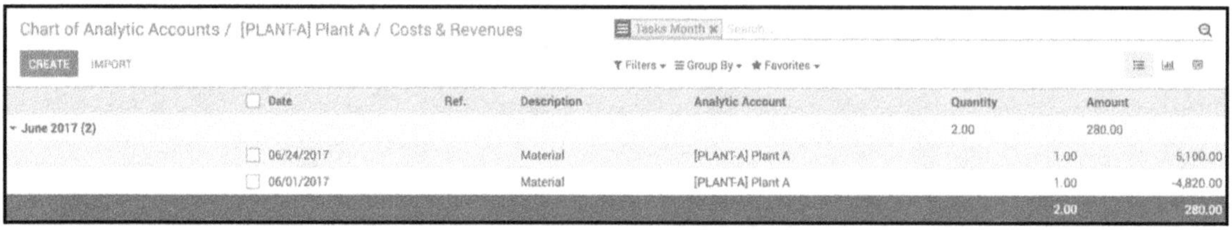

6. You can remove the grouping by month, and apply other groupings to get the different reports.

There's more...

Create an analytic account and link that analytic account with financial transactions, which are income or expenses for that analytic account. The cost-versus-revenue report will be generated, and we can come to know about profit or loss for that analytic account. We can set the customer-on-customer field on the analytic account to get the profitability by customer. There are various ways of using the analytic account in Odoo.

Analytic account on the sales order

The invoice can be automatically created from the **Sales** order; an accountant has to verify and confirm the invoice. On the invoice, the analytic account has to be set on every line, while on **Sales** order, it is a single field available on the **OTHER INFORMATION** tab:

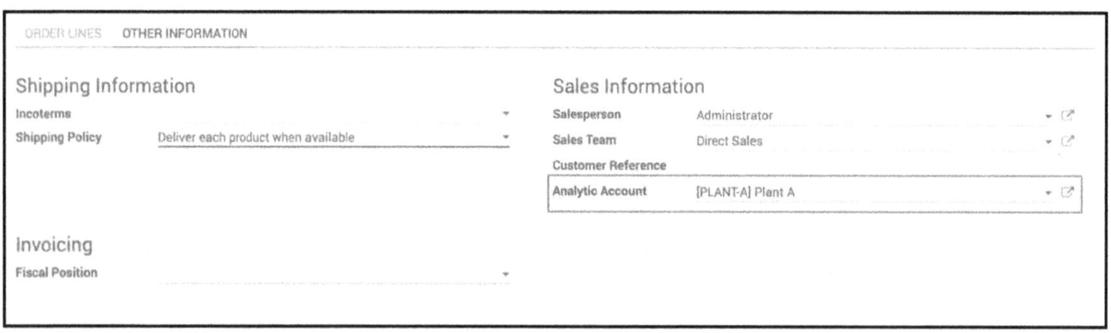

When an analytic account is set on the **Sales** order, it will set automatically on the invoice lines when the invoice is created from the **Sales** order.

The sales order will create an analytic account when you are selling the service type product that needs to be tracked through the project or timesheet. All the costs and revenue should be registered on the same project/analytic account to get the profitability. Using analysis of analytic entries, you can get the detailed statistical reports by a customer or by project/order.

> TIP
>
> Go through `Chapter 5`, *Time Tracking and Invoicing Policy*, to get into the details of how it works. In this chapter, you can jump into details about selling services through Odoo and keeping track of delivery using the analytic account.

Record working hours on analytic account

Odoo has a great feature for the delivery of time and material and tracking the same Timesheet application. You can use the **Timesheet** application to record the time spent by your team on the project, and the cost will be recorded automatically on the analytic account.

> TIP
>
> Go through `Chapter 5`, *Time Tracking and Invoicing Policy*, to get a detailed understanding of the product setup to track time and invoice policy, time tracking while delivering services, and working with the Timesheet application.

Default analytic account

An analytic entry can be created manually or automatically. Most of the time, it is preferable to create an entry automatically. Analytic entry can be set on the invoice automatically if the invoice is created from the sales order, or if you have to set it manually on the invoice lines when the invoice is being created manually. It will be difficult to choose an analytic account from the list of accounts available when you have to choose an account based on the customer or product on the invoice line.

The **Account Analytic Defaults** module allows you to set the default analytic account on the invoice line based on the product, customer, user, company, or time period, and based on the date range. Install the **Account Analytic Defaults** module from Odoo Apps. On successful installation of the application, the **Analytic Defaults** menu can be found by going to **Configuration** | **Settings** in the **Accounting** application.

Click on the **CREATE** button to create a new rule. Let's create a rule to choose **Plant A** as an analytic account when an invoice will be created for the **Material** product. Look at the following screenshot for the rule:

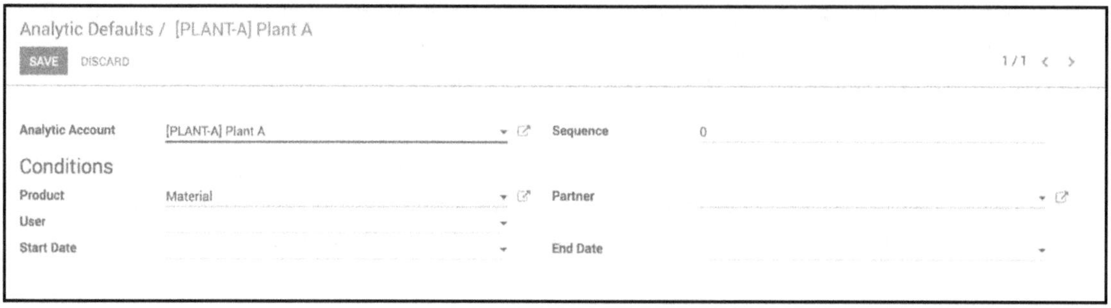

Save the rule and let's create an invoice. Choose the customer, and choose the Material as a product on the invoice line. The **Plant A** analytic account should be selected automatically on that invoice line:

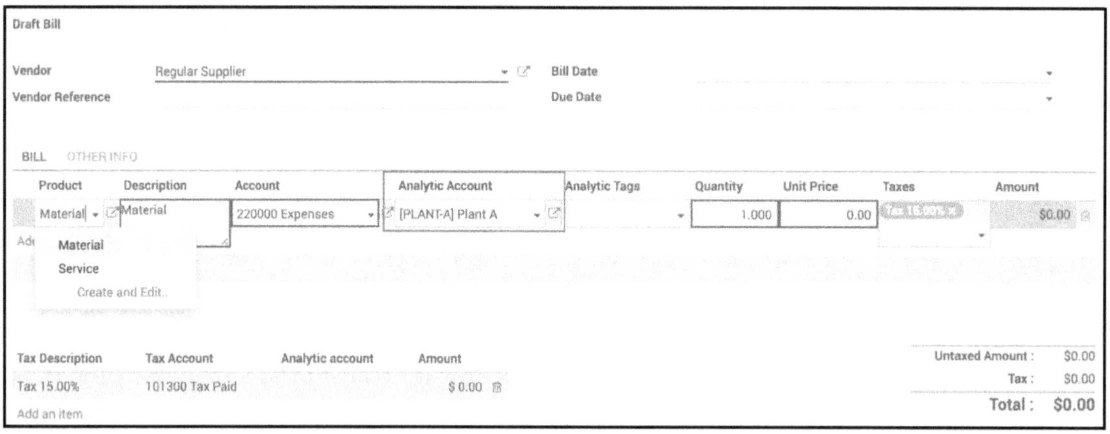

Unlimited rules can be created. Rules created using the analytic default will be applied at the time of creating customer invoices and vendor bills.

If multiple analytic accounts get selected based on the rules, the sequence field will be used to select one account to apply.

Department-wise reports

It is a common requirement in business to view the profitability of the departments or units within a single company. For multi-company, it can be checked easily as every company has their own financial statements that represent the situation. Before Odoo `10.0`, it was not possible to see the profit and loss or balance sheet for the specific department or unit. Odoo version 10.0 allows you to do that.

The Analytic Accounts and Tags can be one of the filters available to set on profit and loss or balance sheet reports. The analytic account is set on all the financial transactions. Thanks to analytic default rules, the reports can be filtered by the analytic accounts or tags.

Let's see the profit and loss report for the **Plant A** and **Plant B** accounts by applying a filter using the analytic account. Look at the following screenshot:

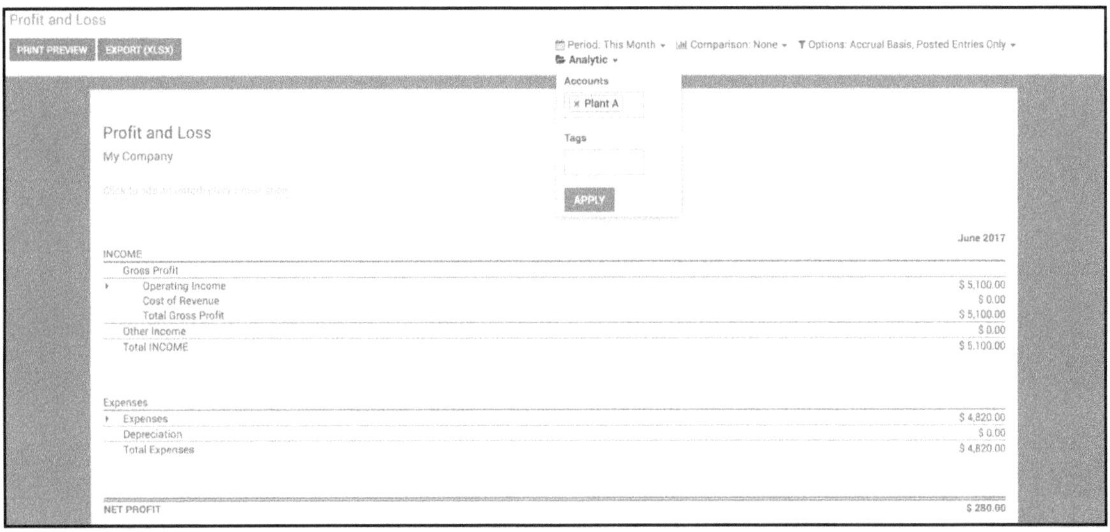

The **INCOME** and **Expenses** field are filtered based on the analytic account linked at the time of registering the income or expense. Look at the following screenshot. It represents the profit and loss account for **Plant B**:

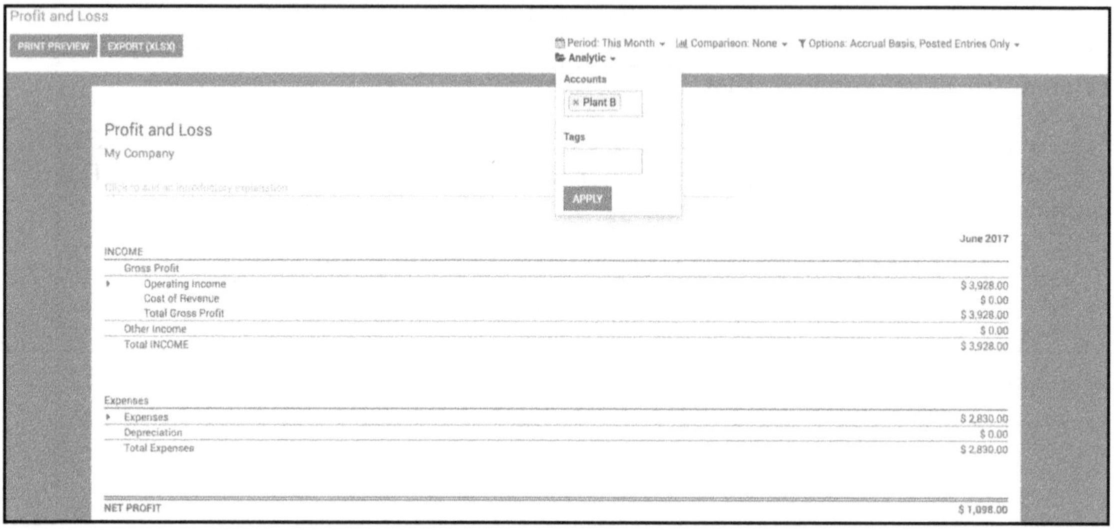

Comparing the profit and loss for **Plant A** with **Plant B**, it is clearly visible that **Plant B** is more profitable. **Plant A** has more turnover with less margin.

Using **Tags**, you can also compare the productivity of the same product in different plants. You can link multiple tags beside the analytic account on every financial transaction.

Using revenue recognition

Selling subscription contracts is one of the possible ways of selling services with the Odoo subscription application. Consider the kind of business where advance payment is received from the customer against the subscription contract. It is a liability and not an actual sale. This customer advance is registered as a deferred revenue instead of being registered as a sale. Every month, liability will decrease and income will be incurred from the advance received. This accounting mechanism is called revenue recognition.

Let's see how we can set up the revenue recognition in Odoo without using subscription application.

How to do it...

1. To enable the **Revenue Recognition** feature for the accounting application, go to **Configuration** | **Settings**. Search for **Revenue Recognition** and select it. Then, click on **APPLY** to activate the feature.
2. The next step is to create a deferred revenue type by going to **Configuration** | **Management** | **Deferred Revenue Type**. **Deferred Revenue Type** has to be configured to define the accounts to be used at the time of sales, to create a liability, to identify the number of entries, and to understand when to recognize the sales, that is, every 1 month or every 2 months. Look at the following screenshot for a 12-month plan:

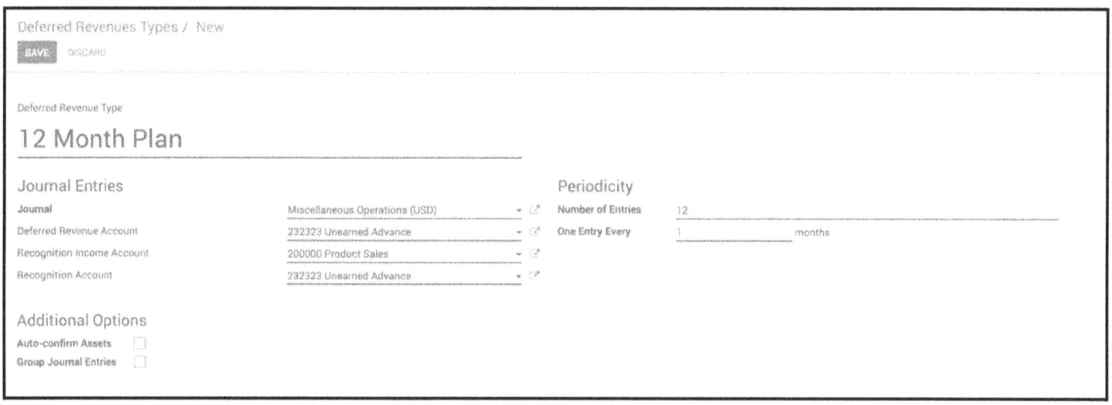

3. The revenue recognition type has to be set on the product so that each invoice created for that product will automatically create the revenue recognition plan.

   Let's set the deferred revenue type on the product. Open the service product from the **Sellable** products from the **Sales** menu. Go to the **INVOICING** tab and select the **12 Month Plan** on the **Deferred Revenue Type** field:

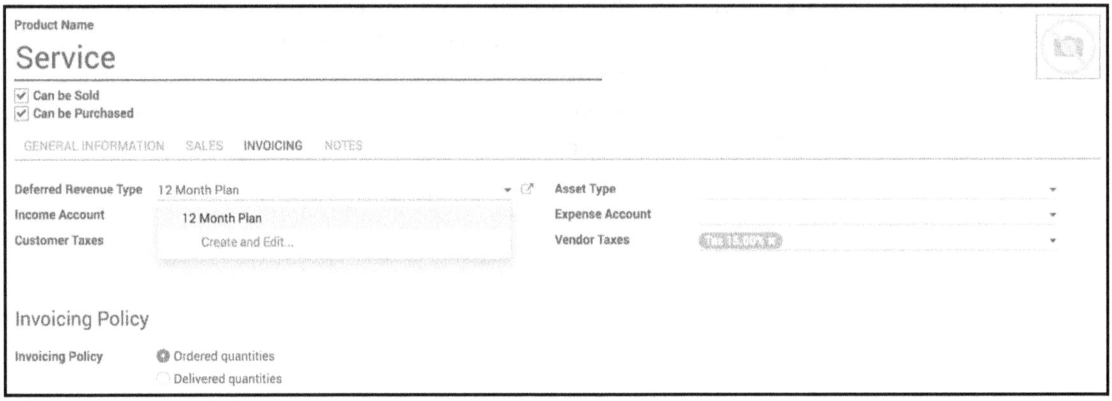

4. To test the **Deferred Revenue Type**, let's create an invoice for the service product:

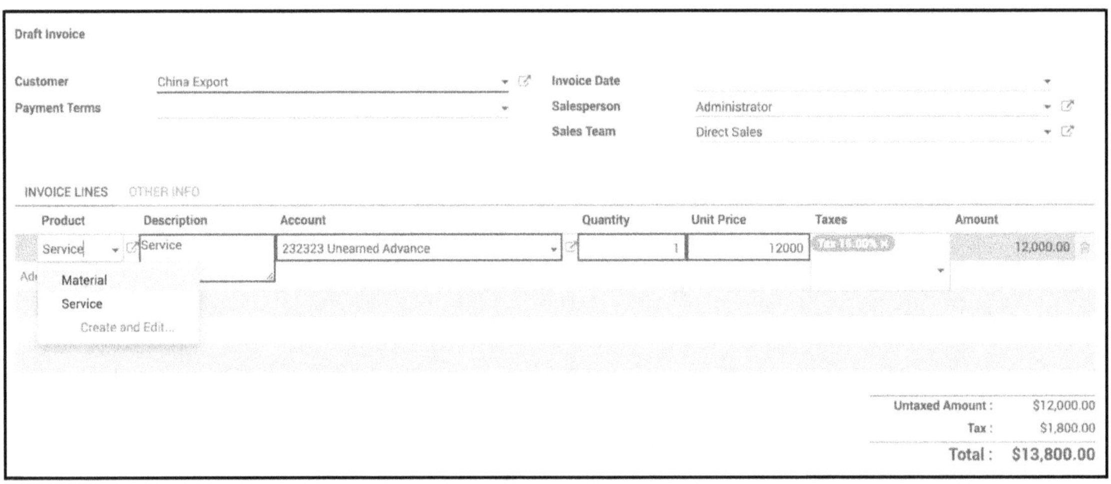

   Look at the preceding screenshot. I have a sales service to **China Export**. As soon as the service product was selected on the invoice line, the account on the invoice line changed to **Unearned Advance**. Now, save and validate the invoice.

5. The draft **Deferred Revenues** will be created by going to **Advisory** | **Deferred Revenues**. If everything goes well, **Deferred Revenues** is a document that contains the details of the number of installments for the revenue recognition, each with a date and amount to be recognized as an income:

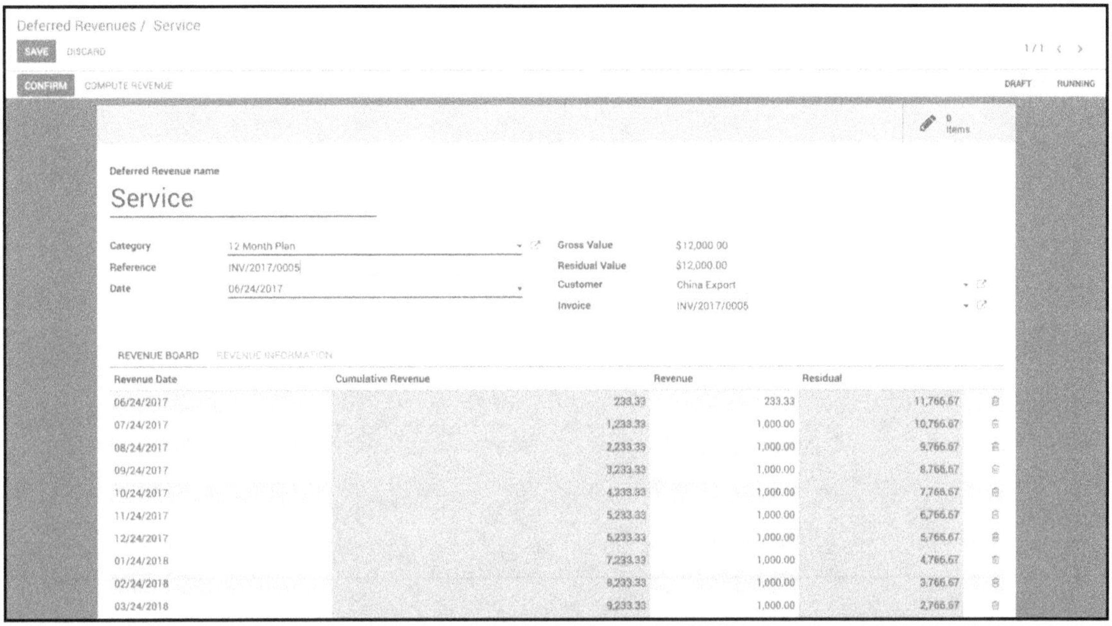

You can get the link to the invoice from where it has been created. The residual value is an amount that still needs to be recognized as an income. By default, all the new **Revenue Recognition** is in draft mode. Click on **CONFIRM** to start the recognition.

6. There is an automated action that takes care to post an entry for all the running **Deferred Revenues**.

You can run the wizard manually. **Generate the Deferred Revenue Entries** can be found in the **Advisory** menu. Enter the debug mode.

7. Each deferred revenue entry generated a color indication that represents the state of the entries itself. This indication will be based on the related accounting entry; if accounting entry was not created, the deferred revenue entry will display the RED signal. It will be in ORANGE when the related accounting entry is created but it will remain as a draft, it will become GREEN only when accounting entry confirms and posts.
8. Look at the following screen, which shows that the accounting entry was created but not posted.

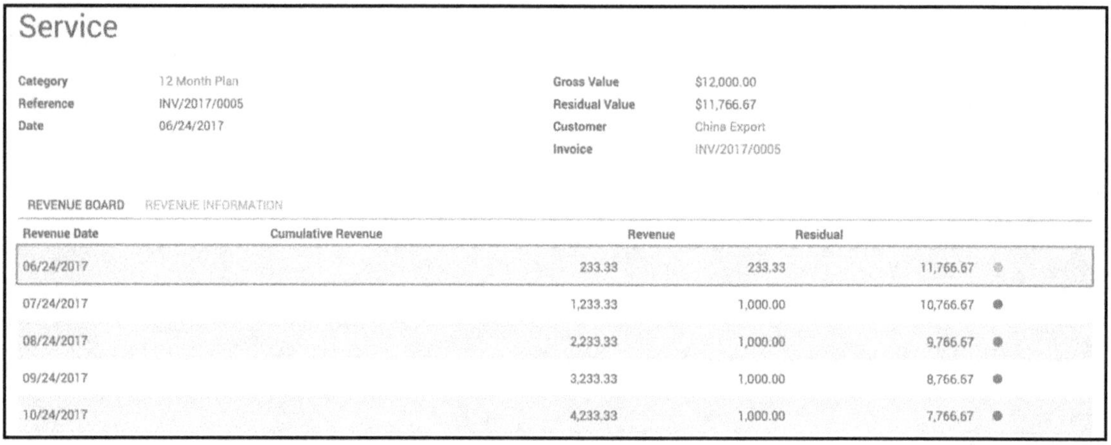

9. An orange signal shows that the entries have been created, but not posted yet. An accountant can review and post the entries. Click on **Items**. The entries created for this deferred revenue can be found here:

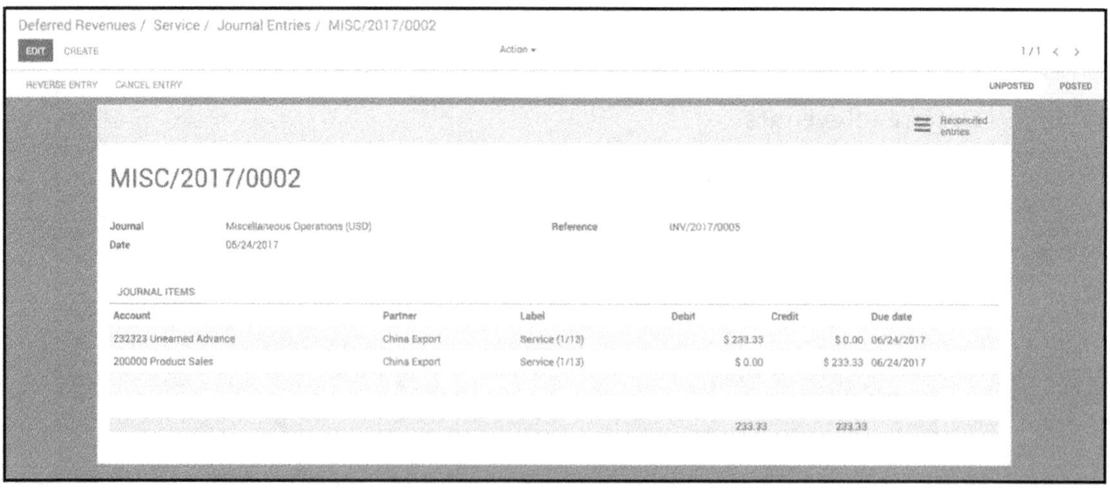

As soon as the entries are posted, they will become green. Look at this screenshot:

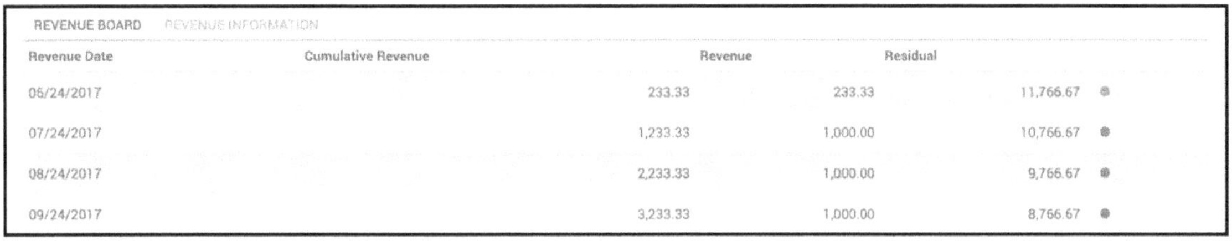

10. **Deferred Revenues** will be closed automatically when all the entries will have the GREEN signal under the **REVENUE BOARD** tab.

There's more...

The deferred revenue mechanism allows you to compute the actual profit or loss incurred at a given period instead of including customer advance as an income on the same day. Let's see how to troubleshoot the creation of automatic entries for the deferred revenue, and analyze the report.

Creating deferred revenue entries manually

Odoo runs a scheduled action to create an accounting entry to recognize the entry. However, you can run the manual wizard to create an entry without waiting for the scheduled action to trigger.

Enter the debug mode. Go through `Chapter 1`, *Getting started with Odoo 10*, to see how to enter and exit from the debug mode. You will get the **Generate Deferred Revenue Entries** menu under the **Advisory** menu. Click on the menu and a popup will appear, asking for the **Account Date,** as follows:

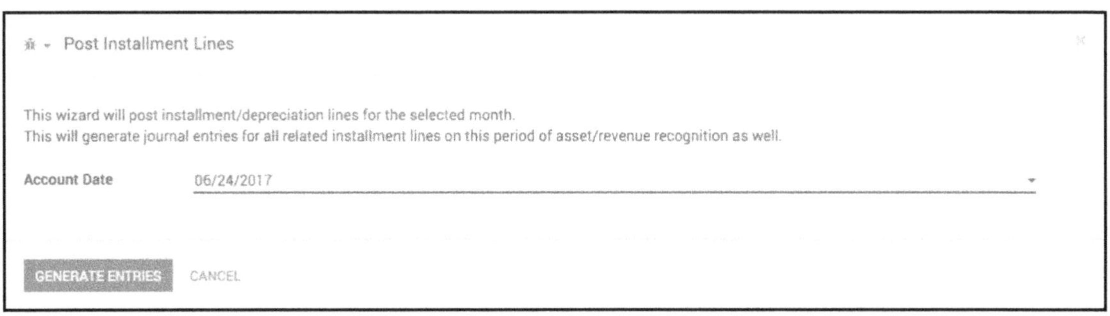

An accounting entry will be created for all the running deferred revenue plans for the selected month. An entry can be created with this wizard if the schedule missed the creation of the entry, or if you want to create an advance entry or a provisional income entry before closing the financial year. On successful creation of the entry, you will be redirected to a list of entries created based on the selected date:

To do the bulk posting, select all those entries and run the wizard from **Action** to **Post Journal Entries**.

Deferred Revenue Analysis

Deferred Revenue Analysis is an analytical report used to analyze **Deferred Revenue** by plans, or across months. You can set the parameters on reports to generate the different statistical reports for the deferred revenue. Look at this screenshot to see the **Revenue-by-Month** report:

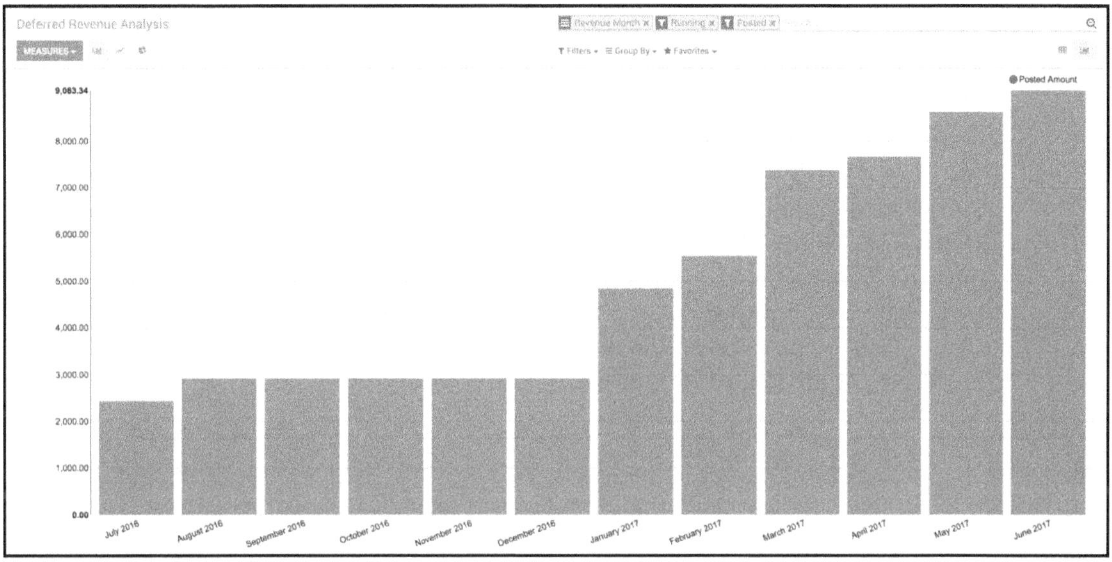

Asset management and depreciation

Asset management refers to the purchase of assets. Define those assets by the correct class or category to compute their life and depreciation. In some countries, the life and rate of depreciation are dependent on the asset category. At the end of life, the asset can either be scrapped or resold to get the money out of it.

Odoo has an **Asset Management** feature built into the accounting system that allows us to define the category of an asset, classify assets to compute the depreciation using different methods, and create an accounting entry for the depreciation at the end of every financial year. The impact of the resale or scrapping of an asset is reflected in the accounting system.

Let's manage the asset and compute the depreciation using the Odoo **Asset Management** feature.

How to do it...

1. The **Asset Management** feature can be activated by going to **Configuration** | **Settings** in the **Accounting** application. Search for **Asset management**, select it, and click on **APPLY** to activate it.
2. The first thing that needs to be configured is the **Asset Type** on successful activation of the feature. Asset type can be a category of the asset based on how the life of an asset or the depreciation computation is defined. For example, we will create a **Computers and Laptops** Asset type. The life of computers and laptops will be of 3 years. The depreciation computation method will be digressive at the rate of 30 percent:

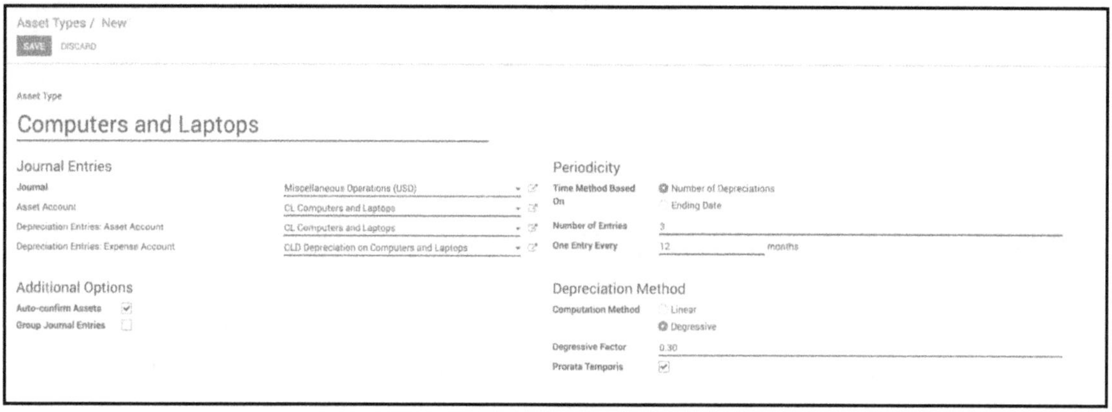

All the accounting entries will be created in the **Miscellaneous Operation** journal. When we buy computers and laptops, the accounting entry will be created in **Computers and Laptops** as a fixed asset-type account, while depreciation will be entered in the **Depreciation on Computers and Laptops** account.

3. Let's buy some computers and laptops, and link the asset category on the invoice line at the time of creating the vendor bill in Odoo:

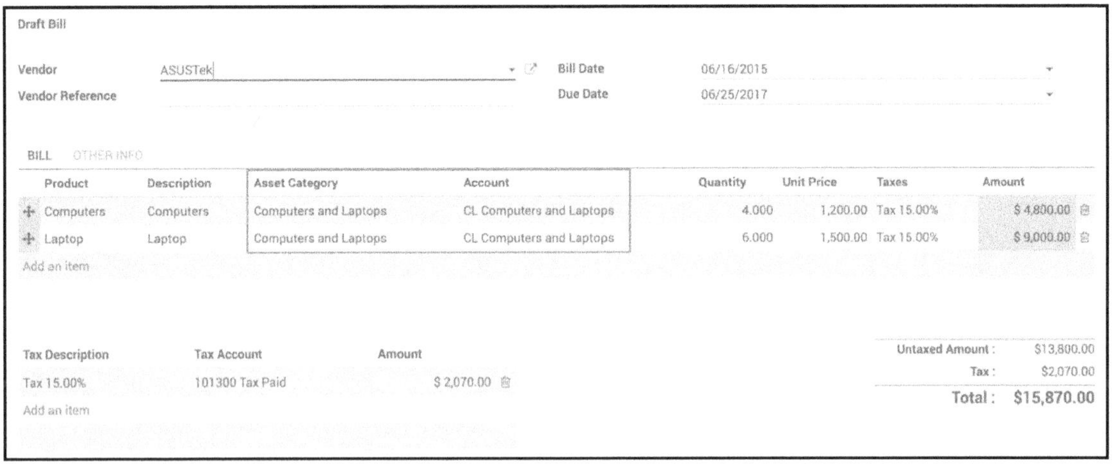

As soon as the vendor bill is created, link the **Asset Category** field to the asset product. In our case, we bought computers and laptops at different prices and both linked to the same asset category group. On selection of the **Asset Category** field, the account on the vendor bill line will be changed automatically to the asset account.

4. Confirm the vendor bill. The assets will be created, and can be accessed through **Advisory** | **Assets** in the **Accounting** application:

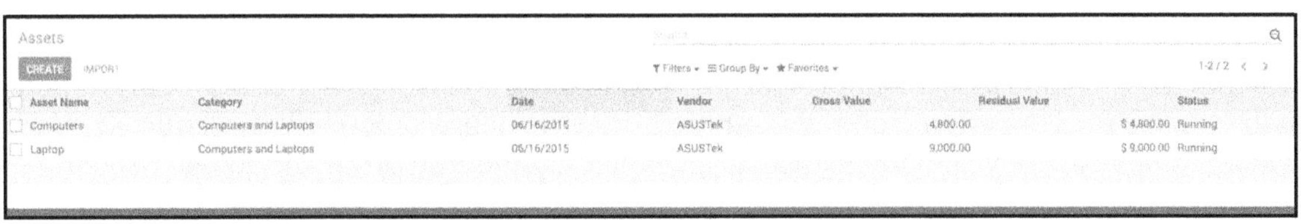

We have purchased computers and laptops that have different values. Therefore, two different types of assets were created. Look at the preceding screenshot showing the list of assets created and confirmed automatically.

5. Open an asset's form view by clicking on its record in list view. You will see the asset category, date of purchase, vendor name, and bill linked to the asset:

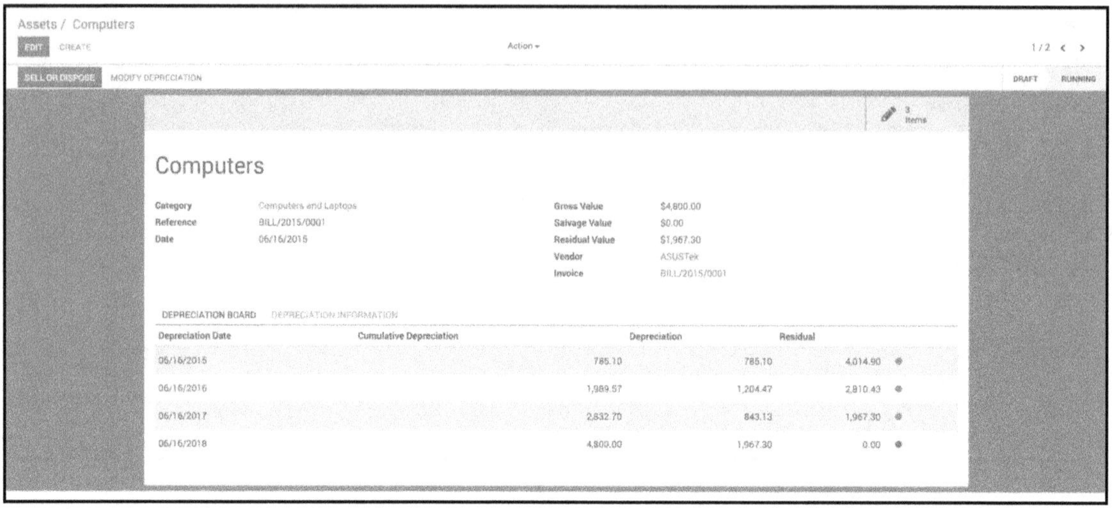

On the right-hand side, you can see the gross value of the asset, residual value, and salvage value. The accounting entries were created automatically by the scheduled action, but, like deferred revenue entries, the depreciation entries can be created manually using the **Generate Asset Entries** wizard, which can be accessed by entering the debug mode.

There's more...

The purchase of new assets will provide an addition to the existing assets. The depreciation will be computed depending on the asset category. The depreciation will be deducted from the asset value every year and claimed as an expense under the profit and loss statement.

Depreciation - accounting entries

Depreciation is computed in advance at the time of configuration of vendor bills, based on the computation method applied to the asset type. An accounting entry will be posted automatically to decrease the value of the asset and write the depreciation expense on the profit and loss account.

Every year, the value of the asset will decrease, as you can verify from the Balance Sheet report. Open the balance sheet report and compare with the previous years. You will find that this year the value has decreased by 30 percent compared to last year, in my case:

Balance Sheet

My Company

	As of 06/25/2017	As of 06/25/2016	%
Current Assets			
Bank and Cash Accounts	$ 32,800.00	$ 0.00	n/a
Receivables	$ 300.00	$ 0.00	n/a
Current Assets	$ 42,870.00	$ 2,070.00	1971.0%
Prepayments	$ 0.00	$ 0.00	n/a
Total Current Assets	$ 75,970.00	$ 2,070.00	3570.0%
Plus Fixed Assets			
100000 Fixed Asset Account	$ 98,000.00	$ 0.00	n/a
CL0000 Computers and Laptops	$ 5,655.99	$ 8,079.99	-30.0%
Total Plus Fixed Assets	**$ 103,655.99**	**$ 8,079.99**	**1182.9%**
Plus Non-current Assets	$ 0.00	$ 0.00	n/a
ASSETS	$ 179,625.99	$ 10,149.99	1669.7%
Current Liabilities			
Current Liabilities	$ 1,450.00	$ 0.00	n/a
Payables	$ 64,870.00	$ 15,870.00	308.8%
Total Current Liabilities	$ 66,320.00	$ 15,870.00	317.9%

As with the balance sheet, open the profit and loss account and compare it with the previous year. The depreciation value would have gone down by 30 percent compared to the previous year. Look at the following report of the profit and loss account:

Profit and Loss

My Company

Click to add an introductory explanation

	2017	2016	%
INCOME			
Gross Profit			
Operating Income	$ 0.00	$ 0.00	n/a
Cost of Revenue	$ 0.00	$ 0.00	n/a
Total Gross Profit	$ 0.00	$ 0.00	n/a
Other Income	$ 0.00	$ 0.00	n/a
Total INCOME	$ 0.00	$ 0.00	n/a
Expenses			
Expenses	$ 688.69	$ 0.00	n/a
Depreciation			
CLD000 Depreciation on Computers and Laptops	$ 2,424.00	$ 3,462.86	-30.0%
Total Depreciation	**$ 2,424.00**	**$ 3,462.86**	**-30.0%**
Total Expenses	$ 3,112.69	$ 3,462.86	-10.1%
NET PROFIT	$ -3,112.69	$ -3,462.86	-10.1%

Scrap or resell the asset

An asset can be scrapped at the end of its life, or it can be resold before the end of its life. We can mark an asset as scrapped or sold by clicking on the **SELL OR DISPOSE** button. Clicking on the button will create a depreciation accounting entry for the residual amount, as shown in the following screenshot:

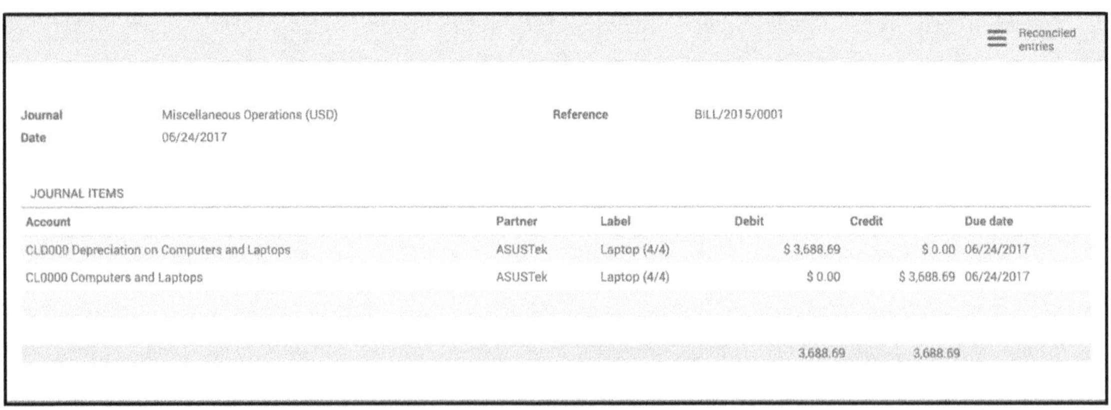

Reconciled entries

Journal: Miscellaneous Operations (USD)
Reference: BILL/2015/0001
Date: 06/24/2017

JOURNAL ITEMS

Account	Partner	Label	Debit	Credit	Due date
CLD000 Depreciation on Computers and Laptops	ASUSTek	Laptop (4/4)	$ 3,688.69	$ 0.00	06/24/2017
CL0000 Computers and Laptops	ASUSTek	Laptop (4/4)	$ 0.00	$ 3,688.69	06/24/2017
			3,688.69	3,688.69	

The residual value is the value of assets as per the books of account. It can be sold either at a higher or lower price than the residual value. If we succeed with selling at a higher price, we may gain a profit, or, if we sold at a lower price than the residual value, we may incur a loss. Let's assume that we sold all the laptops at the value of $3,000 before the end of life. We made a loss of **$688.69** as we get less amount compared to its residual value:

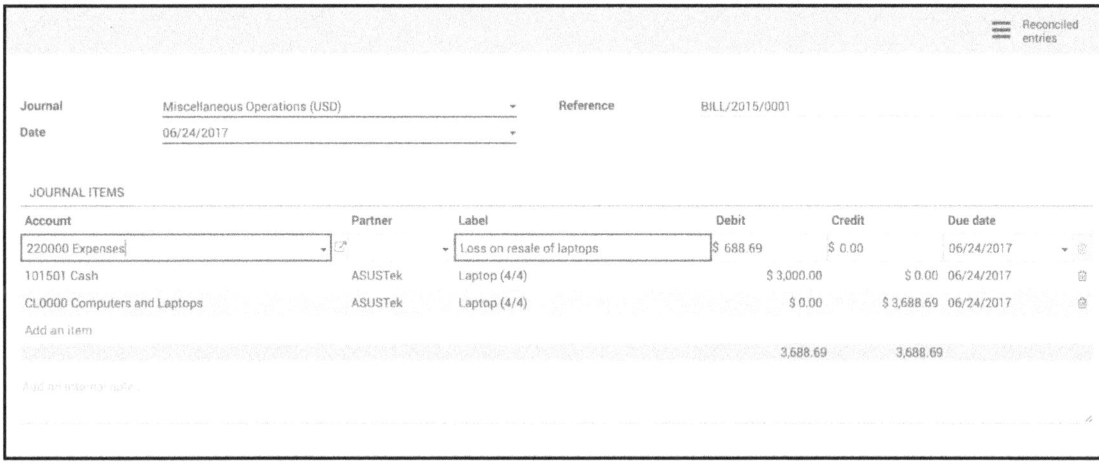

This loss has to be entered at the time of selling the assets. Look at the preceding screenshot. I have changed the accounting entries for the loss, and for receiving cash and a loss.

9
Purchase Management

In this chapter, we will cover the following recipes:

- Complete purchase cycle
- Tenders, choose the best offer
- Controlling invoicing and payments
- Multiple units of measure

Introduction

Odoo Purchase, is one of the core application integrated with the other core applications such as **Sales**, **Inventory**, and **Accounting**. To answer the real business need, Odoo Purchase application manages the different business flows, such as creating a Request For Quotation to confirm the order followed by the goods receipt notes in the warehouse and vendor bills in accounts. Odoo **Purchase** application also allows the large-scale industry to start their buying process with tenders or purchase contracts (blanket orders).

The purchase history allows you to better negotiate on the pricing with your suppliers, or you can be updated with your supplier's price list, which can be imported in Odoo in a single click. The purchase order is created automatically based on the inventory level or on demand when we have a sales order, thanks to wall integration with sales and inventory application.

Let's see all the features of the Odoo **Purchase** application in this chapter, starting from a request for a quotation to confirmation of the order, receiving goods, managing the costing, inventory valuation, and receiving bills in accounting.

Complete the purchase cycle

The material has to be purchased when you confirm the sales unless you want to stock it to answer future demand/sales. According to Odoo, there are two approaches to procure the material, buy on demand or assign from stock, and manage the inventory level based on the minimum order rule.

Let's see the complete purchase flow starting from sales to procurement to procure an order of the material that was configured to be purchased on demand. As soon as the sales confirm the order for the material, a request for a quotation will be generated, the material will be received in the warehouse, the vendor bill will be received, the material will be assigned to the delivery order, and finally, it will be shipped.

How to do it...

1. Like the **Sales** or **Accounting** applications of Odoo, **Purchase Management** is one of the main applications in Odoo. It can be installed form Odoo Apps. Go to **Apps** and search for `Purchase`. Once you find it, click on the **Install** button:

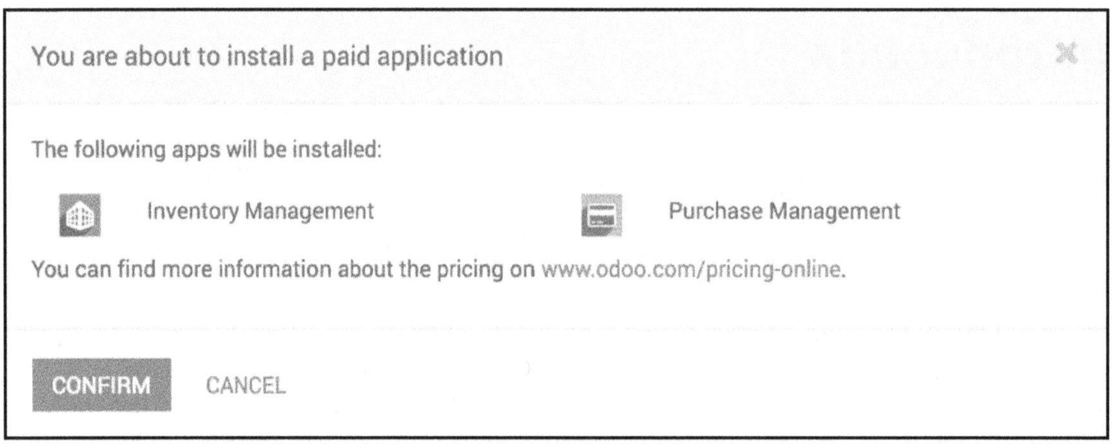

   As soon as you click on the **Install** button, Odoo will confirm with you that the **Inventory** application is going to be installed as the **Purchase** application is dependent on the **Inventory Management** application. This will cost you additionally for **Inventory Management** application.

2. Let's configure the product material so that it can be stockable to maintain the stock for the product. Look at the following screen to configure product as a **Stockable Product**. Change the product type to **Stockable Product**:

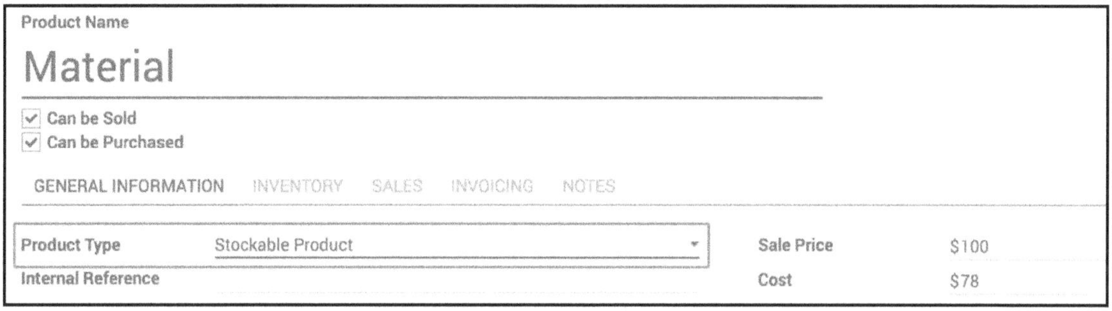

For all the stockable products, the most important configuration to be defined is *procurement method*. In Odoo, it is represented by the routes to be defined in the **INVENTORY** tab on the product form in Odoo:

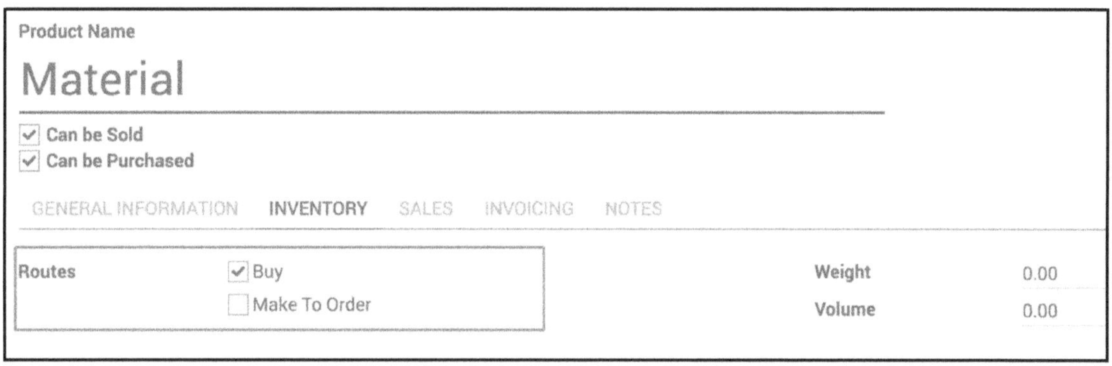

The routes will be available depending on the application installed. In our case, I have installed **Purchase** and **Inventory**. It shows **Buy and Make to Order**; selecting individual Buy and Make to Order has a different meaning or selecting both **Buy** and **Make to Order** have a different meaning. Look at the following options and their business flows listed:

- **Buy**: Assign from the inventory if available; otherwise, process the reorder level point and purchase order created based on that
- **Make to order**: Without checking the inventory, simply create a purchase order for the required quantity

- **Buy** and **Make to Order**: Purchase whatever quantity is required and at the same time, compute the reorder rule and fulfill it with the purchase if required

There is one more route called **Manufacture**, which will be available when we will install the **Manufacture** application. The manufacturing order will be created when a material product is needed.

3. At least one supplier has to be defined in both cases; either you choose to **Buy** or **Make To Order**. In both cases, a purchase order will be created. Odoo creates the request for the quotation for the first supplier listed on the vendor list. Go to the product called **Material**, under the **INVENTORY** tab you will see the list of vendors. Click on the **Add an item** link to create a new vendor for the product **Material**:

Select **Vendor**. You can define the product name and code if a supplier has a different code and name for the material product. The time the supplier will need to deliver the product can be entered in **Delivery Lead Time**. The minimum quantity and its price can be entered along with the validity (date from to date till) for the supplier pricing.

> The vendor information available on the product form under the **INVENTORY** tab is a supplier pricelist, which will give all that information. When you create a purchase order manually, you will get the product name and code as per the supplier, along with the price based on the quantity entered on the purchase order.

4. When you choose to **Buy** as only the one route to procure the material, the reorder rules have to be configured as the purchase will be created based on the reorder rules. Click on the **Reordering Rule** button as shown in the following screenshot. After creating a rule, it will display the min and max quantities on the button:

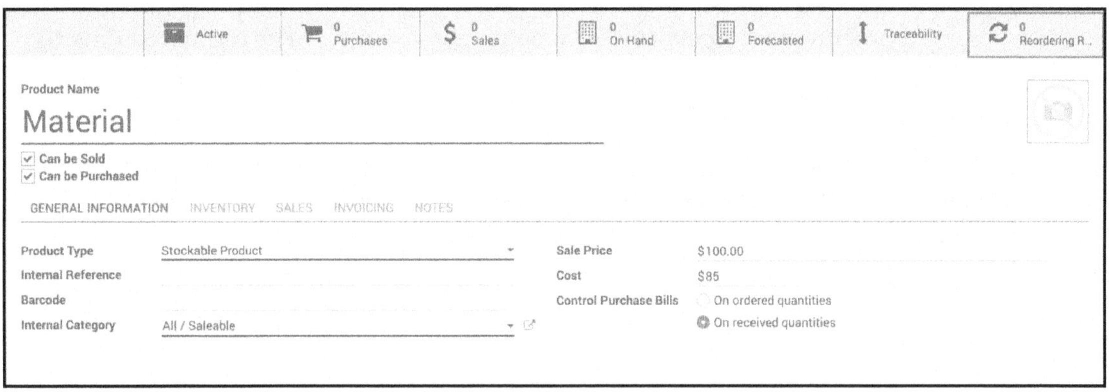

You will be redirected to the list of reordering rules. Create a new rule by clicking on the **CREATE** button. The name of the order point will be set automatically from Order Point OP/ sequence. The warehouse and location will be set automatically to the current warehouse and stock location of that warehouse.

> Odoo allows you to work with multiple locations within the same warehouse. You may want to maintain a minimum stock in different locations. In such a case, you can define the reorder level for those locations.

The important fields are **Minimum Quantity**; if the stock goes below this quantity, Odoo will create a procurement order to make it to **Maximum Quantity * Quantity Multiply**:

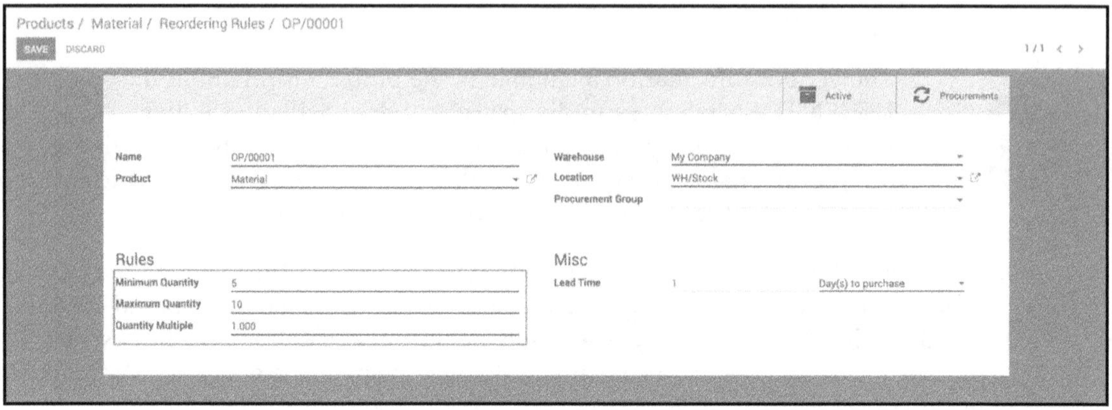

Look at the preceding screen. The ordering rule is for the material product. It will create a procurement to make it `10` when it goes below `5`. The estimated time to fulfill the stock is 1 day, which can be changed in **Lead time** field if it requires more than one day's time.

5. The current **On Hand** stock for the material product is **0** in our inventory; **On Hand** stock can be checked on the product form. Look at the following product screen:

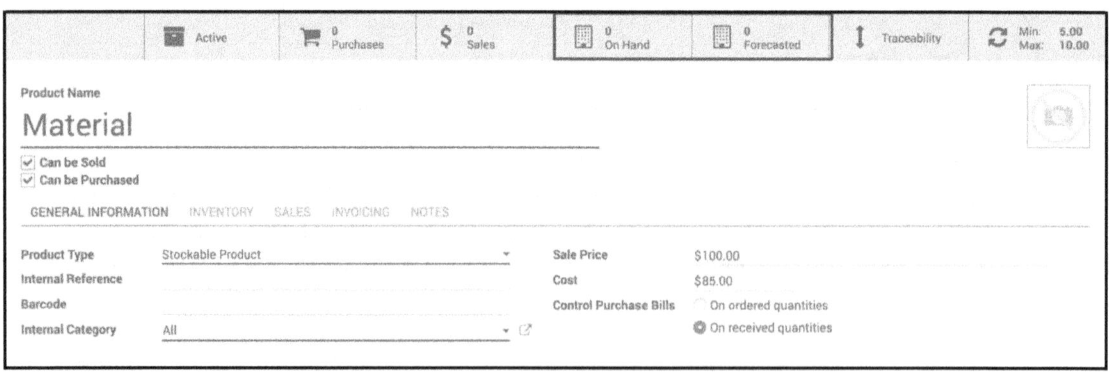

To test the configuration, let's create the sales order to sell two quantities of **Material**. This should create a request for a quotation automatically! The sale will look similar to what is shown in the following screenshot:

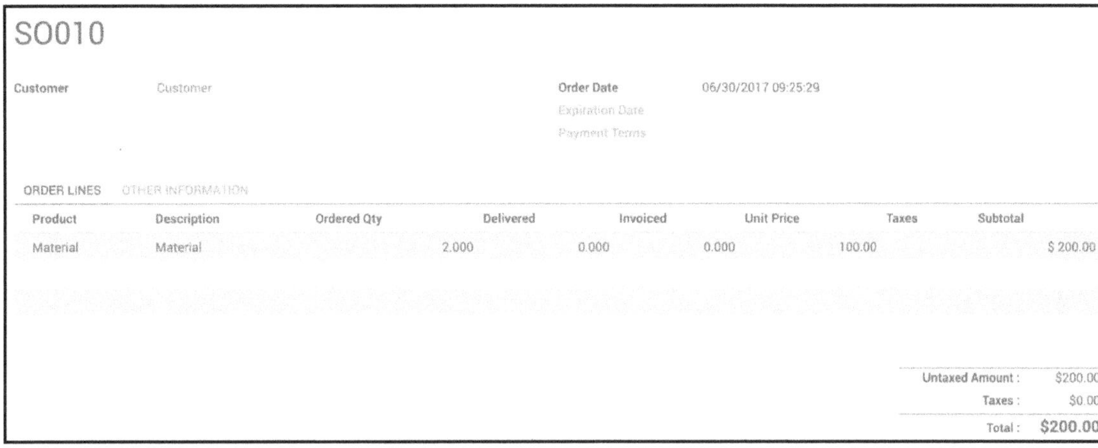

While adding or changing the product or quantity, you may get a **Not enough inventory!** warning, which will look like this:

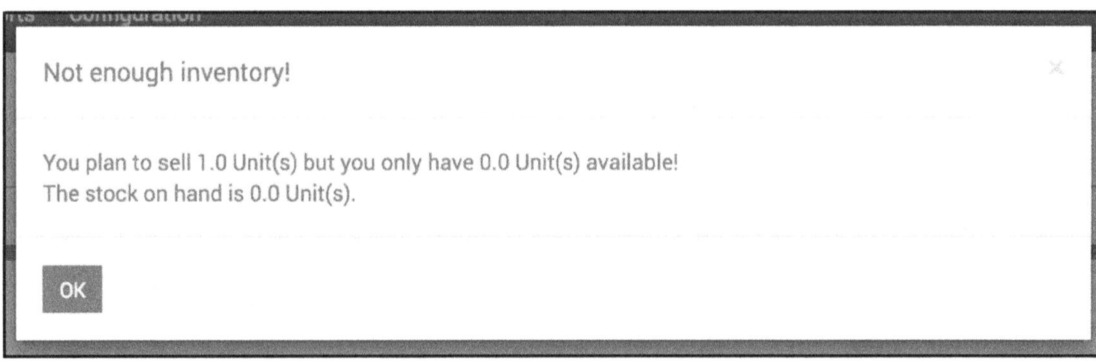

If you don't see **Request for Quotation**, you might need to run the procurement scheduler that actually computes the current stock, quantity required, and reorder point, and triggers the procurement based on the routes selected for the product. In case of Material set **Route** to **Buy**, in our case, the procurement should create the Request for Quotation. To run the scheduler, go to **Inventory** | **Schedulers** | **Run Schedulers**. A wizard will pop up. Now, click on the **RUN SCHEDULERS** button.

6. As soon as the procurement runs, it will compute the reorder rules. As a result, the request for quotation will be created under the **Purchase** application. Review the quantity defined in RFQ document and send to the supplier. Look at the following screen of RFQ created automatically based on the reorder rule:

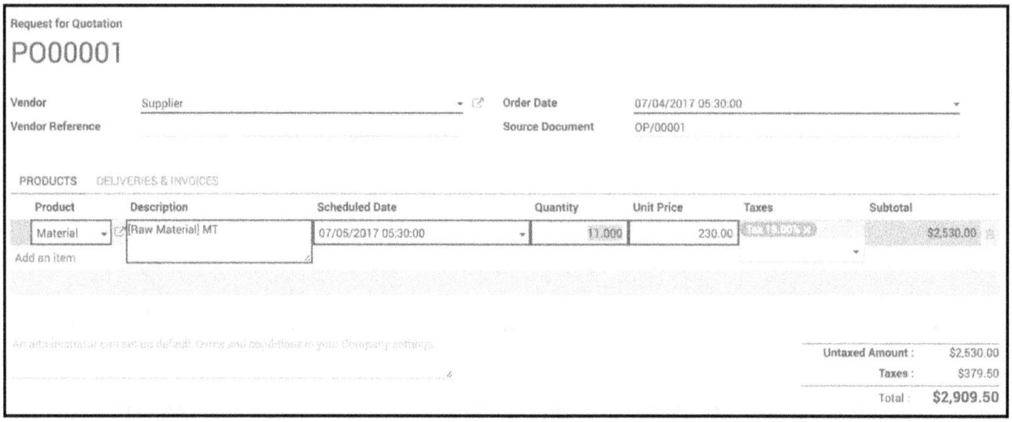

The quantities set on the RFQ document are 11, 10 based on the rule and 1 that is required to fulfill the current sales order **SO010**. The request for quotation can be sent by e-mail or printed on the paper by courier by clicking on the **SEND RFQ BY EMAIL** or **PRINT RFQ** button. Look at the following screen:

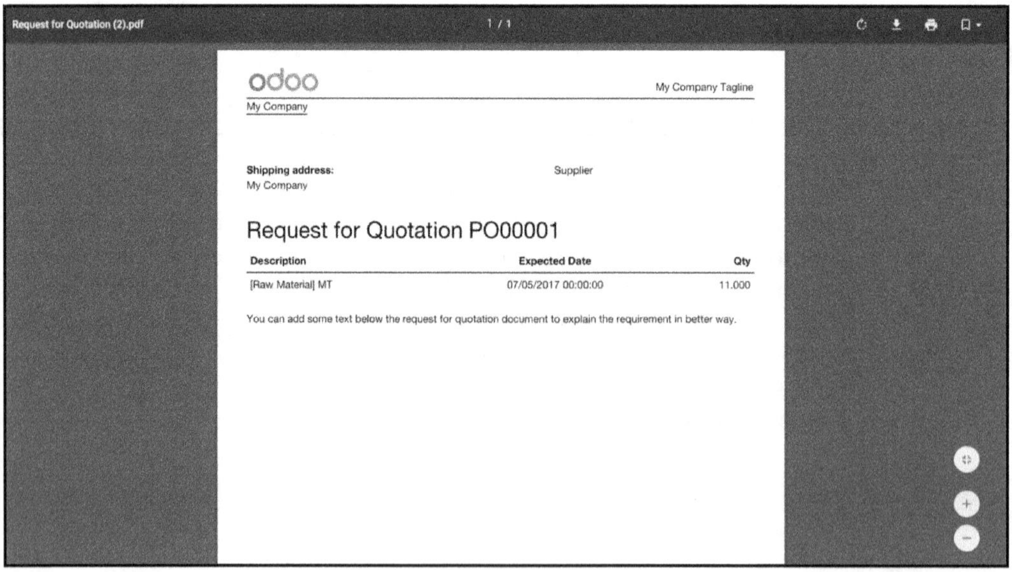

As soon as the RFQ is sent to the supplier, the state of the purchase quotation changes from **RFQ** to **RFQ SENT**, and now, we are waiting for the supplier's price and delivery date confirmation:

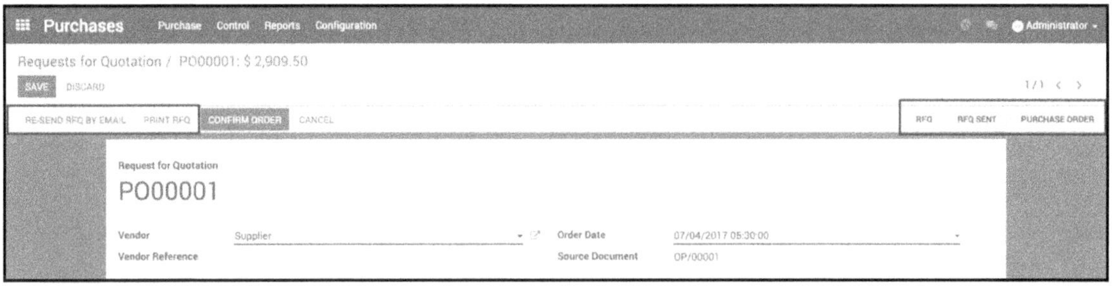

7. Assuming that the supplier supplies the rates, which suits you, change the rates accordingly, confirm the RFQ by clicking on the **CONFIRM ORDER** button and convert to **Confirmed order**:

8. The incoming shipment will be triggered in the warehouse. Process the delivery order as soon as the material is received in the warehouse. Edit the receipt and enter the quantity in the **Done** field, which was received from the supplier. Click on the **VALIDATE** button to process the current receipt:

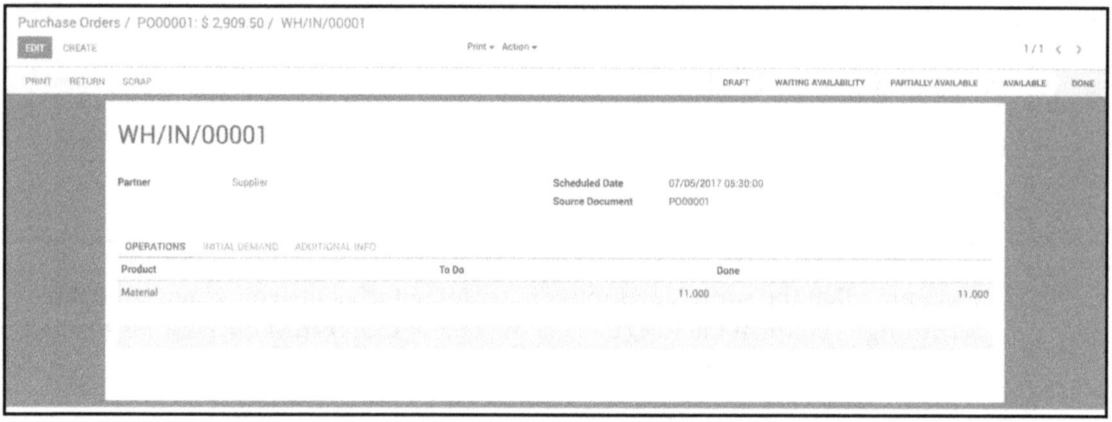

The **OPERATION** line will become green when all the **To Do** quantities will be received and entered in the **Done** field.

9. As an accountant, when you receive the vendor bill against the purchase order, you can create the same in Odoo. Go to **Vendor bill** in the **Accounting** application and create a new vendor bill. You can see the list of purchase order waiting for the vendor invoice in the **Add Purchase Order** field, select the Purchase order from the list:

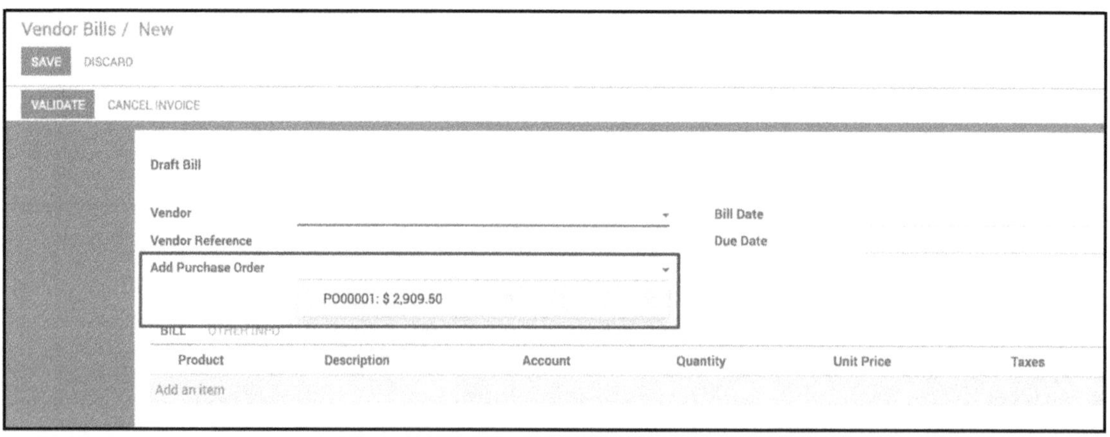

As soon as you choose the **Purchase** order for which you received the invoice, the rest of the information will be filled in automatically. Look at the following screen:

> **TIP:** As soon as you select the purchase order on the **Add Purchase Order** field, the order details are added to the bill and selected purchase order removed from the list. Keep on selecting and adding the multiple purchase order to single vendor bill, when you receive a single bill for the multiple purchase orders.

To process the payment for supplier through a bank check or cash, go through the *Manage vendor bills and payments* recipe in `Chapter 7`, *Set Up Financial Management with Odoo.*

10. To make the delivery, go to the **Inventory** application and click on the **TO DO** button available on the **Delivery Orders** section and search for the delivery of sales order SO010, click on **RESERVE** button to assign the Material just received.
11. As soon as the **Material** assigned, click on the **VALIDATE** button to process the delivery order related to *SO010.*

There's more...

We have gone through the business use case to trigger the purchase order based on the requirement form the current sales order and reorder level rule. In the example, we have seen that we got the RFQ created for 11 quantities, as the warehouse does not have enough stock.

> If you want to configure the business case, that is, assign the material from stock if available or else create a Request for quotation for the requested quantity (sold quantity) only. Edit the reorder rule and set the minimum quantity and maximum quantity to 0.

Let's go through the hidden features of the **Purchase** application that helps you improve and control your purchase process.

Supplier pricelist

The **Purchase** application in Odoo has a great feature to manage the price by product or by the supplier that allows you to keep track of product price just on the product itself in terms of vendors. You can define the vendors with their criteria to supply the goods. Look at the following sample rule:

The vendor price list includes the following criteria:

- **Vendor Product Name**: It is the name given by the vendor in their inventory
- **Vendor Product Code**: It is the product code given as per the vendor inventory
- **Delivery Lead Time**: It is the time required by the vendor to supply the goods
- **Minimal Quantity**: It is the order that cannot be accepted below the stated quantity or may be at different price
- **Price**: It shows the price at which the order for minimal quantity can be accepted
- **Validity**: It is the date range between which this price is valid

Let's create an RFQ to get the price for material (as per our inventory specification). For **China Export**, they named it as **[RM] Raw Material**. The price will be set based on the supplier pricelist:

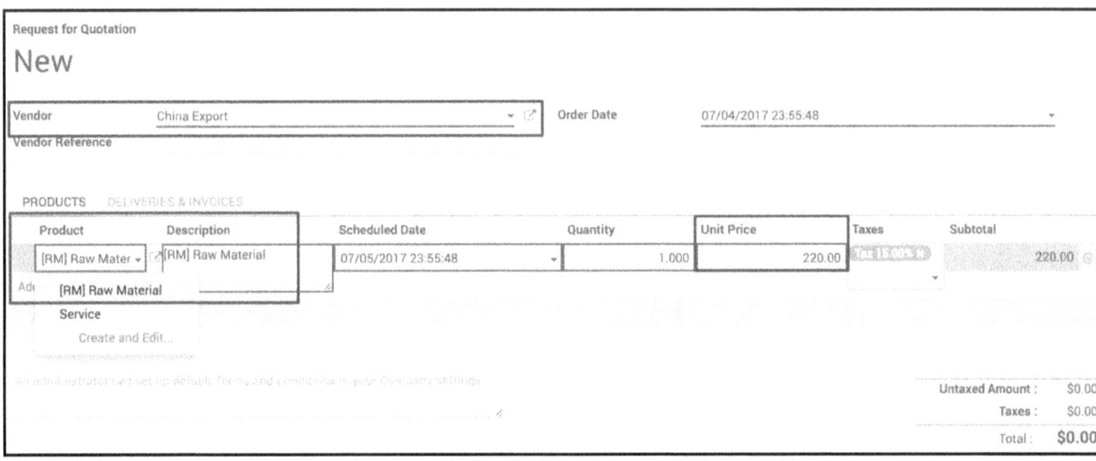

Assuming that we are going to confirm the order for a new supplier, which is not listed on the product vendor list, the price at which the order is confirmed, the details will be automatically added to the Vendor list under the **INVENTORY** tab. This is the only way to remember the last purchase price for a Material product.

Vendor price list can be imported in Odoo using two different file formats; they are Comma Separate Values or XLS. Activate the feature to import the vendor pricelist in Odoo by going to **Configuration** | **Settings** under the **Purchase** application. Search for the **Vendor Pricelists** options and choose **Allow using and importing vendor pricelists**. Click on **APPLY** to save the settings. As soon as the feature has been activated, you will get the menu by going to **Purchase** | **Vendor Pricelists** under the **Purchase** application. Look at the following screen of V**endor Pricelists**:

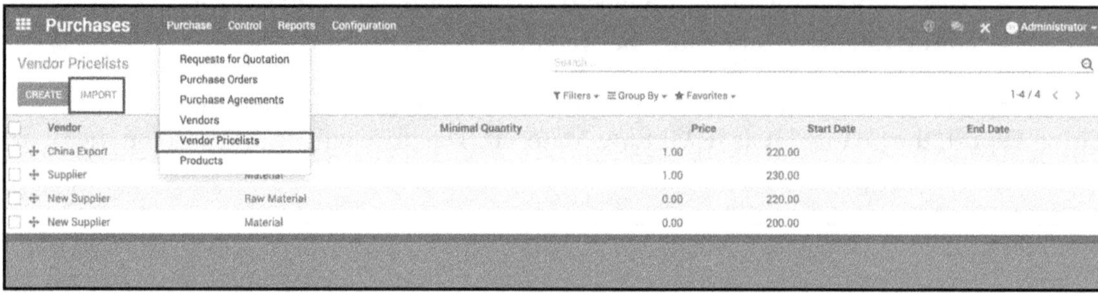

Level of approval

Purchase is a critical process; some companies need a double validation before they confirm the order. By default, the Odoo **Purchase** application is configured to have the single level of validation, but the double validation can be activated to have two levels of validation before confirmation from RFQ to purchase order.

The feature can be activated by going to **Configuration** | **Settings** under the **Purchase** application. Look at the following screen for the setting:

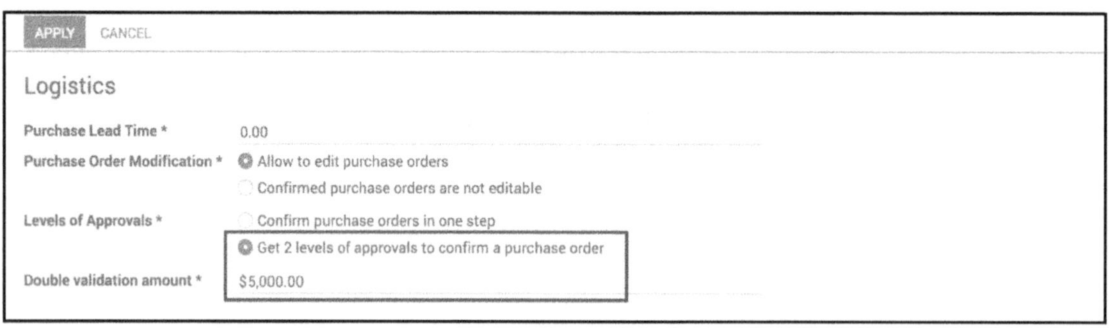

The default option selected was the **Confirm purchase order in one step**. Change that selection to **Get 2 level of approvals to confirm a purchase order**. As soon as this option is selected, the double validation amount field appears. Enter an amount. If the purchase order is greater than amount configured on the **Settings** page, that is, in our case, it is 5000, the order requires the double validation; otherwise, it can be confirmed with single validation.

> Enter `0` in the **Double validation amount** field if you would like to get two levels of validation for all the orders created.

Let's create the RFQ for having an amount of more than $`5000`. Assume that Purchase officer confirms the order by clicking on the **CONFIRM ORDER** button for the first approval. Look at the following screen:

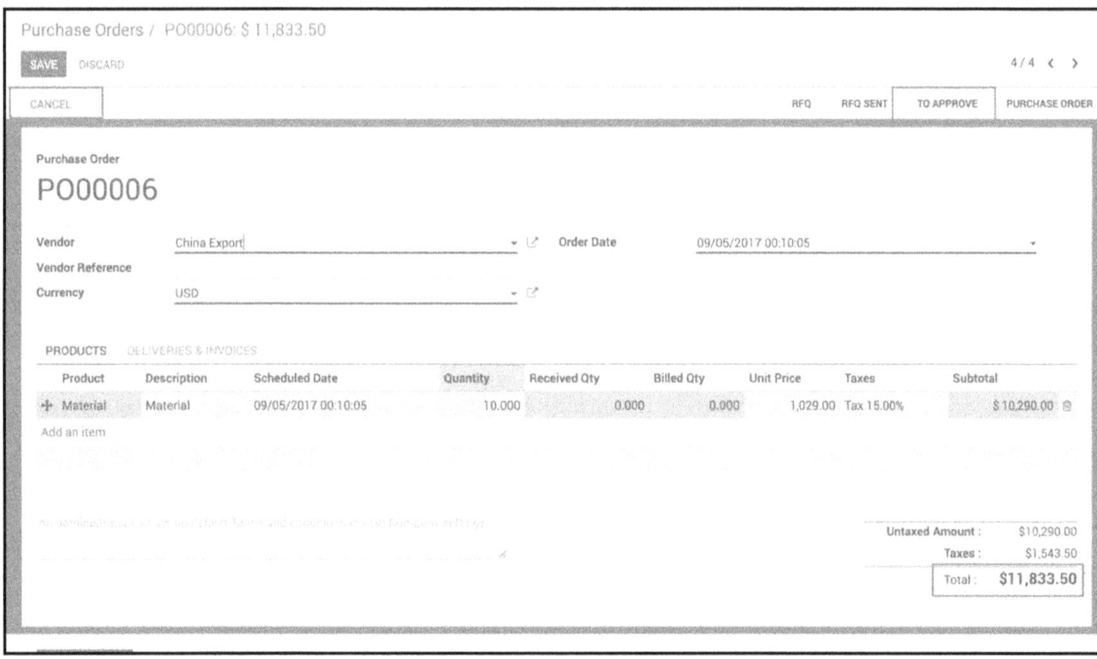

The **APPROVE ORDER** button will appear to the Purchase manager waiting for the second approval; see the following screenshot

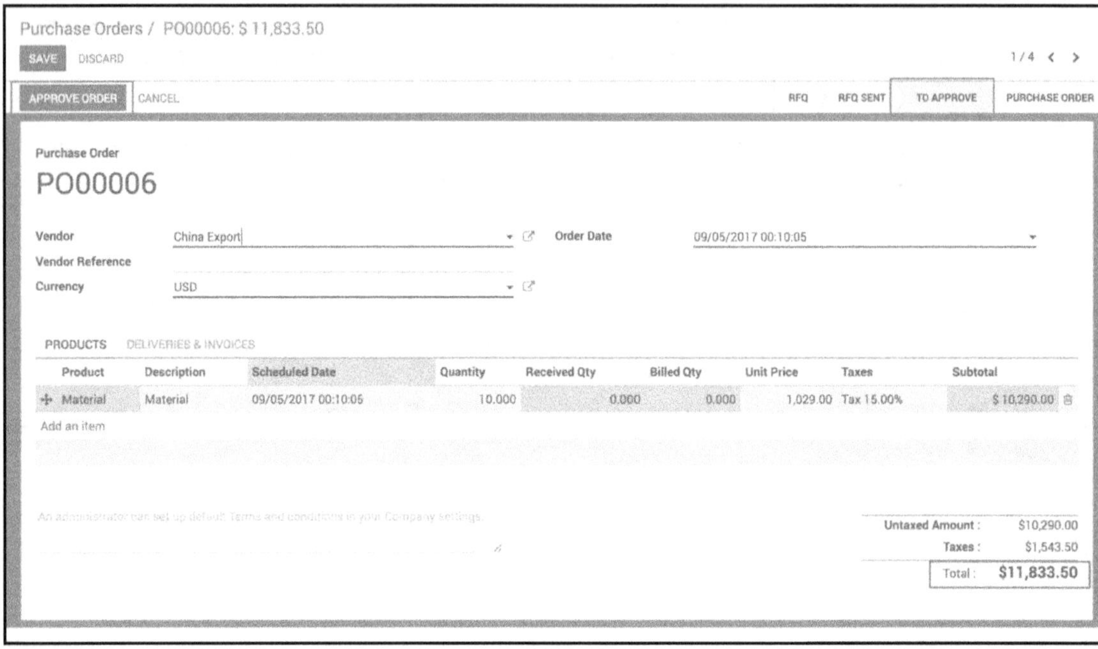

Using Odoo Studio, you can set the visibility by applying **Purchase Manager group** so that only the purchase manager can validate the second approval.

Lock purchase order

Purchase order in Odoo is super flexible; you can increase the quantity after confirmation of the purchase order, even if the receipt or vendor bill is processed for the order. To test the flexibility of the purchase order, let's execute the following business case:

1. Create and confirm the purchase order for the material of 5 quantity. Look at this screenshot:

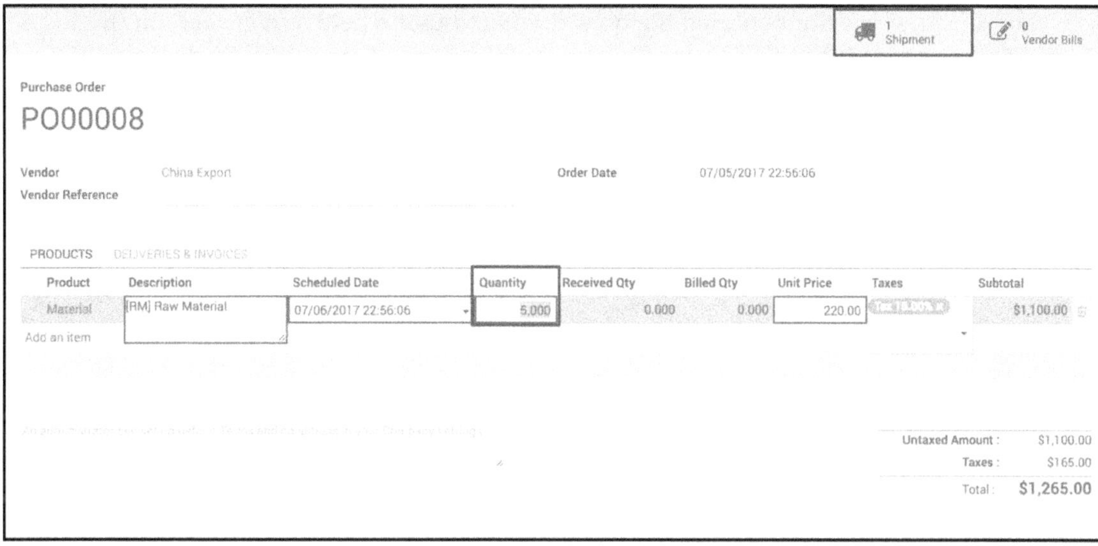

2. Receive 5 quantity of the material. Process the reception of the 5 quantity of material:

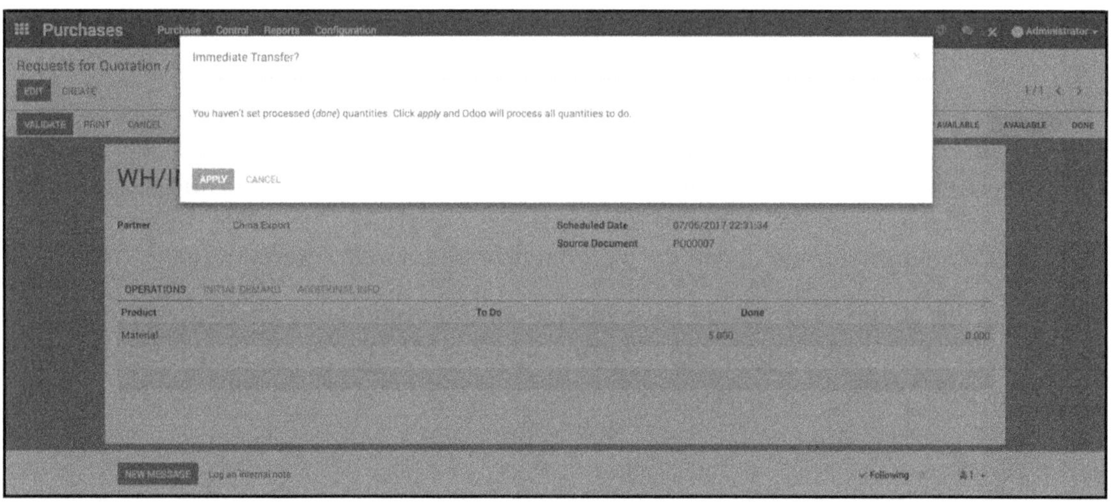

I have not entered the quantity in the **Done** field and clicked on the **VALIDATE** button. So, Odoo will confirm that all the **To do** quantities will be set as **Done**.

3. Open the same purchase order and change the quantity field from `5` to `10` as the quality of the material seems good:

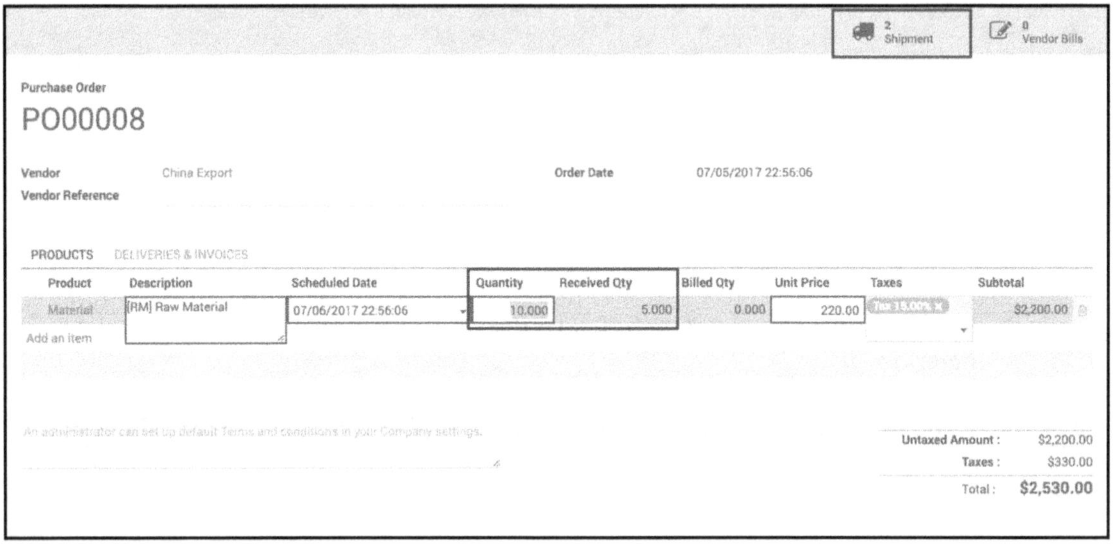

The new incoming shipment for `5` quantity of material is created automatically by clicking on the **SAVE** button after setting the quantity from `5` to `10`. Process the incoming shipment when the material is received in the warehouse.

4. Let's assume that we receive a vendor bill of `10` quantity, it can be created from the vendor bill by going to **Control** | **Vendor Bills** under the **Purchase** application:

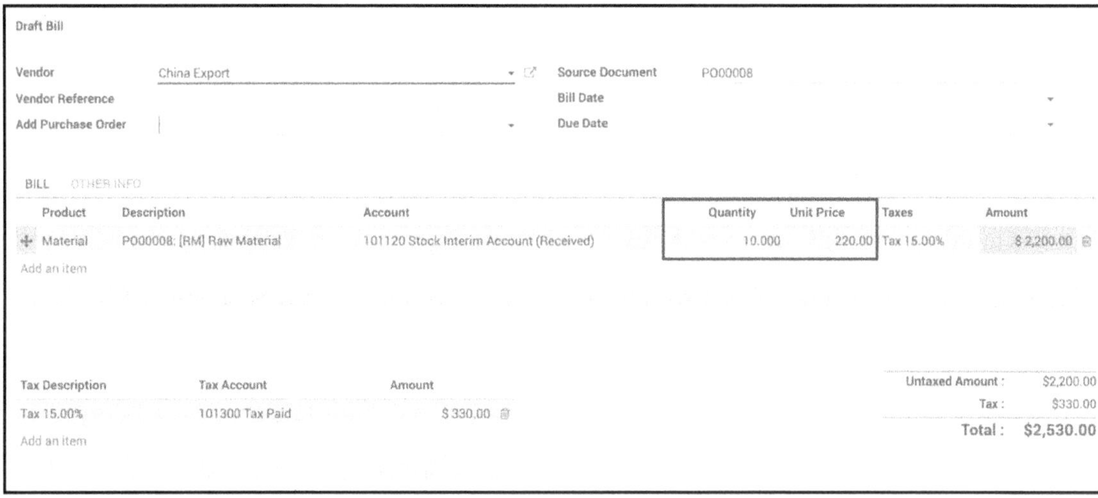

When the vendor bill has been created, the invoiced quantity on the purchase order is set to `10`. Check on the purchase order.

5. If you don't want to allow the modification of the purchase order as soon as the purchase order is confirmed, it has to be set to the **Confirmed purchase orders are not editable** option for the **Purchase Order Modification** field under the **Settings** page of the **Purchase** application, look at the following setting page:

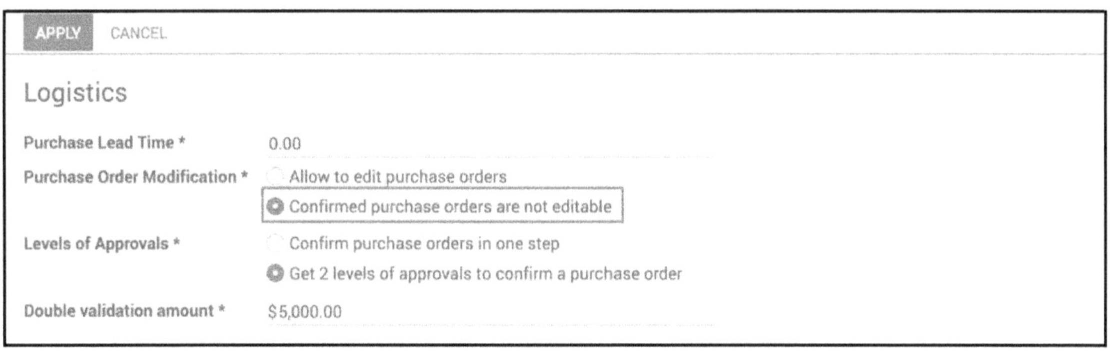

As soon as the **Confirmed purchase orders are not editable** option is selected, you cannot modify the purchase order once it is confirmed.

Warnings on vendors or products

In some business cases, you need to raise an alert or warning message at the time of selecting either product or vendor as you want to inform the users for some business instruction at the time of selecting them in the RFQ document.

Let's activate the warning feature for the purchase order and set some messages that the user has to take care of at the time of buying a material from **China Export**.

To activate the feature, go to **Configuration** | **Settings** under the **Purchase** application and search for the **Warning** option. Choose **An informative or blocking warning can be set on a product or a customer** in the **Warning** field:

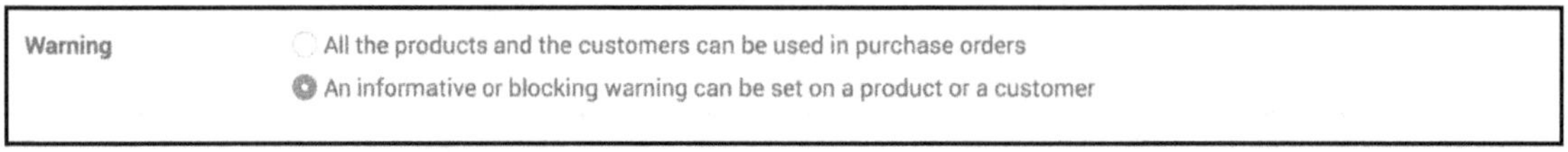

As we have selected the option to have an informative or blocking warning on product or customer, on customer and product form, under **Notes**, the new field can be found with heading **Warning** when purchasing this product. Look at the following screenshot of the product form:

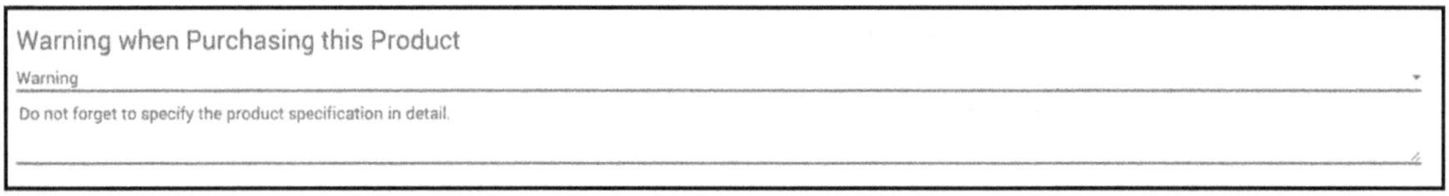

The same kind of warning or blocking warning can be set on the vendor. Look at the following screenshot:

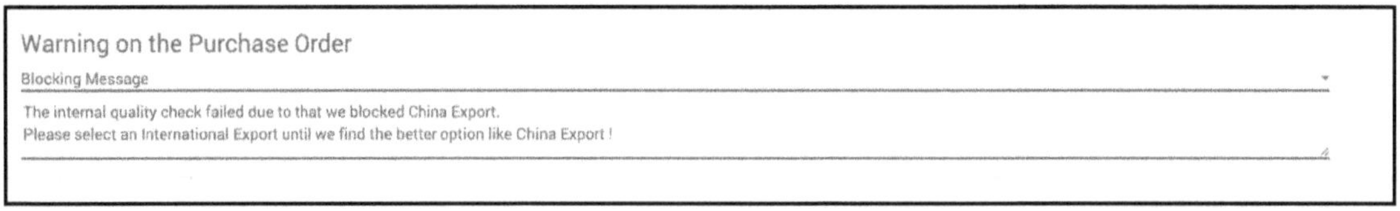

Let's try to create an RFQ for **China Export**. A clear warning will appear and **China Export** will be deselected from the vendor field. Look at the following screenshot:

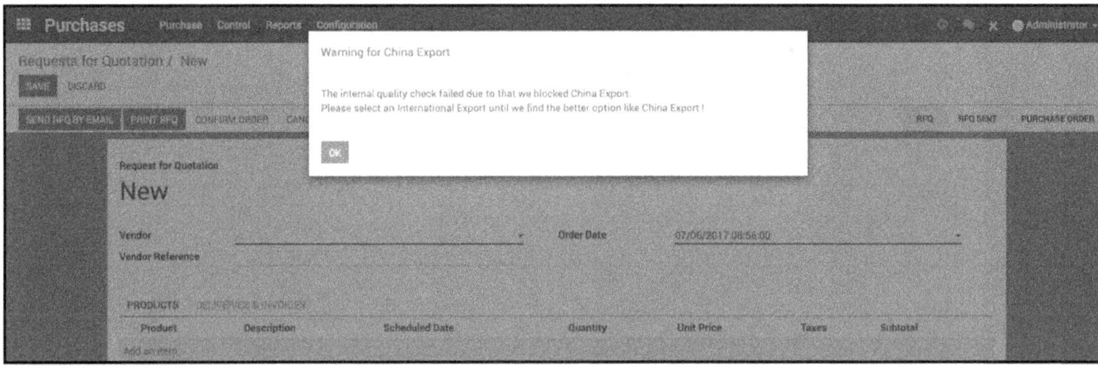

You cannot place the order for **China Export**. Select another suggested supplier. The same kind of warning will appear as soon as you select the material product, but it does not block you:

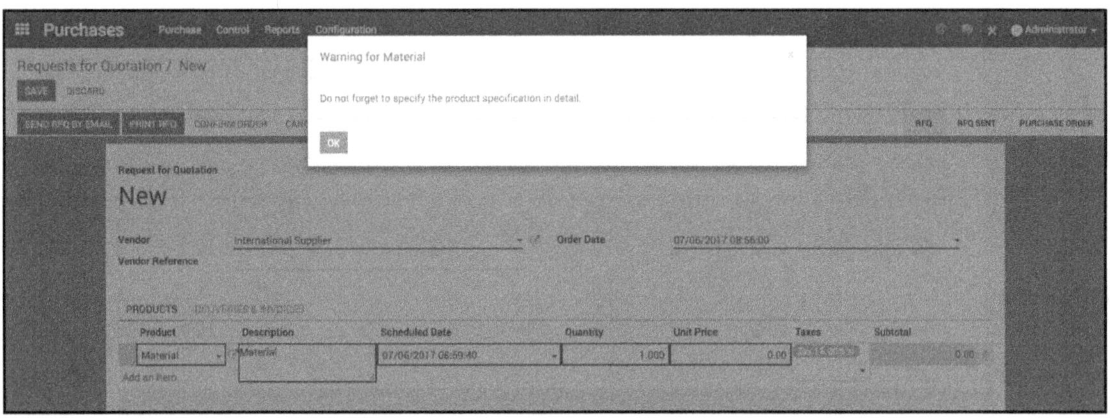

The warning can be useful to block a supplier or product at the time of purchase or remind the user to make sure to explain the requirement in detail while ordering to a specific supplier or purchasing a specific product.

Make to Order versus Make to Stock

There are two routes available on the product for the procurement, **Buy** and **Make to Order**. The **Buy** route is called **Make to Stock**, which means, assign from the stock if available in stock or create a procurement order

According to **Make to Order**, just create a procurement order as and when the product is required. It means that the stock is not maintained in the warehouse. Either the purchase order or manufacturing order will be created when the procurement runs on both the routes.

Let's assume that for some product, you have to set it to **Make to Order** as you do not maintain the stock of material product due to a higher price, fluctuation of the price, or lack of stable demand. In such cases, we buy raw material on demand. In this case, **Make to Order** has to be selected along with the **Buy** route on the **Raw Material** route. Look at the product route configuration in the following screenshot:

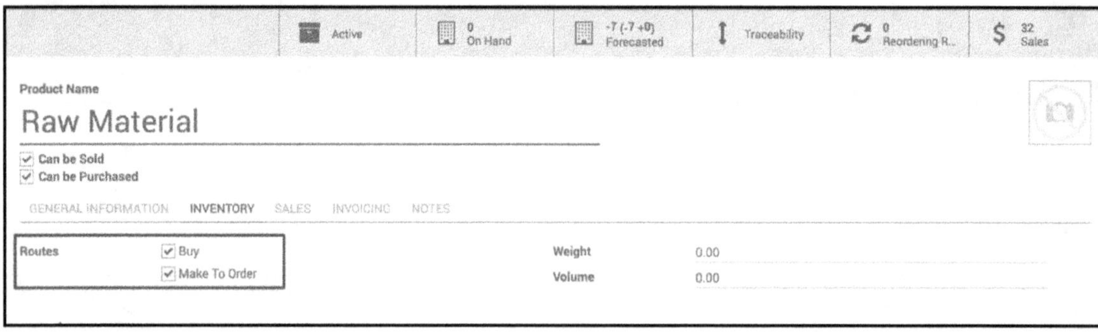

Let's say that you have a customer looking for 20 units. Let's create a sales order for 20 units as soon as the order is confirmed:

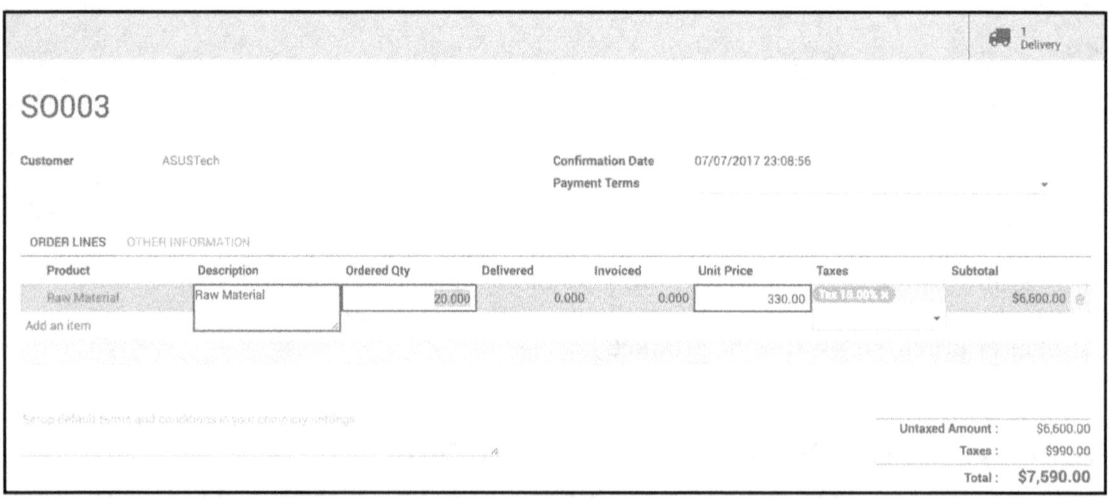

You will get the purchase order for 20 units only, as procurement does not check the stock and does not take care of the reorder rules:

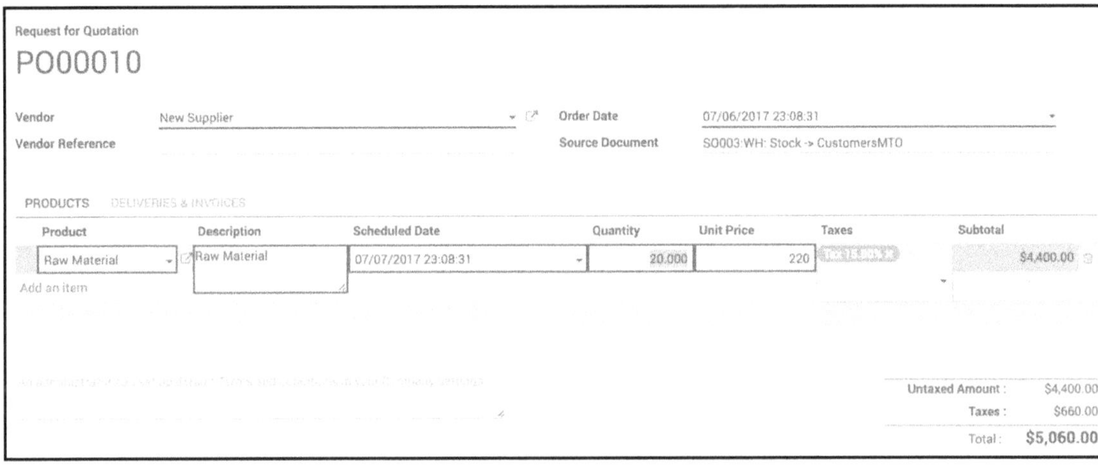

Odoo is not checking for the stock level or reorder level. The procurement order will create a purchase order for the required quantity of the raw material.

If you have selected both routes, **Make to Order** and **Buy**, and also defined the reorder rules, the procurement executes all the routes selected on the Material, which is current units from sales order plus maximum units from the product reorder rule.

Tenders, choose the best offer

The best practice followed by a government or a big organization to procure the material or service for an ongoing or new project is to go with the tendering process. It helps them choose the best supplier at effective rates with the commitment of continuous supply for the material or service.

An open tender process is open for everyone where the announcement will be made in public, and there is no restriction to submit the tender. Whoever wants to supply the material can submit all the required information along with the price. The selective tender is only open to the list of selected suppliers who have already worked previously or who have expertise in such kind of material supply or project work.

Odoo supports both the open and selective tender process. In Odoo, this feature is known as **Call for Tenders**. Almost all the business cases can be managed with the tender process such as purchase contract or blanket order. The tender process can be enabled for selected products only; rest of the products can have their standard purchase flow.

Let's see how to enable this feature, configure the product, and invite the supplier to make their quote. The selection process can be performed based on the many aspects such as price, logistics cost, and so on. The order can be given to a single supplier, or it can be split between multiple suppliers by choosing more than one supplier.

Getting ready

Make sure that you have prepared the list of products or services you would like to procure through the tendering process.

How to do it...

1. The **Calls for Tenders** feature can be activated by going to **Configuration | Settings** under the **Purchase** application. The default option selected is to have a purchase order trigger for a single vendor. Change it to **Allow using call for tenders to get quotes from multiple suppliers (advanced)**, which is an advance purchase process:

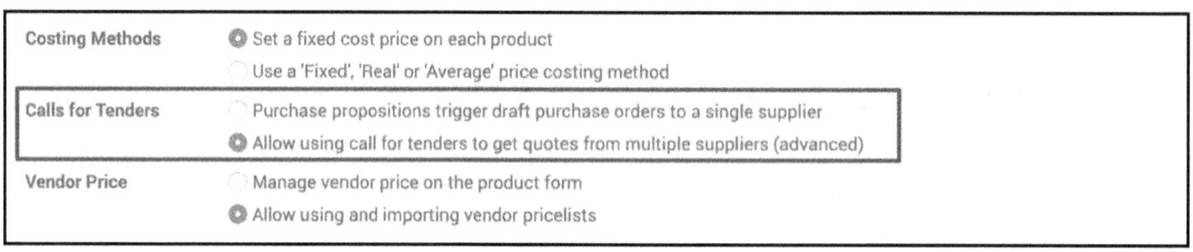

2. The first configuration to be done is to change the procurement option on the product. If you would like to have a tender instead of a purchase order created for the single supplier, select the option **Propose a call for tenders** option for the **Procurement** field:

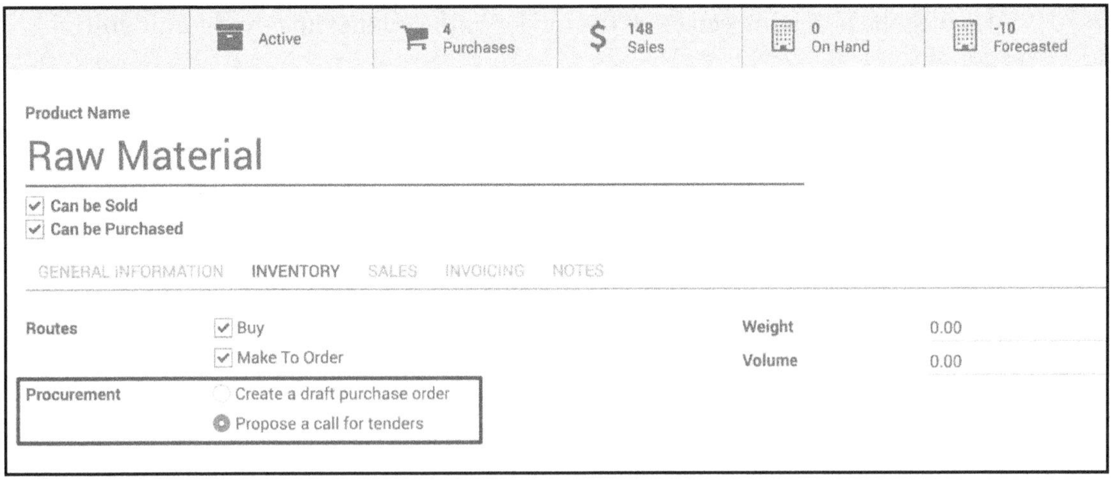

You will have a tender when the raw material is required. You have to choose the list of suppliers manually to send the request for quotation.

3. The tender can be created either manually or automatically through procurement. Let's assume that the manufacturing unit will be going to start a new plant in few weeks, for that they will require lots of material and service, to procure the material and service they open the tender and invite some of the vendors to submit the proposal on the tender.

Create a procurement for the material and service for the new plant about to start. Go to **Purchase** | **Purchase Agreement** under the **Purchase** application. Some important dates to be decided before you open a tender for the vendors are as follows:

- **Agreement Deadline**: This is the last date by which tender will close after accepting the quotations
- **Ordering Date**: After the tender process is closed, the purchase order will be confirmed by this date
- **Delivery Date**: This is the date by which delivery is expected

Look at the following screen of the tender with product lines and terms and conditions:

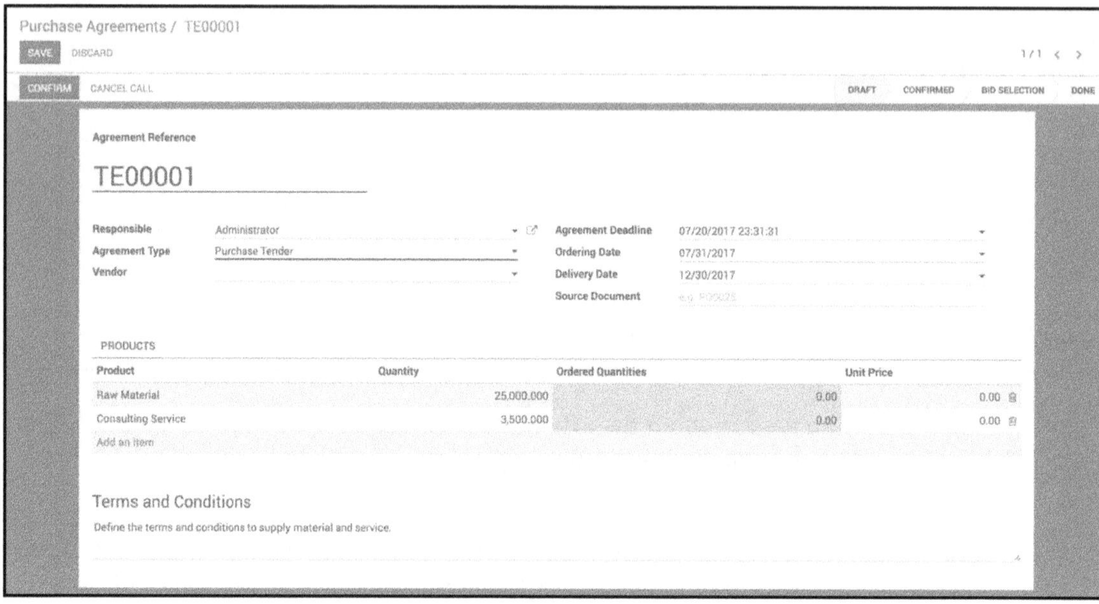

Add the product or service that you are looking to buy through the tender process.

> When you create a tender manually, you can add any product to be purchased through the tender process, no matter how the product has been configured to procure.

The document number will be filled in automatically from the sequence. Select **Purchase Tender** in the tender type.

4. The tender has already been prepared and verified. Now, it's time to confirm and send the request for a quotation to the specific list of vendors to send their proposal. Click on the **CONFIRMED** button to confirm the tender:

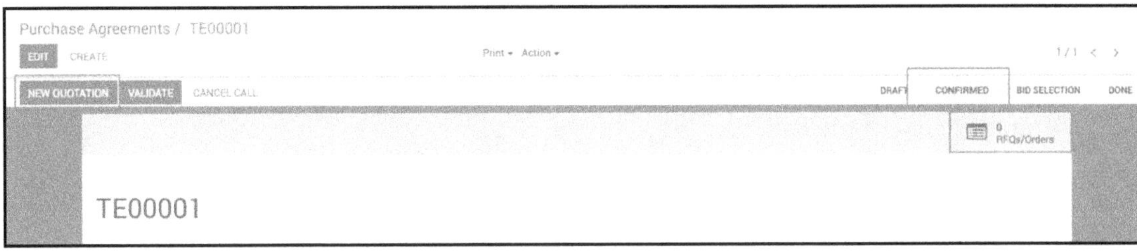

The tender is marked as confirm. The RFQ can be created for individual vendors by clicking on the **NEW QUOTATION** button. Let's create one for **China Export** to supply their quotation:

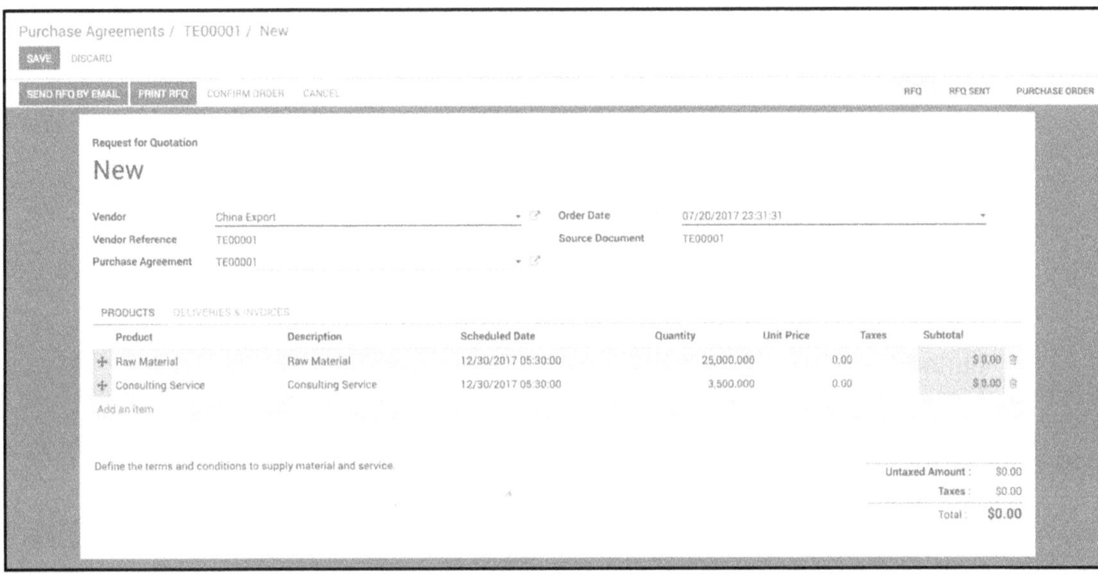

As soon as you click on the **NEW QUOTATION** button, the RFQ will be created and you have to select the vendor name only. Select the vendor name, and rest of the process is the same. You can send the RFQ document by e-mail or a printed copy by courier.

> Create an RFQ for all the vendors shortlisted for the project work, based on their track record or their project expertise.

5. Update the RFQ in Odoo based on the vendor proposal. This will compute the final cost of the full tender. Make sure that you update the supplier lead time to deliver the product. By clicking on the **RFQ/Orders action** button, you will be redirected to the list:

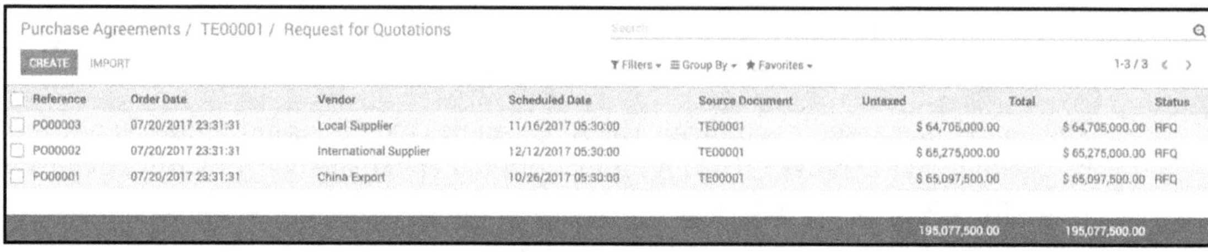

You can keep on updating the proposals coming from vendors. Look at the preceding screenshot having the list of proposals.

Odoo's chatter system helps a lot to communicate with vendors and preserve all the communication related to the pricing, and terms and condition.

6. As soon as the last date is reached for receiving the proposal, you can start the selection process and stop receiving the proposal by clicking on the **VALIDATE** button:

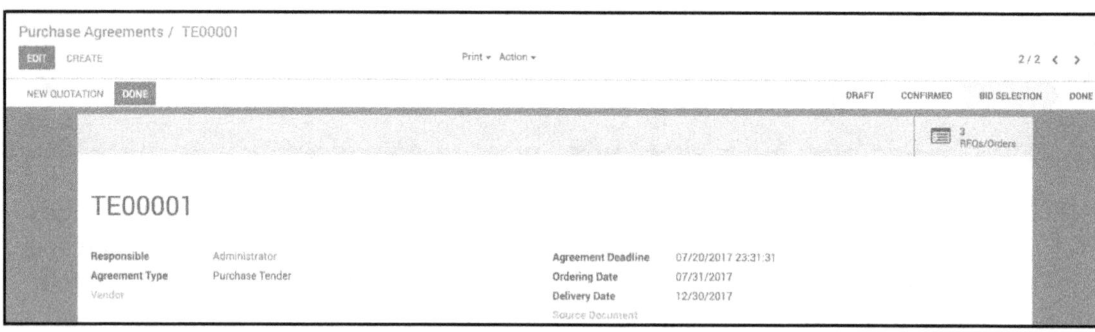

Select the best tender based on the detailed comparison. The comparison cannot be done only based on the price and quantity. There are many other parameters that affect the cost price of the material or service:

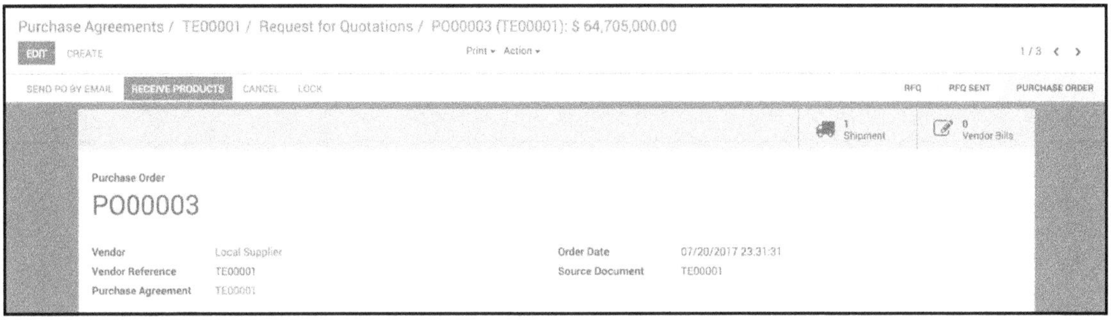

If your requirement can be fulfilled by the single supplier selected, you can reject all the other RFQs and mark the tender as done by clicking on the **DONE** button.

7. The tender process is used to select the best vendor proposal, as soon as the vendor confirmed, the request for quotation will be converted to the purchase order, the remaining process such as process the incoming shipment, checking the quality of the material, and vendor bill control and payment will remain the same.

There's more...

Odoo's **Call For Tender** feature manages much more than what we have gone through in the few steps from creating a tender and asking the price from different vendors, and comparing them and selecting the best one.

Purchase agreements

Odoo allows you to answer all questions related to the business case with a few configurations using **Agreement Type**. In the previous example, we have used **Purchase Agreement** in the agreement type that allows you to split a single order into multiple orders between multiple suppliers. Let's see how we can create different types of agreement used for different business cases.

The **Agreement Type / Tender Type** can be created or changed by going to **Configuration** | **Purchase Agreement Type** under the **Purchase** application. You will find two default tender types, **Purchase Tender** and **Blanket Order**:

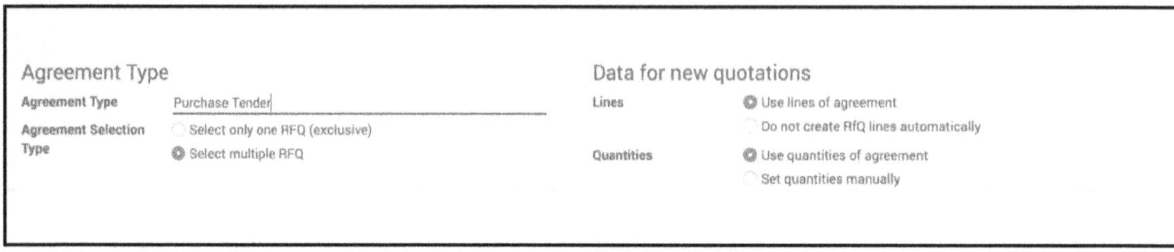

The key configuration fields on the agreement types are as follows:

- **Agreement Type**: This is a name of the type. It should be a meaningful name.
- **Agreement Selection Type**: This refers to the selection of a vendor, which can be exclusive or split order between multiple vendors.
- **Lines**: This is used to control the creation of the RFQ based on the tender. The **Use lines of agreement** options can be chosen if the product or service to buy is fixed. Select **Do not create RFQ line automatically** if you don't know what products are required to complete the project. The vendor will give the details about the product or service required for the project.
- **Quantity**: The field has to be set based on the tender. If we have a large order and it is confirmed that a single vendor cannot complete it, instead of forcing them to put the price, let them give the price and quantity they can supply. If this is the case, select the **Set quantities manually** option. You can restrict the vendor to not allow them to change the quantity by setting the quantity from the agreement. Opt for the **Use quantities of agreement** option in this case.

Configure the preceding key fields to create different types of tenders. Look at the screen of configuring the **Blanket Order** agreement type:

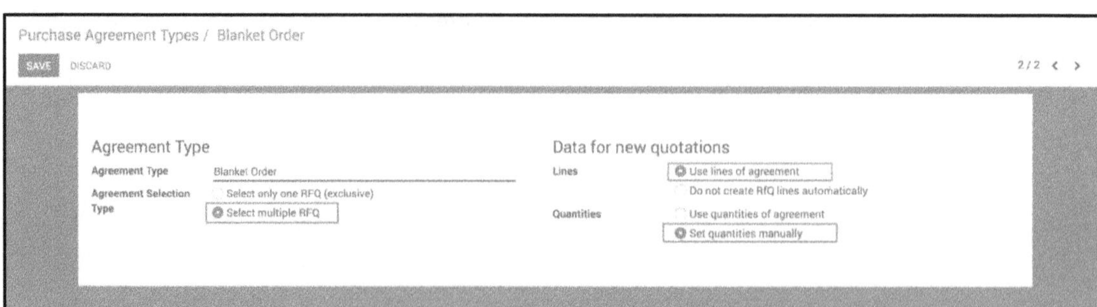

The blanket order is for the huge quantity and it has to be split between multiple vendors to get the required material on-time. Therefore, the product lines will be copied from the agreement but product quantities have to be set manually depending on the vendor's supply capacity.

Let's create a new type called **Purchase Tender (Exclusively)**. This tender can be created to have an exclusive vendor. Look at the following screenshot of exclusive vendor selection:

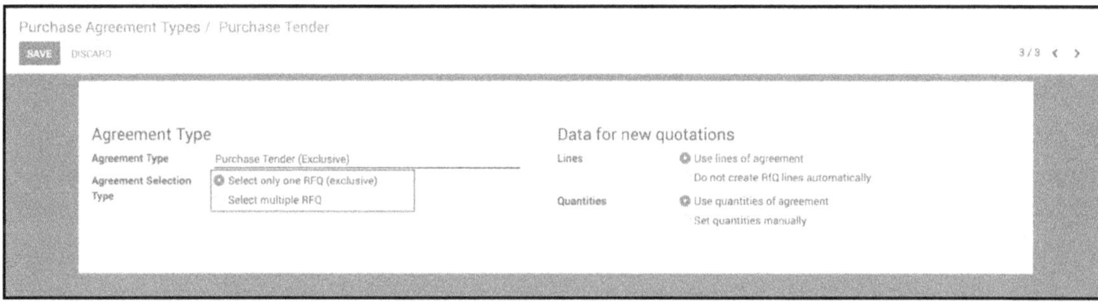

Save the type, and this will be available to create a new type of tender/agreement. Look at the following screen, the tender created with the **Purchase Tender (Exclusive)** option in **Agreement Type**.

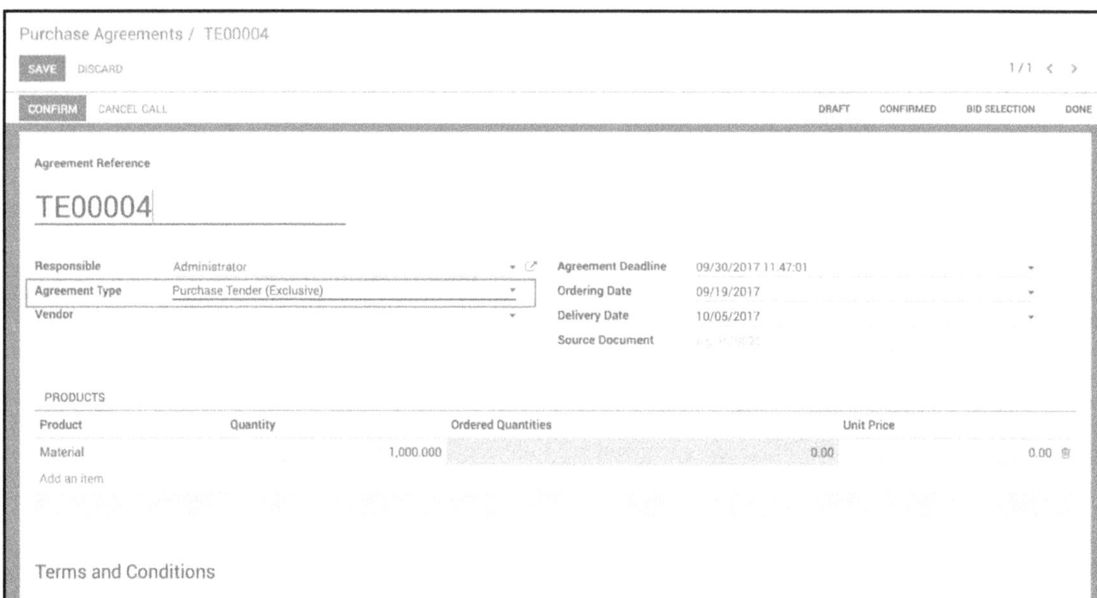

Click on the **CONFIRM** button and send the request for a proposal to different vendors, look at the following screen.

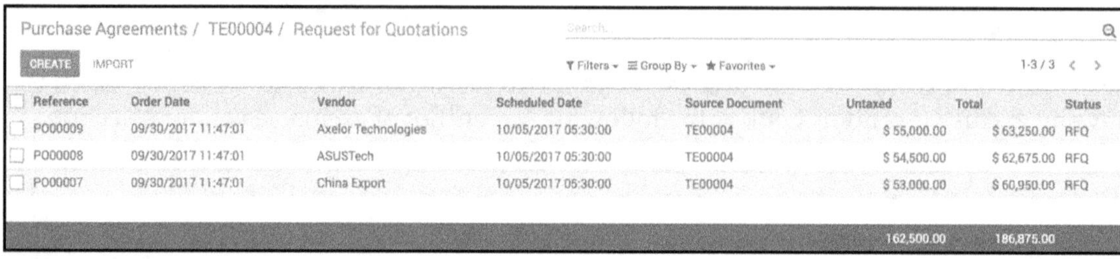

If any of the Purchase quotations are confirmed and converted to purchase order, the other request for quotation for the same purchase tender will be cancelled automatically, look at the following screen as soon as the **China Export**'s proposal selected, others proposal get cancelled:

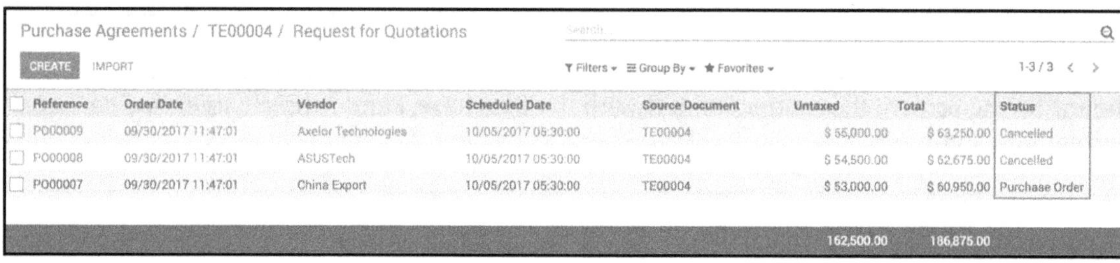

Controlling invoicing and payments

Vendors usually send the bill or invoice along with the delivery of the goods. In some countries, it is mandatory to send the copy of the invoice along with the delivery of goods. All the vendor bills are the part of the purchase process and controlled by the purchase process, before confirming the vendor bill, an accountant has to verify the quantity received in the warehouse and confirm the rates supplied by the vendor in a request for quotation.

Before the vendor bill is confirmed, it has to be verified the rates from the purchase order and quantity received in the warehouse. Imagine if we use Inventory, Purchase, and Warehouse, three different applications they are not integrated with each other, how difficult to verify the vendor bills for rates and quantities received in the accounting application.

The power of Odoo is integration between different business applications and seamless data flow between different business processes. The standard purchase workflow is as follows:

- The request for quotation has been created and sent to vendors.
- Vendor confirms the rates; the RFQ has been converted into a purchase order.
- An incoming shipment is generated by the purchase order for the stockable and consumable items.
- An incoming shipment is received along with the vendor bill, validate the bill with the product received in the warehouse to process further for payment.

We have gone through the purchase process through RFQ or tender in this chapter in the *Complete purchase cycle* and *Tenders, choose the best offer* recipes. Let's see how Odoo creates the vendor bills that are already verified.

Getting ready

With the standard business case, the vendor bill can be created based on the quantity received in the warehouse for specific products after verifying the quantity received. Assumed that you have prepared the list of products for that you would like to control the Purchase Bills and payment process, prepare the products list you would like to control the purchase bills based on the received quantity.

How to do it...

1. Almost all the configurations are done, please verify that the **On receive quantities** option is selected for the **Control Purchase Bills** field under the **GENERAL INFORMATION** on product form:

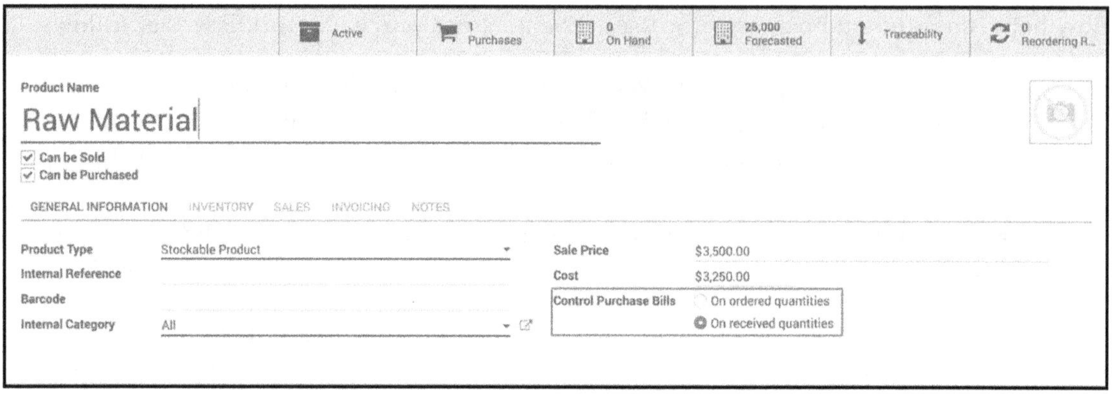

Now, the bill will be generated based on what has been delivered in the warehouse for **Raw Material**.

2. Let's assume that we have a purchase order (blanket order) where the price is fixed for the material in the purchase agreement:

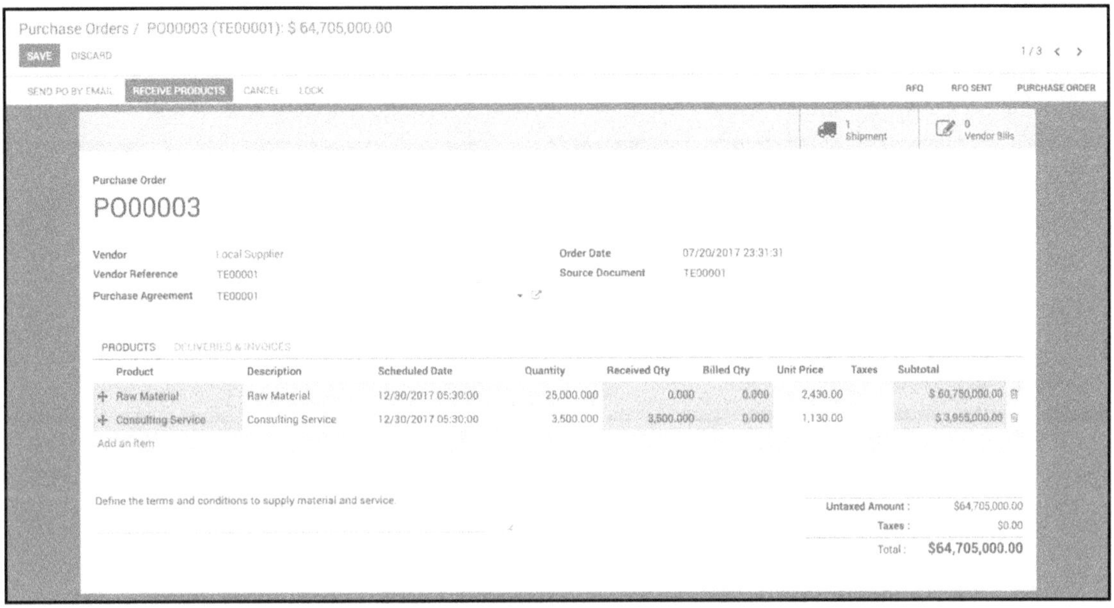

3. Receive the partial incoming shipment in a warehouse for 250 units of **Raw Material** product, look at the following screenshot:

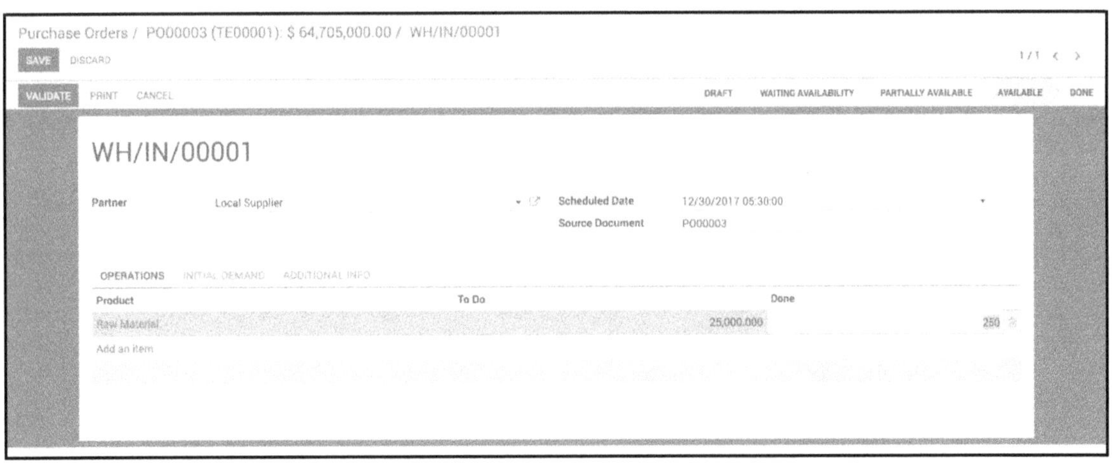

Out of 25,000 units, we received only 250 units, which means we should not receive a bill for more than 250 units. Click on the **VALIDATE** button to process the incoming shipment:

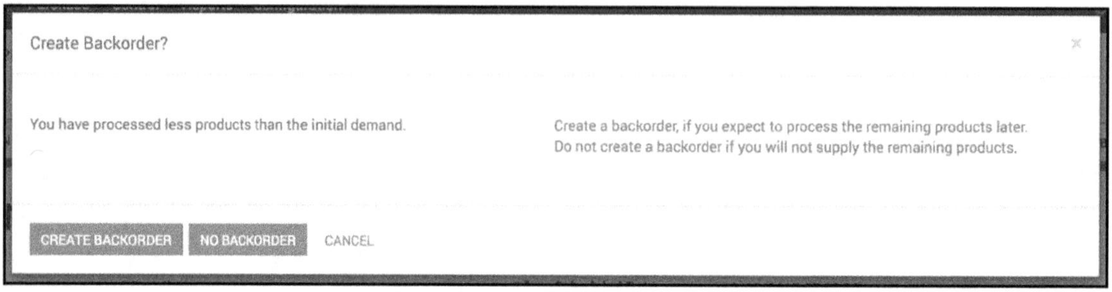

As the full order was not received, it will ask to confirm that it is a partial delivery and whether you would like to create a backorder or not.

4. When the bill is received from the vendor, go to **Control** | **Vendor Bills** under the **Purchase** application and click on the **CREATE** button. Select the purchase order against which the invoice is received:

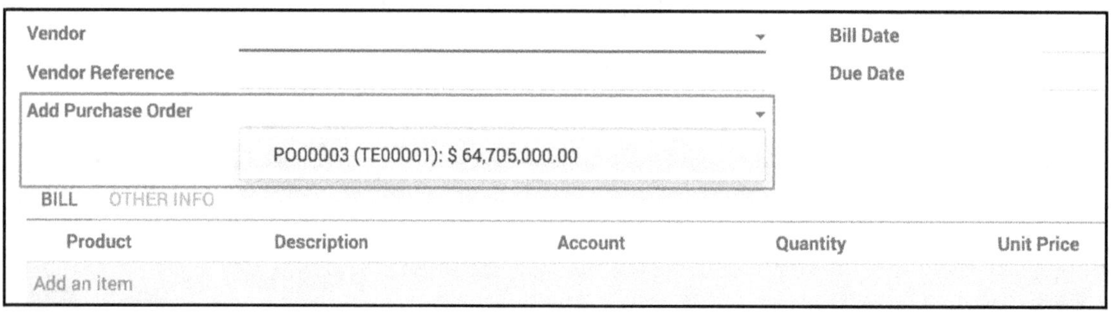

5. As soon as the purchase order is selected, the verification will be done automatically, and the bill will be generated based on what has been received in the warehouse:

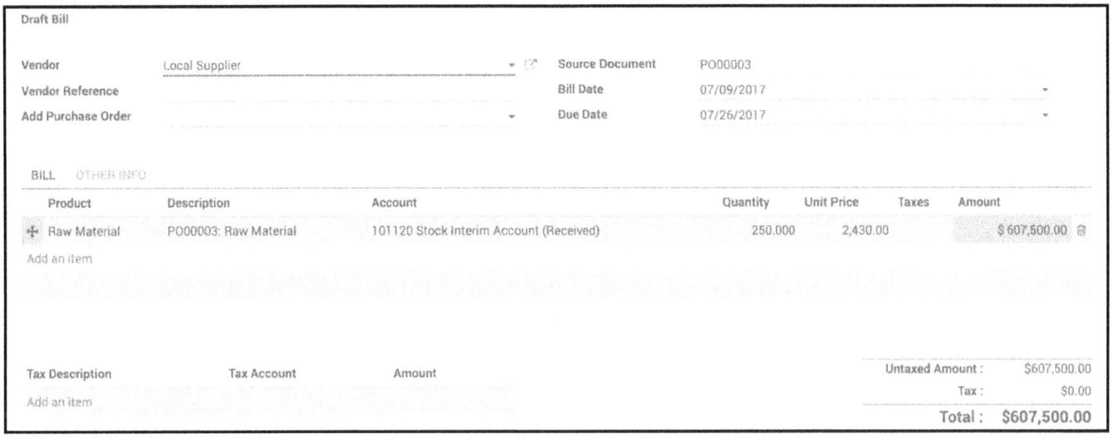

Compare the vendor bill prepared by Odoo with the bill received from the vendor; verify and confirm the bill. You have a full track of the purchase agreement: what has been ordered, received, and invoiced on the purchase order. Look at the this screenshot:

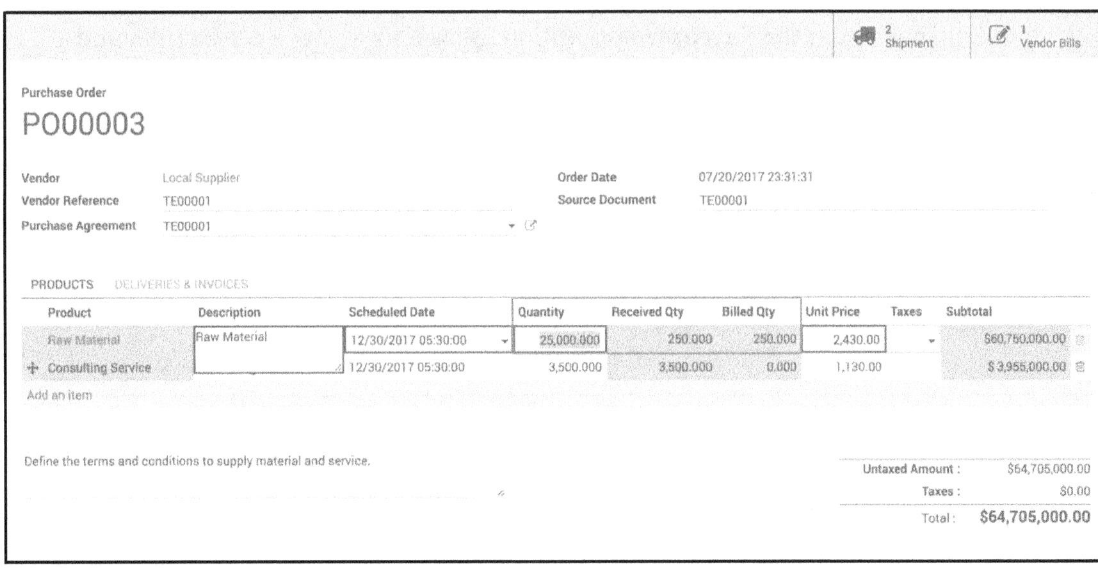

All the shipments received for this purchase order and invoices created based on the incoming shipments are linked on the purchase order and can be viewed.

Multiple units of measures

It is normal in business to deal with the multiple units of measure, purchase in different units, preservation in a different unit in warehouse, and sale in a different unit of measure. Odoo has a feature to manage multiple units of measure for sales, purchase, and inventory efficiently.

There are many business cases where the purchase is done in bulk to get the price benefits and the same product sale in different unit of measure, that is, purchase in pack of 1000 and sale in the pack of 6 or pack of 12, but the stored quantities in warehouse can be identified as a unit only.

Let's see how to activate the multiple units of measure feature in Odoo, purchase in big packs, stored it as a unit, and sell in small packs.

How to do it...

1. The multiple units of measure can be activated by going to **Configuration** | **Settings** under the **Purchase** application. Search for `Unit of Measure` and select **Some products may be sold/puchased in different units of measure (advanced)** option:

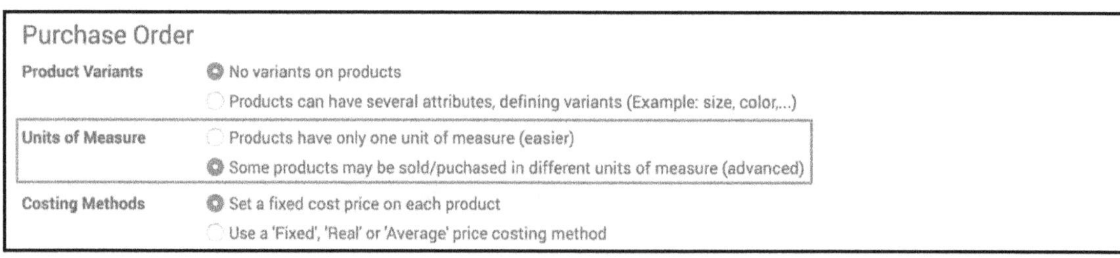

2. As soon as the multiple units of measure are activated, the **Unit of Measure** field will be available on the **Sales** and **Purchase** order:

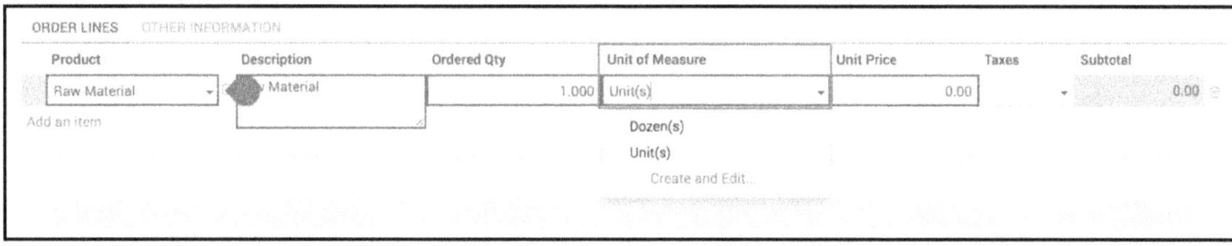

Let's assume that we buy material in a pack of `1000` and sell it in a pack of `5`, `10`, and `20` at different prices. Warehouses keep the stock in unit and not the pack. Look at this screenshot to understand how the product has to be configured:

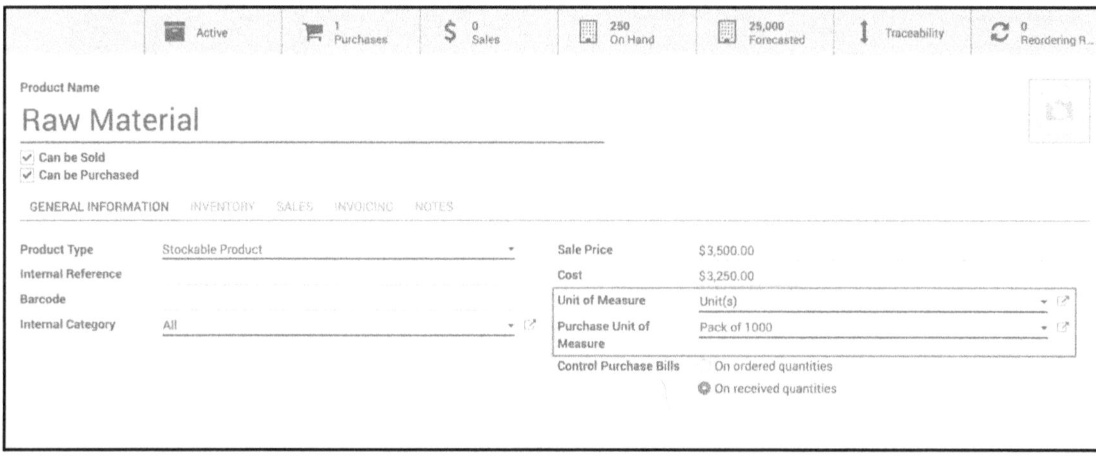

The **Unit of Measure** field is the default that is used to define how it will be stored in the warehouse, while **Purchase Unit of Measure** is used at the time of purchasing the material.

> The sale and cost price defined on the product is for a single unit stored in the warehouse. It will be converted according to the unit of measure selected on the purchase or sale order.

3. As the default purchase of unit is changed, the vendor pricelist has to be updated to match with the new unit of measure.

One unit cost is 3250, but it is beneficial to buy the pack of 1000 to get the advantage of price. The pack of 1000 will cost us 25,00,000.00 which means the pack of one will cost us 2500 instead of 3250:

Let's buy three packs of 1000 from **China Export**. Look at this screenshot of purchase order:

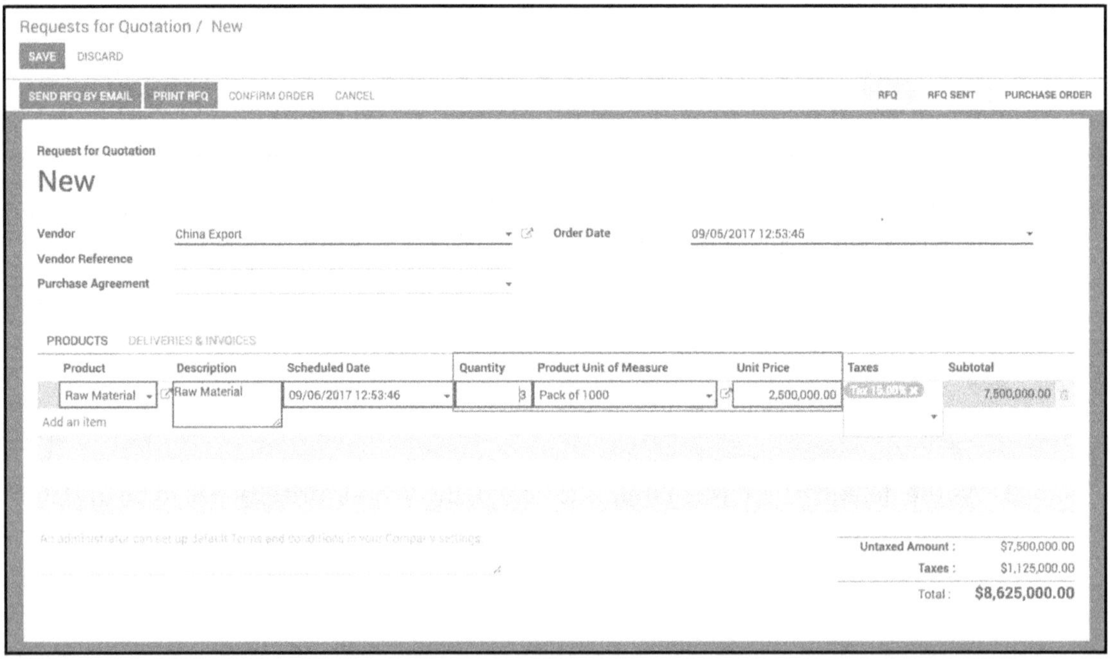

Confirm the purchase order and wait for the material to arrive in the warehouse.

4. As soon as the material arrives in the warehouse, according to the warehouse, we should receive 3000 quantity as per the 3 pack of 1000 unit, the pack of 1000 unit is only for the purchase while it stored as a unit in the warehouse:

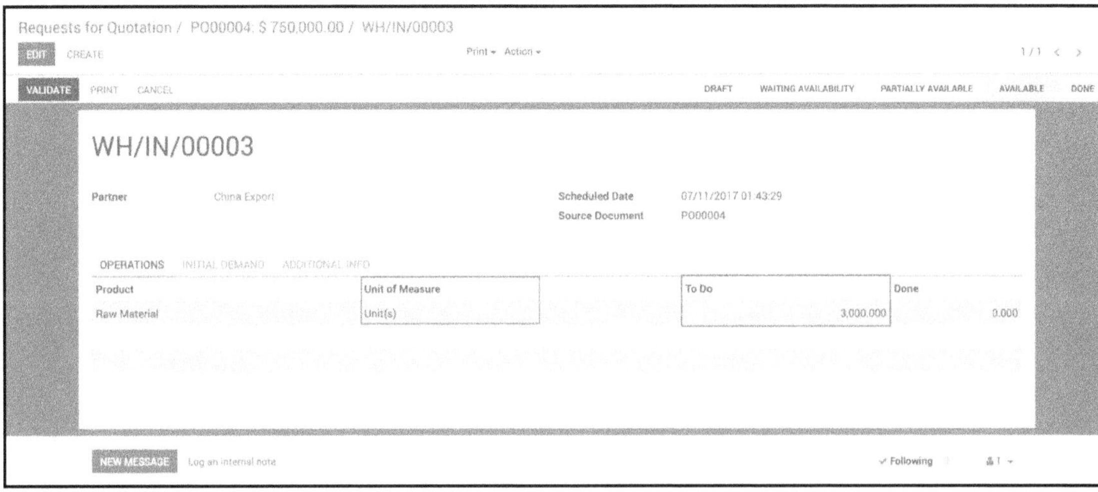

If you look at the **INITIAL DEMAND** tab, you will find that the order was for three packs of 1000.

5. When you receive an invoice, it will be for three packs of 1000, which is correct. Odoo will verify and create an invoice for the three packs of 1000 units only. In this scenario, we will receive the full quantity, so we will get the bill for three packs of 1000:

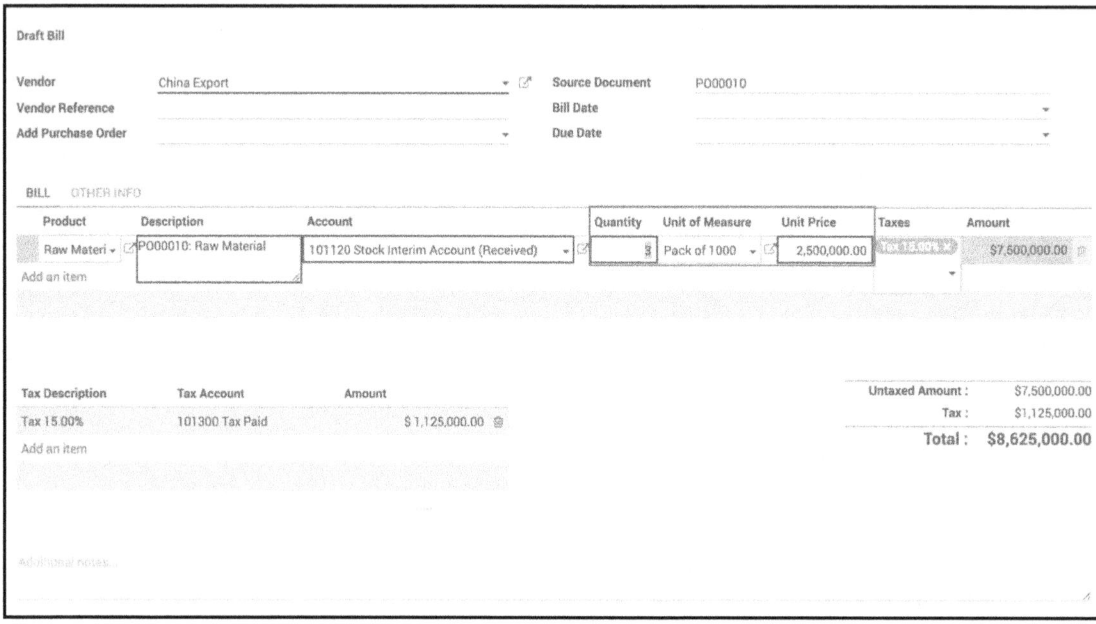

6. Assume that we get the partial delivery along with the invoice. The unit of measure will not change, but the packs will be computed based on the units received in the warehouse and vendor bill be generated based on that. Look at the following screenshot of vendor bill, which was received after the delivery of 1200 units in the warehouse:

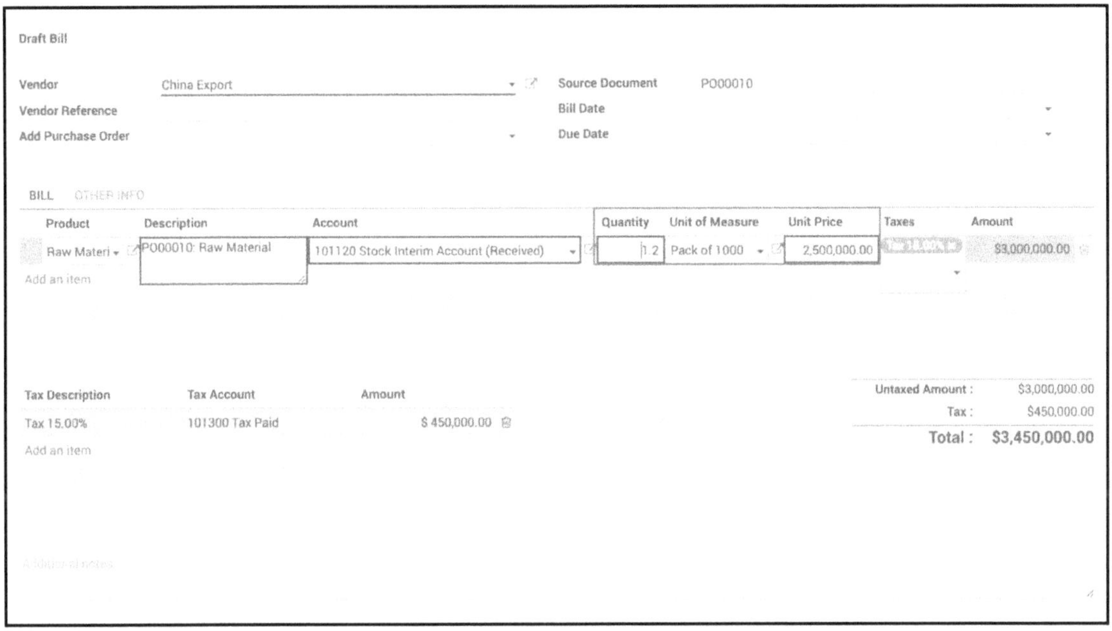

It has been converted to 1.2 packs of 1000, and the bill will be prepared based on the packs received.

How it works...

The conversion between units of measure is done at the time of creating a purchase or receiving a quantity in the warehouse so that the bill can be generated correctly. The new unit or measure can be created by going to **Sales** | **Configuration** | **Products** | **Units of Measure**. Look at the following screenshot of a list of units of measure grouped by their category:

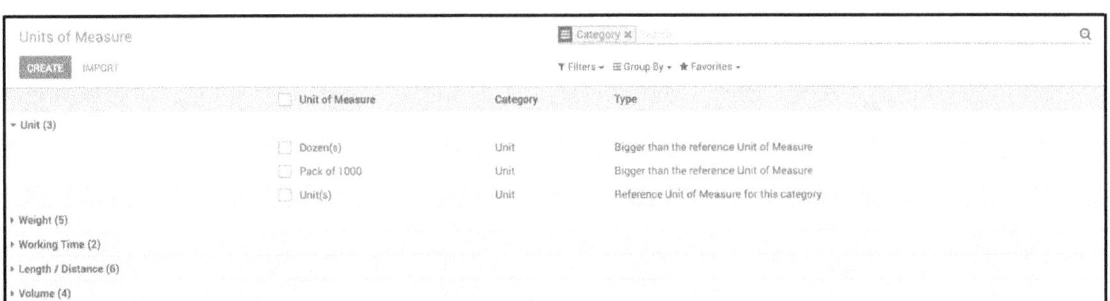

Base Unit of Measure

The value of the **Type** field defines which one is the base (reference) unit in the category. Each category required at least one unit having the **Reference Unit of Measure for this category** type. There are three possible values for **Type**, as listed here:

- **Reference Unit of Measure** for this category
- Smaller than the reference **Unit of Measure**
- Bigger than the reference **Unit of Measure**

For the **Unit** category the base unit of measure is **Unit(s)** as the **Type** is **Reference Unit of Measure for this category** shown in the following screen:

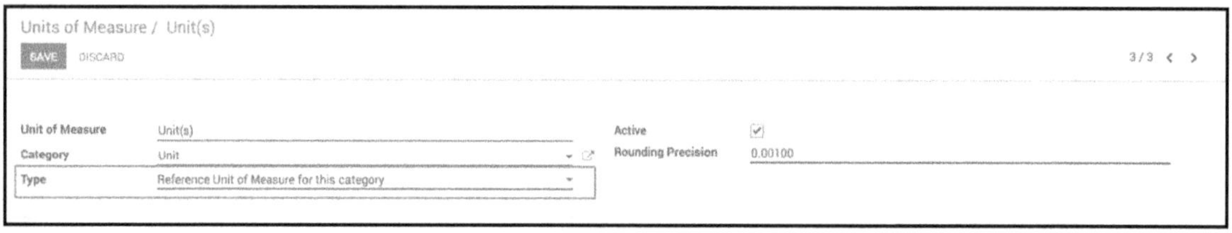

The **Category** field is used to categorize the different units of measures by category such as **Unit**, **Weight**, **Time**, **Volume**, the conversion can be done between the units of measure of the same category, that is, Unit(s), Pack of 1000, Pack of 6, Pack of 12, and so on.

Pack of 1000 and Unit of Measure conversion

Category and **Type** plays an import role in creating a new unit of measure. The conversion between two units is possible when they both belong to the same category.

Look at the following screenshot for the pack of 1000 unit of measure, which belongs to the **Unit** category:

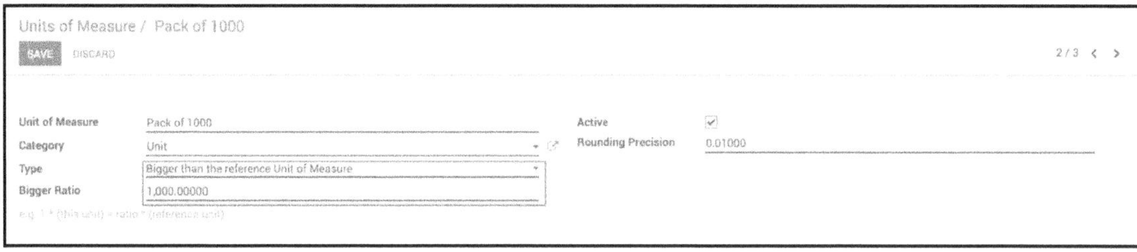

The new unit of measure is 1000 times bigger than the Reference units of measures. Select **Bigger than the reference Unit of Measure** in **Type** and enter 1000 in the **Bigger Ratio** field, which means that the new unit of measure is 1000 times bigger than that Reference units of measures, the reference units of measures always refer to 1.

The conversion will be done at the reception as shown:

```
1 * (this unit) = ratio * (reference unit)
```

In our case `1 * (pack of 1000) = 1000 * (1)`, which means, 1 pack of 1000 is equal to 1000 units.

On purchase order, we have purchased 3 Pack of 1000 which is equal to the 3 * pack of 1000, first it computes the number of units and then multiply with the purchase quantity as shown:

`3 * Pack of 1000 = 3 * 1000 units = 3000 units`, which computes 3000 units on the reception.

There's more...

The Units of measure will also be available in the Sales Order like purchase can be done in different units of measure the sales can be done in different units of measure too.

As soon as the multiple units of measure feature are enabled you will get the Unit of Measure field on the Sales order line. Let's take an example to sale order, where we will sell 1 Dozen of material which was purchased in the Pack of 1000:

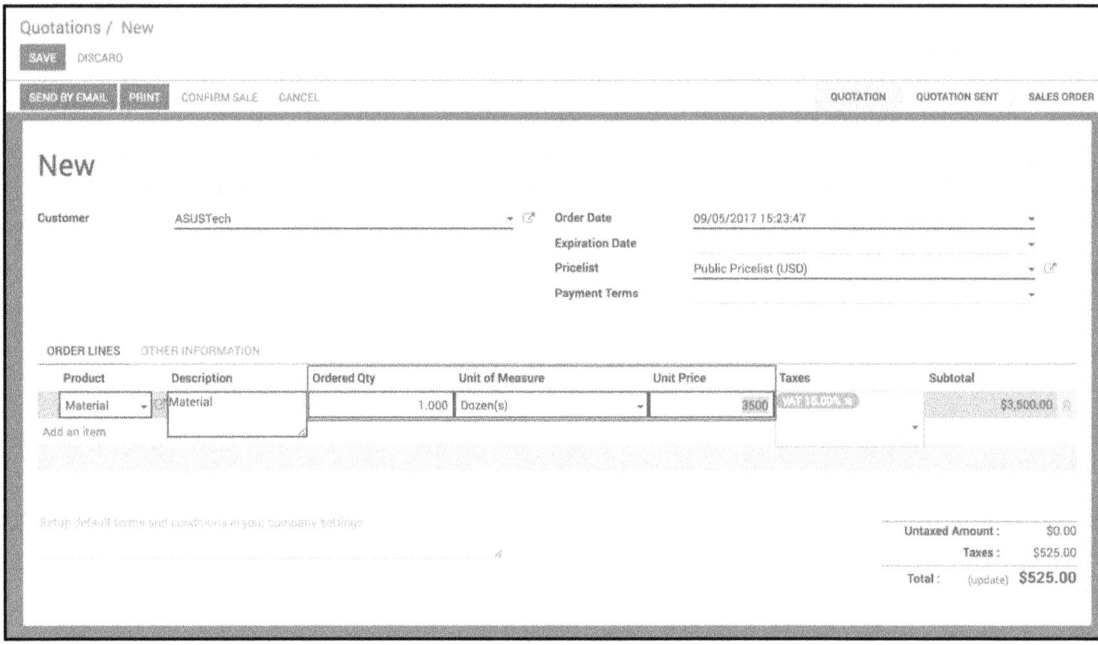

As soon as the **Dozen(s)** selected in the **Unit of Measure** field, the price will be recalculated for the 12 quantity, let's confirm the order by clicking on the **CONFIRM SALE** button.

You will get the delivery order created having 12 units of quantity to be delivered, look at the following screen of the delivery order:

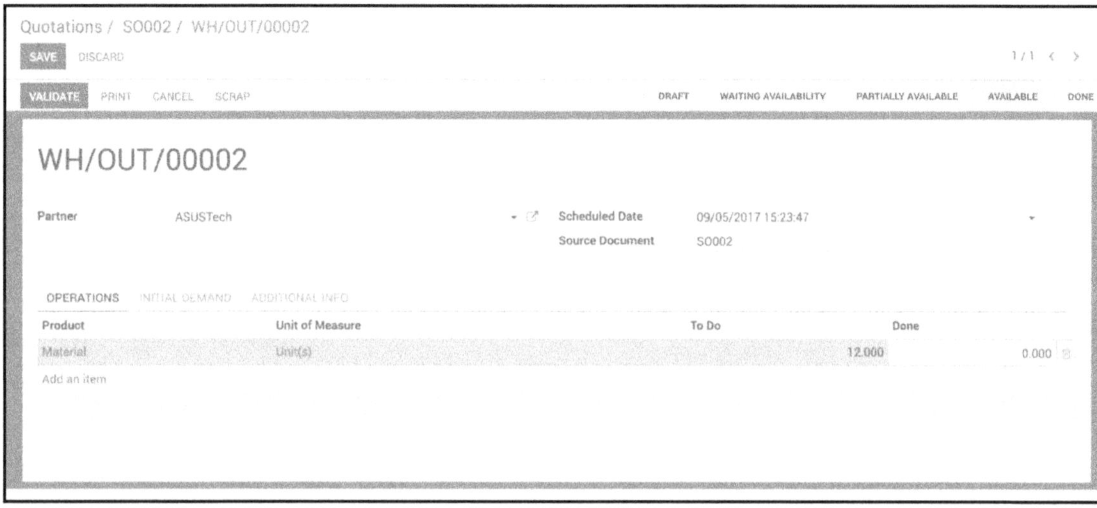

The warehouse maintains the stock in Units, it is just a sales and purchases are done in the different units of measure.

10
Warehouse and Inventory Management

In this chapter we will cover the following recipes:

- Delivery Orders and incoming shipments
- Initializing inventory and periodic verification
- Setting up the warehouses and locations
- Traceability, tracking serials, lots, and packs
- Set up and working with the barcode Interface

Introduction

Like the other Odoo applications the Warehouse Management System can be used alone or integrated with the other applications, it's is one of the most reliable applications supported by the barcode interface which ensuring a smooth running of the warehouse function. The warehouse management application is used to manage the stocks, incoming shipments, delivery orders, maintain minimum stocks depending on the demand, and invoicing based on the delivery or reception, the warehouse application should be connected to all the core business applications such as Sales, Purchasing, and Accounting in order to run the warehouse operation smoothly.

Warehouse application has some advanced features too, such as computing the inventory valuation and updating the balance sheet and profit and loss account based on the inventory movement when the inventory valuation is set to compute automated as Accounting and Warehouse have well-defined integrations.

It is hard to imagine a business being run without integration between warehouse and other core business functions, that is, sales, purchasing, and accounting.

Odoo Warehouse Management is one of the base applications (as important as accounting, sales or purchase) and is fully integrated with those core applications. It manages consumable and stockable products, it computes the inventory valuation efficiently depending on the stockable or consumable items, while the costing can be measured for all the material, either stockable or consumable.

The core functionality of Odoo Warehouse Management is to track incoming shipments and outgoing deliveries, issue materials for internal use, and manage serial numbers, lots and packs. Odoo is powerful and well integrated; it can manage the complex business functions such as stock valuation and real-time linking with balance sheets, compute the cost of goods sold in real time and link them to the profit and loss statement, manage advance routes such as cross-dock or drop shipping, and manage multiple warehouses at multiple locations.

In summary, Odoo warehouse is a simple and powerful application. It can manage a small shop and at the same time, is capable of managing the huge enterprise warehouse.

Let's look at all these features of the Odoo Warehouse Management System in detail and see how easily they can be implemented in your business.

Delivery Orders and incoming shipments

The core function of the warehouse is to manage the delivery schedule and incoming shipments. Odoo manages material procurement efficiently to make sure that you will be able to deliver on-time. It is synchronized with the purchase and sales orders so that you don't need to create Delivery Orders or incoming shipments manually. The pending orders can be tracked easily in the warehouse with urgent orders flagged up as high priority.

Getting ready

It is assumed that you have installed the Sales, Purchase and Accounting applications along with the Inventory Management.

How to do it...

1. Login to Odoo and verify that the Sales, Purchase, Accounting, and Inventory applications have been installed. Enter the Inventory application.
2. Like the other main applications in Odoo such as Sales and Accounting, the Inventory application has its own dashboard. You will see this when you enter the application. The following screenshot with the standard application configuration shows what it will look like:

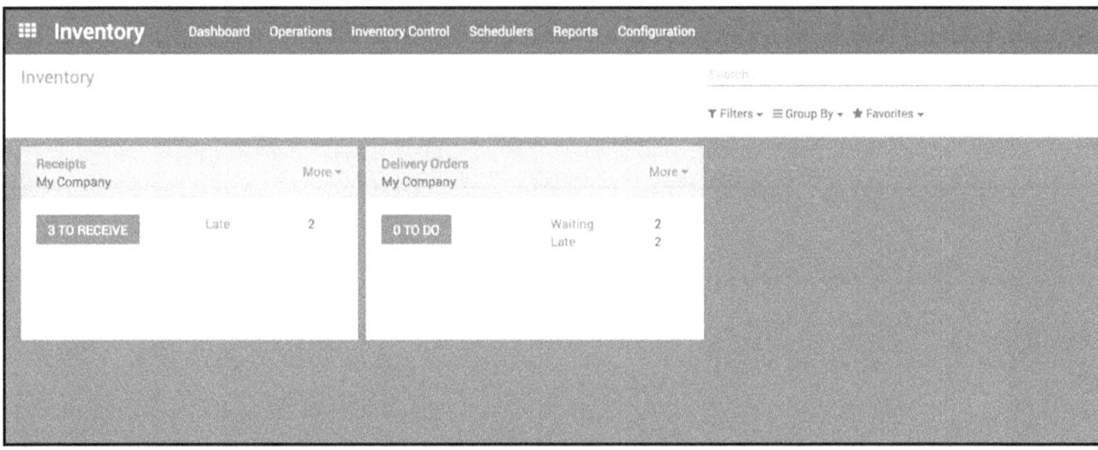

You will see two operations, which are available to you with the default configuration of the application. These are **Receipts** and **Delivery Orders:**

- **Receipts** give the information about the incoming shipments to be processed and any late shipments based on supplier commitments that have not yet been received.
- **Delivery Orders** gives the information about the outgoing shipments--those that have not been processed yet. You can see that either they are late for delivery or waiting for the stock of material to arrive before delivery.

3. Let's assume that we get the incoming shipment from the supplier for which we were waiting. As soon as the shipment arrives, click on the **3 TO RECEIVE** button and go to the list of incoming shipments as shown:

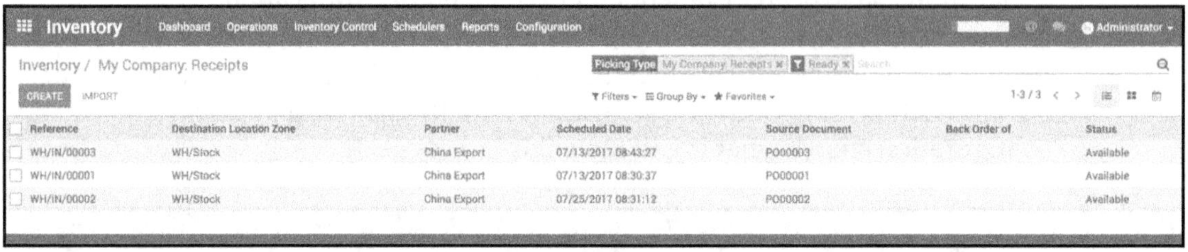

4. Search for the receipt, and open the receipt form view. Click on the **EDIT** button and enter the received quantity in the **Done** field:

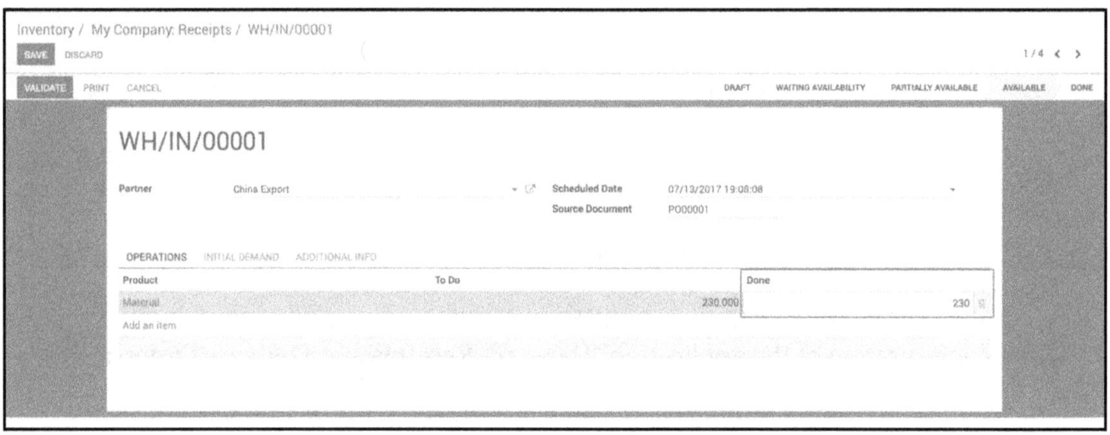

The line will become green. When entered, the quantity is equal to the **To Do** quantity. Click on the **VALIDATE** button to process the receipt.

5. Let's check in the warehouse to see whether all the quantities received are available or not. To check the current stock, go to **Reports** | **Inventory Valuation** under the Inventory application:

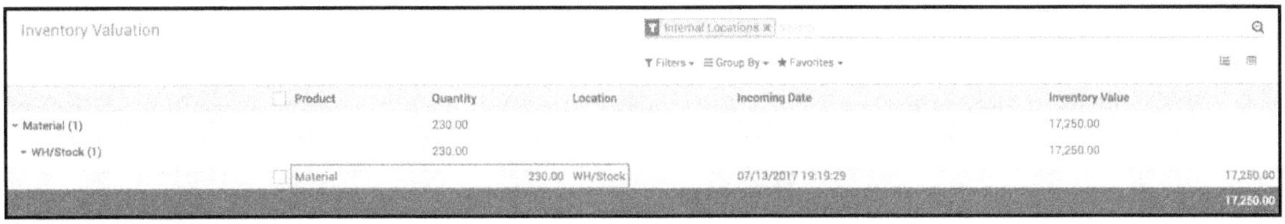

6. As soon as the material is received at the stock location, the Delivery Order will be ready to process. Go back to the **Inventory** dashboard and click on the **To Do** button and get the list of delivery orders ready to dispatch. Look at the list of Delivery Orders ready to process, as shown here:

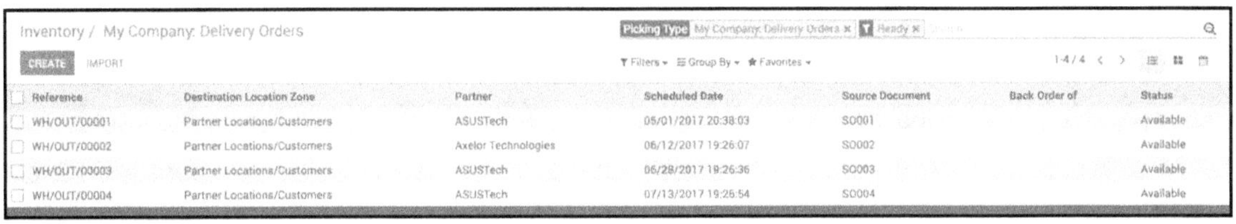

All the lines are red indicating that they were late in being processed. Process one by one and prepare to deliver the material. Edit the Delivery Order and enter the quantity you are going to deliver and click on the **VALIDATE** button:

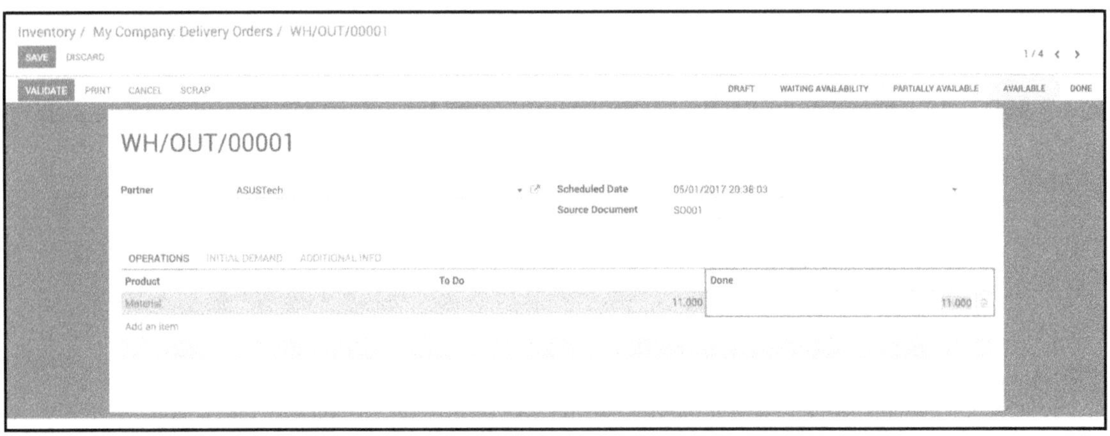

7. Click on the **PRINT** button to print the Delivery Order slip to be attached to the parcel. The delivery slip contains the address for the delivery. Look at the following screen:

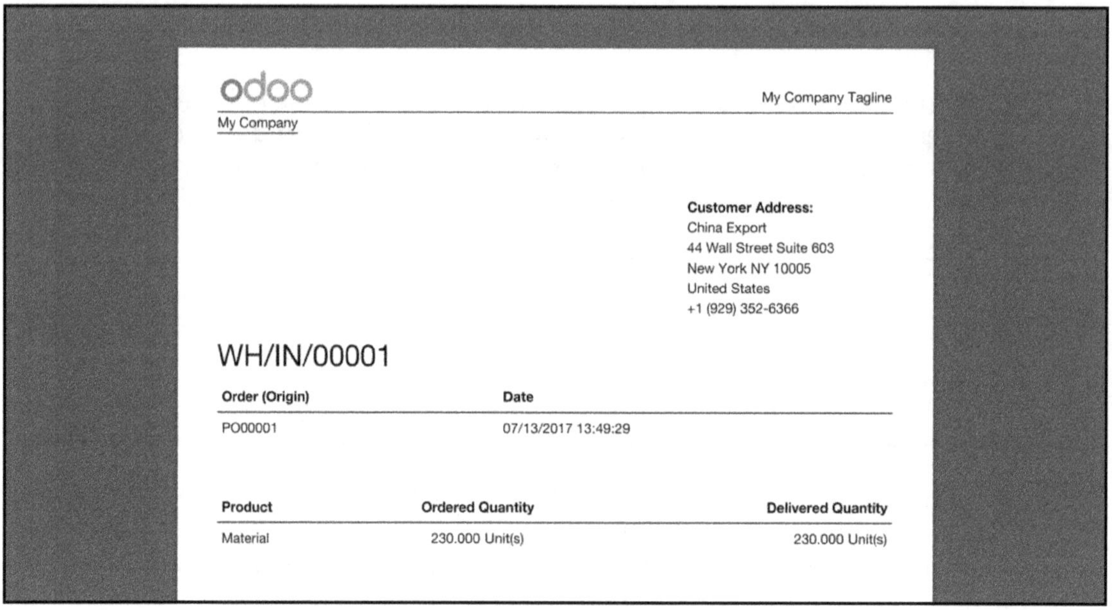
odoo

My Company

My Company Tagline

Customer Address:
China Export
44 Wall Street Suite 603
New York NY 10005
United States
+1 (929) 352-6366

WH/IN/00001

Order (Origin)	Date
PO00001	07/13/2017 13:49:29

Product	Ordered Quantity	Delivered Quantity
Material	230.000 Unit(s)	230.000 Unit(s)

At the reception, the delivery slip will be used to verify the quantity delivered.

> You may wish to do a partial delivery by entering a smaller quantity than is required. In such a case, you will be asked to create a backorder and a partial delivery will be processed.

8. The Delivery Order will be set to **Done** as soon as it is delivered.

There's more...

The Odoo warehouse application dashboard gives you full information about the Delivery Orders and incoming shipments, the late orders can be tracked and processed as a high priority. The Delivery and Reception order can have one of the following statuses: Draft, Waiting Availability, Partial Available, Available and Done. The Delivery and Reception Orders can be processed partially or all at once, depending on the instructions coming from sales or purchase orders.

Let's see in detail how the partial delivery and reception are managed in the Odoo Inventory application.

Partial delivery

The orders in Odoo can be marked as either partially delivered or all at once, depending on what was requested by the customer. Sometimes the customer may have asked to have a partial delivery or sometimes they asked to have the delivery all at once, depending on the logistic costs.

Assuming that the customer asked for delivery of each product when available, this is usually called partial delivery and this instruction can be set from the sales order on the **OTHER INFORMATION** tab. Look at the following screenshot:

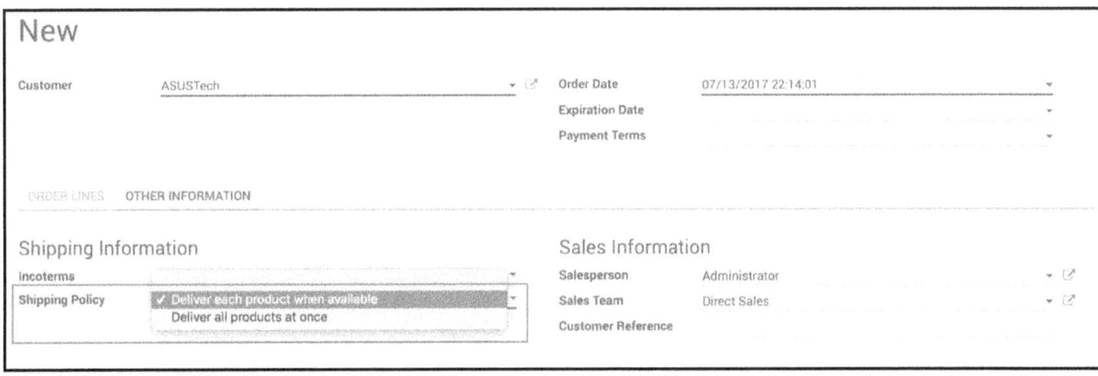

There are two different types of shipping options to choose from in the **Shipping Policy**:

- *Deliver each product when available*: The *Partial* option will be set on the **Delivery Type** field on delivery
- *Deliver all products at once*: The *All at once* option will be set on the **Delivery Type** field on delivery

1. Create a sales order for China Export for 300 units of material though in the warehouse there are only 270 units available.

As soon as the order is confirmed, you will have the delivery order available in the warehouse. Look at the **ADDITIONAL INFO** tab of the Delivery Order, you will see **Partial** in the **Delivery Type** field:

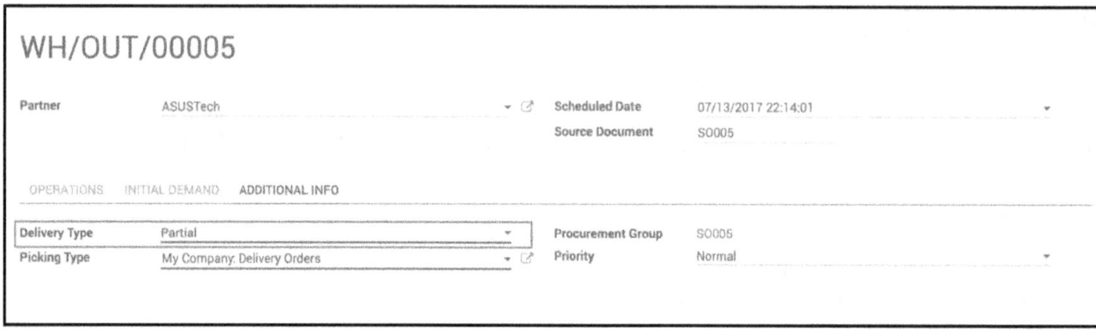

The **INITIAL DEMAND** tab contains the list of items with the quantity ordered, the **OPERATIONS** tab contains the list of items that are available in the warehouse, the **To Do** field contains the quantity available in the warehouse that can be assigned to this order. Look at the following screen:

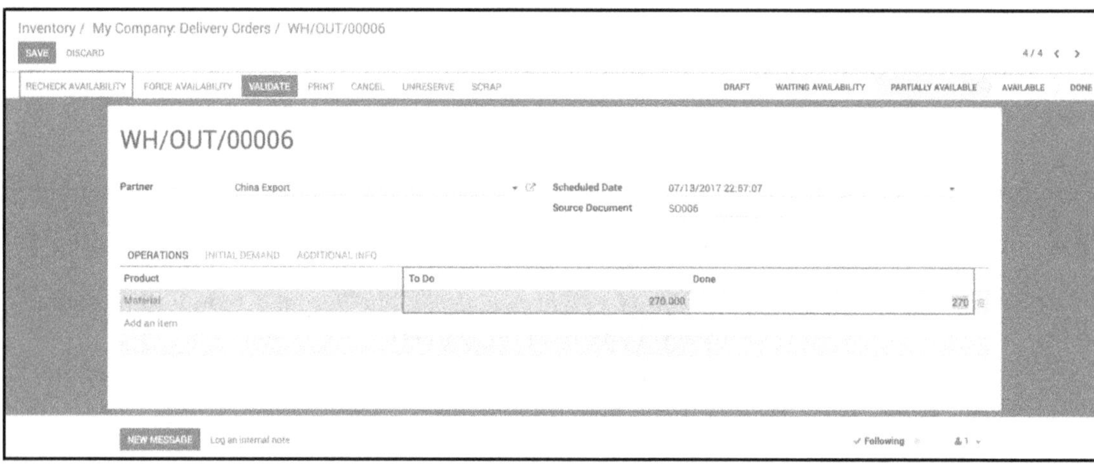

2. Click on the **VALIDATE** button. As the delivering quantity is less than the ordered quantity, Odoo will prompt you to check whether the backorder has to be created or not:

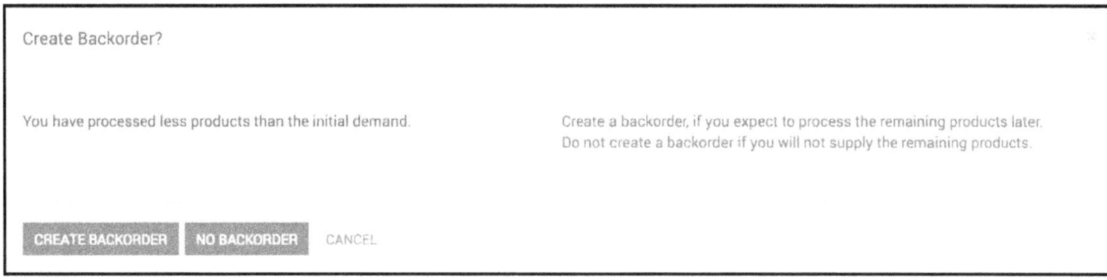

3. Click on the **CREATE BACKORDER** button. If you choose to have a backorder, Odoo will create a backorder with the remaining quantity. Look at the following screen which shows the created backorder:

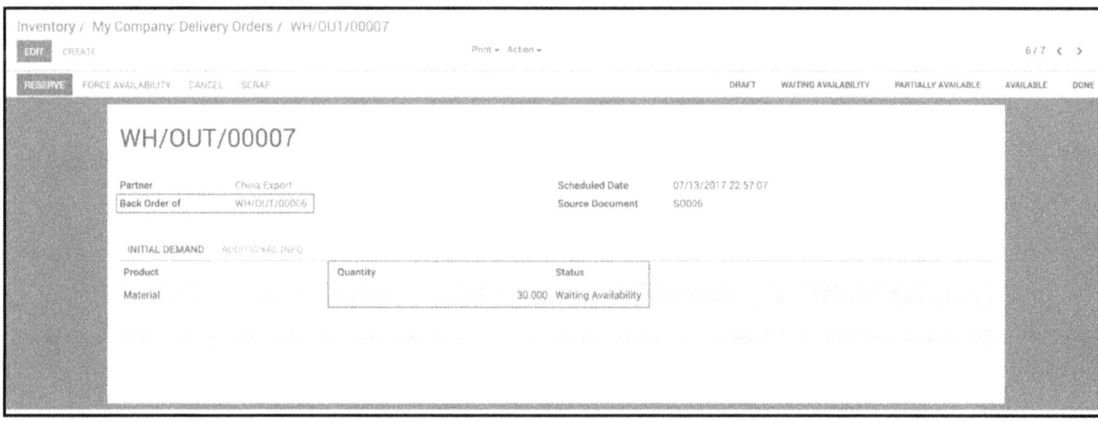

It is clear to see that this order is a backorder of **WH/OUT/00006** order. Out of 300 units, 270 have already been delivered; the backorder was created for the remaining 30 units. The backorders can be tracked using the group by **Back Order of** field as follows:

As soon as you choose to have no backorders by clicking on the button **NO BACKORDER**, Odoo will create a backorder and mark it as **CANCELLED**. If the invoicing policy is based on the Delivery Order, the invoicing will work just fine for the delivered orders; the credit note has to be processed manually for the remaining quantity.

Schedule date

The Purchase Order confirmation date and the schedule date for Reception Order are computed to plan the delivery and incoming receipts. The Odoo scheduler computes the date for the Purchase Order confirmation and the schedule date for the Reception Order. It is computed based on order lines (product) and not per order. The dates that are computed on different documents such as procurement, purchase, incoming shipment and delivery are dependent on the different lead times configured in Odoo such as the delivery lead yime on the vendor pricelist, the lead time on the re-order level and the customer lead time on the product.

Let's take an example of a full sales cycle where the product is configured to be procured by the *Make to Order* and *Buy* **Routes**.

The supplier, **China Export**, according to their price list they need six days from the date of order confirmation to deliver the product:

The **Delivery Lead Time**, **Minimal Quantity** and **Price** are part of the vendor price list supplied by **China Export**. Look at the preceding screenshot.

The **Lead Time** field available on the re-order level is used to compute the **Order Date** for the Purchase Order; the **Order Date** will be computed using the following formula:

Order Date = Date on which the demand generated + Lead Time (from the re-order level)

By default, it is set to `1`. You can set it to `0` if you want to set the **Order Date** on Purchase Order same as the date on which the demand was generated, that is, the date on which Sales Order confirmed:

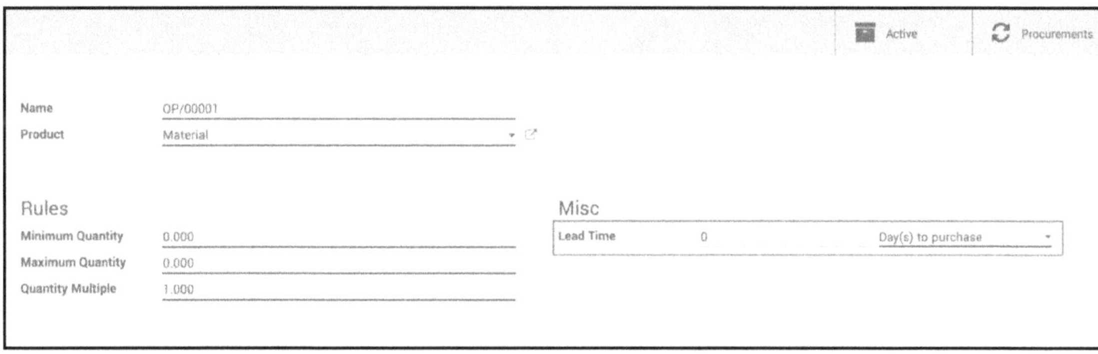

When demand for the product is high, it is advisable to wait for some days before confirming the Purchase Order. Therefore we will confirm the Purchase Order every five days, up until the five days we will keep same Purchase Order and update the quantity of product available after every order (that is, *Sales Order*).

The commitment date we have given to our customer is 10 days, that is, **Customer Lead Time** on the **Product** form. We look at the supplier price list, and according to it the vendor needs six days to deliver the material. Let's assume that the customer confirms the order on July 14, 2017, for the product as shown:

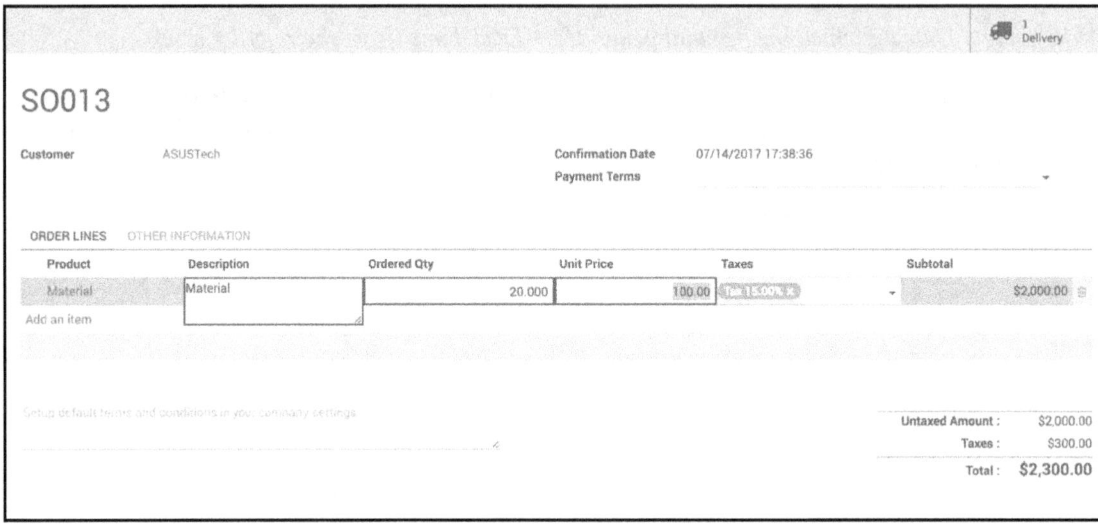

The delivery will be scheduled for July 24 as we need 10 days to deliver the order:

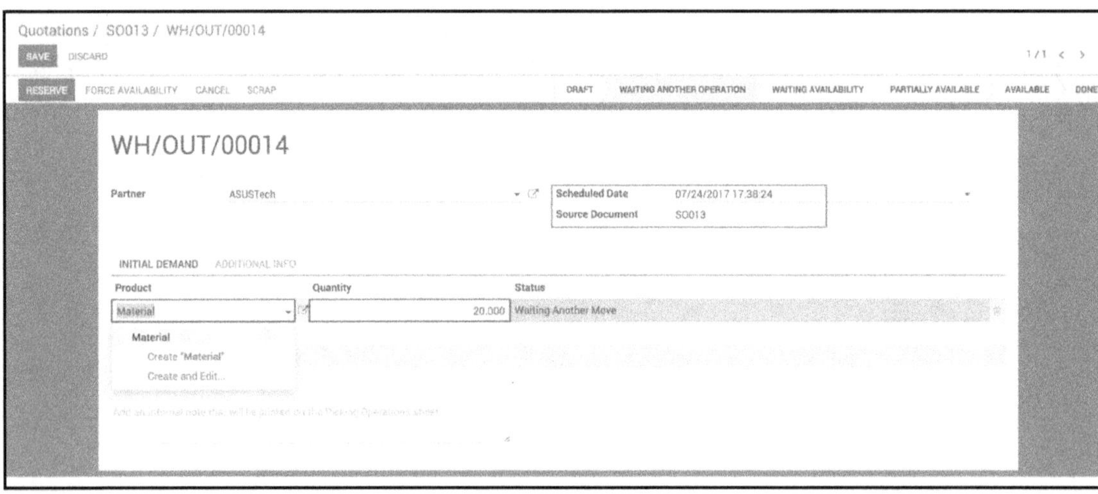

The procurement will trigger the order point as we do not have enough stock in the warehouse. The purchase will be created based on the reorder rules with the estimated reception date:

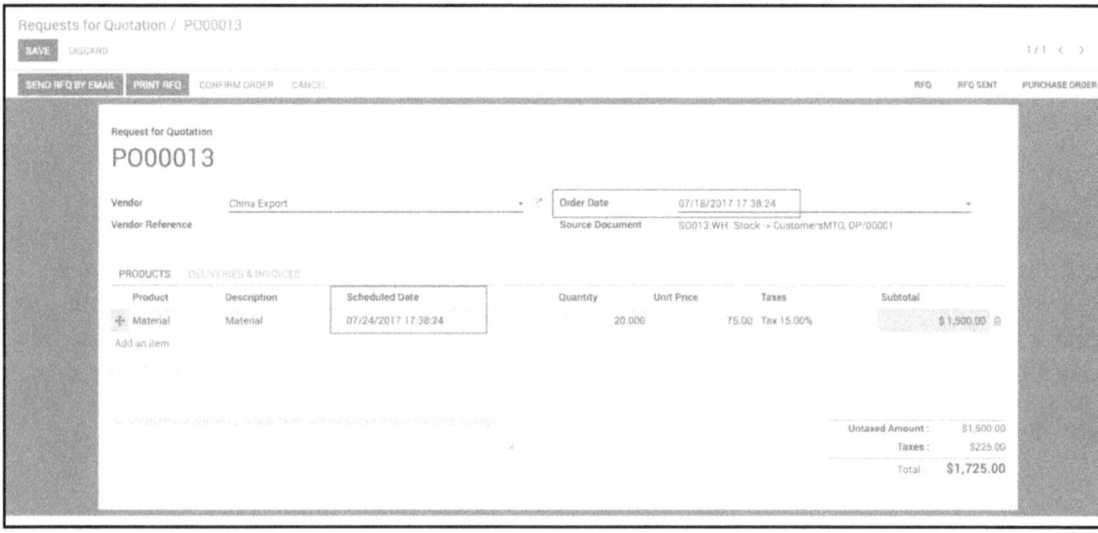

If you look at the preceding Purchase Order closely, you will be noticed that the **Order Date** is July 18, which is six days prior to the date of delivery. It is computed based on the vendor lead time which is six days. The purchase is confirmed on the same date and the delivery will be set to July 24 which means that you will have to make a delivery on the same day when you receive the incoming shipment from the vendor. The Purchase Order date and the reception date is computed based on the delivery schedule date on the Sales Order.

The **Order Date** and the reception date are computed as follows:

```
Purchase Order Date = Delivery Date - Vendor Lead
time
Schedule Date = Delivery Date
```

Purchase Lead Time

Assuming that you would like to keep the buffer days between the incoming shipment and Delivery Order, to cope with any transport delays, it can be set globally for all the Purchase Orders for the company. Go to **Purchase** | **Configuration** | **Settings**, set `1` as the buffer day in the field **Purchase Lead Time ***.

Now the Purchase Order date will be computed as follows:

```
Purchase Order Date = Delivery Date - (Vendor lead
time +
 Purchase Lead Time)
Schedule Date = Delivery Date - Purchase Lead Time
```

So, now your Purchase Order date is July 17 instead of July 18, but the delivery date is still the July 24.

Sales Safety Days

Assuming that you need some time before you deliver the material to the customer for the special packaging and you need one day for the same, as with the **Purchase Lead Time** you can set the **Sales Safety Days** globally for all the purchases that are triggered based on the Sales Order. Go to **Sales** | **Configuration** | **Settings** and enter `1` in **Sales Safety Days** field.

Now the Purchase Order date on will be computed as follows:

```
Purchase Order Date = Delivery Date - (Vendor lead
time +
 Purchase Lead Time + Sales Safety Days)
Schedule Date = Delivery Date - Sales Safety Days
```

So, finally it will work as follows:

- The Sales Order confirmed on July 14
- The delivery will be scheduled for 23 July (`10 days Customer Lead time - 1 day Sales Safety Days`)
- Purchase Order should be confirmed by July 16 (`July 23 - 6 days of Vendor Lead time + 1 day Purchase Lead Time + 1 days Sales Safety Days`)
- Reception of the Purchase Order will be scheduled on July 22 (`July 23 delivery date - 1 days Sales Safety Days`)

Initialize inventory and periodic verification

The inventory has to be initialized as soon as you start managing the inventory with the Odoo inventory application. The Odoo inventory application is flexible; you can start operation before you initializing the inventory, when you start operation before you initialize the inventory, as a result the units and value of the inventory goes negative but as soon as you initialize the inventory the units will be added to the inventory and the inventory value will become positive.

The Odoo inventory follows the double entry system; to increase or decrease the stock at any location you need another location for the counterpart entry. Stock, Input, Output, Customer or Supplier represent locations in Odoo. For example, the delivery operation decreases the stock at Stock location and increases the stock at the Customer location, while the reception operation increases the stock in Stock location and decreases the stock at Vendor location. The main location in Odoo warehouse is Stock where all the stocks are preserved while other locations are virtual locations.

Let's see how the initial inventory can be set up in Odoo warehouse and how to do a periodic verification of the inventory in the warehouse.

Getting ready

We assume that you have already created or imported all the products into Odoo and you are ready with the opening stock of all those products since you started the warehouse operation in Odoo.

How to do it...

1. Make sure that the product list has been imported into Odoo, verify the cost price of the product as the cost price will be used to compute the inventory value in the warehouse:

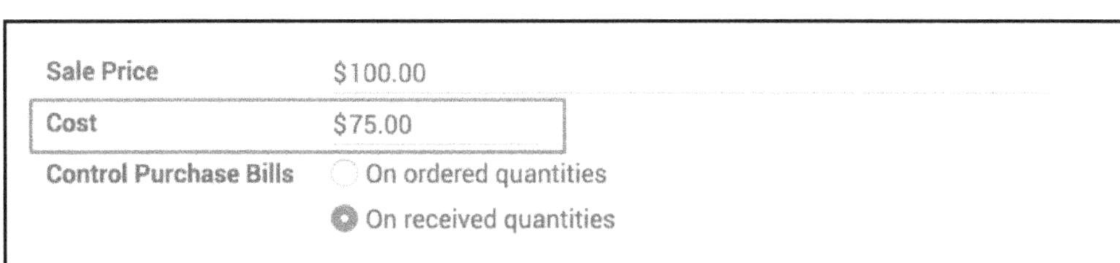

We will see the inventory valuation in detail in the coming topics. The default costing method is Standard Price set on the product Internal Category.

2. To enter the initial inventory in Odoo, go to **InventoryControl | Inventory Adjustments** under the **Inventory** application. Create a new adjustment. Look at the following screenshot:

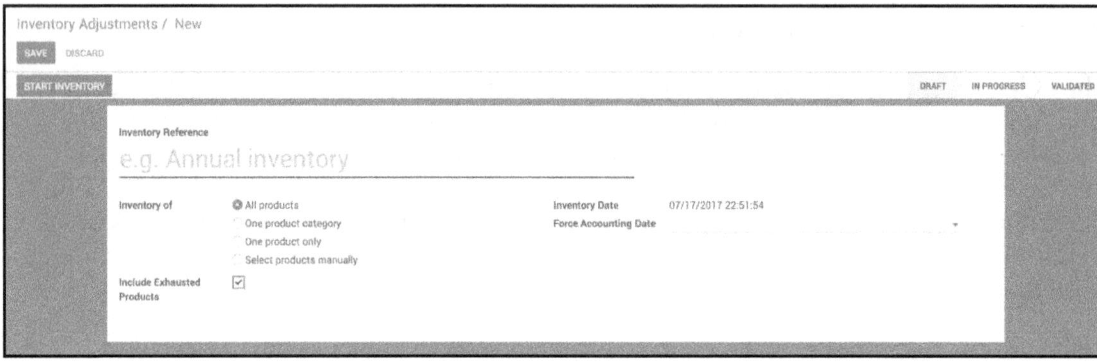

3. Enter the name of the adjustment, **INIT** or **Initial Inventory** could be a perfect name for the initial inventory.

Inventory of is an important field; choose anyone from the list of available options. Let's go through the following list of available options:

- **All products**: automatically adds all the products available in the product catalog, having a current quantity more than 0
- **One product category**: select the list of products belonging to a specific product category
- **One product only**: select any single product for which the inventory has to be updated
- **Select products manually**: you can choose the individual products yourself to update the inventory

Select **All products** for the field **Inventory of**.

4. The field **Include Exhausted Products** will be visible when you choose any one from **All products** or **One product category**. You can select the **Include Exhausted Products** field if you would like to add all the products available in the Product Catalogue even if the stock for those products may not be available.

5. The **Inventory Date** cannot be changed, but **Force Accounting Date** can be changed, as the inventory valuation account in the balance sheet has to be matched with the opening stock in Warehouse on a particular date.
6. Clicking on the **START INVENTORY** button will list all the products available in the Product Catalogue under the **INVENTORY DETAIL** field. The **Theoretical Quantity** will be computed based on the quantity available in the warehouse; **Real Quantity** will have to be filled manually based on the physical checking of the quantity in warehouse:

The **Theoretical Balance** is a quantity computed by Odoo in the warehouse based on the incoming and outgoing shipments; while **Real quantity** has to be entered by the user that represents the actual current quantity in Warehouse.

7. Click on the **VALIDATE INVENTORY** button to confirm the current quantity. The warehouse quantity will be set equal to the value entered in **Real Quantity**:

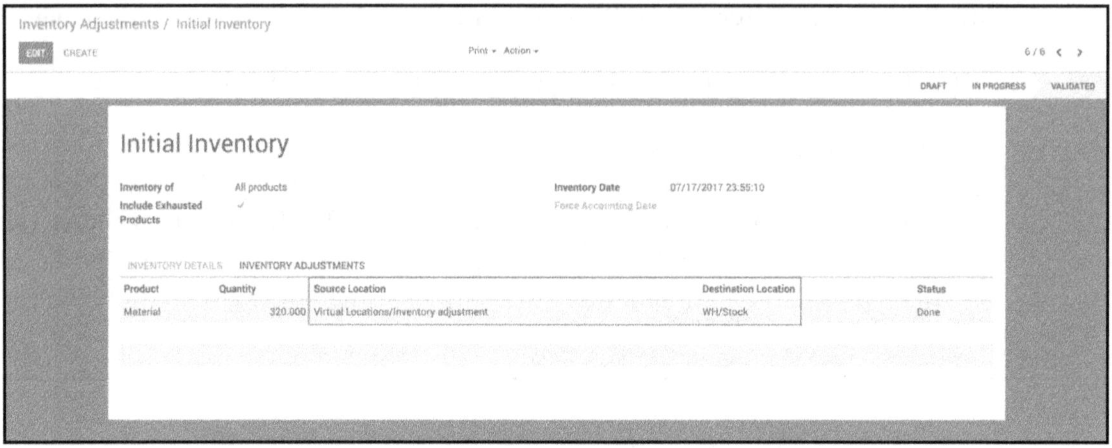

   On the **INVENTORY ADJUSTMENT** tab, the actual inventory transfer movement will be created on confirmation of the inventory. Look at the preceding screenshot.

8. As soon as the initial inventory is confirmed, the real stock of the material will get updated and the inventory valuation will be increased. Look at the following screen of the **Inventory Valuation** after the initial inventory update. The **Inventory Valuation** report can be accessed from the **Reports** | **Inventory Valuation** under the Stock application:

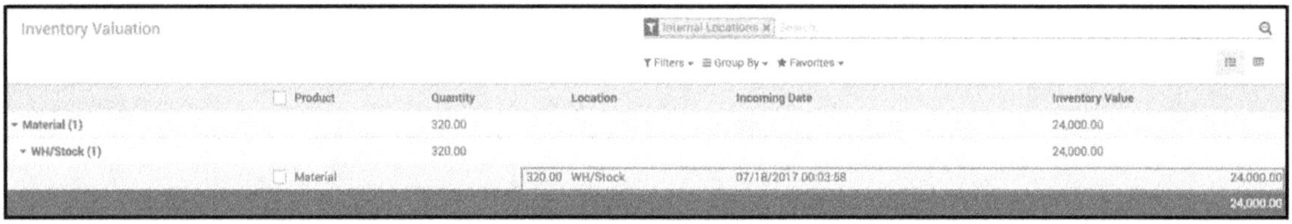

The **Incoming Date** is same as the **Inventory Date**; the valuation is computed based on the quantity entered multiplied by the cost price entered on the **Product Form**.

How it works...

Odoo needs two locations in order to perform any inventory operation such as delivery, incoming shipment or inventory initialization, as Odoo follows the double=entry system to perform the inventory transaction.

The source and a destination location on the initial adjustment will be selected depending on the difference between **Theoretical Quantity** and **Real Quantity**. Let's look at some scenarios explained here.

Real quantity is greater than the theoretical quantity

The Source Location will always be **Inventory adjustment** and the destination will be **Stock**. The quantity will be computed using formula `Real quantity - Theoretical quantity`.

Let's assume that the stock of the material has been updated from `320` to `400`.

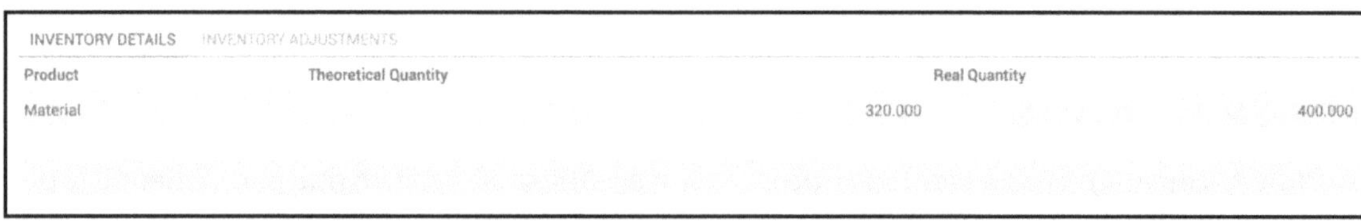

The Inventory Adjustment will be done for the difference of `80` units, `Real quantity (400) - Theoretical quantity (300)`. Look at the following screen for **INVENTORY ADJUSTMENT**.

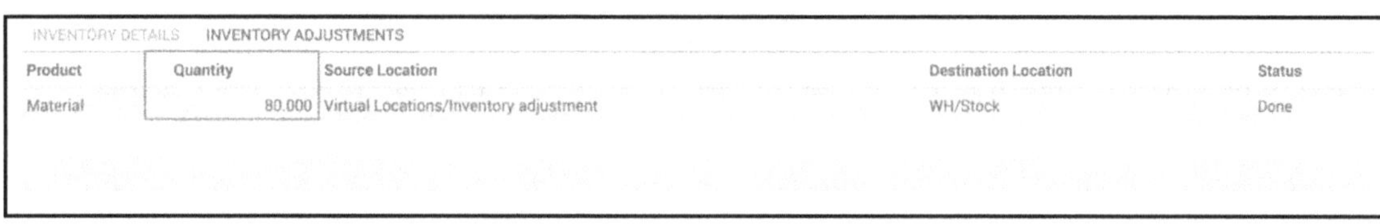

Now, let's move on to the next scenario.

Theoretical quantity is greater than the real quantity

In this case, the **Source Location** will get swapped; the **Source Location** will be **Stock** and the **Destination Location** will be **Inventory adjustment**. The quantity will be computed using the formula `Theoretical quantity - Real quantity.`

Let's assume that the stock of the material has been updated from 400 to 380.

The Inventory Adjustment will be done for the difference of 20 units, `Theoretical quantity (400) - Real quantity (380)`. Look at the following screen for **INVENTORY ADJUSTMENT**:

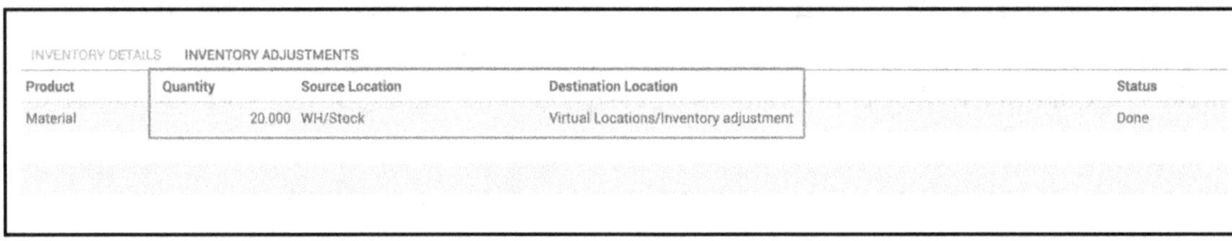

There's more...

Periodic verification is an essential process in a warehouse to be sure that the system is up-to-date with the physical inventory. The periodic verification has to be done to verify that the theoretical quantity, as per the software, matches with the real quantity or not. The real quantity has to be matched with the theoretical quality after every incoming and outgoing quantity is recorded correctly.

The periodic verification process is the same as the inventory initialization; it can be done by selecting all the products, or products by category or a single product or products can be added to be verified manually. You can ignore the products that are out of stock as per the theoretical balance, by unchecking the field **Include Exhausted Products**.

Let's create an inventory adjustment, and name it `Inventory Verification - July 2017`. Select the **All products** for the field **Inventory of**, click on the **START INVENTORY** button to start the verification:

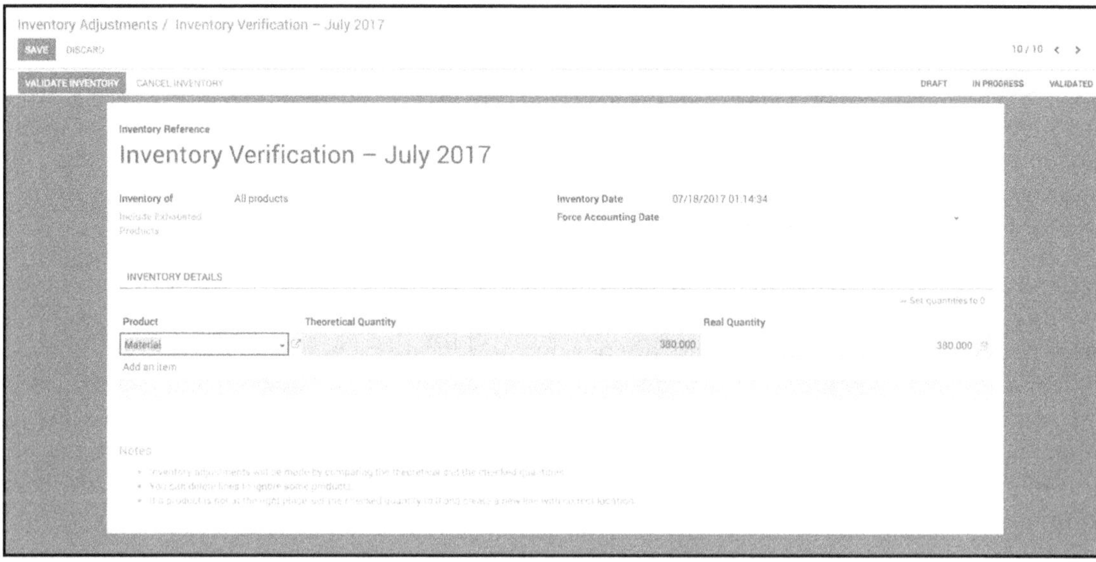

All the products having non-zero stock will be selected in the inventory. Verify the physical inventory and enter the quantity in the **Real Quantity** field. Odoo will create an adjustment entry only in case there is a difference between **Theoretical Quantity** and **Real Quantity**.

The adjustment line will not be created if **Theoretical Quantity** and **Real Quantity** are the same. Or you can delete lines to ignore some products.

The adjustment entry will be created based on which quantity is higher, please go through the *How it works...* section of this recipe to understand how the adjustment entry will be created.

Setting up the warehouse and locations

The warehouse refers to the physical buildings where the stock is stored. You can locate rooms within a building with the logical space called locations. The requirement for a small shop is to have a stock location which is a single location called stock while a big warehouse is required to identify multiple locations such as cold storage and dry locations. A big warehouse wants to drill down the identification of a location by the rooms, cupboards, or racks organized in rows and columns.

Imagine you have a million products stored in a warehouse at thousands of locations. How difficult it would be to organize the warehouse, when you have thousands of locations and each location has to be identified uniquely in the system. It is not about locating the products in the warehouse but assume that you have a variety of products coming in every day and you have to find the correct location to store them, so that they can be retrieved easily when they are needed for delivery. A simple example is when you receive ice-cream or fruit or vegetables; they should go to the cold storage.

In Odoo, the inventory is managed using locations and the warehouse. Some locations point to a physical space like Stock Location while some locations do not exist, but we can still place products in that location. These are not physical locations but virtual locations or logical locations. Inventory Adjustment is an example of a virtual location. Some locations are pointing to the Partner Locations; these are Customer Locations or Supplier Locations which help us to track the incoming and outgoing products. Odoo also supports having multiple warehouses in business, they can be connected to each other to have automatic re-supply between them.

Let's see how we can manage the warehouse, locations and internal transfer between locations or the warehouse, based on such business rules.

Getting ready

I am sure that after looking at the features of the Odoo warehouse application, you would like to scale your warehouse to have multiple locations. It can be identified easily with a unique identification. Logically divide your warehouse into locations and prepare the list of those locations you would like to have in your warehouse.

How to do it...

1. The default warehouse configuration in Odoo is to have a single warehouse with a stock location. This is a perfect fit for a small shop. There are three different options under which a warehouse can be configured.
2. Go to **Configuration** | **Setting** in the Warehouse application. The default option **Manage only 1 Warehouse with only 1 stock location** was selected please select to **Manage several Warehouses, each one composed by several stock locations**:

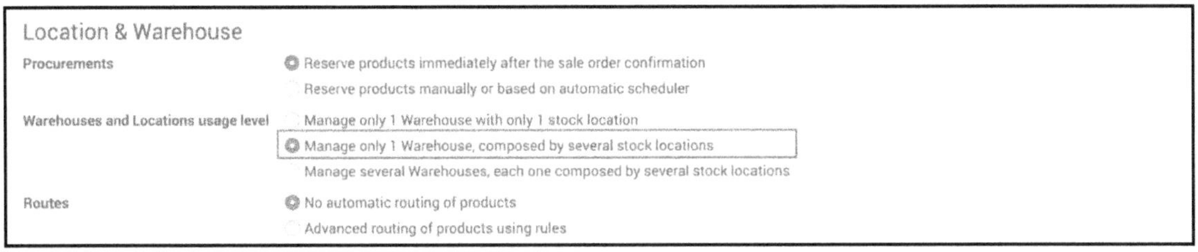

Let's activate multiple locations within a single warehouse so that we can configure either physical or logical location to create the virtual locations in Warehouse to map the physical locations available in the warehouse, that is, bins, shelves, or rooms. Click on **APPLY** to save the configuration:

1. The **Locations** menu will be activated as soon as you enable the option **Manage only 1 Warehouse, composed by several stock locations**. The menu can be accessed from **Configuration** | **Warehouse Management** | **Locations**.

   By default, you can see locations which are Internal, as soon as you remove the **Internal** filter you can see all the locations. Look at the following screen of locations:

2. Let's create a new location which is in the stock but it will be a logical location that represents a physically small part of the **Stock** location within the warehouse. Click on the **CREATE** button to create a new location:

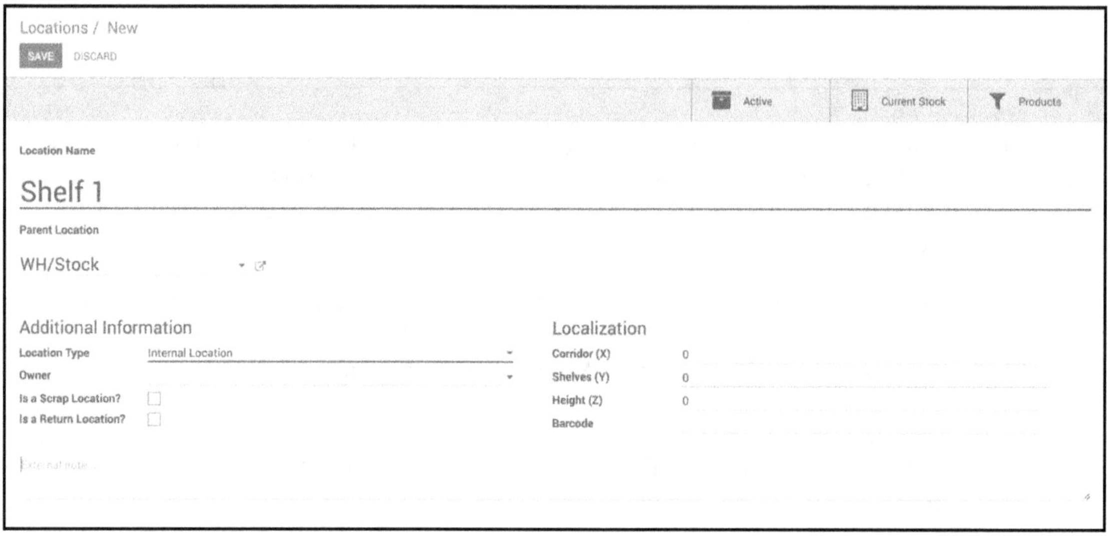

3. Enter the **Name**. As this location will be the stock, select **Stock as a Parent location**. Select the type **Internal Location** as this location's physical location is inside the warehouse.

The locations in Odoo are organized in a hierarchical structure in Warehouse. There are three top-level locations, **Partner Locations**, **Physical Locations**, and **Virtual Locations** in Warehouse. Look at the following screen:

The hierarchical structure of locations is used to compute the stock and inventory valuations.

4. On the **Inventory** dashboard, you will get the new operation type **Internal Transfers**. It will appear as we have activated the multiple locations in Warehouse, and now we can transfer the inventory between different locations within Warehouse:

5. Click on the **TRANSFERS** button in the **Internal Transfer** operation available on the **Inventory** dashboard to see all the internal transfers available within Warehouse. Click on the **CREATE** button to create a new internal transfer. Select the **Source Location Zone** from where the inventory is going to be transferred.

The **Destination Location Zone** is the location where the inventory will be shifted. Enter the **Scheduled Date** on which the internal transfer has to take place:

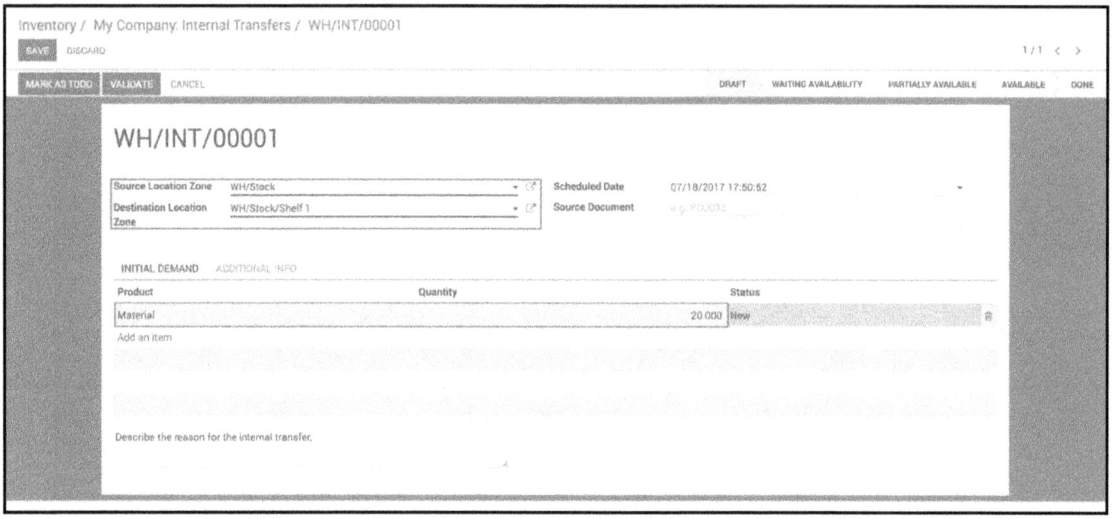

6. Select the product and enter the quantity that you would like to transfer from **Stock** to **Shelf 1**.
7. Click on the **MARK AS TO DO** button, if you would like to process it later. Or you can click on the **VALIDATE** button to process the internal transfer now. As soon as you choose to process the internal transfer later, it will go to the stage **WAITING AVAILABILITY**:

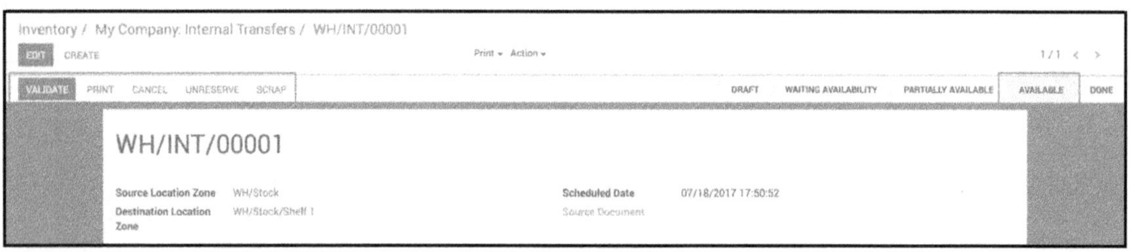

8. The internal transfer will be available, either you check for the stock manually by clicking on the **RESERVE** button or the scheduler assigns the quantity automatically.

9. The rest of the process is the same as the delivery or reception, enter the quantity to be processed in the **Done** field on the operations line and click on the **VALIDATE** button. The transfer will be processed and the internal transfer will be marked as **DONE**.

The inventory can be tracked from the **Inventory Valuation** report available under the **Inventory | Reports** menu. Look at the following screen, Shelf 1 contains 20 units of material available while the Stock location has decreased by 20.

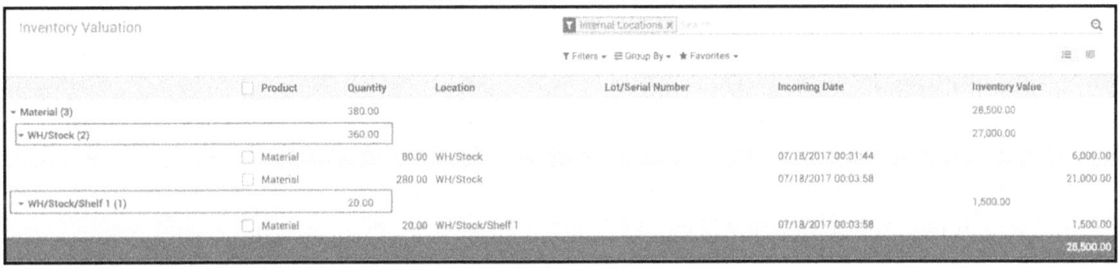

The overall quantity of material is the same as before, what we have changed is just a few units that we have moved to Shelf 1 from the Stock location.

There's more...

You can create unlimited locations within the warehouse or outside the warehouse, by default there are three main types of locations available in Warehouse: *Partner*, *Physical* and *Virtual* locations. There are other types of locations which can be created according to the need, for example, when we set up the manufacturing plant, there could be a **Production** type of location created in Warehouse.

Let's see the different types of location that can be created in Warehouse and how we can configure the minimum stock rules at the location level. We will go through the different strategies at the location level, such as put away and removal strategies.

Types of location

There are eight different types of location that can be created, each having a specific function. The configuration of the location is a critical part of the warehouse configuration.

- **Vendor Location:** Virtual location representing the source location for products coming from your vendors

- **View:** Virtual location used to create a hierarchical structure for your warehouse, aggregating its child locations; can't directly contain products
- **Internal Location:** Physical locations inside your own warehouses
- **Customer Location:** Virtual location representing the destination location for products sent to your customers
- **Inventory Loss:** Virtual location serving as a counterpart for inventory operations used to correct stock levels (physical inventories)
- **Procurement:** Virtual location serving as a temporary counterpart for procurement operations when the source (vendor or production) is not known yet. This location should be empty when the procurement scheduler has finished running
- **Production:** Virtual counterpart location for production operations: this location consumes the raw material and produces finished products
- **Transit Location:** Counterpart location that should be used in inter-companies or inter-warehouse operations

The differences between location types are clear enough, choose the correct location type when you create a new location in Warehouse.

Reorder rules at location level

The reorder rules have to be defined to maintain the minimum stock of the product in the warehouse. We have enabled multiple locations in Warehouse, now it is possible to maintain the minimum stock at the location level.

You can define the location at the time of creating a reorder rule so that you can maintain product stock at different locations:

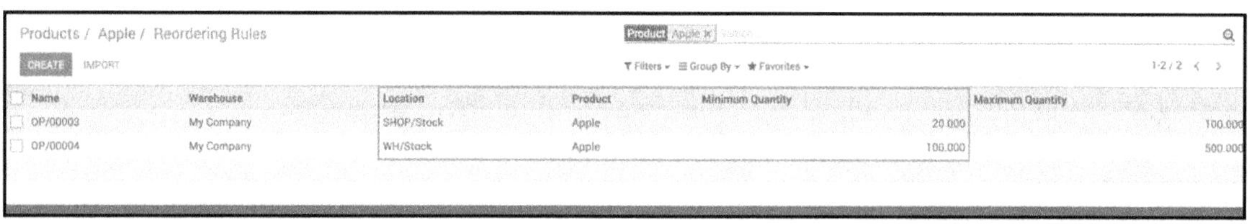

Look at the preceding reorder level rules for Apple configured at two different locations. When the level goes below **20** at **SHOP/Stock** location or **100** at **WH/Stock** location, it will procure and make it available to the maximum limit by creating a procurement. Please go through `Chapter 9`, *Purchase Management* in recipe *Complete purchase cycle.*

Put away strategy

The put away strategy is an advance automation of the internal transfer based on business rules. Let's take an example; you would like to transfer the fruit and vegetables items to the cold storage as soon as they are received in the warehouse.

For all the shipment coming to the stock location, you have to manually transfer the fruit and vegetables to the cold storage. You can automate this based on the put away strategy, so that an automatic transfer is created and it can be transferred to the cold storage:

1. To activate the put away strategy on a location, the advance routes have to be activated for the inventory. The advance routes can be activated from **Configuration** | **Settings** in the **Inventory** application. Choose **Advanced routing of products using rules** instead of **No automatic routing of products,** which is the default option selected on the Routes configuration:

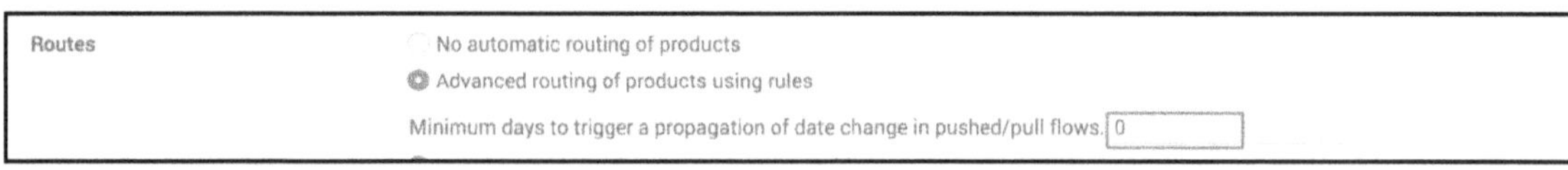

2. Enter the number of days after which the internal transfer should be created, this will be applied to all the product categories defined in the put away strategy.
3. The removal and put away strategy will be created on the location. Please follow the following rules to create a rule on Stock location to transfer the fruits and vegetables items to the cold storage, when received in stock.
4. Go to the locations and search for the **WH/Stock** location. You will be able to see the **Logistics** section on form view in the following screenshot:

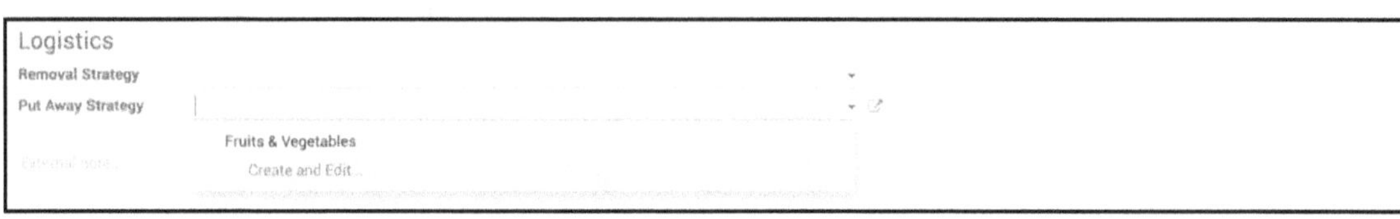

5. Click on the **Create and Edit** link to create a new strategy on the stock location. This will be triggered as soon as stock gets updated with any incoming shipments:

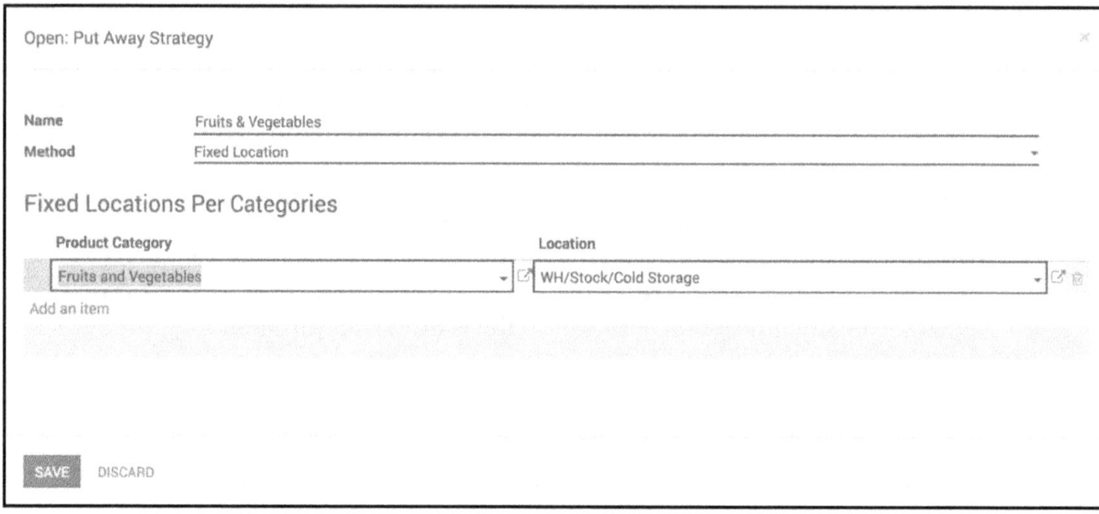

6. Enter the appropriate name, select **Fixed Location** as the method; this is the only method available for the moment. As soon as the method is selected, the category and location mapping list will appear. Enter the product category and select the location to transfer.
7. Organize products category in a better way to have an automatic trigger for a selected group of products when any of them arrive in stock.

To test the strategy, create and process an incoming shipment in Warehouse with a product belonging to the **Fruits and vegetables** category. Look at the following screen where I have created an incoming shipment of `500` quantity of apples:

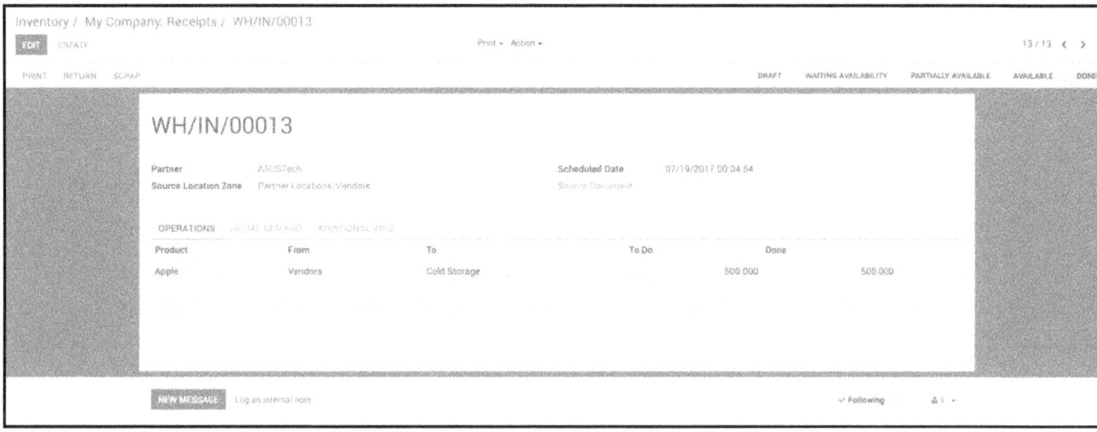

As soon as the incoming shipment is validated, the destination location will be changed to **Cold Storage instead of Stock**.

All the apples are transferred to the Cold Storage automatically, the same can be tracked from the inventory valuation. Look at the following screenshot:

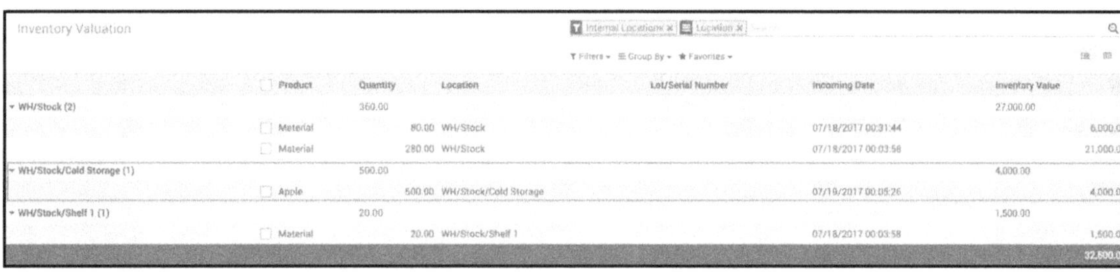

Multiple warehouses and resupply warehouse

Odoo is able to manage multiple warehouses for an organization. It is a standard business case to have more than one warehouse at different locations. The shop gets refilled from the warehouse, where the shop is a small warehouse which asks for re-supply from the big warehouse.

Multiple warehouses can be enabled from the **Settings** page of the **Inventory** application. Activate the third option, *Manage several Warehouses, each one composed by several stock locations* in the **Warehouses and Locations usage level** field:

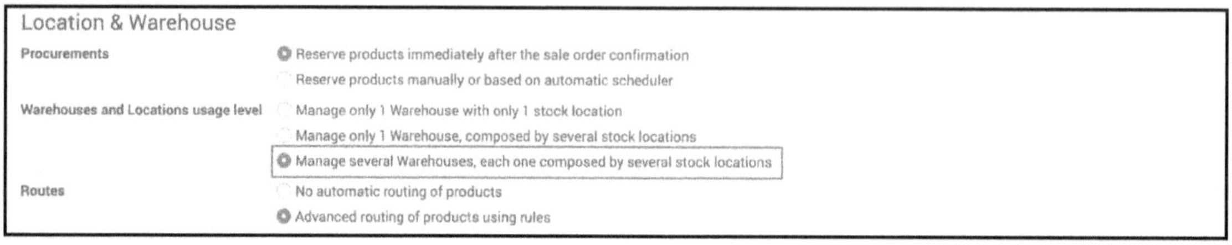

Click on the **APPLY** button and save the settings, the **Warehouse** menu is available under **Inventory | Configuration**.

A new warehouse can be created for the same company. Enter the **Name**, **Short Name**, **Address** and select the resupply method, it can be a purchase or resupply from another warehouse. In case you have a multiple resupply warehouse, the default resupply can be selected. Look at the following screen of the warehouse at the shop, if the stock is needed, it will ask **My Company** warehouse to resupply the required products:

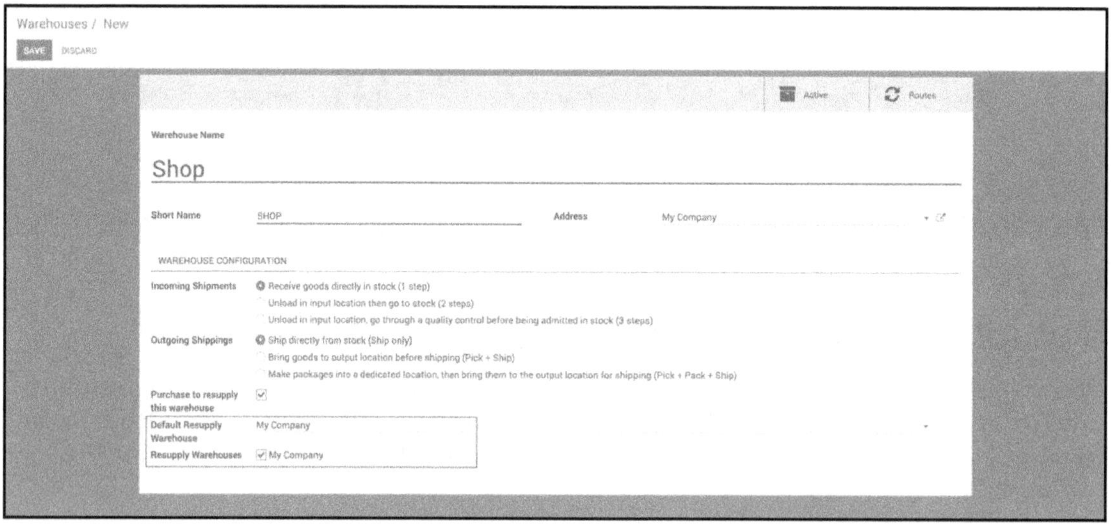

The **Inventory** dashboard gets a new operation as the warehouse is created. Now you have **Receipts, Delivery Orders** and an **Internal Transfer** for the newly created SHOP warehouse:

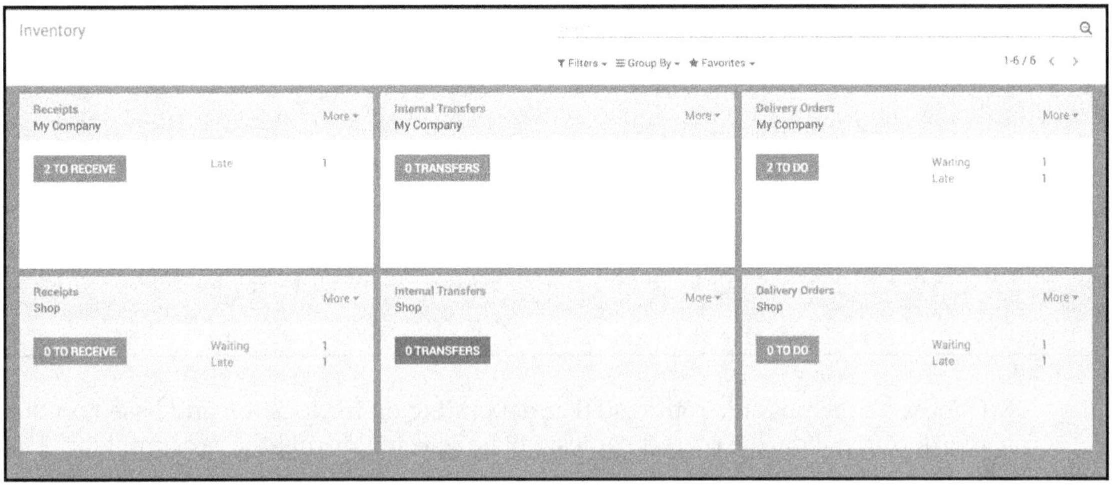

Let's perform the following steps to test the resupply warehouse feature:

1. Create a reorder level for the specific location, in our case SHOP/Stock location. Go to product **Apple** and create a rule as follows:

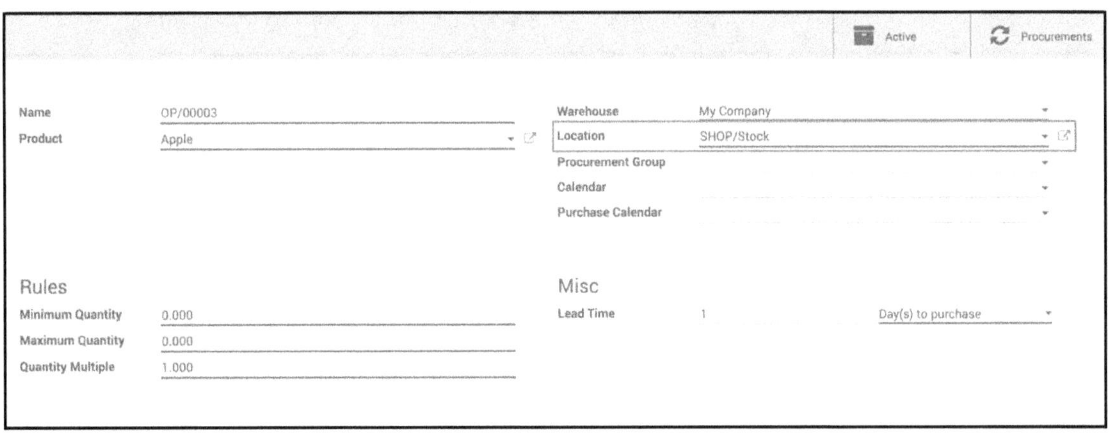

2. Select the routes for the product so that procurement can choose the available and possible routes to procure the stock:

3. Choose all the possible routes so that depending on the location and based on the reordering policy, the correct routes will be selected during the procurement.

In this case, when the stock of **Apple** goes down at the SHOP it will be procured from the **My Company** warehouse and if the stock of **Apple** goes down at **My Company** warehouse it will be procured through the standard purchase process, the Purchase Order will be created for the units defined on the reorder level:

1. Let's create the Delivery Order from the SHOP warehouse:

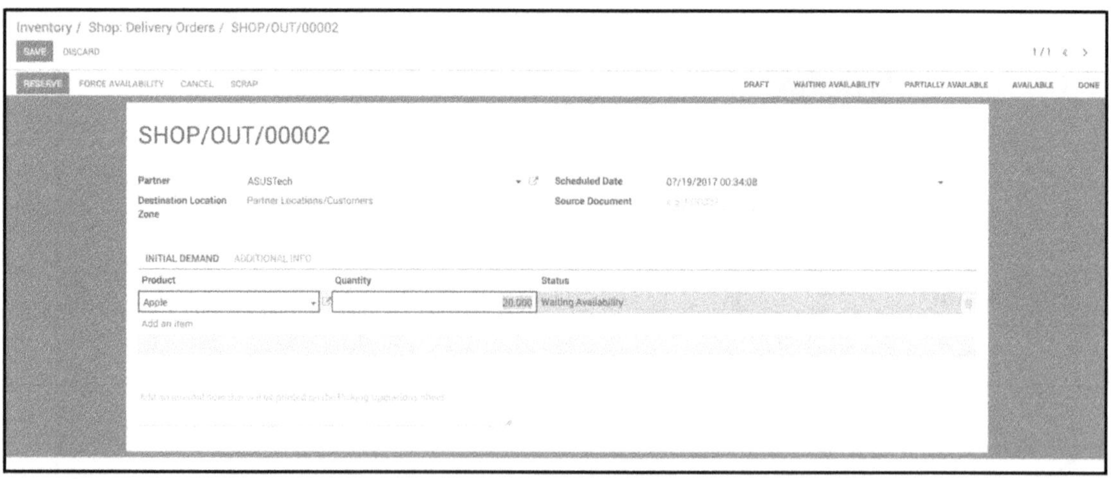

2. The procurement is triggered and the following documents will be created as a result:
    - The Delivery Order in the **My Company** warehouse, the destination location is **My Company: Transit Location**
    - Incoming Shipment in the **SHOP** warehouse, where source location is **My Company: Transit Location**

My Company: Transit Location is a virtual location that work as an intermediate location to transfer products between two different warehouses:

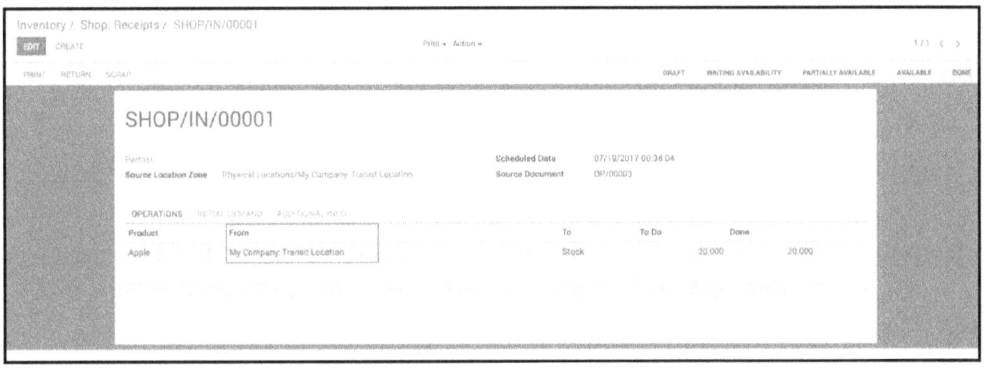

3. Look at the Delivery Order in **My Company** warehouse and assign an **Apple** from Cold Storage. As soon as the Delivery Order is validated in the **My Company** warehouse, the incoming shipment in SHOP warehouse will be marked as available. Look at the following screen for incoming shipment in the SHOP warehouse:

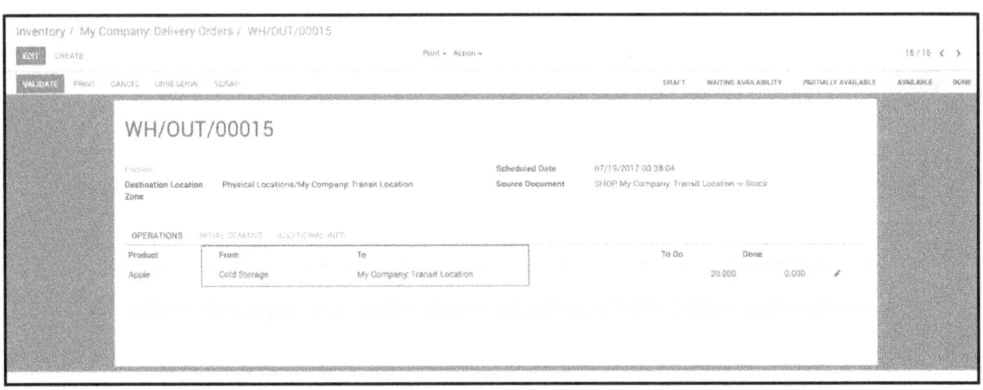

4. Now the Delivery Order in SHOP will be marked available as the stock is available in the SHOP warehouse. Validate the Delivery Order to deliver from the SHOP warehouse.
5. It simulates the real-time business case; the flow is as follows:
    - Sales Order created at the SHOP location
    - Delivery Order created at the SHOP location based on the Sale Order
    - Procurement Order generates the incoming shipment in the SHOP from My Company *(My Company: Transit Location)*
    - Procurement generates the Delivery Order in My Company warehouse. *(Deliver to My Company: Transit Location)*
    - Process delivery from My Company warehouse
    - Incoming shipment ready to process at SHOP warehouse, process the incoming shipment in SHOP
    - Process the Delivery Order in SHOP, as the stock of **Apple** is available at SHOP.

At SHOP, it procures the apples according to the demand, if you would like to maintain the minimum stock at SHOP, make sure that you change the reorder rule at the **Stock location** of SHOP warehouse as follows:

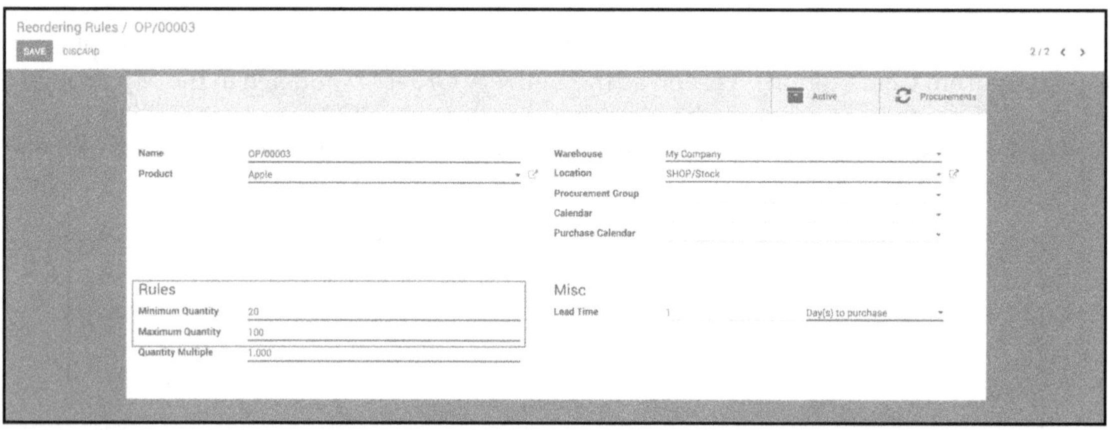

When the stock of **Apple** goes to **20** or below, make it **100** at SHOP warehouse.

Three-step delivery

A small shop processes deliveries order by order. Take the order, prepare the products to be delivered from the warehouse, pack them and deliver them. Odoo calls this operation a Ship only or Ship directly from stock, or sometimes this is called one-step delivery. Assume that you have a big warehouse and you have a team to perform an internal operation such as picking, packing, and delivery of an order.

Picking is an operation that refers to the collecting of products from their location to the packing zone. Packing refers to the packing of the products and at the end, delivery refers to sending the order for delivery. This is usually called three-steps delivery or pick-pack-ship.

Odoo supports the three-step delivery, it can be activated on the warehouse. Before we activate the three-step delivery make sure that advance routes are activated in the Inventory settings page:

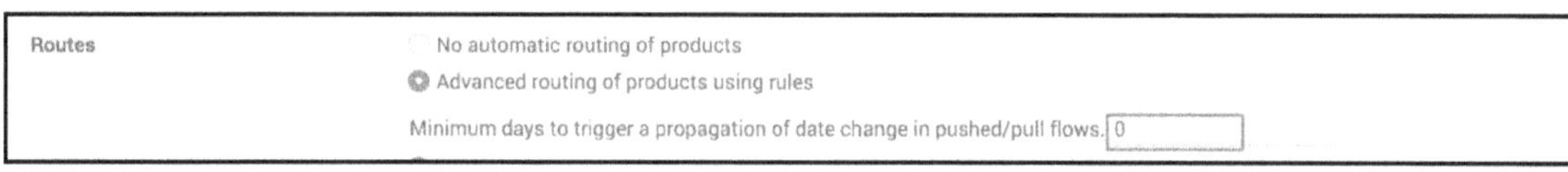

Go to the list of warehouses in **Configuration** | **Warehouses** in the **Inventory** application. Open the warehouse on which you would like to activate the three-step delivery and select the option **Make packages into a dedicated location, then bring them to the output location for shipping (Pick + Pack + Ship)** in the **Outgoing Shippings** field and click on the **SAVE** button to activate it. Look at the following screen for the other options available for the delivery and incoming shipments:

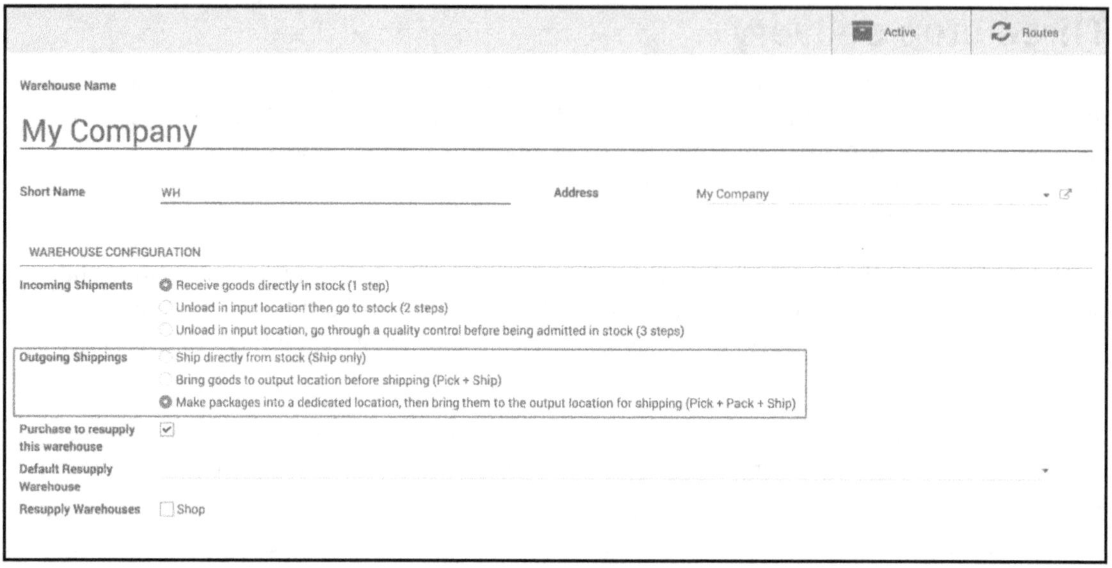

As soon as the **Pick** + **Pack** + **Ship** option is activated for the warehouse, you will find two new Internal Locations. **Packing Zone** and **Output** added to the list of locations. Also, two new picking operations are available on the **Inventory** dashboard for the **My Company** warehouse:

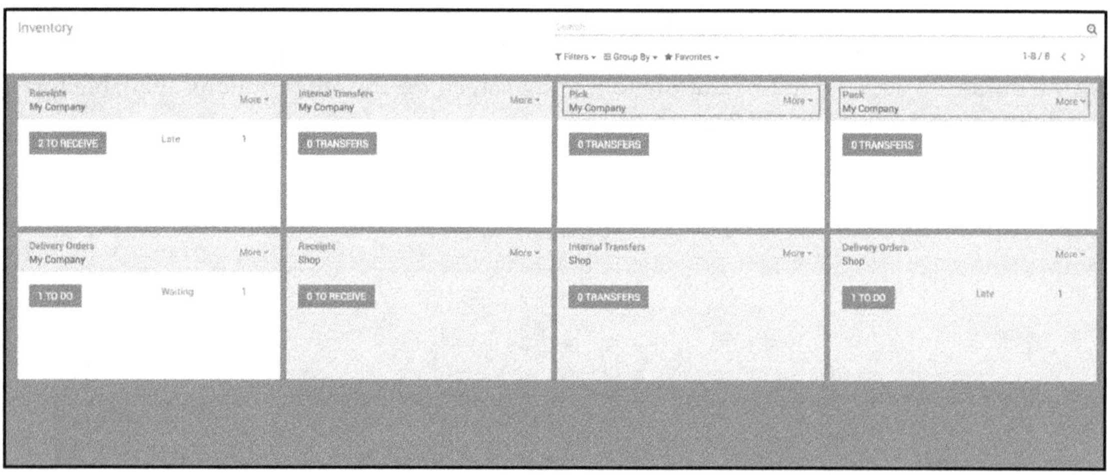

Let's see, with an example how the **Pick** + **Pack** + **Ship** operation works. To test the flow, create a sales order of five units of material and confirm the Sales Order. Look at the following screenshot of the confirmed Sales Order:

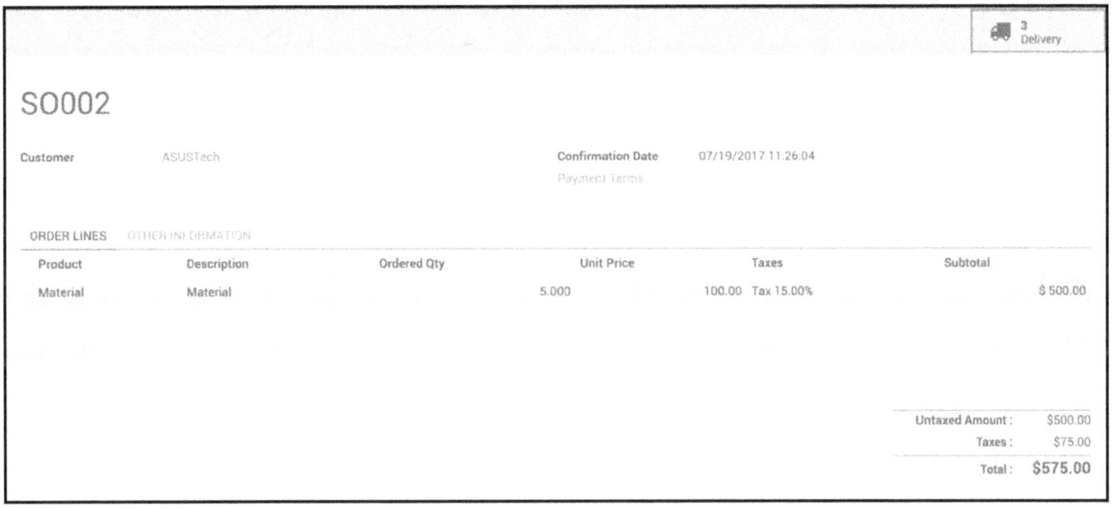

Look at the action button **3 Delivery** closely, it shows 3 instead of 1 Delivery Order. Out of 3 transfers, two are internal transfers which transferred from Picking Order (Stock | Packing) and Packing Order (Picking Zone | Output). The **Picking Order** is marked as **Available** as the material was assigned from the stock:

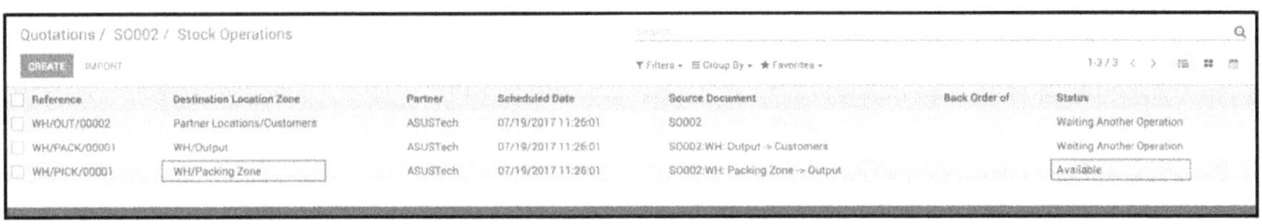

The **Packing Order** will be marked as available as soon as you process the **Picking order**. It means that someone has transferred the material from stock to the packing zone:

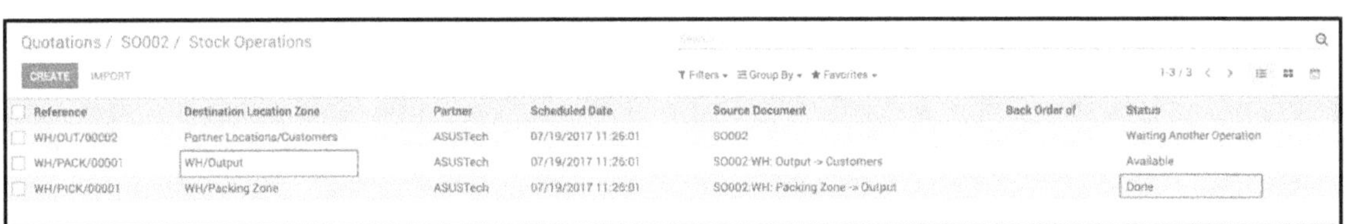

Process the **Packing** Order, it will trigger the Delivery Order and the Delivery Order will be marked as available and ready to process which actually transfers the material from **Output** location to **Customer** location:

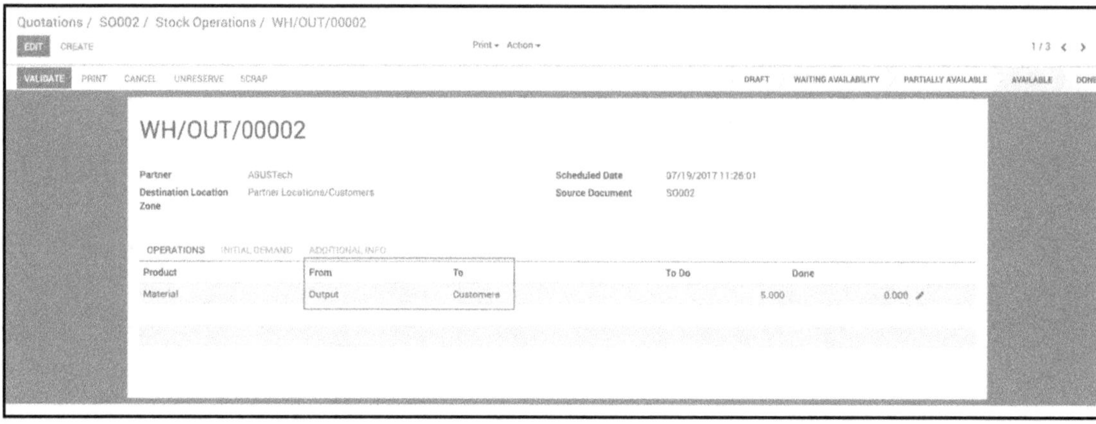

So, the delivery will be completed as soon as you process the Delivery Order. This is called three-step delivery or **Pick + Pack + Ship** delivery. Look at the following table to see how **Pick + Pack + Ship** options executes in Warehouse:

Seq	Operation	Source Location	Destination Location
1	Picking	Stock	Packing Zone
2	Packing	Packing Zone	Output
3	Shipping	Output	Customers

Three-step reception

Unlike the three-step delivery, it is possible to have a three-step reception where all incoming products are first unloaded to the input location, transferred to quality check and finally, transferred to the stock.

Activate the option **Unload in input location, go through a quality control before being admitted in stock (3 steps)** on the warehouse **Incoming Shipments** field.

To test the flow, let's create a Purchase Order for the **Material** product. Look at the following screenshot of the order:

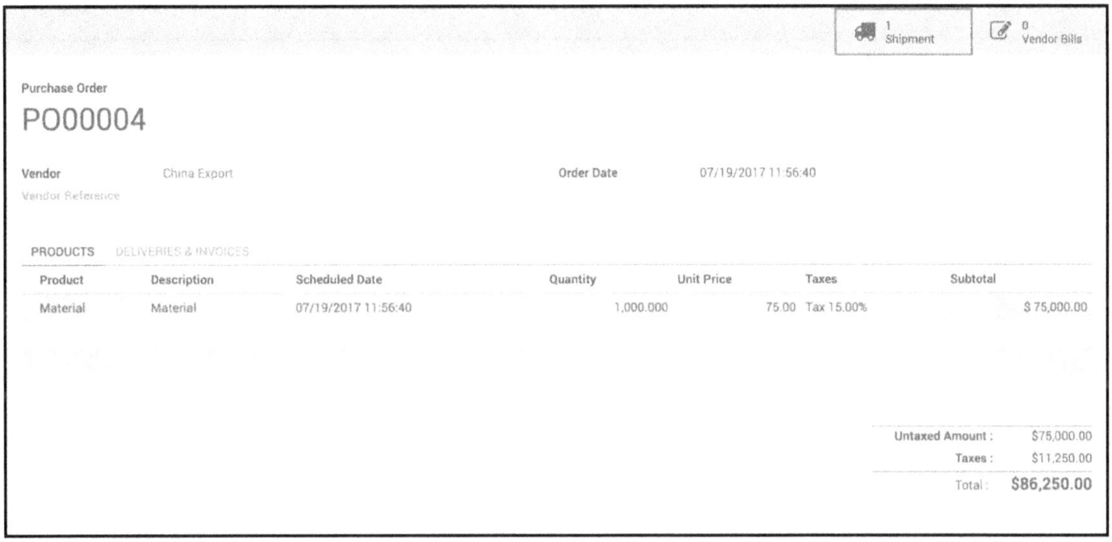

You will be able to see the incoming shipment ready for processing which receives the material from the vendor and unloads the **Material** from **Vendor Location** to **Input Location**. There will be two internal moves created as soon as the Reception Order is validated:

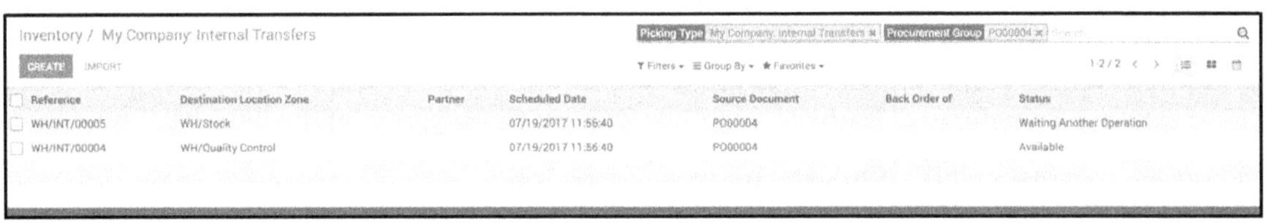

The incoming shipment has to be processed when the material is received from the vendor, after the processing of the incoming shipment, the material will be available at the **Input** Location.

Process the second internal transfer **WH/INT/00004** which will transfer the **Material** from **Input** Location to the **Quality Control** Location. Assume that all the material has passed through the quality check process and is ready to move to the Stock Location:

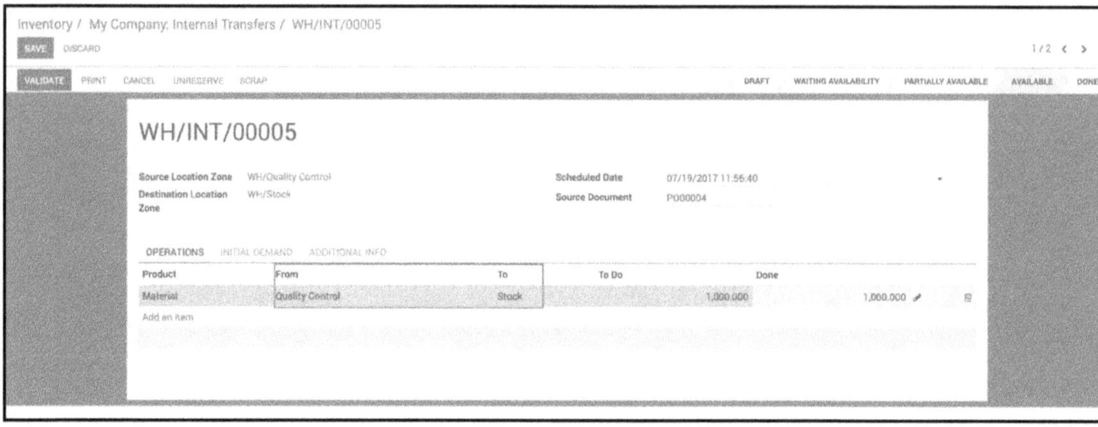

The last internal transfer **WH/INT/00005** will be ready to process and finally, it will transfer all 1,000 units to the Stock Location, see the preceding image of the internal transfer.

So, the incoming shipment will be completed as soon as you process the last internal transfer which actually transfers material to the Stock Location. This is called three-step reception. Look at the following operation to see how it works internally in Warehouse:

Seq	Operation	Source Location	Destination Location
1	Reception	Vendor	Input
2	Internal Transfer	Input	Quality Control
3	Quality Check (INT)	Quality Control	Stock

Traceability, tracking serials, lots, and packs

A warehouse cannot be managed efficiently without having traceability in place. Assume that you buy laptops of the same brand in bulk from different dealers and you're selling them to your customer in a retail business. A customer comes with a complaint about the laptop and asks for a replacement. How can you verify that the laptop is still under warranty or not? Which supplier should you contact and ask for a replacement? If you have not maintained the tracking with a laptop serial number, you will not get the correct supplier from where this defective laptop comes from.

For the manufacturer, it is compulsory to manage the serial numbers or lots of the consumed items and assign a new serial or lot number for the manufactured items so that both way tracing is possible. For example, what is the raw material used in the manufacturing item and where does it come from? For the trading or retail business to keep the tracing based on the serial or lot number, it is as important as the manufacturing business.

Odoo has powerful features for managing and tracing, based on the serial or lot number. It is fully integrated with the barcode scanner; many processes can be automated with the barcode scanner. It will not only speed up the process but it will make sure that the right product is assigned to the right order with 100% accuracy. Like the serials and lots, Odoo also allows you to manage the tracing based on the expiry date for the food, beverages, fruit, and vegetables.

Let's see how we can activate the serial and lot number features and get upstream and downstream tracing.

Getting ready

We assume that you have the barcode scanner available.

How to do it...

1. The **Traceability** feature can be activated from the **Inventory** | **Configuration** | **Settings** page. Choose the **Track lots or serial numbers** option for the first field **Lots and Serial Numbers** under the **Traceability**:

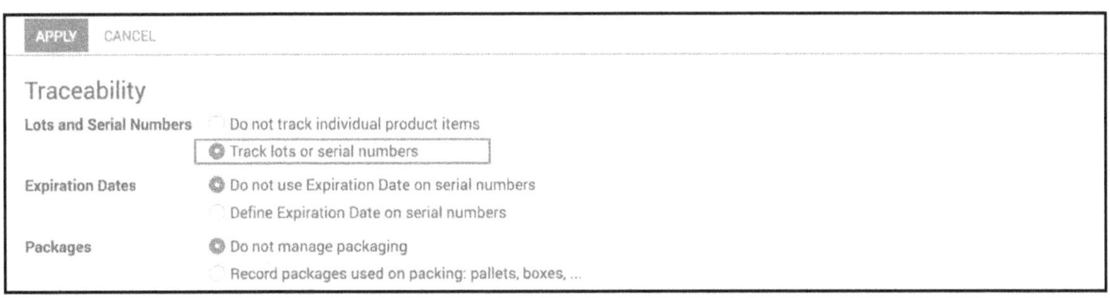

2. You are ready to track the product movement either, with serial or using lots numbers. The product has to be configured once to see how it will be traced:

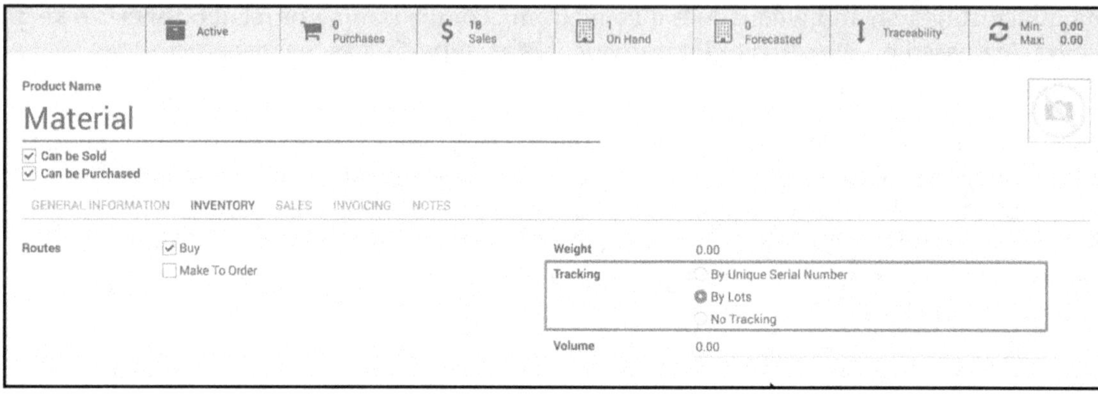

The **Tracking** field is available on the **INVENTORY** tab, where you can choose to track by serial or by lots or no tracking. I choose to have **By Lots.**

3. Let's assume that you have an incoming shipment, and each time you have a new shipment, the lot has to be created in Odoo. Enter your own number or just enter the same lot number supplied by the vendor:

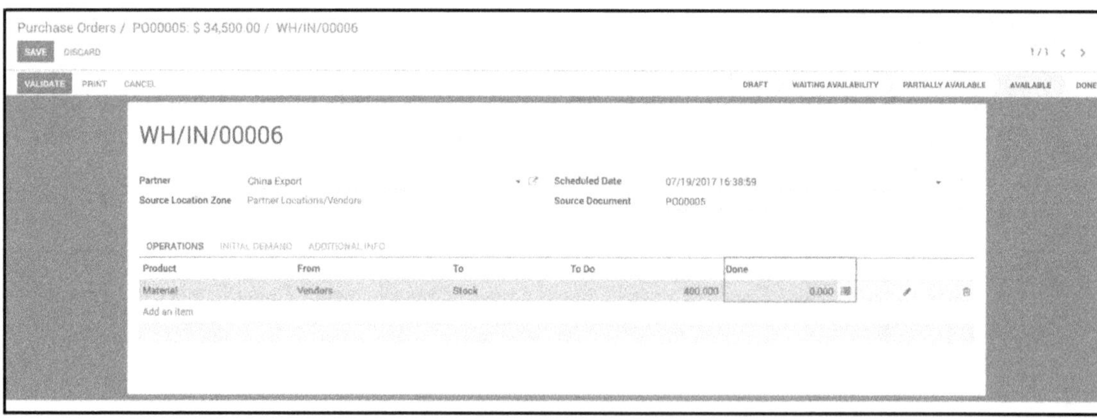

4. The **Done** quantity field has been changed to have details of the quantity instead of just a number field. Click on the Split Lot icon, you will be asked to enter the lot number and quantity per lot in case you're mapping the same lot number supplied by the vendor and you receive different lots. Look at the following image of entering the lot numbers:

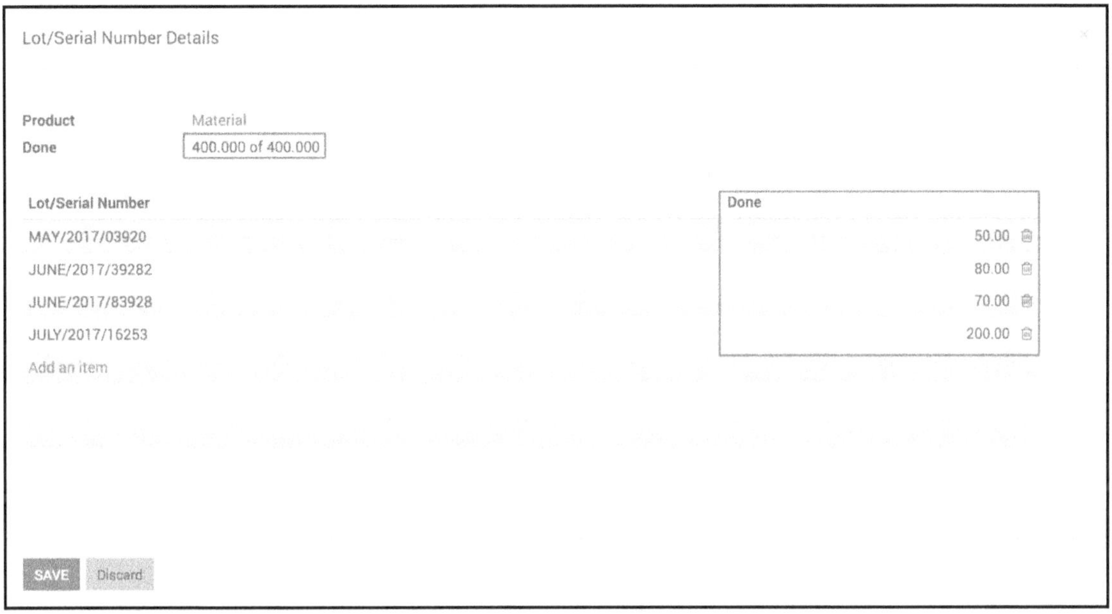

To enter the lot numbers, you can use the barcode scanner. Assume that we have four different lots coming from the vendor and we enter the same.

5. Click on the **SAVE** button, and click on the **VALIDATE** button to process the incoming shipment.
6. The lot detail is already printed on the product. If not, you can go to **Inventory** | **Inventory Control Lots /Serial Numbers** to get the print of the lot numbers. Select the lot and from the Print menu, select the report **Lot Bar Code**:

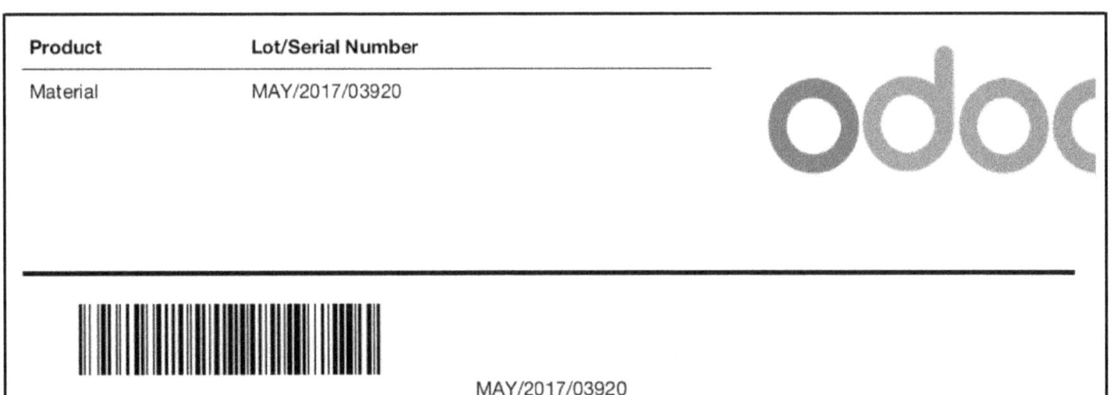

Print the label and it can be fixed on the product, so it can be easily identified which lot this product belongs to in the warehouse.

7. Look at the warehouse; you have a clear indication that you have four different lots available of the same product. Look at the **Inventory Valuation** list in the following screenshot:

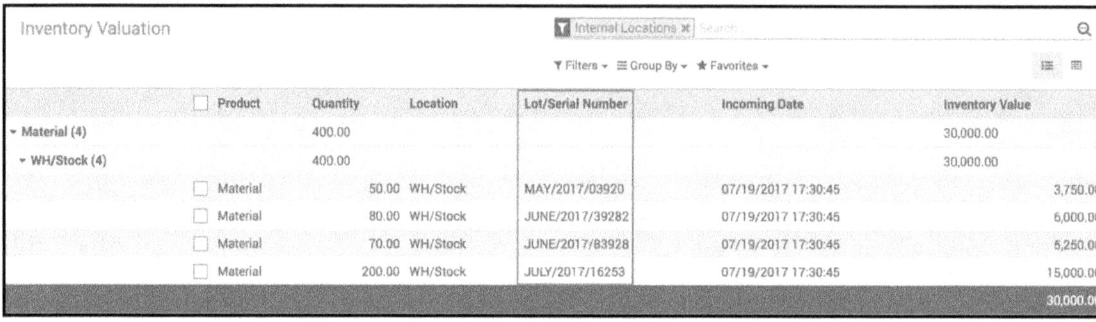

Let's assume that you have a Delivery Order that required 65 units of **Material.** We have 4 different lots available with a quantity on each of 50, 80, 70 and 200. Go to the warehouse and check the Delivery Order, it is marked as **AVAILABLE** as in a total of 65 units are available in stock:

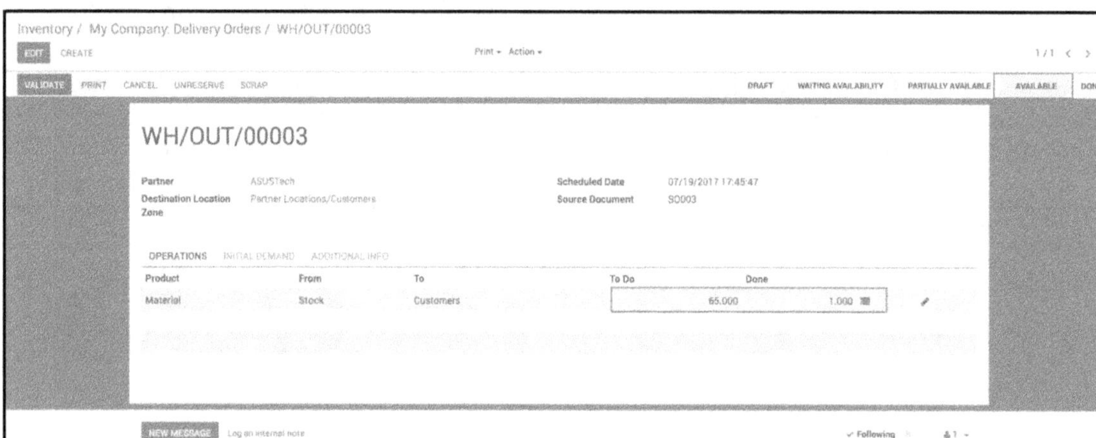

8. Click on the Split Lot icon, you will find that Odoo has proposed the lots with the right quantity of material that can be assigned to fulfill the order:

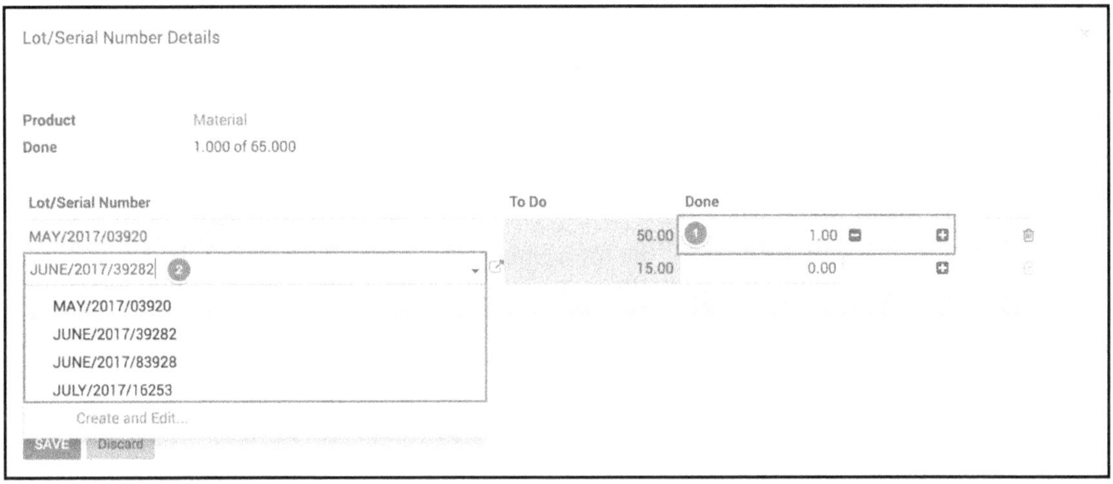

Odoo will propose the lots with a quantity based on the **FIFO** (**First In First Out**) method, you can assign the same by clicking on the plus icon or enter the quantity in the **Done** field. If you want to change the lot, you can select it from the drop-down list and change the **quantity** and then click on the plus icon to assign the quantities from the proposed lots.

When all the required quantity is assigned from the lots, both the lines will become **GREEN**, and you are ready to process the Delivery Order.

The tracing can be done from the **Lot/Serial Number**, open the lot you would like to see the tracing on:

Click on the **Traceability** action button available on the lot number **JUNE/2017/39282**, to see the tracking of the incoming to the outgoing operation that occurred for the lot number.

There's more...

We have gone through an example of the lot number, unlike the lot number the serial number works the same way, the only difference is that each serial number represents one quantity. Let's see in detail how serial numbers can be assigned at incoming shipment and assign the same serial numbers at the delivery.

Serial numbers

The **Track Lots or Serial numbers** feature is already activated on the Inventory application; choose the product you would like to track through the serial number:

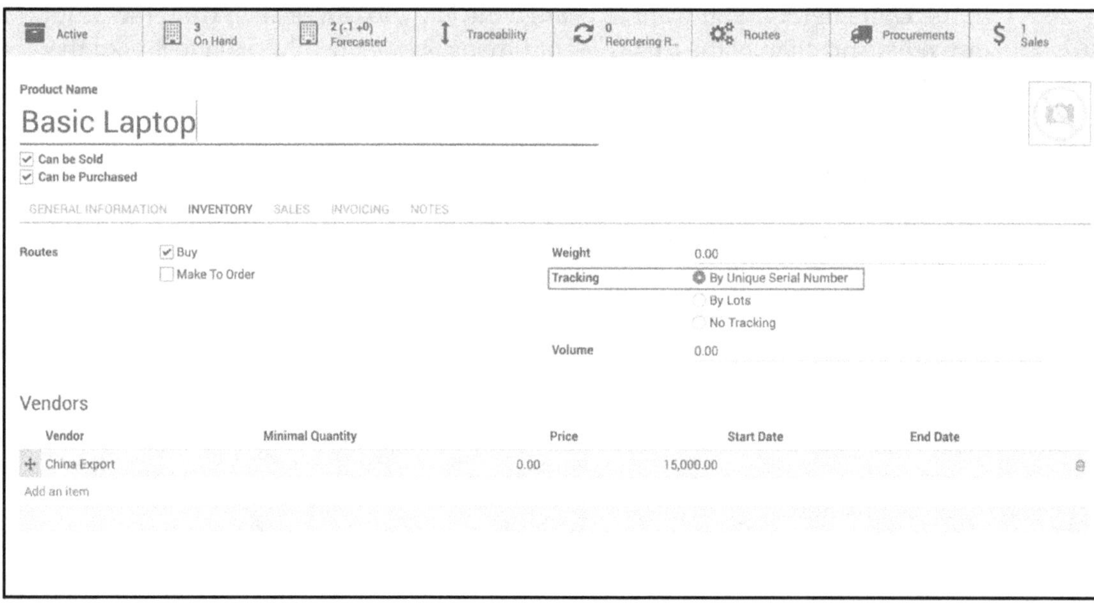

Assume that we have an incoming Reception Order for the **Basic Laptop**, having **3** units:

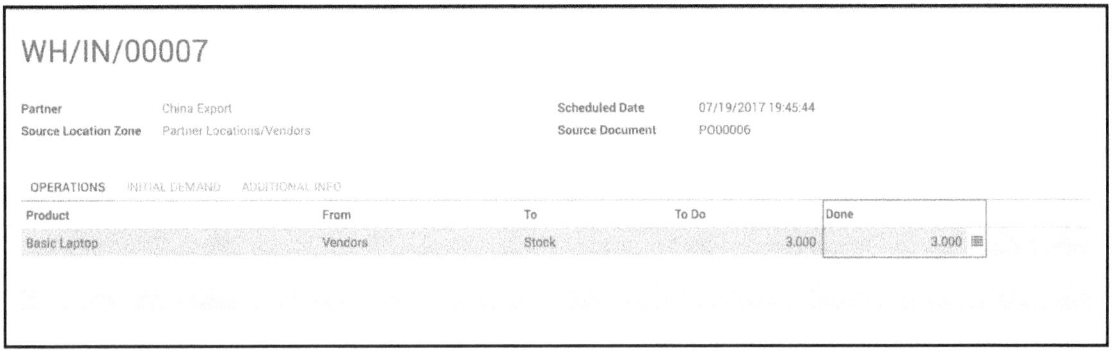

Either enter the product's serial number manually or scan the product serial number through the barcode scanner:

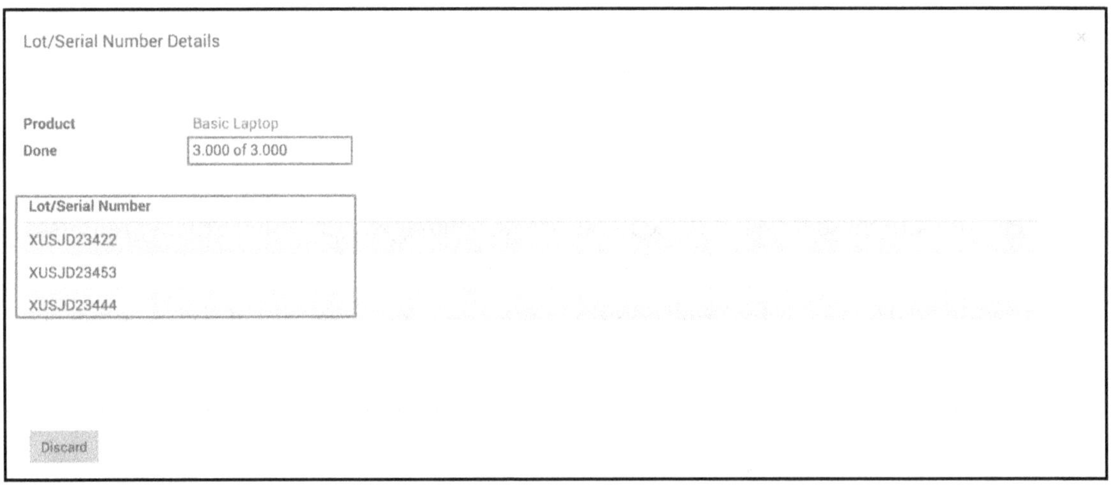

Process the incoming shipment by clicking on the **VALIDATE** button; all the serials are available under the **Lots/Serial Number**. Look at the following screen of serial and lots available in the Inventory:

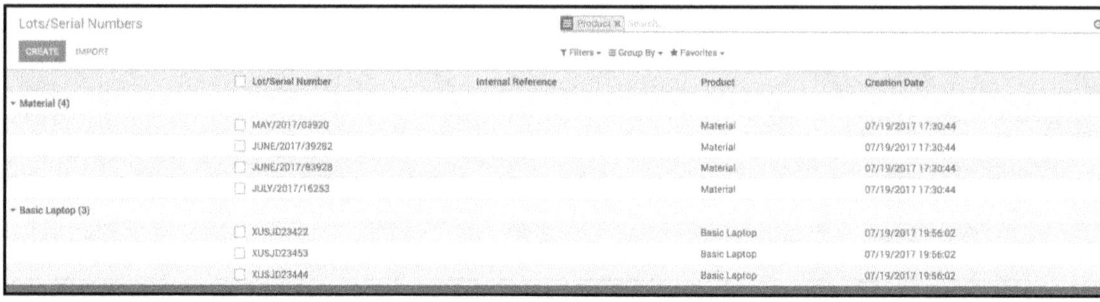

For the Delivery Order, the process is the same as the lot number. Odoo will propose the serial number based on the FIFO method, however, it can be changed at the time of delivery.

Track expired inventory

It is difficult to track the expiry date for milk, fruit, vegetables and other food items in the inventory. The life of such items is not so long, however, to meet the demand we have to keep some stock of these items. If these items are not managed correctly in the warehouse, we could incur a loss as we may get the information late about the expiry of such products.

Odoo Version 10.0 has a workaround solution to the manage inventory of fast-moving items. Few days have to be decided in advance as a part of the configuration of each product about their life. The feature can be activated from the **Inventory** | **Configuration** | **Setting** page:

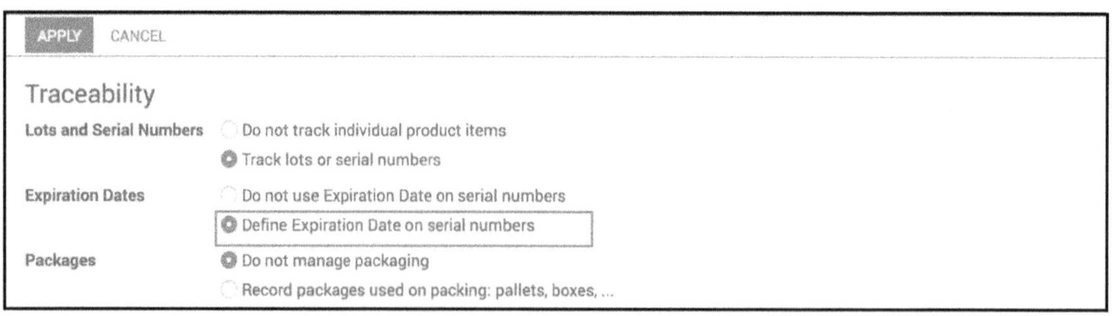

The expiry date feature works when you assign a serial or lot number to the incoming shipment. The **End of Life Date** will be computed based on the configuration done on the product form:

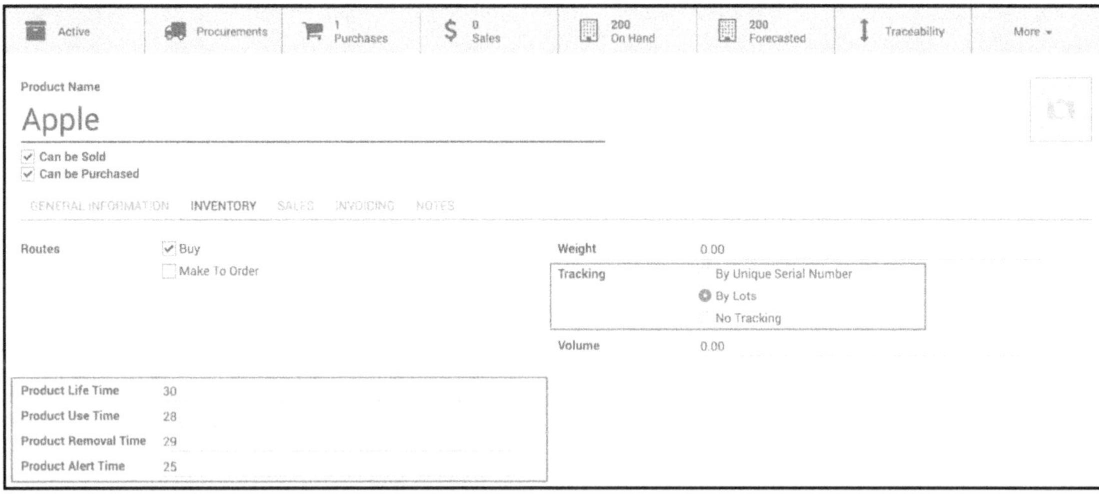

The time is set in number of days; before setting the number of days, please go through the usage of each time period fields:

- **Product Life Time:** this refers to the number of days before the goods become dangerous for consumption. It is estimated based on the period when the serial number was issued.
- **Product Use Time:** this is the number of days before the goods start deteriorating, without being dangerous yet. It is estimated based on the period when the serial number was issued.
- **Product Removal Time**: this is the number of days before the goods should be removed from the stock. It is estimated based on the period when the serial number was issued.
- **Product Alert Time:** this is the number of days before an alert should be raised. It is estimated based on the period when the serial number was issued.

Let's test the automatic assignment of **End of Life Date**, on lot number. We would like to verify that each lot has its own expiry date depending on the date of purchase.

We have an incoming shipment of 200 apples, at the time of reception, just assign the lot number so that the apples can be identified with a unique number in Warehouse. Process the incoming shipment by clicking on the **VALIDATE** button.

The lot will be created in Odoo, it can be accessed from the **Inventory Control | Lots/Serial Numbers** under the **Inventory** application:

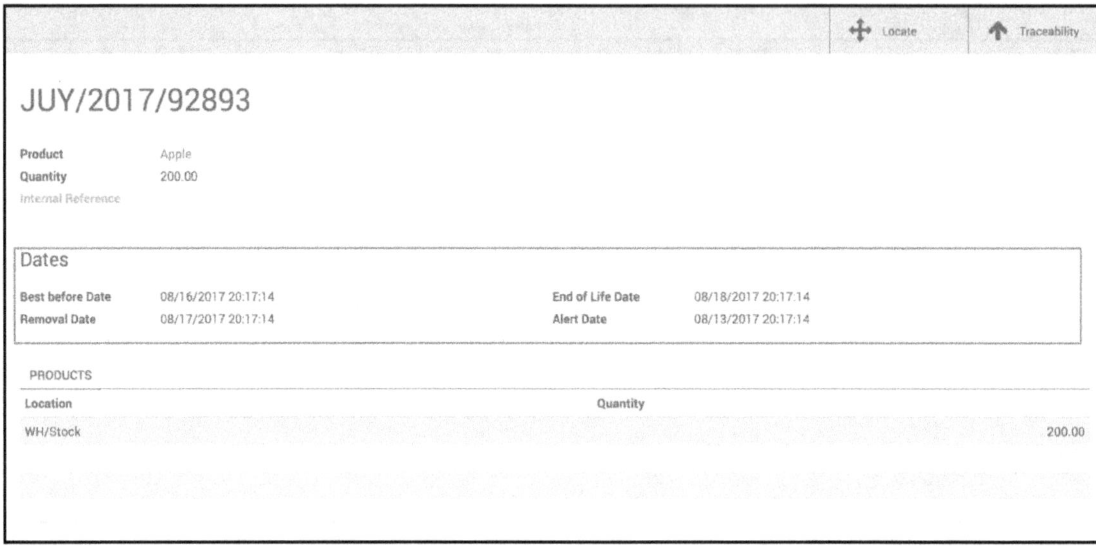

There are four dates computed on the serial or lot number based on the time defined on the product form, that is, the Product Life Time, Use Time field, Product Removal Time, Product Alert Time field on the product form. Here is an explanation as to how these dates are computed:

- **End of Life Date:** This is the date on which the goods with this Serial Number may become dangerous and must not be consumed. Computed based on the **Product Life Time** field on the product configuration.
- **Best before Date:** This is the date on which the goods with this Serial Number start deteriorating, without being dangerous yet. Computed based on the **Product Use Time field**, available on the product configuration.
- **Removal Date:** This is the date on which the goods with this Serial Number should be removed from the stock. The **Product Removal Time** field is used to compute this date. It is available in the product configuration.
- **Alert Date**: This is the date on which an alert should be notified about the goods with this Serial Number. The **Product Alert Time** field is used to compute this date. It is available in the product configuration.

> **TIP:** This feature is a workaround solution for the moment, as the **End of life** cannot be computed based on the fixed number of days. Most of the time we have an expiry date printed on the product label, which has to be entered in the inventory and other dates should be computed based on the expiry date. This feature is improved a lot in Odoo Version 11.

Setting up the removal strategy

Like the put away strategy, the removal strategy is an advanced algorithm used to select the lot/serial of the product on Delivery Order based on the business rules. The business rules are as follows:

- FIFI - (First In First Out)
- LIFO - (Last In First Out)
- FEFO - (First Expire First Out)

The removal strategy is already activated if you have configured the put away strategy, if not please go through the recipe *Multiple warehouse and resupply warehouses* in this chapter.

The removal strategy can be configured on location. On each location, you can configure the removal strategy as to where you store the products and the strategy you would like to use, other than the FIFO strategy which is the default:

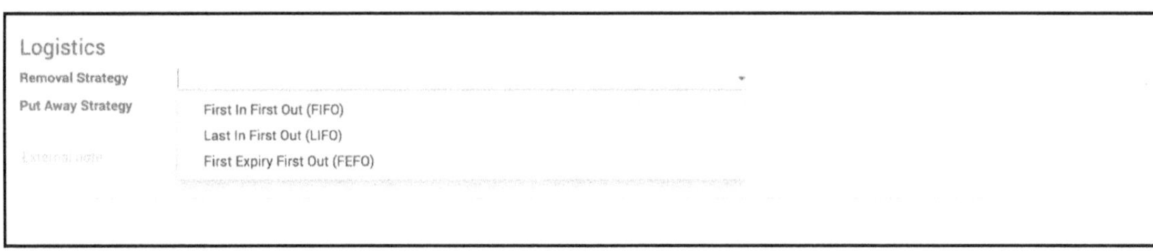

> **TIP:** If you would like to have a different removal strategy based on the product or product category, create separate locations to store those products, define the removal strategy on those locations, create a put away strategy on the stock to distribute specific products to their relevant location.

You can choose any one algorithm for a single location to apply the removal strategy. However, the default strategy is FIFO if no strategy is selected on the Removal Strategy field on the location.

You can test how the different strategy works, by performing the following steps:

- Create a few incoming shipments (create some Purchase orders)
- Receipt the incoming shipment, create a new lot each time
- Create a delivery order (create a sales order and confirm it)
- Check which lot is suggested by the warehouse, the suggestion is based on the removal strategy

You should see the different lot proposal on each removal strategy.

Tracking packages

The packaging itself is a huge topic to discuss, in Odoo packaging is used in many ways, but let's discuss the business need. A package can be created by putting many different products in the same pack, all those which are relevant to the same order. It is easy for the delivery service to transfer big packages instead of multiple small packages. Of course, the delivery price plays an important role in the packaging.

Let's see how a package can be created along with its label to fix on the package for the delivery service to track the package easily.

The packaging feature can be activated from the **Settings** page of the Inventory application. Look at the following screen:

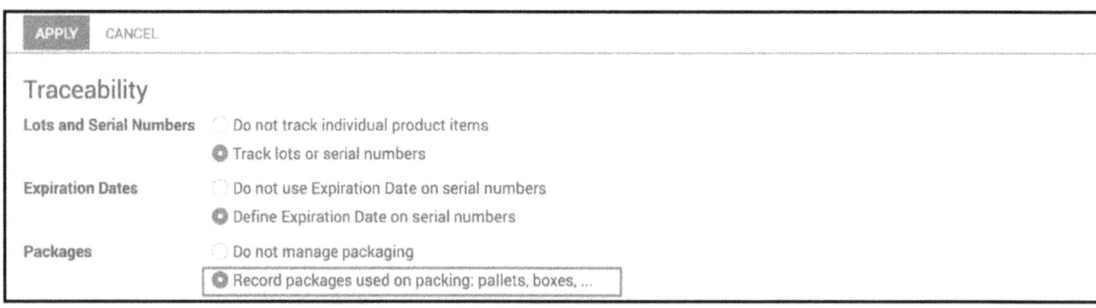

Let's assume that we have a Delivery Order in which we have to deliver two units of the Basic Laptop, instead of sending two separate laptops, it's better to create a package of consisting of two laptops and send it for delivery:

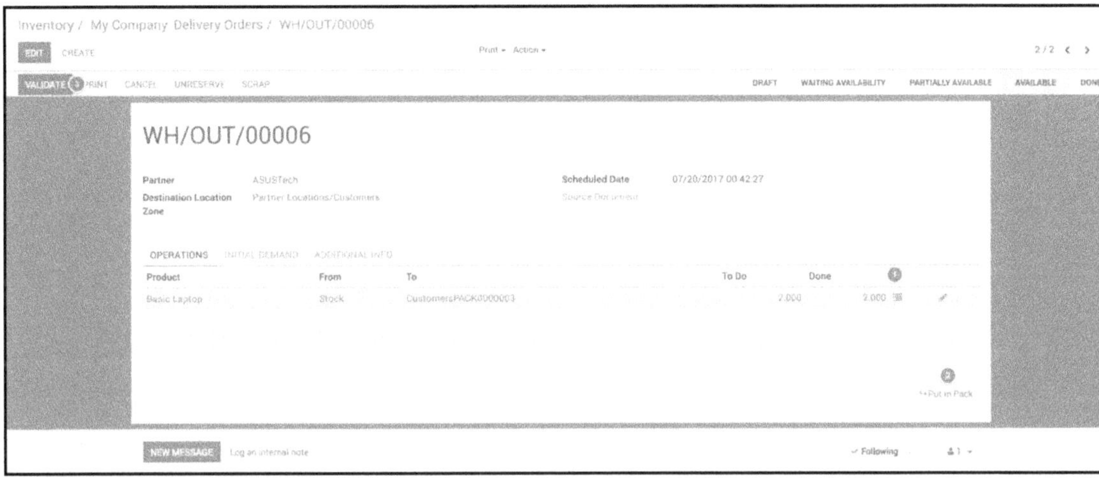

Look at the preceding image of the Delivery Order. I have followed three simple steps listed here to create the package:

1. Assign the Basic Laptops based on the serial numbers proposed by the inventory.
2. Click on **Put in Pack** link, to create the package of the two assigned laptops.
3. Click on the **VALIDATE** button to process the Delivery Order.

As soon as I clicked on the **Put in Pack** link, the package was created and clicking on **VALIDATE** will actually put the product in the pack. The barcode for the package can be printed from the **Inventory Control | Package** under the **Inventory** application:

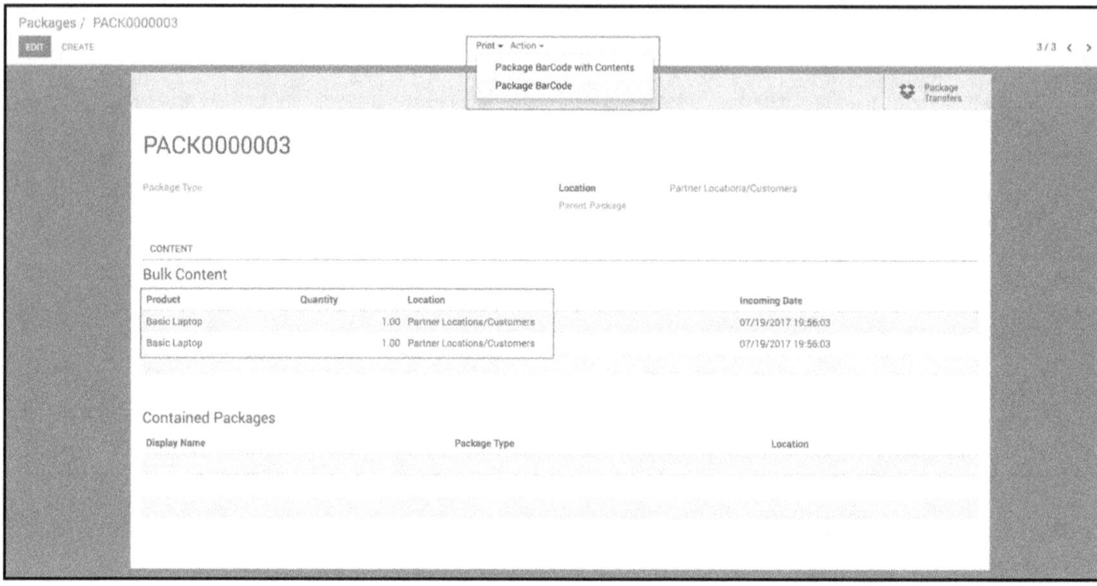

Click on the **Package Barcode** with Contents, you will get the following printed report:

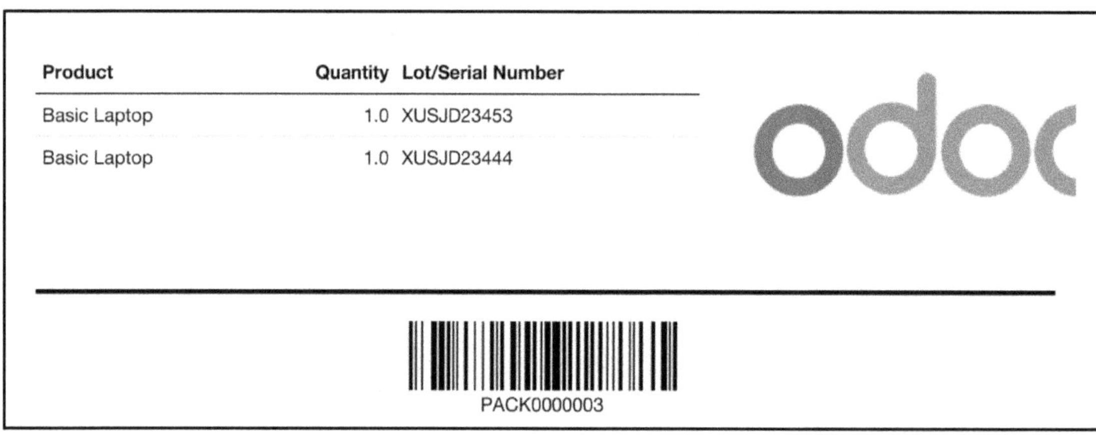

Product	Quantity	Lot/Serial Number
Basic Laptop	1.0	XUSJD23453
Basic Laptop	1.0	XUSJD23444

PACK0000003

This can be pasted on the pack to provide detailed information about the package.

Set up and working with the barcode interface

You will be surprised to know, but it's true that a single-screen barcode interface is capable of managing all the warehouse operation we have gone through till now. Using the barcode interface means you can process the incoming shipment or delivery with serial and lots, the packaging can be created from the interface, you can transfer stock between two locations, and the inventory initialize or verification can be done using the barcode interface, too. The barcode interface is a great feature, if you are using serial, lots, package, and products with barcode, and other than barcode scanner there is no special requirement for setting up and working with the barcode interface.

Getting ready

We assume that you have a barcode scanner available and have set up correctly with a computer or laptop.

How to do it...

1. The barcode interface is an application that adds full barcode support to the Inventory application. This can be activated from the setting page of the Inventory application:

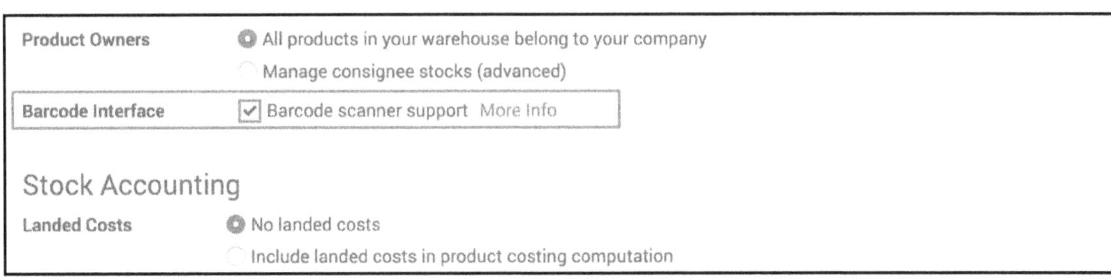

2. Select **Barcode scanner support** and click on the **APPLY** button to activate the feature. The new application Barcode will be added to the Odoo home screen.

3. Click on the **Barcode** application, you will enter a single screen, as shown here:

It is waiting for the barcode scan; it will perform the operation depending on what you scan on this screen. Keep the printout of the list of commands that are used to instruct Odoo through the barcode scanner, such as **VALIDATE**, **MENU**, **PRINT**, and more.

The pdf file with the list of commands can be found in the **Planner**, go to the **Making an Inventory** section to download the barcode screen commands. Look at the following sample command:

O-CMD.MAIN-MENU

O-CMD.CANCEL

O-CMD.EDIT

O-CMD.SAVE

Keep this page ready for fast processing through the barcode scanning interface.

4. Make sure that all the products have barcode configured on them, if not please go through the planner **Product Configuration** section to get the detailed instructions. Click on the **fast scanning interface** link to the screen, using that means the product's barcode can be added quickly. Look at the following screen of lists of products with barcode editable fields:

Place the cursor on the **Barcode** field at the first record and scan the barcode using scanner, the barcode will be scanned and you will automatically go to the next product barcode field. Continue scanning the product's barcodes one by one, according to the product sequence.

5. Now, you are ready to process the incoming shipment using the barcode interface. Let's assume that you receive five **Basic laptops** from the vendor. To process using the barcode interface, you must have the **Picking Operations** for incoming shipments:

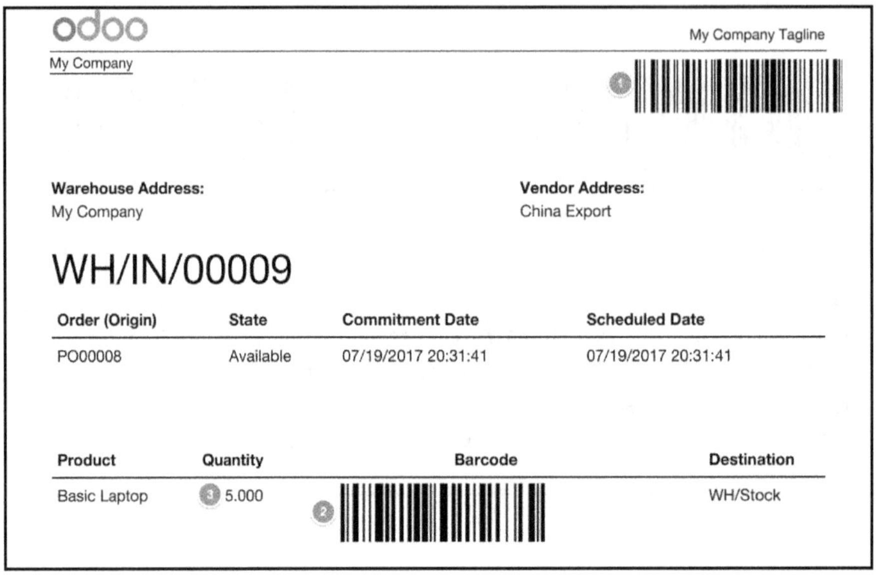

My picking operations page looks like the preceding image.

6. Follow the order of the scan as per the preceding image. First scan the reception document barcode, it will automatically open the Reception Order on screen. The reception operation will be open in edit mode:

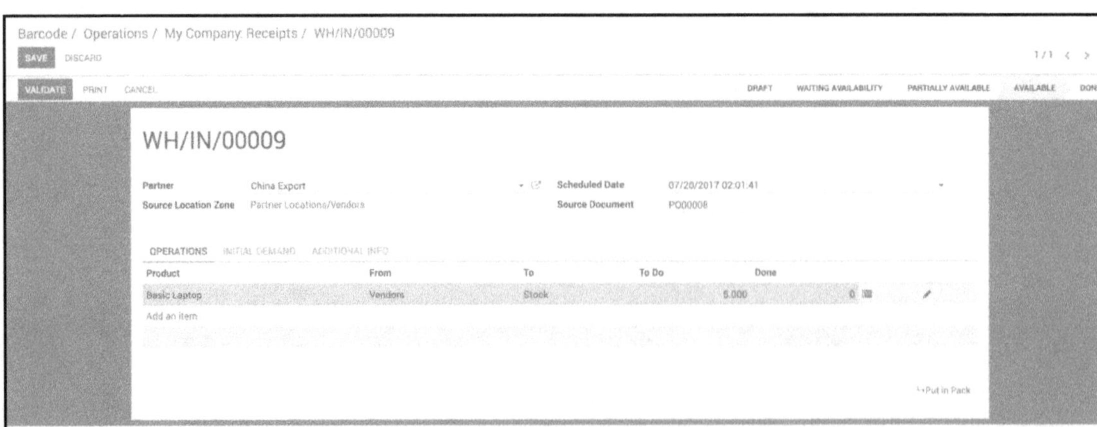

7. Scan the product barcode. As the laptop is tracked by the serial number, it will open a popup to ask for the serial number. Look at following screen:

8. Scan the serial numbers from the laptop package, one by one for all the five laptops. Odoo will create the same serial number in the inventory so that it can be tracked easily in the inventory:

9. Scan the **SAVE** command from the command sheet, you will arrive at the reception form view.

   If you would like to put all the five laptops in a single package, scan the barcode command **BTN-put-in-pack** from the command sheet. A pack will be created and all five laptops will be placed in that package:

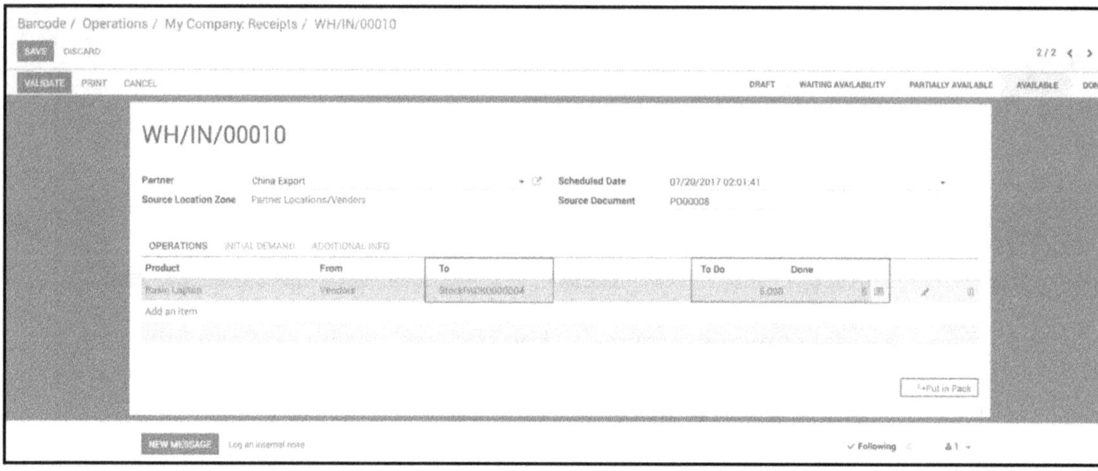

10. Scan the **VALIDATE** command from the command sheet. The incoming reception will be validated.
11. Scan **CMD- Main - Menu** to come back to the Barcode application main interface. You are ready to start a new operation from this screen.

There's more...

The barcode interface is super smart; it understands the operation to be performed based on the barcode scanned. It identifies the reception or delivery operation and opens that operation quickly in edit mode, you just need to print the **Picking Operation** for all the incoming shipment and delivery orders: the reports are available under the **Print** option.

The internal transfer can be created directly from the barcode interface screen; you just need to scan the source and destination locations and products to be transferred, it will automatically create an internal transfer and you will be redirected to that screen. The rest of the process will remain the same to scan the product and serial or lot numbers.

Let's set up barcode on the location before we proceed for an internal transfer of products using the barcode interface:

1. Go to the list of locations through **Configuration** | **Warehouse Management** | **Locations.** It is advisable to set the barcode for all the locations, so that you can transfer the stock between them, or you can choose a few locations and set the barcode on those for which you would like to allow the transfer using the barcode interface:

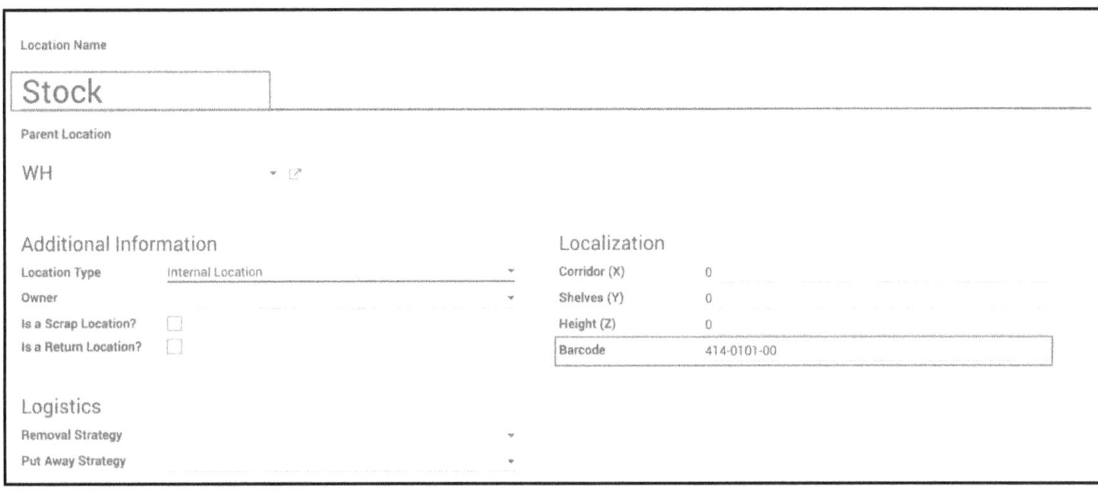

2. Open the form view of location and set the barcode on it, the number for the location has to be started with the specific digits according to the Barcode Nomenclatures. A single screen scans the different barcodes; there should be some coding system to identify which operation has been initiated. The Barcode Nomenclatures defines those coding systems, either you can use existing or you can change those at your convenience.

The Barcode Nomenclatures can be accessed from **Inventory** | **Configuration** | **Barcode Nomenclatures**, after entering into the debug mode:

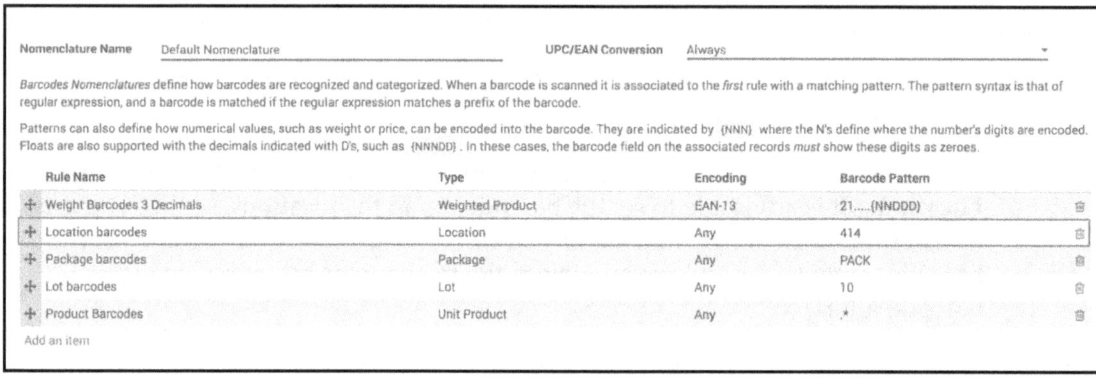

This was the reason I have entered the location code 414-0101-00, which actually starts with 414.

I will not go into much detail, I will let you explore this by yourself, it is easier to identify what could be the code that you should use for Serial, Lot, Location, and more.

Internal transfer using the barcode Interface

As soon as the barcode is set for all the locations, you are ready to transfer the product stock from one location to an other location using the barcode interface. Here are the steps to perform an internal transfer:

1. Scan the source location barcode from the home screen of the barcode application.
2. Scan the barcode of the product you want to transfer, scanning multiple times the same product to increase the quantity.

Scan the serial/lot number, if the product has to be tracked using the serial or lot number:

3. Scan the destination location, once the product scanning completes:

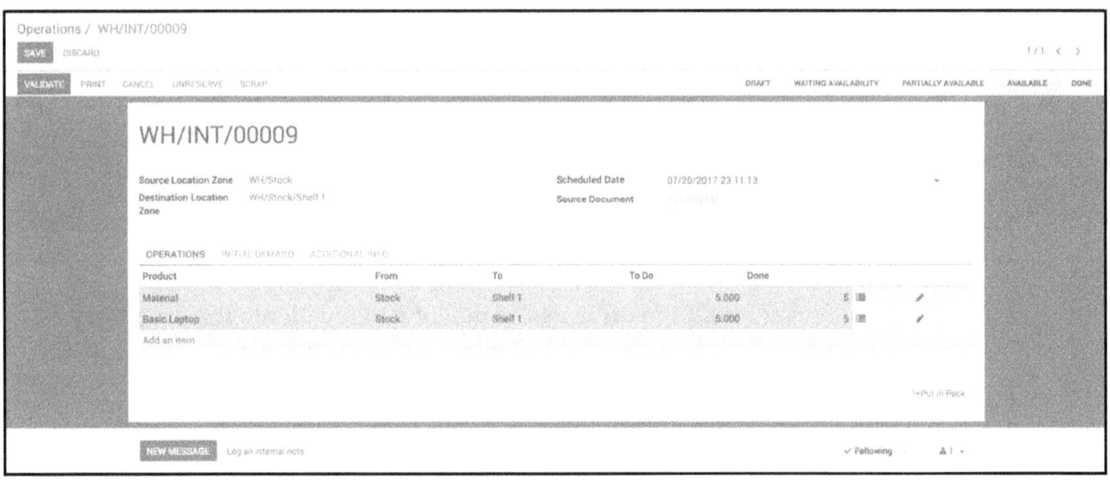

4. Scan the **VALIDATE** command from the list of barcode commands.

Initialize or adjust inventory using the barcode Interface

The inventory initialization or adjustment can be done from the barcode interface by performing the following steps:

1. Click on the **INVENTORY** button from the main screen of the barcode interface.
2. Start scanning the product barcode, if you have more than one quantity, scan multiple times or use the keyboard to change the quantity, scan the **serial/lot number**:

3. When you've scanned all the products of the location, validate the inventory manually or by scanning the **VALIDATE** barcode command.

Reference barcodes

I have used the following barcodes for the products and locations, serial and lot numbers during the test cases:

Product Barcodes:

8 200538 000325

8 200538 000165

8 200538 000127

Lot Numbers for Martial Product:

MAY/2017/039201

JUNE/2017/39282

JUNE/2017/83928

JULY/2017/16253

Laptop Serial Numbers:

XUSJD23422

XUSJD23453

XUSJD23444

Location Barcode:

414-0101-00

414-0101-01

414-0101-02

11
Advanced Warehouse Management

In this chapter, we will cover the following recipes:

- Product costing and inventory valuation
- Managing transportation costs
- Quality control in Warehouse

Introduction

We have seen in the previous chapter how the Warehouse is integrated with sales and purchase applications. When a sales order is confirmed, the delivery order is generated in Warehouse automatically with the estimated delivery date. Warehouse also keeps a track record and schedule for all the incoming shipments as incoming shipments are created when the purchase order gets confirmed.

Warehouse should have integration with the accounting application too. To have the accurate stock valuation in the balance sheet as and when a product is sold, it should be reflected in the profit and loss under the Cost of Goods Sold. Let's assume that if Warehouse is not integrated with the accounting application, you cannot have a real-time inventory valuation and cost of goods in accounting. Big Warehouses need real-time accounting integration, along with integration with sales and purchase as they have a lot of incoming and outgoing shipments to process every day.

Odoo Warehouse Management is able to manage Warehouses for a small shop, and the same Warehouse application can be scaled up to manage the big Warehouses. It has all the capabilities to manage the big Warehouses efficiently with multiple locations, different strategies such as put away strategy and removal strategies, reordering level at the Warehouse, or individual location levels. Let's go through some of the advanced features of Warehouse such as computing the cost of a product, when it will be sold or consumed in manufacturing and adding the logistic costs to the cost of the product to get the correct inventory valuation, or the cost of goods sold. Compute the inventory valuation and cost of goods sold, set up the quality check process at the reception, and return the product if it has not passed the quality check. Check the quality when transferring products to other locations such as production plants, and scrap the product if it is not used or if it has reached the end of its life.

Product costing and inventory valuation

For any trading or manufacturing business, it is a necessity to compute the cost of the product consumed to get the value of the current inventory available in the Warehouse. There are different methods available to compute the product cost, and the valuation of the inventory depends on that. Odoo has three different methods to compute the cost of consumed products--**Standard**, **Average**, and **Real-time**. It has valuation methods, **Periodic (Manual)** and **Perpetual (Automated)**. The inventory valuation can be computed automatically in Warehouse, but it can be linked to the balance sheet and profit and loss when it is set to **Perpetual (Automated)**, or else accounts have to be updated manually when it is set to **Periodic (Manual)**.

Let's see all the costing methods, how they can be activated, how they work, and computes. Also, let's see how to link inventory valuation with accounting, either manually or automatically. You can decide which method to use to compute the product cost and valuation of the inventory in Warehouse.

Getting ready

We assume that you have imported all your products into Odoo and have set the correct **Product Type** *(stockable products, consumables, and services)* and **Internal Category** on all the products.

How to do it...

1. Let's take an example of the product **Material**, which is a **Stockable Product** and its **Internal Category** is **Saleable**. The **Cost Price** o **Material** that is set for the product is **60**, and the **Sale Price** is **100**. You can select an appropriate product from your product list:.

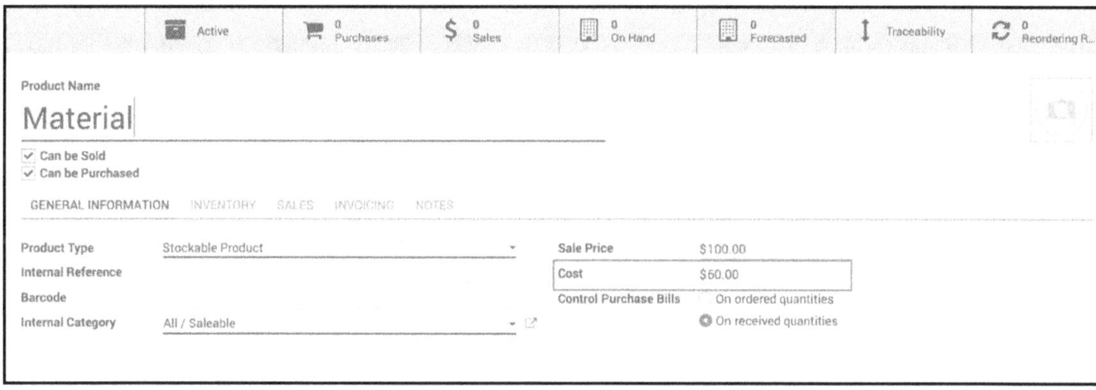

Look at the preceding screenshot of the product configuration that I have in my example.

2. Let's assume that we have an urgent demand for 100 materials, and to fulfill the demand, we buy it from the vendor **China Export** at the rate of **70** instead of **60**:

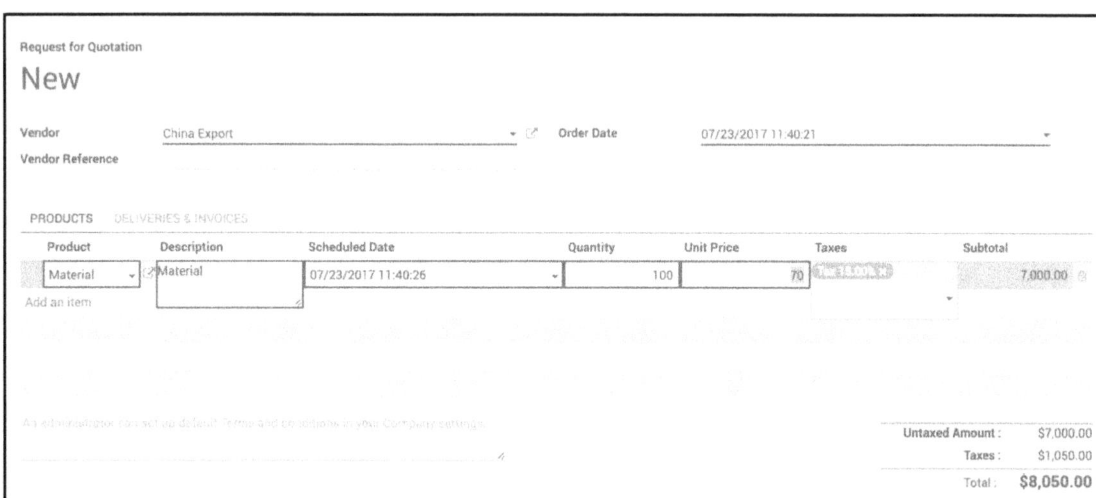

Confirm the order and process the incoming shipment.As soon as you receive the stock in the Warehouse, you can check the **Inventory Valuation** in Warehouse. Go to **Inventory | Reports | Inventory Valuation**:

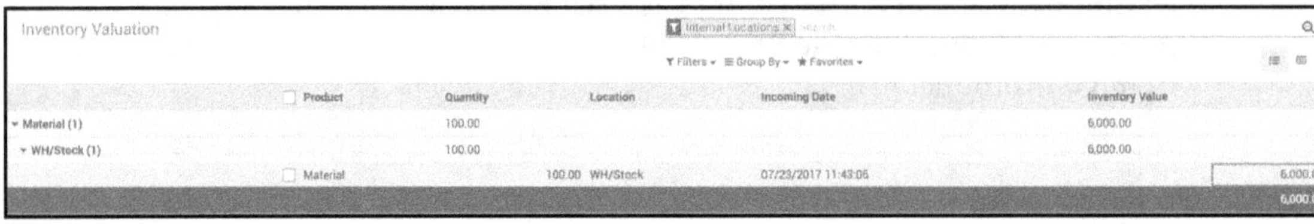

The material valuation is 6,000 in Warehouse, which shows the valuation based on the standard *price* costing method set in the product category.

The default costing method applied is **Standard Price**.If you change the **Cost price** on the product form, the inventory value will be recomputed based on the new cost price.

3. Go to **Purchase | Configuration | Settings** to enable other costing methods. Search for the **Costing Methods** field and select the **Use a 'Fixed', 'Real' or 'Average' price costing method** option on the field. Look at the following screenshot of the configuration page:

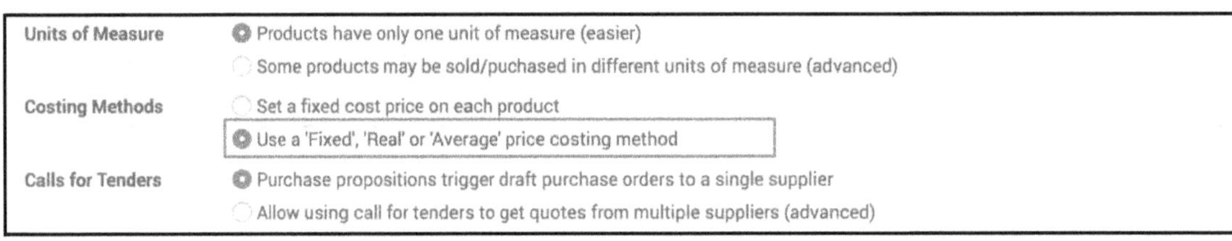

4. Click on the **APPLY** button to save the settings. Open and edit the product **Material** on the form view:

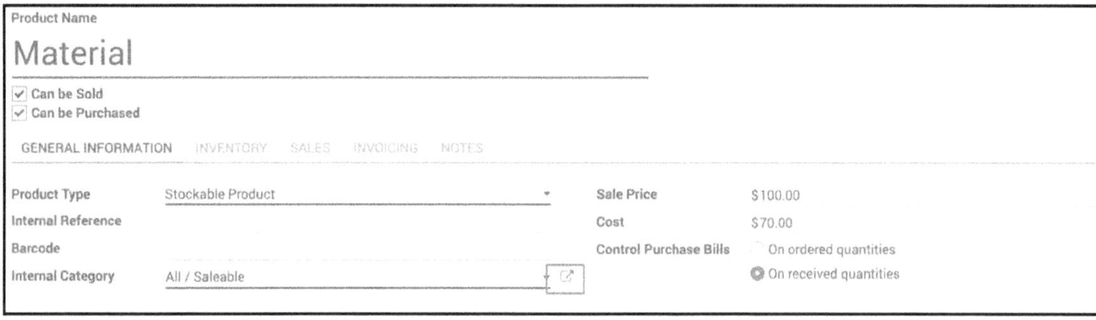

Click on the **Internal category** field to get a detailed view of the *Saleable* **Internal Category**. A detailed view of the internal category will look like this:

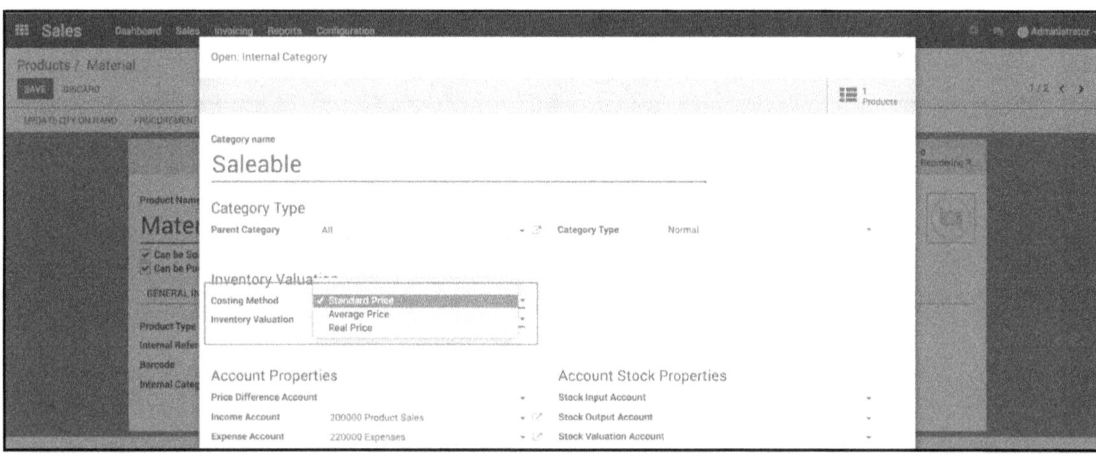

On the *Saleable* **Internal Category** form, you will find the **Costing Method** field, which has three different values. **Standard Price** is the default value. Select **Real Price** and save the form. You will be brought back to the product form.Click on the **SAVE** button of the product form to save the settings.

Just after changing the costing method on **Internal Product**, look at the inventory valuation report again from the **Inventory** application; the inventory value has been changed to 7,000.00:

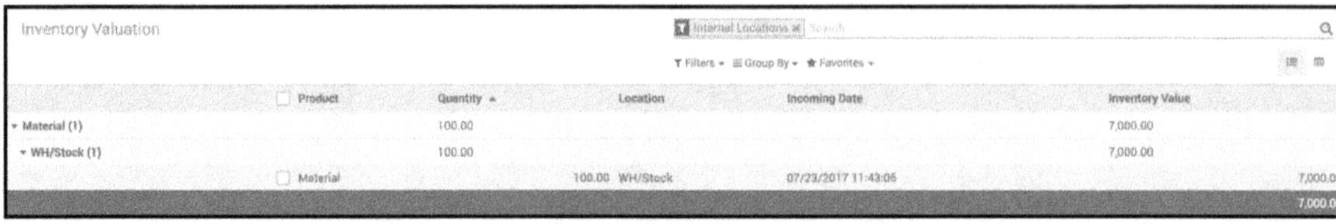

As soon as the costing method is changed to **Real price** on the product category, the inventory re-computes the product cost based on the purchase price. The inventory valuation gets updated; look at the preceding screenshot.

5. Let's assume that for the next demand for **Material**, we have to purchase a quantity of 100 **Material** from **China Export** at the rate of **75**. Confirm the order and process the incoming shipment available after the confirmation of the purchase order:

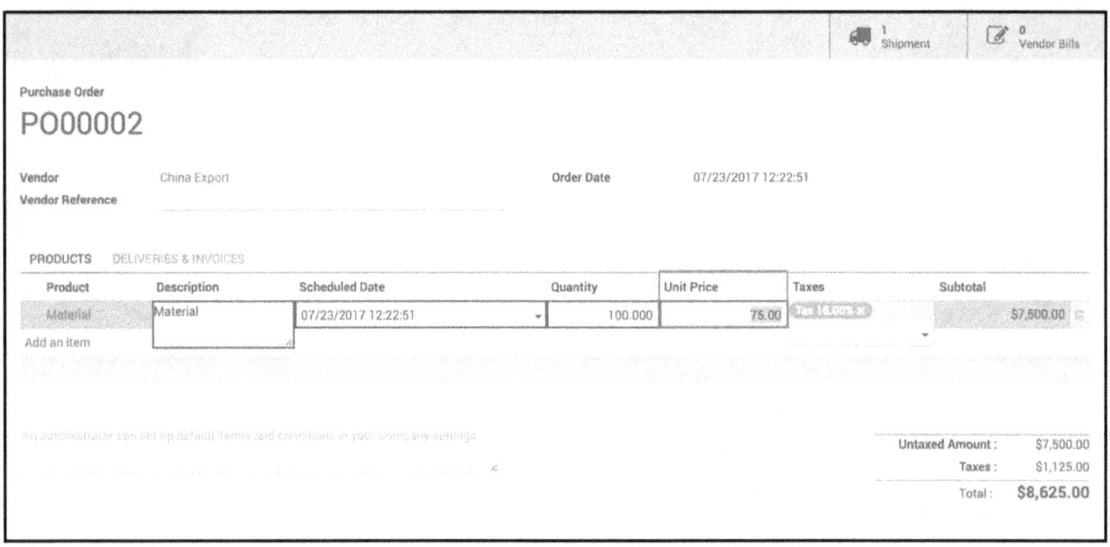

6. Check the inventory valuation once again after the reception has been processed, from the **Inventory** application:

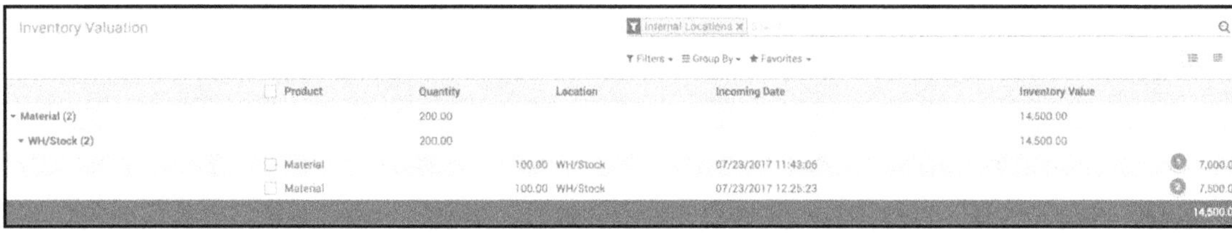

Now, you will have two different lines having two different prices. The total valuation is **14,500**, while individual lots are purchased at different rates. This is called **Real Price** valuation, which keeps track of the purchase price for an individual product in the warehouse.

The cost of the products will be computed based on the purchase price and the cost price of a product in an inventory, and not based on the **Cost** field available for the **Product**. The **Inventory valuation** will be computed based on the cost price of the products. Each purchase has a different cost the inventory valuation will be computed based on the actual cost price; that's why it is known as **Real Price**.

7. Now, let's change the product costing methods again from **Real Price** to **Average Price**.You can change it by going to from **Inventory** | **Configuration** | **Products** | **Product Categories**. Search for the **Saleable** category and change **Costing method** to **Average Price**:

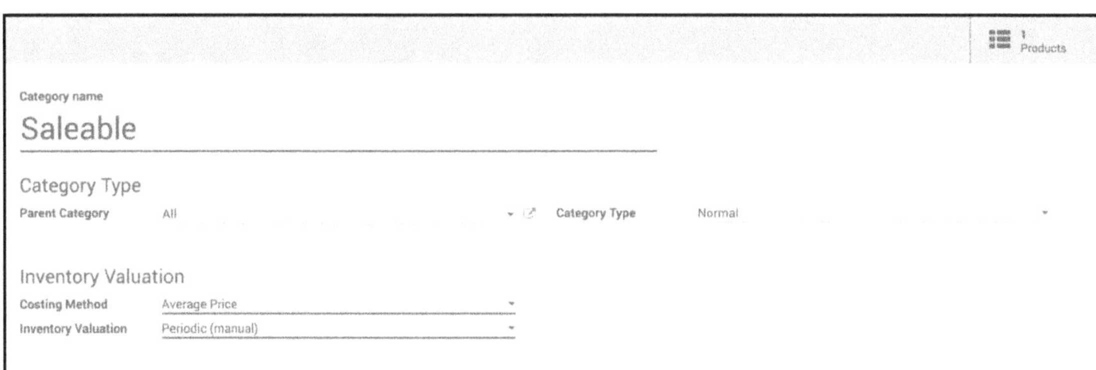

Save the **Product Category** setting, and let's check the inventory valuation again:

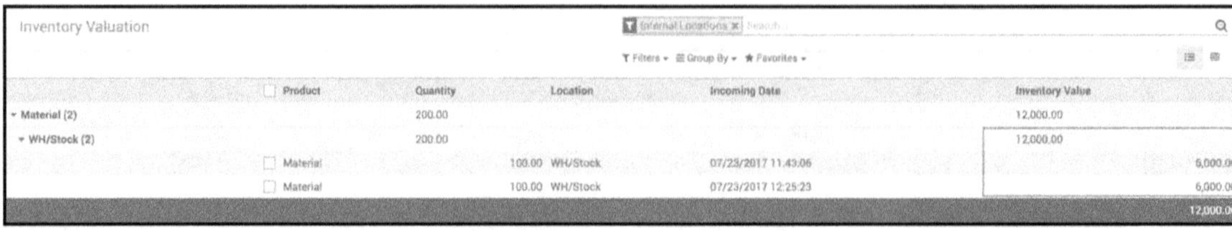

The valuation changed from **14,500** to **12,000**; the inventory valuation has decreased because of the **Average price** methods.The average price will compute the cost of existing stock based on the cost price defined on the product form. The product cost price will be computed again for the next purchase.

> It means for the existing stock, it will compute the valuation based on the product standard cost price; you can change it to have new average cost price.

Let's make a third purchase of a quantity of **100** from the same vendor. This time, the purchase price is **65**. Look at the following screenshot:

Confirm the purchase order and process the incoming shipment. Check the inventory valuation; the valuation should be computed based on the new method set for the **Average Price** product internal category. Look at the following screenshot of inventory valuation:

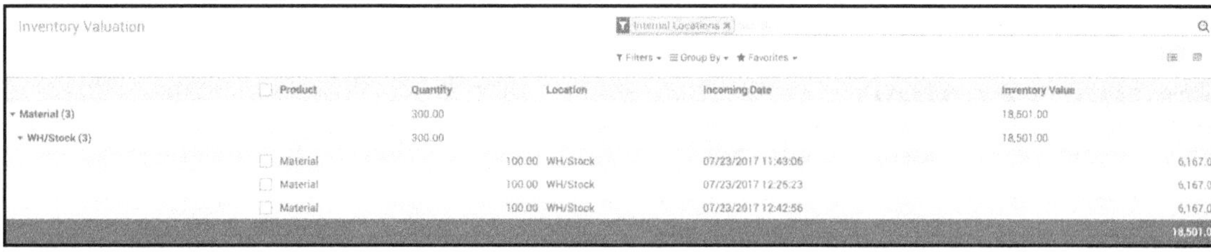

8. For the **Average Price, Costing method**, the new cost price will be computed after every purchase based on the following formula:

cost price = (value of existing stock + value of purchased stock) / (existing quantity + purchased quantity)

The computed cost price, in our case *(12000 + 6500) / (200+100) = 61.67*, will be set to the product **Cost Price** field. Look at the following screenshot of the product form with the computed cost price on it:

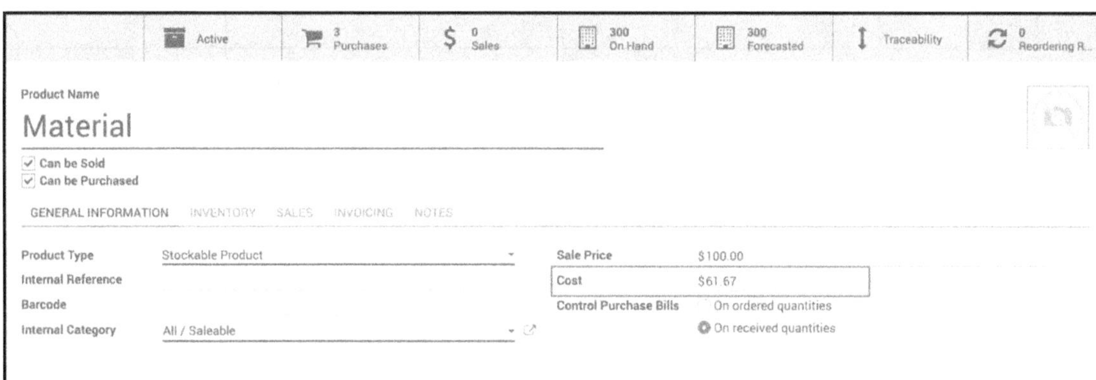

The product **Cost Price** can be changed on the product form the inventory will get updated according to the new **Cost Price**. The cost price can be changed when the costing methods are **Standard** or **Average**; for **Real Price**, it is not advisable to change this on the product cost price field.

How it works...

Consider three concussive purchase orders of a quantity of 100, each with different prices will test this business flow with each costing method. Let's see how each costing method computes the inventory valuation and the new product cost price.

Standard costing

Let's execute the business flow with Standard Price as the costing method for the product internal category:

Seq.	Cost Price of Product	(Sale / Purchase)	Inventory Valuation	Cost Price of Product (after Operation)
1	60	100 quantity at the rate of 70	6,000 100 quantity * 60 product cost price	60
2	60	100 quantity at the rate of 75	12,000 (200 * product cost price)	60
3	60	100 quantity at the rate of 65	18,000 (300 * product cost price)	60
4	70	Change product cost price manually	21,000 (300 * product cost price)	70

Standard Price calculates the inventory valuation based on the cost price defined in the Product Cost Price field, and it does not include the purchase price in computation.

Real-time costing

Let's execute the business flow with Real Price as the costing method for the product internal category:

Seq.	Cost Price of Product	(Sale / Purchase)	Inventory Valuation	Cost Price of Product (after Operation)
1	60	100 quantity at the rate of 70	7,000 100 qty * rate @ 70	60
2	60	100 quantity at the rate of 75	14,500 100 qty * rate @ 70 100 qty * rate @ 75	60
3	60	100 quantity at the rate of 65	21,000 100 qty * rate @ 70 100 qty * rate @ 75 100 qty * rate @ 65	60
4	60	Sale of a quantity of 150 of material	10,250 50 qty * rate @ 75 100 qty * rate @ 65	71.67 (it is the rate at which the quantity of 150 is sold out)

There were three different lots of **Material** that arrived at three different prices-- 70, 75, and 65. The delivery for the sales order will be done based on the FIFO removal strategy, which means the lot purchased at the price of 70 will be out, and the remaining quantity of 50 will be assigned from the second lot, which was bought at the rate of 75:

Cost price (71.67) = (7000 + 3750) / (100 + 50)

The new cost price that will be set for the product is 71.67. It is the cost price computed based on the last lot of products removed from the Warehouse and not based on the products available in the Warehouse.

Average costing

Let's execute the business flow with Average Price as the costing method for the product internal category:

Seq.	Cost Price of Product	(Sale / Purchase)	Inventory Valuation	Cost Price of Product (after Operation)
1	60	100 quantity at the rate of 70	7,000 ((0 + 7000) / (0 + 100)) * 100	70
2	70	100 quantity at the rate of 75	14,500 ((7,000 + 7,500) / (100 + 100)) * 200	72.50
3	72.50	100 quantity at the rate of 65	21,000 ((14,500 + 6,500) / (200 + 100)) * 300	70

The cost price will be computed when the costing method is an average price. It will be computed each time an incoming shipment is received in the Warehouse. Cost price is based on the following formula:

cost price = (value of existing stock + value of purchased stock) / (existing quantity + purchased quantity)

The Inventory valuation for the product can be computed using this following formula:

*Inventory Value = ((value of existing stock + value of purchased stock) / (existing quantity + purchased quantity)) * Total quantity*

There's more...

The costing of the product is computed based on the costing methods available for the product internal category. You can keep the different costing methods for the product category depending on the price fluctuation in the market. The inventory valuation is computed based on the product cost price. However, in the **Inventory** application the inventory valuation is not linked to the balance sheet in accounting when we choose the **Periodic (manual)** option for the **Inventory Valuation** field on the product category; in this case, we have to transfer the inventory valuation manually to the balance sheet.

Let's see how the inventory value can be transferred to the balance sheet when we choose to have a **Periodic (manual)** inventory valuation. It will be linked automatically to the balance sheet when it has the **Perpetual (automated)** option for the **Inventory Valuation** field on the product category:

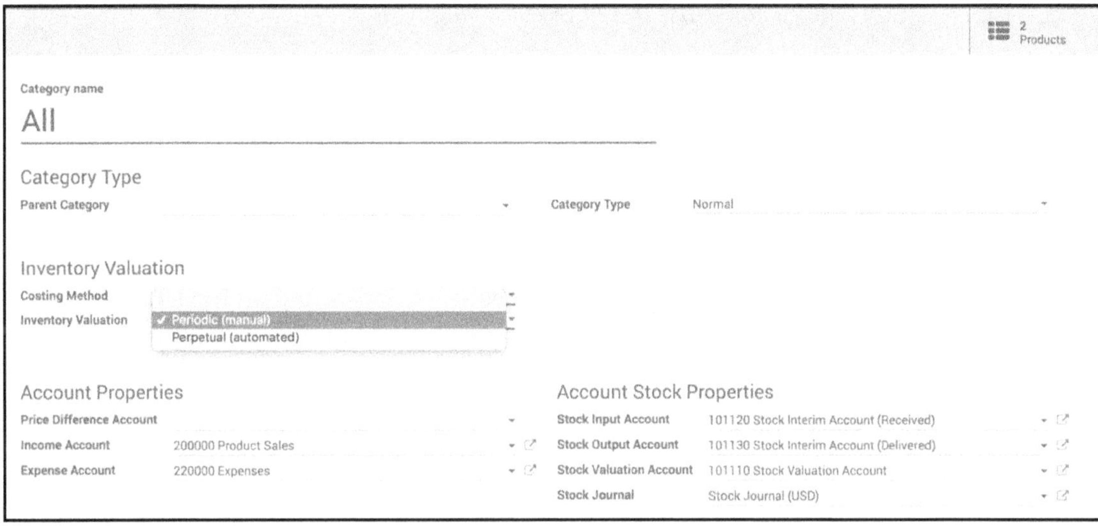

Look at the preceding screenshot of the product internal category. We can configure and link the inventory valuation to financial statements such as **Balance Sheet** or **Profit and Loss** accounts, by selecting the **Perpetual (automated)** option.

Periodic (manual) Inventory Valuation

Make sure that you have created a duplicated database to test this feature. Understand the automatic inventory valuation computation, and manual accounting entries before configuring these in the production instance.

The default option set for the inventory valuation is **Periodic (manual)**.It refers to the manual accounting entries for the books of accounts on periodic intervals. The Inventory valuation is recomputed in Warehouse on every incoming or outgoing shipment.Every time you check the inventory valuation, you will get the latest inventory value. The inventory valuation has to be checked at regular intervals, that is, weekly, monthly, quarterly, or yearly, and the profit and loss account has to be updated manually for the cost of goods sold.

The balance sheet can be updated automatically as soon as we confirm the invoice for the purchase order.

> The vendor bill can be received depending on the **Control Purchase Bills** field available on the product confirmation; it can be set either to *On ordered quantities* or *On received quantities*.

Configure the product internal category before proceeding further. Set the account to **101110 Stock Valuation Account** for **Stock Input Account** instead of **101120 Stock Interim Account (Received)**. When inventory valuation is set to **Periodic (manual),** only the **Stock Input** field account is required.

> I am using the **Generic Chart of Account**; in your case, you have to set the correct **Inventory Valuation** account depending on the **Chart of Account** you choose.

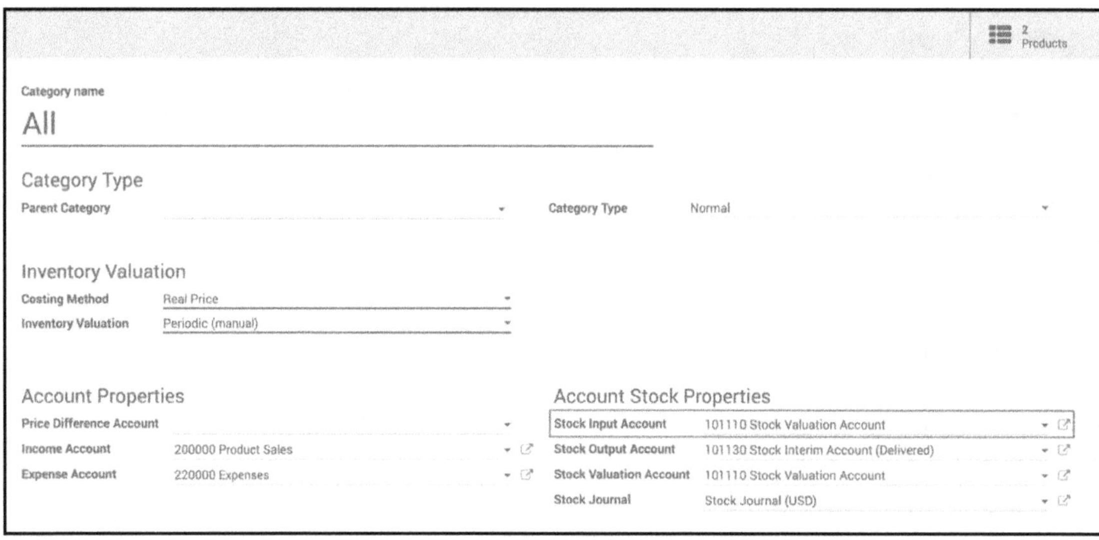

Configure the other options on the product form such as **Control Purchase Bills**. It should be set to *On received quantities*. Create a purchase order and buy a quantity of **100 Material** from **China Export** at the rate of **70**. Look at the following screenshot of the purchase order:

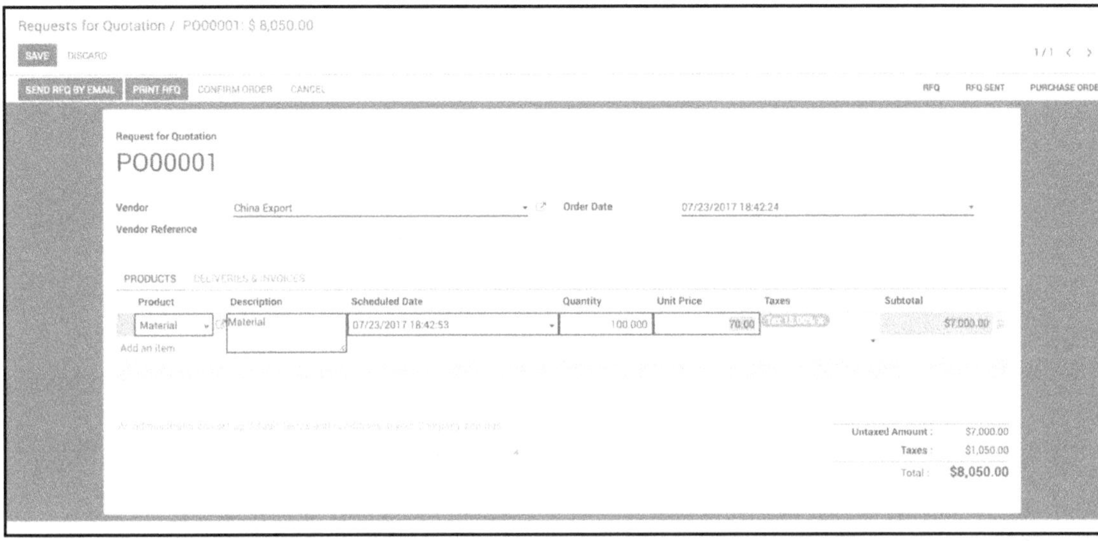

Confirm the order and process the incoming shipment at the reception.As soon as the incoming shipment is processed, the inventory will be updated in Warehouse and the **Inventory Valuation** report will be updated too. Look at this screenshot of the inventory valuation report:

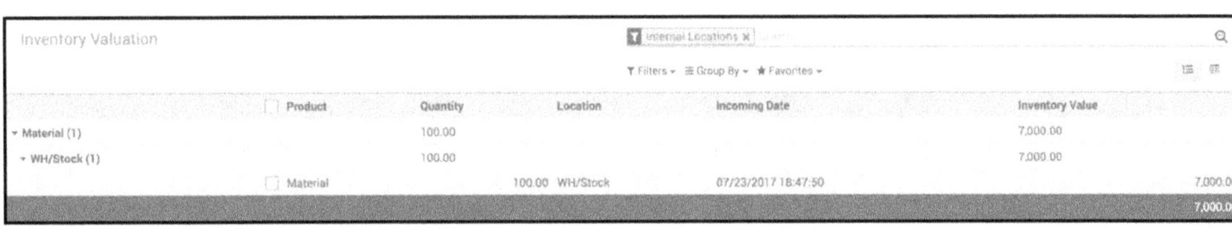

Create a vendor bill as soon as you receive it from the vendor. Look at this screenshot:

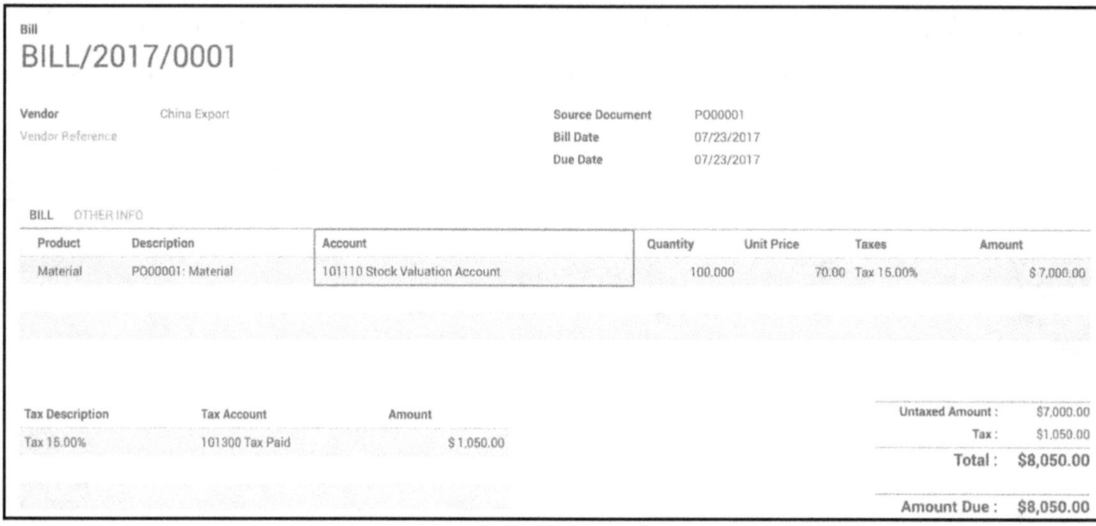

Confirm the vendor bill.The balance sheet will be updated as soon as the vendor bill is validated. The **Stock Valuation Account** will be debited and the vendor payable account will be credited, instead of debiting the cost of goods sold account. As the stock valuation account belongs to the balance sheet, the balance sheet will be updated when the vendor bill is validated. Look at this screenshot of the balance sheet report:

The total of the inventory valuation report and stock valuation on the balance sheet should have the same amount. The stock valuation will be updated automatically for every purchase after receiving and validating the vendor bill.

Let's assume that we have a delivery to process the sales order and we have to deliver a quantity of 40 **Material** from the Warehouse:

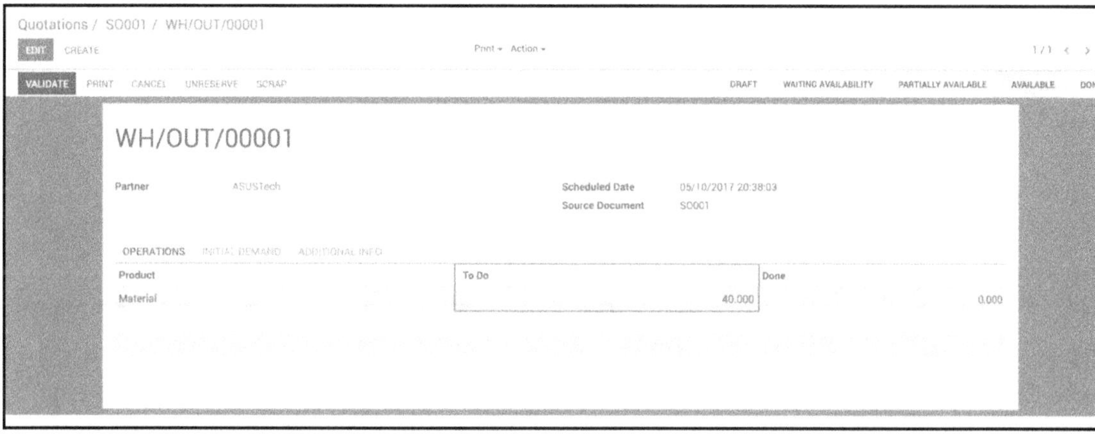

VALIDATE the delivery order; this will assign the quantity of 40 Material from the Warehouse.The quantity decreases from the Warehouse. It will decrease the inventory valuation too. Look at the report; it will look like the following screenshot:

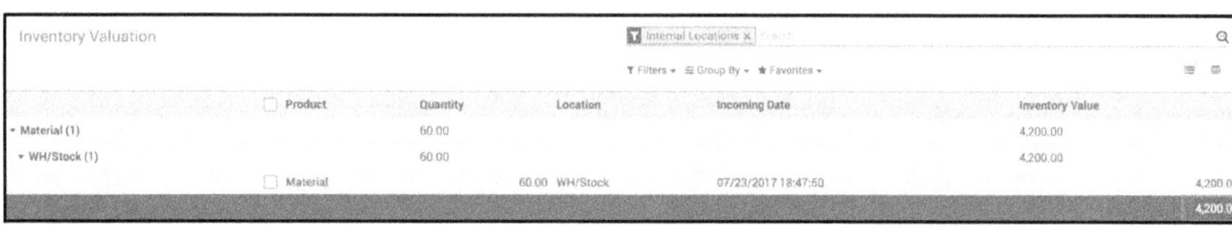

As the delivery is completed, we can create and confirm the customer invoice. On invoice confirmation, it will create the following accounting entry in the book of accounts:

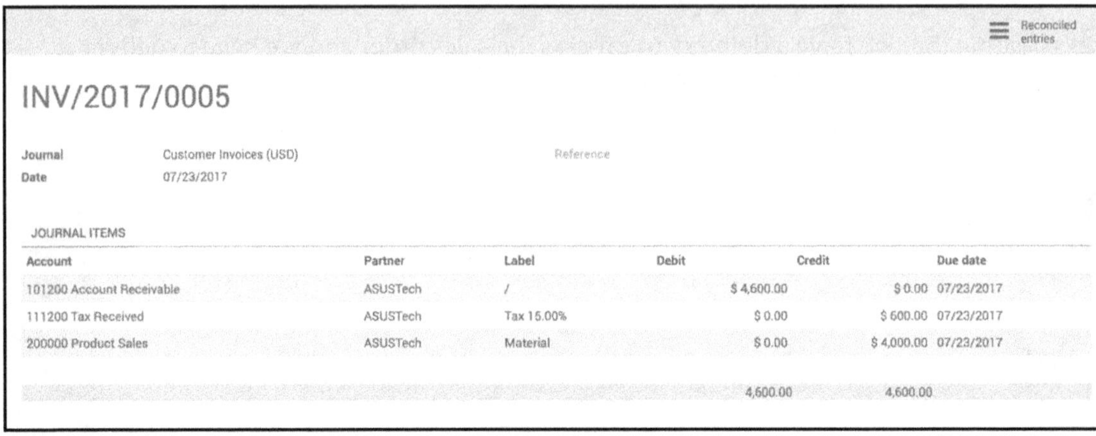

INV/2017/0005

Journal: Customer Invoices (USD)

Date: 07/23/2017

Reference

JOURNAL ITEMS

Account	Partner	Label	Debit	Credit	Due date
101200 Account Receivable	ASUSTech	/	$ 4,600.00	$ 0.00	07/23/2017
111200 Tax Received	ASUSTech	Tax 15.00%	$ 0.00	$ 600.00	07/23/2017
200000 Product Sales	ASUSTech	Material	$ 0.00	$ 4,000.00	07/23/2017
			4,600.00	4,600.00	

This will not affect the inventory valuation.The inventory valuation on the balance sheet has to be updated manually as we choose to update **Periodic (manual)**. Look at the following accounting entry that actually updates the **Inventory Valuation** account and the **Cost of Goods Sold** account, the inventory valuation registers the cost of goods sold, the value will go down, and it will be registered as an expense:

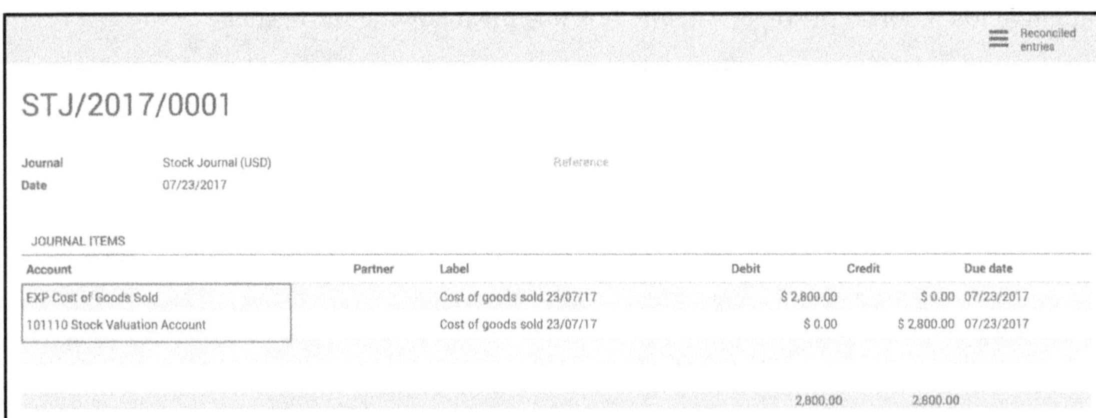

STJ/2017/0001

Journal: Stock Journal (USD)

Date: 07/23/2017

Reference

JOURNAL ITEMS

Account	Partner	Label	Debit	Credit	Due date
EXP Cost of Goods Sold		Cost of goods sold 23/07/17	$ 2,800.00	$ 0.00	07/23/2017
101110 Stock Valuation Account		Cost of goods sold 23/07/17	$ 0.00	$ 2,800.00	07/23/2017
			2,800.00	2,800.00	

The value of **Cost of Goods Sold** can be computed using this formula:

Cost of goods sold (2800) = Stock Valuation Account (balance sheet, 7000) - Value on the Stock Valuation report (4200).

Post the accounting entry and the balance sheet and profit and loss accounts will be updated accordingly. Look at the following screenshot of the balance sheet report:

The **Profit and Loss** account is updated with the **Cost of Goods**. Look at the **Profit and Loss** account report here:

Every time, on the confirmation of the vendor bill, the inventory valuation will get increased. The cost of goods sold has to be computed manually at regular intervals and pass an appropriate accounting journal entry to update the Balance Sheet for the **Inventory Valuation** account and **Profit and Loss** statement for the **Cost of goods sold** account. That's why it's called the **Periodic (manual)** method.

Perpetual (automated)

Make sure that you have created a duplicated database to test this feature. Understand the automatic accounting entries to update the **Inventory Valuation** and **Cost of Goods sold**, before configuring it in the production instance.

When the **Perpetual (automated)** option is set to the **Inventory Valuation** field for the Product Internal Category, it creates and posts an automatic accounting entry for incoming and outgoing shipments. It also computes the cost of goods sold at the time of validating the customer invoice. It updates the profit and loss account and decreases the inventory valuation.

When the inventory valuation is set to P**erpetual (automated)**, you do not need to create an accounting entry manually, as it will create an accounting entry automatically up on the stock movement. The balance sheet will be updated automatically as soon as we purchase the new material, process the incoming shipment, and confirm the invoice.

Let's see how Odoo creates automatic accounting entries on each transaction to compute the real-time inventory valuation on the balance sheet. Check the following configuration of the product category before proceeding:

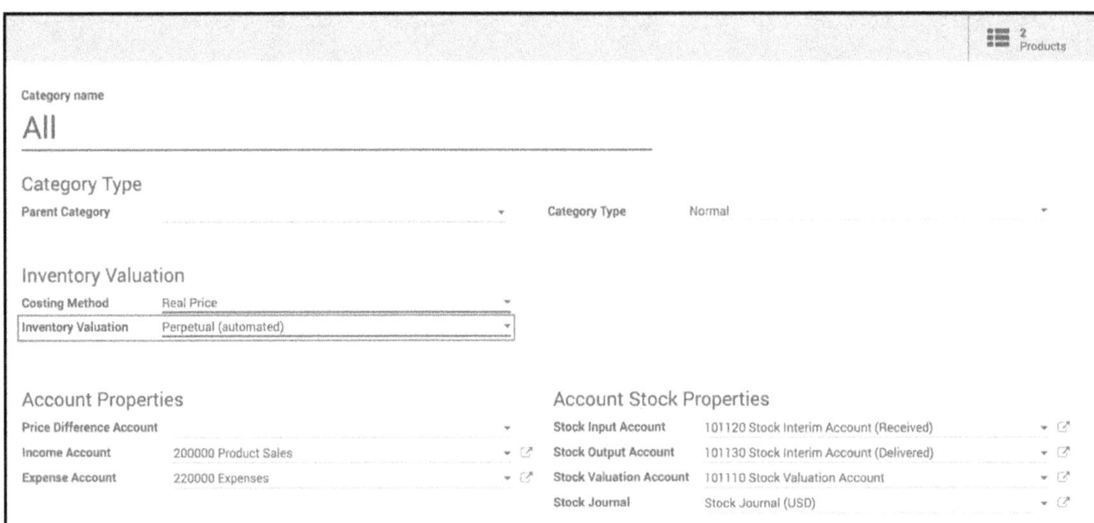

Another option on the product form is **Invoicing Policy**, which is set to *Ordered quantities* and **Control Purchase Bills** is set to *On received quantities*. The costing method is set to **Real price**, the accounts for **Stock Input**, **Stock Output** and **Stock Valuation** available under the **Account Stock Properties**, will be set automatically based on the Chart of Account installed.

Let's see how the inventory value gets updated upon stock movement. Create and confirm the purchase order. Look at the following screenshot of the confirmed purchase order:

Process the incoming shipment in Warehouse. The accounting entry will be created as soon as the incoming shipment is validated. Look at this screenshot of the accounting entry, created after the validation of the incoming reception:

The balance sheet gets updated too. Look at the following screenshot of the balance sheet after the incoming shipment is validated:

The negative balance on **Stock Interim Account (Received)** shows that the vendor bill has to be received. As soon as the vendor bill is received, create and confirm the vendor bill. It will debit **Stock Interim Account (Received),** it will be set to zero, and the payable account will be credited:

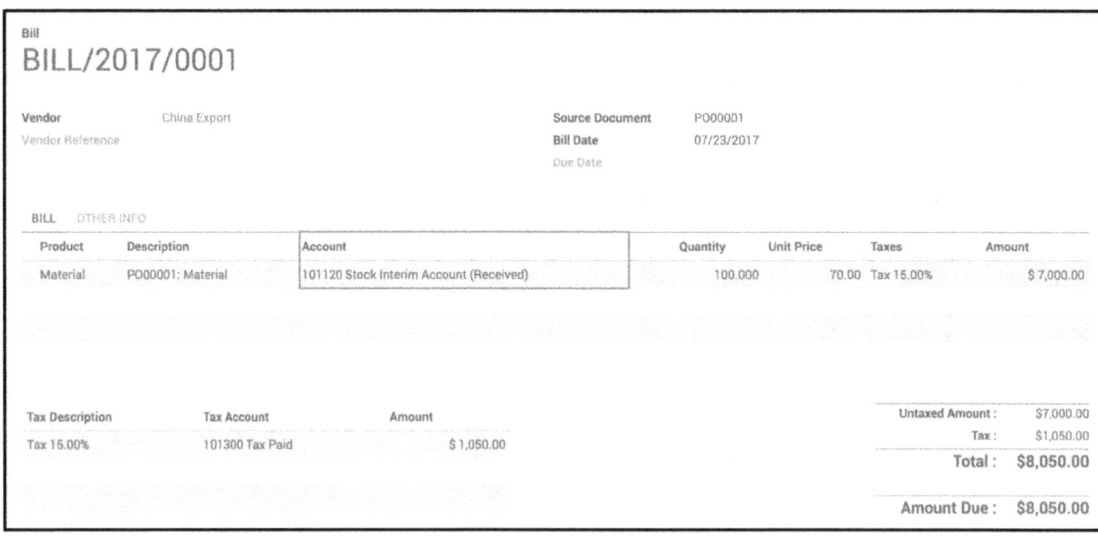

Stock Valuation Account remains as it is. Check the **Current Asset** section under the balance sheet. It will look like this:

Odoo computes the **Cost of Goods Sold** at the time of creating a customer invoice.It will decrease the inventory valuation by that price and update the balance sheet.

Create and confirm the sales order for a quantity of 40 **Material** at the rate of **100**:

Process the delivery order in Warehouse. As soon as the delivery order is processed, it will create the following accounting entries based on the stock movement in the Warehouse:

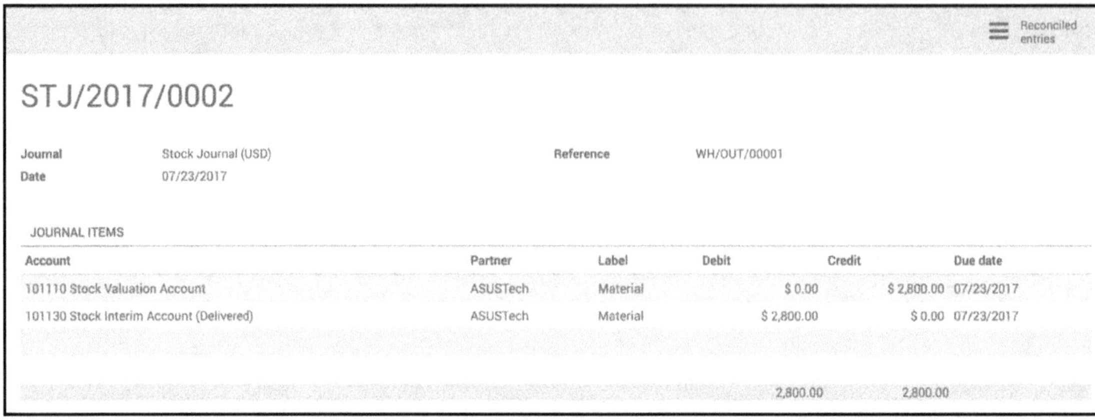

The balance sheet will get impacted after the delivery order is processed. It credits **Inventory Valuation Account** and debits **Stock Interim Account (Delivered)**:

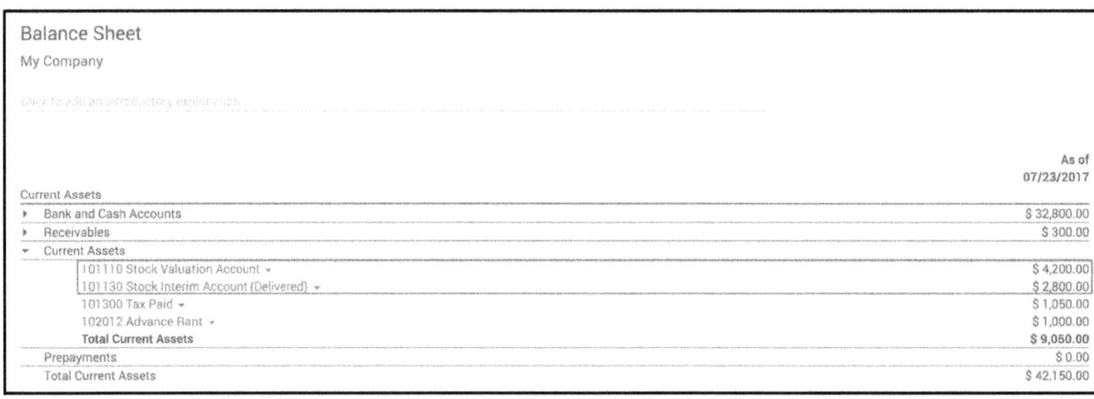

The positive balance on the **Stock Interim Account (Delivered)** shows that the delivery was processed but the customer invoice has not been prepared yet. Let's create and confirm the customer invoice. It will create the following accounting entry as soon as the invoice is confirmed:

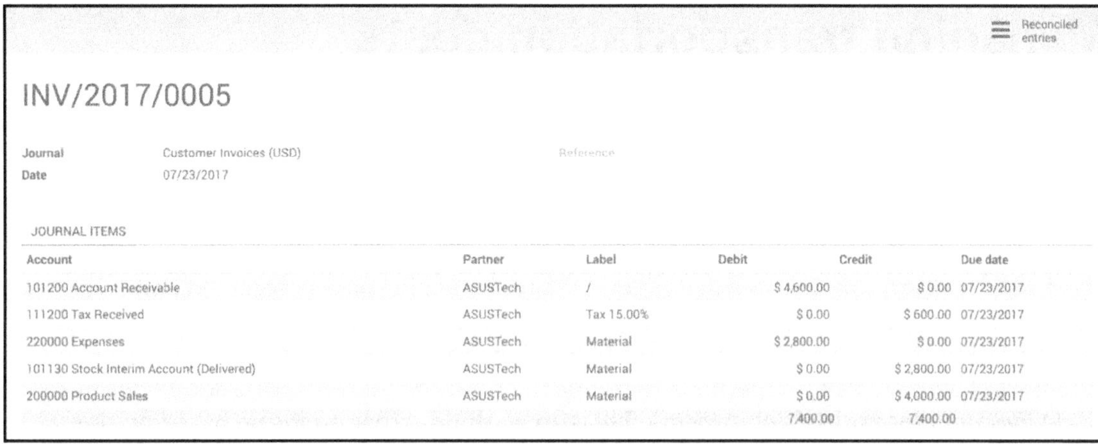

The sales will be credited and the customer receivable account will be debited. Also, it computes the cost of goods sold and creates the accounting entry for the cost of goods sold.

The **Stock Interim Account (Delivered)** will be credited, and the **Cost of Goods Sold** will be debited. Look at the **Profit and Loss** account displayed on the screen, as shown here:

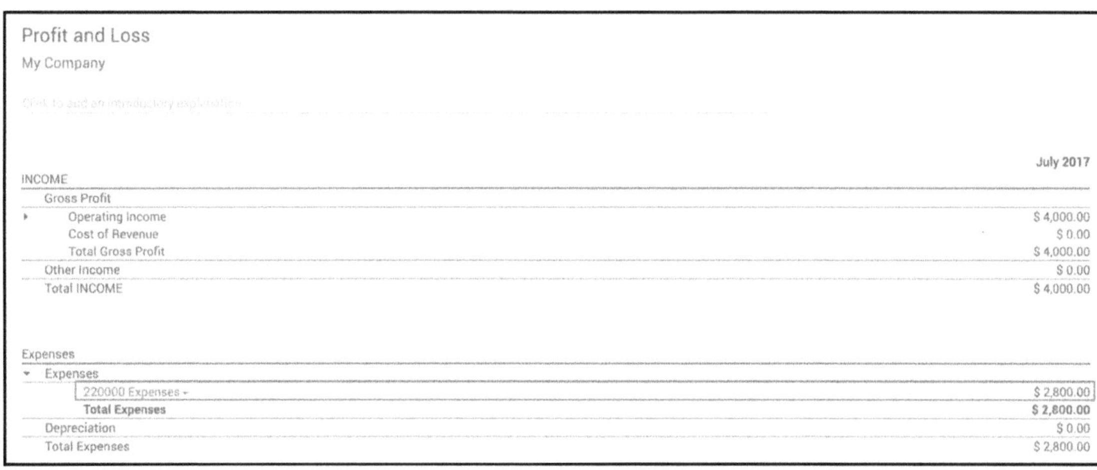

The **Perpetual (automated)** method does automatic accounting entries. So, no need to do periodic accounting entries, as it will be done automatically.

For small businesses, it is always advisable to use the **Periodic (manual)** valuation method for small inventory, while for big Warehouse, **Perpetual (automated)** method is suitable.

Managing transportation costs

Most of the time, the transportation cost has to be borne by the customer in business. When we buy from our vendor, the vendor sends the goods along with the copy of the invoice, while the cost of the logistics comes from the logistics provider. The transportation cost can be a fixed or variable depending on the goods to be delivered. The transportation cost can be paid in cash or bank check or any other payment methods.

The cost of transportation is divided among the number of products received and added to the cost of products that have been received through the number of shipments in the same transportation cost. So the cost of the product will increase, which increases the cost of the inventory. There are certain methods to divide the total cost of transportation between the stocks received for multiple shipments. This can be divided per quantity, based on the weight or volume.

Odoo has a built-in feature to divide the cost of transportation between the received stock based on the different computation methods. This feature is known as landed cost in Odoo. Let's see how the landed cost has been divided between the arrived products, based on the quantity, weight, or volume, and added to the cost of products.

Getting ready

The landed cost only works with the specific **Costing Method** and **Inventory Valuation** method. Make sure that you choose **Real Price** in the **Costing Method** and **Perpetual (automated)** in the **Inventory Valuation** field on the Product Internal Category. Look at the following screenshot for the detailed configuration:

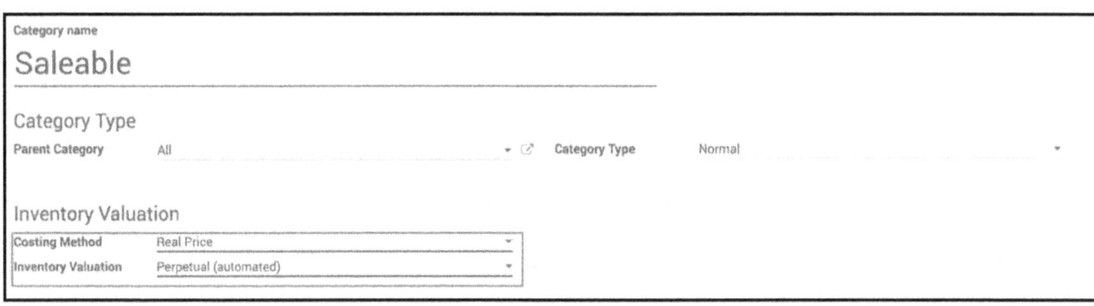

Products related to other categories that do not have **Real Price** in the **Costing Method** and **Perpetual (automated)** in the **Inventory Valuation** will not be included at the time of splitting the landed cost.

How to do it...

1. The landed cost feature can be activated by going to **Configuration** | **Settings** under the **Inventory** application:

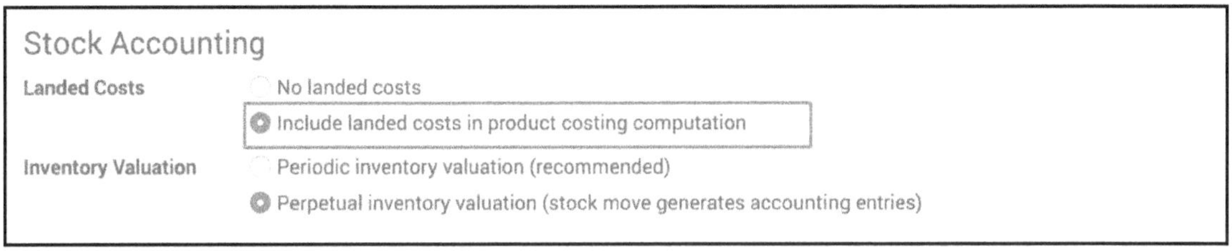

   Select the **Include landed costs in product costing computation** option for the **Landed Cost** field and click on the **APPLY** button to enable the feature.

2. Before we proceed with creating the landed cost, we require at least one **Landed Costs** product. The landed cost product can be created by going to **Inventory** | **Configuration** | **Warehouse Management** | **Landed Cost Type**.

   Create a new product by clicking on the **CREATE** button. Enter the appropriate **Name** such as `Domestic Carrier`, set **Product Type** to **Service**, and **Split Method** and **Cost** can be kept as they are, **Equal** and `0`, respectively. This can be changed at the time of splitting the landed cost:

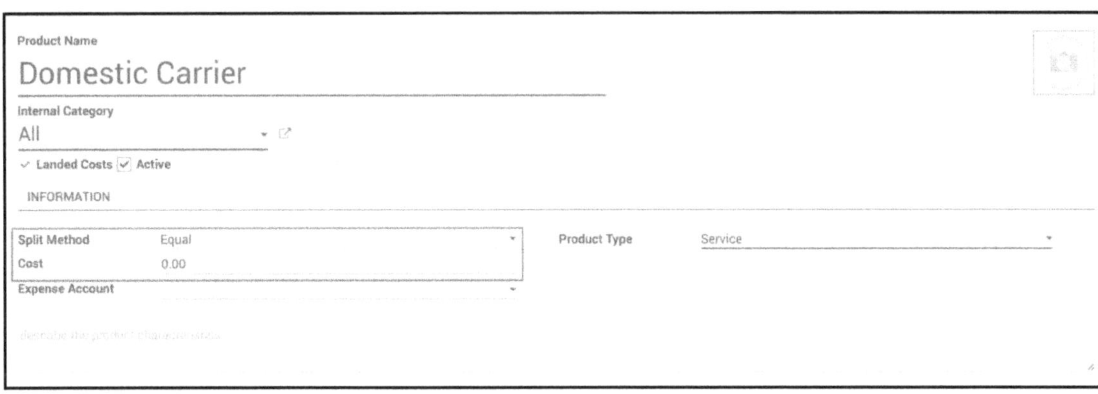

   The expense account can be set, or it will take the default expense account from the Product Internal Category at the time of splitting the landed cost.

3. You are ready to compute the **Landed Costs** before we move forward look at the product's configuration I have used in this example:

Product	**Purchase Price**	**Weight**	**Volume**
Material	70	2	4
Finished Product	60	4	2

Make sure that both the products are linked to the same category, with **Costing Method** is set to **Real Price** and **Inventory Valuation** is set to **Perpetual (automated)**.

Create a purchase order for a quantity of 100 Material and a quantity of 50 **Finished Product** and confirm the order.

4. You have an incoming shipment for the confirmed order, which was already processed at the reception. Look at the following screenshot of the processed incoming shipment:

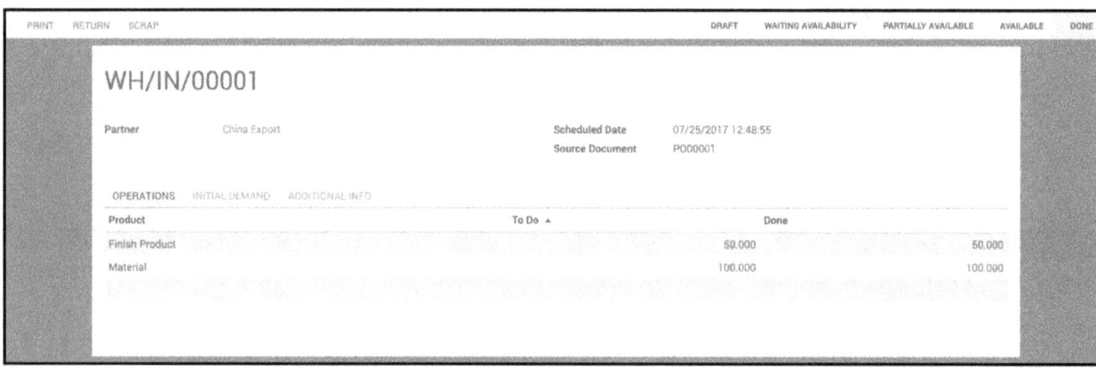

Also, look at the **Inventory Valuation** report. It has already computed the cost of the product and valuation based on it:.

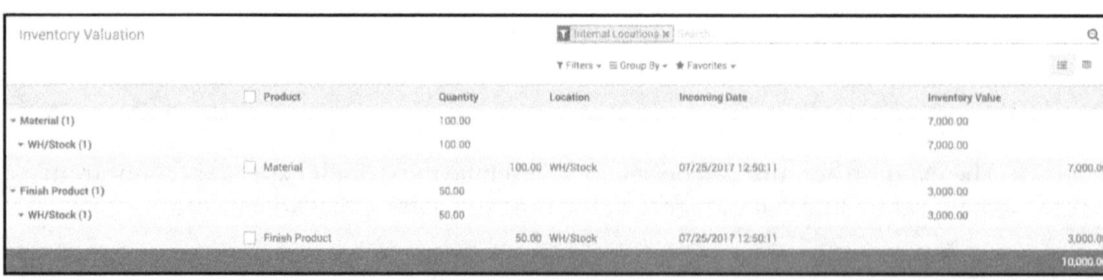

5. The carrier service provider comes up with the transportation bill at the reception, that has to be paid and registered as an expense. Also, it should be added to the product cost. Go to the Landed costs through **Inventory | Inventory Control | Landed Costs** and create a new landing cost by clicking on the **CREATE** button. Select the **Pickings**, in this case, **WH/IN/00001** and, set the **Accounting journal** to *Stock Journal*:.

   Cost Lines has to be created manually, click on **Add an Item**, select the Product Domestic Carrier (other fields will be filled automatically) set the **Split Method** to *By quantity* and enter the total cost incurred for the transportation, assuming it is **500**:

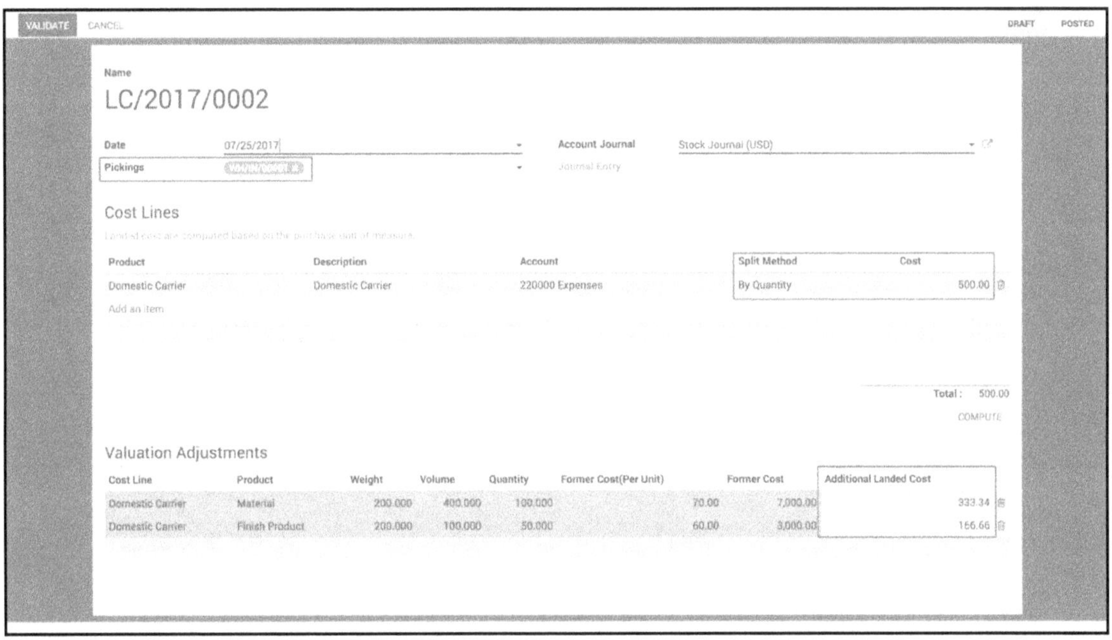

The **Cost Lines** has to be created manually. Click on **Add an Item**, select the **Product, Domestic Carrier** (other fields will be filled automatically), set **Split Method** to **By quantity**, and enter the total cost incurred for the transportation, assuming it was **500**.

As soon as you ready with the **Cost Lines**, click on the **COMPUTE** button, it will compute the cost by the selected method and **Valuation Adjustments** line will be created as a result.

> The cost entered on the Landed cost form, is the total cost of the logistics. The split method computes the cost based on the selected splitting method.

6. The accounting entry will be created in *Stock Journal* as soon as the Landed Cost will be validated by clicking on the **VALIDATE** button. It debited the inventory valuation and credited the expense. Look at the following accounting entry:

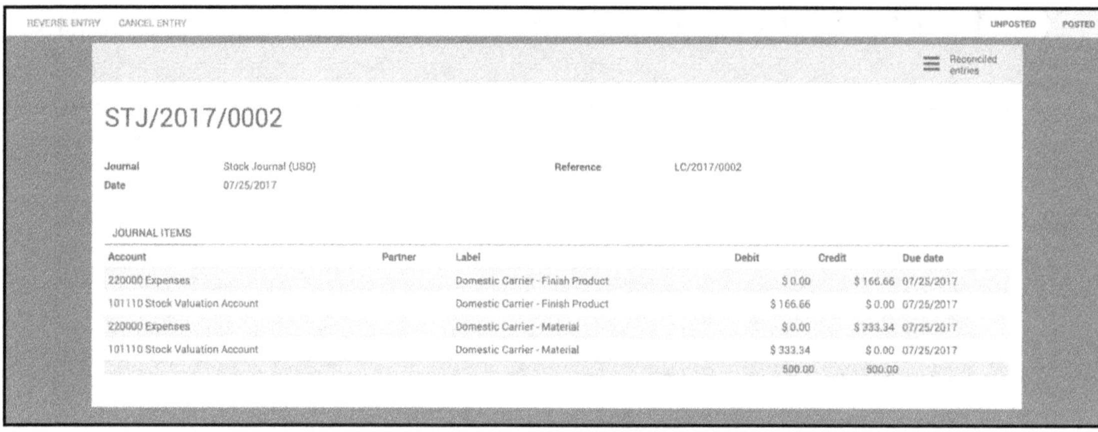

The inventory value also gets increased in Warehouse. Look at the **Inventory Valuation** report shown here:

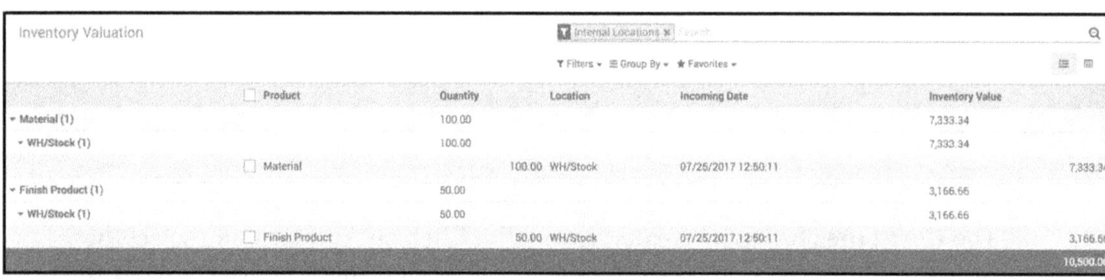

> When Purchase UoM is different from the UoM, the landed cost will be calculated based on Purchase UoM, and **Inventory Valuation** will be displayed based on the default UoM.

7. As soon as the landed cost is applied to the existing stock, along with the inventory, the balance sheet also gets updated. Check the **Profit and Loss** account. It should be credited to the **Expense** account, which shows that we have to process the payment:

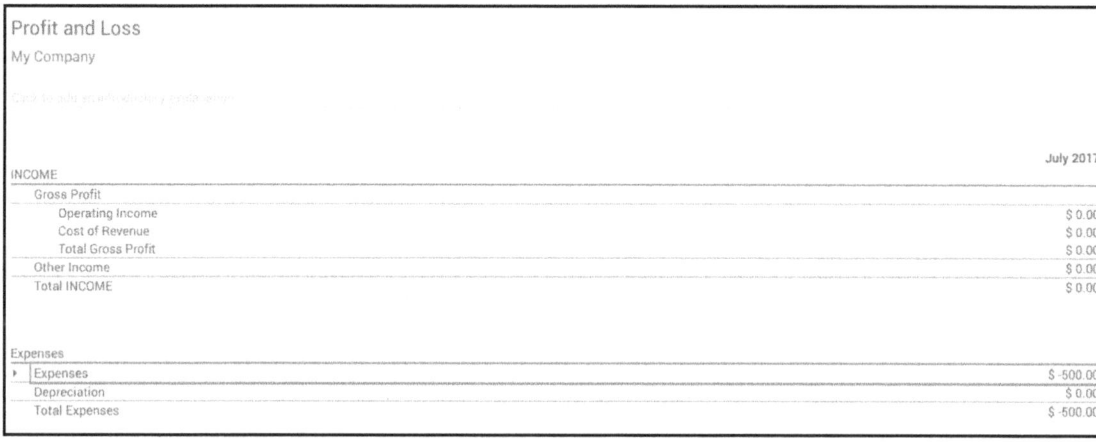

8. The next step is either to make the payment, or if the payment is to be processed by check or bank transfer, it has to be credited to the supplier account. Let's assume that it is a small amount paid by cash. The following entry has to be passed to the books of accounts:

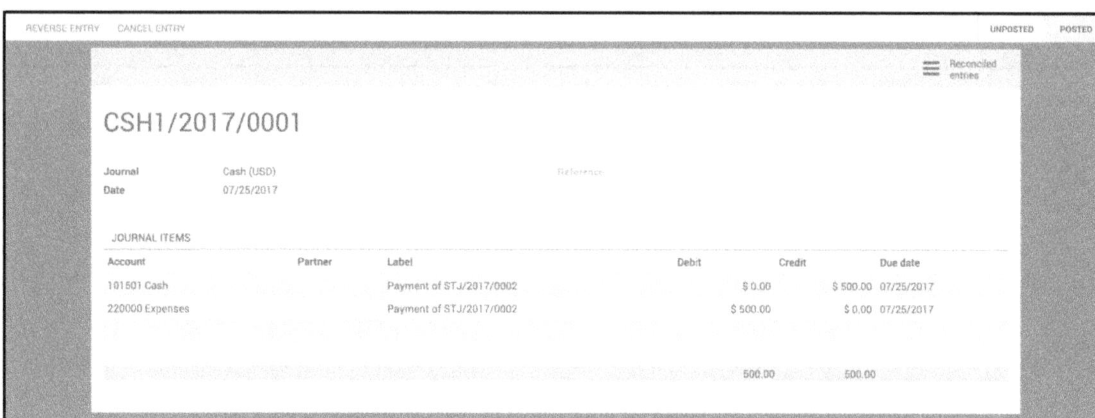

Finally, the **Expenses** account in your Profit and Loss statement will be set to **zero**. As and when we sell the product, the end entry for the cost of product will be created, which includes the cost of product plus the cost of transportation.

The payment entry for the landing cost has to be paid manually. However, there is no automation for processing the payments of the landing cost.

Using the landed cost feature, the cost of the transportation can be divided between the different products by quantity, weight, or volume.It will also create an accounting entry to register the transportation expense, and also increase the inventory valuation.

How it works...

The landing cost methods compute the splitting of costs between different products, or by quantity, weight, or volume. The correct methods have to be chosen to split the cost among the products and quantity.

Let's see an example with two products listed here:

Product	Purchase Price	Weight	Volume
Material	70	2	4
Finished Product	60	4	2

Let's assume that we have the **Purchase Order** as shown here, then confirm the order is created, confirmed and the delivery order is confirmed; process the incoming shipment:

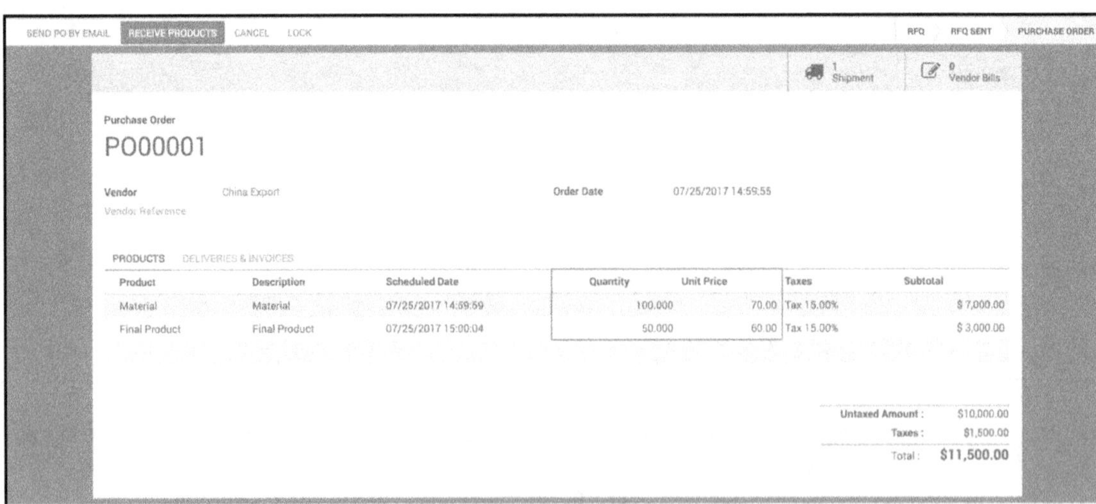

Let's check how the landed cost is split and will be computed using different methods.

Equal method

The equal split method divides the cost between different products available at the time of cost splitting. The total cost will be divided among the number of different products available:

The total cost of 500 will be divided between two products equally--250 per product. Then it will be allocated per quantity. The inventory valuation will look like this:

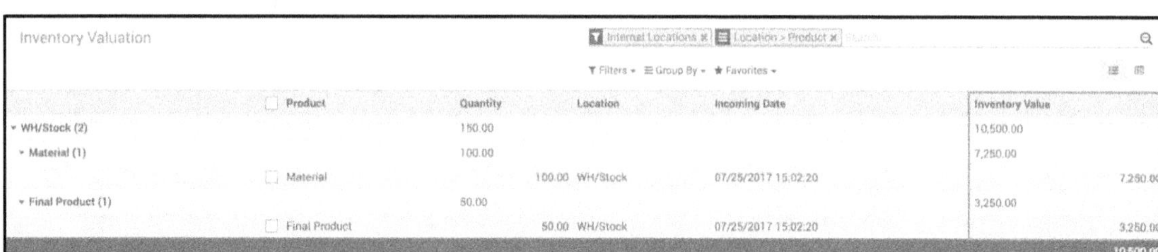

The cost per one quantity will be computed in inventory to compute the cost price. It will look like this:

Product	Rate	Qty	By Method	Cost/Qty
Material	70	100	250	72.50
Finished Product	50	50	250	65

By Quantity

The **By Quantity** method divides the total cost proportionate to the total quantity of products available on the **Value Adjustment** lines. Look at the following screenshot to understand how it divides between a quantity of 100 Material and a quantity of 50 final products:

The total cost of 500 will be divided between two products at equally--250 per product. Then, it will be allocated per quantity. The inventory valuation will be look like this:

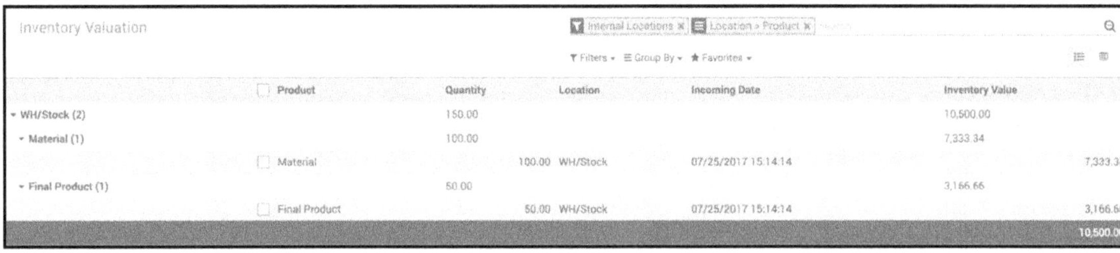

The cost per one quantity will be computed in the inventory to compute the cost price. It will look like this:

Product	Rate	Qty	By Method	Cost/Qty
Material	70	100	333.34	73.33
Finished Product	50	50	166.66	63.33

By Current Cost

The **By Current Cost** method divides the total cost proportionate to the former cost of products available on the **Value Adjustment** lines. Look at the following screenshot to understand how it divides between the 7,000 former cost of the Material and the 300 former cost of the final products:

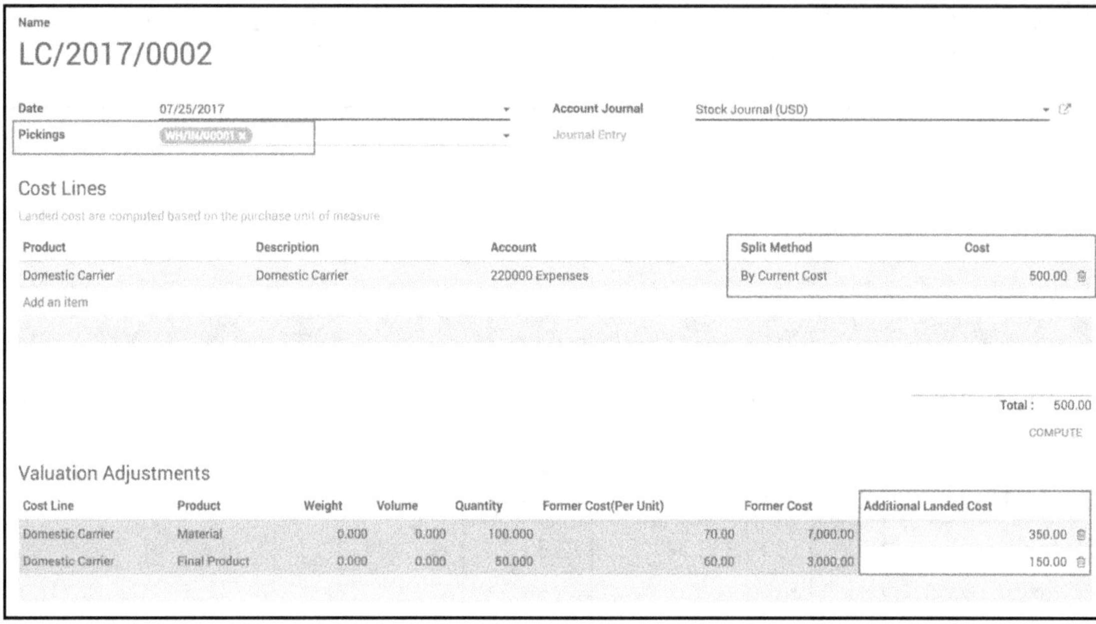

The total cost of 500 will be divided between the products equally 250 per product. Then, it will be allocated per quantity. The inventory valuation will be look like this:

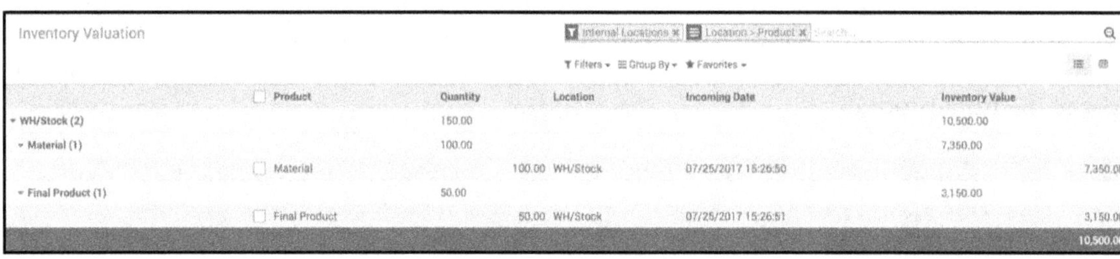

The cost per one quantity will be computed in the inventory to compute the cost price. It will look like this:

Product	Rate	Qty	By Method	Cost/Qty
Material	70	100	350	73.50
Finished Product	50	50	150	63

Likewise, you can check out the other two methods, **By Weight** and **By Volume**. Configure the **Weight** and **Volume** fields in the product **INVENTORY** tab:

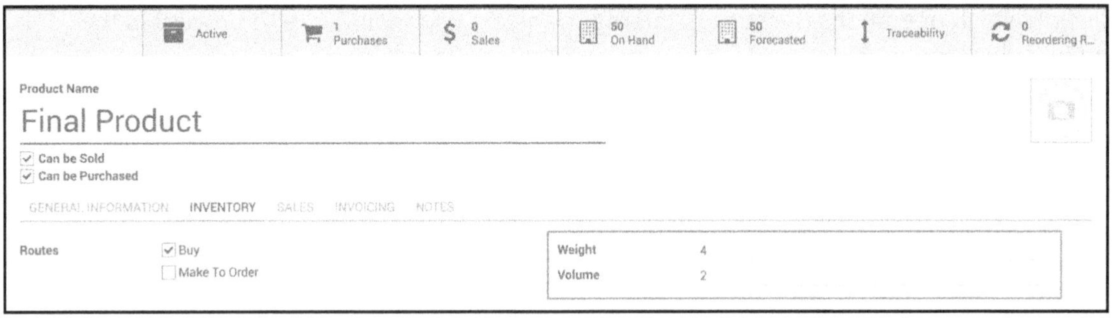

Quality control in Warehouse

Checking the quality of the products at the reception is a standard practice in Warehouse management. Manufacturing plants check the quality of the material when it is assigned from the Warehouse for the consumption, so the quality check is not only limited to the incoming shipment at the reception, but it is important internally too.

Quality control is not only limited to checking the quality of manufactured products; it should find the defects in raw material and initiate the return process and scrap it if not in warranty period. It should also identify the root cause of the problem and resolve the issue that initiated the quality issue. The solution may be to change the supplier or change the product specification.

Quality application in Odoo is an independent yet integrated application within Warehouse and manufacturing. It can be used with manufacturing or just integrated with Warehouse to check the quality of the incoming shipment or to check the quality of the internal transfers. Quality alerts can be generated for the issues that are found frequently. The goal is to identify the root cause and solve the quality issue permanently.

Let's see how to activate the feature and set up the quality check at different operations in Warehouse.

Getting ready

Make sure you are ready with the list of products and quality checks related to it. Also, decide which operations (reception, internal transfer) you would like to process in the quality check.

How to do it...

1. The quality control application can be activated by going to **Settings** under the **Inventory** application. It is an extra feature of the Inventory application:

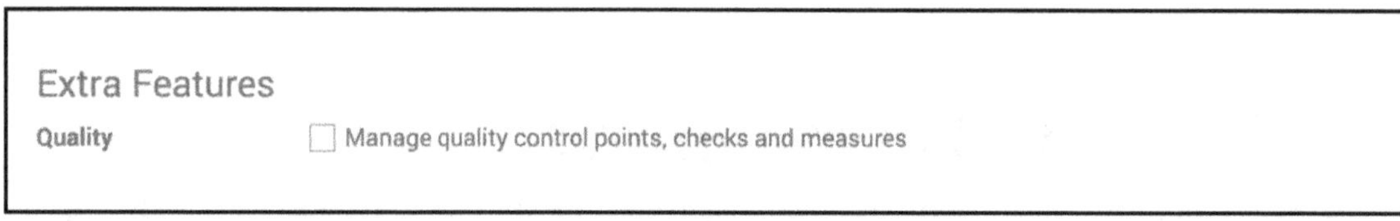

   Select the feature and click on the **APPLY** button to activate it. You will get a new application called **Quality** on your home screen.

2. Like other Odoo applications, the **Quality** application also has its own dashboard. The list of the quality team will appear on the dashboard. The quality team actually processes the quality checks and either passes or fails the product. They also work on quality alerts to identify the root cause of the problems:

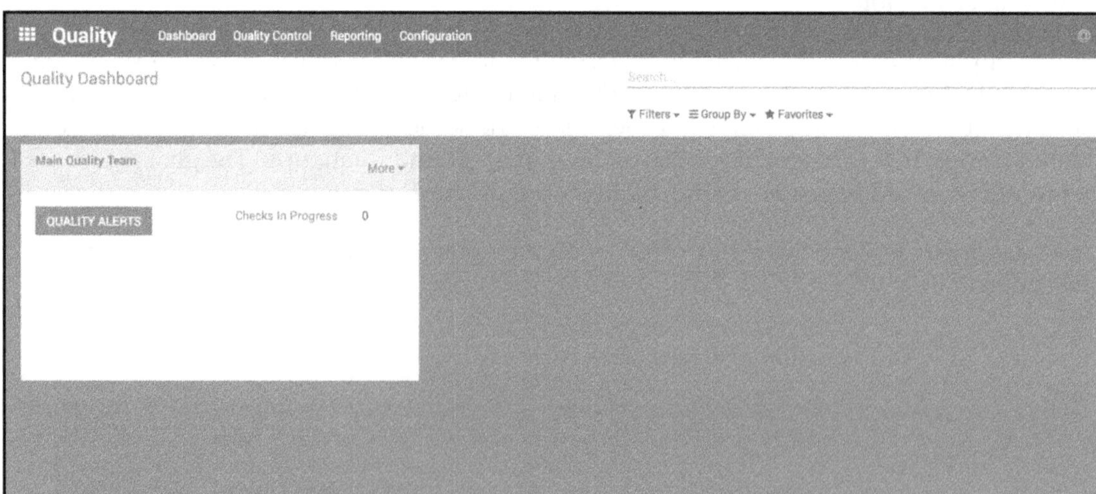

Each team has their own quality alerts to work on, and **Checks in Progress** can be tracked on each team.

3. The quality point has to be configured. To set up the quality control, go to **Quality Control** | **Quality Points** and create a new quality point. The form will look like this:

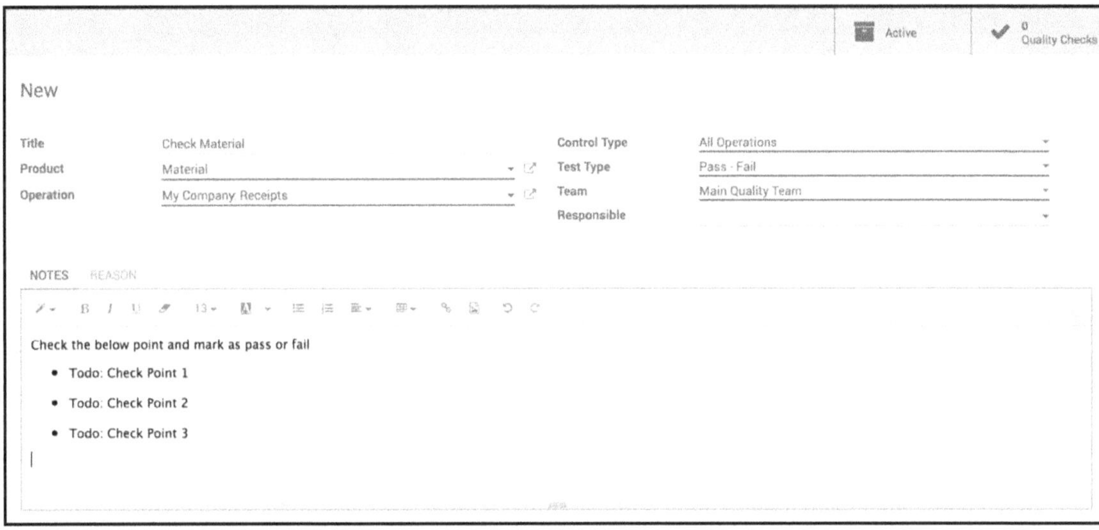

Enter the other details as follows:

- **Title**: The name of the quality check
- **Product**: The product that has to be checked
- **Operation**: Select one from **Reception**, **Delivery**, or **Internal Transfer**
- **Control Type**: How frequently the quality has been checked; select anyone from **All Operations**, **Randomly**, or **Periodically**.
- **Test Type**: The test type can be either pass/fail based on the measure
- **Quality Team**: Select the team that has to perform the quality check

4. The quality has been activated for the **Material** product at the reception. Any incoming shipment having a **Material** product cannot be processed until the quality team performs the check:

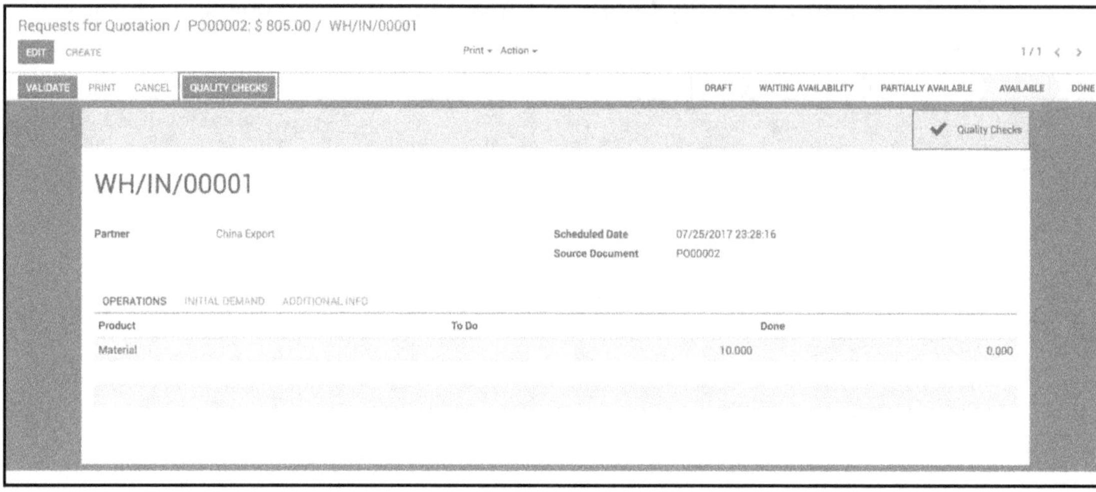

The quality check will be created automatically for incoming shipment if there is **Material** coming at the reception. By clicking on the **QUALITY CHECKS** button, you will be prompted for the quality check instructions and asked for the result. You can click on the **Quality Checks** action button to see the list of checks to be performed for the **Material** product.

We can create multiple checkpoints for the same products in the same operation. For example, **Material** can be tested at reception by different teams for different quality tests.

5. The quality check team starts checking the **Material** and marks it either **PASS** or **FAIL**:

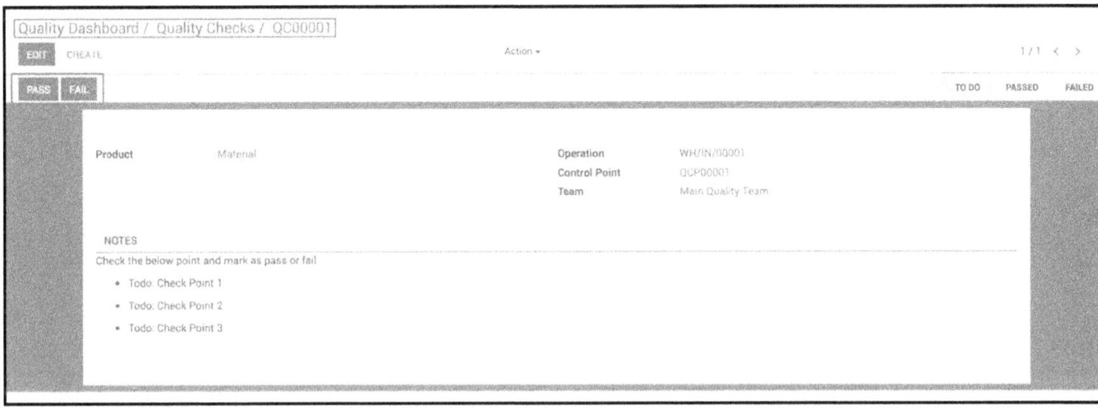

Take the sample and check the quality. If it passes, click on the **PASS** button to mark it as pass, or if it doesn't, then click on **FAIL** to mark it as fail.

6. As soon as the quality team processes the incoming shipment at the reception and the product passes the quality check, it can be received in the Warehouse:

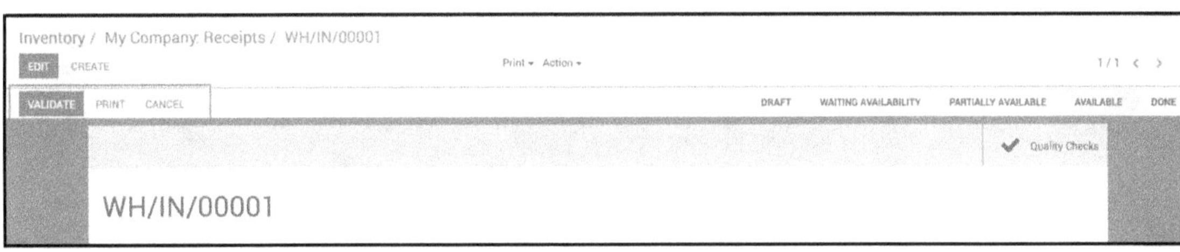

The incoming shipment has to be rejected manually at the reception if the quality check fails.

7. If the quality check fails, it can be marked as failed by clicking on the **FAIL** button. If the quality issue is frequent, a quality alert can be raised from the quality check itself:

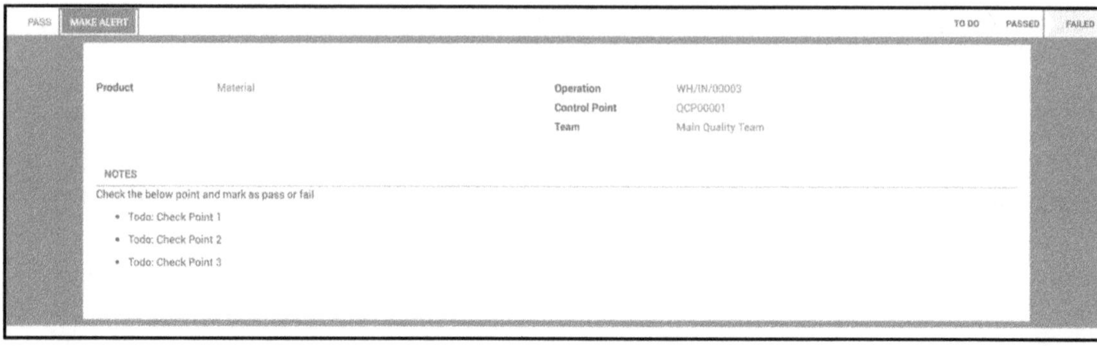

8. Click on the **QUALITY ALERT** button to raise a quality alert. It will create an alert for the **Main Quality Team**:

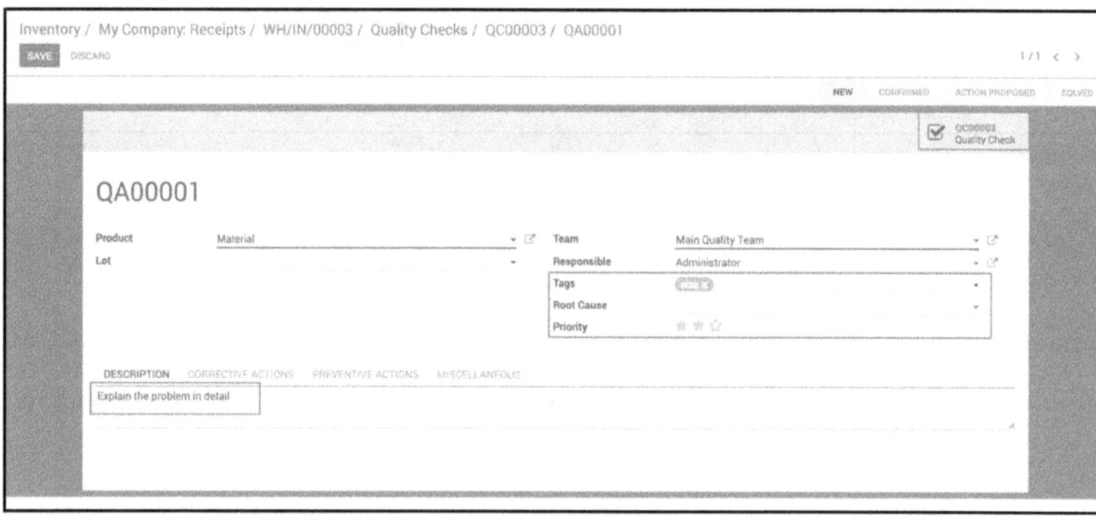

Explain the problem in the description. Set the tags, if any, and set the priority depending on the need. The quality check document also links from where the alert was created.

9. The quality team actually starts working on the alert. First, they qualify the problem and start the investigation to identify the root cause. Look at the following screenshot of the quality alert pipe, where multiple quality alerts are being processed:

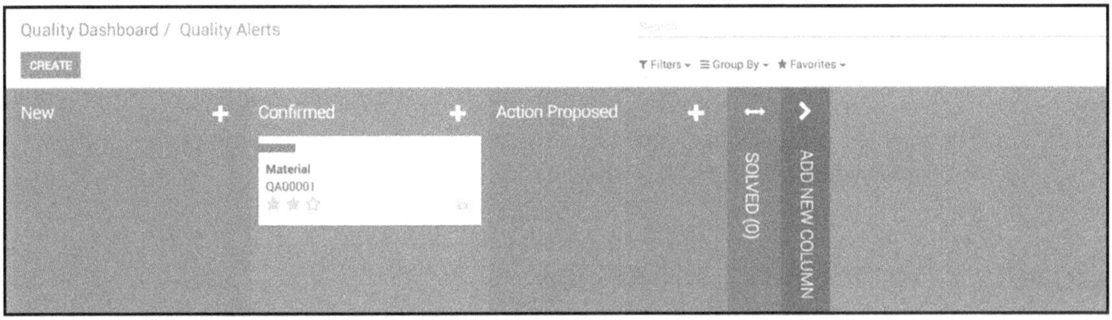

10. As soon as the root cause is identified, the team or individual sets the **Root Cause** on the alert and describes the solution that has to be taken by the purchasing office at the time of purchasing the material:

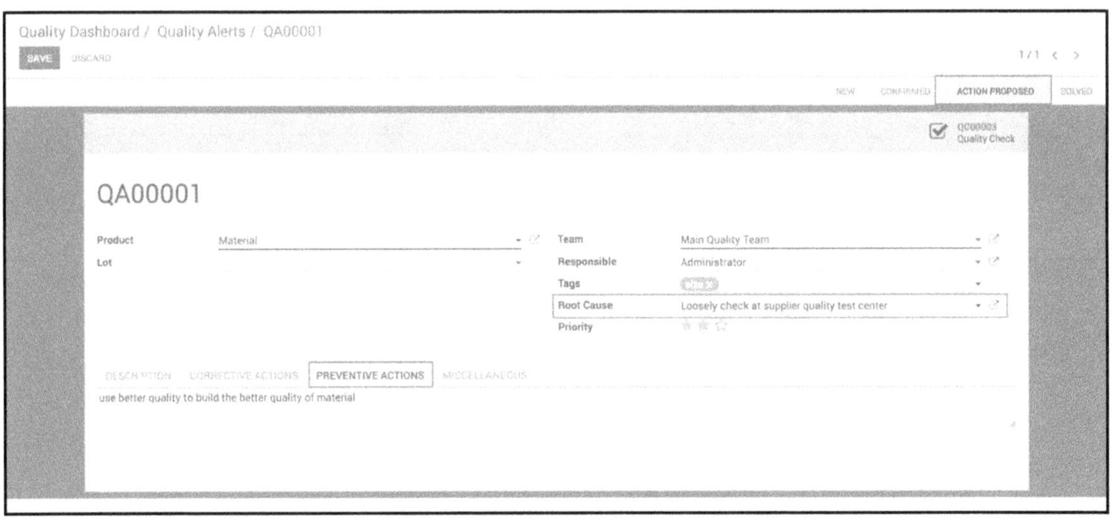

The alert can be marked as **Solved** or **Action Proposed**.

There's more...

A quality check results in either **PASS** or **FAIL**. Material can be accepted either if quality check PASSED or even with an exception. If it FAILED, the decision has to be taken with manual interruption. Odoo will not force you to return the product or reject the incoming shipment.

However, we can process the return of the product manually if it failed at the reception, or we do not have a choice other than scrapping the product if the warranty has passed. Let's see how we can set the quality check based on the measure and process the return and scrapping of product in Inventory when the quality check fails.

Quality check using measure

The quality check is not only limited to the **PASS** or **FAIL**. It can be based on the measure where you can define the normal value which is acceptable from minimum to maximum tolerance:

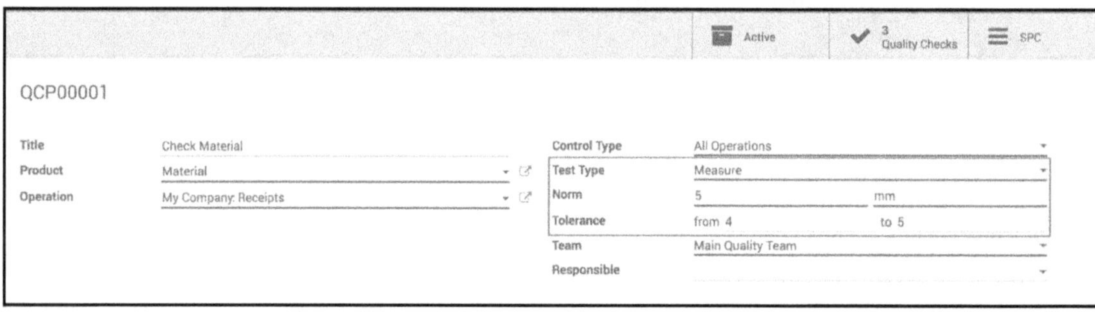

At the quality checks, it will prompt for the measurement, as soon as the measurement is entered after the check, it checks if it is normal. If equal, it will be marked as **PASS:**

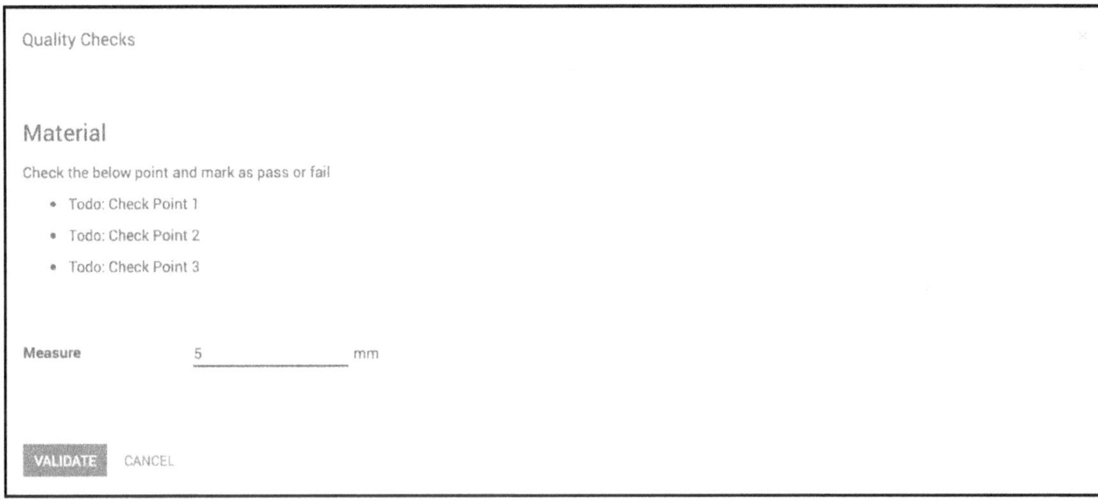

If it is not equal to the normal, it checks whether it is in-between the acceptable tolerance value or not, and the quality will be marked accordingly. In this case, it is marked as **PASS**. Look at the following quality check screen:

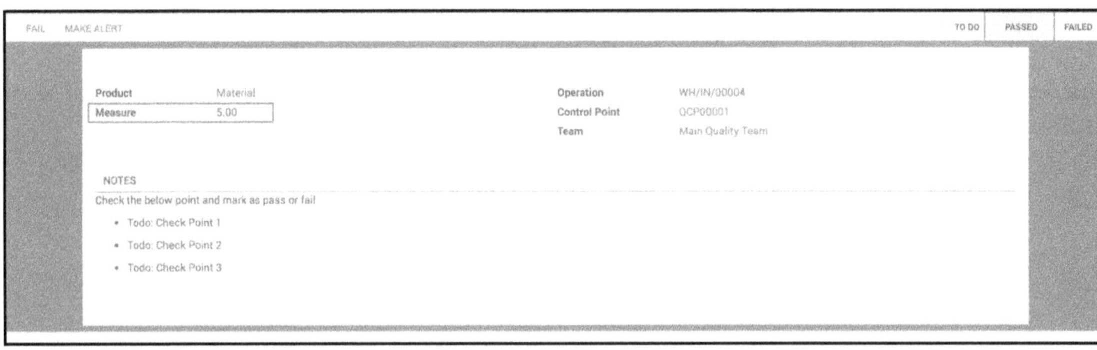

Return product

Every operation can be reverted in the Warehouse by initiating the return process; either it's a reception or it can be a delivery order and both can be returned.

Let's take an example of incoming shipment. As soon as the incoming shipment is processed, the **RETURN** button will appear on the picking. By clicking on that, the return process can be initiated; look at the following screenshot:

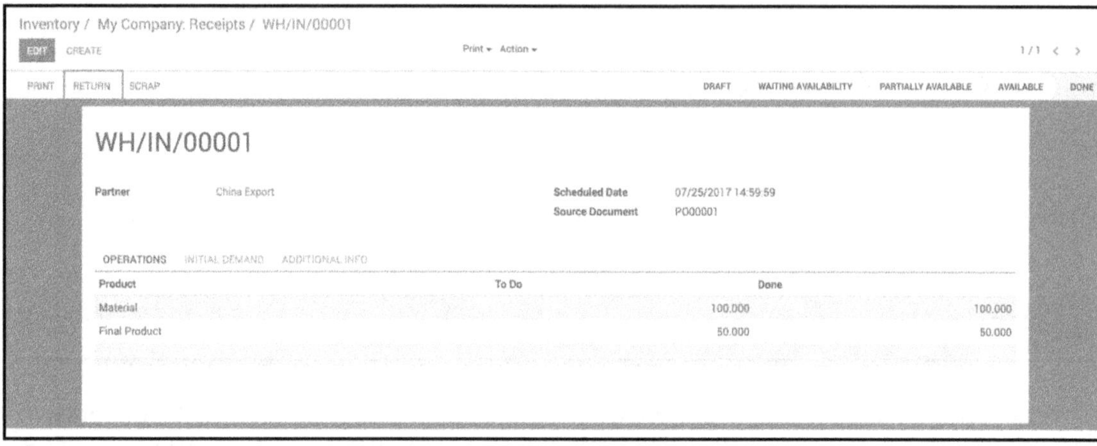

Click on the **RETURN** button to initiate the return process. It will initiate the return process and a popup will allow you to choose what you want to return. Look at the following screenshot:

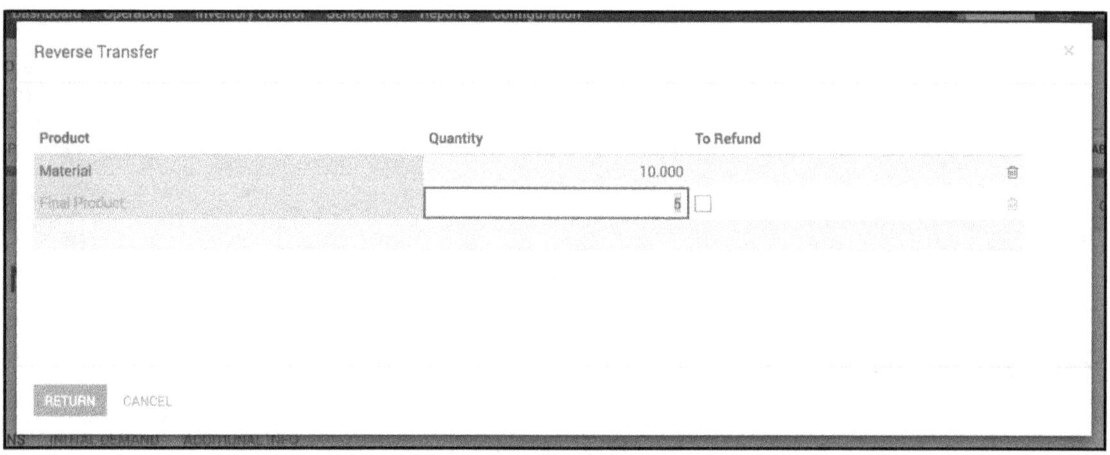

You have to enter the quantity that will be returned. If the vendor bill has not been paid, untick the **To Refund** check box; otherwise, you can select it. However, the refund of the invoice has to be processed manually. Click on the **RETURN** button. It will create the shipment for the return. Look at the following screenshot of return picking:

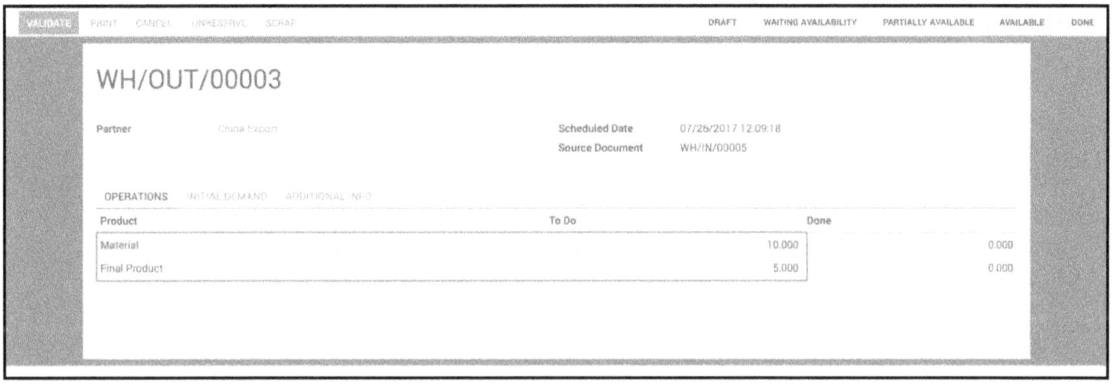

Verify the return picking and click on the **VALIDATE** button to process the return picking. This will decrease the stock in the Warehouse and transfer it to the vendor location. It will update the stock valuation in the inventory and in the balance sheet if the inventory valuation is kept automated.

12
Setup your Manufacturing Process

In this chapter, we will cover the following recipes:

- Completing the first manufacturing order
- Configuring the assembly line and work centers
- Master production schedules
- Sale combo products using kit

Introduction

Businesses evolve every year, but not business software. As a result, today you can see software that is too complex, too rigid in nature, and which requires lots of training to start working with. For those who don't know about the RP process and department, take a look at the following table to see what the documents managed by various departments are, and the software that helps to manage them:

Department	Document	Software to manage it
Engineering	Bill of Material	PLM
Manufacturing-Engineering	Work-center and Routing	MRP
Manufacturing	Manufacturing Order or Work Order	MRP
Quality	Quality checkpoints and Checks	Maintenance
Maintenance	Requests	Maintenance

Supply Chain	Purchase Order	ERP
Inventory	Reception and Delivery	ERP
After Sales	Issue	Helpdesk

The manufacturing process involves a lot of different processes like engineering, manufacturing, quality, maintenance, logistics, supply chain, and so on. There are so many people who have to work together, and you need a good software that communicates with them. The key to success in the manufacturing industry is how efficiently you can make these people work together.

A small change needs the engagement of different people and strong communication between them. Imagine that your manufacturing process has a set up with the following software infrastructure, where each business process is managed with a different software, and they are not connected well:

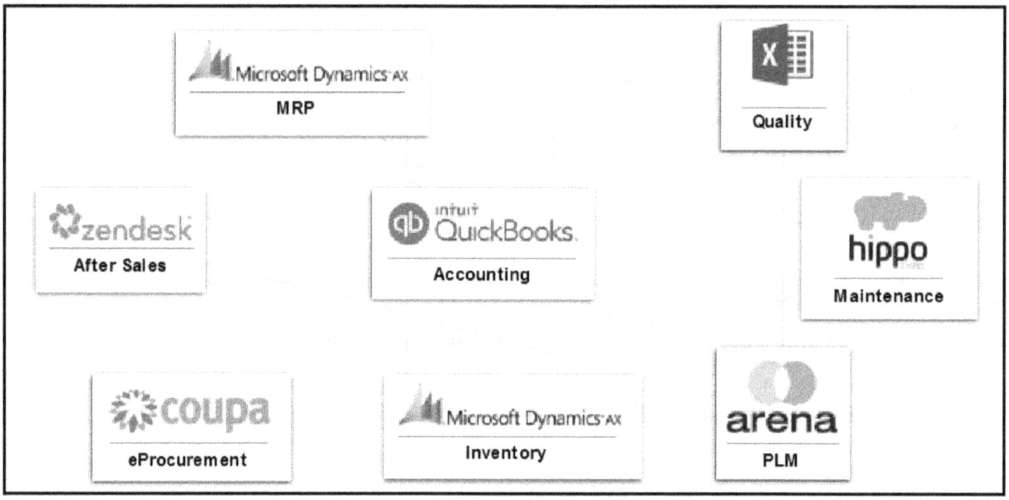

If we have an engineering change in order, this requires the computation of BOM, which has to verify the manufacturing engineering, purchase, logistics, and quality.

Odoo has a single software for all your needs, which is easy and powerful. It helps manage various processes like Engineering, Manufacturing Engineering, Manufacturing, Supply chain, Quality, and Maintenance. You don't need to integrate all those apps, as they are part of Odoo and well integrated.

Let's see how the manufacturing process can be set up with the Odoo Manufacturing module that helps to manage the manufacturing process, which is well integrated with other core business activities such as sales, purchase, accounting, and inventory.

Complete the first manufacturing order

The Odoo manufacturing application is fully integrated with sales and inventory applications—like the other stockable products, the manufactured products can be stocked in an inventory, or it can be manufactured on demand. Let's see an example of on-demand manufactured products, where the manufacturing starts as and when we confirm the sales.

Let's manufacture the Computer Desk. To build the desk, we need four lags, a desktop, and some bolts for the fittings; we will build the desk on demand.

Getting ready

It is assumed that you understand the difference between components, finished products, and semi-finished products and that we need to prepare the bill of material for each manufactured product.

How to do it...

1. Unlike the other Odoo main applications such as Sales, Purchase, Accounting, and Inventory, **Manufacturing** is a major application. The **Manufacturing** application can be installed from the apps.

2. As soon as the **Manufacturing** application is installed, you can see the application icon on the home screen of your instance. By clicking on the icon, you will enter into the application, and you will get the list of manufacturing orders.

3. The product that we are going to manufacture is a **Computer Desk**. Let's create the **Computer Desk** as a manufactured product, and configure the raw material of the desk as the components.

4. On the **INVENTORY** tab, select **Make to Order** on **Routes**.
5. Click on Bill of Material; you will be redirected to the bill of the material list created for the **Computer Desk**. Click on the **CREATE** button to create a bill of the material.

   Computer Desk will be selected in the **Product** field, the **Quantity** field will be set to one, which indicates that one quantity of **Computer Desk** can be made up with the raw materials listed in the **COMPONENTS** list.

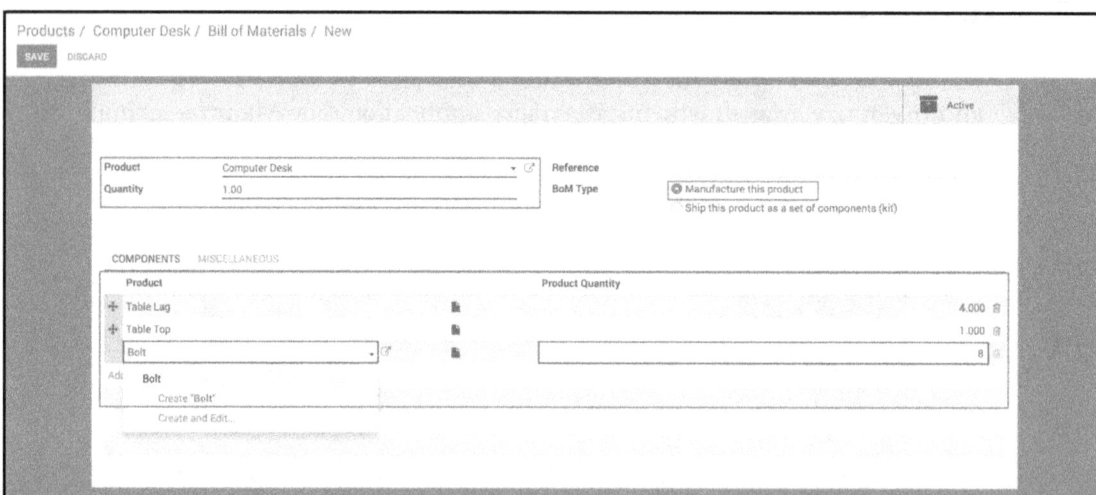

You now have to create the components for the **Computer Desk**—enter the name of the component (**Bolt** in this case), and select the option **Create "Bolt"** in the list. All the components have to be listed on the bill of material. Those components will be used to manufacture the **Computer Desk**. The default configuration will be set to the type of Stockable Product, and **Buy** will be the default routs selected for all the components created directly on the bill of material.

6. As we maintain sufficient stock, let's assume that the stock of all the required components is available in the inventory. Look at the inventory of the components in the following screenshot:

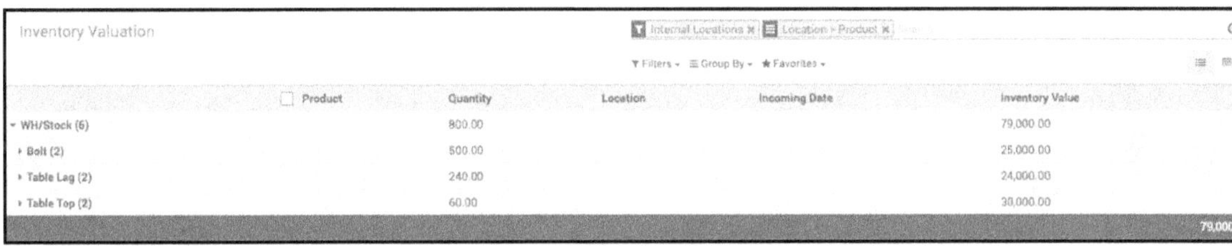

7. The configuration has been compiled; we are now ready to sell the **Computer Desk**, so create the sales order for the **Computer Desk**.

Look at the preceding screenshot. It shows that the order has been confirmed and delivery order created and is waiting for the **Computer Desk** to be produced.

8. Now it's time to start the production for the **Computer Desk**. Let's go to the **Manufacturing** application; you will find the manufacturing order created automatically. The **Source** field contains **SO002:WH: Stock -> CustomersMTO**, which indicates that the order has been created from the sales order **SO002**.

Click on the **CHECK AVAILABILITY** button on the manufacturing order, as we have already purchased and received the raw material; the manufacturing order now goes to the **CONFIRMED** stage, and it will be ready to be produced.

9. The manufacturing process can be started by clicking on the **PRODUCE** button. A popup will appear asking you to enter the quantity that is currently in production:

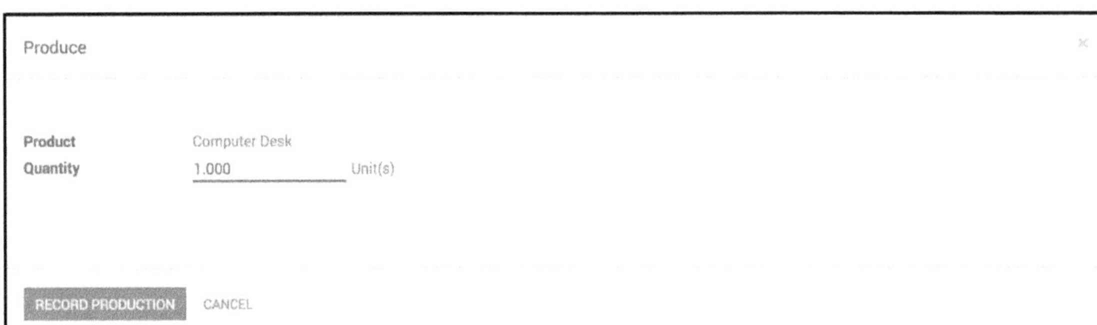

Click on the **RECORD PRODUCTION** button to start the production on one quantity of **Computer Desk**; the raw material will be marked as consumed on the **CONSUMED MATERIALS** tab:

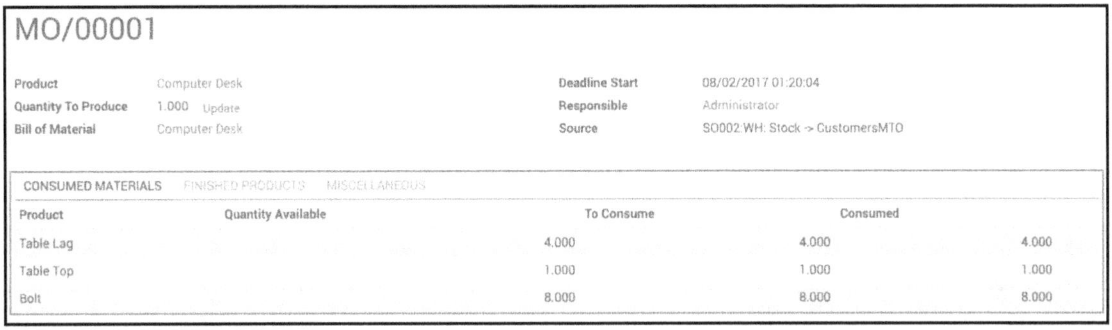

In the **FINISHED PRODUCTS** tab, you can see that one table is going to be produced upon the completion of this manufacturing process:

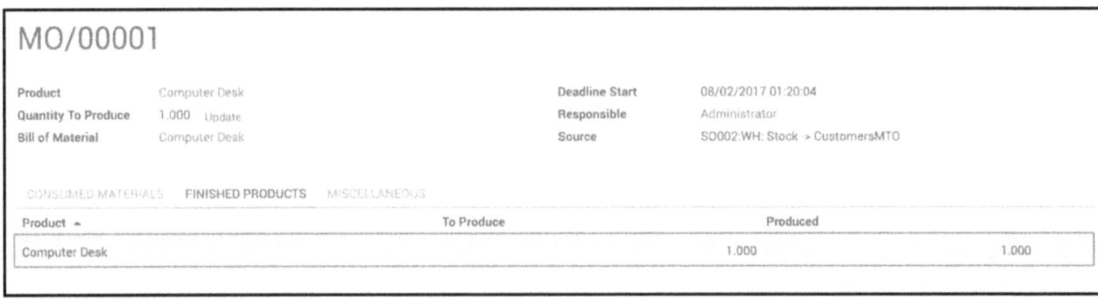

10. Finally, click on the **MARK AS DONE** button to record the production as completed; it will transfer the produced **Computer Desk** to the warehouse:

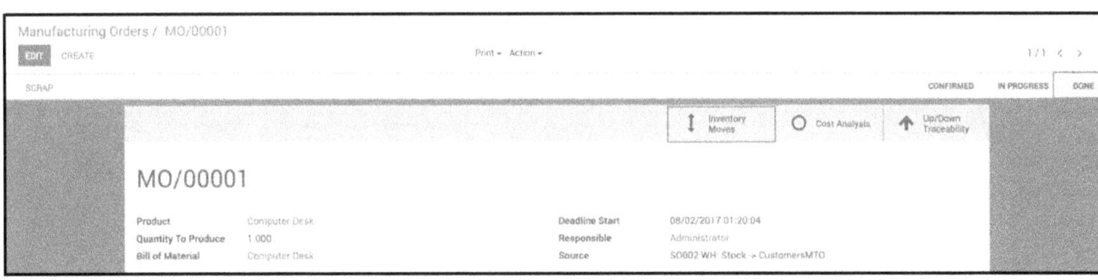

The movement of the material and final product can be tracked from the **Inventory Movement**. Look at the next screenshot of the inventory movement:

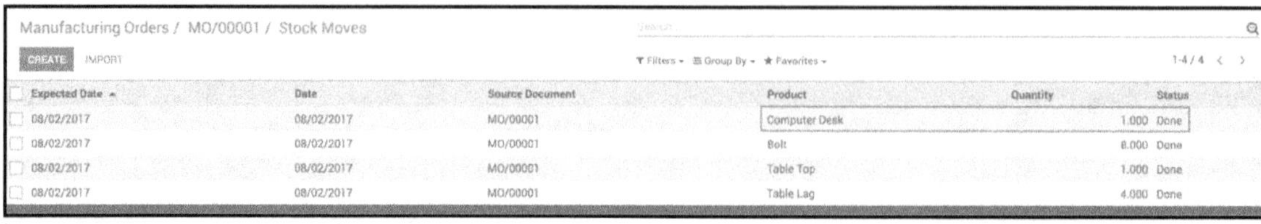

By clicking on the **Up/Down** Traceability action button on the manufacturing order, you can track the movement of the raw material and the finished product related to that manufacturing order, as shown in this screenshot:

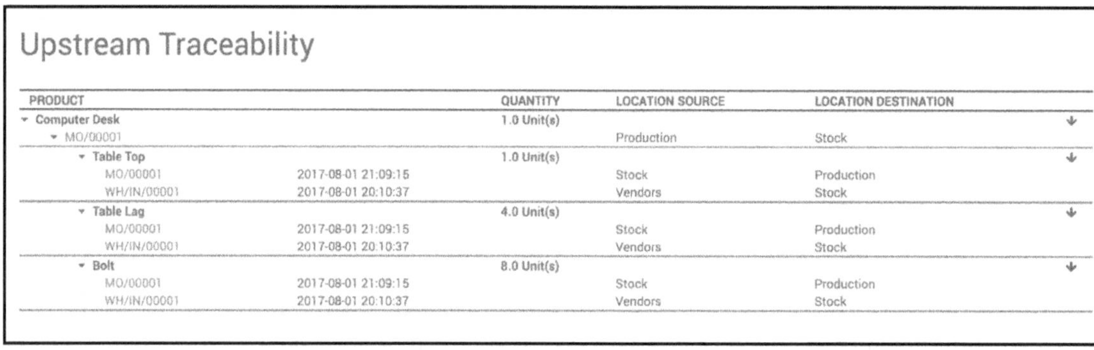

11. Go to the **Sales** order SO002 under the sales application, and go to the delivery order. The **Computer Desk** will be assigned from the stock which was just produced and will be ready for delivery:

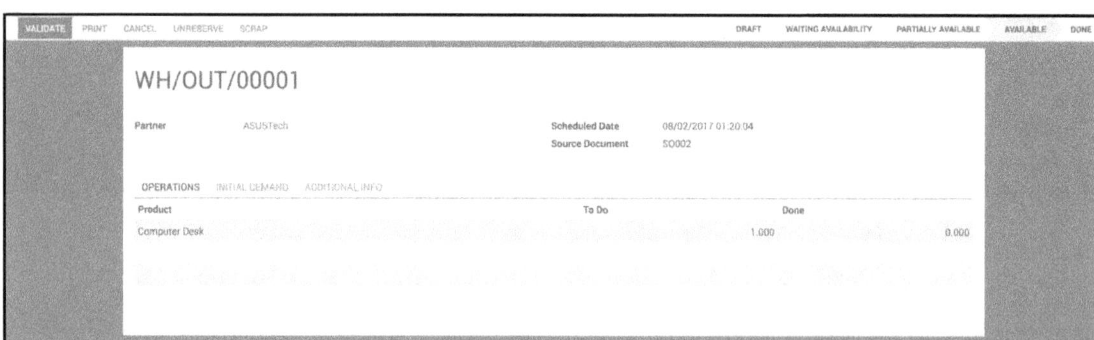

Process the delivery order by clicking on the **VALIDATE** button. Finally, we have delivered the **Computer Desk**, which was produced on demand.

> The Manufacturing order can be created manually, or based on the reorder level with minimum and maximum quantity. This will automatically trigger the manufacturing order for the specific number of **Computer Desks** to be produced.

How it works...

Various configurations are involved in setting up and running the manufacturing unit, and in processing the first successful manufacturing order. To process the first successful manufacturing order, you need to configure the correct configuration for the following:

- Product (Components and Finished Product): Routes, reorder level, vendor of components
- Bill of Material: Composition of the products in order to build the finished product

Procurement

Each demand generated in Odoo creates procurement. The routes defined for the product decides the procurement flow, and the Make to Order decides whether we should first check the stock or not.

We have already gone through the **Buy** and **Make to Order** routes in `Chapter 9`, *Purchase Management* in the recipe *Complete purchase cycle*. Manufacturing is the new route enabled when the manufacturing application is installed in an instance.

The **Manufacture** route can be used either alone to define the product manufactured, or it can be used with the **Make to Order** route to automatically trigger the **Manufacturing** order as and when we have a demand.

Look at the following screenshot of the **Routes** configuration for the **Computer Desk** product:

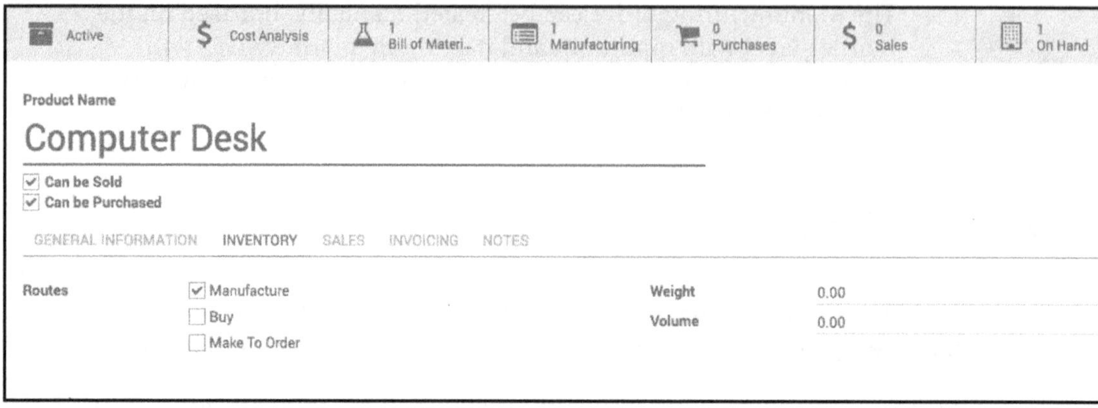

The **Manufacture** route is enabled; it defines that the product has to be produced through the manufacturing process, as only the **Manufacture** route is selected. It specifies that we may have the stock of **Computer Desk** produced from continuous manufacturing, or based on the order point defined for **Computer Desk**. Look at this screenshot of an order point for **Computer Desk**:

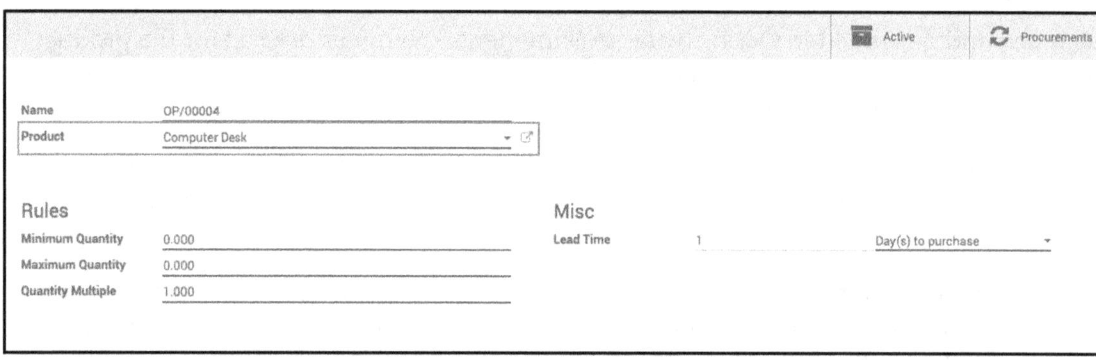

The order point is set to zero for the **Minimum** and **Maximum** quantity, which means that it will create the procurement for the demanded quantity only. If you would like to maintain the stock of **Computer Desk**, it is recommended to set the **Minimum** and **Maximum** quantity on the order point; the maximum quantity of the reorder level will be your batch size.

For this example, it is recommended to select the routes **Manufacturing** and **Make to Order** if you do not maintain the stock of **Computer Desk**.

Look at the following table to understand how manufacturing order triggers depending on the configuration—the scheduler creates the manufacturing order, considering the reorder level or **Make to Order**:

Manufacturing	Make to Order	Order Point	Demand	Trigger
True	False	Min: 0 Max: 0	3	Create a manufacturing order of a quantity of 3
True	False	Min: 5 Max: 10	2	Create a manufacturing order of a quantity of 10
True	True	Min: 5 Max: 10	3	Create a manufacturing order of a quantity of 10

In our case, **Computer Desk** is set to **Manufacturing** and **Make to Order**, which means that it will directly create the manufacturing order for the demanded quantity, and not consider the order point minimum and maximum quantity to maintain. We will go through the **Master Production Schedule** (**MPS**) in a later part of this chapter, where the procurements for the production and purchases will be triggered by the Master Production Schedule.

Bill of Materials

The bill of material defines the list of components to be used to manufacture the finished product; in our case, the finished product is **Computer Desk**, and the components are **Table Top**, **Table Lag**, and **Bolt**. The bill of material can be accessed from **Manufacturing** | **Master Data** | **Bill of Materials**. Have a look at the bill of material for Computer Desk in the following screenshot:

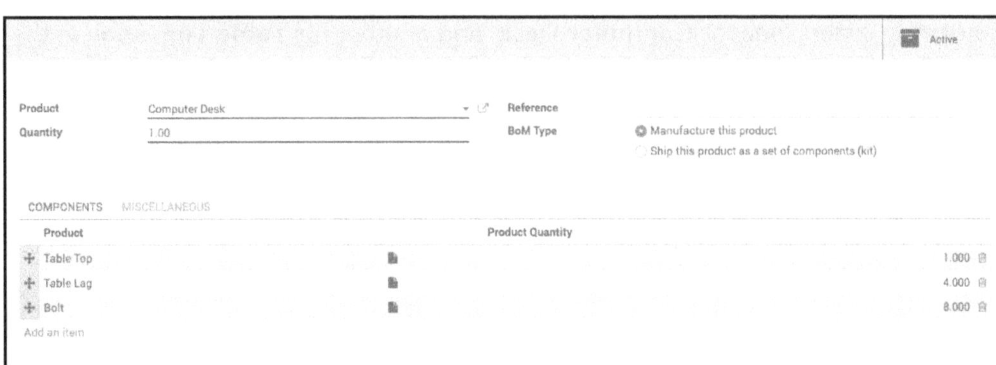

To produce one quantity of **Computer Desk**, we need components that are listed on the **COMPONENTS** tab.

It may be possible that the components are manufacturing products; such components are called semi-finished products. For example, to provide a configurable **Table Top**, we start manufacturing the **Table Top** ourself, depending on the requirement, and then the semi-finished component will be used to produce the **Computer Desk**.

We should first create the bill of material for **Table Top** by adding the **Wooden Sheet** and **Color Laminate** as a component on it, and later, the **Table Top** can be used as a component in the **Computer Desk** bill of material:

BOM Structure

BOM Name	Quantity	BOM Ref
Computer Desk	**1.00**	
Table Top	1.0	
Wooden sheet	1.0	
Color laminate	1.0	
Table Lag	4.0	
Bolt	8.0	

The bill of material structure can be printed from **Print** à **BOM Structure**. The menu is available in the bill of material from view. The preceding screenshot shows the bill of material for **Computer Desk**.

Let's try to sell the **Computer Desk**. If everything is configured well, you will get two manufacturing orders, one for **Computer Desk**, and another for **Table Top**. Look at the screenshot for the list of manufacturing orders. The manufacturing order for Table Top has to be processed first—we cannot produce the Computer Desk without Table Top, as Table Top is one of the raw materials:

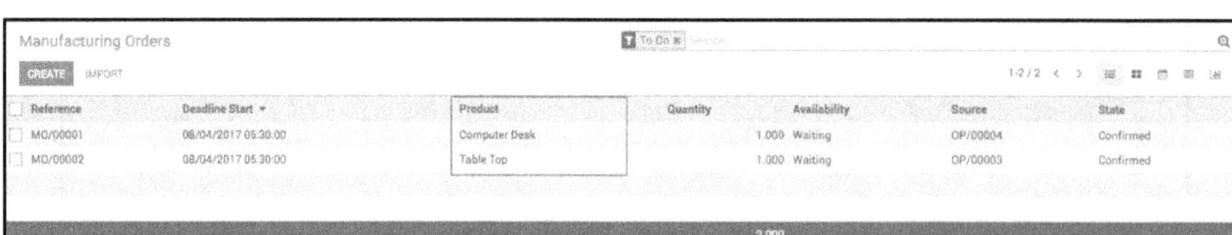

You will also get the request for a quotation for all the raw materials that are required to produce the **Table Top** and **Computer Desk**.

Orders may vary depending on the vendor configuration for the product. For me, the whole order goes to a single vendor, as the same vendor is configured on all the components, as you can see in the following purchase order:

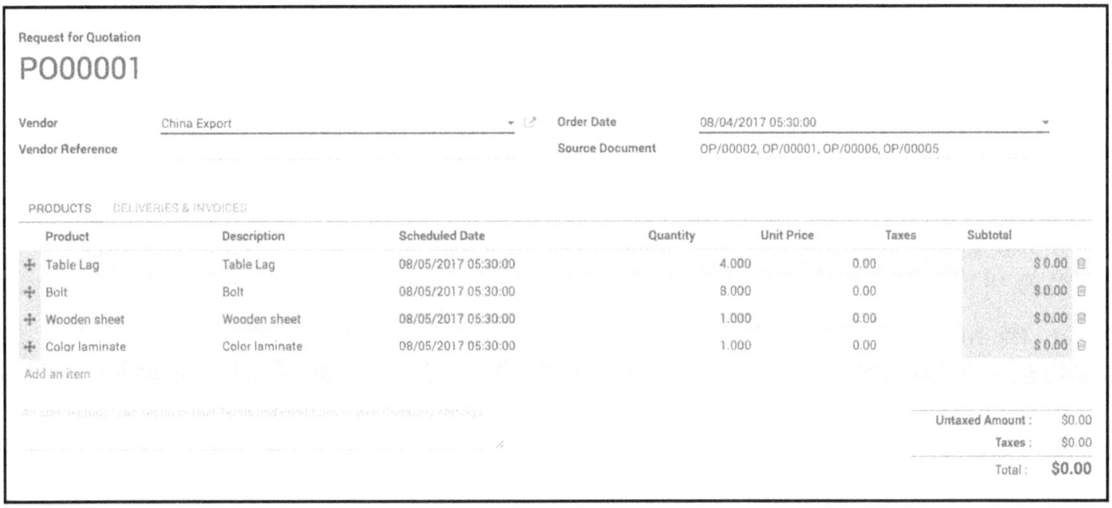

The bill of material has an important role in the manufacturing process; the modification in the bill of material requires input from the different departments to verify and confirm the availability of components or a process design.

There's more...

Manufacturing is a complex process, which involves many different departments and people. Let's take a simple example of the finance people. They may want to know the cost of a finished product by batch or the average of all the quantities produced. The material used in the manufacturing may be purchased at a different rate, so we may have a different cost of production by batch. Let's take another example: the helpdesk people may want to verify a product and its components to resolve a customer issue, so they need full traceability over the manufacturing and purchase process.

Let's see how we can set up traceability in the purchase, manufacturing, and sales processes by either using serials or lots and also compute the cost of the finished product based on the components used in production. This cost will depend on the different costing methods configured for the product.

Traceability in manufacturing

Better *after-sales-service* is really essential to gain customer satisfaction. Traceability of components is used to identify the components used during manufacturing. It is also used to identify the root cause and replace the components—if the damaged components are still under warranty, we can ask the vendor to give a replacement too.

All the products are either components or finished products, and they can be tracked with serial or lot numbers. Please go through `Chapter 10`, *Warehouse and Inventory Management*, and the recipe *Traceability tracking serial, lots and packs* to understand how serial and lot numbers can be traced in Inventory.

Assuming that each **Computer Desk** procured has a unique serial number, and the components used to produce the **Computer Desk** are tracked by the purchase lots, we can have traceability from the purchase of components to consumption in manufacturing, and delivery of the final product to the customer.

To see the full traceability, let's create a sales order and sell a **Computer Desk**. It is configured to be produced on demand by setting the routes to **Manufacturing** and **Make to Order** on the **Computer Desk** product:

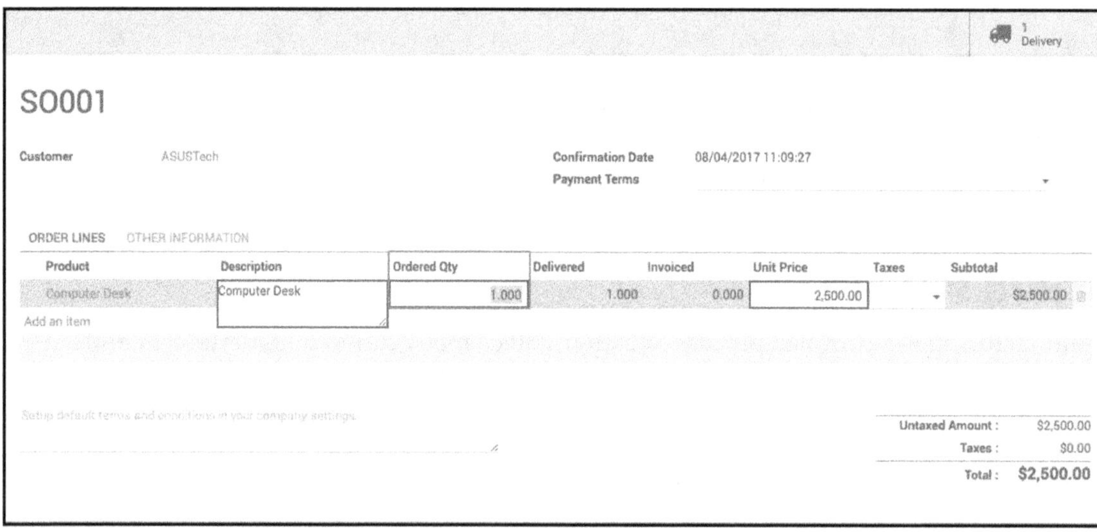

As soon as the order gets confirmed, it will trigger procurement to procure the **Computer Desk**, which will result in a manufacturing order producing the desk. Complete the procurement cycle starting from purchasing the components, assign it to the manufacturing order, and produce the order.

At each inventory operation, you will be asked for either a serial number or lot number. At the reception and at production, you have to create a lot for the incoming component products and a serial number for the finished product, **Computer Desk**.

Let's consume that the components assigned to the manufacturing order produce the Desk. The serial or lot numbers for the components are proposed based on the removal strategy. However, you can change it at the time of assigning the component in the manufacturing order if you plan to assign a component other than the proposed serial or lot number. Look at the following screenshot, which assigns the **Table Top** from the available lot in the inventory:

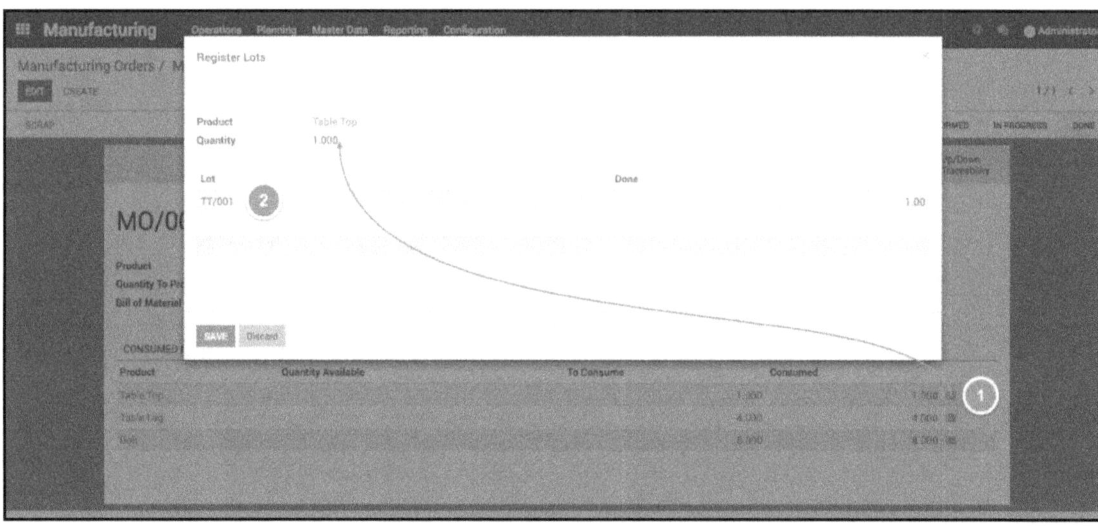

Click on the **Serial/Lot** icon visible on the right-side of the product quantity; a popup will appear with the proposed lot number, so click on the plus sign to consume it into the manufacturing order.

When all the components are assigned to the order, the order is ready to produce the final product. You can start producing the **Computer Desk** by clicking on the **PRODUCE** button. You will be asked for the **Serial/Lot** number for the finished product, as shown in the following screenshot:

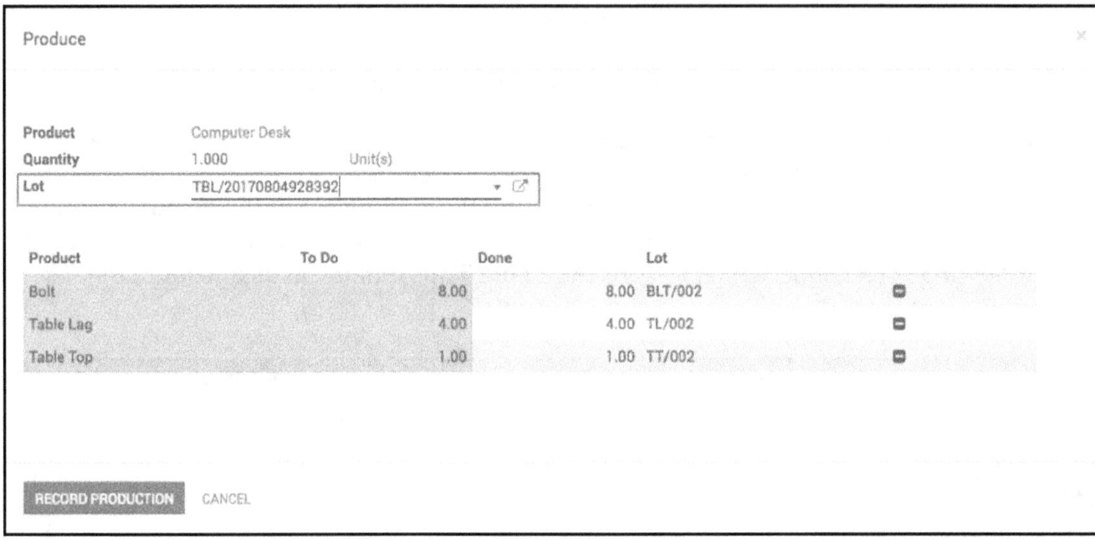

Produce the Desk and transfer it to the warehouse by clicking on the **MARK AS DONE** button in the manufacturing order:

The **Computer Desk** is now available for delivery. Assign it from the warehouse based on the serial number, and process the delivery order:

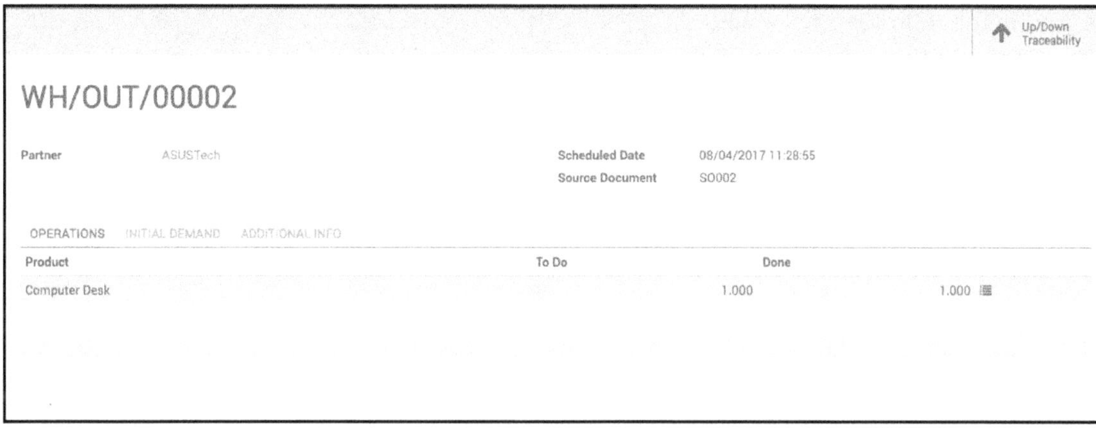

By clicking on the **Up/Down Traceability** button available in the delivery order, you will be able to trace which components are used in the manufacturing of the **Computer Desk** and from where the component arrived into the warehouse.

Traceability will give you complete details of every inventory movement for the component used in the manufacturing of the finished product-**Computer Desk**:

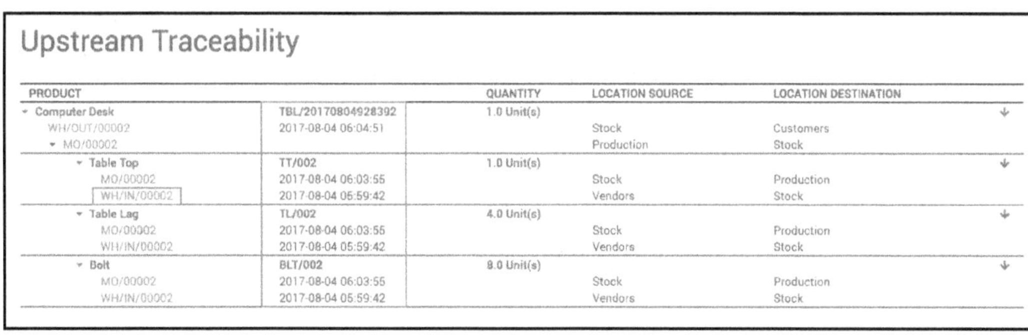

When a customer comes up with an issue in the product or parts, you can have the full trace based on the serial and lot number to identify which part comes from which vendor, so that you can improve the quality checking for that vendor. In case the root cause of the issue lies with the manufacturing process, the engineering manufacturing department can improve it.

The document that does the component movement can be viewed by clicking on the document number link, for example, by clicking on **WH/IN/00002**, you will be redirected to the incoming shipment which received the **Table Top**, along with the other raw materials, as seen in the following screenshot:

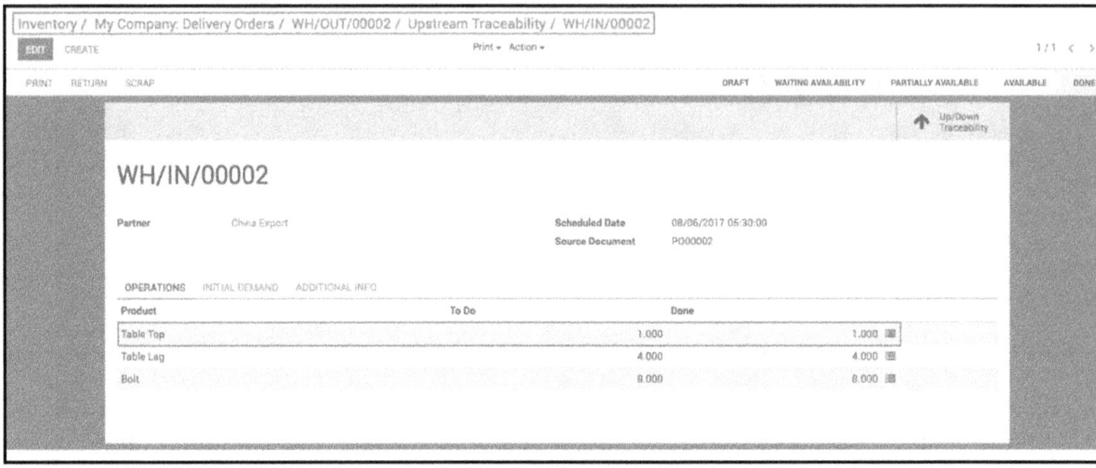

Quality check in Manufacturing

Quality is still individually integrated with the warehouse and manufacturing applications in Odoo, as we saw during `Chapter 11`, *Advance Warehouse Management* in recipe *Quality control in warehouse*. Quality can be checked at any inventory operation: either at the reception or at the delivery order. Let's see how we can implement quality check during the manufacturing operation.

Create a quality point in the **Manufacturing operation**, select the product you would like to check, and apply the quality parameters. You can create multiple quality points to be checked for the **Manufacturing operation** for the same product:

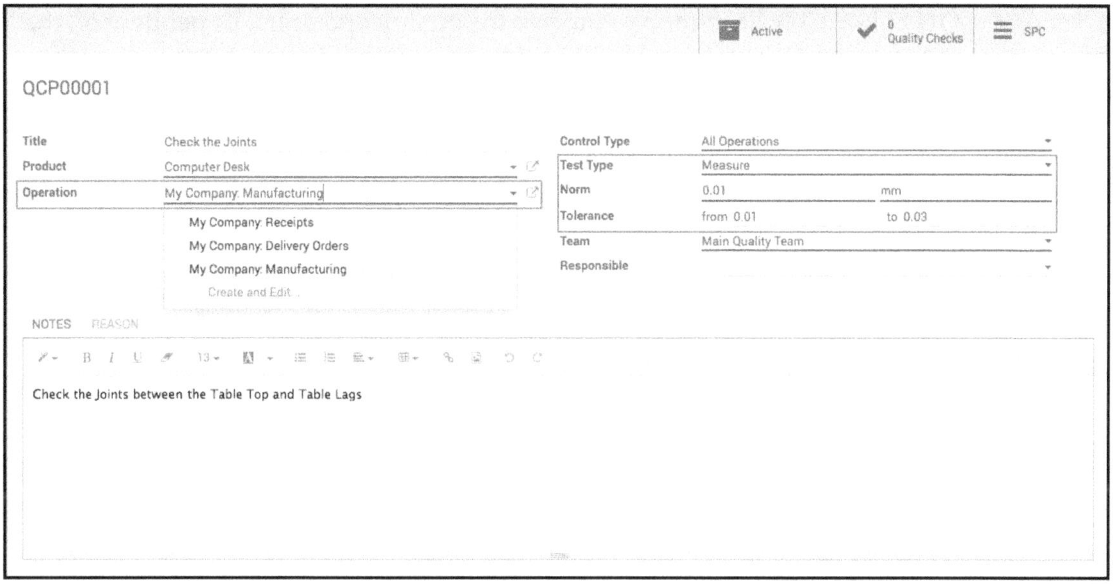

As soon as the material is available and the manufacturing process begins, the **QUALITY CHECK** button will appear in the **Manufacturing** order:

Click on the **QUALITY CHECK** button to process the quality operation. Depending on the parameters set for the quality point, you will be asked to enter the measurement or simply mark the quality check as PASS or FAIL:

If the quality point is configured to check the measurement, the result will be computed and the quality check attached to the manufacturing order. Look at the following screenshot of a quality check and its result:

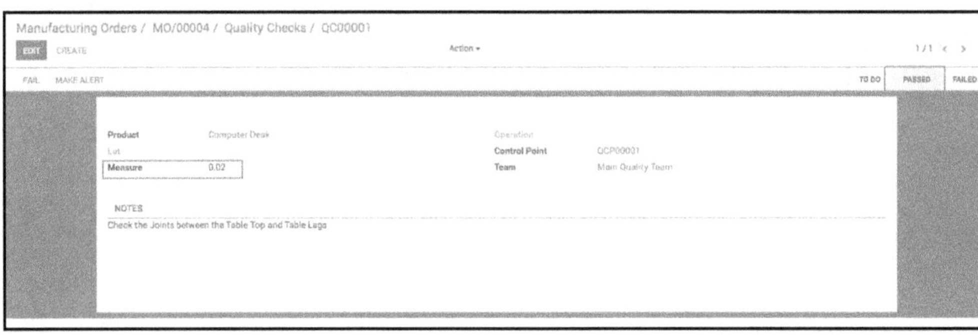

The quality alert can be created by the worker by clicking on the **QUALITY ALERT** button if any critical issue is found in production.

Finished product costing

Computing the cost of the finished product is a really challenging and difficult job. There are various costing methods used to compute the cost of components like Standard, Average, or Real Price. The cost of the finished product can be computed based on the cost of components used in the bill of material, labor, electricity, or any direct or indirect cost incurred during production.

Let's see how to compute the cost of the final product based on the cost of the components. If you would like to understand how different costing methods work, please go through the *Product costing and Inventory Valuation* recipe in `Chapter 11`, *Advanced Warehouse Management*.

Assuming that the costing method for all the components is set to Real Price, for the following example, the route for the manufactured product, **Computer Desk**, is set to **Manufacturing** and **Make to Order**.

We are going to create two manufacturing orders. Each manufacturing order produces one quantity of **Computer Desk**. The components will be purchased at different rates each time when needed.

Assume that the components are bought at the price shown in the following table for the two different manufacturing orders:

Component	**Cost Price for MO/00001**	**Cost Price for MO/00002**
Table Top	490	510
Table Lag	100	95
Bolt	16	18
Total Cost to Produce 1 Table	1018	1034

Create the manufacturing order, process the procurements, confirm the purchase orders, receive in the warehouse, and issue components for the production. Now, process two different manufacturing orders as shown earlier.

The costing can be analyzed using the manufacturing order for all the quantities produced:

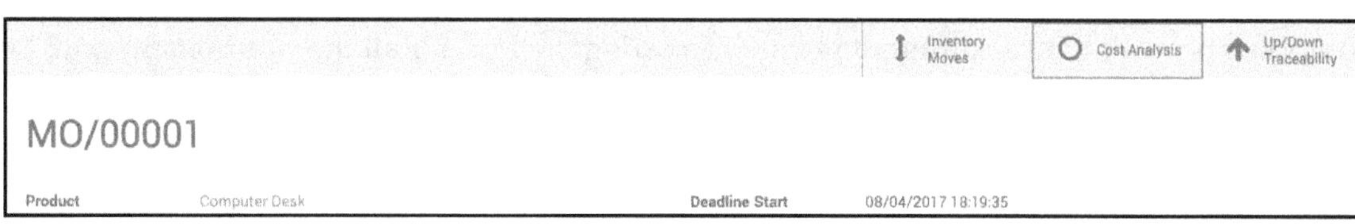

Click on the **Cost Analysis** state button available in the manufacturing order as seen in the preceding screenshot, and you will get the cost analysis for *MO/00001*. Look at the following screenshot:

Computer Desk

1.0 Unit(s), from 1 manufacturing order(s).

Cost Structure

Raw Materials	Quantity	Unit Cost	Total Cost
Bolt	8.0 Unit(s)	16.00 ₹	128.00 ₹
Table Top	1.0 Unit(s)	490.00 ₹	490.00 ₹
Table Lag	4.0 Unit(s)	100.00 ₹	400.00 ₹
		Total Cost of Raw Materials	**1,018.00 ₹**
		Unit Cost	**1,018.00 ₹**

The costing report can be printed by clicking on the **PRINT** button. The cost of the components used to manufacture one **Computer Desk** is 1018.

In the same way, process *MO/00002*; click on the Cost Analysis button to check the Cost Analysis report. It will look like the following screenshot:

Computer Desk

1.0 Unit(s), from 1 manufacturing order(s).

Cost Structure

Raw Materials	Quantity	Unit Cost	Total Cost
Bolt	8.0 Unit(s)	18.00 ₹	144.00 ₹
Table Lag	4.0 Unit(s)	95.00 ₹	380.00 ₹
Table Top	1.0 Unit(s)	510.00 ₹	510.00 ₹
		Total Cost of Raw Materials	**1,034.00 ₹**
		Unit Cost	**1,034.00 ₹**

The cost of the manufacturing order **MO/0002** is different than Order **MO/0001**, as the components are bought at different rates. The costing method for all the components and the finished product is set to **Real Price**.

There are two **Computer Desks** produced with components bought at different rates, thus, the cost price for both desks is different in the inventory. You can check this from the **Inventory Valuation** report. It will look like the screen shown in this screenshot:

Inventory Valuation

Internal Locations × | Location × | Search

Filters ▾ Group By ▾ Favorites ▾

	Product	Quantity	Location	Incoming Date	Inventory Value
▾ WH/Stock (2)		2.00			2,052.00
	Computer Desk	1.00	WH/Stock	08/04/2017 18:24:40	1,018.00
	Computer Desk	1.00	WH/Stock	08/04/2017 18:26:05	1,034.00
					2,052.00

The **Inventory Valuation** shows the different values for each table, as the cost price of the desk is computed at **Real Price** too. However, you can get the average cost price for the Desk from the **Cost Analysis** report available for the product.

> The costing of the finished product will be computed based on the costing of the components. If you change the costing of the components to Average or Standard, the cost price for the Desk will be computed accordingly.

Go to **Computer Desk**, and click on the **Cost Analysis** action button; the report will look like the following screenshot:

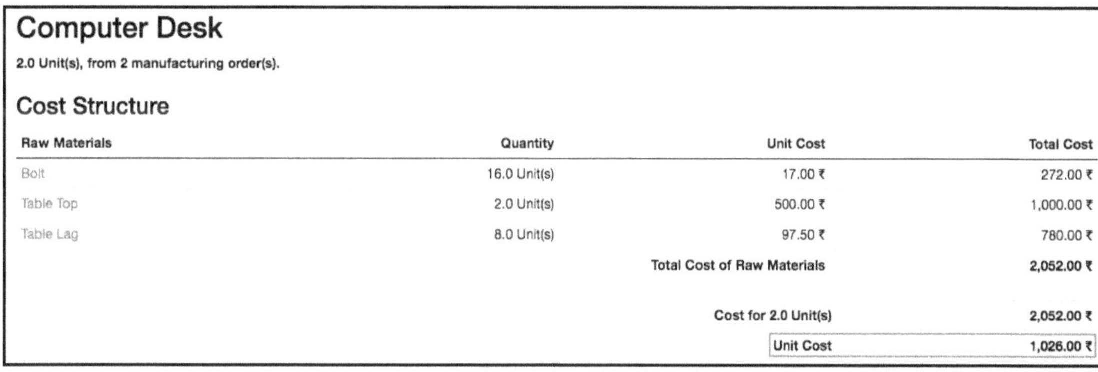

Computer Desk

2.0 Unit(s), from 2 manufacturing order(s).

Cost Structure

Raw Materials	Quantity	Unit Cost	Total Cost
Bolt	16.0 Unit(s)	17.00 ₹	272.00 ₹
Table Top	2.0 Unit(s)	500.00 ₹	1,000.00 ₹
Table Lag	8.0 Unit(s)	97.50 ₹	780.00 ₹
		Total Cost of Raw Materials	2,052.00 ₹
		Cost for 2.0 Unit(s)	2,052.00 ₹
		Unit Cost	1,026.00 ₹

The average cost price will be computed based on the number of desks produced at the time of printing the report. In the preceding example, we have seen that the cost of the finished product is based on the cost of the components used in the bill of material. We will see later in this book how to add additional costs such as such as electricity and labor to the cost of the finished product.

Unbuild Order

Unbuild Order is a reverse process of manufacturing. Of course, it is not possible for all types of products, but for assembled products, it is possible to unassemble the components. When the manufacturing order is processed, it consumes the components, and produces the final product. Let's take the example of **Computer Desk**. When it was manufactured, it consumed one quantity of Table Top, four quantities of Leg and sixteen quantities of Bolt.

The unbuild operation consumes the **Computer Desk**, and gets its components back after the unbuild operation.

Let's see the current status of the inventory in the warehouse before we process the unbuild operation. Look at the following screenshot of the current inventory:

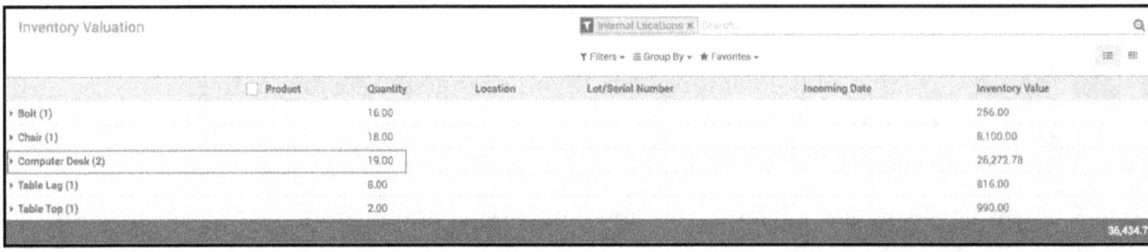

We have 19 **Computer Desks** available in the warehouse. To unbuild the order, go to **Operations | Unbuild Orders**.

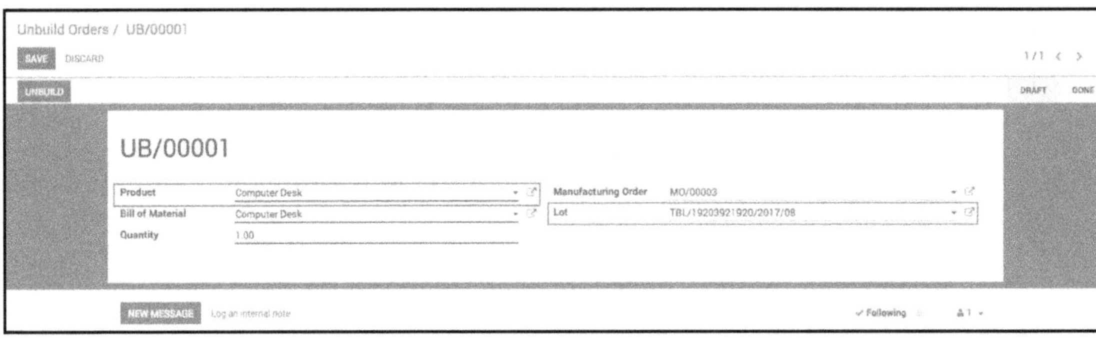

Select the product, manufacturing order number, and **Lot** number. Enter the number of the quantities to unbuild. You can choose between a partial or full unbuild. Click on the **UNBUILD** button to process the order, and unbuild the product.

Check the **Inventory Valuation** report again after processing the unbuild operation. Look at the following **Inventory Valuation** report:

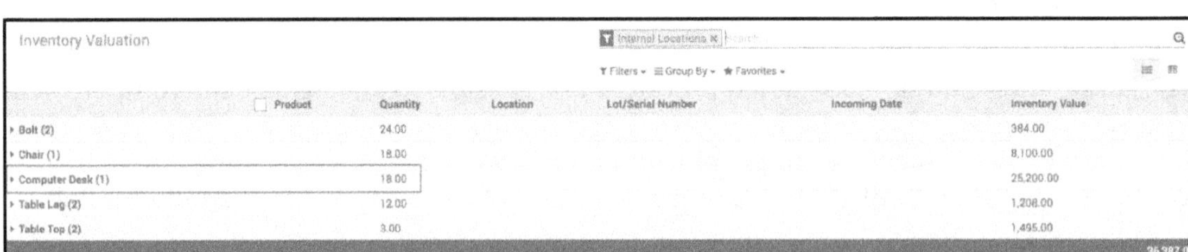

The **Computer Desk** stock is decreased, and the stock of the respective components increases after the unbuild operation.

Configuring assembly line and work centers

A series of machines and workers organized in a factory is called an assembly line. They are organized as work centers dedicated to performing specific operations. The assembled product passes through these work centers in a sequence. At each work center, a new part can be added or processed until the finished product is ready.

The engineering manufacturing department is responsible to design and set up the assembly line. A typical assembly line looks like the following image:

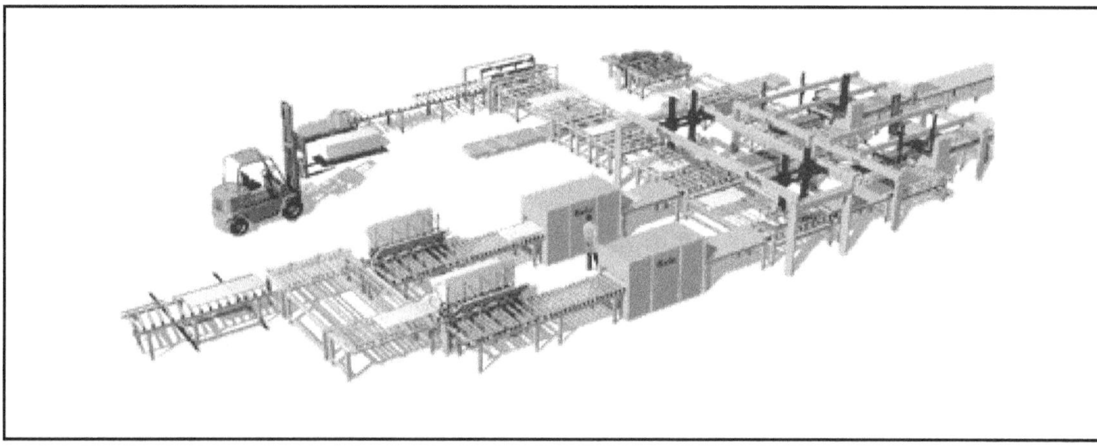

The assembly line to produce the **Computer Desk** can be divided into three different work centers. It starts with **Cutting**, followed by **Drilling**, and ends with **Fitting**.

At the Cutting center, we process the **Table Top** and make the required size as per the specifications. At Drilling, we drill the **Table Top** to join the top and legs, and finally, at Fitting, we assemble the Top with the Legs using Bolts.

Let's set up the work centers and assembly line for the **Computer Desk** in Odoo.

How to do it...

1. In the first recipe, we managed the manufacturing process by the manufacturing orders without the work centers and assembly line. To set up the assembly line, we have to activate the production by work orders instead of the manufacturing order.

   Go to **Manufacturing** | **Configuration** | **Settings**, and select *Manage production by work orders* on the **Routings & Planning** field:

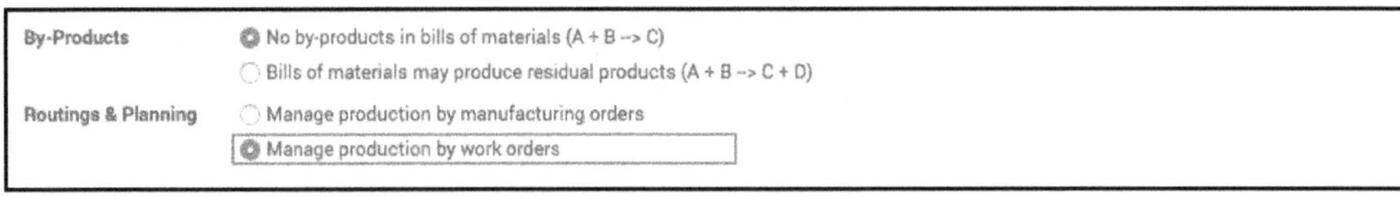

   Click on the **APPLY** button to activate the **Work Centers** and Routing features.

2. As soon as the feature is activated, the dashboard will be enabled for the **Manufacturing** application. It displays the list of work centers and their current status. It is super easy for the production manager to track and resolve these if there are any issues in any work center.

   To create a new work center, go to **Master Data** | **Work Centers** under the **Manufacturing** application. Click on the **CREATE** button to create a work center:

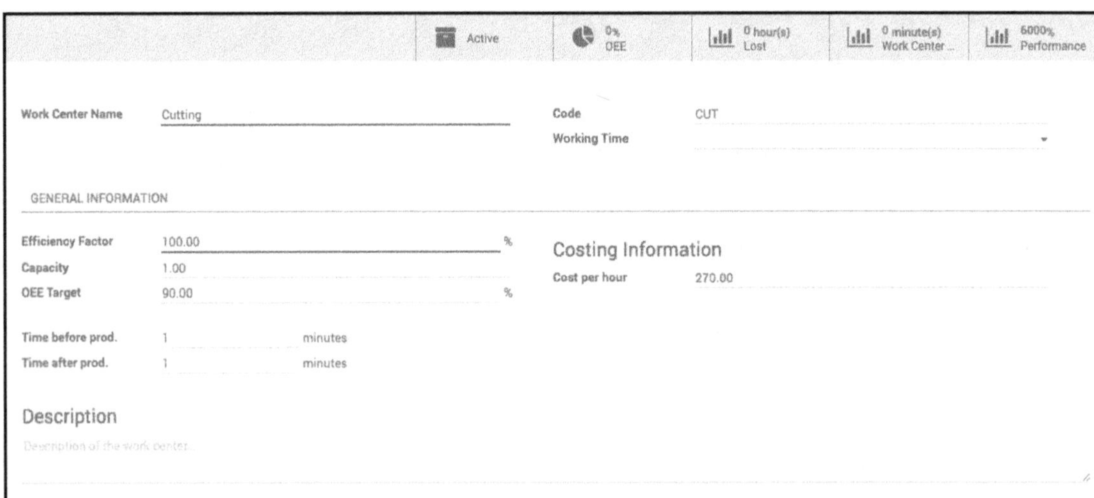

A work center can be a set of workers and/or machines which are used for task assignment as well as capacity and planning forecast. Enter the name and code of the work center. We will see the other fields in detail under the *There's more...* section of this recipe. Create the other work centers needed to set up the assembly line for **Computer Desk such** as Drilling and Fitting.

3. Work centers will be available on the **Manufacturing** dashboard. It will look like the screenshot shown next:

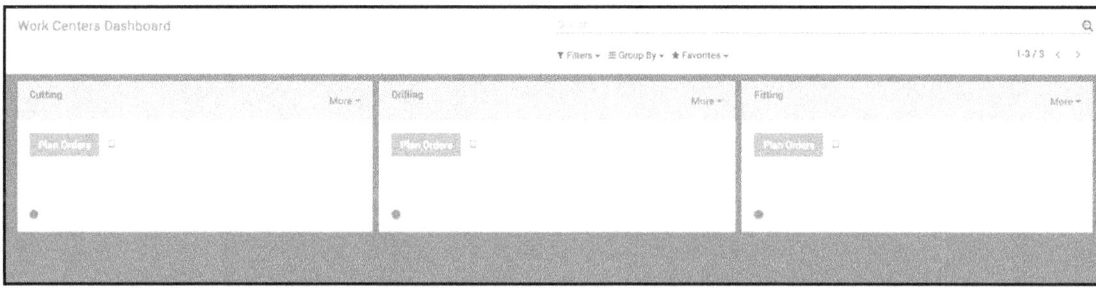

Routing defines the sequence of the operation with time specifications; in our case, there are three operations arranged in a sequence as **Cutting** | **Drilling**| **Fitting**. The routing can be created from **Master Data** | **Routings**:

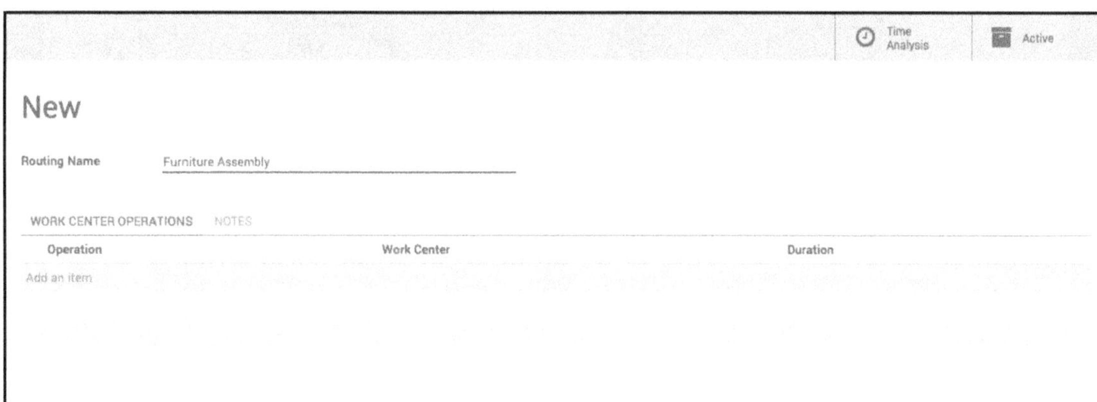

We have created **Furniture Assembly** to define the manufacturing process of **Computer Desk**. Click on **Add an item** to add the new operation on the assembly line. The operations are arranged in sequence. Each operation is linked to the center:

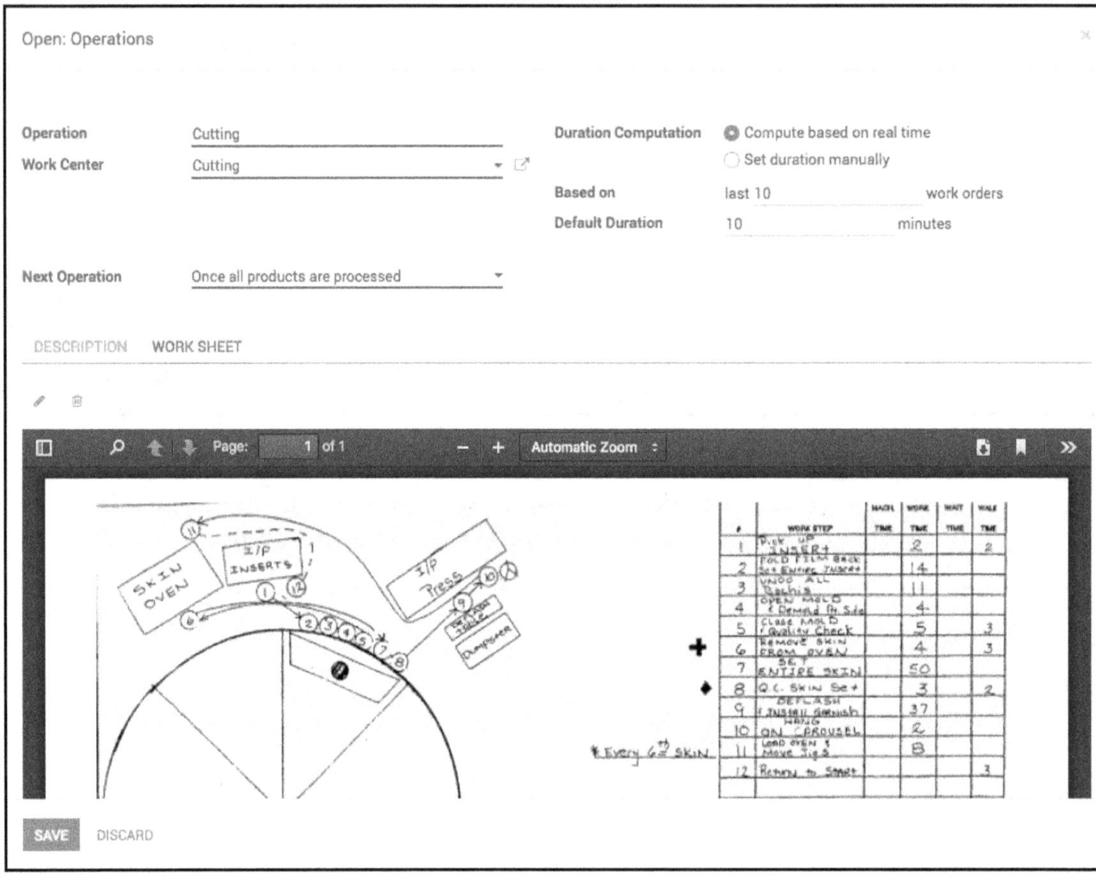

Enter the name in the operation field, select the work center for this operation, and select the operation specification on the **WORK SHEET** tab.

Create other operations such as **Drilling** and **Fitting**. Upon successful creation of all the operations, your routing will look as follows:

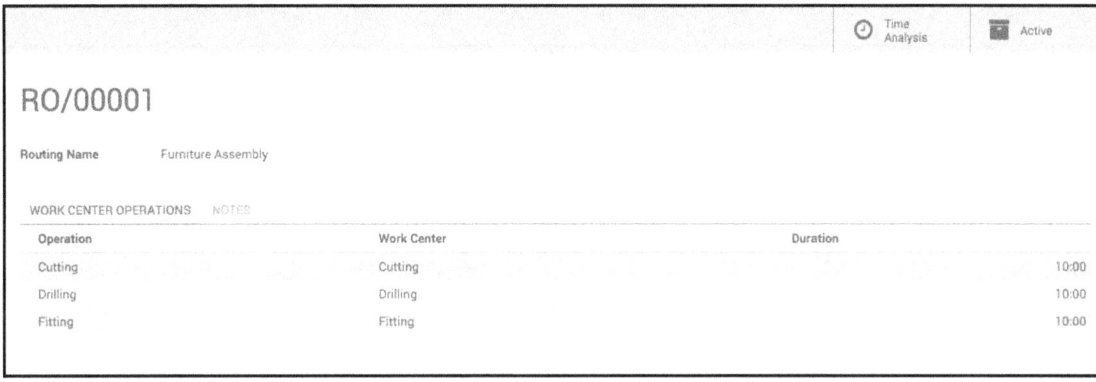

4. Finally, attach the routing on the bill of material of the **Computer Desk**. All the manufacturing orders can be planned and created to produce the **Computer Desk**:

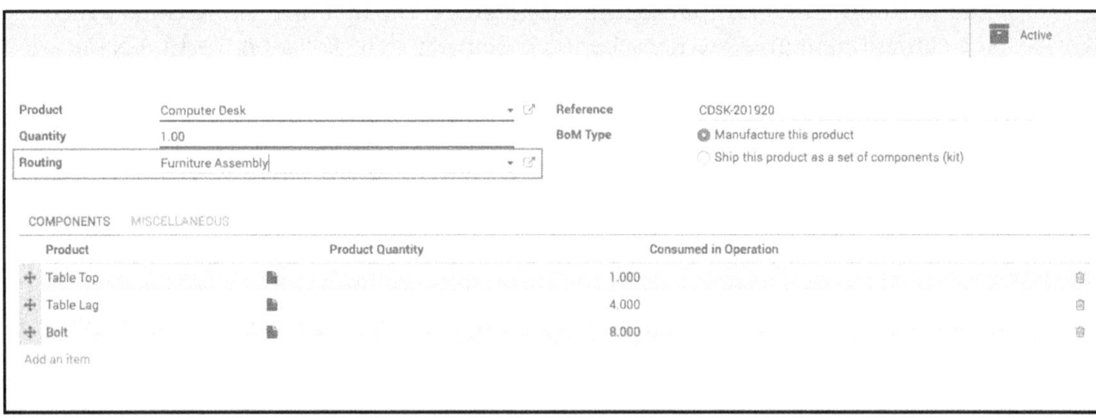

Open the bill of material for **Computer Desk**, and select **Furniture Assembly** on the **Routing** field, as displayed in the preceding screenshot.

5. Assuming all the components are available in the inventory, let's create a manufacturing order and save it. The planning can be done as soon as the manufacturing order is created:

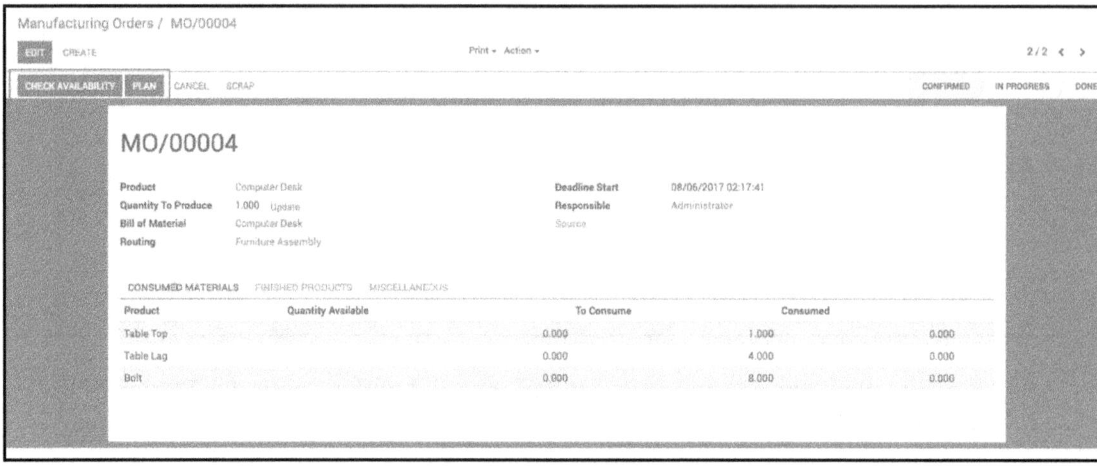

The schedule counts the **Deadline Start** date on the manufacturing order based on the commitment given to the scheduled delivery date. Click on the **PLAN** button to schedule the order.

6. The work order has been created for the manufacturing order. The first operation has to be launched at **Cutting**. It's indicated in the dashboard, as shown in the following screenshot:

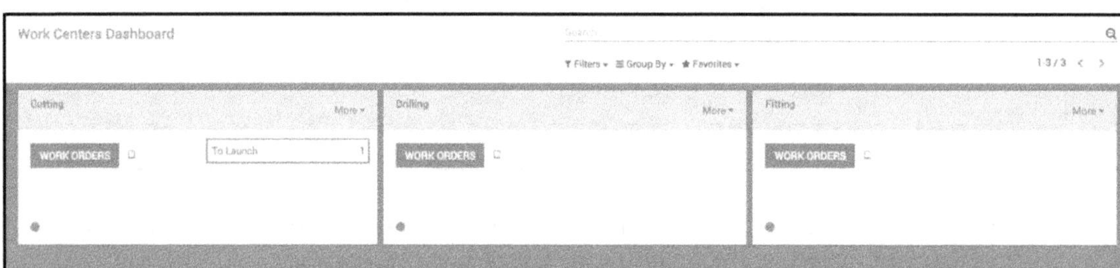

Click on the **To Launch** link to get the work order ready to work on. Open the form view, and click on the **START WORKING** button:

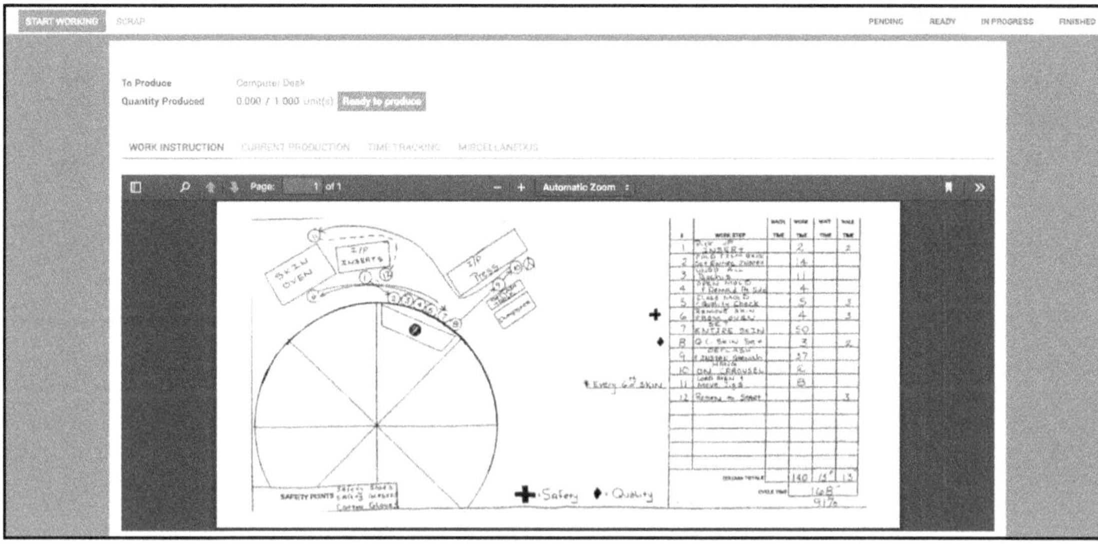

7. As soon as the worker starts working on the work order, the timer starts to record the time, and it is tracked under the **TIME TRACKING** tab. Time is tracked to compute the efficiency of the operation and the work center:

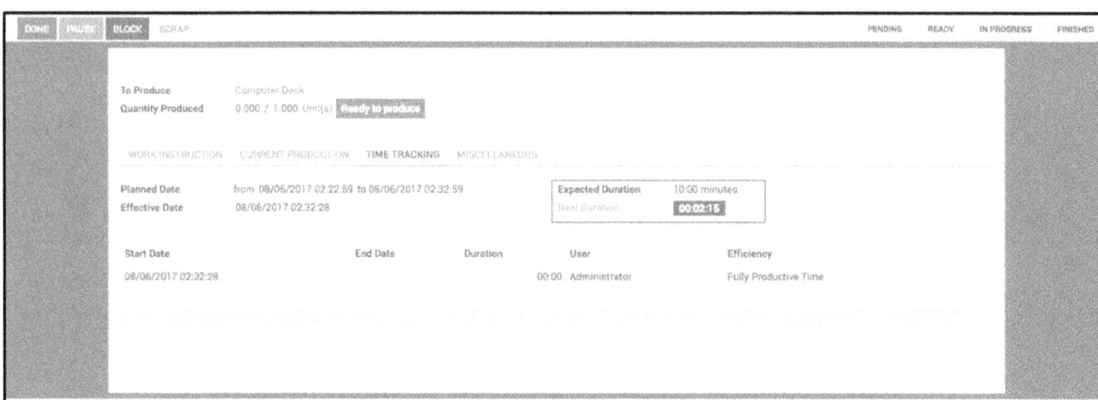

The work log will be generated automatically in the operation as a work log. As the operation time is within the **Expected Duration**, the work log will be created as a **Fully Productive Time**. The time spent to finish the work order, if it is more than the Expected time, it will be logged as Reduced Speed.

The operation can be paused by clicking on the **PAUSE** button in case it has to be stopped for a small break other than the failure of the machine. This time will not be recorded.

The production manager has a clear indication that the operation is ongoing at the **Cutting** work center. Look at this screenshot of the dashboard:

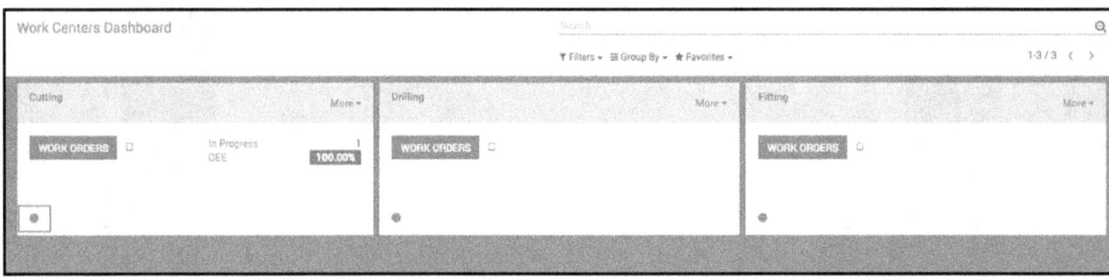

8. Click on the **DONE** button as soon as the operation has completed in the **Cutting** work center. The work order status is set to **FINISHED** when it is marked as **DONE**.

The manufacturing dashboard will be updated. The **Cutting** work center will become available and require planning for the new manufacturing order.

The **Overall Equipment Efficiency** (**OEE**) will be computed and updated for the **Cutting** work center based on the time spent to finish the operation:

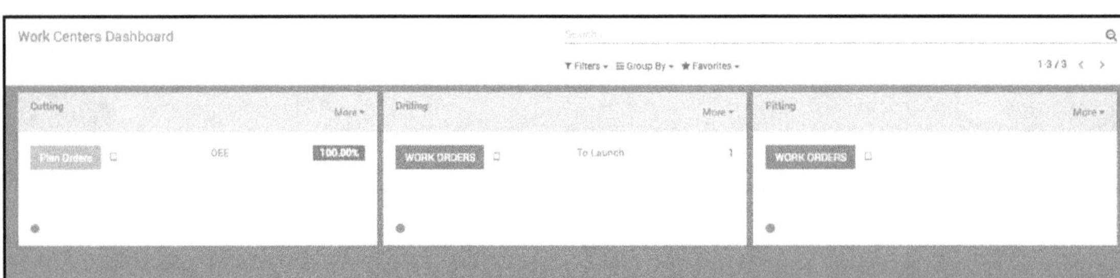

Drilling and **Fitting** still have work to be performed to finish the production of **Computer Desk**. Let's process the work order in the **Drilling** and then **Fitting** work centers.

9. All the work centers will become free when all the work orders are marked as done. Finally, go to the manufacturing order and click on **MARK AS DONE** to update the inventory of the finished product:

10. Finally, we have completed the manufacturing of **Computer Desk** on the Furniture Assembly line using work centers and work orders. Look at the next screenshot of **Inventory Valuation** after completing the manufacturing order:

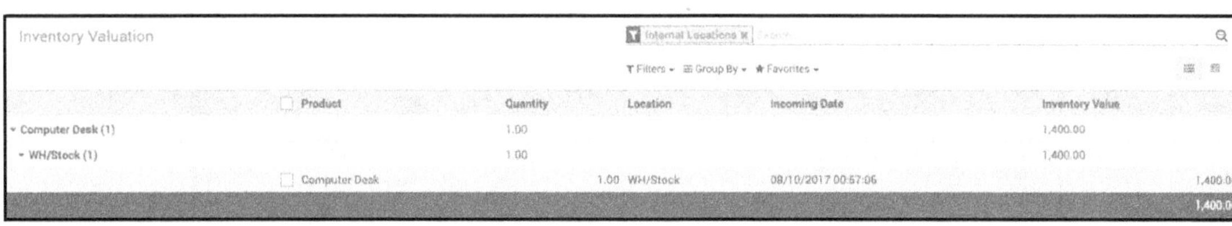

There's more...

We have set up the assembly line called *Furniture Assembly* that streamlines the manufacturing process of **Computer Desk**. The work order is generated for each work center in the assembly line as soon as the manufacturing order is planned for **Computer Desk**.

The Overall Equipment Efficiency will be measured by Odoo to compute the effectiveness of the work center. When there is any problem, we have to see the root cause of the problem to fix it. There are major problems such as material unavailability, slow production cycles, or the rejection of the finished product due to the use of bad quality of material.

Let's see how to enter into the tablet view for the workers, compute the operation time and costing by work centers, set up the consumption of the components, and set the alert message on the work centers.

Worker view (tablet view)

It is recommended to have individual logins for the workers working in the work centers for better accountability, and to understand individual capacity and performance.

The workers may use the same computer with their logins to work on the work orders at the work centers. However, a better, and recommended, the way is to assign a tablet to each worker with a limited access, simplified screen. Click on the tablet icon available in the work center:

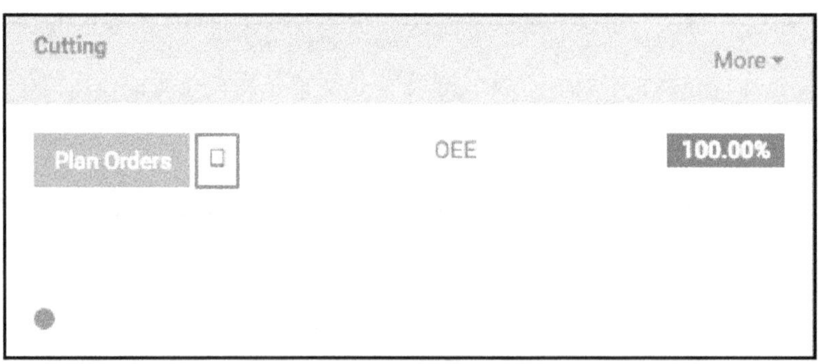

Each worker connects to the work center they belong to and gets the list of work orders to be processed. The next screenshot shows the work orders for the **Cutting** work center:

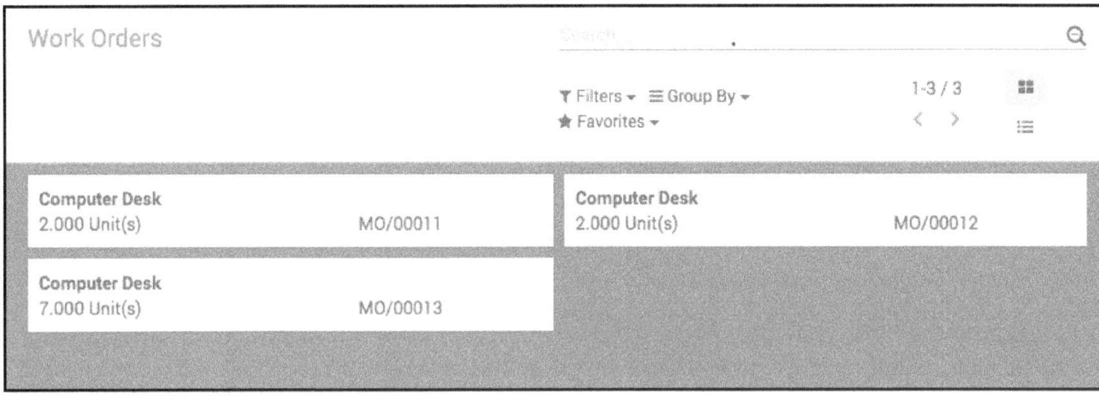

Open the work order by clicking on it. Click on the **START WORKING** button to start working on the work order:

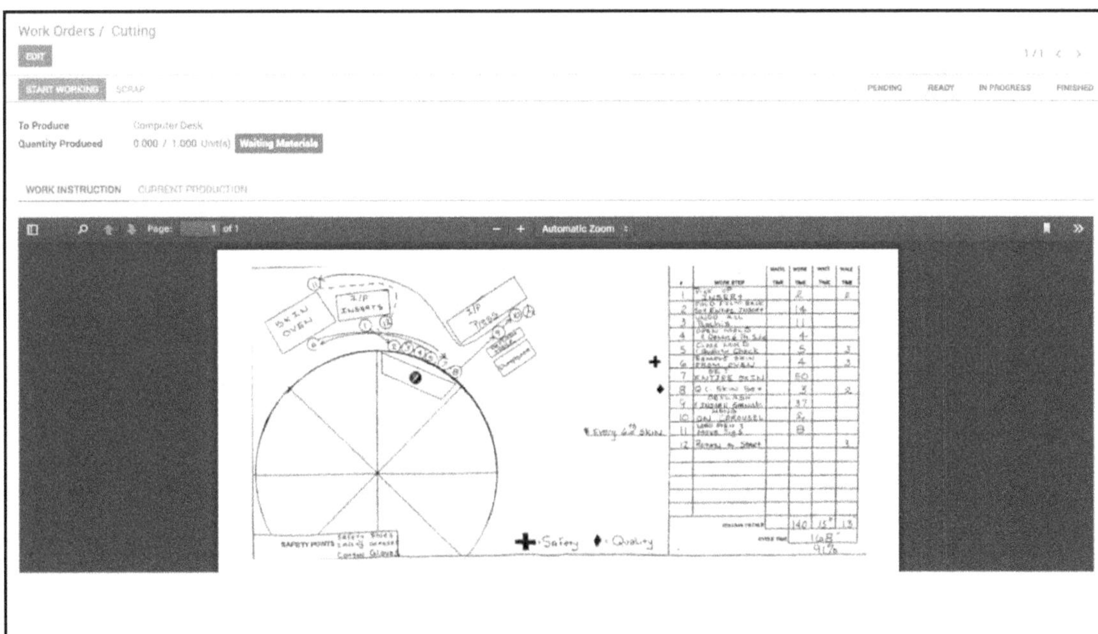

Time tracking starts in the operation; it can be tracked on the **CURRENT OPERATION** tab. The tablet view has a minimal set of operations that the workers have to perform to keep it simple and fast to access.

Scheduling and planning

The Odoo inventory has a built-in scheduler that computes the delivery date or incoming reception date based on the commitment date given to the customer and that we got from the vendors. We computed the delivery date and reception dates in the *Delivery orders and incoming shipments* recipe in `Chapter 10`, *Warehouse and Inventory Management*, based on the commitment date given to the customer.

Let's see how the Odoo scheduler computes the delivery date. Procurement creates the manufacturing order and the manufacturing start date is computed.

Assume that the routes set on the **Computer Desk** are *Manufacture* and *Make to Order*. The **Deadline Start** date on the manufacturing order will be computed by the scheduler based on the Manufacturing Lead time. The delivery date is computed based on the Customer Lead Time, and the Vendor Lead time is used to compute the reception date for the incoming shipment.

The **Customer Lead Time** is set to 15 days, and the **Manufacturer Lead Time** is set to four days on Computer Desk. Look at the following screenshot of product configuration:

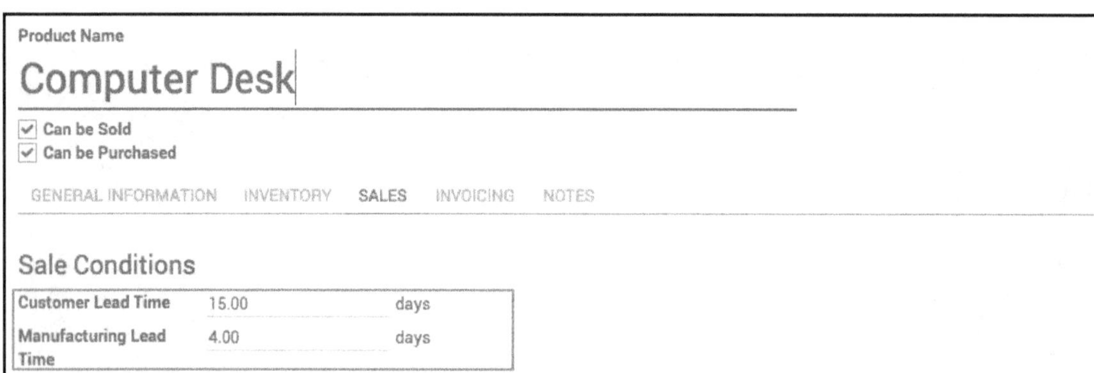

Let's assume that there is a sales order created and confirmed. The sales order Configuration Date is August 11, 2017. The next screenshot shows the sales order:

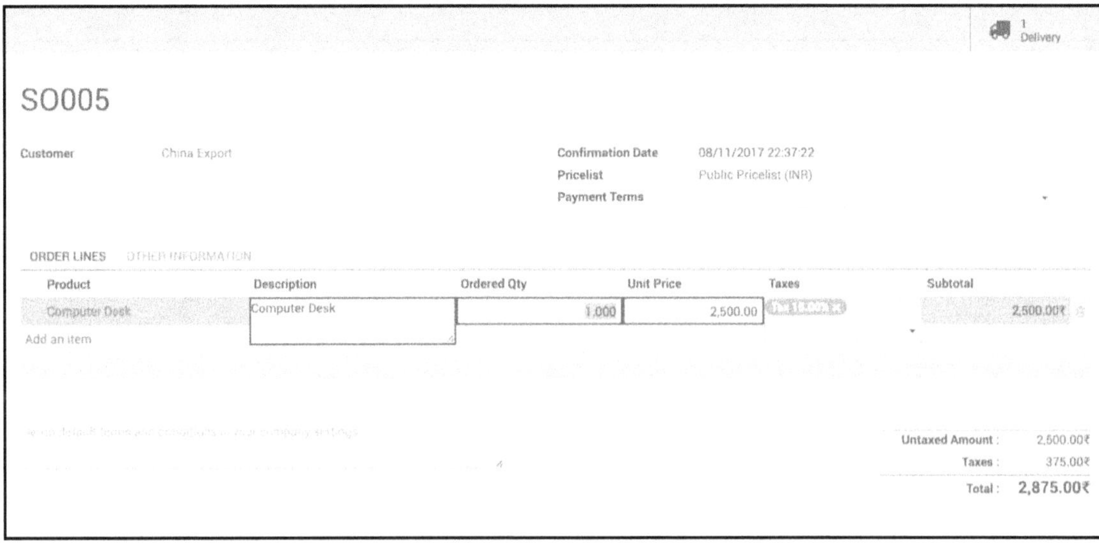

The delivery date will be computed based on **Customer Lead Time**. It will be set to August 26, 2017:

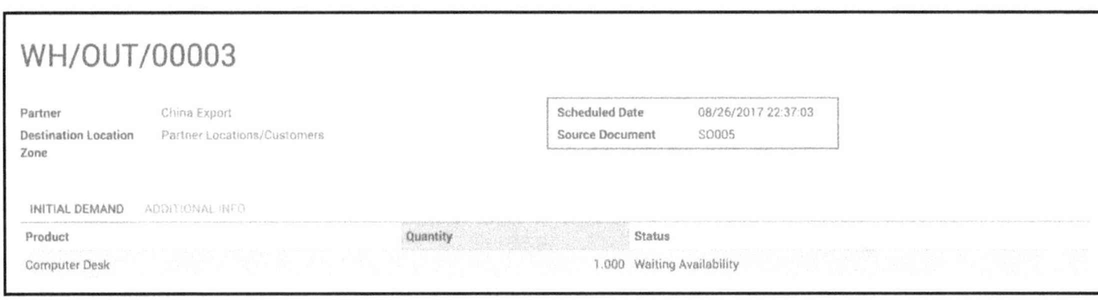

The procurement computes the **Deadline Start** field in the manufacturing order. It will be computed based on the **Manufacturer Lead Time**. The manufacturing order should start at least four days before the delivery date:

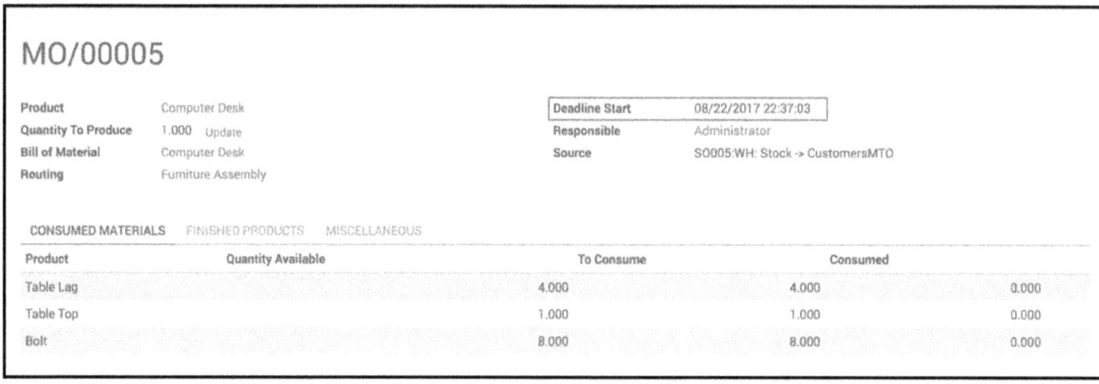

The manufacturing order **Deadline Start** is set to August 22, 2017. The manufacturing has to be planned for the production based on the assembly line and work center's capacity, and the working schedule. Click on the **PLAN** button; it will be assigned a scheduling date by which the production will be started and finished:

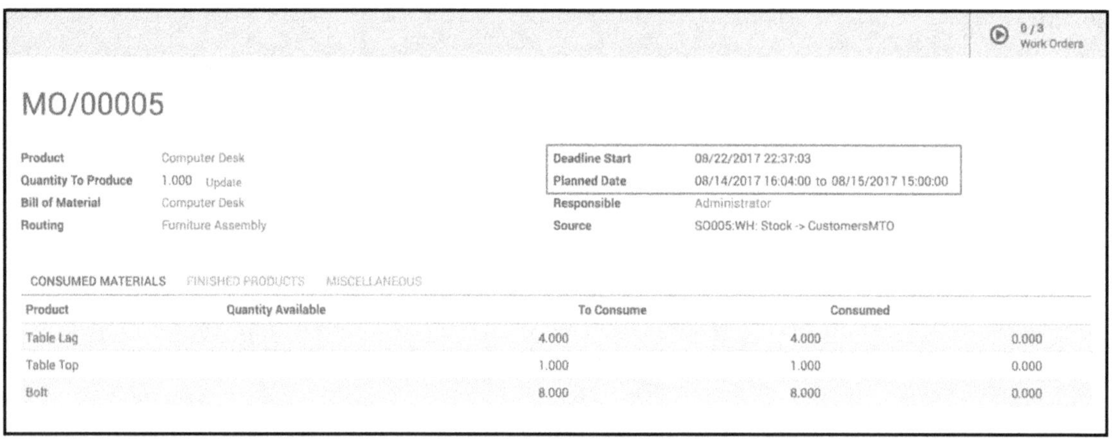

However, if you would like to change the planning of jobs in assembly, it can be done using the Gantt chart production order or work center. Planning by Production can be accessed by going to **Planning | Planning by Production** under the **Manufacturing** application:

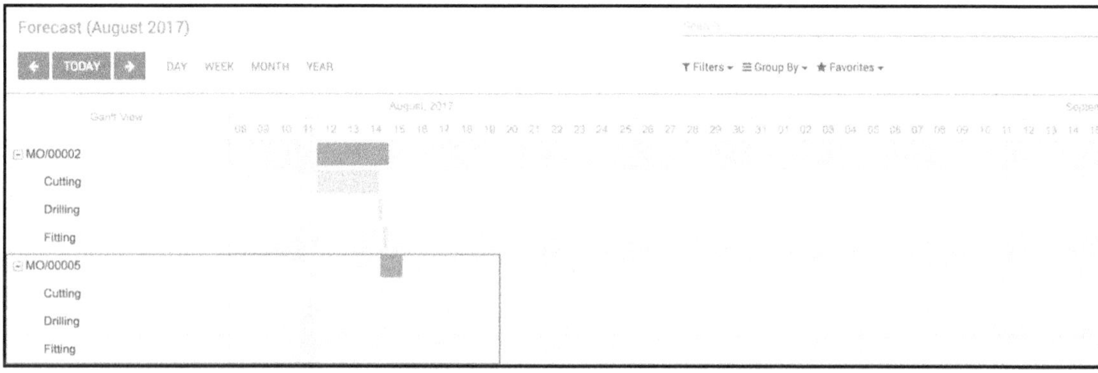

The work order can be planned by dragging and dropping the work order in the Gantt view. Planning can be done based on the capacity of the work centers. The working time is attached to the work center. The following is a screenshot of the work center:

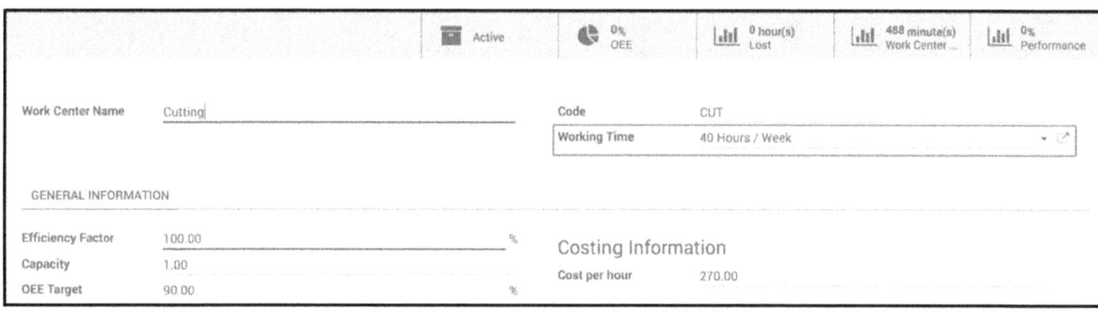

The capacity of the work center can be increased or decreased by changing the working time in Working Schedule, the work centers will be working depending on the working schedule:

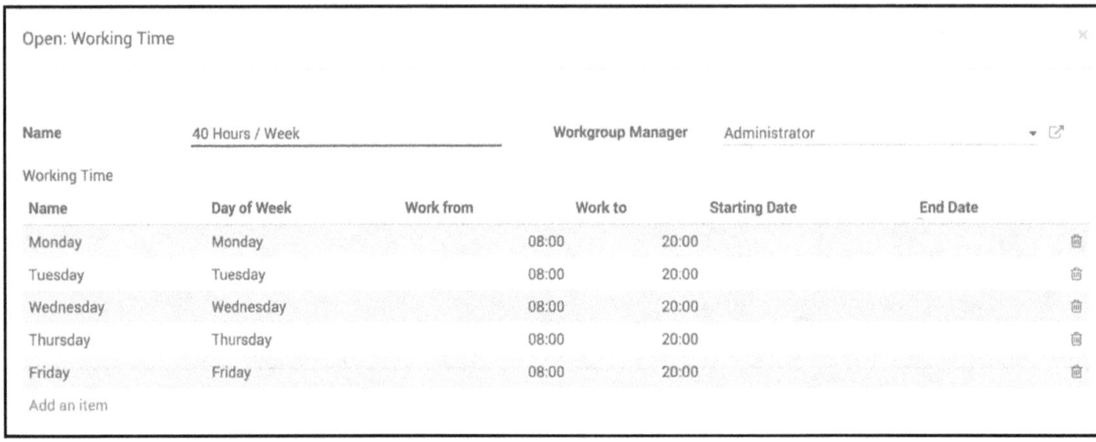

Scheduling is done by the Odoo scheduler, while planning of the manufacturing can be done by the work center or manufacturing order.

Operation time

Fully Productive Time is time recorded in the work order which was actually spent working on the operation at the work center. Odoo records the different types of times in the work order depending on the worker's activity. Other than Fully Productive Time, there are other times recorded such as **Material Availability**, **Equipment Failure**, **Setup and Adjustments,** which block operations, and affect the efficiency of the work center. The blocking time is also recorded in the work center, and it affects the OEE.

Let's jump into the configuration related to the time in the work center and routing to process the operation or job at the work center.

The time required to ready the work center before starting the job, or the time spent after completing the job to clean the work center, has to be configured on the work centers. The following screenshot shows the configuration of the **Cutting** work center:

Efficiency Factor indicates the efficiency of a machine. In the case of machines, it can be 100% when it is new, or it has to be measured from time to time and the correct efficiency is set to get the accurate performance of the work center.

Capacity represents the capability of the work centers to execute a number of parallel operations. Set it to five if you have five work centers that perform the same operation in parallel.

OEE is computed by Odoo based on the productive and unproductive times; the OEE achieved at the work center should be more than or equal to the **OEE Target**.

The operating time can be configured in routing; it is the time given at the work center to complete an operation, and can be set as a fixed time or computed dynamically based on some of the past operations performed at the work center.

Some assembly lines set a fixed time for operations. In the next screenshot, the operation time configuration is fixed to 10 minutes to perform the **Cutting** operation:

If you would like to set the operation duration based on real-time data available based on the past operations, you can set the **Duration Computation** field to **Compute based on real time**. Set the number of past operations in the **Based on** the field to compute the average time to be given to the next operation performed at the work center. In the following screenshot, the real-time data is computed **Based on** the **last 30** operations:

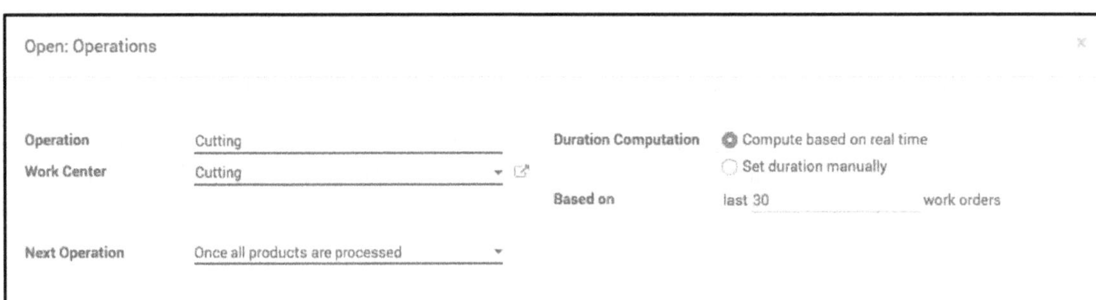

So, the expected duration will be computed based on the last 30 operations. We may have some workers who are super fast, while some may be slower. The average time will be computed based on their operation duration.

Let's check the status on the dashboard for the OEE of the work centers. I have processed some manufacturing orders to simulate the actual process, as seen in this screenshot:

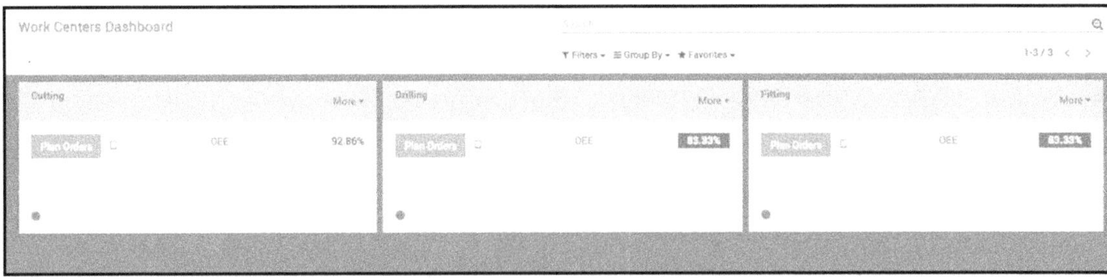

The **Cutting** work centers have an OEE of 92.86%, which is normal, as it is above expectation. The expected OEE is *90%*. **Drilling** and Fitting have an OEE of *83.33%* and shows an alert as they are below the expected OEE.

The duration will be computed automatically on the routing based on the last 30 work orders processed at the work centers. Look at the following screenshot of routing:

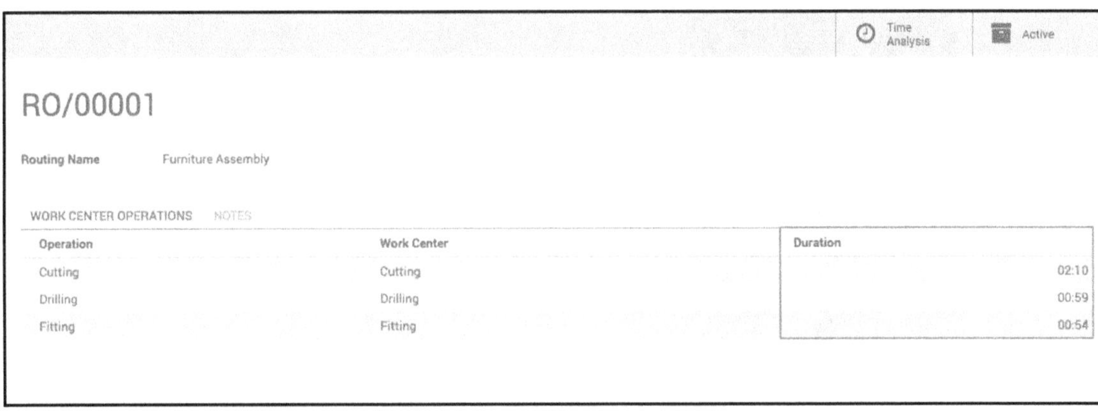

For the next work order created for **Computer Desk**, the operation time for the work centers will be taken from the duration computed in the routing. The time computed on the routing does not include the time required to be spent before and after production.

Assuming that the order has been planned but the material has not arrived, or it has arrived but with a different size and shape, we have to wait until the required material arrives. Until then, it has to be marked as time lost due to material unavailability. Click on the gray icon visible on the work center screen; a popup will appear asking you for the **Loss Reason** and **Description** of blocking, as seen in this screenshot:

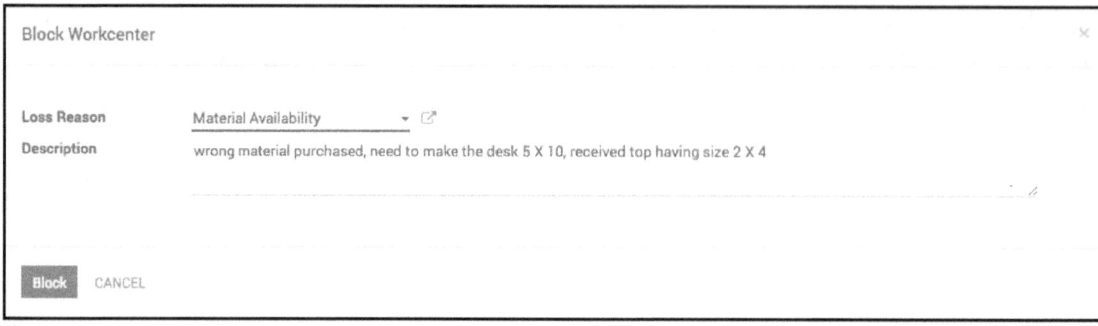

Select the reason, enter the description, and click on the **Block** button. The work center goes to the block stage, and you cannot process any work orders on that work center. When you check the OEE report, a **Material Availably** of a one-time loss is recorded at the work center, which affects the overall work center OEE, as seen in this screenshot:

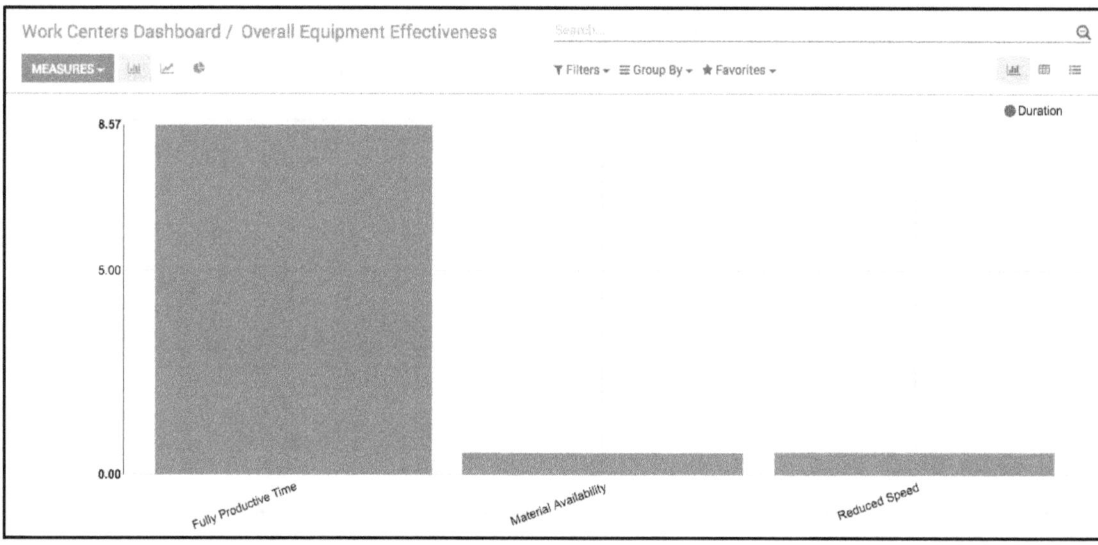

Cost of operations - operating cost

Each business is required to add the operational cost to the cost of the finished product to get the correct cost of the finished product. We have already seen how to compute the cost of a finished product by adding the cost of the components in the *Complete the first manufacturing order* recipe earlier.

Let's see how to add the operations cost to the cost of the components so that we can have the final cost of the product.

The cost of operations includes the cost of electricity, labor, or any other additional direct or indirect costs incurred to complete the manufacturing operation.

The operations cost can be configured at the work center; you have to derive the **Cost per hour** for each work center. It includes all the operational **Costs per hour** for a work center. The following is a screenshot of a **Cutting Work Center** having a cost of 270 per hour:

The cost per hour will be used to compute the cost of operations based on the time taken to complete the operation at the work center.

Assume that the costing method for all the components, and the final product, **Computer Desk**, is set to **Real Price**. On top of that, we have three work centers each consuming electricity and labor. Based on these costs, we compute the **Cost per hour** for each work center, as shown in this table:

Number	Work Center	Cost / hour	Duration
1	Cutting	270	4:24
2	Drilling	250	00:49
3	Fitting	460	1:02

Let's process a manufacturing order which was completed in some minutes. Look at the duration in which **Computer Desk** was produced in the preceding table. The **Cost Analysis** report will be generated as soon as you click on the **MARK AS DONE** button. The following screenshot shows the cost report:

Computer Desk

1.0 Unit(s), from 1 manufacturing order(s).

Cost Structure

Raw Materials	Quantity	Unit Cost	Total Cost
Bolt	8.0 Unit(s)	$ 18.00	$ 144.00
Table Top	1.0 Unit(s)	$ 510.00	$ 510.00
Table Lag	4.0 Unit(s)	$ 95.00	$ 380.00
		Total Cost of Raw Materials	**$ 1,034.00**

Cost of Operations

Operator	Operation	Working Time	Cost/hour	Total Cost
Administrator	Cutting	0.0358333333333 hours	$ 270.00	$ 9.68
Administrator	Drilling	0.0628333333333 hours	$ 250.00	$ 15.71
Administrator	Fitting	0.0458333333333 hours	$ 460.00	$ 21.08
			Total Cost of Operations	$ 46.47
			Unit Cost	**$ 1,080.47**

We have two different types of costs listed in the report: the cost of components and the cost of operation depending on the time spent on each operation.

The average cost of **Computer Desk** produced in our plant can be printed from the **Cost Analysis** report available on the product form. The total cost of production can be divided by the number of units produced. This will help us achieve the average cost per unit produced in the plant.

Let's take an example of two manufacturing orders. The components are bought at different rates for the two different manufacturing orders, and the operations are performed within different durations at each work center. This is shown in the following table:

Component	Cost Price for MO/00001	Cost Price for MO/00002
Table Top	490	510
Table Leg	100	95
Bolt	16	18

The following report is printed from the **Computer Desk** product after successfully completing the two manufacturing orders listed earlier:

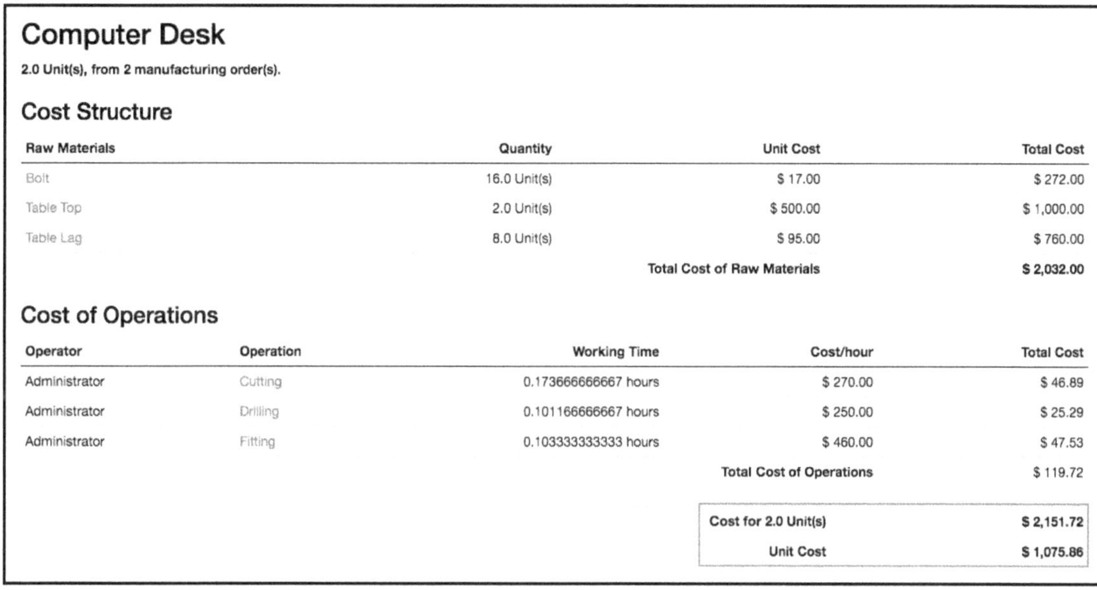

Computer Desk

2.0 Unit(s), from 2 manufacturing order(s).

Cost Structure

Raw Materials	Quantity	Unit Cost	Total Cost
Bolt	16.0 Unit(s)	$ 17.00	$ 272.00
Table Top	2.0 Unit(s)	$ 500.00	$ 1,000.00
Table Lag	8.0 Unit(s)	$ 95.00	$ 760.00
		Total Cost of Raw Materials	**$ 2,032.00**

Cost of Operations

Operator	Operation	Working Time	Cost/hour	Total Cost
Administrator	Cutting	0.173666666667 hours	$ 270.00	$ 46.89
Administrator	Drilling	0.101166666667 hours	$ 250.00	$ 25.29
Administrator	Fitting	0.103333333333 hours	$ 460.00	$ 47.53
			Total Cost of Operations	$ 119.72

Cost for 2.0 Unit(s)	**$ 2,151.72**
Unit Cost	**$ 1,075.86**

Aside from the **Cost Analysis** report, but the **Inventory Valuation** report also includes the cost of **Computer Desk** as per the costing computed during production. Let's check the Inventory Valuation report under the **Inventory** application. We will have two **Computer Desks** having two different values as per the manufacturing cost:

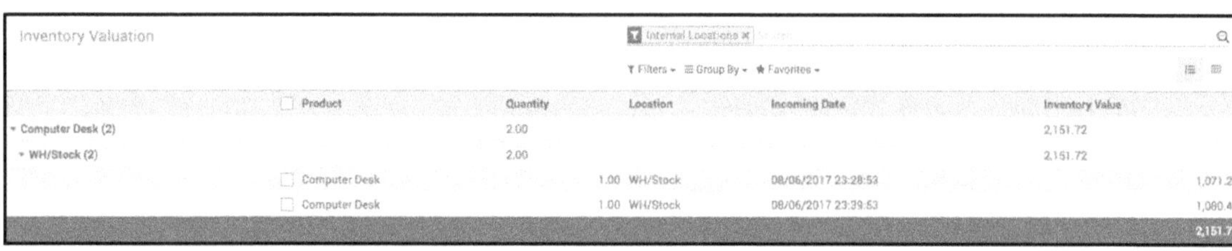

Inventory Valuation

Internal Locations

Filters Group By Favorites

	Product	Quantity	Location	Incoming Date	Inventory Value	
Computer Desk (2)		2.00			2,151.72	
WH/Stock (2)		2.00			2,151.72	
	Computer Desk	1.00	WH/Stock	08/06/2017 23:28:53		1,071.25
	Computer Desk	1.00	WH/Stock	08/06/2017 23:39:53		1,080.47
						2,151.72

The average cost price will be available in the cost analysis report no matter which costing method is set to compute the costing for the finished product.

Component consumption

A complex assembly line has many work centers, and each work center consumes one or many components. The components have to be added to build the final product, assuming that hundreds of components are added to complete the final product.

It would be too difficult to keep track of the sequences in which the components are added. You can actually define which component has to be added at which work center to define the sequence of adding the components to the final product.

Let's take the example of **Computer Desk**. We have three components, and each component is required at a specific work center. You can define which component will be consumed during which operation. Look at the following bill of material configuration, where I have configured which component will be consumed during which operation:

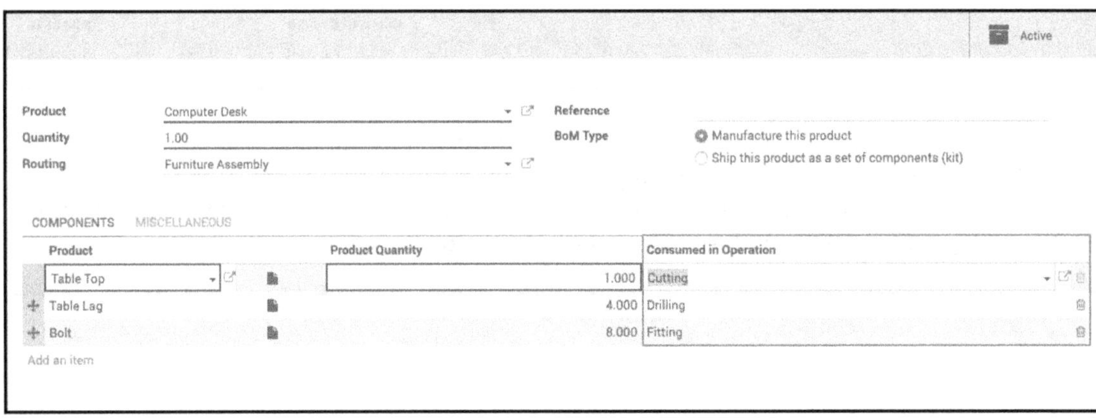

Save the bill of material and you are ready to test the flow in production. Let's create the manufacturing order for one quantity of **Computer Desk**. Look at the next screen of the manufacturing order that I have created. The components are not available yet. It can be scheduled for production, and the schedule will create the procurement order to purchase the components. Later, it can be started at the work center when the components are available:

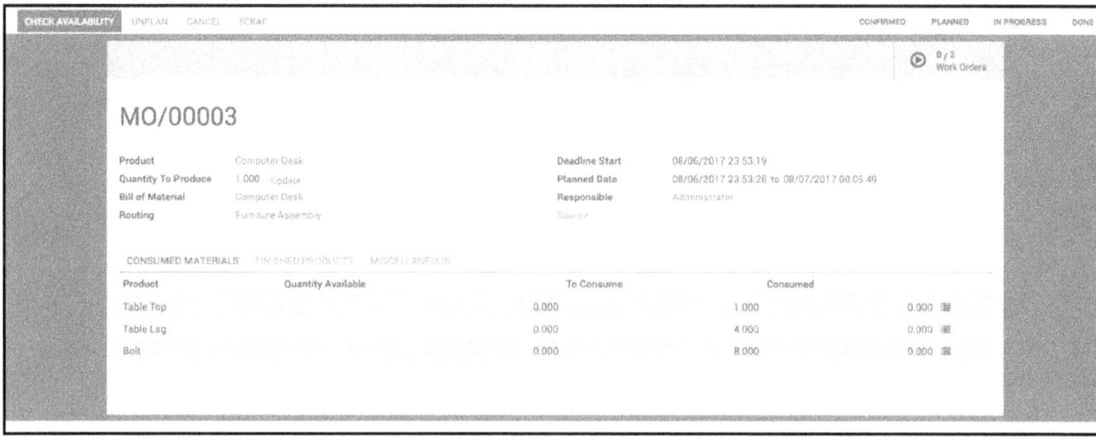

Process the procurement, and receive the components. As soon as the components are received, the manufacturing order will be ready to be produced.

Make sure that you have enabled the feature **Track lot and serial numbers** in the Inventor application, and configure the components to be tracked by Lot, and the final product **Computer Desk** to be tracked by unique serial number.

Go to the **Cutting** work center and open the work order; it will be ready to be worked on as soon as the components are available:

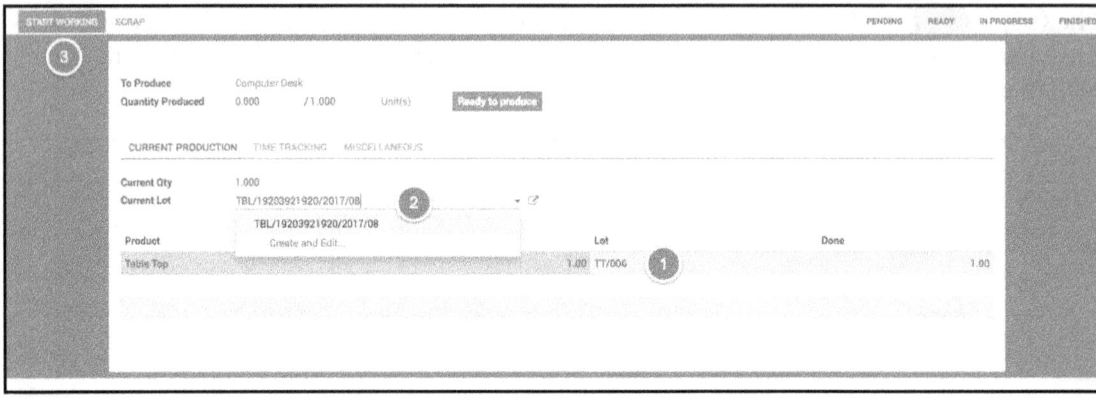

As we have enabled the component consumption at the operation level, we will get the list of components that will be consumed during the **Cutting** operation. The first step is to select the lot/serial number for the component assigned from the inventory.

The final product is tracked by unique serial number. Please assign a serial number by creating a new serial number. Finally, click on the **START WORKING** button to start production. You will be asked to select the component by assigning the correct serial or lot number for each operation; complete all the operations.

Complete the manufacturing process in the end by clicking on the **MARK AS DONE** button. This will also update the quantity of finished products in the inventory.

In the case that work item has more than one quantity, all the quantities can be processed at once if the final product is tracked by the lot number. The **Computer Desk** is tracked by a unique serial number, so only one quantity can be processed for each operation at a time.

Each time, assign the **serial/lot** number for the component, create a new serial for the **Computer Desk**, and start the operation. When you finish the process of one quantity, you will be asked to assign the component and serial number for the next quantity to be produced:

Take a look at the preceding screenshot of an operation where one quantity is already produced. The operation asks you to assign the lot for the Table Top and serial number for the final product to be produced next.

Workorder messages

When workers work at the same work center for a long time, it becomes a routine for them, and as a result, sometimes they may make a mistake when there is a small change in the bill of material or the process.

Most of the time, the worksheet is attached to the operation, but it's still possible to have such small mistakes, which can lead to quality issues.

A warning message can be raised for the workers at a specific work center when they are working on a specific product. It will be helpful to attract the worker's attention to the message before they proceed further. The worker order message will look as shown in the following screenshot:

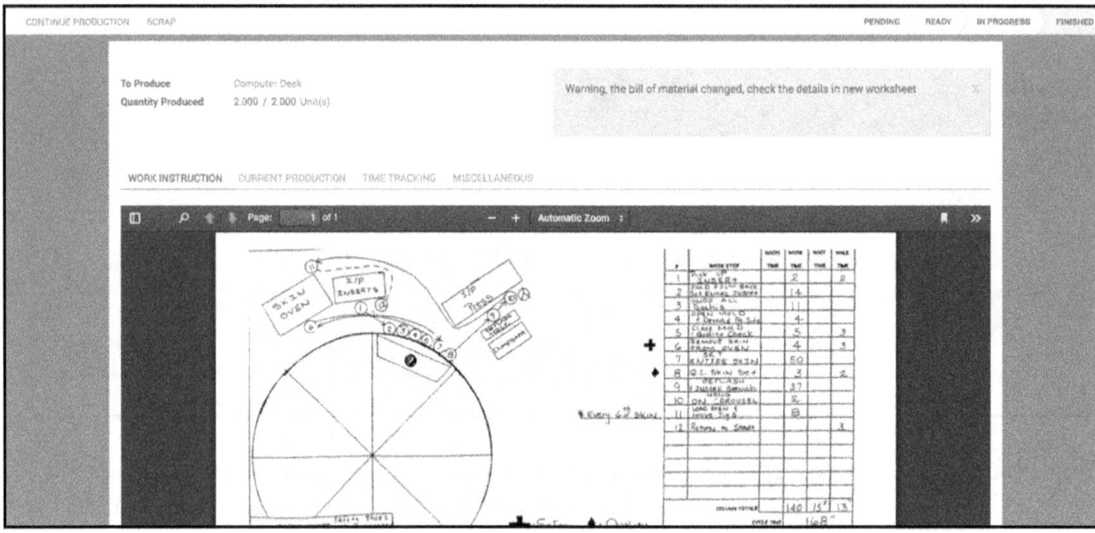

The alert message can be viewed easily. It encourages workers to check the worksheet carefully, and thus reduces the chance of making mistakes.

The warning message can be created by clicking on **Operations** | **Workorder Message** under the **Manufacturing** application. Click on the Create button to create a new Message. The following is a screenshot of the workorder message creation:

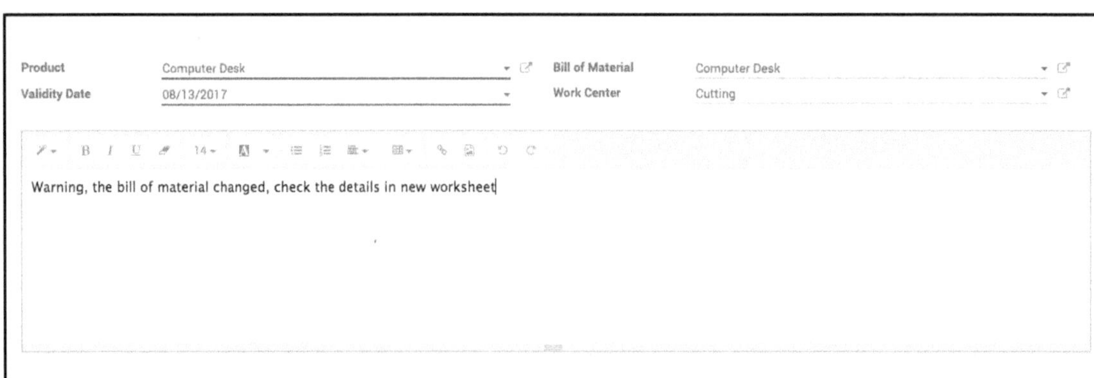

The message will be displayed on the work order when the selected work center processes the selected product with the selected bill of material. The message is displayed for one week from the date of creation. You can change **Validity Date** to change the duration.

> **TIP:** The quality department uses this system to issue a quality alert that informs the workers to double check for defects in the components until they find the root cause of the quality issue. The maintenance department may issue a warning for some work centers which need special treatment to run until they find the root cause of the problem in the machine.

Master production schedule

Scheduling and planning of manufacturing orders can be done either automatically or manually. Automatic planning is managed by the Odoo scheduler—it computes the expected manufacturing order start date based on the customer commitment date. The automatic scheduling of the manufacturing order is perfect for the production unit, which produces the product on demand.

Imagine a factory which works 24/7; they have to plan in different ways instead of schedules based on demand. They have to plan based on the sales forecasts and expectations so that all the components are available in time to meet the sales forecasting.

Take the example of a **Computer Desk—**the Table Top is supplied by the vendor. They need six days to deliver the Top, while other components take only four days to be delivered. If any of the components are not available, they cannot be on time for production, which impacts the targeted sales.

Let's see how the Master Production Schedule (MPS) helps us to trigger the procurements for the finished product, and the purchase order to buy the components based on sales forecasting.

Getting ready

Before we start scheduling the purchase or manufacturing using the master production schedule, it is assumed that you have deep knowledge of the vendor price list and Delivery Lead Time.

How to do it...

1. The Master Production Schedule is an additional feature; it can be activated from the **Configuration** | **Settings** page of the **Manufacturing** application.

   By default, the **Master Production Schedule** is not activated. Select **Use Master Production Schedule in order to create procurements based on forecasts** option in the **Master Production Schedule** field, available under **Extra Features**, and click on the **APPLY** button to activate the feature.

2. On the **Master Production Schedule**, a new menu will be added under the Reporting of Manufacturing application. Click on it, and you will see this screen:

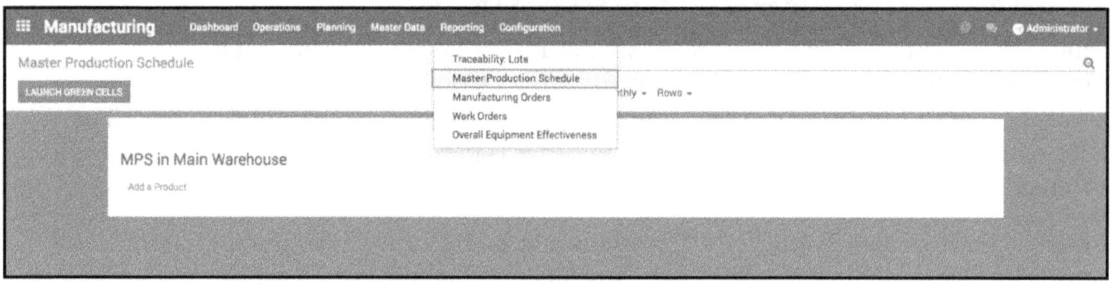

   Click on the **Add a Product** link to add the product to the **Master Production Schedule**. A popup will appear asking you to select the product.

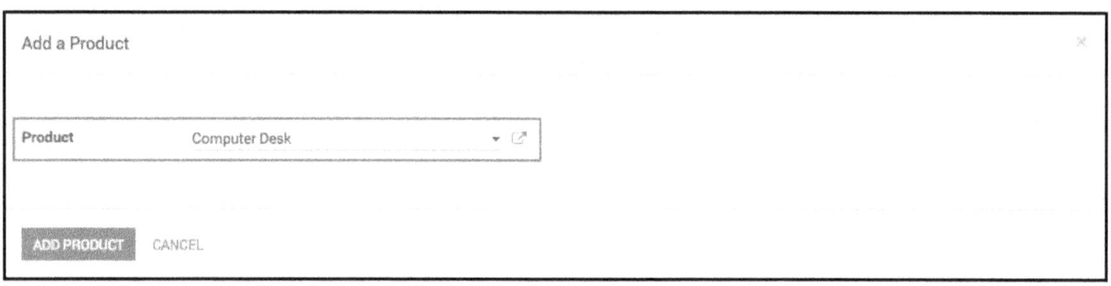

   Select the product you want to add to the scheduling and click on the **ADD PRODUCT** button.

The **Computer Desk** product will be added to the Master Production Schedule; in the same way, it adds the components that are used to build the **Computer Desk**. Look at following screenshot of the **Master Production Schedule**:

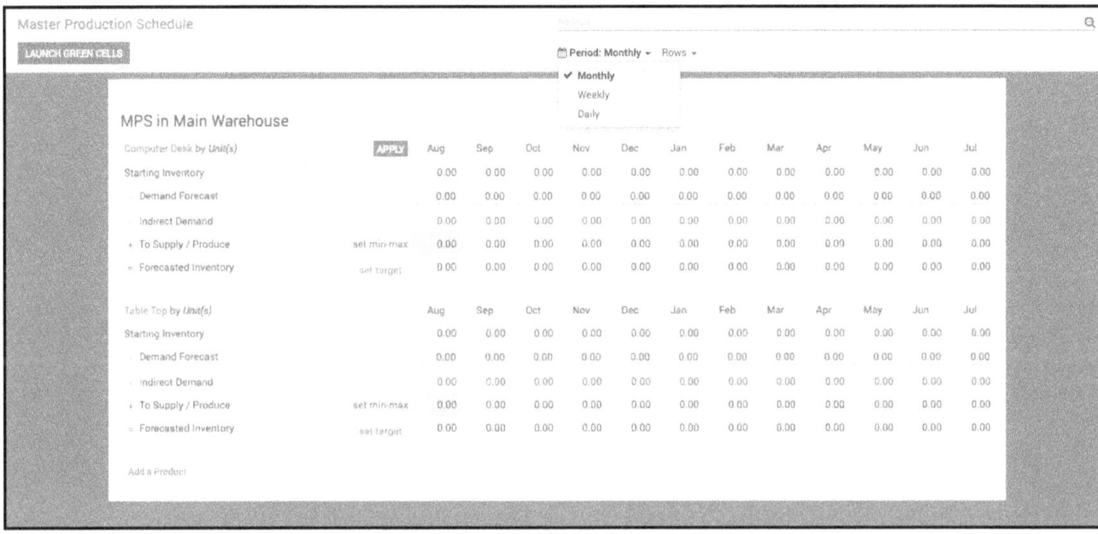

3. The **Master Production Schedule** can be prepared on a **Monthly**, **Weekly**, or **Daily** basis depending on the industry. Each product has the **Starting Inventory**, **Demand Forecast**, **Indirect Demand**, plus **Supply or Produce**. In the end, **Forecasted Inventory** is the closing stock to be secured in an inventory:
    - **Starting Inventory**: This is the opening stock in the warehouse
    - **Demand Forecast**: This refers to the expected demand or sales forecasting
    - **Indirect Demand**: This refers to the product which is used as a component for the final product—depending on the demand of the final product, the indirect demand for the component is generated
    - **To Supply/Produce**: This is the number or quantity that has to be bought or produced; it is determined based on customer demand or sales forecasting
    - **Forecasted Inventory**: This is the closing inventory stock for the product, also known as the buffer stock

Choose the period by which you would like to do the planning; I have selected **Monthly**.

4. The first thing that needs to be set is the **min-max** and **target** for all the products. Based on this, the quantity on the production schedule will be computed.

   Clicking on **min-max** or **set target**, you will be able to set the **Forecasted Inventory** and Minimum and Maximum to supply or produce depending on the product routes configuration:

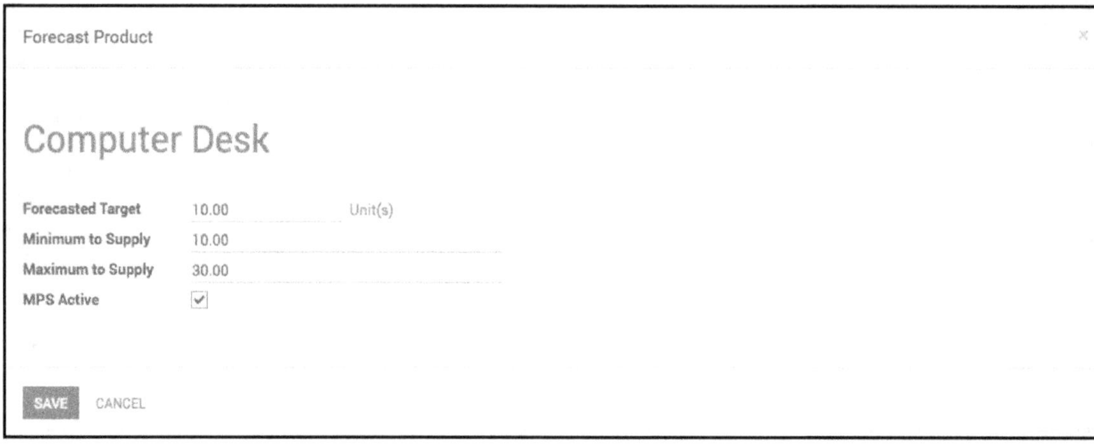

   Forecasted Inventory is set to 10, which means that at the end of the month, we want to keep 10 quantities as buffer stock. This will become the **Starting Inventory** for the next month. Minimum and Maximum actually represent the capacity of the production:

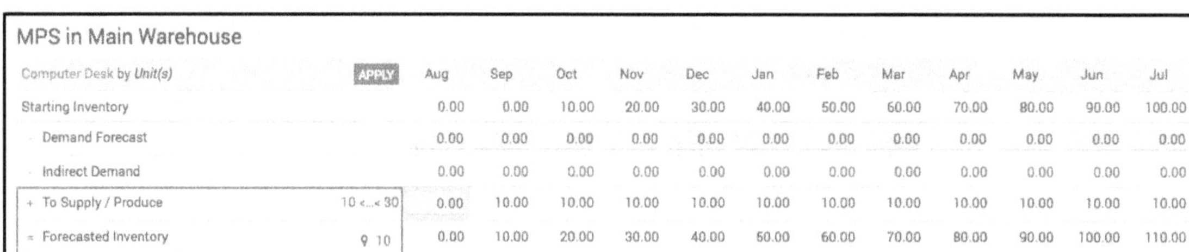

Computer Desk by *Unit(s)*	APPLY	Aug	Sep	Oct	Nov	Dec	Jan	Feb	Mar	Apr	May	Jun	Jul
Starting Inventory		0.00	0.00	10.00	20.00	30.00	40.00	50.00	60.00	70.00	80.00	90.00	100.00
- Demand Forecast		0.00	0.00	0.00	0.00	0.00	0.00	0.00	0.00	0.00	0.00	0.00	0.00
- Indirect Demand		0.00	0.00	0.00	0.00	0.00	0.00	0.00	0.00	0.00	0.00	0.00	0.00
+ To Supply / Produce	10 <...< 30	0.00	10.00	10.00	10.00	10.00	10.00	10.00	10.00	10.00	10.00	10.00	10.00
= Forecasted Inventory	10	0.00	10.00	20.00	30.00	40.00	50.00	60.00	70.00	80.00	90.00	100.00	110.00

   Likewise, set the min-max and target for all the products added onto the master production schedule. In case the product is a component, the min and max is the capacity given by the vendor for the accepting the order or delivery. After setting the **min-max** and **target** it will look like the preceding screen.

5. Before you start, make sure that all the vendors and their price lists are configured correctly with the **Delivery Lead Time** for all the components.

Component	**Delivery Lead time**	**Price**
Table Top	6 Days	500
Table Lag	4 Days	100
Bolt	4 Days	16

Let's schedule **Computer Desk**, the finished product, and the demand for the component will be scheduled automatically. Start filling the **Demand Forecast**, the sales forecasting, or sales target for **Computer Desk** by month. Look at the schedule I have created based on the sales forecasting:

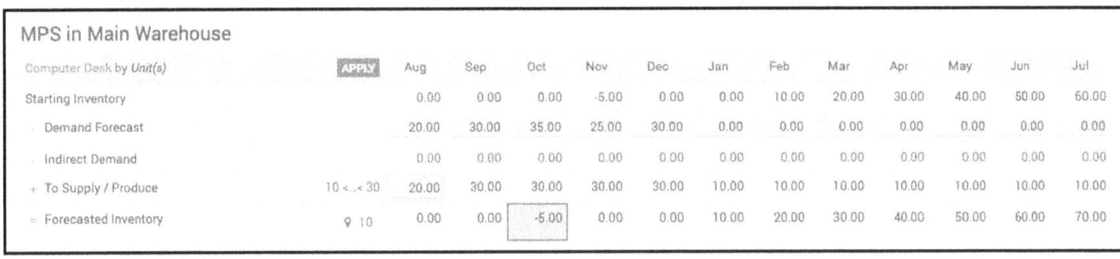
MPS in Main Warehouse

Computer Desk by *Unit(s)*	APPLY	Aug	Sep	Oct	Nov	Dec	Jan	Feb	Mar	Apr	May	Jun	Jul
Starting Inventory		0.00	0.00	0.00	-5.00	0.00	0.00	10.00	20.00	30.00	40.00	50.00	60.00
- Demand Forecast		20.00	30.00	35.00	25.00	30.00	0.00	0.00	0.00	0.00	0.00	0.00	0.00
- Indirect Demand		0.00	0.00	0.00	0.00	0.00	0.00	0.00	0.00	0.00	0.00	0.00	0.00
+ To Supply / Produce	10 <...< 30	20.00	30.00	30.00	30.00	30.00	10.00	10.00	10.00	10.00	10.00	10.00	10.00
= Forecasted Inventory	10	0.00	0.00	-5.00	0.00	0.00	10.00	20.00	30.00	40.00	50.00	60.00	70.00

There is a problem in the month of October. We have a negative closing stock.

We have a demand of 20 in August, 30 in September, and we produce 20 in August and 30 in September, which is same as the demand, and, as a result, we do not have any buffer stock at the end of August and September.

6. The rest of the month's schedule asks us to produce only 10 products, which is the lower capacity of the production plant. We cannot produce more than 30, as it is the maximum capacity of the production plant per month.

The actual problem starts from the month of August, as we did not maintain the buffers stock. October is the month when we have a high demand, which means that we should have the buffer stock in September. In the month of September, we run with the full capacity, and thus do not have more capacity to generate the buffer stock.

August is the only month in which we can still produce more than 10 quantities and keep the buffer stock to meet the future demand.

Let's change **To Supply/Produce** to 30 instead of 20 in the month of August, as shown in the following screenshot:

MPS in Main Warehouse

Computer Desk by *Unit(s)*	APPLY	Aug	Sep	Oct	Nov	Dec	Jan	Feb	Mar	Apr	May	Jun	Jul
Starting Inventory		0.00	10.00	10.00	5.00	10.00	10.00	20.00	30.00	40.00	50.00	60.00	70.00
- Demand Forecast		20.00	30.00	35.00	25.00	30.00	0.00	0.00	0.00	0.00	0.00	0.00	0.00
- Indirect Demand		0.00	0.00	0.00	0.00	0.00	0.00	0.00	0.00	0.00	0.00	0.00	0.00
+ To Supply / Produce	10 <...< 30	30.00	30.00	30.00	30.00	30.00	10.00	10.00	10.00	10.00	10.00	10.00	10.00
= Forecasted Inventory	10	10.00	10.00	5.00	10.00	10.00	20.00	30.00	40.00	50.00	60.00	70.00	80.00

It is just the perfect idea to increase production by 10 more quantities in the month of August.

There are two ways of scheduling in Odoo: automatic scheduling using the scheduler and minimum stock rules using the reorder level, or manual scheduling using the master production schedule. Make sure that when you do the master production schedule, the reorder level should not be created or configured for the products managed by the Master Production Schedule.

7. Finally, we succeed in scheduling the forecast with a buffer stock to meet the future demand.

Click on the **APPLY** button available beside the product name. It will propagate the demand for the components added to the Master Production Schedule so that the indirect demand is generated for those components, and **To Supply/Produce** will be computed based on that:

MPS in Main Warehouse

Computer Desk by *Unit(s)*		Aug	Sep	Oct	Nov	Dec	Jan	Feb	Mar	Apr	May	Jun	Jul
Starting Inventory		0.00	10.00	10.00	5.00	10.00	10.00	20.00	30.00	40.00	50.00	60.00	70.00
- Demand Forecast		20.00	30.00	35.00	25.00	30.00	0.00	0.00	0.00	0.00	0.00	0.00	0.00
- Indirect Demand		0.00	0.00	0.00	0.00	0.00	0.00	0.00	0.00	0.00	0.00	0.00	0.00
+ To Supply / Produce	10 <...< 30	30.00	30.00	30.00	30.00	30.00	10.00	10.00	10.00	10.00	10.00	10.00	10.00
= Forecasted Inventory	10	10.00	10.00	5.00	10.00	10.00	20.00	30.00	40.00	50.00	60.00	70.00	80.00

Table Top by *Unit(s)*		Aug	Sep	Oct	Nov	Dec	Jan	Feb	Mar	Apr	May	Jun	Jul
Starting Inventory		0.00	0.00	0.00	0.00	0.00	0.00	0.00	0.00	0.00	0.00	0.00	0.00
- Demand Forecast		0.00	0.00	0.00	0.00	0.00	0.00	0.00	0.00	0.00	0.00	0.00	0.00
- Indirect Demand		30.00	30.00	30.00	30.00	30.00	10.00	10.00	10.00	10.00	10.00	10.00	10.00
+ To Supply / Produce	set min-max	30.00	30.00	30.00	30.00	30.00	10.00	10.00	10.00	10.00	10.00	10.00	10.00
= Forecasted Inventory	set target	0.00	0.00	0.00	0.00	0.00	0.00	0.00	0.00	0.00	0.00	0.00	0.00

8. Finally, it's the time to launch the procurements. The procurements can be launched by clicking on the green dots.

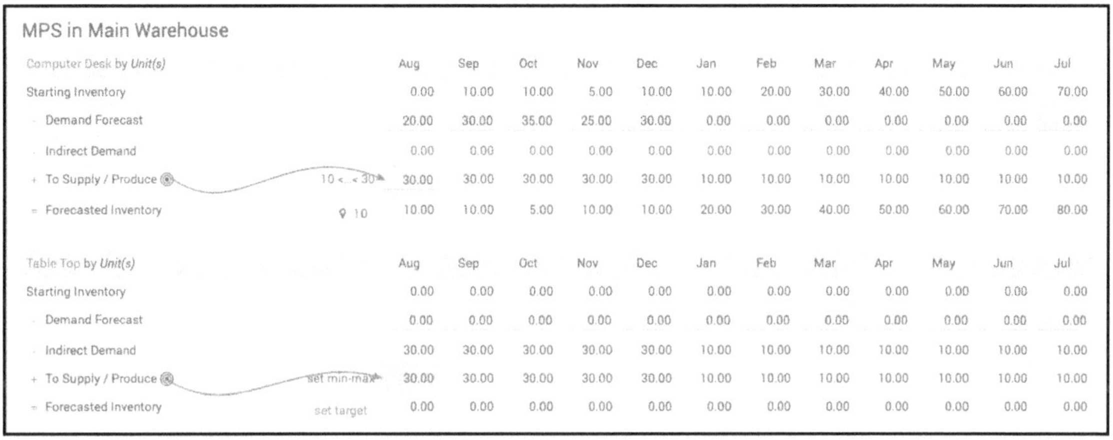

MPS in Main Warehouse

Computer Desk by *Unit(s)*		Aug	Sep	Oct	Nov	Dec	Jan	Feb	Mar	Apr	May	Jun	Jul
Starting Inventory		0.00	10.00	10.00	5.00	10.00	10.00	20.00	30.00	40.00	50.00	60.00	70.00
- Demand Forecast		20.00	30.00	35.00	25.00	30.00	0.00	0.00	0.00	0.00	0.00	0.00	0.00
- Indirect Demand		0.00	0.00	0.00	0.00	0.00	0.00	0.00	0.00	0.00	0.00	0.00	0.00
+ To Supply / Produce	10 <...< 30	30.00	30.00	30.00	30.00	30.00	10.00	10.00	10.00	10.00	10.00	10.00	10.00
= Forecasted Inventory	10	10.00	10.00	5.00	10.00	10.00	20.00	30.00	40.00	50.00	60.00	70.00	80.00

Table Top by *Unit(s)*		Aug	Sep	Oct	Nov	Dec	Jan	Feb	Mar	Apr	May	Jun	Jul
Starting Inventory		0.00	0.00	0.00	0.00	0.00	0.00	0.00	0.00	0.00	0.00	0.00	0.00
- Demand Forecast		0.00	0.00	0.00	0.00	0.00	0.00	0.00	0.00	0.00	0.00	0.00	0.00
- Indirect Demand		30.00	30.00	30.00	30.00	30.00	10.00	10.00	10.00	10.00	10.00	10.00	10.00
+ To Supply / Produce	set min-max	30.00	30.00	30.00	30.00	30.00	10.00	10.00	10.00	10.00	10.00	10.00	10.00
= Forecasted Inventory	set target	0.00	0.00	0.00	0.00	0.00	0.00	0.00	0.00	0.00	0.00	0.00	0.00

It is recommended to click all the green dots individually to launch the procurement for an individual product. It will launch the procurement of only the cells having a green background.

There is also a way to launch all the green cells by clicking on the **LAUNCH GREEN CELLS** button available at the top of the screen.

9. Once the procurement is launched for the green cells, the cells will be locked and we cannot modify them. Make sure you schedule everything correctly before launching it.

For the current month, the procurement is launched for **Computer Desk**, and it creates the manufacturing order for the current month. Look at the following screenshot of the manufacturing order:

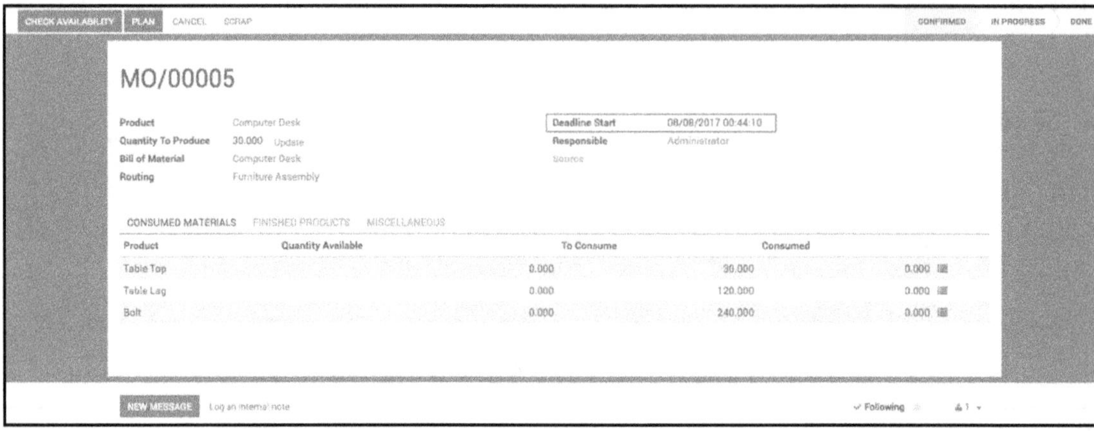

The launching of the green cells for the components will trigger the procurement. It will create the purchase order to procure the components. The following screenshot shows a request for a quotation:

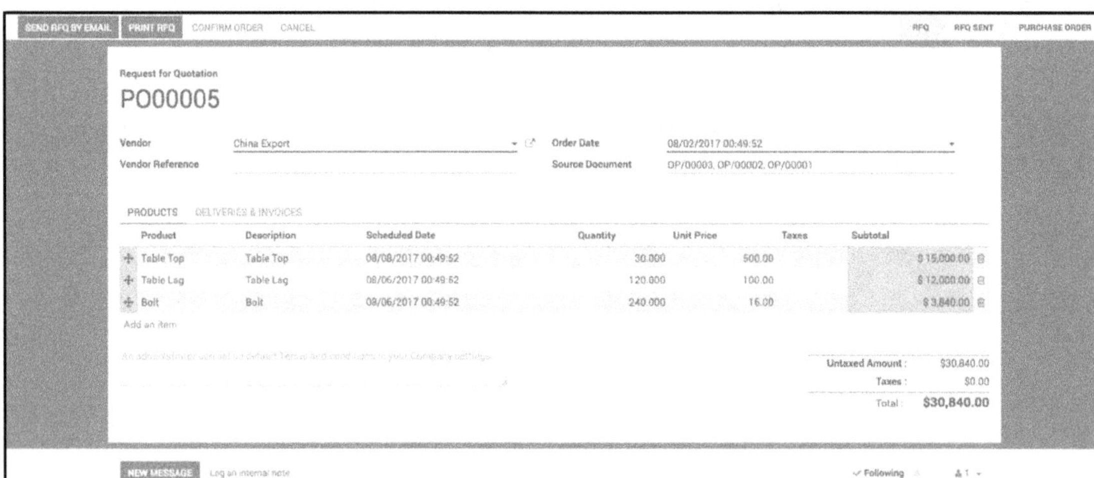

There's more...

There are many different departments involved in the production. Each one should be updated about the schedule and the target for the production and the purchase department should know about the purchase forecast.

The document can be printed from the scheduling, and rows can be chosen in printing depending on the responsibility. Rows can be selected from the **Rows** menu available on the top so that only required rows can be kept, and the rest will be hidden in the report.

Look at the following screenshot, where the rows are selected to be printed in the **Master Production Schedule** report for the production department. They don't take the Demand Forecast or Forecasted Inventory into consideration:

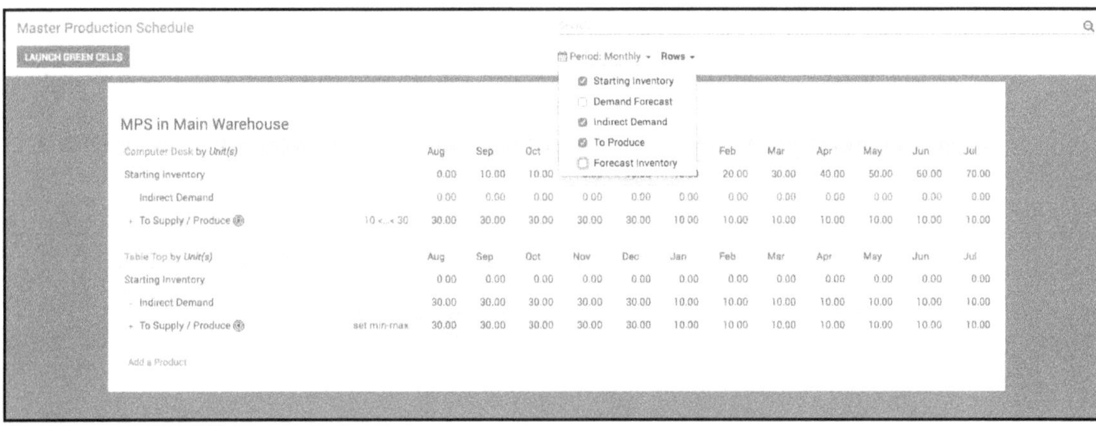

The report can be configured and printed for the relevant people or department depending on the rows selected for the report.

Selling combo products using kit

Selling kits or combo products is normal in business. Preparing kits is not a standard production process. It is just a way to combine different products together and name it as a new product.

Products which are used together can be grouped and sold as a kit, for example, selling a keyboard and a mouse with a laptop as a combo product, or selling a chair with a Computer Desk. The kit or combined products help to increase the sales.

A sales order is required to sell the kit product, and a delivery order delivers the components of the kit product. The stock of the kit product is not maintained in the warehouse. In the warehouse, we have the stock of the components. The invoice will be created for the kit product and not for the components.

Let's see how the kit product is configured, sold, delivered, and invoiced in Odoo.

How to do it...

1. The required features are already activated. It requires the **Sales**, **Inventory**, and **Manufacturing** applications to sell a kit or combo product. Create a new product which you would like to sell as a kit from **Sales** | **Sales** | **Product**. I am going to create a combo product of **Computer Desk + Chair**, as I would like to offer a chair at a lower price if it is purchased along with a computer desk:

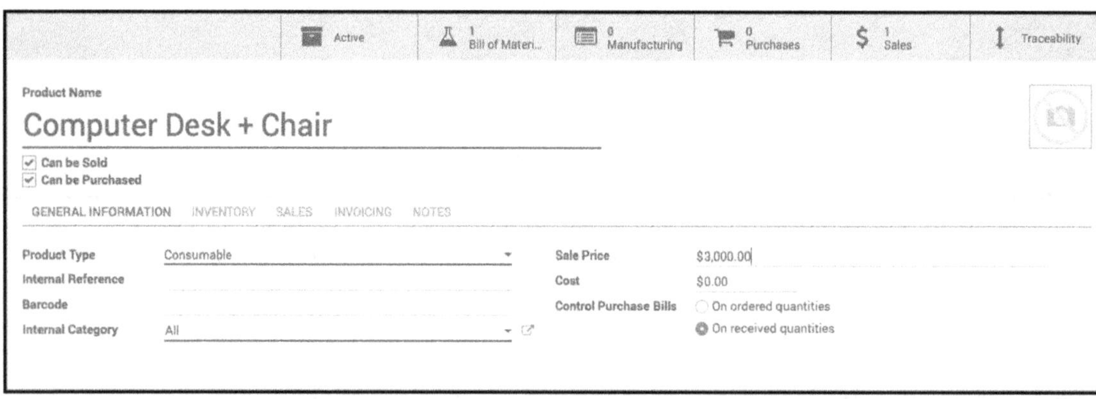

If someone buys a chair, it will cost them 650, but if they buy it along with the computer desk, it will cost them only 500.

2. The kit product can be created from **Master Data** à **Bill of Material**. Create a new bill of material, select the product **Computer Desk + Chair**, and add the Components as **Computer Desk** and **Chair**. The **BoM Type** should be switched to **Ship this product as a set of components (kit)** instead of *Manufacture this product*.

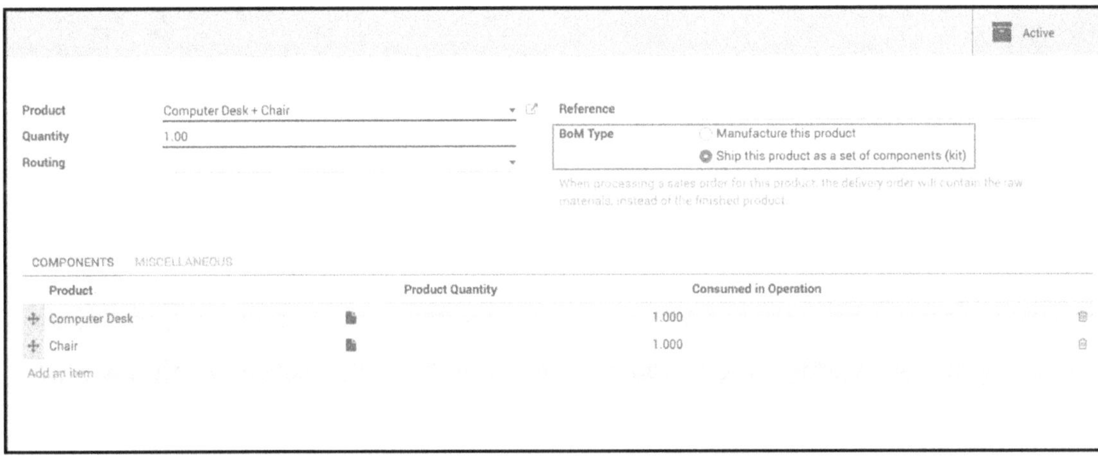

You don't need to define the routing on the kit product, as this does not follow the manufacturing process. The route is set on the kit product to buy and not to manufacture the computer Desk + Chair.

3. Assume that there is an enough stock available for the desk and chair in the inventory. Let's create a sales order and sell one quantity of the Computer Desk + Chair product.

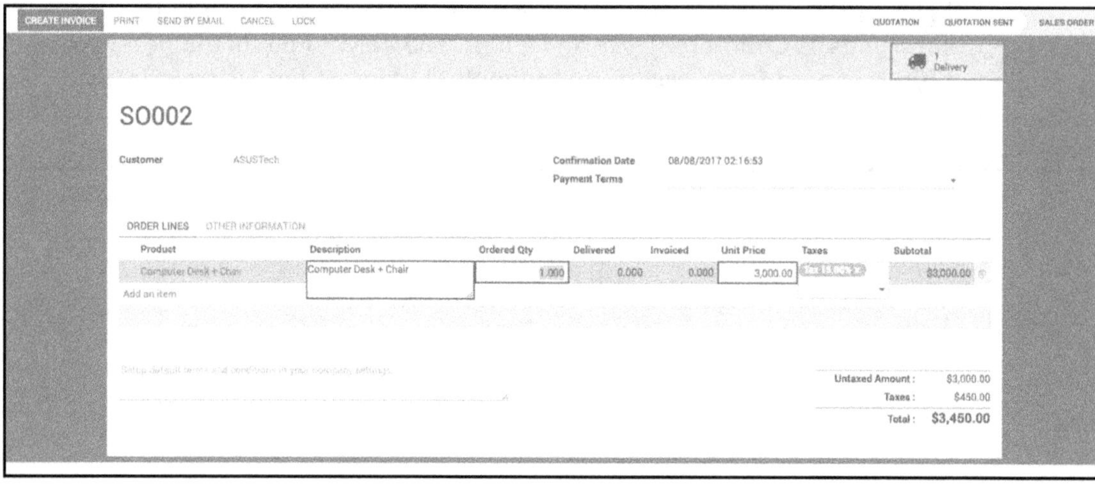

Confirm the order. The preceding screenshot shows the page for confirming the sales order.

4. Click on the **Delivery** action button to process the delivery order. You will get the delivery order with two items to be delivered from the warehouse.

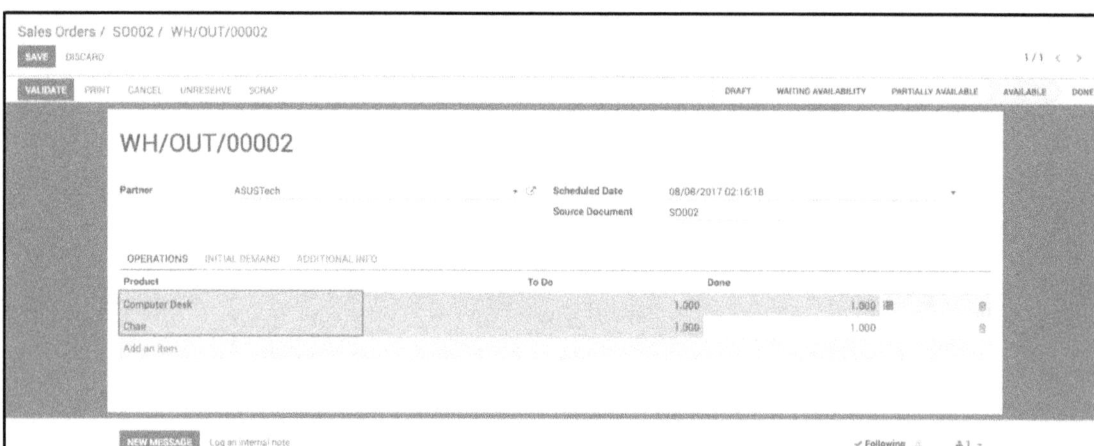

5. **Computer Desk + Chair** is a kind of a virtual product. The system finds the bill of material for the **Computer Desk + Chair** product, which is a type of kit.

After processing the delivery order, it's time to create an invoice. Click on the **CREATE INVOICE** button, keep the default option in the wizard, and click on the **CREATE AND VIEW INVOICES** button.

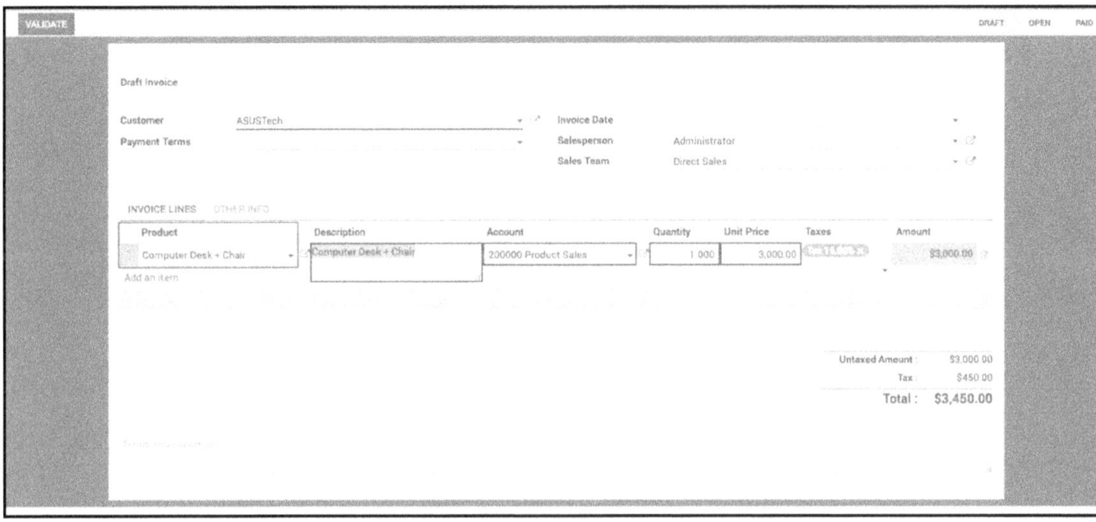

The invoice is created for the **Computer Desk + Chair** product which was actually sold in the sales order.

There's more...

I'm not sure that it can be a real business case, but with the Odoo product kit, we buy the kit product from the vendor and receive the components of the kit product in the warehouse. But the kit is a product which is created by us to increase the sales.

You can create a purchase order for the kit product **Computer Desk + Chair**. As soon as you confirm the purchase order, you will have the incoming reception created with its component. The next screenshot shows the reception order:

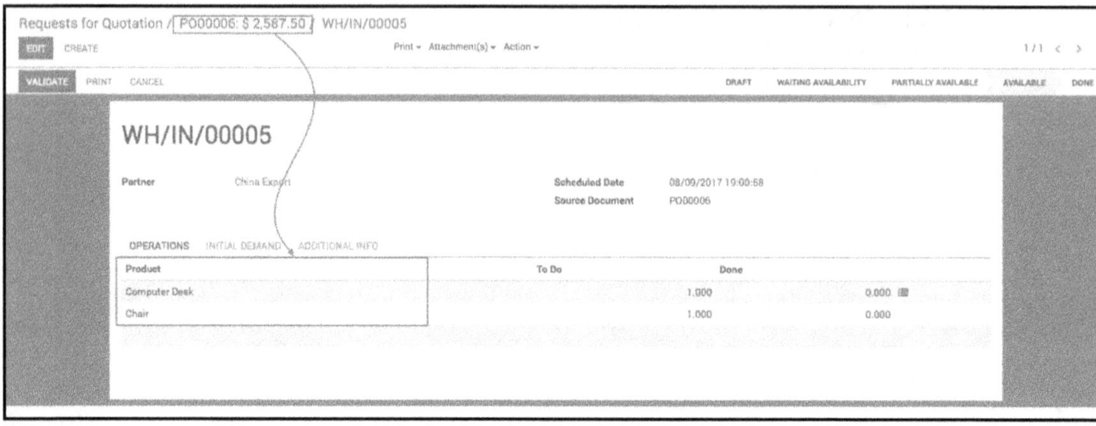

13

Product Life Cycle Management and Maintenance

In this chapter, we will cover the following recipes:

- Product lifecycle management
- Maintenance management

Introduction

The manufacturing process involves many different departments and people to work together. The key to success in quality manufacturing processes depends on the information flow and integration between them.

Assume that the quality department detects a defect in the finished product. Until the quality department identifies the root cause, the production has to be blocked. The root cause is identified. For example, one of the raw materials, the bolt, has a quality problem. Either quality checking has to be improved at the reception for every purchase of a bolt in the warehouse or the purchase department may decide to change the vendor of that part.

A small defect in a finished product leads to the involvement of many different people. It may be possible that the product manager may change the design in the table that leads to the engineering manufacturing change and needs to change the bill of material routing.

Let's see how Odoo manages the engineering change in the product that either makes changes in the component or routing process. Let's also understand how Odoo manages the corrective and preventive maintenance of the work center and equipment of the work center.

Product lifecycle management

Designing a new product requires the involvement of many different departments, starting from setting up the bill of materials, the assembly line, the purchase of quality components, and scheduling the reception, which requires the involvement of the purchase and warehouse department. Collaboration among them can help us better plan the manufacturing orders and deliver the finished product to the customers on time.

Let's see how Odoo product lifecycle management can help us design the bill of materials or assembly line, get the involvement and approval from different departments and people, and put the product changes or assembly changes in production.

How to do it...

1. The Product Lifecycle Management feature has to be activated from **Configuration | Settings** under the **Manufacturing** application, if you would like to involve all those responsible in the engineering change process:

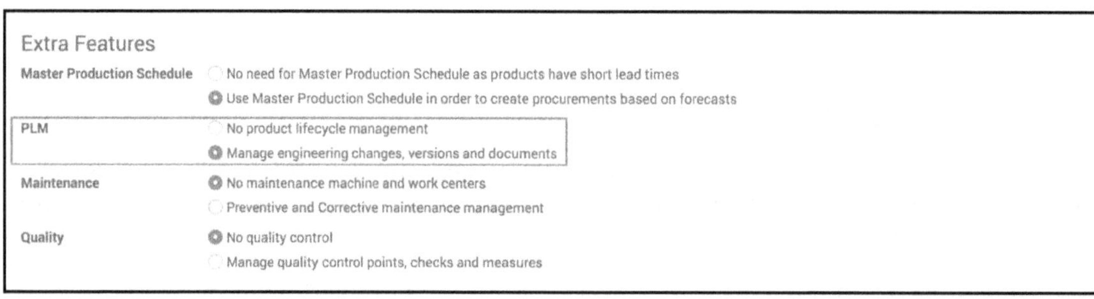

   Click on the **APPLY** button to save and activate the feature.

2. Like the **Manufacturing** application, a new application will be installed called **PLM**. It will be available on your Odoo instance. Clicking on **PLM** will let you enter into the application. You will get the **PML Dashboard** showing different types of engineering change teams:

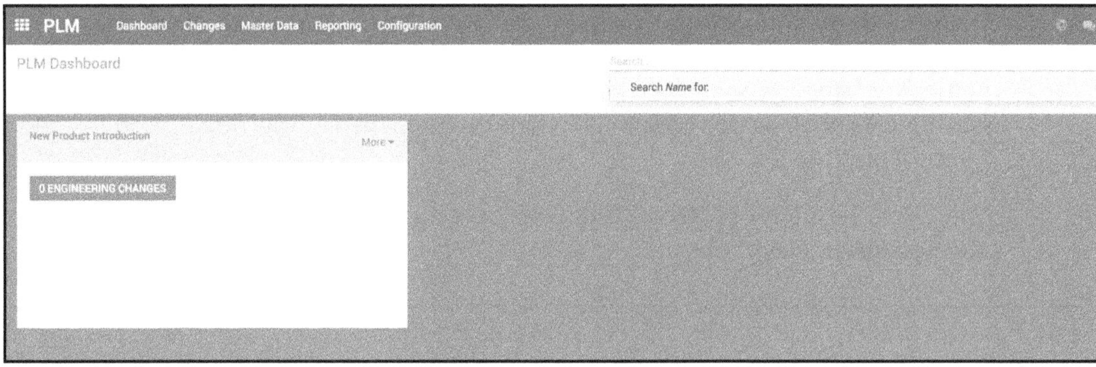

The **Engineering Change Orders** can be tracked by clicking on the **ENGINEERING CHANGES** button of the respective type, or all the engineering change orders can be found by going to **Changes** | **Engineering Change Orders** in the **PLM** application.

3. Let's propose an engineering change to **Computer Desk**. Click on the **CREATE** button to create a new change:

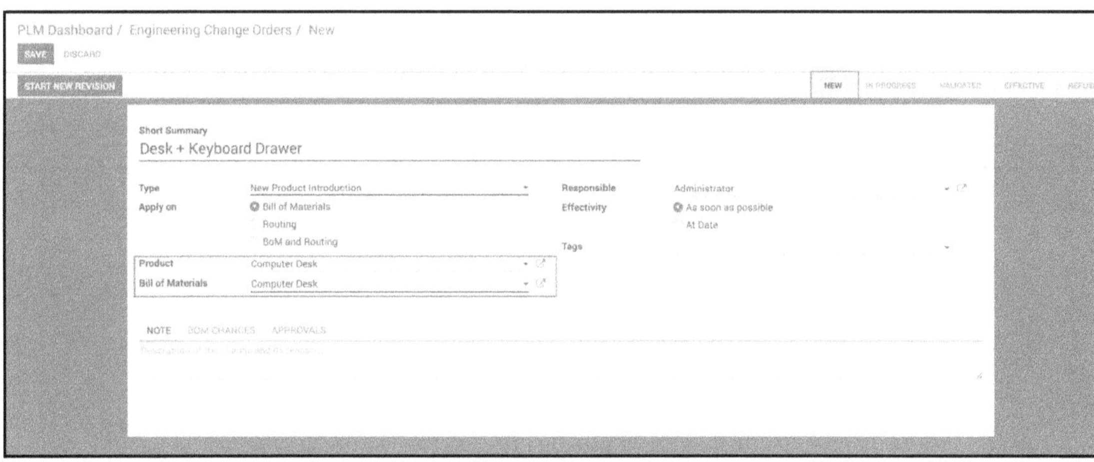

Enter the Engineering Change Order name, select **Type** as `New Product Introduction`, and select the type of changes to be designed and apply them. If change is in the component, select **Bill of Materials**. To change the assembly line, select **Routing** or select **BoM and Routing** to change both **Bill of Materials** and **Routing**.

The **Effectivity** field is important. Select the **At Date** option if the change is approved. The production starts based on the new design depending on a particular date of yours. It can be selected by choosing the option **At Date** or selecting **As soon as possible** to start production when all the departments agree on the change order.

4. Click on **START NEW REVISION** to propose a change to the bill of materials of the **Computer Desk** product:

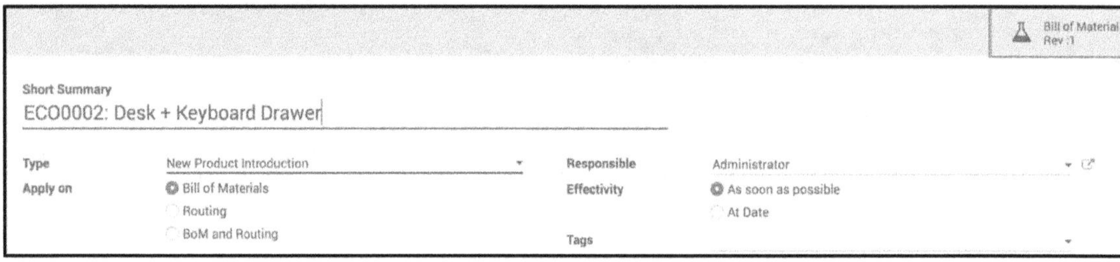

A new bill of material with the revision number 1 will be created and attached to the engineering change order of **Computer Desk**. Every change will be tracked with the revision number.

5. Click on the **Bill of Materials Rev: 1** action button. It will open the bill of materials created just now to accept the changes:

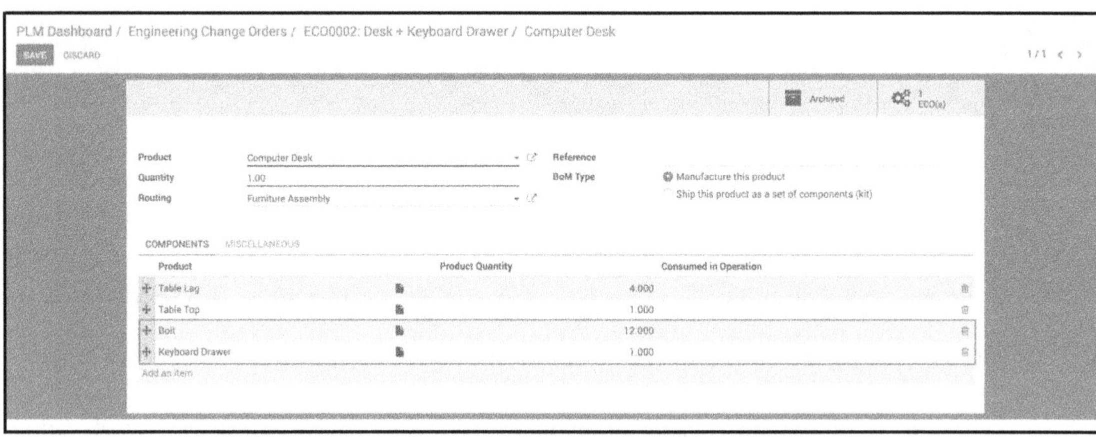

For better comfort, we have added the **Keyboard Drawer** and an additional bolt to fit the drawer. The fitting work center will take care of the fitting of the drawer during the assembly line.

6. Click on the **SAVE** button to save the changes on bill of materials and go back to the engineering change order **ECO0002: Desk + Keyboard Drawer**:

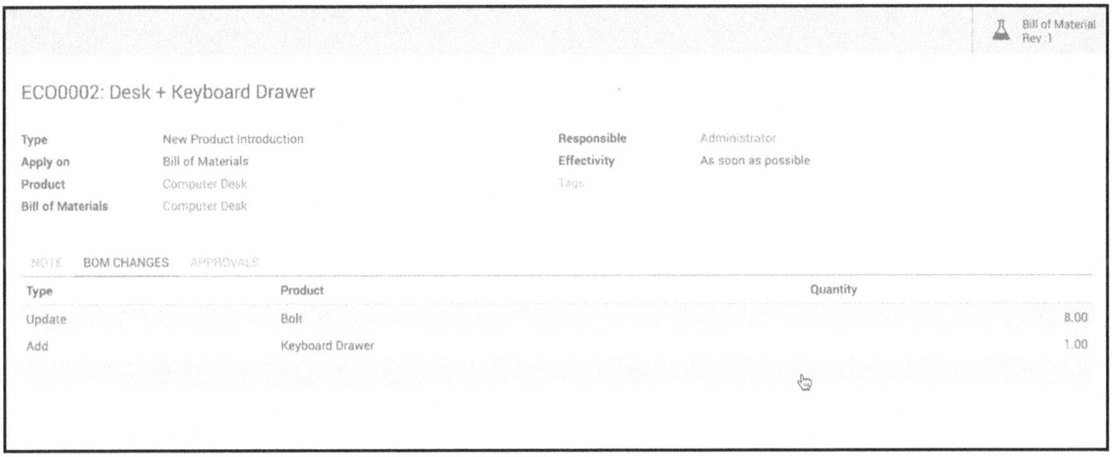

The **BOM CHANGES** tab contains the changes in **Bill of materials Rev:1** compared to the current bill of materials.

7. The BoM changes have to be verified by the concerned department and people and moved forward in the engineering change pipe. By default, it's in a new stage:

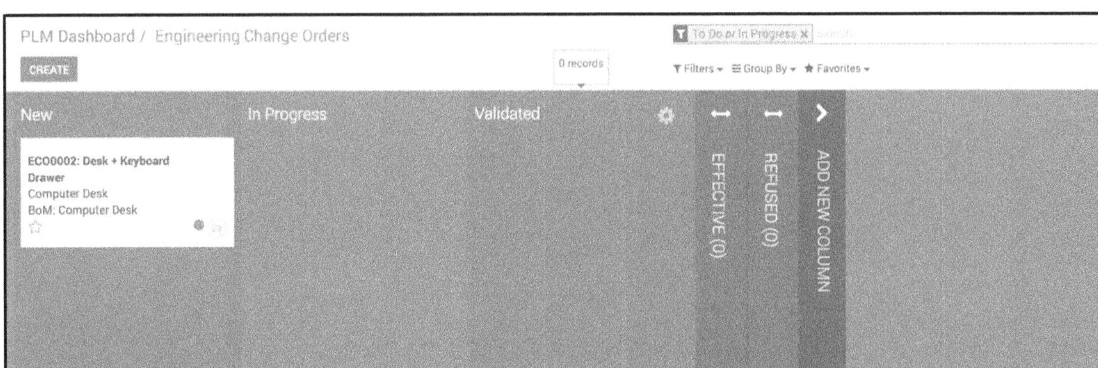

The stage can be changed, either from the engineering change pipe or on the engineering change order, by clicking on the **stage** button:

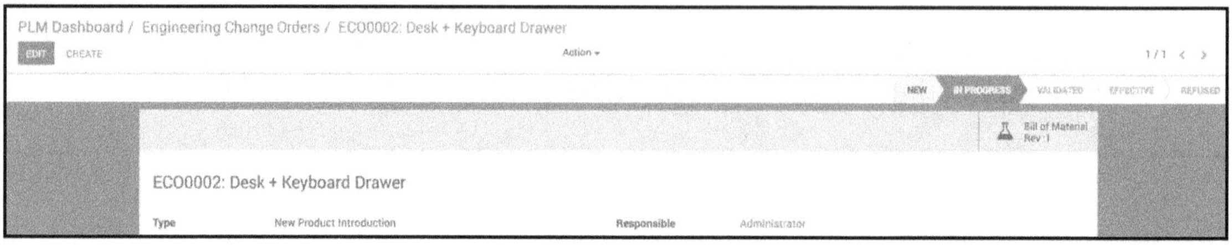

8. Make sure that the change workflow has to be configured before changing the engineering order stage. The workflow can be configured on the stage. Look at the following screenshot that shows how to enter into the stage configuration:

Click on the **configure** icon beside the stage on which you would like to configure the workflow. Click on the **Edit Stage** menu to configure the workflow. Once the engineering change comes to this stage, it requires the acceptance or rejection of the order:

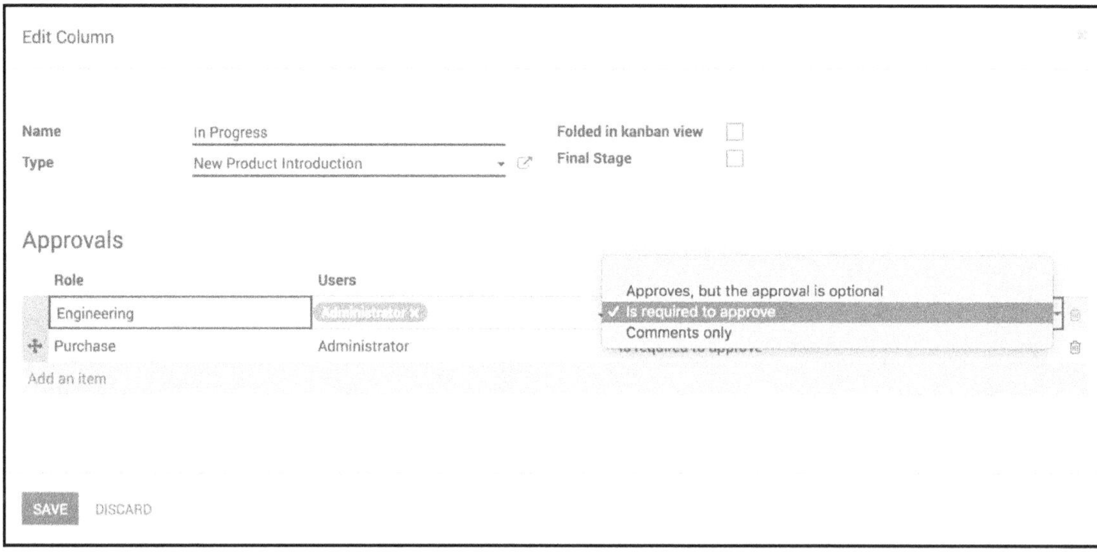

Create the **Role** per line in **Approvals**. Select the list of users who are responsible for accepting or rejecting the changes of the engineering change order.

There are three different **Approval Types**; either approval is optional. Approval is compulsory to move forward, or some departments may not take part in approval or rejection, but they have to give feedback on the engineering change. For them, keep **Comments only**.

9. As soon as the engineering change workflow is configured, the engineering change order can be moved forward to the **In Progress** stage. All the departments and people will get notified by Odoo's global notification system:

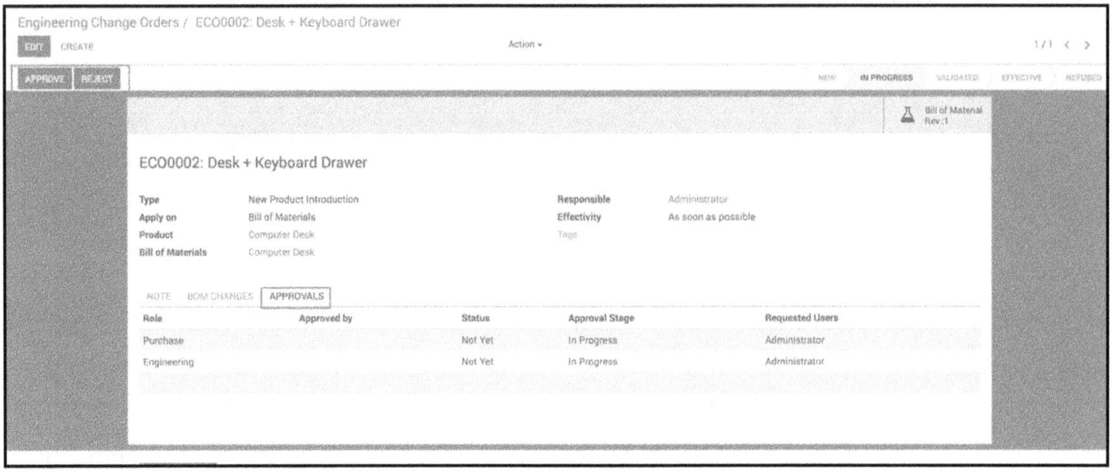

The approval workflow will be generated based on the workflow configuration. Each department either has to approve, reject, or make the notes on those changes.

10. Assuming all the departments approve the engineering change, it can be moved forward to the next stage to validate and apply in the production:

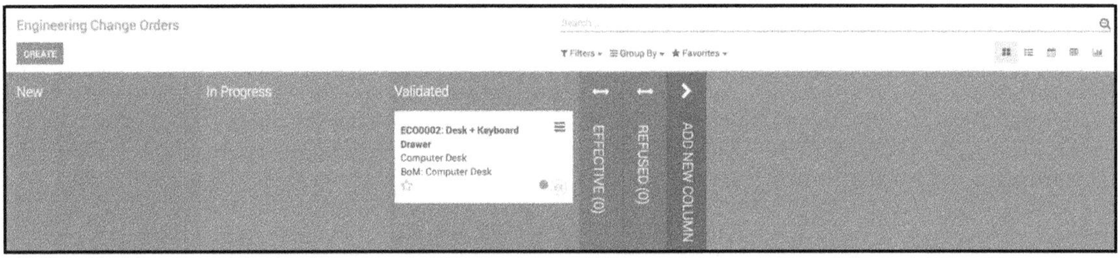

Move to the next stage as displayed in the preceding screenshot and click on the **Engineering Change Order** to get the form view:

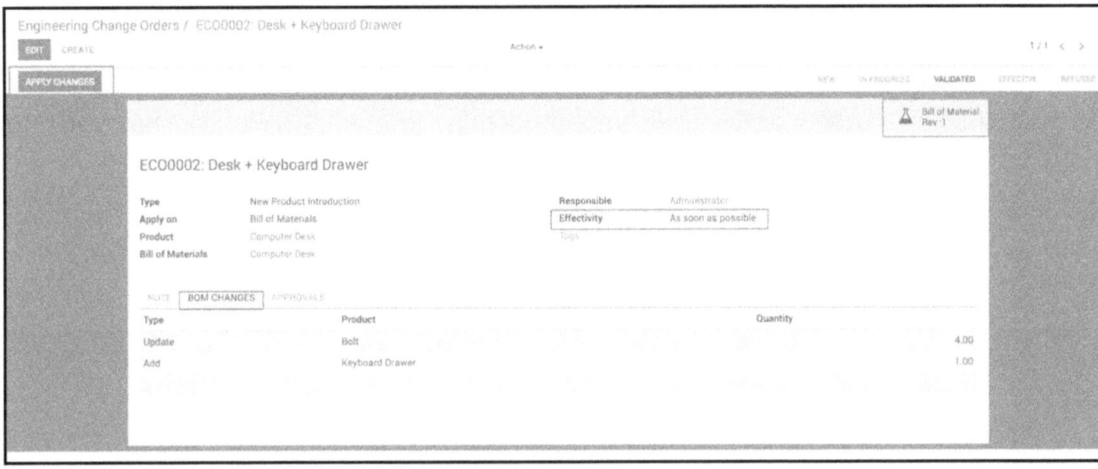

Finally, click on the **APPLY CHANGES** button to apply changes and put the **Bill of Materials Rev:1** in the production. The next manufacturing order will use the new bill of materials, just created after the **Engineering Change Order** was applied in the production.

11. Create a new manufacturing order for **Computer Desk**. You will see the component based on the new bill of material specification. Look at the following screenshot:

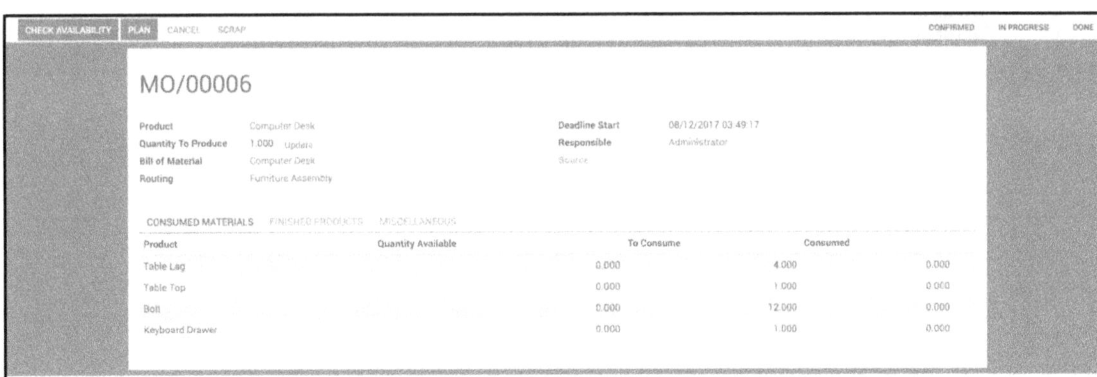

There's more...

The workers sometimes may not notice the new bill of material applied to the improved product with better design or the new components to be attached. An alert can be created to notify the workers who are working so that they can notice the change easily.

Go to the confirmed **Engineering Change Order**, and click on the **CREATE ALERT** button. A popup will appear asking for the alert message. Look at the following screenshot of the pop-up window asking for the message:

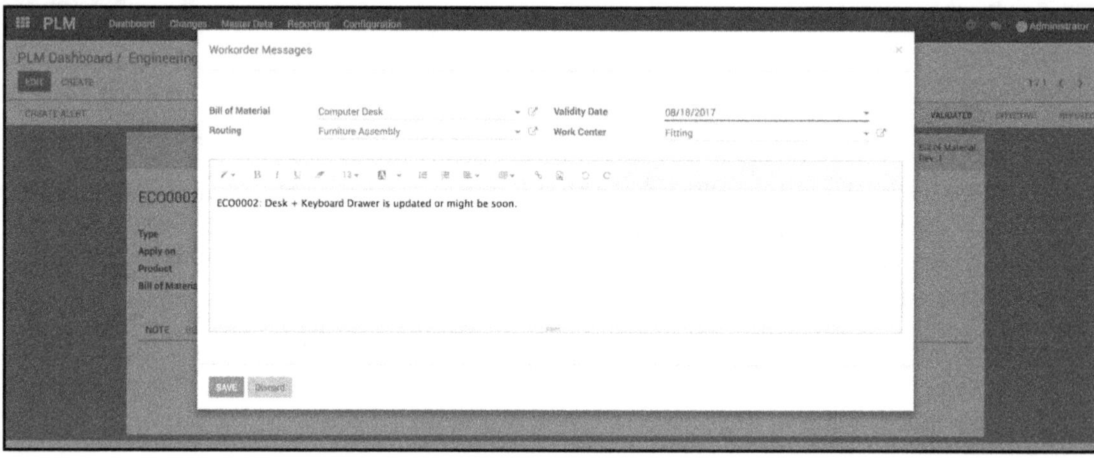

Click on **SAVE** to create an alert message. The message will be visible to the workers until **Validity Date** is defined on the alert.

The alert message will look as follows on the work order at the **Fitting** work center:

>

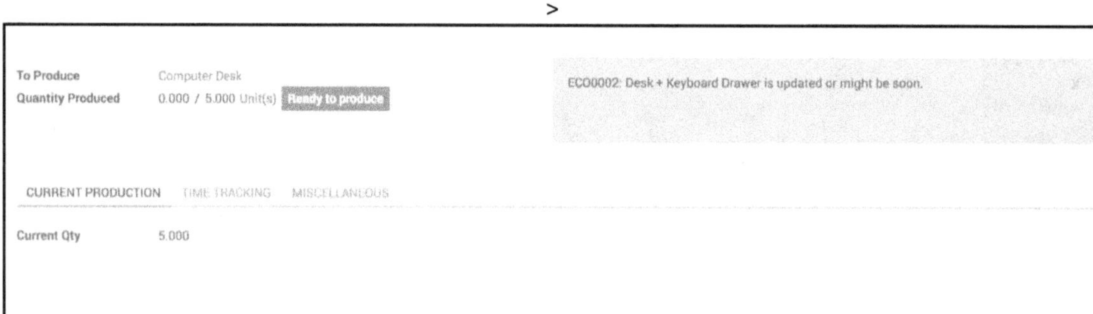

Maintenance management

Work centers are a part of the assembly line. There are various tools such as barcode scanners, drilling machines, and display panels and machines that are fixed. The machines are used to perform specific tasks. Let's take an example of a drill machine. It is a tool that has to be issued at the drilling work center to perform the drilling operation.

The maintenance of the drill machine has to be done at every fixed interval. This is called preventive maintenance. If the drill machine fails during the operation, the maintenance team has to be informed to perform the corrective maintenance.

Let's see how Odoo manages the issue and tracks tools and machines to the work centers to plan the preventive maintenance. The workers may create a maintenance request for the corrective maintenance if tools or machines fail during the operation.

Getting ready

If you would like to use the preventive or corrective maintenance for the tools or machine in your assembly line, prepare the list of tools or machine you have and make a note of the work centers they are issued to. It is advisable to give a unique identification number to each tool or machine if you have multiple tools or machines of the same type or if they do not have the serial number by the manufacturer.

How to do it...

1. Activate the preventive and corrective maintenance management from the **Configuration** | **Settings** page. It is available under **Extra Features**:

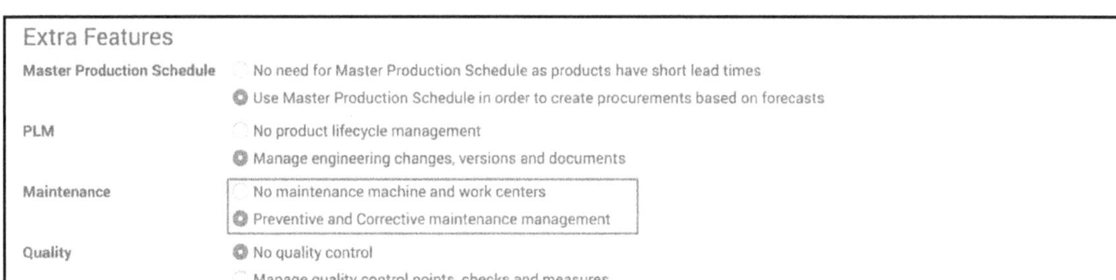

Click on **APPLY** to activate the feature. The new application will be installed, and you will have the **Maintenance** application available on the home of your instance.

2. The first configuration that has to be done after the installation of the **Maintenance** application is to create the tools or machines available in the plant. In a later step, we will see how to issue those tools or material to the work centers.
3. The tools can be created from **Equipments** | **Machines & Tools** available under the **Maintenance** application. Click on the **CREATE** button to create a new tool or machine:

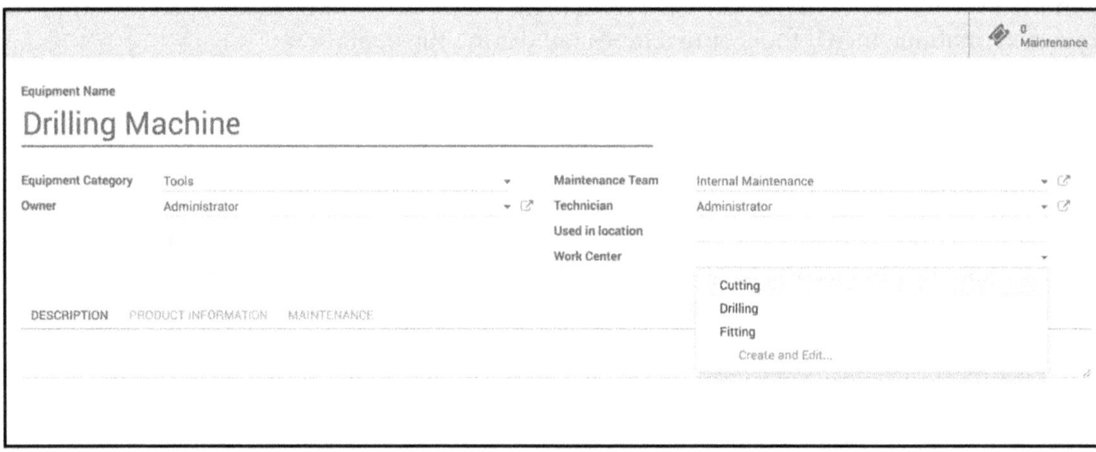

Enter the name of the equipment. Select the **Category** from the existing one or create a new one. On the right-hand side of the form, fill in the information such as **Maintenance Team** and **Technician** who will take care of the tool in case it requires the maintenance.

Select the Work Centre in the field **Work Center** where the equipment is issued.

Enter the product information under the **PRODUCT INFORMATION** tab. Look at the following screenshot of the product information of the equipment:

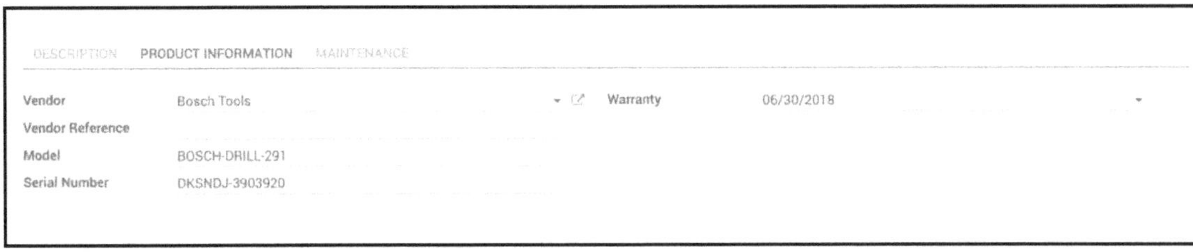

The corrective and preventive maintenance details have to be entered in the **MAINTENANCE** tab. Enter **Preventive Maintenance Frequency**, **Maintenance Duration**, and **Expected Mean Time Between Failure** depending on the equipment maintenance guideline:

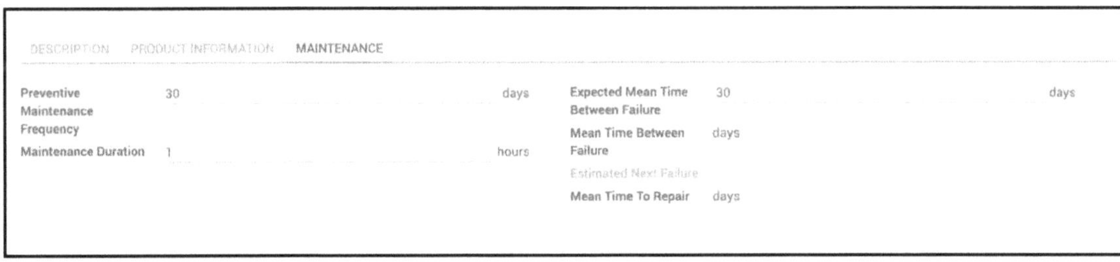

4. The **Next Preventive Maintenance** date will be computed based on the current date. **Estimated Next Failure** will be computed based on the last three consecutive corrective maintenance requests:

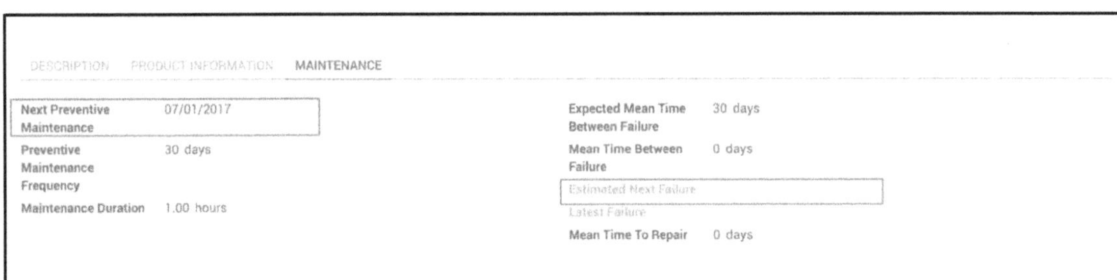

Assume that the equipment was created on June 1, 2017.

You can see the **Next Preventive Maintenance** date on all the equipment that requires preventive maintenance on the list of equipment. Look at this screenshot:

5. Assume that we have a problem with the drill machine while we are working on the Work Order at the drilling work center. Look at the Work Order screen here:

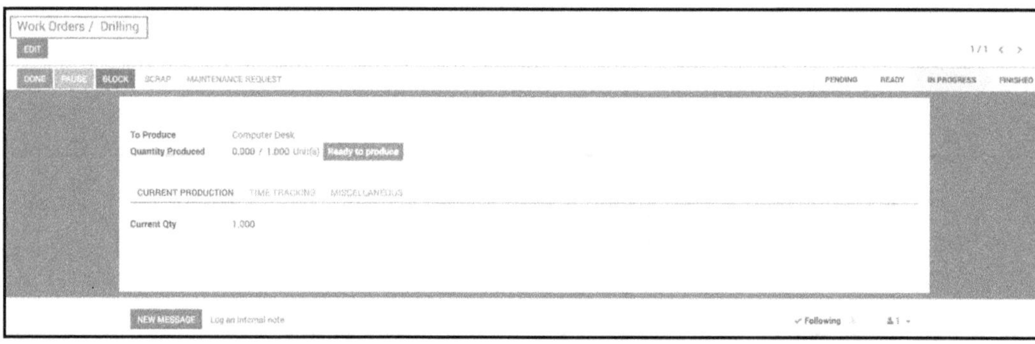

6. Click on the **MAINTENANCE REQUEST** button to raise a corrective maintenance request to the team:

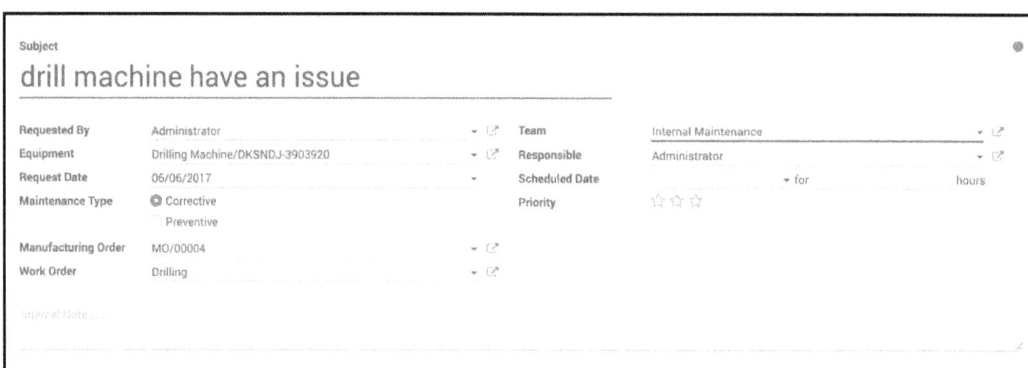

All the details will be filled automatically except equipment; the equipment has to be selected manually and other details such as the **Team** and **Responsible** fields will be filled automatically. Click on the **SAVE** button to save the maintenance request.

7. Go back to the work center and click on the **BLOCK** button to block the current operation as until the drill machine is fixed, we cannot continue the drilling operation:

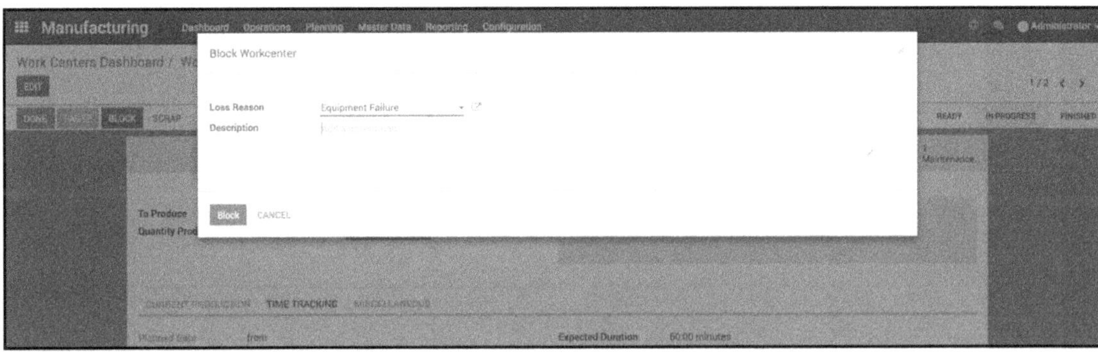

8. The **Internal Maintenance** team will get notified on their dashboard about the request. Like other Odoo applications, the **Maintenance** application also has its own dashboard where different teams are available to take care of the different types of equipment. Go to the **Maintenance** application and click on the **TO DO** button available on the **Internal Maintenance** team:

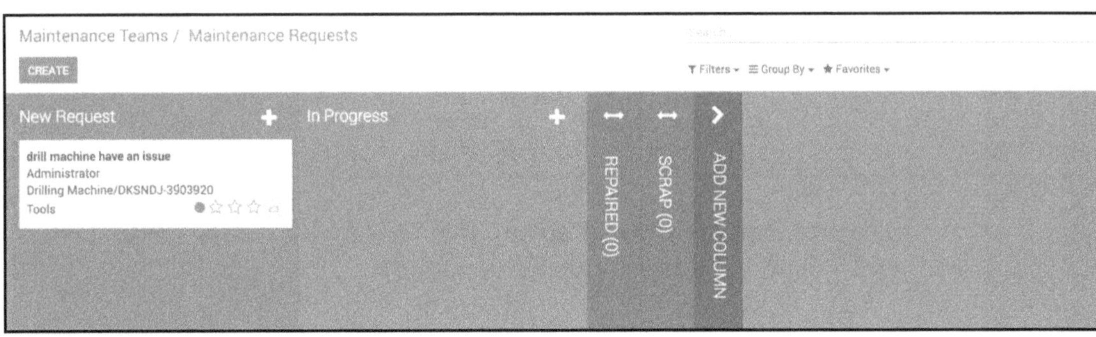

The responsible team confirms whether that the drilling machine is having an issue or not. As soon as the issue gets verified, it has to be scheduled for the maintenance and marked as green for the next step:

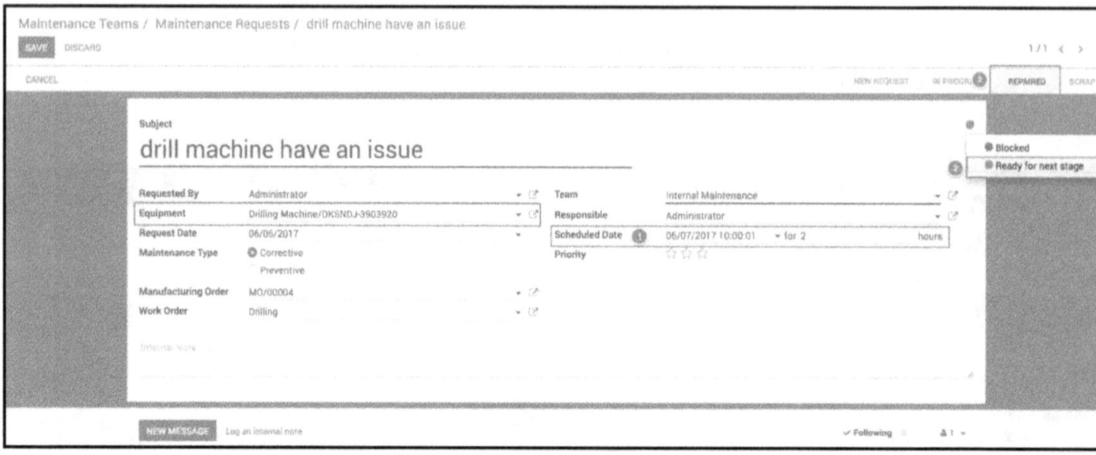

Assume that it has been fixed the next day morning, and we are ready to continue the operation. The maintenance request is set to the **REPAIRED** stage when the issue with the equipment has been fixed. Look at the equipment **MAINTENANCE** tab after fixing the first issue:

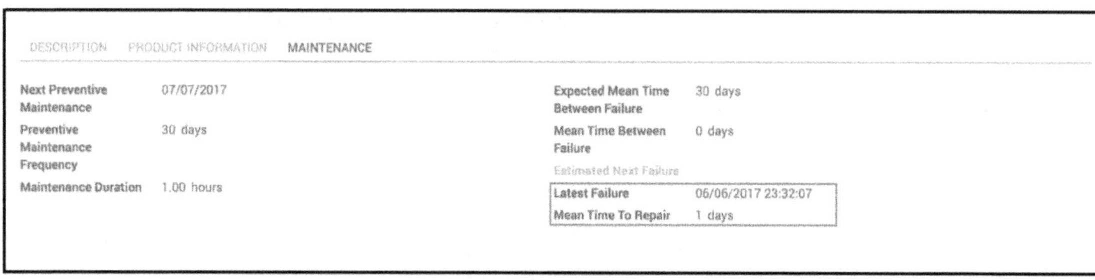

It computes the **Latest Failure** and **Mean Time To Repair** based on the first issue raised and the date and time when it was resolved.

9. Continue the working of the drilling work center by clicking on the **UNLOCK** button. Assume that the drilling work center faces three to four problems in the future. Let's see based on the past data how the **Estimated Next Failure** will be computed. Look at the drill machine history of issue date and resolution date in the following table:

Problems Reported	**Date of Issue**	**Resolved**	**Repair Time**
Drill machine has an issue	6/6/2017	7/6/2017	2 hours
Issue in drill machine	21/6/2017	21/6/2017	2 hours
Issue in drilling	20/7/2017	21/7/2017	1 hour

The **Estimated Next Failures** date and time will be computed based on the past tickets. We can also have the **Mean Time Between Failure** computed. Look at the following screenshot of the drilling machine computed maintenance plan based on the corrective maintenance of past issues:

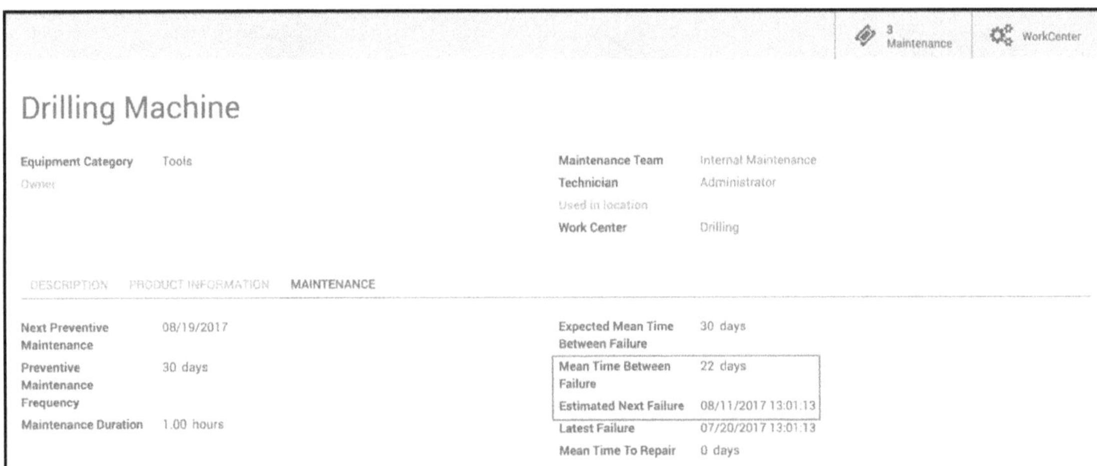

You can analyze the preceding maintenance data of the drill machine. The preventive maintenance says that every 30 days, the drill machine has to be serviced, but based on the last corrective maintenance tickets, it computes the **Mean Time Between Failure** as 22 days and **Estimated Next Failure** on 11/08/2017 13:01:13

10. Based on the corrective maintenance forecast, it would be good to improve the preventive maintenance plan. You can actually compare the two forecasting dates, Next Preventive Maintenance date, and Estimated Next Failure date, and plan the maintenance based on the earliest date for the better prevention.

There's more...

Failure of equipment affects the overall equipment efficiency. The failure of equipment blocks ongoing operation on the work center. Blocking of the drilling work center due to the failure of the drill machine affects the overall efficiency. The overall equipment effectiveness can be checked either directly from the work center or from **Reporting | Overall Equipment Effectiveness** under the **Manufacturing** application. Look at the following report generated from the reporting menu:

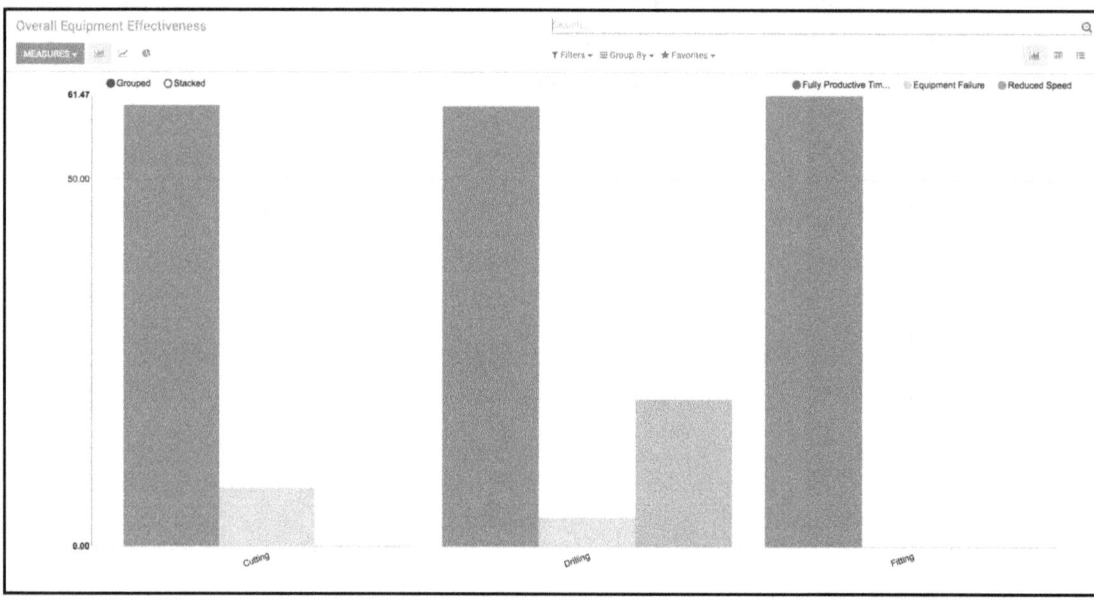

We can track from the graph that the drilling work center is mostly affected by the equipment failure.

14

Implement Project Management

In this chapter, we will cover the following recipes:

- Set up a project and manage tasks
- Project forecasting
- Managing project issues and rating

Introduction

Usually, people relate the term project management to a software project, but in the real world, it is not like that. Most businesses in any domain do their business activities in a series, which ultimately becomes one project. For example, the construction of a building becomes a project for the construction company.

In the process of construction, a company has to design many phases starting from preparing the underground parking, the construction base, and structure for the 10 floors, to interior planning. A long-term project requires the forecasting and planning of the workforce as it requires engagement from different people or teams to work on it. The phases have an estimated duration for work completion work, which is further divided into small parts of work with an estimated start date to work on and finish date. This is called a task.

Let's see how we can manage the project and task using the Odoo Project application. We can create and manage the project, define stages to manage the tasks and also forecast the tasks and plan the resources for the long-term project.

Set up a project and manage tasks

Managing a project is important in the business of a service company. A project can be anything for the service company—building construction projects for the construction company, a software project is a project for an IT company. Sometimes, the project can be used as a cost center to compute the cost of manpower.

Let's see, using the Odoo project management application how we can set up projects and manage tasks within the projects using stages, compute the cost of manpower, engage in the project using the timesheet, and get customer feedback on the different stages of the project.

How to do it...

1. Project is an independent yet integrated application just like other applications. It can be found under Apps. Go to **Apps** and search for the **Project** application. Click on **INSTALL** to install the application. It is assumed that **Project** is your first application you are going to install in the instance:

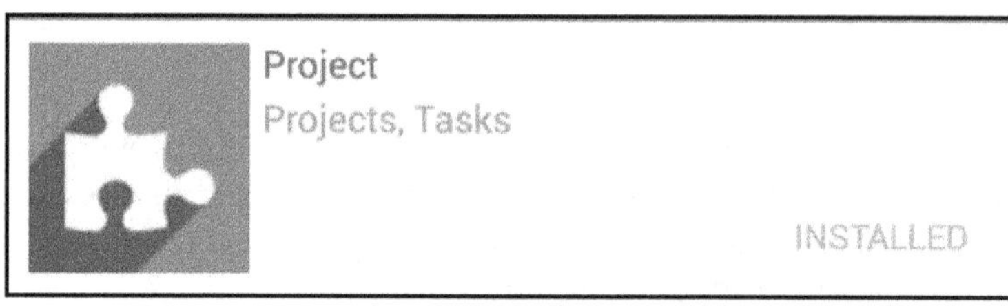

2. Like many other applications, such as **Sale**, **Purchase**, **Inventory**, and **Accounting**, the **Project** application has its own dashboard. Click on the **Project** application, and you will be redirected to the **Project** dashboard. Look at the following screenshot of the dashboard:

3. Let's create a new project and try to configure the project for internal use. Click on the **CREATE** button to create a new project on the **Project** dashboard. A popup will appear asking you the name of the project. Enter a suitable project name and click on the **CREATE** button:

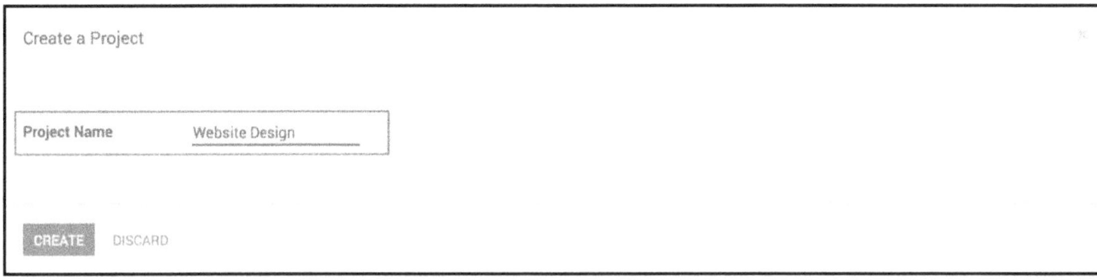

As soon as you click on the **CREATE** button, the project will be created and will appear on the dashboard. Look at the project on the dashboard:

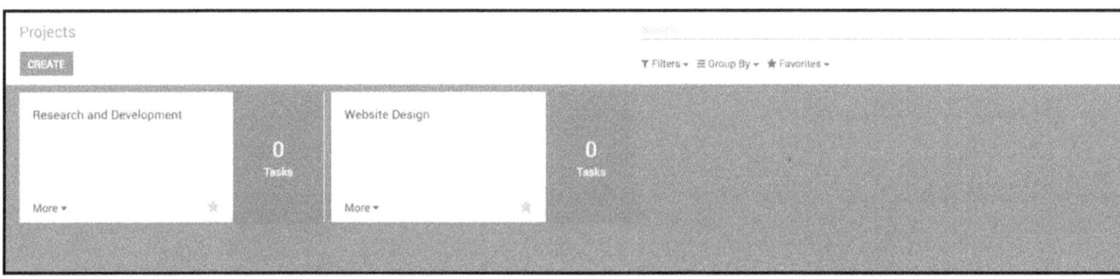

4. Like **Website Design**, let's create one more project called **Research and Development**. For both the projects, the default label is **Tasks**. It would be great to have a label based on the project. For example, for **Research and Development**, the **Tasks** label seems relevant. Also for **Website Design**, the label Websites seems more relevant.

To change the label for the tasks, the option can be found on the **Project** under the **more** option. Click on **More** and get the **Setting** to open the project settings page. It will look like this:

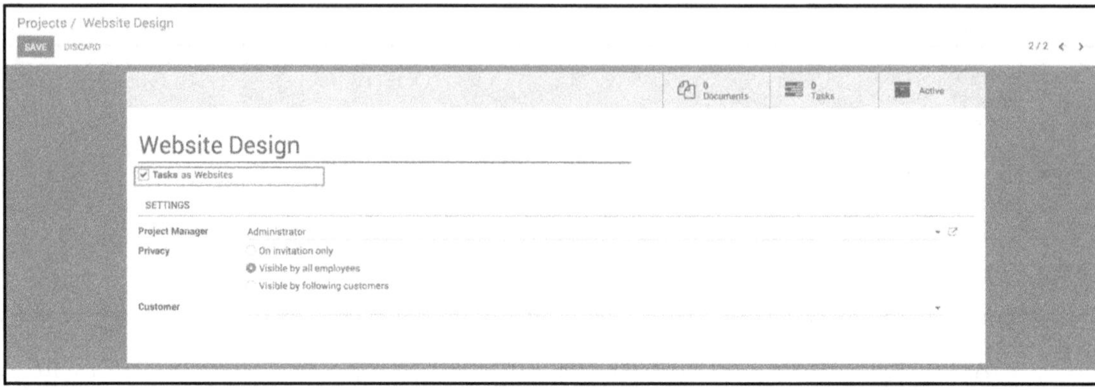

You can see that the **Task** is enabled on the **Project**, and it is identified as **Tasks**. Change it to **Websites** and click on the **SAVE** button. After that, your dashboard will get updated, and on **Website Design**, you can see **0 Websites**:

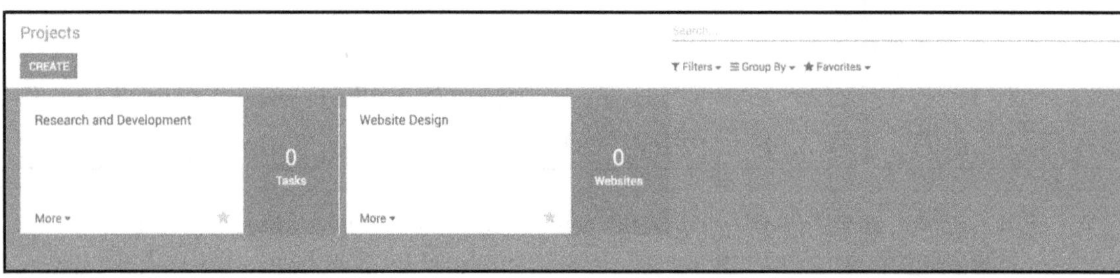

5. Let's create some tasks to design the websites. Each task represents the design of one website and assigns the designer to work on it. Click on **0 Websites**. You will be redirected to the project pipe where you have to define the standard flow (Stages) to manage the website designing process; the process starting from website design to customer delivery.

Follow the pink bubble. It will assist you in creating the stages. Click on the **ADD NEW COLUMN** column. This will allow you to enter a name/heading of a stage. As our first stage is "Idea," enter the string `Idea` and press the **Enter** key. The keyboard focus will go to the next column and ask you to create a new stage. Likewise, you can create all the stages. Look at the following screenshot. It will look like the following screenshot after creating all the stages:

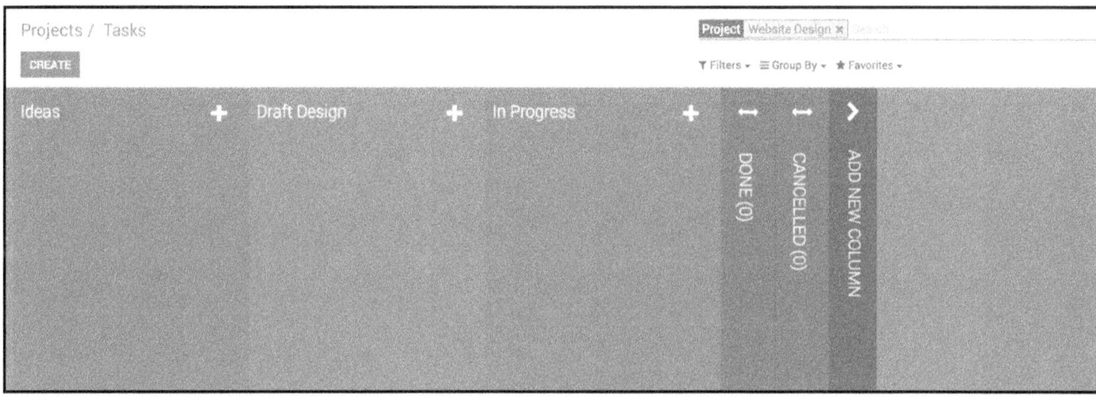

6. A task can be created by clicking on the **CREATE** button or clicking on the **+** button available on the **Idea** column:

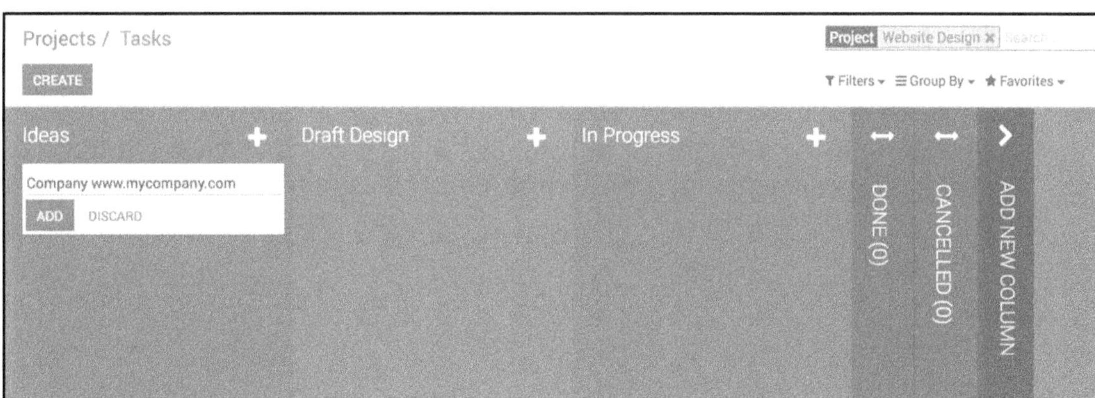

All the tasks have to be passed through the stages from Ideas to **Done** or **Cancelled**. However, the task can be created in any stage (**Draft Design** or **In Progress** stage). In the middle of the process, the task will follow the website design process for the next stage, that is, the task can be created in the **Draft Design** stage. It will follow the next stages (**In Progress** and **Done**).

7. Click on the task to get the details of the task. By clicking on the task, you can enter the **Form View** of the task where you can see **DESCRIPTION**, **Deadline** of the **Task Title**, and **Tags** related to the task:

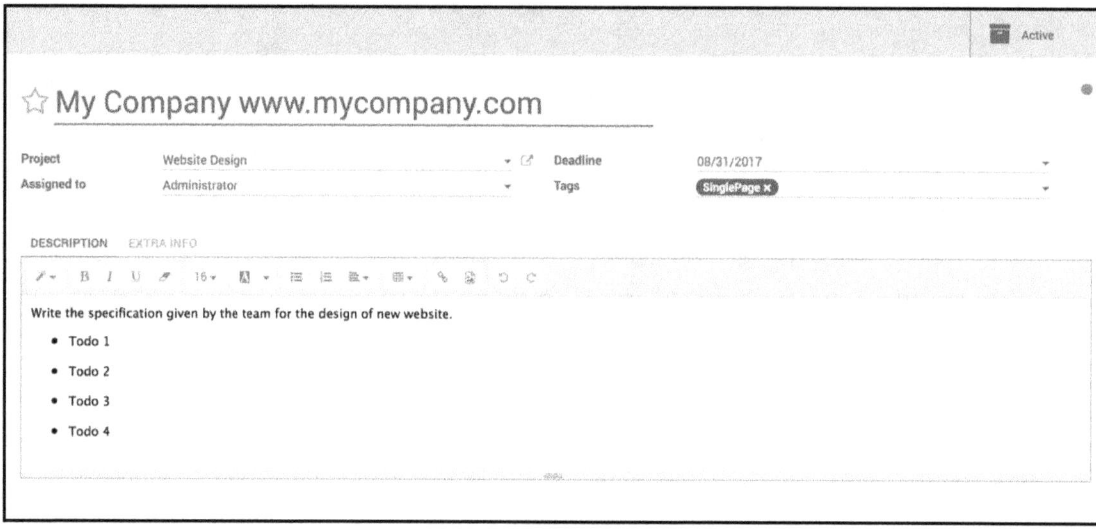

8. As soon as the specification is ready for the idea, it can be marked as **GREEN**, and it is ready to move forward. We can also set the priority for the task:

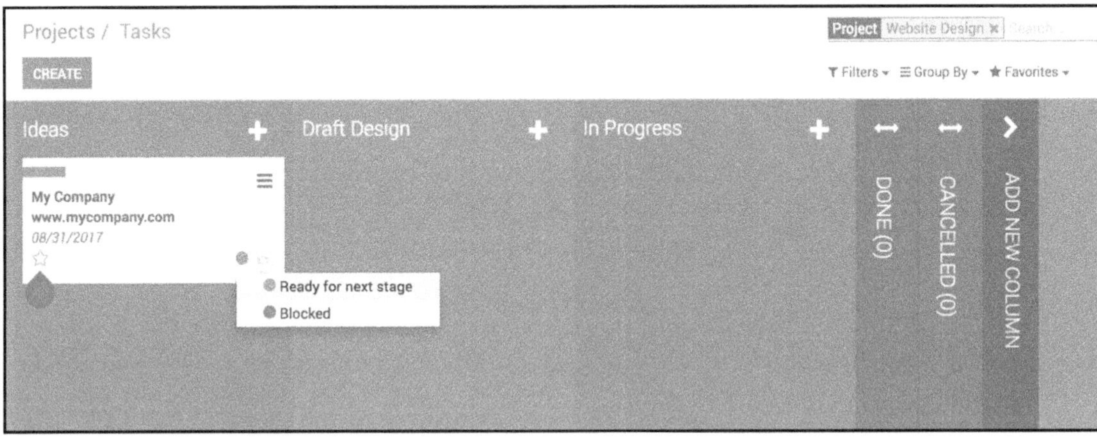

The deadline can be visible on each task. Once it is marked as green, it is a signal to the team to move this task forward. It can go to the **Draft Design** stage. Drag and drop the task **My Company - www.mycompany.com** to the **Draft Design** stage, where the designer will create the draft design for the website:

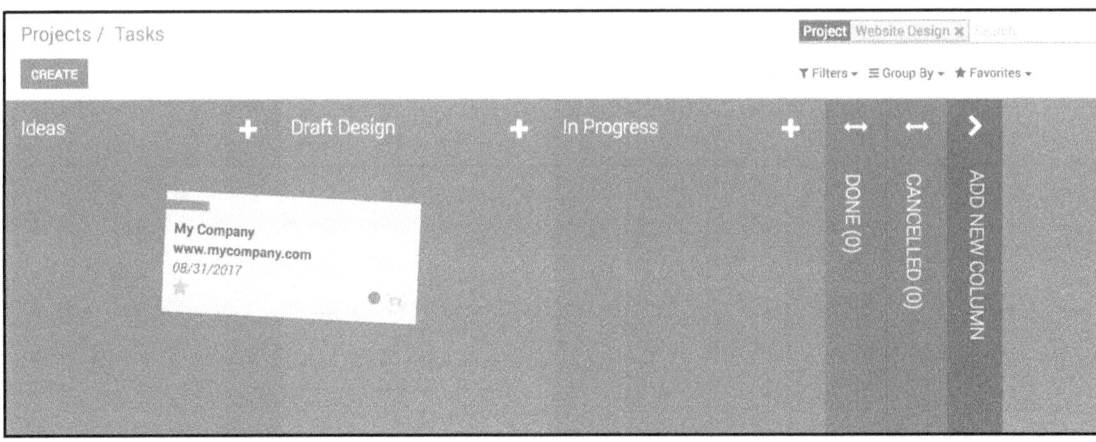

9. Once the design is ready, it can be attached to the task by attaching an image of the website on the attachment of that task. Click on the task, open the **Form View**, and from the attachment menu, click on the **Add...** button visible at the top:

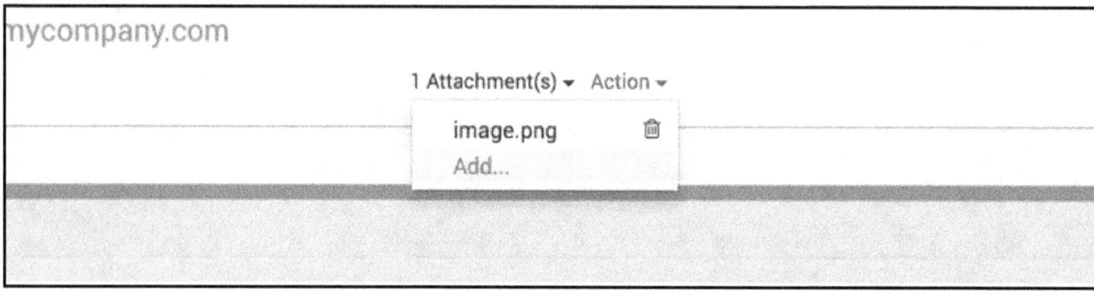

Make sure that you have installed the **App** that supports attachments on any document. If not, go to **Apps**, search for **Attachments List** and **Document Indexation**, and install it.

Go to the Kanban view, click on the options menu on the task, and then, click on the **Set Cover Image** option. A popup will appear asking you to select the cover image from the list of images attached to the task:

You can select the image or remove the image from the task. Look at this screenshot of the task having the image attached on it:

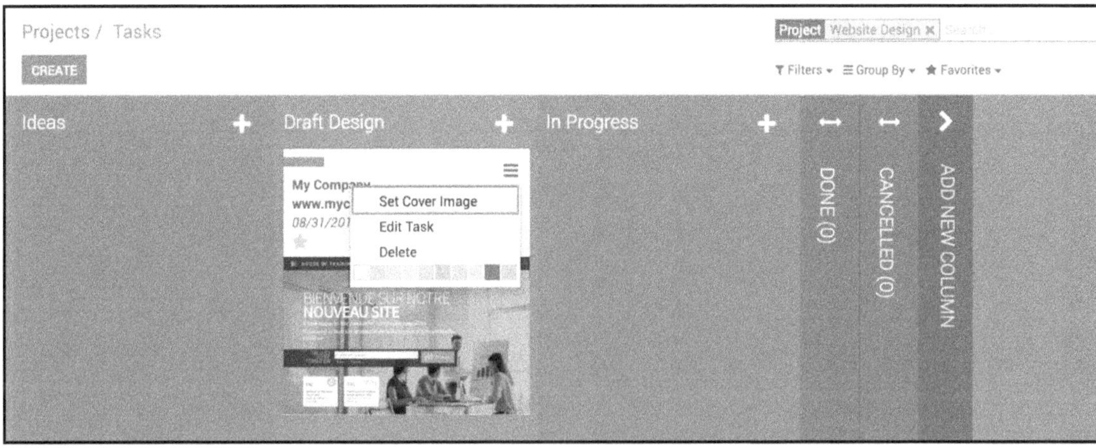

There's more...

Project management in Odoo is not limited to managing customer projects and tasks, it is also used to manage internal projects and tasks, such as **Annual Party**. The **Timesheet** application can be used with the **Project** application. The integration between timesheet and project applications allows you to allows you to track the time spent on each task. Timesheet entries are later used to create an invoice based on the time spent for the project. To see how it works, go through `Chapter 5`, *Time Tracking and Invoicing Policy*.

Let's go through some additional features available on the **Project** application such as **Create a task from an incoming e-mail**, **State vs Stage of Tasks**, **Managing Customer Projects**, **Deadline on the Task**, **Managing time on task**, **Ratings on the Task**, and so on.

Create a task from an incoming e-mail

Odoo allows you to create a task either manually or from an incoming e-mail. We have seen how to create a task manually and manage through the project stages. In Odoo, we can set up an e-mail alias for each project. As a project manager, we can configure a project alias. Open the project setting and go to the **EMAILS** tab:

To configure the setting for an incoming e-mail, we can configure it either to create a task or an issue from an incoming e-mail.

Enter **Email Alias**. To define the e-mail alias, visit `website@mycompany.odoo.com`. It is a `Website Design` project only. Select the `Tasks` in the **Incoming Emails create** field to create a task from the e-mail. We can set the security on the e-mail address in the **Accept Emails From** field by setting any one of the following values:

- **Everyone**: Anyone can mail at the e-mail address that will create a task/issue
- **Authenticated Partners**: Only authenticated partners of Odoo, usual customers in project management, will mail at an e-mail address that will create a task/issue
- **Followers only**: Only employees who are assigned to the tasks of this project can send an e-mail that will create a task/issue

The task will be created from an incoming e-mail arrived at the `website@mycompany.odoo.com` alias. All the followers will be added automatically to the new task created:

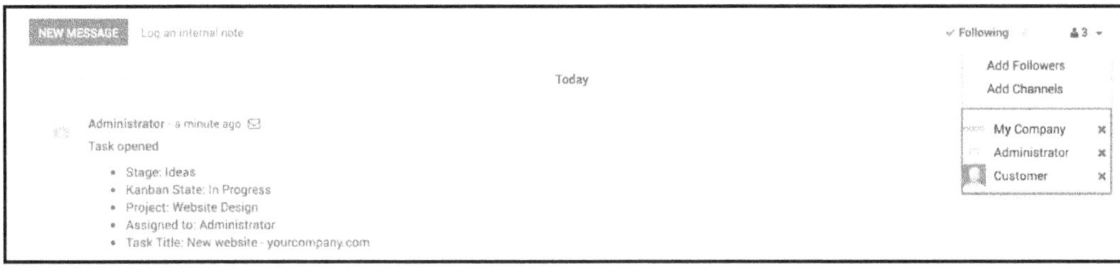

By default, **Tasks** will be created. However, if your project has enabled issue management, it will give two options, **Tasks** and **Issues**, to choose from. We can choose either **Task** or **Issues** to be created from incoming e-mails.

State versus Stage of Tasks

The project has different stages for managing the tasks. The task has the state in each stage that is used to give the signal to the team of the project.

This has to be managed individually at each stage. Click on the setting button beside the stage name. Click on the **Edit Stage** menu. A popup will appear to configure the stage:

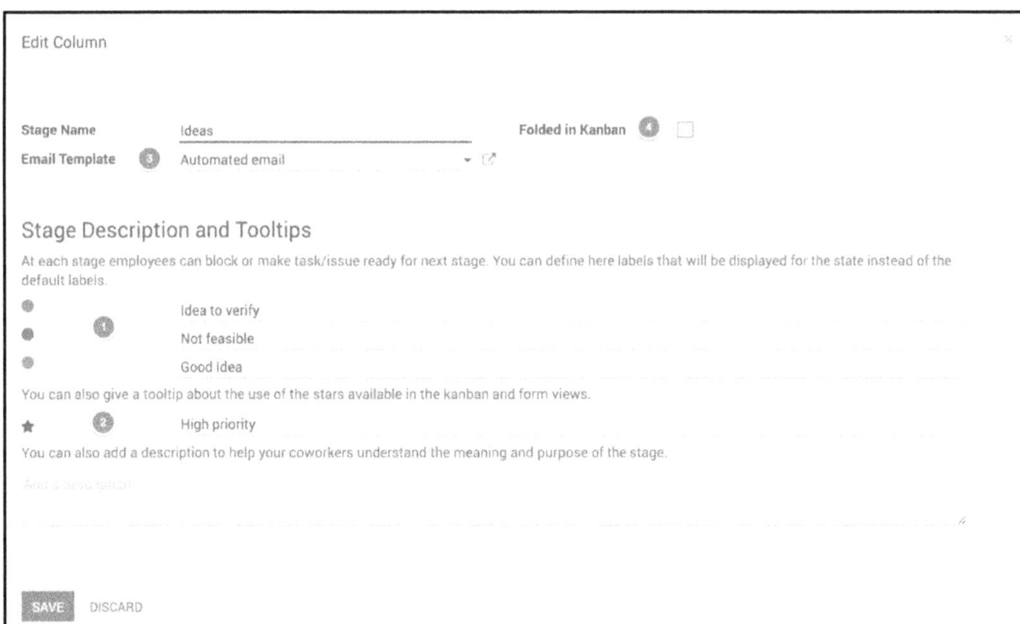

There are three different states, Gray, Green, and Red. We can define the meanings of each state for each stage. We can define the text for high priority. We can define **Email Template** that will be sent to all the followers of the task when the task comes to the **Ideas** stage. Select the **Folded in Kanban** checkbox if you would like to fold this stage in the Kanban view:

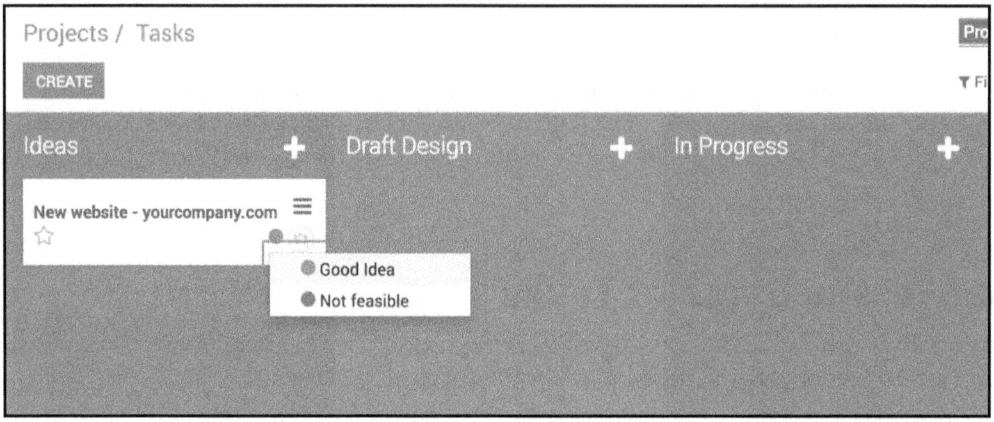

Look at the preceding screenshot, which is how it looks like after setting the meaning of each state on the Ideas stage.

Managing customer projects

Projects can be created for internal use or they can be a customer-specific external project. We can create a customer project by setting a customer on the project and setting the correct **Privacy** on the project. Let's create a customer project and set the Customer and Privacy field:

Privacy can be managed for the accessibility of the project and its task. We can choose the **Privacy** by setting who can view this project, in terms of an employee of the organization or customer if it is a customer project.

- **On invitation only**: If an employee is the follower of the project, only they can they view this project in their dashboard.
- **Visible by all employees**: This option is selected by default. It means as soon as the project is created, it is visible to all employees in the organization (no restriction).
- **Visible by following customers**: If it is a customer-dedicated project, then you can give access to the customer to see the tasks/issues of the project and give their ratings. In Odoo, it is called giving a portal user access to the customer (in this option also, all employees can see this project).

Select **Visible** by following customers on the **Privacy** field and select the customer in the **Customer** field. On the **EMAILS** tab, it is advisable to set **Authenticated Partners** on the **Accept Emails From** field. Now, the project is ready to accept the tasks from a customer through e-mails in our organization. In our case, **Administrator** is a project manager who will manage the project and project members. The project manager will add team members who will actually work on the task by adding the followers on the project.

Deadline on the task

All the tasks usually have a deadline. In this way, people responsible for the task also know within which time period they have to finish the task as it is not necessary that one responsible have only one task to perform. There can be many tasks running in parallel. In Odoo, it is clearly visible in the **Project** pipe if any of the tasks has passed the deadline. The due date will appear in RED. It will be easy for the project manager to see the tasks that have passed the deadline.

Assume that there are some tasks that have already passed the deadline in the **In-Progress** stage. Let's create two more tasks (assuming today is August 14, 2017), where I set a separate deadline. Then, let's see how the tasks will look once the deadline is passed and how they will look in the Kanban view as well as in the list view:

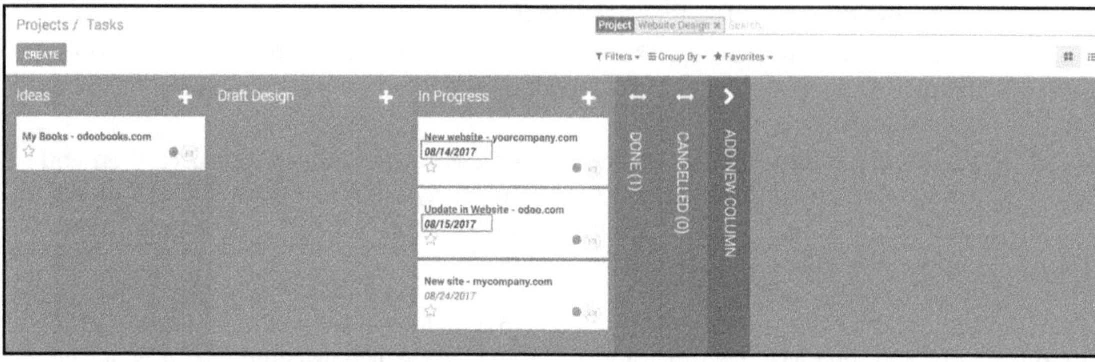

Look at the preceding screenshot, it is easy to track that which tasks crossed the deadline and not finished yet, the deadline date as displayed in RED color, as a project manager you can easily track those tasks and put them high priority.

Managing time on tasks

The time has to be managed on the task for the customer project so that later on it can be used to raise an invoice based on the task. Install the **Timesheet** application in order to activate the time tracking on the project and task. The task may have the planned hours.

Create a task **New website - yourcompany.com**. Set the responsible people in the **Assigned to** field and set the planned hours in the **Initially Planned Hours** field.

The timesheet will be filled by the responsible people who worked on the task. Enter the details of the task done and the **Duration**. The progress on the task will be computed based on the timesheet filled and initially planned hours:

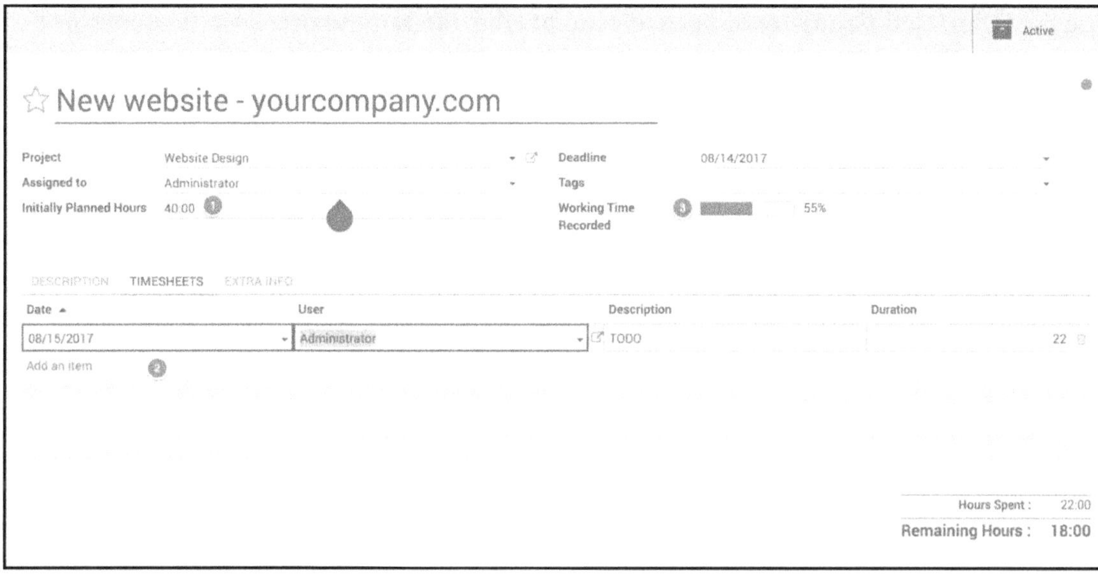

The difference between Initially Planned hours and Duration filled on the timesheet is used to compute the **Remaining Hours**. The timesheet filled on the different tasks in the project can be tracked on the project:

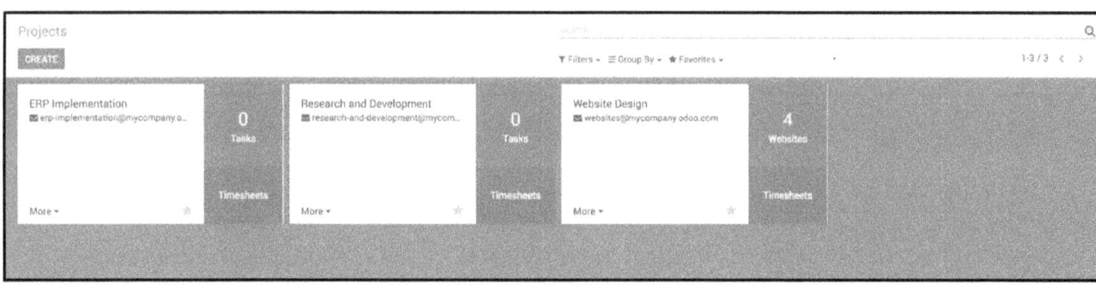

Click on **Timesheet** on the **Website Design** project. You can get the timesheet filled on all the tasks. Look at the following screenshot:

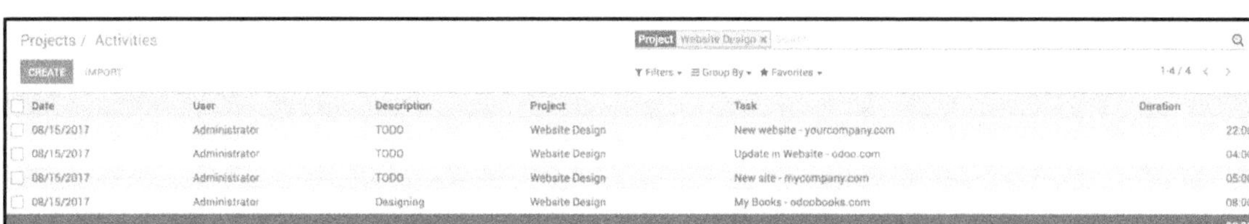

Use the **Filters** and **Group by** options to generate the different reports from the timesheet entries.

Ratings on the task

Customer feedback/rating is always important when doing customer projects. As a project manager, we would always like to get feedback from our customers, which will help us improve our quality if the customer is not happy with the service delivered.

Let's enable the feedback on the task from the **Configuration** | **Setting** page under the **Project** application. Select **Track** customer satisfaction on tasks on the **Rating on task** field:

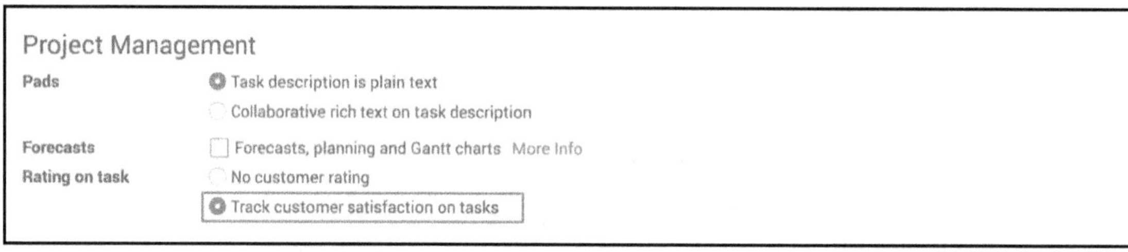

Click on the **APPLY** button to enable the feature. As soon as the feature is enabled, the customer rating can be configured on the project. The rating can be taken when a project changes a stage or period. Choose the configuration on the project. Look at this screenshot:

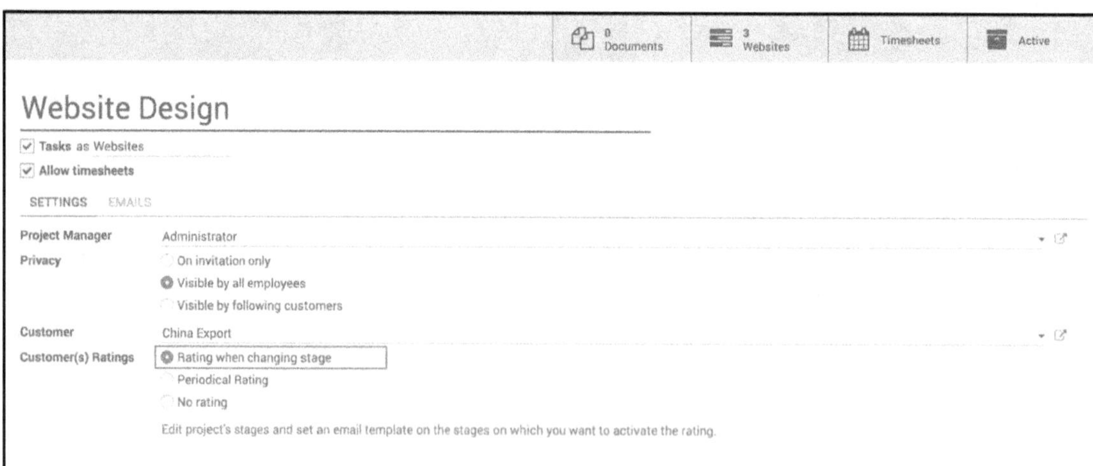

As we choose to get the feedback on stage changed, let's configure the e-mail template on the stage on which we would like to get the feedback:

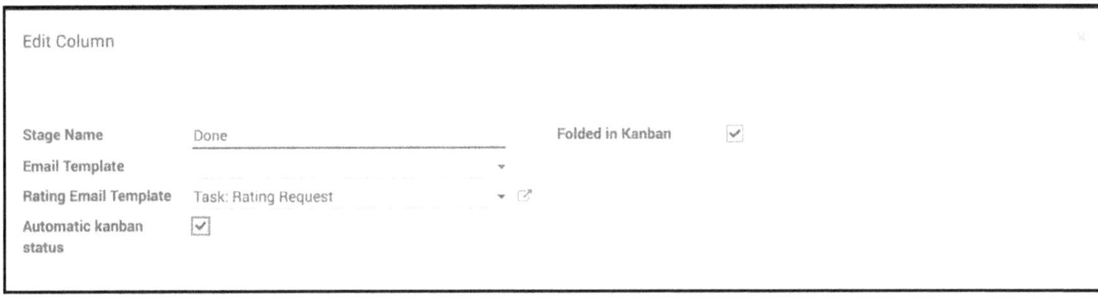

Feedback can be taken from a customer at any stage of the project. Let's set the **Rating Email Template** on the Done stage, which is the last stage of the project.

As soon as the configuration is done, we are ready to take the feedback. When a task lands on the **Done** stage, it will send an automated e-mail to the customer to ask for feedback, as shown here:

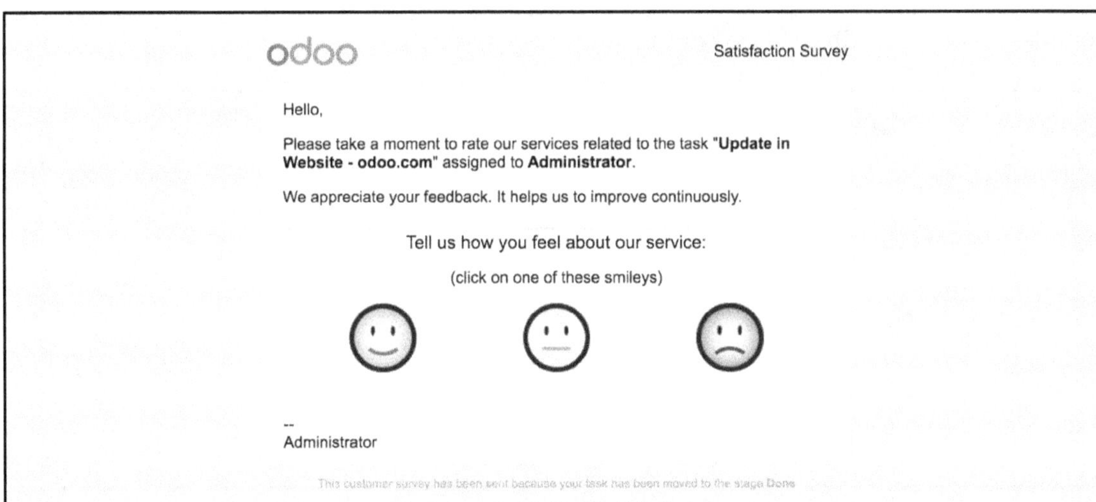

When a customer submits their feeling for the task developed by clicking on the smiley, it will ask for feedback before submitting the review for the task:

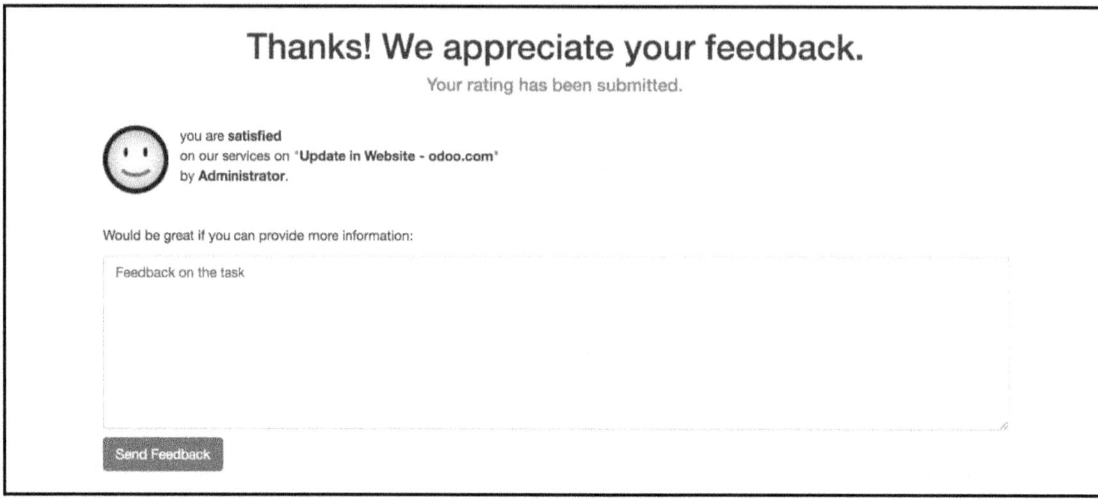

Click on the **Send Feedback** button. You will get a message confirming successful submission of the feedback. Look at the following screenshot:

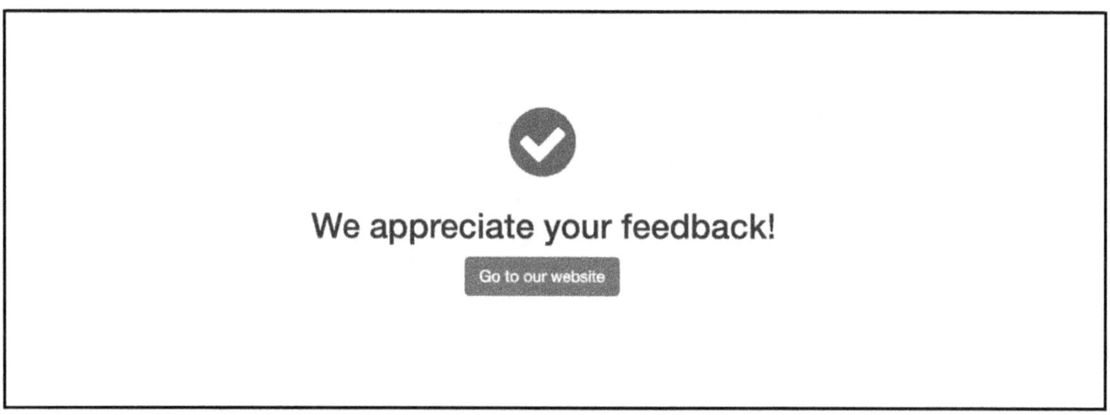

The global rating for the project is computed on the project. It is computed based on all the rating received from the customers on each task. It will be an average of all the ratings received. Look at the `Website Design` project in the following screenshot:

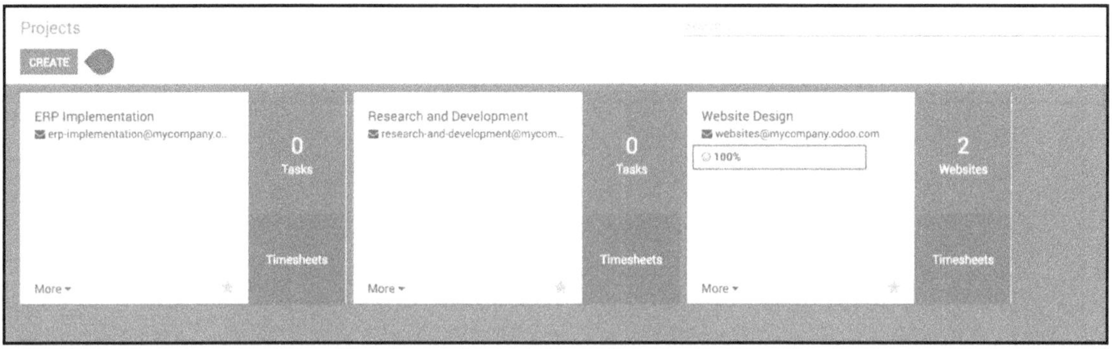

Project forecasting

For a long-term project, it is recommended that you plan future task for better allocation of key resources. This helps a project manager identify the risks in terms of unavailability of the member and resolve the issue by changing the members for the continuous progress of the project. It is a really challenging task for a manager to utilize the time of key resources for the different projects.

Up to now, we have been working with the Kanban view, which shows us the current status of the project and progress of an individual task. The forecasting feature can be enabled for the project. Using the Gantt view, we can plan resource allocation on the task for a specific duration. The planning can be done by week, month, or year depending on the length of the project.

Forecasting includes the availability of a resource from the leave management application so that when a key resource is on leave, for the critical task, we can replace the resource or the task can be delayed for the time being

Getting ready

In order to do the task forecasting and planning, we need to set up and configure an employee, their related user, working time, and holiday as you would like to integrate employee leaves in the planning. Let's create an employee who is required to forecast the tasks:

I have created two employees, Ajay and Vinay, to test the forecasting. We will test **Business Apps Implementation** as a long-term project having various tasks to plan in the next few months.

How to do it...

1. The forecasting feature on the project can be enabled from **Configuration | Settings** of the Project application. Select the checkbox **Forecast, Planning and Gantt charts** under the **Forecasts** section:

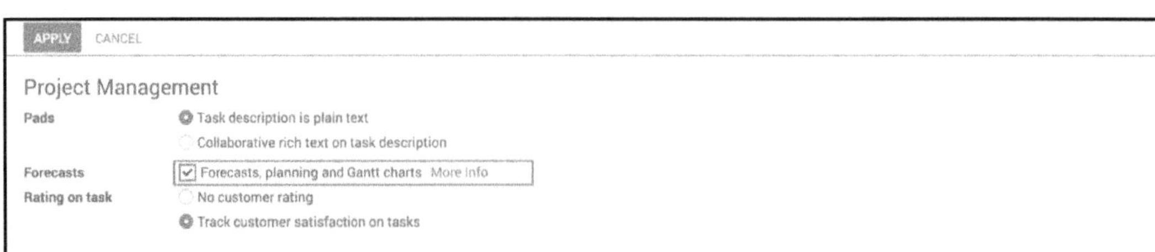

Click on the **APPLY** button to enable the forecasting feature for your projects.

2. Not all projects require forecasting and planning; it is only the long-term projects that require the forecasting feature. Open the settings of the project for which forecasting is required. Select the checkbox **Allow forecast on the project** and click on **SAVE** to save the setting. The forecasting will be enabled for that project.

Let's take an example of the **Business Apps Implementation** project that requires better resource planning as it is a customer project and we would like to meet the deadline:

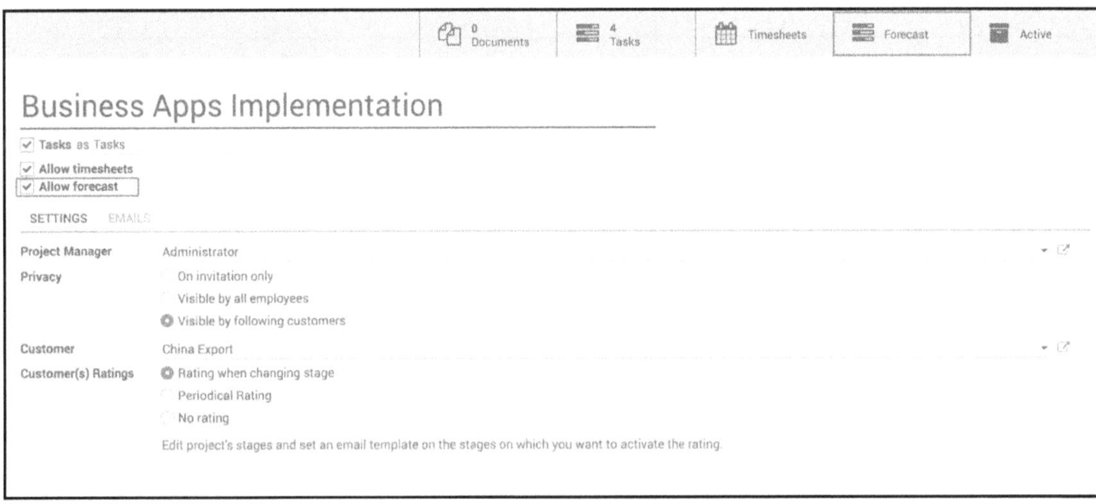

Go to the **Projects** dashboard. You can see that the forecasting section is activated on the projects that have been chosen for forecasting:

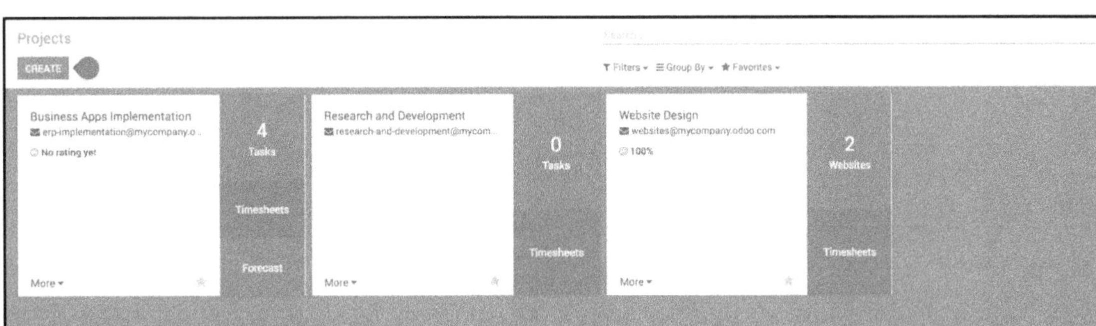

The next step is to create a task and forecast it to allocate the resource and time period to the start date and end date to complete the task.

The critical tasks are required to be forecasted to ensure that the right member is assigned to work on it to complete it on time. The task can be included in the forecasting by creating a plan for the task. It can be done at the time of creating a task or later.

Assume that we have some data import tasks to implement the first business application, which is **Point of Sale**. It can be done by one of the business analysts in our team:

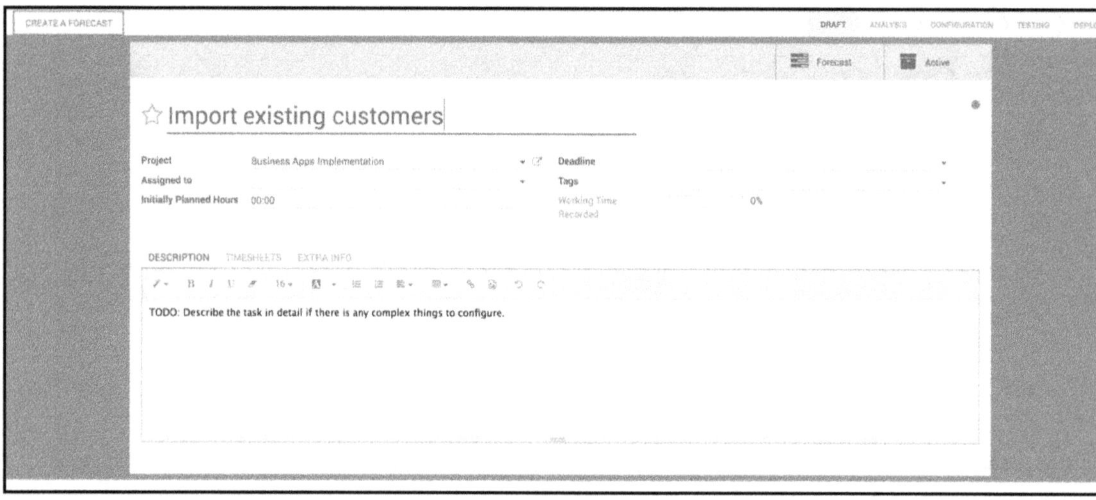

To create the forecasting for the task, click on the **CREATE A FORECAST** button. It will redirect you to the task forecasting window. Look at the following screenshot of planning:

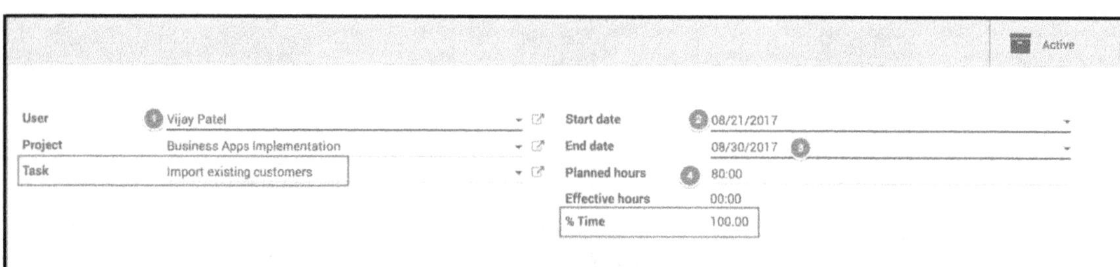

Select the **User** (resource for the planning) to whom we plan to assign the task. A **Start date** is a date by which the task should start and **End date** is the planned deadline date by which the task should be completed. **Planned hours** are allocated to the resource to complete the task.

The **%Time** allocation will be computed based on the dates, hours applicable, and working timesheet attached on the employee. Look at the working timesheet I have created:

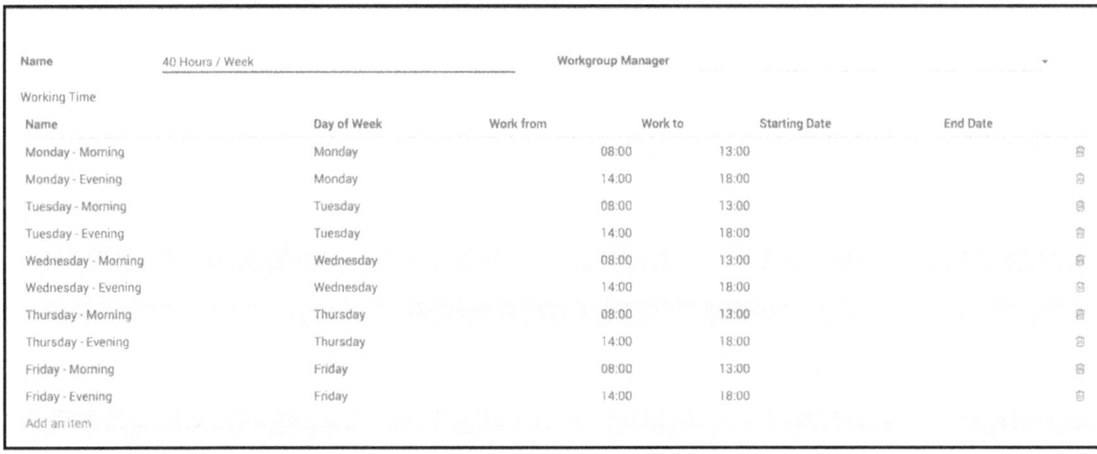

3. Assume that we have some task to be performed to implement the e-commerce application. There are many prerequisites to be configured to launch the point of sale. The tasks are to be performed in the following order:

Sequence	Task Description	Planned Time	Resource
1	Import existing customers	80 hours	Vijay
2	Import brand wise product master	70 hours	Vijay
3	Verify the tax configuration on product	50 hours	Ajay
4	Set up website and e-commerce application	50 hours	Ajay
5	Set up the website theme	50 hours	Ajay and Vijay

Create the preceding tasks and forecasting for the tasks so that we can identify the risk and manage the deadline.

4. We have two consultants who can work parallel for the implementation project. Assume that the forecasting has been created for the task. Assign **Start Date**, **End Date**, **Planned Hours**, and **Resource** on the forecasting.

   Look at the preceding screen. We created the forecasting as soon as the task was created. The initial planning has been done, but there are three problems that have to be fixed. The forecasting can be checked in two ways: **By Project** or **By Users**. Let's go and check the forecasting **By Users** from the **Forecast** menu under the **Project** application:

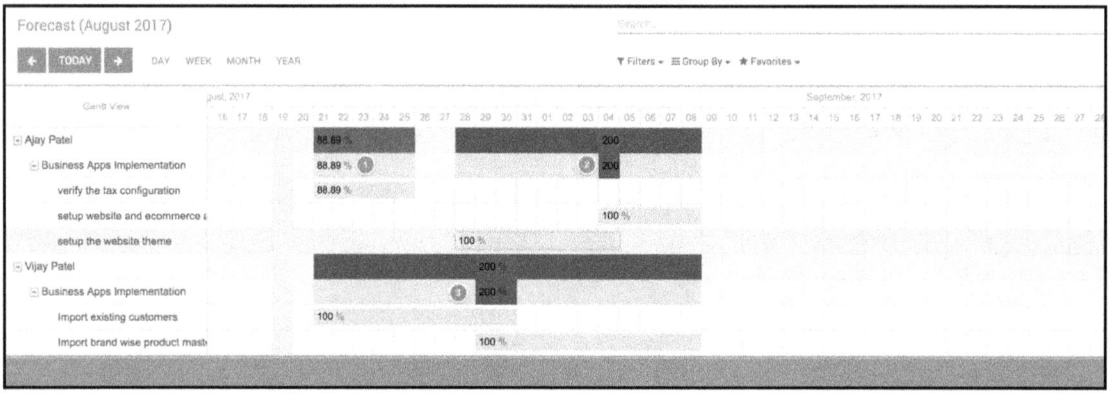

   The first point it suggests is that the resource utilization is not 100 percent during that week. Still, we can use the resource for some other task for 20 percent of the weekly time.

   Other two points indicate a critical problem fix. There are two tasks that overlap for the start date and end date. Those tasks have to be re-planned.

5. To fix the problem, the task has to be dragged and dropped to the correct dates so that we do not have two parallel tasks running for the same user or the time allocation should not be more than 100 percent of the users. Look at the following screenshot after fixing the problem:

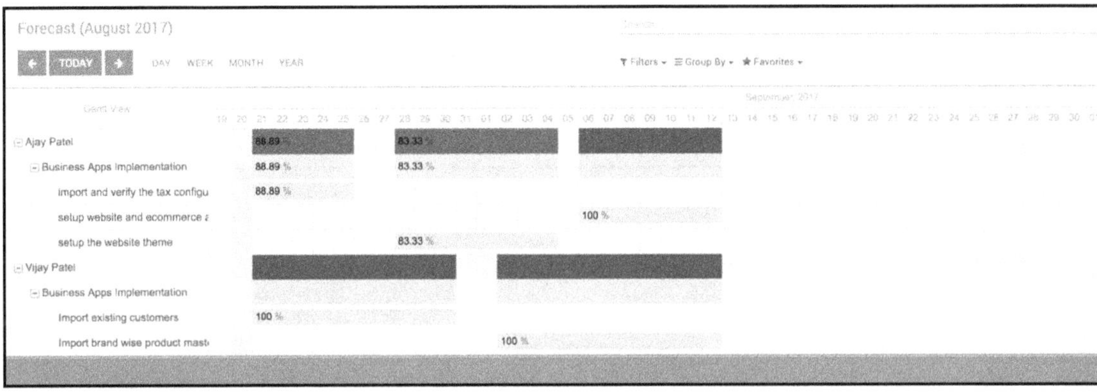

6. The planning can be done by **DAY**, **WEEK**, **MONTH**, or **YEAR**. The current planning was based on **MONTH**. Let's switch to the **WEEK** view. It will look like this:

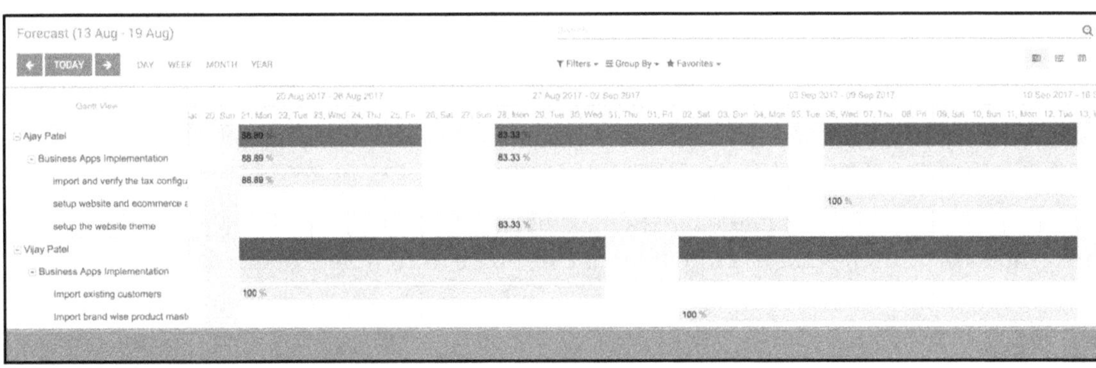

There's more...

As a project manager, we have seen the Gantt views for project forecasting. It can be done **By Project** as well as **By User**. There is a view available in Odoo to do a quick forecasting by Grid view. This view allows you to do a forecasting by Project or Users. On the row, we can have a User/Task/Project depending on the grouping option chosen, and on column, we have **DAY, WEEK,** or **MONTH**. The forecasted hours will be displayed by User/Task/Project. Look at the following screenshot of the yearly planning Group By Task/User. Go to **Forecast** | **Grid** | **By User** to access the grid view of the forecasting:

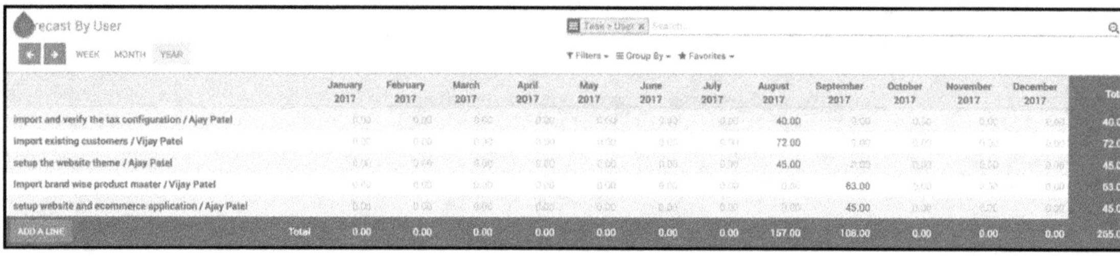

You can get the details of the Planned hours as followed by clicking on the Search icon, available on the left-hand side of the Planned hours:

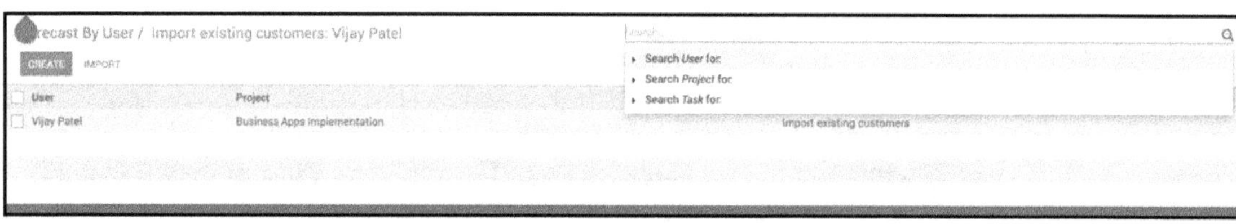

You may need more lines if you have divided 100 percent of resource time between many different tasks or users, that is, more than one resource to complete one task.

Depending on the grouping option, you can see the forecasting. Let's take an example, I have a Group By **User**, my report will look as the following screenshot:

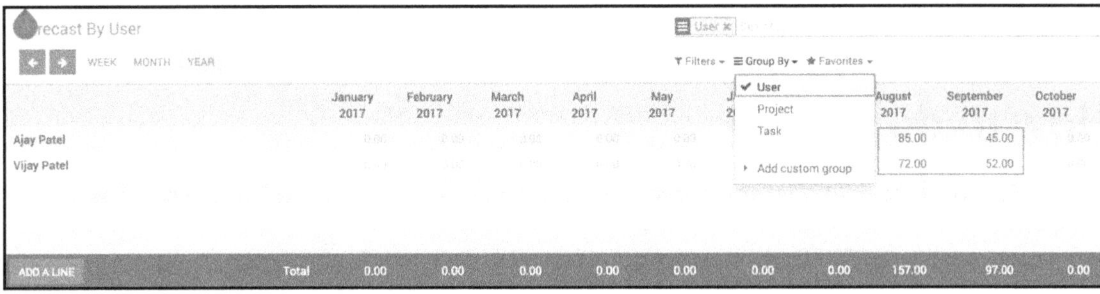

Managing project issues and rating

As soon as a project is completed and the customer reviews on the project have started. The customer may raise an issue for the developed features. Later, it can be decided whether it is a real issue or a change request.

Odoo has an application called **Issue Tracking** supported to the **Project Management**, which allows us to manage these issues. It can be a bug in the system, client complaints, or material breakdown. Issue management allows the project manager to quickly check the issue, assign it to the responsible person, and resolve it as quickly as possible.

The easiest way is to create a new project dedicated to recording the project issues. An issue can come either by e-mail or can be created manually, assigned to the responsible and resolved by the responsible person.

Let's see how the Issue Tracking system manages the Project Issue during the project or after the project completion.

Getting ready

We may have a Task and Issue within the same project, or we may create two different projects, one for Task and another for Issue. It is advisable to create a dedicated project for issues when your issue management team is responsible for solving the issues coming from a different project.

A similar project can be used where your development team is responsible for fixing the issues during the project or after the project completion.

Choose your way of managing the issues depending on your issue management policy.

How to do it...

1. Go to Odoo Apps, and search and install the module called **Issue Tracking**:

   Click on the **INSTALL** button to install the application. This will install **Issue Tracking** in the system.

2. Now, create a project with the name `Support Service` and activate issue management by ticking the **UseIssues** checkbox. Also, select **Allow timesheet** as we would like to measure the time spent on the customer issue:

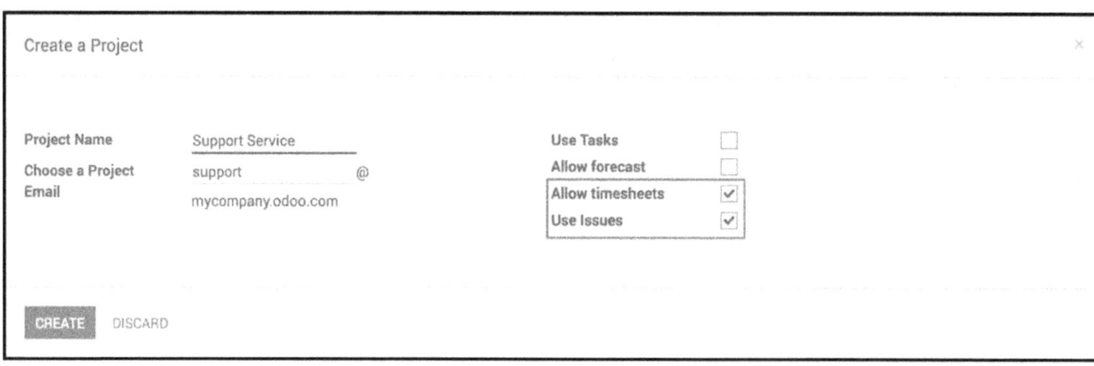

3. As soon as the `Support Service` project is created, it will be available on the dashboard. Go to project settings for more options. Make sure that you have selected Issue to be created on the incoming e-mails in the **EMAILS** tab:

4. The `Support Service` project is different compared to Implementation or `Website Design` project. The issues have to be managed with different stages than the tasks, that is, the task has the stages such as **Ideas**, **Draft Design**, **In Progress**, and more, while the issue has the stages such as **New**, **Confirmed**, **In Progress**, **Waiting Cust. Feedback**, and more.

   Let's go to the `Issues` pipe and create the stages as `New`, `Confirmed`, `In Progress`, `Waiting Cust. Feedback`, `Done`, and `Cancelled`. After creating the stages, the issue pipe will look like this:

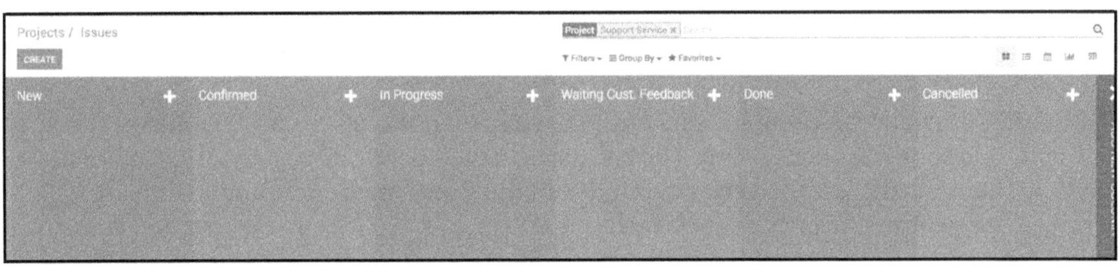

If you choose to manage the Issues within the same project where you manage the tasks, you may have difficulties as your task pipe and issue pipe stages are not the same. You cannot have two different stage pipes for issue and task within the same project.

5. Issues can be created either manually or via an e-mail, just like a task. In our case, if someone sends an e-mail to `support@mycompany.odoo.com`, the issue will be created in the Support Service project:

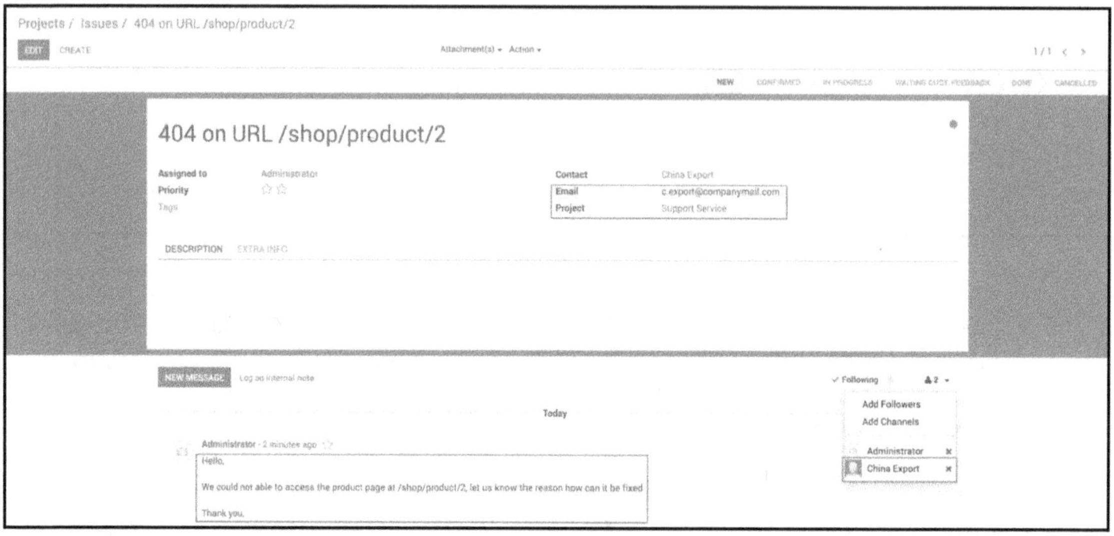

6. The subject of the e-mail will become the **Title of the Issue**. Contact and e-mail will be selected automatically based on the incoming e-mail. The **Contact** is also added to the list of followers. The content of the e-mail body will be added to the chatter.
7. Use chatter to communicate with the customer. It is a standard feature of the Odoo messaging system. The issue has to be routed through the issue pipe. As soon as the issue is verified, move it to the **Confirmed** stage and assign the responsible person on the same:

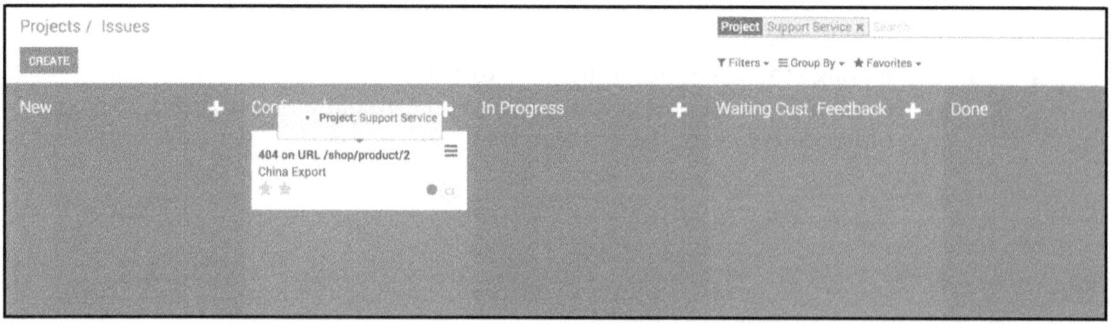

Depending on the stage of the issue, move it to the correct stage. It can be set to **Done** when it's completed, or you can move to **Wait Cust. Feedback** to get customer feedback before you mark it as **Done**.

8. Statistics will be computed for each issue depending on the action taken on the issue. The statistics will be generated based on the date and time on which the action has been taken:

There's more...

Managing an issue and task in Project is similar to each other. Both have to be managed through the stages. The state and stages of the task and issue will be managed in the same way. Let's see how an issue is different from a task.

Timesheet on issue

Just as tasks have a timesheet to compute the time spent on the task, in the same way, we can track the time spent to solve issues. The feature can be activated from the **Project** | **Configuration** | **Settings** page. Select **Activate timesheet on issues** available under the **Timesheets** section:

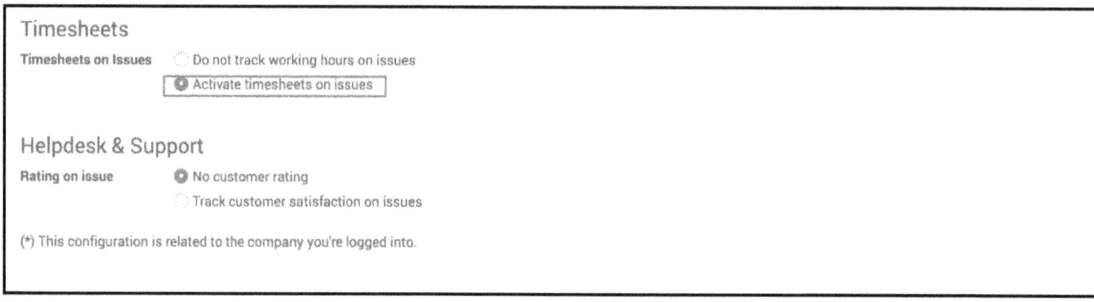

Click on the **APPLY** button to activate the feature. As soon as the timesheet feature is activated for the issue, you will get the **TIMESHEETS** tab on the issue:

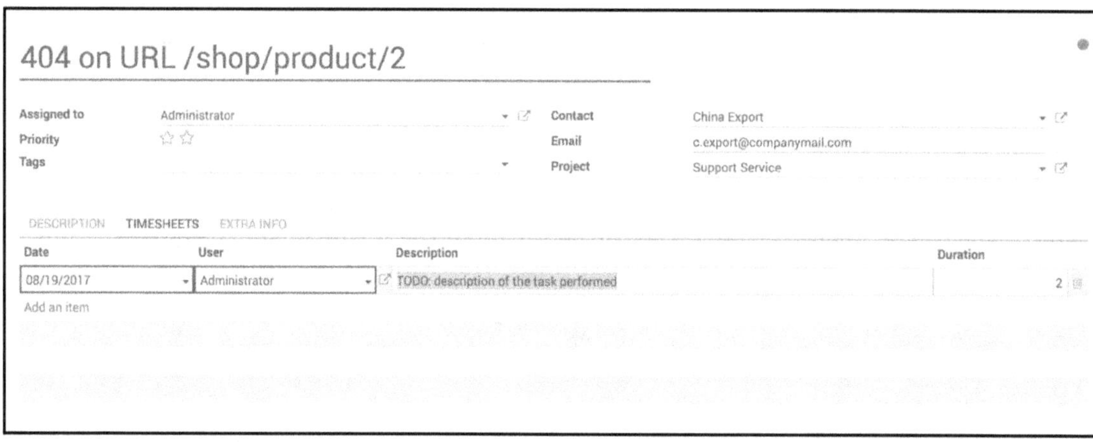

The timesheet line can be added to the issue when the issue is in edit mode. Enter the **Description** and **Duration** on the timesheet line.

The timesheet can be generated for the `Support Service` project by clicking on the `Timesheet` option available on the project under the dashboard:

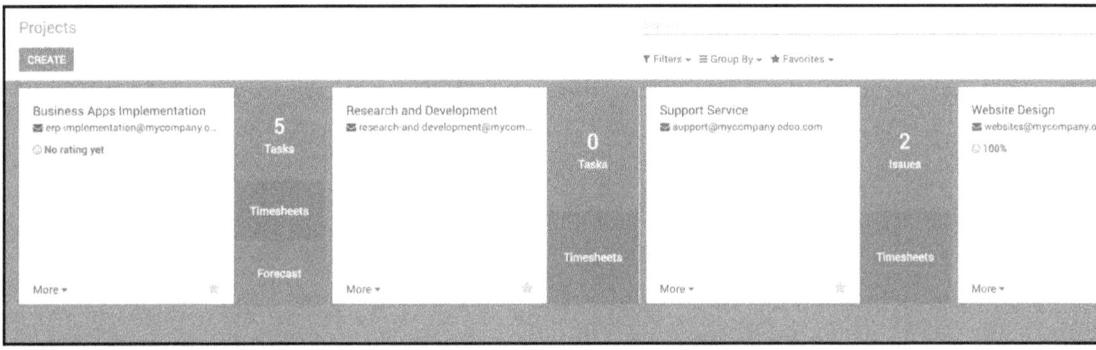

Click on **Timesheets** on the `Support Service` project. You will get the global timesheet for the `Support Service` project. Look at the following screenshot:

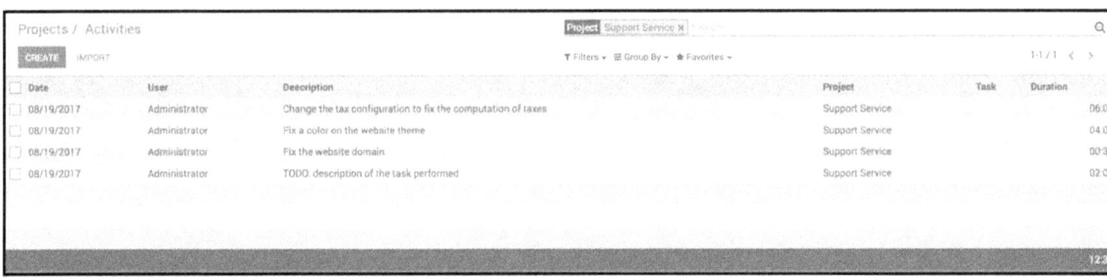

15
Implement Human Resource Applications

In this chapter, we will cover the following recipes:

- Launch employee recruitment
- Managing employees' leave
- HR expenses and reimbursements

Introduction

Managing an employees' activities is as important as tracking a customer's activity. It is essential for the human resource department to manage an employees' activity to be sure that the resources needed to run the business activity they are available and if not we can do the better planning in advance for the smooth business operation.

Assume that some of the employees' planned their holidays in the middle of an ongoing long-term project, and the project manager does not have any information as leave application is not integrated with the core business activity such as Projects. They are not integrated with the payroll. It may be possible that employees' get an incorrect salary as the integration between Payroll, Recruitment, and Leave applications may not be done well. Either it's a business activity or internal company activity related to the employees'; it has to be integrated with the business to have better information flow.

Odoo has applications to manage all the human resource activities and the good thing is they are integrated internally, with the core business activities, which give clear information to identify risks and to better handle any situation.

Let's see how Odoo applications manage the human resource activities starting from recruitment to contract management, appraisal, and the exit process. There are many other processes to manage, such as leave, employee reimbursement, and computing payroll every month.

Launch employee recruitment

Recruiting a skilled workforce is a critical job for the recruiting officer. The recruitment process, starting from launching the job offer, has to be spread widely enough to get enough applicants to choose from. Applications are then collected. After the screening of an applicant, the first round of interviews has to be scheduled, which may be followed by various rounds depending on the job profile or based on policies. The job offer is prepared and sent to candidates who have successfully passed all the interviews. Then an employee record and an employee contract are created in the system, on acceptance of the job offer by the candidate.

Let's see how we can launch the job offer, make the publicity, collect the applications by email, and set the recruitment pipe with different stages. We will also see how it's easy to schedule interviews and propose an employee contract and create an employee record on signing the contract.

Getting ready

By default, when the Odoo instance is set up, we get the feature to manage system users, but the system users are not employees'. To begin working with the **Human Resources** application, we must install the base application, that is, the **Employee Directory** application for the **Human Resource** application:

As soon as you install the **Employee Directory** application, you will see **employees**' as an application on the home screen. Here, you can access the list of employees' and departments:

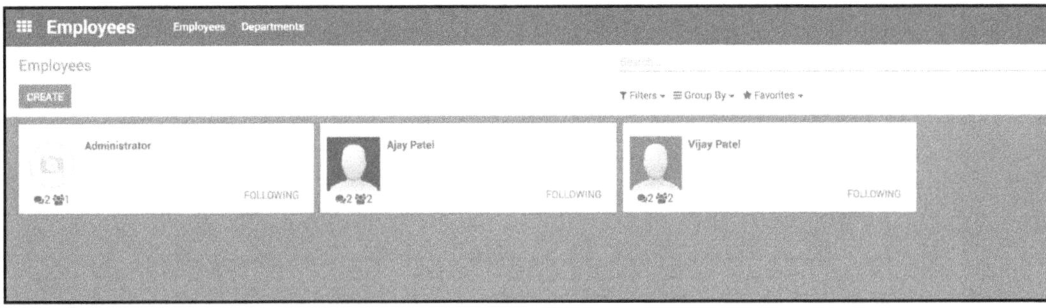

The department can be created from the **Department** menu available under the **employees**' application. Go to **Departments** and create a new department **Sales and Marketing** as we are going to start a new department and launch the recruitment for **Sales Executives**:

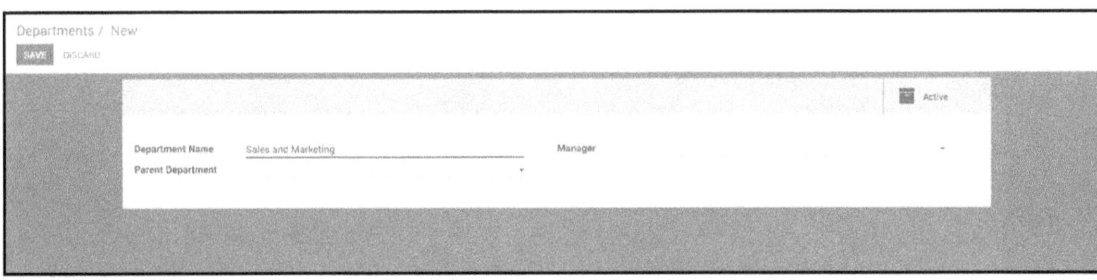

The **Department Name** is a mandatory field. You can keep the other fields empty and create a department. You can create the departments available in your organization or the **Department** in which you launch the job offer.

Let's see how to manage the recruitment process from launching the job offers to create an employee using the Odoo Recruitment application.

How to do it...

1. The first step is to install the **Recruitment** application; it is the same as other Odoo applications. It can be installed from Odoo Apps:

As soon as the **Recruitment Process** application is installed, you will get the Recruitment App icon on your instance home screen. Like other Odoo applications, the **Recruitment** application also has its own dashboard to track the currently launched job positions. Look at the following screenshot. There are no job positions opened yet:

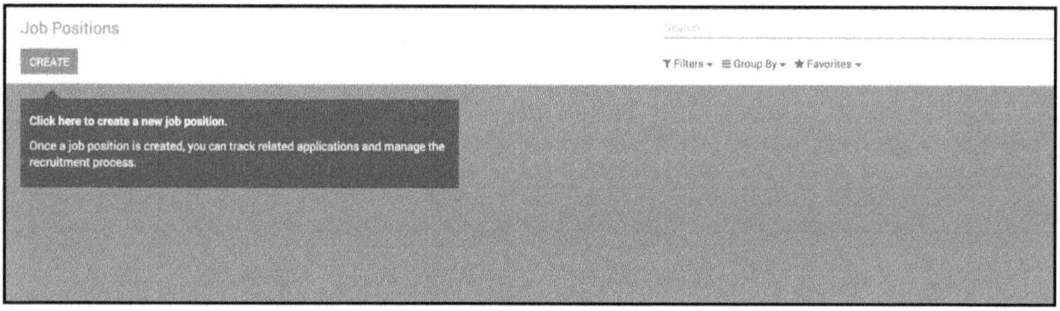

2. Click on the **CREATE** button to create and launch the job position for the **Sales** and **Marketing Department** we just created:

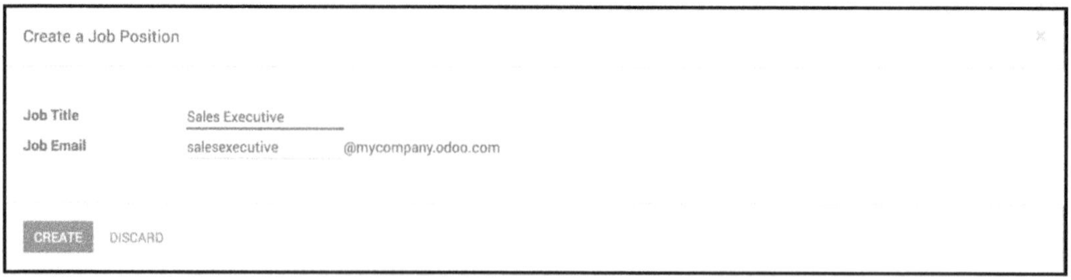

The job e-mail is used to create an e-mail alias in Odoo. When an e-mail is received at `salesexecutive@mycompany.odoo.com` in Odoo, it will create an applicant in the **Sales Executive** job position. Click on the **CREATE** button to create the job position. It will look like this on your **Recruitment** dashboard:

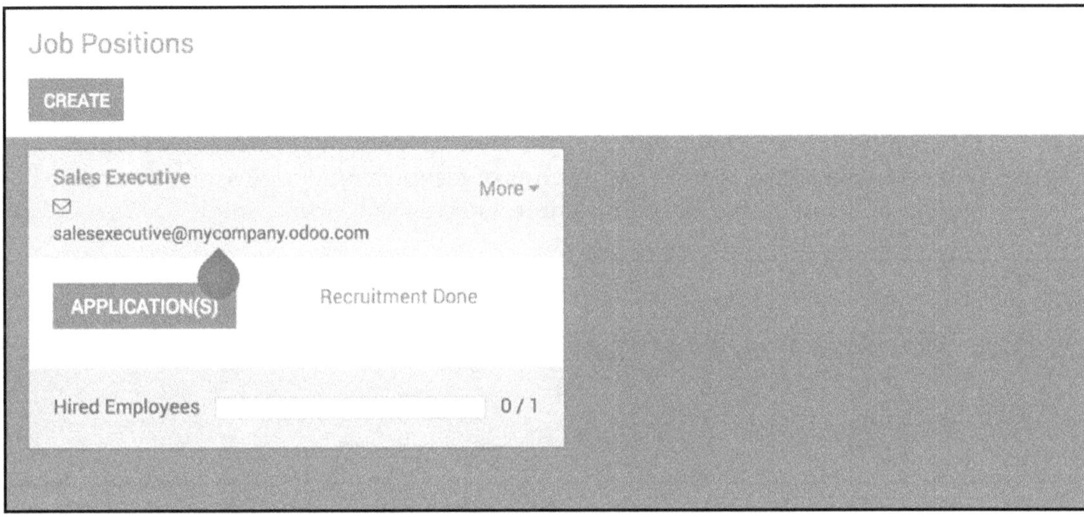

3. As soon as the job position is created, it has to be configured to set the correct department and **Recruitment** responsible. Also, set the number of openings for **Sales Executives**. Look at the following screenshot of the job position configuration. Click on **More** | **Setting** on the **Sales Executive** job position:

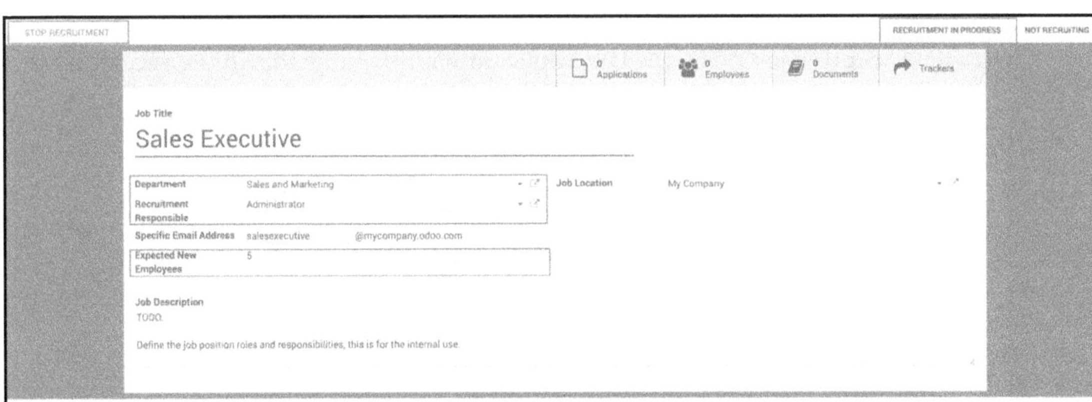

By default, the manager of the department will be set as a **Recruitment Responsible**, as soon as you select the **Department**. However, it can be changed manually if you would like to set someone other than the department manager to conduct the interviews.

4. The next step is to configure the recruitment pipe; we have to configure or fix our recruitment process. This stage will define how the application will be processed for the **Sales Executive** job position.

The application may have different processes depending on the **Job Position**. Some positions may require two rounds of technical interviews, or some may require only one round of technical interviews.

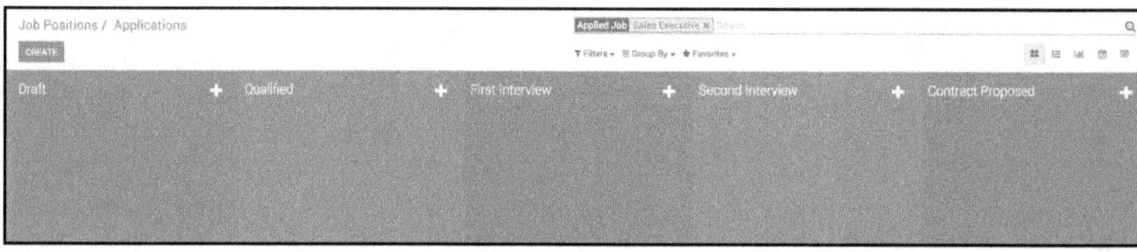

Click on the **APPLICATION(S)** button available on the job position to enter into the pipe and configure the stages. By clicking on the **ADD NEW COLUMN**, we can add a new stage to the recruitment pipe. Look at the preceding screenshot for the **Sales Executive** job position pipe.

5. Assume that we received an e-mail on `salesexecutive@mycompany.odoo.com`, which creates an applicant in the **Sales Executive** job position. The applicant will look like this in the recruitment pipe:

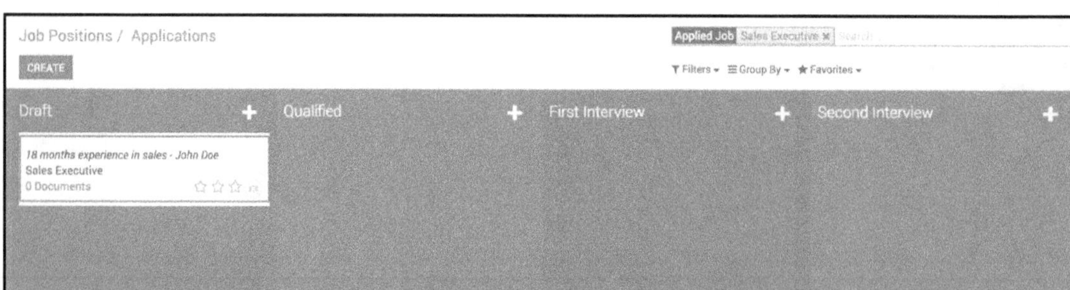

6. Click on the applicant to get more details. You can see the cover letter in the chatter along with the attached resume. Look at the following screenshot:

You can get the resume attached to the e-mail, check the quality of an applicant, and if he/she fits the criteria, you can process them accordingly. If the applicant does not fit the requirements, we can refuse or move forward to the **Qualified** stage:

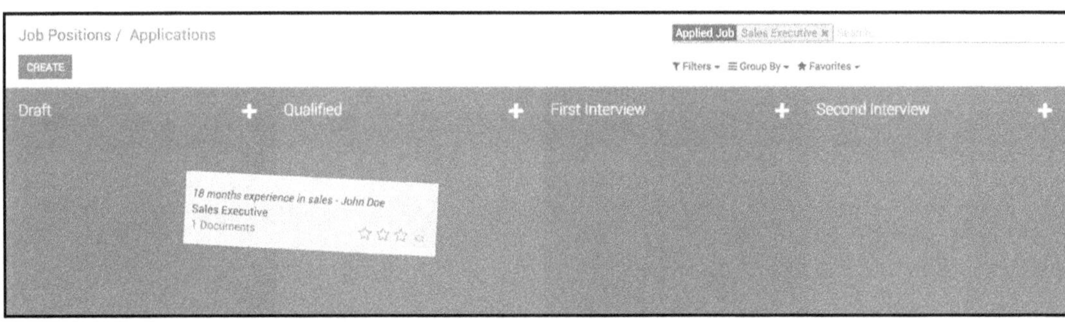

You can drag the applicant and drop him/her to the **Qualified** stage.

7. It's time to update and get more information on the applicant that may not be a part of the resume. Fill the information on the application, such as **Expected Salary**:

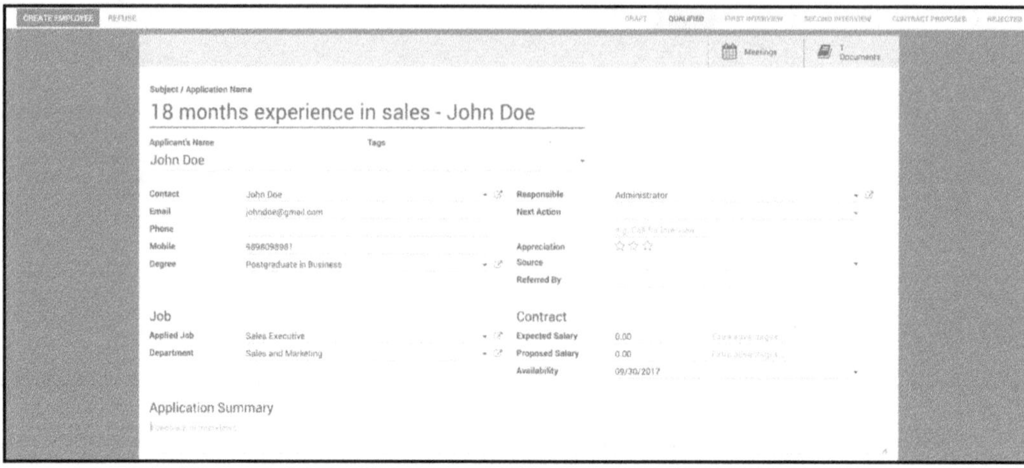

Let's call to collect more information and inform the applicant about the qualification and that they are moving forward for the first round of interviews.

Schedule an interview with the candidate by clicking on **Meeting**. This will redirect you to the **Calendar** view to schedule the meeting:

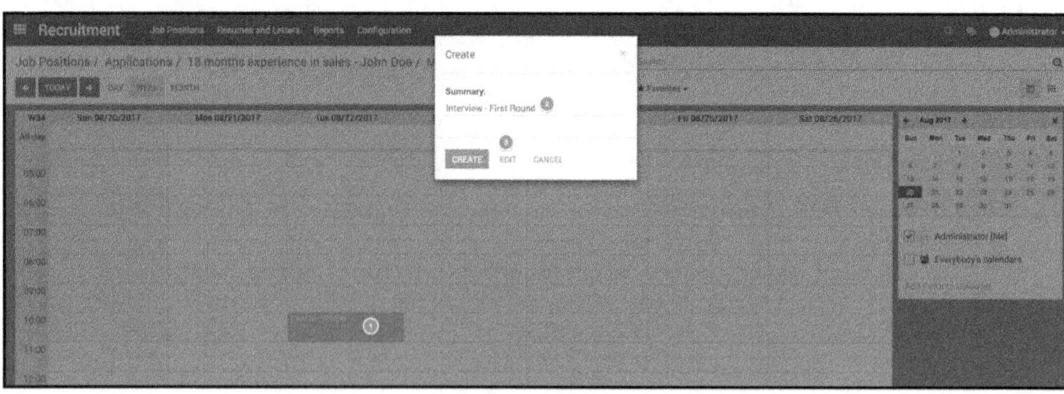

8. To create an appointment, click on the start time and drag to the end time on the date suggested by an applicant. As soon as you release the mouse, a popup will appear asking us to enter the name of the meeting. Enter the name of the meeting and click on the **EDIT** button to add the attendees of the meeting:

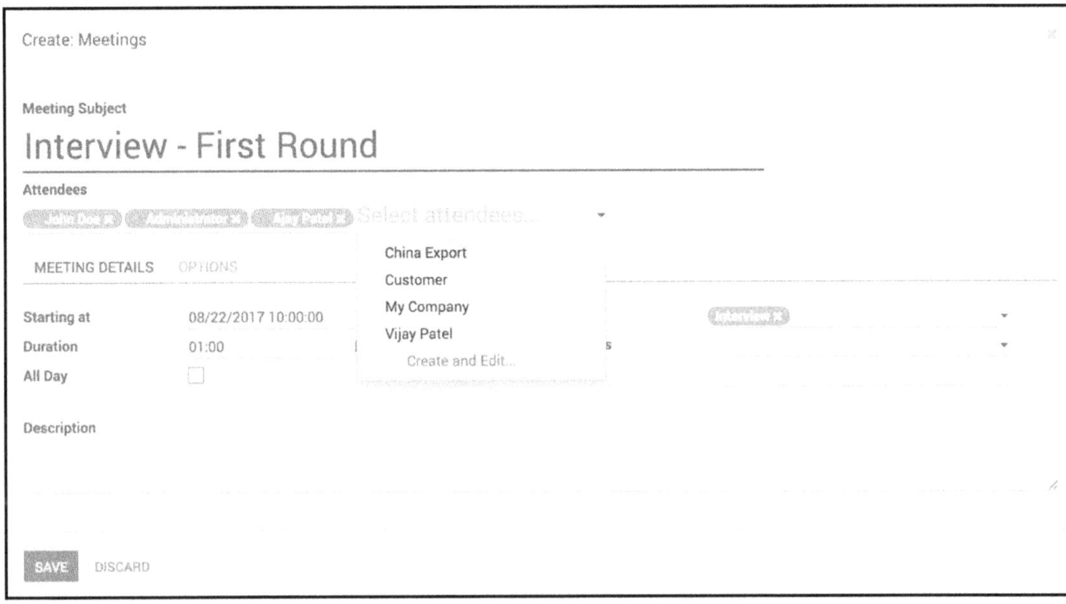

The creator of the meeting and the candidate will be added to the Attendees; we have to add the interviewer manually. Click on **SAVE** when the meeting agenda and attendees have been confirmed. The meeting will appear on everyone's calendar. The candidate will get an e-mail in their mailbox, as shown in the following screenshot. From the e-mail application, the applicant can **Accept** or **Decline** the meeting time to reschedule the meeting, or the applicant may reply to the e-mail to reschedule:

The scheduled interview will appear on the interviewer's calendar as follows; the interviewer can plan the day accordingly if there are many interviews to be conducted:

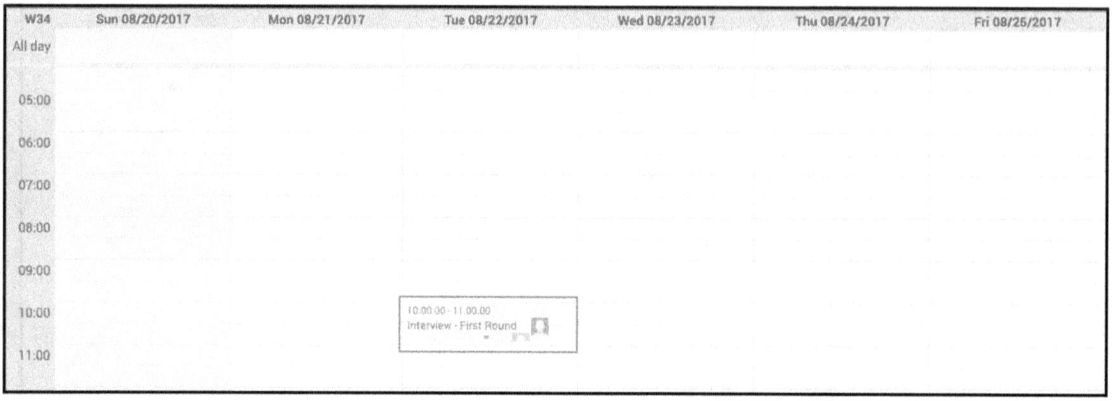

9. On the day of the first interview, the interviewer goes through the standard procedure to check the technical skills and job knowledge, and collect more information along with contractual information. We may have information about the expected benefits and record them on the application.

   Schedule the second round of interviews if needed or propose the contract as an offer. The contractual information can be stored on the application until it gets finalized:

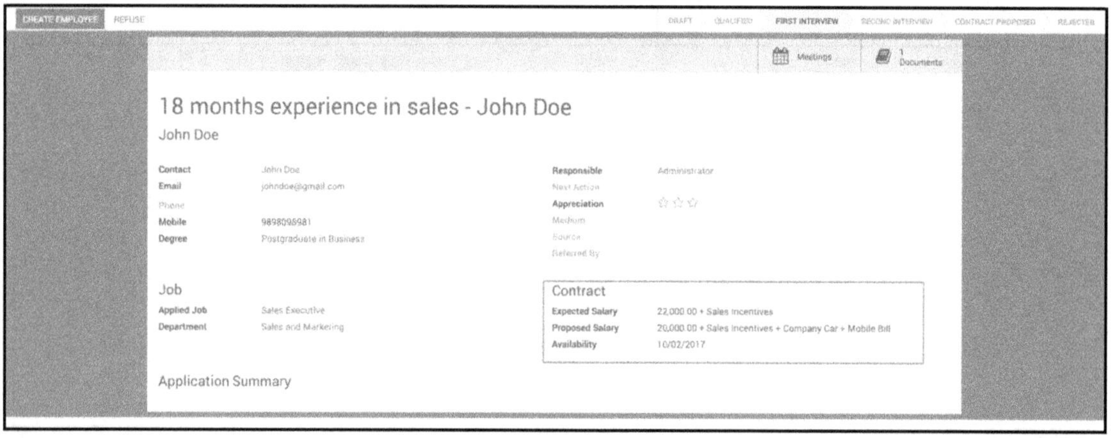

The applicant can either accept the offer or reject it. We may enter into negotiations if the candidate is really a key resource for the required job position or move to the next candidate, depending on the recruitment policy.

10. Click on the **CREATE EMPLOYEE** button available on the application. When a candidate accepts the offer, the employee will be created in the **Employee Directory**:

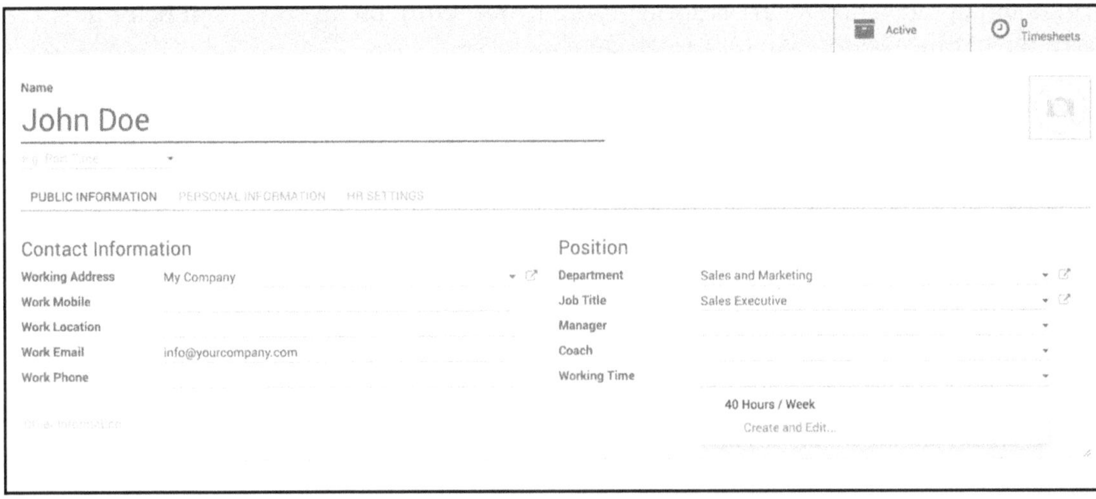

Configure the **Manager**, **Coach**, and **Working Time** under **Position**, and other information on the employee under **PERSONAL INFORMATION**. The most important field is to assign the user to the employee in the **HR SETTINGS** tab.

There's more...

Recruitment starts with launching the job position and ends at employee creation. In between, there are many activities to be performed by many internal resources, such as conducting the first interviews or second round of interviews, preparing the contract and benefits information, and getting a signature on the actual contract.

Let's jump into the details to see how we can organize the internal activities to get the best out of the available features in Odoo.

Launching a job campaign and tracking

It is important for the recruitment office to understand which campaign has brought the right candidate. Tracking the job campaign is the same as tracking the marketing campaign. We should understand which platform gives a better return on investment. It helps the recruitment office better plan for the job campaign.

Tracking can be enabled from the **Trackers** action button available on the job position. The job positions can be accessed from **Configuration** | **Job Positions** under the **Recruitment** application. Let's click on the button to see or create the Tracker for the **Sales Executive** job position:

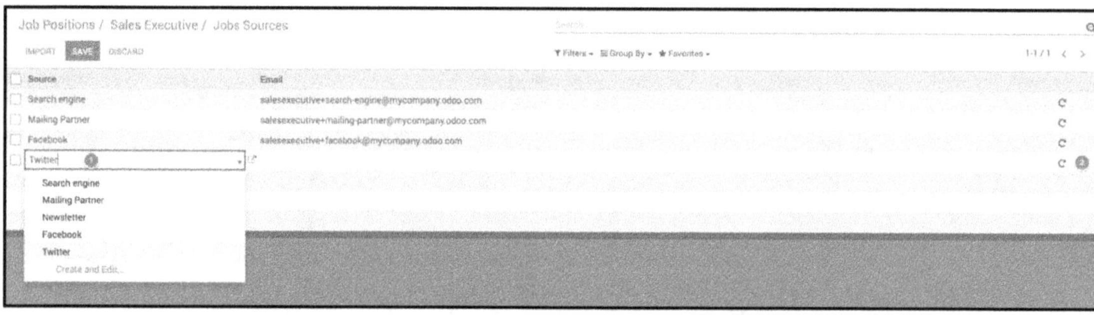

Click on the **CREATE** button, select the **Source**, and click on the **Create alias** button to create an e-mail alias that creates an applicant with tracking information. We just need to share the e-mail alias generated to the correct job campaign. In other words, when we share job information on Facebook, just share the `salesexecutive+facebook@mycompany.odoo.com` e-mail address so that when a candidate sends an e-mail to this e-mail address, we have a candidate created with tracking information as follows:

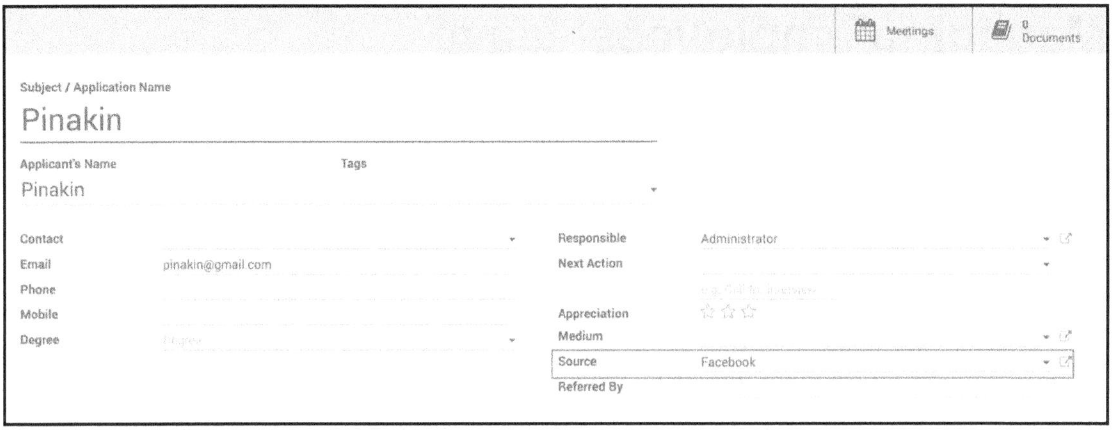

Click on the **Graph** view when you are on the applicant, and apply the grouping on the **Source** field. This will give you analytic information about which source brings more candidates. Look at the following graph report:

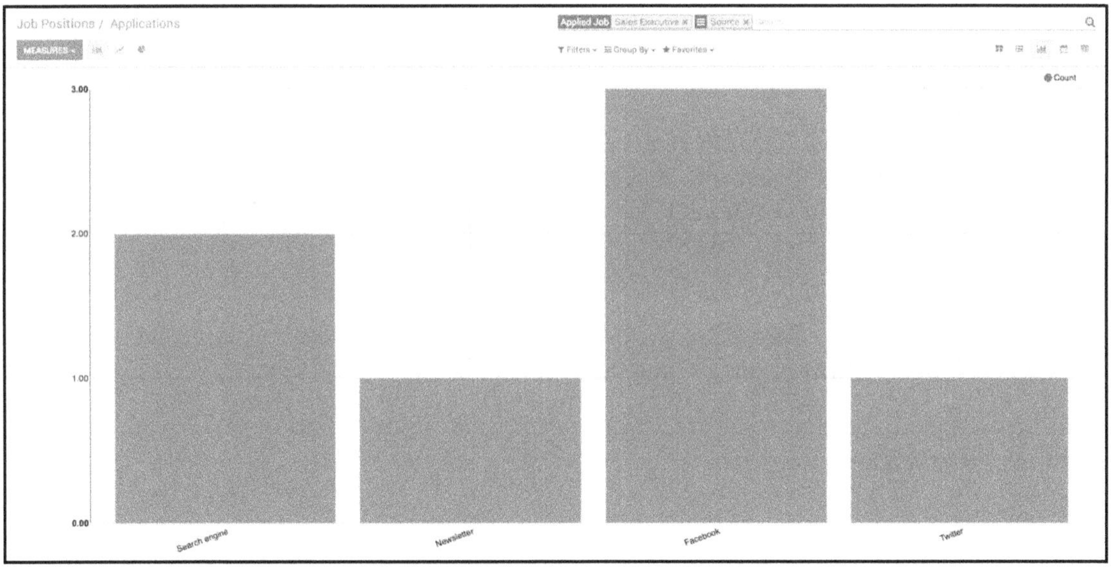

You can add the option from **Filters** to see only selected candidates to check which source brought excellent profiles. Tracking helps a lot to understand where we will get the most return on investment.

Managing employees' leave

Odoo leave management is an application used independently or integrated with other Odoo applications such as Project Management and Manufacturing Applications. The leave management application keeps a track of employee unavailability and keeps other managers informed about the employee availability for a preventive plan.

The Odoo leave application is super flexible. It keeps track of employees' available leave, allocates the leave depending on policy, and manages the work of approval or rejection of the leave application requested by an employee.

The manager is notified about the leave requested by the team members. The leave is either approved or rejected by the manager. Some special leave needs double validation too. A manager can plan the days or weeks depending on the employee leave.

Let's see how the Odoo leave application is easy to get started with allocating the leave to the employee, applying for the leave, managing the approval or rejection workflow, and tracking leave statistics by an employee or by the department.

Getting ready

We assume that you have imported or created the employees' in your instance and set up the correct tags to group the employees'. It will be easier to group similar employees' independently of department or job titles. For example, the Educational staff and Administrative staff can be two different types of employee tags for the educational institutes.

The leave available and allocated to the educational and administrative staff may be different. It is irrespective of the job position or department.

Employee Tags can be created on the **Employee** form as follows. Either select from the existing ones or create a new one:

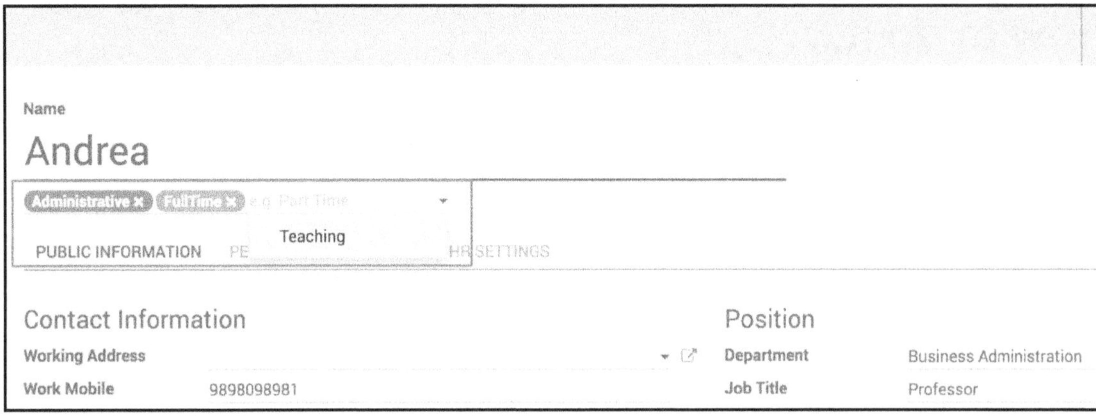

Create and assign the **Tags** to all the employees'. It will be easy to allocate the leave irrespective of the job title or department:

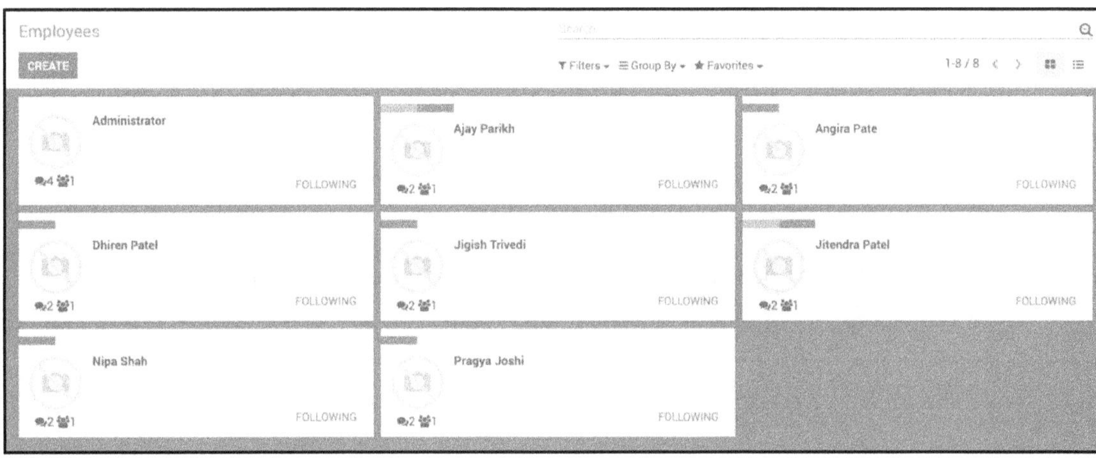

Prepare the list of leave types that are offered by your organization. The leave can be allocated or requested for the leave types. Some of the standard leave types that are offered by almost all the organizations may be as follows:

- Legal leave
- Sick leave
- Unpaid leave
- Compensatory days
- Unpaid

How to do it...

1. The first step is to install the Odoo Leave application. Go to **Apps**, search for the **Leave Management** application, and click on the **INSTALL** button:

   As soon as the **Leave** application is installed, you will get the **leave** application on your home screen.

2. The second configuration to be done is to create the leave types. There are different types of leave allocated to each employee depending on human resource policies. To keep the allocated leave separate, the leave types have to be defined before we allocate the leave. Usual leave types can be **Legal leave**, **Sick leave**, and **Unpaid leave**.

   Go to **leave** | **Configuration** to create the leave types. You will go to the list of **Leave Types**. Click on the **Create** button:

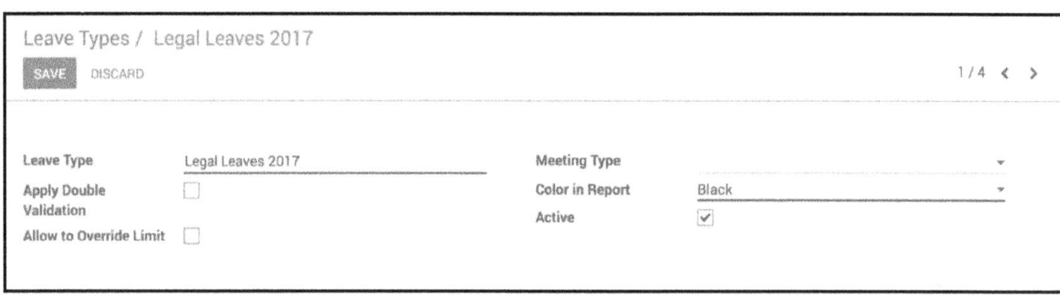

   Enter `Legal leave 2017` in the **Leave Type** field and click on the **SAVE** button.

3. Create all the leave types your organization is offering to all the employees'.

Select the **Allow Double Validation** field if the leave needs to be approved by more than one manager.

Some leaves can be applied for, more than what has been allocated to the employees'. Select the **Allow to Override Limit** field to allow requesting more than the allocated leave to all the employees'. By default, Odoo restricts taking more than allowed leave to the employees'.

4. The next step is to allocate leave to the employee based on the human resource policies. This leave has to be allocated to employees' either at the beginning of the Leave calendar or at regular intervals such as **Half Yearly**, **Quarterly**, or **Monthly**.

For example, let's allocate 15 Legal leave to all Administrative Staff and 12 Legal leave to Academic staff. To allocate leave to the employees', go to **My leave** | **Allocation Request** under the **leave** application.

Click on the **CREATE** button to create a new leave allocation. Enter Administrative Staffs - 15 Legal leave in the **Description** field. Select **Legal leave 2017** in the **Leave Type** field. Enter `12` in the **Duration** field. This is the amount of leave we are going to allocate for the type **Legal leave 2017**:

The leave can be allocated either **By employees'** or **By Employee Tags**. Select By Employee if the leave is being allocated to a single employee or select By Employee Tags in the **Mode** field if the leave is common to more than one employee. In our case, select the employee Tags we have created and allocate to the employees'.

5. Allocate all the different types of leave to employees'. I have allocated *15 Legal leave* to all *Administrative Staff* and 10 days of sick leave.

   Make sure that all the employees' get the correct leave in their accounts. Let's see **leave Summary** for Ajay's account. After successful allocation of leave, it will look like this:

> **TIP:** If any of the employees' are unable to see the allocated leave in their account, there could be two major problems: either the user is not linked to the correct employee or the employee has not been assigned the correct tags; as we have allocated leave by Employee Tags.

6. Let's assume that Ajay has applied for three days of leave from September 4, 2017, to September 6, 2017. To apply for the leave, go to My **leave** | **Leave Request** under the **leave** application. You will get the calendar to select the days in order to apply for the leave.

   Click on a DAY to apply for a single day of leave or click on start day and drag until the end date to apply for multiple days of leave.

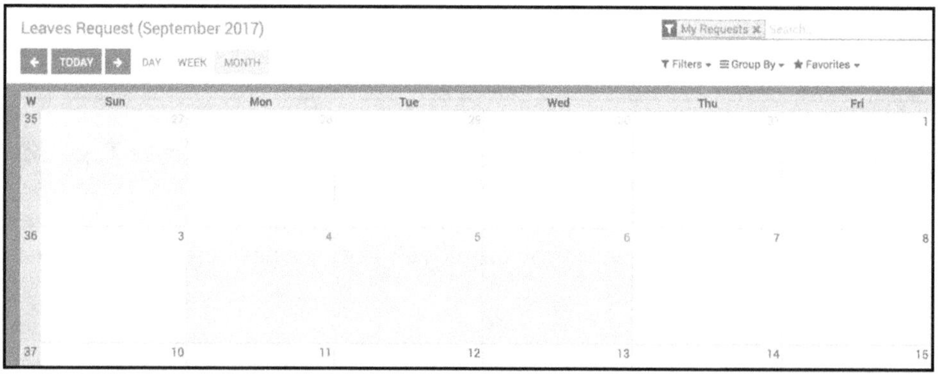

As soon as you leave the mouse, the popup will appear with the **Duration** having the start date and end date. The number of days will be computed automatically. Just select the **Description** and **Leave Type**:

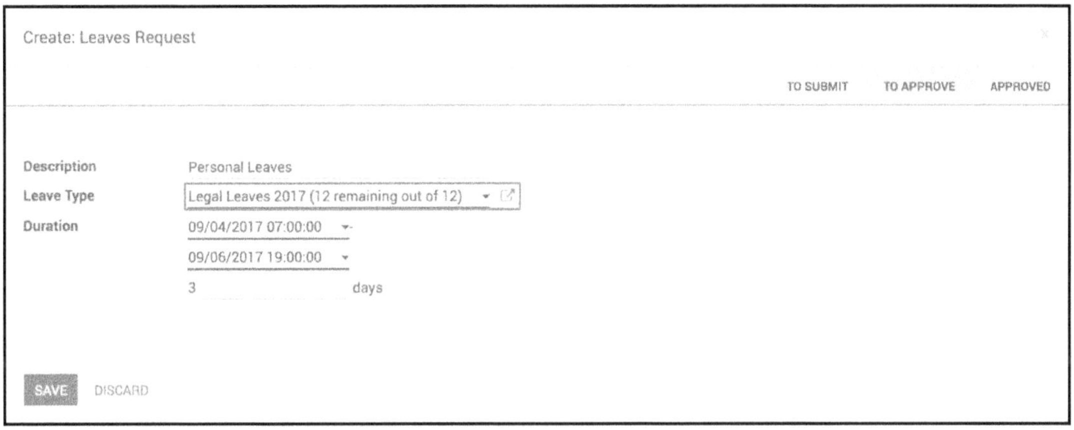

Click on the **SAVE** button. It will create the leave request. Click on the leave under the calendar view. The leave request form will be opened. It will look like this:

It is waiting for the **TO APPROVE** stage as it has already requested for the leave.

7. The manager can see the leave for their department on the Leaves dashboard. Click on the Leaves application to see the manager's dashboard. Look at the dashboard with leave requests for the employees':

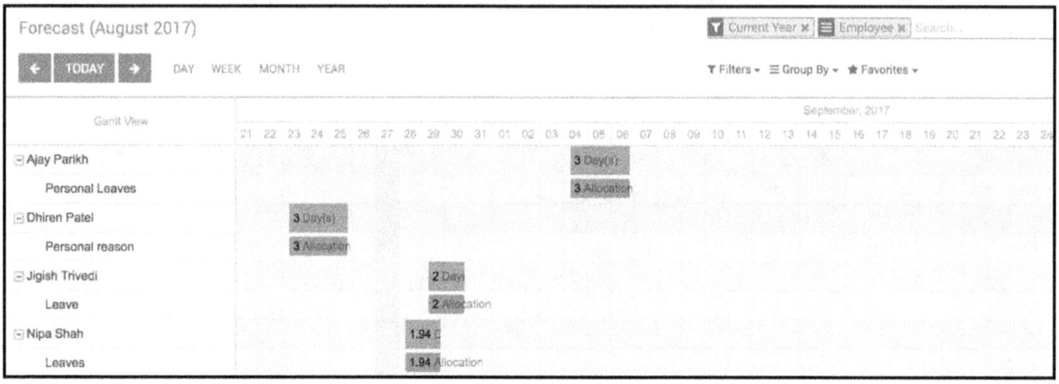

The manager can see the leave applied by the employee and the leave can be Approved or Refused by clicking on the leave:

The manager can also add a comment before approving or rejecting the leave. As soon as the leave is approved, the leave summary will get updated and leave will be deducted from the available leave:

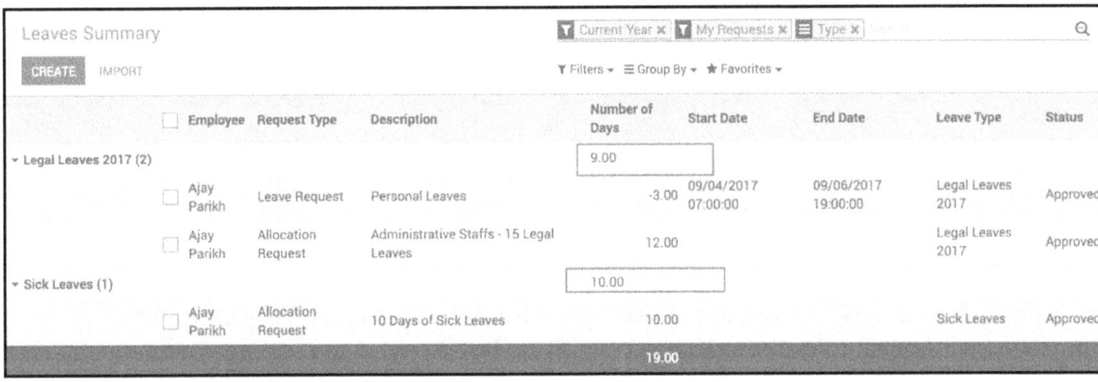

8. The manager may **REFUSE** the leave by adding the reason or asking the employee to apply for other days.

There's more...

We have seen how to create the Leave type, allocate leave to the employees' by **Employee** tags, and check the leave summary and apply for the leave. The manager may approve or reject the leave. This is a standard feature of the leave application.

There are other features available in the Odoo leave application, such as double validation of the leave request, allow employees' to take more than allowed leave by allowing them to override the limit, and link the leave request with the global calendar. Let's see how to configure these features in the Leave application.

Fix leave allocation

Make sure that the **Employee** tags are assigned correctly to each employee once the leave is allocated to the employee by tags.

Click on the **APPROVE** button to approve the leave allocation to the selected employee:

As soon as the leave is approved, the leave allocations will be created by Odoo **By Employee** who falls under the selected **Employee Tag**. Look at the preceding screenshot.

If you find mistakes in the leave allocation, assume *Angira Patel* joined after two months after the academic year started. She should get only 10 leaves instead of 12, depending on the leave policy.

Let's change it. Search the application entry that allocates 12 Legal leave to Angira Patel. Click on **REFUSE** and then on **RESET TO DRAFT** to make the modification. When you modify the leave allocation, Odoo will ask you to pass through the allocation approval or rejection workflow:

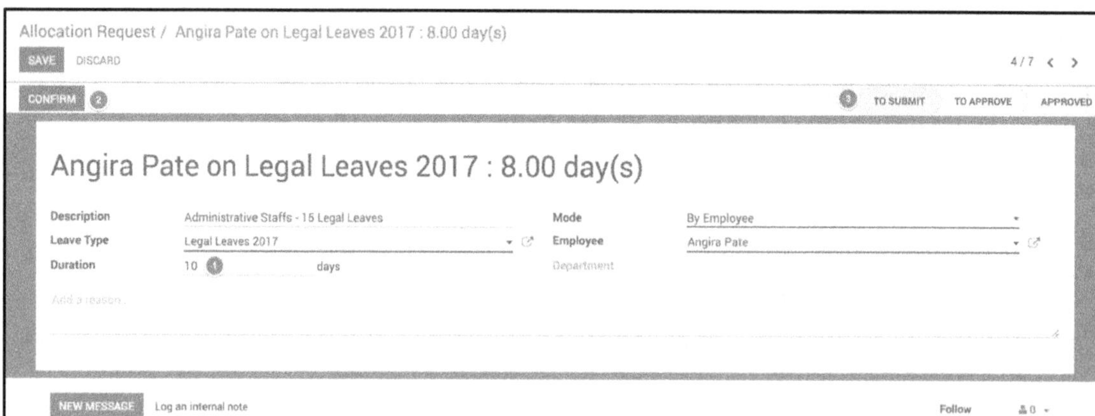

Set **Duration** to **10** instead of **12**, and click on the **CONFIRM** button; the request will go to the **TO APPROVE** stage. As soon as the manager finds it solved, the request can be approved by clicking on the **APPROVE** button.

Double validation

Some types of special leave need double validation before it gets approved. It has to be configured on the **Leave Types**. As soon as the leave is applied by the employee, it asks for approval twice.

Let's configure the **Leave Types** to **Compensatory Days** to have double validation:

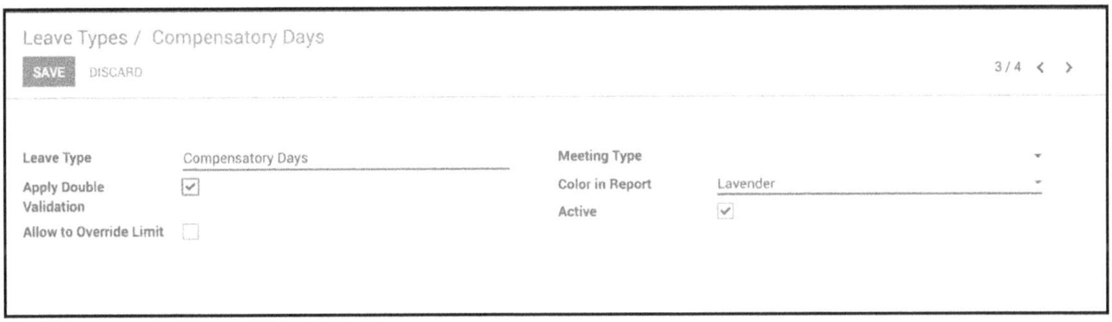

Now, when an employee requests for a leave, it will not be approved until it is approved by a second manager:

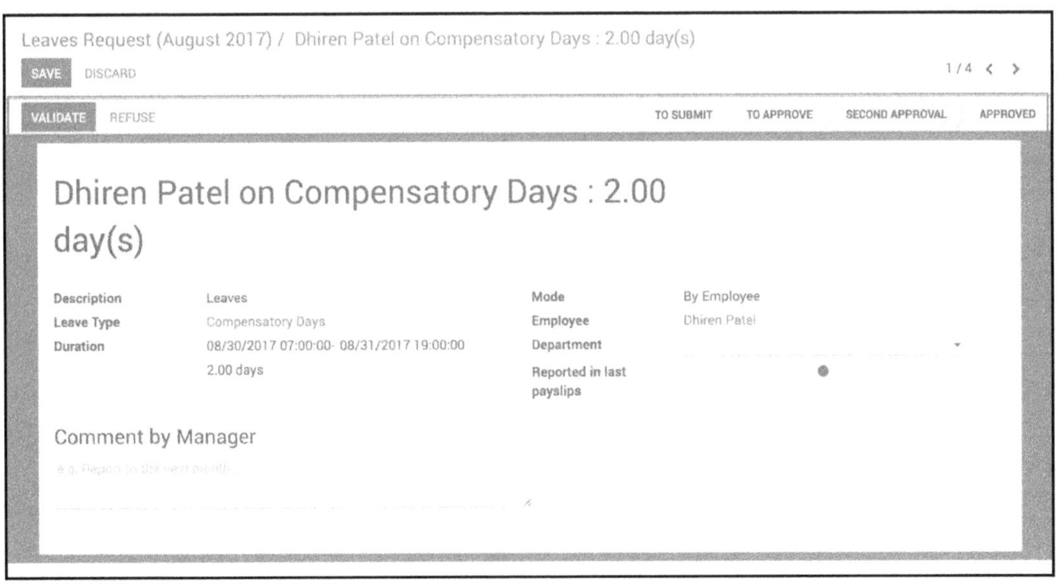

After having the first approval, the **VALIDATE** button will appear, and leave will be waiting for the **SECOND APPROVAL** stage.

Allow overriding the limit

This option is used when we want to allow employees' to take more leave than the available leave in their account. Let's take the example of Pragya. She has only three leave of type **Legal leave** available in her account. When she applies for the leave, she can get the number of leave available for each type of leave:

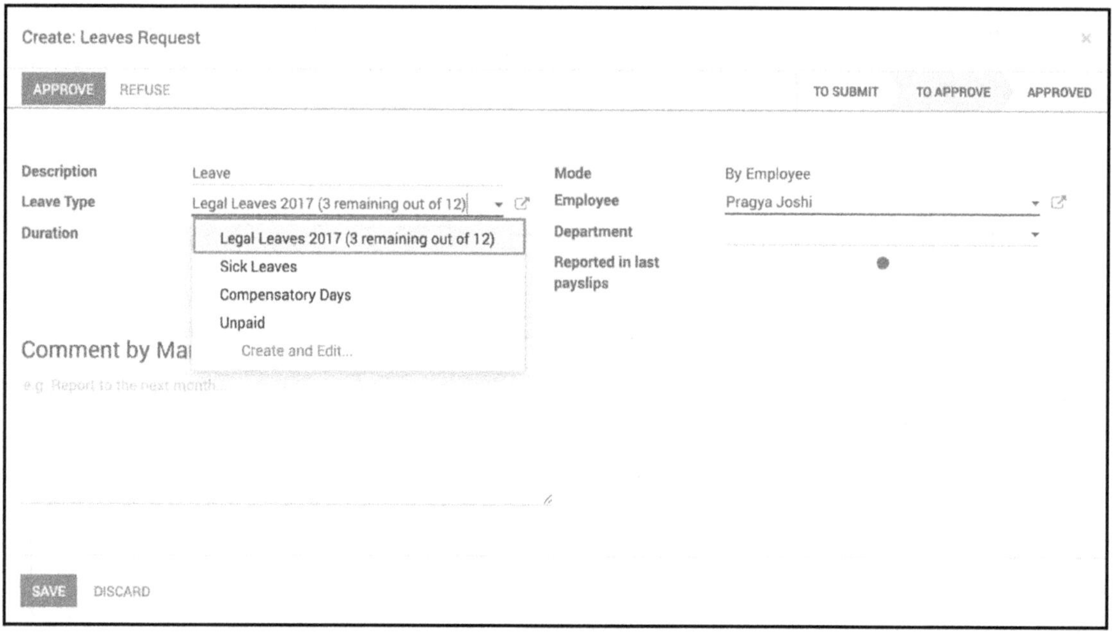

She is going to apply for four days of leave even though she has only three 3 days available. When she tries to save the leave request, she will get a warning message as shown here:

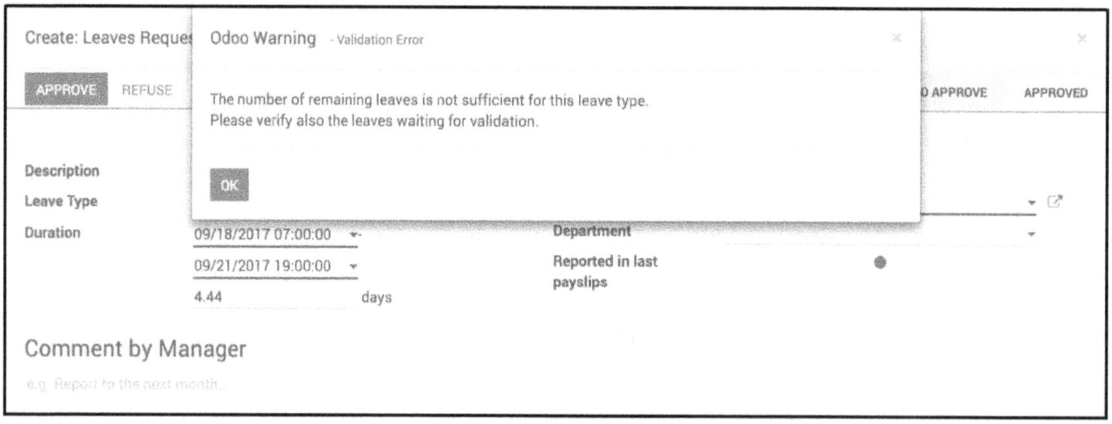

If we would like to allow her to take more than her available leaves, the **Allow to Override Limit** field should be selected on **Leave Type** as **Legal leave 2017**:

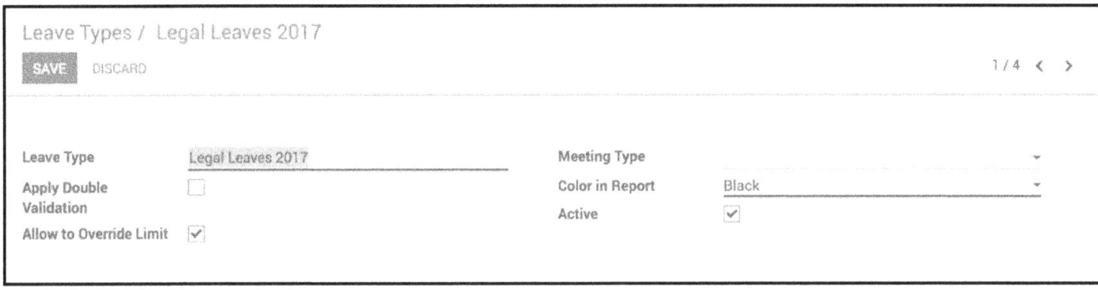

As soon as **Legal leave 2017** is marked as **Allow to Override Limit**, it will not display the available number of leave at the time of the leave request:

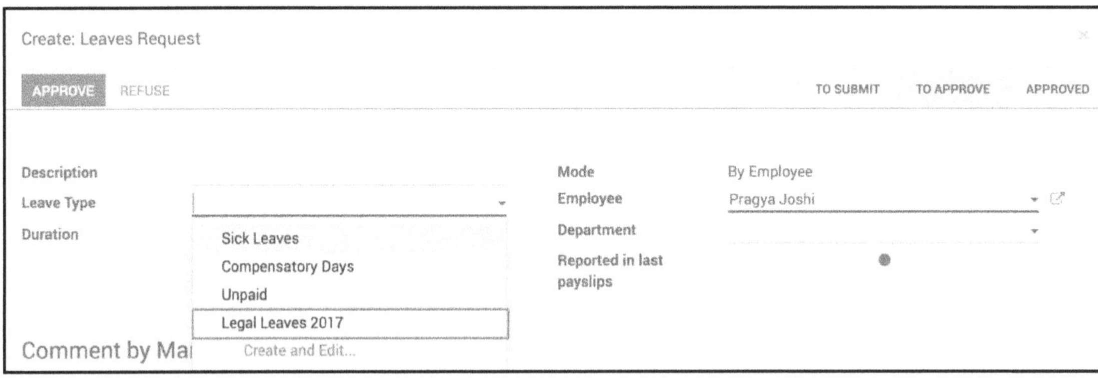

Absent today

The employee directory is accessible to all employees' in an organization. The filter will be applied based on the accessibility. By default, all employees' can see their colleagues, that is, a list of employees' from the same department.

Absent employees' can be filtered from the list by applying the **Absent Today** filter. When an employee applies this filter, they can see the absent employees' within their department, but when the human resource manager applies this filter, they can get list of absent employees' from the entire organization as they have access to the full employee list:

By applying the **Absent Today** filter, we will get the list of employees' who are absent today. The leave type will appear as a label on the employee such as **Legal leave 2017**, **Sick leave**. Look at the preceding screenshot.

HR expense and reimbursements

It is a common requirement in many businesses that some employees' are allowed to do expenses on behalf of the company such as purchase books, CDs, software subscription services, or expenses for travel and accommodation during business trips.

There are two ways expenses can be registered, either by creating an expense line in the expense sheet or by sending an e-mail to the e-mail address that will create an expense line automatically. The expenses can be paid by the employee initially, and it can be reimbursed later by the company, or some employees' can have a company card to pay for expenses. They would just need to submit the valid bills for the expenses.

Usually, an expense that was incurred by an employee has to be verified by the related manager, and later, the accountant processes the reimbursement. Sometimes, the manager may disagree on some expenses too, which will be rejected, and the employee may not get the reimbursement or may get a partial payment.

Let's see how the Odoo Expense management application manages the employee expenses, passes them through the approval system, and the employee gets the reimbursement. Some expenses may be recovered from the customer as part of the contract. We will also see how to get employee expenses refund from the customer.

Getting ready

Assume that you have prepared the list of products or services that can be offered under employee expenses or reimbursement. Some of the employee expense products or services are listed here:

- Hotel accommodation
- Air ticket
- Cab service
- Lunch or dinner

Some products may have a fixed cost price, while some products' cost price cannot be fixed. For example, for cab services, we can fix the cost price per kilometer, while the cost of the air ticket cannot be fixed.

How to do it...

1. Expense Tracker is an independent application like leave. It can be found and installed from Apps. Go to **Apps** and search for **Expense Tracker**. Then, click on the **INSTALL** button:

As soon as the **Expense Tracker** application is installed, the new application **Expenses** can be found on your instance home page.

2. The first step is to set up the expense products. It can be created or imported in Odoo. It is a special type of product used to register the employees' expense. Expense products can be created from **Expense** | **Configuration** | **Expense Products**.

Let's take an example of a cab service. When employees' went onsite for a customer meeting, they may have to hire a car to commute to the customer location:

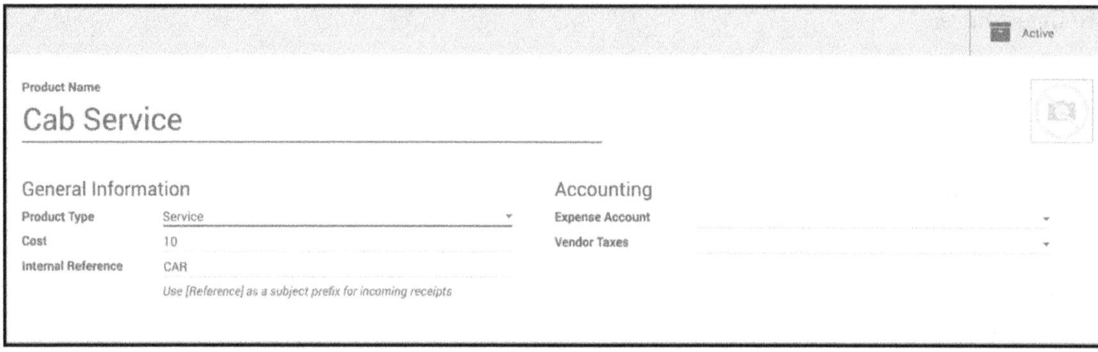

In Odoo, we can create an expense product with a predefined cost price. This will help us approve or reject the expense bills. Look at the preceding screenshot. We created the **Cab Service** as an expense product. We will allow the maximum cost price at the rate of 10 per kilometer.

Likewise, you can create other services or products such as Hotel Accommodation, Air Ticket, and Lunch or Dinner.

3. Assume that we have to send one of our employees' onsite to work on a customer project. This mission is about five days. As soon as the employee comes back, he/she will submit expenses for the five days. The expenses can be created from **My Expense** | **Expenses to Submit** under the **Expense** application:

The expenses can be processed in four steps. Let's create an expense by clicking on the **CREATE** button:

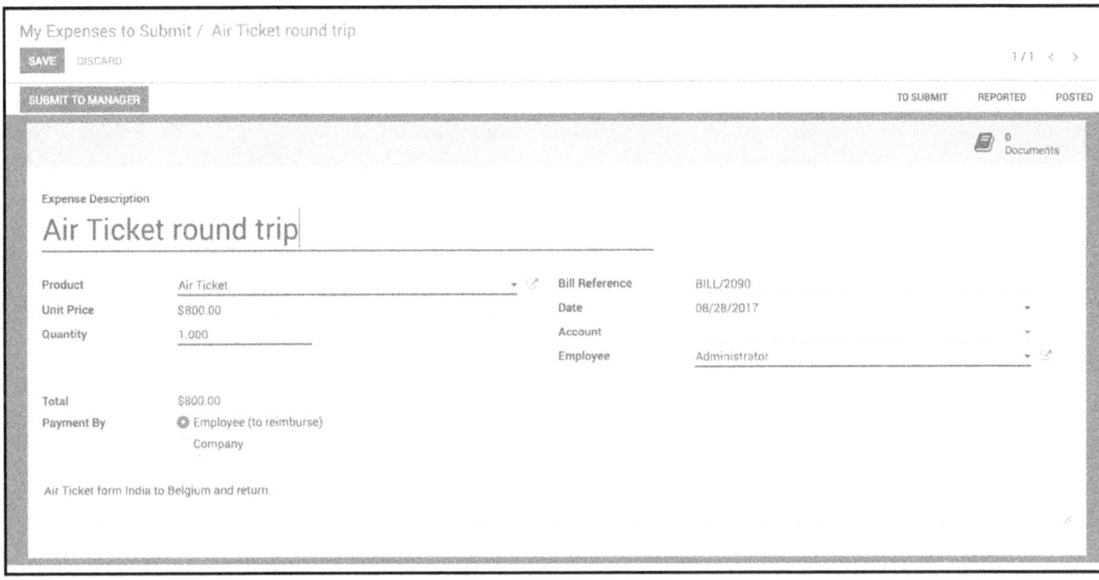

4. The related document can be attached on the expense by clicking on the **Documents** action button. Click on **CREATE**, enter a file name, and upload the file by clicking on the **UPLOAD YOUR FILE** button:

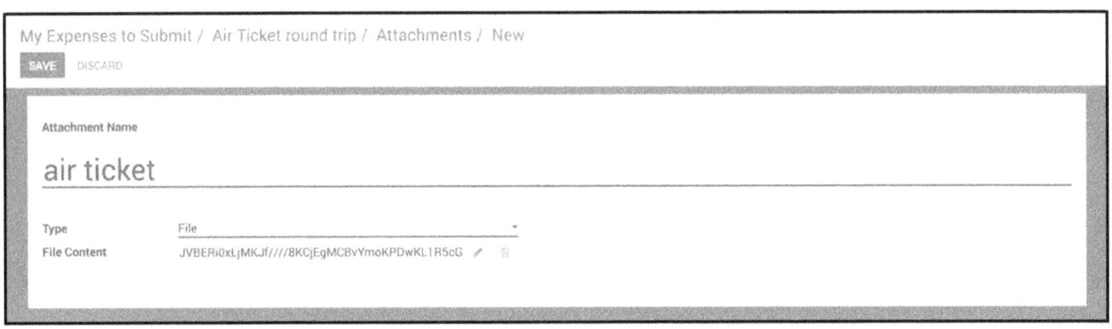

Click on the **SAVE** button to attach the new document on the expense.

5. The expense can be applied for the approval of a manager. If the employee has to submit only one expense, it can be submitted to the manager by clicking on the **SUBMIT TO MANAGER** button or the employee can apply for more than one expense in a single sheet. First, create all the expenses for the single business trip:

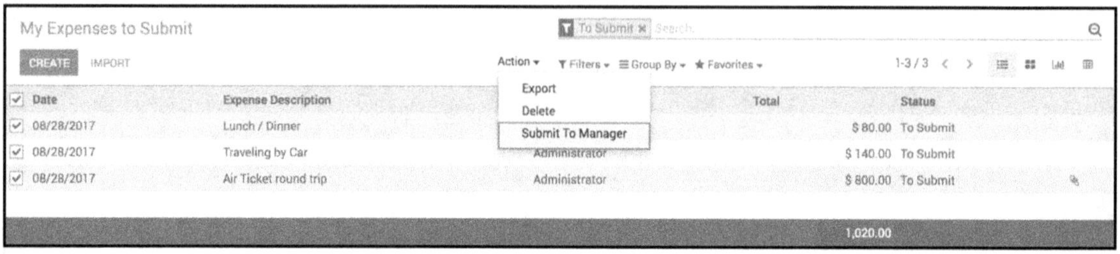

The expense lines will look as displayed in the preceding screenshot. Select the expense lines to apply for the reimbursement and click on the **Submit To Manager** menu available under **Actions**:

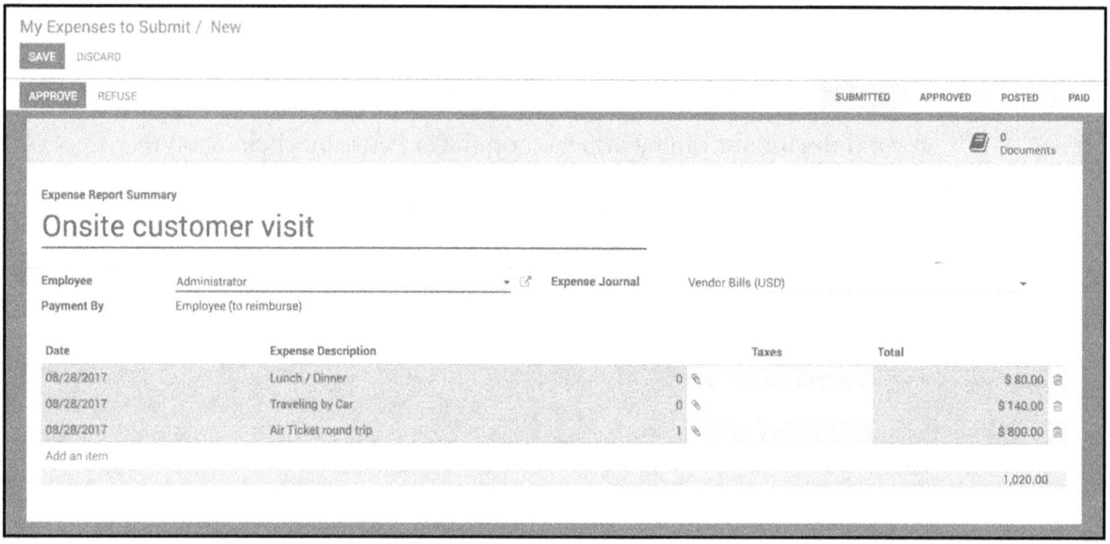

The expense sheet will be created with the list of expense lines selected. Enter the name of the sheet. I have entered `Onsite customer visit` and clicked on **SAVE** to save the sheet.

6. The status of the sheet is marked as **SUBMITTED** as the sheet is submitted to the manager for approval. All the expenses waiting for manager approval can be found under **To Approve** | **Expense Reports** to the **Approve** menu available under the **Expenses** applications.

   The manager may approve or reject the expense depending on the policy. The sheet can be approved by clicking on the **APPROVED** button:

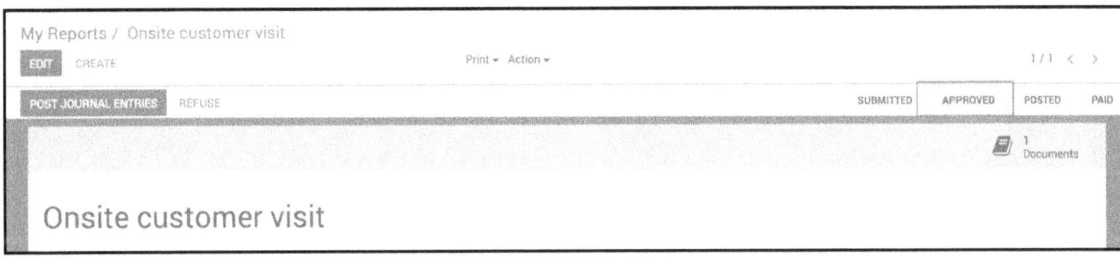

   As soon as the sheet is approved, it goes to the **APPROVED** stage, and it will wait for **Accountant** approval.

7. The account can find all the sheets that are approved by the manager and waiting to be posted in the accounts under the **Accountant** | **Expense Reports To Post** menu under the **Expenses** application:

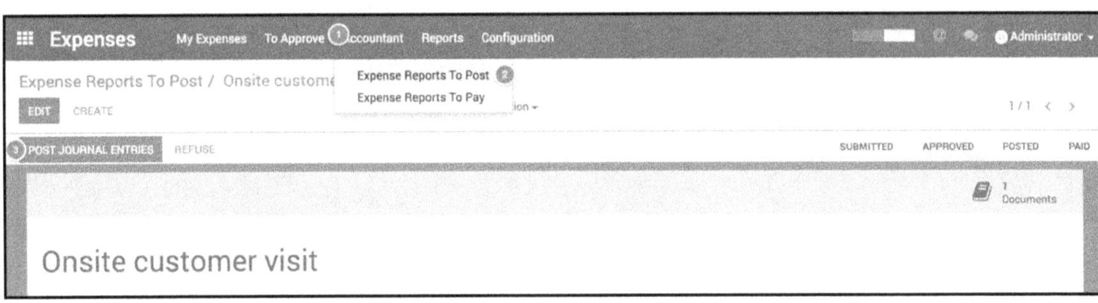

   The accountant has to post accounting entries by clicking on the **POST JOURNAL ENTRIES** button available on the expense sheet. The sheet will go to the **POSTED** stage once the accountant clicks on the **JOURNAL ENTRIES** button.

8. The next step is to pay the expenses to the employee. All the posted expense sheets are waiting for payment. It can be found under **Accountant | Expense Reports To Pay** menu under the **Expenses** application:

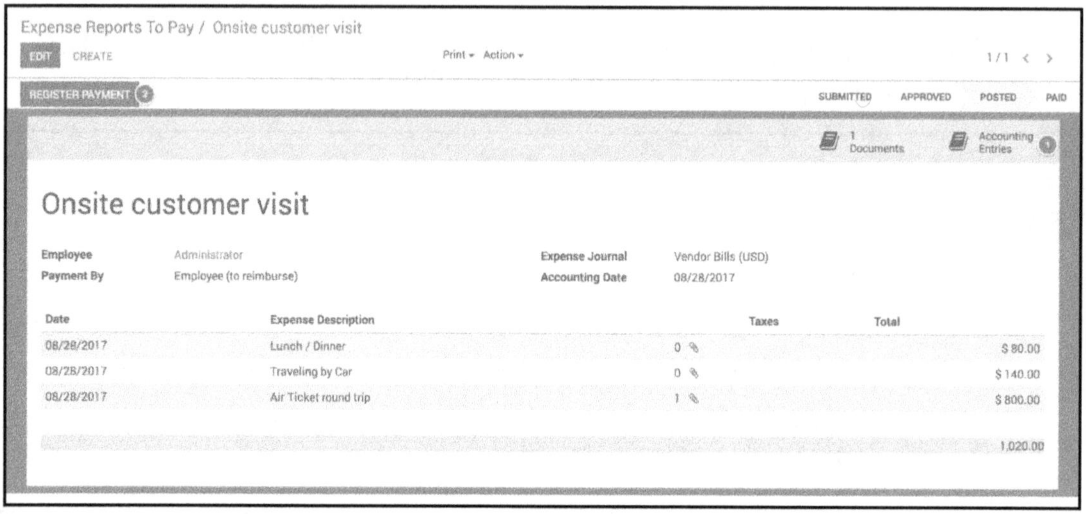

Open the sheet to make the payment. To register the payment, click on the **REGISTER PAYMENT** button. A popup will appear asking you to select the mode of payment. The amount will be filled automatically:

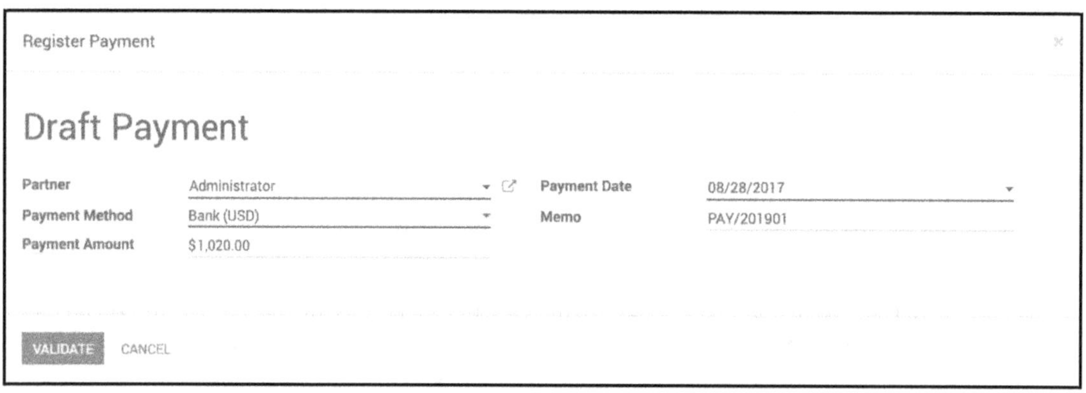

Click on **VALIDATE** to pay the reimbursement to the employee. The payment will be registered and the expense sheet will go to the PAID stage.

Make sure that you have linked an employee with a partner. As in Odoo, all the financial transactions can be done only with a partner. An employee can be linked with the partner by setting the **Home Address** field on an employee form as shown here:

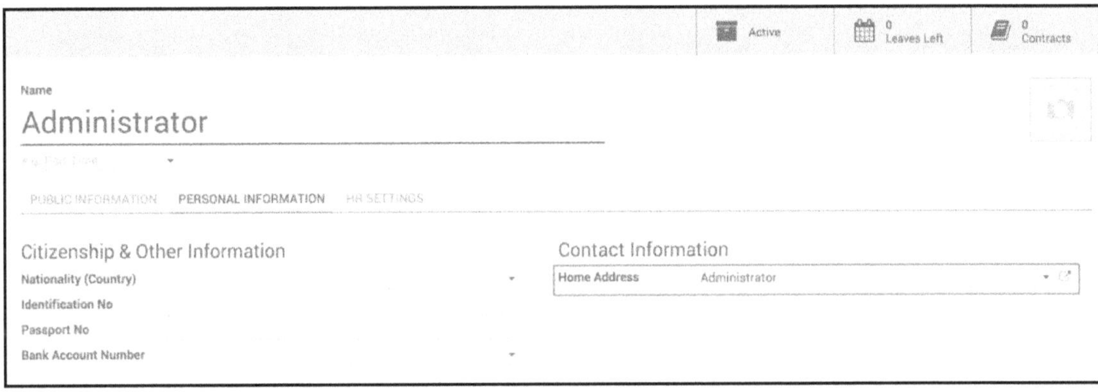

There's more...

We have seen the standard flow of employee reimbursement. It can be done in four steps. It starts with creating and submitting an expense to the manager, the manager approves or rejects the expense, the accountant posts all the approved and the confirmed expense and makes the payment through bank or by cash.

Odoo has some advanced features other than the standard expense approval flow such as recording an expense by e-mail, registering an expense paid by the company card, or the employee can re-invoice a customer and get paid from the customer. Let's see how to use some of the advanced features of expense application.

Record expenses by e-mail

When an employee is onsite, it can be too difficult for them to keep a copy of each invoice or bill. Sometimes, employees' lose a bill and are not able to apply for reimbursement as the company policy requires them to submit the bill.

Odoo has a built-in feature to create an expense along with a copy of bills from an incoming e-mail. An employee just has to click a photo of a bill and send an e-mail to the expense gateway to register the expense. If an employee forgets to preserve the copy of a bill, it will not be an issue as the bill is already submitted to the expense application by e-mail.

To enable the registration of an expense based on an e-mail, the first step to configure is the e-mail gateway available at **Configuration** | **Settings** of the **Expenses** application:

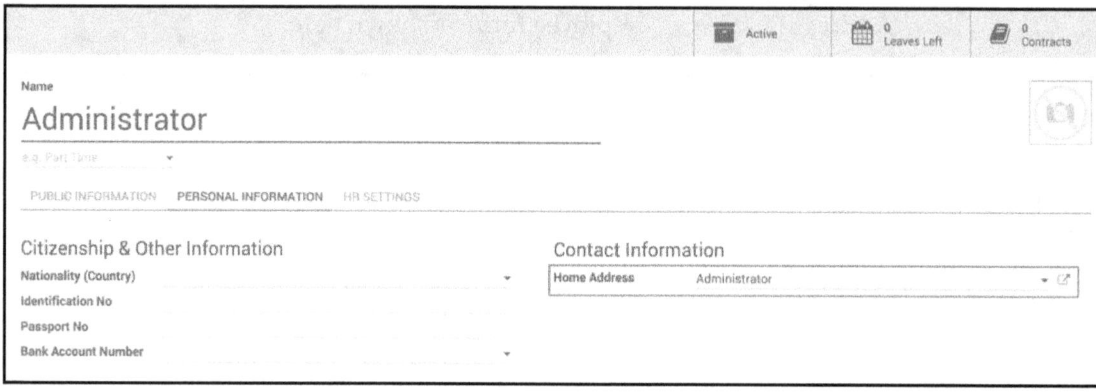

The default e-mail gateway is `expense@mycompany.odoo.com`. Change it if you want a different e-mail gateway.

The second step is to configure the product code to link the product automatically on an incoming e-mail. The price be can be set later based on the attached bill available in an e-mail:

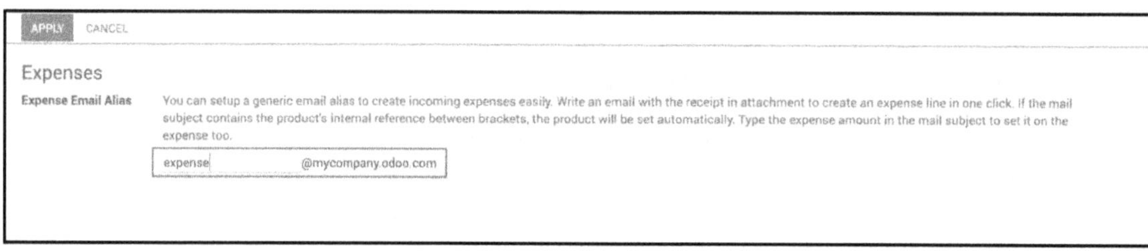

Now, we are ready to receive an e-mail to register an employee expense.

Let's assume that the employee captures the bill and sends a copy of the bill to the e-mail gateway. The employee writes an e-mail with the receipt as an attachment to create an expense in one click.

If the email subject contains the product's internal reference between brackets as [**LUNCH**], the product will be set automatically. The expense amount is typed in the mail subject to set it on the expense too. In our case, the subject can be [**LUNCH**] lunch with customer 192:

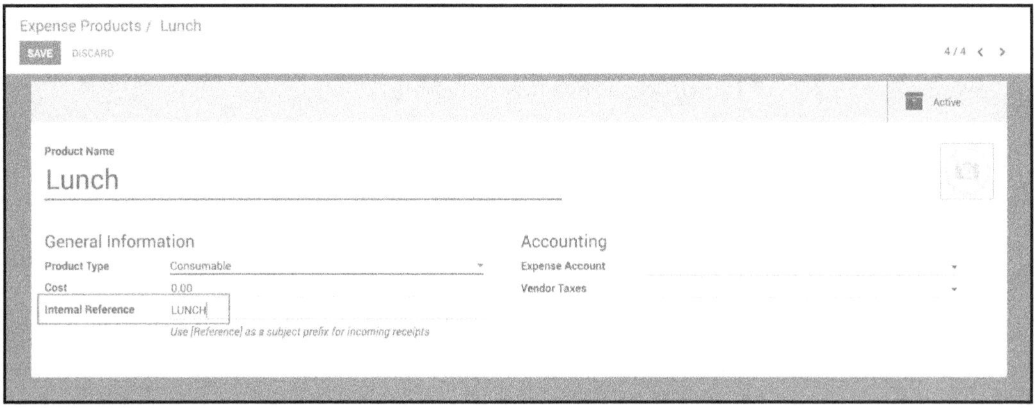

The e-mail will be received by the gateway; it will create an expense entry as follows:

It is advisable to send all the expenses along with the expense receipt by e-mail. It will be used to verify the expense amount before preparing the sheet to apply for the reimbursement. The rest of the process remains the same.

Expenses paid by company card

Some of the employees' in a company have access to a company card. They can pay big expenses using the company card for air ticket, hotel bills, and so on.

Where expenses are paid by company card, the employee needs to submit the bills only. There is no reimbursement process. However, the bill's validation process remains the same:

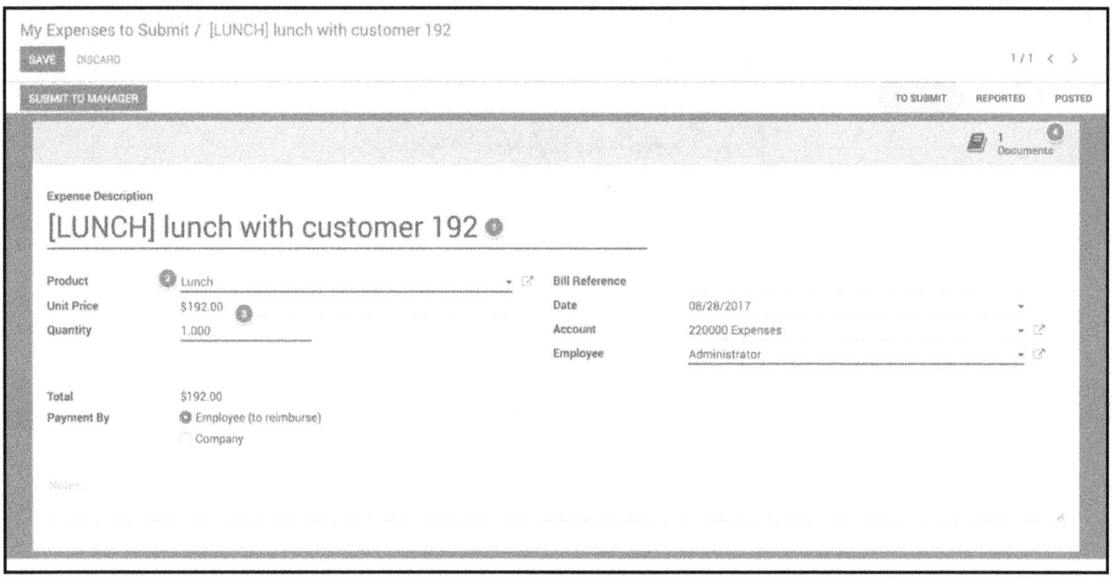

Select **Company** in the **Payment By** field at the time of creating an expense. In case the expense is registered by e-mail, this has to be set manually before submitting it to the manager.

As soon as the accountant clicks on the **POST JOURNAL ENTRIES** button, the expenses will directly go to the **PAID** stage.

Reinvoicing expenses to the customer

Sending an employee onsite to work on a customer project is necessary as part of a project contract. Of course, sometimes, customers are ready to pay the lodging and boarding expenses for an employee.

Most of the time, expenses such as air tickets and hotel accommodation are paid by the company, while traveling and lunch and dinner bills have to be submitted by the employee. The project manager verifies and approves all the bills and an accountant processes payment to the employee.

Later, the full expenses of the onsite visit can be invoiced to the customer for an ongoing project. Do not forget to configure the **Re-invoicing Expense** field under the **Invoicing Policy** section on the **Product** form:

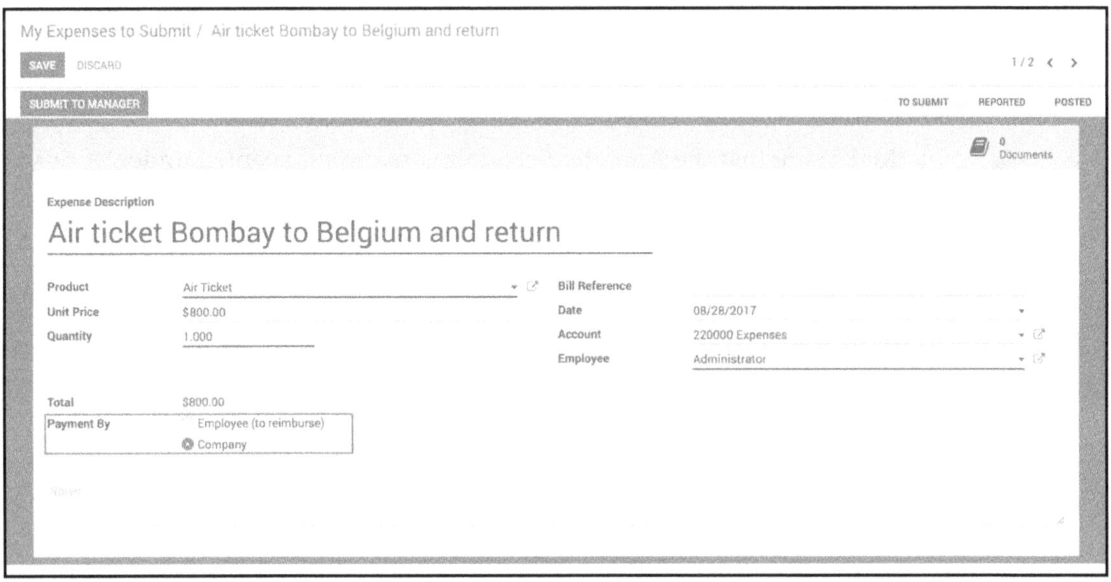

The employee expenses can be reinvoiced either at cost or as the sale price. I choose to reinvoice at cost. We will raise an invoice at the same rate it costs us. In some business cases, it can be set to at sale price if the fixed price is proposed to the customer.

Let's assume that you have installed the **Sales** and **Timesheet** applications on your instance. The Consulting Project is a service type product, and the **Track Service** field is set to **Timesheets** on the project.

To test this feature, let's create a sales order with at least one service type product in the sales order. Look at the sales order in the following screenshot:

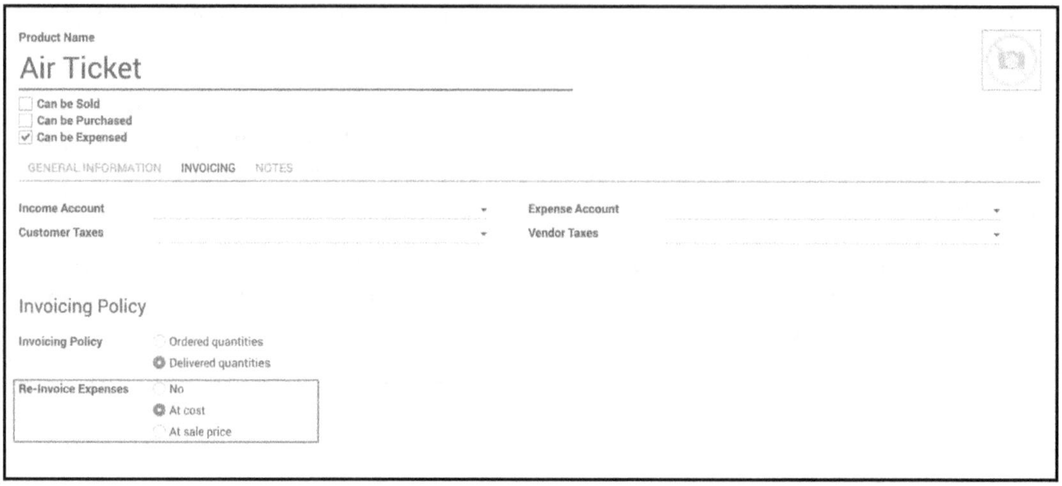

Make sure that the Analytic Accounting feature is enabled under **Configuration** | **Settings** under the **Accounting** application.

Confirm the sales order. This will create an analytic account having the name as `Sales Order number` - **Customer name**, that is, `SO001` - **China Export**. This analytic account will be linked to the **Analytic Account** field available under the **OTHER INFORMATION** tab:

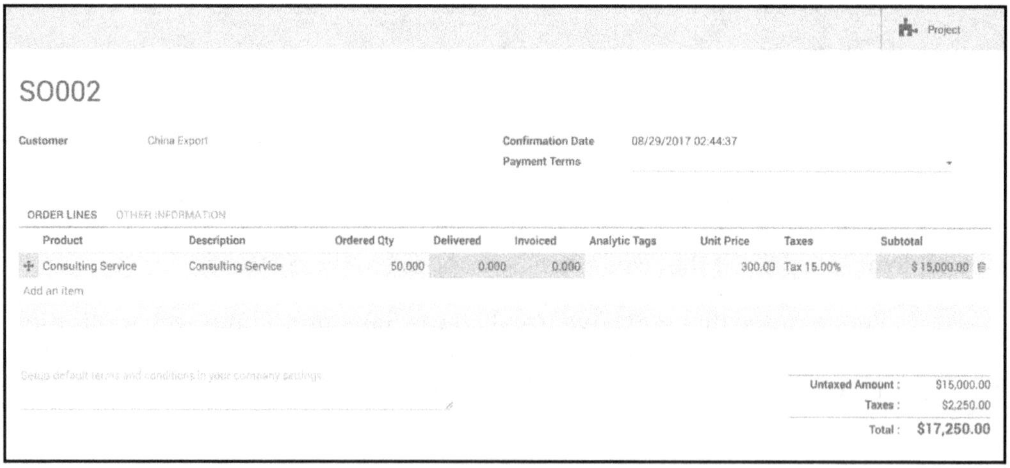

Now, link all the expenses incurred during the onsite visit for the customer project to get the correct analytic account. Look at the following screenshot:

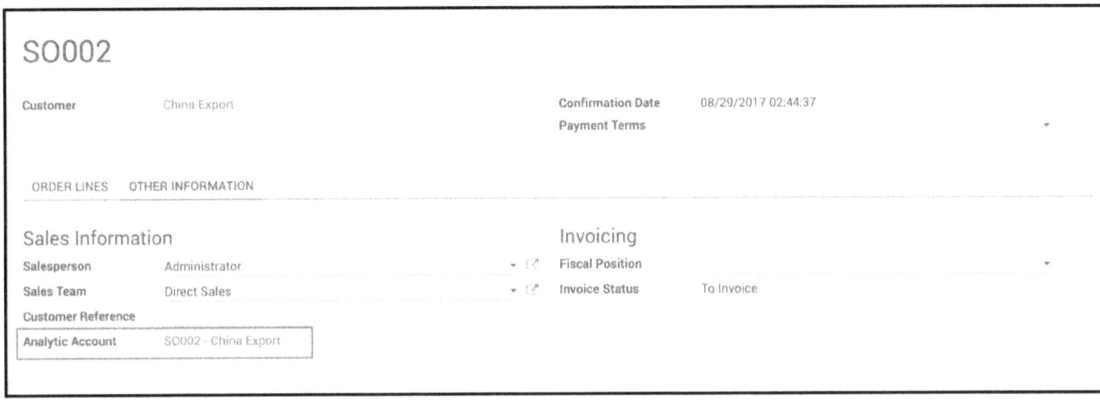

Link all the expenses to the `SO001 - China Export` analytic account at the time of creating an expense. The further process is to select the list of expenses and create an expense sheet to submit to the manager. It will remain the same.

Create an expense sheet. It will look like the following screenshot. It will be easy for the project manager to verify that it is linked to the correct analytics account:

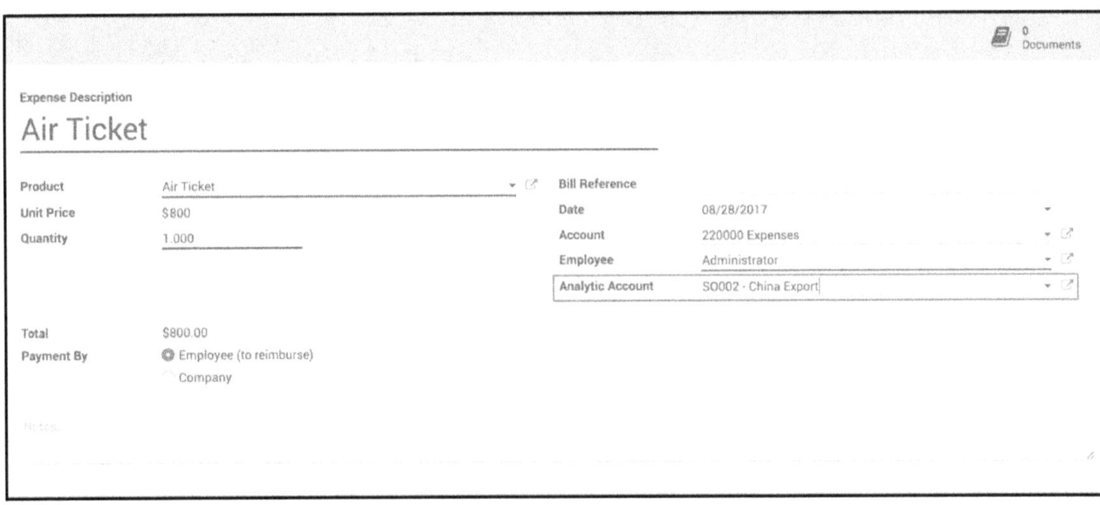

As soon as the expense sheet is approved and an accountant posts the journal entries, the sales order gets updated and the employee expense lines will be injected into the sales order to reinvoice to the end customer:

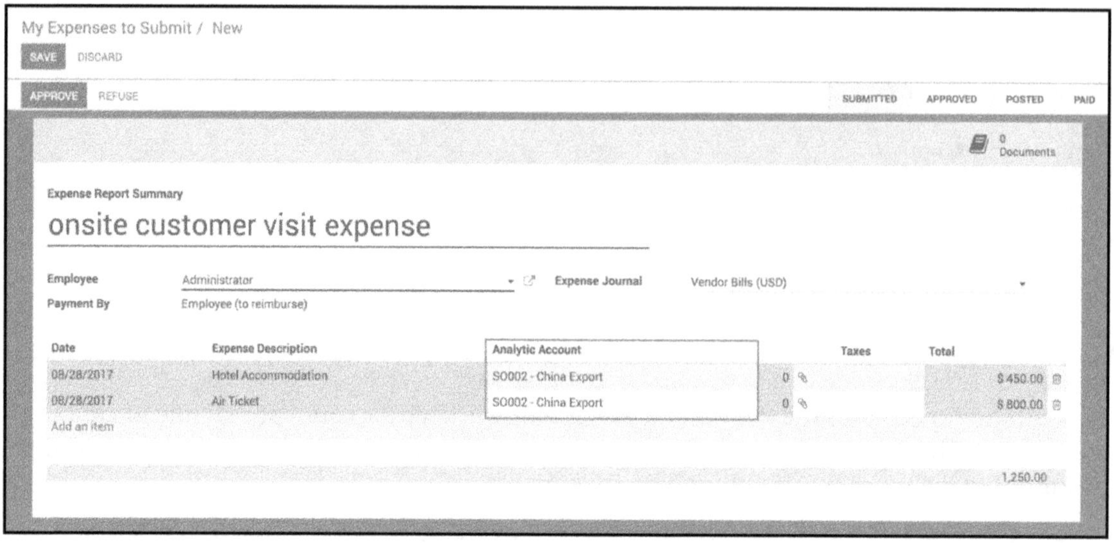

As the lines are in blue, we can create an invoice and ask for the payment to get the reimbursement for the additional employee expense.

16
Installation of Odoo on Ubuntu

In this chapter, we will cover the following recipe:

- Using Odoo onsite for custom needs

Introduction

Odoo can be installed on various platforms, including Windows, Mac, and Linux; however, in order to test Odoo, you just need a web browser on any operating system. If you are looking for the Odoo Instant demonstration, you can quickly go to `https://www.odoo.com/start` to get the Odoo Online Demo. The production environment can be set up on the Linux server either by hosting it on cloud or onsite.

Odoo can be installed on various Linux operating systems; however, we suggest that you use Ubuntu if you are a beginner to the Linux operating system. Setting up the Odoo production platform onsite is not easy, as it requires technical knowledge and the setting up of multiple servers. Test and Production are the minimal servers to be set up to use the Odoo onsite.

Let's see how to set up the production server onsite using Ubuntu Server or using the Odoo Pass service to set up the Odoo instance with full control.

Using Odoo onsite for custom needs

To use Odoo onsite, Ubuntu Server edition is the recommended operating system. With a little technical knowledge, anyone can start working with the Linux operating system. The setting, running, and maintaining Odoo on Ubuntu Linux is easier compared with other Linux operating systems.

Let's set up the database and other required dependencies to run the Odoo Server on Ubuntu Server edition.

Getting ready

We assume that you have chosen the correct hardware and downloaded the Ubuntu Server edition operation. Also, make sure that you choose the LTS version to get a minimum of three years, supports the operating system.

It is assumed that you have the password for the root user, as it is required to install the various dependency libraries and configurations.

In my case, the Linux username is **odoo**.

How to do it...

1. The first step is to update the package list on your Ubuntu Server or desktop using the following command. First, enter the **root** user so that each time you don't need to execute all the installation commands. Using **sudo**, enter the **apt-get update** command to update the package list:

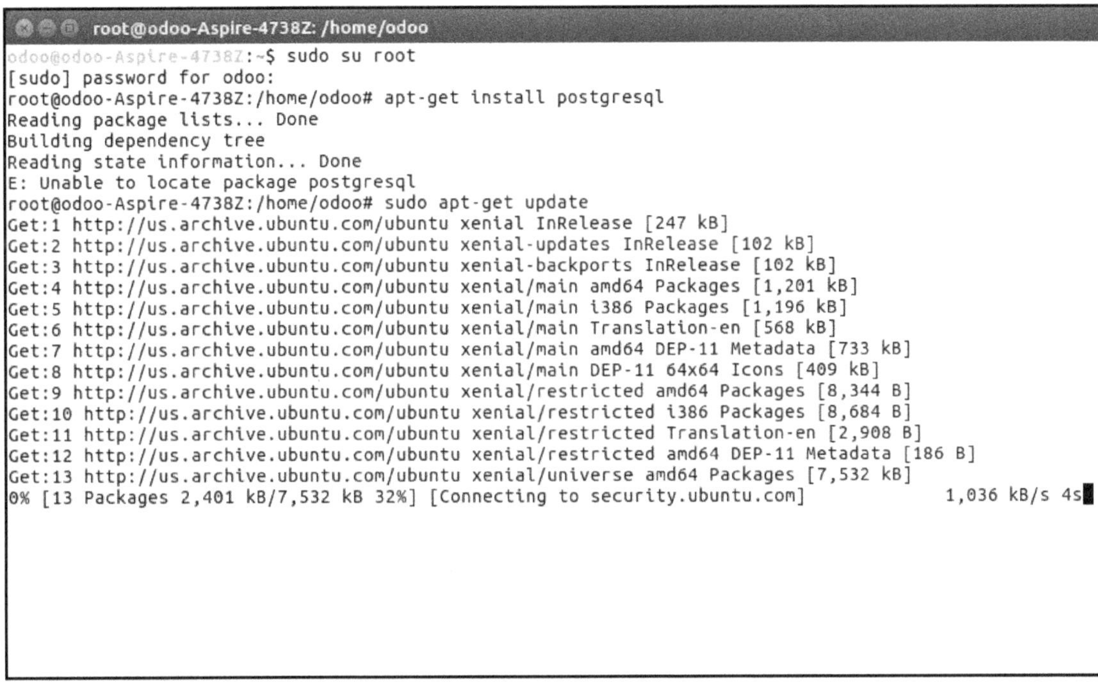

```
root@odoo-Aspire-4738Z: /home/odoo
odoo@odoo-Aspire-4738Z:~$ sudo su root
[sudo] password for odoo:
root@odoo-Aspire-4738Z:/home/odoo# apt-get install postgresql
Reading package lists... Done
Building dependency tree
Reading state information... Done
E: Unable to locate package postgresql
root@odoo-Aspire-4738Z:/home/odoo# sudo apt-get update
Get:1 http://us.archive.ubuntu.com/ubuntu xenial InRelease [247 kB]
Get:2 http://us.archive.ubuntu.com/ubuntu xenial-updates InRelease [102 kB]
Get:3 http://us.archive.ubuntu.com/ubuntu xenial-backports InRelease [102 kB]
Get:4 http://us.archive.ubuntu.com/ubuntu xenial/main amd64 Packages [1,201 kB]
Get:5 http://us.archive.ubuntu.com/ubuntu xenial/main i386 Packages [1,196 kB]
Get:6 http://us.archive.ubuntu.com/ubuntu xenial/main Translation-en [568 kB]
Get:7 http://us.archive.ubuntu.com/ubuntu xenial/main amd64 DEP-11 Metadata [733 kB]
Get:8 http://us.archive.ubuntu.com/ubuntu xenial/main DEP-11 64x64 Icons [409 kB]
Get:9 http://us.archive.ubuntu.com/ubuntu xenial/restricted amd64 Packages [8,344 B]
Get:10 http://us.archive.ubuntu.com/ubuntu xenial/restricted i386 Packages [8,684 B]
Get:11 http://us.archive.ubuntu.com/ubuntu xenial/restricted Translation-en [2,908 B]
Get:12 http://us.archive.ubuntu.com/ubuntu xenial/restricted amd64 DEP-11 Metadata [186 B]
Get:13 http://us.archive.ubuntu.com/ubuntu xenial/universe amd64 Packages [7,532 kB]
0% [13 Packages 2,401 kB/7,532 kB 32%] [Connecting to security.ubuntu.com]          1,036 kB/s 4s
```

2. Once you update the package list, you will have to install the PostgreSQL database, as Odoo uses the PostgreSQL database server to store the data. Run the following command on your terminal to install the **postgresql** server and related dependencies:

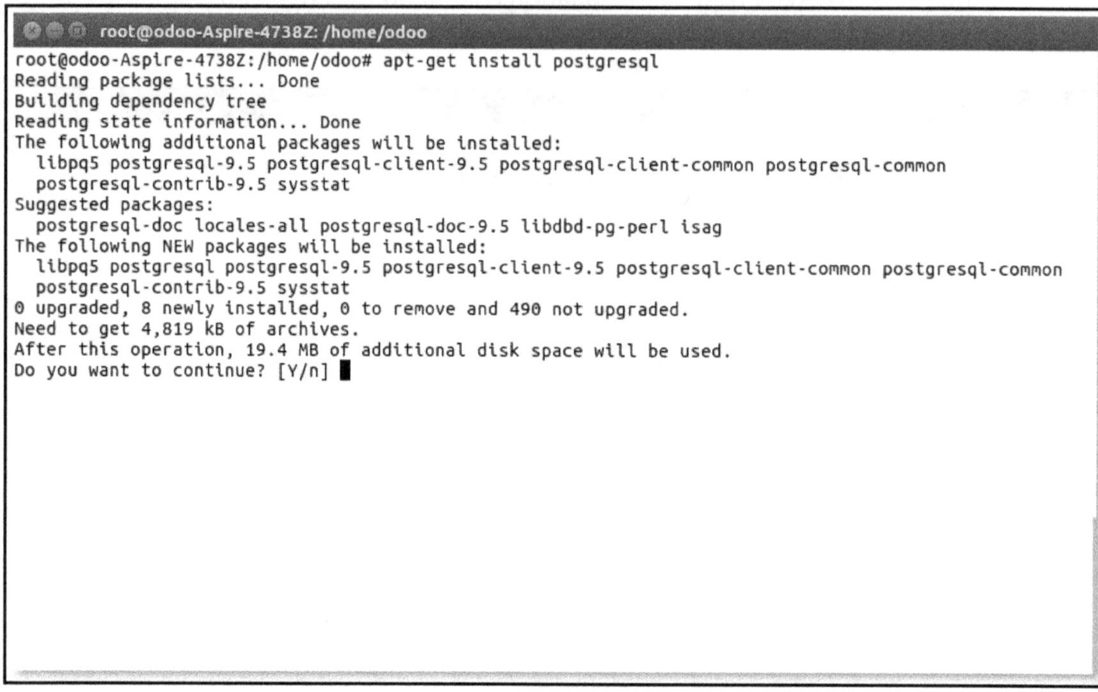

Along with **postgresql**, it will install the dependencies. You will be prompted for confirmation; enter Y to continue the installation along with the dependencies.

3. We have to create a new role in PostgreSQL server as Odoo will not allow you to access the database using **postgres** which is the default role. Create a new role in PostgreSQL with the same server as your Linux user. By default, **postgres** is the only user created by PostgreSQL and this user is not allowed to be used on Odoo. You need the role in PostgreSQL to be the same as the Linux user so that the UNIX socket can be used without a password:

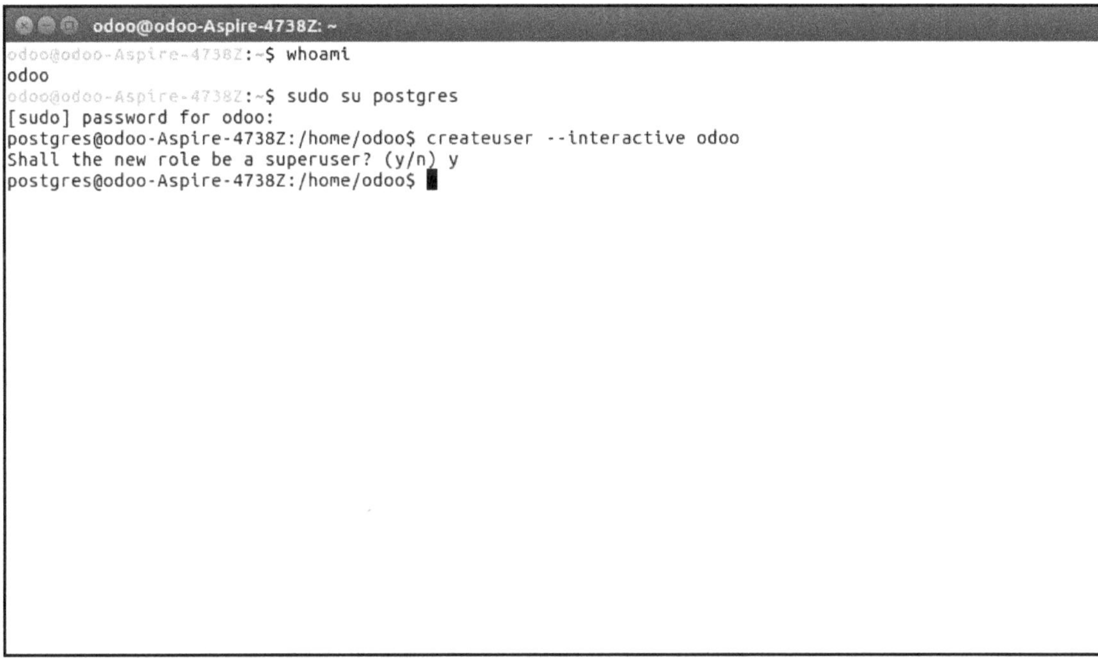

In my case, I have created **odoo** as a Linux user; you can check your username from the fresh terminal using the **whoami** command. Use the preceding command to create the role in the PostgreSQL server.

4. Verify that the normal user (a new role created in PostgreSQL) has access to the PostgreSQL server; to test this try to get the database list using the following command:

```
odoo@odoo-Aspire-4738Z: ~
odoo@odoo-Aspire-4738Z:~$ whoami
odoo
odoo@odoo-Aspire-4738Z:~$ sudo su postgres
[sudo] password for odoo:
postgres@odoo-Aspire-4738Z:/home/odoo$ createuser --interactive odoo
Shall the new role be a superuser? (y/n) y
postgres@odoo-Aspire-4738Z:/home/odoo$ exit
exit
odoo@odoo-Aspire-4738Z:~$ psql --list
                                  List of databases
   Name    |  Owner   | Encoding |   Collate   |    Ctype    |   Access privileges
-----------+----------+----------+-------------+-------------+-----------------------
 postgres  | postgres | UTF8     | en_US.UTF-8 | en_US.UTF-8 |
 template0 | postgres | UTF8     | en_US.UTF-8 | en_US.UTF-8 | =c/postgres          +
           |          |          |             |             | postgres=CTc/postgres
 template1 | postgres | UTF8     | en_US.UTF-8 | en_US.UTF-8 | =c/postgres          +
           |          |          |             |             | postgres=CTc/postgres
(3 rows)

odoo@odoo-Aspire-4738Z:~$
```

5. Look at the suggested installation steps from the Odoo installation documentation:

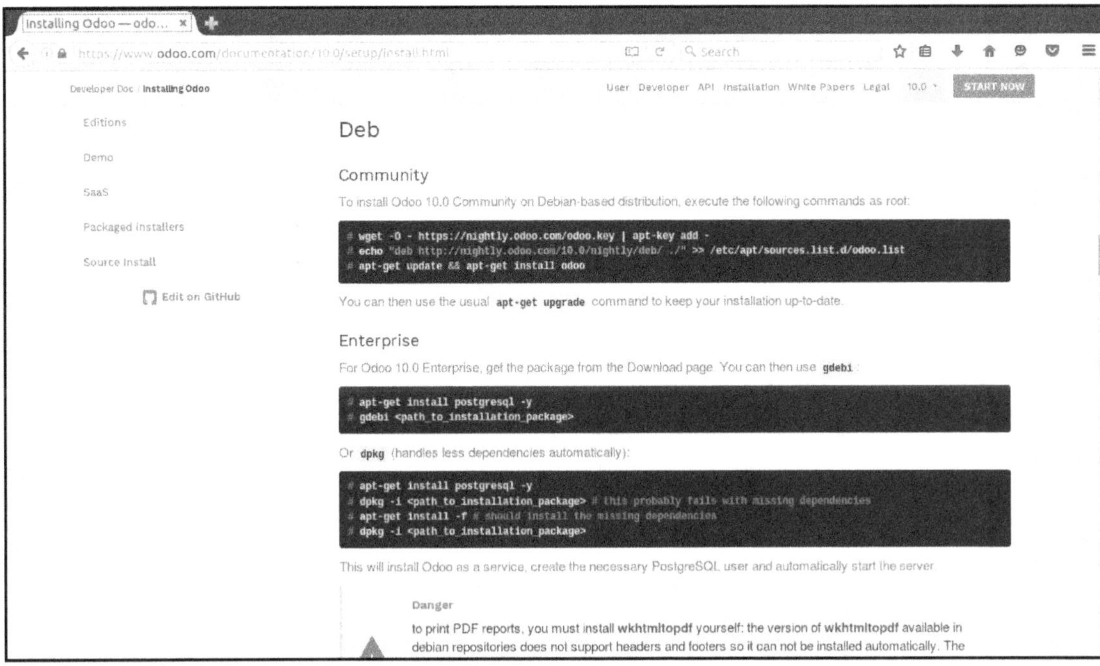

The Odoo software can be installed using the Debian package from the nightly packaging system, which allows you to have continuous updates and fixes for bugs and security issues. To install Odoo, run the following command on the Terminal with root access:

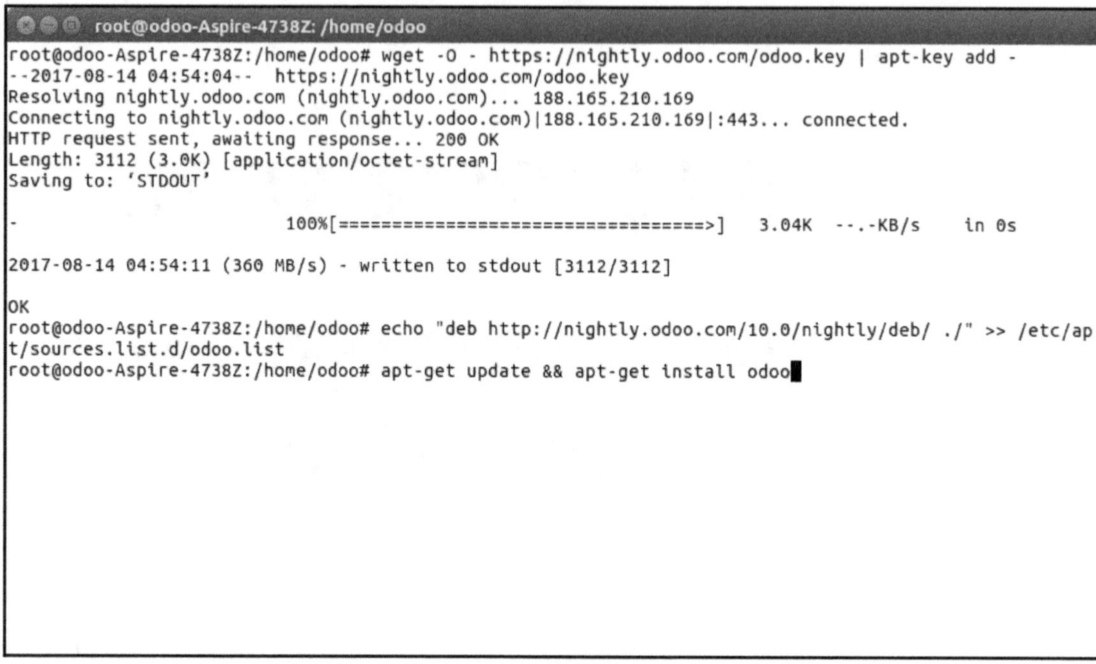

6. As soon as the package list is updated, the installation of the Odoo package begins. You will be prompted for a confirmation when additional dependencies required by the Odoo package will be installed:

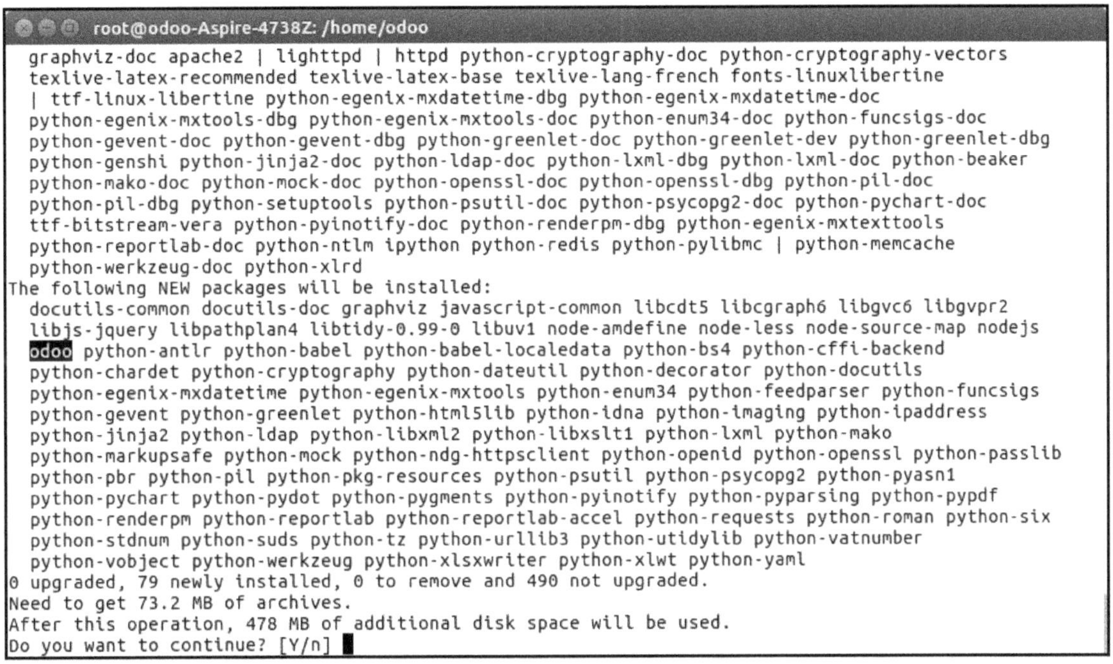

7. On the successful installation of Odoo and the related dependencies, you are ready to launch the Odoo server as a service:

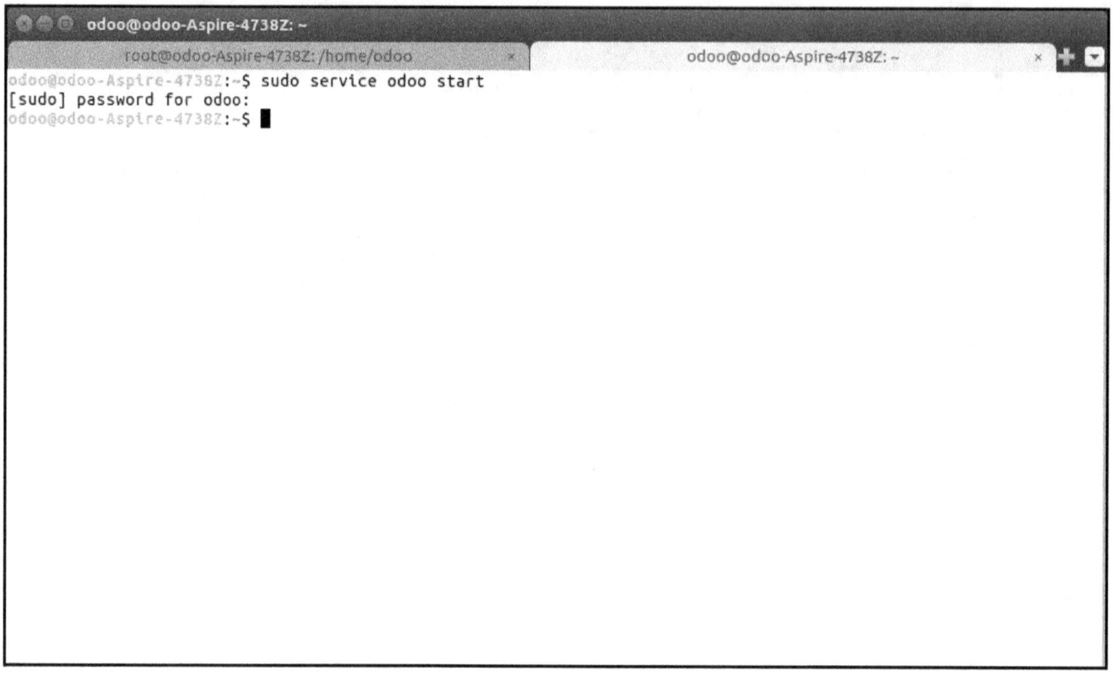

8. Open your web browser and enter the URL, http://localhost:8069; you should see the following screen:

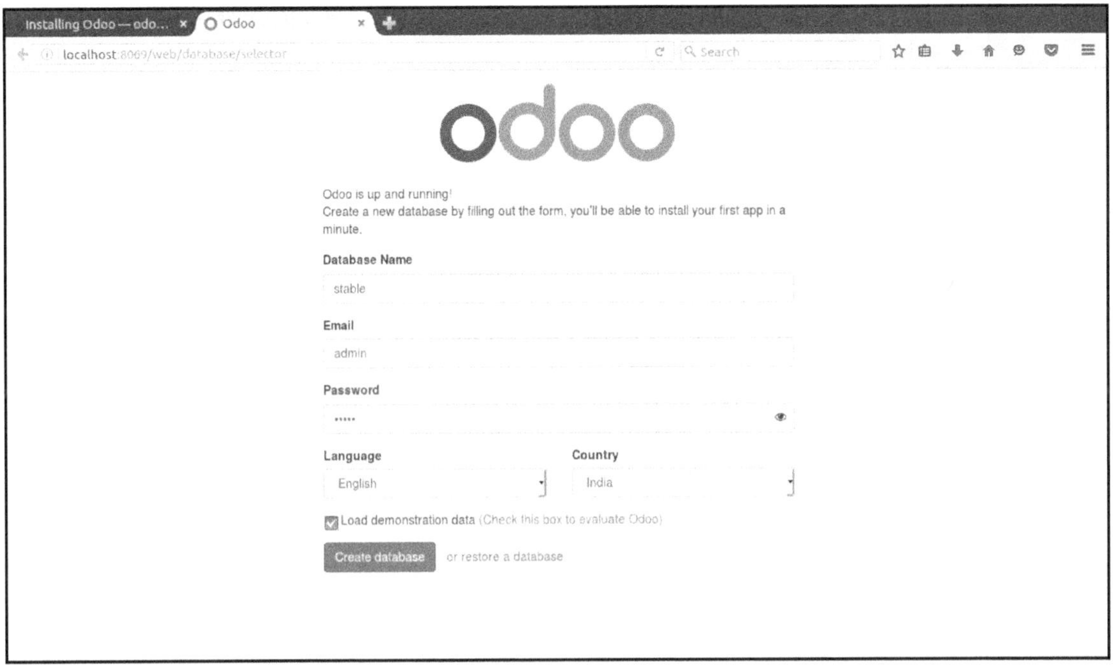

Initially, you will be redirected to the database creation page, as there is no database available. Enter the **Database Name**, **Email** and **Password**. An email will be sent to your username on the database. Select the default Language for the database (instance) and country. If you would like to create a database for the test use, select the **Load demonstration data** checkbox and click on the **Create database** button. It may take some time to create and set up the database.

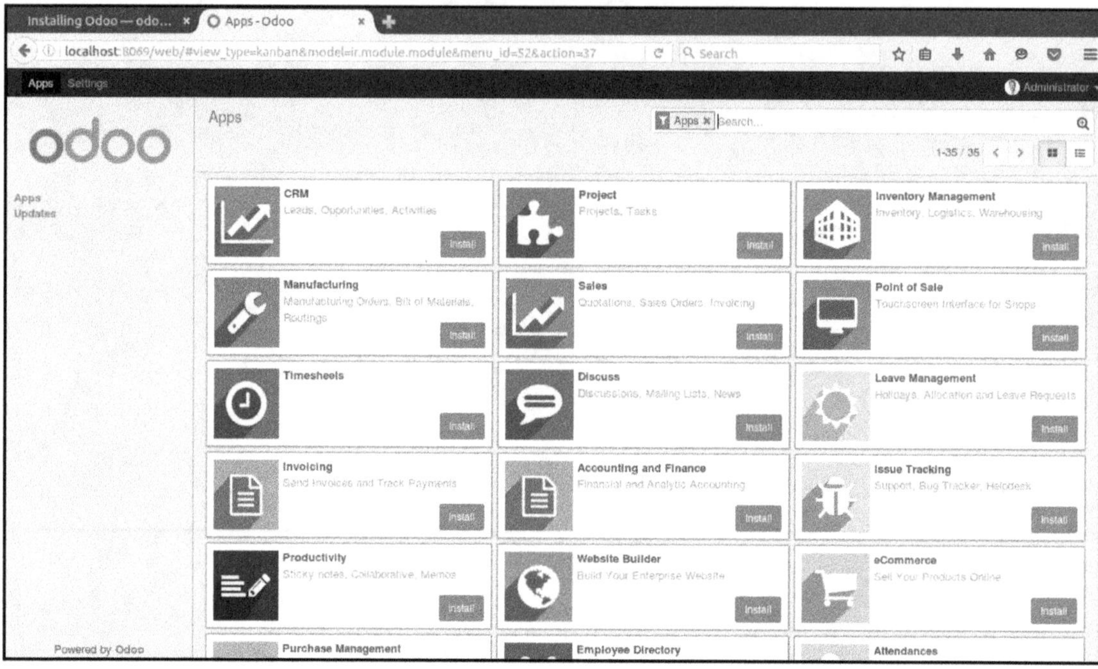

9. You should see the preceding screen on the successful creation of the first database. However, this is the Community Edition. If you have already bought the Enterprise Edition, go to the download page and log in to odoo.com using your username and password to **DOWNLOAD** the Enterprise Edition:

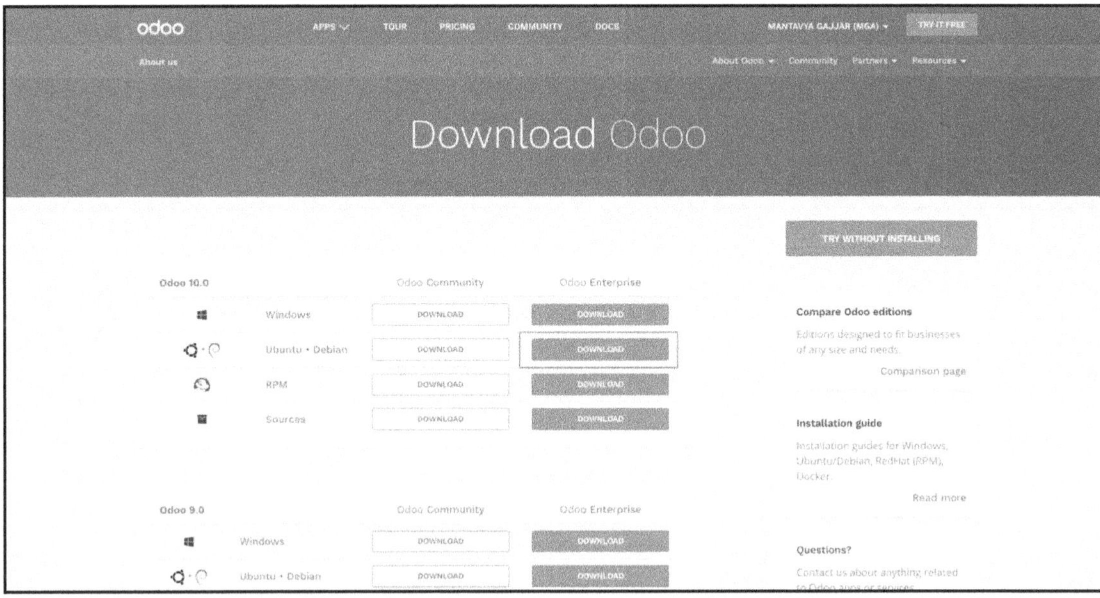

For Odoo 10.0 Enterprise, get the package from the **Download** page. You can then use **gdebi** or **dpkg**. The **gdebi** package manager manages the automatic installation of the dependencies while **dpkg** handles fewer dependencies automatically.

There's more...

There are a few things that need to be configured after the installation, such as the installation of the **wkhtmltopdf** tool, which is required to print the reports and configure Odoo to run on the load-balancing server with multi-processes using worker's parameter of Odoo server.

Let's configure Odoo for production use.

Install the wkhtmltopdf tool

The only package **wkhtmltopdf** required to print the reports has to be installed manually as the installation of this package is not managed automatically by the Odoo package installation process. The default version of **wkhtmltopdf** that is available in Debian repositories does not support headers and footers, so it cannot be installed automatically.

The recommended version is **0.12.1**, and it is available on the **wkhtmltopdf** download page in the **Archive** section. Select the package based on the version of Ubuntu you have installed:

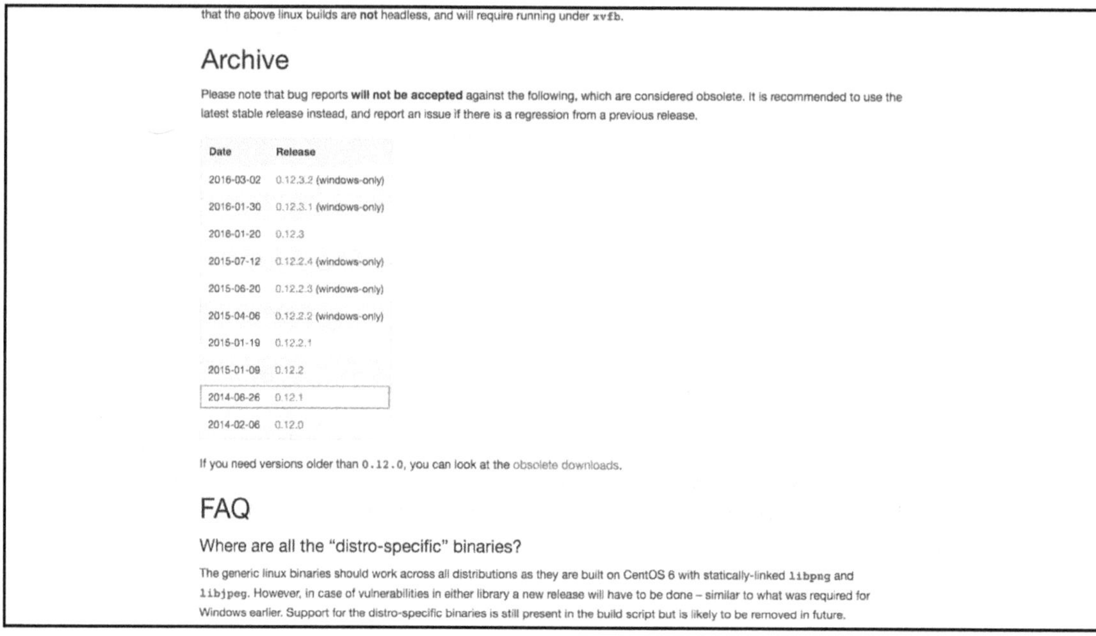

As there is no official release for Xenial Xerus, you can use the package available for Trusty Tahr. Download the installation file using the **gdebi** manager for better dependency management.

Odoo configuration parameters

The Odoo configuration file can be found at **/etc/odoo/odoo.conf**; open the configuration file using the **gedit** editor with the following command:

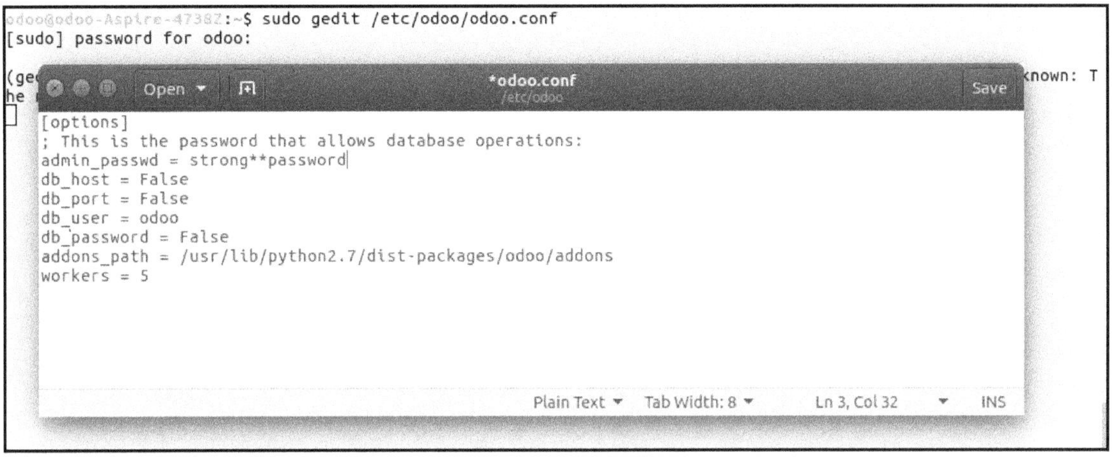

Set **admin_passwd**, which is the master password for managing databases from the Odoo interface. The second parameter to be added is the **workers** parameter; I set it to **5**, as my server has two cores. The workers can be set based on the following calculation:

*Workers = (2 * number or core) + 1*

Restart the Odoo service after changing any parameters to the configuration file.

Index

A

B

C

D

E

F

G

H

I

J

K

L

M

O

P

U

V

W

www.ingramcontent.com/pod-product-compliance
Lightning Source LLC
LaVergne TN
LVHW060007210926
848481LV00013B/3665